AA

# THE
# B&B
# GUIDE

Published by AA Publishing, which is a trading name of AA Media Limited whose registered office is: Fanum House, Basing View, Basingstoke, Hampshire RG21 4EA. Registered number 06112600

48th edition published 2017
© AA Media Limited 2017

The contents of this publication are believed correct at the time of printing. Nevertheless the Publisher cannot be held responsible for any errors or omissions or for changes in the details given in this guide or for the consequences of any reliance on the information provided in the same. This does not affect your statutory rights. Assessments of AA inspected establishments are based on the experience(s) of the hotel and restaurant inspectors on the occasion(s) of their visit(s), therefore the descriptions in this guide represent an element of subjective opinion that may not reflect a reader's own opinion on another occasion.

AA Media Limited strives to ensure accuracy of the information in this guide at the time of printing. Due to the constantly evolving nature of the subject matter the information is subject to change. AA Media Limited gratefully receive advice from readers of any necessary updates.

For queries relating to this guide, please contact:
lifestyleguides@theAA.com

Website addresses are included in some entries and specified by the respective establishment. Such websites are not under the control of AA Media Limited and as such AA Media Limited will not accept any responsibility or liability in respect of any and all matters whatsoever relating to such websites including access, content, material and functionality. By including the addresses of third party websites the AA does not intend to solicit business or offer any security to any person in any country, directly or indirectly.

Image credits:
The Automobile Association wishes to thank the following photographers and organisations for their assistance in the preparation of this book. Abbreviations for the picture credits are as follows – (t) top; (b) bottom; (l) left; (r) right; (c) centre; (AA) AA World Travel Library.

3 Courtesy of The Durham Ox, Crayke ; 4 AA/Stockbyte Royalty Free; 9 Courtesy of The Old Hall Inn, Chinley; 10 Courtesy of The Lion Inn, Chelmsford; 12-16 BG Photodisc; 12 Courtesy of Glenegedale House, Glenegedale; 13l Courtesy of Maiden's Tower at Leeds Castle, Maidstone; 13r Courtesy of Nanny Brow, Ambleside; 14l Courtesy of Pool House, Poolewe; 14r Courtesy of Mansion House Llansteffan, Llansteffan; 24-25 AA/A Burton; 211 AA/J Hunt; 329 Gordon Shoosmith / Alamy Stock Photo; 330-331 AA/J Smith; 358-359 AA/M Bauer; 391 AA/M Bauer; 392-393; AA/C Jones; 407 AA/K Blackwell

Every effort has been made to trace the copyright holders, and we apologise in advance for any unintentional omissions or errors. We would be pleased to apply any corrections in a following edition of this publication.

Photographs in the gazetteer are provided by the establishments.

This guide was compiled by the AA Lifestyle Guides team.

Maps prepared by the Mapping Services Department of AA Publishing.

Maps © AA Media Limited 2017.

Contains Ordnance Survey data © Crown copyright and database right 2017.

This is based upon Crown Copyright and is reproduced with the permission of Land & Property Services under delegated authority from the Controller of Her Majesty's Stationery Office.
© Crown copyright and database rights 2017 PMLPA No. 100497

Republic of Ireland mapping based on © Ordnance Survey Ireland/Government of Ireland Copyright Permit number MP0000117

A CIP catalogue record for this book is available from the British Library.

Printed in Italy by Printer Trento SRL, Trento

ISBN: 978-0-7495-7887-9

# Contents

# Welcome to the AA B&B Guide

For almost half a century, our readers have been using *The AA B&B Guide* to find many different types of accommodation, for a multitude of reasons. As the AA inspects such a wide range of establishments, we hope that this guide will prove an invaluable asset in helping you to find the right place to stay.

## Who's in the guide?

From the most stylish and sophisticated urban boutique accommodation to family-run homes in the countryside; from ultra-chic luxury to charmingly rustic home-from-home comfort and many points between, *The AA B&B Guide* has it all. Throughout the year, our specially trained team of expert inspectors are visiting, grading and advising the Guest Accommodation that appears in this guide. Each one is judged on its presentation, quality of accommodation, leisure facilities, breakfasts and evening meals, service, hospitality, conference facilities and cleanliness and housekeeping. They are then rated according to our classification system (pages 8 and 9).

Our inspectors also choose their Guest Accommodation of the Year for England, Scotland, Wales, and Northern Ireland, as well as the Friendliest B&B of the Year, the Unique B&B of the Year and the Restaurant with Rooms of the Year.

## Gold Stars

All of the Guest Accommodation in this guide is of a high standard, but some are a cut above, and those with Gold Stars are in the top ten percent of their Star rating. At these establishments you can expect a little more of everything: more comfort, more extras, and more attention. From three to five Gold Stars, this is the best of British Guest Accommodation.

## Silver Stars

These properties offer a superior level of quality within their Star rating, high standards of hospitality, service and cleanliness.

## Premier Collection

All five-Star establishments, whether Gold, Silver or Black Stars, are part of the Premier Collection, and these entries are highlighted in the guide. This allows the reader to see at a glance those Guest Accommodations that have met all the criteria required by the Guest Accommodation Scheme and reached the highest rating possible.

## Rosettes

Some of the B&Bs in this guide have their own restaurants, and many of them serve food that has been awarded AA Rosettes; including a few that have reached the four and five Rosette level, making them among the finest restaurants in the world. These are regularly visited by the AA Inspectorate who award Rosettes strictly on the basis of the inspector's experience alone.

Many establishments designated as Restaurants with Rooms have been awarded AA Rosettes for the quality of their food.

## Anonymous inspection

Any Guest Accommodation applying for AA recognition receives an unannounced visit by one of the AA's professional inspectors to check standards. The inspector pays his or her own bill (rather than it being paid by the establishment).

After staying overnight at the Guest Accommodation, the inspector will make themselves known to a member of staff and ask to speak to the manager. Once a rating is awarded, regular visits are made by our inspectors to check that standards are being maintained.

If the accommodation changes hands, the new owners must reapply for classification, as AA recognition is not transferable.

### Tell us what you think

We welcome your feedback-- you can email us at **lifestyleguides@theaa.com**

The B&Bs are visited throughout the year by our team of inspectors. For the very latest updates visit **www.theaa.com/bed-and-breakfasts**

# How to use the AA B&B Guide

**1.** ▪ CAMBRIDGE       Map 12 TL45

## Benson House

**2.** ★★★★ ⌂ GUEST HOUSE

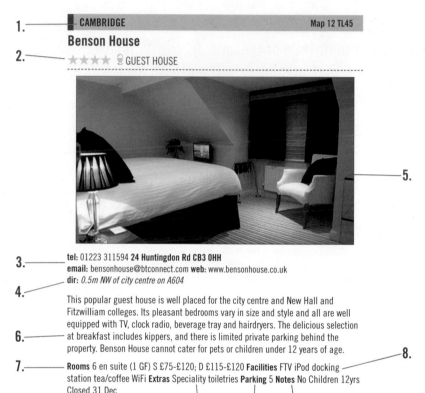

**5.**

**3.** **tel:** 01223 311594 **24 Huntingdon Rd CB3 0HH**
**email:** bensonhouse@btconnect.com **web:** www.bensonhouse.co.uk
**4.** **dir:** *0.5m NW of city centre on A604*

**6.** This popular guest house is well placed for the city centre and New Hall and Fitzwilliam colleges. Its pleasant bedrooms vary in size and style and all are well equipped with TV, clock radio, beverage tray and hairdryers. The delicious selection at breakfast includes kippers, and there is limited private parking behind the property. Benson House cannot cater for pets or children under 12 years of age.

**7.** **Rooms** 6 en suite (1 GF) S £75-£120; D £115-£120 **Facilities** FTV iPod docking station tea/coffee WiFi **Extras** Speciality toiletries **Parking** 5 **Notes** No Children 12yrs Closed 31 Dec

**8.**

**9.**      **10.**      **11.**

## 1. Location, map reference & name

Each country is listed in alphabetical order by county then location. The Channel Islands follow the England section and the Scottish Islands follow the Scotland section. Establishments are listed alphabetically in descending order of Stars, with Gold Stars appearing first in each rating.

The map page number refers to the atlas at the back of the guide and is followed by the National Grid Reference. To find the location, read the first figure across and the second figure vertically within the lettered square.

You can find routes at **theAA.com** or **www.AAbookings.ie**. London has its own Plans (see end of atlas), and London establishments have a Plan number based on these.

## 2. Classification & designator

See pages 8 and 9.

Five-Star establishments are highlighted as Premier Collection, and they are listed on pages 17–22.

◉ **Rosettes** The AA's food award, see page 11.

⌂ **Egg cups and** ⌂ **pies** These symbols indicate that, in the experience of the inspector, either breakfast or dinner (or both) are really special, and have an emphasis on freshly prepared local ingredients.

## 3. Email address & website

Email and website addresses are included where they have been specified by the establishment. Such websites are not under the control of AA Media Limited, who cannot accept any responsibility or liability in respect of any and all matters whatsoever relating to such websites.

## 4. Directions & distances

Distances in **directions** are given in miles (m) and yards (yds), or kilometres (km) and metres (mtrs) in the Republic of Ireland.

## 5. Photographs

Establishments may choose to include a photograph.

## 6. Description

Written by the inspector at the time of his or her visit.

## 7. Rooms

The number of letting bedrooms (rms), or rooms with a bath or shower en suite are shown. Bedrooms that have a private bathroom (pri facs) adjacent are indicated.

The number of bedrooms in an annexe of equivalent standard are also shown. Charges are per night:

**S** bed and breakfast per person
**D** bed and breakfast for two people

sharing a room. If an asterisk (*) follows the prices this indicates 2017 prices.

The euro € is the currency of the Republic of Ireland.

Prices are indications only, so check before booking. Some places may offer free accommodation to children provided they share their parents' room.

## 8. Facilities

Most bedrooms will have TV. If this is important to you, please check when booking. If **TV4B** appears, this means that there are TVs in four bedrooms.

If **Dinner** is shown, you may have to order in advance. Please check when booking.

For other abbreviations and symbols, see panel on the right of this page.

## 9. Extras

Anything the establishment offers in rooms that are more than expected e.g. speciality toiletries, trouser press, mineral water, home-made biscuits etc.

## 10. Parking

Parking is usually followed by the number of spaces. Motorists should be aware that some establishments may charge for parking. Please check when booking.

## 11. Notes

**No children** children cannot be accommodated, or a minimum age may be specified, e.g. No Children 4yrs means no children under four years old.

Establishments with special facilities for children (**ch fac**) may include a babysitting service or baby-intercom system, playroom or playground, laundry facilities, drying and ironing facilities, cots, high chairs and special meals. If you have very young children, check facilities before booking.

Additional facilities such as lifts or any leisure activities available are also listed.

**LB** indicates that Short or Leisure Breaks are available. Contact the establishment for details.

Establishments are open all year unless **Closed** days/dates/months are shown. Some places are open all year but offer a restricted service (**RS**) in low season. If the text does not say what the restricted services are you should check before booking.

**Civ Wed 50** The establishment is licensed for civil weddings and can accommodate 50 guests for the ceremony.

**Smoking** Since 1 July 2007 smoking has been banned by law in all public places in the United Kingdom and Ireland. However, the proprietor can designate one or more bedrooms with ventilation systems where the occupants can smoke, but communal areas must be smoke-free. Communal areas include the interior bars and restaurants in pubs and inns. We indicate number of smoking rooms (if any).

**Conference facilities Conf** indicates that facilities are available. The total number of delegates that can be accommodated is shown, plus maximum numbers in various settings (theatre, classroom and boardroom).

## Key to symbols and abbreviations

| | |
|---|---|
| ★★★ | Classification (see page 8–9) |
| ◉ | AA Rosette award (see page 11) |
| Ⓐ | Associate entry (see page 9) |
| Ⓤ | Unclassified rating (see page 9) |
|  | A very special breakfast, with an emphasis on freshly prepared local ingredients |
|  | A very special dinner, with an emphasis on freshly prepared local ingredients |
| S | Single room |
| D | Double room (2 people sharing) |
| pri fac | Private facilities |
| fmly | Family bedroom |
| GF | Ground floor bedroom |
| LB | Short/Leisure breaks |
| * | 2017 prices |
| ch fac | Special facilities for children |
| TVL | Lounge with television |
| Lounge | Lounge without television |
| TV4B | Television in four bedrooms |
| STV | Satellite television |
| FTV | Freeview television |
| WiFi | Wireless internet |
| tea/coffee | Tea and coffee-making facilities |
| Conf | Conference facilities |
| rms | Bedrooms in main building |
| fr | From |
| RS | Restricted service |
|  | Secure storage |
|  | Indoor swimming pool |
|  | Heated indoor swimming pool |
|  | Outdoor swimming pool |
|  | Heated outdoor swimming pool |
|  | Croquet lawn |
|  | Tennis court |
|  | Golf (followed by number of holes) |

# AA Inspected Guest Accommodation

The AA inspects and classifies more than 1,900 guest houses, farmhouses, inns and restaurants with rooms for its Guest Accommodation Scheme, under common quality standards agreed between the AA, VisitBritain, VisitScotland and VisitWales. AA recognised establishments pay an annual fee according to the classification and the number of bedrooms. The classification is not transferable if an establishment changes hands.

The AA presents several awards within the Guest Accommodation Scheme, including the **AA Friendliest B&B of the Year**, which showcases the very finest hospitality in the country; **AA Guest Accommodation of the Year Awards**, presented to establishments in England, Scotland, Wales, and Northern Ireland, **AA Unique B&B of the Year**, and **AA Restaurant with Rooms of the Year**. See pages 12-15 for this year's winners.

## Stars

AA Stars classify guest accommodation at five levels of quality, from one at the simplest, to five offering the highest quality. In order to achieve a one-Star rating an establishment must meet certain minimum entry requirements. For example:

- A cooked breakfast or substantial continental option is provided
- The proprietor and/or staff are available for your arrival, departure and at all meal times
- Once registered, guests have access to the establishment at all times unless previously notified
- All areas of operation meet minimum quality requirements for cleanliness, maintenance and hospitality as well as facilities and the delivery of services
- A dining room or similar eating area is available unless meals are served in bedrooms

To obtain a higher Star rating, an establishment must provide increased quality standards across all areas, with particular emphasis in four key areas:
- Cleanliness and housekeeping
- Hospitality and service
- Quality and condition of bedrooms, bathrooms and public rooms
- Food quality

There are also particular requirements in order for an establishment to achieve three, four or five Stars, for example:
**Three Stars and above**
- access to both sides of all beds for double occupancy
- bathrooms/shower rooms cannot be used by the proprietor
- there is a washbasin in every guest bedroom (either in the bedrooms or the en suite/private facility)

**Four Stars**
- half of bedrooms must be en suite or have private facilities

**Five Stars**
- all bedrooms must be en suite or have private facilities

Establishments applying for AA recognition are visited by one of the AA's qualified accommodation inspectors as a mystery guest. Inspections are a thorough test of the accommodation, food, and hospitality. The inspector completes a full report, resulting in a recommendation for the appropriate Star rating. After this first visit, the establishment will receive a regular visit to check that standards are maintained. If it changes hands, the new owners must re-apply for classification, as standards can change.

Guests can expect to find the following minimum standards at all levels:

- Pleasant and helpful welcome and service, and sound standards of housekeeping and maintenance
- Comfortable accommodation equipped to modern standards
- Bedding and towels changed for each new guest, and at least weekly if the room is taken for a long stay
- Adequate storage, heating, lighting and comfortable seating
- A sufficient hot water supply at reasonable times
- A full cooked breakfast. (If this is not provided, the fact must be advertised and a substantial continental breakfast must be offered.)

When an AA inspector has visited a property, and evaluated all the aspects of the accommodation for comfort, facilities, attention to detail and presentation, you can be confident the Star rating will help you make the right choice.

### ★ Gold Star Award

AA Gold Stars are awarded to the very best Guest Accommodation within the three, four, or five Star ratings.

### ★ Silver Star Award

Guest Accommodation with Silver Stars offer a superior level of quality within their Star rating, high standards of hospitality, service and cleanliness.

## Accommodation Designators

Along with the Star ratings, six designators have been introduced. The proprietors, in discussion with our inspectors, choose which designator best describes their establishment:

### Bed & Breakfast

A private house run by the owner with accommodation for no more than six paying guests.

### Guest House

Run on a more commercial basis than a B&B, the accommodation provides for more than six paying guests and there are usually more services; for example staff as well as the owner may provide dinner.

### Farmhouse

The B&B or guest house accommodation is part of a working farm or smallholding.

### Inn

The accommodation is provided in a fully licensed establishment. The bar will be open to non-residents and can provide food in the evenings.

### Restaurant with Rooms

This is a destination restaurant offering overnight accommodation, with dining being the main business, and open to non-residents. The restaurant should offer a high standard of food and restaurant service at least five nights a week. A liquor licence is necessary and there is a maximum of 12 bedrooms.

### Guest Accommodation

Any establishment that meets the minimum entry requirements is eligible for this general category.

### U Unclassified entries

A small number of establishments in this guide have this symbol because their Star classification was not confirmed at the time of going to press. This may be due to a change of ownership or because the establishment has only recently joined the AA rating scheme. For up-to-date information on these and other new establishments check **theAA.com**.

### A Associate entries

These establishments have been inspected and rated by VisitBritain, VisitScotland or VisitWales, and have joined the AA scheme on a marketing-only basis.

### AA Advertised

These establishments are not rated or inspected by the AA, but are displayed for advertising purposes only.

# Useful information

What follows is a selection of things we think it is worth bearing in mind when planning a stay. We hope you'll find them useful.

### Arriving at the accommodation
There may be restricted access to some establishments, particularly in the late morning and the afternoon, so do check when booking.

### Booking
Book as early as possible, particularly for the peak holiday period (early June to the end of September) and for Easter and other public holidays. In some parts of Scotland the skiing season is also a peak holiday period.

Some establishments only accept weekly bookings from Saturday, and some require a deposit on booking.

A very small number of establishments may not accept credit cards. If you plan on paying this way, then check when booking. Where credit cards are accepted there may be an extra charge for their use.

### Food Allergies
From December 2014 an EU regulation came into force making it easier for those with food allergies to make safer food choices when eating out. There are 14 allergens listed in the regulation, and pubs and restaurants are required to list any of these that are used in the dishes they offer. These may be highlighted on the menus or customers can ask staff for full information. Remember, if you are allergic to a food and are in any doubt speak to a member of staff. For further information see:
www.food.gov.uk/science/allergy-intolerance/label/labelling-changes

### Prices
Minimum and maximum prices are shown for one (S) and two people (D) per night and include a full breakfast. If dinner is also included this is indicated in brackets (incl dinner). Where prices are for the room only, this is indicated.

Prices in the guide include VAT (and service where applicable), except the Channel Islands where VAT does not apply.

Where proprietors have been unable to provide us with their 2018 charges we publish the 2017 price as a rough guide (shown by an asterisk *). Where no prices are given, please make enquiries direct.

### London prices
London prices tend to be higher than outside the capital, and normally only bed and breakfast is provided, although some establishments do provide a full meal service.

### Cancellation
If you have to cancel a booking, let the proprietor know at once. If the room cannot be re-let you may be held legally responsible for partial payment; you could lose your deposit or be liable for compensation, so consider taking out cancellation insurance.

### Dogs
Although many establishments allow dogs, they may be excluded from some areas of the accommodation and some breeds, particularly those requiring an exceptional license, may not be accepted at all. Under the Equality Act 2010, access should be allowed to guide dogs and assistance dogs. Please check the establishment's policy when making your booking.

### Food and drink
Some guest accommodation provides evening meals, ranging from a set meal to a full menu. Some even have their own restaurant. You may have to arrange dinner in

advance, at breakfast or on the previous day, so do ask when booking.

If you book on bed, breakfast and evening meal terms, you may find that the tariff includes only the set menu. If there is a carte you may be able to order from this and pay a supplement.

On Sundays, many establishments serve the main meal at midday, and provide only a cold supper in the evening. In some parts of Britain, particularly in Scotland, high tea (i.e. a savoury dish followed by bread and butter, scones and cakes) is sometimes served instead of, or as an alternative to, dinner.

**Farmhouses:** Sometimes the land has been sold and only the house remains, but many are working farms and some farmers are happy to allow visitors to look around, or even to help feed the animals. However, you should always exercise care and never leave children unsupervised. Although the directory entry states the acreage and the type of farming, do check when booking to make sure that it matches your expectations. The farmhouses are listed under towns or villages, but do ask for directions when booking.

**Inns:** Traditional inns often have a cosy bar, convivial atmosphere, good beer and hearty pub food. Those listed in the guide will provide breakfast in a suitable room, and should also serve light meals during licensing hours. The character of the properties vary according to whether they are country inns or town establishments. Check before you book, including arrival times as these may be restricted to licensed opening hours. When it comes to coaches, Inns have well-defined legal obligations towards travellers; in the event of a query the customer should contact the proprietor or local licensing authority.

## Facilities for disabled guests

The Equality Act 2010 details the legal rights of disabled people, including access to goods, services and facilities, and means that service providers may have to consider making adjustments to their premises. For more information about the Act see www.gov.uk/definition-of-disability-under-equality-act-2010 or www.gov.uk/government/policies/creating-a-fairer-and-more-equal-society.

Under the Equality Act 2010, access should be allowed to guide dogs and assistance dogs. Please check the establishment's policy when making your booking.

We recommend that you always telephone in advance to ensure that the establishment you have chosen has appropriate facilities. The establishments in this guide should be aware of their obligations under the Act.

**Please note:** AA inspectors are not accredited to make inspections under the National Accessibility Scheme. We indicate in entries if an establishment has ground floor rooms; and if a B&B tells us they have disabled facilities this may be included in the description.

## AA Rosette Awards

The AA awards Rosettes to over 2,000 restaurants that we regard as the best in the UK & Ireland

Excellent local restaurants serving food prepared with care, understanding and skill, using good quality ingredients.

Excellent local restaurants serving food prepared with care, understanding and skill, using good quality ingredients.

The best local restaurants, which aim for and achieve higher standards and better consistency, and where a greater precision is apparent in the cooking. There will be obvious attention to the selection of quality ingredients.

Outstanding restaurants that demand recognition well beyond their local area.

Among the very best restaurants in the British Isles, where the cooking demands national recognition.

The finest restaurants in the British Isles, where the cooking compares with the best in the world.

11

# AA Bed &Breakfast Awards 2017–18

Each year the AA celebrates the best that our Guest Accommodation Scheme has to offer. Our inspectors nominate those places that they feel to be a cut above the rest, and award winners are chosen from these nominations. Held this year at The Landmark London Hotel, the AA Bed & Breakfast Awards 2017–18 recognised and rewarded almost 30 very deserving finalists, for demonstrating all-round excellence and unfailing standards, and for providing outstanding service to their guests. All finalists were treated to a drinks reception, followed by a formal four-course celebratory luncheon. They also received a personalised certificate and an engraved Villeroy & Boch decanter.

## FRIENDLIEST B&B OF THE YEAR

### GLENEGEDALE HOUSE ★★★★★
**GLENEGEDALE, ISLE OF ISLAY – PAGE 356**

Emma and Graeme Clark run the 5 Gold Star Glenegedale House on the beautiful Isle of Islay, which lies in the heart of whisky country. They are incredibly helpful, from planning and booking whisky tours or wildlife trips, to advice on other activities on the island. It seems that nothing is too much trouble for these friendly hosts. Cakes and refreshment are offered as a matter of course, and the smell of baking wafts through the house. So many extra little touches are provided here, right down to the zip-lock bags at the breakfast buffet, so that guests can take a selection of the home-baking away. Graeme and Emma strive to ensure every guest's stay at Glenegedale House is the best they have ever had. The individually designed, sumptuous bedrooms all have TVs, beautiful Egyptian cotton bed linen and luxurious white fluffy towels. Guests can relax in the morning room or sitting room and marvel at the stunning views over the Mull of Oa and the Atlantic Ocean. Graeme and Emma are on hand to offer advice on planning days out to make the most of a stay on wonderful Islay. With award-winning breakfasts, using locally sourced ingredients, guests are truly set up for their day exploring the stunning countryside.

## UNIQUE B&B OF THE YEAR

### MAIDEN'S TOWER AT LEEDS CASTLE ★★★★★
**MAIDSTONE, KENT – PAGE 168**

Guests at Maiden's Tower get the chance to experience life as a royal for the duration of their stay. The 16th-century stone tower on Castle Island is surrounded by the tranquil waters in the moat and set within glorious grounds. Each of the five luxury en suite bedrooms, named after the medieval queens who owned Leeds Castle, are beautifully decorated in period style and have opulent bathrooms and stunning views. Those who stay on a Sunday night are offered a free hawk walk with the castle falconers, while midweek guests can take a complimentary punt around the moat giving them a unique angle of this historic castle. Manager, Debbie Matthews said, 'I am delighted that Maiden's Tower has won the title of AA Unique Bed & Breakfast of the Year 2017. The team here are passionate about providing a memorable stay to our guests and this accolade is a testament to their cheerful and polite approach. Whether we're welcoming guests on arrival, serving them breakfast or looking after the cleanliness of their bedrooms. We could not have asked for more than to know the AA, as a well-beloved institution, recognise our service as being unique and special.'

## GUEST ACCOMMODATION OF THE YEAR FOR ENGLAND

### NANNY BROW ★★★★★ ♀
**AMBLESIDE, CUMBRIA – PAGE 65**

Susan Robinson and her family moved to Nanny Brow in 2009 and since then, she has worked tirelessly to create an establishment that fully reflects her desire for a luxurious and peaceful haven in the heart of the Lake District. Set in five acres of grounds, Nanny Brow sits on its own crag with unrivalled views of the Brathay Valley, the hills behind Tarn Hows, Wrynose Pass and the high fells of Langdale. Built in 1904, the house is one of the finest Arts and Crafts properties in the area and has been painstakingly refurbished by Susan. The period features are offset by modern luxuries with beautiful en suite bathrooms, sumptuous beds and free WiFi. Guests also enjoy the award-winning breakfasts served in the original dining room. Nanny Brow is a lifelong passion for Susan and nothing is too much trouble for any of her guests. Of her award she said, 'We are shocked but deeply honoured and thrilled to be held in such high esteem by an organisation such as the AA. I am grateful to my loyal and dedicated staff who have worked so hard over the years and without whom we wouldn't be receiving this award.'

# AA Bed &Breakfast Awards 2017–18

## GUEST ACCOMMODATION OF THE YEAR FOR SCOTLAND

### POOL HOUSE ★★★★★ 🛏 ☕
**POOLEWE, HIGHLAND – PAGE 348**

Peter and Margaret Harrison met 58 years ago when they both worked at The Midland Hotel in Manchester. With 60 years of experience in the hospitality industry, they are now ably assisted by daughters Elizabeth and Mhairi who can themselves boast over 30 years of looking after guests. Pool House is over 300 years old and was a hunting lodge for the chieftain of the Clan Mackenzie and, during WW2 was the HQ for the Russian Arctic and North Atlantic convoys leaving Loch Ewe. In the most beautiful Highland mountain location, the house has stunning sea and rivers views from all the bedrooms and there's an air of calm and tranquillity for all who stay there.

Peter Harrison said, 'What a huge surprise the family had when we opened the mail. A cold "dreich" day in Scotland became so much better. The family are delighted to receive this prestigious award and look forward to sharing this fabulous news with our guests.'

## GUEST ACCOMMODATION OF THE YEAR FOR WALES

### MANSION HOUSE LLANSTEFFAN ★★★★ ◉◉
**LLANSTEFFAN, CARMARTHENSHIRE – PAGE 362**

David and Wendy Beaney quite literally fell in love at Mansion House at their wedding 21 years ago. Little did they know that after 15 years of travelling the world that when they decided to return to Wales it would be as owners of their wedding venue. With breathtaking views of the Towy Estuary and stunning architecture, Mansion House has a sense of grandeur. All rooms have been individually designed to make the most of the original features such as fireplaces, cornicing and tall Georgian windows. Guests not only receive a warm, friendly welcome from their hosts, but also benefit from a two AA Rosette restaurant.

David said, 'We never imagined, whilst building our business plan on the dining table in Australia five years ago, that we would achieve such an accolade in such a short space of time. We have defined strong financial targets for ourselves each year, and slowly incorporated realistic professional goals for the team and the business. This award had not even come onto our goal list yet! We are grateful for the support of our strong team of professionals and our wonderful families.'

## GUEST ACCOMMODATION OF THE YEAR FOR NORTHERN IRELAND

### THE OLD SCHOOLHOUSE INN ★★★★ ◉◉ ⌂
**COMBER, COUNTY DOWN – PAGE 394**

Terry and Avril Brown purchased The Old Schoolhouse when it was still a school back in 1984 and transformed it into a lovely, luxurious inn, set in extensive grounds. Situated just a 20-minute drive from Belfast, and the airport, the inn is easy to reach. It's also very easy to so enjoy the beautiful countryside that surrounds it. Each of the bedrooms here is named after an American President who was of Ulster descent.

Guests not only benefit from a genuine Irish welcome, but also from Avril's sumptuous breakfasts, that include her famous Guinness wheaten bread. They can also stay in for dinner in the two AA Rosette restaurant run by Terry and Avril's son, Will Brown, and his partner Karena. Nothing is too much bother for the team who aim to make all their guests feel right at home thoughout their stay.

On receiving the news of the award, Avril said, 'We are highly elated and delighted to have won this prestigious award.'

## RESTAURANT WITH ROOMS OF THE YEAR

### PADSTOW TOWNHOUSE ★★★★★ ◉◉◉◉ ⌂
**PADSTOW, CORNWALL – PAGE 53**

The 18th-century Padstow Townhouse, in the old part of town, is a collection of six individually styled suites that provide comfort and added little luxuries. Each of the luxurious and quirky suites is named after a confectionery treat – Marshmallow, Toffee Apple, Honeycomb, Bon Bon, Popcorn, and Rhubarb and Custard. If you find it difficult to decide when booking, you can always ask a member of staff which one will be the perfect choice.

Guests can choose between an extensive Townhouse breakfast served in their suite, or a table in Rojano's in the Square for a full Cornish breakfast. And if you're keen to go out and explore the area, they will prepare a tailored-made picnic basket for you. Then in the evening, guests can choose to dine at the much acclaimed four AA Rosette restaurant, Paul Ainsworth at No. 6, or at Rojano's in the Square that holds one AA Rosette. All the staff go out of their way to make their guests happy.

# AA B&B Story of the Year 2017–18

Sponsored by eviivo

Entrants for the AA B&B Story of the Year, told us about their journey to becoming the establishment that they are today. We chose the one we liked the best.

## THE GROVE CROMER

CROMER, NORFOLK – PAGE 197

For the past 81 years, The Grove has been providing guests with the highest quality accommodation. More recently it has become known for fine dining, earning two AA Rosettes for culinary excellence in 2013, retaining them in 2016. The Grove has 16 bedrooms and six self-catering cottages, an indoor pool and three acres of gardens. There is also a private entrance into Warren Woods leading onto Cromer's cliffs and beaches.

The Grove has only ever been owned by five families, three of which were cousins, who went onto form Barclays Bank. It was re-built as a family bolt-hole by the Gurney family in 1797. The Graveling family took it over in 1936.

Robert and Hilda Graveling were from farming stock and always fancied running a small holding of their own. In 1936, they sold their shop and house, and moved into The Grove.

Chris Graveling, takes up the story: "According to Grandad, old Mr Barclay begged him to take it off his hands. The Grove had about eight acres at the time, and Grandad kept pigs, cows, goats and chickens, as well as farming the top field for arable crops. But the house was expensive to run, so they decided to let some of the spare rooms; apart from a couple of years for the war, when it was used as an army store, it hasn't closed its doors, since."

Since then, the Graveling family have striven to maintain a welcoming, family feel to the house, the main aim is that everyone leaving has had an enjoyable and relaxing time. John and Ann took over in 1978 and their five children, Richard, Chris, Liz, Hannah and Ruth, formed a partnership in 2010.

Now, three generations on, The Grove has converted the aisled barns into self-catering cottages, there is also an indoor pool. As well as a fine-dining restaurant, which gained two rosettes from the AA in 2013.

Also, in 2013, a quiet corner of the garden was converted into five oak-framed, cedar-clad rooms; The Orchard Rooms, which won an architects' award for outstanding craftsmanship on completion.

"Our restaurant focuses on fresh local produce." Chris continues, "Norfolk is very lucky to have such wonderful local produce on our doorstep. Our crabs and lobsters come from the local fishermen, who have been fishing out of Cromer for generations, I recently heard a story about Grandad and the uncle of our crab fishermen going out on a boat and how they shared the fish out according to who could shout the loudest."

The Grove sources meat from the local butcher, farmed from places such as Gunton, Hevingham and Gressingham, all just a few miles away. "We also have a large kitchen garden which adds to our dishes, so some items on the plate are still growing hours before they are eaten." Chris adds.

In 2015, The Grove Glamping, the brainchild of Ruth Graveling, was started, with five heated yurts going up on the top field, and a new shower and toilet block built.

"It's strange to think back that despite us all having our own careers, we were all informally trained in hospitality from a very early age, we all worked at The Grove as teenagers, either in the kitchen, housekeeping or waiting. And as soon as we were old enough to answer the phone, we were taking bookings. On family holidays, we were always asked to analyse what the hotel or restaurant was doing well or wrong and what we could learn from it. We all seem to be just as comfortable dealing with guests in The Grove as we are in our own homes. It's a very natural thing for us."

The Grove is ideal for a wonderful meal out, a private dining venue, a short romantic break, a holiday with the kids, or can even be booked exclusively.

# ★★★★★ The Premier Collection

## ENGLAND

### BERKSHIRE

**HURLEY**
Hurley House
The Olde Bell Inn

**WARGRAVE**
Copperfields

### BRISTOL

**BRISTOL**
Berwick Lodge

### BUCKINGHAMSHIRE

**BEACONSFIELD**
Crazy Bear Beaconsfield

**MEDMENHAM**
The Dog and Badger

### CAMBRIDGESHIRE

**ELTON**
The Crown Inn

### CHESHIRE

**BURWARDSLEY**
The Pheasant Inn

**CHESTER**
Mitchell's of Chester
Stone Villa Chester

**WARMINGHAM**
The Bear's Paw

### CORNWALL & ISLES OF SCILLY

**BUDE**
Pot and Barrel B&B

**FALMOUTH**
Anacapri

**LAUNCESTON**
Wheatley Farm

**LOOE**
The Beach House

**LOSTWITHIEL**
The Old Chapel B&B

**MEVAGISSEY**
Pebble House
Portmellon Cove Guest House

**PADSTOW**
Padstow Townhouse
Penjoly Guest House
St Petroc's Bistro
The Seafood Restaurant

**PENZANCE**
Camilla House

**PERRANUTHNOE**
Ednovean Farm

**POLPERRO**
Trenderway Farm

**PORT GAVERNE**
Port Gaverne

**ST AUSTELL**
Anchorage House
Lower Barns Boutique Bed &
   Breakfast and Wedding Venue

**ST IVES**
The Gannet Inn

**ST MELLION**
Pentillie Castle & Estate

**WADEBRIDGE**
Wadebridge Bed and Breakfast

### CUMBRIA

**AMBLESIDE**
Nanny Brow

**ASKHAM**
Askham Hall

**BORROWDALE**
Hazel Bank Country House

**BRAMPTON**
Lanercost Bed and Breakfast

**BROUGH**
The Inn at Brough

**CARTMEL**
L'Enclume

**CROSTHWAITE**
The Punchbowl Inn
   at Crosthwaite

**GLENRIDDING**
Glenridding House

**GRASMERE**
Moss Grove Organic

**GRIZEDALE**
Grizedale Lodge

**KIRKBY LONSDALE**
Hipping Hall
Plato's
The Sun Inn

**LUPTON**
Plough Inn

**NEAR SAWREY**
Ees Wyke Country House

**NEWBY BRIDGE**
The Knoll Country House

**PENRITH**
Brooklands Guest House
River Garth

**TROUTBECK**
Broadoaks Country House

**WINDERMERE**
Applegarth Villa & Restaurant
The Howbeck
Lindeth Fell Country House
Windermere Suites

### DERBYSHIRE

**BELPER**
Bridge Hill House
Dannah Farm Country House

**BRADWELL**
The Samuel Fox Country Inn

**DARLEY DALE**
Ashford Grange

**HOPE**
Underleigh House

### DEVON

**AXMINSTER**
Kerrington House

**BRATTON FLEMING**
Bracken House

**CHILLATON**
Tor Cottage

**CULLOMPTON**
Muddifords Court Country House

**DARTMOUTH**
Mounthaven
Strete Barton House

**DOLTON**
The Rams Head Inn

**ERMINGTON**
Plantation House

**ILFRACOMBE**
The Habit Boutique Rooms

**LUSTLEIGH**
Eastwrey Barton

# ★★★★★ The Premier Collection *continued*

**LYNMOUTH**
The Heatherville

**LYNTON**
Highcliffe House

**NEWTON ABBOT**
Bulleigh Barton Manor

**PAIGNTON**
The P&M Paignton RESIDENCE

**SIDMOUTH**
The Salty Monk

**TEDBURN ST MARY**
Frogmill Bed & Breakfast

**TIVERTON**
Fernside Bed and Breakfast

**TORQUAY**
The Albaston
Carlton Court
The Cary Arms
Kingston House
Linden House
The 25 Boutique B&B
Tyndale B&B

**TOTNES**
Stoke Gabriel Lodgings -
  Badgers Retreat

## DORSET

**BRIDPORT**
The Shave Cross Inn

**BROADWINDSOR**
The Old George

**CHRISTCHURCH**
The Lord Bute & Restaurant

**CRANBORNE**
10 Castle Street

**DORCHESTER**
Little Court

**SHERBORNE**
The Kings Arms
Munden House
The Rose and Crown Inn, Trent

**SWANAGE**
Swanage Haven
2@2 Rabling Road

**WIMBORNE MINSTER**
Les Bouviers Restaurant
  with Rooms

## ESSEX

**DEDHAM**
The Sun Inn

**GESTINGTHORPE**
The Pheasant

**GREAT YELDHAM**
The White Hart

**WIX**
Dairy House Farm

## GLOUCESTERSHIRE

**BARNSLEY**
The Village Pub

**BLAISDON**
Blaisdon House B&B

**BOURTON-ON-THE-WATER**
The Dial House

**CHELTENHAM**
The Bradley
Cleeve Hill House

**CIRENCESTER**
The Fleece at Cirencester

**LOWER SLAUGHTER**
The Slaughters Country Inn

**NETHER WESTCOTE**
The Feathered Nest Country Inn

**STOW-ON-THE-WOLD**
Old Stocks Inn
The Porch House

## HAMPSHIRE

**BARTON-ON-SEA**
Pebble Beach

**SOUTHAMPTON**
Ennio's Restaurant
  & Boutique Rooms
THE PIG in the Wall

**WINCHESTER**
Giffard House

## HEREFORDSHIRE

**BOLSTONE**
Prickett's Place

**HEREFORD**
Somerville House

**LEINTWARDINE**
The Lion
Upper Buckton

**LEOMINSTER**
Hills Farm

**ROSS-ON-WYE**
Wilton Court Restaurant
  with Rooms

## HERTFORDSHIRE

**WELWYN**
The Wellington

## ISLE OF WIGHT

**NITON**
Enchanted Manor

**TOTLAND BAY**
Sentry Mead

**VENTNOR**
The Hambrough
The Leconfield

## KENT

**DEAL**
Sutherland House

**DOVER**
The Marquis at Alkham

**EGERTON**
Frasers

**MAIDSTONE**
Maiden's Tower at Leeds Castle

**MARDEN**
Merzie Meadows

**TUNBRIDGE WELLS (ROYAL)**
Danehurst House

**WOODCHURCH**
Brook Farm Bed & Breakfast

## LANCASHIRE

**BLACKBURN**
The Millstone at Mellor

**CLITHEROE**
The Assheton Arms

**GREAT ECCLESTON**
The Cartford Inn

**ORMSKIRK**
Moor Hall Restaurant
  with Rooms

**WHITEWELL**
The Inn at Whitewell

## LINCOLNSHIRE

**HEMSWELL**
Hemswell Court

HORNCASTLE
Magpies Restaurant with Rooms

HOUGH-ON-THE-HILL
The Brownlow Arms

MARKET RASEN
The Advocate Arms

STAMFORD
Meadow View

WINTERINGHAM
Winteringham Fields

## LONDON POSTAL DISTRICTS

LONDON SW3
San Domenico House
Sydney House Chelsea

LONDON SW7
The Exhibitionist

LONDON W1
The Marble Arch by Montcalm
The Piccadilly London West End

LONDON W2
Park Grand London
   Lancaster Gate

## NORFOLK

BLAKENEY
Blakeney House

CLEY NEXT THE SEA
Old Town Hall House

NORWICH
Brasteds
38 St Giles

SHERINGHAM
The Eiders Bed & Breakfast

THORPE MARKET
The Green House B&B

THURSFORD
Holly Lodge

## NORTHUMBERLAND

BELFORD
Market Cross Guest House

BERWICK-UPON-TWEED
The Captain's Quarters

MORPETH
Eshott Hall

STOCKSFIELD
The Duke of Wellington Inn

## NOTTINGHAMSHIRE

ELTON
The Grange

NOTTINGHAM
Restaurant Sat Bains
   with Rooms

RETFORD
Blacksmiths

## OXFORDSHIRE

ABINGDON-ON-THAMES
B&B Rafters

FARINGDON
Buscot Manor B&B

KINGHAM
The Wild Rabbit

OXFORD
Burlington House

STADHAMPTON
The Crazy Bear

WITNEY
Old Swan & Minster Mill

WOODSTOCK
The Glove House

## SHROPSHIRE

LUDLOW
The Charlton Arms
The Clive Bar & Restaurant
   with Rooms
Old Downton Lodge

MARKET DRAYTON
Ternhill Farm House

OSWESTRY
Greystones

SHREWSBURY
Darwin's Townhouse
Drapers Hall

WELLINGTON
The Old Orleton Inn

## SOMERSET

AXBRIDGE
The Oak House

BACKWELL
The Rising Sun

BATH
Apple Tree Guest House
Apsley House
Chestnuts House
Dorian House
River House and Friary
   Coach House
Tasburgh House
Waterhouse
The Windsor Townhouse

CHEW MAGNA
The Bear & Swan

CORTON DENHAM
The Queens Arms

FIVEHEAD
Langford Fivehead

FROME
Lullington House

HATCH BEAUCHAMP
Frog Street Farmhouse

HOLCOMBE
The Holcombe Inn

SOMERTON
Cartways Bed and Breakfast

WESTON-SUPER-MARE
Church House

WITHYPOOL
Kings Farm

YEOVIL
Little Barwick House

## STAFFORDSHIRE

LICHFIELD
Netherstowe House
Pipe Hill House

TAMWORTH
Oak Tree Farm

## SUFFOLK

BURY ST EDMUNDS
The Bannatyne Spa
The Northgate

ELVEDEN
The Elveden Inn

IXWORTH
Ixworth House

LAVENHAM
Lavenham Great House
   'Restaurant With Rooms'

LONG MELFORD
Long Melford Swan

MILDENHALL
The Bull Inn

**NEWMARKET**
The Packhorse Inn

**ORFORD**
The Crown & Castle

**SOUTHWOLD**
Sutherland House

**STOKE-BY-NAYLAND**
The Angel Inn

**THORNHAM MAGNA**
Thornham Hall

**YAXLEY**
The Auberge

## SURREY

**CHIDDINGFOLD**
The Crown Inn

## SUSSEX, EAST

**BOREHAM STREET**
Boreham House

**DITCHLING**
The Bull

**EASTBOURNE**
Ocklynge Manor

**HASTINGS & ST LEONARDS**
The Cloudesley
Stream House

**LEWES**
Broadacres

**NORTHIAM**
Knelle Dower B&B

**RYE**
Jeake's House
Manor Farm Oast
Willow Tree House

## SUSSEX, WEST

**CHICHESTER**
Rooks Hill

**CHILGROVE**
The White Horse

**LITTLEHAMPTON**
Berry House
Glendales

**LODSWORTH**
The Halfway Bridge Inn

**SIDLESHAM**
The Crab & Lobster

## WARWICKSHIRE

**ILMINGTON**
The Howard Arms

**STRATFORD-UPON-AVON**
Arden House

## WEST MIDLANDS

**SOLIHULL**
Hampton Manor

## WILTSHIRE

**BOX**
The Northey Arms

**BURTON**
The Old House at Home

**CORSHAM**
The Methuen Arms

**DEVIZES**
Blounts Court Farm
The Peppermill

**EDINGTON**
The Three Daggers

**PEWSEY**
Troutbeck Guest House
  at the Red Lion Freehouse

## WORCESTERSHIRE

**ABBERLEY**
The Manor Arms

**BEWDLEY**
Kateshill House

**BROADWAY**
Abbots Grange
Mill Hay House
Russell's

## YORKSHIRE, EAST RIDING OF

**BEVERLEY**
Newbegin House

**BRIDLINGTON**
Marton Grange

**SOUTH DALTON**
The Pipe and Glass Inn

## YORKSHIRE, NORTH

**AMPLEFORTH**
Shallowdale House

**ASENBY**
Crab Manor

**AUSTWICK**
The Traddock

**BAINBRIDGE**
Yorebridge House

**CLAPHAM**
The New Inn

**CRAYKE**
The Durham Ox

**FILEY**
All Seasons Guesthouse

**GOLDSBOROUGH**
Goldsborough Hall

**GRASSINGTON**
Ashfield House
Grassington House

**HARROGATE**
The Grafton Boutique B&B

**HETTON**
The Angel Inn

**KEXBY**
Kexby House

**KIRKBY FLEETHAM**
Black Horse Inn

**KNARESBOROUGH**
General Tarleton Inn

**LEEMING BAR**
Little Holtby

**LEYBURN**
Braithwaite Hall
Low Mill Guest House
The Old Town Hall

**MIDDLEHAM**
The Saddle Room

**MIDDLETON TYAS**
The Coach House

**OLDSTEAD**
The Black Swan at Oldstead

**OSMOTHERLEY**
The Cleveland Tontine

**PICKERING**
17 Burgate

**RIPON**
Mallard Grange
The Old Coach House

WEST WITTON
The Wensleydale Heifer

YORK
The Judge's Lodging

## YORKSHIRE, WEST

HAWORTH
Ashmount Country House

HUDDERSFIELD
315 Bar and Restaurant

KIRKBURTON
Woodman Inn

# CHANNEL ISLANDS

## JERSEY

ST AUBIN
The Panorama

# SCOTLAND

## ABERDEENSHIRE

ELLON
Aikenshill House

## ANGUS

INVERKEILOR
Gordon's

## ARGYLL & BUTE

BARCALDINE
Ardtorna

OBAN
Blarcreen House

## DUMFRIES & GALLOWAY

PORTPATRICK
Knockinaam Lodge

## EDINBURGH, CITY OF

EDINBURGH
Kew House
21212
The Witchery by the Castle

## FIFE

PEAT INN
The Peat Inn

## HIGHLAND

BRACHLA
Loch Ness Lodge

CROMARTY
The Factor's House

DORNOCH
Links House at Royal Dornoch
2 Quail

GRANTOWN-ON-SPEY
The Dulaig

INVERNESS
Daviot Lodge
Trafford Bank

NAIRN
Boath House

POOLEWE
Pool House

## LOTHIAN, WEST

LINLITHGOW
Arden Country House

## PERTH & KINROSS

ALYTH
Tigh Na Leigh Guesthouse

PERTH
The Townhouse

## SCOTTISH BORDERS

MELROSE
Fauhope Country House

PEEBLES
Kingsmuir House

## STIRLING

STIRLING
Victoria Square Guest House

STRATHYRE
Creagan House

# SCOTTISH ISLANDS

## ISLAY, ISLE OF

GLENEGEDALE
Glenegedale House

## SKYE, ISLE OF

STRUAN
Ullinish Country Lodge

# WALES

## ANGLESEY, ISLE OF

BEAUMARIS
The Bull - Beaumaris

## CARMARTHENSHIRE

LLANARTHNE
Llwyn Helyg Country House

ST CLEARS
Coedllys Country House

## CEREDIGION

ABERAERON
Feathers Royal

ABERYSTWYTH
Awel-Deg

CARDIGAN
Caemorgan Mansion

EGLWYS FACH
Ynyshir

## CONWY

ABERGELE
The Kinmel Arms

BETWS-Y-COED
Penmachno Hall

CONWY
The Groes Inn
Sychnant Pass Country House

LLANDUDNO
Bryn Derwen

LLANDUDNO JUNCTION
Queens Head

RHOS-ON-SEA
Plas Rhos

TAL-Y-CAFN
Bodnant Welsh Food Centre

TREFRIW
Yr Hafod Country House

## DENBIGHSHIRE

LLANDYRNOG
Pentre Mawr Country House

RUTHIN
Firgrove Country House B&B

ST ASAPH
Tan-Yr-Onnen Guest House

## GWYNEDD

**ABERDYFI**
Penhelig Arms

**CAERNARFON**
Plas Dinas Country House

**DOLGELLAU**
Tyddynmawr Farmhouse

**PWLLHELI**
The Old Rectory

## MONMOUTHSHIRE

**USK**
Newbridge on Usk

**WHITEBROOK**
The Whitebrook

## PEMBROKESHIRE

**EGLWYSWRW**
Ael y Bryn

**FISHGUARD**
Erw-Lon Farm

**HAVERFORDWEST**
Roch Castle
Slebech Park Estate

**ST DAVIDS**
Penrhiw
Ramsey House

**SOLVA**
Crug Glas Country House

**TENBY**
Trefloyne Manor

## POWYS

**BRECON**
Peterstone Court

**MONTGOMERY**
The Nags Head Inn

## SWANSEA

**REYNOLDSTON**
Fairyhill

## VALE OF GLAMORGAN

**HENSOL**
Llanerch Vineyard

**PENARTH**
Restaurant James Sommerin

# NORTHERN IRELAND

## COUNTY ANTRIM

**BUSHMILLS**
Causeway Lodge
Whitepark House

# REPUBLIC OF IRELAND

## COUNTY CLARE

**LAHINCH**
Moy House

## COUNTY CORK

**KINSALE**
Friar's Lodge

**SHANAGARRY**
Ballymaloe House

## DUBLIN

**DUBLIN**
Glenogra Town House
Harrington Hall

## COUNTY KERRY

**DINGLE**
Castlewood House
Gormans Clifftop House
 & Restaurant

**KILLARNEY**
Fairview Guest House

**KILLORGLIN**
Carrig House Country House
 & Restaurant

## COUNTY MEATH

**SLANE**
Tankardstown

## COUNTY MONAGHAN

**GLASLOUGH**
The Castle at Castle
 Leslie Estate

## COUNTY TIPPERARY

**THURLES**
The Castle

## COUNTY WEXFORD

**GOREY**
Clonganny House

**WEXFORD**
Killiane Castle Country House
 & Farm

# AA WALKING GUIDES

## The 50 Best Walks of 2–10 Miles by Region and City

- Easy-to-follow directions with clear waypointed maps
- Colour-coded routes – pick from easy strolls through to more challenging walks
- Fascinating background reading for every walk
- Advice for dog owners
- Great for a full day out with recommended sights and attractions plus places to eat and drink

# England

## BEDFORDSHIRE

### HENLOW
Map 12 TL13

## The Crown
★★★★ ⊛ INN

tel: 01462 812433 **2 High Street SG16 6BS**
email: rooms@crownpub.co.uk web: www.crownpub.co.uk
dir: *On B659 (High St)*

The Crown is situated on the High Street in Henlow with easy access from the A1. It's a traditional pub with a modern feel and an attractive beer garden where guests can relax in the summer. Bedrooms all have plenty of useful features such as smart TV, free WiFi, hair straighteners and Nespresso coffee machines. Guests can enjoy dinner in the restaurant which makes good use made of high quality, seasonal ingredients.

**Rooms:** 5 annexe en suite (1 fmly) (5 GF) **Facilities:** STV FTV Lounge tea/coffee Dinner available WiFi **Extras:** Speciality toiletries, mineral water, fresh milk **Parking:** 72 **Notes:** Closed 25–26 Dec

### LEIGHTON BUZZARD
Map 11 SP92

## The Heath Inn
★★★ INN

tel: 01525 237816 & 237390 **76 Woburn Road, Heath and Reach LU7 0AR**
email: enquiries@theheathinn.com web: www.theheathinn.com

Situated in the quiet village of Heath and Reach, close to Leighton Buzzard, this traditional inn offers comfortable accommodation. Good quality dishes and a range of cask ales are available in both the bar and restaurant.

**Rooms:** 16 en suite (5 fmly) (8 GF) **Facilities:** FTV TVL tea/coffee Dinner available WiFi 🐾 **Parking:** 50

## BERKSHIRE

### BEENHAM
Map 5 SU56

## The Six Bells
★★★★ ⊜ INN

tel: 0118 971 3368 **The Green RG7 5NX**
email: info@thesixbells.co.uk web: www.thesixbells.co.uk
dir: *Exit A4 between Reading & Newbury, follow signs for Beenham*

Not far from Thatcham and Newbury, The Six Bells is a friendly, traditional pub with comfortable, well-appointed bedrooms and good service. The restaurant serves a range of excellent, well-prepared dishes, dinner is recommended.

**Rooms:** 4 en suite **Facilities:** FTV tea/coffee Dinner available **Conf:** Max 40 Thtr 40 Class 40 Board 25 **Parking:** 20 **Notes:** No children 16yrs

### BOXFORD
Map 5 SU47

## Bell @ Boxford
★★★ ⚠ INN

tel: 01488 608721 **Lambourn Road RG20 8DD**
email: paul@bellatboxford.com web: www.bellatboxford.com
dir: *M4 junct 14, A338 towards Wantage. Right onto B4000 to x-rds signed Boxford*

Paul and Helen Lavis have been the hosts at this traditional Berkshire inn for over 20 years. The restaurant offers a varied and comprehensive menu, seven days a week, along with relaxed service and good value prices. The bedrooms all come complete with power shower, HDTV, WiFi, trouser press and hairdryers, and the location is ideal for Newbury and Hungerford.

**Rooms:** 9 en suite (4 GF) **S** £48–£85 **Facilities:** FTV DVD tea/coffee Dinner available Direct dial WiFi Pool table **Conf:** Max 12 Board 12 **Parking:** 35

### CHIEVELEY
Map 5 SU47

## Crab & Boar
★★★★ ⊛⊛ RESTAURANT WITH ROOMS

tel: 01635 247550 **Wantage Road RG20 8UE**
email: info@crabandboar.com web: www.crabandboar.com
dir: *1.5m W of Chieveley on B4494*

Part of The Epicurean Collection, this former pub has been appointed to a very high standard and bedrooms include a full range of modern amenities. Some ground floor rooms have a small private patio area complete with a luxury private hot tub. The warm and cosy restaurant offers an extensive and award-winning range of dishes, using the best suppliers in the south.

**Rooms:** 9 en suite 5 annexe en suite (8 GF) **Facilities:** FTV tea/coffee Dinner available Direct dial WiFi Hot tub suites **Extras:** Home-made biscuits **Conf:** Max 14 Thtr 14 Class 14 Board 14 **Parking:** 80 **Notes:** LB

## Ye Olde Red Lion

★★★★ ☕ INN

tel: 01635 248379 & 07764 579808 **Green Lane RG20 8XB**
**email:** redlion@toucansurf.com **web:** www.yeolderedlion.com
**dir:** *M4 junct 13 N towards Oxford for 300yds, onto slip road signed Chieveley.
Left at junct, 300yds on left*

Situated in the quiet village of Chieveley, just five miles north of Newbury, this traditional inn offers comfortable en suite accommodation in the adjoining 15th-century house. The cosy pub offers a good range of real ales, and dinner can be enjoyed in the restaurant where good use is made of local and seasonal produce.

**Rooms:** 5 annexe en suite (3 GF) **S** £85–£95; **D** £95–£105* **Facilities:** FTV tea/coffee Dinner available WiFi **Parking:** 30 **Notes:** No children 14yrs

## Queens Arms

★★★★ INN

tel: 01488 648757 & 649590 **RG17 7ET**
**email:** info@queensarmseastgarston.co.uk **web:** www.queensarmseastgarston.co.uk
**dir:** *M4 junct 14 onto A338 to Great Shefford. Turn left signed East Garston & Lambourn.
Queens Arms on right*

The perfect choice for lovers of country pursuits, the Queens Arms is located in the beautiful Lambourn Valley. The individually themed bedrooms are well appointed and offer sumptuous beds, flat-screen TVs and WiFi. Four-legged guests are welcomed too in both the bar and the rooms. The bar is well stocked, and the restaurant serves good British dishes created from local produce. The Queens Lodge, across the road, is perfect for weddings, private dinners and special occasions. There is ample parking at both venues.

**Rooms:** 7 en suite 5 annexe en suite (1 fmly) (5 GF) **S** £85–£105; **D** £120–£140*
**Facilities:** FTV tea/coffee Dinner available WiFi **Extras:** Speciality toiletries
**Conf:** Max 100 Thtr 70 Class 50 Board 30 **Parking:** 80

## The Swan Inn

★★★★ ☕ INN

tel: 01488 668326 **Craven Road, Inkpen RG17 9DX**
**email:** enquiries@theswaninn-organics.co.uk **web:** www.theswaninn-organics.co.uk
**dir:** *3.5m SE of Hungerford. S on Hungerford High St past rail bridge, left to Hungerford
Common, right signed Inkpen*

This delightful village inn dates back to the 17th century, has open fires and beams in the bar, and the bonus of a smart restaurant. Bedrooms are generally spacious and well equipped. Organic produce is available from the on-site farm shop, so the bar, restaurant and breakfast menus all feature local organic produce too.

**Rooms:** 10 en suite (2 fmly) **S** £75–£80; **D** £85–£105* **Facilities:** FTV Lounge tea/coffee Dinner available Direct dial WiFi 🦮 **Extras:** Trouser press **Conf:** Max 40 Thtr 40 Class 40 Board 12 **Parking:** 50 **Notes:** Closed 25–26 Dec RS 23–24 & 27–31 Dec

### Premier Collection

## Hurley House

★★★★★ ◉◉ 🍴 RESTAURANT WITH ROOMS

tel: 01628 568500 **Henley Road SL6 5LH**
**email:** hello@hurleyhouse.co.uk **web:** www.hurleyhouse.co.uk

Hurley House is a beautiful restaurant with rooms located in a quiet village. The 10 stunning bedrooms vary in size, but all have air conditioning, underfloor heating, mini-bar, coffee machine and extremely comfortable king-size beds. Bathrooms are equipped to the same high standard all with luxurious towels and high quality toiletries. There is a popular and characterful bar with snug and private dining areas. There is also a wood-burning stove, flagstone floors and plenty of relaxed and comfortable seating of different styles. Expect fine ales, beer, spirits and there is an excellent wine list too. In the restaurant the menu showcases the finest local produce in the modern British style. Snacks are also available in the bar and outside areas which are covered and heated. WiFi is available throughout, there is a treatment room and there is also plenty of convenient parking.

**Rooms:** 10 en suite **S** £160–£285; **D** £170–£295* **Facilities:** Dinner available Spa facilities WiFi 🦮 **Extras** Mini-bar Coffee machine **Parking**

HURLEY *continued*

Premier Collection

## The Olde Bell Inn

★★★★★ ◎◎ INN

**tel:** 01628 825881 **High Street SL6 5LX**
**email:** oldebellreception@coachinginn.co.uk **web:** www.theoldebell.co.uk
**dir:** *M4 junct 8/9 follow signs for Henley. At rdbt take A4130 to Hurley,*
*turn right to Hurley Village, 800yds on right*

Dating in part to 1135, this charming coaching inn has lots of original features, with timber framed buildings and extensive landscaped gardens. Dinner can be enjoyed in the award-winning restaurant, and the kitchen uses some of the inn's own home-grown seasonal produce. There is a range of individually-styled bedrooms, each with a modern well-equipped bathroom. Both The Tithe Barn and Malthouse cater for functions and private parties, and there is a range of business facilities.

**Rooms:** 11 en suite 37 annexe en suite (21 GF) **S** £175; **D** £49–£225*
**Facilities:** FTV tea/coffee Dinner available Direct dial WiFi ☺ ⚓ ⚓18
**Conf:** Max 130 Thtr 130 Class 80 Board 52 **Parking:** 80 **Notes:** LB Civ wed 160

---

### KINTBURY                                  Map 5 SU36

## The Dundas Arms

★★★★ ⚓ INN

**tel:** 01488 658263 **53 Station Road RG17 9UT**
**email:** info@dundasarms.co.uk **web:** www.dundasarms.co.uk
**dir:** *A34 onto A4, turn left, signed Kintbury, into Station Rd*

Part of The Epicurean Collection, The Dundas Arms is quite a unique property; the location next to the canal is inviting, with service of food and drinks to the canal side being available. There are also extensive garden areas and ample car parking. The en suite bedrooms are comfortable and well equipped; some have their own private waterside patio areas. Food is a highlight of the stay with local produce featuring highly on the menu.

**Rooms:** 8 en suite (2 fmly) (5 GF) **Facilities:** FTV Lounge tea/coffee Dinner available Direct dial WiFi Fishing **Conf:** Max 16 **Parking:** 60 **Notes:** LB

---

### MAIDENHEAD                               Map 6 SU88

## Pinkneys Court Mews

★★★★ ⚓ BED AND BREAKFAST

**tel:** 01628 633253 & 07989 572167 **Lee Lane SL6 6PE**
**email:** pinkneyscourtmews@outlook.com **web:** www.bedbreakfastmaidenhead.co.uk
**dir:** *M4 junct 8/9 onto A404(M) to Maidenhead West. Exit after 2m & at rdbt onto A4*
*towards Maidenhead. Left at next rdbt, then right to Pinkneys Green. At Pinkneys Arms*
*pub left into Lee Ln, on left*

Situated within easy reach of Henley, Marlow, Maidenhead and Windsor, this attractive country house bed and breakfast offers convenient but quiet and tranquil surroundings. Attractively furnished bedrooms with designer fabrics provide a homely touch. Finish your stay with an enjoyable breakfast featuring locally sourced, fresh ingredients. A conservatory, terrace and garden are available.

**Rooms:** 4 en suite **Facilities:** FTV DVD Lounge tea/coffee WiFi ⚓18 **Extras:** Speciality toiletries, snacks **Parking:** 4 **Notes:** No children 12yrs

---

### NEWBURY                                   Map 5 SU46

## Rookwood Farm House

★★★★ GUEST ACCOMMODATION

**tel:** 01488 608676 & 07770 435621 **Stockcross RG20 8JX**
**email:** charlotte@rookwoodhouse.co.uk **web:** www.rookwoodhouse.co.uk
**dir:** *2m W of Newbury, at junct A4 & A34 onto B4000, 0.75m to Stockcross,*
*1st right signed Woodspeen, bear left, 1st on right*

Rookwood Farm House enjoys wonderful views and is very much a family home. Bedrooms are attractively presented and feature fine pieces of furniture. Breakfast is served at one large table in the kitchen. The coach house has a kitchen and sitting room and, during the summer, visitors can enjoy the beautiful gardens and outdoor pool.

**Rooms:** 2 rms (1 en suite) (1 pri facs) 2 annexe en suite (1 fmly) **S** £85; **D** £110
**Facilities:** TVL tea/coffee WiFi ⚓ ⚓ ⚓9 ⚓ **Conf:** Max 16 Board 16 **Parking:** 4
**Notes:** Civ wed 200

---

## Pilgrims Guest House

★★★★ GUEST ACCOMMODATION

**tel:** 01635 40694 **Oxford Road RG14 1XB**
**email:** office@pilgrimsgh.co.uk **web:** www.pilgrimsnewbury.co.uk
**dir:** *In Newbury exit A4 at Waitrose rdbt onto B4494 towards Wantage, 0.5m on left*

Located close to the town centre, this smartly presented house has comfortable bedrooms with modern bathrooms; some rooms are located in an annexe. WiFi is provided throughout the property and breakfast is served in the bright dining room. Parking is available.

**Rooms:** 13 rms (9 en suite) 4 annexe en suite (1 fmly) (3 GF) **S** £47–£67;
**D** £65–£75* **Facilities:** FTV Lounge tea/coffee WiFi ⚓ **Parking:** 17
**Notes:** Closed 24 Dec–2 Jan

---

### PANGBOURNE                                Map 5 SU67

## Weir View House

★★★★ GUEST ACCOMMODATION

**tel:** 0118 984 2120 **9 Shooters Hill RG8 7DZ**
**email:** info@weirview.co.uk **web:** www.weirview.co.uk
**dir:** *A329 N from Pangbourne, after mini rdbt under rail bridge, opposite The Swan pub*

A warm welcome is guaranteed at this delightful house, overlooking the River Thames in the village of Pangbourne. The spacious modern bedrooms have been finished to a very high standard and the thoughtful extras include a well-stocked mini-bar. A continental breakfast is served in the bright and airy dining room, and freshly cooked meals can be delivered to your room from the pub across the road.

**Rooms:** 9 en suite (6 fmly) (3 GF) **Facilities:** FTV DVD TVL tea/coffee Direct dial WiFi ⚓ **Extras:** Mini-bar chargeable; robes/slippers in some rooms **Conf:** Max 10 Board 10 **Parking:** 10

## READING
Map 5 SU77

### The French Horn
★★★★ ◎◎ RESTAURANT WITH ROOMS

**tel:** 0118 969 2204 **Sonning RG4 6TN**
**email:** info@thefrenchhorn.co.uk **web:** www.thefrenchhorn.co.uk
**dir:** *From A4 into Sonning, follow B478 through village over bridge, on right, car park on left*

This long-established Thames-side establishment has a lovely village setting and retains the traditions of classic hospitality. The restaurant is a particular attraction and has been awarded two AA Rosettes. Bedrooms, including four cottage suites, are spacious and comfortable; many offer stunning views over the river. A private boardroom is available for corporate guests.

**Rooms:** 12 en suite 8 annexe en suite (4 GF) **Facilities:** FTV iPod docking station Lounge tea/coffee Dinner available Direct dial WiFi ↟18 Fishing ⚷ **Extras:** Speciality toiletries, safe, mineral water **Conf:** Max 14 Board 14 **Parking:** 43 **Notes:** Closed 1–2 Jan RS 25 Dec eve closed for dinner

## SLOUGH
Map 6 SU97

### Furnival Lodge
★★★★ Ⓐ GUEST HOUSE

**tel:** 01753 570333 **53-55 Furnival Avenue SL2 1DH**
**email:** info@furnival-lodge.co.uk **web:** www.furnival-lodge.co.uk
**dir:** *Just off A355 (Farnham Rd), adjacent to BP garage*

In operation for more than 20 years, Furnival Lodge offers modern and spacious rooms, complete with power showers in the en suite bathrooms. Bedrooms are pleasantly decorated and guests have the use of a comfortable lounge.

**Rooms:** 10 en suite (1 fmly) (3 GF) **Facilities:** TVL WiFi **Parking:** 7

## THATCHAM
Map 5 SU56

### The Bunk Inn
★★★★★ ◎◎ INN

**tel:** 01635 200400 **Curridge RG18 9DS**
**email:** info@thebunkinn.co.uk **web:** www.thebunkinn.co.uk

The Bunk Inn is a quintessential English pub set in the pretty village of Curridge, close to Newbury Racecourse. The en suite bedrooms have plenty of character and offer impressive quality and comfort. Great beers and ales are served in peak condition in the characterful bar and great food is served, both at breakfast and at dinner, which has achieved two AA Rosettes. Private parties can be accommodated and there is plenty of parking.

**Rooms:** 9 en suite **Facilities:** tea/coffee Dinner available WiFi **Extras:** Speciality toiletries **Parking**

## WARGRAVE
Map 5 SU77

**Premier Collection**

### Copperfields
★★★★★ BED AND BREAKFAST

**tel:** 0118 348 4791 & 07802 483044 **15 Dark Lane RG10 8JU**
**email:** robertdavis48@hotmail.co.uk

An impressive house surrounded by manicured lawns, Copperfields is located in a quiet residential area and only a few miles from Henley-on-Thames. The four rooms have been very well appointed and differ in style and size; the smaller double has a private bathroom. Breakfast is served at the communal table overlooking the garden. Secure parking and free WiFi available.

**Rooms:** 4 rms (2 en suite) (2 pri facs) S £75–£95; D £85–£110* **Facilities:** FTV TVL WiFi ⚹ ⚷ **Parking:** 5

## WINDSOR
Map 6 SU97

### Rainworth House
★★★★ GUEST ACCOMMODATION

**tel:** 01753 856749 **Oakley Green Road SL4 5UL**
**email:** info@rainworthhouse.com **web:** www.rainworthhouse.com
**dir:** *Off A308 Windsor to Maidenhead road. Take 1st left into Oakley Green Rd*

In well-kept grounds near Windsor, this smart property has six individually-styled bedrooms. The richly decorated rooms are well equipped and are ideal for both business and leisure guests. Public areas include a comfortable lounge, and the dining area is a sociable setting for breakfast. Parking is available.

**Rooms:** 6 rms (5 en suite) (1 pri facs) (2 fmly) S £68–£90; D £98–£125 **Facilities:** FTV Lounge tea/coffee Direct dial WiFi ⚷ **Parking:** 10

### Innkeeper's Lodge Old Windsor
★★★★ INN

**tel:** 08451 551551 *(Calls cost 2p per minute plus your phone company's access charge)* **Staright Road, Old Winsdor SL4 2RR**
**email:** info@innkeeperslodge.com **web:** www.innkeeperslodge.com

At Innkeeper's Lodge you'll find accommodation with comfort and character in equal measure, and everything needed for a relaxing stay, from easy check-in and free parking to complimentary breakfast and a cosy pub serving great value food and drink on the doorstep. Each Lodge has quality rooms, and there are Lodges in a variety of locations from towns and cities to countryside settings across the UK.

**Rooms:** 15 en suite (2 fmly) (7 GF) **Facilities:** FTV tea/coffee Dinner available WiFi

WINDSOR *continued*

## 76 Duke Street B&B

★★★★ BED AND BREAKFAST

tel: 01753 620636 & 07884 222225 **76 Duke Street SL4 1SQ**
email: bedandbreakfast@76dukestreet.co.uk web: www.76dukestreet.co.uk
dir: *M4 junct 6 onto A332. Keep in left lane, take 1st slip road into Maidenhead Rd. At rdbt turn left, at 2nd set of lights turn left into Vansittart Rd. Duke St 1st turn on right, No 76 5th house on left*

A Victorian property situated in a quiet residential area of Windsor, just 200 metres from the River Thames and a 10-minute walk along the riverside into the centre. A warm welcome can be expected and lots of thoughtful accessories are available along with free WiFi. Guests can enjoy a selection of freshly cooked items at breakfast, made with fresh quality ingredients.

**Rooms:** 1 rm (1 pri facs) **D** £85–£95 **Facilities:** FTV Lounge TVL tea/coffee WiFi
**Extras:** Chocolates, home-made biscuits/cakes, fresh fruit

## The Windsor Trooper

★★★ INN

tel: 01753 670123 **97 St Leonards Road SL4 3BZ**
email: thewindsortrooper@live.co.uk web: www.thetrooperinnwindsor.com
dir: *M4 junct 6, at rdbt follow signs for Windsor, then straight over next 2 rdbts signed Staines-on-Thames, take 1st road on left*

Located close to many popular attractions and within walking distance of the town centre, this traditional inn provides comfortable annexed accommodation, including a family room. Dinner is served in the bright and airy conservatory, where a range of daily specials are often available. A freshly prepared breakfast is served and limited secure parking is available.

**Rooms:** 4 en suite 4 annexe en suite (1 fmly) (3 GF) **S** £70–£90; **D** £70–£90 (room only)* **Facilities:** FTV tea/coffee Dinner available WiFi Pool table **Extras:** Speciality toiletries **Parking:** 5 **Notes:** LB

| WOKINGHAM | Map 5 SU86 |

## Quarters

★★★★ GUEST ACCOMMODATION

tel: 0118 979 7071 **14 Milton Road RG40 1DB**
email: elaineizod@hotmail.com web: www.quarterswokingham.com
dir: *From town centre on A321 towards Henley & Twyford. Left at 1st mini rdbt into Milton Rd*

Located just a short walk from the town centre, a warm welcome is assured at Quarters. Stylishly decorated bedrooms are well equipped and spacious. A hearty breakfast is served around the communal dining table.

**Rooms:** 3 en suite **Facilities:** FTV DVD iPod docking station tea/coffee WiFi
**Notes:** No children 12yrs

## The Emmbrook Inn

★★★ INN

tel: 0118 978 2552 **Emmbrook Road RG41 1HG**
email: embrookinn@btconnect.com web: emmbrookinn.com
dir: *M4 junct 10 onto A329, 2m to inn*

Situated close to the M4, with direct routes to London and the southwest, this traditional English inn offers comfortable en suite accommodation, situated adjacent to the pub. Home-cooked meals can be enjoyed, along with a good range of real cask conditioned ales. An enclosed garden and front patio are available for summer drinks. Ample parking to the rear.

**Rooms:** 12 en suite (6 GF) **S** £77.50–£98.50; **D** £87.50–£108.50* **Facilities:** STV FTV tea/coffee Dinner available WiFi **Parking:** 24 **Notes:** No children 14yrs

| BRISTOL |

| BRISTOL | Map 4 ST57 |

| Premier Collection |

## Berwick Lodge

★★★★★ ◉◉ RESTAURANT WITH ROOMS

tel: 0117 958 1590 **Berwick Drive, Henbury BS10 7TD**
email: info@berwicklodge.co.uk web: www.berwicklodge.co.uk
dir: *M5 junct 17, A4018 (Westbury-on-Trym). At 2nd rdbt 1st left (Westbury-on-Trym). At next rdbt double back on dual carriageway (signed M5 (M4)). Left after brown Clifton RFC sign. At x-rds straight on, follow Berwick Lodge signs*

This delightful building was built in the late 1890s as a private manor house and is surrounded by rose and woodland gardens. The five-year renovation project has now been completed to provide very high standards of quality and comfort throughout the building, with luxurious bedrooms and bathrooms offered in a range of shapes and sizes. Fine dining can be experienced in the opulent restaurant where both dinner and breakfast will be sure to delight the most discerning of guests.

**Rooms:** 12 en suite 2 annexe en suite (2 fmly) **S** £85; **D** £99–£130* **Facilities:** STV FTV DVD Lounge tea/coffee Dinner available Direct dial Lift WiFi ⬆
**Extras:** Robes, fruit **Conf:** Max 100 Thtr 100 Class 60 Board 30 **Parking:** 100
**Notes:** LB Civ wed 100

## Valley Farm

★★★★ BED AND BREAKFAST

tel: 01275 332723 & 07799 768161 **Sandy Lane BS39 4EL**
email: valleyfarm2010@btinternet.com
dir: *Exit B3130 into Stanton Drew, right into Sandy Ln*

*(For full entry see Stanton Drew (Somerset))*

## The Washington

★★★ GUEST HOUSE

**tel:** 0117 973 3980 **11-15 St Pauls Road, Clifton BS8 1LX**
**email:** washington@cliftonhotels.com
**web:** www.cliftonhotels.com/bristolhotels/washington
**dir:** *A4018 into city, right at lights opposite BBC, house 200yds on left*

This large terraced house is within walking distance of the city centre and Clifton Village. The bedrooms are well equipped for business guests. Public areas include a modern reception lounge and a bright basement breakfast room. The property has secure parking and a rear patio garden.

**Rooms:** 46 rms (40 en suite) (4 fmly) (10 GF) **Facilities:** FTV tea/coffee Direct dial Licensed WiFi Reduced rate pass local health club & Bristol Zoo **Extras:** Fresh fruit – complimentary **Parking:** 16 **Notes:** Closed 23–31 Dec

## BUCKINGHAMSHIRE

### AMERSHAM                                                                 Map 6 SU99

## The Crown

★★★★ INN

**tel:** 01494 721541 **16 High Street HP7 0DH**
**email:** reception@thecrownamersham.com **web:** www.thecrownamersham.com
**dir:** *M40 junct 2 onto A355, continue to Amersham. Onto Gore Hill, left into The Broadway*

Originally a 16th-century coaching inn, The Crown now offers a mix of quirky, modern minimalist style blended with the character of the original building. High quality food is served daily along with a notable breakfast that will set your day off to a good start.

**Rooms:** 29 en suite 16 annexe en suite (1 fmly) (14 GF) **S** £120–£300; **D** £120–£300* **Facilities:** FTV tea/coffee Dinner available Direct dial WiFi ⛳ Spa facility access **Extras:** Speciality toiletries, snacks, wine – complimentary **Parking:** 38 **Notes:** Civ wed 60

## The Potters Arms

★★★ INN

**tel:** 01494 726222 **Fagnall Lane, Winchmore Hill HP7 0PH**
**email:** info@pottersarms.co.uk **web:** www.pottersarms.co.uk
**dir:** *From Beaconsfield on A355, left into Magpie Ln. Follow road to Winchmore Hill*

Situated in a rural location in Buckinghamshire, close to Amersham, this traditional pub offers comfortable accommodation. A warm welcome will be received, and guests can enjoy a range of classic pub favourites in the bar and restaurant. The inn has become well known for its popular Comedy Nights, attracting some top comedians.

**Rooms:** 4 en suite **Facilities:** FTV TVL tea/coffee Dinner available WiFi **Parking:** 20

### ASTON CLINTON                                                             Map 5 SP81

## Innkeeper's Lodge Aylesbury (East)

★★★★ INN

**tel:** 08451 551551 *(Calls cost 2p per minute plus your phone company's access charge)* **London Road HP22 5HP**
**email:** info@innkeeperslodge.com **web:** www.innkeeperslodge.com

At Innkeeper's Lodge you'll find accommodation with comfort and character in equal measure, and everything needed for a relaxing stay, from easy check-in and free parking to complimentary breakfast and a cosy pub serving great value food and drink on the doorstep. Each Lodge has quality rooms, and there are Lodges in a variety of locations from towns and cities to countryside settings across the UK.

**Rooms:** 11 en suite (4 fmly) (3 GF) **Facilities:** FTV tea/coffee Dinner available Direct dial WiFi

### AYLESBURY                                                                 Map 11 SP81

## Innkeeper's Lodge Aylesbury (South)

★★★★ INN

**tel:** 08451 551551 *(Calls cost 2p per minute plus your phone company's access charge)* **40 Main Street, Weston Turville HP22 5RW**
**email:** info@innkeeperslodge.com **web:** www.innkeeperslodge.com

At Innkeeper's Lodge you'll find accommodation with comfort and character in equal measure, and everything needed for a relaxing stay, from easy check-in and free parking to complimentary breakfast and a cosy pub serving great value food and drink on the doorstep. Each Lodge has quality rooms, and there are Lodges in a variety of locations from towns and cities to countryside settings across the UK.

**Rooms:** 16 en suite (5 GF) **Facilities:** FTV tea/coffee Dinner available Direct dial WiFi

### BEACONSFIELD                                                             Map 6 SU99

#### Premier Collection

## Crazy Bear Beaconsfield

★★★★★  GUEST ACCOMMODATION

**tel:** 01494 673086 **75 Wycombe End, Old Town HP9 1LX**
**email:** enquiries@crazybear-beaconsfield.co.uk **web:** www.crazybeargroup.co.uk
**dir:** *M40 junct 2, 3rd exit from rdbt, next rdbt 1st exit. Over 2 mini rdbts, on right*

Located in the heart of the old town, this former inn dating from Tudor times has been completely restored to create an exciting and vibrant environment. Award-winning cuisine in both the Thai and the English restaurants, classic cocktails and an extensive wine list can all be enjoyed. The Terrace and the Moroccan-style lounge offer a calming environment in which to relax. The bedrooms are individually appointed with unusual fabrics and dazzling colour schemes. Resident guests can also enjoy the swimming pool and Jacuzzi. The Crazy Bear Beaconsfield is well equipped to cater for private parties, weddings and business meetings. Limited secure parking available.

**Rooms:** 6 en suite 27 annexe en suite (2 GF) **Facilities:** STV Dinner available Direct dial Licensed WiFi ⬆ Jacuzzi **Extras:** Mineral water – complimentary **Conf:** Max 100 Thtr 100 Class 100 Board 60 **Parking:** 12 **Notes:** Civ wed 100

## The Pheasant

★★★★ INN

**tel:** 01844 239370 **39 Windmill Street HP18 9TG**
**email:** info@thepheasant.co.uk **web:** www.thepheasant.co.uk
**dir:** *M40 junct 7, take A329 Thame, A418 Aylesbury. At next rdbt take B4011,*
*through Long Crendon, right signed Brill*

The Pheasant is a popular local pub with well-appointed rooms some of which offer views of the Grade II listed windmill. The mill is owned by the village and is open to the public at certain times of the year. At The Pheasant all the rooms have been nicely configured to offer comfort and practicality. Real ale and cocktails are served at the bar, while the restaurant offers simple yet delicious dishes using local produce. Free parking and WiFi is available.

*The Pheasant*

**Rooms:** 2 en suite 2 annexe en suite (1 GF) **S** £75–£85; **D** £95–£110* **Facilities:** FTV Lounge tea/coffee Dinner available WiFi **Notes:** RS 25–26 Dec rooms available, no bkfst

***See advert below***

## Poletrees Farm

★★★★ FARMHOUSE

**tel:** 01844 238276 **Ludgershall Road HP18 9TZ**
**email:** poletrees.farm@btinternet.com
**dir:** *Exit S from A41 signed Ludgershall/Brill, after railway bridge 0.5m on left*

Located between the villages of Ludgershall and Brill, this 16th-century farmhouse retains many original features including a wealth of exposed beams. The bedrooms are in converted outbuildings, and the cosy dining room is the setting for a wholesome breakfast.

**Rooms:** 4 annexe en suite (2 fmly) (4 GF) **Facilities:** FTV TVL tea/coffee 🔒 **Parking:** 6
**Notes:** LB 110 acres sheep

| CHALFONT ST GILES | Map 6 SU99 |

## The Ivy House

★★★ 🛏 INN

**tel:** 01494 872184 **London Road HP8 4RS**
**email:** alfie@theivyhousechalfont.co.uk **web:** www.ivyhousechalfontstgiles.co.uk

This popular traditional English inn is more than 250 years old, and has retained some lovely period features. Situated in the heart of the Chiltern Vale surrounded by countryside it makes a popular venue for walkers or even for those heading to London, which is only 40 minutes away. Rooms are comfortably equipped and guests can enjoy dinner in the attractive restaurant, which also has a very good range of real ales and wines.

**Rooms:** 5 en suite **S** £70–£80; **D** £80–£90* **Facilities:** FTV tea/coffee Dinner available WiFi ⛳18 **Parking:** 40

| DENHAM | Map 6 TQ08 |

## The Falcon Inn

★★★★ 🛏 INN

**tel:** 01895 832125 **Village Road UB9 5BE**
**email:** mail@falcondenham.com **web:** www.falcondenham.com
**dir:** *M40 junct 1, follow A40 & Gerrards Cross signs. Approx 200yds, right into Old Mill Rd, pub opposite village green*

This 18th-century inn stands in the heart of the picturesque village of Denham, opposite the green. The en suite bedrooms, with smart shower rooms, are well equipped and display original features. Carefully prepared dishes, together with a good selection of wines, are served at both lunch and dinner in the cosy restaurant.

**Rooms:** 4 en suite **S** £65–£89; **D** £75–£99 (room only)* **Facilities:** FTV DVD tea/coffee Dinner available WiFi ⛳18 🔒 **Extras:** Fresh fruit, bottled water, speciality toiletries – complimentary **Notes:** LB No children 10yrs RS 24–26 & 31 Dec no accommodation

| GREAT MISSENDEN | Map 6 SP80 |

## Nags Head Inn & Restaurant

★★★★ ◉ INN

**tel:** 01494 862200 **London Road HP16 0DG**
**email:** goodfood@nagsheadbucks.com **web:** www.nagsheadbucks.com
**dir:** *N of Amersham on A413, left at Chiltern hospital into London Rd signed Great Missenden*

This delightful 15th-century inn, located in the picturesque Chiltern Hills, has a great reputation locally thanks to its extensive menu of local produce and carefully prepared dishes. Individually-designed bedrooms are comfortable with a modern twist ensuring a home-from-home feel. Ample parking is available.

**Rooms:** 6 en suite (1 fmly) **Facilities:** FTV DVD tea/coffee Dinner available WiFi 🔒 **Extras:** Speciality toiletries, mineral water – complimentary **Conf:** Max 50 **Parking:** 40 **Notes:** Closed 25 Dec

---

## HIGH WYCOMBE Map 5 SU89

### Clifton Lodge

★★★ GUEST HOUSE

---

**tel:** 01494 440095 **210 West Wycombe Road HP12 3AR**
**email:** mail@cliftonlodgehotel.com **web:** www.cliftonlodgehotel.com
**dir:** *A40 from town centre towards Aylesbury, on right after BP station & opposite phone box*

Located west of the town centre, this long-established, owner-managed guest house provides a range of bedrooms, popular with a regular commercial clientele. Public areas include an attractive conservatory-dining room and a cosy lounge. Ample parking behind the property.

**Rooms:** 32 en suite (1 fmly) (7 GF) **S** £45–£60; **D** £55–£70 (room only)*
**Facilities:** FTV Lounge tea/coffee Licensed WiFi **Conf:** Max 25 Thtr 25 Class 20 Board 15 **Parking:** 28 **Notes:** LB

---

### Fox Country Inn

★★★ INN

---

**tel:** 01491 638814 **Ibstone HP14 3XT**
**email:** info@foxcountryinn.co.uk **web:** www.foxcountryinn.co.uk
**dir:** *M40 junct 5 follow signs to Ibstone, 1.5m on left*

This contemporary inn enjoys a peaceful rural location on the outskirts of High Wycombe. The bedrooms are all attractively presented and have a host of thoughtful little extras. Free WiFi is available throughout. The bar and restaurant are contemporary and open-plan in style yet they retain some of the original features, with food served all day in the bar and on the terrace during the warm months of the year. Secure parking available.

**Rooms:** 18 en suite (2 fmly) (10 GF) **S** £40–£75; **D** £50–£85* **Facilities:** FTV Lounge TVL tea/coffee Dinner available Direct dial WiFi **Conf:** Max 25 Thtr 25 Class 20 Board 20 **Parking:** 23 **Notes:** Civ wed 50

---

## MARLOW Map 5 SU88

### The Prince of Wales

★★★ INN

---

**tel:** 01628 482970 **1 Mill Road SL7 1PX**
**email:** prince-of-wales@tiscali.co.uk **web:** www.the-prince-of-wales.co.uk

The Prince of Wales offers well-appointed bedrooms that meet the needs of both business and leisure travellers; some rooms are annexed and have private access. The traditional inn offers a range of ales and an appealing Thai and British menu. There is a large patio that proves ideal for relaxation in the warmer months. Ample secure parking is available.

**Rooms:** 3 en suite 3 annexe en suite (1 GF) **Facilities:** FTV tea/coffee Dinner available WiFi **Parking:** 22

---

## MEDMENHAM Map 5 SU88

### Premier Collection

### The Dog and Badger

★★★★★ ⑳ RESTAURANT WITH ROOMS

---

**tel:** 01491 579944 **Henley Road SL7 2HE**
**email:** reservations@thedogandbadger.com **web:** www.thedogandbadger.com

The Dog and Badger is a beautifully restored restaurant located in the quiet village of Medmenham. The stunning bedrooms are located in a separate cottage; all are spacious and highly comfortable with smart TVs, air conditioning, mini bars and coffee machines as standard. Bathrooms are equipped to the same high standard, all with soft fluffy towels and high quality toiletries. There is a popular feature bar, which serves a great range of wines, spirits, beers and cocktails and throughout the property there's contemporary art, which blends with original features such as exposed brick, a wood-beamed ceiling and decorative floor tiles. In the restaurant, guests are treated to a range of crowd-pleasing dishes all served in a relaxed and informal setting. WiFi is available throughout and outside seating is plentiful. There is also plenty of parking.

**Rooms:** 6 en suite **D** £195–£250 (room only)* **Facilities:** Dinner available WiFi **Extras:** Mini-bar Coffee machine

---

## NEWTON BLOSSOMVILLE Map 11 SP95

### The Old Mill

★★★ INN

---

**tel:** 01234 881273 **Clifton Road MK43 8AN**
**email:** enquiries@oldmill.uk.com **web:** www.oldmill.uk.com
**dir:** *M1 junct 14 onto A509 towards Wellingborough. In Emberton right into Newton Rd*

In the quiet and attractive village of Newton Blossomville, in the Borough of Milton Keynes, this traditional inn offers comfortable accommodation. The inn remains a friendly locals' pub and guests can also enjoy a game of skittles. A traditional pub menu offers a good range of dishes, and a selection of real ales is on offer.

**Rooms:** 5 en suite (2 fmly) **Facilities:** FTV tea/coffee Dinner available WiFi ⛹ **Extras:** Bottled water, fresh milk **Notes:** LB

---

## WADDESDON Map 11 SP71

### The Five Arrows

★★★★ ⑳⑳ ⛩ RESTAURANT WITH ROOMS

---

**tel:** 01296 651727 **High Street HP18 0JE**
**email:** reservations@thefivearrows.co.uk **web:** www.waddesdon.org.uk/fivearrows
**dir:** *On A41 in Waddesdon. Into Baker St for car park*

This Grade II listed building with its elaborate Elizabethan-style chimney stacks stands at the gates of Waddesdon Manor and was named after the Rothschild family emblem. Individually styled en suite bedrooms are comfortable and well appointed. Friendly staff are on hand to offer a warm welcome. Alfresco dining is possible in the warmer months.

**Rooms:** 8 en suite 8 annexe en suite (2 fmly) (3 GF) **S** £70–£130; **D** £95–£235*
**Facilities:** FTV tea/coffee Dinner available WiFi ⛹ **Conf:** Max 20 Thtr 20 Class 20 Board 20 **Parking:** 40 **Notes:** Civ wed 60

## WOOBURN GREEN
Map 6 SU98

# The Old Bell

★★★★ 🛏 INN

tel: 01628 523117 **HP10 0PL**
email: oldbellwooburn@hotmail.co.uk **web:** www.oldbellwooburn.co.uk
dir: *M40 junct 2, A355 towards Beaconsfield. Take A40 through Beaconsfield. Left onto B4440 to Wooburn Green. At T-junct left into Town Ln. Old Bell on left*

Dating back to the 16th century, this former coaching inn retains many of its original features, with low beams and real fires in the cosy bar. The Old Bell has a very good range of real ales, including guest ales, while the award-winning restaurant features some excellent local produce. Bedrooms are very stylish and retain many of the period features that make this place unique. Free WiFi along with ample secure parking is available for guests.

**Rooms:** 6 en suite 1 annexe en suite (2 fmly) (1 GF) **S** £90–£95; **D** £99–£140*
**Facilities:** FTV tea/coffee Dinner available WiFi ⅃18 **Parking:** 14 **Notes:** LB
Closed 1 Jan RS 25–26 Dec Bar & restaurant closes at 4pm

## CAMBRIDGESHIRE

## BALSHAM
Map 12 TL55

# The Black Bull Inn

★★★★ ❀ INN

tel: 01223 893844 **27 High Street CB21 4DJ**
email: info@blackbull-balsham.co.uk **web:** www.blackbull-balsham.co.uk
dir: *From S: M11 junct 9 towards Newmarket, exit signed Balsham, in centre of village. From N: M11 junct 10, A505 signed Newmarket (A11), exit signed Balsham*

This privately owned 16th-century, Grade II listed free house is set in the pretty village of Balsham. There are five spacious en suite bedrooms located alongside the pub which provide very high levels of quality and comfort. Excellent food is served at lunch and dinner every day.

**Rooms:** 5 annexe en suite (1 fmly) (5 GF) **Facilities:** FTV DVD Lounge tea/coffee Dinner available WiFi ⅄ **Conf:** Max 30 Thtr 30 Class 24 Board 20 **Parking:** 20
**Notes:** LB

## BURWELL
Map 12 TL56

# Deerview

★★★★ BED AND BREAKFAST

tel: 01638 741885 & 07554 300501 **133A North Street CB25 0BB**
email: bookings@deerview.biz **web:** www.deerview.biz
dir: *A14 junct 35 onto A1303 then B1102. Through Burwell, take last turn on right, at end turn left, 500yds to Deerview*

Deerview enjoys a prominent position in the heart of the peaceful village of Burwell. Bedrooms are all spacious, attractively presented and very well equipped. A warm welcome is guaranteed from the friendly owners, and the freshly prepared breakfasts are not to be missed. The house is 10 minutes from the famous Wicken Fen and a short drive from Newmarket, Ely, and Cambridge. Secure parking is available, and there is free WiFi for guests.

**Rooms:** 4 en suite (1 fmly) (2 GF) **S** fr £45; **D** fr £85* **Facilities:** FTV DVD tea/coffee WiFi ⅄ **Extras:** Bottled water, snacks – complimentary **Parking:** 4

## CAMBRIDGE
Map 12 TL45

# Benson House

★★★★ 🛏 GUEST HOUSE

tel: 01223 311594 **24 Huntingdon Road CB3 0HH**
email: bensonhouse@btconnect.com **web:** www.bensonhouse.co.uk
dir: *0.5m NW of city centre on A604*

This popular guest house is well placed for the city centre and New Hall and Fitzwilliam colleges. Its pleasant bedrooms vary in size and style and all are well equipped with TV, clock radio, beverage tray and hairdryers. The delicious selection at breakfast includes kippers, and there is limited private parking behind the property. Benson House cannot cater for pets or children under 12 years of age.

**Rooms:** 6 en suite (1 GF) **S** £75–£120; **D** £115–£120* **Facilities:** FTV iPod docking station tea/coffee WiFi **Extras:** Speciality toiletries **Parking:** 5
**Notes:** No children 12yrs Closed 31 Dec

CAMBRIDGE *continued*

## Hamden Guest House

★★★ GUEST HOUSE

**tel:** 01223 413263 & 07543 049010 **89 High Street, Cherry Hinton CB1 9LU**
**email:** info@hamdenguesthouse.co.uk **web:** www.hamdenguesthouse.co.uk
**dir:** *3m SE of city centre. From M11 exit A1134 to Cherry Hinton; from A14 exit N on A1303 signed Cambridge & Cherry Hinton*

Expect a warm welcome at this small, family-run guest house, which is just a short drive from the city centre. The pleasant bedrooms are generally quite spacious and equipped with many thoughtful extras. Public rooms include a large kitchen-dining room where breakfast is served at individual tables.

*Hamden Guest House*

**Rooms:** 5 en suite (2 fmly) (1 GF) **Facilities:** FTV tea/coffee WiFi **Parking:** 6 **Notes:** LB No children 5yrs

*See advert below*

## The Alpha Milton Guest House

★★★ GUEST ACCOMMODATION

**tel:** 01223 311625 **61-63 Milton Road CB4 1XA**
**email:** info@alphamilton.com **web:** www. alphamilton.com
**dir:** *0.5m NE of city centre*

The Alpha Milton Guest House is in a residential area just a short walk from the city centre. The attractive lounge-dining room overlooks the rear garden, and the pleasant bedrooms all have a good range of facilities.

**Rooms:** 8 rms (7 en suite) (1 pri facs) (2 fmly) (2 GF) **S** £60–£90; **D** £70–£90 (room only)* **Facilities:** FTV DVD tea/coffee WiFi **Parking:** 8

## The Carpenters Arms

★★★ ❀ INN

**tel:** 01223 367050 **182-186 Victoria Road CB4 3DZ**
**email:** hello@carpentersarmscambridge.co.uk **web:** www.carpentersarmscambridge.co.uk
**dir:** *Phone for directions*

The Carpenters Arms is a family-friendly gastro pub, located only 10 minutes' walk from the centre of Cambridge. Accommodation is available, and guests can enjoy award-winning meals in the vibrant and friendly restaurant below, alongside a good selection of real ales and craft beers. Guests can also enjoy home-made stone-baked pizza from the wood-burning pizza oven.

**Rooms:** 5 rms (2 en suite) (3 pri facs) (3 fmly) **Facilities:** FTV tea/coffee Dinner available WiFi ❧ **Conf:** Max 30 Thtr 30 Class 15 Board 15 **Parking:** 6 **Notes:** LB

---

**ELTON** Map 12 TL09

### Premier Collection

## The Crown Inn

★★★★★ ♌ ☞ INN

**tel:** 01832 280232 **8 Duck Street PE8 6RQ**
**email:** inncrown@googlemail.com **web:** www.thecrowninn.org
**dir:** *A1 junct 17, A605 W. In 3.5m right signed Elton, 0.9m, left signed Nassington. On village green*

Expect a warm welcome at this delightful village pub, situated opposite the village green. The property dates back to the 16th century. It retains many of its original features, such as a large inglenook fireplace and oak-beamed ceilings. The smartly decorated bedrooms are tastefully appointed and thoughtfully equipped. Public rooms include a large open-plan lounge bar, a small relaxed dining area to the front, and a tastefully appointed circular restaurant.

**Rooms:** 3 en suite 5 annexe en suite (3 fmly) (5 GF) **S** £73–£105; **D** £125–£200* **Facilities:** FTV tea/coffee Dinner available Direct dial WiFi ♿ **Conf:** Max 40 Thtr 25 Class 40 Board 25 **Parking:** 15 **Notes:** RS Sun eve & Mon (ex BH) & 1st week Jan Restaurant only closed

---

**ELY** Map 12 TL58

## Lazy Otter Pub Restaurant

★★★★ INN

**tel:** 01353 649780 **Cambridge Road, Stretham CB6 3LU**
**email:** thelazyotter@btconnect.com **web:** www.lazy-otter.com

The Lazy Otter enjoys an idyllic position, nestled on the banks of the River Ouse, ideally located between Cambridge and Ely. Comfortable bedrooms are all of a high standard. The restaurant overlooks the river with its boats and barges, and enjoys some lovely Fen scenery. The bar offers a range of real ales and guests can relax by roaring log fires in the cooler months. There is a very popular restaurant and the freshly cooked breakfasts are enjoyable. This is an ideal base from which to explore the countryside and delightful historic market towns.

**Rooms:** 3 en suite **Facilities:** FTV DVD iPod docking station tea/coffee Dinner available WiFi ❧ **Parking:** 60

## The Anchor Inn

★★★★ ❀ INN

**tel:** 01353 778537 **Bury Lane, Sutton Gault CB6 2BD**
**email:** anchorinn@popmail.bta.com **web:** www.anchor-inn-restaurant.co.uk
**dir:** *W of Ely. Sutton Gault signed from B1381 at S end of Sutton*

The Anchor Inn is a 17th-century traditional inn, situated outside the city of Ely, in a quiet riverside location. Bedrooms are modern yet retain some period charm, and guests can enjoy award-winning food in the restaurant.

**Rooms:** 4 en suite **Facilities:** FTV tea/coffee Dinner available Direct dial WiFi **Extras:** Bottled water, fresh milk – complimentary **Parking:** 10 **Notes:** Closed 25–26 Dec

## The Three Pickerels

★★★★ INN

**tel:** 01353 777777 **19 Bridge Road, Mepal CB6 2AR**
**email:** info@thethreepickerels.co.uk **web:** www.thethreepickerels.co.uk

Situated in the tranquil village of Mepal on the outskirts of Ely, this property sits on the banks of the New Bedford River and has views of the surrounding area. Public rooms include a smart bar, a dining room and a lovely lounge overlooking the river. The smartly appointed bedrooms are comfortable and well equipped.

**Rooms:** 4 en suite (1 fmly) **Facilities:** FTV TVL tea/coffee Dinner available WiFi Fishing Pool table **Parking:** 40 **Notes:** LB

## The Village Inn

★★★ INN

**tel:** 01353 663763 **80 Main Street, Witchford CB6 2HQ**
**email:** tarobinson@hotmail.co.uk **web:** www.villageinnwitchford.co.uk

The Village Inn offers two comfortable, well-appointed bedrooms and is located in the peaceful village of Witchford. Dinner is available in the evenings and the bar has a good choice of ales and beers. The historic town of Ely and the city of Cambridge are a short drive away. Free WiFi is available along with secure parking.

**Rooms:** 2 rms **Facilities:** Dinner available WiFi **Parking**

---

**GREAT ABINGTON** Map 12 TL54

## Three Tuns

★★★★ ☞ INN

**tel:** 01223 891467 **75 High Street CB21 6AB**
**email:** email@thethreetuns-greatabington.co.uk
**web:** www.thethreetuns-greatabington.co.uk

Visitors are guaranteed a warm welcome at this charming 16th-century inn set in a prominent position in the heart of the pretty village of Great Abington. The very popular restaurant has a well-deserved reputation for its Thai cuisine and the bar has a good selection of real ales. The purpose-built bedrooms are beautifully presented and offer guests stylish and comfortable accommodation along with high quality bathrooms. Free WiFi is available throughout the property and secure parking is provided.

**Rooms:** 9 annexe en suite (1 fmly) (9 GF) **Facilities:** STV FTV tea/coffee Dinner available WiFi **Extras:** Speciality toiletries **Parking:** 20 **Notes:** Closed 1 Jan

## HINXTON · Map 12 TL44

# The Red Lion Inn

★★★★  INN

tel: 01799 530601 **32 High Street CB10 1QY**
email: info@redlionhinxton.co.uk web: www.redlionhinxton.co.uk
dir: *Nbound only: M11 junct 9, towards A11, left onto A1301. Left to Hinxton.
Or M11 junct 10, A505 towards A11/Newmarket. At rdbt 3rd exit onto A1301,
right to Hinxton*

The Red Lion Inn is a 16th-century free house pub and restaurant, set in the pretty
conservation village of Hinxton and offering high quality purpose-built
accommodation. In the winter guests can relax by the well-stoked fire, while in
summer they can enjoy the attractive walled garden which overlooks the village
church.

**Rooms:** 8 annexe en suite (2 fmly) (8 GF) **S** £99–£129; **D** £129–£149* **Facilities:** FTV
DVD Lounge tea/coffee Dinner available Direct dial WiFi 🔒 **Conf:** Max 20 Thtr 20
Class 15 Board 15 **Parking:** 43 **Notes:** LB

## HUNTINGDON · Map 12 TL27

# The Abbot's Elm

★★★★ ⊛ INN

tel: 01487 773773 **Abbots Ripton PE28 2PA**
email: info@theabbotselm.co.uk web: www.theabbotselm.co.uk
dir: *A1(M) junct 13 onto A14 towards Huntingdon. At 1st rdbt straight on (A141 Spittals
Way). Left at 2nd rdbt signed Abbots Ripton. 3m in village centre*

This Grade II listed thatched country inn is situated in the quiet village of Abbots
Ripton, near the ancient market town of Huntingdon. Bedrooms are modern and
comfortable, and guests can enjoy a range of real ales and fine wines in the
spacious and smartly appointed bar and restaurant.

**Rooms:** 3 en suite 1 annexe en suite (4 GF) **S** £65–£70; **D** £80–£90* **Facilities:** STV
Lounge tea/coffee Dinner available WiFi **Extras:** Robes; filtered water –
complimentary **Parking:** 50

## LITTLEPORT · Map 12 TL58

# The Gate House

★★★★ ⊜ BED AND BREAKFAST

tel: 01353 863840 & 07940 120023 **2B Lynn Road CB6 1QG**
email: edna@thegatehousebandb.co.uk web: www.thegatehousebandb.co.uk
dir: *On A10 between Ely & King's Lynn. Cross railway line in Littleport, next right into Lynn
Rd, last house on left*

This new-build house has a range of beautifully presented, stylish bedrooms and is
a short walk from Littleport railway station. Rear-facing rooms have lovely views of
a spur on the River Great Ouse. Conveniently located close to Cambridge,
Newmarket and Ely, it is an ideal base to explore this lovely region. The freshly
prepared breakfasts include award-winning local produce and should not be
missed. Both ample secure parking and free WiFi are available.

**Rooms:** 3 rms (2 en suite) (1 pri facs) **Facilities:** FTV DVD Lounge tea/coffee WiFi
**Extras:** Robes, slippers, home-made biscuits **Parking:** 4

## MELBOURN · Map 12 TL34

# Sheene Mill

★★★★★ ⊛⊛ RESTAURANT WITH ROOMS

tel: 01763 261393 **39 Station Road SG8 6DX**
email: reservations@sheenemill.com web: www.sheenemill.com
dir: *M11 junct 10 onto A505 towards Royston. Right to Melbourn, pass church on right,
on left before old bridge*

This 16th-century watermill is ideally situated just off the A10, a short drive from
both Cambridge and Royston. The bedrooms are individually decorated and well
equipped; some rooms overlook the mill pond and terrace. Public rooms include
a comfortable lounge, a bar, conservatory and a delightful restaurant overlooking
the pond.

**Rooms:** 10 en suite (4 fmly) **S** £75–£95; **D** £80–£180* **Facilities:** FTV Lounge
tea/coffee Dinner available WiFi ↳18 🔒 **Extras:** Speciality toiletries – complimentary
**Conf:** Max 180 Thtr 120 Class 120 Board 60 **Parking:** 60 **Notes:** Civ wed 120

## UFFORD · Map 12 TF00

# The White Hart

★★★★ ⊜ INN

tel: 01780 740250 **Main Street PE9 3BH**
email: info@whitehartufford.co.uk web: www.whitehartufford.co.uk

Just five miles from Stamford and 10 miles from Peterborough, this charming 17th-
century inn is home to Ufford Ales, which are served in the bar. The property is built
from local stone and retains many of its original features. The delightful bedrooms
are tastefully furnished and thoughtfully equipped. Public rooms include a lounge
bar, conservatory and restaurant.

**Rooms:** 4 en suite 8 annexe en suite (7 GF) **D** £80–£120* **Facilities:** FTV tea/coffee
Dinner available WiFi ↳18 🔒 **Conf:** Max 30 Thtr 30 Class 20 Board 20 **Parking:** 30
**Notes:** Civ wed 50

## WHITTLESFORD · Map 12 TL44

# The Red Lion at Whittlesford Bridge

★★★★ ⊛ INN

tel: 01223 497070 & 497085 **Station Road, Whittlesford Bridge CB22 4NL**
email: reservations@hiexpresscambridgeduxford.co.uk
web: www.redlionwhittlesfordbridge.com

A 13th-century coaching inn with a wealth of charm and character situated in close
proximity to Duxford Air Museum, the major road networks (A11/M11) and
Whittlesford Parkway railway station. The individually designed bedrooms are well
equipped and comfortable; the public areas include a large lounge bar, a
restaurant, and a function suite as well as an outside dining area.

**Rooms:** 18 en suite **Facilities:** FTV iPod docking station Lounge tea/coffee Dinner
available Direct dial WiFi **Conf:** Max 200 Thtr 200 Class 74 Board 40 **Parking:** 80
**Notes:** Civ wed 70

## WOODHURST
Map 12 TL37

### Falcon's Nest
★★★ GUEST ACCOMMODATION

tel: 01487 741140 **The Raptor Foundation, The Heath PE28 3BT**
email: info@raptorfoundation.org.uk **web:** www.raptorfoundation.org.uk
**dir:** *On B1040 between St Ives & Somersham*

Located just a few miles from St Ives, Falcon's Nest is in the grounds of The Raptor Foundation estate. There are eight en suite rooms all with kitchenette facilities. As a resident you also get free entry into the Raptor Centre and can see many different birds of prey. Breakfasts are available at an additional cost and served in the Silent Wings Tea Room.

**Rooms:** 8 en suite (1 fmly) (8 GF) **S** fr £47.50; **D** £47.50–£75 (room only)*
**Facilities:** FTV DVD tea/coffee WiFi ⅃18 Entry to The Raptor Foundation Bird of Prey Park **Parking:** 56 **Notes:** LB

## CHESHIRE

## ALDERLEY EDGE
Map 16 SJ87

### Innkeeper's Lodge Alderley Edge
★★★★ INN

tel: 08451 551551 *(Calls cost 2p per minute plus your phone company's access charge)*
**5-9 Wilmslow Road SK9 7QN**
email: info@innkeeperslodge.com **web:** www.innkeeperslodge.com

Situated between Wilmslow and picturesque Alderley Edge, and only 12 miles from Manchester. Bedrooms are modern and offer good space and comfort. The cosy pub and restaurant offer of wide range of drinks and food. Complimentary WiFi is provided and there is on-site parking.

**Rooms:** 11 en suite (3 fmly) **Facilities:** FTV tea/coffee Dinner available WiFi **Parking:** 50

## Find out more about AA Rosettes
— see page 11

## BURWARDSLEY
Map 15 SJ55

### Premier Collection

### The Pheasant Inn
★★★★★ ⊛ INN

tel: 01829 770434 **Higher Burwardsley CH3 9PF**
email: info@thepheasantinn.co.uk **web:** www.thepheasantinn.co.uk
**dir:** *From A41, left to Tattenhall, right at 1st junct & left at 2nd Higher Burwardsley. At post office left, signed*

This delightful 300-year-old inn sits high on the Peckforton Hills and enjoys spectacular views over the Cheshire Plain. Well-equipped, comfortable bedrooms are housed in an adjacent converted barn. Creative dishes are served either in the stylish restaurant or in the traditional, beamed bar where real fires are lit in the winter months.

**Rooms:** 2 en suite 10 annexe en suite (2 fmly) (5 GF) **Facilities:** FTV tea/coffee Dinner available Direct dial WiFi ⅃18 **Parking:** 80

## CHESTER
Map 15 SJ46

*See also Malpas*

### Premier Collection

### Mitchell's of Chester
★★★★★ ♨ GUEST HOUSE

tel: 01244 679004 **28 Hough Green CH4 8JQ**
email: welcome@mitchellsofchester.com **web:** www.mitchellsofchester.com
**dir:** *1m SW of city centre. A483 onto A5104, 300yds on right in Hough Green*

A warm welcome is assured at this delightfully restored and elegant Victorian house, located on the south side of the Dee, within a 20-minute walk of the city centre. Bedrooms are very well equipped and delightfully furnished; and enjoy stylish en suite bathrooms. Guests have use of a beautiful lounge and dining room, where sumptuous breakfasts, featuring lots of local produce, are served. Both of these rooms reflect the Victorian setting.

**Rooms:** 3 en suite **S** £70–£110; **D** £94–£110* **Facilities:** FTV DVD TVL tea/coffee Licensed WiFi **Extras:** Speciality toiletries – complimentary **Parking:** 5 **Notes:** LB No children 8yrs Closed 21 Dec–2 Jan RS Sun–Wed Closed

CHESTER *continued*

## Stone Villa Chester

★★★★★ ⚇ GUEST ACCOMMODATION

**tel:** 01244 345014 & 07764 282015 **Stone Place, Hoole Road CH2 3NR**
**email:** info@stonevillachester.co.uk **web:** www.stonevillachester.co.uk
**dir:** *0.5m NE of city on A56 Hoole Rd*

Stone Villa Chester is a welcoming retreat, away from the bustling city, yet within walking distance of city centre attractions. Bedrooms have comfortable beds and a wealth of accessories which creates a home-from-home experience. Hearty breakfasts feature local produce and home-made jams. Secure parking is a bonus.

**Rooms:** 14 en suite (2 fmly) (3 GF) **S** £60–£100; **D** £90–£150 **Facilities:** FTV DVD iPod docking station Lounge tea/coffee Licensed WiFi ⚇ **Conf:** Max 10 Board 10 **Parking:** 10

## Coach House Inn

★★★★ INN

**tel:** 01244 351900 & 351143 **39 Northgate Street CH1 2HQ**
**email:** info@coachhousechester.co.uk **web:** www.coachhousechester.co.uk
**dir:** *Phone for detailed directions*

Ideally located in the centre of the city, this inn has been appointed to provide high standards of comfort and good facilities. Its sumptuous bedrooms have a wealth of thoughtful extras; some have views over the Town Hall Square and the cathedral. Staff offer informal service and a warm welcome.

**Rooms:** 8 en suite (3 fmly) **Facilities:** FTV tea/coffee Dinner available Direct dial WiFi **Notes:** Closed 25 Dec

## 80 Watergate Street

★★★★ ⚇ BED AND BREAKFAST

**tel:** 01244 314879 & 07834 042278 **80 Watergate Street CH1 2LF**
**email:** 80watergatestreet@gmail.com **web:** www.80watergatestreet.co.uk
**dir:** *M53 junct 12 onto A56, then A5268. Continue to Watergate St (A548), signed Watergate/Queensferry*

This modern and quirky townhouse is set in central Chester within a stone's throw of the famous racecourse. Guests can be assured of superbly well-equipped rooms, deeply comfortable beds dressed with fine linen and of course a notable breakfast. The top floor suite is particularly spacious. Personal attention is a feature, from tea and cake on arrival through access to the goodies cabinet to a friendly chat at breakfast. 80 Watergate Street was a finalist for the AA Friendliest B&B of the Year 2017–18.

**Rooms:** 3 en suite **Facilities:** FTV iPod docking station Lounge tea/coffee WiFi **Extras:** Snacks, coffee machine **Notes:** No children

## Lavender Lodge

★★★★ GUEST ACCOMMODATION

**tel:** 01244 323204 **46 Hoole Road CH2 3NL**
**email:** bookings@lavenderlodgechester.co.uk **web:** www.lavenderlodgechester.co.uk
**dir:** *1m NE of city centre on A56, opposite All Saints Church*

A warm welcome is assured at this smart, late Victorian house located within easy walking distance of Chester's central attractions. The comfortable bedrooms are equipped with thoughtful little extras and have modern bathrooms. Hearty breakfasts are served in the attractive dining room.

**Rooms:** 5 rms (4 en suite) (1 pri facs) (2 fmly) (2 GF) **S** £50–£60; **D** £75–£100* **Facilities:** FTV tea/coffee WiFi ⚇ **Parking:** 4 **Notes:** LB Closed 24 Dec–2 Jan

## Green Gables

★★★★ GUEST HOUSE

**tel:** 01244 372243 **11 Eversley Park CH2 2AJ**
**email:** perruzza_d@hotmail.com **web:** www.greengableschester.co.uk
**dir:** *Off A5116 Liverpool Rd signed Countess of Chester Hospital, right at 3rd pedestrian lights to Eversley Park*

Green Gables is an attractive Victorian house with pretty gardens, set in a quiet residential area close to the city centre. The well-equipped bedrooms include a family room, and there is a large, comfortable sitting room. The bright breakfast room is strikingly decorated. Off-street parking is a bonus.

**Rooms:** 2 en suite (1 fmly) **S** £50–£60; **D** £80–£85* **Facilities:** FTV DVD TVL tea/coffee WiFi ⚇ **Parking:** 8

## Hamilton Court

★★★★ GUEST HOUSE

**tel:** 01244 345387 **Hamilton Street, Hoole CH2 3JG**
**email:** hamiltoncourth@aol.com **web:** www.hamiltoncourtchester.co.uk
**dir:** *M53 junct 12, over 2 rdbts. Pass All Saints church on left, Hamilton St 2nd on left*

This friendly guest house offers a peaceful street location just a few minutes' walk from Chester railway station and city centre. Bedrooms are spacious and comfortable, and equipped with a range of thoughtful extras. Hearty breakfasts are served in the traditionally decorated dining room. Off-road parking is available.

**Rooms:** 11 en suite (2 fmly) (1 GF) **Facilities:** FTV Lounge tea/coffee Licensed WiFi ⚓18 **Parking:** 6 **Notes:** Closed 22 Dec–3 Jan

## The Old Farmhouse B&B

★★★★ BED AND BREAKFAST

tel: 01244 332124 & 07949 820119 9 Eggbridge Lane, Waverton CH3 7PE
email: jmitchellgreenwalls@hotmail.com web: www.chestereggbridgefarm.co.uk
dir: From A41 at Waverton left into Moor Ln, left into Eggbridge Ln, over canal bridge, house on right before shops

The Old Farmhouse, dating from the 18th century, is located in a village community three miles south of the city centre. The cosy bedrooms are equipped with a wealth of thoughtful extras, and the hearty breakfasts feature local and home-made produce.

Rooms: 2 rms (1 en suite) (1 pri facs) S £35–£45; D £70–£80 Facilities: FTV TVL tea/coffee WiFi 🔒 Parking: 6 Notes: LB No children 7yrs Closed 13–28 Feb RS Xmas & New Year continental breakfast only

## Innkeeper's Lodge Chester Christleton

★★★ INN

tel: 08451 551551 (Calls cost 2p per minute plus your phone company's access charge) Whitchurch Road CH3 6AE
email: info@innkeeperslodge.com web: www.innkeeperslodge.com

Innkeeper's Lodge Chester Christleton (locally known as The Cheshire Cat) offers guests comfortable bedrooms with classic decor and thoughtful amenities; some in the main house, and some in converted cottages alongside the canal. A popular lunch venue with locals, the inn provides well cooked meals served in cosy rooms, each with its own style, and most with a real fire. Large attractive outside areas are available for dining in warmer weather, with access to the canalside to walk off your meal.

Rooms: 14 en suite (3 fmly) (4 GF) Facilities: FTV tea/coffee Dinner available Direct dial WiFi

## Glen Garth

★★★ GUEST ACCOMMODATION

tel: 01244 310260 59 Hoole Road CH2 3NJ
email: glengarthguesthouse@btconnect.com web: www.glengarthguesthouse.co.uk
dir: Exit M53 onto A56, 0.5m E of city

Situated within easy walking distance of the city, family-run Glen Garth provides well-equipped bedrooms, and hearty breakfasts served in the pleasant rear dining room. Friendly, attentive service is a strength here.

Rooms: 5 rms (3 en suite) (2 pri facs) (3 fmly) S £40–£60; D £80–£100* Facilities: FTV DVD tea/coffee WiFi ⚓18 Parking: 5 Notes: LB

### CONGLETON                                                Map 16 SJ86

## The Plough Inn Eaton

★★★★ 🍽 INN

tel: 01260 280207 Macclesfield Road, Eaton CW12 2NH
email: enquiries@theploughinncheshire.com web: www.theploughinncheshire.com
dir: On A536 (Congleton to Macclesfield road), 1.5m from Congleton town centre

In the traditional Cheshire mould of half-brick, half-timber, this rural inn offers modern accommodation and hearty pub food and drink. Bedrooms, in a separate annexe, are spacious and well equipped. The stunning 17th-century barn which serves as a function and wedding suite, was moved here piece-by-piece from Wales. A large garden to the rear is also available for dining or drinks.

Rooms: 17 annexe en suite (2 fmly) (8 GF) S £55–£65; D £75–£85* Facilities: STV FTV tea/coffee Dinner available Direct dial WiFi Conf: Max 105 Thtr 80 Class 80 Board 80 Parking: 90 Notes: Civ wed 70

### CREWE                                                    Map 15 SJ75

## Corner Farm

★★★★ BED AND BREAKFAST

tel: 01270 841429 2 Pit Lane, Hough CW2 5JQ
email: leafarm@hotmail.co.uk web: www.cornerfarmathough.co.uk
dir: M6 junct 16 onto A500 towards Nantwich. 1st rdbt, take 1st left, 2nd rdbt follow signs to Hough. Over railway bridge, pass White Hart pub, left into Pit Ln, Corner Farm immediately on right

This refurbished farmhouse enjoys beautiful scenic views beyond its own large landscaped gardens. It is conveniently situated to explore nearby Chester, and further afield the Potteries. Bedrooms are very comfortably furnished, guests have access to a large well-furnished lounge, and the gardens in warmer months. A warm welcome and hearty breakfast are assured.

Rooms: 3 en suite (1 fmly) S £38–£39; D £64–£65* Facilities: FTV DVD TVL tea/coffee WiFi 🔒 Parking: 8

### FARNDON                                                  Map 15 SJ45

## The Farndon

★★★★ 🍽 INN

tel: 01829 270570 High Street CH3 6PU
email: enquiries@thefarndon.co.uk web: www.thefarndon.co.uk
dir: Just off A534 in village on main street

Located close to Chester and the north Wales coast, The Farndon is a family-run coaching inn that dates in part to the 16th century and offers traditional hospitality with a modern twist. The attractive bedrooms are well equipped, and downstairs the bar offers a selection of real ales and fine wines, together with a wide range of imaginative dishes and welcoming log fires.

Rooms: 5 en suite S £70–£80; D £85–£110* Facilities: STV FTV Lounge TVL tea/coffee Dinner available WiFi Parking: 15 Notes: LB

### KNUTSFORD                                                Map 15 SJ77

## Belle Epoque

★★★★ ⚜⚜ RESTAURANT WITH ROOMS

tel: 01565 633060 60 King Street WA16 6DT
email: info@thebelleepoque.com web: www.thebelleepoque.com

This long established fixture on the north west dining scene has welcomed guests for over 40 years. The opulent, boutique styling lives up to its name throughout the bar and restaurant where imaginative French-leaning cuisine is the centrepiece. Accommodation is in seven rooms of varying size. All are equipped to a modern standard.

Rooms: 7 en suite Facilities: Dinner available

## MALPAS
Map 15 SJ44

# Hampton House Farm

★★★★ ⚬ FARMHOUSE

**tel:** 01948 820588 **Stevensons Lane, Hampton SY14 8JS**
**email:** enquiries@hamptonhousefarm.co.uk **web:** www.hamptonhousefarm.co.uk
**dir:** *2m NE of Malpas. Exit A41 into Cholmondeley Rd, next left*

Hampton House is located on a quiet farm and offers thoughtfully appointed accommodation and a warm welcome. Parts of the house are reputed to date from 1600, and its stylish decor highlights the many period features, including a wealth of exposed beams.

**Rooms:** 2 en suite **S** £55–£80; **D** £80–£85* **Facilities:** TVL tea/coffee WiFi ⚓
**Parking:** 12 **Notes:** No children 12yrs 180 acres mixed

## MOBBERLEY
Map 15 SJ77

# The Tens at Owen House Farm

★★★★ FARMHOUSE

**tel:** 07754 370721 & 01565 873555 **Wood Lane WA16 7NY**
**email:** stay@owenhousefarm.co.uk **web:** www.owenhousefarm.co.uk
**dir:** *At x-rds of Wood Ln, continue on Small Ln. 50mtrs on left*

Owen House Farm, as the name suggests is a working farm which is being converted to a stunning wedding venue in the heart of the Cheshire countryside. Though you don't have to be at a wedding to stay! The Tens accommodation comprises spacious and very well equipped bedrooms within one of the farm's sheds. Breakfast in bed is the order of the day here with a hamper delivered to your door.

**Rooms:** 10 annexe en suite (2 fmly) (10 GF) **S** £75–£90; **D** £90–£120* **Facilities:** FTV tea/coffee Licensed WiFi **Extras:** Speciality toiletries **Parking:** 50 **Notes:** Civ wed 150 150 acres beef

## NANTWICH
Map 15 SJ65

# The Cheshire Cat

★★★★ 🍽 INN

**tel:** 01270 623020 **26 Welsh Row CW5 5ED**
**email:** hello@thecatatnantwich.com **web:** www.thecatat.com
**dir:** *M6 junct 15 follow signs to Nantwich. Left off B5341 onto Welsh Row, right into First Wood St*

Originally built in the early 17th century as almshouses for six widows, this property has been restored with a modern 21st-century twist. The inn offers comfortable, attractive accommodation. Imaginative dinners are served in the restaurant with its oak beams and glass atrium. Weekends are lively with a bustling bar.

**Rooms:** 11 en suite 3 annexe en suite (3 fmly) (5 GF) **Facilities:** FTV TVL tea/coffee Dinner available Direct dial WiFi **Extras:** Speciality toiletries **Conf:** Max 30 **Parking:** 20 **Notes:** LB

## SANDBACH
Map 15 SJ76

# Innkeeper's Lodge Sandbach, Holmes Chapel

★★★ INN

**tel:** 08451 551551 *(Calls cost 2p per minute plus your phone company's access charge)*
**Brereton Green CW11 1RS**
**email:** info@innkeeperslodge.com **web:** www.innkeeperslodge.com

Peacefully located in rural Cheshire, close to historic Sandbach, the lodge provides comfortable, modern bedrooms. It is attached to the Bears Head Vintage Inn, an attractive black-and-white building that has real fires, spacious dining areas and a wide choice of cask ales and food. A continental buffet breakfast is complimentary for all guests.

**Rooms:** 25 en suite (6 fmly) (10 GF) **Facilities:** FTV tea/coffee Dinner available WiFi

## TARPORLEY
Map 15 SJ56

# Alvanley Arms Inn

★★★★ INN

**tel:** 01829 760200 **Cotebrook CW6 9DS**
**email:** info@alvanleyarms.co.uk **web:** www.alvanleyarms.co.uk
**dir:** *M56 junct 10, follow signs for Whitchurch then A49*

This historic inn, bedecked with flowers in summer, dates back to the 17th century and the bar and dining areas still feature the original beams. Bedrooms are well equipped with complimentary WiFi access. The Alvanley Arms offers a wide choice of home-cooked meals that utilise local produce. The inn is perfectly placed for visiting the adjoining Shire Horse Centre and Countryside Park, which is popular with families, and also Delamere Forest Park and Oulton Park race circuit.

**Rooms:** 7 en suite **S** £67; **D** £100–£110* **Facilities:** FTV DVD Lounge TVL tea/coffee Dinner available WiFi ⓵18 ⚓ **Parking:** 30

## WARMINGHAM
Map 15 SJ76

# The Bear's Paw

★★★★★ ◉ INN

**tel:** 01270 526317 **School Lane CW11 3QN**
**email:** info@thebearspaw.co.uk **web:** www.thebearspaw.co.uk
**dir:** *M6 junct 17, A534, A533 signed Middlewich & Northwich. Continue on A533, left into Mill Ln, left into Warmingham Ln. Right into Plant Ln, left into Green Ln*

Located beside a small river in a rural Cheshire village, this fully modernised 19th-century red-brick inn provides spacious boutique bedrooms that have a wealth of practical extras and feature deeply comfortable beds. The friendly team serves imaginative food, which makes use of quality seasonal produce, in an attractive open-plan dining room. Relaxed lounge areas are also available.

**Rooms:** 17 en suite (4 fmly) **Facilities:** STV FTV iPod docking station Lounge tea/coffee Dinner available Direct dial WiFi **Extras:** Apple TV – deposit required **Parking:** 75 **Notes:** LB

## CORNWALL & ISLES OF SCILLY

### BODINNICK
Map 2 SX15

## The Old Ferry Inn

★★★ ⊛ INN

**tel:** 01726 870237 **PL23 1LX**
**email:** info@oldferryinn.co.uk **web:** www.oldferryinn.co.uk
**dir:** *From Liskeard on A38 to Dobwalls, left onto A390. After 3m left onto B3359 signed Looe. Right at sign for Lerryn/Bodinnick/Polruan*

The Old Ferry Inn has stood on the edge of the Fowey Estuary for over 400 years, overlooking the Bodinnick to Fowey ferry service. 'Ferryside', the childhood home of Daphne du Maurier, is at the bottom of the hill. There are plenty of coastal walks, historical buildings, fishing and wildlife nearby, with the famous Eden Project just a few miles away. A range of local beers and Cornish ciders are available, and meals can be enjoyed while gazing out over the amazing river views.

**Rooms:** 12 rms (10 en suite) (2 pri facs) (1 fmly) **S** £80–£105; **D** £80–£150*
**Facilities:** FTV Lounge TVL tea/coffee Dinner available WiFi **Parking:** 8 **Notes:** LB

### BODMIN
Map 2 SX06

## Mennabroom Farm

★★★★ ⊛ ⊛ FARMHOUSE

**tel:** 01208 821272 **Warleggan PL30 4HE**
**email:** enquiries@mennabroom.com **web:** www.mennabroom.co.uk
**dir:** *A30 take exit signed Colliford Lake. After 2.8m turn right signed Mennabroom Farm and Cottages, turn right into Mennabroom*

In the heart of Bodmin Moor, this extremely comfortable farmhouse offers a haven of peace and tranquillity for visitors to the beautiful West Country. Rooms are well appointed with quality furnishings and very comfortable beds. Guests are welcomed with afternoon tea, dinner is available on request and breakfast uses the farm's home-produced eggs, bacon and sausages. Self-catering cottages are also available.

**Rooms:** 2 en suite **S** £70; **D** £90 **Facilities:** FTV DVD Lounge tea/coffee Dinner available WiFi **Extras:** Speciality toiletries – complimentary **Parking:** 6 **Notes:** LB 40 acres sheep/pigs/beef

### BUDE
Map 2 SS20

### Premier Collection

## Pot and Barrel B&B

★★★★★ ⊛ BED AND BREAKFAST

**tel:** 01288 355305 **Crooklets Beach EX23 8NE**
**email:** chris@potandbarrel.co.uk **web:** www.potandbarrel.com
**dir:** *From town centre follow signs for Crooklets Beach. Crooklets Inn on right, turn left towards sea, pass unmade track. Take sharp right hairpin bend, proceed up hill*

Originally an elegant Edwardian gentleman's residence built 1910, the Pot and Barrel offers two well-appointed bedrooms, both furnished and decorated to a high standard. There is a guest lounge, with a cosy fire during the winter months, and the dining room has distracting coastal views. The sun lounge also boasts excellent views. A high quality breakfast with plenty of choice, including daily changing specials, is on offer each morning. Pot and Barrel B&B was a finalist for the AA Friendliest B&B of the Year 2017–18.

**Rooms:** 2 en suite (1 GF) **D** £88–£98 **Facilities:** FTV Lounge TVL tea/coffee WiFi **Extras:** Robes, fresh milk – complimentary **Parking:** 3 **Notes:** LB No children 16yrs

## Bangors Organic

★★★★ ⊛ ⊛ GUEST HOUSE

**tel:** 01288 361297 **Poundstock EX23 0DP**
**email:** info@bangorsorganic.co.uk **web:** www.bangorsorganic.co.uk
**dir:** *4m S of Bude. On A39 in Poundstock*

Situated a few miles south of Bude, this renovated Victorian establishment offers elegant accommodation with a good level of comfort. Bedrooms are furnished to a high standard with bathrooms worthy of special mention, being impressively spacious and luxurious. Breakfast and dinner, featuring organic, local and home-made produce, are served in the pleasant dining room. The establishment is certified as organic by the Soil Association.

**Rooms:** 2 en suite **Facilities:** TVL tea/coffee Dinner available Licensed WiFi **&** Badminton **Parking:** 10 **Notes:** No children 10yrs

## Pencarrol Guest House

★★★★ GUEST HOUSE

**tel:** 01288 352478 **21 Downs View EX23 8RF**
**email:** pencarrol21@gmail.com
**dir:** *0.5m N of Bude. N from Bude into Flexbury village*

This cosy guest house is only a short walk from Bude centre and Crooklets Beach, and has glorious views over the golf course. Bedrooms are attractively furnished and there is a first-floor lounge. Breakfast is served at separate tables in the dining room.

**Rooms:** 5 rms (3 en suite) (2 pri facs) (2 fmly) **S** £35–£37; **D** £74–£78*
**Facilities:** FTV tea/coffee WiFi **&** **Notes:** LB No children 10yrs Closed Nov–Feb

## The Old Wainhouse Inn

★★★ INN

**tel:** 01840 230711 & 07752 190514 **Wainhouse Corner, St Gennys EX23 0BA**
**email:** wainhouse10@yahoo.co.uk **web:** www.oldwainhouseinn.co.uk
**dir:** *On A39 between Bude & Camelford*

This popular roadside pub provides an ideal base from which to explore the wonderful countryside and dramatic coastline; the South West Coast Path is close by. The convivial bar is the focus here, with plenty of friendly banter always on offer and helpful local advice readily available. Bedrooms and bathrooms provide good levels of comfort with simple styling. Food in the bar and restaurant includes a Sunday roast and vegetarian options.

**Rooms:** 4 en suite **Facilities:** FTV tea/coffee Dinner available WiFi Pool table **&**
**Conf:** Max 50 Class 50 **Parking:** 25

## Sea Jade Guest House

★★★ GUEST ACCOMMODATION

**tel:** 01288 353404 & 07737 541540 **15 Burn View EX23 8BZ**
**email:** seajadeguesthouse@yahoo.co.uk **web:** www.seajadeguesthouse.co.uk
**dir:** *A39 turn right follow signs for Bude & golf course*

A warm welcome awaits at this popular establishment which is within a few minutes' walk of both the town and beaches. Bedrooms are light and airy with simple, contemporary styling; some have views across the golf course. Breakfast is a generous offering and guaranteed to get the day off to a satisfying start.

**Rooms:** 8 rms (7 en suite) (1 pri facs) (4 fmly) (2 GF) **S** £40–£45; **D** £78–£84*
**Facilities:** FTV TVL tea/coffee WiFi ♨18 **&** **Notes:** LB

| CALLINGTON | Map 3 SX36 |

## Woodpeckers

★★★★ GUEST HOUSE

**tel:** 01579 363717 **Rilla Mill PL17 7NT**
**email:** alisonmerchant@talktalk.net **web:** www.woodpeckersguesthouse.co.uk
**dir:** *5m NW of Callington. Exit B3254 at Upton Cross x-rds for Rilla Mill*

Set in a conservation village, in a wooded valley, by a tumbling stream, this modern, detached house offers cosy, well-equipped bedrooms with numerous thoughtful extras. Home-cooked dinners, using the best of local ingredients, are available by prior arrangement. The hot tub in the garden is an additional feature.

**Rooms:** 3 en suite **D** £75–£80* **Facilities:** STV FTV tea/coffee Dinner available Gym ♨ Spa/Hot tub **Parking:** 7 **Notes:** LB

| CAMELFORD | Map 2 SX18 |

## Toppesfield House B&B

★★★★ BED AND BREAKFAST

**tel:** 01840 211211 & 07789 462559 **26 Mill Lane PL32 9UF**
**email:** karenwilder9@aol.com **web:** toppesfieldhousebnb.co.uk
**dir:** *From High St, turn into Mill Ln (opposite The Masons Arms). Up hill, pass Greenhills on left, fork right, 2nd house on right*

With gardens overlooking Enfield Park, this bed and breakfast offers comfortable and inviting accommodation paired with warm hospitality. The well-presented en suite bedrooms, with garden views, are furnished to a high standard with many thoughtful extras. Private parking available as is a good choice for breakfast, a great way to start the day.

**Rooms:** 3 en suite (2 fmly) **S** £80–£90; **D** £90–£100* **Facilities:** STV FTV tea/coffee WiFi **Parking:** 3 **Notes:** No children 12yrs

| CRAFTHOLE | Map 3 SX35 |

## Little Fox

★★★★ INN

**tel:** 01503 230863 **PL11 3BD**
**email:** info@littlefoxhotel.co.uk **web:** www.littlefoxhotel.co.uk

This attractive, historic 14th-century inn enjoys an imposing position in the rolling Cornish countryside. Bedrooms, many with pleasant views, have a homely feel, and all are comfortable and have impressive modern facilities. Public areas have an engaging charm and the restaurant provides a relaxing environment with an impressive menu selection. Breakfasts are tasty and freshly cooked.

**Rooms:** 7 en suite 4 annexe en suite (5 fmly) (3 GF) **S** £60–£70; **D** £90–£110* **Facilities:** FTV Lounge TVL tea/coffee Dinner available WiFi ♨ ⚓18 ♨ **Conf:** Max 30 Thtr 30 Class 30 Board 30 **Parking:** 60 **Notes:** LB Civ wed 120

| FALMOUTH | Map 2 SW83 |

**Premier Collection**

## Anacapri

★★★★★ GUEST ACCOMMODATION

**tel:** 01326 311454 **Gyllyngvase Road TR11 4DJ**
**email:** anacapri@btconnect.com **web:** www.hotelanacapri.co.uk
**dir:** *A39 (Truro to Falmouth), straight on at lights. Over next 2 rdbts into Melvill Rd, down hill, 2nd right into Gyllyngvase Rd, Anacapri on right*

With stunning views out across the sea and beach, this well managed property offers friendly, attentive service from a young and upbeat team, with jolly managers Peter and June at the helm to oversee guest care. Smart and extremely comfortable bedrooms are spacious, and many rooms enjoying splendid sea views. Public areas are varied and include a smart bar and lounge where guests can enjoy drinks and snacks, and ample seating is provided on the delightful sea facing patio. A superb establishment where guests are made to feel welcome and at home. The hosts are ready to offer all sorts of interesting and additional information on the location and region.

**Rooms:** 16 en suite (3 fmly) (2 GF) **S** fr £35; **D** fr £50* **Facilities:** FTV TVL tea/coffee Licensed WiFi ♨ **Conf:** Max 50 Thtr 50 Class 40 Board 20 **Parking:** 18 **Notes:** LB

## Bosanneth Guest House

★★★★ GUEST ACCOMMODATION

**tel:** 01326 314649 **Gyllyngvase Hill TR11 4DW**
**email:** stay@bosanneth.co.uk **web:** www.bosanneth.co.uk
**dir:** *From Truro on A39 follow signs for beaches/docks, 3rd right mini rdbt Melvil Rd, 3rd right into Gyllyngvase Hill*

This well situated property, just a two-minute walk from the beach, offers stylish and individually decorated bedrooms and a very warm welcome from the friendly hosts. Some bedrooms have a sea view, and dinner is served each evening. A full Cornish breakfast is served in the dining room.

**Rooms:** 8 en suite **Facilities:** FTV Lounge tea/coffee Dinner available Licensed WiFi **Extras:** Speciality toiletries, robes **Parking:** 7 **Notes:** LB No children Closed Nov

## The Rosemary

★★★★ 🍴 GUEST ACCOMMODATION

**tel:** 01326 314669 **22 Gyllyngvase Terrace TR11 4DL**
**email:** stay@therosemary.co.uk **web:** www.therosemary.co.uk
**dir:** *A39 Melvill Rd signed to beaches & seafront, right into Gyllyngvase Rd, 1st left*

Just a short walk from the beach, this welcoming establishment is conveniently located for exploring the local area. The well-equipped bedrooms all provide impressive levels of comfort and quality, with many having the added bonus of wonderful views across Falmouth Bay. Breakfast is a generous and tasty start to the day, and is served in the light and airy dining room. Other facilities include a bar and guest lounge, while outside a decked area and rear garden are also available for guests.

**Rooms:** 8 en suite (2 fmly) **S** fr £50; **D** fr £79* **Facilities:** FTV DVD Lounge tea/coffee Licensed WiFi 🦮 **Extras:** Speciality toiletries **Parking:** 2 **Notes:** LB Closed mid Dec–beginning of Feb

## Melvill House

★★★★ GUEST ACCOMMODATION

**tel:** 01326 316645 **52 Melvill Road TR11 4DQ**
**email:** melvillhouse@btconnect.com **web:** www.melvill-house-falmouth.co.uk
**dir:** *On A39 near town centre & docks*

Well situated for the beach, the town centre and the National Maritime Museum on the harbour, Melvill House is a family-run establishment with a relaxed atmosphere. Some bedrooms have four-poster beds, and breakfast is served in the smart dining room. Ample parking.

**Rooms:** 7 en suite (2 fmly) (1 GF) **S** £40–£55; **D** £75–£95 **Facilities:** FTV TVL tea/coffee WiFi 🦮 **Parking:** 8 **Notes:** LB

## The Rathgowry

★★★★ GUEST HOUSE

**tel:** 01326 313482 **Gyllyngvase Hill TR11 4DN**
**email:** enquiries@rathgowry.co.uk **web:** www.rathgowry.co.uk
**dir:** *A39 into Falmouth, over 1st & 2nd rdbts. After 300mtrs turn right into Gyllyngvase Hill, half way down on left*

Located in a quieter residential area yet only a few minutes' stroll from the beach and 15 minutes from the town centre, this traditionally styled property offers a range of differently sized, well-equipped bedrooms and bathrooms. There are extra thoughtful touches in the rooms, and free WiFi is provided throughout the property. A varied menu is offered at breakfast including ample choice of cereals and preserves, with a bumper full English cooked option.

**Rooms:** 9 rms (7 en suite) (2 pri facs) (1 fmly) **S** £38–£45; **D** £76–£96*
**Facilities:** FTV tea/coffee WiFi **Extras:** Bottled water, fresh milk, chocolate **Parking:** 7 **Notes:** Closed Nov–Mar

## Rosemullion

★★★★ GUEST ACCOMMODATION

**tel:** 01326 314690 **Gyllyngvase Hill TR11 4DF**
**email:** gail@rosemullionhotel.co.uk **web:** www.rosemullionhotel.co.uk

Recognisable by its mock-Tudor exterior, this warm and friendly establishment is well situated for both the town centre and the beach. Some of the comfortable bedrooms are on the ground floor, while a few rooms on the top floor have views to Falmouth Bay. Breakfast, served in the panelled dining room, is freshly cooked and there is a well appointed lounge.

**Rooms:** 13 rms (11 en suite) (2 pri facs) (3 GF) **S** £45–£55; **D** £70–£97
**Facilities:** FTV Lounge tea/coffee WiFi **Parking:** 13 **Notes:** LB No children Closed 23 Dec–3 Jan

## The Westcott Guest House

★★★★ GUEST HOUSE

**tel:** 01326 311309 **Gyllyngvase Hill TR11 4DN**
**email:** thewestcott@outlook.com **web:** www.thewestcottfalmouth.co.uk

The Westcott is a modern guest house situated just minutes from Falmouth beach and within easy walking distance of busy Falmouth harbour with its many interesting shops, art galleries, restaurants and trendy bars, a foodies' paradise. The hosts are friendly and attentive and really know how to make their guests feel at home. The bedrooms are very well appointed; in addition there is a large guest lounge with an honesty bar and lots of extra thoughtful touches. There is some private parking.

**Rooms:** 9 en suite **S** £50–£55; **D** £60–£95* **Facilities:** FTV TVL tea/coffee Licensed WiFi Pool table 🦮 **Extras:** Sweets **Parking:** 7 **Notes:** LB No children 12yrs Closed 14 Dec–14 Jan

## Trevoil Guest House

★★★ GUEST HOUSE

**tel:** 01326 314145 & 07966 409782 **25 Avenue Road TR11 4AY**
**email:** alan.jewel@btconnect.com **web:** www.trevoilfalmouth.co.uk
**dir:** *Exit A39 (Melvill Rd) left into Avenue Rd, 150yds from Maritime Museum*

Located within walking distance of the town centre, the friendly Trevoil is a comfortable and relaxed place to stay. Breakfast is enjoyed in the light, pleasant dining room.

**Rooms:** 8 rms (4 en suite) (3 fmly) (1 GF) **S** £30–£35; **D** £60–£70* **Facilities:** FTV tea/coffee WiFi **Parking:** 7 **Notes:** LB

## GWEEK                              Map 2 SW72

# Black Swan
★★★★ INN

**tel:** 01326 221502 **TR12 6TU**
**email:** bookings@blackswangweek.co.uk **web:** www.blackswangweek.co.uk
**dir:** *In village centre*

The Black Swan inn is in the picturesque village of Gweek, a stone's throw from the popular Cornish Seal Sanctuary. This delightful inn has been restored to its former glory, and the stylish en suite bedrooms are comfortable and enhanced with homely touches. Food is sourced with care, ensuring local produce is used whenever possible; an extensive blackboard menu showcases pub classics and favourites. The selection of Cornish ales is not to be missed.

**Rooms:** 4 en suite **Facilities:** FTV tea/coffee Dinner available WiFi Pool table **Parking:** 15

## HAYLE                                Map 2 SW53

# The Penellen
★★★★ GUEST ACCOMMODATION

**tel:** 01736 753777 **64 Riviere Towans, Phillack TR27 5AF**
**email:** penellen@btconnect.com **web:** www.penellen.co.uk
**dir:** *From A30 onto B3301 through Hayle. Turn opposite petrol station, road bears to left, into private road*

Superbly situated at the water's edge, this personally run, friendly property has splendid views of the beach and coastline. Bedrooms are well equipped and comfortable, many with patio doors and stunning views to wake up to each morning. The dining room is spacious with a bright and airy feel. The cheerful hosts provide attentive service. Food is a strength, with good quality produce on offer.

**Rooms:** 5 en suite (2 fmly) **Facilities:** FTV tea/coffee WiFi **Parking:** 10 **Notes:** Closed Nov–Feb

## LAUNCESTON                          Map 3 SX38

### Premier Collection

# Wheatley Farm
★★★★★ FARMHOUSE

**tel:** 01566 781232 **Maxworthy PL15 8LY**
**email:** valerie@wheatley-farm.co.uk **web:** www.farmstay-cornwall.co.uk
**dir:** *From A39 at Wainhouse Corner follow signs to Canworthy Water. At T-junct, left & after 1.5m turn left at sign to Wheatley Farm. 1st farm on left*

This working dairy farm dates back to 1871 and was originally part of the estate of Lord Bedford. Surrounded by wonderful rolling countryside, the family have been farming here for five generations. A pot of tea is always on offer for arriving guests with every effort made to ensure a relaxing and rewarding stay. Bedrooms all provide high levels of comfort, likewise the modern bathrooms. Breakfast is a treat, served in the lovely dining room complete with original slate floor and imposing granite fireplace. Additional facilities include a guest lounge, heated indoor swimming pool, spa and sauna.

**Rooms:** 4 en suite **S** £50–£60; **D** £82–£84* **Facilities:** FTV DVD TVL tea/coffee WiFi Pool table Spa bath Sauna **Parking:** 4 **Notes:** LB No children Closed Nov–Mar 232 acres dairy

# Hurdon Farm
★★★★ FARMHOUSE

**tel:** 01566 772955 **PL15 9LS**
**email:** hurdonfarm@hotmail.co.uk **web:** www.hurdonfarm.weebly.com
**dir:** *A30 onto A388 to Launceston, at rdbt exit for hospital, 2nd right signed Trebullett, premises 1st on right*

Genuine hospitality is assured at this delightful 18th-century granite farmhouse. The bedrooms are individually furnished and decorated, and equipped with numerous extras. The delicious dinners, which need to be booked in advance, use only the best local produce, and include home-made puddings and the farm's own clotted cream.

**Rooms:** 6 en suite (1 fmly) (1 GF) **Facilities:** FTV TVL tea/coffee Dinner available WiFi **Parking:** 10 **Notes:** LB Closed Nov–Apr 400 acres mixed

# Bradridge Farm
★★★★ FARMHOUSE

**tel:** 01409 271264 & 07748 253346 **PL15 9RL**
**email:** angela@bradridgefarm.co.uk **web:** www.bradridgefarm.co.uk
**dir:** *5.5m N of Launceston. Exit B3254 at Ladycross sign for Boyton, Bradridge 2nd farm on right after Boyton school*

This late Victorian farmhouse stands in glorious countryside on the border of Devon and Cornwall. The well-presented bedrooms have many considerate extras, and the Aga-cooked breakfasts feature farm-fresh eggs.

**Rooms:** 4 rms (3 en suite) (1 fmly) **Facilities:** FTV Lounge TVL tea/coffee WiFi Fishing **Parking:** 6 **Notes:** LB Closed Nov–Mar 250 acres arable/beef/sheep/hens

# Middle Tremollett Farm B&B
★★★★ FARMHOUSE

**tel:** 01566 782416 & 07973 435529 **Coad's Green PL15 7NA**
**email:** btrewin@btinternet.com **web:** www.tremollett.co.uk
**dir:** *A30 onto B3257, through village of Coad's Green. Turn right signed Tremollett, 1st on left at bottom of hill*

Genuine hospitality is assured at this delightful granite farmhouse surrounded with breathtaking views of the countryside. The bedrooms are individually furnished and decorated, and equipped with numerous extras. The delicious breakfasts use only the best local produce, and include home-made produce and the farm's own eggs.

**Rooms:** 2 en suite **S** £38–£42; **D** £72–£84* **Facilities:** FTV TVL tea/coffee WiFi 18 **Extras:** Speciality toiletries **Parking:** 3 **Notes:** LB No children 12yrs Closed Dec–Feb 100 acres arable/beef/sheep

# Tyne Wells House
★★★★ BED AND BREAKFAST

**tel:** 01566 775810 **Pennygillam PL15 7EE**
**email:** btucker@talktalk.net **web:** www.tynewells.co.uk
**dir:** *0.6m SW of town centre. Exit A30 onto Pennygillam rdbt, house off rdbt*

Situated on the outskirts of town, Tyne Wells House has panoramic views over the countryside. There's a relaxed and friendly atmosphere and the bedrooms are neatly furnished. A hearty breakfast is served in the dining room, which overlooks the garden.

**Rooms:** 3 rms (2 en suite) (1 pri facs) (1 fmly) **S** £35–£45; **D** £60–£75 **Facilities:** FTV DVD tea/coffee WiFi **Extras:** Shared fridge **Parking:** 4 **Notes:** LB

## LEEDSTOWN
Map 2 SW63

### Little Pengelly Farm

★★★★ FARMHOUSE

**tel:** 01736 850452 **Trenwheal TR27 6BP**
**email:** maxine@littlepengelly.co.uk **web:** www.littlepengelly.co.uk
**dir:** *From Hayle on B3302 towards Helston. Through Leedstown, after 2m at top of hill turn left. 1st house on right*

Little Pengelly Farm is situated in beautiful countryside about five miles from both the north and south coasts of the Cornish peninsula. B&B and self-catering accommodation are on offer, as well as a tea room serving freshly baked scones with home-made jam. The three guest rooms are bright and comfortable and enjoy views of the garden and courtyard. A farmhouse breakfast is served in the conservatory overlooking the gardens. A laundry service and free WiFi are available, and there is ample parking on site.

**Rooms:** 3 rms (2 en suite) (1 pri facs) (1 fmly) **D** £75–£115* **Facilities:** FTV tea/coffee WiFi **Extras:** Speciality toiletries – complimentary **Parking:** 10
**Notes:** LB Closed 23 Dec–2 Jan 10 acres arable

## LISKEARD
Map 2 SX26

*See also Callington*

### Trecarne House

★★★★ GUEST ACCOMMODATION

**tel:** 01579 343543 & 07950 262682 **Penhale Grange, St Cleer PL14 5EB**
**email:** trish@trecarnehouse.co.uk **web:** www.trecarnehouse.co.uk
**dir:** *B3254 N from Liskeard to St Cleer. 1st right after entering village, 3rd left after church, 2nd right, house on right*

A warm welcome awaits at Trecarne House, a large family home, peacefully located on the edge of the village. The stylish and spacious bedrooms enjoy magnificent country views and have many thoughtful extras. The buffet-style breakfast offers a wide choice, which can be enjoyed in the dining room or bright conservatory overlooking rolling countryside.

**Rooms:** 3 en suite (2 fmly) (1 GF) **S** £65–£105; **D** £85–£120 **Facilities:** FTV DVD iPod docking station TVL tea/coffee Dinner available WiFi **Table tennis Trampoline
**Extras:** Speciality toiletries **Conf:** Max 25 **Parking:** 8 **Notes:** LB

### Cheesewring

★★★ INN

**tel:** 01579 362321 **Minions PL14 5LE**
**email:** thecheesewring@gmail.com **web:** www.cheesewringhotel.co.uk
**dir:** *From Liskeard at rdbt into St Cleer Rd (B3254) (St Cleer). 1m, left signed St Cleer. Through St Cleer. At T-junct right (Minions), 2m to Minions*

This attractive and historic inn has an imposing position on the edge of Dartmoor, a great location for some beautiful walks and observation of the abundant wildlife. Each of the guest rooms is warm and inviting, and all have impressive modern facilities. A good choice of dishes is offered at lunch and dinner in the atmospheric restaurant-bar, and guests can relax in front of lovely open fires.

**Rooms:** 3 en suite **S** £45; **D** £70* **Facilities:** FTV tea/coffee Dinner available WiFi
**Parking:** 30

## LOOE
Map 2 SX25

### The Beach House

★★★★★ GUEST ACCOMMODATION

**tel:** 01503 262598 **Marine Drive, Hannafore PL13 2DH**
**email:** enquiries@thebeachhouselooe.co.uk **web:** www.thebeachhouselooe.co.uk
**dir:** *From Looe W over bridge, left to Hannafore & Marine Drive, on right after Tom Sawyers B&B*

As its name would suggest, this property has panoramic sea views and is just a short walk from the harbour, restaurants and town. Some rooms have stylish hand-made furniture, and the bedrooms are well equipped and have many extras. Hearty breakfasts are served in the first-floor dining room, providing a good start for walking the South West Coast Path which passes right by the house.

**Rooms:** 5 en suite (4 GF) **S** £75–£130; **D** £85–£130 **Facilities:** FTV Lounge tea/coffee WiFi Beauty treatment room **Extras:** Speciality toiletries, fresh fruit – complimentary **Parking:** 6 **Notes:** LB No children 16yrs Closed Xmas

LOOE *continued*

## Bucklawren Farm

★★★★ FARMHOUSE

**tel:** 01503 240738 **St Martin-by-Looe PL13 1NZ**
**email:** info@bucklawren.co.uk **web:** www.bucklawren.co.uk
**dir:** *2m NE of Looe. Off B3253 to Monkey Sanctuary, 0.5m right to Bucklawren, farmhouse 0.5m on left*

This spacious 19th-century farmhouse stands in 400 acres of farmland just a mile from the beach. The attractive bedrooms, including one on the ground floor providing wheelchair access, are well equipped, and the front-facing rooms have spectacular views across fields to the sea. Breakfast is served in the dining room with stunning views of the rolling countryside.

**Rooms:** 6 en suite (3 fmly) (1 GF) **S** £50–£65; **D** £85–£95* **Facilities:** FTV Lounge TVL tea/coffee WiFi ⚓ **Extras:** Speciality toiletries, fridge **Parking:** 6 **Notes:** LB No children 5yrs Closed 20-27 Dec 400 acres arable/beef

## Meneglaze Guest House

★★★★ GUEST HOUSE

**tel:** 01503 269227 & 07717 288497 **Shutta PL13 1LU**
**email:** dannycornwall@outlook.com **web:** www.meneglaze.com
**dir:** *A387, opposite railway station turn into Shutta, 100yds on left*

Built in 1860, this delightful guest house was formerly a sea captain's house. It has a private parking area and offers modern comfort and style just a five-minute, easy walk from the centre of Looe. Meneglaze maintains elements of its seafaring days with hints of the nautical throughout the decor. All rooms have tea and coffee making facilities, mini-bar fridges, sumptuous towelling gowns, Egyptian cotton bedding, flat-screen TV with Freeview and free WiFi. Breakfasts are hearty and proudly Cornish. Expect the best quality home-made marmalades and jams and the finest (award winning) Hog's Pudding available each morning.

**Rooms:** 4 en suite **D** £70–£105* **Facilities:** FTV iPod docking station tea/coffee WiFi ⚓ **Extras:** Safe, fridge, fruit, minibar, home-made biscuits, sweets, flowers **Parking:** 6 **Notes:** LB No children 14yrs

## Trehaven Manor

★★★★ ⚬ ⚮ GUEST ACCOMMODATION

**tel:** 01503 262028 **Station Road PL13 1HN**
**email:** enquiries@trehavenhotel.co.uk **web:** www.trehavenhotel.co.uk
**dir:** *In East Looe between railway station & bridge. Trehaven's drive adjacent to The Globe public house*

Run by a charming family, this former rectory is in a stunning location with magnificent views of the estuary. Many of the attractive bedrooms have views, and all are particularly well equipped. There is also a cosy lounge bar. Dinner, by arrangement, specialises in Oriental cuisine, and breakfast features traditional fare; the meals are memorable.

**Rooms:** 7 en suite (1 fmly) (1 GF) **Facilities:** TVL tea/coffee Dinner available Licensed **Parking:** 8 **Notes:** LB

## Tremaine Farm

★★★★ FARMHOUSE

------------------------------------------------------------------

**tel:** 01503 220417 **Pelynt PL13 2LT**
**email:** rosemary@tremainefarm.co.uk **web:** www.tremainefarm.co.uk
**dir:** *5m NW of Looe. B3359 N from Pelynt, left at x-rds*

Convenient for Fowey, Looe and Polperro, this pleasant working farm offers a relaxing and rewarding stay. The proprietors provide friendly hospitality and attentive service, and the spacious and stylish bedrooms are well equipped with impressive bathrooms. A hearty breakfast is served in the dining room and there is also a spacious and comfortable guest lounge.

**Rooms:** 3 en suite (1 fmly) **S** £40–£45; **D** £80 **Facilities:** FTV DVD iPod docking station TVL tea/coffee WiFi **Extras:** Fridge **Parking:** 6 **Notes:** LB 250 acres arable/sheep

## Trenake Manor Farm

★★★★ FARMHOUSE

------------------------------------------------------------------

**tel:** 01503 220835 & 07812 982775 **Pelynt PL13 2LT**
**email:** lorraine@cornishfarmhouse.co.uk **web:** www.cornishfarmhouse.co.uk
**dir:** *A38 onto A390 then B3359. Right at small x-rds, signed Trenake Farm*

This welcoming 15th-century farmhouse is surrounded by countryside and makes a good base for touring Cornwall. Bedrooms have thoughtful finishing touches and there is a comfortable lounge. Breakfast, using local produce, is served in the cosy dining room. You may see the milking cows passing the end of the garden.

**Rooms:** 3 en suite (1 fmly) **S** £50–£65; **D** £80–£82* **Facilities:** STV FTV Lounge TVL tea/coffee Dinner available WiFi **Parking:** 10 **Notes:** LB 1,000 acres dairy/beef/arable

## Commonwood Manor

★★★★ GUEST ACCOMMODATION

------------------------------------------------------------------

**tel:** 01503 262929 & 07795 258699 **St Martins Road PL13 1LP**
**email:** director@commonwoodmanor.com **web:** www.commonwoodmanor.com
**dir:** *From centre of Looe, on A387, right onto B3253, 200yds on right*

Commonwood Manor is a building steeped in history, with high ceilings, panoramic views of the Looe valley, and grand fireplaces. Refurbishments respect the tradition and history of the building, but you can still look forward to all the comforts you'd expect from a modern guest accommodation. Despite the grand surroundings, the atmosphere is relaxed, with a family-run feel. Bedrooms are situated over three floors offering great views. Breakfast is served daily in the family kitchen, a substantial offering that makes for a great start to the day.

**Rooms:** 7 en suite (3 fmly) **D** £80–£125* **Facilities:** FTV Lounge tea/coffee Licensed WiFi ⊛⬥ ♨18 Pool table **Extras:** Snacks **Conf:** Max 30 Thtr 20 Class 30 Board 12 **Parking:** 14 **Notes:** LB Civ wed 65

## Little Harbour

★★★ GUEST HOUSE

------------------------------------------------------------------

**tel:** 01503 262474 & 07846 575262 **Church Street PL13 2EX**
**email:** littleharbour@btconnect.com **web:** www.littleharbour.co.uk
**dir:** *From West Looe harbour, right into Princess Sq, guest house on left*

Little Harbour is situated almost on Looe's harbour in the historic old town; it is in a pleasant and convenient spot and some parking is available. The proprietors are friendly and attentive, and bedrooms are well appointed and attractively decorated. Breakfast is served, freshly cooked, in the dining room.

**Rooms:** 5 en suite (1 fmly) **S** £45–£60; **D** £54.50–£100* **Facilities:** STV FTV TVL tea/coffee WiFi Gym ⬥ ♨ **Conf:** Max 14 Thtr 14 Class 14 Board 14 **Parking:** 3 **Notes:** LB No children 5yrs

## The Ship Inn

★★★ INN

------------------------------------------------------------------

**tel:** 01503 263124 **Fore Street PL13 1AD**
**email:** reservations@smallandfriendly.co.uk **web:** www.smallandfriendly.co.uk

This lively family pub is located in the very heart of bustling East Looe and has a local following. The bedrooms are comfortable and equipped with all the expected facilities. A wide range of popular dishes is served at lunch and during the evenings, with light refreshments available throughout the day.

**Rooms:** 8 en suite (1 fmly) **Facilities:** FTV tea/coffee Dinner available WiFi Pool table ♨ **Notes:** LB

------------------------------------------------------------------

**LOSTWITHIEL**                 **Map 2 SX15**

**Premier Collection**

## The Old Chapel B&B

★★★★★ GUEST ACCOMMODATION

------------------------------------------------------------------

**tel:** 01579 321260 & 07979 234743 **West Taphouse PL22 0RP**
**email:** enquiries@theoldchapelbandb.co.uk **web:** www.theoldchapelbandb.co.uk
**dir:** *From Bodmin follow signs to Lostwithiel. In town, turn left onto A390. After 3m into West Taphouse, last property on left*

Friendly hosts Greg and Kimberley offer a genuine welcome at The Old Chapel. The beautifully refurbished bedrooms and bathrooms are well equipped with additional thoughtful touches, including chocolates, shortbread biscuits and fresh milk for tea and coffee. The region has much to offer, as sightseeing and activities are plentiful. The hosts have designed their own "Carless breaks" for those who wish to enjoy their trip with the option of leaving the car at home.

**Rooms:** 4 rms (3 en suite) (1 pri facs) **S** £65–£90; **D** £70–£95* **Facilities:** FTV DVD tea/coffee Dinner available WiFi ♨ **Extras:** Home-made biscuits, sweets, flowers – complimentary **Parking:** 6 **Notes:** LB No children 13yrs

## Hazelmere House

★★★★ BED AND BREAKFAST

------------------------------------------------------------------

**tel:** 01208 873315 **58 Grenville Road PL22 0RA**
**email:** hazelmerehouse@aol.com **web:** www.hazelmerehouse.co.uk

Hazelmere House is a professionally run B&B where guests are welcomed with a smile and made to feel at home. The rooms are very well appointed and equipped. All three rooms offer great views over the beautiful Fowey Valley and beyond. The award-winning breakfast is served at the communal table in the formal dining room. The garden offers peace and tranquillity.

**Rooms:** 3 en suite **S** £50–£70; **D** £85–£90* **Facilities:** STV FTV iPod docking station TVL tea/coffee WiFi ⬥ ♨18 **Extras:** Speciality toiletries **Parking:** 6 **Notes:** Closed 23 Dec–2 Jan

**LOSTWITHIEL** *continued*

## Penrose B&B

★★★★ GUEST ACCOMMODATION

**tel:** 01208 871417 & 07766 900179 **1 The Terrace PL22 0DT**
**email:** enquiries@penrosebb.co.uk **web:** www.penrosebb.co.uk
**dir:** *In Lostwithiel on A390 (Edgcumbe Rd) into Scrations Ln, turn 1st right for parking*

Just a short walk from the town centre, this grand Victorian house offers comfortable accommodation and a genuine homely atmosphere. Many of the bedrooms have the original fireplaces and all are equipped with thoughtful extras. Breakfast is a generous offering and is served in the elegant dining room, with views over the garden. WiFi access is also available.

**Rooms:** 6 en suite (3 fmly) (2 GF) **Facilities:** FTV DVD TVL tea/coffee WiFi 🔒
**Extras:** Speciality toiletries, robes, sweets – complimentary **Parking:** 8 **Notes:** LB

## Hartswell Farm

★★★ FARMHOUSE

**tel:** 01208 873419 **St Winnow PL22 0RB**
**email:** hartswell@connexions.co.uk **web:** www.cornish-connexions.co.uk/hartswell
**dir:** *1m E of Lostwithiel. S off A390 at Downend Garage & St Winnow School, farm 0.25m up hill on left*

This 17th-century farmhouse has a wonderfully peaceful setting, and offers generous hospitality and a homely atmosphere. The cosy bedrooms look across rolling countryside, and breakfast includes tasty eggs fresh from the farm. A self-catering barn conversion is available. Hartswell Farm boasts a small herd of Red Poll cattle.

**Rooms:** 2 rms (1 en suite) (1 pri facs) **Facilities:** STV TVL tea/coffee WiFi 🔒 Sailing days for 5 night stays **Parking:** 3 **Notes:** LB No children 6yrs 52 acres sheep

**LUXULYAN** Map 2 SX05

## Ivy Cottage

★★★★ BED AND BREAKFAST

**tel:** 01726 850796 & 07707 038966 **PL30 5DW**
**email:** liz.edwards1@btinternet.com **web:** www.ivycottage-luxulyan.co.uk
**dir:** *A30 exit at Innis Downs onto A391. Follow signs to Eden Project. At rdbt take 1st exit signed Luxulyan. Pass Kings Arms pub, over rail bridge to top of hill. Turn right & at church sharp left, 1st cottage on right*

This welcoming cottage is surrounded by countryside and is an ideal base for touring Cornwall. Bedrooms have thoughtful finishing touches and there is a picturesque garden to relax in with abundant wildlife, and you can watch the friendly cows in the farmers' fields. Breakfast, prepared using local produce, is enjoyed in the cosy dining room. Private parking is provided.

**Rooms:** 2 en suite **Facilities:** FTV TVL tea/coffee Lift WiFi ⤓18 🔒 **Parking:** 3
**Notes:** Closed 15 Oct–Mar

**MARAZION** Map 2 SW53

## The Marazion

★★★★ INN

**tel:** 01736 710334 **The Square TR17 0AP**
**email:** info@marazionhotel.co.uk **web:** www.marazionhotel.co.uk
**dir:** *In village square opposite Out of Blue gallery*

Within 50 metres of one of Cornwall's safest beaches, this family-run establishment offers a relaxed atmosphere with friendly service. The individually furnished and decorated bedrooms are comfortable, and many have the benefit of stunning views across to St Michael's Mount. The Cutty Sark public bar is a great place to sit and enjoy a drink and listen to local banter, while the restaurant provides a wide range of meals to suit all tastes and budgets.

**Rooms:** 11 en suite (1 fmly) **Facilities:** FTV Lounge tea/coffee Dinner available WiFi 🔒 **Parking:** 20 **Notes:** Closed Nov

## Blue Horizon

★★★★ BED AND BREAKFAST

**tel:** 01736 711199 **Fore Street TR17 0AW**
**email:** stay@bluehorizon-marazion.co.uk **web:** www.bluehorizon-marazion.co.uk
**dir:** *E end of village centre*

Located in the heart of this market town, the rear of this establishment is almost at the water's edge and offers superb views of the sea from its garden, some of the bedrooms and the breakfast room. The atmosphere is laid back and relaxed. There are a number of additional facilities available (charged), including a laundry room, sauna cabin and barbecue facilities. Ample parking is also available.

**Rooms:** 5 en suite **D** £85–£105* **Facilities:** FTV tea/coffee WiFi 🔒 Hot tub in cabin **Parking:** 6 **Notes:** Closed Oct–Mar, 23–26 Jun, 26 Jul–7 Aug RS 29 May–5 Jun

## Glenleigh House

★★★ GUEST HOUSE

**tel:** 01736 710308 **Higher Fore Street TR17 0BQ**
**email:** glenleighbandb@hotmail.co.uk **web:** www.glenleigh-marazion.co.uk
**dir:** *A394 to Penzance, opposite Fire Engine Inn*

Glenleigh House, overlooking St Michael's Mount and the sweeping panorama of Mount's Bay, has been owned and run by the Hales family for more than 30 years. With eight comfortable and well-appointed bedrooms (many with views to the Mount and the sea), you can be assured of a comfortable stay. Built in 1898 as the home of a prosperous farmer, the house retains its original Victorian charm while providing modern amenities such as free WiFi. Expect a filling breakfast of your choice to set you up for the day.

**Rooms:** 8 en suite (1 GF) **Facilities:** FTV TVL tea/coffee WiFi **Parking:** 8 **Notes:** LB No children 8yrs Closed Nov–Mar

## MEVAGISSEY
Map 2 SX04

### Premier Collection

## Pebble House
★★★★★ 🍷 GUEST ACCOMMODATION

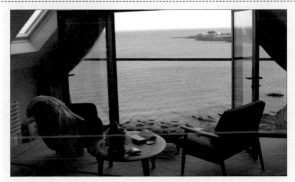

**tel:** 01726 844466 & 07973 714392 **Polkirt Hill PL26 6UX**
**email:** hello@pebblehousecornwall.co.uk **web:** www.pebblehousecornwall.co.uk
**dir:** *B3273 to Mevagissey, into village & follow one-way system. Pass Ship Inn on right, up hill keeping sea on left to T-junct. Pebble House on right*

This property is affectionately known as 'THE house with THE view' which certainly provides an accurate description. Providing boutique-style accommodation, all the rooms are en suite and individual in design – modern, contemporary, quirky, and providing excellent comfort. You can buy pretty much everything you see in the house if you wish. Light snacks, picnics, cream teas and a range of drinks are available, along with a hearty breakfast featuring daily specials. Please note that Pebble House can only accommodate children aged over 16.

**Rooms:** 6 en suite (1 GF) **S** £130–£215; **D** £130–£215* **Facilities:** STV FTV DVD tea/coffee Licensed WiFi 🛎 **Extras:** Speciality toiletries, robes, bottled water **Parking:** 6 **Notes:** LB No children 16yrs

### Premier Collection

## Portmellon Cove Guest House
★★★★★ 🍷 GUEST ACCOMMODATION

**tel:** 01726 843410 & 07747 440002 **121 Portmellon Park, Portmellon PL26 6XD**
**email:** stay@portmellon-cove.com **web:** www.portmellon-cove.com
**dir:** *A390 onto B3273 into Mevagissey. Through village, up Polkirt Hill. 1st left into Porthmellon Rd, pass pub, right into Porthmellon Park, on right*

Portmellon Cove Guest House lies in a quiet, peaceful, sandy cove less than a mile from the pretty fishing village of Mevagissey. This well-run family property offers inviting sea-view rooms, free parking and WiFi. All three rooms are well equipped with a generous mini-bar and beverage tray. Award-winning breakfasts are served in the bright and airy dining room which enjoys views across the garden and out to sea. Close to The Lost Gardens of Heligan, the Eden Project, the coastal path and cycleways, most of Cornwall's many attractions can be reached within an hour.

**Rooms:** 3 en suite **S** £99–£115; **D** £99–£125* **Facilities:** FTV DVD iPod docking station Lounge tea/coffee Licensed WiFi ♨18 🛎 **Extras:** Mini-bar, snacks, robes, fridge, fresh milk –– complimentary; Champagne, chocolates, flowers, fruit bowls, high/cream teas – chargeable **Parking:** 5 **Notes:** LB No children 12yrs Closed Nov–Mar

## Stone's Throw Cottage
★★★★ BED AND BREAKFAST

**tel:** 01726 844605 **5 Polkirt Hill PL26 6UR**
**email:** info@stones-throw-cottage-mevagissey.com
**web:** www.stones-throw-cottage-mevagissey.com
**dir:** *From St Austell take B3273 to Mevagissey*

A beautifully restored fisherman's cottage set in the centre of Mevagissey, a minute's walk from the quaint historic harbour, shops, bars and restaurants. The friendly host offers cheerful hospitality, alongside bedrooms and bathrooms that have been sympathetically refurbished and well equipped. Comfort and quality is assured in the additional thoughtful touches, including chocolates, assorted teas and fresh milk for tea and coffee. Sumptuous beds ensure a good night's sleep. Perfectly located for sightseeing and activities.

**Rooms:** 3 rms (2 en suite) (1 pri facs) **Facilities:** FTV DVD tea/coffee WiFi **Extras:** iPads **Notes:** LB

## MITCHELL
Map 2 SW85

## The Plume of Feathers
★★★★ 🍺 INN

**tel:** 01872 510387 & 511122 **TR8 5AX**
**email:** theplume@hospitalitycornwall.com **web:** www.theplumemitchell.co.uk
**dir:** *Just off A30 & A3076, follow signs*

The Plume of Feathers is a very popular inn, with origins dating back to the 16th century, situated close to Newquay and the beaches. The restaurant offers a varied menu which relies heavily on local produce. The stylish bedrooms are decorated in neutral colours and have wrought-iron beds with quality linens. The garden makes an ideal place to enjoy a meal or a Cornish tea. Staff are very friendly.

**Rooms:** 13 annexe en suite (4 fmly) (10 GF) **Facilities:** FTV tea/coffee Dinner available WiFi **Conf:** Max 65 **Parking:** 40 **Notes:** LB

MORWENSTOW **Map 2 SS21**

## West Point B&B

★★★★ 🍴 BED AND BREAKFAST

**tel:** 01288 331594 & 07443 567963 **West Point, Crimp EX23 9PB**
**email:** bramhill@hotmail.co.uk **web:** www.budebedandbreakfast.co.uk
**dir:** A361 to Barnstaple onto A39 towards Bude. 7m after Clovelly rdbt on right

Ideally placed for exploring the beautiful countryside and coasts of north Cornwall and north Devon, this smartly appointed establishment is surrounded by colourful gardens with far-reaching views to the rear. Guests are assured of a genuine welcome plus the freedom of all-day access. Both bedrooms are comfortable, light and airy; one has a French-style king-size bed and patio doors leading to the garden. Additional facilities include a guest lounge and dining room where local farm produce is on offer whenever possible.

**Rooms:** 2 en suite (1 fmly) (2 GF) **S** £40–£50; **D** £70–£80 **Facilities:** FTV TVL tea/coffee WiFi 🅿 **Extras:** Speciality toiletries, home-made biscuits **Parking:** 4 **Notes:** LB Closed 22 Dec–2 Jan

NEWQUAY **Map 2 SW86**

## Lewinnick Lodge

★★★★ RESTAURANT WITH ROOMS

**tel:** 01637 878117 **Pentire Headland TR7 1QD**
**email:** thelodge@hospitalitycornwall.com **web:** www.lewinnicklodge.co.uk
**dir:** From A392, at rdbt exit into Pentire Rd then Pentire Ave. Turn right to Lewinnick Lodge

Set above the cliffs of Pentire Headland, looking out across the mighty Atlantic, guests are guaranteed amazing coastal views here at Lewinnick Lodge. The bedrooms were designed by Guy Bostock and are modern, spacious, and offer many thoughtful extras; some have open-plan bathrooms. Modern British food (with an emphasis on fresh fish) is served all day.

**Rooms:** 11 en suite (1 fmly) **S** £116–£187.50; **D** £155–£250* **Facilities:** FTV iPod docking station tea/coffee Dinner available Direct dial Lift WiFi Pool table 🅿 Surf board store **Extras:** Speciality toiletries, robes, bottled water – complimentary **Parking:** 50

## The Lyncroft Bed & Breakfast

★★★★ BED AND BREAKFAST

**tel:** 01637 893812 & 07580 109443 **54 Tower Road TR7 1LU**
**email:** info@thelyncroftnewquay.co.uk **web:** www.thelyncroftnewquay.co.uk
**dir:** A392 into Newquay (Trevemper Rd/Gannel Rd). At rdbt, 2nd exit into Higher Tower Rd. On right opposite golf course

The Lyncroft is a 100-year-old, stone-built Cornish house with views out over Fistral beach and along the Cornish coast. All bedrooms have been recently refurbished to a very good standard; contemporary and relaxing. All have en suite shower rooms, TVs, and free WiFi. Five minutes' walk in one direction will take you to Fistral beach, five minutes in the other and you will find Towan beach and the town centre. Dogs allowed upon request; off-street parking available.

**Rooms:** 7 en suite (1 fmly) **S** fr £75; **D** fr £75 **Facilities:** FTV TVL tea/coffee WiFi 🅿 **Extras:** Mineral water **Parking:** 6 **Notes:** LB

## Meadow View

★★★ GUEST ACCOMMODATION

**tel:** 01637 873132 **135 Mount Wise TR7 1QR**
**email:** meadowview135@hotmail.com **web:** www.meadowviewnewquay.co.uk
**dir:** A392 into Newquay to Mountwise, Meadow View on left before rdbt to Pentire

Expect a warm welcome at Meadow View, which is just a short walk from the town centre and Fistral Beach which is famous for surfing. The bedrooms are comfortable and some have countryside views. A hearty breakfast is served in the pleasant dining room and there is a cosy sun lounge to relax in. Waterworld, The Eden Project, and the Pentire peninsula with its rolling green coastline are all just a short drive away.

**Rooms:** 7 en suite (2 fmly) **Facilities:** FTV tea/coffee WiFi 🅿 **Parking:** 7 **Notes:** LB No children 5yrs Closed 7 Nov–mid Feb

## The Three Tees

★★★ GUEST ACCOMMODATION

**tel:** 01637 872055 **21 Carminow Way TR7 3AY**
**email:** greg@3tees.co.uk **web:** www.3tees.co.uk
**dir:** A30 onto A392 signed Newquay. Right at Quintrell Downs rdbt signed Porth, over x-rds, 3rd right

Located in a quiet residential area just a short walk from the town and beach, this friendly family-run establishment is comfortable and well equipped. Guests have use of a lounge, a bar and a sun lounge, and breakfast is served in the dining room, where snacks are available throughout the day. The bar serves light snacks in the evenings. In addition to the bedrooms in the main house, a family annexe is also available, and offers flexible, level-access accommodation.

**Rooms:** 8 rms (7 en suite) (1 pri facs) 1 annexe en suite (4 fmly) (2 GF) **D** £76–£90* **Facilities:** FTV DVD TVL tea/coffee Licensed WiFi 🅿 **Parking:** 9 **Notes:** LB Closed Nov–Feb

## Rolling Waves

★★★ GUEST HOUSE

**tel:** 01637 873236 **Alexandra Road, Porth TR7 3NB**
**email:** enquiries@rollingwaves.co.uk **web:** www.rollingwaves.co.uk
**dir:** A30 onto A392, A3058 towards Newquay. B3276 to Porth, pass Mermaid public house

Rolling Waves is a family-owned and run guest house with great views across the bay. The bedrooms are comfortable, the hosts friendly and welcoming, and dinner is available on request.

**Rooms:** 8 rms (7 en suite) (1 pri facs) (2 fmly) (4 GF) **S** £35–£45; **D** £70–£90* **Facilities:** FTV TVL tea/coffee Dinner available Licensed WiFi **Parking:** 7 **Notes:** LB

## Avalon

★★★ GUEST ACCOMMODATION

**tel:** 01637 877522 & 07870 320346 **4 Edgcumbe Gardens TR7 2QD**
**email:** enquiries@avalonnewquay.co.uk **web:** www.avalonnewquay.co.uk
**dir:** From A30 at Quintrell Downs rdbt onto A3058 signed St Columb Minor. Left in 1m opposite Rocklands

Conveniently situated within walking distance of the town centre and the beaches, in a quiet residential area, Avalon provides comfortable accommodation, and enjoys the benefit of on-site parking. Guests may enjoy the front-facing sun terrace during summer months. Golfing holiday offers are available.

**Rooms:** 6 rms (5 en suite) (1 pri facs) (1 fmly) **S** £30–£40; **D** £60–£70* **Facilities:** FTV tea/coffee WiFi 🅿 **Parking:** 6 **Notes:** LB

**PADSTOW**           Map 2 SW97

### AA RESTAURANT WITH ROOMS OF THE YEAR 2017–18

##### Premier Collection

## Padstow Townhouse

★★★★★ ◉◉◉◉ 🍴 RESTAURANT WITH ROOMS

**tel:** 01841 550950 **16/18 High Street PL28 8BB**
**email:** stay@padstowtownhouse.co.uk **web:** www.paul-ainsworth.co.uk

This cosy 18th-century townhouse offers six individually styled suites, providing all home comforts as well as some extra little luxuries. Each room has its own 40" curved TV complete with Apple TV, as well as free WiFi. Breakfast is served in Rojano's in the Square, and guests are welcome to dine there (it has one AA Rosette) or at the four AA-Rosetted Paul Ainsworth at No.6 restaurant.

**Rooms:** 6 en suite **Facilities:** Dinner available WiFi **Extras:** Speciality toiletries

##### Premier Collection

## Penjoly Guest House

★★★★★ 🍴 GUEST HOUSE

**tel:** 01841 533535 **Padstow Road PL28 8LB**
**email:** penjoly.padstow@btopenworld.com **web:** www.penjolypadstow.co.uk
**dir:** 1m S of Padstow. Off A389 near Padstow Holiday Park

Penjoly is a very professionally run establishment, where attention to detail and quality are noteworthy throughout. Bedrooms are delightfully decorated and complemented by an impressive range of extras. Breakfast is served in the attractive breakfast room or in the conservatory, and a guest lounge is also available. This is a perfect base for exploring the West Country's delights, and for seeking out the great restaurants of Cornwall. Guests have the convenience of off-road parking.

**Rooms:** 3 en suite (3 GF) **S** £90–£99; **D** £100–£110* **Facilities:** STV FTV DVD iPod docking station TVL tea/coffee WiFi **Extras:** Robes **Parking:** 10 **Notes:** No children 16yrs

##### Premier Collection

## The Seafood Restaurant

★★★★★ ◉◉◉ 🍴 RESTAURANT WITH ROOMS

**tel:** 01841 532700 **Riverside PL28 8BY**
**email:** reservations@rickstein.com **web:** www.rickstein.com
**dir:** Into town centre, down hill (Station Rd), follow signs to harbour car park, opposite car park

Food lovers continue to beat a well-trodden path to this famous restaurant. Situated on the edge of the harbour, just a stone's throw from the shops, The Seafood Restaurant offers chic and comfortable bedrooms that boast numerous thoughtful extras; some have views of the estuary and a couple have private balconies with stunning sea views. Service is relaxed and friendly; booking is essential for both accommodation and a table in the restaurant.

**Rooms:** 16 en suite 6 annexe en suite (12 fmly) (3 GF) **Facilities:** FTV DVD tea/coffee Dinner available Direct dial Lift WiFi 🛁 Cookery School **Extras:** Speciality toiletries, robes, mini-bar **Parking:** 13 **Notes:** LB Closed 24–26 Dec RS 24 Dec limited restaurant service times

##### Premier Collection

## St Petroc's Bistro

★★★★★ ◉ RESTAURANT WITH ROOMS

**tel:** 01841 532700 **4 New Street PL28 8EA**
**email:** reservations@rickstein.com **web:** www.rickstein.com
**dir:** A39 onto A389, follow signs to Padstow town centre

One of the oldest buildings in town, this charming establishment is just up the hill from the picturesque harbour. Style, comfort and individuality are all great strengths here, particularly so in the impressively equipped bedrooms. Breakfast, lunch and dinner all reflect a serious approach to cuisine, and the popular restaurant has a relaxed, bistro style. Comfortable lounges, a reading room and lovely gardens complete the picture.

**Rooms:** 10 en suite (2 fmly) **Facilities:** FTV Lounge tea/coffee Dinner available Direct dial WiFi **Parking:** 4 **Notes:** LB Closed 24–26 Dec

## The Old Mill House

★★★★ 🍴 GUEST ACCOMMODATION

**tel:** 01841 540388 **PL27 7QT**
**email:** enquiries@theoldmillhouse.com **web:** www.theoldmillhouse.com
**dir:** 2m S of Padstow. In centre of Little Petherick on A389

The Old Mill House is situated in an Area of Outstanding Natural Beauty, a couple of miles from the busy town of Padstow with its pretty harbour with many shops, bars and restaurants. This 16th-century property, a former corn mill house, has been sympathetically converted and is beautifully decorated and well equipped. Family-run, it offers good levels of comfort and quality. Dinner is served in the restaurant with a good selection of dishes to suits all tastes. Traditional afternoon teas may be served in the garden and a good hearty 'Full Cornish' breakfast is made with locally sourced produce and ingredients.

**Rooms:** 7 en suite (2 fmly) **Facilities:** FTV DVD Lounge tea/coffee Dinner available Licensed WiFi 🛁 Hot tub on request **Extras:** Sherry, fresh milk, snacks **Notes:** LB Closed 20 Dec–1 Feb

## Rick Stein's Café

★★★★ BED AND BREAKFAST

**tel:** 01841 532700 **10 Middle Street PL28 8AP**
**email:** reservations@rickstein.com **web:** www.rickstein.com
**dir:** A389 into town, one way past church, 3rd right

Another Rick Stein success story, this is a lively café by day, restaurant by night, and offers good food and quality accommodation just a short walk from the harbour. Three bedrooms are available – each is quite different but all have high standards of comfort. Friendly and personable staff are always on hand.

**Rooms:** 3 en suite (1 fmly) **Facilities:** FTV DVD tea/coffee Dinner available Direct dial Licensed WiFi 🛁 Cookery school **Extras:** Speciality toiletries; mini-bar – chargeable **Notes:** LB Closed 24–26 Dec RS 24 Dec limited service times

## PAR
Map 2 SX05

# The Britannia Inn & Restaurant

★★★★ 🍴 INN

**tel:** 01726 812889 & 815796 **St Austell Road PL24 2SL**
**email:** info@britanniainn.com **web:** www.britanniainn.com
**dir:** On A390 between Par & St Austell, next to Cornish Market World

This long established inn is situated between Par and St Austell and is just a five-minute drive from The Eden Project. There is a very genuine welcome here and a collective effort to ensure guests are well looked after and enjoy their stay. A choice of bars is available, together with attractive gardens, function room and range of dining options. The extensive menu features plenty of Cornish produce with a range of daily specials also offered. Bedrooms offer contemporary style and comfort with impressive, high quality bathrooms.

**Rooms:** 7 en suite (4 fmly) **S** £60–£85; **D** £80–£155* **Facilities:** FTV tea/coffee Dinner available Direct dial WiFi 🔒 **Conf:** Max 75 Thtr 60 Class 45 Board 50 **Parking:** 105 **Notes:** RS 25 Dec open 12–2 drinks only

# Elmswood House

★★★★ GUEST ACCOMMODATION

**tel:** 01726 814221 **73 Tehidy Road, Tywardreath PL24 2QD**
**email:** info@elmswoodhouse.co.uk **web:** www.elmswoodhouse.co.uk
**dir:** Right from Par station, then 1st left to top of hill, opposite village church

Elmswood House is a fine Victorian building set in the middle of the village opposite the church. Many guests return to stay here time and again. Bedrooms have quality furnishings and many extra facilities, and the attractive dining room and lounge overlook a beautiful garden.

**Rooms:** 6 en suite (1 fmly) (1 GF) **D** £70–£85* **Facilities:** FTV Lounge TVL tea/coffee WiFi **Parking:** 6 **Notes:** No children 10yrs Closed Jan

# The Royal Inn

★★★★ INN

**tel:** 01726 815601 **66 Eastcliffe Road, Tywardreath PL24 2AJ**
**email:** info@royal-inn.co.uk **web:** www.royal-inn.co.uk
**dir:** Adjacent to Par railway station

Situated next to the railway station on the edge of Tywardreath, this free house provides high standards of comfort and quality. Only five minutes from Par Sands and four miles from The Eden Project, it is an ideal base for exploring Cornwall. The open-plan bar area has slate floors and a large open fire; the atmosphere is relaxed and diners can choose from the bar menu or dine more formally in the restaurant or conservatory. All twin rooms have sofa beds (suitable for children under 14), and the family suite is suitable for families of four or five.

**Rooms:** 15 en suite (8 fmly) (4 GF) **S** £55–£65; **D** £65–£80* **Facilities:** STV FTV tea/coffee Dinner available WiFi Pool table **Conf:** Max 20 Thtr 8 Class 8 Board 20 **Parking:** 17 **Notes:** LB Closed 23–26 Dec & 30 Dec–1 Jan

## PENRYN
Map 2 SW73

# Prospect House

★★★★ GUEST ACCOMMODATION

**tel:** 01326 373198 **Commercial Road TR10 8AH**
**email:** stay@prospecthouse-penryn.co.uk **web:** www.prospecthouse-penryn.co.uk
**dir:** Exit A39 at Treluswell rdbt onto B3292, right at Penryn town centre sign. Left at junct to town hall, left into Saint Gluivas St, at bottom on left

Prospect House is an attractive building close to the waterside, and was built in 1820 for a ship's captain. The original charm of the house has been carefully maintained and the attractive bedrooms are well equipped. A comfortable lounge is available, and freshly cooked breakfasts are served in the elegant dining room.

**Rooms:** 3 en suite **D** £80–£85* **Facilities:** FTV Lounge tea/coffee WiFi **Parking:** 4

## PENZANCE
Map 2 SW43

### Premier Collection

# Camilla House

★★★★★ 🍴 GUEST ACCOMMODATION

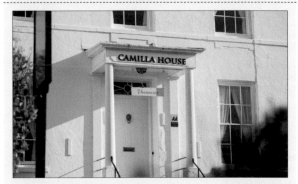

**tel:** 01736 363771 **12 Regent Terrace TR18 4DW**
**email:** enquiries@camillahouse.co.uk **web:** www.camillahouse.co.uk
**dir:** A30 to Penzance, at rail station follow road along harbourfront into Promenade Rd. Opposite Jubilee Bathing Pool, Regent Terrace 2nd right

A warm welcome is assured at this charming Victorian property, located in a quiet residential area facing the sea and only a short walk from Penzance's beach and town centre attractions. Bedrooms, some with views towards the coast, are spacious and attractively appointed. There's a stylish guest lounge with many homely features, and breakfast should not to be missed. Secure car parking is provided.

**Rooms:** 8 rms (7 en suite) (1 pri facs) (1 GF) **Facilities:** FTV DVD Lounge tea/coffee WiFi 🔒 **Parking:** 7 **Notes:** Closed Nov–Mar

### Premier Collection

# Ednovean Farm

★★★★★ 🍴 FARMHOUSE

**tel:** 01736 711883 **TR20 9LZ**
**email:** info@ednoveanfarm.co.uk **web:** www.ednoveanfarm.co.uk

*(For full entry see Perranuthnoe)*

## Mount Royal

★★★★ ☕ GUEST ACCOMMODATION

**tel:** 01736 362233 **Chyandour Cliff TR18 3LQ**
**email:** mountroyal@btconnect.com **web:** www.mountroyalpenzance.com
**dir:** *From A30 onto coast road into town*

Part Georgian and part Victorian, the spacious Mount Royal has splendid views over Mount's Bay and is convenient for the town's attractions. There's a gracious elegance throughout with the impressive dining room retaining its original fireplace and ornate sideboard. Parking available to the rear of the property.

**Rooms:** 6 en suite (1 fmly) (1 GF) **S** fr £115; **D** £115–£140* **Facilities:** FTV Lounge tea/coffee WiFi 🔒 **Extras:** Speciality toiletries **Parking:** 8 **Notes:** LB No children 10yrs Closed Oct–May

## The Dunedin Guest House

★★★★ GUEST ACCOMMODATION

**tel:** 01736 362652 **Alexandra Road TR18 4LZ**
**email:** info@dunedinhotel.co.uk **web:** www.dunedinhotel.co.uk
**dir:** *A30 to Penzance, at rail station along harbour front into Promenade Rd, right into Alexandra Rd, Dunedin on right*

The Dunedin is on a tree-lined avenue just a stroll from the promenade and town centre. The friendly proprietors provide a relaxed atmosphere, and bedrooms that are well equipped and smartly decorated to a high standard. Hearty breakfasts are served in the dining room.

**Rooms:** 8 en suite (2 fmly) (2 GF) **S** £60–£65; **D** £72–£85* **Facilities:** FTV DVD tea/coffee WiFi 🔒 **Extras:** Speciality toiletries **Notes:** LB No children 12yrs Closed 31 Oct–Feb

## The Dolphin Tavern

★★★ INN

**tel:** 01736 364106 **Quay Street TR18 4BD**
**email:** dolphintavern@tiscali.co.uk **web:** www.dolphintavern.co.uk
**dir:** *Opposite Penzance harbour*

The Dolphin Tavern is a traditional inn just a few yards away from Penzance harbour, usefully located for the Scillonian ferry. Rooms are comfortable and well presented, and the staff are friendly and attentive. Food is available in the bar and restaurant daily from a wide menu which also offers daily-changing specials.

**Rooms:** 3 en suite **D** £55–£100* **Facilities:** FTV tea/coffee Dinner available WiFi 🔒 Pool table in winter only

## The Swordfish Inn

★★★ INN

**tel:** 01736 362830 **The Strand, Newlyn TR18 5HN**
**email:** helenmmorris@hotmail.co.uk
**dir:** *1m SW of Penzance*

Situated in the very heart of the fishing village of Newlyn, The Swordfish has been totally renovated to provide modern comforts in a traditional and convivial environment. The spacious, comfortable bedrooms are well appointed, as are the en suite shower rooms. This establishment is a popular venue for locals and tourists alike.

**Rooms:** 4 en suite **D** fr £70* **Facilities:** FTV tea/coffee WiFi **Notes:** RS 25 Dec open 12–2pm only

## The Summer House

**[U]**

**tel:** 01736 363744 & 07768 608439 **Cornwall Terrace TR18 4HL**
**email:** reception@summerhouse-cornwall.com **web:** www.summerhouse-cornwall.com
**dir:** *A30 to Penzance, at rail station follow along harbour onto Promenade, pass Jubilee Pool, right after Queens Hotel. Summer House 30yds on left*

Currently the rating for this establishment is not confirmed. This may be due to a change of ownership or because it has only recently joined the AA rating scheme.

**Rooms:** 5 en suite **Facilities:** FTV DVD TVL tea/coffee Licensed WiFi **Extras:** Fresh milk, chocolates, mini-fridge **Parking:** 5 **Notes:** No children 16yrs Closed Oct–Easter

### PERRANUTHNOE — Map 2 SW52

### Premier Collection

## Ednovean Farm

★★★★★ ☕ FARMHOUSE

**tel:** 01736 711883 **TR20 9LZ**
**email:** info@ednoveanfarm.co.uk **web:** www.ednoveanfarm.co.uk
**dir:** *Off A394 towards Perranuthnoe at Dynasty Restaurant, farm drive on left on bend by post box*

Tranquillity is guaranteed at this 17th-century farmhouse, which looks across the countryside towards Mount's Bay. The bedrooms are individually styled and are very comfortable. The impressive Mediterranean-style gardens are ideal for relaxing and taking in the superb views. In addition to the sitting room, there is also a garden room and several patios. Breakfast is served at a magnificent oak table.

**Rooms:** 3 en suite (3 GF) **S** £100–£140; **D** £100–£140 **Facilities:** FTV DVD iPod docking station Lounge tea/coffee WiFi **Extras:** Speciality toiletries, slippers, robes **Parking:** 4 **Notes:** LB No children 16yrs Closed 24–28 Dec 22 acres grassland/stud

| POLPERRO | Map 2 SX25 |
|---|---|

### Premier Collection

## Trenderway Farm

★★★★★ 🐚 FARMHOUSE

**tel:** 01503 272214 **Pelynt PL13 2LY**
**email:** stay@trenderwayfarm.com **web:** www.trenderwayfarm.co.uk
**dir:** *Take A387 from Looe to Polperro, right at signpost to Pelynt.*
*3rd left at signed junct to farm. Continue down lane to gravel car park*

Warm hospitality awaits at this delightful 16th-century farmhouse set on a 200-acre working farm. Stylish bedrooms, both in the farmhouse and in the adjacent barns, offer high levels of comfort and include WiFi access. Hearty breakfasts are served in the conservatory overlooking the lake, and free-range eggs from the farm, as well as high quality local produce, are served.

**Rooms:** 2 en suite 5 annexe en suite (2 GF) **S** £99–£265; **D** £99–£265*
**Facilities:** FTV DVD TVL tea/coffee Licensed WiFi 🔒 Lakes Falconry school
**Extras:** Speciality toiletries; mini-bar – chargeable **Conf:** Max 100 Thtr 100
Class 50 Board 15 **Parking:** 8 **Notes:** LB No children 16yrs Civ wed 120 200 acres
beef/sheep/orchards

## Penryn House

★★★★ 🐚 GUEST ACCOMMODATION

**tel:** 01503 272157 **The Coombes PL13 2RQ**
**email:** enquiries@penrynhouse.co.uk **web:** www.penrynhouse.co.uk
**dir:** *A387 to Polperro, at mini rdbt left down hill into village (ignore restricted access).*
*200yds on left*

Penryn House has a relaxed atmosphere and offers a warm welcome. Every effort is made to ensure a memorable stay. Bedrooms are neatly presented and reflect the character of the building. After a day exploring, enjoy a drink at the bar and relax in the comfortable lounge.

**Rooms:** 12 en suite (3 fmly) **S** £50–£70; **D** £85–£105 **Facilities:** FTV Lounge
tea/coffee Licensed WiFi 🔒 **Parking:** 13 **Notes:** LB Closed Dec–Feb

| PORT GAVERNE | Map 2 SX08 |
|---|---|

### Premier Collection

## Port Gaverne

★★★★★ 🏅🏅 INN

**tel:** 01208 880244 **PL29 3SQ**
**email:** eat@portgavernehotel.co.uk **web:** www.portgavernehotel.co.uk

This traditional inn is located in a tiny and peaceful cove on Cornwall's dramatic north coast, one headland away and five minutes' walk from Port Isaac. Accommodation is spread over 15 en suite bedrooms, all comfortably furnished, well-maintained, and spotlessly clean. No two are the same. You'll find antique furniture, nooks and crannies, a wonderfully comfortable bed, and good food here. All rooms come complete with full satellite TV, radio, direct-dial telephone and coffee and tea-making facilities. Also available is a relaxing sitting room, outside terrace and sunny beer garden.

**Rooms:** 15 en suite (4 fmly) **S** £85–£140; **D** £95–£170* **Facilities:** STV FTV DVD
iPod docking station Lounge tea/coffee Dinner available Direct dial WiFi ⚓18
🔒 **Extras:** Speciality toiletries, Nespresso coffee machine, chocolates, bottled
water **Conf:** Max 12 Board 12 **Parking:** 17 **Notes:** LB

| PORTHLEVEN | Map 2 SW62 |
|---|---|

## Kota Restaurant with Rooms

★★★ 🏅🏅 RESTAURANT WITH ROOMS

**tel:** 01326 562407 **Harbour Head TR13 9JA**
**email:** kota@btconnect.com **web:** www.kotarestaurant.co.uk
**dir:** *B3304 from Helston into Porthleven. Kota on harbour opposite slipway*

Overlooking the water, this 300-year-old building is the home of Kota Restaurant ('kota' being the Maori word for 'shellfish'). The bedrooms are approached from a granite stairway to the side of the building. The family room is spacious and has the benefit of harbour views, while the smaller, double room is at the rear of the property. The enthusiastic young owners ensure guests enjoy their stay here, and a meal in the two AA Rosette award-winning restaurant should not be missed. Food and drink is also served in the Kota Kai Bar & Kitchen. Breakfast features the best local produce.

**Rooms:** 2 annexe en suite (1 fmly) **S** £65–£90; **D** £75–£100* **Facilities:** FTV DVD
tea/coffee Dinner available WiFi ⚓18 🔒 **Extras:** Fridge **Parking:** 1
**Notes:** Closed Jan–10 Feb

## PORTLOE
Map 2 SW93

## The Lugger

★★★★ ◉◉ ☋ INN

**tel:** 01872 501322 **TR2 5RD**
**email:** reservations.lugger@bespokehotels.com **web:** www.bespokehotels.com/thelugger
**dir:** *A390 to Truro, B3287 to Tregony, A3078 (St Mawes Rd), left for Veryan, left for Portloe*

This delightful inn enjoys a unique setting adjacent to the slipway of the harbour, where fishing boats still come and go. Bedrooms, some in adjacent buildings and cottages, are contemporary in style and are well equipped. There is a sitting room which reflects the original character of the property, with beams and open fireplaces creating a cosy atmosphere. The modern restaurant enjoys superb views, and in warmer months, a sun terrace overlooking the harbour proves a popular place to enjoy a meal.

**Rooms:** 5 en suite 17 annexe en suite (1 GF) **Facilities:** FTV Lounge tea/coffee Dinner available Direct dial WiFi **Parking:** 26 **Notes:** Civ wed 50

## Carradale

★★★★ BED AND BREAKFAST

**tel:** 01872 501508 **TR2 5RB**
**email:** barbara495@btinternet.com **web:** www.carradale-bnb.co.uk
**dir:** *Off A3078 into Portloe, B&B 200yds from Ship Inn*

Carradale lies on the outskirts of this picturesque fishing village, a short walk from the South West Coast Path. It provides warm hospitality, a good level of comfort and well equipped bedrooms. There is an upper-floor lounge with a TV, and breakfast is served around a communal table in the pleasant dining room.

**Rooms:** 2 rms (1 en suite) (1 pri facs) (1 fmly) (2 GF) **S** £45; **D** £75 **Facilities:** TVL tea/coffee WiFi ☋ **Parking:** 5

## REDRUTH
Map 2 SW64

## Old Railway Yard

★★★★ ☋ ⬠ BED AND BREAKFAST

**tel:** 01209 314514 & 07970 595598 **Lanner Hill TR16 5TZ**
**email:** g.s.collier@btinternet.com **web:** www.old-railway-yard.co.uk
**dir:** *A393 Redruth/Falmouth road, at brow of hill before Lanner village, turn right into Tram Cross Ln, 125mtrs on right*

Warm, genuine service and hospitality awaits you at the Old Railway Yard, where a friendly welcome is assured from owners Graham and Suzanne. The Old Railway Yard is located in the heart of Cornwall, minutes away from the A30, perfect for exploring all the region offers. Beautifully equipped rooms provide everything you need, and a superb full Cornish breakfast with many extras will set you up well for the day ahead, especially the freshly prepared home-made bread.

**Rooms:** 3 rms (2 en suite) (1 pri facs) (1 GF) **S** £65; **D** £75–£85* **Facilities:** FTV DVD TVL tea/coffee Dinner available Licensed WiFi ☋ Hot tub **Parking:** 8
**Notes:** No children 6yrs

## Lanner Inn

★★ INN

**tel:** 01209 215611 **The Square, Lanner TR16 6EH**
**email:** info@lannerinn.co.uk **web:** www.lannerinn.co.uk
**dir:** *2m SE of Redruth. In Lanner on A393*

Conveniently situated for access to Redruth and the A30, this traditional inn is situated in the centre of Lanner and has a good local following. The property has a dining room and a bar in addition to the comfortable bedrooms. This inn is owner-run and managed, and the team of staff are very friendly.

**Rooms:** 3 en suite 1 annexe en suite (2 fmly) (1 GF) **Facilities:** FTV tea/coffee WiFi Pool table ☋ **Parking:** 16

## RUAN HIGH LANES
Map 2 SW93

# Trenona Farm Holidays
★★★ FARMHOUSE

**tel:** 01872 501339 & 07775 698953 **TR2 5JS**
**email:** info@trenonafarmholidays.co.uk **web:** www.trenonafarmholidays.co.uk
**dir:** A390 onto A3078, signed St Mawes. 6m on left

Trenona Farm is located on the Roseland Peninsula, surrounded by rolling countryside and close to lots of beautiful sandy beaches. The area provides many attractions, great restaurants and pubs and is very popular with walkers. A warm welcome awaits guests (and well-behaved dogs). Well-equipped rooms are warm and comfortable and a good hearty farmhouse breakfast is provided in the attractive dining room.

**Rooms:** 4 rms (3 en suite) (1 pri facs) (3 fmly) **S** £40–£50; **D** £70–£85*
**Facilities:** FTV TVL tea/coffee WiFi **Extras:** Fridge, fresh milk **Parking:** 8 **Notes:** LB Closed Nov–mid Mar 250 acres arable/beef

## ST AGNES
Map 2 SW75

# Driftwood Spars
★★★★ 🍴 GUEST ACCOMMODATION

**tel:** 01872 552428 **Trevaunance Cove TR5 0RT**
**email:** info@driftwoodspars.co.uk **web:** www.driftwoodspars.co.uk
**dir:** A30 to Chiverton rdbt, right onto B3277, through village. Driftwood Spars 200yds before beach

Partly built from shipwreck timbers, this 18th-century building attracts locals and visitors alike. The attractive bedrooms, some in an annexe, are decorated in a bright, seaside style with many interesting features. Local produce, including delicious seafood, is served in the informal dining room and in the restaurant, together with a range of hand-pulled beers.

**Rooms:** 9 en suite 6 annexe en suite (4 fmly) (5 GF) **S** £52–£100; **D** £93–£150
**Facilities:** FTV tea/coffee Dinner available Direct dial Licensed WiFi Pool table Table football **Conf:** Max 70 Thtr 70 Class 25 Board 20 **Parking:** 40 **Notes:** LB RS 25 Dec no lunch/dinner, no bar in evening Civ wed 76

# Penkerris
★★ GUEST HOUSE

**tel:** 01872 552262 **Penwinnick Road TR5 0PA**
**email:** penkerris@gmail.com **web:** www.penkerris.co.uk
**dir:** A30 onto B3277 to village, Penkerris on right after village sign

Set in gardens on the edge of the village, this Edwardian house has a relaxed and welcoming atmosphere. Period features abound, and the best possible use is made of space in the bedrooms. Home-cooked evening meals are served by prior arrangement. Ample parking is available.

**Rooms:** 7 rms (4 en suite) (3 fmly) **S** £25–£50; **D** £50–£70* **Facilities:** FTV TVL tea/coffee Dinner available Licensed WiFi Badminton Volleyball **Parking:** 9 **Notes:** LB

## ST AUSTELL

Map 2 SX05

### Premier Collection

## Anchorage House

★★★★★ GUEST ACCOMMODATION

**tel:** 01726 814071 **Nettles Corner, Tregrehan Mills PL25 3RH**
**email:** info@anchoragehouse.co.uk **web:** www.anchoragehouse.co.uk
**dir:** *2 m E of town centre off A390, opposite St Austell Garden Centre*

Georgian-style Anchorage House is set in an acre of carefully landscaped gardens at the end of a private lane. Guests are met upon arrival with afternoon tea, often served on the patio. The luxurious and elegant bedrooms are equipped to the highest standard with sumptuous beds, and include satellite TV, fresh fruit, magazines, bottled water and chocolates. Guests also have use of the indoor heated pool, hot tub and gym. The house is a short distance from many of Cornwall's major tourist attractions.

**Rooms:** 3 en suite 1 annexe en suite (1 GF) **S** £85–£120; **D** £125–£145*
**Facilities:** STV FTV DVD Lounge tea/coffee WiFi ⊗Gym Hot tub ⊛
**Extras:** Speciality toiletries **Parking:** 6 **Notes:** No children 16yrs Closed Nov–Mar

### Premier Collection

## Lower Barns Boutique Bed & Breakfast and Wedding Venue

★★★★★ GUEST ACCOMMODATION

**tel:** 01726 844881 & 07825 270962 **Bosue, St Ewe PL26 6ET**
**email:** janie@lowerbarns.co.uk **web:** www.lowerbarns.co.uk
**dir:** *3.5m SW of St Austell. Off B3273 at x-rds signed Lost Gardens of Heligan, Lower Barn signed 1m on right*

Nestled in a corner of south Cornwall, close to the sea and within walking distance of the Lost Gardens of Heligan and the South West Coast Path, Lower Barns is a luxury boutique retreat, ideal for couples who crave a bit of romance. Warm colours throughout create a Mediterranean feel, and staff offer informal and genuine hospitality. Bedrooms have a host of extras. Breakfast is served around a large table or on the patio deck overlooking the garden, which has a hot tub.

**Rooms:** 6 en suite (1 fmly) (1 GF) **Facilities:** FTV DVD tea/coffee Dinner available WiFi ⊛ Hot tub Spa treatments Sauna in Nook Suite **Parking:** 7
**Notes:** LB Closed Jan Civ wed 20

## The Gables

★★★★ ⊜ GUEST ACCOMMODATION

**tel:** 01726 72638 & 07971 821854 **1 Edgcumbe Road PL25 5DU**
**email:** barbara@gablesguesthousebnb.co.uk **web:** www.gablesguesthousebnb.co.uk

A warm welcome is assured at The Gables. The house offers a range of bedrooms with en suite or private facilities. A superb location for those wishing to visit The Eden Project, The Lost Gardens of Heligan and many other Cornish destinations. Memorable breakfasts are served in the conservatory or delightful gardens.

**Rooms:** 4 rms (2 en suite) (2 pri facs) **Facilities:** FTV Lounge tea/coffee WiFi
**Extras:** Home-made biscuits – complimentary **Parking:** 4 **Notes:** No children 12yrs RS Xmas week

## Langdale House

★★★★ BED AND BREAKFAST

**tel:** 01726 71404 & 07764 531050 **1A Southbourne Road PL25 4RU**
**email:** stay@langdalehousecornwall.co.uk **web:** www.langdalehousecornwall.co.uk
**dir:** *On A390 St Austell bypass, 0.5m S of town centre*

Handy for the town centre, this is an ideal choice for both business and leisure guests and a great place to relax, unwind and re-charge the batteries. Quality and comfort levels are high throughout, both in the elegant bedrooms and the impressive bathrooms. The welcome is warm and friendly with every effort made to ensure an enjoyable and rewarding stay. Breakfast is served in the attractive dining room, with a good range of dishes offered. Super-fast WiFi is provided.

**Rooms:** 3 en suite **S** £50–£75; **D** £60–£85* **Facilities:** FTV tea/coffee WiFi ⌁
**Extras:** Speciality toiletries **Parking:** 3 **Notes:** LB No children 5yrs

## Ancient Shipbrokers

★★★★ BED AND BREAKFAST

**tel:** 01726 843370 **1 Higher West End, Pentewan PL26 6BY**
**email:** shipbrokers1@btinternet.com **web:** www.pentewanbedandbreakfast.com
**dir:** *From St Austell on B3273, at Mill Garage turn left signed Pentewan, over bridge bear right & pass Ocean Sports. Next left into private road, Higher West End*

The Ancient Shipbrokers overlooks Pentewan harbour and one of the best sandy beaches in Cornwall. The house has bags of history and character, and has been decorated tastefully and sympathetically. A large area of the garden is given over to wild flowers and trees, and there is also a kitchen garden. The dining room enjoys a wonderful view out across the harbour and the beach, and is the ideal venue for home-cooked breakfasts. Private parking is available on-site or in the village car park. Help with luggage and free WiFi is provided. There is also space for storing bicycles, surf boards and wetsuits. Self-catering is available.

**Rooms:** 3 en suite (1 fmly) **S** £58–£70; **D** £88–£95* **Facilities:** FTV DVD tea/coffee WiFi ⊛ **Parking:** 3 **Notes:** LB Closed 20 Dec–5 Jan

ST AUSTELL *continued*

# Polgreen Farm

★★★★ FARMHOUSE

**tel:** 01726 75151 **London Apprentice PL26 7AP**
**email:** polgreen.farm@btinternet.com **web:** www.polgreenfarm.co.uk
**dir:** *1.5m S of St Austell. Exit B3273, left on entering London Apprentice & signed*

Guests regularly return for the friendly welcome at this peaceful establishment located just south of St Austell. The spacious and well-equipped bedrooms are divided between the main house and an adjoining property, and each building has a comfortable lounge. Breakfast is served in a pleasant conservatory overlooking the garden.

**Rooms:** 2 rms (1 en suite) (1 pri facs) 4 annexe en suite (1 fmly) (1 GF)
**Facilities:** FTV Lounge TVL tea/coffee WiFi **Parking:** 8 **Notes:** LB Closed Nov–Mar
64 acres livestock

# The Bugle Inn

★★★ INN

**tel:** 01726 850307 **57 Fore Street, Bugle PL26 8PD**
**email:** thebugleinn@gmail.com **web:** www.bugleinn.co.uk
**dir:** *A30 onto A391. In Bugle at x-rds*

The Bugle Inn is a warm and inviting establishment, with its origins dating back to the 17th century. It's situated in the heart of the Cornish countryside, between Bodmin and St Austell, handy for The Eden Project. Traditional pub food and drink are served in a characterful building with a lovely open fire. Bedrooms are attractive with a cosy feel.

**Rooms:** 5 en suite (1 fmly) **Facilities:** FTV tea/coffee Dinner available Direct dial WiFi
Pool table

---

**ST BURYAN**      Map 2 SW42

# Tregurnow Farm

★★★★ FARMHOUSE

**tel:** 01736 810255 **TR19 6BL**
**email:** tregurnow@lamorna.biz **web:** www.lamorna.biz
**dir:** *From Newlyn take B3315, after 4m black & white sign on left just past turn for Lamorna Cove*

Tucked away near St Buryan, Tregurnow Farm offers traditional, quality farmhouse bed and breakfast and self-catering facilities. Peace and quiet, stunning views and hearty breakfasts are hallmarks of a stay here. Close to Mousehole, Minack Theatre and Penzance, this is a good base for touring the far southwest of the county.

**Rooms:** 3 en suite **Facilities:** FTV Lounge TVL WiFi Pool table  **Extras:** Fridge
**Parking:** 10 **Notes:** No children 5yrs Closed Xmas 100 acres mixed

---

**ST IVES**      Map 2 SW54

## Premier Collection

# The Gannet Inn

★★★★★ GUEST ACCOMMODATION

**tel:** 01736 795651 & 795311 **St Ives Road, Carbis Bay TR26 2SB**
**email:** info@thegannetinn.co.uk **web:** www.gannetstives.co.uk
**dir:** *From St Ives on A3074 in Carbis Bay*

The Gannet Inn offers high standard bedrooms with a comfy restaurant and bar area, near St Ives in Cornwall. Designed to be a relaxing, stylish place to enjoy good food and a welcoming atmosphere, The Gannet has unique interiors with all the style and finesse of a boutique hotel, while also offering a warm and friendly place to pop in for a catch up or a bite to eat. Part of The Carbis Bay Hotel, Spa & Estate, guests of The Gannet Inn are offered the use of all leisure facilities throughout their stay.

**Rooms:** 16 en suite (4 fmly) **S** £120–£165; **D** £160–£265* **Facilities:** STV Lounge
tea/coffee Dinner available Direct dial Licensed WiFi ⅃18 Fishing Pool table
Leisure facilities available at sister hotel **Extras:** Speciality toiletries
**Conf:** Max 100 Thtr 100 Class 70 Board 60 **Parking:** 30 **Notes:** Civ wed 100

# Downsfield Bed and Breakfast

★★★★ GUEST ACCOMMODATION

**tel:** 01736 796659 **Longstone Hill TR26 2LJ**
**email:** sharonp27@hotmail.com **web:** www.downsfieldbnb.co.uk
**dir:** *On main road between Carbis Bay & St Ives*

A warm welcome awaits you at Downsfield from the lovely hosts Sharon and Phil. Decorated and furnished to an exceptionally high standard this accommodation will feel like a home from home. There is private parking, which is invaluable in St Ives during the summer. Rooms are spacious and well equipped with very good levels of comfort. Within walking distance of St Ives with its many unique shops and restaurants. A great location for exploring the region and stunning coastal attractions.

**Rooms:** 5 en suite (2 fmly) (1 GF) **Facilities:** FTV TVL tea/coffee WiFi  
**Extras:** Speciality toiletries, gowns, chocolate **Parking:** 5 **Notes:** No children 4yrs

## Lamorna Lodge

★★★★ ⌂ GUEST ACCOMMODATION

**tel:** 01736 795967 & 07837 638620 **Boskerris Road, Carbis Bay TR26 2NG**
**email:** lamorna@tr26.wanadoo.co.uk **web:** www.lamorna.co.uk
**dir:** *A30 onto A3074, right after playground in Carbis Bay, establishment 200yds on right*

A warm welcome is assured at Lamorna Lodge, which is just a short walk from Carbis Bay beach. Wonderful views over St Ives Bay to Godrevy Lighthouse can be enjoyed from the spacious lounge, a view also shared by some of the stylish bedrooms. Breakfast makes great use of local Cornish produce and is served in the elegant surroundings of the dining room. The stylish terrace enjoys lovely sea views.

**Rooms:** 9 en suite (2 fmly) (2 GF) **S** £60–£70; **D** £100–£120* **Facilities:** FTV Lounge tea/coffee Licensed WiFi ⚓ **Conf:** Max 18 Thtr 18 Class 18 Board 18 **Parking:** 9
**Notes:** LB Closed 5 Nov–10 Mar

## The Nook

★★★★ GUEST ACCOMMODATION

**tel:** 01736 795913 **Ayr TR26 1EQ**
**email:** info@nookstives.co.uk **web:** www.nookstives.co.uk
**dir:** *A30 to St Ives left at NatWest, right at rdbt & left at top of hill*

The Nook is an ideal base for exploring Cornwall's spectacular coastline, gardens and countryside. The comfortable bedrooms are furnished in a contemporary style and are equipped with numerous facilities. There is a wide variety on offer at breakfast, from full English or continental, to scrambled eggs with smoked salmon.

**Rooms:** 11 en suite (1 fmly) (1 GF) **S** £46–£66; **D** £88–£132 **Facilities:** FTV DVD TVL tea/coffee WiFi **Parking:** 10 **Notes:** LB

## Chypons Farm

★★★★ BED AND BREAKFAST

**tel:** 01736 740303 **Chypons Hill, Nancledra TR20 8NE**
**email:** chyponsfarm@gmail.com **web:** www.cornwallbnb.com

Chypons Farm is a small group of 300-year-old stone barns and self-catering cottages set around a courtyard and bordered by a small river and woodland, sitting on the side of a valley in the village of Nancledra, home to many artists who have escaped the hustle and bustle of nearby St Ives. There is a bus service into St Ives from Nancledra which saves parking in the town. The local pub is less than a mile away if you take the scenic walk through the fields or much less if you take the direct route along the road. Ample parking is available as well as the use of the gardens and summer house.

**Rooms:** 1 en suite

## Count House Cottage B&B

★★★★ GUEST HOUSE

**tel:** 01736 798951 & 07399 592039 **Count House Lane, Carbis Bay TR26 2PZ**
**email:** info@counthousecottagebandb.co.uk **web:** www.counthousecottagebandb.co.uk
**dir:** *In Carbis Bay, on corner of St Ives Rd & Count House Ln*

Count House Cottage is approximately 10 minutes' drive from the A30, and only a few minutes' drive to St Ives. This modern property has undergone a full refurbishment and all five rooms have stunning en suite showers. Three of the rooms have sea views and one room is on the ground floor.

**Rooms:** 5 en suite (1 GF) **D** £75–£109* **Facilities:** FTV tea/coffee WiFi **Parking:** 5
**Notes:** LB No children 16yrs

## The Rookery

★★★★ GUEST ACCOMMODATION

**tel:** 01736 799401 **8 The Terrace TR26 2BL**
**email:** therookerystives@hotmail.com **web:** www.rookerystives.com
**dir:** *A3074 through Carbis Bay, right fork at Porthminster Hotel,
The Rookery 500yds on left*

Aptly named, The Rookery stands in an elevated position overlooking the town and sandy beach. The attractive bedrooms include one which is on the ground floor and a luxurious suite, all of which are well equipped and offer a good level of comfort. Breakfast is served in the first-floor dining room at separate tables.

**Rooms:** 7 en suite (2 fmly) (1 GF) **Facilities:** FTV tea/coffee WiFi ⚓ **Parking:** 7
**Notes:** No children 7yrs

## Coombe Farmhouse

★★★★ BED AND BREAKFAST

**tel:** 01736 740843 **TR27 6NW**
**email:** coombefarmhouse@aol.com **web:** www.coombefarmhouse.com
**dir:** *1.5m W of Lelant. Exit A3074 to Lelant Downs*

Built of sturdy granite, this early 19th-century farmhouse is in a delightful location tucked away at the southern foot of Trencrom Hill, yet convenient for St Ives. The comfortable bedrooms are attractively decorated. There is a conservatory lounge, and substantial breakfasts, featuring farm-fresh eggs, are served in the dining room overlooking the garden.

**Rooms:** 3 rms (2 en suite) (1 pri facs) **S** £50; **D** £80–£86* **Facilities:** FTV Lounge tea/coffee WiFi **Extras:** Bottled water – complimentary **Parking:** 3
**Notes:** No children 16yrs Closed Dec

## The Mustard Tree

★★★★ GUEST HOUSE

**tel:** 01736 795677 & 07840 072323 **Sea View Meadows, St Ives Road TR26 2JX**
**email:** enquiries@mustard-tree.co.uk **web:** www.mustard-tree.co.uk
**dir:** *A3074 to Carbis Bay, The Mustard Tree on right opposite Methodist church*

Set in delightful gardens and with sea views, this attractive house is just a short drive from the centre of St Ives, and the coastal path that leads from Carbis Bay to St Ives. The pleasant bedrooms are very comfortable and have many extras. A splendid choice is offered at breakfast, with vegetarian and continental options.

**Rooms:** 9 rms (8 en suite) (1 pri facs) (1 fmly) (4 GF) **S** £37–£48; **D** £72–£98*
**Facilities:** FTV DVD TVL tea/coffee WiFi ⚓ **Extras:** Guest PC available, fridge
**Conf:** Max 20 **Parking:** 9

## The Old Count House

★★★★ GUEST HOUSE

**tel:** 01736 795369 & 07853 844777 **1 Trenwith Square TR26 1DQ**
**email:** counthouse@btconnect.com **web:** www.theoldcounthouse-stives.co.uk
**dir:** *Follow signs to St Ives, house between leisure centre & school*

Situated in a quiet residential area with on-site parking, The Old Count House is a granite building, where Victorian mine workers collected their wages. Guests are assured of a warm welcome and an extensive choice at breakfast. Bedrooms vary in size, with all rooms being well equipped. The town centre, with all its restaurants, is only a five-minute walk away.

**Rooms:** 10 rms (9 en suite) (1 pri facs) (2 GF) **S** £55–£60; **D** £85–£90*
**Facilities:** FTV DVD Lounge TVL tea/coffee WiFi ⚓ Excercise bike Massage chair
**Parking:** 9 **Notes:** No children Closed Nov, 20–29 Dec & Feb

## ST IVES continued

## Old Vicarage

★★★★ GUEST HOUSE

**tel:** 01736 796124 **Parc-an-Creet TR26 2ES**
**email:** stay@oldvicarage.com **web:** www.oldvicarage.com
**dir:** From A3074 in town centre take B3306, 0.5m right into Parc-an-Creet

This former Victorian rectory stands in secluded gardens in a quiet part of St Ives and is convenient for the seaside, town and Tate St Ives. The bedrooms are enhanced by modern facilities. A good choice of local produce is offered at breakfast, plus home-made yogurt and preserves.

**Rooms:** 6 en suite (4 fmly) **S** £67–£90; **D** £76–£113* **Facilities:** FTV TVL tea/coffee Licensed WiFi **Parking:** 12 **Notes:** LB Closed Dec–Jan Civ wed 35

## The Regent

★★★★ GUEST ACCOMMODATION

**tel:** 01736 796195 **Fernlea Terrace TR26 2BH**
**email:** keith@regenthotel.com **web:** www.regenthotel.com
**dir:** In town centre, near bus & railway station

This popular and attractive property stands on an elevated position convenient for the town centre and seafront. The Regent has well-equipped bedrooms, some with spectacular sea vistas, and the comfortable lounge also has great views. The breakfast choices, including vegetarian, are excellent.

**Rooms:** 10 rms (8 en suite) (1 fmly) **S** £52–£98; **D** £98–£126* **Facilities:** FTV Lounge TVL tea/coffee WiFi **Parking:** 12 **Notes:** LB No children 16yrs

## The Sloop Inn

★★★ INN

**tel:** 01736 796584 **The Wharf TR26 1LP**
**email:** sloopinn@btinternet.com **web:** www.sloop-inn.co.uk
**dir:** On St Ives harbour by middle slipway

This attractive, historic inn has an imposing position on the harbour. Each of the guest rooms has a nautical name, many enjoy pleasant views, and all have impressive modern facilities. A good choice of dishes is offered at lunch and dinner in the atmospheric restaurant-bar.

**Rooms:** 22 en suite (6 fmly) (5 GF) **Facilities:** FTV tea/coffee Dinner available WiFi **Parking:** 8 **Notes:** LB

## ST KEVERNE — Map 2 SW72

## Gallen-Treath Guest House

★★★ GUEST HOUSE

**tel:** 01326 280400 & 07579 967836 **Porthallow TR12 6PL**
**email:** gallentreath@btclick.com **web:** www.gallen-treath.com
**dir:** 1.5m SE of St Keverne in Porthallow

Gallen-Treath Guest House has super views over the countryside and sea from its elevated position above Porthallow. Bedrooms are individually decorated and feature many personal touches. Guests can relax in the large, comfortable lounge complete with balcony. Hearty breakfasts and dinners (by arrangement) are served in the bright dining room.

**Rooms:** 5 en suite (1 fmly) (1 GF) **Facilities:** FTV TVL tea/coffee Dinner available Licensed WiFi **Parking:** 6

## ST KEW — Map 2 SX07

## Tregellist Farm

★★★★ BED AND BREAKFAST

**tel:** 01208 880537 & 07970 559637 **Tregellist PL30 3HG**
**email:** tregellistfarm@btinternet.com **web:** www.tregellistfarm.co.uk
**dir:** On B3314 between Pendoggett & St Endellion, take turn brown signed to St Kew & Tregellist Farm

Tregellist Farm is located in beautiful countryside close to Port Isaac, and convenient for Lanhydrock, Pencarrow, The Lost Gardens of Heligan, Padstow and The Eden Project. All bedrooms are en suite, with flat-screen TVs, hospitality trays with fresh milk daily. Served at separate tables in the dining room, breakfast is sourced locally and includes fresh eggs from the farm.

**Rooms:** 2 en suite 2 annexe en suite (1 fmly) (2 GF) **S** £48–£50; **D** £92–£96* **Facilities:** FTV DVD TVL tea/coffee WiFi **Parking:** 6 **Notes:** Closed Xmas & New Year

## ST MARY'S (ISLES OF SCILLY) — Map 2 SV91

## Crebinick House

★★★★ GUEST HOUSE

**tel:** 01720 422968 **Church Street TR21 0JT**
**email:** aa@crebinick.co.uk **web:** www.crebinick.co.uk
**dir:** House 500yds from quay through Hugh Town; (airport bus to house)

Many guests return time and again to this friendly, family-run house close to the town centre and the seafront. The granite-built property dates from 1760 and has smart, well-equipped bedrooms; two are on the ground floor. There is a quiet lounge for relaxing.

**Rooms:** 4 en suite (2 GF) **S** £54–£64; **D** £78–£98* **Facilities:** FTV Lounge tea/coffee WiFi **Notes:** LB No children 10yrs Closed Nov–Mar

## ST MELLION — Map 3 SX36

### Premier Collection

## Pentillie Castle & Estate

★★★★★ GUEST ACCOMMODATION

**tel:** 01579 350044 **Paynters Cross PL12 6QD**
**email:** contact@pentillie.co.uk **web:** www.pentillie.co.uk
**dir:** From A38 Saltash onto A388 to Callington & St Mellion. After 3.1m right to Cargreen & Landulph. 100yds on left

Pentillie Castle & Estate has a great deal to offer. For a start, it's in a peaceful location in the heart of the Tamar Valley on the Cornwall and Devon border. It has established gardens, formal lawns and breath-taking views stretching over 2,000 acres of land. The property has been lovingly renovated to its former glory; the comfortable and well equipped rooms are warm and inviting. Supper and breakfast are served in the elegant dining room with views of the gardens. The beautifully designed lounge and drawing room are the perfect setting to read the paper or enjoy a glass of wine from the honesty bar.

**Rooms:** 9 en suite (1 GF) **S** £110–£235; **D** £125–£250* **Facilities:** FTV DVD Lounge TVL tea/coffee Dinner available Licensed WiFi ⬆ 36 Pool table Games room **Extras:** Speciality toiletries, robes, slippers, shortbread – complimentary **Conf:** Max 30 Thtr 30 Class 24 Board 24 **Parking:** 100 **Notes:** LB Civ wed 120

## SALTASH
Map 3 SX45

## Smeaton Farm

★★★★ ☒ ⬳ FARMHOUSE

**tel:** 01579 351833 & 07817 419747 **PL12 6RZ**
**email:** info@smeatonfarm.co.uk **web:** www.smeatonfarm.co.uk
**dir:** 1m N of Hatt & 1m S of St Mellion just off A388

This elegant Georgian farmhouse is surrounded by 450 acres of rolling Cornish farmland, providing a wonderfully peaceful place to stay. Home to the Jones family, the atmosphere is relaxed and hospitable, with every effort made to ensure that guests have a comfortable and rewarding break. Bedrooms are spacious, light and airy. Enjoyable dinners often feature home-reared meats, and the sausages at breakfast come highly recommended.

**Rooms:** 3 en suite (1 fmly) **S** £65–£85; **D** £75–£95* **Facilities:** FTV DVD Lounge TVL tea/coffee Dinner available Licensed WiFi ↧18 ☒ Cornish maze Guided farm tours **Extras:** Speciality toiletries, snacks, fruit **Conf:** Max 10 Board 10 **Parking:** 8 **Notes:** LB 450 acres arable/beef/sheep

## Hay Lake Farm Bed & Breakfast

★★★★ BED AND BREAKFAST

**tel:** 01752 851209 & 07989 426306 **Landrake PL12 5AE**
**email:** ianbiffen@hotmail.co.uk **web:** www.haylakefarm.co.uk
**dir:** A38 at Landrake turn into West Ln. 0.75m on left before x-rds

This modern, comfortable bed and breakfast offers spacious and well-equipped en suite accommodation. Hay Lake Farm is ideal for those exploring both north and south coasts of Cornwall, and is within easy reach of many National Trust properties as well as The Eden Project. Stables are available.

**Rooms:** 3 en suite (2 fmly) (1 GF) **S** £50–£60; **D** £85–£95* **Facilities:** FTV DVD tea/coffee WiFi ☒ **Extras:** Speciality toiletries – complimentary **Parking:** 6

## Crooked Inn

★★★★ INN

**tel:** 01752 848177 **Stoketon Cross, Trematon PL12 4RZ**
**email:** info@crooked-inn.co.uk **web:** www.crooked-inn.co.uk
**dir:** 1.5m NW of Saltash. A38 W from Saltash, 2nd left to Trematon, sharp right

The friendly animals that freely roam the courtyard add to the relaxed country style of this delightful inn. The spacious bedrooms are well equipped, and freshly cooked dinners are available in the bar and conservatory. Breakfast is served in the cottage-style dining room.

**Rooms:** 15 annexe en suite (5 fmly) (7 GF) **Facilities:** FTV tea/coffee Dinner available WiFi ↖ **Extras:** Speciality toiletries, fresh milk **Conf:** Max 60 **Parking:** 45 **Notes:** Closed 25 Dec

## ISLES OF SCILLY
*See St Mary's & Tresco*

## TORPOINT
Map 3 SX45

## The Devon and Cornwall

★★★ INN

**tel:** 01752 822320 **1 West Street, Millbrook PL10 1AA**
**email:** thedevonandcornwall@hotmail.co.uk **web:** www.thedevonandcornwall.co.uk
**dir:** From Torpoint Ferry onto A374, follow signs for Antony. Turn left into village & follow road to T-junct. Turn left to Millbrook, follow road

This cosy village inn, popular with the locals, offers a great location for those wishing to explore Devon and the south Cornwall coastline. All bedrooms are en suite, comfortable and modern. Meals are served daily.

**Rooms:** 5 en suite (2 fmly) **Facilities:** FTV tea/coffee Dinner available WiFi ☒ **Notes:** LB

## TRESCO (ISLES OF SCILLY)    Map 2 SV81

### New Inn

★★★★  INN

**tel:** 01720 422849 & 423006 **TR24 0QQ**
**email:** contactus@tresco.co.uk **web:** www.tresco.co.uk
**dir:** *By New Grimsby Quay*

This friendly, popular inn is located at the island's centre point and offers bright, attractive and well-equipped bedrooms, many with splendid sea views. Guests have an extensive choice from the menu at both lunch and dinner and can also choose where they take their meals – either in the airy bistro-style Pavilion, or the popular bar which serves real ales. A heated outdoor pool is also available.

**Rooms:** 16 en suite (2 fmly) (2 GF) **S** £65–£125; **D** £130–£250* **Facilities:** FTV DVD Lounge tea/coffee Dinner available Direct dial WiFi ↖ ⚲ Fishing Pool table Use of local leisure spa **Extras:** Speciality toiletries, fresh ground coffee, home-made shortbread **Notes:** LB

## TRURO    Map 2 SW84

### Bodrean Manor Farm

★★★★ ⚲ FARMHOUSE

**tel:** 07970 955857 **Trispen TR4 9AG**
**email:** bodrean@hotmail.co.uk **web:** www.bodreanmanorfarm.co.uk
**dir:** *3m NE of Truro. A30 onto A39 towards Truro, left after Trispen signed Trehane, farm drive 100yds*

This friendly farmhouse is located in peaceful countryside, convenient for Truro or as a touring base. It has all the charm of an historic house but is styled and fitted with modern facilities. Bedrooms are thoughtfully and extensively equipped, and the bathrooms are well provisioned with soft towels and a host of toiletries. The home-cooked breakfast is served around a large, communal table in the smartly appointed dining room. Storage for motorbikes and cycles is available.

**Rooms:** 3 rms (2 en suite) (1 pri facs) (1 fmly) **S** £48–£50; **D** £76–£78*
**Facilities:** FTV TVL tea/coffee WiFi ⚲ **Parking:** 6 **Notes:** LB  220 acres mixed

### Bissick Old Mill

★★★★ GUEST HOUSE

**tel:** 01726 882557 **Ladock TR2 4PG**
**email:** enquiries@bissickoldmill.plus.com **web:** www.bissickoldmill.co.uk
**dir:** *6m NE of Truro. Exit B3275 in Ladock centre by Falmouth Arms pub*

This charming family-run guest house in a former mill dates back some 300 years. Low ceilings, beams, stone walls and an impressive fireplace all contribute to its

character. Equally inviting is the hospitality extended to guests, who are instantly made welcome. The high-spec bedrooms are all en suite and feature Egyptian cotton sheets along with many extras. The breakfast is a memorable aspect of any stay with the menu offering a range of freshly prepared hot dishes.

**Rooms:** 3 en suite 1 annexe en suite (1 fmly) (1 GF) **Facilities:** FTV DVD TVL tea/coffee Direct dial WiFi **Parking:** 6 **Notes:** LB

### Merchant House

★★★★ GUEST ACCOMMODATION

**tel:** 01872 272450 **49 Falmouth Road TR1 2HL**
**email:** reception@merchant-house.co.uk **web:** www.merchant-house.co.uk
**dir:** *A39 Truro, on approaching centre proceed across 1st & 2nd rdbts onto bypass. At top of hill turn right at twin mini rdbt into Falmouth Rd. 100mtrs on right*

Merchant House is just a short stroll from the city centre. A range of bedrooms is offered – all have good levels of comfort. Public areas are smartly appointed with period features retained where possible. The bar provides an engaging venue for a refreshing glass of something, perhaps accompanied by a tasty dish from the bar menu, and the friendly team are flexible and helpful.

**Rooms:** 30 en suite (2 fmly) (4 GF) **S** £45–£79; **D** £65–£99* **Facilities:** FTV TVL tea/coffee Direct dial Licensed WiFi ⚲ Drying room Launderette Outside heated dog shower **Extras:** Speciality toiletries **Conf:** Max 64 Thtr 64 Class 48 Board 36 **Parking:** 30 **Notes:** LB Closed 24–27 Dec

### Donnington Guest House

★★★ GUEST ACCOMMODATION

**tel:** 01872 222552 & 07787 555475 **43 Treyew Road TR1 2BY**
**email:** info@donnington-guesthouse.co.uk **web:** www.donnington-guesthouse.co.uk

A well located property, just 12 minutes' walk from the city centre. It is actually two houses operating as one, with breakfast being taken in the breakfast room of one of them. Well-appointed bedrooms, a friendly host and good off-road parking make this a very popular venue.

**Rooms:** 14 rms (12 en suite) (2 pri facs) (2 fmly) (2 GF) **Facilities:** FTV DVD tea/coffee ♨18 ⚲ **Extras:** Fridge **Parking:** 11

### Resparveth Farm

★★★ FARMHOUSE

**tel:** 01726 882382 & 07929 234206 **Grampound Road TR2 4EF**
**email:** resparveth.farm@gmail.com **web:** www.resparvethfarmbnb.co.uk
**dir:** *A30 exit signed Fraddon/Grampound Road (B3275). Continue on A3058, through Grampound Road village, turn right at B&B sign*

The young owners of this traditional farmhouse bed and breakfast do all they can to make a stay as comfortable as possible. This is a handy location for St Austell, The Eden Project and Truro, offering comfortable rooms and freshly cooked breakfasts at one large table in the breakfast room featuring an original Cornish range.

**Rooms:** 3 en suite **D** £59–£86* **Facilities:** FTV DVD tea/coffee WiFi ⚲ Feeding of animals Farm experience **Conf:** Max 6 Thtr 6 Class 6 Board 6 **Parking:** 4 **Notes:** LB 60 acres beef/sheep/bees/pigs/chickens/arable

## VERYAN

Map 2 SW93

## Elerkey Guest House

★★★★ GUEST HOUSE

**tel:** 01872 501261 & 501160 **Elerkey House TR2 5QA**
**email:** anne@elerkeyguesthouse.co.uk **web:** www.elerkeyguesthouse.co.uk
**dir:** In village, 1st left after church & water gardens

This peaceful home is surrounded by attractive gardens in a tranquil village. The proprietors and their family provide exemplary hospitality and many guests return time and again. The pleasantly appointed bedrooms have many considerate extras.

**Rooms:** 4 en suite (1 fmly) **S** £65–£90; **D** £70–£90* **Facilities:** FTV DVD Lounge tea/coffee Direct dial WiFi ⚓ Art gallery & gift shop **Extras:** Mineral water **Parking:** 5 **Notes:** LB Closed Xmas–New Year

## WADEBRIDGE

Map 2 SW97

### Premier Collection

## Wadebridge Bed and Breakfast

★★★★★ BED AND BREAKFAST

**tel:** 01208 816837 & 07740 255092 **Orchard House, Elmsleigh Road PL27 7HA**
**email:** info@wadebridgebedandbreakfast.net
**web:** www.wadebridgebedandbreakfast.net
**dir:** From Bodmin A389 into Wadebridge. Pass Trelawney Garden Centre on right, continue to rdbt. Exit onto A39. At next rdbt left into West Hill. After phone box on left, take next left into Elmsleigh Rd, 1st house on left

This contemporary house is just a short walk from the town centre and provides an ideal base from which to explore the area. Bedrooms offer impressive levels of comfort and quality, and one has a balcony with lovely views over the town and countryside. Bathrooms offer all the expected mod cons with underfloor heating, invigorating showers and fluffy towels. Generous and tasty breakfasts are served in the dining room with a garden patio available for alfresco dining. Secure storage is available for bikes and surf boards.

**Rooms:** 3 en suite **S** £70–£100; **D** £80–£120 **Facilities:** FTV DVD TVL tea/coffee WiFi ⚓ **Extras:** Bottled water, fresh milk, speciality toiletries **Parking:** 3 **Notes:** LB No children Closed Jan–Feb

## CUMBRIA

## ALSTON

Map 18 NY74

## Alston House

★★★★ 🍴 RESTAURANT WITH ROOMS

**tel:** 01434 382200 **Townfoot CA9 3RN**
**email:** alstonhouse@fsmail.net **web:** www.alstonhouse.co.uk
**dir:** On A686 opposite Spar garage

Located at the foot of the town, this family-owned restaurant with rooms provides well-equipped, stylish and comfortable accommodation. The kitchen serves both modern and traditional dishes with flair and creativity. Alston House runs a café during the day, serving light meals and afternoon teas.

**Rooms:** 7 en suite (3 fmly) **Facilities:** DVD tea/coffee Dinner available WiFi ⚓9 Fishing **Conf:** Max 70 Thtr 70 Class 30 Board 30 **Parking:** 20 **Notes:** Civ wed

## AMBLESIDE

Map 18 NY30

### AA GUEST ACCOMMODATION OF THE YEAR FOR ENGLAND 2017–18

### Premier Collection

## Nanny Brow

★★★★★ GUEST ACCOMMODATION

**tel:** 015394 33232 & 07746 103008 **Clappersgate LA22 9NF**
**email:** unwind@nannybrow.co.uk **web:** www.nannybrow.co.uk
**dir:** M6 junct 36 onto A590 & A591 through Windermere. At lights bear left onto A593, left again at rugby pitch & left over bridge. Through Clappersgate, 0.5m on right

Nanny Brow provides high quality throughout. Each room is thoughtfully decorated with contemporary furnishings, antique furniture, and original arts and crafts. The property is situated in Clappersgate, close to Ambleside, standing high above the road overlooking the beautiful Langdale Valley. A drink from the bar menu can be enjoyed in the quiet guest lounge where you will find plenty of information about local walks.

**Rooms:** 12 en suite 2 annexe en suite (2 GF) **S** £140–£300; **D** £140–£300* **Facilities:** FTV DVD Lounge tea/coffee Licensed WiFi ⚓ **Extras:** Robes, champagne, chocolates, flowers – chargeable **Conf:** Max 26 Thtr 26 Class 12 Board 12 **Parking:** 15 **Notes:** LB No children 12yrs Civ wed 32

# Symbols and abbreviations
explained on pages 6–7

AMBLESIDE *continued*

## Riverside Bed & Breakfast

★★★★ ⬤ GUEST HOUSE

**tel:** 015394 32395 & 32440 **Under Loughrigg LA22 9LJ**
**email:** info@riverside-at-ambleside.co.uk **web:** www.riverside-at-ambleside.co.uk
**dir:** *A593 from Ambleside to Coniston, over stone bridge, right into Under Loughrigg Ln, Riverside 150yds left*

Riverside is a Victorian house, whose owners offer a most friendly welcome. It is situated on a quiet lane by the River Rothay, below Loughrigg Fell. Bedrooms all have lovely views, are very comfortable and stylishly furnished, and feature many thoughtful extras. A log-burning stove warms the lounge in winter. Guests can use the garden, which has seating for the morning and evening sun. An award-winning hearty Lakeland breakfast is a highlight of any stay and features local produce along with home baking and preserves. Riverside Bed & Breakfast was a finalist for the AA Friendliest B&B of the Year 2017–18.

**Rooms:** 6 en suite **D** £108–£136* **Facilities:** FTV iPod docking station TVL tea/coffee Licensed WiFi ⬤ **Parking:** 6 **Notes:** No children 10yrs Closed 13 Dec–22 Jan

## Innkeeper's Lodge Ambleside, Lake District

★★★★ INN

**tel:** 08451 551551 *(Calls cost 2p per minute plus your phone company's access charge)*
**The White Lion, Market Place LA22 9DB**
**email:** info@innkeeperslodge.com **web:** www.innkeeperslodge.com

Charming 18th-century inn situated in the heart of Ambleside close to Windermere and within easy reach of the M6. The modern, well equipped bedrooms are very well appointed with a range of modern facilities. Public areas include a large open-plan lounge bar with a roaring open fire and a selection of seating options; dinner and full English breakfast are available in the smart dining room.

**Rooms:** 7 en suite (4 fmly) **Facilities:** FTV tea/coffee Dinner available WiFi
**Conf:** Max 20 **Parking:** 7

## The Old Vicarage

★★★★ Ⓐ GUEST ACCOMMODATION

**tel:** 015394 33364 **Vicarage Road LA22 9DH**
**email:** info@oldvicarageambleside.co.uk **web:** www.oldvicarageambleside.co.uk
**dir:** *In town centre. Exit Compston Rd left into Vicarage Rd*

This charming early Victorian house stands in quiet landscaped grounds with private parking, close to the town centre. Bedrooms are mostly spacious, some having four-posters and spa baths, and all have video players, fridges and CD players. There also is a splendid pool, sauna and a hot tub.

**Rooms:** 15 en suite (4 fmly) (2 GF) **Facilities:** FTV DVD Lounge tea/coffee WiFi ⬤ ⬤ Pool table ⬤ Hot tub **Extras:** Mini-fridge **Parking:** 17 **Notes:** LB Closed 23-28 Dec

| ARNSIDE | Map 18 SD47 |
|---|---|

## Ye Olde Fighting Cocks

★★★★ INN

**tel:** 01524 761203 **The Promenade LA5 0HD**
**email:** info@fightingcocksarnside.co.uk **web:** www.fightingcocksarnside.co.uk

A central location on Arnside's seafront gives this popular pub prime position for views over Morecambe bay sands and the Cumbrian fells. Very much a traditional feel inside though bedrooms, spread between the main building and the coach house are modern and well equipped. Food is served daily in the bar and restaurant, whilst hearty breakfasts are served upstairs. Parking available onsite.

**Rooms:** 15 en suite (3 GF) **Facilities:** FTV Lounge TVL tea/coffee Dinner available ⬤ **Conf:** Max 20 Thtr 20 Class 20 Board 20 **Parking:** 15 **Notes:** LB No children 10yrs

| ASKHAM | Map 18 NY52 |
|---|---|

## Askham Hall

★★★★★ ◉◉ GUEST ACCOMMODATION

**tel:** 01931 712350 & 07887 724857 **CA10 2PF**
**email:** enquiries@askhamhall.co.uk **web:** www.askhamhall.co.uk
**dir:** *S of Penrith, follow signs from B5320 to Askham & brown tourist signs*

Askham Hall sits on the edge of the Lake District surrounded by the majestic Cumbrian countryside. This Grade I listed building dates back to the 14th century with only the restaurant being a recent addition to the building. Public areas are warm and welcoming with the open fire adding to the charm.

Bedrooms and their en suites cater well for the modern traveler with many thoughtful extras provided as standard. Award-winning food which uses produce from the kitchen gardens as well as from the farms within the estate. Friendly hands-on team add to this wonderful guest experience.

*Askham Hall*

**Rooms:** 15 en suite (2 fmly) **S** £138–£308; **D** £150–£320* **Facilities:** STV FTV DVD Lounge tea/coffee Dinner available Direct dial Licensed WiFi ↘ ⩗ Fishing Snooker Pool table ⓑ **Extras:** Speciality toiletries, mini-bar, fridge **Notes:** Closed Xmas RS Jan–mid Feb group bookings only Civ wed 150

### BOOT
Map 18 NY10

## Brook House Inn
★★★★ ⬱ INN

**tel:** 01946 723288 **CA19 1TG**
**email:** stay@brookhouseinn.co.uk **web:** www.brookhouseinn.co.uk
**dir:** *In village centre. 0.5m NE of Dalegarth station*

Located in the heart of Eskdale, this impressive inn dates from the early 18th century and has been renovated to offer comfortable accommodation with smart, modern bathrooms for weary walkers and travellers. Wholesome meals using local produce are served in the traditionally furnished dining room or attractive bar – the latter features real ales and country memorabilia.

**Rooms:** 8 en suite (2 fmly) **Facilities:** FTV tea/coffee Dinner available WiFi **Conf:** Max 35 **Parking:** 24 **Notes:** LB Closed 25 Dec

### BORROWDALE
Map 18 NY21

#### Premier Collection

## Hazel Bank Country House
★★★★★ ⬣ ⬱ GUEST ACCOMMODATION

**tel:** 017687 77248 & 07775 701069 **Rosthwaite CA12 5XB**
**email:** info@hazelbankhotel.co.uk **web:** www.hazelbankhotel.co.uk
**dir:** *B5289 from Keswick towards Borrowdale, left after sign for Rosthwaite*

Set on an elevated position surrounded by four acres of gardens and woodland, Hazel Bank Country House enjoys wonderful views of Borrowdale. The approach to this grand Victorian house is impressive, reached via a picturesque hump back bridge and a winding drive. Bedrooms are sumptuous and all are en suite. Carefully cooked dishes are served in the elegant dining room; the daily changing four-course menu features fresh local ingredients. There is a friendly atmosphere here and the proprietors are very welcoming.

**Rooms:** 7 en suite (1 GF) **Facilities:** FTV iPod docking station Lounge tea/coffee Dinner available Licensed WiFi ⩗ **Extras:** Speciality toiletries, chocolates, bottled water **Parking:** 9 **Notes:** LB No children 12yrs Closed 30 Nov–30 Jan

### BOWNESS-ON-WINDERMERE
*See Windermere*

### BRAITHWAITE
Map 18 NY22

## The Cottage in the Wood
★★★★ ⬤⬤⬤ ⬱ RESTAURANT WITH ROOMS

**tel:** 017687 78409 & 07730 312193 **Whinlatter Pass CA12 5TW**
**email:** relax@thecottageinthewood.co.uk **web:** www.thecottageinthewood.co.uk
**dir:** *M6 junct 40, A66 W. After Keswick exit for Braithwaite via Whinlatter Pass (B5292), establishment at top of pass*

This charming property sits on wooded hills with striking views of Skiddaw, and is conveniently placed for Keswick. The owners provide excellent hospitality in a relaxed manner. The award-winning food, freshly prepared and locally sourced, is served in the bright and welcoming conservatory restaurant with its stunning views. The comfortable bedrooms are well appointed and have many useful extras.

**Rooms:** 9 en suite **S** £88–£96; **D** £110–£205* **Facilities:** FTV Lounge tea/coffee Dinner available Direct dial WiFi ⓑ **Parking:** 15 **Notes:** LB No children 10yrs Closed Jan RS Mon closed

### BRAMPTON
Map 21 NY56

#### Premier Collection

## Lanercost Bed and Breakfast
★★★★★ ⬱ ⬱ GUEST ACCOMMODATION

**tel:** 016977 42589 & 07976 977204 **Lanercost CA8 2HQ**
**email:** info@lanercostbedandbreakfast.co.uk
**web:** www.lanercostbedandbreakfast.co.uk
**dir:** *Follow signs to Lanercost Priory, then signs to B&B*

Built in 1840 in the grounds of Lanercost Priory, close to Hadrian's Wall, this property offers individually designed bedrooms of a good size with quality fixtures and fittings. Public areas are welcoming and enhanced with artwork and objets d'art. The hearty, award-winning breakfasts use local produce and make a wonderful start to the day, and dinners are equally good.

**Rooms:** 4 en suite **S** £83–£88; **D** £93–£98* **Facilities:** FTV iPod docking station Lounge tea/coffee Dinner available Licensed WiFi ⌀18 Fishing ⓑ **Extras:** Speciality toiletries, home-made biscuits – complimentary **Conf:** Max 10 Thtr 10 Class 10 Board 10 **Parking:** 10 **Notes:** LB

BRAMPTON *continued*

## Abbey Bridge

★★★★ 🍽 GUEST ACCOMMODATION

**tel:** 016977 3841 **Lanercost CA8 2HG**
**email:** tim@abbeybridge.co.uk **web:** www.abbeybridge.co.uk
**dir:** *M6 junct 43. A69 to Brampton, follow signs for Lanercost Priory. Through town, 2m on left, next to Lanercost Bridge*

The Abbey Bridge has a long history and is a beautifully presented property offering wonderful hospitality and high standards of comfort. Previously an inn and pub but also a Temperance Inn until regaining its license in the 1970s, the property is currently fully licensed, and comprises two buildings, The Blacksmiths and the main house. Walkers are well catered for, with a boot and wet kit room which even boasts boot drying equipment. Located close to Hadrian's Wall and even closer to Lanercost Priory, it's an ideal base to tour the surrounding area with Edinburgh, Newcastle, the North Pennines and the Lakes all within easy reach, as the A69 is just minutes away. Dinner is available by prior arrangement.

**Rooms:** 5 en suite 1 annexe en suite (1 GF) **S** £70–£75; **D** £85–£90* **Facilities:** FTV tea/coffee Dinner available by arrangement Licensed WiFi 🔒 **Parking:** 7 **Notes:** Closed Nov–Mar

## The Blacksmiths Arms

★★★★ INN

**tel:** 016977 3452 & 42111 **Talkin Village CA8 1LE**
**email:** blacksmithsarmstalkin@yahoo.co.uk **web:** www.blacksmithstalkin.co.uk
**dir:** *B6413 from Brampton to Castle Carrock, after level crossing 2nd left signed Talkin*

Dating from the early 19th century and used as a smithy until the 1950s, this friendly village inn offers good home-cooked fare and real ales, with two Cumbrian cask beers always available. Bedrooms are well equipped, and three are particularly smart. An extensive menu and daily specials are offered in the cosy bar lounges or the smart, panelled Old Forge Restaurant.

**Rooms:** 5 en suite 3 annexe en suite (2 fmly) (3 GF) **S** £60–£65; **D** £80–£90 **Facilities:** FTV tea/coffee Dinner available Direct dial WiFi ⌁18 🔒 **Parking:** 20

| BROUGH | Map 18 NY71 |

### Premier Collection

## The Inn at Brough

★★★★★ ⚙ INN

**tel:** 01768 341252 **Main Street CA17 4AX**
**email:** enquiries@theinnatbrough.co.uk **web:** www.theinnatbrough.co.uk
**dir:** *M6 junct 38, A685 to Kirkby Stephen, then Brough. A66 exit to Brough & Kirkby Stephen*

This former 18th-century coaching inn is located in the picturesque Eden Valley and enjoys easy access to the A66. A complete transformation over the past few years has had impressive results. Deeply comfortable bedrooms feature a host of luxury touches, while bathrooms boast Villeroy & Boch fittings and local toiletries. There are contemporary touches throughout the bar and restaurant, and a function suite was also added this year. Any stay here would not be complete without sampling the wonderful food on offer both at dinner and breakfast.

**Rooms:** 14 en suite 2 annexe en suite (2 fmly) (2 GF) **S** £60–£80; **D** £100–£180* **Facilities:** FTV DVD tea/coffee Dinner available WiFi ⌁18 Pool table 🔒 **Extras:** Robes, slippers, soft drinks, home-made biscuits **Conf:** Max 100 Thtr 60 Class 60 Board 30 **Parking:** 40 **Notes:** LB

| CARLISLE | Map 18 NY35 |

*See also Brampton*

## The Angus

★★★★ GUEST ACCOMMODATION

**tel:** 01228 523546 **14-16 Scotland Road CA3 9DG**
**email:** hotel@angus-hotel.co.uk **web:** www.angus-hotel.co.uk
**dir:** *0.5m N of city centre on A7*

Situated just north of the city and built on the actual foundations of Hadrian's Wall, this family-run establishment is ideal for business and leisure. A warm welcome is assured and the accommodation is well equipped. Dinner is available by prior arrangement, providing enjoyable food and home baking. There is also a comfortable lounge available for the guests.

**Rooms:** 10 en suite (2 fmly) **Facilities:** FTV Lounge tea/coffee Dinner available by arrangement Direct dial Licensed WiFi 🔒 **Notes:** LB

| CARTMEL | Map 18 SD37 |

### Premier Collection

## L'Enclume

★★★★★ 🏵🏵🏵🏵🏵 RESTAURANT WITH ROOMS

**tel:** 015395 36362 **Cavendish St LA11 6PZ**
**email:** info@lenclume.co.uk **web:** www.lenclume.co.uk
**dir:** *From A590 turn left for Cartmel before Newby Bridge*

L'Enclume is a delightful 13th-century property in the heart of a lovely village, and offers incredible 21st-century cooking that draws foodies from far and wide. Once the village forge (l'enclume is French for 'the anvil') it's now the location for some of Britain's best food, and Simon Rogan's imaginative and adventurous cooking may be sampled in the stylish restaurant. Individually designed, modern, en suite rooms of varying sizes and styles are in the main property or dotted about the village only a few moments' walk from the L'Enclume restaurant.

**Rooms:** 5 en suite 11 annexe en suite (3 fmly) (2 GF) **S** £130–£175; **D** £170–£395* **Facilities:** STV DVD iPod docking station tea/coffee Dinner available Direct dial WiFi **Extras:** Mini-bar, speciality toiletries **Parking:** 3

## CLIFTON
Map 18 NY52

# George and Dragon, Clifton

★★★★  INN

**tel:** 01768 865381 & 07887 724857 **CA10 2ER**
**email:** enquiries@georgeanddragonclifton.co.uk
**web:** www.georgeanddragonclifton.co.uk
**dir:** On A6 in village of Clifton

The George and Dragon is an 18th-century coaching inn located just south of Penrith, ideally located for the Lakes and surrounding areas. The restored property was is in keeping with its Georgian heritage and retains many of the original features and materials. Comfortable bedrooms are well appointed, catering well for the needs of the modern day guest. The bar is warm and welcoming with a number of real ales on offer. Award-winning food uses predominantly local produce, much of which comes from the owners' estate. The hearty breakfast will provide a great start to the day.

**Rooms:** 11 en suite (2 fmly) **S** £85–£119; **D** £100–£160* **Facilities:** STV FTV Lounge Dinner available WiFi ♨ Fishing ♨ **Extras:** Speciality toiletries **Notes:** Closed 26 Dec

## CROSTHWAITE
Map 18 SD49

### Premier Collection

# The Punchbowl Inn at Crosthwaite

★★★★★ ◎◎  INN

**tel:** 015395 68237 **Lyth Valley LA8 8HR**
**email:** info@the-punchbowl.co.uk **web:** www.the-punchbowl.co.uk
**dir:** M6 junct 36 signed Barrow, on A5074 towards Windermere, turn right for Crosthwaite. At E end of village beside church

Located in the stunning Lyth Valley alongside the village church, this historic inn has been renovated to provide excellent standards of comfort and facilities. Its sumptuous bedrooms have a wealth of thoughtful extras, and imaginative food is available in the elegant restaurant or in the rustic-style bar with open fires. A warm welcome and professional service is assured.

**Rooms:** 9 en suite **S** £82.50–£232.50; **D** £110–£310* **Facilities:** FTV Dinner available Direct dial WiFi ♨ **Extras:** Speciality toiletries, home-made scones & jam **Parking:** 25 **Notes:** Civ wed 48

## GLENRIDDING
Map 18 NY31

### Premier Collection

# Glenridding House

★★★★★  GUEST ACCOMMODATION

**tel:** 017684 82874 & 07966 486701 **CA11 0PH**
**email:** stay@glenriddinghouse.com **web:** www.glenriddinghouse.com
**dir:** M6 junct 40 onto A66, then A592 to Glenridding. Turn sharp second left

Glenridding House is a wonderful Georgian Lakeside villa which sits right on the shores of Ullswater. Used as a holiday home by Charles Darwin, this once derelict building has been lovingly restored. Bedrooms differ in size, and a number boast stunning views of the lake and surrounding fells. An excellent location for those touring this unspoilt area of the Lake District.

**Rooms:** 6 rms (6 pri facs) (1 GF) **Facilities:** FTV Lounge tea/coffee Dinner available Licensed WiFi ♨ Fishing ♨ Packed lunches available **Conf:** Max 30 Thtr 30 Class 30 Board 30 **Parking:** 30 **Notes:** LB No children 18yrs Civ wed 50

## GRANGE-OVER-SANDS      Map 18 SD47

# Birchleigh Guest House

★★★★ GUEST HOUSE

**tel:** 015395 32592 & 07527 844403 **Kents Bank Road LA11 7EY**
**email:** birchleigh@btinternet.com **web:** www.birchleighguesthouse.com
**dir:** M6 junct 36, A590 signed Windermere, then Barrow. At Meathop Rdbt left onto B5277 to Grange-Over-Sands. At 1st rdbt left, at 2nd rdbt right. At T-junct left into Kents Bank Rd. 3rd house on left after car park

This homely and welcoming guest house is situated in the heart of the charming town of Grange-over-Sands, providing four comfortable and tastefully decorated modern bedrooms. Expect a hearty breakfast served in the well-appointed dining room.

**Rooms:** 4 en suite (1 fmly) **S** fr £60; **D** fr £80* **Facilities:** FTV tea/coffee WiFi
🔒 **Extras:** Fresh milk **Parking:** 2

## GRASMERE      Map 18 NY30

### Premier Collection

# Moss Grove Organic

★★★★★ 🍃 GUEST ACCOMMODATION

**tel:** 015394 35251 **LA22 9SW**
**email:** enquiries@mossgrove.com **web:** www.mossgrove.com
**dir:** From S: M6 junct 36 onto A591 signed Keswick. From N: M6 junct 40 onto A591 signed Windermere

Located in the centre of Grasmere, this impressive Victorian house has been appointed using as many natural products as possible, as part of an ongoing dedication to cause minimal environmental impact. The stylish bedrooms are decorated with beautiful wallpaper and natural clay paints, featuring hand-made beds and furnishings. Bose home entertainment systems, flat-screen TVs and luxury bathrooms add further comfort, one room even has a hot tub. Extensive continental breakfasts are served in the spacious kitchen, where guests can help themselves and dine at the large wooden dining table.

**Rooms:** 11 en suite (2 GF) **S** £84–£99; **D** £99–£265* **Facilities:** STV DVD iPod docking station Lounge tea/coffee Licensed WiFi 🔒 **Extras:** Speciality toiletries – complimentary **Parking:** 11 **Notes:** LB No children 14yrs Closed 24–25 Dec

## GRIZEDALE      Map 18 SD39

### Premier Collection

# Grizedale Lodge

★★★★★ 🛏 GUEST HOUSE

**tel:** 015394 36532 **LA22 0QL**
**email:** enquiries@grizedale-lodge.com **web:** www.grizedale-lodge.com
**dir:** From Hawkshead follow signs S to Grizedale. Lodge 2m on right

Set in the heart of Grizedale Forest Park, close to the Go Ape centre and two miles from Hawkshead, this lovely property offers quiet and tranquil surroundings. Hospitality is warm here and Richard and Debs will be keen to welcome you to their home. The comfortable lounge with open log fire and views of the forest, makes this an ideal place to relax. All the rooms are well decorated and some offer four-poster beds. Expect superb home-cooked dinners and appetising breakfasts. Mountain bike storage also available. Grizedale Lodge was a finalist for the AA Friendliest B&B of the Year 2017–18.

**Rooms:** 8 en suite (1 fmly) (2 GF) **D** £66–£160* **Facilities:** FTV DVD Lounge tea/coffee Dinner available Licensed WiFi 🔒 **Extras:** Speciality toiletries **Parking:** 12

## HAWKSHEAD      Map 18 SD39

*See also Near Sawrey*

### Premier Collection

# Ees Wyke Country House

★★★★★ 🌐 🍸 GUEST HOUSE

**tel:** 015394 36393 **LA22 0JZ**
**email:** mail@eeswyke.co.uk **web:** www.eeswyke.co.uk

*(For full entry see Near Sawrey)*

# The Queen's Head Inn & Restaurant

★★★★ 🍴 INN

**tel:** 015394 36271 **Main Street LA22 0NS**
**email:** info@queensheadhawkshead.co.uk **web:** www.queensheadhawkshead.co.uk
**dir:** M6 junct 36, then A590 to Newby Bridge. Over rdbt, 1st right into Hawkshead

This 16th-century inn features a wood-panelled bar with low, oak-beamed ceilings and an open log fire. An excellent selection of quality dishes and local ales are served throughout the day. Accommodation has benefited from a complete refurbishment and bedrooms are comfortable and stylishly decorated with modern amenities.

**Rooms:** 10 en suite 3 annexe en suite (1 fmly) (2 GF) **Facilities:** FTV DVD iPod docking station tea/coffee Dinner available WiFi 🔒 **Extras:** Speciality toiletries, robes, slippers, coffee machine

# Sun Inn

★★★★ 🍴 INN

**tel:** 015394 36236 **Main Street LA22 0NT**
**email:** rooms@suninn.co.uk **web:** www.suninn.co.uk
**dir:** M6 junct 36 onto A591 (Ambleside). Follow signs to Hawkshead, in centre of village

The Sun Inn is a charming 17th-century building located in the heart of the peaceful village of Hawkshead on the quieter side of Windermere. It has retained a great deal of original character, with wooden panelling, oak beams, and stone floors, and exposed brickwork. Bedrooms differ in size but are all well appointed and presented, with local hand-made furniture making the best of the available space. Food is very good, and the bar boasts a number of local real ales, with an open fire adding to the charm in the colder months.

**Rooms:** 8 en suite (1 fmly) **Facilities:** FTV tea/coffee Dinner available WiFi Pool table
🔒 **Extras:** Wine/champagne, flowers, chocolates – chargeable

## Kings Arms

★★★ ⚬ INN

-------------------------------------------------------------

**tel:** 015394 36372 **LA22 0NZ**
**email:** info@kingsarmshawkshead.co.uk **web:** www.kingsarmshawkshead.co.uk
**dir:** *M6 junct 36, A591, left onto A593 at Waterhead. 1m, onto B5286 to Hawkshead, Kings Arms in main square*

The Kings Arms is a traditional Lakeland inn in the heart of a conservation area. The cosy, thoughtfully equipped bedrooms retain much character and are traditionally furnished. A good choice of freshly prepared food is available in the lounge bar and the neatly presented dining room.

**Rooms:** 8 en suite (3 fmly) **S** £60–£72; **D** £90–£104 **Facilities:** FTV DVD tea/coffee Dinner available Direct dial WiFi ⚲ Fishing ⚐ Bowling green **Notes:** LB Closed 25 Dec

---

### ▌ HOLMROOK              Map 18 SD09

## The Lutwidge Arms

★★★★ INN

-------------------------------------------------------------

**tel:** 019467 24230 **CA19 1UH**
**email:** mail@lutwidgearms.co.uk **web:** www.lutwidgearms.co.uk
**dir:** *M6 junct 36, A590 towards Barrow. Follow A595 towards Whitehaven & Workington, property in village centre*

This Victorian roadside inn is family run and offers a welcoming atmosphere. Its name comes from the Lutwidge family of Holmrook Hall, whose lineage included Charles Lutwidge Dodgson, better known as Lewis Carroll. The bar and restaurant offer a wide range of meals during the evening. Bedrooms are smart and comfortable, and the Orangery has transformed the garden and dining areas.

**Rooms:** 11 en suite 5 annexe en suite (5 fmly) (5 GF) **Facilities:** FTV TVL tea/coffee Dinner available WiFi Pool table ⚐ **Conf:** Max 20 Thtr 20 Class 20 Board 20 **Parking:** 30 **Notes:** LB No children 5yrs

---

### ▌ IREBY              Map 18 NY23

## Woodlands Country House

★★★★ ⚲ ⚬ GUEST HOUSE

-------------------------------------------------------------

**tel:** 016973 71791 **CA7 1EX**
**email:** stay@woodlandsatireby.co.uk **web:** www.woodlandsatireby.co.uk
**dir:** *M6 junct 40, A66, pass Keswick, at rdbt right onto A591. At Castle Inn right signed Ireby, 2nd left signed Ireby. Pass church on left, last house in village*

Previously a vicarage, this lovely Victorian home is set in well-tended gardens that attract lots of wildlife. Guests are given a warm welcome by the friendly owner and delicious home-cooked evening meals are available by prior arrangement. A peaceful lounge and cosy bar with snug are also available. Bedrooms are attractively furnished and thoughtfully equipped.

**Rooms:** 4 en suite 3 annexe en suite (3 fmly) (3 GF) **Facilities:** FTV Lounge TVL tea/coffee Dinner available Licensed WiFi **Extras:** Home-made shortbread, sweets, mineral water – complimentary **Parking:** 11 **Notes:** LB

---

### ▌ IRTHINGTON          Map 21 NY46

## The Golden Fleece

★★★★ ◉ INN

-------------------------------------------------------------

**tel:** 01228 573686 & 07766 736924 **Rule Holme CA6 4NF**
**email:** info@thegoldenfleececumbria.co.uk **web:** www.thegoldenfleececumbria.co.uk
**dir:** *M6 junct 44 onto A689 signed Brampton. 1m past Carlisle Airport, on left*

The Golden Fleece is a rural inn set beside the A689, close to Carlisle and Hadrian's Wall. Public areas include a feature bar with local real ales on draught, and a cosy

lounge area with a fire. The dining room is split between several areas helping to create a sense of intimacy. Bedrooms and bathrooms are all modern in appearance. The full Cumbrian breakfasts are not to be missed, and friendly staff provide a true Cumbrian welcome. There is ample parking.

**Rooms:** 8 en suite (4 fmly) **Facilities:** FTV DVD iPod docking station Lounge tea/coffee Dinner available WiFi ⚲18 Fishing ⚐ **Extras:** Speciality toiletries, home-made cakes **Conf:** Max 150 Thtr 120 Class 70 Board 70 **Parking:** 100 **Notes:** Closed 1–8 Jan Civ wed 100

---

### ▌ KENDAL             Map 18 SD59

## The Punch Bowl

★★★★ ⚬ INN

-------------------------------------------------------------

**tel:** 015395 60267 **Barrows Green LA8 0AA**
**email:** punch_bowl@hotmail.co.uk **web:** www.thepunchbowla65.com
**dir:** *M6 junct 36 onto A65 signed Kendal. After 4m, on left*

Expect a warm welcome at this friendly pub within easy reach of local transport links and perfectly situated at the gateway to the Lake District. Two tasteful letting rooms are comfortable and well equipped for the modern traveller. Dinner is traditional and wholesome 'pub grub', and breakfasts are a hearty affair.

**Rooms:** 2 en suite **Facilities:** FTV Lounge TVL tea/coffee Dinner available WiFi Pool table ⚐ **Extras:** Bottled water, Kendal mintcake **Parking:** 40

---

### ▌ KESWICK            Map 18 NY22

## Amble House

★★★★ ⚲ GUEST HOUSE

-------------------------------------------------------------

**tel:** 017687 73288 **23 Eskin Street CA12 4DQ**
**email:** info@amblehouse.co.uk **web:** www.amblehouse.co.uk
**dir:** *400yds SE of town centre. Exit A5271 (Penrith Rd) into Greta St & Eskin St*

An enthusiastic welcome awaits you at this Victorian mid-terrace house, near the town centre and in an ideal location for exploring the Lakes. The thoughtfully equipped bedrooms have co-ordinated decor and are furnished in pine. Healthy breakfasts are served in the attractive dining room. Amble House was a finalist for the AA Friendliest B&B of the Year 2017–18.

**Rooms:** 5 en suite **S** £60–£65; **D** £79–£90 **Facilities:** tea/coffee WiFi ⚐ **Extras:** Speciality toiletries **Notes:** LB No children 16yrs Closed 24–26 Dec

---

## Badgers Wood

★★★★ ⚲ GUEST HOUSE

-------------------------------------------------------------

**tel:** 017687 72621 **30 Stanger Street CA12 5JU**
**email:** enquiries@badgers-wood.co.uk **web:** www.badgers-wood.co.uk
**dir:** *In town centre off A5271 (main street)*

Anne and Andrew at Badgers Wood welcome guests to this delightful Victorian terrace house, located in a quiet area close to the town centre. The smart bedrooms are furnished to a high standard and are well equipped and have lovely views; the attractive breakfast room at the front of the house overlooks the fells. Off-road parking is an added benefit. Special diets gladly catered for.

**Rooms:** 6 en suite **S** £45–£47; **D** £79–£84* **Facilities:** FTV DVD tea/coffee WiFi ⚐ **Parking:** 6 **Notes:** No children 12yrs Closed Nov–Jan

KESWICK *continued*

## Dalegarth House

★★★★ 🍽 GUEST ACCOMMODATION

**tel:** 017687 72817 **Portinscale CA12 5RQ**
**email:** allerdalechef@aol.com **web:** www.dalegarth-house.co.uk
**dir:** *Off A66 to Portinscale, pass Farmers Arms, 500yds on left*

This friendly, family-run establishment stands on an elevated position in the village of Portinscale, and has fine views from the well-tended garden. The attractive bedrooms are well equipped, and there is a peaceful lounge, a well-stocked bar, and a spacious dining room where the resident owner-chef produces hearty breakfasts.

**Rooms:** 8 en suite 2 annexe en suite (1 fmly) (2 GF) **S** £45; **D** £90–£110* **Facilities:** FTV Lounge tea/coffee Licensed WiFi 🎣 **Extras:** Home-made cakes – complimentary **Parking:** 10 **Notes:** LB No children 12yrs Closed 24 Nov–1 Mar

## The Edwardene

★★★★ 🍽 GUEST ACCOMMODATION

**tel:** 017687 73586 **26 Southey Street CA12 4EF**
**email:** info@edwardenehotel.com **web:** www.edwardenehotel.com
**dir:** *M6 junct 40, A66 follow 1st sign to Keswick, right into Penrith Rd. Sharp left by war memorial into Southey St, 150mtrs on right*

Located close to the heart of the town centre, this Victorian Lakeland stone building retains many of its original features. Bedrooms are well equipped, with many thoughtful extras provided throughout. A comfortable lounge is available, and the generous Cumbrian breakfast is served in the stylish dining room. The Edwardene was a finalist for the AA Friendliest B&B of the Year 2017–18.

**Rooms:** 11 en suite (1 fmly) **S** £54; **D** £96–£120* **Facilities:** FTV Lounge TVL tea/coffee Licensed WiFi 🎣 **Extras:** Speciality toiletries **Parking:** 1 **Notes:** LB No children 2yrs

## Rooms 36

★★★★ GUEST ACCOMMODATION

**tel:** 017687 72764 & 74416 **36 Lake Road CA12 5DQ**
**web:** www.rooms36.co.uk
**dir:** *M6 junct 40, A66 to Keswick. From Main St in Keswick follow Borrowdale (B5289) signs. Right at next mini rdbt into Heads Rd (B5289), 4th right into The Heads, left at end into Lake Rd*

Refurbished to a high standard, Rooms 36 overlooks Hope Park at the end of Lake Road. Modern bedrooms feature iPod docking stations, Tassimo coffee machines, comfortable beds and Herdwick wool carpets as standard. En suites are well appointed and public area decor is enhanced with wonderful artwork by local artist Tessa Kennedy.

**Rooms:** 6 en suite (4 fmly) **Facilities:** STV FTV iPod docking station Lounge TVL tea/coffee WiFi 🎣 **Extras:** Tassimo coffee machines **Parking:** 2

## Brundholme

★★★★ 🍽 GUEST ACCOMMODATION

**tel:** 017687 73305 & 07739 435401 **The Heads CA12 5ER**
**email:** bazaly@hotmail.co.uk **web:** www.brundholme.co.uk

Centrally located, overlooking Hope Park with some bedrooms boasting wonderful views of surrounding fells, this Victorian property is just minutes' walk from the town centre in one direction and the theatre in the other. Limited off-road parking is available. Bedrooms are comfortable and well appointed, and the well cooked traditional Lakeland breakfast will set you up for the day. Service is relaxed and friendly.

**Rooms:** 4 en suite (1 GF) **D** £80–£85* **Facilities:** FTV tea/coffee WiFi **Extras:** Fridges **Parking:** 6

## Cragside

★★★★ GUEST ACCOMMODATION

**tel:** 017687 73344 **39 Blencathra Street CA12 4HX**
**email:** cragside-keswick@hotmail.com **web:** www.cragside-keswick.co.uk
**dir:** *A591 Penrith Rd into Keswick, under rail bridge, 2nd left*

Expect warm hospitality at Cragside, located within easy walking distance of the town centre. The attractive bedrooms are well equipped, and many have fine views of the fells. Hearty Cumbrian breakfasts are served in the breakfast room, which overlooks the small front garden. Visually or hearing impaired guests are catered for, with Braille information, TVs with teletext, and a loop system installed in the dining room.

**Rooms:** 4 en suite (1 fmly) **S** £60–£65; **D** £70–£90* **Facilities:** FTV DVD tea/coffee WiFi **Notes:** No children 5yrs

## Eden Green Guest House

★★★★ GUEST HOUSE

**tel:** 017687 72077 **20 Blencathra Street CA12 4HP**
**email:** enquiries@edengreenguesthouse.com **web:** www.edengreenguesthouse.com
**dir:** *A591 Penrith Rd into Keswick, under railway bridge, 2nd left, house 500yds on left*

This mid-terrace house, faced with local stone, offers well-decorated and furnished bedrooms, some with fine views of Skiddaw. Traditional English and vegetarian breakfasts are served in the neat breakfast room, and packed lunches can be provided on request.

**Rooms:** 5 en suite (1 fmly) (1 GF) **Facilities:** FTV DVD iPod docking station tea/coffee WiFi 🎣 **Notes:** LB No children 8yrs

## The George

★★★★ 🍺 INN

**tel:** 017687 72076 **Saint Johns Street CA12 5AZ**
**email:** rooms@thegeorgekeswick.co.uk **web:** www.thegeorgekeswick.co.uk
**dir:** *M6 junct 40, A66, take left filter road signed Keswick, pass pub on left. At x-rds left into Station St, 150yds on left*

Located in the centre of town, this property is Keswick's oldest coaching inn. There is an abundance of character with wooden beamed bar, cosy seating areas and an atmospheric, candle-lit dining room. Food is a highlight with a wide choice of freshly prepared dishes. Bedrooms are simply presented and comfortable. Parking permits and storage for cycles are available.

**Rooms:** 12 en suite (2 fmly) **Facilities:** FTV tea/coffee Dinner available 🎣 **Parking:** 4

## Skiddaw Croft B&B

★★★★ GUEST ACCOMMODATION

**tel:** 017687 72321 **Portinscale CA12 5RD**
**email:** info@skiddawcroft.co.uk **web:** www.skiddawcroft.co.uk
**dir:** *A66 past Keswick, turn left signed Portinscale. Pass Farmers Arms pub, over brow of hill, 3rd property on left*

Located in the peaceful village of Portinscale, just a few hundred metres away from the majestic Derwentwater, Skiddaw Croft was built in 1913 but has enjoyed extensive investment, with numerous projects taking place inside and out. A warm, genuine welcome awaits all guests on arrival, with the offer of refreshments and home baking. Well appointed, modern bedrooms enjoy a variety of views; the lake from the front, and sometimes Cat Bells (depending on the time of year), while from the rear you can see Skiddaw. Off road car parking is a bonus, and Portinscale is handy for the A66, Keswick and further afield.

**Rooms:** 6 rms (4 en suite) (1 fmly) **S** £42–£45; **D** £77–£89* **Facilities:** FTV Lounge tea/coffee WiFi ♨ **Extras:** Speciality toiletries – complimentary **Parking:** 5 **Notes:** No children 8yrs Closed 18 Dec–Jan RS 1–17 Dec & 1–18 Feb Open weekends only

## Claremont House

★★★★ GUEST ACCOMMODATION

**tel:** 017687 72089 **Chestnut Hill CA12 4LT**
**email:** info@claremonthousekeswick.co.uk **web:** www.claremonthousekeswick.co.uk
**dir:** *A591 N into Chestnut Hill. Pass Manor Brow on left, Claremont House 100yds on right*

This impressive 19th-century house has commanding views over Keswick and beyond and is set in mature grounds where red squirrels regularly visit. It is within walking distance of the town and is ideal for walkers or those looking for relaxation. Guests can expect comfortable bedrooms, a hearty breakfast, and friendly service with tea and cake on arrival.

**Rooms:** 6 en suite (1 fmly) (1 GF) **Facilities:** FTV tea/coffee WiFi ♨ **Extras:** Flowers, wine, chocolate – chargeable **Parking:** 8 **Notes:** LB No children 8yrs Closed 24-26 Dec

## Craglands Guest House

★★★★ GUEST ACCOMMODATION

**tel:** 017687 74406 **Penrith Road CA12 4LJ**
**email:** craglands@msn.com **web:** www.craglands-keswick.co.uk
**dir:** *0.5m E of Keswick centre on A5271 (Penrith Rd) at junct A591*

This Victorian house occupies an elevated position within walking distance of the town centre. The good value accommodation provides attractive, well equipped bedrooms. Pauline and Mark offer a warm welcome and serve delicious breakfasts with local produce and home-made breads.

**Rooms:** 7 rms (5 en suite) **Facilities:** FTV tea/coffee WiFi ♨ **Parking:** 6 **Notes:** LB No children 8yrs

## Dorchester House

★★★★ GUEST ACCOMMODATION

**tel:** 017687 73256 **17 Southey Street CA12 4EG**
**email:** dennis@dorchesterhouse-keswick.co.uk **web:** www.dorchesterhouse-keswick.co.uk
**dir:** *200yds E of town centre. Exit A5271 (Penrith Rd) into Southey St, 150yds on left*

Mr and Mrs Banner offer a warm welcome at Dorchester House, just a short stroll from the town centre and its amenities. The comfortably proportioned, well-maintained bedrooms offer pleasing coordinated decor and a few have views of the surrounding fells. Hearty breakfasts are served in the attractive ground-floor dining room.

**Rooms:** 8 rms (7 en suite) (1 pri facs) (2 fmly) **S** £48–£60; **D** £96–£100 **Facilities:** FTV tea/coffee WiFi **Notes:** LB No children 6yrs

## Elm Tree Lodge

★★★★ GUEST ACCOMMODATION

**tel:** 017687 71050 & 07980 521079 **16 Leonard Street CA12 4EL**
**email:** info@elmtreelodge-keswick.co.uk **web:** www.elmtreelodge-keswick.co.uk
**dir:** *Exit A66, pass ambulance depot, left before pedestrian crossing, left into Southey St. 3rd left into Helvellyn St, 1st right into Leonard St, property 3rd on right*

Close to the town centre, Elm Tree Lodge is a tastefully decorated Victorian house that offers a variety of rooms. Bedrooms feature stripped pine, period furniture, crisp white linen and modern en suites or private shower room. Hearty breakfasts are served in the charming dining room and feature local produce. A friendly welcome is guaranteed.

**Rooms:** 4 rms (3 en suite) (1 pri facs) **D** £69–£85* **Facilities:** FTV tea/coffee WiFi ♨ **Parking:** 2 **Notes:** LB No children 8yrs

## Hedgehog Hill Guest House

★★★★ GUEST HOUSE

**tel:** 017687 80654 & 07944 580959 **18 Blencathra Street CA12 4HP**
**email:** moorhouse43@gmail.com **web:** www.hedgehoghill.co.uk
**dir:** *From A5271 (Penrith Rd) via either Southey St or Greta St into Blencathra St*

Hedgehog Hill Guest House offers high standards of hospitality along with great customer care awareness. Hedgehog Hill, like many properties in this location, is a Victorian terrace house where stairs have to be negotiated but in Keswick the higher the room the better the view generally is. This property is convenient for the town centre, local attractions and many walks. Bedrooms are comfortably equipped and offer thoughtful extras. Hearty breakfasts are served in the light and airy dining room with vegetarians well catered for.

**Rooms:** 6 rms (4 en suite) **S** £35; **D** £78–£80 **Facilities:** FTV tea/coffee WiFi ♨ **Notes:** No children 12yrs

## Rickerby Grange

★★★★ GUEST ACCOMMODATION

**tel:** 017687 72344 **Portinscale CA12 5RH**
**email:** stay@rickerbygrange.co.uk **web:** www.rickerbygrange.co.uk
**dir:** *W of Keswick on A66, turn left at Portinscale junct. Pass The Farmers public house, then 2nd right into Rickerby Ln. 50yds on right*

Rickerby Grange is ideally positioned in a private lane in the pretty village of Portinscale one mile from Keswick. This family-run property offers a genuine warm welcome to all, including walkers and cyclists (by prior arrangement). Even dogs are welcome. Bedrooms are pleasantly furnished and most are en suite. A small but well-stocked bar is available, and drinks can be enjoyed in the lounge area or in the garden.

**Rooms:** 9 rms (8 en suite) (1 pri facs) 1 annexe en suite (3 fmly) (1 GF) **S** £50–£60; **D** £85–£95* **Facilities:** FTV tea/coffee Licensed WiFi ♨ **Parking:** 14 **Notes:** LB

KESWICK *continued*

## The Royal Oak at Keswick

★★★★ INN

**tel:** 017687 74584 **Main Street CA12 5HZ**
**email:** relax@royaloakkeswick.co.uk **web:** www.royaloakkeswick.co.uk
**dir:** *M6 junct 40, A66 to Keswick town centre to war memorial x-rds. Left into Station St. Inn 100yds*

Located on the corner of the vibrant market square this large, friendly 18th-century coaching inn offers a wide range of meals throughout the day and evening. There is a fully stocked bar complete with well-kept cask ales. Bedrooms vary in size but all are contemporary, smartly presented and feature quality accessories such as LCD TVs. There is also a drying room.

**Rooms:** 19 en suite (2 fmly) **Facilities:** FTV tea/coffee Dinner available **Notes:** LB

## Springs Farm B&B

★★★ FARMHOUSE

**tel:** 017687 72144 & 07816 824253 **Springs Farm, Springs Road CA12 4AN**
**email:** springsfarmkeswick@gmail.com **web:** www.springsfarmcumbria.co.uk
**dir:** *A66 into Keswick, left at T-junct onto Chestnut Hill. After 200yds right on Manor Brow, then left into Springs Road. 0.5m at end of road*

Part of a working beef farm, the farmhouse was built around 150 years ago. Guests can expect comfortable accommodation and a well-cooked breakfast with eggs from the farm's own hens. Springs Farm B&B is ideally located in the heart of the countryside but surprising close to the town centre, which is an easy 10-minute walk away.

**Rooms:** 2 en suite **S** £45—£47; **D** £86—£90* **Facilities:** STV FTV DVD tea/coffee WiFi ☕ Farm shop Tea room **Extras:** Fresh milk **Parking:** 6 **Notes:** LB Closed 19—29 Dec 180 acres beef

### KIRKBY IN FURNESS      Map 18 SD28

## Low Hall Farm

★★★★ FARMHOUSE

**tel:** 01229 889220 **LA17 7TR**
**email:** tracey.edmondson@btinternet.com **web:** www.low-hall.co.uk
**dir:** *M6 junct 36 onto A590. At rdbt signed Workington follow A595, through Askam in Furness. After 2.5m turn right, signed Low Hall Farm then 1st left*

Low Hall is a lovely Victorian farmhouse owned by Holker Hall Estates and run by Peter and Tracey Edmondson. The farm is a working beef and sheep farm set in peaceful countryside, offering spectacular views of the Duddon Estuary and Lakeland fells. Low Hall is a very spacious farmhouse, with all rooms offering high quality furnishings. English breakfast is served in the bright and airy dining room, and there is a comfortable living room with wood-burning stove. Ironing facilities are available.

**Rooms:** 3 en suite **S** £40; **D** £65* **Facilities:** FTV TVL tea/coffee WiFi **Extras:** Speciality toiletries — complimentary **Parking:** 4 **Notes:** No children 14yrs 366 acres beef/sheep

### KIRKBY LONSDALE      Map 18 SD67

#### Premier Collection

## Hipping Hall

★★★★★ ◉◉◉ ☕ RESTAURANT WITH ROOMS

**tel:** 015242 71187 **Cowan Bridge LA6 2JJ**
**email:** info@hippinghall.com **web:** www.hippinghall.com
**dir:** *M6 junct 36, A65 through Kirkby Lonsdale towards Skipton. On right after Cowan Bridge*

Close to the market town of Kirkby Lonsdale, Hipping Hall offers spacious bedrooms, designed using soft shades with sumptuous textures and fabrics; the bathrooms use natural stone, slate and limestone to great effect. There are also three spacious cottage suites that create a real hideaway experience. The sitting room, with large, comfortable sofas has a traditional feel. The three AA Rosette restaurant is a 15th-century hall with tapestries and a minstrels' gallery that is as impressive as it is intimate.

**Rooms:** 7 en suite 8 annexe en suite (5 GF) **Facilities:** FTV Lounge Dinner available Direct dial WiFi ☕ **Extras:** Speciality toiletries, fruit **Parking:** 30 **Notes:** No children 12yrs Civ wed 42

#### Premier Collection

## The Sun Inn

★★★★★ ◉◉ ☕ RESTAURANT WITH ROOMS

**tel:** 015242 71965 **6 Market Street LA6 2AU**
**email:** email@sun-inn.info **web:** www.sun-inn.info
**dir:** *From A65 follow signs to town centre. Inn on main street*

The Sun is a 17th-century inn situated in the destination market town of Kirkby Lonsdale and overlooking St Mary's Church. The atmospheric bar features stone walls, wooden beams and log fires with real ales available. Delicious meals are served in the bar or in the relaxed and modern 'Carters at the Sun Inn' restaurant. Traditional and modern styles are blended together in the beautifully appointed rooms with excellent en suites.

**Rooms:** 11 en suite (1 fmly) **S** £82—£145; **D** £88—£158* **Facilities:** FTV tea/coffee Dinner available Direct dial WiFi ☕ 🛏18 **Extras:** Bath robes, speciality toiletries **Notes:** LB

#### Premier Collection

## Plato's

★★★★★ ☕ 🍴 RESTAURANT WITH ROOMS

**tel:** 015242 74180 **2 Mill Brow LA6 2AT**
**email:** hello@platoskirkby.co.uk **web:** www.platoskirkbylonsdale.co.uk
**dir:** *M6 junct 36, A65 Kirkby Lonsdale, after 5m at rdbt take 1st exit, onto one-way system*

Tucked away in the heart of this popular market town, Plato's is steeped in history. Recently refreshed bedrooms have a wealth of thoughtful extras and personal touches. Imaginative food is available in the elegant restaurant with its open-plan kitchen or downstairs in the vaulted cellar. The lounge bar has a more relaxed vibe with open fires and soft seating. A warm welcome and professional service is always assured.

**Rooms:** 8 en suite **Facilities:** FTV DVD iPod docking station TVL tea/coffee Dinner available WiFi 🛏18 **Notes:** LB

## Pheasant Inn

★★★★ ⊛ INN

**tel:** 015242 71230 **Casterton LA6 2RX**
**email:** info@pheasantinn.co.uk **web:** www.pheasantinn.co.uk
**dir:** *M6 junct 36, A65 for 7m, left onto A683 at Devils Bridge, 1m to Casterton centre*

A friendly, family-run dining pub with rooms, this is perfectly situated near the picturesque market town of Kirkby Lonsdale. Real ales are a key feature here along with hearty but refined cooking served in the oak-panelled dining room. Spacious and comfortable accommodation is varied but always ship shape.

**Rooms:** 10 en suite (1 GF) **Facilities:** FTV Lounge tea/coffee Dinner available Direct dial **Parking:** 20 **Notes:** Closed Jan

## The Copper Kettle

★★★ ⬛ GUEST ACCOMMODATION

**tel:** 015242 71714 **3-5 Market Street LA6 2AU**
**email:** gamble_p@btconnect.com **web:** www.copperkettlekirkbylonsdale.co.uk
**dir:** *In town centre, down lane by Post Office*

Built between 1610 and 1640 The Copper Kettle is situated in the heart of this small quaint market town, which nestles on the banks of the River Lune. The bedrooms, all of which retain their old world 17th-century charm, are comfortable and atmospheric. Home-cooked meals and hearty breakfasts are served in the cosy restaurant.

**Rooms:** 5 en suite (2 fmly) **S** £40; **D** £57–£67* **Facilities:** FTV tea/coffee Dinner available Licensed WiFi ⬛ **Parking:** 3 **Notes:** LB

■ **KIRKBY STEPHEN** Map 18 NY70

## Tranna Hill

★★★★ ⬛ GUEST ACCOMMODATION

**tel:** 015396 23227 & 07989 892368 **Newbiggin-on-Lune CA17 4NY**
**email:** trannahill@hotmail.com **web:** www.trannahill.co.uk
**dir:** *M6 junct 38 onto A685 towards Brough. After 5m turn left towards Great Asby then immediately left to Kelleth. 100mtrs on right*

Tranna Hill is set in its own grounds on the edge of the village of Newbiggin-on-Lune, a short distance from the M6 and A66. This period building offers fantastic views of the surrounding fells. Bedrooms are comfortable, well appointed and equipped with lots of books, maps and guides. The sitting/dining room has a log-burning stove and the gardens have seating on the patio.

**Rooms:** 3 en suite (1 fmly) **S** £56–£65; **D** £70–£76* **Facilities:** FTV TVL tea/coffee WiFi ⅃9 ⬛ **Extras:** Speciality toiletries **Parking:** 8 **Notes:** LB

■ **LITTLE LANGDALE** Map 18 NY30

## Three Shires Inn

★★★★ ⬛ INN

**tel:** 015394 37215 **LA22 9NZ**
**email:** enquiry@threeshiresinn.co.uk **web:** www.threeshiresinn.co.uk
**dir:** *Exit A593, 3m from Ambleside at 2nd junct signed Langdales. 1st left after 0.5m, 1m along lane*

Enjoying an outstanding rural location, this family-run inn was built in 1872. The brightly decorated bedrooms are individual in style and many offer panoramic views. The attractive lounge features a roaring fire in the cooler months and there

is a traditional bar with a great selection of local ales. Meals can be taken in either the bar or cosy restaurant.

**Rooms:** 10 en suite (1 fmly) **D** £90–£170 **Facilities:** FTV Lounge tea/coffee Dinner available WiFi ⬛ Use of local country club **Parking:** 15 **Notes:** LB Closed 25 Dec RS Dec & Jan wknds & New Year only

■ **LONGTOWN** Map 21 NY36

## The Sycamore Tree

★★★★ ⬛ GUEST ACCOMMODATION

**tel:** 01228 791919 **40/42 Bridge Street CA6 5UD**
**email:** jfothergill2008@googlemail.com **web:** www.sycamoretreelongtown.co.uk
**dir:** *On A7*

The Sycamore Tree is located on the high street of Longtown just four miles from Gretna and the Scottish border. Choose from a four-poster or a king-size family room. If you are staying on one of the 'steak nights' be sure to reserve a table for dinner.

**Rooms:** 2 en suite (2 fmly) **S** £45; **D** £70* **Facilities:** FTV tea/coffee Dinner available Licensed WiFi **Extras:** Robes, slippers, bottled water – complimentary **Notes:** Closed 1st 2 weeks Sep & 26 Dec

■ **LOWESWATER** Map 18 NY12

## Kirkstile Inn

★★★★ ⬛ INN

**tel:** 01900 85219 **CA13 0RU**
**email:** info@kirkstile.com **web:** www.kirkstile.com
**dir:** *A66 onto B5292 into Lorton, left signed Buttermere. Follow signs to Loweswater, left signed Kirkstile Inn*

This historic 16th-century inn lies in a valley surrounded by mountains. Serving great food and ale, its rustic bar and adjoining rooms are a mecca for walkers. There is also a cosy restaurant offering a quieter ambiance. Bedrooms retain their original character. There is a spacious family suite in an annexe, with two bedrooms, a lounge and a bathroom.

**Rooms:** 7 en suite 3 annexe en suite (1 fmly) (2 GF) **S** £63.50–£90; **D** £107–£117* **Facilities:** TVL tea/coffee Dinner available WiFi **Parking:** 30 **Notes:** LB Closed 25 Dec

## Grange Country House

★★★★ ⬛ GUEST ACCOMMODATION

**tel:** 01946 861211 & 861570 **CA13 0SU**
**email:** info@thegrange-loweswater.co.uk **web:** www.thegrange-loweswater.co.uk
**dir:** *Exit A5086 for Mockerkin, through village. After 2m left signed Loweswater Lake. Grange Country House at bottom of hill on left*

The delightful Grange Country House is set in extensive grounds in a quiet valley at the northwestern end of Loweswater and proves popular with guests seeking peace and quiet. It has a friendly, relaxed atmosphere and cosy public areas which include a small bar serving a great range of local beers; a residents' lounge and an attractive dining room with dinner served by prior arrangement. The bedrooms are well equipped and comfortable, some with four-poster beds.

**Rooms:** 8 en suite (2 fmly) (1 GF) **Facilities:** FTV Lounge TVL tea/coffee Dinner available by arrangement Licensed WiFi ⬛ **Extras:** Speciality toiletries **Conf:** Max 25 Thtr 25 Class 25 Board 25 **Parking:** 20 **Notes:** LB

| **LUPTON** | Map 18 SD58 |

## Premier Collection

### Plough Inn

★★★★★ ◉ INN

**tel:** 015395 67700 **Cow Brow LA6 1PJ**
**email:** info@theploughatlupton.co.uk **web:** www.theploughatlupton.co.uk
**dir:** *M6 junct 36 onto A65 towards Kirkby Lonsdale. Through Nook, up hill, inn on right*

This delightful inn's interior is open plan and a real delight; modern but with a rustic farmhouse appearance. There are large beams, and a log-burning stove in the lounge surrounded by comfortable sofas where you can relax and read the papers. The bedrooms are well proportioned and reflect the inn's high standards; all have feature bathrooms with roll-top baths and walk-in showers. The staff are excellent and guests are made to feel like part of the family. The inn is open all year and serves food every day.

**Rooms:** 6 en suite (1 fmly) **Facilities:** FTV Lounge tea/coffee Dinner available Direct dial WiFi ☪18 ☻ **Extras:** Speciality toiletries **Parking:** 50

| **NEAR SAWREY** | Map 18 SD39 |

## Premier Collection

### Ees Wyke Country House

★★★★★ ◉ ☟ GUEST HOUSE

**tel:** 015394 36393 **LA22 0JZ**
**email:** mail@eeswyke.co.uk **web:** www.eeswyke.co.uk
**dir:** *On B5285 on W side of village*

A warm welcome awaits at this elegant Georgian country house with views over Esthwaite Water and the surrounding countryside. The thoughtfully equipped bedrooms have been decorated and furnished with care. There is a charming lounge with an open fire, and a splendid dining room where a carefully prepared five-course dinner is served. Breakfasts have a fine reputation due to the skilful use of local produce.

**Rooms:** 8 en suite (1 GF) **S** £102.50–£117.50; **D** £125–£145* **Facilities:** FTV Lounge tea/coffee Dinner available Licensed WiFi ☻ **Extras:** Sherry, peanuts **Parking:** 12 **Notes:** LB No children 12yrs

| **NEWBY BRIDGE** | Map 18 SD38 |

## Premier Collection

### The Knoll Country House

★★★★★ ☟ ☞ GUEST ACCOMMODATION

**tel:** 015395 31347 **Lakeside LA12 8AU**
**email:** info@theknoll-lakeside.co.uk **web:** www.theknoll-lakeside.co.uk
**dir:** *A590 W to Newby Bridge, over rdbt, signed right for Lake Steamers, house 0.5m on left*

This delightful Edwardian villa stands in a leafy dell on the western side of Windermere. Public areas have many original features, including open fires in the cosy lounge and dining room. The attractive bedrooms vary in outlook, and are all very stylish. Proprietor and chef Jenny Mead and her enthusiastic team extend a very caring and natural welcome. Jenny also prepares a good range of excellent dishes at breakfast.

**Rooms:** 8 en suite 1 annexe rm (1 pri facs) **S** £80–£110; **D** £95–£160 **Facilities:** STV FTV DVD iPod docking station Lounge TVL tea/coffee Direct dial Licensed WiFi ☻ **Extras:** Fruit & wine in 1 room **Conf:** Max 30 Thtr 30 Class 18 Board 12 **Parking:** 9 **Notes:** LB No children 16yrs Closed 24–26 Dec

### Lyndhurst Country House

★★★★ ☟ GUEST HOUSE

**tel:** 015395 31245 **LA12 8ND**
**email:** chris@lyndhurstcountryhouse.co.uk **web:** www.lyndhurstcountryhouse.co.uk
**dir:** *On junct of A590 & A592 at Newby Bridge rdbt*

This 1920s house is situated close to the southern tip of Lake Windermere. Accommodation consists of three comfortable, tastefully decorated bedrooms, each with en suite shower room. Hearty breakfasts feature local produce and are served in the pleasant dining room, which also has a lounge area opening onto the garden.

**Rooms:** 3 en suite **D** £85–£95* **Facilities:** FTV Lounge tea/coffee WiFi ☻ **Parking:** 3 **Notes:** LB No children 8yrs Closed 23–28 Dec

| **PENRITH** | Map 18 NY53 |

## Premier Collection

### Brooklands Guest House

★★★★★ ☟ GUEST HOUSE

**tel:** 01768 863395 **2 Portland Place CA11 7QN**
**email:** enquiries@brooklandsguesthouse.com **web:** www.brooklandsguesthouse.com
**dir:** *M6 junct 40, follow sign for TIC, left at town hall, 50yds on left*

In the bustling market town of Penrith, this beautifully appointed house offers individually furnished bedrooms with high quality accessories and some luxury touches. Nothing seems to be too much trouble for the friendly owners and, from romantic breaks to excellent storage for cyclists, all guests are very well looked after. Delicious breakfasts featuring Cumbrian produce are served in the attractive dining room.

**Rooms:** 6 en suite (1 fmly) **S** £45–£75; **D** £85–£95* **Facilities:** FTV iPod docking station tea/coffee WiFi Cycle storage ☻ **Extras:** Speciality toiletries, fresh fruit – complimentary **Parking:** 2 **Notes:** LB No children 3yrs Closed 24 Dec–4 Jan

## River Garth

★★★★★ 🛏 GUEST HOUSE

**tel:** 01768 863938 & 07718 763273 **Eamont Bridge CA10 2BH**
**email:** rivergarth@hotmail.co.uk **web:** www.rivergarth.co.uk
**dir:** *M6 junct 40, A66 E towards Scotch Corner. At rdbt 4th exit to Shap,*
*150yds over bridge & continue for 200yds, turn right at "Keep Clear" road marking.*
*Last bungalow facing river with balconies*

The River Garth is in an elevated position overlooking the River Eamont.
Spacious and well-presented bedrooms cater well for the needs of the guest,
and two of them have balconies looking out on the river. The lounge dining room
is comfortable and breakfast uses the finest local produce.

**Rooms:** 3 en suite (1 fmly) **S** £50–£65; **D** £72–£90ᴬ **Facilities:** STV FTV TVL
tea/coffee WiFi 🛁 **Extras:** Speciality toiletries, bottled water, sweets –
complimentary **Parking:** 6 **Notes:** LB

## Albany House

★★★★ 🛏 🍴 GUEST HOUSE

**tel:** 01768 863072 **5 Portland Place CA11 7QN**
**email:** info@albany-house.org.uk **web:** www.albany-house.org.uk
**dir:** *Left at town hall into Portland Place. 30yds on left*

A well-maintained Victorian house close to Penrith town centre. Bedrooms are
comfortable and thoughtfully equipped. Wholesome breakfasts using local
ingredients are served in the attractive breakfast room. Good quality dinners are
served at the weekend – advance bookings are required.

**Rooms:** 5 rms (3 en suite) (2 pri facs) (1 fmly) **D** £70–£85* **Facilities:** FTV tea/coffee
Dinner available at weekends by arrangement WiFi 🛁 **Extras:** Speciality toiletries,
bottled water, chocolates **Notes:** LB

## Brandelhow Guest House

★★★★ 🛏 GUEST HOUSE

**tel:** 01768 864470 **1 Portland Place CA11 7QN**
**email:** enquiries@brandelhowguesthouse.co.uk **web:** www.brandelhowguesthouse.co.uk
**dir:** *In town centre on one-way system, left at town hall*

Situated within easy walking distance of central amenities, this friendly guest
house is also convenient for the Lakes and M6. The bedrooms are thoughtfully
furnished and some are suitable for families. Breakfasts, make great use of quality
local produce, are served in a Cumbria-themed dining room overlooking the pretty
courtyard garden. Afternoon and high teas are available by arrangement.

**Rooms:** 5 rms (4 en suite) (1 pri facs) (2 fmly) **Facilities:** FTV tea/coffee WiFi
**Notes:** Closed 31 Dec & 1 Jan

## Glendale Guest House

★★★★ GUEST HOUSE

**tel:** 01768 210061 **4 Portland Place CA11 7QN**
**email:** info@glendaleguesthouse.com **web:** www.glendaleguesthouse.com
**dir:** *M6 junct 40, follow town centre signs. Pass castle, turn left before town hall*

The Glendale Guest House is a friendly, family-run property, part of a Victorian
terrace only a stroll from the town centre, and convenient for the Lakes and Eden
Valley. Bedrooms vary in size, but all are attractive, well equipped, well presented
and cater well for the modern traveler. Hearty breakfasts are served at individual
tables in the charming ground-floor dining room. Walkers and cyclists will be
pleased to know that drying facilities are available.

**Rooms:** 7 en suite (3 fmly) **Facilities:** FTV WiFi Drying facilities 🛁
**Notes:** No children 5yrs

## Stoneybeck Inn

★★★★ 🌐 INN

**tel:** 01768 862369 **Bowscar CA11 8RP**
**email:** reception@stoneybeckinn.co.uk **web:** www.stoneybeckinn.co.uk

This inn enjoys panoramic views over the Cumbrian Fells, and is ideally located
for easy access to the M6, and as a base for touring the Lakes and beyond.
Bedrooms are finished to an impressive standard with a number
of luxurious touches. The inn has built up a strong following locally for both its food
and drink. Monthly pudding nights and the Sunday carvery are not to be missed.
Extensive conference and banqueting facilities are also on site, as well as
complimentary parking.

**Rooms:** 7 en suite (2 GF) **Facilities:** FTV Lounge tea/coffee Dinner available WiFi
🛁 **Conf:** Max 200 Thtr 200 Class 130 Board 60 **Parking:** 50 **Notes:** Civ wed 200

### ▌POOLEY BRIDGE                                        Map 18 NY42

## The Crown Inn

[U]

**tel:** 01768 425869 **Finkle Street CA10 2NP**
**email:** relax@crowninnpooleybridge.co.uk **web:** www.crowninnpooleybridge.co.uk
**dir:** *Follow A592 from Penrith. Take B5320 to Pooley Bridge*

Currently the rating for this establishment is not confirmed. This may be due to a
change of ownership or because it has only recently joined the AA rating scheme.

**Rooms:** 17 en suite (3 fmly) (1 GF) **D** £68–£199* **Facilities:** tea/coffee Dinner
available WiFi 🛁 **Notes:** LB

### ▌RAVENGLASS                                           Map 18 SD09

## The Inn at Ravenglass

[U]

**tel:** 01229 717230 **Main Street CA18 1SQ**
**email:** gm@penningtonhotels.com **web:** www.theinnatravenglass.co.uk

Currently the rating for this establishment is not confirmed. This may be due to a
change of ownership or because it has only recently joined the AA rating scheme.

**Rooms:** 1 en suite **S** £90–£110; **D** £110–£180*

## RAVENSTONEDALE
Map 18 NY70

## The Black Swan

★★★★ 🛜 🍴 INN

tel: 015396 23204 **CA17 4NG**
email: enquiries@blackswanhotel.com web: www.blackswanhotel.com
dir: *M6 junct 38. Black Swan on A685, W of Kirkby Stephen*

Set in the heart of this quiet village, the inn is popular with visitors and locals and offers a very friendly welcome. Bedrooms are individually styled and comfortably equipped. There is an informal atmosphere in the bar areas and home-made meals can be taken in the bar or the stylish dining room. Relax by the fire in the cooler months and enjoy the riverside garden in the summer.

**Rooms:** 10 en suite 6 annexe en suite (3 fmly) (3 GF) **S** £75–£165; **D** £95–£165*
**Facilities:** FTV iPod docking station Lounge tea/coffee Dinner available WiFi ▒ ⌗9 Fishing Snooker 🔒 **Extras:** Speciality toiletries, snacks, water, robes **Conf:** Max 14 Thtr 14 Class 14 Board 14 **Parking:** 20 **Notes:** LB

## The Fat Lamb

★★★★ 🍴 INN

tel: 015396 23242 **Crossbank CA17 4LL**
email: enquiries@fatlamb.co.uk web: www.fatlamb.co.uk
dir: *On A683, between Kirkby Stephen & Sedbergh*

Solid stone walls and open fires feature at this 17th-century inn. The bedrooms are comfortable and all are en suite. An accessible ground-floor room with en suite wet room is available. Guests can enjoy a choice of dining options: well-cooked dishes using local produce are served in either the traditional bar or the more formal dining room. There is also a beer garden.

**Rooms:** 12 en suite (4 fmly) (5 GF) **S** £55–£69; **D** £90–£108* **Facilities:** Lounge tea/coffee Dinner available WiFi ⌗18 🔒 Private 5-acre nature reserve **Parking:** 60 **Notes:** LB

## RYDAL
*See Ambleside*

## SHAP
Map 18 NY51

## Brookfield Guest House

★★★★ GUEST HOUSE

tel: 01931 716397 **CA10 3PZ**
email: info@brookfieldshap.co.uk web: www.brookfieldshap.co.uk
dir: *M6 junct 39, A6 towards Shap, 1st accommodation off motorway, on right*

In a quiet rural location within easy reach of the M6, inviting Brookfield Guest House stands in well-tended, attractive gardens. Bedrooms are thoughtfully appointed and well maintained. There is a comfortable lounge, and a small bar area next to the traditional dining room where substantial, home-cooked breakfasts are served at individual tables.

**Rooms:** 4 rms (3 en suite) (1 pri facs) **Facilities:** FTV TVL tea/coffee Licensed WiFi 🔒 **Parking:** 20 **Notes:** No children 12yrs Closed Nov–1 Mar

## TEMPLE SOWERBY
Map 18 NY62

## The Kings Arms

★★★★ 🍴 INN

tel: 017683 62944 **CA10 1SB**
email: enquiries@kingsarmstemplesowerby.co.uk
web: www.kingsarmstemplesowerby.co.uk
dir: *M6 junct 40, E on A66 to Temple Sowerby, Kings Arms in village*

The Kings Arms is located in the peaceful village of Temple Sowerby, just a couple of minutes from the A66 bypass and a short drive from Center Parcs. The property dates back over 400 years and offers a good deal of charm and character. Quality food is served in the small restaurant or in the bar itself which has an open fire. Comfortable, well-appointed accommodation makes this an ideal base for touring this delightful area.

**Rooms:** 8 en suite (5 fmly) **S** £55–£70; **D** £90–£120* **Facilities:** FTV Lounge tea/coffee Dinner available WiFi Fishing 🔒 **Parking:** 20 **Notes:** LB

## Skygarth Farm

★★★ FARMHOUSE

**tel:** 017683 61300 **CA10 1SS**
**email:** skygarth@outlook.com **web:** www.skygarth.co.uk
**dir:** *Off A66 at Temple Sowerby for Morland, Skygarth 500yds on right, follow signs*

Skygarth is just south of the village, half a mile from the busy main road. The house stands in a cobbled courtyard surrounded by cowsheds, with gardens to the rear, where red squirrels feed. There are two well-proportioned bedrooms and an attractive lounge where tasty breakfasts are served.

**Rooms:** 2 rms (2 fmly) **S** £40–£45; **D** £64–£68* **Facilities:** FTV TVL tea/coffee WiFi
🏃 **Extras:** Bottled water, biscuits – complimentary; robes **Parking:** 4
**Notes:** Closed Dec–Jan 200 acres mixed

### TROUTBECK (NEAR WINDERMERE)　　　Map 18 NY40

#### Premier Collection

## Broadoaks Country House

★★★★★ 🍴 GUEST ACCOMMODATION

**tel:** 015394 45566 **Bridge Lane LA23 1LA**
**email:** enquiries@broadoakscountryhouse.co.uk
**web:** www.broadoakscountryhouse.co.uk
**dir:** *Exit A591 junct 36 pass Windermere. Filing station on left, 1st right 0.5m*

This impressive Lakeland stone house has been restored to its original Victorian grandeur and is set in seven acres of landscaped grounds with stunning views of the Troutbeck Valley. Individually furnished bedrooms are well appointed and en suite bathrooms feature either whirlpool or Victorian roll top baths. Spacious day rooms include the music room, featuring a Bechstein piano. Meals are served by friendly and attentive staff in the elegant dining room.

**Rooms:** 11 en suite 9 rms annexe (8 en suite) (1 pri facs) (9 fmly) (8 GF) **S** £120–£300; **D** £169–£350* **Facilities:** STV FTV DVD iPod docking station tea/coffee Dinner available Direct dial Licensed WiFi 🎣 Fishing Arrangement with local leisure facility & spa **Extras:** Speciality toiletries **Conf:** Max 62 Thtr 40 Class 45 Board 45 **Parking:** 40 **Notes:** LB Civ wed 100

### ULVERSTON　　　Map 18 SD27

## Virginia House

★★★ ◉◉ RESTAURANT WITH ROOMS

**tel:** 01229 584844 & 07495 128499 **24 Queen Street LA12 7AF**
**email:** contact@virginiahouseulverston.co.uk **web:** www.virginiahouseulverston.co.uk
**dir:** *M6 junct 36 onto A590 towards Barrow-in-Furness. In Ulverston take 3rd exit at Tank Square rdbt & follow one-way system. 1st exit at mini rdbt into King St, then Queen St. 200mtrs on right*

A warm, personal welcome is guaranteed at this family-run restaurant with rooms. The restaurant is at the heart of the property with award-winning meals served in modern and comfortable surroundings. All meals highlight very good quality local produce. The gin parlour has a selection of over 100 gins to choose from. Bedrooms are comfortable and well appointed. Complimentary WiFi is available throughout. There is no parking on-site, but there is provision within a short walking distance.

**Rooms:** 8 en suite **S** £65–£75; **D** £99 **Facilities:** FTV iPod docking station tea/coffee Dinner available WiFi 🏃 **Extras:** Speciality toiletries, home-made biscuits **Conf:** Max 30 Thtr 30 Class 11 Board 16

### WASDALE HEAD　　　Map 18 NY10

## Wasdale Head Inn

★★★★ INN

**tel:** 019467 26229 & 26333 **CA20 1EX**
**email:** reception@wasdale.com **web:** www.wasdale.com
**dir:** *Exit A595 (towards S) at Santon Bridge or Gosforth towards S. Follow signs for Wasdale Head*

Wasdale Head is known as the birthplace of British climbing for good reason. The setting of this popular inn is breathtaking, surrounded by the fells with the brooding Wast Water close by. Inside, the decor is enhanced with objets d'art and photos of climbers and mountains. Bedrooms and public areas are comfortable, and the service is relaxed and informal. Real ales and good food are served in the rustic bar while a separate restaurant is available for residents.

**Rooms:** 11 en suite 9 annexe en suite (2 fmly) (5 GF) **Facilities:** FTV Lounge tea/coffee Dinner available Direct dial WiFi 🏃 **Conf:** Max 20 Thtr 20 Class 20 Board 20 **Parking:** 30 **Notes:** LB Civ wed 50

### WINDERMERE　　　Map 18 SD49

#### Premier Collection

## Applegarth Villa & Restaurant

★★★★★ ◉ 🍴 GUEST ACCOMMODATION

**tel:** 015394 43206 **College Road LA23 1BU**
**email:** info@lakesapplegarth.co.uk **web:** www.lakesapplegarth.co.uk
**dir:** *M6 junct 36, A591 towards Windermere. On entering town left after NatWest Bank into Elleray Rd. 1st right into College Rd, Applegarth on right*

This period building in the heart of Windermere offers elegantly furnished accommodation with luxurious bathrooms in the main house. Seven brand new suites in the adjacent former coach house feature modern accommodation and features such as hot tubs on each balcony. The attractive conservatory dining room offers stunning views of the mountains and serves locally sourced produce. Alternatively, the oak-panelled bar has an open fire and is a perfect retreat to while away a winters evening. Private off-road parking is guaranteed.

**Rooms:** 15 en suite 7 annexe en suite (2 GF) **S** £90–£140; **D** £140–£475* **Facilities:** FTV iPod docking station tea/coffee Dinner available Direct dial Licensed WiFi 🏃 7 suites with outdoor hot tubs **Extras:** Speciality toiletries, bottled water, fruit – complimentary **Parking:** 27 **Notes:** LB No children 18yrs

WINDERMERE *continued*

## Lindeth Fell Country House

★★★★★ GUEST ACCOMMODATION

tel: 015394 43286 & 44287 **Lyth Valley Road, Bowness-on-Windermere LA23 3JP**
email: kennedy@lindethfell.co.uk **web:** www.lindethfell.co.uk
*dir: 1m S of Bowness on A5074*

Lindeth Fell offers luxury bed and breakfast accommodation, perfectly located overlooking Lake Windermere. This elegant, stylishly restored Edwardian country house is owned and managed by the Kennedy family, who combine a warm, friendly welcome with five-star service. The 14 individually-designed bedrooms have crisp Egyptian cotton bed linen, deluxe fluffy towels, robes and slippers, complimentary sherry decanters, DAB radio, WiFi, and flat-screen TV. Many rooms have superb lake views; all have tea trays and Nespresso coffee machines. Tea and home-made scones are offered in the elegant lounge on arrival. There are cosy log fires in winter, while in summer you can explore the stunning gardens, complete with a private lake.

**Rooms:** 14 en suite (1 fmly) (1 GF) **S** £95–£100; **D** £190–£250* **Facilities:** FTV iPod docking station Lounge tea/coffee Direct dial Licensed WiFi 🎲 🔒 Use of leisure facilities at nearby hotel **Extras:** Speciality toiletries, robes, slippers, sherry, Nespresso coffee machine – complimentary **Conf:** Max 12 Class 12 Board 12 **Parking:** 20 **Notes:** LB Closed Jan

## Windermere Suites

★★★★★ 🛏 BED AND BREAKFAST

tel: 015394 47672 **New Road LA23 2LA**
email: vicky@windermeresuites.co.uk **web:** www.windermeresuites.co.uk
*dir: Through village on one-way system towards Bowness-on-Windermere. 50mtrs past The Ellerthwaite*

Placed between Windermere and Bowness, Windermere Suites is a very special boutique town house which offers eight individual suites, all combining contemporary designer furniture with cutting edge entertainment technology and sheer elegance. Each suite has its own lounge area and the bathrooms have large spa baths complete with TV, mood lighting and power showers. Rooms also have mini-bars, and room service is available up to 10pm.

**Rooms:** 8 en suite (3 GF) **Facilities:** STV FTV DVD iPod docking station TVL tea/coffee Licensed WiFi Free use of nearby spa & leisure club **Extras:** Mini-bar, safe **Parking:** 9 **Notes:** LB

## The Howbeck

★★★★★ GUEST HOUSE

tel: 015394 44739 **New Road LA23 2LA**
email: relax@howbeck.co.uk **web:** www.howbeck.co.uk
*dir: A591 through Windermere town centre, left towards Bowness*

The Howbeck is a delightful Victorian villa, convenient for the village and the lake. Bedrooms are well appointed and feature lovely soft furnishings, along with luxurious spa baths in some cases. There is a bright lounge with internet access and an attractive dining room where home-prepared hearty Cumbrian breakfasts are served at individual tables.

**Rooms:** 10 en suite 1 annexe en suite (3 GF) **Facilities:** STV FTV TVL tea/coffee Dinner available Licensed WiFi Free membership to nearby spa & leisure club **Parking:** 12 **Notes:** LB Closed 24–25 Dec

## Dene House

★★★★ GUEST ACCOMMODATION

tel: 015394 48236 **Kendal Road LA23 3EW**
email: denehouse@ignetics.co.uk **web:** www.denehouse-guesthouse.co.uk
*dir: From Lake Rd, turn opposite St Martins Church into Kendal Rd. 400yds on right*

Detached period property situated on the edge of the village just a short walk from pubs, restaurants and of course Lake Windermere. Bedrooms are individually furnished and tastefully decorated. Deeply comfortable beds are crisply dressed and one room is situated on the ground floor offering ease of access. Breakfast is served at individual tables in the smart dining room and the property has a beautiful terrace garden.

**Rooms:** 7 rms (6 en suite) (1 pri facs) (1 GF) **Facilities:** FTV iPod docking station tea/coffee WiFi Use of pool and gym at nearby hotel – charges apply **Parking:** 7 **Notes:** LB No children 12yrs

## Fairfield House and Gardens

★★★★ ⚲ GUEST HOUSE

**tel:** 015394 46565 **Brantfell Road, Bowness-on-Windermere LA23 3AE**
**email:** tonyandliz@the-fairfield.co.uk **web:** www.the-fairfield.co.uk
**dir:** *Into Bowness town centre, turn opposite St Martin's Church & sharp left by The Arts Bar & Grill, house 200mtrs on right*

This Lakeland country house is tucked away in half an acre of secluded, peaceful gardens yet in the heart of Bowness. The house combines Georgian and Victorian features with stylish, contemporary design. Guests are shown warm hospitality and can relax either in the bright lounge or eponymous gardens. Bedrooms are well furnished, varying in size and style with some featuring luxurious bathrooms. Delicious breakfasts are served in the attractive dining room or on the terrace in warmer weather.

**Rooms:** 8 en suite 1 annexe en suite (3 GF) **S** £72–£140; **D** £90–£140*
**Facilities:** FTV DVD Lounge tea/coffee Licensed WiFi 🛁 🏌18 🍽 **Conf:** Max 20 Thtr 20 Class 10 Board 12 **Parking:** 10 **Notes:** LB No children 10yrs Closed Xmas

## Glenville House

★★★★ ⚲ GUEST HOUSE

**tel:** 015394 43371 **Lake Road LA23 2EQ**
**email:** mail@glenvillehouse.co.uk **web:** www.glenvillehouse.co.uk
**dir:** *At Windermere station/tourist info centre, turn left into village. Straight through, on right opposite vets*

Glenville House is very conveniently located in a pleasant area, and good parking is a bonus. The house is well appointed and the bedrooms have comfortable beds and many accessories to make your stay relaxing and enjoyable. The friendly proprietors make guests welcome, and breakfast is taken in a pleasant room at individual tables.

**Rooms:** 7 en suite (1 GF) **D** £75–£110* **Facilities:** FTV iPod docking station tea/coffee WiFi **Parking:** 7 **Notes:** I B No children 18yrs Closed 6–30 Jan

## The Hideaway at Windermere

★★★★ ⚲ GUEST ACCOMMODATION

**tel:** 015394 43070 **Phoenix Way LA23 1DB**
**email:** eatandstay@thehideawayatwindermere.co.uk
**web:** www.thehideawayatwindermere.co.uk
**dir:** *Exit A591 at Ravensworth B&B, into Phoenix Way, The Hideaway 100mtrs on right*

Quietly tucked away, this beautiful Victorian Lakeland house is personally run by owners Richard and Lisa. Delicious food, individually designed bedrooms and warm hospitality ensure an enjoyable stay. There is a beautifully appointed lounge looking out to the garden, and the dining area is split between two light and airy rooms. Breakfast is freshly prepared using the best local ingredients and service is attentive and friendly. Bedrooms vary in size and style; the larger rooms feature luxury bathrooms. Tea and home-made cake is included and served each day.

**Rooms:** 10 en suite 1 annexe en suite **S** £80–£160; **D** £90–£170* **Facilities:** FTV Lounge tea/coffee Direct dial Licensed WiFi 🧖 Off-site spa facilities available **Parking:** 15 **Notes:** LB No children 16yrs Closed Jan–mid Feb

## Who are the AA's award-winning B&Bs?
— see pages 12–15

WINDERMERE *continued*

## Holly-Wood Guest House

★★★★ ⚬ GUEST HOUSE

**tel:** 015394 42219 **Holly Road LA23 2AF**
**email:** info@hollywoodguesthouse.co.uk **web:** www.hollywoodguesthouse.co.uk
**dir:** *M6 junct 36 left onto A590 signed Kendal then A591 towards Windermere, left into town, left again into Ellerthwaite Rd, next left into Holly Rd*

This attractive Victorian end terrace is located in a quiet residential area just a few minutes' walk from Windermere town centre. Guests are offered a friendly welcome, comfortable, well equipped bedrooms and a freshly prepared breakfast. Limited off-street parking is also available.

**Rooms:** 6 en suite **Facilities:** FTV iPod docking station tea/coffee WiFi ⬧
**Extras:** Speciality toiletries, home-made snacks – complimentary **Parking:** 3
**Notes:** No children 18yrs Closed 23–27 Dec

## Rockside Guest House

★★★★ ⚬ GUEST HOUSE

**tel:** 015394 45343 **25 Church Street LA23 1AQ**
**email:** enquiries@rockside-guesthouse.co.uk **web:** www.rockside-guesthouse.co.uk

Rockside Guest House was built from Lakeland stone in 1847, and is owner-managed by Martin and Caroline. They have modernised the building yet kept many original features. Situated at the head of the village, Rockside is a short stroll from local transport links, restaurants, pubs and shops, and only 20 minutes' walk from Lake Windermere. Breakfast something for all tastes, from a substantial full breakfast to lighter bites and vegetarian alternatives, all prepared with quality local produce and served with home-made marmalade and jams. Rockside Guest House was a finalist for the AA Friendliest B&B of the Year 2017–18.

**Rooms:** 9 en suite **Facilities:** FTV tea/coffee WiFi **Parking:** 9 **Notes:** No children 18yrs Closed Nov–Feb

## The Wild Boar Inn, Grill & Smokehouse

★★★★ ⊛ INN

**tel:** 015394 45225 **Crook LA23 3NF**
**email:** thewildboar@englishlakes.co.uk **web:** www.thewildboarinn.co.uk
**dir:** *2.5m S of Windermere on B5284. From Crook 3.5m, on right*

Steeped in history, this former coaching inn enjoys a peaceful rural location close to Windermere. Public areas include a welcoming lounge and a cosy bar where an extensive choice of wines, ales and whiskies are served. The Grill & Smokehouse features quality local and seasonal ingredients. Bedrooms, some with four-poster beds, vary in style and size. Leisure facilities are available close by.

**Rooms:** 34 en suite (2 fmly) (9 GF) **S** £103–£331; **D** £118–£346* **Facilities:** FTV DVD tea/coffee Dinner available Direct dial WiFi Use of leisure facilities at sister hotel **Extras:** Speciality toiletries **Parking:** 60 **Notes:** LB Civ wed 100

## The Haven

★★★★ ⚬ BED AND BREAKFAST

**tel:** 015394 88583 **10 Birch Street LA23 1EG**
**email:** info@thehavenwindermere.co.uk **web:** www.thehavenwindermere.co.uk
**dir:** *On A5074 enter one-way system, 3rd left into Birch St*

Built from Lakeland slate and stone, The Haven is just a 50-metre stroll from the town centre and shops. The bright, spacious bedrooms offer en suite facilities and one has a Victorian brass bed. A hearty Cumbrian breakfast is served in a very well-appointed dining room. The Haven benefits from limited off-road parking, available on a first come first served basis. The pretty hanging baskets and planters outside set the scene for a warm and genuine welcome from the owners.

**Rooms:** 4 en suite (1 fmly) **Facilities:** FTV DVD Lounge tea/coffee WiFi ⬧ **Parking:** 3 **Notes:** LB No children 7yrs

## Blenheim Lodge

★★★★ GUEST ACCOMMODATION

**tel:** 015394 43440 **Brantfell Road, Bowness-on-Windermere LA23 3AE**
**email:** enquiries@blenheim-lodge.com **web:** www.blenheim-lodge.com
**dir:** *From Windermere to Bowness village, left at mini rdbt, next left, next left again, to top of Brantfell Rd & turn right*

From a peaceful position above Bowness, Blenheim Lodge has stunning panoramic views of Lake Windermere. Bedrooms are well equipped featuring antique furnishings and pocket-sprung mattresses. Most beds are antiques themselves and include two William IV four-posters and three Louis XV examples. There is a comfortable lounge and a beautifully decorated dining room.

**Rooms:** 11 rms (10 en suite) (1 pri facs) (1 fmly) (2 GF) **S** £60–£65.50; **D** £90–£155* **Facilities:** FTV TVL tea/coffee Licensed WiFi ⬧ Free fishing permits **Parking:** 11 **Notes:** LB No children 8yrs Closed 25 Dec RS 24–27 Dec may open, phone for details

## The Old Court House

★★★★ GUEST HOUSE

**tel:** 015394 45096 **Lake Road LA23 3AP**
**email:** alitheoch@gmail.com **web:** www.theoch.co.uk
**dir:** *On Windermere-Bowness road at junct Longlands Rd*

Guests are given a warm welcome at this attractive former Victorian police station and courthouse, located in the centre of Bowness. Comfortable, pine-furnished bedrooms offer a good range of extra facilities. Freshly prepared breakfasts are served in the bright ground-floor dining room.

**Rooms:** 6 en suite (2 GF) **S** £45–£90; **D** £70–£100* **Facilities:** FTV tea/coffee WiFi **Parking:** 6 **Notes:** LB No children 10yrs

## Bonny Brae Guest House

★★★ GUEST HOUSE

**tel:** 015394 22699 & 07765 778046 **West Beck, 11 Oak Street LA23 1EN**
**email:** stay@bonnybraewindermere.com **web:** www.bonnybraewindermere.com

A warm and genuine welcome awaits you at Bonny Brae, situated in the heart of Windermere village, just a short walk from cafés, shops and travel links. Accommodation is comfortable, and breakfast makes good use of local produce.

**Rooms:** 5 en suite (1 fmly) **S** £70; **D** £82–£86* **Facilities:** FTV DVD iPod docking station tea/coffee WiFi 🔒 **Notes:** No children 7yrs

## Brook House

★★★ GUEST HOUSE

**tel:** 015394 44932 **30 Ellerthwaite Road LA23 2AH**
**email:** stay@brookhouselakes.co.uk **web:** www.brookhouselakes.co.uk
**dir:** M6 junct 36, A591, through one-way system. Ellerthwaite Rd 2nd left, 200yds on right

Brook House is a Lakeland stone Victorian guest house set in a quiet part of Windermere and offers a very relaxed friendly atmosphere. Accessible with or without a car and close to all amenities, it is a perfect base for exploring the Lake District. Bedrooms include a family room and a single. Private parking and a guest lounge are also available. 'Whisky Warmer' weekends are run throughout the winter.

**Rooms:** 5 en suite (1 fmly) **Facilities:** FTV Lounge tea/coffee WiFi **Extras:** Speciality toiletries – complimentary **Parking:** 5 **Notes:** No children 8yrs

## Ellerdene Guesthouse

★★★ GUEST HOUSE

**tel:** 015394 43610 **12 Ellerthwaite Road LA23 2AH**
**email:** info@ellerdene.co.uk **web:** www.ellerdene.co.uk
**dir:** M6 junct 36 follow signs for Kendal then Windermere (A591). Follow one-way system, take 2nd left after pedestrian crossing into Ellerthwaite Rd. On right opposite Holly Rd

Ellerdene is a welcoming guest house situated in the heart of Windermere village, perfectly situated for all local amenities. Accommodation features modern, stylishly designed rooms which are comfortable and thoughtfully equipped. Expect a generous, freshly-cooked breakfast served in the bright and spacious dining room.

**Rooms:** 6 rms (5 en suite) (1 pri facs) (1 GF) **S** £34–£40; **D** £64–£86* **Facilities:** FTV DVD tea/coffee WiFi 🔒 **Extras:** Fridge **Notes:** LB No children 6yrs Closed 6 Nov–16 Jan

## Adam Place Guest House

★★★ GUEST HOUSE

**tel:** 015394 44600 & 07484 826762 **1 Park Avenue LA23 2AR**
**email:** adamplacewindermere@yahoo.co.uk **web:** www.adamplacelakedistrict.co.uk
**dir:** Exit A591 into Windermere, through town centre, left into Ellerthwaite Rd & Park Av

Located in a mainly residential area within easy walking distance of lake and town centre, this stone-built Victorian house has been renovated to provide comfortable and homely bedrooms. Comprehensive breakfasts are served in the cosy dining room and there is a pretty patio garden.

**Rooms:** 5 en suite (2 fmly) **S** £40–£52; **D** £70–£77* **Facilities:** FTV DVD tea/coffee WiFi 🔒 **Notes:** LB No children 6yrs

## Green Gables Guest House

★★★ GUEST HOUSE

**tel:** 015394 43886 **37 Broad Street LA23 2AB**
**email:** info@greengablesguesthouse.co.uk **web:** www.greengablesguesthouse.co.uk
**dir:** A591 into Windermere, 1st left after pelican crossing, opposite car park

Aptly named, Green Gables is a friendly guest house looking onto Elleray Gardens. Just a short walk from the centre, the house is attractively furnished and offers bright, fresh and well appointed bedrooms. There is a comfortable bar-lounge, and substantial breakfasts are served in the spacious dining room.

**Rooms:** 7 rms (4 en suite) (3 pri facs) (2 fmly) (1 GF) **S** £40–£55; **D** £60–£85* **Facilities:** FTV TVL tea/coffee Licensed WiFi **Notes:** LB Closed 23–27 Dec

### ▌ WORKINGTON
Map 18 NY02

## The Sleepwell Inn

★★★★ GUEST ACCOMMODATION

**tel:** 01900 65772 **Washington Street CA14 3AX**
**email:** info@washingtoncentralhotel.co.uk **web:** www.washingtoncentralhotel.co.uk
**dir:** M6 junct 40, W on A66. At bottom of Ramsay Brow left into Washington St, 300yds on left opposite church

The Sleepwell Inn offers comfortable and well-appointed accommodation and is situated just 100 metres from its sister property, the Washington Central Hotel. Guests have full use of the Washington's facilities and that is where breakfast is served. Off-road parking is available to the rear. Rooms differ in size and style at The Sleepwell, with some inter-connecting rooms available. A calming, natural colour scheme has been used in the bedrooms to create a chic, contemporary feel.

**Rooms:** 24 en suite (4 fmly) (12 GF) **S** £55–£65; **D** £80 (room only)* **Facilities:** FTV Lounge TVL tea/coffee Dinner available Direct dial Licensed WiFi ♨18 🔒 Facilities available at Washington Central Hotel **Parking:** 32 **Notes:** LB Civ wed 300

### ▌ DERBYSHIRE

### ▌ ASHBOURNE
Map 10 SK14

## Compton House

★★★★ GUEST ACCOMMODATION

**tel:** 01335 343100 **27-31 Compton DE6 1BX**
**email:** jane@comptonhouse.co.uk **web:** www.comptonhouse.co.uk
**dir:** A52 from Derby into Ashbourne, over lights at bottom of hill, house 100yds on left opposite garage

Within easy walking distance of the central attractions, this conversion of three cottages has resulted in a house with good standards of comfort and facilities. Bedrooms are filled with homely extras and comprehensive breakfasts are served in the cottage-style dining room. Parking available.

**Rooms:** 5 en suite (1 fmly) (1 GF) **S** £50–£55; **D** £70–£80* **Facilities:** FTV TVL tea/coffee WiFi 🔒 **Parking:** 5

ASHBOURNE *continued*

## Mercaston Hall

★★★★ FARMHOUSE

**tel:** 01335 360263 & 07836 648102 **Mercaston DE6 3BL**
**email:** mercastonhall@btinternet.com **web:** www.mercastonhall.com
**dir:** *Exit A52 in Brailsford into Luke Ln, 1m, right at 1st x-rds, house 1m on right*

Located in a pretty hamlet, this medieval building retains many original features. Bedrooms are homely, and additional facilities include an all-weather tennis court and a livery service. WiFi access is also available. This is a good base for visiting local stately homes, the Derwent Valley mills and Dovedale.

**Rooms:** 3 en suite **S** £60–£70; **D** £75–£85* **Facilities:** FTV DVD Lounge tea/coffee WiFi ⌣ Fishing ⚓ **Extras:** Fridge **Parking:** 3 **Notes:** Closed Xmas  60 acres mixed

---

| BEELEY | Map 16 SK26 |

## The Devonshire Arms at Beeley

★★★★★ ⚜ INN

**tel:** 01629 733259 & 01756 718111 **Devonshire Square DE4 2NR**
**email:** enquiries@devonshirebeeley.co.uk **web:** www.devonshirebeeley.co.uk
**dir:** *B6012 towards Matlock, pass Chatsworth House. After 1.5m turn left, 2nd entrance to Beeley*

The Devonshire Arms at Beeley is a charming 18th-century village inn, located on the Chatsworth Estate, with Chatsworth House itself only a short drive away. With 14 stylish and well-appointed rooms and suites, this is the ideal place to stay for exploring one of Britain's best-loved stately homes, the pretty villages on the estate, and the wild and natural beauty of the Peak District National Park. Local produce is fully evident on the menu, and the inn serves an array of dishes. Eat in the cosy bar area, The 'Malt Vault' – a private seating area suited to groups of up to 12; or the contemporary, colourful Brasserie. In the summer months there is a terrace for alfresco dining too, with parasols beside the brook.

**Rooms:** 4 en suite 10 annexe en suite (2 fmly) (5 GF) **Facilities:** FTV DVD tea/coffee Dinner available Direct dial WiFi **Parking:** 30

---

| BELPER | Map 11 SK34 |

### Premier Collection

## Dannah Farm Country House

★★★★★ ⚱ GUEST ACCOMMODATION

**tel:** 01773 550273 & 550630 **Bowmans Lane, Shottle DE56 2DR**
**email:** slack@dannah.co.uk **web:** www.dannah.co.uk
**dir:** *A517 from Belper towards Ashbourne, 1.5m right into Shottle after Hanging Gate pub on right, over x-rds & right*

Part of the Chatsworth Estates at Shottle, in an elevated position with stunning views, this impressive Georgian house and its outbuildings have been renovated to provide luxurious, individually styled bedrooms. Two have private hot tubs, one has a sauna, and there is a Spa Cabin and 'Secret Garden' hot tub that can be booked separately. The elegant dining room is the setting for memorable breakfasts, which make use of the finest local produce. Excellent supper platters are also available by prior arrangement.

**Rooms:** 8 en suite (1 fmly) (2 GF) **S** £95–£110; **D** £185–£295* **Facilities:** FTV DVD iPod docking station Lounge tea/coffee Licensed WiFi ⚓ Spa cabin with hot tub **Extras:** Bath robes, speciality toiletries, honesty bar **Parking:** 20 **Notes:** LB Closed 24–26 Dec

---

### Premier Collection

## Bridge Hill House

★★★★★ ⚱ GUEST ACCOMMODATION

**tel:** 07931 931011 & 01773 599859 **34a Lodge Drive DE56 2TP**
**email:** info@bridgehillhouse.co.uk **web:** www.bridgehillhouse.co.uk
**dir:** *In town centre turn onto A517 signed Ashbourne. After 350mtrs right into Belper Ln, then left into Lodge Drive. Continue up hill, right into drive alongside Number 34*

Bridge Hill House is a modern property designed by its owners and built using local stone on what used to be part of the extensive Strutt family estate. Some evidence of its former life remains, including the ice house and underground arched tunnels which are now listed. A warm welcome is assured, and home-made afternoon bakes and cakes are not to be missed. Award-winning breakfasts are served in the open-plan family room which has far-reaching views across Belper and beyond. Attractively presented en suite accommodation is all located on the ground floor, and rooms are decorated in soft tones with a host of thoughtful extras provided. Local guided tours by prior arrangement.

**Rooms:** 4 en suite (4 GF) **S** £76–£129; **D** £86–£149* **Facilities:** FTV Lounge tea/coffee WiFi ⚓ **Extras:** Mineral water, fresh milk, sweets, fruit – complimentary **Parking:** 4 **Notes:** LB No children 16yrs Closed Nov–Feb

---

| BIRCH VALE | Map 16 SK08 |

## Ladygate Farm Bed and Breakfast

★★★★ ⚱ BED AND BREAKFAST

**tel:** 01663 745562 & 07885 593123 **Briargrove Road SK22 1AY**
**email:** liz@ladygatefarm.co.uk **web:** www.ladygatefarm.co.uk
**dir:** *From Marple Bridge follow signs to Mellor/New Mills. After 3m left into Briargrove Rd, 0.5m on left at bottom of hill*

Beautifully restored, this former farm house is both peaceful and homely, and is surrounded by picturesque Derbyshire countryside. Known as the location for the BBC drama *The Village*, Hayfield is just two miles away. Lyme House, Kinder Scout and the start of the Pennine Way are also within easy reach. Stylish bedrooms are well equipped with comfortable beds, a wealth of thoughtful extras and smart modern bathrooms. Served at the large dining table, Aga-cooked breakfasts include sausage and bacon from a local award-winning butcher. Hosts Liz and Dave will be happy to recommend a number of local dining options.

**Rooms:** 3 rms (2 en suite) (1 pri facs) **Facilities:** FTV DVD TVL tea/coffee WiFi ⚓ **Extras:** Robes, fruit, fresh flowers, speciality toiletries **Parking:** 3 **Notes:** LB No children 12yrs

---

| BRADWELL | Map 16 SK18 |

### Premier Collection

## The Samuel Fox Country Inn

★★★★★ ⚙⚙ INN

**tel:** 01433 621562 **Stretfield Road S33 9JT**
**email:** enquiries@samuelfox.co.uk **web:** www.samuelfox.co.uk
**dir:** *M1 junct 29, A617 towards Chesterfield, A619 signed Baslow & Buxton, 2nd rdbt A623 for 7m, take B6049 to Bradwell, through village on left*

Named after Bradwell's most famous son, industrial magnate Samuel Fox, who built the steelworks at Stocksbridge, The Samuel Fox Country Inn is modern and stylish yet retains its rustic charm. Bedrooms are both immaculately presented and extensively equipped, and service is highly attentive. The restaurant has breathtaking views and serves modern British cuisine, awarded two AA Rosettes.

**Rooms:** 4 en suite **D** £125–£135 (room only)* **Facilities:** FTV tea/coffee Dinner available WiFi ♨18 **Extras:** Home-made chocolates, hand-made cookies, sherry **Conf:** Max 20 Thtr 12 Class 12 Board 10 **Parking:** 15 **Notes:** LB Closed 2–17 Jan

---

### BUXTON
Map 16 SK07

## Alpine Lodge Guest House

★★★★ GUEST HOUSE

**tel:** 01298 26155 & 07808 283408 **1 Thornsett, Hardwick Mount SK17 6PS**
**email:** sales@alpinelodgebuxton.co.uk **web:** alpinelodgebuxton.co.uk
**dir:** A515 onto Hardwick St. Take right hand fork into Hardwick Mount, just past church on left

Alpine Lodge is particularly welcoming to walkers and cyclists. It offers elegant, stylishly furnished accommodation on a tree-lined residential road, close to the town centre. All rooms have en suite shower facilities or private bathrooms with large baths, separate showers and luxurious toiletries. A hospitality tray with fresh milk is provided in each room. Non-allergenic duvets and pillows are available on request, and all beds have fresh crisp cotton sheets and duvet covers. Buxton Opera House and the tranquil Pavilion Gardens are 10 minutes' stroll away. The Peak District National Park and Derbyshire Dales are on the doorstep.

**Rooms:** 5 rms (4 en suite) (1 pri facs) (1 fmly) **S** £65–£70; **D** £85–£95*
**Facilities:** FTV tea/coffee WiFi **Extras:** Speciality toiletries, bottled water – complimentary **Parking:** 4 **Notes:** No children 1yr

## Roseleigh Guest House

★★★★ GUEST ACCOMMODATION

**tel:** 01298 24904 **19 Broad Walk SK17 6JR**
**email:** enquiries@roseleighhotel.co.uk **web:** www.roseleighhotel.co.uk
**dir:** A6 to Morrisons rdbt, into Dale Rd, right at lights, 100yds left by Swan pub, down hill, right into Hartington Rd

This elegant property has a prime location overlooking Pavilion Gardens, and the quality furnishings and decor highlight the many original features. The thoughtfully furnished bedrooms have smart modern shower rooms, and a comfortable lounge is also available.

**Rooms:** 14 rms (12 en suite) (2 pri facs) (1 GF) **Facilities:** FTV Lounge tea/coffee WiFi **Parking:** 9 **Notes:** No children 6yrs Closed 6 Dec–20 Jan

---

### CASTLETON
Map 16 SK18

## Innkeeper's Lodge Castleton, Peak District

★★★ INN

**tel:** 08451 551551 *(Calls cost 2p per minute plus your phone company's access charge)*
**Castle Street S33 8WG**
**email:** info@innkeeperslodge.com **web:** www.innkeeperslodge.com

This property enjoys an excellent location, nestled amongst the hills of Hope Valley and surrounded by the wild moors and sheer rock edges. Dating back to the 1800s this coaching inn provides modern spacious accommodation. The welcoming lounge bar is a popular place to eat with food served all day. Free WiFi available along with on-site car parking.

**Rooms:** 15 en suite (4 fmly) (3 GF) **Facilities:** FTV tea/coffee Dinner available Direct dial WiFi

---

### CHESTERFIELD
Map 16 SK37

## Church Villa B&B

★★★ BED AND BREAKFAST

**tel:** 01246 850254 **29 Church Lane, Temple Normanton S42 5DB**
**email:** churchvilla@btinternet.com **web:** www.churchvilla29.co.uk
**dir:** M1 junct 29 onto A617. After 2m turn to Temple Normanton. Take 3rd right signed Holmewood, right again into Birkin Ln. Next right into Church Ln, opposite church notice board

Church Villa B&B is a charming cottage situated on the outskirts of Chesterfield, ideally placed for visiting the Peak District. It has comfortable, well-equipped bedrooms which come complete with many thoughtful extras. Breakfast and home-cooked dinners are served in the dining room, which has a 100-year old vine, and overlooks the country garden. A guest lounge is also available.

**Rooms:** 3 en suite **S** £54–£59; **D** £64–£79 **Facilities:** FTV DVD TVL tea/coffee Dinner available WiFi **Extras:** Robes **Parking:** 3 **Notes:** LB

---

### CHINLEY
Map 16 SK08

## The Old Hall Inn

★★★★ Ⓐ INN

**tel:** 01663 750529 **Whitehough SK23 6EJ**
**email:** info@old-hall-inn.co.uk **web:** www.old-hall-inn.co.uk

This 16th-century, family-run inn is located in some prime walking country. The rooms are all en suite and one has a balcony overlooking the garden. All rooms have flat-screen TVs and WiFi. Breakfast comes as full English or continental style, while other meals can be eaten in the Old Hall's Minstrel Gallery restaurant. The bar features many ales from local breweries as well as an extensive wine list.

**Rooms:** 7 en suite 4 annexe en suite **S** £65–£90; **D** £79–£140 **Facilities:** FTV DVD tea/coffee Dinner available WiFi **Conf:** Max 16 Board 16 **Parking:** 20 **Notes:** LB

## CROMFORD
Map 16 SK25

# Alison House
★★★★ GUEST ACCOMMODATION

**tel:** 01629 822211 **Intake Lane DE4 3RH**
**email:** info@alison-house-hotel.co.uk **web:** www.alison-house-hotel.co.uk
**dir:** *From A6, SE of Cromford, right into Intake Ln*

This well furnished and spacious 18th-century house stands in seven acres of well-tended grounds just a short walk from the village. Public rooms are comfortable and charming, and bedrooms come in a variety of sizes. All are furnished to a high standard, and The Arkwright Suite is a favourite with honeymooners.

**Rooms:** 15 en suite (2 fmly) (4 GF) **S** £65–£85; **D** £79–£120 **Facilities:** TVL tea/coffee Dinner available Licensed WiFi 🅿 **Conf:** Max 60 Thtr 60 Class 40 Board 40 **Parking:** 30 **Notes:** LB Civ wed 80

## DARLEY DALE
Map 16 SK26

### Premier Collection

# Ashford Grange
★★★★★ BED AND BREAKFAST

**tel:** 01629 732178 **Oakwood Drive DE4 2BT**
**email:** info@ashfordgrange.co.uk **web:** www.ashfordgrange.co.uk
**dir:** *N of Matlock on A6, pass Old Hackney Ln on right, next right into Darley Lodge Drive & Oakwood Drive*

Located in the Derwent Valley and built in the grounds of the former manor house using local stone, Ashford Grange is a modern house full of creature comforts, and a warm welcome is assured. Rooms are spacious and attractively decorated in co-ordinating colours, and all offer high quality en suite facilities. The Hayloft located in the adjacent building has its own private entrance. Home baked afternoon treats and breakfasts are served in the dining room overlooking the garden and hills beyond, or weather permitting on one of the garden terraces.

**Rooms:** 2 en suite 1 annexe en suite **S** £100–£140; **D** £115–£160 **Facilities:** FTV tea/coffee WiFi ⬇18 🅿 Fly fishing available **Extras:** Speciality toiletries, flowers, robes, slippers, cream tea on arrival **Parking:** 3 **Notes:** LB No children Closed Xmas–New Year

## DERBY
Map 11 SK33

*See also Belper & Melbourne*

# The Derby Conference Centre
★★★★ GUEST ACCOMMODATION

**tel:** 01332 861842 & 861831 **London Road DE24 8UX**
**email:** enquiries@thederbyconferencecentre.com
**web:** www.thederbyconferencecentre.com
**dir:** *M1 junct 25, A52 towards Derby. Filter left onto A5111 signed Ring Road. At Raynesway Park rdbt 3rd exit signed Ring Road/Alvaston. At next rdbt A6 towards Derby centre. Pass Wickes, left into entrance*

Formerly a railway training centre, this Grade II listed art deco building has modern public areas, meeting rooms and accommodation, yet original features such as the wall paintings by Norman Wilkinson still remain. Extensive conference facilities include a lecture theatre. Complimentary WiFi and on-site parking available.

**Rooms:** 50 en suite (10 GF) **S** £50–£65; **D** £60–£75* **Facilities:** FTV Lounge TVL tea/coffee Dinner available Licensed WiFi ⬇18 🅿 **Conf:** Max 1000 Thtr 350 Class 60 Board 40 **Parking:** 200 **Notes:** Closed 24 Dec–4 Jan

# A38 Woodlands B&B
★★ BED AND BREAKFAST

**tel:** 01332 293658 & 07792 547964 **300 Burton Road DE23 6AD**
**email:** info@a38woodlands.com **web:** www.a38woodlands.com
**dir:** *From city centre on A5250 to Littleover, opposite Stone Hill Rd, above the International Hotel*

Run by a friendly husband and wife team, the A38 Woodlands B&B is situated within easy walking distance of Derby city centre. This Victorian town house provides a choice of en suite room configurations; singles to large family accommodation. All offer microwaves and refrigeration; however some have additional kitchen facilities on prior request. A hearty home-cooked breakfast is provided in the small conservatory. WiFi available. Limited on-site parking.

**Rooms:** 10 en suite (3 fmly) (4 GF) **S** £28–£40; **D** £38–£50 (room only)*
**Facilities:** FTV tea/coffee WiFi 🅿 **Extras:** Fridge, microwave **Parking:** 6 **Notes:** LB

## EDALE
Map 16 SK18

### Stonecroft Country Guesthouse
★★★★ 🕮 GUEST HOUSE

**tel:** 01433 670262 **Stonecroft S33 7ZA**
**email:** enquiries@stonecroftguesthouse.co.uk **web:** www.stonecroftguesthouse.co.uk
**dir:** *From A6187 in Hope follow signs for Edale. After 4.5m, pass large car park on right, turn right (marked No Through Road). 3rd house after church*

A warm welcome awaits you at this beautifully located guest house in the quiet village of Edale. Bedrooms are comfortable and feature luxurious extras such as fluffy bathrobes and well equipped beverage trays. Award-winning breakfasts are served around a communal breakfast table, and dietary requirements are especially well catered for. A large lounge area is provided with a roaring log fire, perfect for those winter evenings. A limited amount of on-site parking is available. Stonecroft Country Guesthouse was a finalist for the AA Friendliest B&B of the Year 2017–18.

**Rooms:** 3 rms (2 en suite) (1 pri facs) **S** £55–£65; **D** £100–£110 **Facilities:** FTV iPod docking station TVL tea/coffee WiFi 🛁 **Extras:** Robes, speciality toiletries, fruit, chocolates, fresh flowers **Parking:** 3 **Notes:** LB No children 15yrs Closed Xmas

## EYAM
Map 16 SK27

### Barrel Inn
★★★ 🍺 INN

**tel:** 01433 630856 **Bretton S32 5QD**
**email:** barrelinn@btconnect.com **web:** www.thebarrelinn.co.uk
**dir:** *From Baslow on A623, turn right signed Foolow. At next T junct, turn left & immediately right opposite pond. 1m on left*

Laying claim to be the highest pub in Derbyshire, the Barrel Inn dates back to 1597 and provides the visitor with a warm and homely base from which to explore the area. Oak-beamed ceiling and flagstones are a feature in the bar area, while the restaurant offers a wide selection of meals. On a clear day it is possible to see five counties.

**Rooms:** 4 annexe en suite (1 fmly) (3 GF) **Facilities:** DVD tea/coffee Dinner available WiFi **Parking:** 20

## FOOLOW
Map 16 SK17

### The Bulls Head Inn
★★★★ INN

**tel:** 01433 630873 **S32 5QR**
**email:** wilbnd@aol.com **web:** www.thebullatfoolow.co.uk
**dir:** *Off A623 into Foolow*

Located in the village centre, this popular inn retains many original features and offers comfortable, well-equipped bedrooms. Extensive and imaginative bar meals are served in the traditionally furnished dining room or in the cosy bar areas. The inn welcomes well-behaved dogs in the bar (and even muddy boots on the flagstone areas).

**Rooms:** 3 en suite (1 fmly) **Facilities:** tea/coffee Dinner available 🛁18 **Parking:** 20

## FROGGATT
Map 16 SK27

### The Chequers Inn
★★★★ ◉◉ 🕮 INN

**tel:** 01433 630231 **S32 3ZJ**
**email:** info@chequers-froggatt.com **web:** www.chequers-froggatt.com
**dir:** *On A625 between Sheffield & Bakewell, 0.75m from Calver*

The Chequers Inn is a very popular 16th-century inn offering an extensive range of interesting two AA Rosette-worthy dishes, with a clear focus on local produce. The bedrooms are comprehensively equipped with all modern comforts and the hospitality is warm and sincere. This is a good location for touring Derbyshire and the Peak District National Park, and visiting Chatsworth.

**Rooms:** 7 en suite **D** £125–£135* **Facilities:** FTV tea/coffee Dinner available WiFi **Parking:** 45 **Notes:** LB Closed 25 Dec

## GREAT HUCKLOW
Map 16 SK17

### The Queen Anne
★★★ 🍺 INN

**tel:** 01298 871246 **SK17 8RF**
**email:** angelaryan100@aol.com **web:** www.queenanneinn.co.uk
**dir:** *Exit A623 onto B6049 to Great Hucklow*

Set in the heart of this pretty village, The Queen Anne has been a licensed inn for over 300 years and to this day acts a hub for the local community. Meals are served in the cosy bar and dining room which benefits from a wealth of original features. During summer months meals can be taken in the pretty garden with far reaching views across Derbyshire countryside. Bedrooms are tucked away to the rear of the property in a separate building with direct access. Both rooms are comfortable and have modern shower rooms en suite. Ample parking and free WiFi are available.

**Rooms:** 2 annexe en suite (2 GF) **Facilities:** FTV DVD TVL tea/coffee Dinner available WiFi **Parking:** 20 **Notes:** LB No children 10yrs Closed Xmas & New Year

## HATHERSAGE
Map 16 SK28

### The Plough Inn
★★★★ ◉ INN

**tel:** 01433 650319 & 650180 **Leadmill Bridge S32 1BA**
**email:** sales@theploughinn-hathersage.co.uk
**web:** www.theploughinn-hathersage.co.uk
**dir:** *1m SE of Hathersage on B6001. Over bridge, 150yds beyond at Leadmill*

This delightful 16th-century inn with beer garden has an idyllic location by the River Derwent. A selection of real ales and imaginative food is served in the spacious public areas, and original fireplaces and exposed beams have been preserved. The attractive, well-equipped bedrooms include several luxury rooms, and WiFi access is available throughout.

**Rooms:** 3 en suite 3 annexe en suite (3 fmly) (2 GF) **S** £85–£150; **D** £110–£150* **Facilities:** FTV DVD iPod docking station tea/coffee Dinner available Direct dial WiFi 🛁18 🛁 **Extras:** Fruit, water — complimentary **Parking:** 50 **Notes:** LB Closed 25 Dec

## HOPE
Map 16 SK18

### Premier Collection

## Underleigh House

★★★★★ GUEST ACCOMMODATION

**tel:** 01433 621372 **Lose Hill Lane S33 6AF**
**email:** info@underleighhouse.co.uk **web:** www.underleighhouse.co.uk
**dir:** *From village church on A6187 into Edale Rd, 1m left into Lose Hill Ln*

Situated at the end of a private lane, surrounded by glorious scenery, Underleigh House was converted from a barn and cottage that dates from 1873, and now offers carefully furnished and attractively decorated bedrooms with modern facilities. Several rooms have private lounge areas and some also have access to the gardens. There is a very spacious lounge with comfortable chairs and a welcoming log fire. Memorable breakfasts are served at one large table in the dining room.

**Rooms:** 4 en suite (1 GF) **S** £75–£105; **D** £95–£125* **Facilities:** FTV DVD TVL tea/coffee Direct dial Licensed WiFi ⬥ **Extras:** Speciality toiletries, fruit, sweets – complimentary **Parking:** 6 **Notes:** LB No children 12yrs Closed Xmas, New Year & Jan

## Stoney Ridge

★★★★ GUEST ACCOMMODATION

**tel:** 01433 620538 **Granby Road, Bradwell S33 9HU**
**email:** info@stoneyridge.org.uk **web:** www.stoneyridge.org.uk
**dir:** *From N end of Bradwell on B6049 into Gore Ln, uphill, pass Ye Olde Bowling Green Inn, left into Granby Rd*

This large, split-level bungalow stands in attractive mature gardens at the highest part of the village and has extensive views. Hens roam freely in the landscaped garden, and their fresh eggs add to the hearty breakfasts. Bedrooms are attractively furnished and thoughtfully equipped, and there is a spacious comfortable lounge to relax in.

**Rooms:** 4 rms (3 en suite) (1 pri facs) **S** £65–£75; **D** £66–£84 **Facilities:** STV FTV TVL tea/coffee WiFi ⬥ **Extras:** Sweets **Parking:** 6 **Notes:** LB No children 14yrs RS Nov proprietors' holiday

## Round Meadow Barn

★★★ BED AND BREAKFAST

**tel:** 01433 621347 & 07836 689422 **Parsons Lane S33 6RB**
**email:** geof@harrisrmb.freeserve.co.uk **web:** www.mysite.freeserve.com/rmbarn
**dir:** *Exit A625 (Hope Rd) N onto Parsons Ln, over rail bridge, in 200yds right into hay barnyard, through gates, across 3 fields, house on left*

This converted barn, with original stone walls and exposed timbers, stands in open fields in the picturesque Hope Valley. The bedrooms are large enough for families and there are two modern bathrooms. Breakfast is served at one large table adjoining the family kitchen.

**Rooms:** 3 rms (1 en suite) (2 pri facs) (1 fmly) **Facilities:** FTV tea/coffee Direct dial WiFi ⬥ **Parking:** 8 **Notes:** LB

## MARSH LANE
Map 16 SK47

## Ravencar Farm Bed and Breakfast

★★★★ FARMHOUSE

**tel:** 01246 433717 & 07786 911950 **Main Road S21 5RH**
**email:** helenmrshcfish@aol.com **web:** www.ravencarbandb.co.uk

A warm welcome awaits you at this friendly family-run farmhouse which is conveniently located on the border between South Yorkshire and Derbyshire and close to the M1. Bedrooms are well appointed and provide a number of modern accessories such as in-room fridges, well-stocked hospitality trays and TVs. Breakfasts are served in the dining room which overlooks the gardens. Full cooked breakfasts are available as well as a wide range of lighter options.

**Rooms:** 3 en suite (1 fmly) (1 GF) **Facilities:** FTV DVD tea/coffee WiFi ⬥ **Extras:** Fruit juice, mineral water, fridge – complimentary **Parking:** 12 **Notes:** LB 6 acres non-working farm/horses

## MARSTON MONTGOMERY
Map 10 SK13

## The Crown Inn

★★★★ INN

**tel:** 01889 591430 & 07860 342514 **Riggs Lane DE6 2FF**
**email:** enquiries@thecrowninnderbyshire.co.uk **web:** www.thecrowninnderbyshire.co.uk

The Crown Inn in the village of Marston Montgomery has been purchased by one of the villagers and tastefully refurbished to provide somewhere to eat, drink and stay for locals and guests alike, in a comfortable and friendly environment. The food is often locally sourced and has a range of specials on offer that change frequently. The decor has a subtly contemporary feel but keeps traditional features. The rooms (all named after people that have lived in the village for a long time) are well-furnished and comfortable. The outdoor space provides another comfortable and well-furnished area to sit – whatever the weather.

**Rooms:** 7 en suite 1 annexe en suite (3 fmly) **Facilities:** STV FTV tea/coffee Dinner available WiFi ⬥ **Conf:** Max 30 Thtr 30 Class 30 Board 30 **Parking:** 20

## MATLOCK
Map 16 SK35

## Castle Green B&B

★★★★ BED AND BREAKFAST

**tel:** 01629 581349 & 07584 162988 **Butts Drive DE4 3DJ**
**email:** john@castlegreenbandb.co.uk **web:** www.castlegreenbandb.co.uk
**dir:** *A615 into Matlock, pass British Red Cross on left, opposite Castle Green & Butts Drive*

Located in the peaceful grounds of the former Ernest Bailey mansion, the property is nestled in a wooded valley with views of Riber Castle; the house is within walking distance of Matlock. A warm welcome awaits and the accommodation is well equipped and very comfortable. Breakfast is served in the dining room on the ground floor. Other facilities include WiFi and on site parking.

**Rooms:** 6 en suite (1 fmly) (1 GF) **S** fr £55; **D** fr £87* **Facilities:** FTV tea/coffee WiFi ⬥ **Extras:** Speciality toiletries, fridge, fresh milk **Parking:** 8 **Notes:** LB

## The Pines

★★★★ 🐾 BED AND BREAKFAST

**tel:** 01629 732646 & 07796 437333 **12 Eversleigh Road, Darley Bridge DE4 2JW**
**email:** info@thepinesbandb.co.uk **web:** www.thepinesbandb.co.uk
**dir:** *From Bakewell or Matlock take A6 to Darley Dale. Turn at Whitworth Hotel onto B5057, pass Square & Compass pub & The 3 Stags Heads, The Pines on right*

Dating from the 1820s, this home as been authentically restored and stands in a secluded and pretty garden. Three spacious en suite bedrooms are stylishly furnished using rich fabrics. Comprehensive breakfasts, making use of quality local produce, offer a hearty start to the day. The Pines makes an ideal location for visiting the Peak District.

**Rooms:** 3 en suite **S** £50–£60; **D** £80–£90* **Facilities:** FTV DVD tea/coffee Dinner available WiFi 🛁 **Extras:** Bottled water, fruit **Parking:** 5 **Notes:** LB

## The Red Lion

★★★ INN

**tel:** 01629 584888 **Matlock Green DE4 3BT**
**email:** info@theredlionmatlock.co.uk **web:** www.theredlionmatlock.co.uk
**dir:** *500yds SE of town centre on A632*

This comfortable free house is a good base for exploring Matlock and the surrounding Derbyshire countryside. Each bedroom is comfortably furnished, and one comes complete with a four-poster. Public areas include a games area with open fires, and a restaurant where a wide selection of meals is on offer. Private parking is a bonus.

**Rooms:** 6 en suite **S** £50; **D** £70* **Facilities:** tea/coffee Dinner available WiFi Pool table **Parking:** 20 **Notes:** No children

### MELBOURNE — Map 11 SK32

## The Coach House

★★★★ BED AND BREAKFAST

**tel:** 01332 862338 **69 Derby Road DE73 8FE**
**email:** enquiries@coachhouse-hotel.co.uk **web:** www.coachhouse-hotel.co.uk
**dir:** *Off B587 in village centre*

The Coach House sits in the heart of a conservation area, close to Donington Park and East Midlands Airport. This traditional cottage has been restored to provide good standards of comfort and facilities. Bedrooms are thoughtfully furnished, and a lounge and secure parking are available.

**Rooms:** 6 en suite (1 fmly) (3 GF) **S** £50–£57; **D** £72–£82* **Facilities:** FTV TVL tea/coffee WiFi 🛁 **Parking:** 5 **Notes:** LB

## Harpur's of Melbourne

★★★★ 🍴🍴 INN

**tel:** 01332 862134 **2 Derby Road DE73 8FE**
**email:** info@harpursofmelbourne.co.uk **web:** www.harpursofmelbourne.co.uk
**dir:** *From A50 exit signed Melbourne/Swadlincote. Continue for 5m, in centre of Melbourne on left*

Starting life back in the late 18th century as two houses, before becoming the Melbourne Hotel in the mid-19th century, Harpur's continues to welcome guests from far and wide. After extensive refurbishment this is now a modern inn and restaurant, with an increasingly strong following not only for its ales but also for its food; dishes use some of the finest local ingredients. Situated in the attractive Georgian town of Melbourne and steeped in history, Harpur's offers comfortably appointed en suite accommodation within easy reach of the National Forest.

**Rooms:** 4 en suite **Facilities:** FTV tea/coffee Dinner available WiFi 🛁 **Conf:** Max 50 Thtr 50 Class 30 Board 30 **Parking:** 20 **Notes:** LB

### MICKLEOVER — Map 10 SK33

## The Great Northern

★★★★ INN

**tel:** 01332 514288 **Station Road DE3 9FB**
**email:** greatnorthernderby@yahoo.co.uk **web:** www.thegreatnorthern.co.uk
**dir:** *From N: A38 to Markeaton Island, take 3rd exit. Then 2nd left into Radbourne Ln, 3rd left into Station Rd*

Bedrooms at The Great Northern are in a converted barn; the three boutique-style rooms are well appointed and thoughtfully equipped. This modern inn with friendly staff provides imaginative food, and a selection of local cask ales. Free WiFi and ample parking are provided. A meeting room is available for small parties and can be used for private dining.

**Rooms:** 3 en suite (1 fmly) (1 GF) **S** £80; **D** £80–£100* **Facilities:** FTV DVD tea/coffee Dinner available WiFi **Conf:** Max 80 Thtr 80 Class 50 Board 25 **Parking:** 80

### NEW MILLS — Map 16 SK08

## Pack Horse Inn

★★★★ 🅰 INN

**tel:** 01663 742365 **Mellor Road SK22 4QQ**
**email:** info@packhorseinn.co.uk **web:** www.packhorseinn.co.uk

The Pack Horse Inn sits on the edge of the Peak District, ideally located within easy reach of Stockport, Manchester and Sheffield. Some bedrooms are in a converted barn and still have original oak beams. The other rooms are in the main building. The friendly bar has at least three hand-pulled, regularly changing guest ales together with Tetley bitter. Traditional bar meals and snacks are available, or a more formal meal is served in the dining room which overlooks the patio area, where guests can eat and drink in the warmer weather.

**Rooms:** 7 en suite 5 annexe en suite **S** £70–£90; **D** £90–£110* **Facilities:** tea/coffee Dinner available WiFi **Extras:** Speciality toiletries, fruit, speciality teas **Parking:** 60

### PILSLEY — Map 16 SK27

## The Devonshire Arms at Pilsley

★★★ INN

**tel:** 01246 583258 **The High Street DE45 1UL**
**email:** res@devonshirehotels.co.uk **web:** www.devonshirepilsley.co.uk
**dir:** *From A619, in Baslow, at rdbt take 1st exit onto B6012. Follow signs to Chatsworth, 2nd right to Pilsley*

Part of the Devonshire Hotels and Restaurants group, The Devonshire Arms at Pilsley is just two miles from Chatsworth House, and also a minute's walk from the Chatsworth farm shop which provides much of the food served. It is an intimate yet traditional 18th-century village inn with a selection of cosy bedrooms, some in the inn and some in the farmhouse next door. The inn has a bartering system in place, allowing locals to exchange home-grown fruit and veg for a pint or two of local ale at the bar.

**Rooms:** 7 en suite 6 annexe en suite (2 fmly) (3 GF) **Facilities:** FTV Lounge tea/coffee Dinner available WiFi 🛁 **Parking:** 16 **Notes:** RS 24–26 Dec & 31 Dec–1 Jan Xmas & New Year packages

## REPTON
Map 10 SK32

# The Boot Inn
★★★★ ❀ INN

**tel:** 01283 346047 **12 Boot Hill DE65 6FT**
**email:** info@thebootatrepton.co.uk **web:** www.thebootatrepton.co.uk
**dir:** *From Repton Cross into Brook End, The Boot on right*

The Boot can trace its history back to the 17th century when it was a coaching inn, and was also used for legal sessions and proceedings prior to the completion of the Court House opposite, which now forms part of Repton School. It is a delightful village inn, and has recently undergone a complete refurbishment to provide a contemporary dining area and bar, made homely with attractive artwork, exposed original features and wood-burning stoves. The Boot also has its own microbrewery, producing brews like Boot Beer, Tuffer's Old and Clod Hopper. En suite bedrooms are individually decorated, each tastefully furnished with an emphasis on comfort. Carefully prepared dishes make great use of quality, local produce at breakfast and dinner. Free WiFi and on-site parking are available.

**Rooms:** 9 en suite (4 fmly) **S** £79–£120; **D** £79–£120 (room only)* **Facilities:** FTV DVD tea/coffee Dinner available WiFi **Parking:** 8 **Notes:** LB

## WILLINGTON
Map 10 SK22

# The Dragon
★★★★ 🍽 INN

**tel:** 01283 704795 **11 The Green DE65 6BP**
**email:** info@thedragonatwillington.co.uk **web:** www.thedragonatwillington.co.uk
**dir:** *Junct of A50/A38 follow signs for Willington. At mini rdbt turn left, The Dragon on left*

Situated on the bank of the Trent and Mersey canal, this village inn has been welcoming guests by land and water for over 150 years. It's ideally situated for those wishing to explore south Derbyshire's attractions and unspoilt countryside. The beautifully appointed en suite rooms are located in the neighbouring cottage and benefit from private parking and complimentary WiFi. A cooked breakfast includes award-winning local sausages which are a must!

**Rooms:** 7 annexe en suite (2 GF) **S** £49.95–£69; **D** £49.95–£79 (room only)* **Facilities:** FTV tea/coffee Dinner available WiFi 🔒 **Conf:** Max 50 Thtr 50 Class 45 Board 45 **Parking:** 20 **Notes:** LB

## WINSTER
Map 16 SK26

# Brae Cottage
★★★★ 🅰 GUEST ACCOMMODATION

**tel:** 01629 650375 **East Bank DE4 2DT**
**web:** www.braecottagewinster.co.uk
**dir:** *A6 onto B5057, driveway on right past pub*

Brae Cottage lies in the heart of this Peak District village, a stone's throw from the Old Bowling Green Inn. The bedrooms are in converted outbuildings and have a wealth of thoughtful extras. Comprehensive breakfasts, featuring home-made or local produce, are served at an antique table in the carefully furnished cottage.

**Rooms:** 2 annexe en suite (1 fmly) (2 GF) **S** £55–£65; **D** £65* **Facilities:** tea/coffee 🔒 **Extras:** Mineral water – complimentary **Parking:** 2 **Notes:** No children 11yrs Closed Nov–Feb

## YOULGREAVE
Map 16 SK26

# The George
★★★ INN

**tel:** 01629 636292 **Church Street DE45 1UW**
**dir:** *3m S of Bakewell in Youlgreave, opposite church*

The public bars of the 17th-century George are popular with locals and tourists. Bedroom styles vary, and all have shower rooms en suite. Breakfast is served in the lounge bar, and a range of bar meals and snacks is available.

**Rooms:** 3 en suite (1 fmly) **Facilities:** FTV DVD tea/coffee Dinner available WiFi Fishing 🔒 **Parking:** 12 **Notes:** LB

# DEVON

## ASHBURTON
Map 3 SX77

# Greencott
★★★★ GUEST HOUSE

**tel:** 01803 762649 **Landscove TQ13 7LZ**
**web:** www.stayawhile.co.uk/southwest/Greencott/Greencott.html
**dir:** *3m SE of Ashburton. Exit A38 at Peartree junct, Landscove signed on slip road, village green 2m on right, opposite village hall*

Greencott is in a peaceful village location and has superb country views. Your hosts extend a very warm welcome and there is a relaxed home-from-home atmosphere. The service is attentive and caring, and many guests return time and again. The bedrooms are attractive, comfortable and very well equipped. Delicious breakfasts are served around an oak dining table.

**Rooms:** 2 en suite **S** £27.50–£30; **D** £55–£60* **Facilities:** FTV TVL tea/coffee 🔒 **Parking:** 3 **Notes:** LB Closed 25–26 Dec

# Gages Mill Country Guest House
★★★★ GUEST ACCOMMODATION

**tel:** 01364 652391 **Buckfastleigh Road TQ13 7JW**
**email:** katestone@gagesmill.co.uk **web:** www.gagesmill.co.uk
**dir:** *Off A38 at Peartree junct, turn right then left at fuel station, Gages Mill 500yds on left*

Conveniently situated within easy reach of the A38, this Grade II listed building was formerly a woollen mill. Very much a family home, there is a relaxed and welcoming feel here and every effort is made to ensure a rewarding and memorable stay. The bedrooms provide good standards of comfort and many have lovely views across the surrounding fields. Breakfast provides a substantial and enjoyable start to the day, with plenty of choice for all appetites.

**Rooms:** 7 en suite (1 fmly) (1 GF) **S** fr £70; **D** fr £80* **Facilities:** iPod docking station TVL tea/coffee Licensed WiFi 🌀 **Parking:** 7 **Notes:** Closed Nov–Feb

## ATHERINGTON                                    Map 3 SS52

# West Down

★★★★ 🔒 🍽 FARMHOUSE

**tel:** 01769 560551 **Little Eastacombe EX37 9HP**
**email:** info@westdown.co.uk **web:** www.westdown.co.uk
**dir:** 0.5m from Atherington on B3227 to Torrington, turn right, 100yds on left

Set within 25 acres of lush Devon countryside, this farmhouse makes a good base for exploring the area. A peaceful atmosphere and caring hospitality are assured. Bedrooms are equipped with a host of thoughtful extras, and every effort is made to ensure an enjoyable stay. One bedroom has wheelchair access and a large wet room. A choice of homely lounges is available; breakfast and very good dinners are served in the sun lounge.

**Rooms:** 1 en suite 2 annexe en suite (2 GF) **S** £54–£56; **D** £88–£92* **Facilities:** FTV Lounge TVL tea/coffee Dinner available WiFi 🌀 **Parking:** 8 **Notes:** LB 25 acres sheep/chickens

## AXMINSTER                                    Map 4 SY29

### Premier Collection

# Kerrington House

★★★★★ 🔒 🍽 GUEST ACCOMMODATION

**tel:** 01297 35333 **Musbury Road EX13 5JR**
**email:** info@kerringtonhouse.com **web:** www.kerringtonhouse.com
**dir:** 0.5m from Axminster on A358 towards Seaton, house on left

This former Victorian gentleman's residence has been decorated and furnished to very high standards to make guests as comfortable as possible. Bedrooms and bathrooms include a range of welcome extras. Afternoon tea may be enjoyed in the comfortably furnished lounge or, in the warmer months, outside overlooking the landscaped gardens. Locally sourced produce is used both at breakfast and at dinner, which is available by prior arrangement.

**Rooms:** 5 en suite (2 fmly) (2 GF) **S** £87; **D** £132* **Facilities:** FTV DVD iPod docking station Lounge tea/coffee Dinner available Licensed WiFi 🌀 **Extras:** Speciality toiletries, sherry, chocolates – complimentary **Conf:** Max 12 Board 12 **Parking:** 6 **Notes:** LB

# Tytherleigh Arms

**[U]**

**tel:** 01460 220214 **Tytherleigh EX13 7BE**
**email:** info@tytherleigharms.com **web:** www.tytherleigharms.com

Currently the rating for this establishment is not confirmed. This may be due to a change of ownership or because it has only recently joined the AA rating scheme.

**Rooms:** 6 annexe en suite

## BAMPTON                                    Map 3 SS92

# The Swan

★★★★★  INN

**tel:** 01398 332248 **Station Road EX16 9NG**
**email:** info@theswan.co **web:** www.theswan.co

The Swan is a traditional hostelry offering good food, good beer and a wide selection of wines coupled with comfortable, well-equipped bedrooms and en suite bathrooms. Each bedroom has a flat-screen TV, and other modern media staples. Staff are very friendly and do all they can to make a stay comfortable. Breakfast is a hearty affair using good local ingredients, and the menu in the evening, which has been awarded two AA Rosettes, offers a great choice for all.

**Rooms:** 3 en suite **Facilities:** FTV iPod docking station tea/coffee Dinner available WiFi Fishing Gym 🌀 **Extras:** Speciality toiletries, espresso machine, snacks **Notes:** LB Closed 25–26 Dec

# Weston House

★★★★ BED AND BREAKFAST

**tel:** 01398 332094 & 07958 176799 **6 Luke Street EX16 9NF**
**email:** peter@westonhousedevon.co.uk **web:** www.westonhousedevon.co.uk
**dir:** On B3227, in village, opposite church

Located in the heart of Bampton within easy reach of many local attractions and gardens, Weston House offers comfortable, well-equipped bedrooms and hearty breakfasts using quality local ingredients. Owner Catherine Stott is an artist who teaches, and many of her pieces are tastefully displayed throughout the house. Public parking is available within a few minutes' walk.

**Rooms:** 3 rms (2 en suite) (1 pri facs) **S** £60; **D** £75–£90* **Facilities:** FTV DVD tea/coffee WiFi 🌀 Drying facilities **Extras:** Speciality toiletries, home-made biscuits – complimentary **Notes:** LB Closed 20–28 Dec

## BARNSTAPLE                                    Map 3 SS53

# The Spinney

★★★★ 🔒 GUEST ACCOMMODATION

**tel:** 01271 850282 & 07775 335654 **Shirwell EX31 4JR**
**email:** stay@thespinneyshirwell.co.uk **web:** www.thespinneyshirwell.co.uk
**dir:** From Barnstaple on A39, past hospital towards Lynton

This elegant 18th-century former rectory is located in the heart of north Devon, three miles from the historic market town of Barnstaple. The Spinney offers stylishly decorated, en suite accommodation in muted colours, with thoughtful extras. Local farm sausages feature at breakfast which is served in the conservatory. Ample private parking is available. The Spinney was a finalist for the AA B&B Friendliest B&B of the Year 2017–18.

**Rooms:** 5 rms (4 en suite) (1 pri facs) (1 fmly) **S** £70–£80; **D** £80–£98* **Facilities:** FTV DVD Lounge tea/coffee WiFi 🌀 **Extras:** Chocolates, water – complimentary **Parking:** 7 **Notes:** LB No children 10yrs RS Dec–1 Mar winter opening times may vary

---

## BEESANDS        Map 3 SX84

### The Cricket Inn

★★★★  INN

**tel:** 01548 580215 **TQ7 2EN**
**email:** enquiries@thecricketinn.com **web:** www.thecricketinn.com
**dir:** *From Kingsbridge follow A379 towards Dartmouth, at Stokenham mini rdbt turn right for Beesands*

Dating back to 1867 this charming seaside inn is situated almost on the beach at Start Bay. The well-appointed bedrooms have fantastic views, comfortable beds and flat-screen TVs. The daily-changing fish menu includes locally-caught crabs, lobster and perhaps hand-dived scallops.

**Rooms:** 7 en suite (1 fmly) **Facilities:** FTV tea/coffee Dinner available WiFi
**Parking:** 30

---

## BIDEFORD        Map 3 SS42

### The Pines at Eastleigh

★★★★ GUEST ACCOMMODATION

**tel:** 01271 860561 **The Pines, Eastleigh EX39 4PA**
**email:** info@thepinesateastleigh.co.uk **web:** www.thepinesateastleigh.co.uk
**dir:** *A39 onto A386 signed East-the-Water. 1st left signed Eastleigh, 500yds next left, 1.5m to village, house on right*

This charming Grade II listed house is set in seven-acre grounds with lovely views across rolling farmland towards Lundy Island and Hartland Point. This makes a wonderful location from which to explore this beautiful area, and your welcoming hosts will help with any local information required. The bedrooms are located both in the main house and adjacent courtyard – all provide impressive levels of quality and comfort and have stylish bathrooms. Tasty breakfasts are served in the elegant dining room; a guest lounge, with an honesty bar, is also available.

**Rooms:** 10 en suite (1 fmly) (5 GF) **S** £80–£83; **D** £95–£105* **Facilities:** FTV DVD TVL tea/coffee Licensed WiFi Pool table 🔒 **Conf:** Max 25 Thtr 20 Board 20 **Parking:** 10
**Notes:** LB No children 9yrs

---

## BISHOPSTEIGNTON        Map 3 SX97

### Cockhaven Arms

★★★★ INN

**tel:** 01626 775252 **Cockhaven Road TQ14 9RF**
**email:** contact@cockhavenarms.co.uk **web:** www.cockhavenarms.co.uk
**dir:** *From A381 follow brown tourist signs*

Cockhaven Arms is a friendly, family-run inn that dates back to the 16th century. Following extensive refurbishment bedrooms now offer impressive levels of comfort and quality, all of which are well equipped and many enjoy views across the beautiful Teign estuary. A choice of dining options is offered, with traditional favourites and daily specials, locally caught fish as a speciality.

**Rooms:** 10 en suite (2 fmly) **Facilities:** FTV tea/coffee Dinner available WiFi 🎣 18
**Conf:** Max 144 Thtr 100 Class 100 Board 24 **Parking:** 30 **Notes:** LB Closed 26 Dec
Civ wed 80

---

## BLACKAWTON        Map 3 SX85

### The George Inn

★★★ INN

**tel:** 01803 712342 **Main Street TQ9 7BG**
**email:** tgiblackawton@yahoo.co.uk **web:** www.blackawton.com
**dir:** *From Totnes on A381 through Halwell. Left onto A3122 towards Dartmouth, turn right to Blackawton*

Situated in the heart of Blackawton, this village local offers a warm welcome to all. A proper, unspoilt pub, it enjoys an engaging traditional atmosphere and a real sense of community. Bedrooms offer good levels of comfort and quality, likewise the modern bathrooms; while public areas have an inviting, rustic charm. A wide range of food options are offered, with local produce used as much as possible. Lovely views across the rolling countryside can be enjoyed from the terrace and garden.

**Rooms:** 4 en suite (1 fmly) **Facilities:** FTV DVD tea/coffee Dinner available WiFi
🔒 **Parking:** 12 **Notes:** LB

---

## BOVEY TRACEY        Map 3 SX87

### Courtenay House

★★★ BED AND BREAKFAST

**tel:** 01626 835363 & 07774 260446 **76 Fore Street TQ13 9AE**
**email:** info@courtenayhouse.co.uk **web:** www.courtenayhouse.co.uk
**dir:** *A38 from Exeter towards Plymouth. Follow B3344 Chudleigh Knighton signs. At T-junct in Bovey Tracey, right, follow Town Centre signs into Fore St. House on left after Orchard Terrace*

Courtenay House is located in the heart of the historic town of Bovey Tracey and is the perfect base to explore the area. The bedrooms are well furnished and equipped with a range of useful amenities. A freshly cooked breakfast is served in the tea room just off the antique shop.

**Rooms:** 3 rms (2 en suite) (1 pri facs) (1 GF) **S** fr £45; **D** £75–£80* **Facilities:** FTV tea/coffee WiFi **Notes:** LB No children 16yrs Closed 24 Dec–6 Jan

---

## BRATTON FLEMING        Map 3 SS63

### Premier Collection

### Bracken House

★★★★★ BED AND BREAKFAST

**tel:** 01598 711810 & 07970 275881 **EX31 4TG**
**email:** info@brackenhouse.co.uk **web:** www.brackenhouse.co.uk
**dir:** *From M5 (junct 27) A361 to South Molton, right on A399 for 7m, left to Bratton Fleming for 2m. Sign end of drive opposite Baptist Chapel*

Bracken House, a former Victorian rectory, has four en suite bedrooms and is situated on the edge of the popular north Devon village of Bratton Fleming. It is within easy driving distance of the spectacular coast, Exmoor and many other local attractions, including National Trust properties, the gardens at RHS Rosemoor, Castle Hill, Marwood and Tapeley Park. The drawing room, with its cosy open fire, has lovely views over the garden and towards Hartland through the large bay window. The dining room, where a full English breakfast is served each morning, has a wood-burner which is lit during those cooler mornings.

**Rooms:** 4 en suite (1 fmly) (1 GF) **S** £75–£125; **D** £95–£125* **Facilities:** FTV DVD Lounge tea/coffee WiFi 🌿 🔒 **Extras:** Speciality toiletries **Parking:** 6
**Notes:** Closed 23–26 Dec Civ wed 20

## BRIXHAM
Map 3 SX95

### Anchorage Guest House

★★★★ ⌖ GUEST HOUSE

tel: 01803 852960 & 07950 536362 **170 New Road TQ5 8DA**
email: enquiries@brixham-anchorage.co.uk web: www.brixham-anchorage.co.uk
dir: *A3022, enter Brixham, left at lights at junct with Monksbridge Rd. Pass Toll House immediately on right*

Conveniently located within walking distance of the town centre and harbour, this is an excellent choice for anyone looking to explore the many attractions of this popular holiday area. The dining room and the bedrooms have a light, bright contemporary style, with many extra facilities provided to ensure a comfortable stay. Guests are welcome to use the delightful garden, and on-site parking is a bonus.

**Rooms:** 7 rms (6 en suite) (1 pri facs) (4 GF) **S** £34–£40; **D** £65–£80* **Facilities:** FTV tea/coffee WiFi ⌖ **Parking:** 6

### The Melville

★★★★ GUEST HOUSE

tel: 01803 852033 **45 New Road TQ5 8NL**
email: info@themelville.co.uk web: www.themelvillebrixham.co.uk

Situated in Brixham, The Melville is close to the harbour, as well as having easy access to Dartmoor and other local attractions. The comfortable en suite rooms have digital TVs and tea/coffee making facilities, making The Melville a relaxing base for your holiday or short break.

**Rooms:** 7 en suite (1 fmly) **Facilities:** STV FTV Lounge tea/coffee Licensed WiFi **Extras:** Filtered water **Parking:** 4 **Notes:** LB No children 6yrs Closed Nov

## BUCKFAST
Map 3 SX76

### Furzeleigh Mill

★★★ GUEST ACCOMMODATION

tel: 01364 643476 **Old Ashburton Road TQ11 0JP**
email: enquiries@furzeleigh.co.uk web: www.furzeleigh.co.uk
dir: *Exit A38 at Dartbridge junct, right at end slip road, right signed Ashburton/Prince Town (NB do not cross River Dart bridge), 200yds right*

This Grade II listed, 16th-century converted corn mill stands in its own grounds and is a good base for touring Dartmoor. Spacious family rooms are available as well as a lounge and a bar. All meals are served in the dining room and use local produce.

**Rooms:** 14 en suite (2 fmly) **Facilities:** FTV TVL tea/coffee Dinner available Licensed WiFi ⌖ **Conf:** Max 20 Thtr 20 **Parking:** 32 **Notes:** LB No children 6yrs Closed 23 Dec–2 Jan

## BUCKFASTLEIGH
Map 3 SX76

### Kilbury Manor

★★★★ ⌖ GUEST ACCOMMODATION

tel: 01364 644079 **Colston Road TQ11 0LN**
email: info@kilburymanor.co.uk web: www.kilburymanor.co.uk
dir: *Off A38 onto B3380 to Buckfastleigh, left into Old Totnes Rd, at bottom turn right, Kilbury Manor on left*

Dating back to the 17th century, this charming Devon longhouse is situated in the tranquil surroundings of the Dart Valley with access to the river across the meadow. Bedrooms have an abundance of character and are located in the main house and in adjacent converted barns; all provide high levels of comfort. The stylish

bathrooms are also appointed to impressive standards. Breakfast is served in the elegant dining room with local produce very much in evidence.

**Rooms:** 4 rms (3 en suite) (1 pri facs) (1 GF) **Facilities:** FTV DVD tea/coffee WiFi **Parking:** 5 **Notes:** No children 7yrs

## CHILLATON
Map 3 SX48

### Premier Collection

### Tor Cottage

★★★★★ ⌖ GUEST ACCOMMODATION

tel: 01822 860248 **PL16 0JE**
email: info@torcottage.co.uk web: www.torcottage.co.uk
dir: *A30 Lewdown exit through Chillaton towards Tavistock, 300yds after Post Office right signed 'Bridlepath No Public Vehicular Access' to end*

Tor Cottage, located in its own valley with 18 acres of grounds, is a welcome antidote to the fast pace of everyday life. Rooms are spacious and elegant; the cottage-wing bedroom has a separate sitting room, and the garden rooms have their own wood-burners. The gardens are delightful, with a stream and heated outdoor pool. An exceptional range of dishes is offered at breakfast, which can be enjoyed either in the conservatory dining room or on the terrace.

**Rooms:** 1 en suite 3 annexe en suite (3 GF) **S** £98; **D** £150–£155 **Facilities:** FTV DVD TVL tea/coffee WiFi ⌕ ⌖ **Parking:** 8 **Notes:** LB No children 14yrs Closed mid Dec–beginning Feb

## CHRISTOW
Map 3 SX88

### Hyner Farm

★★★★ FARMHOUSE

tel: 01647 252923 & 07781 186133 **EX6 7NT**
email: preston916@btinternet.com web: www.hynerfarm-bandb-devon.co.uk
dir: *A38 take exit signed Teign Valley. Follow brown tourist signs for Canonteign Falls. Turn sharp left signed No Through Road at Canonteign Falls exit*

This beautiful rural farmhouse, located in the middle of the Teign Valley has three highly individual bedrooms. All are richly decorated and well equipped; ideal for business or leisure use. Public areas include a comfortable lounge and a dining area with inglenook fire place; a sociable setting for breakfast. There is also parking, all in characterful grounds.

**Rooms:** 3 en suite **S** £45–£50; **D** £80–£100* **Facilities:** FTV DVD TVL tea/coffee WiFi ⌖18 ⌖ **Parking:** 3 **Notes:** LB 120 acres beef/grass

## CHULMLEIGH
Map 3 SS61

### The Old Bakehouse

★★★★ ⌖ GUEST HOUSE

tel: 01769 580074 & 580137 **South Molton Street EX18 7BW**
email: holly@oldbakehousedevon.co.uk web: www.oldbakehousedevon.co.uk
dir: *A377 onto B3096 into village centre, left into South Molton St, 100yds on left*

This 16th-century thatched house is situated in the centre of Chulmleigh, a hilltop town which stands above a beautiful river valley. The charming bedrooms are equipped with many extras such as DVD players (library available) and are located across a pretty, secluded courtyard garden in the former village bakery. A wealth of beams, thick cob walls and wood-burning stove all contribute to the character and comfort. A generous choice is offered at breakfast with an emphasis on excellent local produce.

**Rooms:** 3 en suite (1 GF) **S** £60; **D** £73.75–£90 **Facilities:** FTV DVD Lounge tea/coffee ⌖18 ⌖ **Extras:** Home-made biscuits, cafetière, flowers **Notes:** LB No children 11yrs

## CLOVELLY                                    Map 3 SS32

# East Dyke Farmhouse

★★★★ 🛏 FARMHOUSE

**tel:** 01237 431216 **East Dyke Farm, Higher Clovelly EX39 5RU**
**email:** helen.goaman@btinternet.com **web:** www.bedbreakfastclovelly.co.uk
**dir:** A39 onto B3237 at Clovelly Cross rdbt, farm 500yds on left

Adjoining an Iron Age hill fort, this working farm has glorious views of Bideford Bay in the distance. The farmhouse has a friendly atmosphere and the open fires, beams and stone floors add to its charm and character. The three bedrooms are spacious and furnished in co-ordinated fabrics with thoughtful little extras. A key feature here is the breakfast – local produce and delicious home-made preserves are served around one large table.

**Rooms:** 3 rms (2 en suite) (1 pri facs) (1 fmly) **S** £45–£55; **D** £65–£75*
**Facilities:** FTV TVL tea/coffee WiFi 🔒 **Extras:** Fridge **Parking:** 6 **Notes:** Closed 24–26 Dec RS Dec–Feb Advance bookings only 350 acres beef/arable

# Red Lion

★★★★ INN

**tel:** 01237 431237 **The Quay EX39 5TF**
**email:** stay@clovelly.co.uk **web:** www.clovelly.co.uk
**dir:** Exit A39 at Clovelly Cross onto B3237. Pass visitor centre, 1st left by white rails to harbour

'Idyllic' is the word that best describes the harbour-side setting of this charming 18th-century inn, with the famous fishing village forming a spectacular backdrop. Bedrooms are stylish and enjoy delightful views. The inn's relaxed atmosphere is conducive to relaxation, even when the harbour comes alive with the activities of the local fishermen during the day.

**Rooms:** 17 en suite (5 fmly) (2 GF) **Facilities:** Sea fishing Diving Tennis Spa treatments can be arranged **Notes:** Civ wed 70

# New Inn

★★★ INN

**tel:** 01237 431303 **High Street EX39 5TQ**
**email:** newinn@clovelly.co.uk **web:** www.clovelly.co.uk
**dir:** At Clovelly Cross, exit A39 onto B3237. Follow down hill for 1.5m. Right at 'All vehicles for Clovelly' sign

Famed for its cobbled descent to the harbour, this fascinating fishing village is a traffic-free zone. Consequently, luggage is conveyed by sledge or donkey to this much-photographed inn. Carefully renovated bedrooms and public areas are smartly presented with quality, locally-made furnishings. Meals may be taken in the elegant restaurant or the popular Upalong bar.

**Rooms:** 8 en suite (1 fmly) (1 GF) **S** £40; **D** £80* **Facilities:** Lounge tea/coffee Dinner available Direct dial WiFi Sea fishing Diving Tennis can be arranged **Notes:** Civ wed 50

## COLEFORD                                    Map 3 SS70

# The New Inn

★★★★ INN

**tel:** 01363 84242 **EX17 5BZ**
**email:** enquiries@thenewinncoleford.co.uk **web:** www.thenewinncoleford.co.uk
**dir:** Exit A377 into Coleford, 1.5m to inn (signed)

Originally dating back to the 13th century, The New Inn is a charming thatched village inn with much to offer, and is a relaxing base from which to explore this

beautiful corner of Devon. Bedrooms are spacious, comfortable and well appointed with lovely beds and lots of period features. Roaring fires, flagged floors, and Captain the resident parrot, all combine to create an engaging atmosphere. A choice of carefully prepared dishes is on offer in the restaurant and bar lounges, with local produce strongly featured.

**Rooms:** 6 en suite (4 fmly) (1 GF) **S** fr £72; **D** fr £95 **Facilities:** FTV DVD tea/coffee Dinner available Direct dial WiFi ♨18 🔒 **Extras:** Bottled water – complimentary **Parking:** 50 **Notes:** LB Closed 25–26 Dec

## CREDITON                                    Map 3 SS80

# The Lamb Inn

★★★★ 🛏 INN

**tel:** 01363 773676 **The Square, Sandford EX17 4LW**
**email:** thelambinn@gmail.com **web:** www.lambinnsandford.co.uk

The Lamb Inn is the sort of quintessential local which any village would be proud to have. This is a proper unpretentious pub with a very welcoming and engaging atmosphere, where good-natured banter will accompany a refreshing pint. Food is not to be missed; accomplished cooking makes good use of quality, local produce, and breakfasts are generous. Bedrooms and bathrooms offer impressive levels of quality with contemporary styling.

**Rooms:** 7 en suite **Facilities:** Dinner available

## CROYDE                                      Map 3 SS43

# The Whiteleaf

★★★★ 🎤 🛏 GUEST HOUSE

**tel:** 01271 890266 **Croyde Road EX33 1PN**
**email:** bookings@thewhiteleaf.co.uk **web:** www.thewhiteleaf.co.uk
**dir:** On B3231 entering Croyde, on left at 'Road Narrows' sign

A warm family welcome awaits guests at this attractive house within easy walking distance of the pretty village and the sandy beach. Each of the well-equipped bedrooms has its own charm, and three rooms have decked balconies. Ambitious and imaginative dinners, using fresh seasonal produce, are served in the elegant restaurant.

**Rooms:** 5 en suite (2 fmly) **S** £68–£98; **D** £82–£140* **Facilities:** FTV Lounge tea/coffee Dinner available Direct dial Licensed WiFi 🔒 **Extras:** Mini-bar **Parking:** 10 **Notes:** LB Closed 24–27 Dec

## CULLOMPTON                                  Map 3 ST00

### Premier Collection

# Muddifords Court Country House

★★★★★ 🛏 GUEST ACCOMMODATION

**tel:** 01884 820023 & 07890 273730 **Willand EX15 2QG**
**email:** info@muddifords.co.uk **web:** www.muddifordscourt.co.uk
**dir:** M5 junct 27 onto A38 (Wellington). After 1m at rdbt right onto B3181, at rdbt (4m) right signed Halberton/Willand. Over mini rdbt, 500mtrs turn right (Sampford Peverell). 200mtrs on right

Muddifords Court has been developed into a high quality establishment, with the added benefit of a range of flexible meeting space to accommodate weddings, conferences and special events. The rooms have been finished to a high standard and are sumptuously appointed; some offer attractive views over the Culm Valley and beyond. A choice of freshly prepared breakfasts is served in the main dining room. Self-catering huts are available in the private copse.

**Rooms:** 5 en suite 2 annexe en suite (1 GF) **D** £70–£145 (room only)*
**Facilities:** FTV DVD TVL tea/coffee Licensed WiFi 🔒 **Extras:** Sherry **Conf:** Max 100 Thtr 100 Class 80 Board 60 **Parking:** 70 **Notes:** Closed 24 Dec–2 Jan Civ wed 120

## Weir Mill Farm

★★★★ FARMHOUSE

**tel:** 01884 820803 **Jaycroft, Willand EX15 2RE**
**email:** rita@weirmill-devon.co.uk **web:** www.weirmill-devon.co.uk
**dir:** *2m N of Cullompton. M5 junct 27, B3181 to Willand, left at rdbt onto B3340 signed Uffculme, 50yds right into Willand Moor Rd, after Lupin Way left into lane*

Set in extensive farmland, this charming 19th-century farmhouse offers comfortable accommodation with a relaxed and homely atmosphere. The spacious bedrooms are attractively decorated and equipped with an impressive range of thoughtful extras. A good choice is offered at breakfast in the well-appointed dining room.

**Rooms:** 3 en suite (1 fmly) **S** £50; **D** £75* **Facilities:** FTV tea/coffee WiFi 🔒 **Parking:** 5 **Notes:** 100 acres arable/beef

---

**DARTMEET** Map 3 SX67

## Brimpts Farm

★★★ GUEST ACCOMMODATION

**tel:** 01364 631450 **PL20 6SG**
**email:** info@brimptsfarm.co.uk **web:** www.brimptsfarm.co.uk
**dir:** *Dartmeet at E end of B3357, establishment signed on right at top of hill*

A popular venue for walkers and lovers of the great outdoors, Brimpts Farm is peacefully situated in the heart of Dartmoor and has been a Duchy of Cornwall farm since 1307. Bedrooms are simply furnished and many have wonderful views across the moor. Additional facilities include a sauna and spa, and a children's play area.

**Rooms:** 10 en suite 3 annexe rms (3 pri facs) (2 fmly) (7 GF) **S** £40; **D** £70*
**Facilities:** Lounge TVL tea/coffee Licensed WiFi Pool table 🔒 Farm walks & trails Hot tub **Conf:** Max 60 Thtr 60 Class 40 Board 25 **Parking:** 50 **Notes:** LB

---

**DARTMOUTH** Map 3 SX85

## Strete Barton House

★★★★★ 🔒 GUEST HOUSE

**tel:** 01803 770364 **Totnes Rd, Strete TQ6 0RU**
**email:** info@stretebarton.co.uk **web:** www.stretebarton.co.uk
**dir:** *From Dartmouth on A379, off coastal road into village, just below church*

This delightful 16th-century former farmhouse blends stylish accommodation with original character. The bedrooms are very comfortably furnished and well equipped with useful extras. Breakfast makes good use of quality local produce and is served in the spacious dining room. Guests are also welcome to use the comfortable lounge, complete with log-burning stove. The village lies between Dartmouth and Kingsbridge and has easy access to the beautiful South Hams as well as many local pubs and restaurants.

**Rooms:** 5 rms (4 en suite) (1 pri facs) 1 annexe en suite **Facilities:** FTV DVD iPod docking station Lounge tea/coffee WiFi 🛝18 🔒 **Extras:** Speciality toiletries, guest fridge **Parking:** 2 **Notes:** LB No children 8yrs

---

## Mounthaven

★★★★★ BED AND BREAKFAST

**tel:** 01803 839061 & 07919 274751 **Mount Boone TQ6 9PB**
**email:** enquiries@mounthavendartmouth.co.uk
**web:** www.mounthavendartmouth.co.uk
**dir:** *A379, right into Townstal Rd, opposite Royal Naval College gates. 1st left into Mount Boone, halfway down on right*

Set on the hillside of Mount Boone, Mounthaven has a superb view of the town and the estuary yet is only a few minutes' walk from the town centre. The hosts are experienced and professional and a very warm welcome is assured. Bedrooms are individually decorated and each enjoys a view of historic Dartmouth or the sea.

**Rooms:** 3 en suite **D** £100–£125* **Facilities:** STV FTV DVD TVL tea/coffee WiFi 🛝18 🔒 **Parking:** 5 **Notes:** LB No children 16yrs

DARTMOUTH *continued*

## Hill View House

★★★★ GUEST ACCOMMODATION

**tel:** 01803 839372 **76 Victoria Road TQ6 9DZ**
**email:** enquiries@hillviewdartmouth.co.uk **web:** www.hillviewdartmouth.co.uk
**dir:** *Phone for detailed directions*

Centrally located, Hill View House is a fully refurbished five-storey late Victorian town house. A warm welcome is guaranteed and the house is located only minutes from the heart of Dartmouth. Bedrooms are comfortably furnished, serviced to a high standard, and come equipped with a range of accessories. Breakfast is served in the light and airy dining room. Free WiFi is accessible throughout.

**Rooms:** 4 en suite 1 annexe en suite **S** £42–£47; **D** £60–£70* **Facilities:** TVL tea/coffee WiFi ⚓18 **Extras:** Speciality toiletries **Parking:** 3 **Notes:** No children 14yrs

## Bayards Cove Inn

★★★★ 🍽 GUEST ACCOMMODATION

**tel:** 01803 839278 **27 Lower Street TQ6 9AN**
**email:** bayardscove@gmail.com **web:** www.bayardscoveinn.co.uk

There is a real sense of history at this charming waterside establishment, once a Tudor merchant's house, located a few steps from where the Pilgrims set sail on the Mayflower in 1621. Every effort is made to ensure guests have a relaxed and rewarding stay. A café and wine bar by day; evening opening times vary, with a tapas menu available on selected nights. Bedrooms are comfortable, and individually styled. Bathrooms provide all the expected modern necessities with cosseting towels and quality toiletries. Breakfast is a generous affair, with a range of continental and cooked options, all showcasing the best of local produce.

**Rooms:** 7 en suite (2 fmly) **Facilities:** FTV DVD Lounge tea/coffee Dinner available Licensed WiFi ⚓18 ⚓ **Extras:** Magazines, speciality toiletries – complimentary **Parking:** 1

## Cherub's Nest

★★★★ GUEST ACCOMMODATION

**tel:** 01803 832482 & 07816 762799 **15 Higher Street TQ6 9RB**
**email:** cherubsnest4bb@aol.com **web:** www.cherubsnest.co.uk
**dir:** *From Lower Dartmouth ferry along Lower St, left into Smith St, left into Higher St, Cherub's Nest 50yds on left*

Dating from 1710, this former merchant's house, bedecked with flowers during the summer, is located in the very heart of historic Dartmouth. Full of character, the individually decorated bedrooms vary in size, but all are attractive and well equipped. A choice of breakfasts is served in the cosy dining room.

**Rooms:** 3 en suite **S** £75–£85; **D** £70–£95* **Facilities:** FTV tea/coffee WiFi **Notes:** LB No children 10yrs

---

## The Nobody Inn

★★★★ ◉ INN

**tel:** 01647 252394 **EX6 7PS**
**email:** info@nobodyinn.co.uk **web:** www.nobodyinn.co.uk
**dir:** *From A38 turn off at top of Haldon Hill, follow signs to Doddiscombsleigh*

Dating back to the 16th century, this fascinating inn is something of a mecca for lovers of wine, whisky and local ale – the choices are extensive. Let's not forget the impressive food, much of which is sourced locally including an extensive cheese selection. Bedrooms and bathrooms have been appointed to provide high levels of quality, comfort and individuality. Reassuringly, the bars and lounges remain unchanged with charmingly mismatched furniture, age-darkened beams and an inglenook fireplace.

**Rooms:** 5 rms (4 en suite) (1 pri facs) **S** £50–£79; **D** £99–£105* **Facilities:** FTV DVD tea/coffee Dinner available Direct dial WiFi ⚓ **Conf:** Max 24 **Parking:** 25 **Notes:** No children 5yrs Closed 25 Dec

---

### Premier Collection

## The Rams Head Inn

★★★★★ ◉◉ INN

**tel:** 01805 804255 **South Street EX19 8QS**
**email:** info@theramsheadinn.co.uk **web:** www.theramsheadinn.co.uk

The Rams Head is a beautifully restored and refurbished 17th-century coaching inn in Dolton; set between Exmoor and Dartmoor. All nine bedrooms have been refurbished to high standards and include antique furniture. Award-winning food is offer, as is a full Devon breakfast each morning, which is a great start to the day.

**Rooms:** 9 rms (8 en suite) (1 pri facs) (3 fmly) (2 GF) **S** £59–£69; **D** £84–£89* **Facilities:** FTV tea/coffee Dinner available WiFi **Parking:** 15 **Notes:** LB

## DUNKESWELL
Map 3 ST10

### The Old Kennels
★★★★ BED AND BREAKFAST

**tel:** 01823 681138 **Stentwood EX14 4RW**
**email:** info@theoldkennels.co.uk **web:** www.theoldkennels.co.uk

Located in the heart of the beautiful Blackdown Hills, on the Devon-Somerset border, the Old Kennels is in a quiet rural location and makes an ideal base for exploring this vibrant area. Accommodation includes a cosy two-bedroom loft apartment, furnished with antique furniture and vintage details. It also has a compact lounge area and fully fitted kitchen. A continental breakfast hamper is delivered to the apartment, allowing the flexibility to enjoy breakfast at your own pace, perhaps outside on the terrace with lovely views across the fields.

**Rooms:** 2 rms annexe (1 en suite) (1 pri facs annexe) (1 fmly) **S** £85–£100; **D** £100  £120 (room only)^ **Facilities:** FTV TVL tea/coffee WiFi ↕18 ▲ 25 acres of woodland Arts & crafts courses **Extras:** Fresh milk **Conf:** Max 12 Board 12 **Parking:** 10 **Notes:** LB

## ERMINGTON
Map 3 SX65

### Premier Collection

### Plantation House
★★★★★ ◉◉ RESTAURANT WITH ROOMS

**tel:** 01548 831100 & 830741 **Totnes Road PL21 9NS**
**email:** info@plantationhousehotel.co.uk **web:** www.plantationhousehotel.co.uk

Peacefully situated in the picturesque South Hams, this former rectory provides an intimate and relaxing base from which to explore the area. Quality, comfort and individuality are hallmarks throughout, with bedrooms offering impressive standards and a host of thoughtful extras. The stylish bathrooms come equipped with fluffy towels, robes and underfloor heating. A drink beside the crackling log fire is the ideal prelude to dinner, where skill and passion underpin menus focusing upon wonderful local produce. Breakfast is equally enjoyable, with superb eggs provided by the resident hens.

**Rooms:** 8 en suite **S** £80–£120; **D** £110  £230* **Facilities:** FTV DVD iPod docking station Lounge tea/coffee Dinner available Direct dial WiFi ➌ ↕18 Fishing Massage & Therapies **Extras:** Speciality toiletries, fruit, robes, mineral water, fresh milk **Conf:** Max 16 **Parking:** 30 **Notes:** LB

## EXETER
Map 3 SX99

### Chi Restaurant & Bar with Accommodation
★★★★ ⊜ RESTAURANT WITH ROOMS

**tel:** 01626 890213 **Fore Street, Kenton EX6 8LD**
**email:** enquiries@chi-restaurant.co.uk **web:** www.chi-restaurant.co.uk
**dir:** 5m S of Exeter. M5 junct 30, A379 towards Dawlish, in village centre

This former pub has been spectacularly transformed into a chic and contemporary bar, allied with a stylish Chinese restaurant. Dishes are beautifully presented with an emphasis on quality produce and authenticity, resulting in a memorable dining experience. Bedrooms are well equipped and all provide good levels of space and comfort, along with modern bathrooms.

**Rooms:** 5 en suite (1 fmly) **S** £50–£126; **D** £63–£140 (room only)* **Facilities:** FTV DVD Lounge TVL tea/coffee Dinner available WiFi ▲ **Parking:** 26 **Notes:** Closed Sun–Mon

### Innkeeper's Lodge Exeter, Clyst St George
★★★ INN

**tel:** 08451 551551 (Calls cost 2p per minute plus your phone company's access charge) **Clyst St George EX3 0QJ**
**email:** info@innkeeperslodge.com **web:** www.innkeeperslodge.com

This welcoming inn is just a short drive from the centre of Exeter and very convenient for access to the M5. Surrounded by rolling fields, this is an excellent base for exploring the East Devon coast, with Exmouth close by and Topsham also worth a visit. Bedrooms all provide impressive levels of comfort and quality with all the requirements for the business and leisure guest. The pub has a warm and inviting atmosphere with crackling log fires and cosy hideaways, so sit back and enjoy a drink and a satisfying meal.

**Rooms:** 21 en suite (6 fmly) (8 GF) **Facilities:** FTV tea/coffee Dinner available Direct dial WiFi

### Innkeeper's Lodge Exeter, Middlemoor Lodge
★★★ INN

**tel:** 08451 551551 (Calls cost 2p per minute plus your phone company's access charge) **Rydon Lane, Middlemoor EX2 7HL**
**email:** info@innkeeperslodge.com **web:** www.innkeeperslodge.com
**dir:** M5 junct 29 onto A30 towards Honiton/Exeter Airport. Right into Honiton Rd, take 1st exit at next 2 rdbts, then 2nd exit at next rdbt, property on left

This conveniently located establishment is ideally suited for both business and leisure guests. It's just a short drive from the city centre, and is also close to the airport and Digby and Sowton station. Contemporary styled bedrooms offer good levels of comfort and quality. A Toby Carvery is adjacent.

**Rooms:** 1 en suite 37 annexe en suite (1 fmly) (28 GF) **Facilities:** FTV tea/coffee Dinner available WiFi **Conf:** Max 40 **Parking:** 200

## EXMOUTH                                     Map 3 SY08

# The Devoncourt

★★★ GUEST ACCOMMODATION

**tel:** 01395 272277 **16 Douglas Avenue EX8 2EX**
**email:** enquiries@devoncourt.com **web:** www.devoncourthotel.com
**dir:** *M5/A376 to Exmouth, follow seafront to Maer Rd, right at T-junct*

The Devoncourt stands in four acres of mature, subtropical gardens, sloping gently towards the sea and overlooking two miles of sandy beaches. It offers extensive leisure facilities, and the smartly furnished bedrooms are exceptionally well equipped. The spacious public areas are available to timeshare owners as well as guests. For meals there is a choice between the informal bar and the restaurant.

**Rooms:** 52 en suite 2 annexe en suite (35 fmly) (8 GF) **Facilities:** FTV DVD TVL tea/coffee Dinner available Direct dial Lift Licensed WiFi 🕐 ⚓ 🦢 🏊 ⛳18 Snooker Gym Sun shower Jacuzzi **Parking:** 50 **Notes:** LB Civ wed 100

## HAYTOR VALE                                 Map 3 SX77

# Rock Inn

★★★★★  INN

**tel:** 01364 661305 & 661465 **TQ13 9XP**
**email:** inn@rock-inn.co.uk **web:** www.rock-inn.co.uk
**dir:** *A38 onto 382 to Bovey Tracey, in 0.5m left onto B3387 to Haytor*

Dating back to the 1750s, this former coaching inn is in a pretty hamlet on the edge of Dartmoor. Each named after a Grand National winner, the individually decorated bedrooms have some nice extra touches. Bars are full of character, with flagstone floors and old beams, and offer a wide range of dishes, cooked with imagination. The food has been awarded two AA Rosettes.

**Rooms:** 9 en suite **Facilities:** FTV DVD Lounge tea/coffee Dinner available Direct dial WiFi ⚓ **Parking:** 10 **Notes:** LB Closed 25–26 Dec

## HOLSWORTHY                                  Map 3 SS30

# Barton Gate Farm Guesthouse

★★★ BED AND BREAKFAST

**tel:** 07768 402640 & 07831 739206 **Pancrasweek EX22 7JT**
**email:** paularaefrancis@me.com **web:** www.bartongatedevon.co.uk
**dir:** *From Holsworthy take A3072 to Bude, 3.1m on right*

This relaxed and welcoming establishment is ideally located for exploring and is within easy access of the coast. Every effort is made to ensure guests enjoy a rewarding stay with plenty of local information always on offer. Hospitality is also extended to animals, with anything from a hamster to a horse more than welcome. Bedrooms are located in a converted stable block, all offering good levels of comfort, and the advantage of inter-connecting doors for families. A choice of continental or traditional English breakfast is served in the light and airy dining room. Additional facilities include a games room, lounge, nail bar and a large exercise field for dogs.

**Rooms:** 3 en suite (3 fmly) (3 GF) **Facilities:** FTV DVD Lounge TVL tea/coffee Pool table ⚓ Table tennis 4G WiFi **Parking:** 30 **Notes:** LB

## HONITON                                     Map 4 ST10

# Threshays

★★★ BED AND BREAKFAST

**tel:** 01404 43551 & 07811 675800 **Awliscombe EX14 3QB**
**email:** threshays@btinternet.com **web:** www.stayat.co.uk/threshays
**dir:** *2.5m NW of Honiton on A373*

A converted threshing barn, situated on a non-working farm, Threshays has wonderful views over open countryside. With tea and cake offered on arrival, this family-run establishment provides comfortable accommodation in a friendly atmosphere. The lounge-dining room is a light and airy setting for enjoying breakfasts. Ample parking is a bonus.

**Rooms:** 2 rms (1 fmly) **S** fr £37; **D** fr £64 **Facilities:** TVL tea/coffee WiFi **Parking:** 4

## HOPE COVE                                    Map 3 SX64

# Cottage

★★★★ 🍽 GUEST ACCOMMODATION

**tel:** 01548 561555 **TQ7 3HJ**
**email:** info@hopecove.com **web:** www.hopecove.com
**dir:** *From Kingsbridge on A381 to Salcombe. 2nd right at Marlborough, left for Inner Hope*

Glorious sunsets can be seen over the attractive bay from this popular accommodation. Friendly and attentive service from the staff and management mean many guests return here. Bedrooms, many with sea views and some with balconies, are well equipped. The restaurant offers an enjoyable dining experience.

**Rooms:** 32 rms (31 en suite) (1 pri facs) (5 fmly) (5 GF) **Facilities:** FTV DVD Lounge TVL tea/coffee Dinner available Direct dial Licensed WiFi ⛳18 ⚓ Table tennis **Conf:** Max 70 Thtr 60 Class 60 Board 30 **Parking:** 50 **Notes:** LB Closed early Jan–early Feb

## ILFRACOMBE
Map 3 SS54

### Premier Collection

## The Habit Boutique Rooms

★★★★★ ⌂ GUEST ACCOMMODATION

**tel:** 01271 863272 & 07931 551487 **46-48 Fore Street EX34 9DN**
**email:** info@thehabitboutiquerooms.com **web:** www.thehabitboutiquerooms.com
**dir:** *Into Ilfracombe on A361, continue to High St until road splits. Take slight left, 100yds on left*

The Habit Boutique Rooms occupy a fully refurbished grand old Victorian building close to Ilfracombe seafront. The rooms, many offering stunning views over the Bristol Channel, are of high quality throughout. There is also a large bar, and a lounge area with soaring ceilings extending out on to a large deck; and a fully equipped Pilates studio and beauty treatment rooms.

**Rooms:** 11 en suite (4 fmly) **D** £150–£230* **Facilities:** FTV Lounge tea/coffee Dinner available Licensed WiFi ⌂ Well-being studio **Extras:** Speciality toiletries, robes, slippers, mini-bar **Conf:** Max 28 Thtr 28 Class 16 Board 12 **Notes:** LB

## Marine Court

★★★★ ⌂ GUEST HOUSE

**tel:** 01271 862920 & 07791 051778 **Hillsborough Road EX34 9QQ**
**email:** info@marinecourthoteldevon.co.uk **web:** www.marinecourthoteldevon.co.uk
**dir:** *M5 junct 27, A361 to Barnstaple, continue to Ilfracombe*

Marine Court is a well-established guest house offering comfortable, well appointed rooms in a handy location. Guests are assured a very warm welcome from the hosts who do all they can to ensure a comfortable stay. Guests have use of a small bar lounge where drinks can be served, and off-road parking is a bonus.

**Rooms:** 8 en suite **Facilities:** FTV DVD iPod docking station Lounge tea/coffee Licensed WiFi **Extras:** Mini-bar **Parking:** 8 **Notes:** No children 16yrs Closed Nov–Mar

## The Olive Branch

★★★★ ◉◉◉ ⌂ GUEST ACCOMMODATION

**tel:** 01271 879005 & 07860 418343 **56 Fore Street EX34 9DJ**
**email:** enquiries@olivebranchguesthouse.co.uk **web:** www.olivebranchguesthouse.co.uk
**dir:** *A361 into Ilfracombe, through lights into High St. At end, fork left into Fore St, continue straight down, pass no entry signs, on left hand side*

A Georgian Grade II listed building situated in the heart of Ilfracombe with easy access to the seafront and only minutes away from all local amenities. Bedrooms are all en suite and decorated to high standards, all offering very good comfort.

The restaurant has been awarded three AA Rosettes, and the excellent breakfast is a great way to start the day.

**Rooms:** 5 en suite **S** £50; **D** £94–£110* **Facilities:** FTV DVD tea/coffee Dinner available WiFi ⌂ **Extras:** Speciality toiletries, bottled water, magazines **Notes:** LB No children 15yrs Closed Nov–Feb

## Collingdale Guest House

★★★★ ⌂ GUEST HOUSE

**tel:** 01271 863770 & 07768 522323 **13 Larkstone Terrace EX34 9NU**
**email:** thecollingdale@gmail.com **web:** www.thecollingdale.co.uk
**dir:** *Take A399 E through Ilfracombe, on left past B3230 turning*

Overlooking the harbour, this terraced Victorian guest house is within easy walking distance of the town centre and seafront. The well-presented bedrooms, many with sweeping sea views, are furnished to a high standard with many thoughtful extras. Two rooms have their own balcony. The comfortable lounge and elegant breakfast room share the magnificent views. A cosy bar is available for a tipple before bedtime. Collingdale Guest House was a finalist for the AA Friendliest B&B of the Year 2017–18.

**Rooms:** 9 rms (8 en suite) (1 pri facs) (3 fmly) **D** £80–£99 **Facilities:** FTV TVL tea/coffee Licensed WiFi ⌂18 **Extras:** Mineral water – complimentary **Notes:** LB No children 8yrs Closed Nov–Feb

## LEWDOWN
Map 3 SX48

## Lobhill Farmhouse

★★★★ BED AND BREAKFAST

**tel:** 01566 783542 & 07817 244687 **EX20 4DT**
**email:** jane.colwill@btopenworld.com **web:** www.lobhillbedandbreakfast.co.uk
**dir:** *Exit A30 at Sourton Cross, follow signs for Lewdown onto old A30. Lobhill 1m before Lewdown*

Ideally situated for easy access to moorland and the Devon and Cornwall coasts, this stone farmhouse dates back some 130 years. Peacefully located, its renovation has resulted in impressive levels of quality, yet it still retains a reassuringly traditional and homely feel. Bedrooms (including one on the ground floor with separate access) have free WiFi and views of the countryside. Tasty and satisfying breakfasts are cooked on the Aga and served either in the dining room or at the kitchen table. Guests are welcome to make use of the lovely gardens and summerhouse, or explore the woodland walks.

**Rooms:** 4 en suite (1 fmly) (1 GF) **S** £55–£65; **D** £85–£95* **Facilities:** FTV DVD iPod docking station Lounge tea/coffee WiFi Fishing ⌂ Vineyard tours **Extras:** Home-made biscuits, local fudge **Parking:** 8 **Notes:** LB

## LUSTLEIGH — Map 3 SX78

### Premier Collection

### Eastwrey Barton

★★★★★ 🍽 GUEST ACCOMMODATION

**tel:** 01647 277338 **Moretonhampstead Road TQ13 9SN**
**email:** info@eastwreybarton.co.uk **web:** www.eastwreybarton.co.uk
**dir:** *On A382 between Bovey Tracey & Moretonhampstead, 6m from A38
(Drumbridges junct))*

Warm hospitality and a genuine welcome are hallmarks at this family-run
establishment, situated inside the Dartmoor National Park. Built in the 18th
century, the house retains many original features and has views across the Wray
Valley. Bedrooms are spacious and well equipped, while public areas include a
cosy lounge warmed by a crackling log fire. Breakfast and dinner showcase local
produce with an impressive wine list to accompany the latter.

**Rooms:** 5 en suite (1 fmly) **D** £130–£140* **Facilities:** FTV Lounge tea/coffee
Dinner available Licensed WiFi 🐾 **Parking:** 18 **Notes:** No children 10yrs

## LYNMOUTH — Map 3 SS74

### Premier Collection

### The Heatherville

★★★★★ 🍽 🍴 GUEST ACCOMMODATION

**tel:** 01598 752327 & 753893 **Tors Park EX35 6NB**
**email:** theheatherville@aol.com **web:** www.heatherville.co.uk
**dir:** *Exit A39 into Tors Rd, 1st left fork into Tors Park*

This wonderful Victorian establishment stands high above Lynmouth, and the
views across the wooded valley are quite superb. There is an abundance of
charm and quality here at The Heatherville, and bedrooms are individually styled
with comfort and character. Public rooms are also inviting with an elegant
lounge and snug bar, while the dining room is the attractive venue for skilfully
prepared dinners and substantial breakfasts.

**Rooms:** 6 en suite **D** £95–£135* **Facilities:** FTV DVD Lounge tea/coffee
Dinner available Licensed WiFi 🐾 **Parking:** 6 **Notes:** LB No children 16yrs
Closed Nov–Mar

### Rising Sun

★★★★ 🏅🏅 🍴 INN

**tel:** 01598 753223 **Harbourside EX35 6EG**
**email:** reception@risingsunlynmouth.co.uk **web:** www.risingsunlynmouth.co.uk
**dir:** *M5 junct 23, A39 to Minehead. On harbourside*

The Rising Sun is a delightful thatched establishment, once a smugglers' inn, that
sits on the harbour front. Popular with locals and guests alike, there is the option of
eating in either the convivial bar or the restaurant; a comfortable, quiet lounge is
also available. Bedrooms, located in the inn and adjoining cottages, are
individually designed and have modern facilities.

**Rooms:** 10 en suite 4 annexe en suite (1 fmly) (1 GF) **D** £125–£200* **Facilities:** FTV
Lounge tea/coffee Dinner available Direct dial **Notes:** Closed 25 Dec

## LYNTON — Map 3 SS74

### Premier Collection

### Highcliffe House

★★★★★ 🅰 BED AND BREAKFAST

**tel:** 01598 752235 & 07889 574005 **Sinai Hill EX35 6AR**
**email:** info@highcliffehouse.co.uk **web:** www.highcliffehouse.co.uk
**dir:** *From B3234 follow signs to Lynton (Station Hill). Turn right into Sinai Hill*

Highcliffe House prides itself in offering superb luxury accommodation. This
Exmoor bed and breakfast promises boutique-style rooms and panoramic views
of the north Devon coastline while you eat your breakfast.

**Rooms:** 6 en suite **D** £100–£150* **Facilities:** FTV iPod docking station Lounge
Licensed WiFi **Extras:** Slippers, robes **Parking:** 10 **Notes:** LB No children 18yrs
Closed 31 Nov–10 Feb

### Gable Lodge Guest House

★★★★ 🍽 🍴 GUEST ACCOMMODATION

**tel:** 01598 752367 & 07811 031270 **35 Lee Road EX35 6BS**
**email:** gablelodge@btconnect.com **web:** www.gablelodgelynton.co.uk
**dir:** *M5 junct 23 onto A39 to Lynmouth. Right up hill to Lynton, right at top of hill signed
Lynton. Continue through town, Gable Lodge on right*

Gable Lodge is a Grade II listed, family-run Victorian establishment just a short
stroll from the centre of this small town. The welcome is warm and genuine with
plenty of local information, help and advice always available to help ensure a
memorable stay. Bedrooms all provide good levels of comfort and quality with lovely
views an added bonus. Generous breakfasts are served in the dining room, and
evening meals also available on request. Additional facilities include a guest
lounge and parking.

**Rooms:** 6 en suite (2 fmly) **S** £42–£46; **D** £64–£72* **Facilities:** FTV DVD iPod docking
station TVL tea/coffee Dinner available Licensed WiFi 🐾 **Extras:** Mini-fridge, fresh
milk **Parking:** 5 **Notes:** LB Closed Xmas

## Rockvale

★★★★  GUEST ACCOMMODATION

**tel:** 01598 752279 **Hollerday Drive, Lee Road EX35 6HQ**
**email:** enquiries@rockvalelynton.com **web:** www.rockvalelynton.com
**dir:** *From A39 follow signs to Lynton, then town hall. In Lee Rd, turn opposite Costcutter supermarket into Hollerday Drive*

Rockvale was once the residence of a Victorian merchant, and now offers all the comforts of home, with accommodation to suit families, couples and single travellers. Rockvale has a warm, friendly atmosphere, great views, and good food, with a licensed bar. Guests have use of a lounge with log fire, and evening meals are served at 7pm, though an earlier sitting may sometimes be arranged if necessary. This is an ideal base for exploring, close to the North Devon coast and with easy access to the stunning countryside of the Exmoor National Park.

**Rooms:** 7 rms (6 en suite) (1 pri facs) (3 fmly) **S** £35–£45; **D** £65–£95*
**Facilities:** STV Lounge TVL tea/coffee Dinner available Licensed WiFi ☕ **Parking:** 7
**Notes:** Closed 31 Oct–13 Mar

## The Fernery

★★★ 🍴 BED AND BREAKFAST

**tel:** 01598 753265 & 07970 857459 **Lydiate Lane EX35 6AJ**
**email:** info@thefernerylynton.com **web:** www.thefernerylynton.com
**dir:** *B3234 to Lynton into Castle Hill. Then Lee Rd, turn left into Cross St. Left into Lydiate Ln, 300mtrs on right*

Nestled in a quiet street within a few minutes' walk of the town centre, The Fernery provides a comfortable, convenient base for exploring the North Devon coast and Exmoor. Rooms are bright and have very comfortable beds, and breakfast features local quality produce. There is on-street parking nearby and two public car parks not far away.

**Rooms:** 3 en suite **Facilities:** FTV DVD Lounge tea/coffee WiFi ☕

---

**MEDDON**                                        Map 2 SS21

## The West Country Inn

★★★ INN

**tel:** 01237 441724 & 07977 496535 **Bursdon Moor EX39 6HB**
**email:** thewestcinn@aol.com **web:** www.westcountryinn.co.uk
**dir:** *On A39 S of Clovelly*

Originally a coaching inn, dating back to the 16th century, this traditional and welcoming establishment is ideally placed for exploring this picturesque area. The bedrooms provide good levels of comfort and have all that's needed to ensure a relaxing stay. The well-stocked bar has a range of local ales and provides a convivial focal point with plenty of good-natured banter always on offer. A range of good, honest dishes are served either in the bar or adjacent dining room. Additional facilities include a spa and gym.

**Rooms:** 9 en suite (1 fmly) **S** £59; **D** £85–£120* **Facilities:** FTV Lounge TVL tea/coffee Dinner available WiFi Gym Pool table ☕ Hot tub **Conf:** Max 100 Thtr 100 Class 70 Board 70 **Parking:** 100

---

**NEWTON ABBOT**                                  Map 3 SX87

### Premier Collection

## Bulleigh Barton Manor

★★★★★ 🍴 BED AND BREAKFAST

**tel:** 01803 873411 & 07973 422678 **Ipplepen TQ12 5UA**
**email:** liz@escapetosouthdevon.co.uk **web:** www.escapetosouthdevon.co.uk
**dir:** *From A381 follow signs to Bulleigh and Compton Castle. Bear left along narrow lane, after 1.5m Bickley Mill signed on left, drive directly opposite turning*

Warm hospitality and a genuine welcome are both hallmarks at this family-run establishment. This wonderful house dates back to the 1400s and is steeped in history. Today it offers en suite bedrooms providing comfortable accommodation in a peaceful countryside location. Breakfast is a hearty affair featuring locally sourced produce. Bulleigh Barton Manor was a finalist for the AA Friendliest B&B of the Year 2017–18.

**Rooms:** 3 en suite **S** £72–£105; **D** £81–£125* **Facilities:** FTV DVD Lounge tea/coffee WiFi ⚡ ☕ **Extras:** Home-made fudge & cakes, fresh milk – complimentary **Parking:** 4 **Notes:** LB No children 16yrs

## Bulleigh Park Farm

★★★★ 🍴 FARMHOUSE

**tel:** 01803 872254 **Ipplepen TQ12 5UA**
**email:** southdevonaccommodation@gmail.com
**web:** www.southdevonaccommodation.co.uk
**dir:** *3.5m S of Newton Abbot. Exit A381 at Parkhill Cross, by petrol station, for Compton, 1m, signed*

Bulleigh Park is a working farm; stock includes a rare breed of sheep, the Devon Closewool. Expect a warm friendly welcome at this family home set in glorious tranquil countryside, but centrally located for the coast and Dartmoor. The breakfasts are notable for their wealth of fresh, local and home-made produce, and the porridge is cooked using a secret recipe. Home-made tea and cakes greet guests on arrival. The local inn is just a short stroll away.

**Rooms:** 2 en suite (1 fmly) **S** £50–£55; **D** £80–£90 **Facilities:** FTV iPod docking station Lounge TVL tea/coffee WiFi ☕ **Extras:** Mini-fridge **Parking:** 6 **Notes:** LB No children 5yrs Closed Nov–1 Mar 60 acres beef/sheep/hens

## OKEHAMPTON — Map 3 SX59

*See also Holsworthy*

### Meadowlea Guest House

★★★★ GUEST HOUSE

**tel:** 01837 53200 **65 Station Road EX20 1EA**
**email:** meadowlea65@btinternet.com **web:** www.meadowleaguesthouse.co.uk
**dir:** *From A30 onto B3260, after 2m left at lights, then 3rd right into Station Rd. 200yds on left*

A well-presented period house, Meadowlea has been modernised over the years but still retains its Victorian essence. A range of comfortably appointed rooms for all budgets, some with shared facilities, is offered. There is a well appointed sitting room in which to relax and local produce is used on the breakfast menu. Should you wish to eat in, after a long day exploring the local area, guests are welcome to use the breakfast room, which is suitably equipped. Secure storage for bicycles is available.

**Rooms:** 7 rms (4 en suite) (1 fmly) **S** £38–£55; **D** £65–£80* **Facilities:** FTV Lounge tea/coffee WiFi ❄ Drying room for boots & coats, Cycle storage **Extras:** Bottled water – complimentary **Parking:** 2

## OTTERY ST MARY — Map 3 SY19

### Fluxton Farm

★★ BED AND BREAKFAST

**tel:** 01404 812818 **Fluxton EX11 1RJ**
**email:** ann@fluxtonfarm.co.uk **web:** www.fluxtonfarm.co.uk
**dir:** *2m SW of Ottery St Mary. B3174, W from Ottery over river, left, next left to Fluxton*

A haven for cat lovers, Fluxton Farm offers comfortable accommodation with a choice of lounges and a large garden, complete with pond and ducks. Set in peaceful farmland four miles from the coast, this 16th-century longhouse has a wealth of beams and open fireplaces.

**Rooms:** 7 en suite **S** £27.50–£35; **D** £55–£70* **Facilities:** FTV Lounge tea/coffee WiFi ❄ **Parking:** 15 **Notes:** LB No children 8yrs RS Nov–Apr pre-booked & wknds only

## PAIGNTON — Map 3 SX86

### Premier Collection

### The P&M Paignton RESIDENCE

★★★★★ BED AND BREAKFAST

**tel:** 01803 523118 & 07803 290568 **2 Kernou Road TQ4 6BA**
**email:** mail@paignton-residence.com **web:** www.paignton-residence.com
**dir:** *Follow signs to seafront, into Kernou Rd, close to cinema*

A warm welcome is guaranteed in this smart B&B, very conveniently located within walking distance of Paignton seafront. All eight bedrooms are comfortably furnished, serviced to a high standard, and come equipped with a range of accessories. Breakfast is served in the light and airy dining room. Free WiFi is available throughout.

**Rooms:** 8 en suite (1 GF) **D** £90–£135 **Facilities:** FTV DVD iPod docking station tea/coffee WiFi ❄ Sauna in 1 room **Extras:** Bottled water **Conf:** Max 10 Thtr 10 Class 10 Board 10 **Parking:** 2 **Notes:** No children 16yrs

### Devon House Guest House

★★★★ GUEST HOUSE

**tel:** 01803 528080 & 07777 642340 **20 Garfield Road TQ4 6AX**
**email:** dhgh@btconnect.com **web:** www.devonhouseguesthouse.co.uk
**dir:** *In Paignton follow signs to seafront & Esplanade Rd. Into Torbay Rd, then Garfield Rd*

Devon House has been lovingly restored and is conveniently located to explore Paignton and its surrounding areas. All rooms offer comfortable beds and a range of facilities to meet the needs of a varied clientele, including families. A freshly cooked breakfast is served in the attractive dining room on the ground floor.

**Rooms:** 8 en suite (2 fmly) **D** £72–£87* **Facilities:** FTV tea/coffee WiFi

# Two Beaches

★★★★ ☙ GUEST ACCOMMODATION

tel: 01803 522164 & 07787 517421 **27 St Andrews Road TQ4 6HA**
email: stay@twobeaches.co.uk **web:** www.twobeaches.co.uk
**dir:** *A380 onto A3022 signed Paignton seafront, Apollo complex on left. At end of road, turn right at rdbt, St Andrews Rd 2nd on left. Two Beaches 400yds on left*

Quietly located in a residential area, this is an ideal base from which to explore the many delights of Paignton, Brixham and Torquay. A warm welcome is assured and there is always help on hand for suggestions for local days out. Bedrooms provide impressive levels of comfort with all the essentials required for a relaxing stay. Breakfast is a real treat with quality produce ensuring a tasty and satisfying start to the day. Additional facilities include a guest lounge, honesty bar and lovely garden. Private parking is available for all guests.

**Rooms:** 7 en suite (2 GF) **S** £45; **D** £78–£88 **Facilities:** FTV Lounge TVL tea/coffee Licensed WiFi **Parking:** 7 **Notes:** No children 8yrs Closed Dec–Mar

# Beaches

★★★★ BED AND BREAKFAST

tel: 01803 665448 & 07854 940747 **9 Manor Road TQ3 2HT**
email: mikemitchell21@hotmail.com **web:** www.beachesbandb.co.uk
**dir:** *From A38 follow signs to Torquay, then Paignton, then Preston. Take one way system at sea front, right into Manor Rd*

Situated just a few hundred metres from Paignton seafront, this bed and breakfast offers bright, spacious, well-equipped rooms with comfortable beds. Breakfast is served in the light, airy breakfast rooms and guests have use of complimentary WiFi, a well-appointed guest lounge, and free off-road parking.

**Rooms:** 6 en suite (2 fmly) **Facilities:** FTV TVL tea/coffee WiFi ☖ **Extras:** Speciality toiletries **Parking:** 4 **Notes:** LB RS Oct–Jan weekends only

# Lazy Days

★★★★ ☙ GUEST ACCOMMODATION

tel: 01803 520854 & 07787 438172 **10 Queens Road TQ4 6AT**
email: irenewolf777@gmail.com **web:** www.lazydaysguesthousepaignton.co.uk

Handily placed for access to the seafront and the town, this recently refurbished establishment is an ideal base from which to explore the area or venture further afield to enjoy the delights of South Devon. A warm welcome is assured and help is always on offer regarding planning day trips or the best places to eat locally. Bedrooms all provide impressive quality and comfort, with snuggly beds ensuring

a peaceful night's sleep. Bathrooms are modern and well appointed. Additional facilities include a lounge and a galley area where guests can make drinks and prepare light snacks if required. Breakfast is a treat, with a range of tasty options available.

**Rooms:** 6 rms (5 en suite) (1 pri facs) **S** £50; **D** £60–£85* **Facilities:** FTV TVL tea/coffee WiFi **Extras:** Bottled water, sweets, fresh milk **Parking:** 2 **Notes:** No children 14yrs Closed Dec & Jan

# The Clydesdale

★★★★ GUEST HOUSE

tel: 01803 558402 & 07939 147013 **5 Polsham Park TQ3 2AD**
email: theclydesdale@hotmail.co.uk **web:** www.theclydesdale.co.uk
**dir:** *Exit A3022 (Torquay Rd) into Lower Polsham Rd, 2nd right into Polsham Park*

Tucked away in a quiet residential area, this is an ideal location from which to explore the varied attractions of Paignton and the wider Torbay area. The welcome is warm and genuine, with every effort made to ensure a relaxed and rewarding stay. The bedrooms are well appointed and provide all the expected modern comforts. Breakfast is served in the dining room; a separate guest lounge is also available.

**Rooms:** 7 en suite (1 fmly) (2 GF) **S** £27–£40; **D** £54–£80* **Facilities:** FTV TVL tea/coffee WiFi ☖ **Parking:** 5 **Notes:** LB No children 3yrs Closed Xmas & New Year RS Nov–Feb open by prior arrangement

# Merritt House Bed & Breakfast

★★★★ ☙ GUEST ACCOMMODATION

tel: 01803 528959 **7 Queens Road TQ4 6AT**
email: bookings@merritthouse.co.uk **web:** www.merritthouse.co.uk
**dir:** *From Paignton seafront, right into Torbay Rd, 1st left into Queens Rd, house on right*

Handily located for the town centre and the lovely beach, this is an ideal choice from which to explore this popular holiday area. A warm welcome is assured along with a slice of cake, the perfect way to start a relaxing break. Bedrooms provide good levels of comfort with ground floor rooms available. Breakfast is a treat, with a range of tantalising options on offer. Off-road parking available.

**Rooms:** 7 en suite (3 GF) **S** £37–£49; **D** £60–£74* **Facilities:** FTV DVD tea/coffee WiFi ☖ **Parking:** 4 **Notes:** LB No children 12yrs

# Merriedale Guest House

★★★ GUEST HOUSE

tel: 01803 553013 & 07443 541162 **21 Garfield Road TQ4 6AX**
email: merriedale@gmx.co.uk **web:** www.merriedale.com
**dir:** *A380 to Torquay, 2nd exit at rdbt (Kerswell Gdns). 1st exit at next rdbt Churscombe Cross into Marldon Rd (B3060). Right into Torquay Rd (A3022), bear left into Hyde Rd, left into Torbay Rd & left into Garfield Rd*

Overlooking Victoria Park, this friendly and welcoming establishment is perfectly situated to explore the local area, as it's just a short walk from the town centre and the wonderful sandy beach. Every effort is made to help guests enjoy a relaxing stay, with local information and advice readily offered. Bedrooms and bathrooms all offer good levels of quality and all the expected comforts. Breakfast is a satisfying start to the day and is served in the well-appointed dining room.

**Rooms:** 6 rms (5 en suite) (1 pri facs) **S** £30–£34; **D** £56–£64* **Facilities:** FTV tea/coffee WiFi **Extras:** Bottled water – complimentary **Parking:** 6 **Notes:** LB No children 14yrs

PAIGNTON *continued*

## The Park

★★★ GUEST ACCOMMODATION

tel: 01803 557856 **Esplanade Road TQ4 6BQ**
email: stay@theparkhotel.net **web:** www.theparkhotel.net
dir: *On Paignton seafront, nearly opposite pier*

This large establishment has a prominent position on the seafront with excellent views of Torbay. The pleasant bedrooms are spacious, and available in a number of options; several have sea views. Entertainment is provided in the lounge on some evenings. Dinner and breakfast are served in the spacious dining room, which overlooks the attractive front garden.

**Rooms:** 47 en suite (5 fmly) (3 GF) **Facilities:** tea/coffee Dinner available Lift Licensed WiFi 🐾 Games room with 3/4 snooker table & table tennis **Conf:** Max 120 Thtr 80 Class 120 Board 40 **Parking:** 38 **Notes:** LB

| PLYMOUTH | Map 3 SX45 |

## Jewell's

★★★★ GUEST ACCOMMODATION

tel: 01752 254760 **220 Citadel Road, The Hoe PL1 3BB**
email: jewellsguest@btconnect.com **web:** www.jewellsguesthouse.com
dir: *A38 towards city ccntre, follow sign for The Barbican, then The Hoe. Left at lights, right at top of road into Citadel Rd. Jewell's 0.25m*

This smart, comfortable, family-run establishment is only a short walk from The Hoe and is convenient for the city centre, the Citadel and the Barbican. Bedrooms come with a wide range of extra facilities, and breakfast is served in the pleasant dining room. Some secure parking is available.

**Rooms:** 10 rms (7 en suite) (1 fmly) (1 GF) **S** £40–£60; **D** £70–£80* **Facilities:** FTV tea/coffee WiFi **Notes:** LB

## Rainbow Lodge Guest House

★★★★ GUEST HOUSE

tel: 01752 229699 & 07584 472723 **29 Athenaeum Street, The Hoe PL1 2RQ**
email: stay@rainbowlodgeplymouth.co.uk **web:** www.rainbowlodgeplymouth.co.uk
dir: *A38 onto A374. Follow City Centre signs for 3m, into Exeter St. Bear left into Breton Side at lights, follow road, left into Athenaeum St at Walrus pub*

Located in a peaceful area of Plymouth, Rainbow Lodge Guest House is within easy walking distance of the town centre, the Barbican and harbour. Service is the highlight of the stay, ensuring that all needs and wants are catered for. The 10 guest bedrooms are all en suite and provide a comfortable night's sleep. Free WiFi is available and a full English breakfast is offered daily in the delightful breakfast room.

**Rooms:** 10 rms (6 en suite) (1 pri facs) (2 fmly) (1 GF) **S** fr £46; **D** fr £54*
**Facilities:** FTV tea/coffee WiFi **Notes:** No children 5yrs Closed 21 Dec–1 Jan

## The Firs Guest Accommodation

★★★ GUEST ACCOMMODATION

tel: 01752 262870 & 300010 **13 Pier Street, West Hoe PL1 3BS**
email: thefirsguesthouseinplymouthdevon@hotmail.com
web: www.thefirsinplymouth.co.uk
dir: *A374 into city centre, follow signs to The Hoe. Continue on Hoe Rd, with sea on left, 1st right at mini rdbt into Pier St*

A well located and well established house on the West Hoe with convenient on-street parking. Friendly owners and comfortable rooms make it a popular destination. Dogs are permitted in bedrooms by prior arrangement.

**Rooms:** 7 rms (3 en suite) (2 fmly) **S** £35–£45; **D** £55–£95* **Facilities:** FTV tea/coffee Dinner available WiFi 🐾 Fishing trips can be arranged **Notes:** LB

## The Lamplighter

★★★ GUEST ACCOMMODATION

tel: 01752 663855 **103 Citadel Road, The Hoe PL1 2RN**
email: stay@lamplighterplymouth.co.uk **web:** www.lamplighterplymouth.co.uk
dir: *Near war memorial*

With easy access to The Hoe, The Barbican and the city centre, this comfortable house provides a good base for leisure or business. Bedrooms, including family rooms, are light and airy and furnished to a consistent standard. Breakfast is served in the dining room, which has an adjoining lounge area.

**Rooms:** 9 rms (7 en suite) (2 pri facs) (2 fmly) **S** £40; **D** £60* **Facilities:** FTV TVL tea/coffee WiFi 🐾 **Parking:** 4

| SEATON | Map 4 SY29 |

## Mariners

★★★★ 🏵 GUEST ACCOMMODATION

tel: 01297 20560 **East Walk Esplanade EX12 2NP**
email: mariners.hotel@btconnect.com **web:** www.marinershotelseaton.co.uk
dir: *Off A3052 signed Seaton, Mariners on seafront*

Located just yards from the beach and cliff paths, this comfortable establishment has a friendly and relaxed atmosphere. Bedrooms, some with sea views, are well equipped, and public rooms are light and airy. The dining room is the venue for enjoyable breakfasts that utilise quality local produce; afternoon teas are also available on the seafront terrace.

**Rooms:** 5 en suite **Facilities:** FTV tea/coffee WiFi 🐾 **Parking:** 5 **Notes:** LB No children 5yrs Closed Nov–Feb

## Beaumont Guest House

★★★★ GUEST HOUSE

**tel:** 01297 20832 & 07775 713667 **Castle Hill EX12 2QW**
**email:** beaumont.seaton@btconnect.com **web:** www.beaumont-seaton.co.uk
**dir:** *In Seaton, from Harbour Rd head W to Marine Place on seafront. Beaumont Guest House at beginning of Castle Hill*

Dating back to the days of Victorian splendour, this elegant establishment is just a few steps away from the wonderful beach at Seaton. A warm and genuine welcome awaits, with plenty of helpful local advice always on offer. Bedrooms have great sea views and provide all the expected modern comforts, with a ground floor room also available. Breakfast provides a tasty start to the day, served in the attractive dining room.

**Rooms:** 5 en suite (1 fmly) (1 GF) **S** £60–£65; **D** £75–£95* **Facilities:** FTV tea/coffee WiFi **Parking:** 6 **Notes:** LB Closed Xmas & New Year

### SHALDON
*See Teignmouth*

### SIDMOUTH                                             Map 3 SY18
*See also Ottery St Mary*

## The Salty Monk

★★★★★ ◉◉ ♨ RESTAURANT WITH ROOMS

**tel:** 01395 513174 **Church Street, Sidford EX10 9QP**
**email:** saltymonk@btconnect.com **web:** www.saltymonk.co.uk
**dir:** *On A3052 opposite church in Sidford*

Set in the village of Sidford, this attractive property dates from the 16th century. There's plenty of style and appeal here and each bedroom has a unique identity. Bathrooms are equally special with multi-jet showers, spa baths and cosseting robes and towels. The output from the kitchen is impressive with excellent local produce very much in evidence, served in the elegant surroundings of the restaurant. A mini-spa facility is available.

**Rooms:** 5 en suite 1 annexe en suite (3 GF) **S** £85–£120; **D** £105–£190* **Facilities:** FTV Lounge tea/coffee Dinner available WiFi ♨18 Gym ♨ Outdoor hot tub Massage therapists Mini-spa **Extras:** Speciality toiletries, bottled water, snacks – complimentary **Parking:** 20 **Notes:** LB Closed 1 week Nov & Jan

## The Groveside

★★★★ GUEST HOUSE

**tel:** 01395 513406 **Vicarage Road EX10 8UQ**
**email:** info@thegroveside.co.uk **web:** www.thegroveside.co.uk
**dir:** *0.5m N of seafront on A375*

Conveniently situated a short, level walking distance from the town centre, The Groveside offers boutique-style accommodation. A number of influences, such as art deco, have been used to impressive effect in the bedrooms, while bathrooms also show individuality and flair. Guests are assured of attentive service and a relaxed and friendly atmosphere. On-site parking is a bonus.

**Rooms:** 9 en suite **Facilities:** FTV Lounge tea/coffee WiFi **Conf:** Max 14 Class 14 Board 14 **Parking:** 9 **Notes:** LB No children 12yrs

## Mincombe Barn Bed & Breakfast

★★★★ ♨ BED AND BREAKFAST

**tel:** 01395 597858 & 07753 747941 **Roncombe Lane, Sidbury EX10 0QN**
**email:** mincombebarn@outlook.com **web:** www.mincombebarn.com
**dir:** *N of Sidmouth on A375, through Sidbury, right to Roncombe (1.5m)*

Set in 20 acres of peaceful pasture and woodland, Mincombe Barn is midway between Honiton and Sidmouth, within the East Devon Area of Outstanding Natural Beauty, a UNESCO World Heritage Site, with the Blackdown Hills just to the north. Each room is individually designed to be elegant, comfortable and practical. All rooms can be made as either a twin or double. Breakfast is served daily with ingredients sourced locally along with fresh eggs daily on site.

**Rooms:** 3 en suite (3 GF) **Facilities:** FTV Lounge tea/coffee WiFi ♨18 ♨ **Extras:** Home-made biscuits, fridge, robes, slippers **Parking:** 8 **Notes:** LB

## The Old Farmhouse

★★★★ GUEST ACCOMMODATION

**tel:** 01395 512284 **Hillside Road EX10 8JG**
**web:** www.theoldfarmhousesidmouth.co.uk
**dir:** *A3052 from Exeter to Sidmouth, right at Bowd x-rds, 2m left at rdbt, left at mini rdbt, next right, over hump-back bridge, bear right on the corner*

This beautiful 16th-century thatched farmhouse, in a quiet residential area just a stroll from the Esplanade and shops, has been lovingly restored. Bedrooms are attractively decorated, and the charming public rooms feature beams and an inglenook fireplace. The welcoming proprietors provide memorable dinners, (by prior arrangement) using traditional recipes and fresh local ingredients.

**Rooms:** 3 en suite 3 annexe en suite (1 fmly) (1 GF) **D** £72–£80* **Facilities:** FTV Lounge TVL tea/coffee Dinner available WiFi ♨18 **Extras:** Speciality toiletries **Parking:** 4 **Notes:** LB No children 12yrs Closed Nov–Feb

## Glendevon

★★★★ GUEST ACCOMMODATION

**tel:** 01395 514028 & 07960 052475 **Cotmaton Road EX10 8QX**
**email:** enquiries@glendevonsidmouth.co.uk **web:** www.glendevonsidmouth.co.uk
**dir:** *A3052 onto B3176 to mini rdbt. Right, house 100yds on right*

Located in a quiet residential area just a short walk from the town centre and beaches, this stylish Victorian house offers neat, comfortable bedrooms. Guests are assured of a warm welcome from the resident owners.

**Rooms:** 8 en suite **S** £42–£47; **D** £84–£92* **Facilities:** FTV DVD TVL tea/coffee WiFi ♨18 ♨ **Notes:** No children 10yrs

## SOURTON
Map 3 SX59

# Bearslake Inn

★★★★ ⌨ INN

**tel:** 01837 861334 **Lake EX20 4HQ**
**email:** enquiries@bearslakeinn.com **web:** www.bearslakeinn.com
**dir:** A30 from Exeter onto A386 signed Sourton & Tavistock, 2m on left from junct

Situated on the edge of the Dartmoor National Park, this thatched inn is believed to date back to the 13th century and was originally part of a working farm. There is character in abundance here with beams, flagstone floors and low ceilings, all of which contribute to an engaging atmosphere. Bedrooms have great individuality and provide period features combined with contemporary comforts. Local produce is very much in evidence on the menu, with dinner served in the attractive Stable Restaurant. The beer garden is bordered by a moorland stream with wonderful views across open countryside.

**Rooms:** 6 en suite (3 fmly) (1 GF) **S** £95–£110; **D** £130–£145* **Facilities:** FTV DVD tea/coffee Dinner available Direct dial WiFi ⓐ **Parking:** 35 **Notes:** LB

# Collaven Manor

★★★★ ⌕ ⌨ GUEST ACCOMMODATION

**tel:** 01837 861522 **EX20 4HH**
**email:** collavenmanor@gmail.com **web:** www.collavenmanor.co.uk
**dir:** A30 onto A386 to Tavistock, 2m on right

This delightful 15th-century manor house is quietly located in five acres of well-tended grounds. The friendly proprietors provide attentive service and ensure a relaxing environment. Charming public rooms have old oak beams and granite fireplaces, provide a range of comfortable lounges, and include a well stocked bar. In the restaurant, a daily-changing menu offers interesting dishes.

**Rooms:** 8 en suite (1 fmly) **S** £80–£95; **D** £98–£148* **Facilities:** FTV Lounge Dinner available Direct dial Licensed WiFi ⚑ Bowls **Conf:** Max 14 Thtr 14 Class 14 Board 14 **Parking:** 50 **Notes:** LB Closed Dec–Jan

## SOUTH BRENT
Map 3 SX66

# Woodland Barton Farm

★★★ FARMHOUSE

**tel:** 01364 73460 & 07837 928588 **Avonwick TQ10 9EZ**
**email:** christine@woodlandbartonfarm.co.uk **web:** www.woodlandbartonfarm.co.uk
**dir:** Exit A38 at Marleyhead junct, follow signs for South Brent, then signs for Avonwick. At Avon Inn turn right, 0.5m on right

Situated on the outskirts of Avonwick, this family farmhouse is the perfect choice for those wanting a base from which to explore the many attractions of South Devon. The welcome is warm and genuine with every effort made to ensure a relaxing and rewarding stay. Bedrooms offer good levels of comfort with a family room available, both rooms offering views over the farm and surrounding countryside. Breakfast is served in the dining room with eggs fresh from the resident hens, a great way to start the day.

**Rooms:** 2 en suite (1 fmly) **S** £40–£50; **D** £60–£70* **Facilities:** FTV DVD TVL tea/coffee WiFi **Parking:** 3 **Notes:** LB 400 acres beef/sheep

## SOUTH MOLTON
Map 3 SS72

# Sampson Barton Guest House

★★★★ ⌨ GUEST HOUSE

**tel:** 01769 572466 **Kings Nympton EX37 9TG**
**email:** mail@sampsonbarton.co.uk **web:** www.sampsonbarton.co.uk
**dir:** From South Molton follow signs for George Nympton & Kings Nympton. Through George Nympton, down hill, over bridge, 1st right into lane signed Sampson & Sletchcott. Up hill, 0.75m on left

Dating back some 400 years, this charming former farmhouse is the perfect place to relax. A reviving cup of tea on arrival in front of the warming wood-burner sets the scene, with helpful local information always on hand. Bedrooms offer good levels of comfort, likewise the contemporary bathrooms. Dinner is a treat, with wonderful local produce on offer. Breakfast is also impressive, and eggs are supplied by the resident hens. A stroll around the wonderful gardens is a must; find a peaceful vantage point and gaze over the rolling Devon countryside.

**Rooms:** 5 en suite (1 fmly) **S** £60–£65; **D** £84–£90* **Facilities:** FTV TVL tea/coffee Dinner available Licensed WiFi ⓐ **Extras:** Speciality toiletries – complimentary **Parking:** 6 **Notes:** LB

# The Coaching Inn

★★★ INN

**tel:** 01769 572526 **Queen Street EX36 3BJ**
**email:** jayne.coach@googlemail.com **web:** www.thecoaching-inn.co.uk
**dir:** In town centre

This long-established former coaching inn has been providing a warm welcome to weary travellers for many years. Situated in the heart of this bustling town, guests are assured of a relaxing stay in a genuine, family-friendly atmosphere. Bedrooms provide good levels of comfort. An extensive menu is provided with an emphasis on quality and value for money.

**Rooms:** 10 en suite (2 fmly) **S** £35–£45; **D** £70* **Facilities:** FTV tea/coffee Dinner available WiFi Pool table ⓐ **Conf:** Max 100 Thtr 80 Class 50 Board 60 **Parking:** 40

## SOUTH POOL
Map 3 SX74

# The Millbrook Loft

Ⓤ

**tel:** 01548 531581 & 07967 046770 **The Millbrook Inn TQ7 2RW**
**email:** info@millbrookinnsouthpool.co.uk **web:** www.millbrookinnsouthpool.co.uk

Currently the rating for this establishment is not confirmed. This may be due to a change of ownership or because it has only recently joined the AA rating scheme.

**Rooms:** 1 en suite **D** £120–£150* **Facilities:** FTV TVL tea/coffee Dinner available Licensed WiFi **Notes:** LB No children over 2yrs

## SOUTH ZEAL
Map 3 SX69

# The Oxenham Arms and Restaurant

★★★★ ⌨ INN

**tel:** 01837 840244 **EX20 2JT**
**email:** lyn@theoxenhamarms.com **web:** www.theoxenhamarms.com
**dir:** From A30, follow signs for A382 Moreton Hampstead/Winkleigh/Torrington. Over mini rdbt towards South Zeal, after 2m, right into village, opposite village shop & post office

Dating back to the 12th century, there is a tangible sense of the past at this fascinating inn. Still very much the village local, it was first licensed in 1477, and boasts a standing stone dating back some 5000 years. Extensive refurbishment has blended contemporary styling with the historic features. Bedrooms have plenty of character and no two are alike, with a number of four-posters available. The stylish restaurant offers accomplished cuisine with a range of dishes, all making good use of quality, local produce. In summer, meals can be taken in the extensive garden with stunning views of Dartmoor.

**Rooms:** 7 en suite (4 fmly) **S** £95–£128; **D** £95–£143* **Facilities:** FTV DVD Lounge TVL tea/coffee Dinner available WiFi ⌣ ⚓18 Fishing ⚓ Free loan of bicycles **Extras:** Bottled water, chocolate **Conf:** Max 50 Thtr 30 Class 25 Board 40 **Parking:** 7 **Notes:** LB

### STRETE
*See Dartmouth*

### TAVISTOCK
Map 3 SX47

#### Premier Collection

## Tor Cottage
★★★★★ ⌣ GUEST ACCOMMODATION

**tel:** 01822 860248 **PL16 0JE**
**email:** info@torcottage.co.uk **web:** www.torcottage.co.uk

*(For full entry see Chillaton)*

### TEDBURN ST MARY
Map 3 SX89

#### Premier Collection

## Frogmill Bed & Breakfast
★★★★★ ⌣ BED AND BREAKFAST

**tel:** 01647 272727 & 24088 **EX6 6ES**
**email:** frogmillbandb@btinternet.com **web:** www.frogmillbandb.co.uk
**dir:** From A30 take exit signed Cheriton Bishop. Take Tedburn road, then left towards Crediton. After 1m left to Froggy Mill, 1m on left

Situated in the heart of Devon, this former mill house is as picturesque as can be, complete with thatch and a babbling brook. The grounds are spectacular, with around 10 acres of woodland and pasture. The welcome is just as impressive; a cream tea in the garden is offered on arrival. The comfortable bedrooms offer quality and individuality and include a separate, self-contained suite away from the main building; the bathrooms have soft towels and invigorating showers. Food is a real treat here – the eggs for breakfast provided by the resident hens. In addition to the elegant dining room, a lounge, with deep leather sofas and a wood-burner, is provided.

**Rooms:** 2 en suite 1 annexe en suite (1 fmly) (1 GF) **S** £65–£70; **D** £85–£95* **Facilities:** FTV iPod docking station Lounge tea/coffee WiFi ⚓ **Extras:** Fruit, chocolates – complimentary; robes **Parking:** 6 **Notes:** LB

### TEIGNMOUTH
Map 3 SX97

## Potters Mooring
★★★★ GUEST ACCOMMODATION

**tel:** 01626 873225 **30 The Green, Shaldon TQ14 0DN**
**email:** info@pottersmooring.co.uk **web:** www.pottersmooring.co.uk
**dir:** A38 onto A380 signed Torquay, B3192 to Teignmouth & Shaldon, over river, follow signs to Potters Mooring

A former sea captain's residence dating from 1625, Potters Mooring has been appointed to provide charming accommodation of a very high standard, including a four-poster room. The friendly proprietors make every effort to ensure an enjoyable stay, and the Captain Potter's breakfast features tasty local produce.

**Rooms:** 9 en suite

### TIVERTON
Map 3 SS91

#### Premier Collection

## Fernside Bed and Breakfast
★★★★★ ⌣ BED AND BREAKFAST

**tel:** 01884 860025 & 07885 192331 **Fernside Cottage, Templeton EX16 8BP**
**email:** enquiries@fernsidecottage-bed-and-breakfast.co.uk
**web:** www.fernsidecottage-bed-and-breakfast.co.uk
**dir:** M5 junct 27, A361 signed Barnstaple. In approx 12m at Stonelands Cross left signed Rackenford & Templeton. Left at T-junct signed Templeton. 2nd right. In Templeton Bridge at T-junct right signed Witheridge. B&B up hill on right

This charming thatched cottage is within easy reach of Tiverton and the M5, and sits in rolling countryside, a haven of peace and tranquillity. Expect high quality bedrooms with wonderful beds, smart bathrooms, Aga-cooked breakfasts and a really warm welcome from two very caring hosts.

**Rooms:** 2 en suite **D** £99–£105* **Facilities:** FTV iPod docking station Lounge tea/coffee WiFi ⚓ **Extras:** Speciality toiletries, robes, home-made biscuits, bottled water, guest fridge **Parking:** 3 **Notes:** No children 18yrs

### TORBAY
*See Brixham, Paignton and Torquay*

### TORQUAY
Map 3 SX96

#### Premier Collection

## Carlton Court
★★★★★ BED AND BREAKFAST

**tel:** 01803 297318 & 07794 613051 **18 Cleveland Road TQ2 5BE**
**email:** stay@carlton-court.co.uk **web:** www.carlton-court.co.uk
**dir:** A380 onto A3022, straight ahead at 3 sets of lights. Stay in left lane, straight ahead at 2 sets of lights. Into right lane at Torre station, down hill. After 100yds left into Cleveland Rd, straight over at x-rds, 700yds on right

This elegant detached Victorian villa has been sensitively refurbished to provide impressive levels of quality and comfort, while retaining many original period features. Service and hospitality are hallmarks here, and every effort is made to ensure guests feel both welcomed and relaxed, with helpful local information always on offer. Bedrooms provide high standards with a range of types available, including suites and ground-floor rooms. Quality is equally high in bathrooms, with lovely warm towels and robes. All rooms also feature chiller fridges. Breakfast is served in the well-appointed dining room, overlooking the garden, and provides a wonderful start to the day.

**Rooms:** 6 en suite (2 GF) **S** £79–£104; **D** £94–£112* **Facilities:** FTV DVD tea/coffee WiFi **Extras:** Fresh milk, bottled water, fridge, speciality toiletries **Parking:** 7 **Notes:** No children 16yrs

TORQUAY *continued*

## Premier Collection

### The Cary Arms

★★★★★  INN

**tel:** 01803 327110 **Babbacombe Beach TQ1 3LX**
**email:** enquiries@caryarms.co.uk **web:** www.caryarms.co.uk
**dir:** *A380 at Ashcombe Cross onto B3192 to Teignmouth. Right at lights to Torquay on A379, left at lights to Babbacombe. Left into Babbacombe Downs Rd, left into Beach Rd*

Located on the water's edge at Babbacombe, this seaside retreat is very well appointed; the rooms have sea views and nearly all have terraces or balconies. Bedrooms and bathrooms are fitted to a high standard with many thoughtful extras and unique touches to make a stay memorable. This is a popular dining venue whether eating inside, or on the terraces that lead down to the water's edge; in summer there's a barbecue and wood-fired oven. The dedicated staff will assist in planning your day, or simply share local knowledge.

**Rooms:** 12 en suite (4 fmly) (3 GF) **Facilities:** FTV Lounge tea/coffee Dinner available WiFi ♨18 Fishing Pool table Spa treatment room Sea fishing **Extras:** Speciality toiletries, sloe gin, confectionery **Conf:** Max 24 Thtr 24 Class 24 Board 24 **Parking:** 15 **Notes:** LB Civ wed 42

## Premier Collection

### Kingston House

★★★★★  GUEST ACCOMMODATION

**tel:** 01803 212760 **75 Avenue Road TQ2 5LL**
**email:** stay@kingstonhousetorquay.co.uk **web:** www.kingstonhousetorquay.co.uk
**dir:** *From A3022 to Torquay, turn right at Torre Station down Avenue Rd, Kingston House approx 0.4m on left*

Dating from around 1870, this elegant Victorian house, just a short stroll from the seafront, is well positioned for those visiting the area on business or for pleasure. There is always plenty of helpful advice and information readily available. Tea and cakes are served on arrival in the inviting guest lounge; an ideal way to start a relaxing break. Bedrooms offer impressive quality with wonderfully comfortable beds; likewise bathrooms come equipped with cosseting towels and robes. Breakfast offers a number of tasty options, served in the well-appointed dining room.

**Rooms:** 5 en suite (1 GF) **S** £80–£105; **D** £90–£120* **Facilities:** FTV iPod docking station TVL tea/coffee WiFi **Extras:** Speciality toiletries, chocolates, home-made cakes, bottled water **Parking:** 5 **Notes:** No children 16yrs Closed Dec–Feb

## Premier Collection

### The 25 Boutique B&B

★★★★★  BED AND BREAKFAST

**tel:** 01803 297517 **25 Avenue Road TQ2 5LB**
**email:** stay@the25.uk **web:** www.the25.uk
**dir:** *A3022 into Torquay, pass railway station, into Avenue Rd. Just past lights*

The 25 Boutique B&B is located within easy walking distance of Torquay's Abbey Sands beach, town centre and harbour. A warm and friendly atmosphere, with attention to detail and attentive yet unobtrusive service is on offer from the proprietors. The six rooms and suites are named after local beaches, and all benefit from individual design, modern en suites and amenities, free WiFi, and fridges with fresh milk and bottled water. Each room is individually designed

combining the latest trends with a classic twist to highlight the period features. A full English breakfast is served in the light and contemporary breakfast room. Off-street parking is available.The 25 Boutique B&B was a finalist for the AA Unique B&B of the Year 2017–18.

**Rooms:** 6 en suite **S** £99–£149; **D** £115–£175* **Facilities:** FTV DVD iPod docking station Lounge tea/coffee Licensed WiFi ⚓ **Extras:** Speciality toiletries, home-made biscuits, robes, slippers, Nespresso machine, fresh milk, sweets, bottled water, iPad, fridge **Parking:** 6 **Notes:** LB No children 18yrs Closed Xmas & New Year

## Premier Collection

### The Albaston

★★★★★  GUEST ACCOMMODATION

**tel:** 01803 212100 **27 St Marychurch Road TQ1 3JF**
**email:** contact@albastonhotel.co.uk **web:** www.albastonhotel.co.uk
**dir:** *A380 to centre (Riviera Way), left onto B3119. Over 1st rdbt & 2nd double rdbt, straight ahead at lights. Turn right into St Marychurch Rd, 0.5m on left*

The Albaston is a detached Victorian residence offering quality guest accommodation, suitable for either business or pleasure. Located in the heart of Torquay, it's an ideal base for exploring the English Riviera. The town centre, harbour and beach are within walking distance, as is Babbacombe Bay, and The Albaston is one of the closest properties to the International Language Schools. On offer are the guest lounge, private south facing Japanese-style decking area and Oscars bar, local beers, lager and wine all on offer. Breakfast is served in the dining room, all freshly cooked with locally sourced or produced ingredients. CCTV-monitored parking and unrestricted on-street parking available.

**Rooms:** 9 en suite **D** £80–£135* **Facilities:** FTV DVD Lounge TVL tea/coffee Licensed WiFi **Parking:** 6 **Notes:** No children 14yrs

## Premier Collection

### Linden House

★★★★★  GUEST ACCOMMODATION

**tel:** 01803 212281 & 07786 075359 **31 Bampfylde Road TQ2 5AY**
**email:** susanelliott488@btinternet.com **web:** www.lindenhousetorquay.co.uk
**dir:** *Phone for directions*

This grand Victorian house has timeless elegance and charm, and offers impressive levels of contemporary comfort combined with stylish period features. Tea and cake is always available on arrival, along with a friendly welcome and the offer of help with local information and advice. Bedrooms and bathrooms offer high levels of quality with individual styling, and everything necessary to ensure a relaxing and rewarding stay. Spacious public areas include a lovely lounge with views over the garden; and the airy dining room is the venue for the wonderful breakfasts that are guaranteed to get the day off to a tasty and satisfying start.

**Rooms:** 6 en suite 1 annexe en suite (1 GF) **Facilities:** FTV TVL tea/coffee WiFi **Extras:** Home-made chocolates **Parking:** 6 **Notes:** LB No children 16yrs Closed 21 Dec–6 Jan

## Premier Collection

## Tyndale B&B

★★★★★ 🛏 BED AND BREAKFAST

**tel:** 01803 380888 **68 Avenue Road TQ2 5LF**
**email:** tyndaletorquay@btinternet.com **web:** www.tyndaletorquay.com
**dir:** *A380 onto A3022, follow seafront signs into Avenue Rd, on right side of 1st lights*

A warm and genuine welcome is extended to all guests arriving at Tyndale. The location is very convenient, being within walking distance of the town and beach, with good off-road parking. Bedrooms have been recently refurbished to create impressive levels of comfort and quality, likewise the stylish bathrooms, complete with cosseting towels and snuggly robes. Breakfast is a real treat with a number of options to tantalise the taste buds, a tasty and fulfilling start to the day.

**Rooms:** 4 en suite (1 GF) **S** £70–£105; **D** £80–£115* **Facilities:** FTV iPod docking station tea/coffee WiFi **Extras:** Speciality toiletries, chocolates, robes, slippers, fridge, bottled water, iPad **Parking:** 7 **Notes:** LB No children 15yrs

## The Cleveland

★★★★ 🛏 GUEST ACCOMMODATION

**tel:** 01803 297522 **7 Cleveland Road TQ2 5BD**
**email:** info@clevelandbandbtorquay.co.uk **web:** clevelandbandbtorquay.co.uk
**dir:** *A3022 into Torquay, at lights by Torre Station take right hand fork. 1st left into Cleveland Rd, at far end on left*

Located in a peaceful area of Torquay, this family-run guest accommodation is within easy walking distance of Abbey Sands beach, town centre and harbour. Service is the highlight of any stay, ensuring that all needs and wants are catered for. The seven guest bedrooms are all en suite, and are ideal for a comfortable night's sleep. A south-facing sun terrace and garden are also on offer for guest use. There is also a fully licensed bar and lounge. Free WiFi and off-street parking are available, with a full English breakfast offered daily within a delightful breakfast room.

**Rooms:** 7 en suite (2 fmly) (1 GF) **S** £38–£50; **D** £58–£115* **Facilities:** FTV Lounge tea/coffee Licensed WiFi **Extras:** Bottled water, robes in suites, speciality toiletries, home-made fudge **Parking:** 7

## The Downs, Babbacombe

★★★★ 🛏 🍽 GUEST ACCOMMODATION

**tel:** 01803 328543 **41-43 Babbacombe Downs Road, Babbacombe TQ1 3LN**
**email:** manager@downshotel.co.uk **web:** www.downshotel.co.uk
**dir:** *From Torquay, A329 to Babbacombe. Off Babbacombe road turn left into Princes St. Left into Babbacombe Downs Rd, 20mtrs on left*

Built in the 1850s, this elegant building forms part of a seafront terrace with direct access to the promenade and Babbacombe Downs. The warm welcome is matched by attentive service, with every effort made to ensure a rewarding and relaxing stay. Bedrooms offer impressive levels of comfort and most have spectacular views across Lyme Bay with balconies being an added bonus. For guests with limited mobility, assisted access is available to the first floor. Additional facilities include the convivial lounge/bar and spacious restaurant where enjoyable dinners and breakfasts are offered.

**Rooms:** 12 en suite (4 fmly) **Facilities:** FTV TVL tea/coffee Dinner available Direct dial Licensed WiFi **Parking:** 8 **Notes:** LB

## Headland View

★★★★ 🛏 BED AND BREAKFAST

**tel:** 01803 312612 **37 Babbacombe Downs Road, Babbacombe TQ1 3LN**
**email:** reception@headlandview.com **web:** www.headlandview.com
**dir:** *A379 into Babbacombe, follow signs for sea front. Into Babbacombe Downs Rd*

With a Victorian heritage, this elegant establishment is located in Babbacombe and looks out over the stunning expanse of Lyme Bay. Many period features have been retained which add a sense of history and the charm of yesteryear. Bedrooms are furnished for comfort with thoughtful extras and sumptuous beds, four of the rooms also have balconies offering spectacular sea views. Every effort is made to ensure a relaxed and rewarding stay with many guests returning several times a year to de-stress and unwind. Breakfast features daily specials alongside the ever popular and indulgent, traditional English offering. Off-road parking is available.

**Rooms:** 6 rms (4 en suite) (2 pri facs) **Facilities:** FTV DVD iPod docking station Lounge tea/coffee WiFi **Parking:** 3 **Notes:** No children 13yrs

## Orestone Manor

★★★★ 🏵🏵 🛏 RESTAURANT WITH ROOMS

**tel:** 01803 328098 **Rockhouse Lane, Maidencombe TQ1 4SX**
**email:** info@orestonemanor.com **web:** www.orestonemanor.com
**dir:** *N of Torquay on A379, on sharp bend in village of Maidencombe*

Set in a fabulous location overlooking the bay, Orestone Manor has a long history of providing fine food and very comfortable accommodation, coupled with friendly, attentive service. Log fires burn in cooler months, and there is a conservatory, a bar and a sitting room for guests to enjoy. AA Rosettes have been awarded for the uncomplicated modern cuisine which is based on quality local produce.

**Rooms:** 11 en suite 3 annexe en suite (6 fmly) (3 GF) **S** £85–£140; **D** £120–£350* **Facilities:** STV FTV iPod docking station Lounge tea/coffee Dinner available Direct dial WiFi 🏊 **Extras:** Speciality toiletries, bottled water **Conf:** Max 90 Thtr 90 Class 60 Board 30 **Parking:** 38 **Notes:** LB Closed 3–29 Jan Civ wed 90

**TORQUAY** *continued*

## Garway Lodge Guest House

★★★★ ≋ GUEST HOUSE

**tel:** 01803 293126 & 07711552878 **79 Avenue Road TQ2 5LL**
**email:** info@garwaylodge.co.uk **web:** www.garwaylodge.co.uk
**dir:** *On A3022, 100mtrs past Torre Station on left*

Garway Lodge is in the heart of Torquay and offers accommodation exclusively for adults. The bedrooms are spacious and stylish, and include a ground floor room. Business guests are particularly welcomed and there is free on-site parking and free WiFi. Residents have use of a small honesty bar, and an extensive breakfast menu is offered. The seafront and harbourside restaurants are a level walk away.

**Rooms:** 6 en suite (1 GF) **S** £35–£45; **D** £68–£80* **Facilities:** FTV DVD iPod docking station tea/coffee Licensed WiFi 🛇 **Extras:** Speciality toiletries, honesty bar **Parking:** 6 **Notes:** LB No children

## The Iona

★★★★ GUEST ACCOMMODATION

**tel:** 01803 294918 **5 Cleveland Road TQ2 5BD**
**email:** stay@hoteliona.co.uk **web:** www.hoteliona.co.uk
**dir:** *A380 to Riviera rdbt, 1st exit onto A3022 towards seafront. Take left into Vine Rd, right into Cleveland Rd*

Dating back to the 1860s, this grand Victorian villa is situated in a quiet location just a short stroll from the town centre, harbour and many attractions. A variety of bedroom sizes is offered; all provide good levels of comfort and the expected necessities. Public areas are elegant with a number of period features retained. Dinner and breakfast are served in the light and airy conservatory.

**Rooms:** 8 en suite **Facilities:** FTV DVD iPod docking station Lounge TVL tea/coffee WiFi 🛇 **Parking:** 8 **Notes:** LB No children 5yrs Closed 31 Dec–1 Mar

## Kelvin House

★★★★ GUEST ACCOMMODATION

**tel:** 01803 209093 **46 Bampfylde Road TQ2 5AY**
**email:** kelvinhousehotel@hotmail.com **web:** www.kelvinhousehotel.co.uk
**dir:** *M5 junct 31, A380, A3032 (Newton Rd) into Torquay. At lights at Torre Station right into Avenue Rd. Bampfylde Rd on left*

This attractive Victorian house was built in the 1880s and sits on a lovely tree-lined road. It is a family-run property with a relaxed, friendly home-from-home atmosphere. All bedrooms are en suite and have been appointed to a high standard with many extras. A large elegant sitting room is available for guests, and hearty breakfasts are served in the dining room, or on the patio in good weather. Close to good transport links, it makes an ideal base for touring the Torquay Riviera.

**Rooms:** 8 en suite (1 fmly) (2 GF) **Facilities:** FTV TVL tea/coffee Licensed WiFi **Parking:** 6 **Notes:** LB No children 12yrs

## Kingsholm

★★★★ GUEST ACCOMMODATION

**tel:** 01803 297794 **539 Babbacombe Road TQ1 1HU**
**email:** thekingsholm@virginmedia.com **web:** www.kingsholmhotel.co.uk
**dir:** *From A3022 left onto Torquay seafront, left at clock tower rdbt, Kingsholm 400mtrs on left*

An elegant, personally-run establishment situated in a conservation area, only 350 metres from the bustling harbour, this fine Edwardian house offers excellent accommodation that is appointed to a high standard; many rooms overlook Torwood Gardens. All bedrooms have Freeview TV, free WiFi, hairdryers and hospitality trays.

There is also a guest lounge, a spacious dining room with separate tables and a licensed bar. Parking is free. Owners June and Carl offer a friendly welcome.

**Rooms:** 9 en suite **S** £38–£40; **D** £68–£78* **Facilities:** FTV TVL tea/coffee Licensed WiFi **Parking:** 9 **Notes:** No children 10yrs Closed 17 Nov–1 Mar

## Peppers

★★★★ GUEST ACCOMMODATION

**tel:** 01803 293856 **551 Babbacombe Road TQ1 1HQ**
**email:** enquiries@hotel-peppers.co.uk **web:** www.hotel-peppers.co.uk
**dir:** *A3022 to seafront, left on to B3199 towards harbour. At clock tower rdbt, turn left, 250mtrs on left*

Dating back to the Edwardian era, Peppers has much to offer and is conveniently located just a short walk from the harbour. Hospitality is assured with every effort made to ensure a relaxing and rewarding stay. Bedrooms are elegantly appointed and all provide impressive levels of quality and comfort. Additional facilities include a spacious guest lounge and intimate bar. The contemporary styled dining room is the venue for tasty breakfasts with a generous choice on offer. At the rear of the property, a sun terrace leads to the car park.

**Rooms:** 10 rms (9 en suite) (1 pri facs) **Facilities:** FTV TVL tea/coffee Licensed WiFi **Extras:** Bottled water – complimentary **Parking:** 9 **Notes:** LB No children 10yrs Closed 18 Dec–18 Jan

## The Robin Hill

★★★★ GUEST ACCOMMODATION

**tel:** 01803 214518 & 07940 559925 **74 Braddons Hill Road East TQ1 1HF**
**email:** reservations@therobinhill.co.uk **web:** www.robinhillhotel.co.uk
**dir:** *From A38 to seafront then left to Babbacombe. Pass theatre to Clock Tower rdbt, take 1st exit & through 2 sets of lights, Braddons Hill Road East on left after museum*

Dating back to 1896, this fascinating building has character in abundance and is located a short stroll from the harbour and shops. Every effort is made to ensure a stay is enjoyable; assistance is readily available at all times. Bedrooms, in varying styles, provide all the expected necessities. Public areas include the inviting lounge, plus a light and airy dining room where breakfast is served.

**Rooms:** 12 en suite (3 fmly) (1 GF) **S** £60–£90; **D** £70–£110* **Facilities:** FTV iPod docking station Lounge TVL tea/coffee Licensed WiFi 🛇 **Conf:** Max 32 Thtr 32 Class 32 Board 28 **Parking:** 10 **Notes:** LB Closed 20 Dec–4 Jan

## Aveland House

★★★★ ≋ GUEST ACCOMMODATION

**tel:** 01803 326622 **Aveland Road, Babbacombe TQ1 3PT**
**email:** avelandhouse@aol.com **web:** www.avelandhouse.co.uk
**dir:** *A3022 to Torquay, left onto B3199 (Hele Rd) into Westhill Rd. Then Warbro Rd, 2nd left into Aveland Rd*

Set in well-tended gardens in a peaceful area of Babbacombe, close to the South West Coast Path, beaches, shops and attractions, Aveland House is within easy walking distance of Torquay harbour and town. This family-run house offers warm and attentive service. The attractive bedrooms are well equipped, with free WiFi throughout. A pleasant bar and two comfortable TV lounges are available. Hearing-impaired visitors are especially welcome, as both the proprietors are OCSL signers. Evening meals and bar snacks are available by arrangement. Coeliacs and special diets can be catered for.

**Rooms:** 10 en suite **Facilities:** Lounge TVL tea/coffee Dinner available Licensed WiFi 🛇 **Parking:** 10 **Notes:** LB No children 12yrs RS Sun no evening meals

## Barclay Court Guest House

★★★★ GUEST ACCOMMODATION

**tel:** 01803 292791 **29 Castle Road TQ1 3BB**
**email:** enquiries@barclaycourt.co.uk **web:** www.barclaycourtguesthouse.co.uk
**dir:** *M5 onto A38 then A380 to Torquay. A3022 Newton Rd left onto Upton Rd, right towards Lymington Rd. Right to Castle Circus, Castle Rd on left*

The delightful, personally-run Barclay Court is within easy walking distance of Torquay's attractions and offers a friendly, relaxed atmosphere. Individually decorated rooms vary in size, but all are en suite and well equipped. There is a games room on the lower-ground floor and the garden is a quiet retreat, especially in the summer months.

**Rooms:** 11 en suite (1 fmly) (1 GF) **S** £30–£35; **D** £60–£70* **Facilities:** FTV tea/coffee WiFi 🔒 **Parking:** 7 **Notes:** Closed 23–28 Dec RS Nov–Feb Limited number of rooms available

## The Coppice

★★★★ GUEST ACCOMMODATION

**tel:** 01803 297786 & 211085 **Barrington Road TQ1 2QJ**
**email:** reservations@coppicehotel.co.uk **web:** www.coppicehotel.co.uk
**dir:** *1m from harbour on Babbacombe Rd, opposite St Matthias Church*

Friendly and comfortable, The Coppice is a popular choice and occupies a convenient location within walking distance of the beaches and shops. In addition to the indoor and outdoor swimming pools, evening entertainment is often provided in the spacious bar. Bedrooms are bright and airy with modern amenities.

**Rooms:** 39 en suite (10 fmly) (28 GF) **S** £35–£65; **D** £70–£130 **Facilities:** FTV Lounge tea/coffee Dinner available Licensed WiFi 🔆🏊 Gym Pool table **Conf:** Max 60 Thtr 60 Class 60 Board 60 **Parking:** 20 **Notes:** LB

## The Elmington

★★★★ GUEST ACCOMMODATION

**tel:** 01803 605192 **St Agnes Lane, Chelston TQ2 6QE**
**email:** mail@elmington.co.uk **web:** www.elmington.co.uk
**dir:** *At rear of rail station*

Set in sub-tropical gardens with views over the bay, this splendid Victorian villa has been lovingly restored. The comfortable bedrooms are brightly decorated and vary in size and style. There is a spacious lounge, bar and dining room. Additional facilities include an outdoor pool and terrace.

**Rooms:** 19 en suite **Facilities:** FTV Lounge TVL tea/coffee Licensed WiFi 🏊 Pool table 🔒 **Parking:** 24 **Notes:** LB No children 6yrs Closed Nov–Mar

## Harmony Bed & Breakfast

★★★★ GUEST ACCOMMODATION

**tel:** 01803 293918 **67 Avenue Road TQ2 5LG**
**email:** enquiries@theharmonytorquay.co.uk **web:** www.theharmonytorquay.co.uk
**dir:** *A380 onto A3022 (Riviera Way). At Torre Station, right onto A3022 (Avenue Rd). On left at junct with Vine Rd*

Harmony is a family-run establishment within walking distance of the town and a level walk from the seafront. A warm welcome is extended to all guests and every effort made to ensure a relaxing and rewarding stay. All the bedrooms provide impressive levels of quality including wonderful comfy beds and all necessities required. Breakfast is a tempting and tasty offering that uses local produce whenever possible – a great start to the day. Ample parking space is also an asset here.

**Rooms:** 8 en suite (2 GF) **S** £50–£60; **D** £65–£85* **Facilities:** FTV DVD Lounge tea/coffee Licensed WiFi **Extras:** Mineral water, sweets – complimentary **Parking:** 10 **Notes:** LB No children 16yrs Closed 24–26 Dec

## Newton House

★★★★ GUEST ACCOMMODATION

**tel:** 01803 297520 **31 Newton Road TQ2 5DB**
**email:** newtonhouse_torquay@yahoo.com **web:** www.newtonhouse-tq.co.uk
**dir:** *From Torre station bear left at lights, Newton House 40yds on left*

You are assured of a warm welcome at Newton House, which is close to the town centre and attractions. The comfortable bedrooms, some on the ground floor, have thoughtful extras, and a lounge is available. Breakfast is enjoyed in the pleasant dining room.

**Rooms:** 9 en suite (3 fmly) (5 GF) **Facilities:** FTV Lounge tea/coffee WiFi 🔒 Drying room for hikers **Extras:** Snacks, chocolate, sweets – complimentary **Parking:** 15 **Notes:** LB

## The Norwood

★★★★ Ⓐ GUEST ACCOMMODATION

**tel:** 01803 294236 & 07444 741409 **60 Belgrave Road TQ2 5HY**
**email:** stay@norwoodhoteltorquay.co.uk **web:** www.norwoodhoteltorquay.co.uk
**dir:** *From Princess Theatre towards Paignton, at 1st lights right into Belgrave Rd, over x-rds, 3rd building on left*

The Norwood is just a short walk from the seafront, town centre and Conference Centre. All the individually decorated bedrooms are en suite and four-poster rooms are available. There are excellent choices at breakfast, from traditional full English to lighter options, and the hosts are happy to cater for special dietary requests. Packed lunches and takeaway breakfasts are also available.

**Rooms:** 9 en suite (5 fmly) (1 GF) **S** £40–£50; **D** £60–£75* **Facilities:** FTV tea/coffee WiFi **Extras:** Speciality toiletries – complimentary **Parking:** 3 **Notes:** LB

| TOTNES | Map 3 SX86 |
|---|---|

### Premier Collection

## Stoke Gabriel Lodgings - Badgers Retreat

★★★★★ 🏡 BED AND BREAKFAST

**tel:** 01803 782003 & 07785 710225 **2 Orchard Close, Stoke Gabriel TQ9 6SX**
**email:** info@stokegabriellodgings.com **web:** www.stokegabriellodgings.com
**dir:** *In Stoke Gabriel, pass Baptist church, take left fork into Paignton Rd. 100mtrs to entrance on left by public bench, travel to top of hill*

Stoke Gabriel Lodgings is an attractive example of contemporary architecture, positioned high above the River Dart just outside Stoke Gabriel, near Totnes. The property was designed to take full advantage of its location. David and Helen offer a warm welcome as well as a delicious Devon cream tea on arrival. Bedrooms are spacious and lavishly furnished with comfortable seating, and the en suites have wet shower areas and heated towel rails. Patio doors open to a private balcony overlooking the garden and countryside. Outside, the landscaped garden can be enjoyed from the large terrace or conservatory. Breakfast is a delight, while dinner can be taken at one of many local pubs and restaurants.

**Rooms:** 3 en suite (1 fmly) **S** £74.50–£80; **D** £99–£110* **Facilities:** STV FTV DVD iPod docking station Lounge TVL tea/coffee WiFi 🐾 🔒 **Extras:** Speciality toiletries, fruit/snacks, mineral water **Parking:** 6

## TOTNES *continued*

### Dartington Hall

★★★★ ◉◉ GUEST ACCOMMODATION

**tel:** 01803 847135 & 84170 **The Darington Hall Trust TQ9 6EL**
**email:** reservations@dartingtonhall.com **web:** www.dartingtonhall.com

Dartington Hall is a Grade I listed property set within a 1200-acre estate in the South Hams. It is the HQ of the Dartington Hall Trust, a charity specialising in the arts, social justice and sustainability. Surrounding a distinctive 14th-century courtyard, accommodation offers a mix of heritage and modern day comforts. A full range of facilities are available, along with guest parking. The award-winning White Hart Restaurant serves breakfast, lunch and dinner.

**Rooms:** 50 rms (39 en suite) (11 pri facs) (10 fmly) (10 GF) **S** £66–£131; **D** £94–£175* **Facilities:** STV FTV DVD TVL tea/coffee Dinner available Direct dial Licensed WiFi ↳ ⌘ ⚓ Fishing **Extras:** Speciality toiletries, fruit **Conf:** Max 500 Thtr 300 Class 200 Board 60 **Parking:** 200 **Notes:** LB Civ wed 169

---

### YARCOMBE     Map 4 ST20

### The Belfry at Yarcombe

★★★★ ⌂ BED AND BREAKFAST

**tel:** 01404 861234 **EX14 9BD**
**email:** stay@thebelfryatyarcombe.co.uk **web:** www.thebelfrycountryhotel.com
**dir:** *On A30, in village of Yarcombe opposite church*

Built in the late 1860s and originally the village school, The Belfry at Yarcombe now offers bright and clean accommodation. Six comfortable en suite rooms are on offer along with a pleasant guest lounge and south-facing terrace, views across the village and valley are a highlight. WiFi and off-street parking available.

**Rooms:** 6 en suite (2 GF) **S** £55–£70; **D** £79–£100* **Facilities:** FTV TVL tea/coffee Licensed WiFi ⚓ **Extras:** Speciality toiletries, fresh milk, juice **Conf:** Max 12 Board 12 **Parking:** 7 **Notes:** LB No children 10yrs RS Sun–Fri restaurant closed and only open to groups on Sat

---

### YELVERTON     Map 3 SX56

### Tor Royal

★★★★ ⌂ BED AND BREAKFAST

**tel:** 01822 890189 & 07892 910666 **Princetown PL20 6SL**
**email:** stay@torroyal.co.uk **web:** www.torroyal.co.uk
**dir:** *A38 exit at Ashburton, follow signs to Princetown/Two Bridges. Turn right to Princetown & left opposite Country Charm shop, Tor Royal on right*

This peacefully located Grade II listed former country house is a wonderfully relaxing base from which to explore the picturesque delights of Dartmoor. Parts of the house date back to the 17th century, but modern comforts are now in place, with bedrooms and bathrooms offering high levels of quality and character. Breakfast makes use of excellent local produce, served in the attractive dining room. Guests also have a lovely lounge at their disposal, with an open fire to keep the chill off in cooler months. There is also a large garden.

**Rooms:** 5 en suite (1 GF) **Facilities:** FTV DVD TVL tea/coffee WiFi ⚓ **Conf:** Max 30 Class 25 Board 20 **Parking:** 10 **Notes:** LB RS Xmas & New Year Civ wed 50

---

### Burrator Inn

★★★★ ⌂ ⛾ INN

**tel:** 01822 853121 **Dousland PL20 6NP**
**email:** reservations@theburratorinn.co.uk **web:** www.theburratorinn.com
**dir:** *From Yelverton on B3212 to Dousland*

This lively pub is located in the very heart of Dousland, near Yelverton, and has a good local following. The bedrooms are comfortable and equipped with all the expected facilities. A wide range of popular dishes served all day, and the very cheerful and upbeat staff are ready and willing to meet the needs of their guests. Good selection of wines and local beers. Great for all ages and families.

**Rooms:** 7 en suite (3 fmly) **S** fr £55; **D** £75–£85* **Facilities:** FTV DVD tea/coffee Dinner available WiFi Pool table **Parking:** 40 **Notes:** Closed 25 Dec

## Overcombe House

★★★★ 🅐 GUEST HOUSE

**tel:** 01822 853501 **Old Station Road, Horrabridge PL20 7RA**
**email:** enquiries@overcombehotel.co.uk **web:** www.overcombehotel.co.uk
**dir:** *Signed 100yds off A386 at Horrabridge*

Many guests return on a regular basis to enjoy this delightful, family-run establishment. Genuine hospitality is a great strength, and every effort is taken to ensure an enjoyable and memorable stay. Given its location, this is a perfect base for exploring the rugged beauty of the Dartmoor National Park, just on the doorstep. Bedrooms are all neatly presented; many have lovely views across the countryside.

**Rooms:** 8 en suite (2 GF) **S** £75–£97.50; **D** £85–£107.50 **Facilities:** FTV DVD tea/coffee Licensed WiFi 🔒 **Parking:** 7 **Notes:** No children 12yrs Closed 24 Dec–2 Jan

## DORSET

### ASKERSWELL — Map 4 SY59

## The Spyway Inn

★★★★ 🍷 🍴 INN

**tel:** 01308 485250 **DT2 9EP**
**email:** spywaytim@hotmail.com **web:** www.spyway-inn.co.uk
**dir:** *From A35 follow Askerswell sign, then follow Spyway Inn sign*

Peacefully located in the rolling Dorset countryside, this family-run inn offers a warm and genuine welcome. Bedrooms are spacious and well appointed with a number of extras provided, including bath robes. Real ales are on tap in the bar. Menus feature home-cooked food, with many dishes making use of local produce both at dinner and breakfast. The extensive beer garden, with wonderful views, is popular in summer.

**Rooms:** 3 en suite (1 fmly) **Facilities:** FTV tea/coffee Dinner available WiFi **Extras:** Robes **Parking:** 40 **Notes:** LB

### BEAMINSTER — Map 4 ST40

## Hill Farm B&B

★★ BED AND BREAKFAST

**tel:** 01308 861037 **DT8 3SQ**
**email:** rkpjones1955@yahoo.co.uk **web:** www.hillfarmbandbdorset.com
**dir:** *Off A356 between Crewkerne & Maiden Newton*

Hill Farm offers a peaceful rural setting, and cosy and comfortable accommodation. There is a relaxed atmosphere, and a good hearty breakfast is served in the traditional dining room adorned with historical artefacts and family pictures. This is a perfect spot from which to explore the stunning south coast and surrounding areas.

**Rooms:** 2 rms (1 en suite) (1 pri facs) **S** £65; **D** £90* **Facilities:** TVL tea/coffee WiFi 🔒 **Parking:** 4

### BLANDFORD FORUM — Map 4 ST80

## Portman Lodge

★★★★ BED AND BREAKFAST

**tel:** 01258 453727 **Whitecliff Mill Street DT11 7BP**
**email:** enquiries@portmanlodge.co.uk **web:** www.portmanlodge.co.uk
**dir:** *One-way system, follow signs from town centre to Shaftesbury & hospital. On right past Our Lady of Lourdes church (on left)*

A Victorian building once used as a music school, this substantial detached house now provides elegant accommodation and a warm welcome. All bedrooms and bathrooms are well decorated and comfortably furnished. Breakfast utilises good quality ingredients and is served at a communal table.

**Rooms:** 3 en suite 2 annexe en suite (1 fmly) **S** £65; **D** £80–£85* **Facilities:** STV tea/coffee WiFi 🔒 **Parking:** 8 **Notes:** No children 10yrs

*See advert on following page*

## BOURNEMOUTH
Map 5 SZ09

### Washington House

★★★★ GUEST ACCOMMODATION

**tel:** 01202 556111 **3 Durley Road BH2 5JQ**
**email:** info@washingtonhousehotel.com **web:** www.washingtonhousehotel.com

This Grade II listed Victorian villa has much to offer, not least of which a great location, just a short walk from the seafront and the Bournemouth International Centre. The bedrooms provide individuality, style and comfort, likewise the modern bathrooms. Public areas are equally impressive; the elegant dining room is the venue for breakfast, an extensive continental offering. A guest lounge is also provided, and there is parking available.

**Rooms:** 13 en suite (2 fmly) (4 GF) **Facilities:** FTV Lounge tea/coffee Licensed WiFi **Parking:** 12

### Southern Breeze Lodge

★★★★ ⬤ GUEST HOUSE

**tel:** 01202 427459 & 07806 950168 **20 Southern Road BH6 3SR**
**email:** enquiries@southernbreezelodge.co.uk **web:** www.southernbreezelodge.co.uk
**dir:** *From A35, at Pokesdown Station turn opposite into Seabourne Rd. After 0.5m turn right into Chestnut Ave. Cross Pine Avenue into Southern Rd, 180yds on left*

Situated in a quiet location, close to Southbourne's popular shops and cafés, this warm and welcoming establishment provides an excellent base from which to explore the local area. Just a five-minute stroll from the cliff tops overlooking the Blue Flag beach, the views from which are superb, there is also a pathway down to the beach or alternatively the Cliff Lift. Bedrooms are all furnished with an appealing simplicity, light and airy with a focus upon comfy beds. Breakfast is a generous offering with an impressive selection of both hot and cold options, a real taste of Dorset.

**Rooms:** 6 en suite S £63–£86; D £73–£96* **Facilities:** FTV tea/coffee WiFi **Parking:** 5
**Notes:** LB No children 16yrs Closed 6 Jan–29 Mar

### Trouville Lodge

★★★ GUEST ACCOMMODATION

**tel:** 01202 552262 **9 Priory Road BH2 5DF**
**email:** reception@trouvillehotel.com **web:** www.trouvillehotel.com

Professionally run, this well-managed establishment offers an impressive standard of accommodation and facilities. Bedrooms are situated in an annexe to the Trouville Hotel next door. All rooms are stylishly appointed and comfortably furnished. Facilities are in the hotel. The Deauville restaurant offers a very good menu choice, and the well-stocked Le Café Bar provides an informal and pleasant environment. There is also a large pool and sauna as well as a resident beautician.

**Rooms:** 19 en suite (4 fmly) (4 GF) **Facilities:** FTV tea/coffee Dinner available Licensed WiFi ⬤Gym Leisure facilities available at Trouville Hotel **Parking:** 14
**Notes:** LB

# *Portman Lodge*

Built in 1873, *Portman Lodge* is the main wing and entrance into a large Victorian property, originally part of Lord Portman's estate. It is thought to have been a residence for choristers for St Martin's Church. Many of the original fixtures and fittings remain, in particular the attractive Victorian tiled floor in the entrance hall and corridor.

The individually decorated bedrooms, with twin, double or kingsize beds, are supremely comfortable, with en suite rooms, plentiful hot water, powerful showers and white fluffy towels.

Substantial cooked tasty breakfasts, including a varied range of locally sourced produce, are served around a large table in our lovely dining room.

There is a good choice of pubs and restaurants for lunch and dinner in the beautiful Georgian market town of Blandford, just five minutes walk away, so no need to get into your car.

Recommended in the area: Kingston Lacy, Lulworth Cove, Jurassic Coast, Corfe Castle, Abbotsbury Swannery and Gardens

**Whitecliff Mill Street, Blandford Forum, Dorset DT11 7BP**
**Tel:** 01258 453727
**Mobile:** 07860 424235 (Gerry) • 07785 971743 (Pat)
**Website:** www.portmanlodge.co.uk
**Email:** enquiries@portmanlodge.co.uk

## BRIDPORT
Map 4 SY49

### Premier Collection

### The Shave Cross Inn
★★★★★ INN

**tel:** 01308 868358 **Marshwood Vale DT6 6HW**
**email:** roy.warburton@virgin.net **web:** www.theshavecrossinn.co.uk
**dir:** *From B3165 turn at Birdsmoorgate & follow brown signs*

This historic inn has been providing refreshment to weary travellers for centuries and continues to offer a warm and genuine welcome. The snug bar is dominated by a wonderful fireplace with crackling logs creating just the right atmosphere. Bedrooms are located in a separate Dorset flint and stone building. Quality is impressive throughout with wonderful stone floors and oak beams, combined with feature beds and luxurious bathrooms. Food, using excellent local produce, has a distinct Caribbean and international slant, including a number of authentic dishes.

**Rooms:** 7 en suite (1 fmly) (3 GF) **Facilities:** STV FTV tea/coffee Dinner available Direct dial WiFi Pool table **Parking:** 29 **Notes:** LB No children RS Mon (ex BH) closed for lunch & dinner

### Oxbridge Farm
★★★★ FARMHOUSE

**tel:** 01308 488368 & 07766 086543 **DT6 3UA**
**email:** jojokillin@hotmail.com **web:** www.oxbridgefarm.co.uk
**dir:** *From A3066 Bridport to Beaminster. Take 1st right signed Oxbridge 1m*

Oxbridge Farm sits in the rolling hills of west Dorset in an Area of Outstanding Natural Beauty. The bedrooms are well equipped and offer a very good level of comfort. A hearty breakfast is served in the attractive dining room which benefits from wonderful countryside views.

**Rooms:** 4 rms (3 en suite) (1 pri facs) (2 fmly) (1 GF) **S** fr £60; **D** fr £100*
**Facilities:** FTV Lounge tea/coffee Dinner available WiFi ⚓18 **Parking:** 6 **Notes:** LB Civ wed 200 40 acres sheep

## BROADWINDSOR
Map 4 ST40

### Premier Collection

### The Old George
★★★★★ GUEST ACCOMMODATION

**tel:** 01308 868434 **The Square DT8 3QD**
**email:** theoldgeorge@gmail.com **web:** www.theoldgeorge-broadwindsor.co.uk

Located in the peaceful and quintessentially English village of Broadwindsor, this comfortable listed Georgian house was converted sympathetically from a pub to a family home 50 years ago, and is an ideal retreat for those seeking peaceful surroundings. King Charles II slept in the adjacent property in 1651. Each of the bedrooms has its own character, and a range of thoughtful extras such as fresh flowers, bottled water and magazines. A pub offering a selection of evening meals is just a stone's throw away. Home-cooked breakfasts are also served in the comfortable dining room.

**Rooms:** 3 en suite **Facilities:** FTV DVD TVL tea/coffee WiFi 🦢 🔒 **Extras:** Speciality toiletries **Parking:** 2 **Notes:** LB

## CHIDEOCK
Map 4 SY49

### The Anchor Inn
★★★★ 🍴 INN

**tel:** 01297 489215 **Seatown DT6 6JU**
**email:** contact@theanchorinnseatown.co.uk **web:** www.theanchorinnseatown.co.uk
**dir:** *Turn off A35 in Chideock into Duck Street, 0.75m down lane to sea*

This long established inn has much to offer, not least of which is its superb position, just a few steps away from the sea. There is a simple and rustic nautical style throughout the bars, combined with an engaging and good humoured atmosphere. Bedrooms are spacious with wonderful bathrooms and the added luxury of quality toiletries and cosseting robes. Food is not to be missed, a varied menu with excellent quality local seafood is always on offer. Breakfast also makes use of impressive local produce.

**Rooms:** 3 en suite (2 fmly) **S** £115–£155; **D** £130–£170* **Facilities:** FTV tea/coffee Dinner available Direct dial WiFi **Extras:** Speciality toiletries, slippers, gowns **Parking:** 8 **Notes:** Closed 24 Dec–1 Jan

## CHRISTCHURCH
Map 5 SZ19

### Premier Collection

### The Lord Bute & Restaurant
★★★★★ ⚫⚫ GUEST ACCOMMODATION

**tel:** 01425 278884 **179-181 Lymington Road, Highcliffe on Sea BH23 4JS**
**email:** mail@lordbute.co.uk **web:** www.lordbute.co.uk
**dir:** *A337 towards Highcliffe*

The elegant Lord Bute stands directly behind the original entrance lodges of Highcliffe Castle, close to the beach and historic town of Christchurch. Bedrooms have been finished to a very high standard with many thoughtful extras including spa baths. Excellent, award-winning food is available in the smart restaurant. Conferences and weddings are catered for.

**Rooms:** 9 en suite 4 annexe en suite (1 fmly) (6 GF) **D** £130–£240* **Facilities:** FTV Lounge tea/coffee Dinner available Direct dial Licensed WiFi **Conf:** Max 25 Thtr 25 Class 15 Board 18 **Parking:** 40 **Notes:** LB RS Mon Restaurant closed (open bkfst) Civ wed 120

CHRISTCHURCH *continued*

## Grosvenor Lodge

★★★★ GUEST HOUSE

**tel:** 01202 499008 **53 Stour Road BH23 1LN**
**email:** bookings@grosvenorlodge.co.uk **web:** www.grosvenorlodge.co.uk
**dir:** *A35 from Christchurch to Bournemouth, at 1st lights left into Stour Rd. Lodge on right*

Grosvenor House is a friendly and popular guest house near the centre of this historic town. The bedrooms are brightly and individually decorated and have lots of useful extras. Hearty breakfasts are served in the cheerful dining room, and there are many local restaurants for lunch and dinner.

**Rooms:** 7 en suite (4 fmly) (1 GF) **S** £37–£70; **D** £65–£135* **Facilities:** FTV DVD iPod docking station tea/coffee WiFi ⚓ **Parking:** 10 **Notes:** LB

## Avon Breeze

★★★★ 🌙 BED AND BREAKFAST

**tel:** 01425 279102 & 07896 128026 **21 Fulmar Road BH23 4BJ**
**email:** info@avonbreeze.co.uk **web:** avonbreeze.co.uk
**dir:** *A35 follow signs for Christchurch. At Sainsburys, signs for Mudeford. At Mudeford quay, turn into Falcon Dr, left & left again*

Avon Breeze is situated on the edge of the New Forest, a few minutes' level walk from the harbour, beach and local pubs. This contemporary home offers two comfortable en suite rooms as well as the use of a conservatory. Breakfast consists of locally-sourced, organic ingredients. Ample off-street parking is available.

**Rooms:** 2 en suite (2 GF) **Facilities:** FTV DVD iPod docking station tea/coffee WiFi ⚓ **Extras:** Bottled water, chocolate – complimentary **Parking:** 3 **Notes:** LB No children Closed Oct–Mar RS Apr 1 room only available

## Riversmead

★★★★ GUEST ACCOMMODATION

**tel:** 01202 487195 **61 Stour Road BH23 1LN**
**email:** riversmead.dorset@googlemail.com **web:** www.riversmeadbb.co.uk
**dir:** *A338 to Christchurch. Left turn to town centre, turn right over railway bridge*

Ideally located close to the town centre, beaches and the New Forest, with excellent access to local transport links, Riversmead is the perfect base for a short break or longer stay. This comfortable house offers a range of facilities including enclosed off-road parking, fridges in rooms, and an excellent breakfast.

**Rooms:** 3 en suite (1 fmly) **S** £45–£65; **D** £65–£80* **Facilities:** FTV DVD tea/coffee WiFi **Parking:** 9 **Notes:** LB No children 10yrs

## The White House

★★★★ GUEST ACCOMMODATION

**tel:** 01425 271279 **428 Lymington Road, Highcliffe on Sea BH23 5HF**
**email:** enquiries@thewhitehouse-christchurch.co.uk **web:** www.thewhitehouse-christchurch.co.uk
**dir:** *Off A35, signs to Highcliffe. After rdbt The White House 200yds on right*

This charming Victorian house is just a short drive from Highcliffe beach, the New Forest, and the historic town of Christchurch. Comfortable, well-appointed accommodation is provided, and a generous, freshly-cooked breakfast is served in the cosy dining room.

**Rooms:** 6 en suite **Facilities:** FTV tea/coffee WiFi **Parking:** 6 **Notes:** LB

## Brantwood Guest House

★★★ GUEST ACCOMMODATION

**tel:** 01202 473446 **55 Stour Road BH23 1LN**
**email:** brantwoodbookings@gmail.com **web:** www.brantwoodguesthouse.com
**dir:** *A338 Bournemouth, 1st exit to Christchurch, right after railway bridge, cross lights, 200yds on right*

Brantwood Guest House offers relaxed and friendly guest accommodation where the proprietors create a home-from-home atmosphere. Bedrooms and bathrooms are all well decorated and comfortably furnished. The town centre is just a stroll away and off-road parking is available.

**Rooms:** 5 en suite (2 fmly) (1 GF) **Facilities:** FTV tea/coffee WiFi **Parking:** 5

| CORFE MULLEN | Map 4 SY99 |

## Kenways

★★★ BED AND BREAKFAST

**tel:** 01202 280620 **90a Wareham Road BH21 3LQ**
**email:** eileen@kenways.com **web:** www.kenways.co.uk
**dir:** *2m SW of Wimborne. Off A31 to Corfe Mullen. Over B3074 rdbt, B&B 0.3m on right*

Expect to be welcomed as one of the family at this homely bed and breakfast situated between Wimborne Minster and Poole. The spacious bedrooms are well provisioned with thoughtful extras, and breakfast is served in the pleasant conservatory overlooking attractive gardens.

**Rooms:** 3 rms (3 pri facs) (1 fmly) (2 GF) **Facilities:** FTV DVD TVL tea/coffee WiFi Table tennis Snooker table **Parking:** 4

## CRANBORNE
Map 5 SU01

### Premier Collection

## 10 Castle Street

★★★★★ 🍴 GUEST ACCOMMODATION

**tel:** 01725 551133 **BH21 5PZ**
**email:** enquiries@10castlestreet.com **web:** www.10castlestreet.com
**dir:** *From centre of village, turn into Castle St (B3078), signed Alderholt & Fordingbridge. On right*

Dating back to the 18th century, this fine country mansion is situated in the tranquil village of Cranborne. Although a grand building, 10 Castle Street has a very engaging, unpretentious and genuinely welcoming atmosphere; the team are sincere and helpful. The charming bedrooms are individually designed and the sumptuous beds ensure a good night's sleep; the impressive bathrooms have cosseting towels, robes and excellent toiletries. The comfortable and elegant public rooms have a wonderful array of eclectic artwork, and accomplished cuisine is offered in the inviting restaurant. The delightful gardens are truly superb.

**Rooms:** 9 rms (8 en suite) (1 pri facs) (2 fmly) **S** £145–£350; **D** £145–£350 (room only)* **Facilities:** FTV iPod docking station Lounge tea/coffee Dinner available Direct dial Licensed WiFi 🍴 ⛳ Pool table 🏊 **Extras:** Speciality toiletries **Parking:** 30 **Notes:** LB Closed 25 & 31 Dec

## The Inn at Cranborne

★★★★ 🍴 INN

**tel:** 01725 551249 **5 Wimborne Street BH21 5PP**
**email:** info@theinnatcranborne.co.uk **web:** www.theinnatcranborne.co.uk
**dir:** *On B3078 in centre of village*

A delightful 17th-century inn, lovingly restored and full of special touches, The Inn at Cranborne is located in a peaceful village just a short drive from the New Forest and the Jurassic Coast. Nine comfortable and beautifully appointed en suite rooms are available. Breakfast (a real treat here), lunch and dinner are served in the bar and dining room areas. Off-street parking is available.

**Rooms:** 9 en suite (2 fmly) **Facilities:** FTV DVD iPod docking station Lounge TVL tea/coffee Dinner available WiFi ⛳18 **Extras:** Speciality toiletries, ground coffee, fresh milk **Conf:** Max 10 Thtr 10 Board 10 **Parking:** 25 **Notes:** LB

## DORCHESTER
Map 4 SY69

### Premier Collection

## Little Court

★★★★★ 🍴 GUEST ACCOMMODATION

**tel:** 01305 261576 **5 Westleaze, Charminster DT2 9PZ**
**email:** info@littlecourt.net **web:** www.littlecourt.net
**dir:** *A37 from Dorchester, 0.25m right at Loders Garage, Little Court 0.5m on right*

Built in 1909 in the style of Lutyens, Little Court sits in over four acres of attractive grounds and gardens, complete with tennis courts and swimming pool. The property has been appointed to a very high standard and the friendly proprietors are on hand to ensure a pleasant stay. A delicious breakfast, including home-grown produce, can be enjoyed in the stylish dining room.

**Rooms:** 8 en suite (1 fmly) **Facilities:** FTV Lounge tea/coffee Licensed WiFi 🐾 🍴 ⛳18 **Parking:** 10 **Notes:** LB Closed Xmas & New Year

## Baytree House Dorchester

★★★★ BED AND BREAKFAST

**tel:** 01305 263696 **4 Athelstan Road DT1 1NR**
**email:** info@baytreedorchester.com **web:** www.bandbdorchester.co.uk
**dir:** *0.5m SE of town centre*

Baytree House Dorchester is a friendly, family-run bed and breakfast situated in the heart of the town, not far from the village of Higher Bockham, birthplace of Thomas Hardy. The bedrooms are furnished in an appealing contemporary style and provide high levels of comfort. Breakfast is served farmhouse style in the open-plan kitchen/dining area. Parking is available.

**Rooms:** 6 en suite **Facilities:** FTV iPod docking station tea/coffee **Parking:** 3 **Notes:** LB

## EVERSHOT
Map 4 ST50

## The Acorn Inn

★★★★ 🍴 INN

**tel:** 01935 83228 **28 Fore Street DT2 0JW**
**email:** stay@acorn-inn.co.uk **web:** www.acorn-inn.co.uk
**dir:** *From A37 between Yeovil & Dorchester, follow Evershot & Holywell signs, 0.5m to inn*

This delightful 16th-century coaching inn is located in the heart of the village. Many of the bedrooms feature interesting four-poster beds, and all the rooms have been individually decorated and furnished. The public areas retain many original features including oak panelling, open fires and stone-flagged floors. Fresh local produce is included on the varied menu.

**Rooms:** 10 en suite (2 fmly) **S** £89–£145; **D** £99–£220 (room only)* **Facilities:** STV FTV TVL tea/coffee Dinner available Direct dial WiFi 🏊 Use of spa opposite – charges apply **Extras:** Speciality toiletries, robes, home-made biscuits **Conf:** Max 30 Thtr 30 Board 30 **Parking:** 40 **Notes:** LB

## FARNHAM                                    Map 4 ST91

# Museum Inn

★★★★ ◉◉ ⬦ INN

**tel:** 01725 812702 **DT11 8DE**
**email:** enquiries@museuminn.co.uk **web:** www.museuminn.co.uk
**dir:** *Off A354 between Salisbury & Blandford Forum*

Part of The Epicurean Collection and located in a peaceful Dorset village, this traditional inn offers cosy log fires, flagstone floors and a welcoming bar combined with efficient service and a friendly welcome. Bedrooms include larger, stylish rooms in the main building or a selection of cosy rooms in an adjacent building. Food here, whether dinner or breakfast, uses the finest quality produce and really should not be missed.

**Rooms:** 4 en suite 4 annexe en suite (2 fmly) (4 GF) **Facilities:** FTV Lounge tea/coffee Dinner available Direct dial WiFi ⬦18 Fishing **Extras:** Speciality toiletries **Conf:** Max 30 Thtr 30 Class 24 Board 20 **Parking:** 24 **Notes:** LB

## HIGHCLIFFE

*See Christchurch*

## LYME REGIS                                  Map 4 SY39

*See also Axminster (Devon)*

# St Cuthberts

★★★★ BED AND BREAKFAST

**tel:** 01297 445901 **Charmouth Road DT7 3HG**
**email:** info@stcuthbertsoflyme.co.uk **web:** www.stcuthbertsoflyme.co.uk
**dir:** *A35 from Dorchester, at Charmouth rdbt onto B3052 for 2m. Establishment on opposite side of road to "Welcome to Lyme Regis" sign*

Located just a ten minute walk above the main town and harbour, this detached home is set within mature gardens and has its own parking. Bedrooms and bathrooms offer plenty of quality and comfort, as well as many thoughtful extras. A lounge with a log-burning stove and a decked terrace are available for guests. Breakfast, served around one large table, offers a varied choice including delicious pancakes with bacon and maple syrup.

**Rooms:** 3 en suite (1 GF) **S** £90–£100; **D** £90–£100* **Facilities:** FTV DVD TVL tea/coffee ⬦18 🔒 **Parking:** 3 **Notes:** No children 7yrs

# Kersbrook

★★★★ ⬦ GUEST ACCOMMODATION

**tel:** 01297 442596 **Pound Round DT7 3HX**
**email:** alex@kersbrook.co.uk **web:** www.kersbrook.co.uk

Just a stroll from the town centre and the famous Cobb, this thatched property provides an excellent base for exploring the fascinating delights of Lyme Regis. Dating back to 1790, there is character and charm in abundance, with facilities including a bar and lounge. Breakfast is a treat, the ideal start to a day of exploration. Bedrooms are traditionally styled, allied with modern bathrooms; an appealing combination.

**Rooms:** 14 rms (13 en suite) (1 pri facs) (1 fmly) (4 GF) **Facilities:** FTV Lounge tea/coffee Licensed WiFi ⬦18 Fishing 🔒 **Parking:** 13 **Notes:** LB

# The Mariners

★★★★ INN

**tel:** 01297 442753 **Silver Street DT7 3HS**
**email:** enquiry@hotellymeregis.co.uk **web:** www.hotellymeregis.co.uk
**dir:** *A35 onto B3165 (Lyme Rd). Mariners is pink building opposite road to The Cobb (Pound Rd))*

This delightful building combines traditional character and ambience with a modern and stylish look. Bedrooms and bathrooms vary in size, but include a range of welcome extras; many have views over the bay. Public areas include a relaxing lounge, comfortable bar and modern restaurant. Guests can choose a full dinner, which makes great use of local fish and seafood, or a varied range of lighter options from the bar menu. Outdoor seating is available.

**Rooms:** 14 en suite (2 fmly) **Facilities:** FTV Lounge tea/coffee Dinner available Direct dial WiFi ⬦18 Fishing **Conf:** Max 30 Thtr 24 Class 16 Board 30 **Parking:** 20 **Notes:** LB

## MILTON ABBAS                                Map 4 ST80

# Hambro Arms

★★★★ INN

**tel:** 01258 880233 **DT11 0BP**
**email:** info@hambroarms.com **web:** www.hambroarms.com
**dir:** *From A354 follow signs for Milton Abbas, in village*

The village of Milton Abbas is something very special. Much admired and featured on many a postcard, it is situated in the heart of Dorset. Identical thatched cottages that once housed the local estate workers line either side of the gently winding road. The Hambro Arms occupies one such thatched building, and is a charming and quintessential village hostelry. Step inside for a genuine welcome and enjoy the refurbished bars, restaurant and lounge, all retaining their original character. Food demonstrates a genuine commitment to quality, local produce; likewise the tasty and substantial breakfast. Impressive bedrooms provide all the expected comforts combined with historic charm.

**Rooms:** 4 en suite (1 fmly) **Facilities:** FTV Lounge tea/coffee Dinner available WiFi 🔒 **Parking:** 15

## MOTCOMBE                                    Map 4 ST82

# The Coppleridge Inn

★★★ ⬦ INN

**tel:** 01747 851980 **SP7 9HW**
**email:** thecoppleridgeinn@btinternet.com **web:** www.coppleridge.com
**dir:** *Exit A350 to Motcombe, under railway bridge, 400yds, right to Mere, inn 300yds on left*

This village inn set in 15 acres offers 10 en suite bedrooms located in a pretty courtyard. All bedrooms have been appointed to a high standard and provide a very comfortable stay. Staff offer a warm welcome, and the inn serves good food with many daily specials. There are tennis courts and boules, plus a children's play area. Clay pigeon shooting can also be arranged.

**Rooms:** 10 en suite (2 fmly) (10 GF) **S** £65; **D** £100* **Facilities:** FTV DVD TVL tea/coffee Dinner available Direct dial WiFi ⬦ 🔒 Boules pitch **Extras:** Mini-bar **Conf:** Max 60 Thtr 60 Class 60 Board 30 **Parking:** 100 **Notes:** LB Civ wed 120

## PLUSH
Map 4 ST70

# The Brace of Pheasants

★★★★ 🍴 INN

**tel:** 01300 348357 **DT2 7RQ**
**email:** info@braceofpheasants.co.uk **web:** www.braceofpheasants.co.uk
**dir:** A35 onto B3142, right to Plush 1.5m

Situated in the heart of Dorset, The Brace of Pheasants is a picturesque thatched pub that offers a warm and genuine welcome to both visitors and locals alike. Very much a traditional inn, its atmosphere is convivial, with plenty of good-natured conversation. Bedrooms are split between the main building and the former skittle alley – all offer exceptional standards of comfort and individual style, with wonderful bathrooms. The food here should not be missed, with excellent local produce used to create an appealing menu.

**Rooms:** 4 en suite 4 annexe en suite (4 GF) **Facilities:** FTV tea/coffee Dinner available Direct dial WiFi **Conf:** Max 14 Board 14 **Parking:** 15 **Notes:** Closed 25 Dec Civ wed 130

## POOLE
Map 4 SZ09

# Acorns Guest House

★★★★ GUEST ACCOMMODATION

**tel:** 01202 672901 **264 Wimborne Road, Oakdale BH15 3EF**
**email:** enquiries@acornsguesthouse.co.uk **web:** www.acornsguesthouse.co.uk
**dir:** On A35, approx 1m from town centre, opposite Esso station

A warm welcome is assured at Acorns Guest House, located with easy access to the town, ferry terminal, business parks and attractions. The bedrooms are furnished to a high standard, and an English breakfast is served in the charming dining room. There is also a quiet cosy lounge.

**Rooms:** 4 en suite (1 GF) **D** £70–£80 **Facilities:** FTV DVD Lounge tea/coffee WiFi **Parking:** 6 **Notes:** LB No children 14yrs Closed 23 Dec–1 Jan

# Seacourt

★★★ GUEST ACCOMMODATION

**tel:** 01202 674995 **249 Blandford Road, Hamworthy BH15 4AZ**
**email:** seacourtguesthouse@hotmail.co.uk
**dir:** Off A3049/A35 signed to Hamworthy

Within a short distance of the ferry port and town centre, this friendly establishment is well maintained and efficiently run. The comfortable bedrooms, some located on the ground floor, are all nicely decorated and equipped with useful extra facilities. Breakfast is served in the pleasant dining room at separate tables.

**Rooms:** 5 en suite (1 fmly) (3 GF) **S** £50; **D** £65* **Facilities:** FTV DVD tea/coffee WiFi **Extras:** Use of microwave & fridge **Parking:** 5 **Notes:** No children 5yrs

## PORTESHAM
Map 4 SY68

# Kings Arms

★★★★ INN

**tel:** 01305 871342 **2 Front Street DT3 4ET**
**email:** info@kingsarmsportesham.co.uk **web:** www.kingsarmsportesham.co.uk
**dir:** On B3157 coastal road

Situated on the coast road, approximately half way between Weymouth and Dorchester, this long-established and popular village local is a great base from which to explore the area. The atmosphere is warm and welcoming with

good-natured banter at the bar. Local produce features on the menu with a range of dishes for all tastes. Bedrooms are located to the side of the pub, all with level access and a private entrance.

**Rooms:** 3 en suite (1 fmly) (3 GF) **Facilities:** tea/coffee Dinner available WiFi **Extras:** Speciality toiletries **Parking:** 20

## PORTLAND
Map 4 SY67

# Queen Anne House

★★★★ GUEST ACCOMMODATION

**tel:** 01305 820028 **2/4 Fortuneswell DT5 1LP**
**email:** margaretdunlop@tiscali.co.uk **web:** www.queenannehouse.com
**dir:** A354 to Portland then Fortuneswell. House on left 200mtrs past Royal Portland Arms

This delightful, Grade II listed building is a charming and comfortable place to stay; particularly delightful are the Italianate gardens to the rear. Ideal for business and leisure travellers, Queen Anne House is close to Portland Bill, Weymouth and Chesil Beach. The bedrooms are particularly attractive and pleasantly furnished. Breakfast, taken at one large table, offers a wide range of options.

**Rooms:** 3 en suite **Facilities:** FTV TVL tea/coffee WiFi 🔒 **Parking:** 4

# Portland Lodge

★★★ GUEST ACCOMMODATION

**tel:** 01305 820265 **Easton Lane DT5 1BW**
**email:** info@portlandlodge.com **web:** www.portlandlodge.com
**dir:** Signs to Easton/Portland Bill, rdbt at Portland Heights Hotel 1st right. Portland Lodge 200yds

Situated on the fascinating island of Portland, this modern, lodge-style establishment provides comfortable accommodation including a number of ground-floor bedrooms. Breakfast is served in the spacious dining room with a friendly team of staff on hand. This is an ideal location for those wishing to explore the World Heritage coastline.

**Rooms:** 30 annexe en suite (15 fmly) (7 GF) **S** £35–£50; **D** £45–£80 (room only)* **Facilities:** FTV tea/coffee WiFi **Parking:** 30 **Notes:** LB

## PUNCKNOWLE
Map 4 SY58

# Offley Bed & Breakfast

★★★★ GUEST ACCOMMODATION

**tel:** 01308 897044 & 07792 624977 **Looke Lane DT2 9BD**
**web:** www.offleybedandbreakfast.info
**dir:** Off B3157 into village centre, left after Crown Inn into Looke Ln, 2nd house on right

With magnificent views over the Bride Valley, this village house provides comfortable, quality accommodation. Guests are assured of a warm, friendly welcome, and this is an ideal base from which to enjoy the numerous local attractions. There are several local inns, one in the village which is just a gentle stroll away.

**Rooms:** 3 rms (2 en suite) (1 pri facs) **S** fr £45; **D** fr £70* **Facilities:** FTV TVL tea/coffee 🔒 **Extras:** Fruit, flowers – complimentary **Parking:** 4 **Notes:** LB Closed 1 week Xmas

## La Fleur de Lys Restaurant with Rooms

★★★★ ⚛⚛ RESTAURANT WITH ROOMS

**tel:** 01747 853717 **Bleke Street SP7 8AW**
**email:** info@lafleurdelys.co.uk **web:** www.lafleurdelys.co.uk
**dir:** *From junct of A30 & A350, 0.25m towards town centre*

Located just a few minutes' walk from the famous Gold Hill, this light and airy restaurant with rooms combines efficient service with a relaxed and friendly atmosphere. Bedrooms, which are suitable for both business and leisure guests, vary in size but all are well equipped, comfortable and tastefully furnished. A relaxing guest lounge and courtyard are available for afternoon tea or pre-dinner drinks. The excellent food has been awarded two AA Rosettes.

**Rooms:** 8 en suite (2 fmly) (1 GF) **S** £85–£120; **D** £100–£170* **Facilities:** FTV Lounge tea/coffee Dinner available Direct dial WiFi ⚓ **Extras:** Home-made biscuits, fresh milk – complimentary **Conf:** Max 12 Board 10 **Parking:** 10 **Notes:** LB RS 1–21 Jan restaurant closed

## The Fontmell

★★★★ ⚬ INN

**tel:** 01747 811441 **Crown Hill, Fontmell Magna SP7 0PA**
**email:** info@thefontmell.com **web:** www.thefontmell.com

This warm and welcoming pub was formerly known as The Crown, but was re-named following extensive refurbishment in 2010. The result is a stylish and comfortable environment, complete with a stream flowing between the bar and the dining room. Relaxation is guaranteed; a great place to linger over a pint at the bar, or curl up on the sofa and peruse the newspapers. Bedrooms offer impressive quality and comfort, and each has its own unique identity. The kitchen presents a range of flavour-packed dishes, based on the best of local, seasonal produce.

**Rooms:** 6 rms (6 pri facs) (1 fmly) **Facilities:** FTV DVD TVL tea/coffee Dinner available Direct dial WiFi ⚓18 Fishing ⚓ **Extras:** Bottled water **Parking:** 30

*See also Corton Denham (Somerset)*

### Premier Collection

## Munden House

★★★★★ ⚬ GUEST ACCOMMODATION

**tel:** 01963 23150 **Munden Lane, Alweston DT9 5HU**
**email:** stay@mundenhouse.co.uk **web:** www.mundenhouse.co.uk
**dir:** *A352 from Sherborne, left onto A3030 to Alweston, at Oxfords Bakery sign, turn left into Mundens Ln. Munden House 100yds on right*

Munden House is a delightful property set in a quiet lane away from the main road, with pleasant views over the surrounding countryside. Bedrooms and bathrooms come in a variety of shapes and styles but all are very well decorated and furnished; the beds are especially comfortable. Guests are welcome to use the lounge and garden. Breakfast includes a selection of high quality hot and cold dishes, all carefully prepared to order.

**Rooms:** 5 en suite 3 annexe en suite (2 fmly) (4 GF) **Facilities:** FTV Lounge tea/coffee Licensed WiFi ⚓ ⚓ **Extras:** Speciality toiletries, mineral water – complimentary **Parking:** 11 **Notes:** LB

### Premier Collection

## The Kings Arms

★★★★★ ⚛ INN

**tel:** 01963 220281 **Charlton Horethorne DT9 4NL**
**email:** admin@thekingsarms.co.uk **web:** www.thekingsarms.co.uk
**dir:** *From A303 follow signs for Templecombe & Sherborne onto B3145 to Charlton Horethorne*

Situated in the heart of this engaging village, The Kings Arms offers impressive standards throughout. The experienced owners have created something for everyone with a convivial bar, snug and choice of dining environments, including the garden terrace with lovely countryside views. Bedrooms have individuality, quality and style with marble bathrooms, robes and wonderful showers. Food is taken seriously here, with an assured team producing a menu showcasing the best of local produce.

*The Kings Arms*

**Rooms:** 10 en suite (1 fmly) **D** £100–£145* **Facilities:** FTV DVD Lounge tea/coffee Dinner available Direct dial Lift WiFi ⛱ ⛳18 **Parking:** 30 **Notes:** Closed 25 Dec RS 26 Dec no dinner served

## The Rose and Crown Inn, Trent

★★★★★ ◎◎ INN

**tel:** 01935 850776 **Trent DT9 4SL**
**email:** info@theroseandcrowntrent.co.uk **web:** www.theroseandcrowntrent.co.uk
**dir:** *Just off A30 between Sherborne & Yeovil*

The Rose and Crown dates from the 14th century and is a quintessential country inn with a long and interesting history. Packed full of character, this is a place where relaxation comes easily, with crackling fires adding to the atmosphere and charm. Bedrooms are accessed externally, and each has high levels of comfort and quality, with stylish bathrooms and cosseting extras. They also have patio areas with lovely views across the rolling countryside. Food is taken seriously here and creative and flavoursome dishes are offered.

**Rooms:** 3 annexe en suite (3 GF) **S** £65–£95; **D** £75–£110 **Facilities:** FTV DVD iPod docking station Lounge tea/coffee Dinner available WiFi ⛱ **Extras:** Speciality toiletries, home-made cookies **Parking:** 30

## The Alders

★★★★ BED AND BREAKFAST

**tel:** 01963 220666 **Sandford Orcas DT9 4SB**
**email:** info@thealdersbb.com **web:** www.thealdersbb.com
**dir:** *3m N of Sherborne. Off B3148 signed Sandford Orcas, near Manor House in village*

Located in the charming conservation area of Sandford Orcas and set in a lovely walled garden, this delightful property offers attractive, well-equipped bedrooms. Guests have their own entrance leading from the garden. A large inglenook fireplace with a wood-burning stove can be found in the comfortable sitting room, which also features the owner's watercolours. Massage therapies are available.

**Rooms:** 3 en suite (1 fmly) **S** £60–£75; **D** £75–£90 **Facilities:** FTV TVL tea/coffee WiFi ⛱ **Parking:** 4

**SWANAGE** Map 5 SZ07

## Swanage Haven

★★★★★ 🍷 ☕ GUEST HOUSE

**tel:** 01929 423088 **3 Victoria Road BH19 1LY**
**email:** info@swanagehaven.com **web:** www.swanagehaven.com

Swanage Haven is a boutique-style guest house close to Swanage beach and the coastal path. Exclusively for adults, the accommodation is contemporary, with many extras such as fluffy robes, slippers, hot tub and WiFi. The hands-on owners provide excellent hospitality with a relaxed and friendly service. The breakfasts are superb – top quality organic and local produce are featured on the extensive menu.

**Rooms:** 8 en suite **Facilities:** FTV iPod docking station TVL tea/coffee Dinner available Licensed WiFi ⛱ Hot tub **Extras:** Honesty bar **Parking:** 7 **Notes:** LB No children 18yrs Closed Nov–weekend nearest to 14 Feb

SWANAGE *continued*

### Premier Collection

## 2@2 Rabling Road

★★★★★ BED AND BREAKFAST

**tel:** 01929 423983 & 07803 182530 **2 Rabling Road BH19 1EE**
**email:** vetbennett.bjb@gmail.com
**web:** www.visit-dorset.com/accommodation/2-rabling-road-bed-and-breakfast-p2073433
**dir:** *A351 into Swanage (Victoria Ave), left into Northbrook Rd. 1st right into Rabling Rd, house on left*

This proud 1930s house is situated just a short stroll from the beach and a level walk to the town centre, thus making a perfect base for exploring the many charms of Swanage. There is an engaging fusion of period features and contemporary styling, all of which contributes to a rewarding and relaxing environment to stay. A warm welcome is assured with helpful advice on the locale always on offer if required. Bedrooms provide impressive levels of comfort with spacious bathrooms, both complete with bath, separate shower and cosseting bathrobes. Breakfast provides a tasty start to the day, served within the elegant dining room, after which, perhaps a few minutes relaxing in the attractive garden may be in order, or a stroll along the shoreline.

**Rooms:** 2 rms (1 en suite) (1 pri facs) **Facilities:** FTV DVD iPod docking station tea/coffee Dinner available WiFi **Extras:** Home-made snacks, bottled water **Parking:** 2 **Notes:** No children 1yr Closed 30 Oct–Mar

## Caythorpe House

★★★★ GUEST ACCOMMODATION

**tel:** 01929 422892 **7 Rempstone Road BH19 1DN**
**email:** enquiries@caythorpehouse.co.uk **web:** www.caythorpehouse.co.uk
**dir:** *A351 to Swanage. Right at lights opposite church, Caythorpe House at junct*

Conveniently located just a short stroll from the seafront and town centre, this elegant Edwardian villa is a perfect place from which to enjoy the many delights Swanage has to offer. A warm and genuine welcome is assured, with every effort made to ensure a relaxing and rewarding break whether for business or pleasure. Bedrooms are light and airy with all the expected comforts, and a variety of configurations to suit all needs. Breakfast is a satisfying start, and helpful advice for the day ahead is always on offer. A guest lounge is also provided and there is ample off-road parking.

**Rooms:** 7 rms (5 en suite) (2 fmly) (2 GF) **S** £44–£56; **D** £80–£92* **Facilities:** FTV DVD iPod docking station TVL tea/coffee WiFi **Parking:** 6 **Notes:** No children 10yrs Closed 17 Oct–1 Apr

## The Limes

★★★★ GUEST HOUSE

**tel:** 01929 422664 **48 Park Road BH19 2AE**
**email:** info@limeshotel.net **web:** www.limeshotel.net
**dir:** *Follow one-way system, signed to Durlston Country Park. Pass Trattoria restaurant on left, right into Park Rd, 200mtrs on right*

Ideally located for both the town centre and the seafront, this comfortable establishment offers a variety of different bedroom shapes and sizes. In addition to the pleasant dining room, guests are free to use a small bar area and a popular games room.

**Rooms:** 12 rms (10 en suite) (7 fmly) **Facilities:** FTV DVD Lounge tea/coffee Licensed WiFi Pool table **Conf:** Max 25 Thtr 25 Class 20 Board 16 **Parking:** 8 **Notes:** LB

| TARRANT MONKTON | Map 4 ST90 |
|---|---|

## The Langton Arms

★★★★ INN

**tel:** 01258 830225 **DT11 8RX**
**email:** info@thelangtonarms.co.uk **web:** www.thelangtonarms.co.uk
**dir:** *Exit A354 in Tarrant Hinton to Tarrant Monkton, through ford, Langton Arms opposite*

Tucked away in a sleepy Dorset village, The Langton Arms offers stylish, light and airy accommodation and is a good base for touring this attractive area. Bedrooms, all at ground-floor level in the modern annexe, are very well equipped and comfortable. Diners can choose between the relaxed bar-restaurant and the more formal Stables Restaurant, which offers innovative and appetising dishes. Breakfast is served in the conservatory dining room just a few steps across the pretty courtyard.

**Rooms:** 6 annexe en suite (6 fmly) (6 GF) **S** fr £90; **D** fr £100* **Facilities:** FTV tea/coffee Dinner available Direct dial WiFi **Conf:** Max 70 Thtr 70 Class 70 Board 70 **Parking:** 100 **Notes:** Closed 25–26 Dec Civ wed 60

| WAREHAM | Map 4 SY98 |
|---|---|

## Kingston Country Courtyard

★★★★ GUEST ACCOMMODATION

**tel:** 01929 481066 **Kingston, Nr Corfe Castle BH20 5LR**
**email:** relax@kingstoncountrycourtyard.com **web:** www.kingstoncountrycourtyard.com
**dir:** *Through Corfe Castle towards Swanage (A351), turn right onto B3069. Through village, up steep hill, sharp left hand bend, Kingston Country Courtyard 0.25m on left*

Situated amid the beautiful Purbeck Hills, the views from this house include historic Corfe Castle and the distant shores of the Isle of Wight. A variety of comfortable guest bedrooms is on offer and breakfast is served in the spacious dining hall.

**Rooms:** 25 en suite (3 fmly) (21 GF) **Facilities:** FTV Lounge tea/coffee Licensed WiFi **Conf:** Max 100 Thtr 100 Class 100 Board 50 **Parking:** 100 **Notes:** LB Closed 24 Dec–3 Jan RS wknds may be closed due to weddings Civ wed 130

## Worgret Manor

★★★★ GUEST ACCOMMODATION

**tel:** 01929 552957 **Worgret Road BH20 6AB**
**email:** admin@worgretmanor.co.uk **web:** www.worgretmanor.co.uk
**dir:** *A351 to Wareham. Take A352 signed Dorchester. 0.5m to manor on left*

Worgret Manor is a grand Georgian manor house perfectly situated for exploration of this beautiful area with the Saxon market town of Wareham just a mile away. Comfortable bedrooms provide good levels of space with period features adding to the character and charm. Breakfast provides a satisfying start to the day and friendly and helpful service is always on offer.

**Rooms:** 3 en suite (1 GF) **Facilities:** FTV tea/coffee Licensed WiFi 🔒 **Parking:** 8 **Notes:** No children 16yrs

## WEST LULWORTH
Map 4 SY88

### Bishops

★★★★ 🛏 GUEST ACCOMMODATION

**tel:** 01929 400552 & 07956 102371 **Lulworth Cove BH20 5RQ**
**email:** bishopscottagelulworth@gmail.com **web:** www.bishopscottage.co.uk

Bishops is located 100 metres from beautiful Lulworth Cove, and offers high quality en suite bedrooms, a bar that opens daily, and a restaurant offering fish and vegetarian dishes. During spring and summer guests can enjoy afternoon tea outside. Breakfast is served in the contemporary dining room, with dishes based on locally sourced ingredients. Additional facilities include an outdoor pool with seating area offering stunning views of the cove.

**Rooms:** 6 en suite 2 annexe en suite (2 fmly) **Facilities:** STV FTV TVL tea/coffee Dinner available Licensed WiFi 🏸 🔒 **Extras:** Robes, snacks **Notes:** Civ wed 150

## WEYMOUTH
Map 4 SY67

*See also Portland*

### Swallows Rest

★★★★ 🛏 BED AND BREAKFAST

**tel:** 01305 785244 & 07747 753656 **Martleaves Farm, South Road DT4 9NR**
**email:** jane.furlong@btinternet.com **web:** www.swallowsrestselfcatering.co.uk
**dir:** *From Weymouth on Portland road, follow brown tourism signs*

This beautiful rural B&B with coastal views has highly individual bedrooms. Each is richly decorated and well equipped; ideal for any type of break. Public areas include a comfortable lounge and the dining area, which is a sociable setting for breakfast. Parking is available, and there is also a campsite, and some self-catering apartments. The owners have their own pigs, chickens, ducks and alpacas, and the grounds are full of character.

**Rooms:** 5 en suite (1 fmly) **S** £60–£70; **D** £90–£120* **Facilities:** FTV TVL tea/coffee WiFi 🔒 **Extras:** Speciality toiletries, home-made cakes, chocolates **Parking:** 16 **Notes:** LB No children 5yrs Closed 24–26 Dec Civ wed 30

### The Esplanade

★★★★ 🍴 GUEST ACCOMMODATION

**tel:** 01305 783129 & 07515 657116 **141 The Esplanade DT4 7NJ**
**email:** stay@theesplanadehotel.co.uk **web:** www.theesplanadehotel.co.uk
**dir:** *On seafront, between Jubilee Clock & pier bandstand*

Dating from 1835, this attractive property is located on the seafront and offers wonderful views from the elegant dining room and stylish first-floor lounge. There's a genuine enthusiasm here, with a warm welcome assured. The comfortable bedrooms are thoughtfully equipped, including Egyptian cotton sheets and towels, and many rooms have sea views. Breakfast is a showcase of local produce with an extensive menu.

**Rooms:** 11 en suite (3 fmly) (2 GF) **Facilities:** FTV TVL tea/coffee Licensed WiFi **Parking:** 9 **Notes:** LB Closed Nov–Feb

### Barnes's Rest Weymouth

★★★★ BED AND BREAKFAST

**tel:** 01305 779354 & 07582 707749 **165 Dorchester Road DT4 7LE**
**email:** barnessrest@hotmail.co.uk **web:** www.bandbbarnessrestweymouth.co.uk
**dir:** *A354 into Weymouth. At Manor rdbt 1st exit onto B3159 (Dorchester Rd), on right just past doctors surgery*

This Victorian family home is ideally located for those visiting Weymouth for either business or pleasure. The welcome is warm and inviting, with every effort made to ensure a relaxing and rewarding stay. The handy location is just a 10 minute stroll from the seafront. Bedrooms and bathrooms are light and airy with modern facilities and all the required necessities. Breakfast is served around the dining table with an ample choice for all appetites. Safe storage facilities are available for bikes and outdoor gear.

**Rooms:** 3 en suite **Facilities:** FTV tea/coffee WiFi 🔒 **Parking:** 2 **Notes:** LB

### Florian Guest House

★★★★ GUEST HOUSE

**tel:** 01305 773836 & 07460 442166 **59 Abbotsbury Road DT4 0AQ**
**email:** enquiryflorian@aol.com **web:** www.florianguesthouse.co.uk
**dir:** *At junct of A354 & A353 into Abbotsbury Rd. 500yds on left after St Pauls Church*

Situated about 10 minutes' walk from the town centre, beach and local attractions, this welcoming property offers bedrooms in a range of shapes and sizes, and is ideally situated for a family seaside holiday or a short break. Breakfast is taken in the comfortably furnished downstairs dining area.

**Rooms:** 6 rms (5 en suite) (1 pri facs) (1 fmly) (1 GF) **Facilities:** FTV DVD tea/coffee WiFi 🔒 **Extras:** Fridge **Parking:** 5 **Notes:** LB

WEYMOUTH *continued*

## Kingswood

★★★★ GUEST ACCOMMODATION

tel: 01305 784926 & 07899 770920 **55 Rodwell Road DT4 8QY**
email: info@kingswoodhotel.com web: www.kingswoodhotel.com
dir: *On A354 up hill towards Portland from inner harbour, on left after lights*

Handily located for both Weymouth and Portland, this welcoming establishment provides spacious guest accommodation, including larger suites with jacuzzi baths. The building has a long and interesting history, including a period when it was commandeered for American officers during World War II. The bedrooms are well appointed and comfortable, as are the public areas. Breakfast is served in the attractive dining room. Just a stroll away is Brewers Quay, a lovely area in which to while away an hour or two.

**Rooms:** 10 rms (9 en suite) (1 pri facs) (2 GF) **Facilities:** FTV Lounge tea/coffee WiFi **Extras:** Fridges in most rooms **Parking:** 20 **Notes:** LB No children Closed Nov–Feb

## St John's Guest House

★★★★ GUEST ACCOMMODATION

tel: 01305 775523 **7 Dorchester Road DT4 7JR**
email: stjohnsguesthouse@googlemail.com web: www.stjohnsguesthouse.co.uk
dir: *Opposite St John's Church*

Located just 70 yards from the beach, St John's is an elegant building from around 1880. Hospitality here is warm and genuine, and the property has an appealing, uncluttered style. Standards are high throughout. Bedrooms have comfy beds and are all well equipped with such extras as DVD players and WiFi access. Breakfast is served in the light and airy dining room, a satisfying and tasty start to the day.

**Rooms:** 7 en suite (2 fmly) (2 GF) **Facilities:** FTV DVD tea/coffee WiFi **Parking:** 10 **Notes:** LB No children 4yrs

## Wadham Guesthouse

★★★ GUEST HOUSE

tel: 01305 779640 & 07375 914381 **22 East Street DT4 8BN**
email: shirleystephenson@btconnect.com web: www.wadhamhouse.co.uk
dir: *Off S end of A353 The Esplanade*

This pleasant town centre property offers a range of rooms, and is a good base for touring or for a short stay. The comfortable bedrooms are attractively decorated, and home-cooked breakfasts are served in the ground-floor dining room. Parking permits are available.

**Rooms:** 9 en suite (1 GF) **S** £40–£48; **D** £76–£86* **Facilities:** FTV tea/coffee WiFi **Notes:** No children 8yrs Closed Xmas & New Year, Jan, Feb RS Mar Limited rooms available

## Beaufort Guesthouse

★★★ GUEST HOUSE

tel: 01305 782088 **24 The Esplanade DT4 8DN**
web: www.beaufortguesthouse.co.uk

Just a few steps from the sandy beach, this friendly, family-run establishment is ideally located for a seaside break. Bedrooms are soundly appointed with all the necessary essentials, likewise the modern showers. Some of the rooms have the added bonus of sea views. Breakfast is served in the lounge diner, which also has a bar to refresh and revive guests after a hard day enjoying the many and varied local attractions.

**Rooms:** 6 rms (5 en suite) (1 pri facs) (2 fmly) **S** £30–£35; **D** £60–£70 **Facilities:** FTV tea/coffee Licensed WiFi **Notes:** LB No children 6mths Closed 23 Dec–1 Jan

## The Cavendale

★★★ BED AND BREAKFAST

tel: 01305 786960 **10 The Esplanade DT4 8EB**
email: thecavendale@gmail.com web: weymouth.co.uk
dir: *Phone for directions*

Conveniently located right on the seafront with splendid views from some of the rooms, this cosy bed and breakfast offers a range of bedroom sizes, some with private bathrooms. Guests are welcome to use the lounge, where in addition to a large range of videos, they can join in with the current on-the-go jigsaw. Helpfully, parking permits for nearby car parks are available.

**Rooms:** 9 rms (6 en suite) (3 pri facs) (5 fmly) **S** £32–£36; **D** £70–£78* **Facilities:** FTV DVD TVL tea/coffee WiFi **Extras:** Fridges in en suite rooms **Notes:** LB No children 5yrs Closed 24 Dec–2 Jan

## The Edenhurst

★★★ GUEST HOUSE

tel: 01305 771255 **122 The Esplanade DT4 7ER**
email: enquiries@edenhurstweymouth.com web: www.edenhurstweymouth.com
dir: *Phone for directions*

Just a step across the road from the beach and within walking distance of the railway and bus stations, this smartly presented establishment is a perfect base from which to explore the local area. A number of bedroom styles are offered, some having balconies and wonderful sea views; all have modern bathrooms. Breakfast is served in the elegant, sea-facing dining room, and a guest lounge is also provided.

**Rooms:** 12 rms (11 en suite) (1 pri facs) (4 fmly) **S** £39–£55; **D** £78–£125* **Facilities:** FTV TVL tea/coffee WiFi **Extras:** Bottled water – complimentary **Notes:** LB

**WIMBORNE MINSTER**          **Map 5 SZ09**

### Premier Collection

## Les Bouviers Restaurant with Rooms

★★★★★ ⚛⚛ RESTAURANT WITH ROOMS

tel: 01202 889555 **Arrowsmith Road, Canford Magna BH21 3BD**
email: info@lesbouviers.co.uk web: www.lesbouviers.co.uk
dir: *A31 onto A349. Left in 0.6m. In approx 1m right into Arrowsmith Rd. Establishment approx 100yds on right*

Les Bouviers is an excellent restaurant with rooms in a great location, set in five and a half acres of grounds. Food is obviously a highlight of any stay here, as is the friendly, attentive service. Chef-patron Leonard James Coward's team turn out impressive cooking, which has been recognised with two AA Rosettes. The bedrooms are extremely well equipped and the beds are supremely comfortable. Cream teas can be taken on the terrace.

**Rooms:** 6 en suite (4 fmly) **S** £70–£150; **D** £80–£220* **Facilities:** FTV DVD Lounge tea/coffee Dinner available Direct dial WiFi All bathrooms have steam showers or air baths **Extras:** Robes, slippers, mineral water **Conf:** Max 120 Thtr 100 Class 100 Board 100 **Parking:** 50 **Notes:** LB RS Sun eve restricted opening & restaurant closed Civ wed 120

## COUNTY DURHAM

### BARNARD CASTLE
Map 19 NZ01

## Three Horseshoes

★★★★ INN

**tel:** 01833 631777 **5-7 Galgate DL12 8EQ**
**email:** info@three-horse-shoes.co.uk **web:** www.three-horse-shoes.co.uk

Three Horseshoes is a family-owned and -run inn. It is modern with very good design throughout the refurbished bedrooms, en suite bathrooms, and public areas. Real ales and home-cooked food are a feature, with an ever-changing menu and competitively priced wine list. Private parking and sun terrace add to the features of this beautifully restored inn.

**Rooms:** 7 en suite 4 annexe en suite (1 fmly) (2 GF) **S** £70–£115; **D** £80–£125*
**Facilities:** FTV DVD tea/coffee Dinner available WiFi ꩜ **Parking:** 12

## Strathmore Lawn East

★★★★ GUEST ACCOMMODATION

**tel:** 01833 637061 & 07790 006920 **81 Galgate DL12 8ES**
**email:** strathmorelawn@gmail.com **web:** www.strathmorelawneast.co.uk
**dir:** From A66 to Barnard Castle, through town centre into Galgate.
On right opposite chemist

Located just five minutes' walk from the main high street, pubs and restaurants, Strathmore Lawn East is a great base for visiting the Yorkshire Dales. Expect a warm and friendly welcome at this Victorian town house, where bedrooms are comfortable, pleasantly furnished and well equipped. Memorable breakfasts with local produce, home-made bread and preserves are served in the pleasant dining room with guests seated at one table. Special dietary requirements and individual preferences are catered for.

**Rooms:** 3 rms (2 en suite) (1 pri facs) 1 annexe en suite **D** £80* **Facilities:** FTV Lounge tea/coffee WiFi ♪18 ꩜ **Extras:** Bottled water, speciality toiletries – complimentary **Notes:** LB No children 2yrs Closed 22 Dec–4 Jan

### CHESTER-LE-STREET
Map 19 NZ25

## The Lambton Worm

★★★★ INN

**tel:** 0191 387 1162 **North Road DH3 4AJ**
**email:** info@thelambton.com **web:** www.thelambton.com
**dir:** A1(M) junct 63 onto A167, 0.7m on left

Named after a local legend that inspired Bram Stoker's 1911 novel, *The Lair of the White Worm*, this boutique inn offers comfortable and well-appointed bedrooms. Real ales come from the local parent company, Sonnet 43 Brew House, while the award-winning food is locally sourced and of a very good standard. The team are friendly and helpful making this property a real little gem.

**Rooms:** 14 en suite (2 fmly) **Facilities:** FTV iPod docking station Lounge tea/coffee Dinner available WiFi ♪18 ꩜ **Parking:** 24 **Notes:** LB

### CROOK
Map 19 NZ13

## The Quarry Burn Guest House and Restaurant

★★★★ GUEST HOUSE

**tel:** 01388 608336 & 07967 826413 **1 Helmington Square, Hunwick DL15 0LH**
**email:** jbell27@sky.com **web:** www.thequarryburn.co.uk

The Quarry Burn Guest House and Restaurant is ideally located in the quiet village of Hunwick, within easy striking distance of Durham city centre and the A1. A family run business, it's a well-established restaurant which has added four contemporary bedrooms. Quality decor, flooring and comfortable beds, with smart TVs and WiFi feature throughout. The lively restaurant serves popular, freshly prepared dishes, and the service is warm and genuine. The secluded beer garden is a real sun trap and a perfect place to sit and have a drink in fine weather.

**Rooms:** 4 en suite (2 fmly) **Facilities:** FTV TVL tea/coffee Dinner available Licensed WiFi **Notes:** RS Mon Pub closed, accommodation available

### DURHAM
Map 19 NZ24

## The Old Mill

★★★★ INN

**tel:** 01740 652928 **Thinford Road, Metal Bridge DH6 5NX**
**email:** office@oldmilldurham.co.uk **web:** www.oldmilldurham.co.uk
**dir:** 5m S of Durham. A1(M) junct 61, A688 S for 1.5m, left at rdbt, sharp right

This traditional, family-owned inn is in a countryside setting yet is only a mile from the A1. There is a friendly atmosphere and the bar and dining areas are full of character. Food is served throughout the day and evening, with the vast menu displayed on blackboards. Bedrooms are spacious and well equipped. Complimentary WiFi is provided.

**Rooms:** 12 en suite **S** £65–£85; **D** £75–£95* **Facilities:** STV FTV DVD tea/coffee Dinner available Direct dial WiFi ꩜ **Conf:** Max 40 Thtr 40 Class 40 Board 25 **Parking:** 40 **Notes:** Closed 26 Dec RS 25 Dec bookings only

## The Kingslodge Inn

★★★ INN

**tel:** 0191 370 9977 **Waddington Street, Flass Vale DH1 4BG**
**email:** enquiries@kingslodgeinn.co.uk **web:** www.kingslodgeinn.co.uk

The Kingslodge Inn enjoys a wonderful location, just minutes away from the city centre but surrounded by woodland offering a peaceful location. The Kingslodge Inn has undergone a massive refurbishment programme with very good results achieved. Modern bedrooms are well appointed offering quality and comfort. The inn offers a wide array of beverages with real ales always on tap. The menu, as with the other properties within The Inn Collection, is very appealing and offers a wide choice and styles of food. Service and hospitality are both warm and genuine. Outdoor seating around the property within the gardens is an added benefit as is the off-road parking.

**Rooms:** 23 en suite (3 fmly) (2 GF) **Facilities:** FTV tea/coffee Dinner available WiFi **Parking:** 25

## HESLEDEN
Map 19 NZ43

### The Ship Inn
★★★★ ⊜ INN

**tel:** 01429 836453 & 07760 767448 **High Hesleden TS27 4QD**
**email:** sheila@theshipinn.net **web:** www.theshipinn.net
**dir:** A19 onto B1281 signed Blackhall. Follow Hesleden signs to High Hesleden

The Ship Inn has some wonderful sea views from its well-appointed and comfortable bedrooms. The bar is cosy and welcoming and has an impressive selection of well-kept real ales. Dinner is served in the spacious, comfortable restaurant and log fires burn brightly on cooler evenings. Sympathetically restored over a number of years, many of the original features of this fine old property are still in place. Free WiFi and secure parking is provided.

**Rooms:** 6 en suite 3 annexe en suite (3 fmly) (6 GF) **Facilities:** STV FTV DVD tea/coffee Dinner available WiFi 🔒 **Extras:** Fruit – complimentary **Conf:** Max 45 Thtr 45 Class 25 Board 25 **Parking:** 25 **Notes:** RS Mon

## LANCHESTER
Map 19 NZ14

### The Old Post Office
★★★★ GUEST HOUSE

**tel:** 01207 528420 & 07917 108481 **27 Front Street DH7 0LA**
**email:** keithgill51@talktalk.net **web:** www.theoldpostofficelanchester.com
**dir:** From Durham on A691, follow signs to Consett. Turn left signed Lanchester village centre, then immediately right into Front St. On right hand side by post box

Located in the historic town of Lanchester, this Grade II listed building dates back to 1788 and has been lovingly restored by the current owners. Bedrooms are spacious and very comfortable, with thoughtful extras provided as standard. Great care has gone into choosing suppliers for breakfast items, and the delightful gardens to the rear add to the quality of this wonderful property.

**Rooms:** 3 en suite (1 fmly) **S** £75; **D** £85 **Facilities:** FTV Lounge tea/coffee WiFi 🔒 **Extras:** Speciality toiletries, chocolate, home-made biscuits – complimentary **Parking:** 3

## PETERLEE
Map 19 NZ44

### The Bell Guest House
★★★★ GUEST HOUSE

**tel:** 0191 586 3863 **Sunderland Road, Horden SR8 4PF**
**email:** info@thebellguesthouse.com **web:** www.thebellguesthouse.com
**dir:** From A19 onto A1086 (Sunderland road)

The Bell Guest House is located in Horden, just a few minutes from the sea. The house gets its name from the previous owner Henry Bell who purchased the property back in 1925. It has recently been refurbished but kept plenty of its charm and character. Bedrooms are well appointed and comfortable, while the coach bar and lounge are warm and welcoming. The Bell Guest House is ideally located for Hartlepool, Sunderland, Newcastle and Durham.

**Rooms:** 9 en suite (2 fmly) **S** £39–£49; **D** £75 **Facilities:** FTV TVL tea/coffee Licensed WiFi 🔒 **Notes:** Closed 24–26 Dec

## SEAHAM
Map 19 NZ44

### The Seaton Lane Inn
★★★★ ⊜ INN

**tel:** 0191 581 2038 **Seaton Lane, Seaton Village SR7 0LP**
**email:** info@seatonlaneinn.com **web:** www.seatonlaneinn.com
**dir:** A19 S of Sunderland on B1404 between Seaham & Houghton

Set on the edge of the quiet village of Seaton, close to Seaham and the A19, the inn is popular with visitors and locals alike and is a blend of modern and traditional. The emphasis is on food here with interesting home-made dishes offered in the restaurant and bar. The bedrooms, located in the adjoining building, are modern, spacious and smartly furnished.

**Rooms:** 18 en suite (9 GF) **Facilities:** FTV TVL tea/coffee Dinner available Direct dial WiFi ⚓18 **Extras:** Speciality toiletries **Parking:** 36

## WHORLTON
Map 19 NZ11

### Fernaville's Rest
★★★★ ⊜ INN

**tel:** 01833 627341 **DL12 8XD**
**email:** thomas@fernavilles.com **web:** www.fernavilles.com

Fernaville's Rest is a Grade II listed inn located in the quiet village of Whorlton but within easy striking distance of Barnard Castle. This family-run operation caters well for the needs of the guest with well appointed en suite bedrooms. Hospitality from the hands on owners and team is very good making for a wonderful guest experience. Dinner offers local quality produce which is accurately cooked and presented. Real ales including a "dog beer" are served from the bar and in winter can be enjoyed in front of the open fire.

**Rooms:** 6 en suite **S** £49.50; **D** £69.50–£89.50* **Facilities:** Dinner available WiFi

# ESSEX

## CHELMSFORD
Map 6 TL70

### The Lion Inn
★★★★ ⊜ INN

**tel:** 01245 394900 **Main Road, Boreham CM3 3JA**
**email:** info@lioninnhotel.co.uk **web:** www.lioninnhotel.co.uk
**dir:** A12 junct 19 onto B1137 to Maldon. 0.75m on right

The Lion Inn offers stylish and comfortably appointed accommodation; well-equipped with flat-screen TVs, free WiFi, and full air-conditioning it appeals to leisure and business guests alike. Many rooms benefit from balconies or direct access to the private garden. The spacious bar and restaurant is open-plan style with additional seating in the Victorian conservatory. Guests can enjoy a wide selection of good classic pub dishes with a continental twist; a cooked and continental breakfast is served daily.

*The Lion Inn*

**Rooms:** 15 en suite 8 annexe en suite (1 fmly) (9 GF) **D** £110–£250
**Facilities:** tea/coffee Dinner available Direct dial WiFi **Conf:** Max 150 Thtr 150 Class 50 Board 20 **Parking:** 150 **Notes:** Closed 24–26 Dec RS All BHs Civ wed 150

## CLACTON-ON-SEA
Map 7 TM11

## The Chudleigh

★★★★ GUEST ACCOMMODATION

**tel:** 01255 425407 **13 Agate Road, Marine Parade West CO15 1RA**
**email:** chudleighhotel@btconnect.com **web:** www.chudleighhotel.com
**dir:** *With sea on left, cross lights at pier, turn into Agate Rd at mini rdbt*

Conveniently situated for the seafront and shops, this immaculate property has been run by the friendly owners Peter and Carol Oleggini for more than 50 years. Bedrooms are most attractive with co-ordinating decor and well chosen fabrics. Breakfast is served in the smart dining room and there is a cosy lounge with plush sofas.

**Rooms:** 10 en suite (2 fmly) (2 GF) **S** £50–£58; **D** £80–£90* **Facilities:** FTV TVL tea/coffee Direct dial Licensed WiFi **Extras:** Speciality toiletries, chocolates – complimentary **Parking:** 7 **Notes:** No children 18mths Closed Oct RS 1 week Mar/Apr

## COLCHESTER
Map 13 TL92

## Black Bond Hall Bed and Breakfast

★★★★ BED AND BREAKFAST

**tel:** 01206 735776 & 07909 516013 **Lodge Lane, Langenhoe CO5 7LX**
**email:** gill@blackbondhall.co.uk **web:** www.blackbondhall.co.uk
**dir:** *A12 junct 26 signed to Mersea (B1025). Through Abberton & Langenhoe pass x-rds & garage, 1st left into School Rd & Fingringhoe Range. 1st right into Lodge Ln, on right*

Black Bond Hall is ideally situated for Colchester and attractions such as The Beth Chatto Gardens, Dedham, Rowhedge, Abberton Reservoir, Mersea Island and Fingringhoe Nature Reserves. The two comfortable double rooms provide tea- and coffee-making facilities, TV, WiFi and hairdryer. Guests can expect a warm welcome, with home-made cake on arrival, as well as tea and coffee. Breakfast is sourced from local produce and is served in either the modern breakfast room overlooking the garden, or the traditional dining room. There are pubs nearby for evening meals.

**Rooms:** 2 en suite **D** fr £90* **Facilities:** FTV tea/coffee WiFi **Extras:** Snacks **Parking:** 8 **Notes:** LB No children 12yrs

## DEDHAM
Map 13 TM03

### Premier Collection

## The Sun Inn

★★★★★ ◎◎ INN

**tel:** 01206 323351 **High Street CO7 6DF**
**email:** office@thesuninndedham.com **web:** www.thesuninndedham.com
**dir:** *In village centre opposite church*

The Sun Inn is a charming 15th-century coaching inn situated in the centre of Dedham, opposite the church. The carefully decorated bedrooms include four-poster and half-tester beds, along with many thoughtful touches. The open-plan public rooms have a wealth of character with inglenook fires, oak beams and fine oak panelling, and the food in the restaurant has been awarded two AA Rosettes.

**Rooms:** 7 en suite **Facilities:** FTV DVD iPod docking station Lounge tea/coffee Dinner available WiFi **Extras:** Speciality toiletries, mineral water **Parking:** 15 **Notes:** LB Closed 25–28 Dec

## GESTINGTHORPE
Map 13 TL83

### Premier Collection

## The Pheasant

★★★★★ ◎ INN

**tel:** 01787 465010 & 461196 **Audley End CO9 3AU**
**email:** thepheasantpb@aol.com **web:** www.thepheasant.net
**dir:** *Phone for directions*

Close to the Suffolk/Essex border, The Pheasant enjoys stunning countryside views and a lovely location in the heart of the village of Gestingthorpe. The bar is charming and features wood-burning stoves, low ceilings and a good choice of local real ales. Dinner is not to be missed and much of the produce is grown on the pub's own plot of land. The five spacious bedrooms in the coach house are beautifully presented and are all individually designed. An ideal base from which to explore the surrounding countryside and pretty Suffolk villages.

**Rooms:** 5 en suite (2 fmly) (2 GF) **Facilities:** FTV tea/coffee Dinner available Direct dial WiFi 18 **Extras:** Speciality toiletries, home-made cookies **Parking:** 25 **Notes:** LB Closed 1st 2 weeks Jan

## GREAT TOTHAM — Map 7 TL81

### The Bull & Willow Room at Great Totham

★★★★  RESTAURANT WITH ROOMS

**tel:** 01621 893385 & 894020 **2 Maldon Road CM9 8NH**
**email:** reservations@thebullatgreattotham.co.uk
**web:** www.thebullatgreattotham.co.uk
**dir:** Exit A12 at Witham junct to Great Totham

A 16th-century former coaching inn located in the village of Great Totham, The Bull is now a very stylish restaurant with rooms that offers en suite bedrooms with satellite TVs with Freeview; WiFi is available throughout. Guests can enjoy dinner in the gastro-pub or in the two AA Rosette award-winning fine dining restaurant, The Willow Room.

**Rooms:** 4 annexe en suite (2 GF) **Facilities:** STV FTV Lounge tea/coffee Dinner available WiFi ℒ18 **Conf:** Max 60 Thtr 40 Class 40 Board 16 **Parking:** 80 **Notes:** LB Closed 25 Dec

## GREAT YELDHAM — Map 13 TL73

### Premier Collection

### The White Hart

★★★★★  INN

**tel:** 01787 237250 **Poole Street CO9 4HJ**
**email:** restaurant@whitehartyeldham.com **web:** www.whitehartyeldham.com
**dir:** On A1017 in village

The White Hart is a large timber-framed character building that includes the main restaurant and bar areas while the bedrooms are located in the converted coach house; all are smartly appointed and well equipped with many thoughtful extras. The comfortable lounge and bar and the beautifully landscaped gardens provide areas for relaxation. Locally sourced produce is used on menus in the main house restaurant which is popular with local residents and guests alike.

**Rooms:** 13 en suite (2 fmly) (6 GF) **Facilities:** FTV TVL tea/coffee Dinner available Direct dial WiFi **Conf:** Max 200 Thtr 200 Class 200 Board 50 **Parking:** 80 **Notes:** LB Closed 1–18 Jan Civ wed 130

## HARWICH — Map 13 TM23

### The Goodlife Guesthouse

★★★ GUEST ACCOMMODATION

**tel:** 01255 556565 & 242440 **162 High Street, Dovercourt CO12 3AT**
**email:** mike@clickyourfingers.com **web:** www.goodlifehotel.co.uk
**dir:** On Dovercourt High Street, opposite park

This seaside establishment is located in the centre of Harwich. The accommodation is modern in style and very spacious, both in the bedrooms and the main dining and lounge areas. There is a private car park located on site, and a park directly opposite with good views of the sea which is only 150 metres from the house. A cooked breakfast is served daily in the dining area.

**Rooms:** 10 en suite (2 fmly) **Facilities:** STV FTV TVL tea/coffee Lift Licensed WiFi ℒ9 Snooker Pool table **Parking:** 24

## HATFIELD HEATH — Map 6 TL51

### Lancasters Farm

★★★★ FARMHOUSE

**tel:** 01279 730220 **Chelmsford Road CM22 7BB**
**email:** lancastersfarm@btconnect.com **web:** www.lancastersfarm.com
**dir:** A1060 from Hatfield Heath for Chelmsford, 1m left on sharp right bend, through white gates

Guests are made to feel at home at this delightfully spacious house, which is at the heart of this large working arable farm close to Stansted Airport. Bedrooms vary in size and style, but all are smartly decorated and thoughtfully equipped. Garaging can be arranged, as can transport to and from the airport.

**Rooms:** 4 rms (3 en suite) (1 pri facs) **S** £54–£60; **D** £108–£120 **Facilities:** FTV Lounge tea/coffee WiFi **Parking:** 6 **Notes:** No children 12yrs Closed 14 Dec–4 Jan 260 acres arable

## MALDON — Map 7 TL80

### The Bell

★★★ GUEST HOUSE

**tel:** 01621 843208 **2 Silver Street CM9 4QE**
**email:** info@thebellmaldon.co.uk **web:** www.thebellmaldon.co.uk
**dir:** Phone for directions

Centrally located to explore the historic town of Maldon and surrounding areas, this attractive guest house used to be a pub in a previous life and many original features can still be found around the property. The bedrooms offer good accommodation, while breakfast is served in the former cellar. Limited parking is available.

**Rooms:** 4 rms (2 en suite) (2 pri facs) **Facilities:** FTV DVD TVL tea/coffee Direct dial WiFi ℒ18 **Parking:** 2 **Notes:** LB No children 6yrs

## MANNINGTREE — Map 13 TM13

### Premier Collection

### Dairy House Farm

★★★★★ FARMHOUSE

**tel:** 01255 870322 & 07749 073974 **Bradfield Road CO11 2SR**
**email:** bridgetwhitworth353@gmail.com **web:** www.dairyhousefarm.info

*(For full entry see Wix)*

## SAFFRON WALDEN — Map 12 TL53

### Bendysh Hall Bed & Breakfast

★★★★ FARMHOUSE

**tel:** 01799 599220 & 07950 750684 **Ashdon Road, Radwinter CB10 2UA**
**email:** info@bendyshhallbedandbreakfast.co.uk
**web:** www.bendyshhallbedandbreakfast.co.uk
**dir:** From Saffron Walden on B1053 towards Radwinter, through village, turn left signed Ashdon. Bendysh Hall 1m on right

Bendysh Hall Bed & Breakfast is located close to Saffron Walden and in this quiet spot offers a comfortable night's sleep. A beautiful Grade II listed building that has been thoughtfully renovated over the years keeping some of the period features of the house. The farm consists of 300 acres of land and guests are welcome to take a walk/cycle through the woods. A hearty breakfast makes good use made of high quality ingredients and eggs from the farm.

**Rooms:** 3 rms (2 en suite) (1 pri facs) **D** £70–£95* **Facilities:** FTV DVD Lounge TVL tea/coffee WiFi Fishing ♨ **Extras:** Snacks – complimentary; robes **Parking:** 10 **Notes:** LB No children 10yrs 300 acres arable/poultry

## The Cross Keys

★★★★ 🛏 INN

**tel:** 01799 522207 **32 High Street CB10 1AX**
**email:** info@theoldcrosskeys.co.uk **web:** www.theoldcrosskeys.co.uk

Enjoying a prominent position in the busy market town of Saffron Walden, The Cross Keys is an authentic coaching inn dating back some 850 years. It offers guests a range of beautifully presented, individually styled bedrooms. The stylish restaurant is very popular and there is a real buzz in the small bar area in the evenings. Free WiFi is available, along with some secure parking.

**Rooms:** 9 en suite **Facilities:** FTV iPod docking station tea/coffee Dinner available WiFi ♨ ♨18 **Parking:** 6

## The Crown Inn

★★★ 🛏 INN

**tel:** 01799 522475 **Little Walden CB10 1XA**
**email:** pippathecrown@aol.com **web:** www.thecrownlittlewalden.co.uk
**dir:** M11 junct 9 follow signs for Saffron Walden. In Saffron Walden, left at lights signed Thaxted. At mini rdbt left towards Little Walden (B1052)

This charming country inn enjoys a prominent position in the pretty village of Little Walden and has a choice of three cosy, comfortable bedrooms. All are individually styled and well equipped. Free WiFi is available throughout the property and there is secure parking for guests. There's a great atmosphere in the authentic bar, and an extensive choice of home-cooked meals on the evening menu.

**Rooms:** 3 en suite **Facilities:** FTV DVD tea/coffee Dinner available WiFi **Conf:** Max 40 Thtr 40 Class 30 Board 30 **Parking:** 30

■ SOUTHEND-ON-SEA                                        Map 7 TQ88

## The Ilfracombe House

★★★★ GUEST ACCOMMODATION

**tel:** 01702 351000 **9-13 Wilson Road SS1 1HG**
**email:** info@ilfracombe-hotel.co.uk **web:** www.ilfracombe-hotel.co.uk
**dir:** 500yds W of town centre. Exit A13 at Cricketers pub into Milton Rd, 3rd left into Cambridge Rd, 4th right, car park in Alexandra Rd

The Ilfracombe House lies in Southend's conservation area, just a short walk from the cliffs, gardens and the beach. The public rooms include a dining room, lounge and a cosy bar, and the well-equipped bedrooms include deluxe options and two four-poster rooms.

**Rooms:** 20 en suite (4 fmly) (2 GF) **Facilities:** STV FTV DVD TVL tea/coffee Dinner available Direct dial Licensed WiFi **Extras:** Mini-fridge **Conf:** Max 15 **Parking:** 9 **Notes:** LB

■ STANSTED AIRPORT                                        Map 6 TL52
*See also Bishop's Stortford (Hertfordshire)*

## The White House

★★★★ GUEST ACCOMMODATION

**tel:** 01279 870257 **Smiths Green CM22 6NR**
**email:** enquiries@whitehousestansted.co.uk **web:** www.whitehousestansted.co.uk
**dir:** M11 junct 8, B1256 towards Takeley. Through lights at Four Ashes x-rds. 400yds, corner of B1256 & Smiths Green

The White House is a delightful 16th-century property situated close to Stansted Airport (but not on the flight path). The stylish bedrooms feature superb beds, luxurious bathrooms and many thoughtful touches. Traditional breakfasts, served in the farmhouse-style kitchen, are made from local ingredients; evening meals are available at the Lion and Lamb, a nearby pub/restaurant owned by the proprietors, who can usually provide transport to and from The White House.

**Rooms:** 3 rms (2 en suite) (1 pri facs) (3 fmly) **Facilities:** FTV DVD tea/coffee Dinner available WiFi ♨ **Extras:** Robes, speciality toiletries, bottled water, Nespresso coffee machine **Conf:** Max 25 **Parking:** 6 **Notes:** Closed 24–25, 31 Dec & 1 Jan

■ THAXTED                                        Map 12 TL63

## The Farmhouse Inn

★★★ INN

**tel:** 01371 830864 **Monk Street CM6 2NR**
**email:** info@farmhouseinn.org **web:** www.farmhouseinn.org
**dir:** M11 to A120 to B184, 1m from Thaxted, between Thaxted & Great Dunmow

This 16th-century inn overlooks the Chelmer Valley, and is surrounded by open countryside. The property is ideally situated in the quiet hamlet of Monk Street about two miles from the historic town of Thaxted. Bedrooms are pleasantly decorated and equipped with modern facilities. Public rooms include a cosy lounge bar and a large, smartly appointed restaurant.

**Rooms:** 11 annexe en suite **Facilities:** FTV tea/coffee Dinner available WiFi **Conf:** Max 80 Thtr 80 Class 60 Board 50 **Parking:** 35

■ THORPE BAY
*See Southend-on-Sea*

## TOPPESFIELD                                    Map 12 TL73

## Ollivers Farm

★★★ BED AND BREAKFAST

**tel:** 01787 237642 **CO9 4LS**
**web:** www.essex-bed-breakfast.co.uk
**dir:** *500yds SE of village centre. Off A1017 in Great Yeldham to Toppesfield, farm 1m on left before T-junct to village*

Full of charm and character, this impressive 16th-century farmhouse is set amid pretty landscaped gardens in a peaceful rural location. Bedrooms are pleasantly decorated and thoughtfully equipped. Public rooms have a wealth of original features including exposed beams and there is a huge open fireplace in the reception hall.

**Rooms:** 3 rms (1 en suite) (1 pri facs) **S** £50; **D** £85–£90 **Facilities:** FTV Lounge tea/coffee WiFi 🚲 Shed for bikes **Parking:** 4 **Notes:** No children 10yrs Closed 23 Dec–1 Jan

## WIX                                            Map 13 TM12

### Premier Collection

## Dairy House Farm

★★★★★ FARMHOUSE

**tel:** 01255 870322 & 07749 073974 **Bradfield Road CO11 2SR**
**email:** bridgetwhitworth353@gmail.com **web:** www.dairyhousefarm.info
**dir:** *Exit A120 into Wix, turn at x-rds to Bradfield, farm 1m on left*

This Georgian house stands amid 550 acres of arable land, and is blessed with stunning views of the surrounding countryside. Extensively renovated in the Victorian style, it has original decorative tiled floors, moulded cornices and marble fireplaces. The spacious bedrooms are carefully furnished and equipped with many thoughtful touches. Breakfast is served in the elegant antique-furnished dining room and there is a cosy lounge.

**Rooms:** 3 en suite **S** £56–£60; **D** £76–£85 **Facilities:** FTV DVD TVL tea/coffee WiFi 🎣 Farm reservoir fishing **Extras:** Home-made cake – complimentary **Parking:** 8 **Notes:** No children 12yrs 550 acres arable

### GLOUCESTERSHIRE

## ALDERTON                                       Map 10 SP03

## Corner Cottage Bed and Breakfast

★★★★ BED AND BREAKFAST

**tel:** 01242 620630 **Stow Road GL20 8NH**
**email:** info@stayatcornercottage.co.uk **web:** www.stayatcornercottage.co.uk
**dir:** *M5 junct 9 E onto A46 to rdbt then B4077 (Stow). Turn left opposite Alderton garage into Willowbank Rd, left again into drive & follow signs to car park*

There is a warm and genuine welcome for all guests arriving at Corner Cottage, with helpful advice on local attractions and places to visit always on offer, if required. The location makes an ideal base from which to explore this picturesque area, with Tewkesbury only a short drive away. The bedrooms offer good levels of comfort, with modern, well-appointed bathrooms. Breakfast is a generous and tasty offering, served around the table in the lounge-diner.

**Rooms:** 4 en suite **D** £70–£85* **Facilities:** FTV TVL tea/coffee WiFi **Parking:** 8 **Notes:** No children 18yrs Closed Xmas/New Year & Jan

## Tally Ho Bed & Breakfast

★★★★ BED AND BREAKFAST

**tel:** 01242 621482 & 07966 593169 **20 Beckford Road GL20 8NL**
**email:** tallyhobb@aol.com **web:** www.cotswolds-bedandbreakfast.co.uk
**dir:** *M5 junct 9, A46 signed Evesham, through Ashchurch. Take B4077 signed Stow-on-the-Wold & Alderton. Left in 1.5m opposite garage signed Alderton. Into village, pass Gardeners pub on right, Tally Ho on left*

Convenient for the M5, this friendly establishment stands in a delightful quiet village. Bedrooms, including two on the ground floor, offer modern comforts and attractive co-ordinated furnishings. Breakfast is served in the stylish dining room, and for dinner, the village pub is just a stroll away.

**Rooms:** 3 en suite (1 fmly) (2 GF) **S** £50–£55; **D** £70–£75* **Facilities:** FTV DVD tea/coffee WiFi **Extras:** Bottled water **Parking:** 3 **Notes:** No children 2yrs

## AMBERLEY                                        Map 4 SO80

## The Amberley Inn

★★★★ INN

**tel:** 01453 872565 **Culver Hill GL5 5AF**
**email:** enquiries@theamberleyinn.co.uk **web:** www.theamberleyinn.co.uk
**dir:** *From A46 follow signs for Amberley, up Culver Hill, in village centre on left*

This delightful inn is just outside Stroud, with walks from the door in all directions across the Woodchester Valley and commons. Pets are especially welcome here. The bedrooms come in a range of sizes, and some are located above the main building while others are in the separate Garden House. A range of real ales and wines is available in the traditional, welcoming bar and a selection of delicious bar and restaurant meals, making good use of fine quality local produce, is offered.

**Rooms:** 8 en suite 5 annexe en suite (2 fmly) (1 GF) **S** £75–£85; **D** £85–£140* **Facilities:** FTV Lounge tea/coffee Dinner available Direct dial WiFi 🎱 £18 🚲 **Extras:** Speciality toiletries, robes **Conf:** Max 30 **Parking:** 7 **Notes:** LB Civ wed 35

## ARLINGHAM                                       Map 4 SO71

## The Old Passage Inn

★★★★ ❀❀ RESTAURANT WITH ROOMS

**tel:** 01452 740547 **Passage Road GL2 7JR**
**email:** oldpassage@btconnect.com **web:** www.theoldpassage.com
**dir:** *A38 onto B4071 through Frampton on Severn. 4m to Arlingham, through village to river*

Delightfully located on the very edge of the River Severn, this relaxing restaurant with rooms combines high quality food with an air of tranquillity. Bedrooms and bathrooms are decorated in a modern style, and have a collection of welcome extras including a well-stocked mini-bar. The menu offers a wide range of seafood and shellfish dishes including crab, oysters and lobsters from Cornwall, kept alive in seawater tanks. An outdoor terrace is available in warmer months.

**Rooms:** 2 en suite **S** £80–£140; **D** £110–£140* **Facilities:** FTV DVD Lounge tea/coffee Dinner available WiFi 🚲 **Extras:** Mini-bar – chargeable **Parking:** 30 **Notes:** Closed 25 & 26 Dec RS Jan–Feb closed for dinner Tue & Wed

## BARNSLEY
Map 5 SP00

### Premier Collection

## The Village Pub
★★★★★ ⌂ 🍴 INN

**tel:** 01285 740000 & 740241 **GL7 5EF**
**email:** reservations@barnsleyhouse.com **web:** www.thevillagepub.co.uk
**dir:** On B4425 in centre of village

With a village location as its name suggests, this delightful establishment provides high quality accommodation and an efficient but relaxed style of hospitality and service. Owned by the same company as Barnsley House Hotel (across the road), guests here can enjoy an informal stay with high standards. The bar-dining room serves an excellent choice of top quality, seasonal produce and a varied choice of wines and ales. The bedrooms and bathrooms come in a range of sizes and all are comfortably furnished and equipped.

**Rooms:** 6 en suite (1 fmly) **S** £94–£154; **D** £104–£174* **Facilities:** STV FTV DVD iPod docking station tea/coffee Dinner available Direct dial WiFi 🦢 🦆 ⚘18 **Parking:** 20 **Notes:** LB

## BERKELEY
Map 4 ST69

## The Malt House
★★★ INN

**tel:** 01453 511177 **22 Marybrook Street GL13 9BA**
**email:** the-malthouse@btconnect.com **web:** www.themalthouse.uk.com
**dir:** A38 into Berkeley, at town hall follow road to right, premises on right past hospital & opposite school

Conveniently located for business and leisure travellers, this family-run inn has a convivial atmosphere. Bedrooms are soundly appointed while public areas include a choice of bars, a skittle alley and an attractive restaurant area. Local attractions include Berkeley Castle, and the Wildfowl & Wetlands Trust at Slimbridge.

**Rooms:** 9 en suite (2 fmly) **Facilities:** FTV tea/coffee Dinner available WiFi Pool table Skittle Alley **Parking:** 30 **Notes:** LB

## BIBURY
Map 5 SP10

## The Catherine Wheel
★★★★ INN

**tel:** 01285 740250 **Arlington GL7 5ND**
**email:** rooms@catherinewheel-bibury.co.uk **web:** www.catherinewheel-bibury.co.uk
**dir:** On B4425 between Burford & Cirencester

This family-run inn provides a pleasant welcome and traditional country pub ambience. A range of seating is available in the cosy bar, or in the more formal dining room where a selection of carefully prepared dishes is offered throughout the day and evening. Bedrooms are in an adjacent building and include smaller standard rooms or larger superior rooms – all comfortably furnished and with some welcome extras.

**Rooms:** 4 annexe en suite (4 GF) **Facilities:** FTV DVD TVL tea/coffee Dinner available WiFi 🐾 **Parking:** 23

## BLAISDON — Map 10 SO71

### Premier Collection

## Blaisdon House B&B

★★★★★ 🍷 BED AND BREAKFAST

tel: 01452 830437 GL17 0AH
email: stay@blaisdonhouse.com web: www.blaisdonhouse.com
dir: *From A4136 follow signs for Blaisdon, opposite pub in village*

This delightful house was previously a vicarage with parts dating back to the 12th century. The owners have spent many months completely renovating and updating the property to provide three high quality bedrooms and bathrooms, with a feel of luxury throughout. Tea is offered in the relaxing lounge on arrival. A carefully prepared delicious breakfast makes good use of local produce, served around a large table in the spacious dining room. There are many local walks from the house and the helpful proprietors are always glad to assist. The village inn is ideal for dinner, and is just opposite.

Rooms: 3 en suite S £80–£100; D £85–£150* Facilities: STV FTV DVD Lounge tea/coffee WiFi 🛁 Extras: Speciality toiletries Parking: 3 Notes: No children 13yrs

## BOURTON-ON-THE-WATER — Map 10 SP12

### Premier Collection

## The Dial House

★★★★★ 🍷 GUEST ACCOMMODATION

tel: 01451 822244 High Street GL54 2AN
email: info@dialhousehotel.com web: www.dialhousehotel.com

With an idyllic location in the middle of the delightful village of Bourton-on-the-Water, this high quality accommodation offers a well judged mix of professional and efficient service with a relaxed and friendly ambience. Bedrooms and bathrooms offer a range of shapes and sizes and all are decorated and maintained to high standards. Off-street car parking and a pleasant garden are provided to the rear of the property.

Rooms: 9 en suite 5 annexe en suite (7 GF) Facilities: FTV DVD Lounge tea/coffee Direct dial Licensed WiFi 🛁 Hot tub Extras: Speciality toiletries Conf: Max 20 Thtr 14 Class 14 Board 16 Parking: 15 Notes: No children 10yrs Closed 1–8 Jan

## The Mousetrap Inn

★★★ INN

tel: 01451 820579 Lansdowne GL54 2AR
email: thebatesies@gmail.com web: www.mousetrap-inn.co.uk

The Mousetrap Inn is a traditional and informal Cotswold hostelry located on the edge of this idyllic village just a few minutes' stroll from the centre. A selection of real ales and also home-cooked dinners (except Sundays and Mondays) are offered in the relaxed bar. Bedrooms and bathrooms vary in size and include three at ground floor level. Breakfast includes home-made sausages and free-range eggs.

Rooms: 10 en suite (3 GF) Facilities: tea/coffee Dinner available WiFi Parking: 10 Notes: No children 10yrs

## CHELTENHAM — Map 10 SO92

### Premier Collection

## The Bradley

★★★★★ 🍷 GUEST ACCOMMODATION

tel: 01242 519077 & 07502 225031 19 Royal Parade, Bayshill Road GL50 3AY
email: enquiries@thebradleyhotel.co.uk web: www.thebradleyhotel.co.uk

The Bradley is a boutique townhouse in the centre of Regency Cheltenham, just a few minutes' stroll from the local shops and the town centre. Bedrooms and bathrooms offer plenty of quality and comfort, and come in a range of shapes and sizes. Breakfast utilises the best quality produce, and is served in the elegant dining room. Parking permits can generally be arranged if booked in advance.

Rooms: 8 en suite (1 fmly) (1 GF) D £95–£230* Facilities: FTV iPod docking station Lounge tea/coffee Dinner available Licensed WiFi Extras: Fresh milk Parking: 3 Notes: No children 12yrs

### Premier Collection

## Cleeve Hill House

★★★★★ 🍷 GUEST ACCOMMODATION

tel: 01242 672052 Cleeve Hill GL52 3PR
email: info@cleevehill-hotel.co.uk web: www.cleevehill-hotel.co.uk
dir: *3m N of Cheltenham on B4632*

Many of the bedrooms and the lounge at this Edwardian property have spectacular views across to the Malvern Hills. Room shapes and sizes vary but all are comfortably furnished with many welcome extras; some have four-poster beds. There is a relaxing guest lounge, and an honesty bar is in place. Breakfast, served in the pleasant conservatory, offers a good selection of carefully presented hot and cold items.

Rooms: 10 en suite (1 GF) Facilities: STV FTV DVD Lounge tea/coffee Direct dial Licensed WiFi Parking: 11 Notes: No children 8yrs

## The Battledown Bed and Breakfast

★★★★ 🍷 BED AND BREAKFAST

tel: 01242 233881 & 07807 142069 125 Hales Road GL52 6ST
email: info@thebattledown.co.uk web: www.thebattledown.co.uk
dir: *0.5m E of town centre. A40 onto B4075, 0.5m on right*

Simon, Sarah and their daughter Isabella welcome you to their home, The Battledown, a French colonial-style villa that was built in 1855. It is conveniently located for the town centre, all of the events in Cheltenham and the surrounding Cotswold countryside.

Rooms: 7 en suite (2 fmly) S fr £65; D fr £85* Facilities: FTV DVD Lounge tea/coffee WiFi 🛁 Parking: 7 Notes: LB

## Clarence Court

★★★★ 🛏 GUEST ACCOMMODATION

**tel:** 01242 580411 **Clarence Square GL50 4JR**
**email:** enquiries@clarencecourthotel.com **web:** www.clarencecourthotel.com

Situated in an attractive, tree-lined Georgian square, this property was once owned by the Duke of Wellington. The building is charming and its elegant public rooms reflect the grace of a bygone age. Spacious bedrooms offer ample comfort and quality, and have many original features. The convenience of the peaceful location is a great asset, only a five-minute stroll from the town centre. A varied range of carefully prepared dishes is offered in the café-restaurant from noon to 9pm.

**Rooms:** 20 en suite (3 fmly) (7 GF) **Facilities:** FTV DVD TVL tea/coffee Dinner available Direct dial Licensed WiFi Free use of Fitness First Leisure Club (adults) **Parking:** 21

## Hope Orchard

★★★★ GUEST ACCOMMODATION

**tel:** 01452 855556 **Gloucester Road, Staverton GL51 0TF**
**email:** info@hopeorchard.com **web:** www.hopeorchard.com
**dir:** A40 onto B4063 at Arlecourt rdbt. Hope Orchard 1.25m on right

Situated midway between Gloucester and Cheltenham, Hope Orchard is a good base for exploring the area. The comfortable bedrooms are next to the main house, all are on the ground floor, and each has its own separate entrance. There is a large garden, and ample off-road parking is available.

**Rooms:** 8 en suite (8 GF) **Facilities:** FTV DVD tea/coffee Direct dial WiFi 🐾
**Extras:** Fridge, microwave **Parking:** 10 **Notes:** Closed 23 Dec–2 Jan

## Malvern View

★★★★ GUEST ACCOMMODATION

**tel:** 01242 672017 & 07917 714929 **Cleeve Hill GL52 3PR**
**email:** info@malvernview.com **web:** www.malvernview.com
**dir:** B4632 from Cheltenham towards Winchcombe & Stratford-upon-Avon. Through Southam & Cleeve Hill, Malvern View on right

Located just outside Cheltenham, most rooms in this comfortable accommodation have delightful views over the countryside towards the Malverns and beyond. Bedrooms and bathrooms here are all comfortably furnished and include some welcome extras. Breakfast is made to order and offers a range of well-presented options. Off-street car parking is another welcome feature.

**Rooms:** 7 rms (6 en suite) (1 pri facs) (1 fmly) **S** £80–£120; **D** £90–£130*
**Facilities:** FTV iPod docking station Lounge tea/coffee Licensed WiFi ♨18 🐾
**Extras:** Honesty bar **Conf:** Max 30 Thtr 18 Class 30 Board 18 **Parking:** 12 **Notes:** LB Closed 4–29 Jan RS weekends (Oct–Mar) min 2 night stay all year

**CHIPPING CAMPDEN** Map 10 SP13

## The Kings

★★★★  RESTAURANT WITH ROOMS

**tel:** 01386 840256 & 841056 **The Square, High Street GL55 6AW**
**email:** info@kingscampden.co.uk **web:** www.kingscampden.co.uk
**dir:** In centre of town square

Located in the centre of this delightful Cotswold town, The Kings effortlessly blends a relaxed and friendly welcome with efficient service. Bedrooms and bathrooms come in a range of shapes and sizes and all are appointed to a high level of quality and comfort. Dining options, whether in the main restaurant or the comfortable bar area, serve a tempting menu to suit all tastes, from light salads and pasta, to meat and fish dishes.

**Rooms:** 13 en suite 5 annexe en suite (3 fmly) (3 GF) **S** £110–£225; **D** £130–£245*
**Facilities:** FTV tea/coffee Dinner available Direct dial WiFi **Parking:** 14 **Notes:** LB Civ wed 60

## Lygon Arms

★★★★ 🛏 INN

**tel:** 01386 840318 & 840089 **High Street GL55 6HB**
**email:** sandra@lygonarms.co.uk **web:** www.lygonarms.co.uk
**dir:** In town centre near church

This charming and welcoming inn sits on Chipping Campden's high street – a tranquil location with lots of tempting antique shops. Well managed by a friendly team, the inn has a cosy bar with open log fires and oak beams. Spacious and very well-appointed accommodation is provided in the main building and in mews houses. Both breakfast and dinner are hearty and should not be missed.

**Rooms:** 10 en suite (3 fmly) (1 GF) **Facilities:** FTV tea/coffee Dinner available Direct dial WiFi **Parking:** 12 **Notes:** LB

## The Seagrave Arms

★★★★ RESTAURANT WITH ROOMS

**tel:** 01386 840192 **Friday Street, Weston-sub-Edge GL55 6QH**
**email:** enquiries@seagravearms.com **web:** www.seagravearms.com
**dir:** From Moreton-in-Marsh take A44 towards Evesham. Approx /m right onto B4081 signed Chipping Campden. Becomes Sheep St. At junct with High Street, left into Dyers Ln. 0.5m over Dovers Hill, into Weston-sub-Edge, becomes Church St. Inn on left

Part of The Epicurean Collection, this Grade II listed, 400-year-old house is set in the heart of the Cotswolds. It offers modern accommodation in the main house and also rooms around the courtyard. The inn is full of character, serving award-winning seasonal food every day of the week, with occasional specialist nights. Staff are warm and friendly, and the bar offers local ales and good wines. There is ample parking and attractive gardens.

**Rooms:** 5 en suite 3 annexe en suite (3 GF) **Facilities:** FTV tea/coffee Dinner available WiFi **Notes:** LB

CHIPPING CAMPDEN *continued*

## Holly House

★★★★ BED AND BREAKFAST

**tel:** 01386 593213 **Ebrington GL55 6NL**
**email:** jeffreyhutsby@yahoo.co.uk **web:** www.hollyhousebandb.co.uk
**dir:** *B4035 from Chipping Campden towards Shipston on Stour, 0.5m left to Ebrington & signed*

Set in the heart of the pretty Cotswold village of Ebrington, this late Victorian house offers thoughtfully equipped accommodation. Bedrooms are housed in buildings that were formerly used by the local wheelwright, and offer level access, seclusion and privacy. Quality English breakfasts are served in the light and airy dining room. For other meals, the village pub is just a short walk away.

**Rooms:** 2 en suite 1 annexe en suite (2 fmly) (3 GF) **S** £60–£80; **D** £85–£90*
**Facilities:** FTV Lounge tea/coffee WiFi **Parking:** 5

CHIPPING SODBURY Map 4 ST78

## The Moda House

★★★★ GUEST ACCOMMODATION

**tel:** 01454 312135 **1 High Street BS37 6BA**
**email:** enquiries@modahouse.co.uk **web:** www.modahouse.co.uk
**dir:** *In town centre*

This popular, Grade II listed Georgian house has an imposing position at the top of the High Street. It has been appointed to provide modern bedrooms of varying shapes and sizes, and has comfortable public areas that have retained many original features. Room facilities include satellite TV and phones.

**Rooms:** 8 en suite 3 annexe en suite (3 GF) **Facilities:** STV FTV Lounge TVL tea/coffee Direct dial Licensed WiFi **Conf:** Max 20 Thtr 10 Board 10 **Notes:** No children 16yrs

CIRENCESTER Map 5 SP00

### Premier Collection

## The Fleece at Cirencester

★★★★★ 🞰 INN

**tel:** 01285 658507 **Market Place GL7 2NZ**
**email:** relax@thefleececirencester.co.uk **web:** www.thefleececirencester.co.uk

Located in the heart of the market town of Cirencester, this country inn has been finished to a high standard with guests and comfort in mind. Bedrooms are sumptuous, and many thoughtful touches add to the stay. Public areas include a traditional bar featuring Thwaites cask ales, a cosy lounge and a popular restaurant.

**Rooms:** 28 en suite (1 fmly) **Facilities:** FTV Lounge tea/coffee Dinner available WiFi **Parking:** 8

## Greensleeves

★★★★ BED AND BREAKFAST

**tel:** 01285 642516 & 07971 929259 **Baunton Lane, Stratton GL7 2LN**
**email:** johnps1@tesco.net **web:** www.greensleeves4u.co.uk
**dir:** *From Cirencester, follow signs for Stratton. Right into Baunton Ln*

Guests are ensured of a warm and friendly welcome from proprietor John, at this delightful property, just a short drive from Cirencester. Smart en suite accommodation, with off-street parking, is well equipped with a host of facilities to ensure both leisure and corporate guests feel at home. Delicious breakfasts feature home-baked bread.

**Rooms:** 3 en suite **Facilities:** FTV DVD tea/coffee WiFi 🛈 🔒 **Parking:** 5

## The Old Brewhouse

★★★★ BED AND BREAKFAST

**tel:** 01285 656099 **7 London Road GL7 2PU**
**email:** info@theoldbrewhouse.com **web:** www.theoldbrewhouse.com

The Old Brewhouse dates back to the 17th century and is situated in the centre of Cirencester, a short walking distance from a range of shops and restaurants. Bedrooms are comfortable, many with original features, and all have good quality en suite bathrooms. The conservatory provides a comfortable seating area and leads onto a pretty courtyard garden, an unusual feature. A small car park is located to the rear of the property.

*The Old Brewhouse*

**Rooms:** 10 en suite (1 fmly) (4 GF) **Facilities:** tea/coffee

## COLEFORD
Map 4 SO51

# The Rock B&B

★★★★ GUEST ACCOMMODATION

**tel:** 01594 83/893 **Hillersland GL16 7NY**
**email:** chris@stayattherock.com **web:** www.stayattherock.com
**dir:** *A40 at Monmouth onto A4136. 5m, left at Five Acres into Park Rd. At Christchurch right, immediately left towards Symonds Yat Rock, 0.75m S of Symonds Yat Rock*

The Rock B&B offers stylish modern accommodation and is located on the outskirts of Coleford, near the famous Symonds Yat Rock. Bedrooms are attractively presented and very comfortable, with the garden rooms making the most of the spectacular views over the Wye Valley. Very popular with walkers, The Rock also caters well for business guests. Breakfasts are served in the spacious dining room overlooking the garden.

**Rooms:** 7 annexe en suite (5 GF) **Facilities:** FTV Lounge tea/coffee WiFi ♨ Hot tub **Parking:** 20 **Notes:** LB No children 12yrs

# The Miners Country Inn

★★★ ⊛ INN

**tel:** 01594 836632 **Chepstow Road, Sling GL16 8LH**
**email:** admin@theminerssling.com **web:** www.theminerssling.co.uk
**dir:** *1m from Coleford town centre*

The Miners is a real family affair, set in the heart of the Forest of Dean. First impressions are of a quintessential pub with beamed ceilings, stone floors and a bar offering an array of local ales. A strong local trade makes for a bustling atmosphere, but really it's the food that's the focus. The chef-patron uses locally sourced ingredients, and suppliers are championed on blackboards and menus, with most supplying the inn exclusively. Dishes are well conceived and offer classic hearty fare with a modern twist. Bedrooms are light and airy, with modern en suite bathrooms.

**Rooms:** 4 en suite **Facilities:** FTV tea/coffee Dinner available

## COWLEY
Map 10 SO91

# The Green Dragon Inn

★★★★ ⊜ INN

**tel:** 01242 870271 **Cockleford GL53 9NW**
**email:** green-dragon@buccaneer.co.uk **web:** www.green-dragon-inn.co.uk

The Green Dragon offers all the charm and character of an English country pub combined with a relaxed atmosphere and carefully prepared food made with local produce; dinner is particularly recommended. Bedrooms, some at ground floor level, are individually furnished and vary in size. There is a terrace at the front where guests may enjoy a drink on warmer days.

**Rooms:** 9 annexe en suite (3 fmly) (4 GF) **S** £70–£195; **D** £95–£195* **Facilities:** STV tea/coffee Dinner available Direct dial WiFi **Extras:** Fresh milk, fruit **Conf:** Max 100 Thtr 100 Class 65 Board 65 **Parking:** 40 **Notes:** LB Closed 25 Dec eve-26 Dec eve & 1 Jan eve

## DIDMARTON
Map 4 ST88

# The Kings Arms

★★★★ ⊜ INN

**tel:** 01454 238245 **The Street GL9 1DT**
**email:** enquiries@kingsarmsdidmarton.co.uk **web:** www.kingsarmsdidmarton.co.uk
**dir:** *M4 junct 18, A46 towards Stroud. 6m, right onto A433. 3m to Didmarton. Kings Arms on left*

Part of The Epicurean Collection, The Kings Arms is a real gem. Bedrooms, converted from the old stables, are extremely comfortable, and are named after hounds who ran with the local hunt. Locally sourced produce is cooked with passion and presented with flair. The inn has been fully restored but retains its stone-flagged floors, heavy wooden tables, rustic walls and simple decoration. Real ales are also a feature. Outside, the garden provides a great space in the summer.

**Rooms:** 6 en suite (1 GF) **S** £60–£80; **D** £95–£130 **Facilities:** FTV tea/coffee Dinner available WiFi **Conf:** Max 30 Thtr 30 Board 18 **Parking:** 29

## EBRINGTON
Map 10 SP14

# The Ebrington Arms

★★★★ ⊛⊛ ⊜ INN

**tel:** 01386 593223 **GL55 6NH**
**email:** info@theebringtonarms.co.uk **web:** www.theebringtonarms.co.uk
**dir:** *From Chipping Campden take B4035 towards Shipston on Stour, left to Ebrington*

Nestled in the quiet, unspoilt village of Ebrington, just a couple of miles from Chipping Campden, this 17th-century inn offers an excellent selection of real ales, fine wines and really enjoyable award-winning cuisine utilising the finest of produce. Food is served in the friendly bar or in the cosy dining room where the open fire roars on chilly days. Bedrooms are full of character and include some welcome extras. A large beer garden and car park are also available.

**Rooms:** 5 en suite **Facilities:** FTV tea/coffee Dinner available WiFi **Extras:** Home-made cookies, sherry – complimentary **Conf:** Max 32 Thtr 32 Class 32 Board 25 **Parking:** 10 **Notes:** LB

## FALFIELD
Map 4 ST69

# The Park

★★★★ 🍽 GUEST ACCOMMODATION

**tel:** 01454 260550 **Gloucester Road GL12 8DR**
**email:** info@theparkfalfield.co.uk **web:** www.theparkfalfield.co.uk
**dir:** M5 junct 14 follow signs for A38 & Falfield (B4509). 1m on left

With easy access to the M5, this stylish accommodation provides high levels of quality and comfort throughout. Bedrooms offer a range of shapes and sizes and an impressive black and white decor theme runs throughout the building. Guests can enjoy breakfast and dinner in the comfortable dining room or a light snack in the bar area. Welcome extras include a full license and ample car parking. The pleasant surrounding gardens with outdoor seating also make this a popular wedding venue.

**Rooms:** 10 en suite (1 fmly) **S** £70–£80; **D** £70–£120* **Facilities:** FTV DVD TVL tea/coffee Dinner available Direct dial Licensed WiFi **Parking:** 50 **Notes:** Civ wed 100

## FRAMPTON MANSELL
Map 4 SO90

# The Crown Inn

★★★★ 🍽 INN

**tel:** 01285 760601 **GL6 8JG**
**email:** enquiries@thecrowninn-cotswolds.co.uk **web:** www.thecrowninn-cotswolds.co.uk
**dir:** Off A419 signed Frampton Mansell, 0.75m at village centre

This establishment was a cider house in the 17th century, and guests today will find that roaring log fires, locally brewed ales and traditional, home-cooked food are all on offer. The comfortable, well-equipped bedrooms are in an annexe, and ample parking is available.

**Rooms:** 12 annexe en suite (1 fmly) (4 GF) **S** £70–£95; **D** £95–£115* **Facilities:** tea/coffee Dinner available WiFi **Conf:** Max 40 **Parking:** 35 **Notes:** LB

## GLOUCESTER
Map 10 SO81

# The Wharf House Restaurant with Rooms

★★★★ ⚛ RESTAURANT WITH ROOMS

**tel:** 01452 332900 **Over GL2 8DB**
**email:** enquiries@thewharfhouse.co.uk **web:** www.thewharfhouse.co.uk
**dir:** From A40 between Gloucester & Highnam exit at lights for Over, Establishment signed

The Wharf House was built to replace the old lock cottage and, as the name suggests, it is located at the very edge of the river; it has pleasant views and an outdoor terrace. The bedrooms and bathrooms have been finished to a high standard, and there are plenty of guest extras. Seasonal, local produce can be enjoyed both at breakfast and dinner in the delightful AA Rosetted restaurant. The Wharf House is owned and run by the Herefordshire and Gloucestershire Canal Trust, and all profits go towards the promotion and restoration of the Hereford and Gloucester Canal.

*The Wharf House Restaurant with Rooms*

**Rooms:** 7 en suite (1 fmly) (1 GF) **Facilities:** STV FTV DVD Lounge tea/coffee Dinner available WiFi Fishing 🅿 **Extras:** Speciality toiletries – complimentary; mini-bar – chargeable **Parking:** 37 **Notes:** Closed 22 Dec–8 Jan RS Sun & Mon Check in before 6pm/restaurant closed evening

*See advert opposite*

## GUITING POWER
Map 10 SP02

# Guiting Guest House

★★★★ BED AND BREAKFAST

**tel:** 01451 850470 **Post Office Lane GL54 5TZ**
**email:** info@guitingguesthouse.com **web:** www.guitingguesthouse.com

Guiting Power is a quintessential, beautiful and peaceful Cotswold village, surrounded by stunning countryside, and well placed for exploring the entire region. Guiting Guest House is very close to the village shop, post office, the church and two excellent pubs. A 16th-century Cotswold-stone farmhouse with warming log fires in the winter, and a delightful garden, it offers comfortable rooms, breakfasts with local produce and home-made bread, and a friendly, peaceful atmosphere; all of which have made it a favourite with guests from all over the world. There are lots of walks right from the garden gate. Some bedrooms have four-poster beds, and baskets of fresh fruit and flowers provide a personal touch. Hairdryer, bathrobes and toiletries are provided for extra comfort.

**Rooms:** 5 rms (4 en suite) (1 pri facs) (2 GF) **S** £90–£110; **D** £90–£110* **Facilities:** FTV Lounge tea/coffee WiFi 🅿 **Extras:** Fresh fruit, flowers, robes – complimentary **Notes:** No children 5yrs Closed 25–26 Dec

## HYDE
Map 4 SO80

# The Ragged Cot

★★★★ 🍽 INN

**tel:** 01453 884643 & 07976 011198 **Cirencester Road GL6 8PE**
**email:** info@theraggedcot.co.uk **web:** www.theraggedcot.co.uk
**dir:** M5 junct 13 onto A419 signed Stroud/Cirencester. At Ashton Down Airfield rdbt, right signed Minchinhampton. 2m on left

Originally a 17th-century coaching inn, the property has been extended and offers a modern, large, airy bar and restaurant with a selection of good quality bedrooms equipped for the modern day traveller. An extensive collection of ever-changing artwork is an interesting feature. This friendly inn serves a wide selection of real ales and a menu focusing on locally sourced ingredients.

**Rooms:** 9 en suite (4 GF) **Facilities:** FTV DVD tea/coffee Dinner available WiFi 🛏36 **Extras:** Speciality toiletries **Parking:** 30

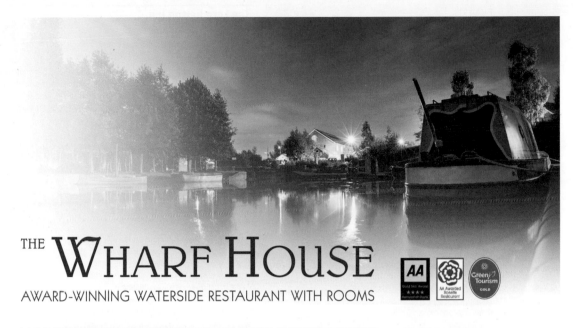

# THE WHARF HOUSE

## AWARD-WINNING WATERSIDE RESTAURANT WITH ROOMS

MODERN BRITISH AND EUROPEAN CUISINE WITH A TWIST

### Tasting Menu at The Wharf House Six Courses only £39.99 per person.

Lighter lunches including paninis from £4.50 and deli boards from £13 now available.

**Luxury accommodation with stunning riverside views.**

# 01452 332 900
## www.thewharfhouse.co.uk

Over, Gloucester, GL2 8DB
enquiries@thewharfhouse.co.uk
Directions: Turn off the A40 at traffic lights
250 yds west of Over Roundabout
(junction A40/A417). GR SO 816197

All profits from The Wharf House will be used for the promotion and restoration of the Hereford & Gloucester Canal.

## LECHLADE ON THAMES      Map 5 SU29

# The Riverside

★★★ INN

tel: 01367 252534 **Park End Wharf GL7 3AQ**
email: riverside@arkells.com **web:** www.riverside-lechlade.com

Located on the banks of the Thames, with an unrivalled position in Lechlade, this traditional inn is within easy reach of Swindon, Cirencester and the Cotswolds. Comfortable accommodation is located adjacent to the inn with its own entrance, all rooms are en suite with some suitable for families. Owned by the Arkell's family brewers, a great range of traditionally brewed beers is available.

**Rooms:** 6 en suite **Facilities:** Dinner available

## LOWER SLAUGHTER      Map 10 SP12

### Premier Collection

# The Slaughters Country Inn

★★★★★ ◉◉ INN

tel: 01451 822143 **GL54 2HS**
email: info@theslaughtersinn.co.uk **web:** www.theslaughtersinn.co.uk
**dir:** *Exit A429 at 'The Slaughters' sign, between Stow-on-the-Wold & Bourton-on-the-Water. In village centre*

This attractive 17th-century inn is set in beautiful grounds beside the River Eye. Inside, contemporary high quality bedrooms, all with modern bathrooms, blend well with the more traditional bar area with its beamed ceilings, open fires, and flagstone floors. The Eton Restaurant is an attractive setting where modern British cooking sits next to more classical dishes and there's a comfortable lounge in which to relax. Parking is a bonus. The Slaughters Country Inn is part of the Andrew Brownsword Hotels group, which is the AA's Hotel Group of the Year 2017–2018.

**Rooms:** 19 en suite 12 annexe en suite (3 fmly) (6 GF) **D** £120–£380*
**Facilities:** FTV DVD tea/coffee Dinner available Direct dial WiFi ⚓ **Parking:** 45
**Notes:** Civ wed 80

## MARSHFIELD      Map 4 ST77

# Snow at the Barn

★★★★ ⬤ BED AND BREAKFAST

tel: 01225 892339 & 07973 382028 **The Barn, Chippenham Road SN14 8NY**
email: snowatthebarn@icloud.com **web:** www.snowatthebarn.co.uk
**dir:** *M4 junct 18, A46 towards Bath. After 3m left at Cold Ashton rdbt onto A420 towards Chippenham. 3m turn right into Tormarton Rd then left into Chippenham Rd, barn on right*

Located in the pleasant village of Marshfield, this friendly accommodation offers a relaxed ambience just a short drive from Bath. Guests are welcomed with tea and cake and are assured of attentive hospitality throughout their stay. Breakfast includes a good selection of carefully-prepared hot and cold dishes, all served around one large table in the comfortable dining room. Off-street car parking is also provided.

**Rooms:** 3 en suite **Facilities:** FTV iPod docking station tea/coffee WiFi ⅃18
⚓ **Parking:** 6

# The Lord Nelson Inn

★★★ INN

tel: 01225 891820 **1 & 2 High Street SN14 8LP**

Popular and traditional style village inn with a good local following and a range of home cooked meals and ales available in the relaxing bar. Bedrooms and bathrooms offer a range of shapes and sizes and are all located above the inn. Parking usually available on the main street right outside the accommodation.

**Rooms:** 3 en suite **Facilities:** Dinner available

## MORETON-IN-MARSH      Map 10 SP23

# Horse and Groom

★★★★ ⬤ ⬤ INN

tel: 01386 700413 **Bourton-on-the-Hill GL56 9AQ**
email: info@horseandgroom.info

Located on the hill at Bourton-on-the-Hill, this relaxing inn offers an ideal base for exploring many famous Cotswold villages and attractions. Bedrooms and bathrooms are very well decorated and furnished and a good selection of real ales is offered in the bar. Both dinner and breakfast are highlights here and offer a range of delicious dishes made from local quality produce. Dinner is by way of blackboard specials to reflect the freshest produce available. A car park and rear garden with seating are both welcome extras.

**Rooms:** 5 en suite **Facilities:** Dinner available **Parking**

## NAILSWORTH      Map 4 ST89

# Wild Garlic Restaurant and Rooms

★★★★ ◉◉ ⬤ RESTAURANT WITH ROOMS

tel: 01453 832615 **3 Cossack Square GL6 0DB**
email: info@wild-garlic.co.uk **web:** www.wild-garlic.co.uk
**dir:** *M4 junct 18, A46 towards Stroud. Enter Nailsworth, left at rdbt, immediately left. Establishment opposite Britannia pub*

Situated in a quiet corner of charming Nailsworth, this restaurant with rooms offers a delightful combination of welcoming, relaxed hospitality and serious cuisine. The spacious and well-equipped bedrooms are situated above the award-winning restaurant. The small and friendly team of staff ensure guests are very well looked after throughout their stay.

**Rooms:** 5 en suite (2 fmly) **S** £80–£160; **D** £85–£160* **Facilities:** STV FTV DVD tea/coffee Dinner available WiFi ⅃18 Fishing Shooting, hot air balloning
**Extras:** Speciality toiletries, spring water – complimentary; mini-bar – chargeable
**Conf:** Max 6 Thtr 6 Class 6 Board 6

## NAUNTON      Map 10 SP12

# Mill View Guest House

★★★★ GUEST HOUSE

tel: 01451 850586 & 07887 553571 **2 Mill View GL54 3AF**
email: patricia@millview.myzen.co.uk **web:** www.millviewguesthousecotswolds.com
**dir:** *Exit B4068 to E end of village*

Mill View Guest House takes its name from the historic watermill opposite, and the owners of this former family home aim to provide every comfort. A warm welcome and attentive care is assured in this non-smoking house, which has one ground floor bedroom, equipped for easier access. The accommodation provides a good base for walkers or for touring Gloucestershire.

**Rooms:** 3 en suite (1 GF) **S** £45–£55; **D** £60–£80* **Facilities:** FTV DVD iPod docking station TVL tea/coffee Dinner available WiFi 🍷 **Extras:** Snacks, sherry – complimentary **Parking:** 4 **Notes:** LB

---

| NETHER WESTCOTE | Map 10 SP22 |
|---|---|

### Premier Collection

## The Feathered Nest Country Inn

★★★★★ 🌐🌐🌐 ⚘ INN

**tel:** 01993 833030 **OX7 6SD**
**email:** info@thefeatherednestinn.co.uk **web:** www.thefeatherednestinn.co.uk
**dir:** A424 between Burford & Stow-on-the-Wold, follow signs

Located in the picturesque Cotswold village of Nether Westcote, with rolling views over the Evenlode Valley, this charming village inn offers a cosy base from which to explore the pretty countryside. There are four luxurious en suite bedrooms, all individually designed combining quality antiques and modern extras. Service is attentive and helpful while food is a delight, offering a selection of carefully crafted dishes using the best of quality, seasonal produce. Fish is delivered fresh from the coast, and meals can be enjoyed on the charming outdoor terrace in warmer weather.

**Rooms:** 4 en suite **Facilities:** STV FTV DVD TVL tea/coffee Dinner available Direct dial WiFi **Extras:** Home-made biscuits, fruit – complimentary; robes **Parking:** 45 **Notes:** Closed 25 Dec RS Mon (ex BHs) Civ wed 200

---

| NEWENT | Map 10 SO72 |
|---|---|

## Kilcot Inn

★★★★ 🍺 INN

**tel:** 01989 720707 **Ross Road GL18 1NA**
**email:** info@kilcotinn.com **web:** www.kilcotinn.com

The inviting Kilcot Inn deals in the best traditions of hospitality, food and drink. From the selection of real ales and local ciders on tap, to the high quality produce used in the delicious dishes in the bar/restaurant there is something for everyone. The bedrooms and bathrooms above the inn provide high levels of quality and comfort. Outdoor seating is also available, including a pleasant garden area to the rear of the property.

**Rooms:** 4 en suite **D** £85–£95* **Facilities:** FTV Lounge tea/coffee Dinner available WiFi 🍷 **Parking:** 40

## Three Choirs Vineyards

★★★★ 🌐 RESTAURANT WITH ROOMS

**tel:** 01531 890223 **GL18 1LS**
**email:** info@threechoirs.com **web:** www.three-choirs-vineyards.co.uk
**dir:** On B4215 N of Newent, follow brown tourist signs

This thriving vineyard continues to go from strength to strength and provides a wonderfully different place to stay. The restaurant, which overlooks the 100-acre estate, enjoys a popular following thanks to well-executed dishes that make good use of local produce. Spacious, high quality bedrooms are equipped with many extras, and each opens onto a private patio area which has lovely views.

**Rooms:** 11 annexe en suite (1 fmly) (11 GF) **S** £135–£195; **D** £145–£195*
**Facilities:** FTV Lounge tea/coffee Dinner available Direct dial WiFi Wine tasting Vineyard Tours **Conf:** Max 20 Thtr 20 Class 15 Board 20 **Parking:** 11 **Notes:** LB Closed 24–26 Dec & 31 Dec–6 Jan

---

| OLD SODBURY | Map 4 ST78 |
|---|---|

## The Sodbury House

★★★★ GUEST HOUSE

**tel:** 01454 312847 **Badminton Road BS37 6LU**
**email:** info@sodburyhouse.co.uk **web:** www.sodburyhouse.co.uk
**dir:** M4 junct 18, A46 N, 2m left onto A432 to Chipping Sodbury, house 1m on left

This comfortably furnished, 19th-century farmhouse stands in six acres of grounds. The bedrooms, some located on the ground floor and some in buildings adjacent to the main house, have many extra facilities. Breakfast offers a varied choice and is served in the spacious breakfast room.

**Rooms:** 6 en suite 3 annexe en suite (1 fmly) (2 GF) **Facilities:** FTV Lounge TVL tea/coffee WiFi 🐾 🍷 **Parking:** 30 **Notes:** Closed 24 Dec–3 Jan

## PAINSWICK                                    Map 4 SO80

# The Falcon

★★★★ 🍴 🍺 INN

tel: 01452 814222 **New Street GL6 6UN**
email: info@falconpainswick.co.uk **web:** www.falconpainswick.co.uk
**dir:** *On A46 in centre of Painswick*

The Falcon is an imposing Cotswold stone building that dates back to 1554, and sits on the main street of this attractive Cotswold village. Overlooking St Mary's church with its famous clipped yews, it's also within easy driving distance of Cheltenham Racecourse. Bedrooms are all individually designed and well equipped with comfortable beds, crisp white linen and very good quality toiletries. With an eclectic mix of furnishings, and chalky white and muted duck egg blue walls, this popular place has a charming atmosphere with a good mix of locals and tourists. The kitchen serves an accomplished bistro-style menu awash with locally-sourced, seasonal ingredients.

**Rooms:** 8 en suite 3 annexe en suite (1 fmly) (1 GF) **Facilities:** FTV tea/coffee Dinner available WiFi ⅃18 🐾 **Extras:** Speciality toiletries **Conf:** Max 30 Thtr 30 Class 20 Board 20 **Parking:** 20

## PUCKLECHURCH                                Map 4 ST77

# Orchard Cottage Bed & Breakfast

AA ADVERTISED

tel: 0117 937 3284 **18 Homefield Road BS16 9QD**
email: davidmstacey@gmail.com **web:** www.orchardcottagebandb.co.uk

Orchard Cottage is adjacent to Pucklechurch conservation area, and is a completely private duplex apartment with its own entrance and free parking, available for B&B or self-catering. The apartment includes a lounge with designer furniture, LCD TV, WiFi, iPod dock, fridge and tea/coffee making facilities. The bedroom has a round window with a lovely view of the conservation area barn. The apartment is suitable for adults only.

**Rooms:** 1 en suite **S** £62.10–£69; **D** £71.10–£79* **Facilities:** STV FTV DVD iPod docking station TVL tea/coffee WiFi 🐾 **Parking:** 4 **Notes:** No children 18yrs

## SELSLEY                                      Map 4 SO80

# The Bell Inn

★★★★ ◉◉ INN

tel: 01453 753801 **Bell Lane GL5 5JY**
email: info@thebellinnselsley.com **web:** www.thebellinnselsley.com

This traditional 16th-century, Grade II listed country inn has been refurbished to provide relaxing quality and comfort throughout. Guests can chose from a selection of real ales in the bar or enjoy the surrounding countryside views from the pleasant garden with seating. A separate gin bar has also been recently opened offering guests a choice of around 30 gins. The food here should not be missed, with a range of carefully selected and locally sourced produce.

**Rooms:** 2 en suite **S** £65–£105; **D** £70–£120 (room only)* **Facilities:** FTV Dinner available WiFi **Extras:** Nespresso machines **Parking:** 12 **Notes:** No children RS winter closed between 3pm & 5pm

## STOW-ON-THE-WOLD                             Map 10 SP12

### Premier Collection

# Old Stocks Inn

★★★★★ ◉ 🍴 RESTAURANT WITH ROOMS

tel: 01451 830666 **The Square GL54 1AP**
email: info@oldstocksinn.com **web:** www.oldstocksinn.com
**dir:** *From A429 turn into Market Sq, located opposite Town Hall*

Old Stocks Inn has been lovingly restored, and offers a mix of modern facilities and 17th-century charm. Bedrooms are well designed and make good use of space; there are some unique features in the 'great' rooms. Cuisine is at the heart of the operation, with a café, restaurant and bar making up the impressive ground floor. Award-winning breakfasts are served in the restaurant, while lunch and dinner also offer award-winning dining.

**Rooms:** 13 en suite 3 annexe en suite (4 fmly) (3 GF) **D** £99–£279* **Facilities:** FTV iPod docking station Lounge tea/coffee Dinner available Direct dial WiFi 🐾 **Extras:** Mini-bar, Nespresso machine **Conf:** Max 16 Thtr 10 Board 16 **Parking:** 10 **Notes:** Closed 25 Dec RS 24 Dec no accommodation

## The Porch House

★★★★★ ◎◎ 🍴 INN

**tel:** 01451 870048 **Digbeth Street GL54 1BN**
**email:** book@porch-house.co.uk **web:** www.porch-house.co.uk/home
**dir:** *Short walk from main square, on left*

Originally built in 975 AD, The Porch House is reputed to be England's oldest inn, and many of the original features can be seen today in the beautifully presented public areas. The inn has 13 individually styled bedrooms, all equipped to a high standard, with WiFi available throughout. Guests have a choice of cosy authentic bars — with exposed stone walls and log fires — for casual dining. The award-winning restaurant is very well appointed and the unmissable breakfast features lots of local produce.

**Rooms:** 13 en suite (2 fmly) (2 GF) **Facilities:** STV FTV Lounge TVL tea/coffee Dinner available WiFi 🔔 **Conf:** Max 12 **Parking:** 4

## Woodlands Guest House

★★★★ 🍴 GUEST ACCOMMODATION

**tel:** 01451 832346 **Upper Swell GL54 1EW**
**email:** amandak247@talktalk.net **web:** www.woodlands-guest-house.co.uk
**dir:** *Upper Swell 1m from Stow-on-the-Wold, take B4077 (Tewkesbury Road)*

Situated in the small hamlet of Upper Swell, Woodlands provides an ideal base for exploring the many charming nearby villages. This establishment enjoys delightful rural views and has comfortably appointed bedrooms with a good range of extra accessories. Breakfast is served in the welcoming dining room around the communal dining table. Off-road parking is available.

**Rooms:** 4 en suite (2 GF) **Facilities:** FTV tea/coffee WiFi **Parking:** 8 **Notes:** LB

## Sheep on Sheep Street

★★★★ INN

**tel:** 01451 830344 **Sheep Street GL54 1AG**
**email:** info@thesheepstow.co.uk **web:** www.thesheepstow.co.uk
**dir:** *From A429 onto A436 (Sheep Street)*

The attractive 17th-century buildings that make up the Sheep on Sheep Street have undergone a sympathetic, stylish and sophisticated refurbishment. Rooms are well-appointed and attractively furnished. All have modern en suite facilities supplied with luxurious toiletries. On the ground floor, the bar and dining area provide a relaxed and casual dining experience, with a wood-fired oven offering a wide range of speciality pizzas alongside à la carte dishes. Car parking is available at the rear of the building. Complimentary WiFi is available throughout.

**Rooms:** 22 en suite (1 fmly) (3 GF) **Facilities:** Lounge tea/coffee Dinner available Direct dial WiFi **Extras:** Speciality toiletries **Parking:** 22 **Notes:** LB

## Aston House

★★★★ BED AND BREAKFAST

**tel:** 01451 830475 **Broadwell GL56 0TJ**
**email:** fja@astonhouse.net **web:** www.astonhouse.net
**dir:** *A429 from Stow-on-the-Wold towards Moreton-in-Marsh, 1m right at x-rds to Broadwell, Aston House 0.5m on left*

Peacefully located on the edge of the village of Broadwell, this is an ideal base from which to explore the Cotswolds. A warm and genuine welcome is guaranteed and every effort is made to ensure a relaxed and enjoyable stay. Great care and attention are hallmarks here, and bedrooms come equipped with many thoughtful extras such as electric blankets.

**Rooms:** 2 en suite **D** £90–£95* **Facilities:** FTV tea/coffee WiFi 🔔 Stairlift **Extras:** Chocolates **Parking:** 2 **Notes:** No children 10yrs Closed Nov–Feb

## Corsham Field Farmhouse

★★★★ FARMHOUSE

**tel:** 01451 831750 **Bledington Road GL54 1JH**
**email:** farmhouse@corshamfield.co.uk **web:** www.corshamfield.co.uk
**dir:** *A436 from Stow towards Chipping Norton. After 1m bear right onto B4450 (Bledington Rd), 1st farm on right in 0.5m, opposite Oddington turn*

This charming farmhouse offers superb views over the peaceful Cotswold countryside and has comfortable, well furnished bedrooms located in the main house or an adjoining cottage. The garden, with relaxing chairs and tables, provides a lovely spot for picnics and observing the wildlife. Freshly prepared breakfast is served in the spacious dining room/lounge, and the local pub is only five minutes' walk away for dinner.

**Rooms:** 7 rms (6 en suite) (1 pri facs) (2 fmly) (2 GF) **S** £55–£70; **D** £70–£90* **Facilities:** FTV Lounge tea/coffee WiFi **Extras:** Speciality toiletries, sweets **Parking:** 10 **Notes:** LB No children 5yrs 100 acres arable

## The Kings Head Inn

★★★★ ◎ INN

**tel:** 01608 658365 **The Green, Bledington OX7 6XQ**
**email:** info@kingsheadinn.net **web:** www.kingsheadinn.net
**dir:** *4m SE off B4450*

In prime position on the delightful village green near the river, this 16th-century inn has spacious public areas with open fires, uneven floors, beams and wood furnishings. The comfortable restaurant offers an excellent dining experience and the bedrooms have been creatively decorated and well furnished; some rooms are in a converted annexe.

**Rooms:** 6 en suite 6 annexe en suite (3 GF) **S** £75–£105; **D** £100–£135* **Facilities:** FTV TVL tea/coffee Dinner available WiFi **Extras:** Speciality toiletries **Parking:** 24 **Notes:** Closed 25–26 Dec RS weekdays

## THORNBURY                                                    Map 4 ST69

# Thornbury Lodge
★★★★ GUEST ACCOMMODATION

**tel:** 01454 281144 **Bristol Road BS35 3XL**
**email:** info@thornburygc.co.uk **web:** www.thornburygc.co.uk
**dir:** *M5 junct 16, A38 towards Thornbury. At lights (Berkeley Vale Motors) turn left, 1m on left*

With good access to both the M4 and M5, this lodge offers a popular retreat for both business and leisure guests, and is surrounded by pleasant scenery including a golf course. Dinner and breakfast can be enjoyed in the clubhouse-style dining area where an abundant choice is offered. Spacious and comfortable bedrooms are located in a lodge adjacent to the main clubhouse. An excellent golf driving range is also available.

**Rooms:** 7 en suite 4 annexe en suite (11 fmly) (7 GF) **Facilities:** FTV TVL tea/coffee Dinner available Direct dial Licensed WiFi ₤36 Driving range Practice putting green **Conf:** Max 165 Thtr 165 Class 60 Board 40 **Parking:** 200 **Notes:** LB Closed 25 Dec Civ wed 120

## WICK                                                         Map 4 ST77

# Blue Lodge Farm
★★★★ FARMHOUSE

**tel:** 0117 937 2254 & 07748 733740 **Lodge Road, Abson BS30 5TX**
**email:** info@bluelodgefarm.co.uk **web:** www.bluelodgefarm.co.uk
**dir:** *Phone for directions*

Peacefully located and surrounded by countryside, this pleasant farm offers a relaxed environment and yet is only a short drive from Bath or Bristol. Bedrooms and bathrooms are spacious and comfortable and all have their own front door, being located in a modern, purpose-built annexe. A garden and car park are both available for guest use. Breakfast make use of good quality produce and is served in the main building.

**Rooms:** 3 annexe en suite (1 fmly) (3 GF) **Facilities:** FTV Lounge WiFi 🛁
**Extras:** Speciality toiletries, fruit – complimentary **Parking:** 6 **Notes:** 52 acres beef

## WINCHCOMBE                                                   Map 10 SP02

# The Lion Inn
★★★★ ◉ INN

**tel:** 01242 603300 **37 North Street GL54 5PS**
**email:** reception@thelionwinchcombe.co.uk **web:** www.thelionwinchcombe.co.uk
**dir:** *In town centre (parking in Chandos St)*

This 15th-century inn is situated in the centre of historic Winchcombe, a pretty Cotswold village. The accommodation has been recently updated to offer comfortable bedrooms that make the most of the historic elements of the property. Close by is Sudeley Castle, where Queen Katherine Parr, sixth wife of Henry VIII, is buried, while Cheltenham Racecourse is not far away. A seasonal menu is offered in the award-winning restaurant enhanced by daily-changing dishes. Parking is available in the pay and display car park to the rear of the property.

**Rooms:** 8 en suite (1 fmly) (1 GF) **D** £110–£195* **Facilities:** Dinner available Direct dial WiFi **Extras:** Speciality toiletries – complimentary **Conf:** Max 20 Thtr 20 Class 12 Board 20 **Notes:** RS 25 Dec evening closed

# Sudeley Hill Farm
★★★★ 🏡 FARMHOUSE

**tel:** 01242 602344 **GL54 5JB**
**email:** sudeleyhillfarm@gmail.com
**dir:** *Exit B4632 in Winchcombe into Castle St. White Hart Inn on corner, farm 0.75m on left*

Located on an 800-acre mixed arable and sheep farm, this 15th-century stone farmhouse is full of original features including fireplaces and exposed beams. Genuine hospitality is always on offer here together with a relaxed and welcoming atmosphere. The comfortable bedrooms are filled with thoughtful extras, and memorable breakfasts are served in the elegant dining room that overlooks the immaculate gardens.

**Rooms:** 3 en suite (1 fmly) **S** £55–£60; **D** £75–£80* **Facilities:** FTV DVD TVL tea/coffee WiFi 🛁 **Parking:** 10 **Notes:** Closed Xmas 800 acres sheep/arable/pigs

# Wesley House
★★★★ ◉◉ 🏡 RESTAURANT WITH ROOMS

**tel:** 01242 602366 **High Street GL54 5LJ**
**email:** enquiries@wesleyhouse.co.uk **web:** www.wesleyhouse.co.uk
**dir:** *In town centre*

This 15th-century, half-timbered property is named after John Wesley, founder of the Methodist Church, who stayed here while preaching in the town. Bedrooms are small and full of character. In the rear dining room, where the food has been awarded two AA Rosettes, a unique lighting system changes colour to suit the mood required, and also highlights the various floral displays created by a world-renowned flower arranger. A glass atrium covers the outside terrace.

**Rooms:** 5 en suite **S** £75–£85; **D** £95–£110* **Facilities:** FTV Lounge tea/coffee Dinner available WiFi 🛁 **Notes:** RS Sun eve & Mon Restaurant closed Civ wed 60

## GREATER MANCHESTER

### ALTRINCHAM
Map 15 SJ78

## Ash Farm Country House

★★★★ ⚫ GUEST ACCOMMODATION

**tel:** 0161 929 9290 **Park Lane, Little Bollington WA14 4TJ**
**email:** ashfarm@gmail.com **web:** www.ashfarm.co.uk
**dir:** *M56 junct 7 onto A56 at Lymm Rd 1st right into Park Ln, house at bottom of lane on right, just before The Swan with Two Nicks pub*

A warm welcome is guaranteed at this charming 18th-century National Trust farmhouse, which enjoys a peaceful location along a quiet country lane. The bedrooms are attractively presented and public areas include a book-filled lounge with its crackling log fire and cosy sofas. Free WiFi is available and the house is equally popular with business and leisure guests. Dunham Massey Hall and Deerpark is a short stroll from the house while Manchester Airport is just a 15-minute drive away.

**Rooms:** 3 rms (2 en suite) (1 pri facs) 1 annexe en suite (1 GF) **Facilities:** FTV Lounge tea/coffee Licensed WiFi ⓦ **Extras:** Robes, mineral water, chocolates **Conf:** Max 10 Class 10 **Parking:** 12 **Notes:** No children 12yrs Closed 22 Dec–2 Jan

### ASHTON-UNDER-LYNE
Map 16 SJ99

## Broadoak

★★★★ ⚫ INN

**tel:** 0161 330 2764 **69 Broadoak Road OL6 8QD**
**email:** broadoakhotel@googlemail.com **web:** www.broadoakhotel.co.uk
**dir:** *M60 junct 23 follow signs to Oldham (A627). Right at lights into Wilshaw Ln. Right at rdbt, Broadoak on right*

This inn is popular with locals, and ideally situated for Manchester, with excellent transport links to the ring road, and trams into the city. Hearty meals are served in the pub restaurant by the friendly team. Accommodation is bang up to date; stylish with a range of modern amenities including complimentary WiFi and large TVs. Family suite available. Functions are also catered for.

**Rooms:** 7 en suite (1 fmly) **Facilities:** FTV Lounge TVL tea/coffee Dinner available Direct dial WiFi ⓦ **Conf:** Max 100 Thtr 100 Class 50 Board 50 **Parking:** 25 **Notes:** LB

### DELPH
Map 16 SD90

## The Old Bell Inn

★★★★ ⚫ INN

**tel:** 01457 870130 **5 Huddersfield Road OL3 5EG**
**email:** info@theoldbellinn.co.uk **web:** www.theoldbellinn.co.uk
**dir:** *M62 junct 22 onto A672. In Denshaw onto A6052, through Delph to x-rds with A62. Turn left, 100yds on left*

Formerly a coaching inn, dating back to 1835, and situated in a rural village yet close to motorway links, The Old Bell has a quiet ambience allied with refined service. Hospitality is a real strength of the young and enthusiastic team. Bedrooms offer space, quality and comfort. The conservatory lounge is the perfect place to finish the evening after dinner in the modern restaurant.

**Rooms:** 18 en suite (1 fmly) **S** £59.50–£69.50; **D** £95–£125^ **Facilities:** FTV TVL tea/coffee Dinner available Direct dial WiFi **Parking:** 20

### MANCHESTER
Map 15 SJ89

## The Ascott

★★★★ GUEST ACCOMMODATION

**tel:** 0161 950 2453 **6 Half Edge Lane, Ellesmere Park M30 9GJ**
**email:** ascotthotelmanchester@yahoo.co.uk **web:** www.ascotthotelmanchester.co.uk
**dir:** *M602 junct 2, left into Wellington Rd, 0.25m, right into Abbey Grove & left into Half Edge Ln*

Set in a mainly residential area close to major routes, this early Victorian house, once the home of the Mayor of Eccles, provides thoughtfully furnished bedrooms with smart modern bathrooms. A choice of breakfast rooms is available and there is an elegant lounge.

**Rooms:** 14 en suite (1 fmly) (4 GF) **Facilities:** FTV Lounge TVL tea/coffee Direct dial WiFi **Parking:** 12 **Notes:** Closed 22 Dec–2 Jan RS Sun & Fri Closed 1–5pm

### OLDHAM
Map 16 SD90

## The White Hart Inn

★★★★ ⚫⚫ INN

**tel:** 01457 872566 **51 Stockport Road, Lydgate OL4 4JJ**
**email:** bookings@thewhitehart.co.uk **web:** www.thewhitehart.co.uk

Located on the edge of the Pennines in the small village of Lydgate, this inn is the perfect combination of modern style and old-world tradition. A choice of dining options is provided; the Brasserie serving good quality home cooking, and the restaurant, which has been awarded two AA Rosettes and provides a more formal approach. Bedrooms are comfortable and well-appointed with amenities such as TV, complimentary WiFi and well-stocked hospitality trays. Weddings and events are catered for in a purpose-built suite.

**Rooms:** 12 en suite 4 annexe en suite (5 fmly) (2 GF) **S** £145; **D** £185* **Facilities:** FTV DVD Lounge TVL tea/coffee Dinner available Direct dial WiFi **Extras:** Speciality toiletries, home-made biscuits **Conf:** Max 220 Thtr 220 Class 120 Board 60 **Parking:** 65 **Notes:** Closed 24–26 Dec & 1 Jan Civ wed 220

## STOCKPORT
Map 16 SJ89

## Innkeeper's Lodge Stockport
★★★ INN

**tel:** 08451 551551 *(Calls cost 2p per minute plus your phone company's access charge)*
**271 Wellington Road, North Heaton Chapel SK4 5BP**
**email:** info@innkeeperslodge.com **web:** www.innkeeperslodge.com

At Innkeeper's Lodge you'll find accommodation with comfort and character in equal measure, and everything needed for a relaxing stay, from easy check-in and free parking to complimentary breakfast and a cosy pub serving great value food and drink on the doorstep. Each Lodge has quality rooms, and there are Lodges in a variety of locations from towns and cities to countryside settings across the UK.

**Rooms:** 22 en suite (1 fmly) (1 GF) **Facilities:** FTV tea/coffee Dinner available WiFi

## HAMPSHIRE

## ALTON
Map 5 SU73

## The Anchor Inn
★★★★ ◉◉ INN

**tel:** 01420 23261 **Lower Froyle GU34 4NA**
**email:** info@anchorinnatlowerfroyle.co.uk **web:** www. anchorinnatlowerfroyle.co.uk
**dir:** *From A3 follow Bentley signs & inn signs*

The Anchor Inn is located in the tranquil village of Lower Froyle. Luxury rooms are designed to reflect the traditional English inn style with charming decor, pictures, and a selection of books. The restaurant welcomes both residents and non-residents with classic pub cooking, which has been awarded two AA Rosettes, served in impressive surroundings, with feature wooden floors and period furnishings.

**Rooms:** 5 en suite **S** £90–£210; **D** £90–£210* **Facilities:** FTV DVD tea/coffee Dinner available Direct dial WiFi **Extras:** Mini-fridge **Conf:** Max 40 Thtr 40 Class 30 Board 24 **Parking:** 30 **Notes:** RS 25–26 Dec, 31 Dec–1 Jan Civ wed 45

## ANDOVER
Map 5 SU34

## The George and Dragon
★★★★ ◉ INN

**tel:** 01264 736277 **The Square, Hurstbourne Tarrant SP11 0AA**
**email:** info@georgeanddragon.com **web:** www.georgeanddragon.com
**dir:** *N of Andover on A343, in middle of village*

With a history dating back to the 16th century, this former coaching inn was recently given a new lease of life with a complete renovation. The results are impressive, with wonderfully comfortable beds, stylish decor and contemporary bathrooms. The bar is the focus downstairs, where a pre-dinner drink can be enjoyed before sampling the very enjoyable output from the kitchen. Crackling fires and low beams add to the charm of this revitalised village local.

**Rooms:** 8 en suite (1 fmly) **Facilities:** FTV tea/coffee Dinner available WiFi ⊕
**Conf:** Max 22 Board 22 **Parking:** 17

## The Hatchet Inn
★★★ INN

**tel:** 01264 730229 **Lower Chute SP11 9DX**
**email:** info@thehatchetinn.co.uk **web:** www.thehatchetinn.co.uk
**dir:** *A303 exit signed Weyhill/Monxton onto A343. Follow signs for The Chutes*

Dating back to the 13th century, this picturesque thatched inn is very much the traditional village local, providing a warm welcome to all. Bedrooms offer good levels of comfort with all the essentials for a relaxing and rewarding stay. A good choice is offered at dinner, while breakfast provides a tasty start to the day. Many original features remain in the bar and public areas, all adding to the unique charms of this popular hostelry. Additional facilities include gun cabinets for those shooting in the area.

**Rooms:** 7 annexe en suite (2 fmly) (3 GF) **S** £70; **D** £80* **Facilities:** FTV TVL tea/coffee Dinner available WiFi ⊕ **Conf:** Max 20 Board 20 **Parking:** 50 **Notes:** LB

## ASHURST
Map 5 SU31

## Forest Gate Lodge
★★★★ BED AND BREAKFAST

**tel:** 023 8029 3026 **161 Lyndhurst Road SO40 7AW**
**email:** forestgatelodge161@hotmail.co.uk **web:** www.forestgatelodge.co.uk

Forest Gate Lodge is located in Ashurst, just a short drive from all that the New Forest has to offer. Bedrooms have modern decor, furnishings and come equipped with digital TV, DVD and free WiFi access. There is a guest lounge on the ground floor and guests can enjoy a cooked or continental breakfast in the dining room. Off-road parking is available, and there are restaurants and pubs within a short walking distance of the property.

**Rooms:** 5 en suite **D** £75–£85* **Facilities:** FTV DVD iPod docking station TVL tea/coffee WiFi ⊕ **Parking:** 6 **Notes:** LB No children 5–12yrs

## BARTON-ON-SEA
Map 5 SZ29

### Premier Collection

## Pebble Beach
★★★★★ ◉ RESTAURANT WITH ROOMS

**tel:** 01425 627777 **Marine Drive BH25 7DZ**
**email:** mail@pebblebeach-uk.com **web:** www.pebblebeach-uk.com
**dir:** *A35 from Southampton onto A337 to New Milton, left into Barton Court Av to clifftop*

Situated on the clifftop, the restaurant at Pebble Beach boasts stunning views towards The Needles. Bedrooms and bathrooms (situated above the restaurant) are well equipped and provide a range of accessories. A freshly cooked breakfast is served in the main restaurant, or outside on the wonderful terrace. Next door, Petit Pebbles delicatessen is well worth a visit.

**Rooms:** 4 rms (3 en suite) (1 pri facs) **D** £79.95–£349.95* **Facilities:** FTV tea/coffee Dinner available Direct dial WiFi **Extras:** Speciality toiletries
**Conf:** Max 8 Thtr 8 Class 8 Board 8 **Parking:** 20 **Notes:** RS 25 Dec & 1 Jan dinner not available

## BASINGSTOKE
Map 5 SU65

### Innkeeper's Lodge Basingstoke

★★★ INN

**tel:** 08451 551551 *(Calls cost 2p per minute plus your phone company's access charge)*
**Andover Road, Clerken Green RG23 7EP**
**email:** info@innkeeperslodge.com **web:** www.innkeeperslodge.com

Located on the quiet outskirts of the town, Innkeeper's Lodge Basingstoke provides a good level of comfort and quality through the accommodation and public areas. Bedrooms are well appointed and fitted with extras tailored to the modern traveller. Meals and drinks are served in The Beach Arms, adjacent to the Lodge; a wide choice on the menu is sure to suit any appetite and all tastes.

**Rooms:** 22 en suite (4 fmly) (22 GF) **Facilities:** FTV tea/coffee Dinner available Direct dial WiFi **Parking:** 45

## BRANSGORE
Map 5 SZ19

### Tothill House

★★★★ BED AND BREAKFAST

**tel:** 01425 674414 **Black Lane, off Forest Road BH23 8EA**
**email:** enquiries@tothillhouse.com **web:** www.tothillhouse.com
**dir:** *M27 onto A31 or A35, between Burley & Bransgore*

Built for an admiral in 1908, Tothill House is located in the southern part of the New Forest. The garden backs on to the forest, and is frequently visited by deer, ponies and other wildlife. The spacious bedrooms are furnished to a high standard, reflecting the character of the house. There is an elegant library, and a generous breakfast is served in the dining room.

**Rooms:** 3 rms (2 en suite) (1 pri facs) **D** fr £80* **Facilities:** Lounge tea/coffee WiFi 🔒 **Parking:** 6 **Notes:** No children 16yrs Closed Nov–Feb

## BROCKENHURST
Map 5 SU30

### The Filly Inn

★★★★ INN

**tel:** 01590 623449 **Lymington Road SO42 7UF**
**email:** www.thefillyinn.co.uk **web:** www.thefillyinn.co.uk

Conveniently located in the New Forest, this traditional inn offers a characterful restaurant and bar, and has retained many original features. All the bedrooms are en suite with stylish decor and very comfortable furnishings. There is plenty of parking on site and a large garden for guests to enjoy. Both cooked and continental breakfasts are served in the main restaurant.

**Rooms:** 5 en suite **Facilities:** FTV Dinner available

## BROOK
Map 5 SU21

### The Bell Inn

★★★★ ⚜ INN

**tel:** 023 8081 2214 **SO43 7HE**
**email:** bell@bramshaw.co.uk **web:** www.bellinnbramshaw.co.uk
**dir:** *M27 junct 1 onto B3079, 1.5m on right*

This delightful inn is part of the Bramshaw Golf Club and is an ideal base for visiting the New Forest. Bedrooms are spacious and have been refurbished to a high standard. Public areas are full of character, and there is a welcoming bar, a popular restaurant and a comfortable lounge.

**Rooms:** 26 en suite 2 annexe en suite (2 fmly) (8 GF) **S** £69–£79; **D** £99–£179*
**Facilities:** TVL tea/coffee Dinner available Direct dial WiFi ⌁36 🔒 Boules Garden chess **Conf:** Max 40 Thtr 40 Class 16 Board 24 **Parking:** 150 **Notes:** LB Civ wed 50

## BURGHCLERE
Map 5 SU46

### Carpenters Arms

★★★ INN

**tel:** 01635 278251 **Harts Lane RG20 9JY**
**email:** thecarpenters.burghclere@arkells.com
**web:** www.carpentersarms-burghclere.co.uk
**dir:** *A34 Newbury Tothill Services, at rdbt take 2nd exit signed Burghclere. At end of road, turn left, 200m on right.*

Located in a tranquil setting just a couple of miles outside Newbury, this traditional inn offers comfortably appointed bedrooms boasting some traditional features and modern furnishings. All rooms are annexed, plenty of on-site parking available and guests can enjoy breakfast, lunch or dinner with a range of traditional pub dishes in the conservatory restaurant or bar.

**Rooms:** 4 annexe en suite (1 fmly) **Facilities:** FTV tea/coffee Dinner available **Parking:** 18

## COSHAM
Map 5 SU60

### Innkeeper's Lodge Portsmouth, Cosham

★★★★ GUEST ACCOMMODATION

**tel:** 0845 155 1551 *(Calls cost 2p per minute plus your phone company's access charge)*
**The Red Lion, London Road PO6 3EE**
**email:** info@innkeeperslodge.com **web:** www.innkeeperslodge.com
**dir:** *From A27 follow signs for Cosham (A397 Northern Rd) to London Rd*

This lodge is an ideal venue for business meetings or a base for exploring local attractions. Convenient for the M3 and M27, Cosham and Portsmouth & Southsea railway stations. It has fresh and contemporary, comfortable en suite bedrooms, attractive public areas and friendly, welcoming staff. The Red Lion offers a variety of drinks and a menu that includes handmade stone-baked pizzas. Free WiFi and on-site parking are a plus.

**Rooms:** 16 en suite **S** £69–£89; **D** £69–£89* **Facilities:** FTV Lounge TVL tea/coffee Dinner available Licensed WiFi **Parking:** 16

## DUMMER — Map 5 SU54

### Tower Hill House

★★★ BED AND BREAKFAST

**tel:** 01256 398340 **Tower Hill, Winchester Road RG25 2AL**
**email:** martin.hyndman@virgin.net **web:** www.accommodationinbasingstoke.co.uk
**dir:** *In village. M3 junct 7, A30 towards Winchester, 2nd left, opposite sign for North Waltham*

Ideally situated for access to the M3 and A30, while overlooking fields and countryside, this family-run bed and breakfast is in the pretty village of Dummer, just 10 minutes away from the centre of Basingstoke. Bedrooms are simply but comfortably furnished and a well-prepared breakfast is served in the cheerful dining room.

**Rooms:** 4 en suite **Facilities:** tea/coffee WiFi **Parking:** 6

## EMSWORTH — Map 5 SU70

### 36 on the Quay

★★★★ ◉◉◉ RESTAURANT WITH ROOMS

**tel:** 01243 375592 & 372257 **47 South Street PO10 7EG**
**email:** info@36onthequay.co.uk **web:** www. 36onthequay.co.uk
**dir:** *Last building on right in South St, which runs from square in centre of Emsworth*

Occupying a prime position with far-reaching views over the estuary, this 16th-century house is the scene for some accomplished and exciting cuisine. The elegant restaurant occupies centre stage with peaceful pastel shades, local art and crisp napery together with glimpses of the bustling harbour outside. The contemporary bedrooms offer style, comfort and thoughtful extras.

**Rooms:** 4 en suite **Facilities:** FTV iPod docking station tea/coffee Dinner available WiFi **Parking:** 6 **Notes:** LB Closed 3 weeks Jan, 1 week late May

### The Jingles

★★★★ 🍷 GUEST ACCOMMODATION

**tel:** 01243 373755 **77 Horndean Road PO10 7PU**
**email:** info@thejingles.co.uk **web:** www.thejingles.co.uk
**dir:** *A3 (M) junct 2, follow signs for Emsworth, 4m, 1st building in Emsworth on right*

The Jingles is a family-run business, located in the charming maritime village of Emsworth. Situated adjacent to open farmland, it's a great location for exploring both Portsmouth and Chichester. All bedrooms are en suite and decorated to a high standard. The dining room is the setting for a cooked English breakfast, and a drawing room is available for relaxing in. WiFi is available if required.

**Rooms:** 28 en suite (2 fmly) (7 GF) **Facilities:** FTV Lounge tea/coffee Licensed WiFi 🔒 **Extras:** Bottled water – complimentary **Parking:** 35 **Notes:** LB Closed 24 Dec–2 Jan

### The Crown

★★★ INN

**tel:** 01243 372806 **High Street PO10 7AW**
**email:** thecrownemsworth@aol.com **web:** www.thecrownemsworth.com

A historic property conveniently located in the centre of town with ample parking at the back. Long winding stairs and uneven corridors lead to well-appointed bedrooms which offer a range of amenities such as TVs and WiFi. Freshly prepared food is served in the well-stocked bar and the restaurant.

**Rooms:** 9 rms (7 en suite) (2 pri facs) (2 fmly) **Facilities:** FTV tea/coffee Dinner available WiFi ⅃18 **Conf:** Max 48 Thtr 48 Class 36 Board 24 **Parking:** 16

## FARNBOROUGH — Map 5 SU85

### The Alexandra Pub

★★★ INN

**tel:** 01252 519964 **74 Victoria Road GU14 7PH**
**email:** thealex@alexandrapub.co.uk **web:** www.alexandrapub.co.uk
**dir:** *M3 junct 4 onto A331 (Farnborough), at 1st rdbt take 2nd exit. Follow signs for A331 Hawley/Farnborough, at next rdbt 3rd exit. At next rdbt 1st exit onto Farnborough Rd (A325). 3rd exit at next rdbt into Victoria Rd*

Named after a young Danish princess who became a much loved queen, The Alexandra Pub remains at the heart of the local community. The inn has been refurbished to a good standard and retains its warm and welcoming feel. There are three well equipped en suite rooms offering comfortable accommodation. The bar is well stocked and secure parking is provided at the rear of the inn, as well as a dedicated smoking area.

**Rooms:** 3 en suite **S** £50–£75; **D** £50–£75* **Facilities:** STV FTV DVD Lounge TVL tea/coffee WiFi Pool table **Parking:** 16 **Notes:** Closed 24–25 Dec RS Xmas

## HAWKLEY — Map 5 SU72

### The Hawkley Inn

★★★★ 🍺 INN

**tel:** 01730 827205 **Pococks Lane GU33 6NE**
**email:** info@hawkleyinn.co.uk **web:** www.hawkleyinn.co.uk
**dir:** *A3 Liss rdbt towards Liss B3006. Right at Spread Eagle, follow brown tourist signs. After 3m, left to village centre*

The Hawkley Inn captures all that is required of a traditional inn and more. There are five beautifully appointed double rooms, which offer all the comforts required by discerning travellers. The bar is well stocked including a range of real ales while the chef-proprietor is passionate about local produce and prepares award-winning dishes. The rear garden is a haven of tranquillity.

**Rooms:** 5 en suite (1 fmly) **S** £95; **D** £95–£105* **Facilities:** STV FTV tea/coffee Dinner available WiFi ⅃18 **Extras:** Speciality teas **Parking:** 4

## HAYLING ISLAND
Map 5 SU70

### Ravensdale

★★★★ BED AND BREAKFAST

**tel:** 023 9246 3203 & 07802 188259 **19 St Catherines Road PO11 0HF**
**email:** phil.taylor@tayloredprint.co.uk **web:** www.ravensdale-hayling.co.uk
**dir:** *A27 onto A3023 at Langstone, cross Hayling Bridge, 3m to mini rdbt, right into Manor Rd, 1m. Right by Barley Mow into Station Rd, 3rd left into St Catherines Rd*

A warm welcome awaits you at this comfortable home, quietly situated near the beach and golf course. Bedrooms are attractive, very comfortable and enhanced with numerous thoughtful extras. One room is a triple and has its own separate facilities. Home cooking can be enjoyed at breakfast in the dining room, and there is also a lounge area.

**Rooms:** 3 rms (2 en suite) (1 pri facs) (1 fmly) **S** £50–£55; **D** £80–£88 **Facilities:** FTV DVD TVL tea/coffee WiFi **Extras:** Flowers, chocolates – complimentary **Parking:** 4 **Notes:** No children 8yrs Closed last 2 weeks Dec & 1st 2 weeks Jan

## HIGHCLERE
Map 5 SU45

### The Yew Tree

★★★★ ◉◉ RESTAURANT WITH ROOMS

**tel:** 01635 253360 **Hollington Cross RG20 9SE**
**email:** info@theyewtree.co.uk **web:** www.theyewtree.co.uk
**dir:** *1m S of Highclere village*

Part of The Epicurean Collection, this attractive 17th-century country inn has comfortable bedrooms, decorated with William Morris print wallpaper and retaining traditional features, giving it an overall cosy feel. Great British cooking can be enjoyed in the attractively-decorated restaurant, where good use is made of high-quality produce and fresh ingredients. The garden, with its own bar and dining areas, is a real bonus.

**Rooms:** 6 en suite 2 annexe en suite **S** £95–£125; **D** £95–£125 **Facilities:** FTV Lounge tea/coffee Dinner available WiFi ✿ **Parking:** 35

## HOOK
Map 5 SU75

### Innkeeper's Lodge Hook

★★★★ INN

**tel:** 08451 126077 & 551551 *(Calls to both numbers cost 2p per minute plus your phone company's access charge)* **The White Hart, London Road RG27 9DZ**
**email:** info@innkeeperslodge.com **web:** www.innkeeperslodge.com
**dir:** *M3 junct 5, follow signs for Hook (B3349). At next rdbt, 1st exit into Station Rd. Next rdbt 3rd exit into London Rd (A30), on right*

This recently refurbished inn is located in the centre of Hook, between Basingstoke and Fleet. Bedrooms are modern in style and very comfortably appointed, ideal for both leisure and corporate guests alike. All rooms are well equipped with Hypnos beds, digital TVs and free WiFi throughout. A cooked or continental breakfast is served in the restaurant, where guests can also relax in the evening for dinner.

**Rooms:** 21 en suite (4 fmly) (21 GF) **S** £69–£79; **D** £69–£79* **Facilities:** FTV Lounge tea/coffee Dinner available WiFi **Parking:** 21 **Notes:** LB

## HURSLEY
Map 5 SU42

### The Kings Head

★★★★ ◉ INN

**tel:** 01962 775208 **Main Road SO21 2JW**
**email:** enquiries@kingsheadhursley.co.uk **web:** www.kingsheadhursley.co.uk
**dir:** *M3 junct 11, follow signs for A3090 & Hursley*

Part of The Epicurean Collection, The Kings Head is a traditional inn a short drive from Winchester in an idyllic quiet village. The bar and restaurant areas are smart yet cosy, and quality food is available. Rooms are exceptionally well presented with comfortable beds and a host of extras to make your stay even more enjoyable. A full English breakfast can be enjoyed each morning in the Snug.

**Rooms.** 7 en suite 1 annexe en suite **S** tr £75; **D** fr £115* **Facilities:** FTV Lounge tea/coffee Dinner available WiFi Skittle alley **Conf:** Max 50 **Parking:** 30

## LEE-ON-THE-SOLENT
Map 5 SU50

### West Wind Guest House

★★★★ GUEST ACCOMMODATION

**tel:** 023 9255 2550 & 07748 010102 **197 Portsmouth Road PO13 9AA**
**email:** info@west-wind.co.uk **web:** www.west-wind.co.uk
**dir:** *M27 junct 11 follow Gosport & Fareham signs, B3385 for Lee-on-the-Solent. At seafront left along Marine Pde, 600mtrs left into Portsmouth Rd. West Wind on right*

This family-run guest accommodation is found in a quiet, residential area within walking distance of the beach and town centre. The bedrooms are comfortable and nicely appointed, some with TV and all with free WiFi. There is an attractive breakfast room and off-street parking.

**Rooms:** 6 en suite (1 GF) **S** fr £55; **D** fr £70 **Facilities:** FTV DVD iPod docking station tea/coffee WiFi **Parking:** 6 **Notes:** No children 8yrs

## LISS
Map 5 SU72

### The Jolly Drover

★★★★ INN

**tel:** 01730 893137 **London Road, Hillbrow GU33 7QL**
**email:** thejollydrover@googlemail.com **web:** www.thejollydrover.co.uk
**dir:** *From Liss on B3006, at junct with B2070*

Situated on the West Sussex/Hampshire border this traditional inn prides itself on local ales, good home-cooked food and a warm welcome. It is popular with both business and leisure guests due to its close proximity to Petersfield and transport links. Rooms are situated in the traditional outbuildings, and have been fitted in a comfortable modern style with all expected guest amenities. Free WiFi is available. A large beer garden to the rear of the inn is the perfect place to enjoy a summer's day, and ample parking is available.

**Rooms:** 6 annexe rms (6 pri facs) (1 fmly) (6 GF) **Facilities:** FTV tea/coffee Dinner available WiFi **Extras:** Bottled water **Parking:** 48 **Notes:** LB Closed 25–26 Dec & 1 Jan

## LYMINGTON
Map 5 SZ39

### Britannia House

★★★★ 🛏 BED AND BREAKFAST

**tel:** 01590 672091 & 07808 792639 **Station Street SO41 3BA**
**email:** enquiries@britannia-house.com **web:** www.britannia-house.com
**dir:** *Follow signs to railway station, at corner of Station St & Mill Ln*

Built in 1865 as the Britannia Commercial Hotel, Britannia House occupies a quiet location only two minutes' walk from the quay, waterfront and the High Street with its many shops, pubs and restaurants. Rooms are elegant with a refined air, there is a charming lounge and breakfast is taken in the homely kitchen.

**Rooms:** 3 en suite 2 annexe en suite (2 GF) **S** £75–£119; **D** £99–£124 **Facilities:** FTV Lounge tea/coffee WiFi 🅿 **Parking:** 4 **Notes:** LB No children 8yrs

### The Mayflower

★★★★ 🏵 INN

**tel:** 01590 672160 **King's Saltern Road SO41 3QD**
**email:** info@themayflowerlymington.co.uk **web:** www.themayflowerlymington.co.uk

Set just behind the Royal Lymington Yacht Club and just a short walk from the centre of Lymington, this property offers impressive levels of quality and comfort within a bustling pub environment. There are six beautiful en suite bedrooms, all with a nautical theme, some with feature baths set in the bedroom and all dressed with Egyptian cotton linen bedding and thoughtful extras. The bar and dining areas both have open fires, and there is an extensive garden to be enjoyed in the warmer months. The Mayflower is also dog friendly.

**Rooms:** 6 en suite **Facilities:** Dinner available

### The Elderflower Restaurant

★★★★ 🏵🏵🏵 RESTAURANT WITH ROOMS

**tel:** 01590 676908 **4-5 Quay Street SO41 3AS**
**email:** reservations@elderflowerrestaurant.co.uk **web:** www.elderflowerrestaurant.co.uk
**dir:** *Phone for directions*

Situated on the cobbled streets in the heart of Lymington, just moments from the quay and a short drive into the New Forest National Park. Owned and run by a husband and wife team, The Elderflower is the realisation of a lifelong dream. Bedrooms and bathrooms are well appointed and situated above the restaurant. Cuisine is a real treat, with the team preparing modern British food with French influences using only the very best of locally sourced, sustainable produce. Parking is available nearby in the town's many car parks.

**Rooms:** 2 en suite **S** fr £85; **D** £95–£100* **Facilities:** FTV tea/coffee Dinner available WiFi **Notes:** No children 12yrs (weekend only) Closed 26 Dec

## LYNDHURST
Map 5 SU30

### The Rufus House

★★★★ 🛏 GUEST ACCOMMODATION

**tel:** 023 8028 2930 **Southampton Road SO43 7BQ**
**email:** stay@rufushouse.co.uk **web:** www.rufushouse.co.uk
**dir:** *From Lyndhurst centre onto A35 (Southampton Rd), 300yds on left*

Located on the edge of town, this delightful family-run Victorian property is well situated for exploring the New Forest. The brightly decorated bedrooms are appointed to a high standard, while the turret lounge and the garden terrace are great spots for relaxing.

**Rooms:** 10 en suite (1 fmly) (2 GF) **S** £45–£80; **D** £80–£120* **Facilities:** FTV tea/coffee WiFi ⚓18 🅿 **Parking:** 12 **Notes:** LB No children 5yrs

### Temple Lodge

★★★★ 🛏 GUEST ACCOMMODATION

**tel:** 023 8028 2392 **2 Queens Road SO43 7BR**
**email:** templelodge@btinternet.com **web:** www.templelodge-guesthouse.com
**dir:** *M27 junct 2/3 onto A35 to Ashurst & Lyndhurst. Temple Lodge on 2nd corner on right, opposite forest*

Temple Lodge is a well appointed Victorian house with very friendly hosts, who welcome back returning guests year after year. Guests will enjoy easy access to the New Forest and Lyndhurst town centre, with good off-road parking. The bedrooms are furnished with comfort in mind and feature lots of thoughtful extras including mini-bars, and some bedrooms have sofas too. The breakfasts should not be missed.

**Rooms:** 6 en suite (1 fmly) **D** £70–£120* **Facilities:** FTV DVD TVL tea/coffee WiFi 🅿 **Extras:** Mini-fridge with snacks/soft drinks – chargeable **Parking:** 6 **Notes:** LB No children 13yrs

### Whitemoor House B&B

★★★★ 🛏 GUEST ACCOMMODATION

**tel:** 023 8028 3043 **Southampton Road SO43 7BU**
**email:** whitemoorhouse@talktalk.net **web:** www.whitemoorhouse.co.uk
**dir:** *0.5m NE of town centre on A35 towards Southampton*

Situated just on the edge of Lyndhurst, this very well run establishment offers comfortable, smartly-decorated bedrooms, well equipped and all en suite. Breakfast is impressive, with home-made preserves and an extensive selection of cold items; there are plenty of hot options too, most sourced from local suppliers. Guests can relax in the cosy lounge, which opens on to the patio overlooking the well-kept grounds. There is also an honesty bar, free WiFi and parking on site.

**Rooms:** 7 en suite **S** £57–£65; **D** £76–£96 **Facilities:** FTV DVD TVL tea/coffee Licensed WiFi ⚓18 🅿 **Extras:** Mini-bar – chargeable; home-made cake on arrival **Parking:** 7 **Notes:** No children 12yrs Closed Nov–Jan

### Clayhill House

★★★★ BED AND BREAKFAST

**tel:** 023 8028 2304 **SO43 7DE**
**email:** clayhillhouse@tinyworld.co.uk **web:** www.clayhillhouse.co.uk
**dir:** *Exit M27 junct 2. A35 to Lyndhurst then A337 signed Brockenhurst, 0.75m*

Set at the edge of this attractive town, and convenient for visiting the New Forest and coastal attractions nearby, Clayhill House is a well-appointed property, which offers friendly service and comfortable accommodation. The bedrooms are particularly well equipped with thoughtful extras. Freshly cooked breakfasts are served in the dining room.

**Rooms:** 3 en suite (1 fmly) **Facilities:** FTV tea/coffee WiFi 🅿 **Parking:** 6 **Notes:** LB No children 14yrs Closed 22 Dec–4 Jan

## NORTHINGTON
Map 5 SU53

### The Woolpack Inn

★★★★ 🏵 🛏 INN

**tel:** 01962 734184 **Totford SO24 9TJ**
**email:** info@thewoolpackinn.co.uk **web:** www.thewoolpackinn.co.uk
**dir:** *On B3046 S of Basingstoke*

Part of The Epicurean Collection, this attractive country inn, tucked away in Hampshire's Candover Valley, offers a traditional feel with lots of character. The flint and brick building dates back to 1880 and many original features can be seen throughout. The inviting bar has flagstone floors, leather armchairs and open fires, while the dining room features smart fabrics, candle-lit tables and the same relaxed, friendly atmosphere. There is also a wood-fired outdoor kitchen and a small private dining room. Bedrooms, each named after a game bird, are richly furnished and very well equipped. All of them have a contemporary en suite bath or shower room.

**Rooms:** 7 en suite (1 fmly) (4 GF) **Facilities:** FTV tea/coffee Dinner available Direct dial WiFi ⅃⅃18 Fishing Pool table **Conf:** Max 15 Thtr 15 Class 12 Board 12 **Parking:** 50

## PETERSFIELD
Map 5 SU72

## The Old Drum
★★★★ ⊚ INN

**tel:** 01730 300208 **16 Chapel Street GU32 3DP**
**email:** info@theolddrum.com **web:** www.theolddrum.com

Located in the very centre of Petersfield, this inn offers stylish and contemporary accommodation. The bar is open daily and has an inviting ambience, busy with residents and locals alike. Breakfast, lunch and dinner are available daily in the restaurant. There is an outside courtyard with seating, perfect for the summer months. There's no parking on site; however a large carpark to the rear of the inn is less than a minute's walk away.

**Rooms:** 5 en suite (1 fmly) **S** £100–£120; **D** £120–£135* **Facilities:** STV FTV Lounge TVL tea/coffee Dinner available WiFi 🏌 **Extras:** Speciality toiletries, fruit, Nespresso machine **Conf:** Max 25 Class 25 **Notes:** LB Closed 25 Dec & 1–3 Jan

## RINGWOOD
Map 5 SU10

## Moortown Lodge
★★★★ GUEST ACCOMMODATION

**tel:** 01425 471404 **244 Christchurch Road BH24 3AS**
**email:** enquiries@moortownlodge.co.uk **web:** www.moortownlodge.co.uk
**dir:** 1m S of Ringwood. Exit A31 at Ringwood onto B3347, follow signs to Sopley. Lodge adjacent to David Lloyd Leisure Club

Moortown Lodge was originally a Georgian hunting lodge and is conveniently located ten miles from the Dorset coast, not far from Christchurch, and just five minutes south of Ringwood. A warm welcome is assured, with every effort made to ensure a relaxed and rewarding stay. Bedrooms offer impressive levels of comfort combined with individual styling and a host of additional facilities. The elegant dining room is the venue for satisfying breakfasts which make use of local New Forest produce. Moortown Lodge is a very convenient base for exploring this delightful area.

**Rooms:** 7 en suite (1 fmly) (2 GF) **Facilities:** FTV DVD Lounge tea/coffee Direct dial WiFi Reduced rates at local David Lloyd Leisure Club **Extras:** Speciality toiletries, robes, bottled water **Parking:** 7 **Notes:** No children 5yrs

## Lamb Inn
★★★ INN

**tel:** 01425 473721 **2 Hightown Road BH24 1NW**
**email:** anitaandbrum@gmail.com **web:** www.lambinnringwood.co.uk

This traditional inn is situated in the market town of Ringwood and provides a convenient location for exploring the beautiful New Forest. A very warm and genuine welcome is always on offer, with a helpful team to ensure your stay is relaxed and rewarding. Bedrooms provide good levels of comfort, and two rooms are located externally with separate entrance. The bar is the hub of activity with friendly banter to accompany the good choice of food and drink on offer.

**Rooms:** 3 rms (2 en suite) (1 pri facs) 2 annexe en suite (2 GF) **Facilities:** FTV tea/coffee Dinner available WiFi Pool table **Parking:** 6 **Notes:** LB No children

## ST MARY BOURNE
Map 5 SU45

## Bourne Valley Inn
★★★★ ⊚ INN

**tel:** 01264 738361 **SP11 6BT**
**email:** enquiries@bournevalleyinn.com **web:** www.bournevalleyinn.com
**dir:** S of St Mary Bourne on B3048

Part of The Epicurean Collection, the Bourne Valley Inn is located in the rural village of St Mary Bourne. Ample customer car parking and large riverside beer gardens are real features. The inn is both child and dog friendly, and accommodation is all en suite and in keeping with the style of this rustic building. Food is a highlight with mostly local produce being used; Sunday lunch is a real treat. Hospitality from the young and enthusiastic management and team is excellent.

**Rooms:** 9 en suite (3 GF) **S** £75–£100; **D** £85–£120* **Facilities:** FTV Lounge tea/coffee Dinner available WiFi Fishing **Conf:** Max 80 **Notes:** LB

## SOUTHAMPTON
Map 5 SU41

### Premier Collection

## Ennio's Restaurant & Boutique Rooms
★★★★★ ⍟ ⌂ RESTAURANT WITH ROOMS

**tel:** 023 8022 1159 & 07748 966113 **Town Quay Road SO14 3AS**
**email:** info@ennios.co.uk **web:** www.ennios.co.uk
**dir:** Opposite Red Funnel Ferry terminal

This fine property, lovingly converted from a former Victorian warehouse, offers luxurious accommodation on Southampton's waterfront. All rooms are en suite and are furnished to a very high standard, including mini-bars and over-sized showers. Downstairs, the popular Ennio's Restaurant and bar is the ideal setting in which to dine, offering an authentic Italian atmosphere and a wonderful selection of dishes. There is limited parking available to the rear of the building.

**Rooms:** 10 en suite **Facilities:** FTV iPod docking station tea/coffee Dinner available WiFi **Extras:** Speciality toiletries, mini-bar **Parking:** 6 **Notes:** LB Closed 24–26 Dec

### Premier Collection

## THE PIG in the Wall
★★★★★ ⌂ INN

**tel:** 023 8063 6900 **8 Western Esplanade SO14 2AZ**
**email:** info@thepiginthewall.com **web:** www.thepighotel.com

Located close to the city centre, this beautifully restored property has high quality bedrooms in all shapes and sizes, all with air-conditioning, some with roll-top baths, all with their own larder of goodies and Nespresso machine. There is secure parking and the deli-bar showcases local produce. Its homely, relaxed, 'shabby-chic' in style and there is an extensive continental breakfast available to guests each morning.

**Rooms:** 12 en suite (2 GF) **Facilities:** FTV DVD Lounge tea/coffee Dinner available Direct dial WiFi **Extras:** Nespresso – complimentary; stocked larder – chargeable **Parking:** 12

## SOUTHAMPTON *continued*

### Alcantara Guest House

★★★★ ☺ GUEST ACCOMMODATION

**tel:** 023 8033 2966 **20 Howard Road, Shirley SO15 5BN**
**email:** alcantaraguesthouse@sky.com **web:** www.alcantaraguesthouse.co.uk
**dir:** *0.5m NW of city centre. Exit A3057 into Howard Rd*

A warm welcome is assured at this Victorian property, named after an ocean liner to reflect the establishment's shipping connections. Bedrooms are comfortable and well decorated and have many thoughtful extras. An appetising breakfast can be served in the bright and airy dining room. Secure off-road parking is available.

**Rooms:** 9 rms (6 en suite) (1 fmly) (2 GF) **S** fr £40; **D** fr £78* **Facilities:** FTV tea/coffee WiFi ⏏ **Parking:** 7 **Notes:** No children 12yrs RS 2 weeks Xmas

### Prince Consort

★★★ INN

**tel:** 023 8045 2676 **Victoria Road, Netley SO31 5DQ**
**email:** info@theprinceconsortpub.co.uk **web:** www.theprinceconsortpub.co.uk
**dir:** *Premises situated next to main entrance of Royal Victoria Country Park*

The Prince Consort is situated just five minutes' walk from the seafront, and enjoys a friendly atmosphere. Food is available every evening in the spacious bar and restaurant. Bedrooms are contemporary and well presented, with smart, fully tiled en suites. Outdoor seating is a real bonus, as is the on-site parking.

**Rooms:** 7 annexe en suite (1 fmly) (5 GF) **S** fr £52.50; **D** fr £67.50* **Facilities:** STV FTV tea/coffee Dinner available WiFi **Conf:** Max 40 Class 40 Board 20 **Parking:** 25

### The Brimar Guest House

★★ GUEST ACCOMMODATION

**tel:** 023 8086 2950 **10-14 High Street, Totton SO40 9HN**
**email:** info@brimar-guesthouse.co.uk **web:** www.brimar-guesthouse.co.uk
**dir:** *3m W of city centre, exit A35 (Totton bypass) into Totton High St*

This property offers practical, comfortable accommodation at reasonable prices. Not all rooms are en suite but bathrooms are well situated. Breakfast is served in the dining room or as a take-away option. The Brimar is well placed for the M27 and Southampton docks, and off-road parking is available.

**Rooms:** 21 rms (8 en suite) (7 pri facs) (2 fmly) (8 GF) **S** £40–£50; **D** £50–£80* **Facilities:** FTV WiFi **Parking:** 20

| STOCKBRIDGE | Map 5 SU33 |
|---|---|

### The Greyhound on the Test

★★★★ ◉◉ ☺ RESTAURANT WITH ROOMS

**tel:** 01264 810833 **31 High Street SO20 6EY**
**email:** info@thegreyhoundonthetest.co.uk **web:** www.thegreyhoundonthetest.co.uk
**dir:** *9m NW of Winchester, 8m S of Andover. Off A303*

This charming restaurant with rooms has the River Test at its rear and the two AA Rosette award-winning food is a real draw. In addition, the luxury bedrooms are generally spacious, beautifully styled and come with a host of extras. Bathrooms are modern and have high quality towels and toiletries. There is also ample parking and well-kept grounds.

**Rooms:** 10 en suite (1 GF) **S** fr £85; **D** £140–£240* **Facilities:** FTV DVD Lounge tea/coffee Dinner available WiFi ⌕18 Fishing **Extras:** Speciality toiletries – complimentary; honesty bar **Conf:** Max 12 Board 12 **Parking:** 28 **Notes:** Closed 24–25 Dec

### The Three Cups Inn

★★★★ ◉ ☺ INN

**tel:** 01264 810527 **High Street SO20 6HB**
**email:** manager@the3cups.co.uk **web:** www.the3cups.co.uk

Standing on Stockbridge high street, The Three Cups Inn dates from the 15th century. A former coaching inn, it has bags of charm and character and there are many cask ales to try in the cosy bar. The bedrooms are individually furnished, comfortable and equipped to a high standard. Excellent food is available every evening, served in both the cosy, snug-like dining room and the Orangery overlooking the garden.

**Rooms:** 8 en suite (3 fmly) **Facilities:** FTV tea/coffee Dinner available WiFi Fishing **Extras:** Speciality toiletries, fresh milk **Parking:** 15

### The Peat Spade Inn

★★★★ ◉ INN

**tel:** 01264 810612 **Village Street, Longstock SO20 6DR**
**email:** info@peatspadeinn.co.uk **web:** www.peatspadeinn.co.uk
**dir:** *M3 junct 8, A303 W approx 15m, then take A3057 Stockbridge/Andover*

In a delightfully tranquil setting between the historic cities of Winchester and Salisbury, Longstock is just north of Stockbridge, in the heart of the Test Valley, known for its fly fishing and picture-postcard villages. The inn has lots of character, with bedrooms located in the main building and the adjacent former peat house; all are comfortable and furnished in a modern style yet in keeping with the date of the original building. The inn is popular for both dining and drinking; the modern British menus are well balanced and use seasonal ingredients sourced from the local area.

**Rooms:** 3 rms (3 pri facs) 5 annexe rms (5 pri facs) (3 GF) **Facilities:** FTV tea/coffee Dinner available Direct dial WiFi ⌕18 Fishing ⏏ Shooting **Extras:** Bottled water, mini-fridge, speciality toiletries **Conf:** Max 16 Board 16 **Parking:** 19

| WARNFORD | Map 5 SU62 |
|---|---|

### George & Falcon

★★★★ ⌕ INN

**tel:** 01730 829623 **Warnford Road SO32 3LB**
**email:** reservations@georgeandfalcon.com **web:** www.georgeandfalcon.com
**dir:** *Adjacent to A32 in village*

Set in the picturesque village of Warnford, close to major transport links to Winchester, Portsmouth and Southampton, the George & Falcon offers tastefully appointed bedrooms that retain the charm and character of a coaching inn yet provide modern facilities. Traditional fare is served in the popular restaurant and bar, and there is a large decking area which proves a useful addition in summer months.

**Rooms:** 6 en suite (1 fmly) **S** £65–£99; **D** £70–£129 (room only)* **Facilities:** FTV Lounge tea/coffee Dinner available WiFi ⌕18 Fishing ⏏ **Extras:** Speciality toiletries, mineral water **Conf:** Max 30 Thtr 30 Class 15 Board 15 **Parking:** 47 **Notes:** LB Civ wed 135

## WHITCHURCH                    Map 5 SU44

# White Hart Whitchurch

★★★ INN

**tel:** 01256 892900 **The Square RG28 7DN**
**email:** thewhitehart.whitchurch@arkells.com **web:** www.whiteharthotelwhitchurch.co.uk

Located in the centre of Whitchurch the White Hart is steeped in history and has served the local community for over 500 years. En suite rooms are well equipped some of which are located in an adjacent building. The inn is very popular with locals and diners alike. A very warm welcome from the friendly team is assured. Owned by Arkell's family brewers, a great range of traditionally brewed beers are available.

**Rooms:** 10 en suite (3 fmly) **Facilities:** FTV tea/coffee Dinner available WiFi **Parking:** 12

## WINCHESTER                    Map 5 SU42

### Premier Collection

# Giffard House

★★★★★ GUEST HOUSE

**tel:** 01962 852628 **50 Christchurch Road SO23 9SU**
**email:** giffardhotel@aol.com **web:** www.giffardhotel.co.uk
**dir:** *M3 junct 11, at rdbt 3rd exit onto A333 (St Cross road) for 1m. Pass BP garage on right, next left, 2nd right. 150mtrs on left*

Expect a warm welcome at Giffard House, a stunning Victorian property, close to the university. The accommodation is luxurious, comfortable and well equipped for both the business and leisure traveller. Beds are made up with crisp linen, and breakfast is served in the dining room. There is also a fully licensed bar in the elegant conservatory. Parking is a real bonus.

**Rooms:** 13 en suite (1 fmly) (4 GF) **S** £83; **D** £109–£166* **Facilities:** STV FTV Lounge tea/coffee Direct dial Licensed WiFi 🔒 **Extras:** Speciality toiletries
**Conf:** Max 15 Thtr 15 Class 15 Board 13 **Parking:** 13 **Notes:** Closed 24 Dec–2 Jan

# The Old Vine

★★★★ INN

**tel:** 01962 854616 **8 Great Minster St SO23 9HA**
**email:** reservations@oldvinewinchester.com **web:** www.oldvinewinchester.com
**dir:** *M3 junct 11 towards St Cross, right at Green Man Pub, left into Symonds St, left into Little Minster St*

Overlooking the cathedral, this Grade II listed 18th-century inn mixes the elegance of days gone by with chic, modern comfort. The beautifully appointed bedrooms are named after designers and blend antique with contemporary, and the attractive dining room serves quality fare using local produce. There is permit parking.

**Rooms:** 5 en suite 1 annexe en suite (2 fmly) **S** £120–£160; **D** £130–£200*
**Facilities:** FTV tea/coffee Dinner available WiFi 🔒 **Extras:** Speciality toiletries, water, fruit juices – complimentary

# The Wykeham Arms

★★★★   🍷 INN

**tel:** 01962 853834 **75 Kingsgate Street SO23 9PE**
**web:** www.wykehamarmswinchester.co.uk
**dir:** *Immediately S of Cathedral, by Kingsgate and opposite Winchester College*

This is one of the oldest and best-loved public houses in Hampshire and is situated just south of the ancient cathedral. All areas are furnished to a high standard with excellent facilities. Dining in the restaurant or bar is recommended – walls are adorned from top to bottom with every kind of bijouterie imaginable and the regularly changing menu uses fresh ingredients.

**Rooms:** 14 en suite **Facilities:** FTV Lounge tea/coffee Dinner available Direct dial WiFi ⚓18 🔒 **Extras:** Mineral water – complimentary; robes in some rooms
**Conf:** Max 20 Thtr 20 Class 20 Board 20 **Parking:** 10 **Notes:** No children 14yrs

# Running Horse Inn

★★★★ @@ INN

**tel:** 01962 880218 **88 Main Road, Littleton SO22 6QS**
**email:** info@runninghorseinn.co.uk **web:** www.runninghorseinn.co.uk
**dir:** *B3049 from Winchester 1.5m, turn right into Littleton after 1m, Running Horse on right*

Situated in a pretty, rural location, yet with easy access to the M3, this is a great location for business and leisure travellers visiting Hampshire. Offering quality accommodation, the Running Horse Inn is minimalist in its design, and provides comfortable beds and a small workstation area. Highlights of a stay here are a meal in the smart restaurant or a drink in the bar.

**Rooms:** 15 annexe en suite (1 fmly) (9 GF) **Facilities:** FTV tea/coffee Dinner available WiFi **Parking:** 40

# The Westgate

★★★★ GUEST ACCOMMODATION

**tel:** 01962 820222 & 07710 545999 **The Westgate SO23 8TP**
**email:** info@westgatewinchester.com
**dir:** *At the top of Winchester High St by Romsey Rd rdbt. Next to The Westgate & The Great Hall*

The Westgate sits in a commanding position at the top of historic Winchester High Street, in the heart of the city and a short stroll from the fortified medieval gateway after which it was named. The 'real' Westgate served as a debtors' prison for 150 years – you can even still read some of the prisoners' graffiti. Good quality interesting menus are served at breakfast, lunch and dinner in the warm and welcoming bar. The extensively renovated Westgate offers light, airy and elegant bedrooms with wonderful views of this beautiful city.

**Rooms:** 10 en suite (3 fmly) **D** £85–£125* **Facilities:** FTV tea/coffee Dinner available Licensed WiFi

**WINCHESTER** *continued*

## 24 Clifton Road

★★★ BED AND BREAKFAST

**tel:** 01962 851620 **SO22 5BU**
**email:** a.williams1997@btinternet.com
**dir:** *500yds NW of city centre. B3090 Romsey Rd W from city centre, Clifton Rd 2nd right*

This delightful house is in a quiet residential area close to the railway station and High Street. It combines town-house elegance with a homely cottage charm, and is handy for local walks. The bedroom is comfortably furnished and the bathroom has a deep claw-foot bath. There is a lounge and a dining room.

**Rooms:** 1 rms (1 pri facs) **S** £45; **D** £70* **Facilities:** TVL tea/coffee WiFi 🔒 **Parking:** 2 **Notes:** No children 6yrs

## HEREFORDSHIRE

| AYMESTREY | Map 9 SO46 |

## The Riverside at Aymestrey

★★★★ ◉◉ INN

**tel:** 01568 708440 **HR6 9ST**
**email:** enquiries@riversideaymestrey.co.uk **web:** www.riversideaymestrey.co.uk
**dir:** *On A4110, just before arched bridge*

The Riverside sits alongside the River Lugg in this rural part of Herefordshire, offering peace and tranquility for guests. The larger centres of Ludlow, Leominster and Hereford are easily accessed by car. This 16th-century black-and-white inn offers a range of comfortable bedrooms including suites, which successfully bring together traditional features with a more contemporary feel. Dinner is a labour of love for chef-patron Andy Link, and should not be missed. Local sourcing and home-grown produce are key to the ethos here, with a large kitchen garden providing the majority of the fruit, vegetables and herbs used in the kitchen.

**Rooms:** 4 en suite 2 annexe en suite (2 fmly) (1 GF) **S** £65–£75; **D** £75–£130* **Facilities:** FTV Dinner available WiFi Fishing **Extras:** Speciality toiletries, robes, mini-bar, fresh coffee & milk **Conf:** Max 40 Thtr 40 Class 25 Board 25 **Parking:** 30 **Notes:** RS Mon closed for lunch

| BODENHAM | Map 10 SO55 |

## The Coach House at England Gate's Inn

★★★★ 🍴 INN

**tel:** 01568 797286 **HR1 3HU**
**email:** englandsgate@btconnect.com **web:** www.englandsgate.co.uk
**dir:** *Just off A417*

This fine black-and-white 16th-century inn is run by the McNeil family, who pride themselves on quality service. It is set in attractive gardens which are ideal for alfresco dining on warmer days. The detached coach house has comfortable bedrooms with modern en suite facilities; the views are spectacular from the upstairs rooms. Continental breakfast is served in the coach house dining area on weekdays, and a full cooked breakfast is available at weekends.

**Rooms:** 7 en suite (2 fmly) (1 GF) **S** £68–£75; **D** £70–£123* **Facilities:** FTV DVD tea/coffee Dinner available Direct dial WiFi 🔒 **Extras:** Bottled water **Conf:** Max 12 Board 12 **Parking:** 30

| BOLSTONE | Map 10 SO53 |

## Prickett's Place

★★★★★ 🍴 BED AND BREAKFAST

**tel:** 01432 870221 **HR2 6LZ**
**email:** prickettsplace@btinternet.com **web:** www.prickettsplace.com
**dir:** *M50 junct 4 onto A49, right towards Hoarwithy. Follow signs for Cottage of Content public house, turn left then turn right, Prickett's Place on left*

Surrounded by magnificent countryside in the beautiful Wye Valley, Prickett's Place is peacefully located just seven miles from Hereford and nine miles from Ross-on-Wye. Bedrooms are very well furnished and equipped with welcome extras. Guests can enjoy tea in the garden upon arrival and also have use of a comfortable lounge. An excellent selection of high-quality ingredients is offered at breakfast.

**Rooms:** 1 en suite 1 annexe en suite (1 fmly) **S** £55; **D** £72–£78 **Facilities:** FTV DVD TVL tea/coffee WiFi 🔒 Canoeing **Extras:** Speciality toiletries, fruit, fridge in annexe **Parking:** 6 **Notes:** LB No children 7yrs Closed Xmas & New Year

| BREDWARDINE | Map 9 SO34 |

## Red Lion

★★★ INN

**tel:** 01981 500303 **HR3 6BU**
**email:** info@redlion-hotel.com **web:** www.redlion-hotel.com
**dir:** *Off A438, Hereford to Brecon road*

This traditionally styled inn is set in a pleasant village and provides an ideal base for exploring the local countryside and river walks. Popular with anglers, the inn has a fishing theme running throughout the public areas. Bedrooms offer a range of shapes and sizes, and are located either above the inn or in an adjacent annexe. Home-cooked meals are served at both lunch and dinner.

**Rooms:** 7 en suite 3 annexe en suite (1 fmly) (2 GF) **S** fr £60; **D** fr £80 **Facilities:** FTV TVL tea/coffee Dinner available WiFi Fishing 🔒 **Parking:** 20 **Notes:** LB Closed Dec–1 Mar RS Mar–May closed Sun eve to Wed am

| EWYAS HAROLD | Map 9 SO32 |

## The Temple Bar Inn

★★★★ ◉◉ INN

**tel:** 01981 240423 **HR2 0EU**
**email:** phillytemplebar@btinternet.com **web:** www.thetemplebarinn.co.uk
**dir:** *From Pontrilas (A465) onto B4347 signed Ewyas Harold. After 1m left into village. On right in 0.1m*

Standing in the centre of the village, The Temple Bar Inn was lovingly refurbished and brought back to life by the owners, with the help of local craftsmen, making it the hub of the community. Smart bedrooms are well equipped for the modern traveller and complemented by modern en suite bathrooms. There is a bustling bar area with a separate games room and a small dining room serving high quality, locally sourced seasonal dishes.

**Rooms:** 3 en suite (1 fmly) **S** £65; **D** £90* **Facilities:** FTV tea/coffee Dinner available WiFi Pool table **Extras:** Speciality toiletries, fresh milk – complimentary; hairdryer, iron **Conf:** Max 45 Thtr 45 Class 24 Board 16 **Parking:** 10 **Notes:** Closed 25 Dec RS 1 week Nov & 1 week Jan/Feb no lunch or dinner available No evening meals (all year) Sun–Tue

## GARWAY                                        Map 9 SO42

# Garway Moon Inn

★★★★ ⬜ INN

**tel:** 01600 750270 **HR2 8RQ**
**email:** info@garwaymooninn.co.uk **web:** www.garwaymooninn.co.uk
**dir:** *From Hereford, S on A49. Right onto A466, right again onto B4521.*
*At Broad Oak turn right to Garway*

This traditional old hostelry is situated in peaceful and picturesque surroundings. Bedrooms are located above the inn and provide good quality and comfort. This 'proper' pub offers a selection of real ales and ciders, with a relaxed and welcoming ambience in the bar. Dinner should not be missed with high quality produce from local suppliers – many of whom might be found sitting in the bar. The home-made burgers are especially recommended.

**Rooms:** 3 en suite (2 fmly) **D** £80–£100* **Facilities:** STV FTV DVD Lounge tea/coffee Dinner available WiFi **Extras:** Bottled water – complimentary **Conf:** Max 12 Board 12 **Parking:** 20

## HEREFORD                                      Map 10 SO53

### Premier Collection

# Somerville House

★★★★★ ⬜ GUEST ACCOMMODATION

**tel:** 01432 273991 **12 Bodenham Road HR1 2TS**
**email:** enquiries@somervillehouse.net **web:** www.somervillehousehereford.co.uk
**dir:** *A465, at Aylestone Hill rdbt towards city centre, left at Southbank Rd,*
*leading to Bodenham Rd*

Situated in a quiet, tree-lined residential road, Somerville House is a detached late-Victorian villa that provides a boutique-style experience. Expect a warm and friendly welcome from Rosie and Bill who offer quality accommodation with high standards of luxury and comfort. All bedrooms are spacious, with a good range of quality extras. Breakfast is served at individual tables in the light and contemporary dining room. There is a terraced garden to the rear where guests can sit and relax, or indoors, they can make use of the comfortable lounge. There is ample parking.

**Rooms:** 12 en suite (2 fmly) (1 GF) **S** £65; **D** £85–£125* **Facilities:** FTV DVD Lounge tea/coffee Licensed WiFi ⬤ Arrangement with health spa **Extras:** Speciality toiletries, chocolate, bottled water – complimentary; mini-bar with drinks/snacks – chargeable **Conf:** Max 10 Thtr 10 Class 10 Board 10 **Parking:** 10 **Notes:** LB

# No 21

★★★★ GUEST ACCOMMODATION

**tel:** 01432 279897 & 07967 525403 **21 Aylestone Hill HR1 1HR**
**email:** jane@21aylestonehill.co.uk **web:** www.21aylestonehill.co.uk
**dir:** *On A4103 from Worcester to rdbt at approach to Hereford.*
*Take 1st exit to town centre (A465)*

A warm welcome awaits visitors to this peaceful detached property, not far from the train station and the centre of Hereford. All the bedrooms and smart modern bathrooms are appointed to a high standard. The bedrooms are spacious with many extras; one ground-floor room, with a wet room, is ideal for guests that have difficulty with stairs. Breakfast is served in the spacious dining room at the front of the property, and there is ample secure parking.

**Rooms:** 4 en suite (1 fmly) (1 GF) **Facilities:** FTV TVL tea/coffee WiFi ⬤ **Extras:** Orange juice, bottled water, fresh milk – complimentary **Parking:** 8

# Sink Green Farm

★★★★ FARMHOUSE

**tel:** 01432 870223 **Rotherwas HR2 6LE**
**email:** enquiries@sinkgreenfarm.co.uk **web:** www.sinkgreenfarm.co.uk
**dir:** *3m SE of city centre. Exit A49 onto B4399 for 2m*

This charming 16th-century farmhouse stands in attractive countryside and has many original features, including flagstone floors, exposed beams and open fireplaces. Bedrooms are traditionally furnished and one has a four-poster bed. The pleasant garden has a comfortable summer house, hot tub and barbecue.

**Rooms:** 3 en suite **S** £45–£60; **D** £80–£100 **Facilities:** FTV iPod docking station Lounge TVL tea/coffee WiFi ⬤ Hot tub **Extras:** Home-made biscuits **Parking:** 10 **Notes:** LB 180 acres beef

# The Bay Horse Inn

★★★★ INN

**tel:** 01432 273351 **236 Kings Acre Road HR4 0SD**
**email:** info@bayhorseinnhereford.co.uk **web:** www.bayhorseinnhereford.co.uk
**dir:** *On A438, pass Wyevale garden centre, 100yds on left*

Located just outside the city centre, The Bay Horse Inn combines comfortable bedrooms and bathrooms with an excellent range of food available during the day and evening. There is a relaxed ambience and welcoming service throughout. Guests also benefit from the use of a car park and a range of outdoor seating in warmer weather. A good selection of real ales, wine and bottled ciders are available.

**Rooms:** 8 annexe en suite (3 fmly) (4 GF) **S** fr £59; **D** fr £69 **Facilities:** STV FTV TVL tea/coffee Dinner available WiFi **Conf:** Max 60 Thtr 35 Class 60 Board 20 **Parking:** 56 **Notes:** Closed 26 Dec

# Heron House

★★★ ⬛ BED AND BREAKFAST

**tel:** 01432 761111 **Canon Pyon Road, Portway HR4 8NG**
**email:** info@theheronhouse.com **web:** www.theheronhouse.com
**dir:** *A4103 onto A4110 to Portway x-rds, Heron House 200yds on left*

Originally an 18th-century cottage, Heron House was considerably extended about 30 years ago. It is quietly located at Burghill, some four miles north of Hereford. The accommodation consists of one twin and one double room, both with modern furnishings and equipment. Separate tables are provided in the breakfast room.

**Rooms:** 2 rms (1 en suite) **Facilities:** DVD tea/coffee **Parking:** 5 **Notes:** No children 10yrs

## KIMBOLTON
Map 10 SO56

# Grove Farm B&B

★★★ FARMHOUSE

**tel:** 01568 613425 & 07890 471314 **Grove Farm HR6 0HE**
**email:** fiona@grovefarmdirect.co.uk **web:** www.grovefarmdirect.co.uk
**dir:** *A49 N of Leominster onto A4112, signed Leysters. Into Kimbolton, turn left at pub, 500mtrs on left*

Located in the Herefordshire countryside, this working farm offers a proper farmhouse feel with plenty of animals around and a friendly welcome, with tea and cake on arrival. Bedrooms offer a range of shapes and sizes including one on the ground floor. Breakfast includes home-produced sausages and bacon in addition to apple juice from a nearby farm. For dinner, the local pub is just a few minutes stroll along the lane, or you could prepare something yourself in the guest kitchen which has a microwave and a fridge/freezer among other useful things. Dogs are welcome.

**Rooms:** 3 en suite (1 fmly) (1 GF) **Facilities:** FTV Lounge tea/coffee Dinner available WiFi ⚓18 ⚾ Table tennis **Extras:** Fresh milk, home-made cakes **Conf:** Max 20 Thtr 20 Class 20 Board 20 **Parking:** 6 **Notes:** LB 40 acres pigs/sheep/orchard

## LEINTWARDINE
Map 9 SO47

### Premier Collection

# The Lion

★★★★★ ⓦ 🍽 RESTAURANT WITH ROOMS

**tel:** 01547 540203 & 540747 **High Street SY7 0JZ**
**email:** enquiries@thelionleintwardine.co.uk **web:** www.thelionleintwardine.co.uk
**dir:** *Beside bridge on A4113 (Ludlow to Knighton road) in Leintwardine*

This quiet country restaurant with rooms in the picturesque village of Leintwardine, set beside the River Teme, is just a short distance from Ludlow and Craven Arms. The interior is stylish and the contemporary bedrooms are all en suite. Dining is taken seriously here and the modern, imaginative food uses the freshest local ingredients. The well-stocked bar offers a selection of real ales and lagers and there is a separate drinkers' bar too. The Lion is particularly popular with families as the garden has a secure children's play area, and in warmer months guests can eat alfresco. The friendly staff help to make any visit memorable.

**Rooms:** 8 en suite (1 fmly) **S** £75–£95; **D** £100–£120* **Facilities:** FTV Lounge tea/coffee Dinner available WiFi Fishing ⚾ **Extras:** Home-made shortbread – complimentary **Conf:** Max 25 Class 25 Board 25 **Parking:** 25 **Notes:** Closed 25 Dec

### Premier Collection

# Upper Buckton

★★★★★ ⚍ FARMHOUSE

**tel:** 01547 540634 **Buckton SY7 0JU**
**email:** ghlloydco@btconnect.com **web:** www.upperbuckton.co.uk
**dir:** *From Leintwardine on A4113 to Walford. Right into narrow road signed Buckton. 2nd farm on left*

Upper Buckton is a Georgian house surrounded by beautiful grounds that slope gently down to the mill stream and out to the motte. Beyond this lies the ha-ha, old fashioned meadowland, the River Teme and the forested Wigmore Rolls. The house is comfortably furnished with interesting paintings and antique furniture. Of the three bedrooms, two have an en suite bathroom and one has private facilities, and beds are fitted with electric blankets. An enjoyable home-cooked dinner is available by prior arrangement. In the cooler months the sitting room is a pleasant place to take afternoon tea and enjoy an after-dinner coffee around the log fire.

**Rooms:** 3 rms (2 en suite) (1 pri facs) **D** £100–£120* **Facilities:** FTV Lounge tea/coffee Dinner available Licensed WiFi Table tennis **Extras:** Speciality toiletries **Parking:** 3 **Notes:** LB 360 acres arable/potatoes/sheep

## LEOMINSTER
Map 10 SO45

### Premier Collection

# Hills Farm

★★★★★ 🍽 FARMHOUSE

**tel:** 01568 750205 **Leysters HR6 0HP**
**email:** stay@thehillsfarm.co.uk **web:** www.thehillsfarm.co.uk
**dir:** *Off A4112 (Leominster to Tenbury Wells), on outskirts of Leysters*

Set in a peaceful location with views over the countryside, this property dates in part from the 16th century. The friendly, attentive proprietors provide a relaxing and homely atmosphere. The attractive bedrooms, in the converted barns, are spacious and comfortable. Breakfasts, served in the dining room and conservatory, feature fresh local produce.

**Rooms:** 3 annexe en suite (1 GF) **D** £92–£94* **Facilities:** FTV iPod docking station Lounge tea/coffee WiFi ⚾ **Extras:** Fridge, microwave, crockery, cutlery **Parking:** 8 **Notes:** No children 12yrs Closed Nov–Mar 120 acres arable

## ROSS-ON-WYE                                            Map 10 SO52

### Premier Collection

## Wilton Court Restaurant with Rooms

★★★★★ ⚘⚘ ☕ RESTAURANT WITH ROOMS

**tel:** 01989 562569 **Wilton Lane HR9 6AQ**
**email:** info@wiltoncourthotel.com **web:** www.wiltoncourthotel.com
**dir:** *M50 junct 4, A40 towards Monmouth at 3rd rdbt left signed Ross-on-Wye, 1st right, on right*

Dating back to the 16th century, Wilton Court has great charm and a wealth of character. Standing on the banks of the River Wye, just a short walk from the town centre, there is a genuinely relaxed, friendly and unhurried atmosphere created by hosts Roger and Helen Wynn and their reliable team. Bedrooms are tastefully furnished and well equipped, while public areas include a comfortable lounge, traditional bar and pleasant restaurant with a conservatory extension overlooking the garden. High standards of food, using fresh, locally sourced ingredients, are offered.

**Rooms:** 11 en suite (1 fmly) (1 GF) **S** £100–£155; **D** £135–£185* **Facilities:** FTV DVD Lounge tea/coffee Dinner available Direct dial WiFi ⚓ ⚓18 Fishing ⚓ **Extras:** Kimonos, bottled water **Parking:** 20 **Notes:** LB Closed 3–15 Jan

## Glewstone Court Country House

★★★★★ ⚘⚘ ☕ RESTAURANT WITH ROOMS

**tel:** 01989 770367 **Glewstone HR9 6AW**
**email:** info@glewstonecourt.com **web:** www.glewstonecourt.com
**dir:** *From Ross-on-Wye market place follow A40/A49 Monmouth/Hereford signs, over Wilton Bridge to rdbt, left onto A40 towards Monmouth, in 1m right for hotel*

This charming country house enjoys an elevated position with views over Ross-on-Wye, and is set in well-tended gardens. The owners ensure guests are well looked after from the moment of arrival. Bedrooms come in a variety of sizes and are tastefully furnished and well equipped. An excellent choice of dishes utilising high quality ingredients should not be missed at dinner.

**Rooms:** 9 en suite (2 fmly) **S** £99–£169; **D** £114–£184* **Facilities:** Dinner available ⚓ **Notes:** Closed 2–18 Jan RS Nov-Feb Civ wed 70

## Forest View Guest House

★★★★ BED AND BREAKFAST

**tel:** 01600 890210 & 07881 247068 **Symonds Yat East HR9 6JL**
**email:** steve-jose@mail.com **web:** www.forestviewguesthouse.co.uk
**dir:** *A40 onto B4229 signed Goodrich, then B4432 for Symonds Yat East*

Delightfully located on the banks of the river, guests can take part in a range of activities such as walking and canoeing, right on the doorstep. Bedrooms and bathrooms are comfortably furnished and most have views over the river and the forest beyond. In addition to the carefully prepared breakfast, guests can take advantage of the free transfer to the sister property for dinner. A small bar and lounge is provided.

**Rooms:** 10 en suite (2 GF) **Facilities:** FTV DVD Lounge TVL tea/coffee Dinner available Licensed WiFi ⚓18 Fishing ⚓ **Extras:** Speciality toiletries, snacks **Conf:** Max 20 Thtr 20 Class 20 Board 20 **Parking:** 15 **Notes:** No children 12yrs

## Lea House

★★★★ ☕ GUEST ACCOMMODATION

**tel:** 01989 750652 & 07495 713603 **Lea HR9 7JZ**
**email:** enquiries@leahouse.co.uk **web:** www.leahouse.co.uk
**dir:** *4m SE of Ross on A40 towards Gloucester, in Lea*

This former coaching inn, near Ross-on-Wye, has a relaxed atmosphere and makes a good base for exploring the Forest of Dean and the Wye Valley. The individually furnished bedrooms are thoughtfully equipped and very homely. Breakfast in the oak-beamed dining room offers home-made breads, freshly squeezed juice, fresh fruit platters, local sausages and fish choices.

**Rooms:** 3 en suite (1 fmly) **Facilities:** FTV DVD TVL tea/coffee WiFi ⚓ **Parking:** 4 **Notes:** LB

## Thatch Close

★★★★ GUEST ACCOMMODATION

**tel:** 01989 770300 **Llangrove HR9 6EL**
**email:** info@thatchclose.co.uk **web:** www.thatchclose.co.uk
**dir:** *Off A40 at Symonds Yat West/Whitchurch junct to Llangrove, right at x-rds after Post Office & before school. Thatch Close 0.6m on left*

Standing in 13 acres, this sturdy 18th-century farmhouse is full of character. Expect a wonderfully warm atmosphere with a genuine welcome from your hosts. The homely bedrooms are equipped for comfort with many thoughtful extras. Breakfast is served in the elegant dining room, and a lounge is available. The extensive patios and gardens are popular in summer, providing plenty of space to find a quiet corner and relax with a good book.

**Rooms:** 3 en suite **S** £55–£70; **D** £80–£95* **Facilities:** FTV TVL tea/coffee WiFi ⚓ **Extras:** Snacks – complimentary **Parking:** 8 **Notes:** LB

## SYMONDS YAT [EAST]                                     Map 10 SO51
*See also Coleford (Gloucestershire)*

## The Royal Lodge

★★★★ ☕ ⚘ GUEST ACCOMMODATION

**tel:** 01600 890238 **HR9 6JL**
**email:** info@rhhotels.co.uk **web:** www.rhhotels.co.uk
**dir:** *Midway between Ross and Monmouth exit A40 at signs for Goodrich & B4229 to Symonds Yat East*

The Royal Lodge stands at the top end of the village overlooking the River Wye. Bedrooms are spacious and comfortable, and come complete with TVs and many guest extras; the bathrooms offer modern facilities. There is a cosy lounge with an open fireplace and two bars are available. Meals are offered in the welcoming restaurant, which provides carefully prepared meals using fresh and local ingredients. Staff are pleasant and friendly.

**Rooms:** 24 en suite (5 fmly) **S** £40–£65; **D** £69–£139* **Facilities:** FTV DVD TVL tea/coffee Dinner available Direct dial Licensed WiFi Fishing ⚓ **Extras:** Mineral water **Conf:** Max 120 Thtr 120 Class 80 Board 80 **Parking:** 150 **Notes:** LB Civ wed 150

SYMONDS YAT [EAST] *continued*

## Saracens Head Inn

★★★★ 🛏 🍺 INN

**tel:** 01600 890435 **HR9 6JL**
**email:** contact@saracensheadinn.co.uk **web:** www.saracensheadinn.co.uk
**dir:** *Exit A40 at South Herefordshire Motorcaravan Centre, signed Symonds Yat East, 2m*

Dating from the 16th century, the friendly, family-run Saracens Head faces the River Wye and has wonderful views. The well-equipped bedrooms are decorated in a cottage style, and there is a cosy lounge, an attractive dining room, and a popular public bar that leads onto a riverside patio. All meals are offered from a regularly changing and comprehensive menu that includes locally-sourced produce.

**Rooms:** 7 en suite 2 annexe en suite (1 GF) **S** £65–£85; **D** £100–£140*
**Facilities:** FTV TVL tea/coffee Dinner available Direct dial WiFi Fishing 🛁
**Conf:** Max 25 Thtr 25 Class 25 Board 25 **Parking:** 35 **Notes:** No children 12yrs

*See advert opposite*

| UPPER SAPEY | Map 10 SO66 |

## The Baiting House

★★★★ 🍽🍽 INN

**tel:** 01886 853201 & 07825 232843 **Stourport Road WR6 6XT**
**email:** info@baitinghouse.co.uk **web:** www.baitinghouse.co.uk
**dir:** *On B4203 between Bromyard & Great Witley*

Dating back to the 1800s, The Baiting House is a quintessential country inn brought right up to date. Purchased by a local couple to avoid redevelopment, this inn has been completely refurbished and is a popular place, where locals and visitors alike are welcomed by the friendly team. Local sourcing is very important here, not only the food but also the cask ales and ciders. A separate 'clubhouse' with traditional pub games can also be used for private dining.

Dinner is not to be missed, with a constantly changing menu of exciting dishes showcasing the best the area has to offer. Three bedrooms are located in the main building with three ground floor rooms offered in the annex. A spacious terrace affords stunning views over the surrounding countryside a perfect spot for an alfresco dinner.

**Rooms:** 3 en suite 3 annexe en suite (1 fmly) (3 GF) **S** £65–£130; **D** £65–£130*
**Facilities:** FTV tea/coffee Dinner available WiFi ♪27 Pool table **Conf:** Max 20 Class 20 Board 20 **Parking:** 60 **Notes:** LB

| WHITCHURCH | Map 10 SO51 |

## Norton House

★★★★ 🛏 BED AND BREAKFAST

**tel:** 01600 890046 & 07948 079660 **Old Monmouth Road HR9 6DJ**
**email:** lynda.mwhittle@gmail.com **web:** www.norton-house.com

Built as a farmhouse, Norton House dates back some 300 years and has retained a lot of character, with flagstone floors and beamed ceilings. A warm and friendly welcome awaits all guests from hosts Lynda and David. The bedrooms, including a four-poster room, are individually styled and furnished for maximum comfort. Charming public areas include a snug with a wood-burning stove and comfortable lounge, a perfect location to enjoy the home-baked cakes on arrival. Excellent local produce is used to create an imaginative range of breakfast dishes. Parking is off-road, and self-catering cottages are also available.

**Rooms:** 3 en suite **Facilities:** FTV iPod docking station Lounge TVL tea/coffee WiFi 🛁 **Extras:** Fruit, biscuits **Parking:** 5 **Notes:** LB No children 13yrs

| WHITNEY-ON-WYE | Map 9 2024 |

## Rhydspence Inn

★★★★ 🍺 INN

**tel:** 01497 831262 **HR3 6EU**
**email:** info@rhydspence.com **web:** www.rhydspence.com
**dir:** *On A438 between Hereford & Brecon, on right at England/Wales border*

The Rhydspence Inn is full of character and history. Spanning the Wales-England border this popular property is ideally located for Hay-on-Wye and Hereford. Parts of the building date from 1380, and extensions were added in the 17th to 20th centuries. A friendly welcome and relaxing ambience are provided in both the bar and the dining room where locals and guests mingle. Bedrooms offer a variety of shapes and sizes and are all located above the inn. Both dinner and breakfast offer a good selection of home-made, carefully prepared dishes.

**Rooms:** 8 en suite **Facilities:** FTV Lounge TVL tea/coffee Dinner available WiFi Fishing **Extras:** Speciality toiletries **Conf:** Max 30 Thtr 30 Class 30 Board 30 **Parking:** 30 **Notes:** LB

| YARKHILL | Map 10 SO64 |

## Garford Farm

★★★★ FARMHOUSE

**tel:** 01432 890226 **HR1 3ST**
**email:** garfordfarm@btconnect.com
**dir:** *Exit A417 at Newtown x-rds onto A4103 for Hereford, farm 1.5m on left*

This black-and-white, timber-framed farmhouse, set on a large arable holding, dates from the 17th century. Its character is enhanced by period furnishings, and fires burn in the comfortable lounge during colder weather. The traditionally furnished bedrooms, including a family room, have modern facilities.

**Rooms:** 2 en suite (1 fmly) **S** fr £45; **D** fr £70 **Facilities:** FTV Lounge tea/coffee WiFi 🛁 **Parking:** 6 **Notes:** No children 2yrs Closed 25–26 Dec 200 acres arable

## HERTFORDSHIRE

### BISHOP'S STORTFORD
Map 6 TL42

## The PitStop

★★★★ GUEST ACCOMMODATION

**tel:** 01279 725725 & 725007 **The Morgan Garage, Little Hallingbury CM22 7RA**
**email:** mr@melvyn-rutter.net **web:** www.the-pitstop.net
**dir:** *3m S of Bishop's Stortford, signed Melvyn Rutter Ltd – Morgan Garage*

The PitStop offers four individually styled en suite rooms. Located above The Morgan Garage, guests can enjoy a good night's sleep, and hire a modern classic Morgan car for the day. All rooms are very well equipped and meet the needs of a varied clientele. Self-service continental breakfast can be taken in the American-style diner.

**Rooms:** 4 en suite (1 fmly) **S** £95; **D** £89–£99* **Facilities:** FTV iPod docking station TVL Lift WiFi Hire of Morgan sports cars **Extras:** Fruit, snacks – complimentary **Parking:** 30

## Bonningtons Guest House

★★★ GUEST HOUSE

**tel:** 01279 507472 & 07815 704830 **George Green, Little Hallingbury CM22 7SP**
**email:** info@bonningtons.net **web:** www.bonningtons.net
**dir:** *M11 junct 8 onto A120 towards Bishop's Stortford. Left at next rdbt, at lights left onto A1060 towards Hatfield Heath. In centre of Little Hallingbury, turn right opposite The George pub*

Set in its own grounds, Bonningtons is a stylish guest house with a range of individually designed modern bedrooms. All bedrooms are well equipped, and free WiFi is available along with secure parking. Stansted Airport is a short drive away and daily rates for parking are available. Continental-style breakfasts are provided and there is a very good choice on offer. An ideal base from which to explore the Cambridgeshire and Essex countryside.

**Rooms:** 6 annexe en suite (1 fmly) (4 GF) **S** £47.50–£52.50; **D** £55–£69.99
**Facilities:** FTV Lounge tea/coffee WiFi **Extras:** Chocolates **Parking:** 20
**Notes:** No children 5yrs

### BUNTINGFORD
Map 12 TL32

## Sword Inn Hand

★★★★ INN

**tel:** 01763 271356 **Westmill SG9 9LQ**
**email:** theswordinnhandrestaurant@gmail.com **web:** www.theswordinnhand.co.uk
**dir:** *In Westmill, off A10 S of Buntingford*

Set within the peaceful village of Westmill amid rolling countryside, this charming 14th-century inn offers excellent accommodation in a friendly and relaxed atmosphere. The purpose-built, ground-floor bedrooms are located just off the rear gardens; all are very well-equipped and carefully appointed and have their own access. Character public rooms offer a choice of restaurant and bar dining options, along with a choice of draught ales.

**Rooms:** 4 en suite (4 GF) **Facilities:** STV FTV TVL tea/coffee Dinner available **Parking:** 25

### MUCH HADHAM
Map 6 TL41

## High Hedges Bed & Breakfast

★★★★ BED AND BREAKFAST

**tel:** 01279 842505 **High Hedges, Green Tye SG10 6JP**
**email:** info@high-hedges.co.uk **web:** www.high-hedges.co.uk
**dir:** *From B1004 turn off to Green Tye at Prince of Wales pub, turn into private road, 1st on right*

Expect a warm welcome at High Hedges, a family-run B&B conveniently located for Stansted Airport, and convenient for visiting London and Cambridge. Bedrooms are well presented and comfortable, and come with many thoughtful extra touches. A substantial breakfast is served in the pleasant dining room.

**Rooms:** 3 rms (2 en suite) (1 pri facs) (1 fmly) (1 GF) **S** £60; **D** £75–£80*
**Facilities:** FTV tea/coffee WiFi **Parking:** 3 **Notes:** Closed 25–26 Dec & 31 Dec–1 Jan

## NUTHAMPSTEAD — Map 12 TL43

### The Woodman Inn
★★★ INN

**tel:** 01763 848328 **SG8 8NB**
**email:** enquiries@thewoodman-inn.co.uk **web:** www.thewoodman-inn.co.uk
**dir:** *M11 junct 20, A505 towards Royston, left onto B1368 to Barkway, 1st left past Tally Ho, right in 2m. Inn on left. Or from Royston take A505 signed motorway (M11) & Newmarket. Right onto B1368 & then as above*

This 17th-century inn has many fine features, and is close to the Duxford Imperial War Museum. The practical bedrooms are decorated in a traditional style. The kitchen offers a good range of British meals, plus a generous breakfast.

**Rooms:** 2 annexe en suite (2 GF) **Facilities:** FTV tea/coffee Dinner available WiFi ♿ 18 Pool table Shooting range by arrangement **Parking:** 30 **Notes:** RS Sun eve–Mon bar & restaurant closed

## ST ALBANS — Map 6 TL10

### Innkeeper's Lodge St Albans, London Colney
★★★★ INN

**tel:** 08451 551551 *(Calls cost 2p per minute plus your phone company's access charge)*
**Barnet Road, London Colney AL2 1BL**
**email:** info@innkeeperslodge.com **web:** www.innkeeperslodge.com

Conveniently located close to the historic town of St Albans, The Colney Fox is a favourite with leisure and business guests. The charming original bar is warm and welcoming, and the log fires burn brightly on cooler evenings. This is a very popular dining venue, and the extensive dinner menu caters for most tastes. The stylish bedrooms are all attractively presented while still retaining many of the inn's original features. Free WiFi is provided, ample secure parking is available and the M25 is close by.

**Rooms:** 13 en suite **Facilities:** FTV tea/coffee Dinner available WiFi

## WELWYN — Map 6 TL21

### Premier Collection

### The Wellington
★★★★★ ⬡ INN

**tel:** 01438 714036 **High Street AL6 9LZ**
**email:** info@wellingtonatwelwyn.co.uk **web:** www.wellingtonatwelwyn.co.uk
**dir:** *A1(M) junct 6 follow signs to Welwyn. In the High St opposite St Mary Church*

Enjoying a prominent position in the heart of the pretty village of Welwyn, The Wellington offers a range of beautifully presented, individually styled bedrooms. The most is made of the eye-catching original features in the charming restaurant, and log fires on colder evenings add to the ambience. There is a cosy bar area along with a sheltered terrace at the rear of the property. Ample secure parking is available along with free WiFi for guests.

**Rooms:** 6 en suite **Facilities:** FTV DVD iPod docking station tea/coffee Dinner available WiFi **Extras:** Bottled water **Parking:** 34

### The White Hart
★★★★ ⬡ INN

**tel:** 01438 715353 **2 Prospect Place AL6 9EN**
**email:** info@whitehartwelyn.co.uk **web:** www.whitehartwelyn.co.uk

Period charm and character are plentiful throughout this inn, which in parts dates back to the 13th century. The spacious bedrooms are individually decorated and thoughtfully equipped, some in a boutique style and those in the stable block in a more traditional style. Public rooms include a cosy bar, which has a great range of quality wines, ales and gins, and the atmospheric restaurant with inglenook fireplace and flagstone floors. There is also a function room and convenient parking on-site.

**Rooms:** 13 en suite **S** £69–£125; **D** £79–£135* **Facilities:** Dinner available

## ISLE OF WIGHT

## BEMBRIDGE — Map 5 SZ68

### The Spinnaker
★★★★ 🍴 INN

**tel:** 01983 873572 & 872840 **1 Steyne Road PO35 5UH**
**email:** info@thespinnakeriow.co.uk **web:** www.thespinnakeriow.co.uk
**dir:** *From A3055 take B3395 (Sandown Rd) towards Bembridge. After rdbt becomes Steyne Rd*

A beautifully restored Edwardian inn, set in the heart of Bembridge, open from 9am daily for breakfast, lunch and dinner. The 14 en suite rooms are appointed with modern amenities, while the decor retains the character and charm of this grand building. The bar has a fabulous snug area, chart room and many other cosy corners. The menu uses local produce and island suppliers where possible. There are two intimate function rooms available to hire. Flexible, tailor-made packages are available and advance booking is recommended.

**Rooms:** 14 en suite (2 fmly) **Facilities:** FTV DVD iPod docking station tea/coffee Dinner available WiFi ♿ 9 **Conf:** Max 100 Thtr 100 Class 60 Board 50 **Parking:** 30 **Notes:** LB Civ wed 50

## CHALE — Map 5 SZ47

### The Old House
★★★★ 🏠 BED AND BREAKFAST

**tel:** 01983 551368 & 07746 453398 **Gotten Manor, Gotten Lane PO38 2HQ**
**email:** aa@gottenmanor.co.uk **web:** www.gottenmanor.co.uk
**dir:** *1m N of Chale. Turn right from B3399 into Gotten Ln (opposite chapel), house at end*

Located in countryside close to the coast, this 17th-century house has 18th- and 19th-century additions. The charming rustic bedrooms have antique bathtubs. Comprehensive breakfasts using the finest ingredients are served in the cosy dining room, and there is a spacious lounge with an open fire.

**Rooms:** 2 en suite **S** £70–£95; **D** £80–£115 **Facilities:** STV FTV iPod docking station Lounge tea/coffee WiFi ♿ **Parking:** 3 **Notes:** LB No children 12yrs

**COWES** Map 5 SZ49

## Duke of York Inn

★★★ INN

**tel:** 01983 295171 **Mill Hill Road PO31 7BT**
**email:** bookings@dukeofyorkcowes.co.uk **web:** www.dukeofyorkcowes.co.uk

This family-run inn is situated very close to the centre of Cowes. Comfortable bedrooms are divided between the main building and a separate annexe only seconds away. Home-cooked meals, with a number of fish and seafood dishes, feature on the menu every evening and are served in the bar and dining area; outdoor covered dining is also an option. Parking is a bonus.

**Rooms:** 8 en suite 5 annexe en suite (1 fmly) (1 GF) **S** £59; **D** £79* **Facilities:** FTV tea/coffee Dinner available WiFi **Parking:** 10

**FISHBOURNE** Map 5 SZ59

## The Fishbourne

★★★★ INN

**tel:** 01983 873572 & 882823 **111 Fishbourne Lane PO33 4EU**
**email:** info@thefishbourne.co.uk **web:** www.thefishbourne.co.uk
**dir:** Off A3054 (Newport to Ryde road), adjacent to Wightlink ferry terminal

The Fishbourne is conveniently located just by the Wightlink ferry terminal. The inn offers five stylishly decorated bedrooms with light and airy decor and modern fixtures, including LCD TV and free WiFi. Guests can enjoy breakfast, lunch or dinner served in the open-plan bar and restaurant area. On offer are a wide range of traditional pub dishes, with all produce locally sourced.

**Rooms:** 5 en suite (2 fmly) **Facilities:** FTV DVD iPod docking station tea/coffee Dinner available WiFi ᨠ9 **Parking:** 40 **Notes:** LB

**NEWPORT** Map 5 SZ58

## Bank Cottage B&B

★★★★ BED AND BREAKFAST

**tel:** 01983 822255 & 07796 945019 **Dodnor Lane PO30 5TD**
**email:** bankcottagebnb@gmail.com **web:** www.bankcottagebandb.co.uk

Bank Cottage offers a one bedroom suite with private facilities and a private terrace on which to relax in warmer months. This is an ideal place for those searching for a quiet location to unwind and recharge their batteries. The suite has been well designed and can be configured to accommodate families or friends travelling together. In-room breakfast is served at the dining table, and guests can choose from a well-written breakfast menu the night before for a prompt delivery in the morning. The suite also offers all mod cons including free WiFi. Secure parking is available.

**Rooms:** 1 rm (1 pri facs) (1 fmly) **Facilities:** FTV TVL tea/coffee WiFi
**Extras:** Slippers **Parking:** 3

## Castle Lodge

★★★ GUEST ACCOMMODATION

**tel:** 01983 527862 & 07789 228203 **54 Castle Road PO30 1DP**
**email:** castlelodge@hotmail.co.uk **web:** www.castlelodgeiow.co.uk
**dir:** 0.5m SW of town centre. On B3323 towards Carisbrooke Castle

Well-presented Castle Lodge is located in a quiet residential area within close walking distance of the famous Carisbrooke Castle. A comfortable stay is assured in attractive and restful bedrooms, together with a bright and airy dining room where a substantial breakfast can be enjoyed.

**Rooms:** 2 en suite 5 annexe en suite (1 fmly) (5 GF) **S** £38–£59; **D** £50–£75* **Facilities:** FTV DVD tea/coffee WiFi **Parking:** 5

**NITON** Map 5 SZ57

### Premier Collection

## Enchanted Manor

★★★★★ GUEST ACCOMMODATION

**tel:** 01983 730215 **Sandrock Road PO38 2NG**
**email:** info@enchantedmanor.co.uk **web:** www.enchantedmanor.co.uk

Enchanted Manor is a delightful property, set in charming grounds, and enjoys an enviable location within walking distance of the sea. The unusual theme of magic and enchantment prevails throughout the beautifully appointed suites and spacious public areas, all of which are furnished and decorated to a very high standard. A host of extra touches are provided such as DVD players, well-stocked mini-fridges and welcome baskets. Friendly, attentive service is assured.

**Rooms:** 7 en suite (2 GF) **Facilities:** STV FTV DVD Lounge tea/coffee Licensed WiFi Snooker Pool table Spa/hot tub Massage beauty treatment room **Conf:** Max 30 Board 30 **Parking:** 15 **Notes:** LB No children Civ wed 50

**SANDOWN** Map 5 SZ58

## The Wight

★★★★ GUEST ACCOMMODATION

**tel:** 01983 403722 **11 Avenue Road PO36 8BN**
**email:** enquiries@wighthotel.co.uk **web:** www.wighthotel.co.uk
**dir:** 100yds after mini rdbt between High St & Avenue Rd

A family establishment, set in secluded grounds, only a short walk from Sandown's beach and high street shops. Bedrooms are very welcoming and are either on the ground or first floor. There's a heated swimming pool and a spa facility; there's also evening entertainment in the bar. A plentiful breakfast is served in the colourful dining room.

**Rooms:** 41 en suite (17 fmly) (18 GF) **Facilities:** FTV Lounge TVL tea/coffee Licensed WiFi ⓈSnooker Gym Pool table Steam room Jacuzzi **Parking:** 36 **Notes:** LB Civ wed 80

## SEAVIEW
Map 5 SZ69

# The Boathouse

★★★★ 🛏 INN

**tel:** 01983 873572 & 01938 810616 **Springvale Road PO34 5AW**
**email:** info@theboathouseiow.co.uk **web:** www.theboathouseiow.co.uk
**dir:** *From Seaview follow sea road, The Boathouse on corner of Springvale Rd & Puckpool Hill*

This very pleasant inn has a shore-side location and is a relaxing, friendly and comfortable place to stay. Food is a focus here with fresh, local produce and speciality lobster and crab dishes. The inn provides a contemporary style throughout; bedrooms are pleasantly spacious and most have beach views. There is ample parking and a garden, where in warmer times food and drink are served.

**Rooms:** 4 en suite (1 fmly) **Facilities:** FTV DVD iPod docking station tea/coffee Dinner available WiFi **Parking:** 20 **Notes:** LB

## SHANKLIN
Map 5 SZ58

# Fernbank

★★★★ 🖺 GUEST ACCOMMODATION

**tel:** 01983 862790 **6 Highfield Road PO37 6PP**
**email:** fernbank2010@btconnect.com **web:** www.fernbank-iow.co.uk
**dir:** *Approaching Shanklin on A3020, right into Highfield Rd. 300yds on left*

Located in Shanklin Old Village, Fernbank offers modern, comfortable and spacious accommodation. Home-made refreshments are available throughout the afternoon and guests can enjoy a wide range of both cooked and continental breakfasts in the airy dining room. There is an indoor swimming pool and plenty of outside space within the landscaped gardens in which to relax. Free WiFi is available throughout.

**Rooms:** 17 en suite (1 fmly) (2 GF) **S** £52; **D** £88–£112* **Facilities:** FTV DVD tea/coffee Licensed WiFi 🏊Petanque **Parking:** 13 **Notes:** LB No children 12yrs Closed Nov–Feb

# The Birkdale

★★★★ GUEST ACCOMMODATION

**tel:** 01983 862949 & 07508 591889 **5 Grange Road PO37 6NN**
**email:** birkdale-iow@hotmail.co.uk **web:** www.birkdalehotel.com
**dir:** *Follow signs for Shanklin Old Village, Grange Rd opposite car park. The Birkdale on right opposite dance school*

Located right in the heart of Shanklin Old Village, The Birkdale offers spacious and stylishly decorated accommodation, well equipped and with well-stocked beverage trays, digital TV and free WiFi access. There is a traditional guest lounge and extensive range of both cooked and continental dishes for breakfast. Ample off-road parking is available, and a number of shops, cafés, pubs and restaurants are right on the doorstep of this establishment.

**Rooms:** 7 en suite (3 GF) **D** £64–£76* **Facilities:** STV DVD TVL tea/coffee WiFi 🔒 **Parking:** 7 **Notes:** LB No children 16yrs

# The Rowborough

★★★★ GUEST ACCOMMODATION

**tel:** 01983 866072 **32 Arthurs Hill PO37 6EX**
**email:** info@rowboroughhotel.com **web:** www.rowboroughhotel.com
**dir:** *Off A3055 Sandown Rd, on corner of Arthurs Hill & Wilton Park Rd*

A warm welcome is guaranteed at this family-run Victorian house, set in beautifully tended gardens within walking distance of Shanklin Village, Chine and beaches. All nine bedrooms are comfortably furnished, serviced to a high standard, and come equipped with Freeview TV and DVD player. Breakfast and dinner are served in the light and airy dining room, which has doors leading out to the patio and gardens. Guests can enjoy a drink at the well-stocked bar or simply relax in either the guest lounge or modern conservatory. Free WiFi is accessible throughout. Children over the age of three and small dogs are welcome.

**Rooms:** 9 en suite (2 fmly) (1 GF) **S** £35–£45; **D** £70–£90* **Facilities:** FTV DVD Lounge TVL tea/coffee Dinner available Licensed WiFi **Extras:** Speciality toiletries **Parking:** 5 **Notes:** LB No children 3yrs Closed Nov–Feb

# The Belmont

★★★★ 🖺 GUEST ACCOMMODATION

**tel:** 01983 862864 & 867875 **8 Queens Road PO37 6AN**
**email:** enquiries@belmont-iow.co.uk **web:** www.belmont-iow.co.uk
**dir:** *From Sandown (on A3055), half turn left at Fiveways lights signed Ventnor. Belmont 400mtrs on right, opposite St Saviour's Church*

Situated less than 10 minutes' walk from Shanklin beach and only five minutes from Shanklin Old Village, The Belmont offers comfortable accommodation and several rooms with stunning sea views. The Belmont is licensed, and drinks and sandwiches are available during the day and evening. Off-road parking is a benefit, and during summer months guests can enjoy the outdoor swimming pool.

**Rooms:** 12 en suite (2 GF) **D** £70–£114* **Facilities:** FTV TVL tea/coffee Dinner available Licensed WiFi 🏊 🔒 **Parking:** 9 **Notes:** LB No children 16yrs

# The Grange

★★★★ GUEST ACCOMMODATION

**tel:** 01983 867644 **9 Eastcliff Road PO37 6AA**
**email:** info@thegrangebythesea.com **web:** www.thegrangebythesea.com
**dir:** *Off A3055, High St*

This delightful house specialises in holistic breaks and enjoys a tranquil yet convenient setting among manicured grounds, close to the seafront and village centre. Care has been taken over the beautifully presented bedrooms and spacious public areas. Breakfast is taken en famille (outside in fine weather).

**Rooms:** 16 en suite (2 fmly) (6 GF) **Facilities:** Lounge TVL tea/coffee Licensed WiFi Beauty treatments & massage **Extras:** Speciality toiletries **Parking:** 10 **Notes:** LB Civ wed 100

## Hayes Barton

★★★★ 🍴 GUEST ACCOMMODATION

**tel:** 01983 867747 **7 Highfield Road PO37 6PP**
**email:** enquiries@hayesbarton.co.uk **web:** www.hayesbarton.co.uk
**dir:** A3055 onto A3020 Victoria Ave, 3rd left

Hayes Barton has the relaxed atmosphere of a family home and provides well-equipped bedrooms and a range of comfortable public areas. Dinner is available from a short selection of home-cooked dishes, and there is a cosy bar-lounge. Shanklin Old Village, beach and promenade are all within walking distance.

**Rooms:** 9 en suite (2 fmly) (2 GF) **S** £48–£53; **D** £84–£94^ **Facilities:** FTV DVD TVL tea/coffee Dinner available Licensed WiFi **Parking:** 9 **Notes:** LB No children 3yrs Closed Oct–Apr

## The St Leonards

★★★★ GUEST HOUSE

**tel:** 01983 862121 **22 Queens Road PO37 6AW**
**email:** info@thestleonards.co.uk **web:** www.thestleonards.co.uk
**dir:** Off A3055 into Queens Rd

The St Leonards is located in the heart of Shanklin just a short walk away from Shankin Old Village and nearby beach. This traditional guest accommodation offers spacious and comfortably appointed rooms, all well equipped with well-stocked beverage trays, free WiFi access and digital TV. There is a comfortable guest lounge and bar on the ground floor where guests can enjoy refreshments on arrival. Breakfast is served daily and offers a good selection of both cooked and continental dishes. Off-road parking is also available.

**Rooms:** 7 en suite (2 fmly) **Facilities:** FTV Lounge TVL tea/coffee Licensed WiFi 🔒 **Parking:** 6 **Notes:** LB

---

**TOTLAND BAY**        Map 5 SZ38

### Premier Collection

## Sentry Mead

★★★★★ 💡 🍴 GUEST ACCOMMODATION

**tel:** 01983 753212 **Madeira Road PO39 0BJ**
**email:** info@sentrymead.co.uk **web:** www.sentrymead.co.uk
**dir:** From Yarmouth onto A3054 to Freshwater, 2m, straight over at rdbt, right at next rdbt into Madeira Rd, 300yds on right

This country house is located in Totland Bay, in the west of the island. Bedrooms have been tastefully decorated to offer guests traditional yet stylish accommodation, all well equipped with WiFi and digital TV. Public areas are spacious; guests can relax in the main lounge or conservatory area, both with views of the large, well-tended garden. A selection of cooked breakfasts and continental dishes is available each morning in the dining room.

**Rooms:** 9 en suite **S** £65–£80; **D** £90–£120* **Facilities:** FTV DVD iPod docking station Lounge TVL tea/coffee Dinner available Licensed WiFi ↓18 🔒 Day membership to West Bay Country Club **Extras:** Speciality toiletries, robes **Parking:** 9 **Notes:** LB

## The Hoo

★★★★ BED AND BREAKFAST

**tel:** 01983 753592 **Colwell Road PO39 0AB**
**email:** the.hoo@btinternet.com **web:** www.thehoo.co.uk
**dir:** From Yarmouth ferry right onto A3054, 2.25m enter Colwell Common. The Hoo on corner of Colwell Rd & Warden Rd

Located close to the port and beaches, this friendly family home provides a peaceful setting. The house has many Japanese features and guests are asked to wear slippers. The spacious bedrooms are well equipped and comfortably furnished. English breakfast is most enjoyable and is served overlooking the gardens.

**Rooms:** 3 rms (1 en suite) (1 pri facs) (2 fmly) **D** £60–£80* **Facilities:** FTV tea/coffee WiFi **Parking:** 1 **Notes:** No children 5yrs

## The Hermitage

★★★ GUEST ACCOMMODATION

**tel:** 01983 752518 **Cliff Road PO39 0EW**
**email:** blake_david@btconnect.com **web:** www.thehermitagebnb.co.uk
**dir:** From Church Hill (B3322), right into Eden Rd, left into Cliff Rd, 0.5m on right

The Hermitage is an extremely pet- and people-friendly establishment which occupies a stunning and unspoilt location near to the cliff top in Totland Bay. Extensive gardens are well maintained and off-road parking is a bonus. Rooms are comfortable and guests are assured of a genuinely warm welcome here. A range of delicious items at breakfast provide a substantial start to the day.

**Rooms:** 6 rms (5 en suite) (1 pri facs) (1 fmly) **Facilities:** FTV Lounge TVL tea/coffee Dinner available WiFi 🔒 **Parking:** 6 **Notes:** LB

TOTLAND BAY *continued*

## The Highdown Inn

★★★ INN

tel: 01983 752450 & 07964 322044 **Highdown Lane PO39 0HY**
email: susan@highdowninn.com web: www.highdowninn.com

This traditional country pub and restaurant is located on a quiet crossroads, only a few minutes from nearby beaches, stunning bay views and the iconic Needles. Walkers and cyclists are welcome, as are dogs (in the bar). The bar offers real ales, an open fire and a wide range of dishes including local seafood. There is also a smartly presented dining room. There is a sunny garden with decking, vegetable plot and a children's play area.

**Rooms:** 3 en suite **S** £55–£70; **D** £70–£85* **Facilities:** FTV DVD tea/coffee Dinner available WiFi ₺18 ♠ **Extras:** Robes **Parking:** 30 **Notes:** LB

### VENTNOR                                                Map 5 SZ57

#### Premier Collection

## The Hambrough

★★★★★ 🦢 GUEST ACCOMMODATION

tel: 01983 856333 **Hambrough Road PO38 1SQ**
email: info@thehambrough.com web: www.thehambrough.com

A former Victorian villa set on the hillside above Ventnor and with memorable views out to sea, The Hambrough has a modern, stylish interior with well-equipped and boutique-style accommodation. Afternoon tea is available in the bar from Tuesday to Saturday.

**Rooms:** 7 en suite (3 fmly) **Facilities:** STV DVD Lounge tea/coffee Direct dial Licensed WiFi ♠ **Extras:** Speciality toiletries – complimentary; mini-bar – chargeable **Conf:** Max 40 Thtr 40 Class 20 Board 24 **Notes:** LB Civ wed 40

#### Premier Collection

## The Leconfield

★★★★★ 🌐 🦢 GUEST ACCOMMODATION

tel: 01983 852196 **85 Leeson Road, Upper Bonchurch PO38 1PU**
email: enquiries@leconfieldhotel.com web: www.leconfieldhotel.com
dir: *On A3055, 3m from Shanklin Old Village*

This country house is situated on an elevated position with panoramic sea views over the historic village of Bonchurch. Luxury bedrooms and suites are spacious and individually styled. Public rooms include two lounges and a conservatory, in addition to the Sea Scape restaurant, where freshly prepared breakfast and imaginative dinner menus are served. Additional facilities include the outdoor pool, terrace area and ample off-road parking.

**Rooms:** 6 en suite 5 annexe en suite (3 GF) **S** £60–£160; **D** £70–£200* **Facilities:** FTV DVD iPod docking station Lounge tea/coffee Dinner available Licensed WiFi ⤻ ♠ **Extras:** Bath robes – complimentary **Parking:** 14 **Notes:** LB No children 16yrs Closed 24–26 Dec & 3–27 Jan

## Little Rannoch

★★★★ 🦢 BED AND BREAKFAST

tel: 01983 852263 **1 Steephill Court Road PO38 1UH**
email: littlerannoch@btinternet.com web: www.littlerannoch.co.uk
dir: *From Ventnor town centre onto A3055 to St Lawrence. After 1.3m turn right after botanic gardens into Steephill Court Rd, on left*

Little Rannoch is a south-facing bungalow less than a mile from Ventnor, close to Ventnor Botanic Gardens, Cricket Ground and Steephill Cove. The accommodation comprises one self-contained suite comprising of double bedroom, dining room/kitchenette, shower room and patio with garden and sea views. The resorts of Shanklin and Sandown are within eight miles of Little Rannoch. Breakfast features local and home-made items. Off-street parking available.

**Rooms:** 1 en suite (1 GF) **S** £80; **D** £110* **Facilities:** STV FTV iPod docking station tea/coffee ♠ **Extras:** Snacks, home-made biscuits **Parking:** 1 **Notes:** No children Closed Nov–1 Mar

## St Maur

★★★★ GUEST ACCOMMODATION

tel: 01983 852570 & 853645 **Castle Road PO38 1LG**
email: info@stmaur.co.uk web: www.stmaur.co.uk
dir: *Exit A3055 at end of Park Av into Castle Rd, premises 150yds on left*

A warm welcome awaits at this Victorian villa, which is pleasantly and quietly located in an elevated position overlooking the bay. The well-equipped bedrooms are traditionally decorated, while public areas include a spacious lounge and cosy residents' bar. The gardens here are a delight.

**Rooms:** 8 en suite (2 fmly) **Facilities:** STV FTV Lounge tea/coffee Dinner available Licensed WiFi ♠ **Extras:** Speciality toiletries **Parking:** 8 **Notes:** LB No children 4yrs Closed Dec

### KENT

### BENENDEN                                               Map 7 TQ83

## Apple Trees B&B

★★★★ BED AND BREAKFAST

tel: 01580 240622 **Goddards Green TN17 4AR**
email: garryblanch@aol.com web: www.appletreesbandb.co.uk
dir: *3m E of Cranbrook. Exit A262 at Sissinghurst S into Chaple Ln, over x-rds, 2m left to Goddards Green, 1m on right*

This spacious cottage is situated in the heart of the Kentish countryside, and is convenient for those visiting Sissinghurst Castle and Great Dixter. Bedrooms are attractively presented and include plenty of thoughtful extras such as flat-screen TVs and internet connection. Breakfast is served in the rustic dining room overlooking the garden.

**Rooms:** 3 rms (1 en suite) (2 pri facs) (3 GF) **S** £60–£75; **D** £70–£85* **Facilities:** TVL tea/coffee WiFi ₺18 ♠ **Parking:** 6

## BOUGHTON STREET
Map 7 TR05

## The White Horse Inn

★★★★ 🍴 INN

**tel:** 01227 751343 **246 The Street, Boughton-under-Blean ME13 9AL**
**email:** whitehorseinn@live.co.uk **web:** www.whitehorsecanterbury.co.uk
**dir:** *M2 junct 7, slip road left towards Channel Tunnel/Canterbury/Dover. At rdbt 4th exit onto A2 then slip road left to Boughton. On left on entering village*

This traditional inn is located in the picturesque village of Boughton-under-Blean, just a short drive from Canterbury city centre. The White Horse Inn has a spacious pub and restaurant area where lunch, dinner and breakfast are served daily. Bedrooms are all modern in style and comfortably appointed, and come well equipped with digital TV and free WiFi.

**Rooms:** 13 en suite (3 fmly) (2 GF) **S** £60–£90; **D** £80  £120* **Facilities:** FTV Lounge TVL tea/coffee Dinner available Direct dial WiFi ⬇18 🔒 **Extras:** Speciality toiletries, water – complimentary; slippers **Parking:** 31 **Notes:** LB

## BROADSTAIRS
Map 7 TR36

## The Victoria Bed and Breakfast

★★★★ BED AND BREAKFAST

**tel:** 01843 871010 **23 Victoria Parade CT10 1QL**
**email:** helkemp2@gmail.com **web:** www.thevictoriabroadstairs.co.uk
**dir:** *A299 into Broadstairs, pass train station & continue on High St. Turn right into Charlotte St, 1st left then right into Victoria Parade*

The Victoria Bed and Breakfast offers very comfortable seaside accommodation in an excellent location. The breakfast room/lounge and top floor bedroom have stunning sea views and the house is just 30 metres from the beach. All bedrooms are well furnished with en suite bathrooms, Freeview TV and tea/coffee making facilities. Breakfast is cooked to order, and a range of breakfast options is available with most items locally sourced. Private parking or nearby permit parking available at no charge.

**Rooms:** 3 en suite (1 fmly) **S** £75–£110; **D** £90–£130* **Facilities:** FTV DVD Lounge tea/coffee WiFi 🔒 **Extras:** Fridge, fresh milk & mineral water – complimentary **Parking:** 1 **Notes:** LB RS Xmas

**Find out more**
about the AA's B&B rating
scheme on pages 8–9

## CANTERBURY
Map 7 TR15

## Renville Oast

★★★★ BED AND BREAKFAST

**tel:** 01227 830932 & 07754 243819 **Renville, Bridge CT4 5AD**
**email:** jamesokeeffe3710@gmail.com **web:** www.renvilleoast.co.uk
**dir:** *M2 junct 7 onto A2 (Boughton bypass) signed Canterbury/Dover. Take exit signed Bridge (immediately after Canterbury exit). At T junct, turn right over the bridge; right at next fork; right at T-junct. Fork left (on A2 slip road), 200yds on left exit into farm road, 2nd property on left*

This recently refurbished oast house offers three comfortably appointed bedrooms; all have been revamped with modern decor and high quality soft furnishings. Rooms are all well equipped with free WiFi, comfortable seating and views of the surrounding countryside. Guest can enjoy a hearty breakfast in the dining room. Located in a quiet and tranquil position, yet just off the A2 and within five minutes of Canterbury City Centre.

**Rooms:** 3 en suite (3 fmly) **S** £64–£93; **D** £80–£107* **Facilities:** FTV Lounge tea/coffee WiFi **Extras:** Snacks, robes, bottled water **Parking:** 3 **Notes:** Closed 22–28 Dec

## The White House

★★★★ GUEST ACCOMMODATION

**tel:** 01227 761836 **6 St Peters Lane CT1 2BP**
**email:** info@whitehousecanterbury.co.uk **web:** www.whitehousecanterbury.co.uk
**dir:** *A2 into Canterbury. At London Rd rdbt take 2nd exit (A2050), at next rdbt 1st exit into St Peters Pl. Right at Westgate Tower rdbt, right before next rdbt. Left at end, St Peters Ln on right*

The White House is an ideally located Regency property in the heart of Canterbury, within a two-minute walk of the famous cathedral. All bedrooms are modern with bright, airy decor and have LCD TVs and WiFi. Breakfast can be enjoyed in the ground-floor dining room and there's additional space for guests to relax during their stay.

**Rooms:** 7 en suite **Facilities:** FTV DVD tea/coffee WiFi **Notes:** No children 16yrs Closed Jan

CANTERBURY *continued*

## Yorke Lodge

★★★★ GUEST ACCOMMODATION

**tel:** 01227 451243 **50 London Road CT2 8LF**
**email:** info@yorkelodge.com **web:** www.yorkelodge.com
**dir:** *M2 junct 7, A2, exit left signed Canterbury. At 1st rdbt turn left into London Rd*

Yorke Lodge stands in a tree-lined road just a 10-minute walk from the town centre and railway station. The spacious bedrooms are thoughtfully equipped and carefully decorated using a calming palette of neutral and pastel shades. Some rooms have four-poster beds. The stylish dining room leads to a conservatory which opens onto a superb terrace.

**Rooms:** 8 en suite (1 fmly) **S** £63–£75; **D** £85–£130* **Facilities:** FTV Lounge tea/coffee WiFi **Parking:** 5 **Notes:** LB No children 5yrs

## The Corner House

★★★★ RESTAURANT WITH ROOMS

**tel:** 01227 780793 & 01843 823000 **1 Dover Street CT1 3HD**
**email:** matt@cornerhouserestaurants.co.uk **web:** www.cornerhouserestaurants.co.uk

Located right in the city centre, The Corner House has benefited from a complete refurbishment. It now offers three stylishly decorated bedrooms, all of which are very spacious and showcase some of the buildings original features. Breakfast, lunch and dinner are available in the restaurant, though dinner is not available on a Monday.

**Rooms:** 3 en suite **S** £79–£130; **D** £79–£130* **Facilities:** FTV DVD tea/coffee Dinner available WiFi **Extras:** Fridge **Conf:** Max 20 Class 20 Board 10

## The Duke William

★★★★ 🛏 INN

**tel:** 01227 721308 **Ickham CT3 1QP**
**email:** info@thedukewilliamickham.com **web:** www.thedukewilliamickham.com
**dir:** *A257 (Canterbury to Sandwich) into Littlebourne, left opposite The Anchor into Nargate St. 0.5m, right into Drill Ln, right into The Street*

Located in the quiet village of Ickham, this village pub has been completely revamped; the public areas still offer a traditional style with exposed beams and roaring wood fires, though decor and furnishings have been modernised, including a comfortable bar and restaurant area. Bedrooms enjoy stylish decor and contemporary furnishings offering guests high quality and comfort; ideal for both leisure and corporate guests. The location here is quiet, yet is just a short drive from Canterbury.

**Rooms:** 4 en suite **S** £110; **D** £110 **Facilities:** FTV tea/coffee Dinner available WiFi **Extras:** Speciality toiletries – complimentary

## Canterbury Lodge

★★★★ GUEST ACCOMMODATION

**tel:** 01227 768767 **63 London Road CT2 8JZ**
**email:** info@canterburylodge.uk **web:** www.canterburylodge.uk
**dir:** *M2 onto A2, 1st exit signed Canterbury. At 1st rdbt, left into London Rd*

Conveniently located on the London Road in the centre of Canterbury, this spacious establishment offers comfortably appointed accommodation with en suite facilities. Rooms are well equipped and modern in style yet still show many of the building's original features. Free WiFi and parking available. Guests can enjoy a hearty cooked and continental breakfast served daily in the dining room on the ground floor.

**Rooms:** 10 en suite (2 fmly) **S** £60–£80; **D** £70–£90 **Facilities:** FTV Lounge TVL tea/coffee WiFi 🅿 **Parking:** 9 **Notes:** LB No children 5yrs

## Peregrine House

★★★★ GUEST ACCOMMODATION

**tel:** 01227 761897 **18 Hawks Lane CT1 2NU**
**email:** enquiries@castlehousehotel.co.uk **web:** www.theperegrinehouse.co.uk

Peregrine House is centrally located right in the heart of Canterbury. This is a sister property to Castle House. Guests register at Castle House (at 28 Castle Street) and then take a short walk to Peregrine House, alternatively a courtesy car is available to help transport guests and their luggage. Bedrooms and bathrooms offer clean, modern comfortable accommodation. Close to the main high street, cathedral, shops and restaurants.

**Rooms:** 13 rms (11 en suite) (2 pri facs) (5 fmly) (3 GF) **Facilities:** TVL tea/coffee Dinner available Licensed WiFi **Parking:** 14

## Cathedral Gate

★★★ GUEST ACCOMMODATION

**tel:** 01227 464381 **36 Burgate CT1 2HA**
**email:** cathedralgatehotel@btconnect.com **web:** www.cathgate.co.uk
**dir:** *In city centre. Next to main gateway into cathedral precincts*

Dating from 1438, this house has an enviable central location next to the cathedral. Old beams and winding corridors are part of the character of the property. Bedrooms are traditionally furnished, equipped to modern standards and many have cathedral views. Luggage can be unloaded at reception before parking in a nearby car park.

**Rooms:** 12 rms (2 en suite) 12 rms annexe (10 en suite) (1 fmly) **S** £50; **D** £70–£120 **Facilities:** FTV Lounge tea/coffee Direct dial Licensed WiFi **Notes:** Closed 20–27 Dec

## St Stephens Guest House

★★★ GUEST ACCOMMODATION

**tel:** 01227 767644 **100 St Stephens Road CT2 7JL**
**email:** info@ststephensguesthouse.co.uk **web:** www.ststephensguesthouse.co.uk
**dir:** *A290 from city, Westgate & sharp right into North Ln, 2nd rdbt left into St Stephens Rd, right into Market Way, car park on right*

St Stephens Guest House offers well-appointed accommodation. Rooms are well equipped. It is located just 10 minutes' walk from Canterbury town centre and conveniently located near the University of Kent and Christchurch College. The dining room is traditionally decorated and has views of the garden; guests can enjoy a cooked or continental breakfast.

**Rooms:** 1 en suite 8 annexe en suite (2 fmly) (3 GF) **S** fr £52; **D** fr £73* **Facilities:** FTV tea/coffee WiFi **Parking:** 6 **Notes:** Closed mid Dec–mid Jan

## Innkeeper's Lodge Canterbury

★★★ INN

**tel:** 08451 551551 *(Calls cost 2p per minute plus your phone company's access charge)*
**162 New Dover Road CT1 3EL**
**email:** info@innkeeperslodge.com **web:** www.innkeeperslodge.com

At Innkeeper's Lodge you'll find accommodation with comfort and character in equal measure, and everything needed for a relaxing stay, from easy check-in and free parking to complimentary breakfast and a cosy pub serving great value food and drink on the doorstep. Each Lodge has quality rooms, and there are Lodges in a variety of locations from towns and cities to countryside settings across the UK.

**Rooms:** 9 en suite (1 fmly) **Facilities:** FTV tea/coffee Dinner available WiFi

---

**DARTFORD**      Map 6 TQ57

## The Rising Sun Inn

★★★ INN

**tel:** 01474 872291 **Fawkham Green DA3 8NL**
**email:** admin@risingsun-fawkham.com **web:** www.risingsun-fawkham.com
**dir:** *M25 junct 3, A20 Brands Hatch. Turn into Scratchers Ln until sign for Fawkham. Left into Brandshatch Rd, Inn on left*

This popular inn overlooks the village green and is just a short drive from Brands Hatch. All the en suite bedrooms are spacious, pleasantly decorated and comfortable. There is a busy character bar, restaurant, and a patio for alfresco dining in warmer weather.

**Rooms:** 5 en suite (1 fmly) (2 GF) **S** £55–£65; **D** £75–£85 **Facilities:** FTV tea/coffee Dinner available WiFi **Extras:** Bottled water – complimentary **Parking:** 20

---

**DEAL**      Map 7 TR35

## Sutherland House

★★★★★ GUEST ACCOMMODATION

**tel:** 01304 362853 **186 London Road CT14 9PT**
**email:** info@sutherlandhouse.fsnet.co.uk **web:** www.sutherlandhousehotel.co.uk
**dir:** *0.5m W of town centre/seafront on A258*

This stylish accommodation demonstrates impeccable taste with its charming, well-equipped bedrooms and a comfortable lounge. A fully stocked bar, books, free WiFi, Freeview TV and radio are some of the many amenities offered. The elegant dining room is the venue for a hearty breakfast and dinner is available by prior arrangement.

**Rooms:** 4 en suite (1 GF) **S** £70–£80; **D** £85–£95* **Facilities:** FTV DVD iPod docking station Lounge tea/coffee Dinner available Direct dial Licensed WiFi 🔒 **Extras:** Speciality toiletries, honesty bar **Conf:** Max 12 Thtr 12 Class 12 Board 12 **Parking:** 7 **Notes:** LB No children 5yrs

---

**DOVER**      Map 7 TR34

## The Marquis at Alkham

★★★★★ ❀❀ RESTAURANT WITH ROOMS

**tel:** 01304 873410 & 822945 **Alkham Valley Road, Alkham CT15 7DF**
**email:** info@themarquisatalkham.co.uk **web:** www.themarquisatalkham.co.uk
**dir:** *A256 from Dover, at rdbt 1st exit into London Rd, left into Alkham Rd, Alkham Valley Rd. Establishment 1.5m after sharp bend*

Located between Dover and Folkestone, this contemporary restaurant with rooms offers luxury accommodation with modern features; flat screen TVs, WiFi, monsoon showers and bathrobes, to mention a few. All the stylish bedrooms are individually designed and have fantastic views of the Kent Downs. The award-winning restaurant, open for lunch, afternoon tea and dinner, specialises in modern British cuisine with a strong emphasis on locally sourced ingredients. Both continental and a choice of cooked breakfasts are offered.

**Rooms:** 10 en suite (3 fmly) (1 GF) **S** £69–£139; **D** £99–£169* **Facilities:** FTV DVD Lounge tea/coffee Dinner available Direct dial WiFi **Extras:** Speciality toiletries **Conf:** Max 20 Thtr 20 Class 20 Board 16 **Parking:** 22 **Notes:** LB Civ wed 55

DOVER *continued*

## Castle Guest House

★★★★ GUEST HOUSE

**tel:** 01304 201656 **10 Castle Hill CT16 1QW**
**email:** info@castle-guesthouse.com **web:** www.castle-guesthouse.co.uk
**dir:** *A20 Dover, follow signs for Dover Castle. At foot of hill, on right*

Castle Guest House is located in the centre of Dover just minutes from the town centre, Dover ferry port and Channel Tunnel terminal. Bedrooms are modern and comfortably appointed and include digital TV and free WiFi access. A cooked and continental breakfast is served daily in the dining room. Free off-road parking available and secure parking is available for motorbikes or bicycles (on request).

**Rooms:** 6 en suite (2 fmly) **S** £40–£45; **D** £70–£85 **Facilities:** FTV DVD tea/coffee WiFi 🅿 **Parking:** 1 **Notes:** LB Closed Xmas

## Maison Dieu Guest House

★★★★ GUEST ACCOMMODATION

**tel:** 01304 204033 **89 Maison Dieu Road CT16 1RU**
**email:** info@maisondieu.co.uk **web:** www.maisondieu.co.uk
**dir:** *M20/A20 to Dover. Left into York St, at rdbt 2nd exit. Right at lights into Ladywell, right at next lights, 100yds on left*

Maison Dieu is ideally located to offer the perfect stopover en route to and from Dover and mainland Europe. Dover ferry and cruise terminals and The White Cliffs of Dover are just five minutes away and the Channel Tunnel is 10 minutes by car. Bedrooms are comfortably decorated and come well equipped with WiFi and digital TV. Guests can enjoy a cooked or continental breakfast daily in the dining room.

**Rooms:** 6 rms (4 en suite) (2 pri facs) (4 fmly) **S** £38–£40; **D** £62–£77 (room only)\* **Facilities:** FTV tea/coffee WiFi 🅿 **Parking:** 6 **Notes:** LB No children 4yrs Closed 30 Dec–15 Feb

## Bleriot's

★★★ GUEST ACCOMMODATION

**tel:** 01304 211394 **Belper House, 47 Park Avenue CT16 1HE**
**email:** info@bleriotsguesthouse.co.uk **web:** www.bleriotsguesthouse.co.uk
**dir:** *A20 to Dover, left into York St, right at lights into Ladywell. Left at next lights into Park Avenue*

This large, family-run Victorian property is convenient for the ferry port and town centre. Guests receive a warm welcome and can enjoy a range of comfortable, spacious en suite bedrooms. The attractive dining room is the venue for a wholesome breakfast to set you up for the day.

**Rooms:** 8 en suite (2 fmly) **S** £38–£39; **D** £66–£68 (room only) **Facilities:** FTV Lounge tea/coffee WiFi 🅿 **Extras:** Bottled water **Parking:** 8 **Notes:** LB

## Ardmore Guest House

★★★ GUEST ACCOMMODATION

**tel:** 01304 205895 **18 Castle Hill Road CT16 1QW**
**email:** res@ardmoreph.co.uk **web:** www.ardmoreph.co.uk
**dir:** *On A258 by Dover Castle*

Dating from 1796, this delightful house is adjacent to Dover Castle. Convenient for the town centre and ferry port, the Ardmore offers comfortable accommodation and friendly hospitality. The non-smoking bedrooms are spacious and airy. Public rooms include a comfortable lounge and a well-appointed breakfast room.

**Rooms:** 4 en suite (1 fmly) **Facilities:** FTV Lounge tea/coffee WiFi **Notes:** Closed Xmas

## St Martins Guest House

★★★ GUEST ACCOMMODATION

**tel:** 01304 205938 **17 Castle Hill Road CT16 1QW**
**email:** res@stmartinsgh.co.uk **web:** www.stmartinsgh.co.uk
**dir:** *On A258 by Dover Castle*

Located close to the castle, ferry port and town centre, this smart guest accommodation offers a friendly welcome. The thoughtfully equipped en suite bedrooms are attractively decorated, and most rooms enjoy a sunny aspect. Breakfast is served in the pine-furnished dining room, and there is also a comfortable lounge.

**Rooms:** 6 en suite (3 fmly) **Facilities:** FTV Lounge tea/coffee WiFi **Notes:** Closed Xmas

---

**EGERTON** Map 7 TQ94

**Premier Collection**

## Frasers

★★★★★ ◉◉ ☺ GUEST ACCOMMODATION

**tel:** 01233 756122 **Coldharbour Farm, Barhams Mill Road TN27 9DD**
**email:** lisa@frasers-events.co.uk **web:** www.frasers-events.co.uk
**dir:** *Please contact Frasers for detailed directions*

Frasers is nestled at the end of a private drive on a working farm set deep in beautiful Kent countryside, halfway between Maidstone and Ashford. Bedrooms are spacious and individual in style with excellent quality furnishings ensuring a comfortable stay. Guests can enjoy an extensive cooked or continental breakfast in the main restaurant; this is also where the AA Rosette-worthy dinner is served.

**Rooms:** 8 en suite **D** fr £100 **Facilities:** FTV DVD iPod docking station tea/coffee Dinner available Licensed ⚓18 Fishing **Extras:** Speciality toiletries, robes, slippers **Conf:** Max 150 Thtr 150 Class 50 Board 50 **Parking:** 50 **Notes:** LB Civ wed 100

## FAVERSHAM
Map 7 TR06

### Faversham Creek & Red Sails Restaurant

★★★★ ◉ RESTAURANT WITH ROOMS

**tel:** 01795 533535 & 534689 **Conduit Street ME13 7BH**
**email:** office@favershamcreekhotel.co.uk **web:** www.favershamcreekhotel.co.uk
**dir:** *M2 junct 6 onto A251. At T-junct left then right into The Mall. Pass railway station, continue on B2041. Left into Quay Ln*

Located in the heart of Faversham and adjacent to the Creek, this restaurant with rooms offers modern accommodation with its own individual style, and rooms named after characters from the Faversham area. Bedrooms are well equipped and ideal for both business and leisure guests alike. There is a courtyard terrace where guests can enjoy lunch or pre-dinner drinks before dining in the award-winning Red Sails Restaurant. Parking is available on site.

**Rooms:** 6 en suite (4 fmly) **S** £75–£105; **D** £85–£175* **Facilities:** STV FTV Lounge tea/coffee Dinner available Direct dial WiFi **Parking:** 4

## FOLKESTONE
Map 7 TR23

### Rocksalt Rooms

★★★★ ◉◉ RESTAURANT WITH ROOMS

**tel:** 01303 212070 **2 Back Street CT19 6NN**
**email:** info@rocksaltfolkestone.co.uk **web:** www.rocksaltfolkestone.co.uk
**dir:** *M20 junct 13 follow signs to harbour (A259). At harbour left onto Fish Market*

Overlooking the busy harbour, often crowded with small leisure boats, and with wonderful sea views, Rocksalt enjoys a great location in Folkestone. Bedrooms are stylish, well-appointed with original antique beds and equipped with a host of thoughtful little extras. Continental breakfasts are delivered promptly to the guests' rooms each morning, and dinner is served in the award-winning restaurant, also blessed with panoramic views.

**Rooms:** 4 en suite (1 fmly) **Facilities:** FTV iPod docking station tea/coffee Dinner available WiFi **Extras:** Nespresso machine, fruit, speciality toiletries

### The Relish

★★★★ GUEST ACCOMMODATION

**tel:** 01303 850952 **4 Augusta Gardens CT20 2RR**
**email:** reservations@hotelrelish.co.uk **web:** www.hotelrelish.co.uk
**dir:** *M20 junct 13 onto A2034 (0.6m), then B2064 (0.6m). Right into Earls Avenue, then left into Bouverie Rd West, right into Trinity Gardens*

Expect a warm welcome at this impressive Victorian terrace property, which overlooks Augusta Gardens in the fashionable West End of town. The bedrooms feature beautiful, contemporary natural-wood furniture, lovely co-ordinated fabrics and many thoughtful extras such as DVD players and free WiFi. Public rooms include a modern lounge-dining room, and a sun terrace where breakfast is served in the summer.

**Rooms:** 10 en suite **Facilities:** FTV DVD Lounge tea/coffee Direct dial WiFi **Extras:** Home-made cake, bottled water – complimentary **Conf:** Max 12 Thtr 9 Class 9 Board 12 **Notes:** Closed 23–31 Dec

## GOUDHURST
Map 6 TQ73

### The Star & Eagle

★★★★ ⇔ INN

**tel:** 01580 211512 **High Street TN17 1AL**
**email:** starandeagle@btconnect.com **web:** www.starandeagle.co.uk
**dir:** *Off A21 to Hastings rd, take A262, inn at top of village next to church*

A warm welcome is assured at the 15th-century Star & Eagle, located in the heart of this delightful village. Within easy reach of Royal Tunbridge Wells and the Weald, this is a great base for walkers. Both bedrooms and public areas boast original features and much character. A wide range of delicious home-made dishes is available in the restaurant and bar.

**Rooms:** 10 rms (8 en suite) (2 pri facs) **S** £95–£160; **D** £95–£160 **Facilities:** FTV tea/coffee Dinner available Direct dial WiFi ⚓ **Extras:** Speciality toiletries, home-made shortbread **Conf:** Max 30 Thtr 30 Class 15 Board 12 **Parking:** 20 **Notes:** RS 25–26 Dec eve closed Civ wed 50

## GRAFTY GREEN
Map 7 TQ84

### Who'd A Thought It

★★★★ ◉◉ GUEST ACCOMMODATION

**tel:** 01622 858951 **Headcorn Road ME17 2AR**
**email:** joe@whodathoughtit.com **web:** www.whodathoughtit.com
**dir:** *M20 junct 8 onto A20 towards Lenham. After 1m take turn signed Grafty Green, follow brown tourism signs for 4-5m*

The unusually named Who'd A Thought It is located in the quiet village of Grafty Green, convenient for both Maidstone and Ashford. Bedrooms and bathrooms are spacious and individually designed, using eclectic furnishings and stylish decor. Bathrooms feature hot tubs or jacuzzi baths, along with speciality toiletries. The restaurant has been awarded two AA Rosettes and offers an intimate and comfortable ambience. Meals are served daily in the restaurant and there is also a bar menu available.

**Rooms:** 19 annexe en suite (19 GF) **S** £70–£120; **D** £100–£475* **Facilities:** STV FTV DVD iPod docking station Lounge tea/coffee Dinner available Licensed WiFi ⌖18 Fishing **Extras:** Chocolates, champagne, bottled water, robes **Conf:** Max 30 Thtr 30 Class 30 Board 20 **Parking:** 40

## HALSTEAD
Map 6 TQ46

### 7 Motel Diner

★★★★ GUEST ACCOMMODATION

**tel:** 01959 535890 **London Road, Polhill TN14 7AA**
**email:** reservations@7hoteldiner.co.uk **web:** www.7hoteldiner.co.uk
**dir:** *M25 junct 4, 2m towards Sevenoaks*

This guest accommodation is conveniently located off the M25 and is just a short drive from Sevenoaks. The well-equipped bedrooms have been stylishly decorated to offer modern, comfortable accommodation; all have custom-made furniture, TVs and free WiFi. The lounge has a huge 50" TV with BT Sport coverage. There is an American-themed diner complete with authentic jukebox and leather booths, and all-day dining is available from 7am to 9.30pm.

**Rooms:** 26 en suite (2 fmly) (6 GF) **S** £59–£79; **D** £79–£139 (room only)* **Facilities:** FTV TVL tea/coffee Dinner available Direct dial Licensed WiFi ⌖ **Parking:** 50

## HAWKHURST     Map 7 TQ73

# The Queen's Inn

★★★★ INN

**tel:** 01580 754233 **Rye Road TN18 4EY**
**email:** info@queensinn.co.uk **web:** www.thequeensinnhawkhurst.co.uk
**dir:** *From M25 junct 5 take A21 to Flimwell. Turn left at lights to Hawkhurst*

The Queen's Inn was carefully and sympathetically refurbished by the current owners after years of decline. The rooms have been individually styled in a traditional yet contemporary style, all offering en suite facilities, deep and comfortable beds and home-made goodies. The restaurant uses local seasonal produce with many items such as breads, jams and marmalade made on-site by the talented co-owner and Head Chef. Free WiFi is offered in the public areas. Parking provided.

**Rooms:** 7 en suite (2 fmly) **S** £90–£100; **D** £100–£185* **Facilities:** FTV iPod docking station Lounge tea/coffee Dinner available Direct dial WiFi **Extras:** Home-made brownies, fresh milk, robes – complimentary **Conf:** Max 100 Thtr 100 Class 50 Board 50 **Parking:** 30

# Applebloom Bed and Breakfast

★★★★ BED AND BREAKFAST

**tel:** 01580 753347 **White Rose Cottage, Conghurst Lane TN18 5DZ**
**email:** enquiries@applebloom.co.uk **web:** www.applebloom.co.uk
**dir:** *A21 onto A268 at Flimwell. Through Hawkhurst, after 1.1m turn right at x-rds into Conghurst Ln. 400mtrs on right*

Applebloom Bed and Breakfast is set in its own attractive garden and surrounded by the beautiful Kent countryside. The two bedrooms are individually appointed and offer style, quality and comfort. Guests can relax either in the lounge, or in the garden during the warm months of the year. Breakfast is served at a communal table overlooking the garden; expect home-made and locally sourced items of the highest quality.

**Rooms:** 2 rms (1 en suite) (1 pri facs) **S** £60–£85; **D** £70–£95 **Facilities:** FTV Lounge tea/coffee WiFi **Parking:** 2 **Notes:** No children 12yrs

## HERNE COMMON     Map 7 TR16

# Westgrange House B&B

★★★ GUEST ACCOMMODATION

**tel:** 01227 740663 **42 Bushyfields Road CT6 7LJ**
**email:** westgrangebandb@ymail.com **web:** www.westgrangehouse.co.uk

Located in a quiet and tranquil area, this family-run bed and breakfast offers comfortable rooms, all equipped with WiFi and TVs. Off-road parking is available for all guests and a cooked and continental breakfast is served daily in the dining room. Herne Bay with its shops, bars and restaurants, is only a 10-minute drive away.

**Rooms:** 4 rms **Facilities:** WiFi

## LEYSDOWN-ON-SEA     Map 7 TR07

# The Ferry House Inn

★★★★ ◉ INN

**tel:** 01795 510214 **Harty Ferry Road ME12 4BQ**
**email:** info@theferryhouseinn.co.uk **web:** www.theferryhouseinn.co.uk
**dir:** *A249 over Sheppey Bridge, follow signs for Leysdown. Past Eastchurch, turn right before Leysdown*

The Ferry House Inn is on the Isle of Sheppey, and offers spacious and comfortable accommodation as well as some fantastic views. All rooms have modern fixtures, fittings and decor. Guests can enjoy dinner in the main restaurant or in the bar area with lots of local produce sourced from surrounding farms. A cooked or continental breakfast is served daily.

**Rooms:** 5 en suite **Facilities:** FTV DVD iPod docking station Lounge tea/coffee Dinner available WiFi **Conf:** Max 80 Thtr 80 Class 40 Board 40 **Parking:** 50 **Notes:** LB No children 12yrs Closed 24–30 Dec Civ wed 150

## MAIDSTONE     Map 7 TQ75

*See also Marden*

### AA UNIQUE B&B OF THE YEAR
### 2017–18

### Premier Collection

# Maiden's Tower at Leeds Castle

★★★★★ GUEST ACCOMMODATION

**tel:** 01622 767823 & 765400 **Leeds Castle Estate ME17 1PL**
**email:** accommodation@leeds-castle.co.uk **web:** www.leeds-castle.com
**dir:** *M20 junct 8, follow brown tourist signs. After 3rd sign, continue over rdbt on A20. Pass Park Gate Inn on right, turn next right signed Broomfield*

The Maiden's Tower was built as an annexe to the castle and used for house parties when the castle was still a private residence. Today, it offers five beautifully appointed bedrooms – all with stunning views. All rooms are en suite and are equipped with modern amenities. The venue can be hired for exclusive use for family parties or intimate ceremonies. Breakfast and dinner are served in the 17th-century, oak-beamed Fairfax Restaurant. Guests are free to explore the castle, grounds and gardens while in residence. Free parking is offered.

**Rooms:** 5 en suite **D** £235–£275* **Facilities:** FTV DVD tea/coffee Dinner available Direct dial Licensed WiFi ♨9 ☕ Facilities available within Leeds Castle grounds **Extras:** Speciality toiletries, robes, slippers, coffee machine **Conf:** Max 100 Thtr 100 Class 40 Board 30 **Parking:** 15 **Notes:** Closed 25–26 Dec Civ wed 100

# The Black Horse Inn

★★★★ ◎ INN

**tel:** 01622 737185 **Pilgrims Way, Thurnham ME14 3LD**
**email:** info@wellieboot.net **web:** www.wellieboot.net
**dir:** *M20 junct 7, N A249. Right into Detling, opposite pub into Pilgrims Way for 1m*

This charming inn dates from the 17th century, and the public areas showcase a wealth of oak beams, exposed brickwork and open fireplaces. The stylish bedrooms are in a series of cosy cabins behind the premises; each one is attractively furnished and thoughtfully equipped, and the bathrooms are of an equally high standard.

**Rooms:** 27 annexe en suite (8 fmly) (27 GF) **S** £75–£85; **D** £90–£110* **Facilities:** FTV tea/coffee Dinner available WiFi ❀ **Conf:** Max 80 Thtr 80 Class 40 Board 28 **Parking:** 40 **Notes:** LB Closed 24–27 Dec Civ wed 100

## Stable Courtyard at Leeds Castle

★★★★ GUEST ACCOMMODATION

**tel:** 01622 767823 & 767786 **Leeds Castle Estate ME17 1PL**
**email:** accommodation@leeds-castle.co.uk **web:** www.leeds-castle.com
**dir:** M20 junct 8, follow brown tourist signs. After 3rd sign, continue over rdbt on A20. Pass Park Gate Inn on right, turn next right signed Broomfield

Stable Courtyard is located right in the heart of the grounds at Leeds Castle. The stylishly appointed bedrooms are spacious, and many benefit from excellent views of the formal gardens and lake. Guests are welcome to explore the grounds and castle as part of their stay. Dinner and breakfast are served just opposite in The Great British Kitchen Restaurant.

**Rooms:** 17 annexe en suite (1 fmly) (5 GF) **S** £85–£100; **D** £100–£190*
**Facilities:** FTV DVD tea/coffee Dinner available Direct dial Licensed WiFi ❀9
**Extras:** Robes, slippers **Conf:** Max 90 Thtr 90 Class 40 Board 30 **Parking:** 30
**Notes:** Closed 25–26 Dec Civ wed 100

## Innkeeper's Lodge Maidstone

★★★ INN

**tel:** 08451 551551 *(Calls cost 2p per minute plus your phone company's access charge)*
**Sandling Road ME14 2RF**
**email:** info@innkeeperslodge.com **web:** www.innkeeperslodge.com

Known as The White Rabbit Sandling, this Innkeeper's Lodge is situated close to the centre of town, and dates back to 1797 when it was built to house the officers' quarters of the Invicta Barracks. Lodge bedrooms are modern, spacious and well appointed with a good range of facilities. Public rooms feature plush seating and dining areas where a good choice of food is available.

**Rooms:** 12 en suite (1 fmly) **Facilities:** FTV tea/coffee Dinner available WiFi

### MARDEN                                               Map 6 TQ74

### Premier Collection

## Merzie Meadows

★★★★★ BED AND BREAKFAST

**tel:** 01622 820500 & 07762 713077 **Hunton Road TN12 9SL**
**email:** pamela@merziemeadows.co.uk **web:** www.merziemeadows.co.uk
**dir:** A229 onto B2079 for Marden, 1st right into Underlyn Ln, 2.5m at large Chainhurst sign, right onto drive

Merzie Meadows is a detached property set in 20 acres of mature gardens in the Kent countryside. The generously proportioned bedrooms are housed in two wings, which overlook a terrace; each room is carefully decorated, thoughtfully equipped and furnished with well-chosen pieces. The attractive breakfast room has an Italian tiled floor and superb views of the garden.

**Rooms:** 2 en suite (1 fmly) (2 GF) **S** £98–£100; **D** £115–£120* **Facilities:** STV FTV TVL tea/coffee WiFi **Extras:** Speciality toiletries, chocolates, magazines – complimentary **Parking:** 4 **Notes:** No children 15yrs Closed mid Dec–mid Feb

### NEW ROMNEY                                            Map 7 TR02

## The Ship

★★★ INN

**tel:** 01797 362776 **83 High Street TN28 8AZ**
**email:** theshiphotelandrestaurant@gmail.com **web:** www.the-ship-hotel.co.uk
**dir:** M20 junct 10 onto A2070 to Brenzett. At rdbt 1st exit onto A259 to New Romney. Next to petrol station on right

This traditional inn is located in the very centre of Romney Marsh, bedrooms are traditional in style and are all located above the main pub area. The restaurant is spacious, seating up to 70 people, and is ideal for events and functions. Main bar area, conservatory and fully heated patio offer a good array of seating areas for guests to enjoy. Breakfast, lunch and dinner are served here daily.

**Rooms:** 10 en suite (1 fmly) **S** £45–£60; **D** £65–£90* **Facilities:** FTV DVD tea/coffee Dinner available WiFi ❀18 Pool table ❀ **Conf:** Max 130 Thtr 130 Class 80 Board 40 **Parking:** 20 **Notes:** LB

### PEMBURY                                               Map 6 TQ64

## Camden Arms

★★★★ INN

**tel:** 01892 822012 **1 High Street TN2 4PH**
**email:** food@camdenarms.co.uk **web:** www.camdenarms.co.uk
**dir:** Off A21, opposite village green

Located in a central position and just a couple of minutes' drive from Tunbridge Wells, this inn offers comfortable, well-equipped accommodation with LCD TVs, free WiFi throughout, and spacious en suite bathrooms. The large garden has outdoor seating, and the restaurant and bar area serve a large variety of local beers which change on a regular basis and pub meals are available seven days a week. Guests can enjoy a continental breakfast in the morning, or, for an extra charge, a hearty traditional English breakfast.

**Rooms:** 15 annexe en suite (1 fmly) (8 GF) **Facilities:** FTV tea/coffee Dinner available WiFi ❀ **Extras:** Trouser press **Conf:** Max 50 Thtr 50 Class 24 Board 16 **Parking:** 68

### PLUCKLEY                                              Map 7 TQ94

## Elvey Farm

★★★★ GUEST ACCOMMODATION

**tel:** 01233 840442 **Elvey Lane TN27 0SU**
**email:** bookings@elveyfarm.co.uk **web:** www.elveyfarm.co.uk
**dir:** M20 junct 8 onto A20 to Charing. Right into Station Road signed Pluckley. At bottom of Forge Hill turn right. 1st right into Mundy Bois Road, then 1st right into Elvey Lane

Located in a very quiet and picturesque part of the Kentish countryside, a number of period outbuildings have been converted to offer stylish and comfortable accommodation. There is a restaurant on site, with an outside seating area, open for afternoon tea and dinner every night. Meeting rooms make this ideal for small functions, weddings or business meetings. A hearty cooked or continental breakfast is served daily in the main restaurant.

**Rooms:** 11 en suite (3 fmly) (6 GF) **S** £55–£100; **D** £90–£275* **Facilities:** FTV DVD Lounge tea/coffee Dinner available Licensed WiFi ❀ **Conf:** Max 20 Thtr 20 Class 15 Board 12 **Parking:** 30 **Notes:** Civ wed 100

## QUEENBOROUGH
Map 7 TQ97

### Queen Phillippa B&B

★★★★ GUEST ACCOMMODATION

**tel:** 01795 228756 **High Street ME11 5AQ**
**email:** queenphillippabedandbreakfast@gmail.com **web:** www.queenphillippa.com
**dir:** *A249 onto the Isle of Sheppey, follow signs for Queenborough. Located opposite entrance to railway station*

This former pub has recently been completely renovated to provide 10 en suite bedrooms, all have been refurbished throughout with modern decor and stylish furnishings. Rooms are well equipped with free WiFi, digital TV and beverage making facilities. Breakfast is served daily in the dining area on the ground floor where guests can enjoy a cooked or continental breakfast.

**Rooms:** 10 en suite (10 fmly) **Facilities:** FTV TVL tea/coffee WiFi ♨18 **Parking:** 9
**Notes:** LB

## SANDWICH
Map 7 TR35

### The New Inn

★★★ INN

**tel:** 01304 612335 **2 Harnet Street CT13 9ES**
**email:** new.inn@thorleytaverns.com **web:** www.thenewinnsandwich.com
**dir:** *Off A256, one-way system into town centre, inn on right*

The New Inn is situated in the heart of busy Sandwich. The large open-plan lounge bar offers an extensive range of beers and an interesting choice of home-made dishes. Bedrooms are furnished in pine and have many useful extras.

**Rooms:** 5 en suite (3 fmly) **Facilities:** STV tea/coffee Dinner available Direct dial WiFi
🅿 **Parking:** 17

## SITTINGBOURNE
Map 7 TQ96

### Sandhurst Farm Forge

★★★★ BED AND BREAKFAST

**tel:** 01795 886854 **Seed Road, Newnham ME9 0NE**
**email:** rooms.forge@btinternet.com **web:** www.sandhurstfarmforge.co.uk
**dir:** *Exit A2 into Newnham, into Seed Rd by church, establishment 1m on right*

A warm welcome is assured at this peaceful location, which also features a working forge. The spacious bedrooms are in a converted stable block and provide smartly furnished accommodation. Breakfast is served in the dining room adjoining the bedrooms. The owner has won an award for green tourism by reducing the impact of the business on the environment.

**Rooms:** 2 annexe en suite (2 GF) **S** £50–£60; **D** £80–£85* **Facilities:** STV DVD tea/coffee WiFi 🅿 **Extras:** Snacks, bottled water **Parking:** 6 **Notes:** LB
No children 12yrs Closed 23 Dec–2 Jan

## TENTERDEN
Map 7 TQ83

### Little Dane Court

★★★★ BED AND BREAKFAST

**tel:** 01580 763389 & 07776 193399 **1 Ashford Road TN30 6AB**
**email:** littledanecourt@gmail.com **web:** www.littledanecourt.co.uk
**dir:** *A28 to Tenterden, after 1m pass 2 red telephone boxes. Little Dane 4th house on right*

Little Dane Court has a long and fascinating history, and offers a range of well-appointed bedrooms that meet the needs of discerning travellers. All rooms are well equipped. For something a bit more individual, the Japanese-style cottage offers extra privacy and space. Breakfast is served at the communal table in the dining room or in the courtyard during the warm months of the year. The Japanese-style garden is a pocket of tranquillity.

**Rooms:** 3 rms (2 en suite) (1 pri facs) 1 annexe en suite **Facilities:** FTV DVD TVL tea/coffee Dinner available WiFi 🅿 **Conf:** Max 10 Thtr 10 Board 10 **Parking:** 6
**Notes:** LB

## TUNBRIDGE WELLS (ROYAL)
Map 6 TQ53

### Premier Collection

### Danehurst House

★★★★★ 🍽 BED AND BREAKFAST

**tel:** 01892 527739 **41 Lower Green Road, Rusthall TN4 8TW**
**email:** info@danehurst.net **web:** www.danehurst.net
**dir:** *1.5m W of Tunbridge Wells in Rusthall. Exit A264 into Coach Rd & Lower Green Rd*

Situated in pretty gardens in a quiet residential area, this gabled Victorian house is located to the west of the historic spa town. The house retains many original features and is attractively decorated throughout. Public areas include a comfortable lounge with a small bar. The homely bedrooms come with a wealth of thoughtful extras, and excellent breakfasts are served in the conservatory.

**Rooms:** 4 en suite **Facilities:** FTV DVD iPod docking station TVL tea/coffee Licensed WiFi **Extras:** Speciality toiletries, Nespresso coffee machine **Parking:** 6
**Notes:** No children 12yrs Closed Xmas

### Salomons

★★★★ GUEST ACCOMMODATION

**tel:** 01892 515152 **Salomons Estate, Broomhill Road TN3 0TG**
**email:** reception@salomons-estate.com **web:** www.salomons-estate.com
**dir:** *M25 junct 5, A21 signed Hastings. Then A26 (Southborough & Tunbridge Wells). In Southborough right at 2nd lights into Speldhurst Rd. 2nd left into Broomhill Rd, entrance on right*

Salomons is located on a private, 36-acre estate just a short distance from Royal Tunbridge Wells. The bedrooms are all contemporary in style with modern decor and are well equipped ideal for both business and leisure guests. Guests can enjoy breakfast, lunch and dinner in the main Manor House daily. This is also a very popular wedding venue and a great range of conference rooms are available.

**Rooms:** 47 annexe en suite (23 GF) **S** £60–£75; **D** £90–£105* **Facilities:** STV FTV tea/coffee Dinner available Direct dial Licensed WiFi Gym **Extras:** Speciality toiletries **Conf:** Max 230 Thtr 230 Class 77 Board 68 **Parking:** 200 **Notes:** Civ wed 200

## Innkeeper's Lodge Tunbridge Wells

★★★ INN

tel: 08451 551551 *(Calls cost 2p per minute plus your phone company's access charge)*
**London Road, Southborough TN4 0QB**
email: info@innkeeperslodge.com web: www.innkeeperslodge.com

At Innkeeper's Lodge you'll find accommodation with comfort and character in equal measure, and everything needed for a relaxing stay, from easy check-in and free parking to complimentary breakfast and a cosy pub serving great value food and drink on the doorstep. Each Lodge has quality rooms, and there are Lodges in a variety of locations from towns and cities to countryside settings across the UK.

**Rooms:** 14 en suite (2 fmly) **Facilities:** FTV tea/coffee Dinner available WiFi

### WOODCHURCH                              Map 7 TQ93

#### Premier Collection

## Brook Farm Bed & Breakfast

★★★★★ BED AND BREAKFAST

tel: 01233 860444 & 07790 906611 **Brook Street TN26 3SR**
email: reservations@brook.farm web: www.brook.farm
dir: *M20 junct 9 onto A28 south. After 4m turn left signed Woodchurch, 3m to village. Through village to T-junct, turn right onto B2067. 0.5m on right*

Brook Farm offers three cottage-style bedrooms with their own private entrance and convenient parking space. All rooms have been very well configured and appointed to the highest standard to ensure a relaxing and enjoyable stay. Freshly prepared breakfasts are served in the attractive breakfast room in the farmhouse.

**Rooms:** 3 annexe en suite (3 GF) **S** £75; **D** £95 **Facilities:** FTV iPod docking station tea/coffee WiFi ⬩ ⅃18 🔒 **Extras:** Speciality toiletries, Nespresso machine, slippers **Parking:** 4 **Notes:** LB No children 12yrs

### WROTHAM                              Map 6 TQ65

## The Bull

★★★★ ◉◉ INN

tel: 01732 789800 **Bull Lane TN15 7RF**
email: info@thebullhotel.com web: www.thebullhotel.com
dir: *M20 junct 2, A20 signed Paddock Wood, Gravesend & Tonbridge. At rbt take 3rd exit onto A20 signed Wrotham, Tonbridge, Borough Green, M20 & M25. At rdbt take 4th exit into Bull Lane signed Wrotham*

Dating back to 1385 and first licensed in 1495, The Bull offers modern facilities yet retains many traditional features, including original exposed beams. High quality meals can be enjoyed at breakfast, lunch and dinner; the inn sources local produce from nearby farms, south coast landed fish, and real ales from the Dark Star microbrewery. Dinner can be taken in the two AA Rosette award-winning à la carte restaurant, while more relaxed fare is offered in the smokehouse bar. The bedrooms, including one four-poster room, are decorated with modern furnishings. The Buttery function room was originally the village bakery.

**Rooms:** 11 en suite (1 fmly) **S** £69–£139; **D** £79–£159 (room only)* **Facilities:** FTV tea/coffee Dinner available WiFi ⅃18 **Extras:** Speciality toiletries – complimentary **Conf:** Max 100 Thtr 60 Class 60 Board 40 **Parking:** 30 **Notes:** Civ wed 60

### WYE                              Map 7 TR04

## Wife of Bath

★★★★ ◉◉ RESTAURANT WITH ROOMS

tel: 01233 812232 **4 Upper Bridge Street TN25 5AF**
email: info@thewifeofbath.com web: www.thewifeofbath.com
dir: *M20 junct 10, A2070 signed Kennington. At rdbt right onto A28 (Canterbury Road). Right at x-rds into Harville Rd signed Wye. At T-junct (station opposite) right into Bridge Rd, becomes Churchfield Way. Right into Church St. At T-junct left, Wife of Bath on right*

Located in the heart of this picturesque village of Wye, the Wife of Bath has benefited from a complete refurbishment, with the restaurant and the en suite rooms stylish in design. All are very comfortably appointed and still feature the building's original features including exposed oak beams. The restaurant is open daily for breakfast, lunch and dinner.

**Rooms:** 3 en suite 2 annexe en suite (2 GF) **S** £105–£140; **D** £105–£140* **Facilities:** FTV tea/coffee Dinner available WiFi **Extras:** Fruit, snacks, robes **Parking:** 10

## LANCASHIRE

### ACCRINGTON
Map 18 SD72

## The Maple Lodge

★★★★ GUEST ACCOMMODATION

**tel:** 01254 301284 **70 Blackburn Road, Clayton-le-Moors BB5 5JH**
**email:** info@stayatmaplelodge.co.uk **web:** www.stayatmaplelodge.co.uk
**dir:** *M65 junct 7, follow signs for Clitheroe, right at T-junct into Blackburn Rd*

This welcoming house is convenient for the M65 and local business areas and provides modern bedrooms generously equipped with home comforts as well as an inviting lounge with well-stocked bar. Hearty breakfasts are served in the bright dining room.

**Rooms:** 4 en suite 4 annexe en suite (1 fmly) (4 GF) **S** £42–£49; **D** £56–£66*
**Facilities:** FTV DVD TVL tea/coffee Direct dial Licensed WiFi 🚗 **Parking:** 6

## Pilkington's Guest House

★★★ GUEST HOUSE

**tel:** 01254 237032 **135 Blackburn Road BB5 0AA**
**email:** pilkingtonsaccrington@hotmail.com
**web:** www.pilkingtonsbedandbreakfast.webs.com
**dir:** *M65 junct 7 follow signs to Accrington town centre, establishment opposite railway station. M66 onto A56 to Accrington town centre*

Positioned close to the railway station, this family-run property has two comfortable bedrooms in the main house and four further bedrooms in the terrace which is just a short way along the street. Home-cooked breakfasts are served in the main house.

**Rooms:** 6 rms (6 pri facs) (2 GF) **S** £35; **D** £65* **Facilities:** FTV DVD Lounge TVL tea/coffee WiFi 🚗 **Extras:** Slippers, robes **Parking:** 2

### BARLEY
Map 18 SD84

## Barley Mow

★★★★ 🍴 INN

**tel:** 01282 690868 **BB12 9JX**
**email:** info@barleymowpendle.co.uk **web:** www.seafoodpubcompany.com
**dir:** *M65 junct 13, at rdbt exit onto A682. Left into Pasture Ln, right into Ridge Ln, continue on Barley New Rd. Turn right*

This relaxed dining pub is full of stripped back rustic charm. Although managed by the Seafood Pub Company, there is plenty for meat lovers as traditional pub fare with an international twist is also a staple. Six bedrooms upstairs are spacious and equipped with smart-TVs, free WiFi and deeply comfortable beds. A rural location offers a peaceful setting but quick motorway links are also on the doorstep.

**Rooms:** 6 en suite (2 fmly) **Facilities:** FTV tea/coffee Dinner available WiFi **Extras:** Mineral water, fresh milk **Parking:** 10

### BLACKBURN
Map 18 SD62

## The Millstone at Mellor

★★★★★ ◎◎ INN

**tel:** 01254 813333 **Church Lane, Mellor BB2 7JR**
**email:** relax@millstonemellor.co.uk **web:** www.millstonemellor.co.uk
**dir:** *A677 from Blackburn (or from A59) follow signs to Mellor*

Once a coaching inn, The Millstone is situated in a village just outside the town. It provides a very high standard of accommodation and professional and friendly service. Bedrooms, some in an adjacent house, are comfortable and generally spacious, and all are very well equipped. A room for less mobile guests is also available. Meals in the AA Rosetted restaurant make excellent use of the highest quality Ribble Valley produce.

**Rooms:** 17 en suite 6 annexe en suite (5 fmly) (8 GF) **S** £90–£150; **D** £96–£156*
**Facilities:** STV Lounge tea/coffee Dinner available Direct dial WiFi **Conf:** Max 10 Board 10 **Parking:** 40

### BLACKPOOL
Map 18 SD33

## The Fylde International

★★★★ GUEST HOUSE

**tel:** 01253 623735 **93 Palatine Road FY1 4BX**
**email:** fyldeinternationalblackpool@gmail.com
**web:** www.familyaccommodationblackpool.com
**dir:** *A5099 (Central Dr) into town centre, right into Palatine Rd. Property on right before lights*

This family-run guest house has a prime central location, close to all of Blackpool's attractions. Accommodation is comfortable and all rooms are equipped with modern facilities. Families are well catered for with a choice of family rooms and suites available. A spacious lounge and a separate dedicated children's area ensure all guests can enjoy the relaxed and welcoming environment. A substantial buffet breakfast is served. Parking is available. The Fylde International was a finalist for the AA Friendliest B&B of the Year 2017–18.

**Rooms:** 7 en suite (4 fmly) (1 GF) **Facilities:** FTV TVL tea/coffee Licensed WiFi 🚗 **Parking:** 6 **Notes:** LB

## The Berwick

★★★★ GUEST HOUSE

**tel:** 01253 351496 **23 King Edward Avenue FY2 9TA**
**email:** info@theberwickblackpool.co.uk **web:** www.theberwickblackpool.co.uk
**dir:** *From Queen's Promenade turn into King Edward Ave, pass Holmfield Rd, on right before Warbreck Dr*

In a quiet North Shore setting, only a few minutes' walk from the promenade, is this guest house with an interesting history as it was the birthplace of what would become Jaguar Motors. The bodyshop even supplied the first AA Patrol motorcycle sidecars! The welcome and the hospitality offered by Heather is matched by homely cooking, pristine housekeeping and comfortably appointed bedrooms. Private parking is available.

**Rooms:** 8 en suite **Facilities:** FTV TVL tea/coffee Dinner available Licensed WiFi 🚗 **Parking:** 4 **Notes:** LB No children 15yrs Closed Xmas-New Year & 23 Feb–5 Mar

## The Bromley

★★★★ BED AND BREAKFAST

tel: 01253 624171 & 07702 239890 **306 Promenade FY1 2EY**
email: bromleyblackpool@gmail.com web: www.thebromleyhotelblackpool.co.uk
dir: 0.1m N past Blackpool Tower, on right

Located on the North Shore promenade, just a short walk from many of the main attractions, The Bromley offers comfortable, en suite accommodation. There is a licensed bar and lounge on the ground floor. Free WiFi is available in public areas, and off-road parking, provided at the front of the property, is a real bonus. The Bromley was a finalist for the AA Friendliest B&B of the Year 2017–18.

**Rooms:** 13 en suite (3 fmly) (1 GF) **S** £45–£50; **D** £70–£95 **Facilities:** FTV DVD TVL tea/coffee Licensed WiFi 🔒 **Parking:** 14 **Notes:** Closed 21–27 Dec, 26 Jan–23 Feb

## The Craigmore

★★★★ GUEST HOUSE

tel: 01253 355098 **8 Willshaw Road, Gynn Square FY2 9SH**
email: enquiries@thecraigmore.com web: www.thecraigmore.com
dir: 1m N of Tower. A584 N over Gynn rdbt, 1st right into Willshaw Rd. The Craigmore 3rd on left

This friendly and welcoming guest house is in an attractive location overlooking Gynn Square gardens, with the Promenade and tram stops just metres away. Three of the smart and modern bedrooms are suitable for families. There is a comfortable lounge, a separate sun lounge and patio to the front, and the dining room has a small bar.

**Rooms:** 7 en suite (3 fmly) **S** £50–£55; **D** £50–£70* **Facilities:** FTV Lounge TVL tea/coffee Licensed WiFi **Notes:** LB No children 5yrs Closed Nov–Mar

## Pelham Lodge

★★★★ GUEST ACCOMMODATION

tel: 01253 625127 & 07717 342897 **7-9 General Street FY1 1RW**
email: info@pelhamlodge.co.uk web: www.pelhamlodge.co.uk

Situated towards the North End of Blackpool, and close to attractions such as the Winter Gardens and Blackpool Tower, Pelham Lodge is only a five-minute walk from the train station. Good quality and comfortable accommodation is promised and a friendly welcome on arrival guaranteed. Limited parking available to the rear.

**Rooms:** 15 en suite (2 fmly) (2 GF) **S** £35–£45; **D** £55–£70* **Facilities:** FTV TVL tea/coffee WiFi **Extras:** Bottled water - complimentary **Parking:** 4 **Notes:** Closed 24–25 Dec

## Hartshead

★★★ GUEST ACCOMMODATION

tel: 01253 353133 & 357111 **17 King Edward Avenue, North Shore FY2 9TA**
email: info@hartshead-hotel.co.uk web: www.hartshead-hotel.co.uk
dir: M55 junct 4, A583, A584 to North Shore, exit Queens Promenade into King Edward Av

Popular for its location near the seafront on the quieter North Shore, the enthusiastically-run Hartshead has modern bedrooms of various sizes, all equipped with a good range of practical extras. A comfortable sun lounge is available to the front, in addition to a lounge bar. Breakfast and pre-theatre dinners are served in the bright dining room. Guaranteed off-street parking is a bonus.

**Rooms:** 9 en suite (3 fmly) **S** £25–£50; **D** £48–£80* **Facilities:** FTV DVD Lounge tea/coffee Dinner available Licensed WiFi **Parking:** 7 **Notes:** LB

## The Abbotsford

★★★ GUEST HOUSE

tel: 01253 346417 **18 Woodfield Road FY1 6AX**
email: abbotsford-blackpool@outlook.com web: www.abbotsford-blackpool.co.uk
dir: M55 to end of motorway. Over rdbt into Yeadon Way, continue for 1.5m, over 2 rdbts. Turn left at football ground

This friendly, personally-run guest house has a great location close to the promenade and handy for the Pleasure Beach and all of Blackpool's central attractions. Rooms are neat and well equipped and there is a small bar and sun lounge to relax in. Dinner is available on request and a generous breakfast is served in the bright dining room.

**Rooms:** 9 rms (8 en suite) (1 pri facs) (2 fmly) **Facilities:** FTV DVD TVL tea/coffee Dinner available Licensed WiFi Pool table **Notes:** LB Closed 15–28 Dec

## Bianca Guesthouse

★★★ GUEST HOUSE

tel: 01253 752824 **25 Palatine Road FY1 4BX**
email: enquiries@hotelbianca.co.uk web: www.hotelbianca.co.uk

A warm Blackpool welcome awaits at Bianca Guesthouse, situated centrally, and within easy walking distance of all the town's attractions and amenities. Homely accommodation is decorated with modern floral prints. Family rooms are available, as well as a range of cosy doubles fitted with impressively comfortable beds. There is a licensed bar for residents.

**Rooms:** 10 en suite (2 fmly) **S** £25–£30; **D** £40–£55* **Facilities:** FTV tea/coffee Licensed WiFi **Notes:** Closed 20–27 Dec

BLACKPOOL *continued*

## Casablanca

★★★ GUEST HOUSE

tel: 01253 622574 **84 Hornby Road FY1 4QS**
email: jdixon8969@aol.com

This personally-run and homely guest accommodation is perfectly situated within easy reach of all of Blackpool's central attractions. Accommodation is fully en suite and features modern accessories and a choice of room types. There is a comfortable lounge, breakfasts are generous and limited parking is available.

**Rooms:** 9 en suite (2 fmly) **Facilities:** FTV TVL tea/coffee 🔒 **Parking:** 2 **Notes:** LB Closed 20 Dec-4 Jan

## The Derby

★★★ GUEST ACCOMMODATION

tel: 01253 623708 & 07809 143248 **2 Derby Road FY1 2JF**
email: tj52way@yahoo.com web: www.thederbyhotel.co.uk
dir: *From promenade, pass North Pier, heading N. Turn right next to Hilton Hotel into Derby Road, The Derby on right*

The Derby is a family-friendly establishment offering good value, modern accommodation in a variety of sizes. Dinner is available and guests have the use of a comfortable lounge and a separate bar. Breakfast is the highlight of any stay with quality cooking and hearty portions to be expected.

**Rooms:** 9 rms (5 en suite) (4 pri facs) (3 fmly) **S** £25-£40; **D** £45-£65 **Facilities:** FTV TVL tea/coffee Dinner available Licensed WiFi 🔒 **Parking:** 5 **Notes:** LB

## The Fairway

★★★ 🅰 GUEST ACCOMMODATION

tel: 01253 623777 **34-36 Hull Road FY1 4QB**
email: fairwayblackpool@aol.com web: www.fairwayhotelblackpool.co.uk

Close to Blackpool's seafront and Tower, The Fairway is run by friendly owners and is a traditional seaside property. It is ideal for families, or those attending dance festivals, conferences or other Blackpool entertainments. There is a licensed bar, and a games area with a pool table. A full English breakfast is served and free WiFi is a bonus.

**Rooms:** 18 en suite (3 fmly) **D** £50-£55* **Facilities:** FTV DVD TVL tea/coffee Licensed WiFi Pool table **Notes:** LB

### BOLTON-BY-BOWLAND                    Map 18 SD74

## Middle Flass Lodge

★★★★ 🍽 GUEST HOUSE

tel: 01200 447259 **Settle Rd BB7 4NY**
email: middleflasslodge@btconnect.com web: www.middleflasslodge.co.uk
dir: *2m N of Bolton-by-Bowland. Off A59 for Sawley, N to Forest Becks, over bridge, 1m on right*

Set in peaceful countryside in the Forest of Bowland, this traditional house provides a warm welcome for those wishing to get away from it all. Stylishly converted from farm outbuildings, exposed timbers feature throughout. There is an attractive restaurant and a cosy lounge. Bedrooms include a family room, with stairlift access to the first floor. Thanks to the accomplished chef, the restaurant is very popular.

**Rooms:** 5 en suite 2 annexe en suite (1 fmly) **Facilities:** FTV TVL tea/coffee Dinner available Licensed WiFi 🔒 **Extras:** Speciality toiletries – complimentary **Parking:** 14 **Notes:** LB

### CHORLEY
*See Eccleston*

### CLITHEROE                    Map 18 SD74

#### Premier Collection

## The Assheton Arms

★★★★★ ⊚ RESTAURANT WITH ROOMS

tel: 01200 441227 **Downham BB7 4BJ**
email: info@asshetonarms.com web: www.seafoodpubcompany.com
dir: *A59 to Chatburn, then follow Downham signs*

This historic Grade II listed building is located in the conservation village of Downham, with stunning views of Pendle Hill. The inn is owned by the Seafood Pub Company which means you can expect outstanding seafood. The rooms are spacious with traditional fittings yet maintain a modern feel. The team are young, friendly and guarantee a warm welcome.

**Rooms:** 1 en suite 11 annexe en suite (4 fmly) (6 GF) **Facilities:** FTV Lounge tea/coffee Dinner available WiFi 🏌18 🔒 **Extras:** Mineral water, fresh milk **Conf:** Max 20 **Parking:** 18

### ECCLESTON                    Map 15 SD51

## Parr Hall Farm

★★★★ GUEST ACCOMMODATION

tel: 01257 451917 **8 Parr Lane PR7 5SL**
email: enquiries@parrhallfarm.com web: www.parrhallfarm.com
dir: *M6 junct 27, B5250 N for 5m to Parr Ln on right. 1st property on left*

This attractive, well-maintained farmhouse and sometime wedding venue is located in a quiet corner of the village yet close to the M6. Dating back to the 18th century, the majority of bedrooms are located in a sympathetic barn conversion and include luxury en suite bathrooms and lots of thoughtful extras. A comprehensive continental breakfast is included in the room price.

**Rooms:** 10 annexe en suite (1 fmly) (5 GF) **S** £55-£65; **D** £80-£90* **Facilities:** FTV tea/coffee WiFi 🏌9 🔒 Guided Walks **Conf:** Max 15 Class 15 Board 15 **Parking:** 20

### FENCE                    Map 18 SD83

## The Forest

★★★★ INN

tel: 01282 692228 **Cuckstool Lane BB12 9PA**
email: info@forestfence.co.uk
web: www.seafoodpubcompany.com/venue-promotions/forest-fence/

Recently refurbished and relaunched under the Seafood Pub Company banner, this modern dining pub has much to offer. The food has an eclectic Mediterranean focus with local produce and grills cooked over burning coals. Accommodation is contemporary and well equipped. Ample parking on-site and outside dining is a big draw in the summer months.

**Rooms:** 8 en suite **S** £75-£100; **D** £90-£120* **Facilities:** Dinner available **Parking**

## GREAT ECCLESTON
Map 18 SD44

### Premier Collection

# The Cartford Inn
★★★★★ ⊛ INN

**tel:** 01253 670199 **Cartford Lane, Little Eccleston PR3 0YP**
**email:** info@thecartfordinn.co.uk **web:** www.thecartfordinn.co.uk
**dir:** N of A586 (W of Great Eccleston)

This 17th-century inn has undergone many changes through the years and now offers stylish and chic accommodation. Bedrooms are well equipped and comfortable with impressive en suite facilities. Dining is a must here with the team using local produce which they also sell in their on-site deli, Toti (short for Taste of the Inn). Private function room are available for small parties.

**Rooms:** 15 en suite (1 fmly) (3 GF) **S** £75–£130; **D** £125–£230* **Facilities:** FTV tea/coffee Dinner available WiFi ⅃18 🔒 **Conf:** Max 35 Thtr 35 Class 14 Board 16 **Parking:** 50 **Notes:** Closed 25 Dec

## HEYSHAM
Map 18 SD46

# The Royal
Ⓤ

**tel:** 01524 859298 **Main Street LA3 2RN**
**email:** paulturner@theroyalheysham.co.uk **web:** www.theroyalheysham.co.uk
**dir:** A589 follow signs for Heysham Village, then brown tourist signs for St Peter's Church. The Royal is next to church

Currently the rating for this establishment is not confirmed. This may be due to a change of ownership or because it has only recently joined the AA rating scheme.

**Rooms:** 4 en suite 7 annexe en suite (3 GF) **S** £75–£90; **D** £80–£95* **Facilities:** tea/coffee Dinner available Licensed WiFi **Parking:** 30

## LANCASTER
Map 18 SD46

# The Fenwick Steak & Seafood Pub
★★★★ ⊜ INN

**tel:** 015242 21157 **Lancaster Road, Claughton LA2 9LA**
**email:** info@fenwickarms.co.uk **web:** www.fenwickarms.co.uk

This charming roadside dining pub has been stylishly restored in recent years by the growing Seafood Pub Company. The comfortable and character public bar and restaurant areas make the setting for the fish and grill-led menu and a great choice of real ales and wines. The accommodation is modern and comfortable, and suites are available.

**Rooms:** 9 en suite **Facilities:** Dinner available WiFi **Parking**

# Toll House Inn
★★★★ INN

**tel:** 01524 599900 **Penny Street LA1 1XT**
**email:** relax@tollhouseinnlancaster.co.uk **web:** tollhouseinnlancaster.co.uk

Ideally situated in the heart of the city, Toll House Inn has been transformed from a typical Victorian property to one that is fresh and contemporary, yet retains all the elegance of its original era. Bedrooms are modern and very well equipped. The stylish bar and brasserie are popular with both guests and local residents, serving meals and light bites throughout the day.

**Rooms:** 28 en suite (2 fmly) (2 GF) **Facilities:** FTV tea/coffee Dinner available Lift WiFi 🔒 **Conf:** Max 20 Thtr 20 Board 20 **Parking:** 3 **Notes:** LB

## LANESHAW BRIDGE
Map 18 SD94

# The Alma Inn
★★★★ ⊜ INN

**tel:** 01282 857830 **Emmott Lane BB8 7EG**
**email:** reception@thealmainn.com **web:** www.thealmainn.com
**dir:** At end of M65 onto A6068 (Vivary Way) towards Skipton. At 3rd rdbt, 1st exit into Skipton Old Rd, after 0.5m right into Hill Ln. 0.5m on right

A recent addition to the Seafood Pub Company's stable, The Alma Inn is a longstanding gem nestled in the magnificent Pendle countryside. Dating back to 1725, it is a rural coaching inn that features open fires, stone floors and oak beams. Guests can dine well in the lounge-style bars or the more lavishly appointed restaurant. The stylish rooms come in a variety of sizes, and all are thoroughly equipped with Nespresso machines, DAB radio and safes. Function facilities are available along with ample parking and even a helicopter landing pad.

**Rooms:** 9 en suite (8 fmly) **Facilities:** FTV iPod docking station Lounge tea/coffee Dinner available Direct dial WiFi ⅃9 🔒 **Extras:** Speciality toiletries, Nespresso coffee machine **Conf:** Max 150 Thtr 100 Class 50 Board 40 **Parking:** 45 **Notes:** LB Civ wed 200

# Rye Flatt Bed & Breakfast
★★★★ BED AND BREAKFAST

**tel:** 01282 871565 **20 School Lane BB8 7JB**
**email:** info@rye-flatt.co.uk **web:** www.rye-flatt.co.uk
**dir:** M65 onto A6068 towards Keighley. Turn right at Emmott Arms, park on left, immediately after bridge

Situated on the Lancashire and Yorkshire border with great transport links, this B&B operates from a 17th-century farmhouse which has some fantastic original features. Ideally located for business or leisure, the house features cosy bedrooms and well-equipped bathrooms. Warm hospitality and a memorable breakfast are features of any stay here. There is also a garden for sunnier days.

**Rooms:** 2 en suite **S** £50; **D** £80 **Facilities:** FTV Lounge tea/coffee WiFi 🔒 **Parking:** 2

## LONGRIDGE
Map 18 SD63

# Derby Arms
★★★★ ⊜ INN

**tel:** 01772 782370 **Chipping Road PR3 2NB**
**email:** info@derbyarmslongridge.co.uk **web:** www.derbyarmslongridge.co.uk
**dir:** Phone for directions

This relaxed dining pub is managed by the Seafood Pub Company so although classic British pub fare is to be expected, the emphasis is on locally landed fish. Accommodation upstairs is spacious and equipped with smart-TVs. Little luxury extras in the form of toiletries are noteworthy and a deeply comfortable bed is guaranteed. A rural location offers a peaceful setting but quick motorway links are also a boon.

**Rooms:** 6 en suite (1 fmly) **Facilities:** FTV tea/coffee Dinner available ⅃18 🔒 **Conf:** Max 15 Thtr 15 Class 15 Board 15 **Parking:** 50

## LYTHAM ST ANNES — Map 18 SD32

### Innkeeper's Lodge Lytham St Annes

★★★★ INN

**tel:** 0845 112 6078 *(Calls cost 2p per minute plus your phone company's access charge)*
**The County Hotel, Church Road FY8 5LH**
**email:** info@innkeeperslodge.com **web:** www.innkeeperslodge.com
**dir:** *At western end of M55 junct 4 onto A5239 Progress Way, becomes A5230 Squires Gate Lane. At Starr Gate turn left onto A584 Clifton Drive North. Towards Kilgrimol Garden, following A584, left onto Beach St, then right into Henry St. Next left into Church Rd, on left*

The Innkeeper's Lodge Lytham St Annes is ideally situated in the heart of the town between the golf courses and just off the west beach promenade. Recent refurbishment has seen this busy dining pub have fresh and contemporary bedrooms which are well equipped for the modern traveller. The stylish bar and pizza kitchen are popular with both guests and local residents, serving meals and light bites throughout the day.

**Rooms:** 21 en suite (3 fmly) **S** £60–£80; **D** £60–£80* **Facilities:** FTV Lounge tea/coffee Dinner available WiFi **Parking:** 5 **Notes:** LB

### Strathmore

★★★ GUEST ACCOMMODATION

**tel:** 01253 725478 **305 Clifton Drive South FY8 1HN**
**dir:** *In centre of St Annes opposite Post Office*

The long-established, family-run Strathmore has a central location close to the promenade, and offers smartly furnished and well-equipped bedrooms. There is an elegant lounge and a smart dining room.

**Rooms:** 4 en suite **S** £31–£33; **D** £62–£66* **Facilities:** Lounge tea/coffee WiFi **Parking:** 5 **Notes:** LB No children 9yrs

## MORECAMBE — Map 18 SD46

### The Morecambe Hotel

★★★★ INN

**tel:** 01524 415239 & 415515 **25 Lord Street, Poulton LA4 5HX**
**email:** hello@themorecambehotel.co.uk **web:** www.themorecambehotel.co.uk
**dir:** *M6 junct 34 onto A683 to Morecambe. Follow signs for town centre (Lancaster Rd). At rdbt 2nd exit into Thornton Rd, The Morecambe opposite St Mary's Church*

This 18th-century former coaching inn has been lovingly refurbished to a high standard and now provides several en suite bedrooms, a small function room for up to 30 people and an extensive dining area. A large garden to the rear boasts a terrace for alfresco dining and children's play area.

**Rooms:** 7 en suite **Facilities:** FTV DVD iPod docking station Lounge TVL tea/coffee Dinner available WiFi ᴸ18 **Extras:** Speciality toiletries, slippers, robes – complimentary **Conf:** Max 24 Thtr 24 Class 24 Board 24 **Parking:** 10 **Notes:** LB

### Yacht Bay View

★★★★ GUEST HOUSE

**tel:** 01524 414481 **359 Marine Road East LA4 5AQ**
**email:** yachtbayview@hotmail.com **web:** www.yachtbay.co.uk
**dir:** *0.5m NE of town centre on seafront promenade*

This comfortable seafront guest house is situated in pride of place on Morecambe's promenade. Seven guest rooms are available in a range of sizes and all smartly appointed and well equipped. The welcome is warm and generous and breakfast is a highlight of any stay.

**Rooms:** 7 en suite (1 fmly) **S** £40–£45; **D** £70–£80* **Facilities:** FTV DVD TVL tea/coffee WiFi **Extras:** Bottled water, fresh milk

### Beach Mount

★★★ GUEST ACCOMMODATION

**tel:** 01524 420753 **395 Marine Road East LA4 5AN**
**email:** beachmounthotel@aol.com **web:** www.beachmounthotelmorecambe.co.uk
**dir:** *M6 junct 34/35, follow signs to Morecambe. Beach Mount 0.5m from town centre on E Promenade*

This spacious property overlooks the bay and features a range of room styles that includes a junior suite. Guests have use of a comfortable lounge with fully licensed bar, and breakfasts are served in a pleasant separate dining room.

**Rooms:** 10 en suite (1 GF) **S** £28.50–£31.75; **D** £57–£63.50* **Facilities:** FTV DVD Lounge tea/coffee Licensed WiFi **Notes:** LB Closed Nov–Mar

### Silverwell

★★★ GUEST HOUSE

**tel:** 01524 410532 **20 West End Road LA4 4DL**
**email:** silverwell.hotel@btconnect.com **web:** www.silverwellhotel.co.uk
**dir:** *Follow signs to West End, turn right at promenade, take 3rd on right, Silverwell on left*

Silverwell offers comfortable accommodation in a quiet residential street, with rooms in a range of sizes with singles and families catered for. There is a licensed bar and lounge for guests use. Evening meals are available by prior arrangement.

**Rooms:** 14 rms (8 en suite) (6 pri facs) (3 fmly) (4 GF) **S** £28–£40; **D** £56–£80 **Facilities:** FTV Lounge tea/coffee Dinner available Licensed WiFi **Conf:** Max 20 Thtr 15 Class 20 Board 12

*See advert on page 178*

## ORMSKIRK — Map 15 SD40

### Premier Collection

## Moor Hall Restaurant with Rooms

★★★★★ ⚫⚫⚫ 🍽 RESTAURANT WITH ROOMS

**tel:** 01695 572511 & 07817 917868 **Prescot Road, Aughton L39 6RT**
**email:** enquiry@moorhall.com **web:** www.moorhall.com
**dir:** *From M58 junct 1, take 1st exit at rdbt then 1st left. 1.7m. Moor Hall signed on right*

Located within west Lancashire in five acres of gardens with stunning views over a beautiful lake, said to be the remains of a medieval moat. This Grade II listed house has been transformed with care and attention to detail into a true destination restaurant with rooms. Bedrooms are stunning, with many showcasing some of the original features of the house, paired with a new and exciting style. Mark Birchall is at the helm here and has created a refined dining experience in relaxed surroundings. Local provenance is at the forefront of this modern British cuisine; produce grown on the five-acre Moor Hall site or by local suppliers is used whenever possible, naturally reflecting the broad culinary experience Mark has gained over his career. New developments include the addition of The Barn which will offer a more casual dining experience with the same strong ethos. Throughout the establishment, the knowledgeable and friendly team are passionate about what they do.

**Rooms:** 5 en suite 2 annexe en suite (2 fmly) (2 GF) **D** fr £195* **Facilities:** FTV Lounge tea/coffee Dinner available WiFi **Extras:** Fruit, snacks, mini-bar **Parking:** 40 **Notes:** Closed 31 Jul for 2 weeks

## Innkeeper's Lodge Ormskirk

★★★★ INN

**tel:** 08451 551551 *(Calls cost 2p per minute plus your phone company's access charge)*
**Springfield Road, Aughton L39 6ST**
**email:** info@innkeeperslodge.com **web:** www.innkeeperslodge.com

On the edge of the pretty village of Aughton, this luxurious lodge provides smart yet affordable accommodation ideally located for a country escape or as a quiet base away from the hustle and bustle of Liverpool or Southport, and in easy reach of attractions such as Knowsley Safari Park, Chester Zoo, Formby Golf Club and Aintree racecourse. The elegant en suite rooms offer many extras and there's a Miller & Carter steakhouse.

**Rooms:** 12 en suite (1 fmly) **Facilities:** FTV tea/coffee Dinner available Lift WiFi

## PRESTON — Map 18 SD52

## Birch Croft Bed & Breakfast

★★★ BED AND BREAKFAST

**tel:** 01772 613174 & 07761 817187 **Gill Lane, Longton PR4 4SS**
**email:** johnsuts@btinternet.com **web:** www.birchcroftbandb.co.uk
**dir:** *From A59 right at rdbt to Midge Hall. B&B 4th on left*

Situated only 10 minutes away from major motorway links (M6, M65, M61) Birch Croft is on the doorstep of many attractions and close to Southport, Preston and Blackpool. This is a friendly, family-run business which offers comfortable accommodation in a very peaceful location.

**Rooms:** 3 en suite (1 fmly) **S** £48–£52; **D** £62–£68* **Facilities:** FTV DVD Lounge TVL tea/coffee WiFi 🅿 **Parking:** 11 **Notes:** LB

## RILEY GREEN — Map 18 SD62

## Grill & Grain at the Boatyard

Ⓤ

**tel:** 01254 209841 **Bolton Road PR5 0SP**
**email:** markmckeown@grillandgrainboatyard.co.uk
**web:** www.grillandgrainboatyard.co.uk
**dir:** *M65 junct 3 onto A675 signed Houghton Tower. 500mtrs on right*

Currently the rating for this establishment is not confirmed. This may be due to a change of ownership or because it has only recently joined the AA rating scheme.

**Rooms:** 6 annexe en suite (6 GF) **S** £75–£85; **D** £75–£85* **Facilities:** FTV tea/coffee Dinner available Licensed WiFi **Extras:** Bottled water, fresh milk – complimentary **Parking:** 72

## SAMLESBURY                                    Map 18 SD53

### Samlesbury Hall Lodge
★★★★ GUEST ACCOMMODATION

tel: 01254 812010 **Preston New Road PR5 0UP**
email: info@samlesburyhall.co.uk **web:** www.samlesburyhall.co.uk
dir: *M6 junct 31 onto A59 then A677 signed Blackburn*

The gate lodge of Samlesbury Hall provides a cosy getaway for small groups, or couples looking for a romantic retreat. Accommodation comprises a large suite with two sitting rooms on one level, making it accessible for guests with mobility issues. The sitting rooms can be converted, allowing up to six guests. Breakfasts are served in the hall or in the suite by prior arrangement. The Hall serves hearty lunches and has an antiques saleroom and an art gallery, as well as the Hall and gardens themselves to explore.

**Rooms:** 3 en suite (3 fmly) (3 GF) **Facilities:** FTV DVD Lounge TVL tea/coffee Licensed WiFi ⚓ Golf driving range Play trail Historic house Mayflower Playground **Conf:** Max 150 Thtr 150 Class 150 Board 150 **Parking:** 4 **Notes:** Civ wed 120

## WARTON                                        Map 18 SD42

### The Birley Arms
★★★★ INN

tel: 01772 679988 **Bryning Lane PR4 1TN**
email: birley@thebirleyarmshotel.co.uk **web:** www.thebirleyarmshotel.co.uk
dir: *M55 junct 3 (Kirkham), 1st left, then over 3 rdbts. Straight on at mini rdbt, at next rdbt left signed Warton. 2m on left*

The Birley Arms is a smartly appointed inn situated in the charming village of Warton, between Lytham St Annes and Preston. The bedrooms are smartly decorated and equipped with modern facilities. Open-plan public areas are light and airy, and feature a conservatory, lounge bar and a restaurant.

**Rooms:** 16 en suite (1 fmly) (8 GF) **S** £70–£80; **D** £80–£90* **Facilities:** FTV DVD tea/coffee Dinner available WiFi ⚓ **Extras:** Speciality toiletries – complimentary **Conf:** Max 30 Board 30 **Parking:** 60

## WHITEWELL                                     Map 18 SD64

### Premier Collection

### The Inn at Whitewell
★★★★★ ◉ INN

tel: 01200 448222 **Forest of Bowland, Clitheroe BB7 3AT**
email: reception@innatwhitewell.com **web:** www.innatwhitewell.com
dir: *M6 junct 31a, B6243 to Longridge. Left at mini rdbt. After 3 rdbts (approx 3m) sharp left (with white railings), then right. Approx 1m, left, right at T-junct. Next left, 3m to Whitewell*

This long-established culinary destination is hidden away in quintessential Lancashire countryside, just 20 minutes from the M6. The fine dining restaurant is complemented by a warren of cosy bar rooms with roaring fires, real ales and polished service. Bedrooms are richly furnished with antiques and eye-catching bijouterie, while many of the bathrooms have Victorian brass showers.

**Rooms:** 19 en suite 4 annexe en suite (1 fmly) (2 GF) **Facilities:** STV FTV DVD iPod docking station tea/coffee Dinner available Direct dial WiFi ♨18 Fishing ⚓ Horse stabling can be arranged **Extras:** Speciality toiletries – complimentary **Conf:** Max 45 Thtr 45 Board 35 **Parking:** 60 **Notes:** Civ wed 80

## LEICESTERSHIRE

### CROFT
Map 11 SP59

## Fossebrook B&B

★★★★ GUEST ACCOMMODATION

**tel:** 01455 283517 & 07860 762214 **Coventry Road LE9 3GP**
**web:** www.fossebrook.co.uk
**dir:** *From M1 exit junct 21 or M69 exit junct 1 on to A5. 6m SE of village centre on B4114*

Offering friendly guest accommodation, Fossebrook B&B stands in a quiet rural location with good access to major roads. Bedrooms are spacious, very comfortable and offer an excellent range of facilities including a range of videos in all rooms. Breakfast is served in the bright dining room overlooking pleasant gardens and grounds.

**Rooms:** 4 en suite (4 GF) **Facilities:** tea/coffee WiFi 🛇 **Extras:** Snacks – complimentary **Parking:** 16 **Notes:** Closed 24 Dec–2 Jan

### KNIPTON
Map 11 SK83

## The Manners Arms

★★★★ 🍴 RESTAURANT WITH ROOMS

**tel:** 01476 879222 **Croxton Road NG32 1RH**
**email:** info@mannersarms.com **web:** www.mannersarms.com
**dir:** *From A607 follow signs to Knipton; from A52 follow signs to Belvoir Castle*

Part of the Rutland Estate and built as a hunting lodge for the 6th Duke, The Manners Arms offers thoughtfully furnished bedrooms designed by the present Duchess. Public areas include the intimate Beater's Bar and attractive Red Coats Restaurant, popular for its imaginative menus.

**Rooms:** 10 en suite (1 fmly) **Facilities:** FTV TVL tea/coffee Dinner available Direct dial WiFi ⚽18 🛇 **Conf:** Max 50 Thtr 50 Class 25 Board 20 **Parking:** 60 **Notes:** Civ wed 50

### LEICESTER
Map 11 SK50

## Maiyango

★★★★ ⊚ RESTAURANT WITH ROOMS

**tel:** 0116 251 8898 **13–21 St Nicholas Place LE1 4LD**
**email:** reservations@maiyango.com **web:** www.maiyango.com
**dir:** *B4114 Narborough Rd to city centre, right onto A47 King Richard III Rd, keep right into St Nicholas Pl*

Maiyango restaurant with rooms offers a warm welcome and professional service. Access to the public areas is via a discreet foyer adjacent to a Middle Eastern-themed restaurant (under the same ownership), where imaginative food is sure to be a memorable experience. Spacious bedrooms, decorated in minimalist style are enhanced by quality modern art, fine furnishings and superb bathrooms. Parking is available close by.

**Rooms:** 14 en suite **D** fr £79 (room only)* **Facilities:** FTV tea/coffee Dinner available Direct dial Lift WiFi **Notes:** LB Closed 25 Dec, 1–14 Jan

### LONG WHATTON
Map 11 SK42

## The Royal Oak

★★★★ ⊚ 🛇 INN

**tel:** 01509 843694 **26 The Green LE12 5DB**
**email:** enquiries@theroyaloaklongwhatton.co.uk **web:** www.theroyaloaklongwhatton.co.uk

The Royal Oak is a popular gastropub with rooms, located in a small village just four miles from East Midlands Airport. Members of the young team offer a warm welcome and service is attentive. The seven spacious en suite bedrooms are to the rear of the property and have been designed with comfort and style in mind. There is plenty of parking available and a small garden for the warmer months.

**Rooms:** 7 en suite (7 GF) **S** £79–£95; **D** £89–£109* **Facilities:** FTV tea/coffee Dinner available WiFi **Extras:** Speciality toiletries, mineral water **Parking:** 28

### LOUGHBOROUGH
Map 11 SK51

## Charnwood Lodge

★★★★ GUEST HOUSE

**tel:** 01509 211120 **136 Leicester Road LE11 2AQ**
**email:** reservations@charnwoodlodge.com **web:** www.charnwoodlodge.com

Located within easy walking distance of the city's shopping areas and university campus, Charnwood Lodge offers a choice of well-equipped rooms, with some situated on the ground floor having private access. A spacious dining room provides comfortable surroundings for evening meals and home-cooked breakfasts. A large TV lounge and bar with period features are also available. Complimentary WiFi and ample onsite parking is provided.

**Rooms:** 12 rms (10 en suite) (2 pri facs) 2 annexe en suite (2 fmly) (6 GF) **Facilities:** FTV TVL tea/coffee Dinner available Licensed WiFi **Parking:** 30 **Notes:** Closed 21 Dec–5 Jan

### MARKET BOSWORTH
Map 11 SK40

## Softleys

★★★ 🍴 GUEST ACCOMMODATION

**tel:** 01455 290464 **2 Market Place CV13 0LE**
**email:** softleysrestaurant@gmail.com **web:** www.softleys.com
**dir:** *On B585 in Market Place*

Softleys is a Grade II listed building dating back to 1794. The bedrooms are en suite and set on the third floor offering picturesque views over Market Bosworth. Quality food is served using locally sourced ingredients.

**Rooms:** 3 en suite (1 fmly) **Facilities:** FTV tea/coffee Dinner available Direct dial Licensed WiFi **Conf:** Max 26 Thtr 26 Class 26 Board 26 **Notes:** RS Sun eve & Mon no food available

## LINCOLNSHIRE

### ADDLETHORPE                                          Map 17 TF56

## The Kings Head

★★★ INN

tel: 01754 871671 **Orby Road PE24 4TR**
email: addlethorpeleisure@yahoo.co.uk **web:** www.kingsheadaddlethorpe.com

The Kings Head Pub & Campsite is a family run business, situated just off the A52 west of Skegness, near the village of Addlethorpe. A quiet location surrounded by countryside that offers a great venue for families. The accommodation at the inn recently benefited from refurbishment. Guests can also enjoy a wide range of meals, beers and wines in the bar and restaurant.

**Rooms:** 10 en suite (2 fmly) **Facilities:** FTV Dinner available WiFi ⚓9 Pool table
🔒 **Conf:** Max 40 **Parking:** 40 **Notes:** LB

### CLEETHORPES                                          Map 17 TA30

## The Comat

★★★★ GUEST ACCOMMODATION

tel: 01472 694791 & 591861 **26 Yarra Road DN35 8LS**
email: comat-hotel@ntlworld.com **web:** www.comat-hotel.co.uk
dir: *Exit A1098 (Alexandra Rd), left of library*

A short walk from the shops and seafront, the welcoming Comat offers cosy, well-equipped bedrooms. There are a range of rooms, including ground floor bedrooms and a family suite with all bedrooms featuring smart, modern en suite bath or shower rooms. Tasty English breakfasts are served in the bright dining room, and an attractive lounge is also available.

**Rooms:** 5 en suite (2 fmly) (1 GF) **Facilities:** FTV DVD TVL tea/coffee WiFi **Notes:** LB Closed Xmas

## Brier Parks Guest House

★★★★ GUEST HOUSE

tel: 01472 605591 & 07849 639923 **27 Clee Road DN35 8AD**
email: graham.sherwood2@ntlworld.com **web:** www.brierparks-guesthouse.co.uk
dir: *Left at bottom of Isaac's Hill, 150yds on left*

A warm welcome awaits you at this friendly owner-run guest house. All bedrooms are en suite and offer complimentary WiFi, fridges and flat-screen TVs. Breakfast is freshly cooked to order, and there is limited parking in front of the building. The house is just a short stroll from the seafront and town centre.

**Rooms:** 5 en suite (2 GF) **S** £45–£50; **D** £65–£75 **Facilities:** FTV TVL tea/coffee WiFi
**Parking:** 2 **Notes:** LB No children 5yrs

## Ginnie's Guest House

★★★ Ⓐ GUEST HOUSE

tel: 01472 694997 **27 Queens Parade DN35 0DF**
email: enquiries@ginnies.co.uk **web:** www.ginnies.co.uk
dir: *From Kingsway (seafront) into Queens Parade (A1098)*

Ginnie's Guest House is a Victorian terraced house situated in a quiet location close to the Winter Gardens, Playtower, and many other amenities. Well maintained by the resident proprietor who takes pride in the many guests who return for further visits.

**Rooms:** 7 rms (5 en suite) (2 pri facs) (3 fmly) (1 GF) **S** £30–£40; **D** £50–£70
**Facilities:** FTV DVD iPod docking station TVL tea/coffee WiFi 🔒 **Extras:** Speciality toiletries – complimentary **Parking:** 4 **Notes:** LB RS 24–25 & 31 Dec room only

### GRANTHAM                                             Map 11 SK93

## Beaver House

★★★ BED AND BREAKFAST

tel: 01476 565011 & 07779 002206 **School Lane, Old Somerby NG33 4AH**
email: cuttlers@btinternet.com **web:** www.beaverhouse.co.uk
dir: *From Grantham A52 E for 2m. At rdbt take exit signed Old Somerby, then 1st left, 1st house on right*

Beaver House is located on a mainly residential avenue in the quiet village of Old Somerby, just five minutes' drive from Grantham. The accommodation has been thoughtfully designed, and is well equipped and very comfortable. Breakfasts are served in the dining room overlooking the manicured garden, and there is a restaurant within walking distance. A highchair and travel cot can be provided.

**Rooms:** 3 rms (1 en suite) **S** £35–£45; **D** £45–£55* **Facilities:** FTV DVD TVL tea/coffee WiFi 🔒 **Parking:** 3 **Notes:** Closed Owner's holiday (dates vary)

### GREAT LIMBER                                         Map 17 TA10

## The New Inn

★★★★ ⓘⓘ INN

tel: 01469 569998 **2 High Street DN37 8JL**
email: enquiries@thenewinngreatlimber.co.uk **web:** www.thenewinngreatlimber.co.uk
dir: *2m from Humberside Airport on A18*

The New Inn is a Grade II listed building that has been refurbished to a modern standard. It is nestled in the Brocklesby estate, with close links to nearby areas of Grimsby and Hull. Bedrooms are comfortably appointed with modern decor and amenities such as flat-screen TVs and good WiFi connectivity. Dinners served in the restaurant are the highlight of any stay, with an interesting choice of dishes available. Meals can also be enjoyed in the more relaxed bar area. Car parking is available on-site.

**Rooms:** 10 en suite (1 fmly) (3 GF) **S** fr £79; **D** fr £99 (room only)* **Facilities:** FTV Lounge Dinner available WiFi 🔒 **Extras:** Speciality toiletries – complimentary
**Conf:** Max 18 Thtr 18 Class 18 Board 18 **Parking:** 15

### HEMSWELL                                             Map 17 SK99

#### Premier Collection

## Hemswell Court

★★★★★ 🏆 ⌂ GUEST ACCOMMODATION

tel: 01427 668508 **Lancaster Green, Hemswell Cliff DN21 5TQ**
email: function@hemswellcourt.com **web:** www.hemswellcourt.com
dir: *1.5m SE of Hemswell on A631 in Hemswell Cliff*

Originally an officers' mess, Hemswell Court is a popular venue for conferences, weddings or private gatherings. The modern bedrooms and many suites are ideal for families or groups of friends, and all rooms are well equipped. The lounges and dining rooms are enhanced by many antique pieces.

**Rooms:** 25 en suite (3 fmly) (6 GF) **Facilities:** Lounge TVL tea/coffee Dinner available Licensed WiFi 🎱🏓 **Extras:** Slippers **Conf:** Max 200 Thtr 200 Class 150 Board 150 **Parking:** 150 **Notes:** Closed Xmas & New Year Civ wed 200

## HORNCASTLE
Map 17 TF26

### Premier Collection

## Magpies Restaurant with Rooms

★★★★★ ◎◎ RESTAURANT WITH ROOMS

**tel:** 01507 527004 **71–73 East Street LN9 6AA**
**email:** info@magpiesrestaurant.co.uk **web:** www.magpiesrestaurant.co.uk
**dir:** A158 into Horncastle, continue at lights. On left opposite Trinity Centre

This quaint and charming property is nestled in the popular market town of Horncastle. The spacious en suite accommodation features three individually appointed rooms. All provide flat-screen TVs, complimentary WiFi, home-made biscuits, mini-bar and luxurious bathrooms. There is a cosy lounge area with wood-burning stove which is perfect for those winter evenings. The two AA Rosette award-winning restaurant provides a good choice of imaginative dishes at both lunch and dinner, and afternoon tea is also served. On-street parking is available nearby.

**Rooms:** 3 en suite **S** £70–£80; **D** £110–£130* **Facilities:** FTV iPod docking station Lounge tea/coffee Dinner available WiFi **Extras:** Bottled water, home-made biscuits & jam, mini-bar **Notes:** No children Closed 26-30 Dec & 1–7 Jan RS Mon–Tue closed

## HOUGH-ON-THE-HILL
Map 11 SK94

### Premier Collection

## The Brownlow Arms

★★★★★ ◎ INN

**tel:** 01400 250234 **High Road NG32 2AZ**
**email:** armsinn@yahoo.co.uk **web:** www.thebrownlowarms.com
**dir:** Take A607 (Grantham to Sleaford road). Hough-on-the-Hill signed from Barkston

The Brownlow Arms is a beautiful 16th-century property that enjoys a peaceful location in this picturesque village, located between Newark and Grantham. Tastefully appointed and spacious public areas have many original features, and include a choice of luxurious lounges and an elegant restaurant offering imaginative cuisine. The bedrooms are stylish, comfortable and particularly well equipped.

**Rooms:** 4 en suite 1 annexe en suite (1 GF) **S** £75–£85; **D** £120–£130* **Facilities:** FTV DVD tea/coffee Dinner available Direct dial WiFi  **Parking:** 20 **Notes:** No children 8yrs Closed 25–27 Dec & 31 Dec–1 Jan

## LINCOLN
Map 17 SK97

*See also Horncastle & Marton (village)*

## Eagles Guest House

★★★★ GUEST ACCOMMODATION

**tel:** 01522 686346 **552A Newark Road, North Hykeham LN6 9NG**
**email:** eaglesguesthouse@yahoo.co.uk **web:** www.eaglesguesthouse.co.uk
**dir:** A46 onto A1434, signed Lincoln South, North Hykeham & South Hykeham. 0.5m on right opposite Cornflower Way

This large, modern detached house is situated within easy access of the A46 and the historic city of Lincoln. The smartly appointed, thoughtfully equipped bedrooms are bright and fresh in appearance. A substantial breakfast is served in the pleasant dining room and free WiFi is available throughout the property.

**Rooms:** 6 en suite (2 fmly) (2 GF) **S** £45–£55; **D** £62–£75* **Facilities:** FTV tea/coffee WiFi **Parking:** 6 **Notes:** No children 9yrs

## The Loudor

★★★★ GUEST ACCOMMODATION

**tel:** 01522 680333 **37 Newark Road, North Hykeham LN6 8RB**
**email:** info@loudorhotel.co.uk **web:** www.loudorhotel.co.uk
**dir:** 3m from city centre. A46 onto A1434 for 2m, on left opposite shopping centre

The Loudor can be found opposite the Forum shopping centre and a short walk from the sports centre. This friendly place offers well-equipped bedrooms, and breakfast is served at individual tables in the spacious dining room. There is some on-site parking.

**Rooms:** 9 en suite 2 annexe en suite (1 fmly) (2 GF) **S** £42–£46; **D** £63–£68* **Facilities:** FTV Lounge tea/coffee WiFi ✆ **Extras:** Home-made biscuits **Conf:** Max 30 **Parking:** 8

## The Old Bakery

★★★★ ◎◎ RESTAURANT WITH ROOMS

**tel:** 01522 576057 & 07772 667606 **26–28 Burton Road LN1 3LB**
**email:** enquiries@theold-bakery.co.uk **web:** www.theold-bakery.co.uk
**dir:** Exit A46 at Lincoln North follow signs for cathedral. 3rd exit at 1st rdbt, 1st exit at next rdbt

Situated close to the castle at the top of the town, this converted bakery offers well-equipped bedrooms and a delightful dining operation. The cooking has gained two AA Rosettes, and uses much local produce. Expect good friendly service from the dedicated staff.

**Rooms:** 3 rms (2 en suite) (1 pri facs) (1 fmly) **D** £75–£80 **Facilities:** FTV tea/coffee Dinner available WiFi ✆ **Extras:** Bottled water, home-made cookies – complimentary **Notes:** Closed 25–26 Dec, 1–16 Jan, 1–12 Aug RS Sun & Mon closed

## LOUTH — Map 17 TF38

### The Manse B&B

★★★ BED AND BREAKFAST

**tel:** 01507 327495 **Middlesykes Lane, Grimoldby LN11 8TE**
**email:** knowles578@btinternet.com **web:** www.themansebb.co.uk
**dir:** *Grimoldby 4m from Louth on B1200. Into Tinkle St, right into Middlesykes Ln*

Located on a quiet country lane, this pleasantly appointed house offers comfortable accommodation and a friendly, warm welcome. Proprietors are enthusiastic and helpful, ensuring guests enjoy their stay. Bedrooms offer a range of homely extras, and freshly cooked evening meals are available by prior arrangement. The Manse is an ideal location for exploring the delights of the Wolds. The Manse B&B was a finalist for the AA Friendliest B&B of the Year 2017–18.

**Rooms:** 4 rms (3 en suite) (1 pri facs) (1 fmly) (1 GF) **S** £55; **D** £75* **Facilities:** FTV TVL tea/coffee Dinner available WiFi **Parking:** 5 **Notes:** LB No children 5yrs Closed 25 Dec

## MARKET RASEN — Map 17 TF18

### Premier Collection

### The Advocate Arms

★★★★★ ◎◎ RESTAURANT WITH ROOMS

**tel:** 01673 842364 **2 Queen Street LN8 3EH**
**email:** info@advocatearms.co.uk **web:** www.advocatearms.co.uk
**dir:** *In town centre*

Appointed to a high standard, this 18th-century property is located in the heart of Market Rasen and combines historic character with contemporary design. The operation centres around the stylish restaurant where service is friendly yet professional and the food is a highlight. The attractive bedrooms are very well equipped and feature luxury bathrooms.

**Rooms:** 10 en suite (2 fmly) **S** £60–£150; **D** £60–£160 (room only)* **Facilities:** FTV tea/coffee Dinner available WiFi ⌨18 **Conf:** Max 22 Thtr 18 Class 22 Board 18 **Parking:** 6

### Wold View House B&B

★★★ ⌂ BED AND BREAKFAST

**tel:** 01673 838226 & 07976 563473 **Bully Hill Top, Tealby LN8 6JA**
**email:** enquiries@woldviewhouse.co.uk **web:** www.woldviewhouse.co.uk
**dir:** *A46 onto B1225 towards Horncastle, after 7m Wold View House at x-rds*

Situated at the top of Bully Hill with expansive views across The Wold, this smart bed and breakfast offers modern bedrooms and warm hospitality. Ideal for walking, riding, or touring the charming nearby villages and coastline, Wold View House is just a short drive from Lincoln.

**Rooms:** 3 rms (2 en suite) (1 pri facs) (1 fmly) **Facilities:** FTV Lounge TVL tea/coffee Dinner available Licensed WiFi ⊖ **Parking:** 15 **Notes:** LB

## MARTON (VILLAGE) — Map 17 SK88

### Black Swan Guest House

★★★★ GUEST ACCOMMODATION

**tel:** 01427 718878 **21 High Street DN21 5AH**
**email:** info@blackswanguesthouse.co.uk **web:** www.blackswanguesthouse.co.uk
**dir:** *On A156 in village centre at junct A1500*

Centrally located in the village, this 18th-century former coaching inn retains many original features, and offers good hospitality and homely bedrooms with modern facilities. Tasty breakfasts are served in the cosy dining room and a comfortable lounge with WiFi access is available. Transport to nearby pubs and restaurants can be provided.

**Rooms:** 6 en suite 4 annexe en suite (2 fmly) (4 GF) **S** £50–£60; **D** £72–£85* **Facilities:** FTV tea/coffee Licensed WiFi ⊖ **Parking:** 10 **Notes:** LB

## NORTON DISNEY — Map 17 SK85

### Norton Lodge and Conference Centre

★★★ BED AND BREAKFAST

**tel:** 01522 789111 **Old Harbour Farm LN6 9JR**
**email:** norton.lodge@virgin.net **web:** www.nortonlodge.co.uk

This rural property is set in 14 acres of countryside although still close to main road links such as the A1 and A46. Bedrooms are spacious and boast many modern accessories such as TV and complimentary WiFi. Perfect for leisure and business guests alike the property features four conference rooms catering up to 150 guests, as well as being closely situated to the popular market town of Newark-on-Trent. Ample on-site parking is available.

**Rooms:** 8 en suite 14 annexe en suite (2 fmly) (6 GF) **Facilities:** FTV TVL tea/coffee Direct dial Licensed WiFi ⊖ **Conf:** Max 150 Thtr 150 Class 100 Board 40 **Parking:** 100 **Notes:** Civ wed 150

## SCOTTER — Map 17 SE80

### The White Swan

★★★★ ◎ INN

**tel:** 01724 763061 **9 The Green DN21 3UD**
**email:** info@whiteswanscotter.com **web:** www.whiteswanscotter.com

This smartly presented property provides stylish contemporary accommodation in a peaceful village location. The restaurant is modern with vaulted ceilings and is split over three levels, while there is also a traditional pub called The Mucky Duck. A lounge bar and impressive garden add to the range of areas for guests to relax. Weddings and other special events are also well catered for. Accommodation rates include a continental breakfast or a choice of other breakfast options is also available.

**Rooms:** 11 en suite 18 annexe en suite **Facilities:** FTV tea/coffee Dinner available WiFi **Conf:** Max 50 Thtr 50 Class 35 Board 35 **Parking:** 35 **Notes:** Civ wed 110

## SCUNTHORPE
Map 17 SE81

### San Pietro Restaurant Rooms
★★★★ ◉◉ RESTAURANT WITH ROOMS

tel: 01724 277774 **11 High Street East DN15 6UH**
email: info@sanpietro.uk.com web: www.sanpietro.uk.com
dir: *3m from M180, follow signs for Scunthorpe town centre & railway station, left into Brigg Rd/Station Rd. Near windmill*

This family-run restaurant with rooms was purpose-built, and offers comfortable modern accommodation. Bedrooms and bathrooms provide a range of additional extras such as mini-bars, home-made cakes, complimentary WiFi and smart TVs. Dinner and breakfast are served in the annexe Ristorante. Dinner menus have an Italian influence and provide a range of choice including a chef's tasting menu as well as a full à la carte offering. Continental breakfasts are included, with a choice to upgrade to a hearty cooked breakfast.

**Rooms:** 14 en suite (5 GF) **Facilities:** STV FTV iPod docking station tea/coffee Dinner available Direct dial Lift WiFi ♨18 ♨ **Extras:** Speciality toiletries, home-made cake, mini-bar **Conf:** Max 80 Thtr 80 Class 40 Board 30 **Parking:** 25 **Notes:** Closed 25–26 Dec, Sun & BH Mon Civ wed 120

## SKILLINGTON
Map 11 SK82

### The Cross Swords Inn
★★★ ⬭ INN

tel: 01476 861132 **The Square NG33 5HB**
email: harold@thecross-swordsinn.co.uk web: www.thecross-swordsinn.co.uk
dir: *Exit A1 at Colsterworth junct between Grantham & Stamford*

Very popular with the local community, this traditional inn offers three modern, well-equipped bedrooms, housed in an attractive cottage at the top of the courtyard, and named in keeping with the history of the village. All are very comfortable and coupled with smart modern bathrooms. The inn provides imaginative food and a range of real ales in a rustic period atmosphere.

**Rooms:** 3 annexe en suite (3 GF) **S** £75; **D** £82–£85* **Facilities:** FTV tea/coffee Dinner available WiFi Gliding club nearby **Parking:** 12 **Notes:** No children 10yrs RS Sun eve & Mon lunch bar & restaurant closed

## SOUTH FERRIBY
Map 17 SE92

### The Hope and Anchor Pub
★★★★ ◉◉ RESTAURANT WITH ROOMS

tel: 01652 635334 **Sluice Road DN18 6JQ**
email: info@thehopeandanchorpub.co.uk web: www.thehopeandanchorpub.co.uk

This pub dates back to the 19th century and is perfectly situated in the town of South Ferriby, with stunning views of the Humber Bridge. Bedrooms are modern and furnished to a high standard with exceptionally comfortable beds. Modern amenities such as Nespresso machines, TVs and complimentary WiFi. Dinner in the award-winning restaurant will be a highlight as is the hearty breakfast. Staff are friendly and welcoming, and a relaxed atmosphere is guaranteed.

**Rooms:** 5 en suite **S** £95–£115; **D** £95–£115 (room only)* **Facilities:** Dinner available WiFi **Notes:** Closed Sun & Mon **Parking**

| STAMFORD | Map 11 TF00 |
|---|---|

### Premier Collection

## Meadow View

★★★★★ BED AND BREAKFAST

**tel:** 01780 762133 & 07833 972577 **Wothorpe Road PE9 2JR**
**email:** bookings@bedandbreakfast-stamford.co.uk
**web:** www.bedandbreakfast-stamford.co.uk
**dir:** *Off A1 signed Stamford, follow road past entrance to Burley House, bottom of hill, left at lights. Follow road round, 1st house on left*

Meadow View is a stylish property situated just a short walk from the town centre and Burghley House. The tastefully appointed bedrooms are contemporary in style with lovely co-ordinated soft furnishings and many thoughtful touches. Breakfast is served at a large communal table in the open-plan kitchen/dining room, and guests have the use of a smartly appointed lounge with plush sofas.

**Rooms:** 3 en suite **Facilities:** FTV iPod docking station TVL tea/coffee WiFi
**Extras:** Chocolates, sherry, still/sparkling water **Notes:** LB

## The Bull & Swan at Burghley

★★★★★ ⚜ INN

**tel:** 01780 766412 **High Street, St Martins PE9 2LJ**
**email:** enquiries@thebullandswan.co.uk **web:** www.thebullandswan.co.uk
**dir:** *A1 onto Old Great North Rd, left onto B1081, follow Stamford signs*

This delightful inn dates back to the 16th century when it is said to have been a gentlemen's drinking club. The public rooms include a large bar with a range of ales. There is also a separate restaurant serving AA Rosette award-winning food. The stylish bedrooms are extremely well appointed with lovely soft furnishings and a range of thoughtful touches.

**Rooms:** 9 en suite (2 fmly) **Facilities:** FTV iPod docking station tea/coffee Dinner available WiFi ⚓18 **Extras:** Organic vodka **Parking:** 7 **Notes:** LB

## Candlesticks

★★★ RESTAURANT WITH ROOMS

**tel:** 01780 764033 **1 Church Lane PE9 2JU**
**email:** info@candlestickshotel.co.uk **web:** www.candlestickshotel.co.uk
**dir:** *B1081 into Stamford. Left onto A43. Right into Worthorpe Rd, right into Church Ln*

Candlesticks is a 17th-century property situated in a quiet lane in the oldest part of Stamford, just a short walk from the centre of town. The bedrooms are pleasantly decorated and equipped with a good range of useful extras. Public rooms include Candlesticks restaurant and a cosy bar.

**Rooms:** 8 en suite **Facilities:** STV FTV Lounge tea/coffee Dinner available Direct dial WiFi ⚓ **Parking:** 8 **Notes:** LB RS Mon No restaurant or bar service

| WINTERINGHAM | Map 17 SE92 |
|---|---|

### Premier Collection

## Winteringham Fields

★★★★★ ⚜⚜⚜⚜ RESTAURANT WITH ROOMS

**tel:** 01724 733096 **1 Silver Street DN15 9ND**
**email:** reception@winteringhamfields.co.uk **web:** www.winteringhamfields.co.uk
**dir:** *In village centre at x-rds*

This highly regarded restaurant with rooms, located deep in the countryside at Winteringham village, is six miles west of the Humber Bridge. Public rooms and bedrooms, some of which are housed in renovated barns and cottages, are delightfully luxurious. There is an abundance of charm, and period features are combined with rich furnishings and fabrics. The award-winning food is a highlight of any stay and guests can expect highly skilled dishes, excellent quality and stunning presentation.

**Rooms:** 4 en suite 11 annexe en suite (6 fmly) (3 GF) **Facilities:** iPod docking station tea/coffee Dinner available Direct dial WiFi ⚓ **Conf:** Max 50 Thtr 50 Class 50 Board 50 **Parking:** 14 **Notes:** LB Closed 25 Dec for 2 weeks, last week Oct, 2 weeks Aug Civ wed 60

| WOODHALL SPA | Map 17 TF16 |
|---|---|

## Oglee Guest House

★★★★ GUEST HOUSE

**tel:** 01526 353512 **16 Stanhope Avenue LN10 6SP**
**email:** ogleeguesthouse@gmail.com **web:** www.oglee.co.uk
**dir:** *Close to junct of B1191 & B1192*

This Edwardian family home is ideally situated for exploring Lincolnshire. It is also within easy reach of several RAF bases and the well-regarded Hotchkin Golf Course. Spacious bedrooms offer a high level of comfort with modern amenities. Hearty breakfasts use local produce, feature hand-made jams and additional special dishes. Evening meals by prior arrangement.

**Rooms:** 3 en suite (1 fmly) **S** £55; **D** £80* **Facilities:** FTV DVD TVL tea/coffee Dinner available WiFi ⚓ **Extras:** Fruit, bottled water, speciality teas – complimentary **Parking:** 4 **Notes:** LB

| WOOLSTHORPE | Map 11 SK83 |
|---|---|

## Chequers Inn

★★★★ ⚜ INN

**tel:** 01476 870701 **Main Street NG32 1LU**
**email:** justinnabar@yahoo.co.uk **web:** www.chequersinn.net
**dir:** *From Melton Mowbray on A607 towards Grantham, follow brown heritage signs to Belvoir Castle. Turn left at x-rds & follow signs*

Situated in the picturesque village of Woolsthorpe in the unspoilt Vale of Belvoir, the Chequers Inn is a quintessentially English inn dating from the 17th century. It has roaring fires in the winter and a well-maintained garden for alfresco dining in the summer. The snug and bar was once the original village bakery. Bedrooms are situated in the adjacent stables and are tastefully decorated. Good food is served in the bar and in the restaurant.

**Rooms:** 4 annexe en suite (1 fmly) (3 GF) **Facilities:** FTV DVD tea/coffee Dinner available ⚓18 ⚓ **Conf:** Max 80 Thtr 80 Class 80 Board 30 **Parking:** 40 **Notes:** Closed 25 Dec eve, 26 Dec eve & 1 Jan eve Civ wed 80

## LONDON

### E1

## The Culpeper
PLAN 1 G4

★★★★ RESTAURANT WITH ROOMS

**tel:** 020 7247 5371 **40 Commercial Street E1 6LP**
**email:** bookings@theculpeper.com **web:** www.theculpeper.com
**dir:** *From Aldgate East tube station left into Commercial St, The Culpeper on right*

Located on Commercial Street and just a stone's throw from Spitalfields Market and Brick Lane, The Culpeper offers comfortably appointed en suite bedrooms. All showcase stripped-back decor, and some of the building's original features, yet still include some modern furnishings and fixtures. There is a busy pub on the ground floor, a roof-top terrace and conservatory which serves barbecue tapas, and a main restaurant on the second floor which is open for breakfast, lunch and dinner. A real gem in the heart of East London, ideal for leisure and business guests alike.

**Rooms:** 5 en suite **D** £120* **Facilities:** Dinner available **Notes:** Closed 24–30 Dec

### N4

## Best Western London Highbury
PLAN 2 F5

★★★ GUEST ACCOMMODATION

**tel:** 020 8802 6551 **372-374 Seven Sisters Road N4 2PG**
**email:** reservations@highbury.com **web:** www.bwhighbury.com
**dir:** *0.5m from Finsbury Park Station*

Opposite Finsbury Park and only a short tube ride from the centre of London, this establishment offers a range of well-appointed and well-equipped accommodation. There is ample and secure parking and a well-stocked bar. Hot and cold breakfasts are served in the lower-ground floor breakfast room.

**Rooms:** 45 en suite (6 fmly) (7 GF) **S** £95–£155; **D** £115–£175 (room only)*
**Facilities:** STV FTV TVL tea/coffee Direct dial Lift Licensed WiFi 🔒 **Extras:** Chocolates
**Parking:** 20

### NW1

## TheWesley
PLAN 1 C5

★★★★ 🍴 GUEST ACCOMMODATION

**tel:** 020 7380 0001 **81-103 Euston Street NW1 2EZ**
**email:** reservations@thewesley.co.uk **web:** www.thewesley.co.uk
**dir:** *Euston Rd left at lights into Melton St, 1st left into Euston St, 100yds on left*

Located within walking distance of Euston station, this smart property is convenient for central London. Stylish air-conditioned bedrooms are thoughtfully equipped for business and leisure. The airy Atrium Bar and Restaurant offers drinks, light snacks and an evening menu. Extensive conference and meeting facilities are available.

**Rooms:** 100 en suite (2 fmly) **Facilities:** STV FTV iPod docking station TVL tea/coffee Dinner available Direct dial Lift Licensed WiFi **Extras:** Speciality toiletries, safe
**Conf:** Max 150 Thtr 150 Class 50 Board 45 **Notes:** LB Civ wed

### NW3

## The Langorf
PLAN 2 E4

★★★★ GUEST ACCOMMODATION

**tel:** 020 7794 4483 **20 Frognal, Hampstead NW3 6AG**
**email:** info@langorfhotel.com **web:** www.langorfhotel.com
**dir:** *Off A41 (Finchley Rd), near Finchley Road tube station*

Located on a leafy and mainly residential avenue within easy walking distance of shops and restaurants, this elegant Edwardian property has been appointed to provide high standards of comfort and facilities. Bedrooms are furnished with flair and a warm welcome is assured.

**Rooms:** 31 en suite (4 fmly) (3 GF) **Facilities:** STV Lounge TVL tea/coffee Direct dial Lift Licensed WiFi **Conf:** Max 30 Thtr 30 Class 20 Board 15 **Notes:** LB

**LONDON NW3** *continued*

## La Gaffe

PLAN 2 E5

★★★ 🍴 GUEST ACCOMMODATION

**tel:** 020 7435 8965 & 7435 4941 **107–111 Heath Street NW3 6SS**
**email:** info@lagaffe.co.uk **web:** www.lagaffe.co.uk
**dir:** *On A502, 250yds N of Hampstead tube station*

This family-owned and -run guest accommodation, just north of Hampstead High Street, offers charm and warm hospitality. The Italian restaurant, which is open most lunchtimes and for dinner, is popular with locals. Bedrooms are compact, but all are en suite.

**Rooms:** 11 en suite 7 annexe en suite (2 fmly) (2 GF) **S** £80–£110; **D** £105–£130*
**Facilities:** FTV tea/coffee Dinner available Direct dial Licensed WiFi **Conf:** Max 10 Board 10 **Notes:** RS 25–26 Dec Restaurant closed 25 Dec eve & 26 Dec

---

**NW11**

## Martel Guest House

PLAN 2 D5

★★★ GUEST HOUSE

**tel:** 020 8455 1802 & 07587 655181 **27 The Ridgeway NW11 8QP**
**email:** reservations@bedbreakfastlondon.co.uk **web:** www.bedbreakfastlondon.co.uk

Martel Guest House is in a quiet residential area of north London, just a 15-minute underground journey from central London, and only five minutes from the M1. Restaurants and convenience stores are just a short walk away. The accommodation is nicely appointed and offers all modern comforts including air-conditioning and free WiFi. A self-service continental breakfast or a freshly cooked English breakfast are served in the family-style breakfast room overlooking the rear garden. Secure parking offered.

**Rooms:** 9 en suite (2 fmly) (3 GF) **Facilities:** FTV tea/coffee Direct dial WiFi
**Extras:** Fridge, bottled water, canned drinks **Parking:** 7

---

**SE10**

## Innkeeper's Lodge London, Greenwich

PLAN 2 G3

★★★★ INN

**tel:** 08451 551551 *(Calls cost 2p per minute plus your phone company's access charge)*
**291 Greenwich High Road, Greenwich SE10 8NA**
**email:** info@innkeeperslodge.com **web:** www.innkeeperslodge.com

At Innkeeper's Lodge you'll find accommodation with comfort and character in equal measure, and everything needed for a relaxing stay, from easy check-in and free parking to complimentary breakfast and a cosy pub serving great value food and drink on the doorstep. Each Lodge has quality rooms, and there are Lodges in a variety of locations from towns and cities to countryside settings across the UK.

**Rooms:** 24 en suite (3 fmly) **Facilities:** FTV tea/coffee Dinner available Lift WiFi

---

**SW1**

## The Windermere

PLAN 1 C1

★★★★ 🍴 GUEST ACCOMMODATION

**tel:** 020 7834 5163 **142/144 Warwick Way, Victoria SW1V 4JE**
**email:** reservations@windermere-hotel.co.uk **web:** www.windermere-hotel.co.uk
**dir:** *B324 off Buckingham Palace Rd, on Warwick Way, at junct with Alderney St*

The Windermere is a relaxed, informal and family-run establishment within easy reach of Victoria station and many of the capital's attractions. Bedrooms, although varying in size, are stylish, comfortable and well equipped. The Pimlico restaurant serves good quality evening meals and hearty cooked breakfasts.

**Rooms:** 19 en suite (3 fmly) (3 GF) **S** £130–£155; **D** £145–£215* **Facilities:** FTV Lounge TVL tea/coffee Dinner available Direct dial Lift Licensed WiFi
**Extras:** Speciality toiletries **Notes:** No children 5yrs

---

## Best Western Corona

PLAN 1 C1

★★★ GUEST ACCOMMODATION

**tel:** 020 7828 9279 & 7487 0673 **87–89 Belgrave Road SW1V 2BQ**
**email:** info@coronahotel.co.uk **web:** www.coronahotel.co.uk
**dir:** *From Pimlico Station into Tachbrook St. 1st left into Moreton St, 1st right into Belgrave Rd*

Centrally located, this elegant Victorian property is appointed to a high standard. The smart, well-equipped bedrooms offer comfortable, modern accommodation. A continental breakfast is served in the basement dining room, and room service is also available.

**Rooms:** 51 en suite (13 fmly) (7 GF) **Facilities:** FTV Lounge tea/coffee Direct dial Lift WiFi

## The Lidos
PLAN 1 C1

★★★ GUEST ACCOMMODATION

tel: 020 7828 1164 **43–45 Belgrave Road, Victoria SW1V 2BB**
email: reservations@lidoshotel.com **web:** www.lidoshotel.com
dir: *From Victoria railway station exit to Wilton Rd. After 2nd set of lights into Denbigh St. Left at next lights into Belgrave Rd. On left*

The Lidos offers affordable accommodation within walking distance of Victoria Station and the tube. In addition, there's a bus stop right in front of the main entrance making access easy to all major sites. All rooms have en suite facilities and have been equipped with modern amenities. An inclusive continental breakfast is offered to all guests, and a range of restaurants and pubs can be found nearby.

**Rooms:** 39 en suite (2 fmly) (4 GF) **Facilities:** FTV tea/coffee Lift WiFi
**Notes:** Closed 24–26 Dec

## Best Western Victoria Palace
PLAN 1 C1

★★★ GUEST ACCOMMODATION

tel: 020 7821 7113 **60–64 Warwick Way SW1V 1SA**
email: info@bestwesternvictoriapalace.co.uk **web:** www.bestwesternvictoriapalace.co.uk

An elegant, 19th-century building located in the heart of London, near to Belgravia and a five-minute walk from Victoria rail, underground and coach stations. The bedrooms have en suite shower rooms. A buffet-style breakfast is served in the basement dining room.

**Rooms:** 43 en suite 44 annexe en suite (4 fmly) (4 GF) **Facilities:** FTV Lounge tea/coffee Direct dial Lift WiFi

## Comfort Inn Buckingham Palace Road
PLAN 1 C1

★★★ GUEST ACCOMMODATION

tel: 020 7834 2988 **8–12 St George's Drive SW1V 4BJ**
email: info@comfortinnbuckinghampalacerd.co.uk
web: www.comfortinnbuckinghampalacerd.co.uk
dir: *From Buckingham Palace Rd into St George's Dr. Comfort Inn on left*

Located just a short walk south from Victoria station, this establishment is a good base for visiting the capital's attractions. All bedrooms and public areas are smartly appointed and offer very good levels of comfort. An extensive continental breakfast is served.

**Rooms:** 81 en suite (13 fmly) (15 GF) **Facilities:** STV TVL tea/coffee Direct dial Lift WiFi **Conf:** Max 20 Thtr 20 Class 20 Board 20

## Comfort Inn London Westminster
PLAN 1 C1

★★★ GUEST ACCOMMODATION

tel: 020 7834 8036 **39 Belgrave Road SW1V 2BB**
email: stay@comfortinnwestminster.co.uk **web:** www.comfortinnwestminster.co.uk
dir: *Near Victoria station*

Located a short walk from Victoria station, the Comfort Inn London Westminster offers affordable accommodation. Bedroom sizes vary, and each room is suitably appointed, with en suite compact shower rooms. A contemporary lobby is equipped with a large TV and computer desk. A self-service continental breakfast is offered in the dining room on the lower ground floor.

**Rooms:** 54 en suite (4 fmly) **S** £69–£149; **D** £79–£179* **Facilities:** FTV TVL tea/coffee Direct dial Lift WiFi **Notes:** LB

## Comfort Inn Victoria
PLAN 1 C1

★★★ GUEST ACCOMMODATION

tel: 020 7233 6636 **18–24 Belgrave Road, Victoria SW1V 1QF**
email: stay@comfortinnvictoria.co.uk **web:** www.comfortinnvictoria.co.uk

With a prime location close to Victoria station, this property offers brightly appointed en suite accommodation that is thoughtfully equipped for business and leisure guests. A continental breakfast is offered in the basement dining room.

**Rooms:** 50 rms (48 en suite) (16 fmly) (9 GF) **Facilities:** STV FTV TVL tea/coffee Direct dial Lift WiFi

## The Victoria Inn
PLAN 1 C1

★★★ GUEST HOUSE

tel: 020 7834 6721 **65–67 Belgrave Road, Victoria SW1V 2BG**
email: welcome@victoriainn.co.uk **web:** www.victoriainn.co.uk
dir: *On A3213, 0.4m SE of Victoria station, near Pimlico tube station*

A short walk from Victoria station, this Victorian property offers modern, well-equipped accommodation for business and leisure guests. There is a comfortable reception lounge, and a limited self-service buffet breakfast is available in the basement breakfast room.

**Rooms:** 43 en suite (7 fmly) **Facilities:** FTV TVL tea/coffee Direct dial Lift WiFi
**Notes:** LB

## Stanley House
PLAN 1 C1

★★ Ⓐ BED AND BREAKFAST

tel: 020 7834 5042 & 7834 7292 **19–21 Belgrave Road, Victoria SW1V 1RB**
email: cmahotel@aol.com **web:** www.londonbudgethotels.co.uk
dir: *Near Victoria station*

Stanley House is conveniently situated close to Victoria station and with easy access to the West End. Plain, soundly appointed bedrooms of varying sizes are offered, with breakfasts served in the lower ground-floor dining room; guests also have use of a ground-floor TV lounge area.

**Rooms:** 44 rms (41 en suite) (7 fmly) (8 GF) **S** £40–£55; **D** £65–£75* **Facilities:** FTV TVL Direct dial WiFi **Notes:** LB No children 5yrs

## SW3

### Premier Collection

## San Domenico House
PLAN 1 B1

★★★★★ ⌂ GUEST ACCOMMODATION

tel: 020 7581 5757 29–31 Draycott Place SW3 2SH
email: info@sandomenicohouse.com web: www.sandomenicohouse.com

This stunning property in the heart of Chelsea offers beautiful, individually styled bedrooms, all with antique and period pieces, and well appointed en suites complete with Italian Spa toiletries. A sumptuous drawing room with wonderful works of art is available for guests to relax in or maybe to enjoy afternoon tea. Breakfast is served either in guests' bedrooms or in the elegant lower ground-floor dining room. Staff are friendly and attentive.

Rooms: 17 en suite (4 fmly) (1 GF) Facilities: STV Lounge Dinner available Direct dial Lift Licensed

### Premier Collection

## Sydney House Chelsea
PLAN 1 A1

★★★★★ ⌂ GUEST ACCOMMODATION

tel: 020 7376 7711 & 7376 6900 Sydney Street, Chelsea SW3 6PU
email: info@sydneyhousechelsea.co.uk web: www.sydneyhousechelsea.co.uk
dir: A4 Cromwell Rd, pass Natural History Museum on left, turn next right. Sydney St on left

Located in the heart of Chelsea, this smart Grade II listed Georgian town house offers stylish and very comfortable accommodation, well equipped for both corporate and leisure guests. There is a small bar and drawing room and room service is also available. Staff are attentive and are always on hand to ensure guests feel at home. Breakfast is a particular highlight. Sydney House Chelsea is a part of the Andrew Brownsword Hotels group, which is the AA Hotel Group of the Year 2017-2018.

Rooms: 21 en suite S fr £129; D fr £129 (room only)* Facilities: STV FTV DVD Lounge tea/coffee Dinner available Direct dial Lift Licensed WiFi Extras: Still mineral water

## SW5

## Best Western The Boltons
PLAN 2 E3

★★★★ GUEST ACCOMMODATION

tel: 020 7373 8900 19–21 Penywern Road, Earl's Court SW5 9TT
email: london@theboltonshotel.co.uk web: www.theboltonshotel.co.uk
dir: A3220 from Cromwell Rd, follow road past Earl's Court station, 1st right into Penywern Rd. Located on left

Located right in the heart of Earl's Court, and just around the corner from Earl's Court underground station, The Boltons offers modern and comfortably appointed rooms, all with en suite facilities, digital TVs, beverage-making facilities, and free WiFi throughout. There is a cosy dining room on the ground floor where breakfast is served, and a wide range of restaurants, cafés and bars within a short walking distance.

Rooms: 56 en suite (4 fmly) (4 GF) Facilities: FTV iPod docking station Lounge tea/coffee Direct dial Lift WiFi Notes: No children 18yrs

## The Park Grand London Kensington
PLAN 2 E3

★★★★ GUEST ACCOMMODATION

tel: 020 7370 6831 33–37 Hogarth Road SW5 0QQ
email: info@parkgrandlondon.com web: www.parkgrandkensington.co.uk

Well appointed to a high standard, this property has a smart modern feel and is conveniently located for the West End and local transport links. Bedrooms are furnished and decorated to a very high standard, offering guests a comprehensive range of modern facilities and amenities.

Rooms: 132 en suite (7 GF) D £100–£200 (room only)* Facilities: STV FTV iPod docking station tea/coffee Dinner available Direct dial Lift Licensed WiFi Gym Fitness centre Conf: Max 15 Board 15

## SW7

### Premier Collection

## The Exhibitionist
PLAN 1 A2

★★★★★ GUEST ACCOMMODATION

tel: 020 7915 0000 8–10 Queensberry Place, South Kensington SW7 2EA
email: info@theexhibitionisthotel.com web: www.theexhibitionisthotel.com
dir: Exit A4 (Cromwell Rd) opposite Natural History Museum, near South Kensington tube station

The Exhibitionist can be found close to Kensington and Knightsbridge and offers friendly hospitality, attentive service and sumptuously furnished bedrooms; some have a private terrace. Public areas include a choice of lounges (one with internet access) and an elegant bar. There is an option of English or continental breakfast, and 24-hour room service is available.

Rooms: 37 en suite D £199–£349* Facilities: STV FTV iPod docking station Lounge tea/coffee Dinner available Direct dial Lift Licensed WiFi Extras: Speciality toiletries, mineral water Conf: Max 40 Thtr 40 Class 35 Board 30

## The Gainsborough
PLAN 1 A2

★★★★ GUEST ACCOMMODATION

tel: 020 7957 0000 7–11 Queensberry Place, South Kensington SW7 2DL
email: reservations@thegainsboroughhotel.com web: www.thegainsboroughhotel.com
dir: Off A4 (Cromwell Rd) opposite Natural History Museum, near South Kensington tube station

This smart Georgian house is in a quiet street near South Kensington's museums. Bedrooms are individually designed with fine fabrics and quality furnishings in co-ordinated colours. A choice of breakfasts is offered in the attractive dining room. There is also a delightful lobby lounge, and 24-hour room service is available.

Rooms: 48 en suite (5 fmly) (4 GF) Facilities: STV Lounge tea/coffee Dinner available Direct dial Lift Licensed WiFi Conf: Max 40 Class 40 Board 30

## Best Western The Cromwell
PLAN 1 A2

★★★ GUEST ACCOMMODATION

**tel:** 020 7244 1720 **108–112 Cromwell Road SW7 4ES**
**email:** reception@thecromwell.co.uk **web:** www.thecromwell.co.uk
**dir:** M4/A4 towards London, pass Cromwell Hospital, 0.5m

Just minutes away from Gloucester Road tube station and with easy access to all main tourist attractions, this property offers comfortable, modern accommodation. Fully air-conditioned and with free WiFi, this is an ideal location for both leisure and business guests. Amenities include an on-site meeting room, and secure parking is available nearby.

**Rooms:** 85 en suite (11 GF) **Facilities:** STV TVL tea/coffee Direct dial Lift Licensed WiFi Gym Fitness room **Conf:** Max 8 Board 8 **Notes:** LB

### SW14

## The Victoria
PLAN 2 C2

★★★★ ◉◉ RESTAURANT WITH ROOMS

**tel:** 020 8876 4238 **10 West Temple Sheen SW14 7RT**
**email:** reservations@victoriasheen.co.uk **web:** www.victoriasheen.co.uk
**dir:** Off Upper Richmond Rd West into Derby Rd, then into West Temple Sheen

The Victoria is in a quiet residential area close to Richmond Park. The bedrooms are refreshingly stylish and thoughtfully equipped. The public areas consist of a small contemporary seating area, a modern bar, and an award-winning restaurant that serves imaginative and well sourced dishes. Alfresco dining is also an option.

**Rooms:** 7 en suite (2 fmly) (3 GF) **Facilities:** FTV iPod docking station tea/coffee Dinner available Direct dial WiFi 🔒 **Parking:** 10

### W1

### Premier Collection

## The Marble Arch by Montcalm
PLAN 1 B4

★★★★★ GUEST ACCOMMODATION

**tel:** 020 7258 0777 **31 Great Cumberland Place W1H 7TA**
**email:** info@themarblearchlondon.co.uk **web:** www.themarblearchlondon.co.uk

Located just a short walk from Marble Arch, this luxury boutique townhouse property offers elegant, stylish and comfortable accommodation. Bedrooms are well equipped for the modern traveller with all rooms offering media hub, WiFi and mini-bar.

**Rooms:** 43 en suite (1 fmly) **Facilities:** STV FTV TVL tea/coffee Lift Licensed WiFi

### Premier Collection

## The Piccadilly London West End
PLAN 1 D3

★★★★★ GUEST ACCOMMODATION

**tel:** 020 7871 6000 **65–73 Shaftesbury Avenue W1D 6EX**
**email:** reservations@thepiccadillywestend.co.uk
**web:** www.thepiccadillywestend.co.uk
**dir:** From Piccadilly Circus 300yds up Shaftesbury Av, at junct with Dean St

In the centre of the West End, this boutique property offers plenty of warm, traditional hospitality. It's located close to two major underground stations and has a comfortable club lounge, a popular Japanese bar/restaurant, a fitness

room and a small spa. High quality bedrooms and bathrooms come in a variety of sizes, all well-equipped and smartly presented.

**Rooms:** 67 en suite (6 fmly) **Facilities:** FTV iPod docking station TVL tea/coffee Dinner available Direct dial Lift Licensed WiFi Gym Steam room Treatment rooms **Extras:** Fruit – complimentary; Mini-bar – chargeable **Notes:** LB

## The Sumner
PLAN 1 B4

★★★★ GUEST ACCOMMODATION

**tel:** 020 7723 2244 **54 Upper Berkeley Street, Marble Arch W1H 7QR**
**email:** hotel@thesumner.com **web:** www.thesumner.com

Centrally located and just five minutes' walk from Marble Arch, The Sumner is part of a Georgian terrace. Appointed throughout to a very high standard, this delightful property combines much of the original character of the building with modern comfort. The air-conditioned bedrooms have all been designer decorated and feature widescreen LCD TVs as well as a range of traditional amenities. The breakfast buffet is included in the rate.

**Rooms:** 20 en suite **D** £135–£215* **Facilities:** FTV Lounge Direct dial Lift Licensed WiFi **Notes:** No children 5yrs

### W2

### Premier Collection

## Park Grand London Lancaster Gate

★★★★★ GUEST ACCOMMODATION
PLAN 1 A3

**tel:** 020 7262 0111 **14-16 Craven Hill Road, Paddington W2 3DU**
**email:** info@parkgrandlancastergate.co.uk **web:** www.parkgrandlancastergate.co.uk

Close to both Lancaster Gate and Paddington tube stations, this boutique property has a lot to offer. A warm welcome is assured and the team of dedicated staff deliver attentive service. There is a small comfortable club lounge and all day dining is available in the restaurant. In warmer months, drinks and snacks can also be enjoyed outside. High quality, refurbished bedrooms and bathrooms come in a variety of sizes, all well-equipped and smartly presented. WiFi and a high standard of amenities come as standard

**Rooms:** 64 en suite **Facilities:** WiFi

## Best Western Mornington
PLAN 1 A3

★★★★ GUEST ACCOMMODATION

**tel:** 020 7262 7361 **12 Lancaster Gate W2 3LG**
**email:** london@mornington.co.uk **web:** www.morningtonhotel.co.uk
**dir:** N of Hyde Park, off A402 Bayswater Rd

This fine Victorian building is located in a quiet road and close to Lancaster Gate station for easy access to the West End. The bedrooms have been appointed to provide comfortable, stylish accommodation. There is a lounge bar and an attractive dining room where an extensive Scandinavian-style breakfast is served.

**Rooms:** 70 en suite (10 fmly) (4 GF) **Facilities:** STV FTV tea/coffee Direct dial Lift Licensed WiFi **Extras:** Mini-bar **Conf:** Max 14 Thtr 14 Class 14 Board 14

LONDON W2 *continued*

## Park Grand London Paddington

PLAN 1 A4

★★★★ GUEST ACCOMMODATION

tel: 020 7298 9800 **1–2 Queens Gardens W2 3BA**
email: info@parkgrandlondon.co.uk web: www.parkgrandlondon.co.uk
dir: *Exit Paddington station via Praed St, turn right. After 3 sets of lights right into Devonshire Terrace. 100mtrs to Park Grand Paddington*

Park Grand Paddington enjoys a central location, just a moments' walk from Paddington station and Hyde Park, not to mention the city's main shopping districts and attractions. Rooms vary in size and are appointed to a very high standard. A number of stylish suites are also available. The Atlantic bar serves a range of light snacks throughout the day and evening. Additional facilities include state-of-the-art technology with free internet access, TV and fridges.

**Rooms:** 157 en suite (11 fmly) (23 GF) **Facilities:** FTV TVL tea/coffee Dinner available Direct dial Lift Licensed WiFi Fitness room

## Grand Royale London Hyde Park

PLAN 2 E3

★★★★ GUEST ACCOMMODATION

tel: 020 7313 7900 **1 Inverness Terrace W2 3JP**
email: info@shaftesburyhotels.com web: www.shaftesburyhotels.com
dir: *On A40 Bayswater Rd*

Located adjacent to Hyde Park, fashionable Notting Hill and within easy reach of the West End, the Grand Royale combines its rich heritage with the needs of the modern traveller. The accommodation is contemporary in style and very well equipped. Breakfast is served in the staterooms.

**Rooms:** 188 en suite (2 GF) **Facilities:** tea/coffee Direct dial Lift Licensed WiFi **Conf:** Max 20 Thtr 20 Class 20 Board 20

## Hyde Park Radnor

PLAN 1 A4

★★★★ GUEST ACCOMMODATION

tel: 020 7723 5969 **7–9 Sussex Place, Hyde Park W2 2SX**
email: hydeparkradnor@btconnect.com web: www.hydeparkradnor.com
dir: *A402 (Bayswater Rd) into Lancaster Ter & Sussex Gardens, right into Sussex Place*

This family-run property is within walking distance of Paddington station, the Underground and all London's central attractions. There is a choice of well-appointed bedrooms with modern en suites to meet the needs of a varied clientele. All rooms are well equipped with a range of useful amenities including free WiFi. The dining room is located on the lower-ground floor, where a continental buffet and a freshly-cooked breakfast are served daily.

**Rooms:** 36 en suite (10 fmly) (5 GF) **Facilities:** STV FTV TVL tea/coffee Direct dial Lift WiFi **Notes:** LB

## Mercure London Paddington

PLAN 1 A4

★★★★ GUEST ACCOMMODATION

tel: 020 7835 2000 **144 Praed Street, Paddington W2 1HU**
email: stay@mercurepaddington.com web: www.mercurepaddington.com

Contemporary and stylish, Mercure London Paddington enjoys a central location, adjacent to Paddington Station. Bedrooms and en suites vary in size but all are smartly appointed and boast a host of extra facilities including CD players, TVs, room safes and internet access. A small gym, stylish lounge and meeting rooms are also available.

**Rooms:** 86 en suite (12 fmly) **Facilities:** STV TVL tea/coffee Dinner available Direct dial Lift Licensed WiFi Gym **Conf:** Max 22 Thtr 22 Class 20 Board 22

## Park Grand London Hyde Park

PLAN 1 A4

★★★★ GUEST ACCOMMODATION

tel: 020 7262 4521 **78–82 Westbourne Terrace W2 6QA**
email: reservations@londonpremierhotels.co.uk web: www.parkgrandhydepark.co.uk
dir: *A40 into Lancaster Terrace, at crossing left onto slip road*

This attractive property enjoys a central location within easy reach of central London shops and attractions. The en suite bedrooms and public areas have a smart contemporary feel. Although rooms vary in size, all boast many useful facilities such as free internet access, mini-fridges and irons.

**Rooms:** 119 en suite (10 fmly) (19 GF) **Facilities:** FTV Lounge tea/coffee Direct dial Lift Licensed WiFi **Parking:** 11

## Park Grand Paddington Court London

PLAN 1 A4

★★★★ GUEST ACCOMMODATION

tel: 020 7745 1200 **27 Devonshire Terrace W2 3DP**
email: info@paddingtoncourt.com web: www.paddingtoncourt.com
dir: *From A40 take exit before Paddington flyover, follow Paddington Station signs. Devonshire Ter is off Craven Rd*

This establishment benefits from its convenient location, close to Paddington station, which has links to the tube and the Heathrow Express terminal. Situated next to Hyde Park and Kensington Palace Gardens, the guest accommodation comprises smart and comfortable rooms, and a substantial breakfast is offered. Club Rooms are also available with additional extras including the exclusive use of the Club Lounge. A room is available for small meetings by prior arrangement.

**Rooms:** 175 en suite 35 annexe en suite (43 fmly) (45 GF) **Facilities:** STV FTV TVL tea/coffee Dinner available Direct dial Lift Licensed

## Princes Square

PLAN 2 E3

★★★★ GUEST ACCOMMODATION

tel: 020 7229 9876 **23–25 Princes Square, off Ilchester Gardens W2 4NJ**
email: info@princessquarehotel.co.uk web: www.princessquarehotel.co.uk
dir: *From Bayswater 1st left into Moscow Rd, 3rd right into Ilchester Gardens*

This fine building is in a quiet road close to a number of tube stations, with easy access to the West End. The comfortable bedrooms provide stylish accommodation, and are equipped with a range of useful amenities. A continental breakfast is served in the attractive dining room.

**Rooms:** 50 en suite (3 fmly) (6 GF) **Facilities:** STV FTV tea/coffee Direct dial Lift WiFi **Notes:** LB

## Shaftesbury Hyde Park International

PLAN 2 E3

★★★★ GUEST ACCOMMODATION

tel: 020 7985 8300 **52–55 Inverness Terrace W2 3LB**
email: info@shaftesburyhotels.com web: www.shaftesburyhotels.com
dir: *Off A402 (Bayswater Rd)*

A smart, modern establishment near to Bayswater, Queensway and Paddington underground stations, the Shaftesbury Hyde Park International is also within walking distance of a myriad of dining options. Bedrooms and bathrooms are decorated to a very high standard with a good range of in-room facilities including TV, iron and ironing board and complimentary internet or WiFi access. Continental and cooked buffet breakfasts are served daily. There is a limited number of off-road parking spaces.

**Rooms:** 70 en suite (2 GF) **Facilities:** STV TVL tea/coffee Direct dial Lift Licensed WiFi **Extras:** Mini-bar, fruit, snacks **Conf:** Max 12 Thtr 12 Class 8 Board 8 **Parking:** 3

## Shaftesbury Metropolis London Hyde Park
PLAN 1 A4

★★★★ GUEST ACCOMMODATION

**tel:** 020 7723 7723 **78–84 Sussex Gardens, Hyde Park W2 1UH**
**email:** gurpreet@shaftesburymetropolitan.com **web:** www.shaftesburyhotels.com

This establishment is in an ideal location close to Paddington station with express links to Heathrow Airport. Smartly decorated bedrooms with highly comfortable beds are available in a range of sizes, all with stylish en suite provision. On-site facilities include complimentary internet or WiFi, and continental and full English breakfasts are served every day. Reception is staffed 24 hours.

**Rooms:** 90 en suite (14 GF) **Facilities:** STV FTV TVL tea/coffee Direct dial Lift Licensed WiFi Small fitness centre

## Shaftesbury Premier London Paddington
PLAN 1 A4

★★★★ GUEST ACCOMMODATION

**tel:** 020 7723 3434 **55-61 Westbourne Terrace W2 6QA**
**email:** info@shaftesburyhotels.com **web:** www.theshaftesbury.co.uk
**dir:** Exit A40 into Lancaster Terrace

This smart property enjoys a convenient location within walking distance of Hyde Park and of many of London's major shops and attractions. Bedrooms are smartly appointed and boast modern technology. A hearty breakfast is served in the airy dining room. Limited off-street parking (chargeable) is a bonus. The staff are friendly and attentive.

**Rooms:** 118 en suite (7 fmly) (20 GF) **Facilities:** STV TVL tea/coffee Dinner available Direct dial Lift Licensed WiFi **Parking:** 12

## Number 63
PLAN 1 A3

★★★ GUEST ACCOMMODATION

**tel:** 020 7723 8575 **63 Bayswater Road W2 3PH**
**email:** info@number63.co.uk **web:** www.number63.co.uk

Number 63 offers a surprisingly tranquil environment just a minute's walk from Lancaster Gate tube and directly opposite Hyde Park. All bedrooms are comfortable with en suite facilities and consist of a range of singles and twins; there is also a triple room. Hot snacks are available throughout the afternoon and evening (by prior arrangement) and a good continental or cooked breakfast is served in the mornings. A meeting/function room is available. Parking can be arranged.

**Rooms:** 16 en suite (1 fmly) **Facilities:** FTV Lounge TVL tea/coffee Dinner available Direct dial Lift Licensed WiFi **Conf:** Max 32 Thtr 32 Board 24 **Notes:** No children 5yrs Closed 22–27 Dec

## Griffin House
PLAN 1 B4

★★★ GUEST ACCOMMODATION

**tel:** 020 7723 6532 & 7491 0683 **10 Connaught Street, Marble Arch W2 2AH**
**email:** info@griffinhousehotel.co.uk **web:** www.griffinhousehotel.co.uk

A compact establishment, strategically located in the heart of central London, very well connected to the public transport network and with many landmarks just a stone's throw away. Bedrooms are comfortable and have practical amenities. A substantial continental breakfast is served in the lower-ground floor breakfast room, overseen by attentive staff.

**Rooms:** 15 rms **Facilities:** STV Direct dial WiFi 🔒 **Extras:** Mini-bar

## Kingsway Park Guest Accommodation
PLAN 1 A4

★★★ GUEST ACCOMMODATION

**tel:** 020 7723 5677 & 7724 9346 **139 Sussex Gardens W2 2RX**
**email:** info@kingswaypark-hotel.com **web:** www.kingswaypark-hotel.com
**dir:** A40 Ebound junct for Paddington, through to Sussex Gdns

This Victorian property has a central location within walking distance of Marble Arch, Hyde Park and Paddington. Bedrooms offer well-equipped, good value accommodation. Public areas include a reception lounge and a basement breakfast room adorned with interesting artwork. A limited number of parking spaces is available.

**Rooms:** 22 en suite (5 fmly) (2 GF) **Facilities:** STV FTV Lounge TVL tea/coffee Direct dial Licensed **Conf:** Max 30 **Parking:** 3 **Notes:** LB

### W6

## Best Western Plus Seraphine
PLAN 2 D3

★★★★ GUEST ACCOMMODATION

**tel:** 020 8600 0555 & 8741 6464 **84 King Street W6 0QW**
**email:** hammersmith@seraphinehotel.co.uk **web:** www.seraphinehotel.co.uk
**dir:** A4 exit into Hammersmith Bridge Rd before Hammersmith flyover. Left into King St

Located just a short walk from Hammersmith tube station, this establishment is a good base for visiting the capital's attractions. All bedrooms and public areas are smartly appointed and offer very good levels of comfort. Continental and cooked breakfast are served in the open-plan breakfast room. The bar offers a suitable range of drinks and snacks.

**Rooms:** 62 en suite (14 fmly) **S** £90–£150; **D** £100–£299* **Facilities:** STV FTV iPod docking station Lounge TVL tea/coffee Direct dial Lift Licensed WiFi **Extras:** Bottled water **Notes:** LB

### W8

## Best Western Seraphine Kensington Olympia
PLAN 2 E3

★★★★ GUEST ACCOMMODATION

**tel:** 020 7938 5911 **225 Kensington High Street W8 6SA**
**email:** olympia@seraphinehotel.co.uk **web:** www.seraphinehotel.co.uk
**dir:** A4 left onto A330, then right onto A315. On corner of Kensington High St & Abingdon Rd

This chic and intimate property enjoys a prime location in the heart of High Street Kensington, and is ideally positioned for Holland Park, local attractions, shops and museums. Bedrooms vary in size but all are well equipped with interactive TV, iPod docking stations, laptop safes and free WiFi. En suites are modern with powerful showers. An extensive continental breakfast is included and full cooked breakfasts on request.

**Rooms:** 40 en suite (40 fmly) **S** £99–£129; **D** £119–£149* **Facilities:** STV FTV iPod docking station TVL tea/coffee Direct dial Lift Licensed WiFi **Extras:** Bottled water

LONDON W8 *continued*

## Mercure London Kensington

PLAN 2 E3

★★★★ GUEST ACCOMMODATION

**tel:** 020 7244 2400 **1a Lexham Gardens, Kensington W8 5JJ**
**email:** stay@mercurekensington.com **web:** www.mercurekensington.com

Mercure London Kensington enjoys a prime location adjacent to the famous Cromwell Road Hospital, and is within easy reach of the V&A and the chic shops of Knightsbridge and South Kensington. Bedrooms are extremely well equipped and, along with the comfortable public areas, have a stylish, contemporary feel. The smart and popular bar is a feature.

**Rooms:** 82 en suite **Facilities:** STV TVL tea/coffee Dinner available Direct dial Lift Licensed **Parking:** 8

### W9

## The Warrington

PLAN 1 A5

★★★★ INN

**tel:** 020 7286 8282 **93 Warrington Crescent W9 1EH**
**email:** warrington@faucetinn.com **web:** www.faucetinn.com/warrington

The Warrington is a Grade II listed building that has been serving the Maida Vale community since its opening in 1857. It has a rich and intriguing history, which continues to fascinate the locals and might shock new patrons. The interiors are richly furnished with many original features still in place such as the staircase, the bar and the fireplace. There is a large events room on the first floor, while the top floor now houses five beautifully appointed en suite bedrooms; all different in size but equipped with deeply comfortable beds and all modern facilities. The bar is well stocked and the menu offers a choice of old favourites. Barbecues are regularly held during the warm months of the year.

**Rooms:** 5 en suite **Facilities:** tea/coffee Dinner available

### W12

## W12 Rooms

PLAN 2 D3

★★★★ GUEST ACCOMMODATION

**tel:** 020 3658 551 **54 Uxbridge Road, Shepherd's Bush W12 8LP**
**email:** info@w12rooms.co.uk **web:** www.w12rooms.co.uk

The 19 vintage-inspired bedrooms, with a modern twist, at this establishment make a good base for a trip to London. Westfield Shopping Centre is just minutes away, with Portobello Market, Holland Park and famous music and sports venues close by. Most of London's major tourist attractions, including the London Eye, Buckingham Palace and the Shard are also easily accessible. W12 offers comfortable contemporary rooms on a room-only basis, there are various cafés and eateries a short walk away.

**Rooms:** 19 en suite (1 fmly) **Facilities:** FTV TVL tea/coffee WiFi
**Notes:** No children 2yrs

### W13

## Best Western Maitrise Suites

PLAN 2 C3

★★★★ GUEST ACCOMMODATION

**tel:** 020 8799 3850 **50–54 The Broadway, West Ealing W13 0SU**
**email:** info@maitrisesuites.com **web:** www.maitrisesuites.com

This establishment offers fully serviced accommodation. The rooms are made up of studio, one- and two-bedroom apartments, all with kitchens and lounge areas. Bedrooms are stylish and come fully equipped with all modern amenities including digital TV and free WiFi throughout. A continental room service breakfast can be enjoyed daily. This property has parking available and is just 10 minutes from Ealing Broadway tube station.

**Rooms:** 17 en suite (17 fmly) **D** £109–£399 (room only)* **Facilities:** FTV iPod docking station Lounge tea/coffee Direct dial Lift WiFi **Parking:** 8

### WC1

## The George

PLAN 1 D5

★★★ GUEST ACCOMMODATION

**tel:** 020 7387 8777 **58–60 Cartwright Gardens WC1H 9EL**
**email:** reception@georgehotels.co.uk **web:** www.georgehotel.com
**dir:** *From St Pancras 2nd left into Marchmont St & 1st left into Cartwright Gardens*

The George is within walking distance of Russell Square and the tube, and convenient for London's central attractions. The brightly appointed bedrooms vary in size, and some have en suites. A substantial breakfast is served in the attractive ground-floor dining room.

**Rooms:** 41 rms (31 en suite) (10 pri facs) (5 GF) **S** £63.50–£100; **D** £90–£150*
**Facilities:** FTV Lounge TVL tea/coffee Direct dial WiFi

## GREATER LONDON

### BARNET

Map 6 TQ29

## Savoro Restaurant with Rooms

★★★★ ◉ RESTAURANT WITH ROOMS

**tel:** 020 8449 9888 **206 High Street EN5 5SZ**
**email:** savoro@savoro.co.uk **web:** www.savoro.co.uk
**dir:** *M25 junct 23, A1000. Establishment in crescent behind Hadley Green Jaguar Garage*

Set back from the main high street, the traditional frontage of this establishment belies the stylishly contemporary bedrooms within. Several have modern four-poster beds and all have well designed bathrooms. The award-winning restaurant is an additional bonus, serving food which is all freshly prepared in-house, from bread to ice cream.

*Savoro Restaurant with Rooms*

**Rooms:** 11 rms (9 en suite) (2 pri facs) (2 fmly) (3 GF) **Facilities:** FTV tea/coffee Dinner available WiFi **Extras:** Bottled water – complimentary **Conf:** Max 20 Class 20 Board 20 **Parking:** 9 **Notes:** LB

### BECKENHAM

## Innkeeper's Lodge Beckenham
PLAN 2 G1

★★★ INN

tel: 08451 551551 *(Calls cost 2p per minute plus your phone company's access charge)*
**422 Upper Elmers End Road BR3 3HQ**
email: info@innkeeperslodge.com web: www.innkeeperslodge.com

At Innkeeper's Lodge you'll find accommodation with comfort and character in equal measure, and everything needed for a relaxing stay, from easy check-in and free parking to complimentary breakfast and a cosy pub serving great value food and drink on the doorstep. Each Lodge has quality rooms, and there are Lodges in a variety of locations from towns and cities to countryside settings across the UK.

**Rooms:** 24 en suite (1 fmly) (8 GF) **Facilities:** FTV tea/coffee Dinner available Direct dial WiFi **Parking:** 40

### CRANFORD

*See Heathrow Airport*

### CROYDON
Map 6 TQ36

## Kirkdale

★★★ GUEST HOUSE

tel: 020 8688 5898 **22 St Peters Road CR0 1HD**
email: reservations@kirkdalehotel.co.uk web: www.kirkdalehotel.co.uk
dir: *A23 onto A232 W & A212 (Lower Coombe St), 500yds right*

Close to the town centre, this Victorian property retains many original features. Public areas include a small lounge bar and an attractive breakfast room, and the bedrooms have good facilities. There is a sheltered patio for use in the summer.

**Rooms:** 16 en suite (5 GF) **Facilities:** FTV TVL tea/coffee Direct dial Licensed WiFi **Parking:** 12

### HARROW ON THE HILL

## Old Etonian
Plan 2 B5

★★★ ➧ GUEST ACCOMMODATION

tel: 020 8423 3854 & 8422 8482 **36–38 High Street HA1 3LL**
email: info@oldetonian.com web: www.oldetonian.com
dir: *In town centre. On B458 opposite Harrow School*

In the heart of this historic part of London and opposite the prestigious school, this friendly guest accommodation is a delight. Bedrooms are attractive, well appointed and comfortable. A continental breakfast is served in the dining room, which in the evening is home to a lively restaurant. Roadside parking is available.

**Rooms:** 9 en suite (1 GF) **Facilities:** FTV tea/coffee Dinner available Direct dial Licensed WiFi 🔒 **Extras:** Snacks – complimentary **Conf:** Max 30 Thtr 20 Class 20 Board 20 **Parking:** 3

### HEATHROW AIRPORT

## The Cottage
PLAN 2 B3

★★★★ GUEST ACCOMMODATION

tel: 020 8897 1815 **150–152 High Street TW5 9WB**
email: info@the-cottage.eu web: www.the-cottage.eu
dir: *M4 junct 3, A312 towards Feltham, left at lights, left after 1st pub on left*

This beautiful property is a peacefully situated, family-run oasis, within five minutes of Heathrow Airport. It offers comfortable and spacious accommodation, in the tastefully decorated main house and six bedrooms located at the rear of the garden, connected to the main building by a covered walkway overlooking the stunning courtyard.

**Rooms:** 14 en suite 6 annexe en suite (4 fmly) (12 GF) **Facilities:** FTV tea/coffee WiFi **Parking:** 16 **Notes:** Closed 24–26 Dec & 31 Dec–1 Jan

HEATHROW AIRPORT *continued*

## Crompton Guest House
PLAN 2 B2

★★★★ GUEST HOUSE

**tel:** 020 8570 7090 **49 Lampton Road TW3 1JG**
**email:** cromptonguesthouse@btconnect.com **web:** www.cromptonguesthouse.co.uk
**dir:** *M4 junct 3, follow signs for Hounslow. Into Bath Rd (A3005), left at Yates pub. 200yds on right just before bridge*

Located just a moment's walk away from Hounslow underground station this accommodation is popular with both business and leisure travellers. Bedrooms and bathrooms are comfortable and well equipped with good facilities including air conditioning. Breakfast is served in the intimate dining room where a freshly prepared breakfast is served. Parking is a bonus and is free for up to 15 days.

**Rooms:** 11 en suite (7 fmly) (2 GF) **S** £90–£200; **D** £100–£250 **Facilities:** STV FTV DVD iPod docking station tea/coffee Dinner available Direct dial WiFi 🛁
**Extras:** Speciality toiletries, safe, mini-bar **Parking:** 12 **Notes:** LB

## London Plus Heathrow Bed & Breakfast
PLAN 2 B3

★★★ GUEST ACCOMMODATION

**tel:** 020 3475 8421 & 07917 276111 **21 Woodfield Road TW4 6LL**
**email:** info@london-plus.co.uk **web:** www.london-plus.co.uk

This smart and well cared-for property is just a few minutes away from Heathrow Airport and off-street parking is available. The bedrooms vary in size and all are smartly decorated, comfortable and well equipped. Breakfast is served in the bright communal breakfast room and there is also a small garden at the rear of the property.

**Rooms:** 18 en suite (3 fmly) (5 GF) **S** £40–£55; **D** £55–£80* **Facilities:** STV FTV TVL tea/coffee WiFi **Parking:** 14

---

### HORNCHURCH
Map 6 TQ58

## Innkeeper's Lodge Hornchurch

★★★ INN

**tel:** 08451 551551 *(Calls cost 2p per minute plus your phone company's access charge)*
**Station Lane RM12 6SB**
**email:** info@innkeeperslodge.com **web:** www.innkeeperslodge.com

At Innkeeper's Lodge you'll find accommodation with comfort and character in equal measure, and everything needed for a relaxing stay, from easy check-in and free parking to complimentary breakfast and a cosy pub serving great value food and drink on the doorstep. Each Lodge has quality rooms, and there are Lodges in a variety of locations from towns and cities to countryside settings across the UK.

**Rooms:** 12 en suite (1 fmly) **Facilities:** FTV tea/coffee Dinner available WiFi
**Conf:** Max 60 **Parking:** 40

---

### HOUNSLOW
*See Heathrow Airport*

### ILFORD

## Best Western Greater London
Plan 2 H5

★★★★ GUEST ACCOMMODATION

**tel:** 020 8514 0444 **60 Cranbrook Road IG1 4NH**
**email:** info@bestwesterngreaterlondon.com **web:** www.bestwesterngreaterlondon.com

The Best Western Greater London is an ideal base from which to explore the capital. This stylish modern property enjoys a prominent position on the high street in Ilford, and secure parking can be arranged in advance at reception. The popular café serves food throughout the day and there is an extensive choice on offer at breakfast. Comfortable, modern bedrooms are all finished to a high standard and free WiFi is available for guests.

**Rooms:** 22 en suite **Facilities:** tea/coffee WiFi

## Best Western Ilford
Plan 2 H5

★★★ GUEST ACCOMMODATION

**tel:** 020 8911 6083 **3–5 Argyle Road IG1 3BH**
**email:** manager@expresslodging.co.uk **web:** www.expresslodging.co.uk
**dir:** *From A406 E towards Ilford, then A118 & 1st left after Ilford Station*

This establishment is conveniently located for easy access to the Queen Elizabeth II Olympic Park and central London. The accommodation is very comfortable and offers a range of amenities such as free internet and a state-of-the-art media hub. 24-hour room service and parking is also provided.

**Rooms:** 34 en suite 26 annexe en suite (9 fmly) (15 GF) **Facilities:** FTV Lounge TVL tea/coffee Dinner available Direct dial WiFi 🛁 **Conf:** Max 30 Thtr 30 Class 30 Board 30 **Parking:** 12 **Notes:** LB

## Lucky 8
Plan 2 H5

★★★ GUEST ACCOMMODATION

**tel:** 020 8514 5050 & 07450 288336 **21–25 York Road IG1 3AD**
**email:** info@lucky8hotels.com **web:** www.lucky8hotels.com

This accommodation is conveniently located just a short walk from the overground station into central London and offer a range of rooms to suit all budgets. The cosy rooms have comfortable beds, free WiFi and coffee-making facilities. Breakfast is included in the room price. Limited parking is available. A range of restaurants is located within walking distance, as well as convenience stores.

**Rooms:** 38 en suite (4 fmly) (15 GF) **Facilities:** FTV TVL tea/coffee Direct dial WiFi
🔒 **Parking:** 15 **Notes:** LB

## MERSEYSIDE

### BIRKENHEAD                                               Map 15 SJ38

# Shrewsbury Lodge

★★★ GUEST HOUSE

**tel:** 0151 652 4029 & 07912 846197 **31 Shrewsbury Road, Oxton CH43 2JB**
**email:** info@shrewsbury-hotel.com **web:** www.shrewsbury-hotel.com

Modern accommodation situated in a quiet residential area but within easy walking distance of local amenities and close to travel links. Family-run, it provides well-equipped bedrooms and good breakfasts are served in the pleasant dining room. Friendly, attentive service is a strength here.

**Rooms:** 15 rms (12 en suite) (3 pri facs) (3 fmly) (4 GF) **Facilities:** FTV Lounge TVL tea/coffee Licensed WiFi 🏊 ♨18 Fishing **Conf:** Max 20 Thtr 20 Class 20 Board 20 **Parking:** 12 **Notes:** LB

### BOOTLE                                                   Map 15 SJ39

# Breeze Guest House

★★★ GUEST HOUSE

**tel:** 0151 933 2576 **237 Hawthorne Road L20 3AW**
**email:** breezegh@googlemail.com **web:** www.breezeguesthouse.co.uk
**dir:** Phone for directions

This pleasant family-run guest house provides a friendly place to stay. With secure parking and great transport links, it is ideally located for Anfield and Goodison Park as well as being convenient for Aintree. Dinner is available and there is a pleasant bar too. Bedrooms are spacious and comfortable.

**Rooms:** 10 en suite (1 fmly) (1 GF) **S** £40–£70; **D** £80–£150* **Facilities:** FTV DVD TVL tea/coffee Dinner available Licensed WiFi **Extras:** Bottled water **Parking:** 8 **Notes:** LB Closed 20 Dec–5 Jan

### BROMBOROUGH                                              Map 15 SJ38

# Pesto at the Dibbinsdale Inn

★★★★ 🍴 INN

**tel:** 0151 334 9818 **Dibbinsdale Road CH63 0HJ**
**email:** pestodibbinsdale@hotmail.com **web:** www.pestorestaurants.co.uk
**dir:** M53 junct 5 onto A41 towards Birkenhead. After 2m left towards railway station, through 2 sets of lights, 2nd right into Dibbinsdale Rd. 600yds on right

Pesto at the Dibbinsdale Inn offers plenty of those little luxuries you'd expect from a larger establishment, combined with the relaxed comfort of an independently-run inn, all in a peaceful setting. With high standards of comfort and facilities, the stylish en suite bedrooms are equipped for both leisure and business guests. With real ales on tap and open fires, the restaurant also offers Pesto's informal Italian dining experience with its piattini menu of small plates. A special party menu is available for group bookings.

**Rooms:** 12 en suite (1 fmly) **S** £50–£65; **D** £65–£110* **Facilities:** FTV Lounge tea/coffee Dinner available WiFi ♨18 **Parking:** 25 **Notes:** LB RS 25 Dec restaurant closed

### IRBY                                                      Map 15 SJ28

# Manor Garden Lodge

★★★★ BED AND BREAKFAST

**tel:** 0151 648 7212 & 07855 512008 **5 Manor Road CH61 4UA**
**email:** markwhite7212@gmail.com **web:** www.manorgardenlodge.co.uk
**dir:** M53 junct 3 onto A552 towards Heswall. Left into Arrowe Park Rd, then right into Thingwall Rd E. After 1m at T-junct turn right, then 1st right

This is a B&B with a difference located in the heart of the Wirral and handy for local venues and golfing as well as easy transport into Liverpool and Chester. The wooden lodge at the secluded end of the neat garden is split into two spacious and well equipped bedrooms, with modern facilities and thoughtful extras. Breakfast is taken in the main house. A warm and personal welcome and service is guaranteed.

**Rooms:** 2 annexe en suite (2 GF) **S** £70–£75; **D** £70–£85* **Facilities:** FTV iPod docking station tea/coffee WiFi ♨18 **Parking:** 2 **Notes:** LB

### LIVERPOOL                                                 Map 15 SJ39

# Liverpool Gateway B&B

★★★ GUEST ACCOMMODATION

**tel:** 0151 298 2288 & 07714 090842 **95 Saint Oswald's Street L13 5SB**
**email:** info@liverpoolgateway.co.uk **web:** www.liverpoolgateway.co.uk
**dir:** End of M62 through 2 pedestrian lights, through next lights, on right opposite subway

Ideally situated for the M62 and with easy access to the city centre and its attractions, Liverpool Gateway provides comfortable accommodation, facilities and thoughtful extras for the modern traveller. Continental breakfasts are taken in a communal kitchen; secure off-road parking is provided.

**Rooms:** 10 rms (4 GF) **S** £25–£40; **D** £40–£100* **Facilities:** FTV WiFi 🔒 **Parking:** 15 **Notes:** No children 10yrs

### SOUTHPORT                                                 Map 15 SD31

# Bay Tree House B&B

★★★★ 🍴 GUEST ACCOMMODATION

**tel:** 01704 510555 **No1 Irving Street, Marine Gate PR9 0HD**
**email:** info@baytreehousesouthport.co.uk **web:** www.baytreehousesouthport.co.uk
**dir:** 3rd road right off Leicester St, approaching from rdbt off Lord St

A warm welcome is assured at this immaculately maintained house, located a short walk from the promenade and central attractions. Bedrooms are equipped with a wealth of thoughtful extras, and delicious imaginative breakfasts are served in an attractive dining room overlooking the pretty front patio garden.

**Rooms:** 6 en suite **S** £55–£65; **D** £75–£85* **Facilities:** FTV DVD iPod docking station Lounge tea/coffee Licensed WiFi ♨18 Discounts available for local swimming baths & gym **Extras:** Speciality toiletries, mini-bar, snacks, robes, slippers **Parking:** 2 **Notes:** Closed 15 Nov–Jan

SOUTHPORT *continued*

## The Leicester

★★★★ ⌂ GUEST HOUSE

**tel:** 01704 501703 **24 Leicester Street PR9 0EZ**
**email:** relax@theleicester.com **web:** www.theleicester.com

Jayne and Cliff run a comfortable and welcoming Southport guest house situated handily for both the attractions and eateries of Lord Street but also with the promenade close at hand. The 10 guest rooms are available in a range of sizes and all smartly appointed and very well equipped. Breakfast is a highlight of any stay; generous portions and superb local produce are noteworthy.

**Rooms:** 10 en suite **S** £45–£50; **D** £90–£97*

## The Baytrees

★★★★ GUEST ACCOMMODATION

**tel:** 01704 536513 & 07952 963081 **4 Queens Road PR9 9HN**
**email:** baytreeshotel@gmail.com **web:** www.baytreeshotel.co.uk
**dir:** *From B565 (Lord St) towards fire station, right at rdbt into Manchester Rd, left at lights, 200yds on right*

Located a short walk from Lord Street, this elegant late Victorian house has been well appointed to provide thoughtfully furnished bedrooms with smart modern en suite bathrooms. Breakfast is served in the attractive dining room overlooking the pretty rear garden, and a lounge is also available.

**Rooms:** 12 en suite (2 GF) **Facilities:** FTV TVL tea/coffee WiFi Gym ♨ **Parking:** 11

## NORFOLK

| BACTON | Map 13 TG33 |
|---|---|

## The Keswick

★★★★ GUEST ACCOMMODATION

**tel:** 01692 650468 **Walcott Road NR12 0LS**
**email:** margaret@keswickhotelbacton.co.uk **web:** www.keswickhotelbacton.co.uk
**dir:** *On B1159 (coast road)*

This family-run property enjoys lovely sea views and is within easy driving distance of the Broads and the stunning north Norfolk coastline. The individually decorated bedrooms are all well-appointed, have modern facilities and many rooms have sea views. Public areas include a cosy lounge bar with plush, comfortable seating along with stylish conservatory restaurant.

**Rooms:** 12 rms (10 en suite) (2 pri facs) **S** £60; **D** £90* **Facilities:** FTV DVD Lounge TVL Licensed WiFi **Parking:** 100

| BAWBURGH | Map 13 TG10 |
|---|---|

## The Kings Head Bawburgh

★★★★ ⚙⚙ INN

**tel:** 01603 744977 **Harts Lane NR9 3LS**
**email:** anton@kingsheadbawburgh.co.uk **web:** www.kingshead-hawburgh.co.uk
**dir:** *Exit A47 signed university & hospital onto B1108 (Whatton). 500yds right into Stocks Hill. Into centre of Bawburgh, opposite river*

The Kings Head Bawburgh is Grade II listed, was built in 1602 and is situated in the picturesque village of Bawburgh, opposite the river, only a 10-minute drive from the centre of Norwich. The pub boasts six boutique-style bedrooms with modern bathrooms, and high quality fixtures and fittings throughout. The gastro pub below offers award-winning food in a traditional dining area complete with oak beams, inglenook fireplace, and wood-burners. There is also a lovely outside patio where guests can eat or enjoy a drink in the summer, with a good range of real ales available. Nothing is too much trouble for the owners who will ensure all guests feel welcomed.

**Rooms:** 6 en suite (1 fmly) **Facilities:** FTV iPod docking station tea/coffee Dinner available WiFi ♨27 **Extras:** Speciality toiletries, home-made biscuits **Conf:** Max 20 Thtr 20 Class 20 Board 12 **Parking:** 51 **Notes:** LB

| BLAKENEY | Map 13 TG04 |
|---|---|

### Premier Collection

## Blakeney House

★★★★★ GUEST HOUSE

**tel:** 01263 740561 **High Street NR25 7NX**
**email:** admin@blakeneyhouse.com **web:** www.blakeneyhouse.com
**dir:** *In village centre*

Blakeney House is a stunning Victorian manor house set amid two acres of attractive landscaped grounds, just a short walk from the quay and town centre. The stylish, individually decorated bedrooms have co-ordinated fabrics and many thoughtful touches. Breakfast is served at individual tables in the smart dining room, which overlooks the well-stocked front garden.

**Rooms:** 8 rms (7 en suite) (1 pri facs) (1 fmly) **Facilities:** DVD tea/coffee WiFi ♨18 ♨ **Parking:** 8 **Notes:** No children 12yrs

| BROOKE | Map 13 TM29 |
|---|---|

## The Old Vicarage

★★★★ BED AND BREAKFAST

**tel:** 01508 558329 **48 The Street NR15 1JU**
**web:** www.bedandbreakfastdirect.co.uk
**dir:** *From Norwich on B1332, turn left after Kings Head pub. 1st left at fork in road to village. Immediately before church on right*

Set in mature gardens in a peaceful village, this charming house is within easy driving distance of Norwich. The individually decorated bedrooms are thoughtfully furnished and equipped, and one room has a lovely four-poster bed. There is an elegant dining room and a cosy lounge, and dinner is available by arrangement. Service is genuinely helpful, provided in a relaxed and friendly manner.

**Rooms:** 2 en suite **S** £40; **D** £70–£80* **Facilities:** TVL tea/coffee Dinner available **Parking:** 4 **Notes:** LB No children 18yrs

| BURNHAM MARKET | Map 13 TF84 |
|---|---|

## The Nelson Country Inn

★★★★ ⌂ INN

**tel:** 01328 738321 **4 Creake Road PE31 8EN**
**email:** stay@the-nelson.com **web:** www.the-nelson.com
**dir:** *From Market Pl onto Front St (at lower end). 200yds, on Creake Rd*

This country inn is set in the pretty north Norfolk village of Burnham Market, within easy reach of King's Lynn, Norwich, Hunstanton and Cromer. Bedrooms are individually styled and comfortable. Hearty meals are served daily, making good use of local and seasonal produce where possible.

**Rooms:** 5 en suite 2 annexe en suite (2 GF) **Facilities:** FTV tea/coffee Dinner available WiFi ♨ **Extras:** Sweets **Conf:** Max 18 Thtr 12 Class 18 Board 14 **Parking:** 20

## CASTLE ACRE                                                    Map 13 TF81

# Ostrich Inn

★★★★ ⊜ INN

**tel:** 01760 755398 **Stocks Green PE32 2AE**
**email:** info@ostrichcastleacre.com **web:** www.ostrichcastleacre.com
**dir:** *0.3m on right of Castle Acre Priory*

The 15th-century Ostrich Inn is situated adjacent to the village green in the centre of Castle Acre. The warm and inviting public areas have a wealth of original features such as exposed brickwork, oak beams and open fires. The spacious bedrooms are in an adjacent building; each room is equipped with modern facilities.

**Rooms:** 6 en suite (1 fmly) (1 GF) **Facilities:** FTV Lounge tea/coffee Dinner available Direct dial WiFi ☎ **Conf:** Max 25 Thtr 25 Class 25 Board 25 **Parking:** 30 **Notes:** LB

## CLEY NEXT THE SEA                                              Map 13 TG04

### Premier Collection

# Old Town Hall House

★★★★★ ☕ ⊜ GUEST HOUSE

**tel:** 01263 741439 & 07813 335236 **High Street NR25 7RB**
**email:** bookings@oldtownhallhouse.com **web:** www.oldtownhallhouse.com
**dir:** *On A149 in centre of Cley. On High St, opposite old red phone box*

Old Town Hall House is located in the popular little village of Cley next the Sea, which has been designated as an Area of Outstanding Natural Beauty and has a superb bird-watching reserve on its outskirts. The tastefully appointed bedrooms offer luxurious fabrics and retro accessories with a modern touch. Dinner is available on certain nights and guests can enjoy a pre-dinner drink in the lounge beforehand. James has worked in some of the finest restaurants in Europe and only high quality ingredients will be on the menu. Breakfast is equally enjoyable.

**Rooms:** 4 en suite (1 fmly) **Facilities:** Lounge tea/coffee Dinner available Licensed WiFi ⅄18 ☎ **Extras:** Speciality toiletries, fresh milk – complimentary **Notes:** LB

# The George

★★★★ ☕ ⊜ INN

**tel:** 01263 740652 **The High Street NR25 7RN**
**email:** info@thegeorgehotelatcley.co.uk **web:** www.thegeorgehotelatcley.co.uk
**dir:** *On A149 coast road*

The George is located in Cley next the Sea, within easy reach of Blakeney and Holt. This is a great spot for bird watchers, and The George overlooks the Cley marshes and bird reserve, looking out towards Blakeney Harbour. This is a quiet little village without any street lights and retains its original charm complete with red village phone box. The rooms all provide modern amenities and have each been attractively decorated; most overlooking the marshes. Guests can enjoy a range of freshly prepared dishes in the restaurant (where food is served all day in the summer), including a fantastic breakfast.

**Rooms:** 10 en suite (1 fmly) **D** £120–£345 (room only)* **Facilities:** FTV DVD tea/coffee Dinner available WiFi **Extras:** Bottled water – complimentary **Parking:** 10

## CROMER                                                         Map 13 TG24

*See also Sheringham*

### AA B&B STORY OF THE YEAR
### 2017–18

# The Grove Cromer

★★★★★ ◉◉ GUEST ACCOMMODATION

**tel:** 01263 512412 **95 Overstrand Road NR27 0DJ**
**email:** enquiries@thegrovecromer.co.uk **web:** www.thegrovecromer.co.uk
**dir:** *Into Cromer on A149, right at 1st mini rdbt into Cromwell Rd. At double mini rdbt straight over into Overstrand Rd, 200mtrs on left*

A charming Georgian house, The Grove Cromer sits amid several acres of landscaped gardens and is just a short walk from Cromer town centre, cliff walks and the beach. There are several bedroom styles to choose from; the well-appointed comfortable bedrooms in the main house and stylish garden rooms. There is an indoor heated swimming pool available for guests along with a children's play area in the woodland walk. Delicious dinners are served in the restaurant and guests are guaranteed a warm welcome at this fine property.

**Rooms:** 11 en suite 5 annexe en suite (4 fmly) (5 GF) **S** £50–£66; **D** £80–£150* **Facilities:** FTV DVD Lounge TVL tea/coffee Dinner available Direct dial Licensed WiFi ⌚⅄18 ☎ **Conf:** Max 24 Thtr 24 Class 24 Board 18 **Parking:** 25 **Notes:** LB Closed 2–23 Jan Civ wed 25

# The Red Lion Food and Rooms

★★★★ ⊜ INN

**tel:** 01263 514964 **Brook Street NR27 9HD**
**email:** info@redlion-cromer.co.uk **web:** www.redlion-cromer.co.uk
**dir:** *Follow one-way system, pass church on left & take next left into Brook St*

The Red Lion is a charming Victorian inn in an elevated position at the heart of the town centre, overlooking the beach and the sea. The open-plan public areas include a lounge bar, a popular restaurant and sunny conservatory. The spacious bedrooms are tastefully decorated with co ordinated soft furnishings and include many thoughtful touches.

**Rooms:** 14 en suite (3 fmly) **S** £62.50–£95; **D** £115–£180* **Facilities:** FTV DVD iPod docking station tea/coffee Dinner available WiFi ☎ **Extras:** Honesty box including chocolate, wine, snacks **Parking:** 20 **Notes:** LB

# Shrublands Farm

★★★★ ☕ FARMHOUSE

**tel:** 01263 579297 **Church Street, Northrepps NR27 0AA**
**email:** youngman@farming.co.uk **web:** www.shrublandsfarm.com
**dir:** *Exit A149 to Northrepps, through village, past Foundry Arms, cream house 50yds on left*

Expect a warm welcome from the caring host at this delightful 18th-century farmhouse, set in landscaped grounds and surrounded by 300 acres of arable farmland. Public areas include a cosy lounge with a wood-burning stove, and breakfast is served at a communal table in the elegant dining room.

**Rooms:** 2 rms (1 en suite) (1 pri facs) **S** £65; **D** £85* **Facilities:** FTV DVD TVL tea/coffee WiFi ☎ **Extras:** Speciality toiletries, snacks, confectionery – complimentary **Parking:** 5 **Notes:** LB No children 12yrs Closed 25–26 Dec 300 acres arable

CROMER *continued*

## The White Horse Overstrand

★★★★★ ◉◉ INN

**tel:** 01263 579237 **34 High Street, Overstrand NR27 0AB**
**email:** reservations@whitehorseoverstrand.co.uk **web:** www.whitehorseoverstrand.co.uk
**dir:** *From A140, before Cromer, turn right into Mill Rd. At bottom right into Station Rd. After 2m, bear left into High St, White Horse on left*

The White Horse Overstrand is a smartly appointed inn ideally situated in the heart of this popular village on the north Norfolk coast. The modern bedrooms are tastefully appointed and equipped with a good range of useful extras. Public rooms include a large open-plan lounge bar with comfortable seating and a relaxed dining area. Cooking is taken seriously here as is reflected in its award of two AA Rosettes.

**Rooms:** 8 en suite (2 fmly) **Facilities:** STV TVL tea/coffee Dinner available WiFi
Pool table **Parking:** 6 **Notes:** LB

## Homefield Guest House

★★★★ GUEST HOUSE

**tel:** 01263 837337 **48 Cromer Road, West Runton NR27 9AD**
**email:** homefield@hotmail.co.uk **web:** www.homefieldguesthouse.co.uk
**dir:** *On A149 (coast road) between Sheringham & Cromer*

This large Victorian house was previously owned by the Canon of Cromer and is situated in the peaceful village of West Runton between Cromer and Sheringham. The pleasantly co-ordinated bedrooms have many useful extras. Breakfast, which includes locally sourced produce, is served at individual tables in the smart dining room.

**Rooms:** 6 en suite **Facilities:** STV tea/coffee WiFi 🔒 **Parking:** 8 **Notes:** LB
No children 14yrs

## The Sandcliff Guest House

★★★ GUEST HOUSE

**tel:** 01263 512888 **Runton Road NR27 9AS**
**email:** bookings@sandcliffcromer.co.uk **web:** www.sandcliffcromer.co.uk
**dir:** *500yds W of town centre on A149*

Ideally situated on the seafront just a short walk from the town centre, this guest house offers a large lounge with comfortable seating and a spacious dining room where breakfast is served. The bedrooms are pleasantly decorated, thoughtfully equipped and some have superb sea views.

**Rooms:** 23 rms (17 en suite) (6 pri facs) (10 fmly) (3 GF) **S** £39–£99; **D** £39–£99
(room only)* **Facilities:** FTV TVL tea/coffee WiFi ♨18 🔒 **Parking:** 10

## Glendale Guest House

★★★ GUEST HOUSE

**tel:** 01263 513278 **33 Macdonald Road NR27 9AP**
**email:** glendalecromer@btconnect.com **web:** www.glendalecromer.co.uk
**dir:** *A149 (coast road) from Cromer centre, 4th left*

Glendale Guest House is a Victorian property situated in a peaceful side road adjacent to the seafront, just a short walk from the town centre. Bedrooms are pleasantly decorated, well maintained and equipped with a good range of useful extras. Breakfast is served at individual tables in the smart dining room.

**Rooms:** 5 rms (1 en suite) **S** £35–£45; **D** £70–£90 **Facilities:** FTV tea/coffee
**Parking:** 2 **Notes:** LB Closed 13 Oct–30 Mar

| **DEREHAM** | Map 13 TF91 |
|---|---|

## Orchard Cottage

★★★★ BED AND BREAKFAST

**tel:** 01362 860265 **The Drift, Gressenhall NR20 4EH**
**email:** walkers.norfolk@btinternet.com **web:** www.walkers-norfolk.co.uk
**dir:** *2m NE of Dereham. Exit B1146 in Beetley to Gressenhall, right at x-rds into Bittering St, right at x-rds, 2nd right*

Orchard Cottage is an attractive Norfolk flint building situated in the historic village of Gressenhall near Dereham. The comfortable, country style bedrooms are smartly decorated and situated on the ground floor; one of the rooms has a superb wet room. Public rooms include a lounge, a dining room and a study. Dinner is available by arrangement.

**Rooms:** 2 en suite (2 GF) **Facilities:** FTV Lounge TVL tea/coffee Dinner available WiFi
🔒 **Parking:** 2 **Notes:** LB

| **DOWNHAM MARKET** | Map 12 TF60 |
|---|---|

## Crosskeys Riverside House

★★★★ BED AND BREAKFAST

**tel:** 01366 387777 **Bridge Street, Hilgay PE38 0LD**
**email:** crosskeyshouse@aol.com **web:** www.crosskeys.info
**dir:** *2m S of Downham Market. Off A10 into Hilgay, Crosskeys on bridge*

Situated in the small village of Hilgay, in its own grounds on the banks of the River Wissey, this former coaching inn offers comfortable accommodation that includes a number of four-poster bedrooms; all rooms have river views, as well as CD players and free WiFi. Public rooms include a dining room with oak beams and an inglenook fireplace.

**Rooms:** 1 en suite **S** £45–£65; **D** £70–£85 **Facilities:** FTV DVD Lounge tea/coffee WiFi
Fishing 🔒 Rowing boat for guests' use **Extras:** Flowers, champagne – chargeable
**Parking:** 10

| **EDGEFIELD** | Map 13 TG03 |
|---|---|

## Mount Farm Barn Bed & Breakfast

★★★★ ⓖ GUEST ACCOMMODATION

**tel:** 01263 585069 **NR24 2AE**
**email:** david@mountfarmbarn.co.uk **web:** www.mountfarmbarn.co.uk

Just on the outskirts of Holt this sympathetically converted 15th-century barn offers guests high quality accommodation in a peaceful rural setting. The bedrooms overlook the lovely Norfolk countryside; they are beautifully presented and most comfortable. The award-winning breakfast is not to be missed, and all guests are made to feel most welcome, often with tea and home-made cake on arrival. This is an ideal location from which to explore north Norfolk and its lovely coastline. Ample secure parking is available, along with WiFi.

**Rooms:** 2 en suite (2 fmly) **Facilities:** FTV DVD TVL tea/coffee WiFi **Extras:** Fridge, fresh milk **Parking:** 4

### GORLESTON ON SEA — Map 13 TG50

## Avalon

★★★★ GUEST ACCOMMODATION

**tel:** 01493 662114 **54 Clarence Road NR31 6DR**
**email:** avalon.hotel@btinternet.com **web:** www.avalon-gorleston.co.uk
**dir:** *A47 past James Paget Hospital. Take 2nd exit at rdbt towards Gorleston. Next rdbt 2nd exit, 1st right*

This Edwardian terraced house is just a short walk from the promenade and beach. Breakfast is served in the smart dining room. Service is both helpful and friendly. Bedrooms are pleasantly appointed, thoughtfully equipped and well furnished.

**Rooms:** 10 en suite (6 fmly) (1 GF) **S** £40–£50; **D** £60–£70* **Facilities:** FTV tea/coffee WiFi **Notes:** LB

### GREAT ELLINGHAM — Map 13 TM09

## Aldercarr Hall

★★★★ GUEST ACCOMMODATION

**tel:** 01953 455766 & 07710 752213 **Attleborough Road NR17 1LQ**
**email:** bedandbreakfast@aldercarr-limited.com **web:** www.aldercarrhall.co.uk
**dir:** *On B1077 500yds SE of village*

Aldercarr Hall is set in extensive grounds and surrounded by open countryside on the edge of Great Ellingham. Public rooms include a comfortably appointed conservatory and a delightful dining room where breakfast is served around a large table. The excellent facilities include a health, beauty and hairdressing studio, an indoor swimming pool, a jacuzzi and a large function suite.

**Rooms:** 3 annexe en suite (1 fmly) (3 GF) **Facilities:** FTV TVL tea/coffee WiFi 🌊 🎣18 Fishing Pool table 🔒 **Parking:** 200 **Notes:** LB

### GREAT MOULTON — Map 13 TM19

## South Norfolk Guest House

★★★★ GUEST HOUSE

**tel:** 01379 677359 & 07885 351212 **Frith Way NR15 2HE**
**email:** info@sngh.co.uk **web:** www.southnorfolkguesthouse.co.uk
**dir:** *From A140 (N), in Long Stratton turn left at 1st set of lights. Through Wacton, pass sign to Coronation Hall on right. 1st property on right in Great Moulton, past house, turn right & right again*

This former village school enjoys a peaceful rural location yet is only a short drive from Norwich. A warm welcome is guaranteed from the friendly proprietors and bedrooms are all most comfortable. Ample secure parking is available for guests along with free WiFi. Delicious hot breakfasts are served in the conservatory breakfast room.

**Rooms:** 9 en suite (1 fmly) (4 GF) **S** £40–£54; **D** £60–£80* **Facilities:** FTV DVD Lounge tea/coffee WiFi 🔒 **Parking:** 14 **Notes:** LB

### GREAT RYBURGH — Map 13 TF92

## The Blue Boar Inn

★★★ 🍺 INN

**tel:** 01328 829212 **5 Station Road NR21 0DX**
**email:** blueboarinnryburgh@gmail.com **web:** www.blueboar-norfolk.co.uk

Built in 1635, The Blue Boar has been in the heart of village life in Great Ryburgh for over three centuries. The cosy wood-beamed bar has an original inglenook fireplace and guests are guaranteed a warm welcome. Bedrooms are all comfortable, attractively presented and well equipped. The Blue Boar has been sympathetically restored in recent years and the restaurant serves an extensive choice of imaginative dishes using the best in local produce. Hearty breakfasts are cooked to order. Secure parking and free WiFi are available for guests.

**Rooms:** 6 en suite **Facilities:** FTV tea/coffee Dinner available WiFi **Parking:** 40

### GREAT YARMOUTH — Map 13 TG50

## The Classic Lodge

★★★★ BED AND BREAKFAST

**tel:** 01493 852851 **13 Euston Road NR30 1DY**
**email:** classiclodge@uwclub.net **web:** www.classiclodge.com
**dir:** *A12 to A47, follow signs for seafront. Turn left at Sainsbury's, ahead at lights 200mtrs on right, 100mtrs from seafront*

The Classic Lodge is an impressive Victorian villa situated just a short stroll from the seafront and town centre. Breakfast is served at individual tables in the large lounge-dining room, and the spacious bedrooms are carefully furnished and equipped with a good range of facilities. Secure parking is provided at the rear of the property.

**Rooms:** 3 en suite **S** £30–£40* **Facilities:** FTV TVL tea/coffee WiFi **Parking:** 5 **Notes:** LB No children 18yrs Closed Nov–Mar

## Marine Lodge

★★★★ 🍺 GUEST ACCOMMODATION

**tel:** 01493 331120 **19-20 Euston Road NR30 1DY**
**email:** res@marinelodge.co.uk **web:** www.marinelodge.co.uk
**dir:** *Follow signs for seafront, 300mtrs N of Britannia Pier*

This establishment's enviable seafront position has panoramic views of the bowling greens and beach, and is within easy walking distance of Britannia Pier. Bright, modern bedrooms are complemented by smart public areas that include a bar area where light snacks are available during the evening. Guests also have complimentary use of the indoor swimming pool at the sister Palm Court Hotel.

**Rooms:** 40 en suite (5 fmly) (5 GF) **Facilities:** FTV TVL tea/coffee Dinner available Lift Licensed WiFi **Parking:** 38 **Notes:** LB

**GREAT YARMOUTH** *continued*

## Swiss Cottage Bed and Breakfast

★★★★ GUEST ACCOMMODATION

**tel:** 01493 855742 & 07986 399857 **31 North Drive NR30 4EW**
**email:** info@swiss-cottage.info **web:** www.swisscottagebedandbreakfast.co.uk
**dir:** *0.5m N of town centre. Exit A47 or A12 to seafront, 750yds N of pier. Left at Britannia Pier. Swiss Cottage on left opposite Water Gardens*

Swiss Cottage Bed and Breakfast is a charming property situated in a peaceful part of town overlooking the Venetian waterways and the sea beyond. The comfortable bedrooms are pleasantly decorated with co-ordinated fabrics and have many useful extras. Breakfast is served in the smart dining room and guests have use of an open-plan lounge area.

**Rooms:** 8 en suite 1 annexe en suite (2 GF) **S** £48–£58; **D** £77–£100* **Facilities:** FTV Lounge tea/coffee WiFi ⚓ **Extras:** Speciality toiletries **Parking:** 9 **Notes:** LB No children 16yrs Closed Nov–Feb

## The Chequers

★★★★ GUEST HOUSE

**tel:** 01493 853091 **27 Nelson Road South NR30 3JA**
**email:** mitchellsatchequers@hotmail.co.uk **web:** www.thechequersguesthouse.co.uk
**dir:** *Exit A47 signed seafront, right into Marine Parade & Kings Rd, 1st right*

Guests will receive a warm welcome from the caring hosts at this privately-run establishment, situated just a short walk from Wellington Pier and the beach. Public rooms include a cosy bar, residents' lounge and a smart dining room. Bedrooms are cheerfully decorated and have many thoughtful touches.

**Rooms:** 8 rms (7 en suite) (1 pri facs) (2 fmly) **Facilities:** FTV TVL tea/coffee Dinner available Licensed WiFi **Notes:** LB

## The Hamilton

★★★★ GUEST HOUSE

**tel:** 01493 844662 **23–24 North Drive NR30 4EW**
**email:** enquiries@hamilton-hotel.co.uk **web:** www.hamilton-hotel.co.uk

Overlooking the beach with fantastic views of the sea, this property is ideally situated for the theatre, tourist attractions, town centre and Yarmouth Racecourse. Public rooms include a smart lounge bar with plush leather seating, a breakfast room and a residents' lounge with comfy sofas. Bedrooms are bright and airy with many thoughtful touches; most rooms have lovely sea views.

**Rooms:** 21 en suite (4 fmly) (2 GF) **Facilities:** FTV TVL tea/coffee Dinner available Licensed WiFi ⚓18 **Conf:** Max 40 Thtr 40 Class 26 Board 26 **Parking:** 20 **Notes:** LB

## The Winchester

★★★★ ⚇ GUEST ACCOMMODATION

**tel:** 01493 843950 & 07807 733161 **12 Euston Road NR30 1DY**
**email:** enquiries@winchesterprivatehotel.com **web:** www.winchesterprivatehotel.com
**dir:** *A12 onto A47, signs for seafront, left at Sainsbury's over lights, premises 400yds on right*

A warm welcome is assured from the friendly hosts at The Winchester, just off the seafront. The pleasant bedrooms vary in size and style and are thoughtfully equipped. Public rooms include a large lower ground-floor dining room, a small conservatory and a foyer with comfortable sofas.

**Rooms:** 14 en suite (2 fmly) (5 GF) **S** £30–£45; **D** £60–£90 **Facilities:** FTV TVL tea/coffee Dinner available WiFi ⚓ **Parking:** 10 **Notes:** LB No children 12yrs Closed Dec–Jan RS Oct–Easter No evening meals

## Senglea Lodge

★★★ GUEST ACCOMMODATION

**tel:** 01493 859632 & 07775 698819 **7 Euston Road NR30 1DX**
**email:** senglealodge@fsmail.net **web:** www.senglealodge.com
**dir:** *From A4 straight over 1st 2 rdbts. At lights left towards seafront. Through next lights, Lodge on right*

Senglea Lodge is a delightful terrace property situated just off the seafront and very close to the town centre. Bedrooms are pleasantly decorated, have co-ordinated soft furnishings and a good range of useful extras. Breakfast is served at individual tables in the smart open-plan lounge/dining room.

**Rooms:** 6 rms (4 en suite) (2 fmly) **Facilities:** FTV TVL tea/coffee WiFi ⚓ **Notes:** LB Closed 23 Dec–2 Jan

## Haydee

★★★ GUEST HOUSE

**tel:** 01493 844580 **27 Princes Road NR30 2DG**
**email:** info@haydee.co.uk **web:** www.haydee.co.uk
**dir:** *Exit A47 to seafront, Princes Rd opposite Britannia Pier*

The Haydee is in a side road just a stroll from the seafront, pier and town centre. The pleasant bedrooms vary in size and style, and all are well equipped. Breakfast is served in the smart dining room and there is a cosy lounge bar.

**Rooms:** 8 en suite (2 fmly) **S** £25–£30; **D** £50–£56* **Facilities:** FTV DVD TVL tea/coffee Licensed WiFi ⚓ **Notes:** LB

## Silverstone House

★★★ GUEST ACCOMMODATION

**tel:** 01493 844862 **29 Wellesley Road NR30 1EY**
**email:** silverstonehouse@yahoo.co.uk **web:** www.silverstone-house.co.uk
**dir:** *A47 into Great Yarmouth. Over 2 rdbts, left at lights signed seafront. Over next lights, turn left*

A warm welcome is guaranteed at this family-run property. Silverstone House is conveniently located close to the seafront and a short walk to the main shopping district. This four-storey Victorian terraced house has nine well-appointed, comfortable bedrooms. Freshly prepared hot breakfasts are served to individual tables in the charming breakfast room.

**Rooms:** 9 en suite (4 fmly) (1 GF) **S** £25–£30; **D** £45–£55* **Facilities:** FTV tea/coffee WiFi **Extras:** Mini-fridge – complimentary **Notes:** LB

**■ HARLESTON**      **Map 13 TM28**

## Heath Farmhouse

★★★★ BED AND BREAKFAST

**tel:** 01986 788417 **Homersfield IP20 0EX**
**email:** julia.john.hunt@googlemail.com
**dir:** *A143 onto B1062 towards Flixton, over bridge past Suffolk sign, 2nd farm entrance on left at AA sign*

This charming 16th-century farmhouse is set amid attractive landscaped grounds that include a croquet lawn. The property retains much of its original character with exposed beams, open fireplaces and wood-burning stoves. The pleasant bedrooms are carefully furnished and have many thoughtful touches. Breakfast is served in the smart dining room overlooking the garden.

**Rooms:** 2 rms (1 fmly) **S** £40; **D** £75* **Facilities:** Lounge TVL tea/coffee WiFi ⚇ ⚓ Table tennis **Extras:** Mineral water **Parking:** 8

## HINDOLVESTON
Map 13 TG02

### The Old Bakery B&B

★★★★ 🗲 ⊜ BED AND BREAKFAST

tel: 01263 862802 & 07771 391967 **34 The Street NR20 5DF**
email: mike@theoldbakerynorfolk.co.uk web: www.theoldbakerynorfolk.co.uk
dir: *From A148 exit at Little Snoring signed Fulmodeston, follow signs to Hindolveston. At next junct continue for 1.3m, house on corner of turn to Foulsham*

The Old Bakery B&B is a delightful property which was originally the village bakery and dates back to the 17th century. Guests will be welcomed into the property by Mike and Alison, who were winners of the AA Friendliest B&B of the Year 2016-2017. The spacious bedrooms are well-equipped and include many thoughtful touches. Breakfast and dinner are served at a large communal table in the smart dining room, and good use is made of fresh seasonal ingredients.

**Rooms:** 2 en suite **S** £65–£70; **D** £70–£85* **Facilities:** FTV DVD iPod docking station tea/coffee Dinner available WiFi 🌸 🔒 **Extras:** Cakes on arrival – complimentary; fridge **Parking:** 4 **Notes:** LB No children

## HOLT
Map 13 TG03

### The Lawns

★★★★ 🍽 RESTAURANT WITH ROOMS

tel: 01263 713390 **26 Station Road NR25 6BS**
email: info@lawnshotelholt.co.uk web: www.lawnshotelholt.co.uk
dir: *A148 (Cromer road). 0.25m from Holt rdbt, turn left, 400yds along Station Rd*

The Lawns is a superb Georgian house situated in the centre of this delightful north Norfolk market town. The open-plan public areas include a large wine bar, a conservatory and a smart restaurant. The spacious bedrooms are tastefully appointed with co-ordinated soft furnishings and have many thoughtful touches.

**Rooms:** 8 en suite 2 annexe en suite (2 GF) **S** £99; **D** £120–£145 **Facilities:** FTV DVD TVL tea/coffee Dinner available WiFi **Extras:** Speciality toiletries **Conf:** Max 20 Thtr 20 Class 12 **Parking:** 18

### The Feathers

★★★★ INN

tel: 01263 712318 **6 Market Place NR25 6BW**
email: enquiries@thefeathershotel.com web: www.thefeathershotel.com

This former coaching inn enjoys a prominent position in the heart of this pretty village. Bedrooms vary in size but all are well equipped and comfortable. The bar, with its real fire, is extremely popular with locals and the dinner menu offers an extensive choice.

**Rooms:** 13 en suite (2 fmly) **S** £85–£90; **D** £110–£115* **Facilities:** FTV Lounge tea/coffee Dinner available Direct dial WiFi 🔔18 🔒 **Conf:** Max 100 Thtr 100 Class 80 Board 80 **Parking:** 15

### Holm Oaks

★★★★ GUEST HOUSE

tel: 01263 711061 & 07778 600600 **83a Cromer Road NR25 6DY**
email: holmoaks@btinternet.com web: www.holmoaksatholt.co.uk

Holm Oaks enjoys a very convenient location on the outskirts of the Georgian town of Holt. The four bedrooms are all attractively presented and free WiFi is available throughout the house. Breakfast is served at individual tables in the conservatory, which overlooks the landscaped gardens. Secure parking is available. This makes an ideal base from which to explore beautiful north Norfolk.

**Rooms:** 4 en suite (4 GF) **S** fr £40; **D** £75–£90 **Facilities:** FTV DVD Lounge tea/coffee WiFi **Parking:** 5 **Notes:** LB

## HORNING
Map 13 TG31

### Innkeeper's Lodge Norfolk Broads, Horning

★★★ INN

tel: 08451 551551 *(Calls cost 2p per minute plus your phone company's access charge)*
**10 Lower Street NR12 8AA**
email: info@innkeeperslodge.com web: www.innkeeperslodge.com

At Innkeeper's Lodge you'll find accommodation with comfort and character in equal measure, and everything needed for a relaxing stay, from easy check-in and free parking to complimentary breakfast and a cosy pub serving great value food and drink on the doorstep. Each Lodge has quality rooms, and there are Lodges in a variety of locations from towns and cities to countryside settings across the UK.

**Rooms:** 8 en suite (3 fmly) **Facilities:** FTV tea/coffee Dinner available WiFi

## HUNSTANTON
Map 12 TF64

### The Neptune Restaurant with Rooms

★★★★ 🍽🍽🍽 RESTAURANT WITH ROOMS

tel: 01485 532122 **85 Old Hunstanton Road, Old Hunstanton PE36 6HZ**
email: reservations@theneptune.co.uk web: www.theneptune.co.uk
dir: *On A149, past Hunstanton, 200mtrs on left after post office*

This charming 18th-century coaching inn, now a restaurant with rooms, is ideally situated for touring the Norfolk coastline. The smartly appointed bedrooms are brightly finished with co-ordinated fabrics and hand-made New England furniture. Public rooms feature white clapboard walls, polished dark wood floors, fresh flowers and Lloyd Loom furniture. Obviously, the food is very much a draw here with the carefully prepared, award-winning cuisine using excellent local produce; from oysters and mussels from Thornham to quinces grown on a neighbouring farm.

**Rooms:** 5 en suite **S** fr £160; **D** fr £260* **Facilities:** FTV tea/coffee Dinner available Direct dial WiFi 🔒 **Parking:** 6 **Notes:** No children 10yrs Closed 2 weeks Nov & 3 weeks Jan RS Oct–Apr closed Mon

HUNSTANTON *continued*

## Gemini Lodge Guest House

★★★★ GUEST ACCOMMODATION

**tel:** 01485 533902 **5 Alexandra Road PE36 5BT**
**web:** www.geminilodgehunstanton.co.uk

Gemini Lodge Guest House is in an elevated position close to the centre of town and seafront. The bedrooms are smartly decorated in neutral colours with lovely co-ordinated soft furnishings and fabrics; some rooms have lovely views of the sea. Public rooms include a smart lounge with plush sofas, and breakfast is served at a large communal table in the contemporary dining room.

**Rooms:** 3 en suite **Facilities:** FTV TVL tea/coffee **Parking:** 3 **Notes:** LB

## The King William IV Country Inn & Restaurant

★★★★ ⬤ INN

**tel:** 01485 571765 **Heacham Road, Sedgeford PE36 5LU**
**email:** info@thekingwilliamsedgeford.co.uk **web:** www.thekingwilliamsedgeford.co.uk
**dir:** *A149 to Hunstanton, right at Norfolk Lavender in Heacham onto B1454, signed Docking. 2m to Sedgeford*

Tucked away in the village of Sedgeford, close to Norfolk's beautiful coast line, The King William IV Country Inn & Restaurant is a family-run inn that has been welcoming travellers and locals since 1836. The menu offers classic dishes, complemented by daily specials and seasonal offerings, and guests can enjoy a drink outside in summer months. Bedrooms are full of character and offer a comfortable stay.

**Rooms:** 9 en suite (4 fmly) **S** £80–£90; **D** £105–£110* **Facilities:** Lounge tea/coffee Dinner available WiFi ⛳18 ⚿ **Extras:** Speciality toiletries **Parking:** 60 **Notes:** LB

## The White Cottage

★★★ GUEST ACCOMMODATION

**tel:** 01485 532380 **19 Wodehouse Road PE36 6JW**

A charming cottage situated in a quiet side road in Old Hunstanton, The White Cottage has been owned and run by Mrs Burton for 30 years. The spacious bedrooms are attractively decorated, and some have lovely sea views. There is a cosy sitting room with a television.

**Rooms:** 3 rms (1 en suite) (1 pri facs) **D** £76–£80* **Facilities:** TVL tea/coffee WiFi ⚿ **Parking:** 4 **Notes:** LB No children 10yrs

## Old Marine Inn

★★★ INN

**tel:** 01485 533310 **10 St Edmunds Terrace PE36 5EH**
**email:** administrator@marinebar.demon.co.uk **web:** www.marinehotelhunstanton.com

Situated in the centre of Hunstanton, some rooms benefit from sea views, and all generally provide good levels of comfort. A range of dining options are available with either a bar meal in the Marine bar below or for something more special in the Steak and Stilton Restaurant, which offers a good range of à la carte dishes.

**Rooms:** 10 rms **Facilities:** FTV tea/coffee Dinner available WiFi ⛳ **Parking:** 10

**KING'S LYNN** Map 12 TF62

## Linden Bed & Breakfast

★★★★ 🍽 BED AND BREAKFAST

**tel:** 01485 609198 & 07867 686216 **Station Road PE31 6DE**
**email:** info@lindenbedandbreakfast.co.uk **web:** www.lindenbedandbreakfast.co.uk
**dir:** *From A148 onto B1153 signed Congham, 200mtrs on left before St Mary's church*

In a modern house, Linden Bed & Breakfast offers three individual, well-appointed en suite bedrooms along with a spacious guest lounge, a pretty garden overlooking the Norfolk countryside and a family-style breakfast/dining room. In the warmer months, cream teas are available and light suppers can also be arranged with prior notice.

**Rooms:** 3 en suite **S** £55–£70; **D** £70–£85* **Facilities:** FTV iPod docking station TVL tea/coffee WiFi ⚿ **Extras:** Speciality toiletries – complimentary **Parking:** 5 **Notes:** No children 12yrs

**LITCHAM** Map 13 TF81

## Bramley

★★★★ BED AND BREAKFAST

**tel:** 01328 701592 & 07778 783412 **Weasenham Road PE32 2QT**
**email:** bramleybandb@hotmail.co.uk **web:** www.bramley-litcham.co.uk
**dir:** *A1065 onto B1145. Left at x-rds, left at school, 4th house on left*

A warm welcome awaits at Bramley, a delightful detached house, set in a peaceful location on the fringe of the village, with ample safe parking in generous grounds. The mostly spacious bedrooms are thoughtfully furnished to ensure guest comfort and have smartly appointed en suite shower rooms. A hearty, freshly-cooked breakfast is served at individual tables in the separate, elegant dining room.

**Rooms:** 4 en suite (1 fmly) **S** £40–£45; **D** £75–£85* **Facilities:** FTV tea/coffee WiFi ⚿ **Parking:** 4 **Notes:** LB

**LITTLE PLUMSTEAD** Map 13 TG31

## Wayside B&B

★★★★ BED AND BREAKFAST

**tel:** 01603 721827 & 07769 655682 **Honeycombe Road NR13 5HY**
**email:** info@littleplumsteadbedandbreakfast.com
**web:** www.littleplumsteadbedandbreakfast.com
**dir:** *From A47 follow signs for Little Plumstead & Witton. At x-rds in Little Plumstead into Honeycombe Rd, immediately on left*

Wayside B&B is a charming house conveniently located close to Norwich and the Norfolk Broads and is set in the pretty village of Little Plumstead. Bedrooms are comfortable and very well equipped. Guests can relax on the terrace, and the continental breakfast offer a very good choice. Free WiFi is available along with secure parking.

**Rooms:** 3 en suite 3 annexe en suite (2 fmly) (4 GF) **S** £44–£49; **D** £59–£69* **Facilities:** FTV TVL tea/coffee WiFi ⚿ **Conf:** Max 8 Board 8 **Parking:** 6

## LODDON
Map 13 TM39

# The Loddon Swan
★★★★ ◉◉ INN

**tel:** 01508 528039 **23 Church Plain NR14 6LX**
**email:** info@theloddonswan.co.uk **web:** www.theloddonswan.co.uk
**dir:** A146 exit signed High Bungay Rd. Follow road into Loddon High St

The Loddon Swan is situated in the centre of Loddon, just a minute's walk from the River Chet. This popular 18th-century inn offers modern accommodation. Dinner is available in the attractive restaurant overlooking a patio garden, and guests can enjoy viewing the gallery of original artwork. Good use is made of seasonal and local produce in some innovative and enjoyable dishes.

**Rooms:** 7 annexe en suite (5 GF) **D** £80–£130* **Facilities:** FTV tea/coffee Dinner available WiFi Pool table **Conf:** Max 30 Thtr 30 Class 20 Board 20 **Parking:** 20

## NORTH WALSHAM
Map 13 TG23

# Scarborough Hill Country Inn
★★★★ ⬦ INN

**tel:** 01692 402151 **Old Yarmouth Road NR28 9NA**
**email:** reservations@scarboroughhillcountryinn.co.uk
**web:** www.scarboroughhillcountryinn.co.uk

Set in five acres of landscaped gardens, Scarborough Hill Country Inn enjoys a quiet rural setting a short drive from the historic village of North Walsham. The inn offers a range of individually styled well-appointed bedrooms. The charming bar has several local ales, a good wine list and guests can relax by the log fire on colder evenings. Dinner is served in the conservatory restaurant and there is an extensive menu with a strong emphasis on local produce. WiFi is available and there is ample secure parking.

**Rooms:** 8 en suite 1 annexe en suite (1 fmly) (1 GF) **Facilities:** FTV DVD TVL tea/coffee Dinner available Direct dial WiFi ⬥ ⬧ **Extras:** Speciality toiletries, hand-made fudge **Conf:** Max 80 Thtr 60 Class 50 Board 22 **Parking:** 50
**Notes:** Civ wed 70

## NORWICH
Map 13 TG20

### Premier Collection

# Brasteds
★★★★★ ◉◉ ⬧ RESTAURANT WITH ROOMS

**tel:** 01508 491112 **Manor Farm Barns, Fox Road NR14 7PZ**
**email:** enquiries@brasteds.co.uk **web:** www.brasteds.co.uk
**dir:** A11 onto A47 towards Great Yarmouth, then A146. 0.5m, right into Fox Rd, 0.5m on left

Brasteds is a lovely detached property set in 20 acres of mature, landscaped parkland on the outskirts of Norwich. The tastefully appointed bedrooms have beautiful soft furnishings and fabrics along with comfortable seating and many thoughtful touches. Public rooms include a cosy snug with plush sofas, and a smart dining room where breakfast is served. Dinner is available in Brasteds Restaurant, which can be found in an adjacent building.

**Rooms:** 6 en suite (1 fmly) (3 GF) **Facilities:** FTV DVD iPod docking station TVL tea/coffee Dinner available Direct dial WiFi ⬧ **Extras:** Mini-bar **Conf:** Max 120 Thtr 120 Class 100 Board 40 **Parking:** 50 **Notes:** LB Civ wed 160

### Premier Collection

# 38 St Giles
★★★★★ ⬧ GUEST ACCOMMODATION

**tel:** 01603 662944 & 07492 050098 **38 Saint Giles Street NR2 1LL**
**email:** booking@38stgiles.co.uk **web:** www.38stgiles.co.uk

38 St Giles is a stunning Georgian, Grade II listed building that is situated in the centre of Norwich and offers boutique accommodation. All rooms are en suite and have benefited from recent refurbishment. Each contains high quality furnishings, including Bang and Olufsen televisions, and free WiFi. Guests are welcomed with home-made cake on arrival, and breakfast offers a wide selection of locally sourced and organic products.

**Rooms:** 8 en suite (1 fmly) (1 GF) **S** £95–£110; **D** £140–£240* **Facilities:** FTV Lounge tea/coffee WiFi **Extras:** Speciality toiletries, home-made cakes, flowers **Parking:** 3

# Gothic House Bed & Breakfast
★★★★ ⬧ BED AND BREAKFAST

**tel:** 01603 631879 **King's Head Yard, Magdalen Street NR3 1JE**
**email:** charvey649@aol.com **web:** www.gothic-house-norwich.com
**dir:** Follow signs for A147, exit at rdbt past flyover into Whitefriars. Right into Fishergate, at end, right into Magdalen St

Gothic House Bed & Breakfast is an elegant Grade II listed Regency town house set in a quiet courtyard in the heart of Norwich. The property retains much of its original character and the spacious bedrooms are individually decorated and have many thoughtful touches. Breakfast, which includes locally sourced produce, is served in the elegant dining room.

**Rooms:** 2 rms (2 pri facs) **S** £65–£75; **D** £95–£105* **Facilities:** STV FTV tea/coffee WiFi ⬧ **Extras:** Speciality toiletries **Parking:** 2 **Notes:** No children 18yrs Closed Feb

NORWICH *continued*

## The Old Rectory

★★★★ ◉◉ RESTAURANT WITH ROOMS

**tel:** 01603 700772 **103 Yarmouth Road, Thorpe St Andrew NR7 0HF**
**email:** enquiries@oldrectorynorwich.com **web:** www.oldrectorynorwich.com
**dir:** *From A47 southern bypass onto A1042 towards Norwich N & E. Left at slip road onto A1042. Follow signs to 'All routes' & Thorpe St Andrew, at mini rdbt left onto A1242. Straight on at lights, entrance on right*

This delightful Grade II listed Georgian property is ideally located in a peaceful area overlooking the River Yare, just a few minutes' drive from the city centre. Spacious bedrooms are individually designed with carefully chosen soft fabrics, plush furniture and many thoughtful touches; many of the rooms overlook the swimming pool and landscaped gardens. Accomplished cooking is offered via an interesting daily-changing menu, which features skilfully prepared local produce.

**Rooms:** 5 en suite 3 annexe en suite **S** £99–£185; **D** £125–£185* **Facilities:** FTV iPod docking station Lounge tea/coffee Dinner available Direct dial WiFi ↘ ⚄
**Extras:** Robes, speciality toiletries **Conf:** Max 14 Thtr 14 Class 10 Board 14
**Parking:** 12 **Notes:** LB Closed 22 Dec–3 Jan RS Sun–Mon No dinner served

## Old Thorn Barn

★★★★ GUEST ACCOMMODATION

**tel:** 01953 607785 & 07894 203208 **Corporation Farm, Wymondham Road NR14 8EU**
**email:** enquiries@oldthornbarn.co.uk **web:** www.oldthornbarn.co.uk
**dir:** *6m SW of Norwich. Follow signs for Lotus Cars from A11 or B1113, on Wymondham Rd*

Old Thorn Barn is a delightful Grade II listed barn situated in a peaceful rural location just a short drive from the city centre. The property has stylish, thoughtfully equipped bedrooms with polished wood floors and antique pine furniture. Breakfast is served in the open-plan barn, which also has a wood-burning stove and a cosy lounge area.

**Rooms:** 5 en suite 2 annexe en suite (7 GF) **S** £41–£47; **D** £71–£77* **Facilities:** FTV TVL tea/coffee WiFi ⚄ **Parking:** 14

## Cringleford Guest House

★★★★ GUEST HOUSE

**tel:** 01603 451349 & 07775 725933 **1 Gurney Lane, Cringleford NR4 7SB**
**email:** robandkate@cringlefordguesthouse.co.uk **web:** www.cringlefordguesthouse.co.uk
**dir:** *From A11 & A47 Thickthorn rdbt follow signs to Norwich, 0.25m slip road to Cringleford, left at junct into Colney Ln. Gurney Ln 5th on right*

Cringleford Guest House is a delightful property, situated just a short drive from the hospital, University of East Anglia and major roads. The pleasant, well-equipped bedrooms have co-ordinated fabrics and pine furniture. Breakfast is served at individual tables in the smart dining room.

**Rooms:** 5 en suite 1 annexe en suite (3 fmly) (1 GF) **Facilities:** FTV DVD TVL tea/coffee WiFi ⚄ **Conf:** Max 10 Thtr 10 Class 10 Board 10 **Parking:** 6 **Notes:** LB

## Church Farm

★★★★ GUEST ACCOMMODATION

**tel:** 01603 898020 & 898582 **Church Street, Horsford NR10 3DB**
**email:** churchfarmgh@aol.com **web:** www.churchfarmgh.co.uk
**dir:** *5m NW of city centre. A140 onto B1149, right at x-rds*

Church Farm is set in a peaceful rural location just a short drive from Norwich airport and the city centre. The spacious bedrooms are smartly decorated, pleasantly furnished and have many considerate extras. Breakfast is served at individual tables in the conservatory-style lounge-dining room, which overlooks the garden and sun terrace.

**Rooms:** 10 en suite (1 fmly) (3 GF) **Facilities:** FTV TVL tea/coffee WiFi **Parking:** 20

## Salhouse Lodge Inn

★★★★ INN

**tel:** 01603 782828 **Vicarage Road, Salhouse NR13 6HD**
**email:** thelodgeinn@hotmail.co.uk **web:** www.salhouselodge.co.uk
**dir:** *From A1042 (ring road), NE of Norwich centre, exit at lights into Salhouse Rd signed New Rackheath. Through New Rackheath to Salhouse. Left onto B1140 signed Wroxham. Right in Vicarage Rd at sign for inn*

Situated on the outskirts of Norwich, this former rectory has extensive gardens and enjoys a peaceful rural location close to the Norfolk Broads. All the bedrooms are of a high standard and are very well equipped. Evening meals are served available and the log fire really comes into its own on cooler evenings.

**Rooms:** 7 en suite (2 fmly) **Facilities:** FTV tea/coffee Dinner available WiFi ⚲18 Pool table ⚄ **Parking:** 50 **Notes:** LB

## Innkeeper's Lodge Norwich

★★★ INN

**tel:** 08451 551551 *(Calls cost 2p per minute plus your phone company's access charge)*
**18-22 Yarmouth Road NR7 0EF**
**email:** info@innkeeperslodge.com **web:** www.innkeeperslodge.com

Ideally located close to the beautiful city of Norwich, with its medieval architecture, and the Norfolk Broads, this Innkeeper's Lodge has 14 well appointed bedrooms. All are attractively presented and well-equipped, and free WiFi is available. Set beside the banks of the River Yare the large garden is a pleasant place in the warmer months. There is a very popular restaurant and the lounge is spacious and comfortable.

**Rooms:** 14 en suite (5 fmly) **Facilities:** FTV tea/coffee Dinner available WiFi **Parking:** 16

*See also Cromer*

### Premier Collection

## The Eiders Bed & Breakfast

★★★★★ BED AND BREAKFAST

---
**tel:** 01263 837280 **Holt Road, Aylmerton NR11 8QA**
**email:** enquiries@eiders.co.uk **web:** www.eiders.co.uk
**dir:** *From Cromer on A148, enter Aylmerton, pass garage on left. After x-rds, 2nd entrance on right*

The Eiders Bed & Breakfast is just a short drive from the centre of Sheringham and is ideally placed for touring the north Norfolk coast. The tastefully appointed bedrooms have lovely co-ordinated fabrics and many extras. Breakfast is served at individual tables in the conservatory which overlooks the gardens and a duck pond. Guests have the use of a heated swimming pool which is open from May to September.

**Rooms:** 6 en suite (1 fmly) (6 GF) **Facilities:** FTV DVD iPod docking station TVL tea/coffee WiFi ⊀ ⚲ **Extras:** Bottled water – complimentary **Parking:** 7 **Notes:** LB

## Roman Camp Inn

★★★★ ⊜ INN

---
**tel:** 01263 838291 **Holt Road, Aylmerton NR11 8QD**
**email:** enquiries@romancampinn.co.uk **web:** www.romancampinn.co.uk
**dir:** *On A148 between Sheringham & Cromer, approx 1.5m from Cromer*

Roman Camp Inn provides spacious, tastefully appointed bedrooms with a good range of useful facilities including hairdryers. Five rooms are presented as deluxe, and two are suitable for disabled guests. Public rooms include a smart conservatory-style restaurant, a comfortable open-plan lounge/bar and a dining area. Room service is available, guests have complimentary use of local leisure facilities, and there is ample free parking.

**Rooms:** 15 en suite (1 fmly) (10 GF) **S** £75; **D** £120–£160* **Facilities:** FTV DVD Lounge TVL tea/coffee Dinner available Direct dial WiFi Fishing Free use of nearby leisure complex & pool **Extras:** Home-made biscuits **Conf:** Max 20 Thtr 20 Class 20 Board 20 **Parking:** 50 **Notes:** LB Closed 25–26 Dec

## Bay Leaf Guest House

★★★ GUEST HOUSE

---
**tel:** 01263 823779 **10 St Peters Road NR26 8QY**
**email:** bayleafgh@aol.com **web:** www.bayleafbandb.co.uk
**dir:** *A149 Cromer road into Station Rd. 1st left into Station Approach, 2nd right into St Peters Rd*

This lovely Victorian property is ideally situated just a short walk from the golf course, steam railway and town centre. There is a small lounge bar, and breakfast is served in the conservatory-dining room which overlooks the patio. Bedrooms vary in size and style, all are comfortable.

**Rooms:** 7 en suite (2 fmly) (2 GF) **S** £55; **D** £78–£80 **Facilities:** FTV tea/coffee Licensed **Parking:** 5 **Notes:** LB No children 8yrs

## The Rose & Crown

★★★★ ⑧ INN

---
**tel:** 01485 541382 **Old Church Road PE31 7LX**
**email:** info@roseandcrownsnettisham.co.uk **web:** www.roseandcrownsnettisham.co.uk
**dir:** *A149 towards Hunstanton. In village centre into Old Church Rd, 100yds on left*

This lovely village inn provides comfortable, well-equipped bedrooms. A range of quality meals is served in the many dining areas, complemented by a good variety of real ales and wines. Service is friendly and a delightful atmosphere prevails. A walled garden is available on sunny days, as is a children's play area.

**Rooms:** 16 en suite (4 fmly) (2 GF) **S** £100–£125; **D** £120–£140* **Facilities:** FTV Lounge tea/coffee Dinner available WiFi ⚲ ⚲ **Extras:** Speciality toiletries, milk, home-made biscuits **Conf:** Max 80 **Parking:** 60 **Notes:** LB

## Queen Victoria

★★★ INN

---
**tel:** 01485 541344 **19 Lynn Road PE31 7LW**
**email:** info@orchardaccountancy.co.uk **web:** www.queenvictoriasnettisham.com

The Queen Victoria is located in the coastal village of Snettisham, close to the beach, not far from Sandringham. Comfortable accommodation is provided to the rear of the property, and guests can enjoy an evening meal with a good range of cask ales in this traditional inn. In warmer months guests can relax with a drink outside on the terrace, while the children play in the playground with a pirate ship and magic tree.

**Rooms:** 5 rms **Facilities:** Dinner available

## The Ingham Swan

★★★★ ⑧⑧ RESTAURANT WITH ROOMS

---
**tel:** 01692 581099 **Sea Palling Road, Ingham NR12 9AB**
**email:** info@theinghamswan.co.uk **web:** www.theinghamswan.co.uk
**dir:** *From A149 Stalham, into Old Market Rd towards Upper Staithe Rd/Lower Staithe Rd. At rdbt 1st exit, 2nd exit at next rdbt into Ingham Rd. Continue to Town Rd*

The Swan is a charming 14th-century former coaching inn that has been sympathetically restored and enjoys a peaceful rural location in the heart of Norfolk. Stylish, very well equipped bedrooms are most comfortable and the eye-catching original features really add to the presentation. The award-winning restaurant serves the best of Norfolk produce and there is a small bar area for pre-dinner drinks. Secure parking is available along with free WiFi for guests.

**Rooms:** 4 annexe en suite (1 fmly) (2 GF) **S** £105–£115; **D** £125–£145*
**Facilities:** FTV tea/coffee Dinner available WiFi **Parking:** 12 **Notes:** Closed 25–26 Dec

## THORPE MARKET
Map 13 TG23

### Premier Collection

## The Green House B&B

★★★★★ ☕ ☛ GUEST ACCOMMODATION

**tel:** 01263 834701 & 07786 195213 **Cromer Road NR11 8TH**
**email:** greenhouse.norfolk@btinternet.com **web:** www.greenhousenorfolk.co.uk
**dir:** *A140 in village of Roughton, right at mini rdbt into Thorpe Market Rd. After 1.5m turn right at x-rds, 200yds on left*

Situated only four miles away from both Cromer and the beach, a very warm welcome is offered by Rosanna and Simon who have both worked at various top hotels in London. This 16th-century property has been carefully modernised throughout, offering high quality and comfort. Plenty of care has been taken to retain period pieces of the property. Dinner can be pre-arranged and a comfortable lounge and bar area is also available for guests to relax. An attractive garden is also available for guests to use during summer months.

**Rooms:** 5 en suite **S** £85–£99; **D** £85–£99* **Facilities:** FTV DVD iPod docking station Lounge tea/coffee Dinner available Licensed WiFi ♨18 ♨
**Extras:** Speciality toiletries, sweets – complimentary **Parking:** 6
**Notes:** No children 14yrs

## The Barns at Thorpe Market

★★★★ ☕ GUEST ACCOMMODATION

**tel:** 01263 833033 **Common Lane NR11 8TP**
**email:** info@bedbreakfastnorfolk.com **web:** www.bedbreakfastnorfolk.com
**dir:** *A140 at Roughton onto B1436. At end turn right onto A149, onto slip road just past bus stop*

This charming 18th-century converted barn offers a range of beautifully presented bedrooms overlooking a central courtyard. The bedrooms are spacious and very comfortable, and original flint walls are a real feature of the property. Thorpe Market is a short drive from Norwich and is close to the Norfolk Broads as well as a number of National Trust properties. Breakfast is served in the vaulted breakfast room, and features the best in local produce. WiFi is available for guests along with secure bike storage.

**Rooms:** 3 en suite (3 GF) **S** £75–£80; **D** £80–£90* **Facilities:** FTV tea/coffee WiFi ♨ **Extras:** Fridge **Parking:** 3 **Notes:** No children 14yrs

## THURSFORD
Map 13 TF93

### Premier Collection

## Holly Lodge

★★★★★ ☕ ☛ BED AND BREAKFAST

**tel:** 01328 878465 **The Street NR21 0AS**
**email:** info@hollylodgeguesthouse.co.uk **web:** www.hollylodgeguesthouse.co.uk
**dir:** *Exit A148 into Thursford (village green on left) 2nd driveway on left past green*

Holly Lodge is an award-winning 18th-century property situated in a picturesque location surrounded by open farmland. The stylish cottage bedrooms are in a converted stable block, each room individually decorated, beautifully furnished and equipped with many useful extras. The attractive public rooms have a wealth of character, with flagstone floors, oak beams and open fireplaces. There are superb landscaped grounds to enjoy.

**Rooms:** 3 en suite (3 GF) **S** £80–£110; **D** £100–£130* **Facilities:** FTV DVD Lounge TVL tea/coffee Dinner available WiFi ♨ **Extras:** Speciality toiletries, wine, home-made cakes – complimentary **Parking:** 5 **Notes:** LB No children 14yrs

## TIVETSHALL ST MARGARET
Map 13 TM18

## Red House Farm Bed & Breakfast

★★★★ BED AND BREAKFAST

**tel:** 01379 676566 & 07719 437007 **Station Road NR15 2DJ**
**email:** office@redhousefarm.info **web:** www.redhousefarm.info
**dir:** *500mtrs from Pulham rdbt A140*

A warm welcome is assured at this delightful 17th-century barn conversion, situated on a small working farm in a peaceful rural location. The tastefully appointed bedrooms have modern furniture and lovely countryside views. Breakfast, which includes home-grown produce, is served at a large communal table in the smart kitchen.

**Rooms:** 1 en suite 2 annexe en suite (3 GF) **S** £45–£50; **D** £75–£85* **Facilities:** FTV tea/coffee WiFi **Parking:** 4

## WELLS-NEXT-THE-SEA
Map 13 TF94

## Kilcoroon

★★★★ BED AND BREAKFAST

**tel:** 01328 710270 & 07733 112108 **Chancery Lane NR23 1ER**
**email:** terry@kilcoroon.co.uk **web:** www.kilcoroon.co.uk
**dir:** *Exit B1105 into Mill Rd. 3rd right into Buttlands. Property on left of Crown Hotel*

Kilcoroon is a delightful, detached period property situated by the green, just off the Buttlands and a short walk from the town centre. The spacious bedrooms are pleasantly decorated with co-ordinated fabrics and equipped with modern facilities. Breakfast is served at a communal table in the elegant dining room.

**Rooms:** 2 en suite **S** fr £75; **D** £95* **Facilities:** FTV DVD tea/coffee WiFi ♨
**Notes:** No children 10yrs Closed 23–31 Dec

## WIVETON
Map 13 TG04

## Wiveton Bell

★★★★ ⊛ INN

**tel:** 01263 740101 **The Green, Blakeney Road NR25 7TL**
**email:** wivetonbell@me.com **web:** www.wivetonbell.com
**dir:** *1m from Blakeney*

Wiveton Bell is situated in a quiet and scenic part of Norfolk. The luxurious bedrooms come complete with a whole host of accessories including flat-screen TVs, Blu-ray/DVD players, complimentary Prosecco, REN toiletries, and Egyptian cotton linens with duck and goose down bedding. Hampers containing continental breakfasts are delivered to the rooms, including fresh pastries from the local baker, and every room has outside seating. Dinner can be taken in the AA Rosette award-winning restaurant and good use is made of fresh and local ingredients.

**Rooms:** 6 en suite (2 GF) **Facilities:** FTV DVD tea/coffee Dinner available WiFi ♨18
**Extras:** Prosecco, speciality toiletries – complimentary **Parking:** 60
**Notes:** No children Closed 25 Dec

## WRENINGHAM
Map 13 TM19

## The Bird In Hand

★★★★ ⚑ INN

**tel:** 01508 489438 **Church Road NR16 1BJ**
**email:** mail@davidbrake.co.uk **web:** www.birdinhandwreningham.com
**dir:** *S of Norwich on B1113*

The Bird In Hand is a family-run free house and restaurant combining all the atmosphere of a traditional British pub with quality food and drink and comfortable surroundings. You are guaranteed a friendly welcome from the whole team who always work hard to ensure your experience is an enjoyable one. There is a large parking area, indoor and outdoor seating areas, restaurant, bar area and above all a friendly atmosphere.

**Rooms:** 8 annexe en suite (8 GF) **S** £80; **D** £80 (room only)* **Facilities:** FTV tea/coffee Dinner available WiFi **Extras:** Speciality toiletries, mineral water **Conf:** Max 60 Thtr 60 Class 60 Board 30 **Parking:** 90

### WROXHAM
Map 13 TG31

## Delaware
★★★★ BED AND BREAKFAST

**tel:** 01603 781947 & 07805 023249 **Tunstead Road, Hoveton NR12 8QN**
**email:** eilidh_villa@hotmail.co.uk **web:** www.delawarewroxham.co.uk
**dir:** *Into Wroxham on A1151, turn left into Horning Rd, then right into Tunstead Rd*

A charming, family-run B&B that is conveniently located close to the centre of Wroxham and the splendid Norfolk Broads. Norwich is a short drive away and Delaware makes an ideal base from which to explore the lovely county of Norfolk. Bedrooms are all comfortable, and freshly cooked breakfasts are served at individual tables. Parking is available, along with free WiFi for guests.

**Rooms:** 3 rms (2 en suite) (1 pri facs) (1 GF) **D** £65–£75* **Facilities:** FTV tea/coffee WiFi ♨ **Extras:** Sweets **Parking.** 4 **Notes:** LB No children 14yrs Closed Dec–Mar

### NORTHAMPTONSHIRE

### ASHBY ST LEDGERS
Map 11 SP56

## Olde Coach House
★★★★ ⊜ INN

**tel:** 01788 890349 **Main Street, Ashby St Ledgers CV23 8UN**
**email:** info@oldecoachhouse.co.uk **web:** www.oldecoachhouse.co.uk
**dir:** *M1 junct 18 onto A428. Follow signs for Daventry (A361), Ashby St Ledgers signed on left*

The Olde Coach House is a delightful old building, offering public areas in keeping with the age of the surroundings, but with all the modern amenities expected by today's guests. There is a large bar and a spacious raised dining area, with open fires and exposed beams. The accommodation is smartly presented; rooms vary in size but all are equipped to the same high standard with TVs, iPod docking stations

and wonderfully comfortable beds. The property benefits from excellent parking and outside areas for dining and drinking.

*Olde Coach House*

**Rooms:** 4 en suite 11 annexe en suite (6 GF) **S** £65–£95; **D** £85–£95* **Facilities:** FTV iPod docking station Lounge tea/coffee Dinner available Direct dial WiFi ⅃18 **Extras:** Robes, speciality toiletries, snacks **Parking:** 30

### DESBOROUGH
Map 11 SP88

## The R Inn
★★★ INN

**tel:** 01536 648050 & 763510 **11-15 Station Road NN14 2RL**
**email:** enquiries@ketteringvenues.co.uk **web:** www.desboroughhotel.co.uk

The R Inn enjoys a prominent position in the peaceful village of Desborough which is located in the heart of the lovely Ise Valley. There is a popular tapas bar along with well-equipped conference facilities, and a selection of stylish bedrooms that have been refurbished to a high standard. Secure parking is available along with free WiFi for guests.

**Rooms:** 14 en suite (2 fmly) (1 GF) **S** £35–£45; **D** £40–£60 (room only)*
**Facilities:** FTV tea/coffee Dinner available WiFi ♨ **Conf:** Max 600 Thtr 400 Class 300 Board 50 **Parking:** 40 **Notes:** Civ wed 600

### EASTON-ON-THE-HILL
Map 11 TF00

## The Exeter Arms
★★★★ ⊜ INN

**tel:** 01780 756321 **21 Stamford Road PE9 3NS**
**email:** reservations@theexeterarms.net
**dir:** *A1 Nbound take exit signed Easton-on-the-Hill; A1 Sbound take exit signed A47/A43 Corby/Kettering, on left entering village*

This lovely village inn is situated in north-eastern Northamptonshire just a short drive from Stamford. The public rooms have many original features such as stone walls and open fireplaces; they include a lounge bar and the Orangery Restaurant which opens out onto the terrace for alfresco dining. The modern, well-equipped bedrooms are very stylish.

**Rooms:** 5 en suite 1 annexe en suite (2 fmly) **S** £70; **D** £75–£100*
**Facilities:** FTV tea/coffee Dinner available Direct dial WiFi ⅃18 **Parking:** 40

## NASSINGTON
Map 12 TL09

### The Queens Head Inn
★★★★ @ INN

tel: 01780 784006 **54 Station Road PE8 6QB**
email: info@queensheadnassington.co.uk web: www.queensheadnassington.co.uk
dir: *A1 Nbound exit junct 17, follow signs for Yarwell, then Nassington. Queens Head on left on entering the village*

The Queens Head Inn offers a friendly atmosphere and a warm welcome, situated on the banks of the River Nene in the picturesque village of Nassington. The adjacent bedrooms are constructed from local stone; each one is smartly appointed and well equipped. Public rooms include a smart lounge bar, a restaurant and a light-filled conservatory dining room.

**Rooms:** 10 en suite (2 fmly) (10 GF) **Facilities:** FTV tea/coffee Dinner available Direct dial WiFi Fishing ♠ **Extras:** Home-made biscuits **Conf:** Max 50 Thtr 50 Class 20 Board 20 **Parking:** 45 **Notes:** LB Civ wed 70

## NORTHAMPTON
Map 11 SP76

### The Hopping Hare
★★★★ @@ INN

tel: 01604 580090 **18 Hopping Hill Gardens, Duston NN5 6PF**
email: info@hoppinghare.com web: www.hoppinghare.com
dir: *Off A428, 2m from centre of Northampton*

Situated in a quiet location just two miles away from Northampton city centre, this inn provides luxury accommodation meeting the needs of holidaymakers and business travellers. Rooms have been attractively decorated with high quality soft furnishings, TVs and free WiFi. Dinner can be enjoyed in the restaurant where the food has been awarded two AA Rosettes. A very good selection of dishes is available, with good use made of fresh quality ingredients sourced by local suppliers.

**Rooms:** 20 en suite (8 fmly) (1 GF) **S** £60–£70; **D** £65–£95* **Facilities:** FTV tea/coffee Dinner available Direct dial WiFi **Parking:** 40

## WEEDON
Map 11 SP65

### Narrow Boat at Weedon
★★★★ @@ INN

tel: 01327 340333 **Stowe Hill, A5 Watling Street NN7 4RZ**
email: info@narrowboatatweedon.co.uk web: www.narrowboatatweedon.co.uk
dir: *M1 junct 16 follow signs to Flore & Weedon. In Weedon at x-rds turn left up hill, on left*

The Narrow Boat at Weedon has a superb location beside the Grand Union Canal, just off the A5. Close to both Milton Keynes and Northampton, it makes an ideal location for those wishing to visit Silverstone and the Althorp Estate. There are seven very comfortable en suite bedrooms at the rear of the property, each with external access. Modern British cuisine and traditional pub classics can be enjoyed in both the bar and the restaurant, which has been awarded two AA Rosettes, or out on the heated decking area in the garden by the canal, weather permitting of course.

**Rooms:** 7 annexe en suite (7 GF) **Facilities:** FTV DVD tea/coffee Dinner available WiFi **Conf:** Max 30 Class 30 Board 30 **Parking:** 40

## NORTHUMBERLAND

## ALNWICK
Map 21 NU11

### The Hogs Head Inn
★★★ ⌐ INN

tel: 01665 606576 & 0191 580 3610 **Hawfinch Drive, Cawledge NE66 2BF**
email: info@hogsheadinnalnwick.co.uk web: www.hogsheadinnalnwick.co.uk
dir: *A1 to Alnwick, follow signs for Cawledge Park*

Named after the inn featured in the Harry Potter books, the Hogs Head opened in July 2012. It is ideally located just off the A1, on the edge of Alnwick close to the castle and gardens. It offers comfortable, spacious and well-equipped bedrooms, and WiFi throughout the whole property. The bar and restaurant serve tasty dishes in comfortable, informal surroundings. This purpose-built inn also offers external seating and dining.

**Rooms:** 53 en suite (9 fmly) (25 GF) **Facilities:** FTV Lounge TVL tea/coffee Dinner available Lift WiFi ♿18 **Parking:** 125

## BEADNELL
Map 21 NU23

### The Craster Arms
★★★★ INN

tel: 01665 720272 & 07958 678280 **The Wynding NE67 5AX**
email: michael@crasterarms.co.uk web: www.crasterarms.co.uk
dir: *From A1 junct at Brownieside Head East, through Preston and Chathill to Beadnell*

Parts of The Craster Arms date back to the 15th century. The property has it all – open fire, beer garden and spacious well-appointed, comfortable bedrooms. The bar serves real ales along with good quality food using local produce and offers generous portion sizes. Well located in the peaceful village of Beadnell and just a short drive to the beach, Seahouses and Bamburgh with world famous Craster kippers available for breakfast.

**Rooms:** 3 en suite (2 fmly) (1 GF) **Facilities:** FTV TVL tea/coffee Dinner available WiFi ♿18 Pool table **Parking:** 20

## BELFORD
Map 21 NU13

### Premier Collection

### Market Cross Guest House
★★★★★ ♀ GUEST HOUSE

tel: 01668 213013 & 07595 453208 **1 Church Street NE70 7LS**
email: info@marketcrossbelford.co.uk web: www.marketcrossbelford.co.uk
dir: *Exit A1 into village, opposite church*

Market Cross Guest House goes from strength to strength; the owners have added their own personal slant to the property. Comfortable bedrooms have a whole array of personal touches including Nespresso machines, home baking and mini-fridges.

**Rooms:** 4 en suite **S** £60–£100; **D** £70–£110* **Facilities:** FTV iPod docking station tea/coffee WiFi ♠ **Extras:** Home-made snacks, mini-fridge, robes, speciality toiletries **Parking:** 4 **Notes:** No children 10yrs Closed 23–28 Dec

## Post Office House Bed & Breakfast

★★★★ ☕ BED AND BREAKFAST

**tel:** 01668 219622 **2 Church Street NE70 7LS**
**email:** enquiries@postofficehouse.com **web:** www.postofficehouse.com
**dir:** *From A1 follow signs for Belford, into village centre, opposite St Marys Church*

Post Office House was built in 1893 as a dedicated post office with its own sorting room and telegraph facilities. More recently it has been lovingly restored and made into a B&B. Inside are high quality fixtures, fittings and many thoughtful extras. Hospitality is excellent, and enhanced with home baking as well as the offer of some famous Lindisfarne Mead. Breakfast is a highlight of the stay. A wonderful location close to the coastal areas of Bamburgh and Seahouses but just a few minutes from the A1. The Cheviots are also in easy striking distance.

**Rooms:** 3 en suite (1 GF) **S** £75–£85; **D** £85–£95* **Facilities:** FTV tea/coffee WiFi
🔒 **Extras:** Nespresso machine, speciality toiletries, robes, slippers **Parking:** 3
**Notes:** No children 12yrs Closed 24–26 Dec

---

**BERWICK-UPON-TWEED**      **Map 21 NT95**

### Premier Collection

## The Captain's Quarters

★★★★★ GUEST ACCOMMODATION

**tel:** 01289 763209 & 07591 598574 **1 Sallyport, Off Bridge Street TD15 1EZ**
**email:** info@sallyport.co.uk **web:** www.the-captainsquarters.co.uk

The Captain's Quarters is located in the heart of the Old Town, and is a Grade II listed town house dating back to the 17th century. All bedrooms are individually designed and presented to a high standard. Stairs have to be negotiated to all bedrooms, and rooms at the top have sloping roofs. Very good extras are provided as standard with high quality decor, artwork, objets d'art and fittings. Rooms are sold on a room-only basis with breakfast charged and served in your bedroom. Warm and genuine hospitality is a given.

**Rooms:** 5 en suite **S** £95–£120; **D** £95–£120 (room only)* **Facilities:** STV DVD tea/coffee WiFi 🔒

## The Rob Roy Inn

★★★★ INN

**tel:** 01289 306428 **Dock Road, Tweedmouth TD15 2BE**
**email:** therobroy@hotmail.co.uk **web:** www.robroyberwick.co.uk

The Rob Roy Inn enjoys views over the Tweed estuary and across to the historical border town of Berwick-upon-Tweed, this family-run inn offers high standards of accommodation. The small bar is warm and welcoming and well used by guests and locals alike. Dinner (residents only) is served in the Harbour Lights Restaurant, and offers good quality food and great value for money. The town centre is only a five-minute walk whilst Spittle beach and promenade is just 10 minutes in the opposite direction.

**Rooms:** 5 en suite (1 fmly) **S** £50–£70; **D** £70–£75* **Facilities:** tea/coffee Dinner available WiFi 🔒 **Notes:** Closed 25 Dec RS Sun & Mon No evening meal

## Lindisfarne Inn

★★★ INN

**tel:** 01289 381223 **Beal TD15 2PD**
**email:** enquiries@lindisfarneinn.co.uk **web:** www.lindisfarneinn.co.uk
**dir:** *Exit A1 for Holy Island*

The Lindisfarne Inn stands on the site of the old Plough Hotel at Beal, on the road leading to Holy Island. The inn has a traditional bar, rustic-style restaurant and comfortably equipped, courtyard bedrooms in the adjacent wing. Food is available all day.

**Rooms:** 23 annexe en suite (20 fmly) (11 GF) **Facilities:** FTV TVL tea/coffee Dinner available WiFi 🔒 **Parking:** 25

---

**BLYTH**      **Map 21 NZ38**

## The Commissioners Quay Inn

★★★ INN

**tel:** 01670 335060 **Quay Road NE24 3AF**
**email:** enquiries@cqi-blyth.com **web:** www.commissionersquayinn.com

The Commissioners Quay Inn is the latest addition to The Inn Collection. This purpose-built inn offers high levels of comfort and quality along with wonderful hospitality and customer care. Spacious modern bedrooms are well appointed, and some rooms facing the sea have their own private balcony and seating. The large bar and restaurant area serves food all day with a great selection of real ales and cocktails. There is ample car parking, with a charging point available for an electric car.

**Rooms:** 40 en suite (8 fmly) **Facilities:** FTV tea/coffee Dinner available Lift WiFi 🔒 **Parking:** 90

---

**CHATTON**      **Map 21 NU02**

## Percy Arms

★★★★ ☕ ☕ INN

**tel:** 01668 215244 **Main Street NE66 5PS**
**email:** percyarmschatton@gmail.com **web:** www.percyarmschatton.co.uk
**dir:** *From A1 onto B6348 signed Chatton, on Main Rd*

The Percy Arms is ideally located in the tranquil village of Chatton just a short drive from the A1. Alnwick, Seahouses, Bamburgh and Holy Island are all easily accessible, as are some wonderful beaches on the Northumbrian coastline. Refurbished to a very high standard, bedrooms and their en suites are luxurious and comfortable. The pub boasts a number of local real ales and offers a warm welcome. The decor is sympathetic to the age and style of the building, and there is a good mix of locals and residents. The food is good, with the relaxed menu making the best of what local suppliers have to offer.

**Rooms:** 5 en suite (3 fmly) **Facilities:** FTV tea/coffee Dinner available WiFi ⚡18
🔒 **Extras:** Robes **Conf:** Max 40 Thtr 40 Class 40 Board 40 **Parking:** 30 **Notes:** LB Civ wed 60

## CRAMLINGTON  Map 21 NZ27

## Innkeeper's Lodge Cramlington

★★★ INN

**tel:** 08451 551551 *(Calls cost 2p per minute plus your phone company's access charge)*
**Blagdon Lane NE23 8AU**
**email:** info@innkeeperslodge.com **web:** www.innkeeperslodge.com

At Innkeeper's Lodge you'll find accommodation with comfort and character in equal measure, and everything needed for a relaxing stay, from easy check-in and free parking to complimentary breakfast and a cosy pub serving great value food and drink on the doorstep. Each Lodge has quality rooms, and there are Lodges in a variety of locations from towns and cities to countryside settings across the UK.

**Rooms:** 18 en suite (4 fmly) (10 GF) **Facilities:** FTV tea/coffee Dinner available Direct dial WiFi **Parking:** 50

## FALSTONE  Map 21 NY78

## Pheasant Inn

★★★★ ⬚ ⬚ INN

**tel:** 01434 240382 **Stannersburn NE48 1DD**
**email:** stay@thepheasantinn.com **web:** www.thepheasantinn.com
**dir:** *From A69 (N of Hexham) take A6079 signed Otterburn & Bellingham. Left onto B6320 signed Bellingham. Before Bellingham follow Hesleyside sign, then signs for Kielder & Stannersburn*

Pheasant Inn is a traditional, charming country inn; it has character, good food and warm hospitality. Bright modern bedrooms, some with their own entrances, can be found in stone buildings adjoining the inn. Delicious home-cooked meals are served in the bar with its low-beamed ceilings and exposed stone walls, or in the attractive dining room. Dogs are welcome by arrangement.

**Rooms:** 8 annexe en suite (1 fmly) (5 GF) **Facilities:** tea/coffee Dinner available WiFi ⌗18 ⬚ **Extras:** Speciality toiletries **Parking:** 40 **Notes:** LB Closed 4 days Xmas RS Nov–Mar closed Mon & Tue

## The Blackcock Country Inn and Restaurant

★★★★ INN

**tel:** 01434 240200 **NE48 1AA**
**email:** thebcinn@yahoo.co.uk **web:** www.blackcockinn.co.uk
**dir:** *From Hexham take A6079 to Bellingham, then left at church. In village centre, towards Kielder Water*

This traditional, family-run village inn lies close to Kielder Water and offers wonderful hospitality. Inside it is cosy with a homely atmosphere; welcoming fires burning in the colder weather. The bedrooms are very comfortable and well equipped; evening meals are served here or in the restaurant. During the winter months the inn has reduced opening hours, please check ahead.

**Rooms:** 6 rms (4 en suite) (2 pri facs) (1 fmly) **S** £50–£65; **D** £85* **Facilities:** STV TVL tea/coffee Dinner available WiFi ⬚ Fishing Pool table ⬚ Children's play area Clay pigeon shooting **Extras:** Robes, chocolates; pet menus – chargeable **Parking:** 15 **Notes:** LB RS Tue–Wed closed during low season

## FELTON  Map 21 NU10

## Birchwood House

★★★★ ⬚ GUEST ACCOMMODATION

**tel:** 01670 787828 **Kitswell Dene NE65 9NZ**
**email:** gbblewitt@btinternet.com **web:** www.birchwood-house.co.uk
**dir:** *Just off A1. Take 2nd Swarland exit, bear left, left again*

Ideally located for the A1, this spacious house combines very high standards of accommodation with warmth and great hospitality. Modern bedrooms and en suites cater well for the needs of the guest, and a fantastic large lounge is also made available. A well-cooked breakfast will set you up for your day regardless of your planned activities.

**Rooms:** 3 en suite (3 GF) **Facilities:** FTV iPod docking station TVL tea/coffee WiFi **Parking:** 20 **Notes:** No children 14yrs

## The Northumberland Arms

★★★★ ⬚ INN

**tel:** 01670 787370 **The Peth, West Thirston NE65 9EE**
**email:** thenorthumberlandarmsfelton@gmail.com
**web:** www.northumberlandarms-felton.co.uk
**dir:** *From A1, follow signs for coastal route/Felton*

The Northumberland Arms enjoys a wonderful location just a mile away from the A1. Built back in the 1820s by the 3rd Duke of Northumberland as a coaching inn, it overlooks the River Coquet. The standards are high in all areas from the warm and welcoming bar to the conservatory and main restaurant. Bedrooms are very well appointed combining the age and character of the building with quality furniture, fixtures and fittings. Finishing touches are provided with an array of luxurious extras which are the icing on the cake. Look for real ales and award-winning food which uses the best that Northumbria's larder has to offer.

**Rooms:** 6 en suite (1 fmly) **S** £133–£175; **D** £140–£185* **Facilities:** FTV tea/coffee Dinner available Direct dial WiFi ⌗9 **Conf:** Max 35 Thtr 35 Class 35 Board 35 **Parking:** 20 **Notes:** LB Civ wed 40

## FORD  Map 21 NT93

## The Estate House

★★★★ GUEST HOUSE

**tel:** 01890 820668 & 07436 266951 **TD15 2PX**
**email:** admin@theestatehouse.info **web:** www.theestatehouse.info
**dir:** *1m from A697, follow signs to Ford on B6354*

Located in the heart of peaceful Ford village, this Edwardian house is set in its own mature gardens. A pet-friendly house that offers spacious, well-appointed accommodation with well-dressed and comfortable beds. A guests' lounge is available and during the day, the property runs a popular tea room. A wonderful base from which to tour this area of Northumberland.

**Rooms:** 4 rms (3 en suite) (1 pri facs) (1 fmly) **Facilities:** FTV DVD iPod docking station TVL tea/coffee Dinner available Licensed WiFi ⬚ Fishing ⬚ **Extras:** Bottled water – complimentary

*Opposite: Hadrian's Wall, Northumberland*

## HAYDON BRIDGE
Map 21 NY86

# Old Repeater Station

★★★★ BED AND BREAKFAST

tel: 01434 688668 & 07941 238641 **Military Road, Grindon NE47 6NQ**
email: les.gibson@tiscali.co.uk **web:** www.hadrians-wall-bedandbreakfast.co.uk
dir: *See website for directions*

Old Repeater Station started life out as one of a number of buildings used as Repeater Stations for British Telecom on their Newcastle to Carlisle line. Now converted into a bed and breakfast it enjoys an enviable location roughly half way along the world famous Hadrian's Wall. The Old Repeater Station offers simple practical accommodation, an ideal stop off point for people walking the wall or for guests looking to explore this historic area. Dinner by arrangement for walkers and cyclists with drying room facilities available. Family-style breakfast uses quality locally sourced produce. A comfortable lounge is available, as well as seating in the garden overlooking Sewingshield Crags.

**Rooms:** 4 en suite (1 fmly) (2 GF) **S** £65–£69; **D** £79* **Facilities:** FTV TVL tea/coffee Dinner available Licensed WiFi 🔒 **Parking:** 4 **Notes:** Closed Nov–Feb

## LONGFRAMLINGTON
Map 21 NU10

# The Granby Inn

★★★ 🍴 INN

tel: 01665 570228 & 570362 **NE65 8DP**
email: info@thegranbyinn.co.uk **web:** www.thegranbyinn.co.uk
dir: *Off A1 onto A697 signed Coldstream. On right in Longframlington*

The Granby Inn is a traditional, family-run coaching inn dating back over 250 years, situated in the heart of the village. Bedrooms are comfortable and some have wonderful views right to the coast. Food is a real strength here and the team take great pride in their locally sourced produce. The bar is welcoming and reservations to eat are always recommended.

**Rooms:** 5 en suite **S** £45; **D** £55–£85* **Facilities:** FTV DVD tea/coffee Dinner available Direct dial WiFi 🔒 **Parking:** 24 **Notes:** LB Closed 25–26 Dec, 1 Jan

## MORPETH
Map 21 NZ28

### Premier Collection

# Eshott Hall

★★★★★ ◉◉ GUEST ACCOMMODATION

tel: 01670 787454 **Eshott NE65 9EN**
email: info@eshotthall.co.uk **web:** www.eshotthall.co.uk
dir: *A1 Northbound from Morpeth 5m. A1 Southbound from Alnwick 15m*

Eshott Hall dates back to the 16th century and is set behind walled gardens in the heart of Northumberland, just a few miles from the A1. Bedrooms are extremely comfortable and very well appointed in keeping with the style and character of the house. Award-winning food uses the best from the local larder with public areas offering a real 'wow' factor.

**Rooms:** 17 en suite (3 fmly) (3 GF) **Facilities:** Dinner available 🦢 🦆
**Notes:** Civ wed 80

## NEWTON-ON-THE-MOOR
Map 21 NU10

# The Cook and Barker Inn

★★★★ 🍴 INN

tel: 01665 575234 **NE65 9JY**
email: info@cookandbarkerinn.co.uk **web:** www.cookandbarkerinn.co.uk
dir: *North on A1, pass Morpeth. A1 becomes single carriageway for 8m, then dual carriageway. Up slight incline 3m, follow signs on left to Newton-on-the-Moor*

Set in the heart of a quiet village, this inn is popular with visitors and locals. The emphasis is on food here with interesting home-made dishes offered in the restaurant and bar areas. Bedrooms are smartly furnished and well equipped, and are split between the main house and the adjacent annexe.

**Rooms:** 1 en suite 15 annexe en suite (2 fmly) (7 GF) **S** £89–£170; **D** £109–£170* **Facilities:** FTV tea/coffee Dinner available Direct dial WiFi **Conf:** Max 50 Thtr 50 Class 50 Board 25 **Parking:** 64 **Notes:** LB

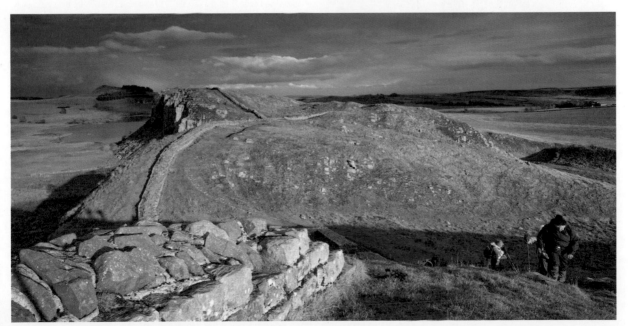

## SEAHOUSES                                   Map 21 NU23

### The Olde Ship Inn
★★★★ 🛏 INN

tel: 01665 720200 **NE68 7RD**
email: theoldeship@seahouses.co.uk web: www.seahouses.co.uk
dir: *Lower end of main street above harbour*

Under the same ownership since 1910, this friendly inn overlooks the harbour and is full of character. Lovingly maintained, its sense of history is evident in the amount of nautical memorabilia on display. Public areas include a character bar, a cosy snug, a restaurant and a guests' lounge. The individual bedrooms are smartly presented. Two separate buildings contain executive apartments, all with sea views.

**Rooms:** 12 en suite 6 annexe en suite (4 GF) **S** £48; **D** £96–£133* **Facilities:** FTV Lounge TVL tea/coffee Dinner available Direct dial WiFi Pool table 🛋 **Parking:** 18 **Notes:** LB No children 10yrs Closed Dec–Jan

### Bamburgh Castle Inn
★★★ INN

tel: 01665 720283 **NE68 7SQ**
email: enquiries@bamburghcastleinn.co.uk web: www.bamburghcastleinn.co.uk
dir: *A1 onto B1341 to Bamburgh, B1340 to Seahouses, follow signs to harbour*

Situated in a prime location on the quayside, this establishment has arguably the best view along the coast. Dating back to the 18th century, the inn has superb dining and bar areas, with outside seating available in warmer weather. There are smart, comfortable bedrooms, many with views of the Farne Islands and the inn's famous namesake, Bamburgh Castle.

**Rooms:** 33 en suite (6 fmly) (8 GF) **Facilities:** FTV TVL tea/coffee Dinner available WiFi ⚓18 🛋 **Parking:** 35 **Notes:** LB

## STOCKSFIELD                                 Map 21 NZ06

### Premier Collection

### The Duke of Wellington Inn
★★★★★ 🍽 🛏 INN

tel: 01661 844446 Newton **NE43 7UL**
email: info@thedukeofwellingtoninn.co.uk web: www.thedukeofwellingtoninn.co.uk
dir: *Off A69, follow signs to Newton, 3m from Corbridge*

Set in the peaceful village of Newton in the Tyne Valley, The Duke of Wellington Inn is reputedly one of Northumberland's oldest pubs. Located close to Corbridge, in Hadrian's Wall country, not far from Newcastle and just minutes from the A69, the inn offers high standards of accommodation, food and hospitality. Generous sized bedrooms have quality beds, bedding and branded toiletries, with every small detail taken care of. The busy bar and restaurant make great used of the best local produce. Terraces outside allow the guest to make the best of the fine weather.

**Rooms:** 7 en suite **S** £85–£95; **D** £110–£140* **Facilities:** FTV DVD iPod docking station tea/coffee Dinner available Direct dial WiFi ⚓36 🛋 **Extras:** Speciality toiletries **Parking:** 30

## THROPTON                                    Map 21 NU00

### The Three Wheat Heads
★★★★ 🛏 INN

tel: 01669 620262 **NE65 7LR**
email: info@threewheatheads.co.uk web: www.threewheatheads.co.uk
dir: *On B6341 2m N of Rothbury*

The Three Wheat Heads is located on the edge of the Northumberland National Park just a few miles from Rothbury. All bedrooms are decorated to a high standard, and most offer picture-postcard views of the local countryside. Good food is served in a choice of areas with a beer garden to the rear also available.

**Rooms:** 5 en suite (1 fmly) **S** £50; **D** £80* **Facilities:** FTV tea/coffee Dinner available WiFi ⚓18 Fishing 🛋 **Parking:** 14 **Notes:** LB

## NOTTINGHAMSHIRE

## BLIDWORTH                                   Map 16 SK55

### The Black Bull
★★★★ ⚫⚫ INN

tel: 01623 490222 Main Street **NG21 0QH**
email: info@blackbullblidworth.co.uk web: www.blackbullblidworth.co.uk
dir: *M1 junct 27, A608 E, left at Derby rdbt, right onto B6020. Into Blidworth, 1st right after St Marys Church*

The Black Bull in the village of Blidworth can trace its history as an ale house back to the 17th century. It has recently been refurbished to a high standard in a contemporary manner, but has still kept many traditional features. The inn provides a comfortable and friendly environment in which to have a drink; the restaurant provides a wide range of well-cooked, good quality, locally-sourced dishes, and the rooms are spacious and encourage a good night's sleep.

**Rooms:** 4 en suite (1 fmly) **Facilities:** FTV iPod docking station tea/coffee Dinner available WiFi ⚓18 🛋 Local cycle hire with discount **Extras:** Bottled water, biscuits **Parking:** 6 **Notes:** Closed 24–25 Dec, 31 Dec

| COTGRAVE | Map 11 SK63 |

## Jerico Farm

★★★★ 🥄 FARMHOUSE

**tel:** 01949 81733 **Fosse Way NG12 3HG**
**email:** info@jericofarm.co.uk **web:** www.jericofarm.co.uk
**dir:** Off A46, signed Kinoulton. N of junct with A606

A friendly relaxed atmosphere is offered at Jerico Farm, an attractive building, which stands in the beautiful Nottinghamshire countryside just off the A46, close to Nottingham, Trent Bridge and the National Water Sports Centre. Day rooms include a comfortable lounge, and a separate dining room in which substantial, tasty breakfasts are served overlooking the gardens. Spacious bedrooms are individually appointed and thoughtfully equipped.

**Rooms:** 3 en suite (1 fmly) **Facilities:** FTV TVL tea/coffee WiFi Fishing
**Extras:** Speciality toiletries **Parking:** 4 **Notes:** No children 10yrs Closed 24 Dec–2 Jan 150 acres mixed

| EDWINSTOWE | Map 16 SK66 |

## The Forest Lodge

★★★★ INN

**tel:** 01623 824443 **Church Street NG21 9QA**
**email:** reception@forestlodgehotel.co.uk **web:** www.forestlodgehotel.co.uk
**dir:** A614 into Edwinstowe. On B6034, opposite St Mary's church

Situated in the heart of Sherwood Forest, The Forest Lodge is a 17th-century coaching inn that provides the visitor with a warm and homely base from which to explore this fascinating and historic area. The bedrooms have been tastefully finished and the bar provides home comforts and good company. Food is served in the bar and in the restaurant.

**Rooms:** 8 en suite 5 annexe en suite (2 fmly) (5 GF) **S** £75; **D** £90* **Facilities:** FTV tea/coffee Dinner available WiFi ♨️36 🛁 **Extras:** Speciality toiletries – complimentary **Conf:** Max 75 Thtr 75 Class 45 Board 50 **Parking:** 37

| ELTON | Map 11 SK73 |

### Premier Collection

## The Grange

★★★★★ BED AND BREAKFAST

**tel:** 07887 952181 **Sutton Lane NG13 9LA**
**email:** d.bmasson@btinternet.com **web:** www.thegrangebedandbreakfastnotts.co.uk
**dir:** From Grantham A1 onto A52 to Elton x-rds, left 200yds, B&B on right

Parts of this lovely house date back to the early 17th century and the rooms command fine views across the gardens and rolling open countryside. Bedrooms contain many thoughtful extras and fine hospitality is assured from the proprietors. There is also a lounge as well as a reading room for residents' use, both furnished in warm tones with welcoming soft sofas and wood-burning stoves.

**Rooms:** 3 en suite **S** £50–£59; **D** £85–£90* **Facilities:** FTV DVD Lounge TVL tea/coffee WiFi 🛁 **Extras:** Chocolate, snacks, orange juice, water – complimentary **Parking:** 8 **Notes:** 🚭

| HOLME PIERREPONT | Map 11 SK63 |

## Holme Grange Cottage

★★★ GUEST ACCOMMODATION

**tel:** 0115 981 0413 **Adbolton Lane NG12 2LU**
**email:** jean.colinwightman@talk21.com **web:** www.holmegrangecottage.co.uk
**dir:** Exit A52 SE of Nottingham onto A6011. After 500yds turn right into Regatta Way, 1.25m on right

Holme Grange Cottage is ideally located in a quiet location opposite the National Water Sports Centre, and only three miles away from Nottingham city centre. The cottage has its own all-weather tennis court – ideal for the active guest. Indeed, when not providing warm hospitality and freshly cooked breakfasts, the proprietor is often on the golf course, and can advise on the best places locally to play.

**Rooms:** 3 rms (1 en suite) (1 fmly) **S** £36–£42; **D** £62–£68* **Facilities:** FTV TVL tea/coffee WiFi ♨️ 🛁 **Parking:** 6 **Notes:** Closed Xmas

| MANSFIELD | Map 16 SK56 |

## Bridleways Holiday Homes & Guest House

★★★★ GUEST HOUSE

**tel:** 01623 635725 **Newlands Road, Forest Town NG19 0HU**
**email:** bridleways@outlook.com **web:** www.stayatbridleways.co.uk
**dir:** From Mansfield take B6030 towards New Clipstone. Right at rdbt, follow Crown Farm Industrial Park sign. 1st left into Newlands Rd. Guest house on left

Beside a quiet bridleway that leads to Vicar Water Country Park and Sherwood Pines Forest Park, this friendly guest house is a good touring base for walking, cycling or sightseeing. The double, twin and family bedrooms are particularly spacious and all are en suite. Lovely breakfasts are served in a cottage-style dining room.

**Rooms:** 9 cn suite (1 fmly) (2 GF) **S** £45; **D** £78* **Facilities:** FTV tea/coffee WiFi 🛁 **Parking:** 14

| NEWARK-ON-TRENT | Map 17 SK75 |

## Compton House

★★★★ 🥄 🍽 GUEST HOUSE

**tel:** 01636 708670 **117 Baldertongate NG24 1RY**
**email:** info@comptonhousenewark.com **web:** www.comptonhousenewark.com
**dir:** 500yds SE of town centre. B6326 into Sherwood Av, 1st right into Baldertongate

Located a short walk from Newark's central attractions, this elegant period house provides high standards of comfort. Individually themed bedrooms come with a wealth of thoughtful extras and smart modern bathrooms. Comprehensive breakfasts, and wholesome dinners (by arrangement), are served in the attractive dining room and a lounge is available.

**Rooms:** 7 rms (6 en suite) (1 pri facs) (1 fmly) (1 GF) **S** £55–£95; **D** £98  £130* **Facilities:** FTV Lounge tea/coffee Dinner available WiFi 🛁 **Extras:** Magazines, mineral water – complimentary **Conf:** Max 10 Thtr 10 Class 10 Board 10 **Parking:** 2 **Notes:** Closed Xmas

NEWARK-ON-TRENT *continued*

## The Hollies

★★★★ BED AND BREAKFAST

**tel:** 01636 707486 & 07880 722323 **41 Victoria Street NG24 4UU**
**email:** caroline@theholliesnewark.co.uk **web:** caroline@theholliesnewark.co.uk
**dir:** *2.4m to A1, 1m from A46*

The Hollies is located in the historical town of Newark. This beautiful Georgian townhouse offers three attractive boutique style bedrooms each with their own private bathroom or en suite. A wonderful breakfast is offered every morning. The attractive drawing room is an ideal venue for weddings and Caroline offers a Bespoke Bridal package.

**Rooms:** 3 rms (2 en suite) (1 pri facs) **S** £75–£95; **D** £95–£115* **Facilities:** FTV Lounge tea/coffee WiFi **Extras:** Snack machine

### NOTTINGHAM                                      Map 11 SK53

*See also Cotgrave*

#### Premier Collection

## Restaurant Sat Bains with Rooms

★★★★★ ◉◉◉◉◉ RESTAURANT WITH ROOMS

**tel:** 0115 986 6566 **Lenton Lane, Trentside NG7 2SA**
**email:** info@restaurantsatbains.net **web:** www.restaurantsatbains.com
**dir:** *M1 junct 24, A453 Nottingham S. Over River Trent into central lane to rdbt. Left, left again towards river. Establishment on left after bend*

This charming restaurant with rooms, a stylish conversion of Victorian farm buildings, is situated on the river and close to the industrial area of Nottingham. The bedrooms create a warm atmosphere by using quality soft furnishings together with antique and period furniture; suites and four-poster rooms are available. Public areas are chic and cosy, and the delightful restaurant complements the truly outstanding, much acclaimed cuisine.

**Rooms:** 7 en suite **Facilities:** STV tea/coffee Dinner available **Parking:** 22 **Notes:** No children 8yrs Closed 1st week Jan & 2 weeks mid Aug

## The Yellow House

★★★★ BED AND BREAKFAST

**tel:** 0115 926 2280 **7 Littlegreen Road, Woodthorpe NG5 4LE**
**email:** suzanne.prewsmith1@gmail.com **web:** www.bandb-nottingham.co.uk
**dir:** *Exit A60 (Mansfield Rd) N from city centre into Thackeray's Ln, over rdbt, right into Whernside Rd to x-rds, left into Littlegreen Rd, house on left*

This semi-detached private house is in an easily-accessible and quiet residential suburb to the north-east of the city. The one purpose-built bedroom contains many thoughtful extras. A warm welcome is assured here and the proprietors' pet dog is also very friendly.

**Rooms:** 1 en suite **S** £50–£60; **D** £60–£80* **Facilities:** FTV tea/coffee WiFi 🐾 **Parking:** 1 **Notes:** No children Closed 24–26 & 31 Dec, 1 Jan

## Innkeeper's Lodge Nottingham, Lowdham

★★★ INN

**tel:** 08451 126116 & 551551 *(Calls to both numbers cost 2p per minute plus your phone company's access charge)* **Old Epperstone Road, Lowdham NG14 7BZ**
**email:** info@innkeeperslodge.com **web:** www.innkeeperslodge.com
**dir:** *From city centre follow A612, signed Southwell onto A6097 (Epperstone bypass). Through Lowdham, left into Old Epperstone Rd*

This very well-presented building has had a makeover, creating a fresh and contemporary look in cream and grey. There is a range of comfortable seating to either relax or dine in, and the menu offers a good range of pub staples or more refined dishes.

**Rooms:** 11 en suite (1 fmly) **S** £59–£69; **D** £59–£69* **Facilities:** FTV tea/coffee Dinner available WiFi **Parking:** 30 **Notes:** LB

### RETFORD                                          Map 17 SK78

#### Premier Collection

## Blacksmiths

★★★★★ ◉◉ RESTAURANT WITH ROOMS

**tel:** 01777 818171 **Town Street, Clayworth DN22 9AD**
**email:** info@blacksmithsclayworth.com **web:** www.blacksmithsclayworth.com
**dir:** *From A631, 2.4m to Clayworth*

Blacksmiths is a modern restaurant with annexed accommodation, situated in the quiet village of Clayworth, and a short drive from Retford. Meals in the restaurant are one of the many highlights of the stay, as are the hearty breakfasts which can be delivered as room-service. Modern gadgets and accessories are provided such as climate control, large widescreen TVs, and WiFi. Thoughtful extras such as fluffy bathrobes and luxurious toiletries add to the experience. A warm welcome is guaranteed at this owner-run establishment.

**Rooms:** 4 en suite (2 fmly) (2 GF) **Facilities:** FTV iPod docking station tea/coffee Dinner available WiFi 🐾 **Conf:** Max 120 Thtr 70 Class 20 Board 20 **Parking:** 31 **Notes:** Civ wed 70

### TORWORTH                                         Map 16 SK68

## The Separatist Inn

★★★★ 🍽 INN

**tel:** 01777 816807 **Great North Road DN22 8NW**
**email:** info@theseparatistinn.com **web:** www.theseparatistinn.com

This modern inn is located in the small village of Torworth. Bedrooms are completed to a high standard and are named after various Pilgrim Fathers. Facilities such as complimentary WiFi, TVs and well-stocked hospitality trays are all offered, as well as a very good range of complimentary toiletries. Award-winning evening meals can be enjoyed in the main restaurant and bar area. On-site parking also provided.

**Rooms:** 6 en suite **S** £70–£150; **D** £70–£150* **Facilities:** FTV tea/coffee Dinner available WiFi **Parking:** 30

## Acorn Lodge

★★★★ GUEST ACCOMMODATION

**tel:** 01909 478383 **85 Potter Street S80 2HL**
**email:** info@acornlodgeworksop.co.uk **web:** www.acornlodgeworksop.co.uk
**dir:** *A1 onto A57. Take B6040 (town centre) through Manton. Lodge on right, 100mtrs past Priory*

Originally part of the community house of the Priory Church, this property has been modernised to offer comfortable, well-appointed accommodation. Good breakfasts are served in the pleasant breakfast room and ample private parking is available at the rear.

**Rooms:** 7 en suite (2 fmly) **S** £50–£60; **D** £70–£80* **Facilities:** FTV tea/coffee WiFi ⚓ **Parking:** 15

## OXFORDSHIRE

### Premier Collection

## B&B Rafters

★★★★★ ⓢ BED AND BREAKFAST

**tel:** 01865 391298 & 07824 378720 **Abingdon Road, Marcham OX13 6NU**
**email:** enquiries@bnb-rafters.co.uk **web:** www.bnb-rafters.co.uk
**dir:** *A34 onto A415 towards Witney. Rafters on A415 in Marcham adjacent to pedestrian crossing, on right*

Set amid immaculate gardens, this modern house is built in a half-timbered style and offers spacious accommodation together with a warm welcome. Bedrooms are stylishly furnished and equipped in a boutique style, and come with a range of homely extras. Comprehensive breakfasts feature local and organic produce when possible.

**Rooms:** 4 en suite **S** £60–£67; **D** £115–£139* **Facilities:** FTV DVD iPod docking station Lounge tea/coffee WiFi **Extras:** Speciality toiletries, bottled water – complimentary **Parking:** 4 **Notes:** No children 12yrs

**Find out more about AA Rosettes**
– see page 11

## Abbey Guest House

★★★★ BED AND BREAKFAST

**tel:** 01235 537020 & 0/976 627252 **136 Oxford Road OX14 2AG**
**email:** info@abbeyguest.uk **web:** www.abbeyguest.uk
**dir:** *1m from A34 Sbound, exit at North Abingdon*

A warm welcome is assured at Abbey Guest House. This well maintained property offers very comfortable, modern bedrooms with many useful extras and a relaxed atmosphere. Terry's business ethos is firmly focused on accessibility, and the guest house's website offers comprehensive information on the facilities available for disabled guests. There are a couple of local pubs nearby as well as very good bus links to Oxford from just outside the property. Freshly prepared breakfasts are served in the airy dining room overlooking the garden. Free WiFi is available throughout the house and off-road parking is provided.

**Rooms:** 7 en suite (2 fmly) (1 GF) **S** £90; **D** £120 **Facilities:** FTV DVD Lounge tea/coffee Lift WiFi ⚓ **Extras:** Use of fridge & microwave, guest PC **Parking:** 7

## The Lambert

★★★★ ⊛ ⓢ INN

**tel:** 01844 351496 **London Road OX49 5SQ**
**email:** info@thelamberthotel.com **web:** www.thelamberthotel.com
**dir:** *M40 junction 6, follow signs to Chinnor (B4009) then left to Thame (A40)*

Retaining original and historical features, this lovely coaching inn combines the feel of an old pub with a modern twist. You'll find a comfortable and friendly bar with log fires, real ales and a mouth-watering array of food, including favourite pub classics using fresh, seasonal locally sourced produce.

**Rooms:** 9 rms (8 en suite) (1 pri facs) 35 annexe en suite (13 fmly) (16 GF) **Facilities:** FTV tea/coffee Dinner available Direct dial Lift WiFi ⅃18 Gym ⚓ **Conf:** Max 140 Thtr 120 Class 62 Board 38 **Parking:** 75 **Notes:** Civ wed 120

## BANBURY
Map 11 SP44

### The Three Pigeons Inn
★★★★ ✿ INN

**tel:** 01295 275220 **3 Southam Road OX16 2ED**
**email:** manager@thethreepigeons.com **web:** www.thethreepigeons.com
**dir:** *M40 junct 11 onto A422 signed Banbury. Left at Southam Road rdbt onto A361. Inn on left at lights*

Located in the centre of Banbury this 17th-century coaching inn offers high levels of quality and comfort. Individually styled bedrooms with well-equipped bathrooms overlook the attractive courtyard garden. Low beams and uneven floors add to the inn's charm. Guests can enjoy a drink in the comfortable bar, and should not miss the carefully prepared dishes at dinner. Free WiFi and on-site parking available.

**Rooms:** 3 en suite (1 fmly) **Facilities:** STV FTV tea/coffee Dinner available Direct dial WiFi **Conf:** Max 20 Thtr 20 Class 20 Board 20 **Parking:** 11

### Ashlea Guest House
★★★★ GUEST HOUSE

**tel:** 01295 250539 & 07818 431429 **58 Oxford Road OX16 9AN**
**email:** enquiry@ashleaguesthouse.co.uk **web:** www.ashleaguesthouse.co.uk
**dir:** *M40 junct 11, follow signs to Banbury. At 2nd rdbt take 1st exit (Concord Avenue), next rdbt 1st exit. Through 3 sets of lights, then into right hand lane at 4th set of lights, opposite junction*

Ashlea Guest House is a family-run establishment where the husband and wife team ensure their guests are warmly welcomed and made to feel at home. There is a choice of well-presented rooms to match all budgets. The guest house is the perfect base to explore the historic town of Banbury or the beautiful Cotswold countryside. Ashlea Guest House was a finalist for the AA Friendliest B&B of the Year award 2017-2018.

**Rooms:** 6 rms (5 en suite) (1 pri facs) 6 annexe en suite (1 fmly) (5 GF)
**Facilities:** FTV DVD tea/coffee WiFi **Parking:** 13 **Notes:** LB

### Horse & Groom Inn
★★★★ ⬚ INN

**tel:** 01295 722142 & 07774 210943 **Milcombe OX15 4RS**
**email:** horseandgroominn@gmail.com **web:** www.thehorseandgroominn.co.uk
**dir:** *M40 junct 11, A422 towards Banbury. Onto A361 signed Chipping Norton, past Bloxham turn right signed Milcombe. At end of village*

This 17th-century coaching house is a traditional village pub with a good atmosphere, friendly service and comfortable, well-appointed bedrooms. The restaurant offers a good choice of well-prepared and tasty dishes. The establishment is convenient for Banbury, Stratford-upon-Avon and the Cotswolds.

**Rooms:** 4 en suite (1 fmly) **Facilities:** FTV DVD iPod docking station tea/coffee Dinner available WiFi ⌁18 Fishing **Conf:** Max 40 Thtr 40 Class 30 Board 20 **Parking:** 20

## BURFORD
Map 5 SP21

### The Angel at Burford
★★★★ ✿ INN

**tel:** 01993 822714 **14 Witney Street OX18 4SN**
**email:** enquiries@theangelatburford.co.uk **web:** www.theangelatburford.co.uk

Just off the high street in the picturesque market town of Burford, this 16th-century coaching inn features beamed ceilings and open fires. Guests can dine well in the restaurant, and the character bedrooms are thoughtfully equipped. Service is friendly here and families, children and dogs are all welcome.

**Rooms:** 3 en suite **D** £110–£140* **Facilities:** FTV DVD iPod docking station Lounge tea/coffee Dinner available WiFi **Extras:** Refreshments – complimentary **Notes:** LB

### The Maytime Inn
★★★★ ⬚ ⬚ INN

**tel:** 01993 822068 **Asthall OX18 4HW**
**email:** info@themaytime.com **web:** www.themaytime.com

This country inn has retained its country charm albeit with some modern enhancement, and is located just a few miles outside Burford, known as 'The gateway to the Cotswolds'. The six en suite bedrooms are all individual in design, and offer a very comfortable stay. Food is available every day.

**Rooms:** 2 en suite 4 annexe en suite (6 GF) **S** £90–£130; **D** £95–£160 **Facilities:** FTV iPod docking station tea/coffee Dinner available Direct dial WiFi **Petanque pitch **Extras:** Speciality toiletries **Conf:** Max 22 Thtr 15 Class 15 Board 22 **Parking:** 30 **Notes:** LB

### The Bull at Burford
★★★★ ✿✿ ⬚ INN

**tel:** 01993 822220 **105 High Street OX18 4RG**
**email:** info@bullatburford.co.uk **web:** www.bullatburford.co.uk
**dir:** *In town centre*

Situated in the heart of a pretty Cotswold town, The Bull was originally built in 1475 as a rest house for the local priory. It now has stylish, attractively presented bedrooms that reflect plenty of charm and character. Dinner is a must and the award-winning restaurant has an imaginative menu along with an excellent choice of wines. Lunch is served daily and afternoon tea is popular. There is a residents' lounge, and free WiFi is available.

**Rooms:** 15 en suite 3 annexe en suite (1 fmly) (3 GF) **S** £69–£85; **D** £85–£130*
**Facilities:** STV FTV Lounge tea/coffee Dinner available WiFi **Parking:** 6 **Notes:** LB

## The Golden Pheasant Inn

★★★★ INN

tel: 01993 823223 **91 High Street OX18 4QA**
email: bournehospitality@hotmail.co.uk web: www.goldenpheasantburford.com

This attractive inn is set on Burford's main street and dates, in part, back to the 16th century. Bedrooms vary in size but are well furnished with attractive fabrics and some period furniture. The bar and open-plan restaurant is full of character, and lunch and dinner are served here daily.

**Rooms:** 12 rms (11 en suite) (1 pri facs) 6 annexe en suite (5 GF) **S** £65–£195; **D** £65–£195 **Facilities:** FTV TVL tea/coffee Dinner available WiFi **Parking:** 8 **Notes:** Closed 24 Dec RS 25 Dec No accommodation, bar open

### CHIPPING NORTON                                      Map 10 SP32

#### Premier Collection

## The Feathered Nest Country Inn

★★★★★   INN

tel: 01993 833030 **OX7 6SD**
email: info@thefeatherednestinn.co.uk web: www.thefeatherednestinn.co.uk

*(For full entry see Nether Westcote (Gloucestershire))*

## Wild Thyme Restaurant with Rooms

★★★★ ◉◉ RESTAURANT WITH ROOMS

tel: 01608 645060 **10 New Street OX7 5LJ**
email: enquiries@wildthymerestaurant.co.uk web: www.wildthymerestaurant.co.uk
dir: *On A44 in town centre off market square*

Set in the bustling Cotswold market town of Chipping Norton, this restaurant with rooms offers three en suite bedrooms that are individually designed, well equipped, and have many thoughtful extras. The restaurant serves exciting Modern British food that is presented with relaxed and friendly service.

**Rooms:** 3 en suite **S** £65–£85; **D** £75–£105* **Facilities:** FTV DVD tea/coffee Dinner available WiFi **Extras:** Mineral water, home-made biscuits

### CULHAM                                                Map 5 SU59

## The Railway Inn

★★★ INN

tel: 01235 528046 **Station Road OX14 3BT**
email: info@railwayinnculham.co.uk web: www.railwayinnculham.co.uk
dir: *2.5m SE of Abingdon-on-Thames on A415. Turn left signed Culham railway station*

The Railway Inn is located beside Culham railway station and is the perfect base to explore Abingdon-on-Thames, Didcot and Oxford. The inn offers a choice of comfortable and affordable rooms, a selection of real ales and home cooked food. In addition, there is a permanent marquee in the garden, which is suitable for all occasions.

**Rooms:** 6 rms (5 en suite) (1 pri facs) 4 annexe en suite (2 fmly) **Facilities:** FTV Lounge TVL tea/coffee Dinner available WiFi ♨ **Parking:** 30

### FARINGDON                                             Map 5 SU29

#### Premier Collection

## Buscot Manor B&B

★★★★★ BED AND BREAKFAST

tel: 01367 252225 & 07973 831690 **SN7 8DA**
email: romneypargeter@hotmail.co.uk web: www.buscotmanor.co.uk

Delightfully located in a peaceful village, Buscot Manor dates from 1692 and is full of character and quality. Guests are welcome to use the two comfortable lounges in addition to the pleasant gardens, where tea may be enjoyed in the summer months. The two upper-floor bedrooms have traditional four-poster beds. A more contemporary room is located on the ground floor. Breakfast is taken around one large table in the elegant dining room.

**Rooms:** 2 en suite 1 annexe en suite (3 fmly) (1 GF) **Facilities:** FTV DVD Lounge TVL tea/coffee WiFi ♨ Fishing Gym ♨ Watersports weekends available **Extras:** Speciality toiletries, fruit, snacks **Conf:** Max 12 Board 12 **Parking:** 30

## The Trout Inn

★★★★ ◉ INN

tel: 01367 870382 **Buckland Marsh SN7 8RF**
email: info@troutinn.co.uk web: www.troutinn.co.uk
dir: *A420 Swindon to Oxford road, turn signed Bampton. Inn 2m on right*

Located in a tranquil location just a couple of miles from the village of Bampton and within a short distance to the Cotswolds, this refurbished inn offers stylish and comfortably appointed accommodation. The inn boasts many original features including original flagstone flooring and exposed beams yet tastefully revamped with modern furnishings and roaring log-burners. Located right on the River Thames with a large beer garden. A hearty breakfast is served daily in the restaurant and lunch and dinner is available throughout the week.

**Rooms:** 6 en suite (1 fmly) (4 GF) **Facilities:** STV tea/coffee Dinner available Direct dial WiFi **Extras:** Speciality toiletries **Conf:** Max 20 Thtr 20 Class 20 Board 20 **Parking:** 25 **Notes:** Civ wed

## The Eagle

★★★★ ◉◉ INN

tel: 01367 241879 **Little Coxwell SN7 7LW**
email: eaglelittlecoxwell@gmail.com web: www.eagletavern.co.uk
dir: *M4 junct 15, A419, A420 signed Oxford, right into village*

Located in the peaceful village of Little Coxwell, in the beautiful Vale of the White Horse, The Eagle is a traditional inn with a welcoming atmosphere and a selection of real ales. The upstairs bedrooms, in a range of shapes and sizes, are very stylish and offer good comfort and ease of use. At both breakfast and dinner there's a variety of carefully prepared, quality dishes to choose from.

**Rooms:** 6 en suite **Facilities:** FTV Lounge tea/coffee Dinner available WiFi ♨ **Notes:** LB

FARINGDON *continued*

## The Bell

★★★ INN

tel: 01367 358050 **13 Market Place SN7 7HP**
email: bellhotelfar@aol.com web: www.thebellhotelonline.co.uk

With a history dating back to the 14th century, this family-run inn is located in the engaging town of Faringdon, a handy base from which to explore the local area. There is character at every turn, with low beams, uneven floors and period features, all contributing to the building's individuality. Bedrooms offer a number of configurations, while public rooms include a choice of dining areas and an atmospheric bar. An extensive menu is offered with popular favourites and daily specials.

**Rooms:** 8 en suite **Facilities:** tea/coffee Dinner available WiFi

| GORING | Map 5 SU68 |
|---|---|

## The Miller of Mansfield

★★★★ ◉◉ RESTAURANT WITH ROOMS

tel: 01491 872829 & 07702 853413 **High Street RG8 9AW**
email: reservations@millerofmansfield.com web: www.millerofmansfield.com
dir: *M4 junct 12, S on A4 towards Newbury. 3rd rdbt onto A340 to Pangbourne. A329 to Streatley, right at lights onto B4009 into Goring*

The frontage of this former coaching inn hides sumptuous rooms furnished in a distinctive and individual style. The two AA Rosette award-winning restaurant serves appealing dishes using locally sourced ingredients, and there is a comfortable bar, which serves real ales, fine wines and afternoon tea; a bar menu provides quick bites to eat.

**Rooms:** 13 en suite (2 fmly) **D** £99–£180* **Facilities:** FTV Lounge tea/coffee Dinner available WiFi Boat hire & beauty therapies can be arranged **Extras:** Speciality toiletries **Conf:** Max 12 Board 12 **Parking:** 2 **Notes:** LB Closed 26–27 Dec

| HENLEY-ON-THAMES | Map 5 SU78 |
|---|---|

## Phyllis Court Club

★★★★ 🛏 GUEST ACCOMMODATION

tel: 01491 570500 **Marlow Road RG9 2HT**
email: enquiries@phylliscourt.co.uk web: www.phylliscourt.co.uk
dir: *A404 onto A4130 into town centre. Follow A4155, 150mtrs on right*

Phyllis Court was founded in 1906 as a private members' club and has welcomed many distinguished visitors over the years. Set in 18 acres, with lawns sweeping down to the Thames, it offers a unique blend of traditional elegance and modern comforts. The club takes centre stage during Henley Royal Regatta week, being positioned opposite the finishing line. The individually styled bedrooms are well appointed and very comfortable. There is restricted meal service two days before and after the regattas in June and July. An excellent range of function venues is available, and the Grade II listed Grandstand Pavilion is perfect for weddings.

**Rooms:** 17 en suite **D** £145–£380* **Facilities:** FTV Lounge TVL tea/coffee Dinner available Direct dial Lift Licensed WiFi 🏃 **Extras:** Speciality toiletries, trouser press, magazines **Conf:** Max 250 Thtr 250 Class 100 Board 30 **Parking:** 200 **Notes:** RS 26–28 Dec, 2–3 Jan, regattas Jun–Jul Civ wed 250

## Badgemore Park Golf Club

★★★★ GUEST ACCOMMODATION

tel: 01491 637300 **Badgemore Park, Badgemore RG9 4NR**
email: info@badgemorepark.com web: www.badgemorepark.com

Located close to Henley-on-Thames, this property offers comfortable accommodation in quiet surroundings within the secluded and private walled gardens, situated just 100 metres away from the main clubhouse. In summer months, dinner and a bar are available until 6pm. The venue also caters well for business meetings complete with own lounge and kitchen. Free WiFi available.

**Rooms:** 8 rms annexe (7 en suite) (1 pri facs) (3 fmly) (3 GF) **Facilities:** FTV TVL tea/coffee Licensed WiFi 🏃18 **Extras:** Bottled water **Conf:** Max 120 Thtr 120 Class 60 Board 45 **Parking:** 120 **Notes:** Closed 25 Dec Civ wed 120

## The Baskerville

★★★★ ❀ INN

**tel:** 0118 940 3332 **Station Road, Lower Shiplake RG9 3NY**
**email:** enquiries@thebaskerville.com **web:** www.thebaskerville.com
**dir:** 2m S of Henley in Lower Shiplake. Exit A4155 into Station Rd, inn signed

Located close to Shiplake station and just a short drive from Henley, this smart pub is perfect for a business or leisure break. The accommodation is well equipped and it is a good base for exploring the Oxfordshire countryside and surrounding areas. The award-winning dinner menu, coupled with daily specials, makes good use of local produce.

**Rooms:** 4 en suite (1 fmly) **S** tr £100; **D** fr £110* **Facilities:** FTV tea/coffee Dinner available WiFi ❀ **Extras:** Bottled water, sweets, speciality toiletries – complimentary **Conf:** Max 15 Thtr 15 Class 15 Board 15 **Parking:** 15 **Notes:** Closed 1 Jan

## The Cherry Tree Inn

★★★★ ❀ INN

**tel:** 01491 680430 **Main Street, Stoke Row RG9 5QA**
**email:** enquiries@thecherrytreeinn.co.uk **web:** www.thecherrytreeinn.co.uk
**dir:** On A4155 from Henley-on-Thames exit B481 to Sonning Common. Follow Stoke Row signs, turn right for inn

This 400 year-old building is located in a pretty village on the outskirts of Henley-on-Thames. There are four en suite bedrooms which offer modern comforts and are set adjacent to the public house. A range of high quality wines complement the menus which often feature local produce.

**Rooms:** 4 annexe en suite (4 GF) **S** £65–£85; **D** £85–£100 **Facilities:** FTV Lounge TVL tea/coffee Dinner available WiFi ⅃18 **Extras:** Bottled water **Parking:** 30 **Notes:** LB

## Leander Club

★★★★ ⬭ GUEST ACCOMMODATION

**tel:** 01491 575782 **Leander Way RG9 2LP**
**email:** events@leander.co.uk **web:** www.leander.co.uk
**dir:** M4 junct 8/9 follow signs for Henley (A404M & A4130). Turn right immediately before Henley Bridge to Club & car park

This historic rowing club has opened its doors and made its delightful facilities available to guests. The location is breathtaking, particularly in the morning, when the rowers can be seen setting out on the river. The rooms are each named after various colleges and universities, and each is packed with interesting photos and memorabilia linking them with the Leander Club. Public areas also feature lots of trophies, pictures and artefacts, and it all makes for a most interesting place to stay.

**Rooms:** 11 en suite (1 fmly) **S** £99–£152; **D** £119–£178 **Facilities:** STV FTV Lounge TVL tea/coffee Dinner available Direct dial Lift Licensed WiFi **Extras:** Snacks – complimentary **Conf:** Max 120 Thtr 120 Class 40 Board 20 **Parking:** 60 **Notes:** No children 10yrs Closed Xmas–New Year RS 1st week Jul Henley Royal Regatta Civ wed 120

| HORNTON | Map 11 SP34 |
|---|---|

## Hornton Grounds Country House

★★★★ FARMHOUSE

**tel:** 01295 678318 **OX15 6HH**
**email:** catherine@horntongrounds.com **web:** www.horntongrounds.co.uk
**dir:** From Banbury onto A422 signed Stratford. Through Wroxton, pass Indian Queen pub, next right & follow long drive

A very warm welcome waits at Hornton Grounds Country House, an impressive retreat set on a busy working farm. It's an ideal setting for those wishing to explore the north Cotswold countryside. Guests are encouraged to enjoy the extensive grounds on foot, or you can even bring your own horse (stabling available). Evening meals are available by prior arrangement.

**Rooms:** 4 rms (2 en suite) (2 pri facs) **S** £39; **D** £90–£110* **Facilities:** TVL tea/coffee Dinner available WiFi ⬭ ⬭ ⅃ ❀ Stabling for guests' horses **Parking:** 8 **Notes:** 200 acres pigs/beef/sheep

| KINGHAM | Map 10 SP22 |
|---|---|

## The Wild Rabbit

★★★★★ ⬤⬤⬤ ⬭ RESTAURANT WITH ROOMS

**tel:** 01608 658389 **Church Street OX7 6YA**
**email:** theteam@thewildrabbit.co.uk **web:** www.thewildrabbit.co.uk

Situated in the idyllic Cotswold village of Kingham, this Grade II listed Georgian building has been lovingly restored and refurbished. The rooms are modern and offer up-to-date technology. The public areas are a real feature with a large bar and open-plan restaurant kitchen. An outside dining area has also been added. The food is exceptional, with many French influences evident in the cooking. Service is informal yet professional and very friendly. Car parking is available.

**Rooms:** 11 en suite 1 annexe en suite (1 fmly) (4 GF) **Facilities:** FTV DVD iPod docking station Lounge tea/coffee Dinner available WiFi ❀ **Extras:** Mini-bar – chargeable **Parking:** 19

KINGHAM *continued*

## The Kingham Plough

★★★★ ⚘⚘⚘ INN

**tel:** 01608 658327 **The Green OX7 6YD**
**email:** book@thekinghamplough.co.uk **web:** www.thekinghamplough.co.uk
**dir:** *From Chipping Norton, take B4450 to Churchill. Take 2nd right to Kingham, left at T-junct in Kingham. Pub on right.*

The Kingham Plough is a quintessential Cotswold inn set in the pretty village of Kingham, just minutes away from the well-known Daylesford Organic Estate. The en suite bedrooms have Cotswold character and offer impressive quality and comfort. The food here is a real draw, and has been recognised by achieving three AA Rosettes; the team deliver excellent results using locally sourced produce.

**Rooms:** 4 en suite 2 annexe en suite (2 fmly) **S** £110–£150; **D** £145–£195*
**Facilities:** FTV DVD iPod docking station Lounge tea/coffee Dinner available WiFi ⌇18 ⚘ Discounted rates at local spa **Extras:** Speciality toiletries, home-made biscuits – complimentary **Parking:** 25 **Notes:** Closed 25 Dec

| MARSTON | Map 5 SP50 |

## Hill Farm

★★★ BED AND BREAKFAST

**tel:** 07976 288329 **Mill Lane OX3 0QF**
**email:** laura@cherbridgecottages.co.uk **web:** www.cherbridgecottages.co.uk

Hill Farm is set in its own extensive grounds yet is conveniently close to Oxford city centre. This 18th-century cottage has many original features and is most comfortable. Bedrooms are very well appointed and there is a four-poster bed in the larger bedroom. Surrounded by open countryside, there is a pretty walk to the rear of the property along with a show jumping ground and working stables. Freshly cooked breakfasts feature the best in local produce and free WiFi is available throughout the house.

**Rooms:** 2 rms (1 en suite) (1 pri facs) **Facilities:** FTV Lounge TVL tea/coffee WiFi ⚘ Conf: Max 80 Thtr 70 Class 60 Board 50 **Notes:** LB Closed 19 Dec–4 Jan

| OXFORD | Map 5 SP50 |

### Premier Collection

## Burlington House

★★★★★ GUEST ACCOMMODATION

**tel:** 01865 513513 **374 Banbury Road, Summertown OX2 7PP**
**email:** stay@burlington-house.co.uk **web:** www.burlington-house.co.uk
**dir:** *Opposite Oxford Conference Centre on A4165 on corner of Hernes Rd & Banbury Rd*

Guests are assured of a warm welcome and attentive service at this smart, beautifully maintained Victorian house, within walking distance of Summertown's fashionable restaurants. Elegant, contemporary bedrooms are filled with a wealth of thoughtful extras, and some open onto a pretty patio garden. Memorable breakfasts, served in the delightful dining room, include home-made preserves, fruit breads, granola and excellent coffee.

**Rooms:** 13 en suite 3 annexe en suite (4 GF) **S** £74–£99; **D** £94–£169*
**Facilities:** FTV tea/coffee Direct dial WiFi ⚘ **Parking:** 5 **Notes:** No children 12yrs Closed 24 Dec–2 Jan

## Galaxie

★★★★ GUEST ACCOMMODATION

**tel:** 01865 515688 **180 Banbury Road OX2 7BT**
**email:** info@galaxie.co.uk **web:** www.galaxie.co.uk
**dir:** *1m N of Oxford centre, on right before shops in Summertown*

In the popular Summertown area of the city, Galaxie has a welcoming atmosphere and good-quality accommodation. The well-equipped bedrooms are all very comfortable and come with a range of extra facilities. The attractive conservatory dining room looks over the Oriental garden.

**Rooms:** 32 rms (28 en suite) (3 fmly) **Facilities:** TVL tea/coffee Direct dial Lift WiFi **Parking:** 30

## The Oxford Townhouse

★★★★ GUEST ACCOMMODATION

**tel:** 01865 511122 **88–90 Abingdon Road OX1 4PX**
**email:** stay@theoxfordtownhouse.co.uk **web:** www.theoxfordtownhouse.co.uk

The Oxford Townhouse overlooks The Queen's College playing fields, and is an ideal base to explore the city. Spread over two Victorian town houses, it offers a range of modern styled spacious bedrooms that have benefited from full refurbishment. Freshly prepared breakfasts are served at individual tables and service is friendly and attentive. WiFi is available throughout the house and there is secure parking.

**Rooms:** 15 en suite **S** £100–£135; **D** £130–£165* **Facilities:** FTV Lounge tea/coffee WiFi **Extras:** Bottled water, soft drinks – complimentary **Parking:** 9 **Notes:** No children 10yrs Closed 24–26 Dec

## Parklands

★★★★ GUEST ACCOMMODATION

**tel:** 01865 554374 **100 Banbury Road OX2 6JU**
**email:** stay@parklandsoxford.co.uk **web:** www.parklandsoxford.co.uk

Parklands enjoys a prominent position along the tree-lined Banbury road and is only a short walk from the city centre. This beautiful Victorian building was once the home of an Oxford Don and has a range of individually designed, spacious bedrooms. Secure parking is available and free WiFi is provided. The walled garden is a peaceful retreat and the residents' lounge is very well appointed.

**Rooms:** 14 rms (13 en suite) (1 pri facs) **S** £64–£89; **D** £94–£149* **Facilities:** FTV Lounge tea/coffee Direct dial Licensed WiFi **Extras:** Bottled water – complimentary **Parking:** 14 **Notes:** No children 18yrs Closed 24–26 Dec

## Red Mullions Guest House

★★★★ GUEST HOUSE

**tel:** 01865 742741 **23 London Road, Headington OX3 7RE**
**email:** stay@redmullions.co.uk **web:** www.redmullions.co.uk
**dir:** *M40 junct 8, A40. At Headington rdbt, 2nd exit signed Headington into London Rd*

Red Mullions Guest House takes its name from the brick columns between the windows of the building. Modern bedrooms provide comfortable accommodation set within easy reach of motorway networks and Oxford city centre. Hearty breakfasts provide a good start to any day.

**Rooms:** 16 rms (15 en suite) (1 pri facs) (3 fmly) (7 GF) **S** £95–£105; **D** £110–£130 **Facilities:** STV FTV DVD tea/coffee WiFi **Extras:** Bottled water – complimentary **Parking:** 11

## Remont Oxford

★★★★ GUEST ACCOMMODATION

**tel:** 01865 311020 **367 Banbury Road OX2 7PL**
**email:** info@remont-oxford.co.uk **web:** www.remont-oxford.co.uk

Remont Oxford is in the popular Summertown area, some two miles from the city centre. The well-equipped bedrooms and bathrooms are modern and stylish and come with TVs, complimentary WiFi and well-stocked beverage trays; rooms all offer high quality and comfort. Parking is available and there is a delightful garden for guests to enjoy. Cooked and continental buffet breakfasts are served in the light and airy dining room.

**Rooms:** 18 en suite 7 annexe en suite (2 fmly) (8 GF) **S** £89–£170; **D** £99–£180*
**Facilities:** FTV Lounge tea/coffee Lift WiFi **Parking:** 18

## Conifers Guest House

★★★★ GUEST ACCOMMODATION

**tel:** 01865 763055 **116 The Slade, Headington OX3 7DX**
**email:** stay@conifersguesthouse.co.uk **web:** www.conifersguesthouse.co.uk
**dir:** Exit ring road onto A420 towards city centre. Left onto B4495 (Windmill Rd), straight over at lights, house on left past Nuffield Orthopaedic Centre

Situated in the Headington area, Conifers is within walking distance of the Headington Hospitals, the BMW plant, Cowley Business Park, and Oxford Brookes, as well as Shotover Country Park. It is an impressive Edwardian house that provides comfortable accommodation in pine-furnished bedrooms. Breakfast is served in a smart, front-facing dining room. A private car park and a large rear garden are bonuses.

**Rooms:** 12 en suite (4 fmly) **Facilities:** FTV tea/coffee WiFi **Parking:** 8

## Cotswold House

★★★★ GUEST ACCOMMODATION

**tel:** 01865 310558 **363 Banbury Road OX2 7PL**
**email:** d.r.walker@talk21.com **web:** www.cotswoldhouse.co.uk
**dir:** A40 onto A423 into city centre, follow signs to Summertown, house 0.5m on right

Situated in a leafy avenue close to the northern ring road and Summertown, this well-maintained house offers comfortable, well-equipped bedrooms and a relaxed atmosphere. Enjoy a traditional, hearty breakfast with vegetarian choices, including home-made muesli and fresh fruit, served in the bright attractive dining room.

**Rooms:** 7 en suite (2 fmly) (1 GF) **S** £78–£95; **D** £125–£135 **Facilities:** FTV Lounge tea/coffee WiFi 🐾 **Parking:** 6 **Notes:** Closed 28 Dec–10 Jan

## Who are the AA's award-winning B&Bs?
— see pages 12–15

## Green Gables

★★★ GUEST ACCOMMODATION

**tel:** 01865 725870 **326 Abingdon Road OX1 4TE**
**email:** enquiries@green.gables.uk.com **web:** www.greengables.uk.com
**dir:** Exit ring road onto A4144 towards city centre, Green Gables 0.5m on left

A warm welcome is assured at Green Gables, located within easy walking distance of the city centre. Bedrooms are equipped with a range of practical and homely extras, and a comprehensive breakfast is served in the cosy dining room. Guests have free access to the internet in the smart conservatory-lounge, and some private parking is available.

**Rooms:** 11 en suite (2 fmly) (4 GF) **S** fr £50; **D** fr £85 (room only)* **Facilities:** FTV Lounge tea/coffee WiFi **Parking:** 9 **Notes:** No children 5yrs Closed 23–31 Dec

## Oxford Guest House

★★★ GUEST HOUSE

**tel:** 01865 308833 & 07855 737373 **228 London Road, Headington OX3 9EG**
**email:** oxfordguesthouse@gmail.com **web:** www.theoxfordguesthouse.co.uk
**dir:** M40 junct 8 onto A40 towards Oxford. At Headington rdbt take 2nd exit signed Headington into London Rd (A420). On left after 2nd set of lights

The modern Oxford Guest House is located in a quiet residential area, and offers well configured rooms finished to a very good standard. All rooms have been equipped with flat-screen TVs and free WiFi. A choice of breakfasts is served daily in the well-appointed breakfast room. Off-street parking is available.

**Rooms:** 6 en suite (1 fmly) (2 GF) **Facilities:** STV FTV tea/coffee WiFi 🐾 **Parking:** 6 **Notes:** LB

**OXFORD** *continued*

## All Seasons Guest House

★★★ GUEST ACCOMMODATION

**tel:** 01865 742215 **63 Windmill Road, Headington OX3 7BP**
**email:** info@allseasonshouse.com **web:** www.allseasonshouse.com
**dir:** *Exit ring road onto A420 towards city centre. 1m, left at lights into Windmill Rd, house 300yds on left*

Within easy walking distance of the suburb of Headington, this double-fronted Victorian house provides comfortable, homely bedrooms equipped with practical and thoughtful extras. The inviting dining room features an original fireplace, and parking is available to the rear of the property.

**Rooms:** 7 rms (5 en suite) (2 pri facs) (1 fmly) (1 GF) **Facilities:** FTV TVL tea/coffee WiFi **Parking:** 6

## Sports View Guest House

★★★ GUEST HOUSE

**tel:** 01865 244268 **106–110 Abingdon Road OX1 4PX**
**email:** stay@sportsviewguesthouse.co.uk **web:** www.sportsviewguesthouse.co.uk
**dir:** *Exit Oxford S at Kennington rdbt towards city centre, 1.25m on left*

This family-run Victorian property overlooks The Queen's College sports ground. Situated south of the city, it is within walking distance of the centre. Rooms are comfortable, and the property benefits from off-road parking.

**Rooms:** 20 rms (19 en suite) (1 pri facs) (4 fmly) (5 GF) **Facilities:** FTV Lounge tea/coffee WiFi 🐾 **Parking:** 7 **Notes:** No children 3yrs Closed 25–26 Dec & 1 Jan

---

**SHRIVENHAM**     Map 5 SU28

## The White Horse View

★★★★ BED AND BREAKFAST

**tel:** 01793 780301 & 07967 497926 **Cherry Bungalow, Station Road SN6 8JL**
**email:** colin@thewhitehorseview.com **web:** www.thewhitehorseview.com

Located in the pretty village of Shrivenham, this bed and breakfast offers four modern en suite bedrooms set away from the main house, each with their own external seating and spectacular countryside views. Breakfasts are served in the conservatory and feature local produce. This is a good location for those wanting to walk the Ridgeway or take in the sights of historic Marlborough.

**Rooms:** 4 en suite (1 fmly) (4 GF) **S** £65–£85; **D** £65–£85* **Facilities:** FTV TVL tea/coffee WiFi Pool table **Parking:** 3

---

**STADHAMPTON**     Map 5 SU69

### Premier Collection

## The Crazy Bear

★★★★★ ◎◎ 🍷 GUEST ACCOMMODATION

**tel:** 01865 890714 **Bear Lane OX44 7UR**
**email:** enquiries@crazybear-stadhampton.co.uk **web:** www.crazybeargroup.co.uk
**dir:** *M40 junct 7, A329. In 4m left after petrol station, left into Bear Ln*

This popular and attractive guest accommodation successfully combines modern chic with old world character. Cuisine is extensive and varied, with award-winning Thai and English restaurants under the same roof (both with AA

Rosettes). Those choosing to make a night of it can enjoy staying in one of the concept bedrooms, all presented to a very high standard and styled with exciting themes; the 'infinity suites' have state-of-the-art facilities.

**Rooms:** 4 en suite 12 annexe en suite (3 fmly) (4 GF) **Facilities:** STV FTV Dinner available Direct dial Licensed WiFi 🐾 **Conf:** Max 40 Thtr 30 Class 30 Board 30 **Parking:** 100 **Notes:** Civ wed 200

---

**SWINBROOK**     Map 5 SP21

## The Swan Inn

★★★★★ ◎◎ INN

**tel:** 01993 823339 **OX18 4DY**
**email:** swaninnswinbrook@btconnect.com **web:** www.theswanswinbrook.co.uk
**dir:** *1m from A40, 2m E of Burford*

The idyllic location and award-winning food are only two of the reasons why this is the perfect place for a comfortable business visit or a relaxed weekend. The bar offers real ales, local lagers and an appealing wine list. The accommodation is sumptuous and combines modern facilities with traditional comfort.

**Rooms:** 6 en suite (1 fmly) (4 GF) **Facilities:** FTV tea/coffee Dinner available WiFi ♨18 **Parking:** 20 **Notes:** Closed 25 Dec

---

**UFFINGTON**     Map 5 SU38

## The Fox and Hounds

★★★★ INN

**tel:** 01367 820680 **High Street SN7 7RP**
**email:** enquiries@uffingtonpub.co.uk **web:** www.uffingtonpub.co.uk
**dir:** *From A420 (S of Faringdon) follow Fernham or Uffington signs. From M4 junct 14 via Lambourn & Kingston Lisle*

The Fox and Hounds is a traditional pub located in the charming village of Uffington, and an ideal base to explore the surrounding area. The two cottage-style bedrooms are well appointed and offer a range of amenities. The beamed bar is well stocked and includes a selection of real ales, while the restaurant offers a daily menu with an oriental twist.

**Rooms:** 4 annexe en suite (3 fmly) (4 GF) **S** £85; **D** £85 (room only)* **Facilities:** FTV DVD tea/coffee Dinner available WiFi 🐾 **Parking:** 14

---

**WANTAGE**     Map 5 SU38

## The Star Inn

★★★★ ◎◎ INN

**tel:** 01235 751873 **Watery Lane, Sparsholt OX12 9PL**
**email:** info@thestarsparsholt.co.uk **web:** www.thestarsparsholt.co.uk
**dir:** *From B4507, 4m W of Wantage turn right to Sparsholt. The Star Inn is signposted*

Located in the picturesque village of Sparsholt, at the foot of the famous Ridgeway. At the heart of the community for over 300 years, The Star Inn offers bedrooms that are peacefully situated in a converted barn at the rear of the property, each providing a very good level of comfort. The two AA Rosette-worthy food is a highlight of any stay; excellent quality ingredients are skilfully prepared and carefully presented.

**Rooms:** 8 en suite (1 fmly) (5 GF) **S** £85–£115; **D** £95–£135* **Facilities:** FTV DVD tea/coffee Dinner available WiFi 🐾 **Extras:** Speciality toiletries **Conf:** Max 30 Board 30 **Parking:** 15

## La Fontana Restaurant with Accommodation

★★★★ 🍽 RESTAURANT WITH ROOMS

**tel:** 01235 868287 & 07836 730048 **Oxford Road, East Hanney OX12 0HP**
**email:** anna@la-fontana.co.uk **web:** www.la-fontana.co.uk
**dir:** *A338 from Wantage towards Oxford. Restaurant on right in East Hanney*

Guests are guaranteed a warm welcome at this family-run Italian restaurant located on the outskirts of the busy town of Wantage. The stylish bedrooms are individually designed, well equipped and very comfortable. Dinner should not be missed – the menu features a wide range of regional Italian specialities.

**Rooms:** 12 en suite 3 annexe en suite (1 fmly) (4 GF) **S** £67.50–£72.50; **D** £87.50–£125* **Facilities:** FTV Lounge tea/coffee Dinner available Direct dial WiFi **Parking:** 30 **Notes:** Civ wed 120

## Hill Barn

★★★ FARMHOUSE

**tel:** 01235 751236 & 07885 368918 **Sparholt Firs OX12 9XB**
**email:** jmw@hillbarn.plus.com **web:** www.hillbarnbedandbreakfast.co.uk
**dir:** *W of B4001 on The Ridgeway, 4m N of Wantage*

This working farm offers en suite bedrooms with beautiful far-reaching views over the countryside. The atmosphere is friendly, and guests are able to relax either in the sitting room or in the garden. Breakfast is a highlight with home-made jams and other produce from the farm (when available).

**Rooms:** 3 rms (2 en suite) (1 pri facs) **S** £45; **D** £85* **Facilities:** Lounge TVL tea/coffee Dinner available WiFi 🦺 **Parking:** 3 **Notes:** LB  100 acres horses

### WATLINGTON
Map 5 SU69

## The Fat Fox Inn

★★★★ 🍽 INN

**tel:** 01491 613040 **13 Shirburn Street OX49 5BU**
**email:** info@thefatfoxinn.co.uk **web:** www.thefatfoxinn.co.uk
**dir:** *M40 junct 6 onto B4009 S for 2.5m. On right in village*

Just 20 minutes out of Oxford city, this inn is conveniently located for both the leisure guest, especially walkers of the nearby Ridgeway and the business traveller looking for a quiet location. Guests can enjoy lunch and dinner in the relaxed bar or in the restaurant, where the kitchen team offers well-sourced, seasonal fare.

**Rooms:** 9 rms (7 en suite) (1 fmly) (5 GF) **S** £69–£115; **D** £89–£125* **Facilities:** FTV tea/coffee Dinner available WiFi 🦺 **Parking:** 20

### WHEATLEY
Map 5 SP50

## Gidleigh House

★★★★ BED AND BREAKFAST

**tel:** 01865 875150 & 07733 026882 **27 Old London Road OX33 1YW**
**web:** www.gidleighhousebb.co.uk
**dir:** *M40 junct 8 follow signs to Wheatley. Pass Asda on left & right turn to Hotton/Waterperry. Next right, marked private road*

You are assured of a warm, personal welcome at this modern home which is located on a private road in a quiet village just 10 minutes from Oxford city centre and has easy access to the M40. The two en suite rooms are spacious, very comfortable and equipped with thoughtful extras. Relax over a newspaper in the conservatory at the family-style table while your breakfast is freshly prepared.

**Rooms:** 2 en suite (2 fmly) **Facilities:** TVL tea/coffee **Extras:** Fruit, chocolates **Parking:** 4 **Notes:** No children 10yrs Closed 18 Dec–5 Jan

### WITNEY
Map 5 SP31

### Premier Collection

## Old Swan & Minster Mill

★★★★★ 🏵  INN

**tel:** 01993 774441 **Old Minster OX29 0RN**
**email:** enquiries@oldswanandminstermill.com **web:** www.oldswanandminstermill.com
**dir:** *Exit A40 signed Minster Lovell, through village right T-junct, 2nd left*

Located within its own stunning grounds and gardens including a private stretch of the River Windrush, the Old Swan & Minster Mill are two distinct accommodation areas, both with quality and individuality. Check-in is at the Minster Mill, where guests are welcomed and escorted to their room or suite. Old Swan rooms are traditional, with old oak beams and fireplaces in some rooms, while Mill rooms are more contemporary in style, many of which feature great views of the river and grounds. Award-winning cuisine is served in the dining room. There is a two-night minimum stay at weekends.

**Rooms:** 60 rms (52 en suite) (4 fmly) (19 GF) **Facilities:** FTV Lounge tea/coffee Dinner available Direct dial WiFi 🏊 🎣 ♨18 Fishing Gym Pool table 🦺 Petanque **Extras:** Speciality toiletries, decanter of sloe gin **Conf:** Max 55 Thtr 55 Class 22 Board 24 **Parking:** 70 **Notes:** LB Civ wed 50

### WOODSTOCK
Map 11 SP41

### Premier Collection

## The Glove House

★★★★★ BED AND BREAKFAST

**tel:** 01993 813475 & 07447 012832 **24 Oxford Street OX20 1TS**
**email:** info@theglovehouse.co.uk **web:** www.theglovehouse.co.uk
**dir:** *M40 junct 8 onto A40, then A44 signed to Evesham/Woodstock. The Glove House is on the right*

The Glove House is a 17th-century Grade II listed property, which has been sympathetically renovated and enjoys a prime location; Blenheim Palace is within walking distance. The two en suite bedrooms are very well appointed and ooze style, quality and comfort. Breakfast can be served in the walled garden during the summer.

**Rooms:** 2 en suite (2 fmly) **S** £155–£205; **D** £170–£220* **Facilities:** FTV DVD iPod docking station Lounge tea/coffee WiFi **Extras:** Speciality toiletries, mini-bar **Notes:** No children 10yrs

## Duke of Marlborough Country Inn

★★★★ INN

**tel:** 01993 811460 **Woodleys OX20 1HT**
**email:** sales@dukeofmarlborough.co.uk **web:** www.dukeofmarlborough.co.uk
**dir:** *1m N of Woodstock on A44 x-rds*

The Duke of Marlborough is just outside the popular town of Woodstock, convenient for local attractions including Blenheim Palace. Bedrooms and bathrooms are in an adjacent lodge-style building and offer high standards of quality and comfort. Dinner includes many tempting home-cooked dishes, complemented by a good selection of ales and wines.

**Rooms:** 13 annexe en suite (2 fmly) (7 GF) **Facilities:** FTV tea/coffee Dinner available Direct dial WiFi 🦺 **Extras:** Snacks **Conf:** Max 20 Thtr 20 Class 16 Board 12 **Parking:** 42 **Notes:** LB

WOODSTOCK *continued*

## The Townhouse

★★★ GUEST ACCOMMODATION

**tel:** 01993 810843 **15 High Street OX20 1TE**
**email:** townhousewoodstock@hotmail.co.uk **web:** www.woodstock-townhouse.com
**dir:** Off A44 into High St

This early 18th-century stone town house is full of character and offers five individually styled, cosy en suite bedrooms. Situated in the heart of the town just a short walk from Blenheim Palace, it is an ideal base for exploring many famous Cotswold locations. Breakfasts are cooked to order and served in the small conservatory room overlooking the walled garden.

**Rooms:** 5 en suite (1 fmly) **S** £65–£70; **D** £83–£93* **Facilities:** FTV TVL tea/coffee WiFi

| WOOTTON | Map 11 SP41 |

## The Killingworth Castle

★★★★ ⓜ INN

**tel:** 01993 811401 & 832849 **Glympton Road OX20 1EJ**
**email:** reservations@thekillingworthcastle.com **web:** www.thekillingworthcastle.com

This 17th-century roadside country inn, located just a few miles from Woodstock and Blenheim Palace, recently underwent a full refurbishment. It has retained its country charm with many modern creature comforts added. There are eight comfortable en suite bedrooms all within a converted Cotswold stone barn less than a stone's throw from the inn, and offer a very comfortable stay in a peaceful setting. A warm welcome is assured and dinner is not to be missed.

**Rooms:** 8 annexe en suite (4 GF) **Facilities:** FTV tea/coffee Dinner available WiFi
**Extras:** Sherry **Parking:** 40 **Notes:** No children 16yrs

| RUTLAND |

| CLIPSHAM | Map 11 SK91 |

## Beech House

★★★★ ⓜⓜ 🍷 INN

**tel:** 01780 410355 **Main Street LE15 7SH**
**email:** info@theolivebranchpub.com **web:** www.theolivebranchpub.com
**dir:** From A1 take B668 signed Stretton & Clipsh–am

Beech House stands over the road from the Olive Branch restaurant. Its bedrooms are furnished with style and finesse, combining crisp linens, natural wood and retro-style accessories with traditional and modern furniture. Breakfasts are served in the Olive Branch and should not be missed. Excellent lunches and dinners are also available.

**Rooms:** 5 en suite 1 annexe en suite (2 fmly) (3 GF) **S** £97.50–£112.50; **D** £115–£205* **Facilities:** FTV DVD tea/coffee Dinner available Direct dial WiFi ♨18 🔒 **Extras:** Speciality toiletries – complimentary; fruit – chargeable **Conf:** Max 20 Thtr 20 Class 12 Board 16 **Parking:** 10 **Notes:** LB

| LYDDINGTON | Map 11 SP89 |

## The Marquess of Exeter

★★★★ ⓜ INN

**tel:** 01572 822477 **52 Main Street LE15 9LT**
**email:** info@marquessexeter.co.uk **web:** www.marquessexeter.co.uk
**dir:** M1 junct 19, A14 to Kettering, then A6003 to Caldecott. Right into Lyddington Rd, 2m to village

Situated in the picturesque Rutland countryside, the inn is appointed with contemporary touches while retaining many original features such as timber beam ceilings, log fires and flagstone floors. The stylish bedrooms, situated across a courtyard, are individually decorated and comfortable. The food is imaginative with the chef's 'sharing dishes' being particularly noteworthy.

**Rooms:** 17 rms (16 en suite) (1 pri facs) (3 fmly) (10 GF) **S** £79.50–£104.50; **D** £99.50–£134.50* **Facilities:** FTV tea/coffee Dinner available Direct dial WiFi **Conf:** Max 50 Thtr 50 Class 40 Board 40 **Parking:** 60

| OAKHAM | Map 11 SK80 |

## Fox & Hounds

★★★★ ⓜⓜ INN

**tel:** 01572 812403 **19 The Green, Exton LE15 8AP**
**email:** info@afoxinexton.co.uk **web:** www.afoxinexton.co.uk
**dir:** From A1, follow signs to Rutland Water on A606. Turn right at Barnsdale Avenue then right towards Exton. On The Green

This 17th-century coaching inn overlooks The Green in the picturesque Rutland village of Exton; the property has been newly refurbished and has four individually designed bedrooms. Public areas include a lounge bar, restaurant and library; the building also has a wealth of original features and landscaped gardens.

**Rooms:** 4 en suite (1 fmly) (1 GF) **S** £130–£165; **D** £130–£165* **Facilities:** STV FTV DVD Lounge tea/coffee Dinner available WiFi ♨18 Fishing 🔒 **Extras:** Speciality toiletries **Conf:** Max 20 Thtr 14 Class 16 Board 20 **Parking:** 20

## Kirkee House

★★★★ BED AND BREAKFAST

**tel:** 01572 757401 **35 Welland Way LE15 6SL**
**email:** carolbeech@kirkeehouse.demon.co.uk **web:** www.kirkeehouse.co.uk
**dir:** S of town centre. Exit A606 (High St) into Mill St, over level crossing, 400yds on left

Located on a leafy avenue a short walk from the town centre, this immaculately maintained modern house provides comfortable bedrooms filled with homely extras. Comprehensive breakfasts, including local sausages and home-made jams, are served in the elegant conservatory-dining room which overlooks the pretty garden.

**Rooms:** 2 en suite **D** £75* **Facilities:** FTV tea/coffee WiFi 🔒 **Parking:** 2 **Notes:** No children 7yrs

| UPPINGHAM | Map 11 SP89 |

## The Lake Isle

★★★★ ⓜⓜ 🍷 RESTAURANT WITH ROOMS

**tel:** 01572 822951 **16 High Street East LE15 9PZ**
**email:** info@lakeisle.co.uk **web:** www.lakeisle.co.uk
**dir:** From A47, turn left at 2nd lights, 100yds on right

This attractive town house centres around a delightful restaurant and small elegant bar. There is also an inviting first-floor guest lounge, and the bedrooms are extremely well appointed and thoughtfully equipped; spacious split-level cottage suites situated in a quiet courtyard are also available. The imaginative cooking and an extremely impressive wine list are highlights here.

**Rooms:** 9 en suite 3 annexe rms (3 pri facs) (1 fmly) (1 GF) **S** £70–£80; **D** £90–£120* **Facilities:** FTV Lounge tea/coffee Dinner available Direct dial WiFi 🛁 **Extras:** Home-made biscuits – complimentary **Conf:** Max 16 Board 16 **Parking:** 7 **Notes:** Closed 1 Jan & BHs RS Sun eve & Mon lunch closed

## The Crown

★★★ INN

**tel:** 01572 822302 **19 High Street, East Uppingham LE15 9PY** **email:** info@thecrownrutland.co.uk **web:** www.thecrownrutland.co.uk

Located on the high street in the centre of Uppingham, this traditional inn dates back to 1739, and with some modernisation to the bedrooms, now offers comfortable accommodation. Guests can enjoy a range of real ales, and a selection of bar meals. There is parking to the rear, and free WiFi is available.

**Rooms:** 7 en suite (1 fmly) **Facilities:** FTV TVL tea/coffee Dinner available WiFi 🛁 **Conf:** Max 25 Thtr 25 Class 25 Board 25 **Parking:** 10

---

| WING | Map 11 SK80 |
|------|-------------|

## Kings Arms Inn & Restaurant

★★★★ ◉◉ ◻ INN

**tel:** 01572 737634 **13 Top Street LE15 8SE** **email:** info@thekingsarms-wing.co.uk **web:** www.thekingsarms-wing.co.uk **dir:** 1.5m off A6003 in village centre

This traditional village inn, with its open fires, flagstone floors and low beams, dates from the 17th century. The restaurant is more contemporary and offers a wide range of interesting, freshly produced dishes. Service is attentive and friendly. The spacious, well-equipped bedrooms are in The Old Bake House and Granny's Cottage, in the nearby courtyard.

**Rooms:** 8 en suite (4 GF) **S** £65–£85; **D** £75–£100 (room only)* **Facilities:** FTV tea/coffee Dinner available WiFi **Parking:** 30

---

| SHROPSHIRE |
|------------|

| BISHOP'S CASTLE | Map 15 SO38 |
|-----------------|-------------|

## The Castle

★★★★ ⊜ INN

**tel:** 01588 638403 **Market Square SY9 5BN** **email:** stay@thecastlehotelbishopscastle.co.uk **web:** www.thecastlehotelbishopscastle.co.uk **dir:** Turn off A488 into Bishop's Castle, at top of High St on left

This medieval town on the England-Wales border is famed for its ale, and is home to the oldest working brewery in the country. Overlooking the historic town with its mixed architecture and unusually painted houses (spotty, jigsaw etc.) sits the remains of a castle. In 1719 much of the stone from this castle was used to create The Castle Hotel, built on the old Baille (or enclosed courtyard) on the instruction of a wealthy landowner. Nearly 300 years on The Castle continues to welcome guests from far and wide. Many of the comfortably furnished rooms have stunning views across the Marches. Hearty meals are served in the bar, dining room and on sunny days on the garden terrace. Offa's Dyke, The Shropshire Way and Kerry Ridgeway are all within easy striking distance.

**Rooms:** 12 en suite (2 fmly) **S** fr £85; **D** £85–£160* **Facilities:** FTV TVL tea/coffee Dinner available WiFi 🛁 **Conf:** Max 24 **Parking:** 25 **Notes:** LB Closed 25 Dec

## The Coach House

★★★★ ◉◉ ◻ RESTAURANT WITH ROOMS

**tel:** 01588 650846 & 07930 694516 **Norbury SY9 5DX** **email:** info@coachhousenorbury.com **web:** www.coachhousenorbury.com **dir:** 3m NE of Bishop's Castle. Exit A488/A489 into Norbury

Located in an Area of Outstanding Natural Beauty this quaint property is in the centre of a pretty Shropshire village and has been welcoming travellers since the 1700s. A warm welcome is assured by the owners. Bedrooms offer comfortable accommodation for guests and are located either in the main building, or the attached coach house annexe which is dog friendly. Cosy lounges with log-burning fires are an ideal place to enjoy a locally-produced beer or one of the quality wines on offer. With Lexi a qualified wine maker, you are assured of something special. Award-winning dinners and breakfast are not to be missed; with an innovative menu showcasing the best local produce.

**Rooms:** 4 rms (3 en suite) (1 pri facs) 3 annexe en suite (1 fmly) (1 GF) **S** £79–£119; **D** £79–£119* **Facilities:** FTV DVD Lounge tea/coffee Dinner available WiFi 🛁 **Extras:** Speciality toiletries, home-made biscuits **Conf:** Max 18 Thtr 18 Class 18 Board 18 **Parking:** 8 **Notes:** LB No children 5yrs Closed 2–31 Jan

---

## Boars Head

★★★★ INN

**tel:** 01588 638521 **Church Street SY9 5AE** **email:** info@boarsheadhotel.co.uk **web:** www.boarsheadhotel.co.uk

The Boars Head is situated in the centre of Bishop's Castle, and is a traditional inn with comfortable and spacious bedrooms in a separate annexe. The inn incorporates a post office with a cash machine and phone top-up facilities. Food is on offer all day. Parking is available to the rear of the inn.

**Rooms:** 4 annexe en suite (1 fmly) (3 GF) **Facilities:** FTV DVD iPod docking station Lounge tea/coffee Dinner available WiFi **Extras:** Fridge, digital safe, mineral water **Parking:** 60

---

| BRIDGNORTH | Map 10 SO79 |
|------------|-------------|

## The Halfway House Inn

★★★ INN

**tel:** 01746 762670 **Pengwern Sports Tours Ltd, Cleobury Road WV16 5LS** **email:** info@halfwayhouseinn.co.uk **web:** www.halfwayhouseinn.co.uk **dir:** 1.5m from town centre on B4363 to Cleobury Mortimer

Located in a rural area, this 16th-century inn has been renovated to provide good standards of comfort, while retaining its original character. The bedrooms, some in converted stables and cottages, are especially suitable for families and groups.

**Rooms:** 10 en suite (10 fmly) (6 GF) **S** £59–£89; **D** £75–£99 **Facilities:** FTV TVL tea/coffee Dinner available WiFi 🎣18 Fishing Pool table 🛁 **Conf:** Max 30 Thtr 30 Class 24 Board 20 **Parking:** 30 **Notes:** LB Closed 25–26 Dec RS Winter Sun eve (ex BHs) from 5pm

## CHURCH STRETTON
Map 15 SO49

### Court Farm
★★★★ ☺ FARMHOUSE

**tel:** 01694 771219 **Gretton SY6 7HU**
**email:** alison@courtfarm.eu **web:** www.courtfarm.eu
**dir:** Turn off B4371 at Longville, left at x-rds, 1st on left

Located in the village of Gretton, this Grade II listed stone-built Georgian house is on a 330-acre working farm, and its bedrooms overlook the pretty gardens. Home to the Norris family since 1898, over the years they have sympathetically restored and modernised the building. Comprehensive breakfasts are served in an elegant dining room, and a comfortable guest lounge is also available. Court Farm is an ideal base for exploring Shropshire and surrounding areas.

**Rooms:** 2 en suite **S** £55–£60; **D** £80–£90* **Facilities:** FTV TVL tea/coffee WiFi ☎ **Parking:** 4 **Notes:** No children 12yrs  330 acres mixed

### Belvedere Guest House
★★★★ GUEST HOUSE

**tel:** 01694 722232 **Burway Road SY6 6DP**
**email:** info@belvedereguesthouse.co.uk **web:** www.belvedereguesthouse.co.uk
**dir:** Exit A49 into town centre, over x-rds into Burway Rd

Popular with walkers and cyclists and peacefully located on the lower slopes of the Long Mynd, this impressive, well-proportioned Edwardian house has a range of homely bedrooms, equipped with practical extras and complemented by modern bathrooms. Ground-floor areas include a cottage-style dining room overlooking the pretty garden and large lounge complete with TV, a large selection of reading material and board games.

**Rooms:** 7 rms (6 en suite) (2 fmly) **S** £35–£41; **D** £60–£72 **Facilities:** TVL tea/coffee WiFi ☎ **Extras:** Mini-fridge, snacks, bottled water – chargeable **Parking:** 9 **Notes:** LB Closed Xmas & Jan

### The Bucks Head
★★★★ INN

**tel:** 01694 722898 & 07811 364416 **42 High Street SY6 6BX**
**email:** lloyd.nutting@btconnect.com **web:** www.the-bucks-head.co.uk
**dir:** A49 N or S, turn into Church Stretton. At top of town turn left, Bucks Head on right

The Bucks Head enjoys a central location in the heart of historic Church Stretton, and is a vibrant modern inn. There are high levels of comfort and up-to-date facilities together with original charm and character. The comfortable bedrooms are complemented by smart en suite bathrooms, and the attractive open-plan public areas are the perfect setting for enjoying food and drinks. The hospitality is warm and genuine.

**Rooms:** 4 en suite **Facilities:** FTV tea/coffee Dinner available WiFi
**Notes:** No children 5yrs

## DORRINGTON
Map 15 SJ40

### Upper Shadymoor Farm
★★★★ FARMHOUSE

**tel:** 01743 718670 **Stapleton SY5 7AL**
**email:** kevan@shadymoor.co.uk **web:** www.shadymoor.co.uk

Upper Shadymoor Farm has it all, the shabby-chic rooms, the formal dining room, the family atmosphere, the tranquil location, the farm animals, the deer park and much more. Expect a warm welcome from the Fox family and a truly enjoyable experience. Produce from the farm is used at dinner and breakfast.

**Rooms:** 3 en suite (1 fmly) **Facilities:** Lounge tea/coffee Dinner available WiFi Fishing ☎ **Parking:** 20 **Notes:** 200 acres beef/mixed/sheep

## GRINSHILL
Map 15 SJ52

### The Inn at Grinshill
★★★★ INN

**tel:** 01939 220410 **The High Street SY4 3BL**
**email:** sales@theinnatgrinshill.co.uk **web:** www.theinnatgrinshill.co.uk
**dir:** N of Shrewsbury on A49, after 7m turn left, inn 500yds on left

This country inn is part Grade II listed and many areas have been uncovered to highlight the original features. It is located under the lee of Grinshill in a delightful village with beautiful countryside close by. The Welsh border is within easy driving distance as are Shrewsbury, Telford and Welshpool. The accommodation is comfortable, and guests are very welcome to make use of the grounds

**Rooms:** 3 en suite **Facilities:** FTV TVL tea/coffee WiFi ☂36 ☎ **Parking:** 30 **Notes:** LB Closed 31 Mar–13 Apr RS Sun, Mon & Tue no accommodation

## IRONBRIDGE
Map 10 SJ60

### Broseley House
★★★★ GUEST HOUSE

**tel:** 01952 882043 & 07790 732723 **1 The Square, Broseley TF12 5EW**
**email:** info@broseleyhouse.co.uk **web:** www.broseleyhouse.co.uk
**dir:** 1m S of Ironbridge in Broseley town centre

A warm welcome is assured at this impressive Georgian house in the centre of Broseley. Quality, individual decor and soft furnishings highlight the many original features, and the thoughtfully furnished bedrooms are equipped with a wealth of homely extras. Comprehensive breakfasts are taken in an elegant dining room; a stylish apartment is also available.

**Rooms:** 6 en suite (2 fmly) (1 GF) **S** £50–£65; **D** £80–£100 **Facilities:** FTV DVD iPod docking station tea/coffee WiFi ☎ **Extras:** Fridge, robes, slippers **Notes:** LB No children 5yrs

## Premier Collection

# Old Downton Lodge

★★★★★  RESTAURANT WITH ROOMS

**tel:** 01568 771826 & 07977 475881 **Downton on the Rock SY8 2HU**
**email:** bookings@olddowntonlodge.com **web:** www.olddowntonlodge.com
**dir:** *From Ludlow onto A49 towards Shrewsbury, 1st left onto A4113. After 1.9m turn
left signed Downton, 3m on single track road. Turn right, signed*

Old Downton Lodge is within easy reach of Ludlow's many attractions, and is in
a peaceful location with good parking, pleasant grounds, ideal for walks and
country pursuits. Originally a farm, this high-end establishment has bags of
character, and is a stylish, comfortable and tranquil place to stay. Bedrooms are
spacious and very well appointed, with comfortable beds and luxurious
bathrooms. There is an honesty bar and excellent wine list. Breakfast should not
be missed, and the three AA Rosette-worthy dinner is a highlight, with an
imaginative five- or seven-course tasting menu using local, seasonal and
foraged produce, served every Tuesday to Saturday evening.

**Rooms:** 10 en suite (5 GF) **S** £99–£250; **D** £99–£250* **Facilities:** FTV DVD Lounge
tea/coffee Dinner available Direct dial WiFi **Extras:** Speciality toiletries,
home-made biscuits **Conf:** Max 40 Thtr 40 Class 40 Board 40 **Parking:** 20
**Notes:** LB No children 13yrs Closed 24–26 Dec Civ wed 60

## Premier Collection

# The Clive Bar & Restaurant with Rooms

★★★★★ RESTAURANT WITH ROOMS

**tel:** 01584 856565 & 856665 **Bromfield SY8 2JR**
**email:** info@theclive.co.uk **web:** www.theclive.co.uk
**dir:** *2m N of Ludlow on A49 in Bromfield*

The Clive is just two miles from the busy town of Ludlow and is a convenient
base for visiting the local attractions or for business. Based at the Ludlow Food
Centre, good use is made of food made on site or from the company farms,
ensuring local seasonal produce at every meal. The bedrooms, located in an
annexe, are spacious and very well equipped; one is suitable for families and
many are on the ground-floor level. Meals are available in the well-known Clive
Restaurant or in the bar areas. The property also has a small meeting room.

**Rooms:** 14 annexe en suite (1 fmly) (10 GF) **Facilities:** FTV tea/coffee Dinner
available Direct dial WiFi ⌁18 **Extras:** Mini-bar with local produce **Conf:** Max 40
Thtr 40 Class 40 Board 24 **Parking:** 80 **Notes:** LB Closed 25–26 Dec

## Premier Collection

# The Charlton Arms

★★★★★ INN

**tel:** 01584 872813 **Ludford Bridge SY8 1PJ**
**email:** reservations@thecharltonarms.co.uk **web:** www.thecharltonarms.co.uk

The accommodation at this riverside inn reflects the character of the
historic building which offers all modern comforts. Diners can enjoy fresh,
locally-sourced ingredients in the dishes they choose and a panoramic view
across the River Teme. As a free house it also offers a fine selection of local
beers. There is one bedroom which has a private terrace and a hot tub, plus
decking areas to enjoy drinks or a meal on warmer days.

**Rooms:** 9 en suite (2 fmly) **S** £90–£140; **D** £100–£160* **Facilities:** FTV tea/coffee
Dinner available WiFi **Conf:** Max 100 Thtr 100 Class 80 Board 70 **Parking:** 30
**Notes:** Civ wed 70

# The Cliffe at Dinham

★★★★ RESTAURANT WITH ROOMS

**tel:** 01584 872063 & 876975 **Halton Lane, Dinham SY8 2JE**
**email:** info@thecliffeatdinham.co.uk **web:** www.thecliffeatdinham.co.uk

This former gentleman's residence is a short stroll from the River Teme, with
magnificent views of Ludlow Castle, just a short walk from the vibrant centre of
Ludlow. The Cliffe is a successful blend of the existing Victorian features and
a more contemporary style. The rooms are comfortable and well equipped. Relaxed
dining from locally sourced ingredients is offered in the attractive dining room, and
there is a pleasant terraced area overlooking the gardens.

**Rooms:** 11 en suite 2 annexe en suite (3 fmly) (1 GF) **S** £65–£85; **D** £80–£160*
**Facilities:** FTV tea/coffee Dinner available Direct dial WiFi ⌁18 **Parking:** 30
**Notes:** LB Closed 25–26 Dec & 1–15 Jan

# Angel House Bed and Breakfast

★★★★ BED AND BREAKFAST

**tel:** 01584 891377 & 07568 142626 **Angel Bank, Bitterley SY8 3HT**
**email:** angelhouse48@gmail.com **web:** www.angelhousecleehill.co.uk
**dir:** *On A4117 towards Kidderminster*

Angel House has a super location, set just outside the busy hustle and bustle of
Ludlow; the house has plentiful parking and super views. The friendly proprietors
are very attentive and provide a comfortable place to stay. Bedrooms are very well
appointed with lots of thoughtful extras. The gardens are spacious and home to the
chickens that provide breakfast eggs.

**Rooms:** 2 en suite (1 fmly) **S** £75; **D** £85–£90 **Facilities:** FTV DVD Lounge
tea/coffee Dinner available WiFi **Extras:** Speciality toiletries **Parking:** 3
**Notes:** No children 7yrs

**LUDLOW** *continued*

# Dinham Hall

★★★★ RESTAURANT WITH ROOMS

**tel:** 01584 876464 **By The Castle SY8 1EJ**
**email:** info@dinhamhall.com **web:** www.dinhamhall.com
**dir:** *In town centre, opposite castle*

Built in 1792, this lovely house stands in attractive gardens immediately opposite Ludlow Castle, and it has a well-deserved reputation for warm hospitality. The well-equipped bedrooms include two in a converted cottage, and some rooms have four-poster beds. The comfortable public rooms are elegantly appointed. Dishes served in the brasserie-style restaurant are based on good, seasonal produce.

**Rooms:** 11 en suite 2 annexe en suite (2 fmly) (2 GF) **S** £99–£119; **D** £119–£239*
**Facilities:** Lounge tea/coffee Dinner available WiFi **Parking:** 13

# 130 Corve Street B&B

★★★★ BED AND BREAKFAST

**tel:** 01584 875548 **130 Corve Street SY8 2PG**
**email:** info@130corvestreet.co.uk **web:** www.130corvestreet.co.uk
**dir:** *N side of town on B4361, adjacent to Tesco supermarket*

Expect a warm welcome at this Grade II listed building, situated within easy access of the town's many amenities and restaurants. The attractive bedrooms, situated on the ground floor at the rear, are comfortable and have independent entrances. Hearty breakfasts are served in the first-floor dining room. There is secure off-road parking next to the property.

**Rooms:** 3 en suite (3 GF) **S** £59–£79; **D** £79* **Facilities:** FTV DVD tea/coffee WiFi **Parking:** 3 **Notes:** No children 12yrs

| MARKET DRAYTON | Map 15 SJ63 |
|---|---|

## Premier Collection

# Ternhill Farm House

★★★★★ ⚜ 🍴 GUEST ACCOMMODATION

**tel:** 01630 638984 **Ternhill TF9 3PX**
**email:** info@ternhillfarm.co.uk **web:** www.ternhillfarm.co.uk
**dir:** *On junct A53 & A41, archway off A53 to back of property*

This elegant Grade II listed Georgian property, once a farmhouse, has been lovingly converted into friendly, family-run guest accommodation. Bedrooms are individually designed and offer high levels of comfort. A choice of cosy lounges is available, and the large garden is a pleasant feature. The Cottage Restaurant is cosy (for parties of up to 22 people) but contemporary. Dinner must be reserved when the room reservation is made, and menu choices are required a minimum of 24 working hours prior to arrival. In addition, The Cottage Restaurant and/or Dining Room may be reserved for pre-booked non-resident parties of between 10 and 24 people.

**Rooms:** 8 rms (7 en suite) (1 pri facs) **S** £55–£85; **D** £75–£105*
**Facilities:** FTV DVD Lounge tea/coffee Dinner available Licensed WiFi
**Extras:** Speciality toiletries, mineral water **Parking:** 16 **Notes:** LB
No children 14yrs RS Sun no dinner available

# The Four Alls Inn

★★★ 🍴 INN

**tel:** 01630 652995 **Woodseaves TF9 2AG**
**email:** inn@thefouralls.com **web:** www.thefouralls.com
**dir:** *On A529 1m S of Market Drayton*

This country inn provides spacious open-plan public areas and has a strong local following for its food and real ales. Bedrooms, which are in a purpose-built chalet block, offer a good balance between practicality and homeliness. The superb beer gardens are adorned with attractive floral displays in summer.

**Rooms:** 9 annexe en suite (4 fmly) (9 GF) **Facilities:** FTV tea/coffee Dinner available Direct dial WiFi 🎱 **Conf:** Max 100 Thtr 100 Class 100 Board 30 **Parking:** 60 **Notes:** LB Closed 24–26 Dec

| MUNSLOW | Map 10 SO58 |
|---|---|

# Crown Country Inn

★★★★ ⚜⚜ 🍴 INN

**tel:** 01584 841205 **SY7 9ET**
**email:** info@crowncountryinn.co.uk **web:** www.crowncountryinn.co.uk
**dir:** *Off B4368 into village*

Located between Much Wenlock and Craven Arms, this impressive pastel-coloured and half-timbered Tudor inn is full of character and charm with stone floors, exposed beams and blazing log fires during winter. The smart pine-furnished bedrooms are in a converted stable block, and the spacious public areas include two dining rooms.

**Rooms:** 3 en suite (1 GF) **S** £68–£125; **D** £99–£125 **Facilities:** FTV DVD tea/coffee Dinner available WiFi ⚓19 🎱 **Conf:** Max 30 Thtr 30 Class 30 Board 20 **Parking:** 20 **Notes:** LB No children 12yrs Closed 25 Dec RS Closed Sun evening & Mon for food & drink

| NORTON | Map 10 SJ70 |
|---|---|

# The Hundred House

★★★★ ⚜⚜ INN

**tel:** 01952 580240 & 0845 644 6100 *(Calls cost 7p per minute plus your phone company's access charge)* **Bridgnorth Road TF11 9EE**
**email:** reservations@hundredhouse.co.uk **web:** www.hundredhouse.co.uk
**dir:** *M54 junct 5, follow signs for Bridgnorth (A442), midway between Bridgnorth & Telford*

This interesting property has a genuine atmosphere of rural charm, setting it apart from the modern style of country 'food destination' pubs. A rabbit warren of public bars and restaurants, it provides respite for weary travellers and locals alike, many of whom come for the excellent meals. Bedrooms are individually designed, with quirky furnishings and decor, and are well equipped. A large beer garden provides for good weather, with well-stocked herb and flower gardens to encourage a wander.

**Rooms:** 9 en suite (4 fmly) **Facilities:** FTV tea/coffee Dinner available Direct dial WiFi ⛳18 🛁 **Extras:** Bottled water, sweets **Conf:** Max 100 Thtr 80 Class 30 Board 35 **Parking:** 50 **Notes:** LB RS 25 Dec Restaurant closed pm Civ wed 120

| OSWESTRY | Map 15 SJ22 |
|---|---|

**Premier Collection**

## Greystones

★★★★★ 🍴 🏡 GUEST HOUSE

**tel:** 07976 740141 **Crickheath SY10 8BW**
**email:** enquiry@stayatgreystones.co.uk **web:** www.stayatgreystones.co.uk
**dir:** From A483 follow B4396, turn right through village take No Through Road, Greystones on right

A warm welcome is assured at this impressive detached house, set in pretty, mature gardens in the hamlet of Crickheath. The bedrooms are equipped with a wealth of thoughtful extras and smart modern bathrooms. Comprehensive breakfasts and imaginative dinners, featuring the best seasonal produce, are available in the elegant dining room. A comfortable guest lounge is also provided. Dogs are allowed by prior arrangement only.

**Rooms:** 4 en suite (1 fmly) (1 GF) **Facilities:** FTV DVD TVL tea/coffee Dinner available Licensed WiFi 🚲 ⛳18 Fishing 🛁 **Extras:** Espresso machine, robes, fridge, fruit **Parking:** 20 **Notes:** LB No children 14yrs

## Sebastians

★★★★★ 🍴🍴 🍴 RESTAURANT WITH ROOMS

**tel:** 01691 655444 **45 Willow Street SY11 1AQ**
**email:** info@sebastians-hotel.com **web:** www.sebastians-hotel.co.uk
**dir:** From town centre, take turn signed Selattyn into Willow St. 400yds from junct on left opposite Willow Street Gallery

Sebastians is an intrinsic part of the leisure scene in Oswestry and has built up a loyal local following. Meals feature French influences, with a multi-choice set menu as well as a simpler market menu. Rooms are set around the pretty terrace courtyard, and provide very comfortable accommodation with all the comforts of home.

**Rooms:** 2 en suite 4 annexe en suite (2 fmly) (2 GF) **S** £75; **D** £85 (room only)* **Facilities:** iPod docking station Lounge tea/coffee Dinner available WiFi **Extras:** Speciality toiletries, fruit, sweets – complimentary **Parking:** 6 **Notes:** Closed Xmas/New Year & BHs

| SHIFNAL | Map 10 SJ70 |
|---|---|

## The Anvil Lodge

★★★★ GUEST ACCOMMODATION

**tel:** 01952 460125 & 07918 163289 **22 Aston Road TF11 8DU**
**email:** michaeldavies234@btinternet.com **web:** www.anvillodge.co.uk

A friendly welcome is assured at The Anvil Lodge, just a short stroll from the market town of Shifnal. Delicious, freshly cooked breakfasts are served around the dining room table. Bedrooms are spacious, fresh in appearance and very comfortable with modern bathrooms complete with bath and separate shower. Secure off-road parking is available.

**Rooms:** 4 annexe en suite (2 fmly) (2 GF) **Facilities:** FTV **Parking:** 8

| SHREWSBURY | Map 15 SJ41 |
|---|---|

*See also Criggion (Powys), Wem & Westbury*

**Premier Collection**

## Drapers Hall

★★★★★ 🍴🍴 🍷 RESTAURANT WITH ROOMS

**tel:** 01743 344679 **10 Saint Mary's Place SY1 1DZ**
**email:** goodfood@drapershallrestaurant.co.uk **web:** www.drapershallrestaurant.co.uk
**dir:** From A5191 (Saint Mary's St) on one-way system into St Mary's Place

Drapers Hall is a 16th-century, timber-framed property situated in the heart of the market town of Shrewsbury. Rooms differ in size, and all offer high levels of comfort and style, including two spacious suites. Bathrooms have a high quality finish and are well equipped for the modern traveller. The original beams and wood panels are complemented by striking art work and large gilt mirrors. A smart modern bar area successfully blends with the original architectural features, and has a great vibe. Accomplished cooking from Nigel Huxley can be enjoyed in a relaxing dining environment. Parking is available on request.

**Rooms:** 6 en suite (2 fmly) **Facilities:** FTV TVL tea/coffee Dinner available WiFi **Conf:** Max 20 Thtr 20 Class 20 Board 20

**Premier Collection**

## Darwin's Townhouse

★★★★★ 🍷 BED AND BREAKFAST

**tel:** 01743 343829 & 07576 076376 **37 St Julians Friars SY1 1XL**
**email:** info@darwinstownhouse.com **web:** www.darwinstownhouse.com
**dir:** Cross English Bridge, bear left (over pedestrian crossing) into Beeches Ln. 1st left into Williams Way, turn 1st left after car park, on left

Darwin's Townhouse is a beautifully restored Georgian property. Although situated in the centre of Shrewsbury, within walking distance of the many shops and restaurants, it sits on a peaceful street near the river. Bedrooms of various sizes are stylish and comfortable, and are located either in the main house or in the garden rooms to the rear of the property. Breakfast is served in the conservatory by the friendly team, using the finest local seasonal produce. There is an honesty bar.

**Rooms:** 12 en suite 8 annexe en suite (1 fmly) (4 GF) **S** £65–£95; **D** £95–£140* **Facilities:** FTV iPod docking station Lounge TVL tea/coffee Licensed WiFi 🛁 **Extras:** Speciality toiletries, robes, slippers; Honesty bar & snacks – chargeable **Conf:** Max 50 Thtr 50 Class 40 Board 30 **Notes:** LB

SHREWSBURY *continued*

## Porter House SY1

★★★★ ◉ RESTAURANT WITH ROOMS

**tel:** 01743 358870 & 761220 **15 Saint Mary's Street SY1 1EQ**
**email:** hello@porterhousesy1.co.uk **web:** www. porterhousesy1.co.uk
**dir:** *Follow one-way system around town, opposite St Mary's church*

This fine property is located in the heart of the town. The name comes from a cut of steak, which is relevant to the style of cuisine here, with a real emphasis on locally sourced, good quality steaks and grills, served in the award-winning vibrant restaurant or bar. The four individually designed bedrooms, including a suite, are very comfortable and have spacious and contemporary bathrooms. Breakfast offers a quality range of dishes. Secure parking is available in a nearby public car park.

**Rooms:** 4 en suite (1 fmly) **S** £65–£110; **D** £95–£140 (room only)*
**Facilities:** tea/coffee Dinner available WiFi **Notes:** LB Closed 25–26 Dec & 1 Jan RS Xmas & New Year

## The Loopy Shrew

★★★★ INN

**tel:** 01743 366505 **15–17 Bellstone SY1 1HU**
**email:** hello@loopyshrew.com **web:** www.loopyshrew.com
**dir:** *In centre of town, follow one-way system*

Sister property to Porter House SY1, The Loopy Shrew offers 12 comfortably furnished en suite rooms in the heart of historic Shrewsbury. The open plan ground floor includes a well-stocked bar, coffee lounge and split level restaurant, all of which have been refurbished in the last few years. Long stay parking is available within a few minutes' walk.

**Rooms:** 12 en suite **S** £60–£110; **D** £90–£130 (room only)* **Facilities:** FTV tea/coffee Dinner available WiFi **Extras:** Speciality toiletries – complimentary **Notes:** LB Closed 25–26 Dec & 1 Jan

## The Old Station

★★★★ BED AND BREAKFAST

**tel:** 01939 290905 & 07714 068305 **Leaton, Bomere Heath SY4 3AP**
**email:** enquiries@theoldstationshropshire.co.uk **web:** www.theoldstationshropshire.co.uk
**dir:** *M54 junct 7 onto A5 then A49 N. At Battlefield (A5124) over rdbt into Huffley Ln, left by cricket field, 100mtrs on right*

This former railway station, built in 1847, is set in the heart of the Shropshire countryside yet just four miles from Shrewsbury. The railway theme continues throughout the rooms, which offer a range of shapes and sizes. Stained-glass windows are a feature throughout the house. Breakfast is served in the well furnished dining room, with some tables located on what was previously the station platform. A garden and a small lounge are provided and there is ample parking.

**Rooms:** 6 en suite (4 fmly) (1 GF) **S** fr £45; **D** fr £75* **Facilities:** FTV TVL tea/coffee Dinner available WiFi ⊛ **Extras:** Fridge in 2 bedrooms **Parking:** 11 **Notes:** LB Closed Dec–Feb

| TELFORD | Map 10 SJ60 |
|---|---|

## The Old Rectory of St James

[U]

**tel:** 01952 598519 & 07747 058512 **Stirchley Village TF3 1DY**
**email:** enquiries@theoldrectoryofstjames.co.uk **web:** www.theoldrectoryofstjames.co.uk
**dir:** *Follow signs for Stirchley, into Stirchley Rd, pass Rose and Crown pub & follow brown signs for St James Church*

Currently the rating for this establishment is not confirmed. This may be due to a change of ownership or because it has only recently joined the AA rating scheme.

**Rooms:** 4 rms (3 en suite) (1 pri facs) **S** fr £75; **D** £90–£105* **Facilities:** FTV DVD Lounge tea/coffee Dinner available WiFi ⊛ **Parking:** 4 **Notes:** No children 16yrs

| UPTON MAGNA | Map 10 SJ51 |
|---|---|

## The Haughmond

★★★★ ◉◉ ⚲ INN

**tel:** 01743 709918 **Pelham Road SY4 4TZ**
**email:** contact@thehaughmond.co.uk **web:** www.thehaughmond.co.uk

This delightful village inn has undergone a complete refurbishment to provide a contemporary dining area and bar with a range of comfortable bedrooms above. All rooms offer welcome extras and WiFi, with large rain showers in the bathrooms. Carefully prepared dishes, making good use of quality, local produce, are served for breakfast and dinner. Car parking, a garden with seating and even the village shop/café are on site. A recent addition is Basil's restaurant (open Thursday to Saturday evenings), located in the former hayloft of a large barn conversion. If you were wondering, Basil is the family dog.

**Rooms:** 5 en suite (1 fmly) **S** £75–£100; **D** £90–£120* **Facilities:** STV FTV iPod docking station Lounge tea/coffee Dinner available WiFi ⚹ ⊛ **Extras:** Smart TVs with Netflix **Conf:** Max 60 Thtr 40 Class 60 Board 30 **Parking:** 30

## WELLINGTON
Map 10 SJ61

### Premier Collection

## The Old Orleton Inn
★★★★★ Ⓐ INN

tel: 01952 255011 & 07515 352538 **Holyhead Road TF1 2HA**
email: info@theoldorleton.com web: www.theoldorleton.com
dir: *M54 junct 7, towards Wellington then 400yds on left on corner of Haygate Rd & Holyhead Rd*

Facing the Wrekin, this impressive 17th-century coaching inn has been appointed in a charming contemporary style. Each of the boutique-style bedrooms is unique in design and character, yet all retain original antique features. The kitchen has a good local reputation and fresh, quality produce, sourced locally whenever possible, is used in everything from snacks to three-course dinners, which are served in the three dining rooms.

**Rooms:** 10 en suite **S** £79–£99; **D** £99–£119* **Facilities:** FTV iPod docking station tea/coffee Dinner available Direct dial WiFi ♪18 Discounted access to local gym/spa **Conf:** Max 15 Thtr 15 Class 15 Board 15 **Parking:** 25 **Notes:** LB No children 5yrs Closed 1st 2 weeks Jan

## The Lord Nelson
★★ GUEST ACCOMMODATION

tel: 01952 240055 **11–13 Park Street TF1 3AE**
web: www.hotelintelford.com
dir: *Contact The Lord Nelson for detailed directions*

This Grade II listed property is located in a quiet residential area close to town. Inside there are a number of eating options, as well as comfortably appointed bedrooms in a range of sizes. There is a large car park to the rear and free WiFi is available throughout.

**Rooms:** 12 en suite **Facilities:** FTV tea/coffee Licensed WiFi **Parking:** 12 **Notes:** Closed 16 Dec–6 Jan

## WEM
Map 15 SJ52

## Aston Lodge Guest House
★★★★ BED AND BREAKFAST

tel: 01939 232577 **Soulton Road SY4 5BG**
email: astonlodge@btconnect.com web: www.aston-lodge.co.uk
dir: *On B5065, close to Wem railway station*

Aston Lodge is an elegant Georgian house situated in a quiet, convenient position close to the train station in the heart of Wem. Some bedrooms are in the main house while the others are found in the adjoining coach house. Of the latter, two are on the ground floor and the other has its own lounge. All rooms are of a high standard and have free WiFi and high quality bathrooms. Breakfast is served in the spacious dining room using fine quality and, where possible, locally-sourced produce. A comfortable lounge is available for guest use. There is ample off-road parking and a pleasant good-sized garden.

**Rooms:** 3 rms (2 en suite) (1 pri facs) 3 annexe en suite (1 fmly) (2 GF) **S** £49–£59; **D** £74–£94 **Facilities:** FTV DVD TVL tea/coffee WiFi **Parking:** 6 **Notes:** No children 10yrs RS 25–26 Dec room only

## WESTBURY
Map 15 SJ30

## Barley Mow House
★★★★ BED AND BREAKFAST

tel: 01743 891234 & 07890 215412 **Aston Rogers SY5 9HQ**
email: colinrigby@astonrogers.fsnet.co.uk web: www.barleymowhouse.co.uk
dir: *2m S of Westbury. Exit B4386 into Aston Rogers, house 400yds opposite Aston Hall*

Dating in part from the 17th century and extended in the 18th, this charming property has been restored to provide comfortable accommodation with modern facilities. The house stands in a peaceful village and is surrounded by beautifully maintained gardens.

**Rooms:** 3 en suite (1 fmly) (1 GF) **Facilities:** FTV TVL tea/coffee WiFi ⚓ **Parking:** 4 **Notes:** LB Closed Dec–1 Mar

### SOMERSET

## AXBRIDGE
Map 4 ST45

### Premier Collection

## The Oak House
★★★★★ ⊚⊚ ♔ RESTAURANT WITH ROOMS

tel: 01934 732444 **The Square BS26 2AP**
email: info@theoakhousesomerset.com web: www.theoakhousesomerset.com
dir: *M5 junct 22, A38 N, turn right towards Axbridge & Cheddar*

This impressive restaurant with rooms is located in the middle of the village and provides a relaxed, high quality experience, whether guests are coming to enjoy the restaurant or to stay in one of the nine bedrooms above. Hospitality and service are delivered in an efficient and helpful manner by a young and enthusiastic team. The kitchen has a serious approach and delivers delightful dishes full of flavour, utilising the best quality produce.

**Rooms:** 9 en suite (2 fmly) **Facilities:** FTV DVD Lounge tea/coffee Dinner available WiFi **Notes:** Closed 2-5 Jan RS Sun eve & Mon eve Restaurant closed

## BABCARY
Map 4 ST52

## The Red Lion Inn
★★★★ ⚘ INN

tel: 01458 223230 **Main Street TA11 7ED**
email: info@redlionbabcary.co.uk web: www.redlionbabcary.co.uk
dir: *Off A303 & A37*

Tucked away in a sleepy village, this engaging country pub has so much to offer and provides an appealing blend of traditional and contemporary styles. The thatched roof, flagstone floors and crackling log fires all set the tone alongside a committed team dedicated to ensuring guests are properly looked after. Bedrooms are located in the adjacent barn and provide impressive levels of comfort and quality, with all the necessities for a thoroughly relaxing stay. Food is not to be missed, as a skilled kitchen team make excellent use of the best the area has to offer. An alternative option in spring and summer is The Den, a stylish function room in the gardens which houses a wood-fired pizza oven.

**Rooms:** 6 annexe en suite (2 fmly) (4 GF) **S** £90–£110; **D** £110–£130* **Facilities:** DVD tea/coffee Dinner available Direct dial WiFi **Extras:** Speciality toiletries, snacks **Parking:** 35

## BACKWELL
Map 4 ST46

### Premier Collection

## The Rising Sun
★★★★★ ⬤ INN

**tel:** 01275 462215 **91 West Town Road BS48 3BH**
**email:** therisingsun@ohhcompany.co.uk **web:** www.ohhpubs.co.uk

Recently refurbished throughout, The Rising Sun has been transformed under the new owners (OHH pub company) and now delivers high quality bedrooms and bathrooms with excellent hospitality and service. Rooms are in a range of shapes and sizes and are all decorated to very comfortable standards. A good selection of real ales and wines are available to accompany the range of tempting dishes from the regularly changing dinner menu. Breakfast also offers a good selection and features high quality produce. A car park, and rear garden with seating are also available.

**Rooms:** 6 en suite **Facilities:** Dinner available **Parking**

## BALTONSBOROUGH
Map 4 ST53

## Lower Farm
★★★★ FARMHOUSE

**tel:** 01458 850206 & 07773 497188 **Lottisham BA6 8PF**
**email:** dboard51@btinternet.com **web:** www.lowerfarmbandb.co.uk
**dir:** From Shepton Mallet take A37 over Wraxall Hill past Queens Arms. Follow road 3rd turning on right to Lottisham, 1st on right

A working farm peacefully located and surrounded by pleasant countryside, where the proprietors offer a genuine welcome and traditional farmhouse hospitality. The one en suite bedroom is spacious and well equipped, and is located on the ground floor at one end of the main building. Breakfast is taken in the comfortable dining room where a wood-burning fire adds to the ambience during the winter.

**Rooms:** 1 en suite (1 GF) **Facilities:** FTV TVL tea/coffee ♿ **Notes:** beef/sheep farm

## BATH
Map 4 ST76
*See also Box (Wiltshire), Bradford-on-Avon (Wiltshire) & Frome*

### Premier Collection

## Apple Tree Guest House
★★★★★ ⬤ GUEST HOUSE

**tel:** 01225 337642 **7 Pulteney Gardens BA2 4HG**
**email:** enquiries@appletreebath.com **web:** www.appletreeguesthouse.com
**dir:** A4 onto A36 into Pulteney Rd. Under railway bridge, take 2nd left into Pulteney Gdns

This charming house is quietly located, and offers a tranquil setting. Some parking is available, and the location is within walking distance of Bath's many attractions. Excellent breakfasts are served in the cosy breakfast lounge. Bedrooms are thoughtfully appointed, and beds are particularly comfortable.

**Rooms:** 4 en suite **Facilities:** FTV tea/coffee WiFi Massage & beauty treatments **Extras:** Speciality toiletries – complimentary **Parking:** 2 **Notes:** No children 11yrs Closed 14 Dec–9 Jan

### Premier Collection

## Apsley House
★★★★★ ⬤ BED AND BREAKFAST

**tel:** 01225 336966 **Newbridge Hill BA1 3PT**
**email:** info@apsley-house.co.uk **web:** www.apsley-house.co.uk
**dir:** 1.3m W of city centre on A431

Built in 1830 by the Duke of Wellington, Apsley House is within walking distance (allow around half an hour) of the city centre. The house is extremely elegant, and the spacious bedrooms have pleasant views. Some rooms have four-poster beds, and there are two family rooms. A smart breakfast room and a delightful lounge are available.

**Rooms:** 11 en suite (2 fmly) (1 GF) **S** £99–£180; **D** £120–£240* **Facilities:** STV FTV DVD iPod docking station Lounge tea/coffee Direct dial Licensed WiFi **Extras:** Speciality toiletries, bottled water, mini-bar **Parking:** 12 **Notes:** LB Closed 3 days Xmas

### Premier Collection

## Tasburgh House
★★★★★ ⬤ GUEST ACCOMMODATION

**tel:** 01225 425096 **Warminster Road BA2 6SH**
**email:** stay@tasburghhouse.co.uk **web:** www.tasburghhouse.co.uk
**dir:** On N side of A36, next to Bathampton Ln junct

Located on the main road just outside Bath, this elegant, detached property has undergone a complete refurbishment and provides high levels of quality and comfort throughout. Relaxing public areas include a guest lounge and the delightful conservatory-style breakfast room. Bedrooms vary in size but each includes a host of extras and very comfortable beds. Guests also have use of outdoor seating on the terrace, the large garden, and off-street parking.

**Rooms:** 15 en suite (3 fmly) (2 GF) **S** £97.50–£112.50; **D** £117–£196* **Facilities:** FTV DVD Lounge tea/coffee Dinner available Direct dial Licensed WiFi ♿ 🏌18 Fishing ⬤ **Extras:** Speciality toiletries, fresh milk – complimentary **Conf:** Max 15 Thtr 10 Class 10 Board 15 **Parking:** 16 **Notes:** No children 6yrs Closed 21–31 Dec RS 2 days per week Jan–Feb

### Premier Collection

## River House and Friary Coach House
★★★★★ GUEST ACCOMMODATION

**tel:** 01225 722252 & 07712 437478 **Friary, Freshford BA2 7UE**
**email:** info@riverhousebath.com **web:** www.riverhousebath.com
**dir:** A36 S of Bath, pass signs for Freshford on left, take left turn at x-rds sign down narrow lane, "No through road"

Set in eleven acres of delightfully peaceful former monastery grounds, River House offers views over the delightful gardens, and is just five miles from Bath. Accommodation consists of five comfortable bedrooms in the main house with lounges and relaxing areas for guests to enjoy, and the separate Friary Coach House: a luxurious, self-contained building adjacent to the main house. Guests in the Coach House have the option of breakfast being delivered to their own dining room. Attentive service and a genuine welcome are assured.

**Rooms:** 5 rms (4 en suite) 1 annexe en suite (2 fmly) (2 GF) **Facilities:** STV FTV DVD iPod docking station Lounge TVL tea/coffee Dinner available Direct dial Licensed WiFi ♿ ♿ Fishing ⬤ Hot tub Badminton Art Nature Trail Clock golf **Extras:** Chocolates, fridge, speciality toiletries, fresh fruit, flowers – complimentary **Parking:** 10 **Notes:** LB

Premier Collection

## Chestnuts House

★★★★★ ☕ GUEST ACCOMMODATION

**tel:** 01225 334279 **16 Henrietta Road BA2 6LY**
**email:** reservations@chestnutshouse.co.uk **web:** www.chestnutshouse.co.uk
**dir:** *Enter Bath on A46, under flyover, right at rdbt. Follow signs for A36 Warminster, over Cleveland Bridge & turn right. 50mtrs on left*

Located just a few minutes' walk from the city centre and appointed using light shades and oak, Chestnuts' accommodation is fresh and airy. Bedrooms are attractively co-ordinated, well equipped and comfortable. Added enhancements such as WiFi make the rooms suitable for both business and leisure guests. Breakfast, which features quite an extensive buffet and daily specials, is served in the dining room that opens onto the pretty rear garden. There is a cosy lounge, and the small car park is a bonus.

**Rooms:** 5 en suite (1 fmly) (2 GF) **Facilities:** STV FTV DVD TVL tea/coffee WiFi **Extras:** Speciality toiletries **Parking:** 5

Premier Collection

## Waterhouse

★★★★★ ☕ GUEST ACCOMMODATION

**tel:** 01225 721999 **Waterhouse Lane, Monkton Combe BA2 7JB**
**email:** waterhouse@wilsher-group.com **web:** www.waterhousebath.co.uk
**dir:** *From Bath on A36 to Monkton Combe, over viaduct, turn right into Waterhouse Ln. From S on A36 turn left into Waterhouse Ln, at bottom of the hill*

This 18th-century manor house is in a peaceful location just a couple of miles outside of Bath. It offers modern bedrooms and bathrooms with plenty of welcome guest extras, and a range of relaxing lounges. Guests can enjoy the garden, and country walks start straight from the front door. Breakfast is served in the contemporary dining room, and meeting rooms are also available.

**Rooms:** 13 en suite (4 fmly) **D** £87–£159 (room only)* **Facilities:** FTV Lounge TVL tea/coffee Direct dial Lift Licensed WiFi ⌁18 Fishing ⚓ **Extras:** Fresh milk, bottled water – complimentary; fridge **Conf:** Max 40 Thtr 40 Class 20 Board 16 **Parking:** 45 **Notes:** LB

Premier Collection

## Dorian House

★★★★★ GUEST ACCOMMODATION

**tel:** 01225 426336 **1 Upper Oldfield Park BA2 3JX**
**email:** info@dorianhouse.co.uk **web:** www.dorianhouse.co.uk
**dir:** *A36 onto A367 (Wells Rd), right into Upper Oldfield Park, 3rd building on left*

This elegant Victorian property has stunning views over the city. The atmosphere is welcoming, and the accommodation high quality. Several of the rooms have fine period four-poster beds and all offer a range of extra facilities. The attractive lounge has an honesty bar and views of the terraced gardens.

**Rooms:** 13 en suite (4 fmly) (2 GF) **Facilities:** FTV iPod docking station Lounge tea/coffee Direct dial Licensed WiFi ⚓ **Parking:** 9 **Notes:** LB Closed 24–26 Dec

Premier Collection

## The Windsor Townhouse

★★★★★ GUEST HOUSE

**tel:** 01225 422100 **69 Great Pulteney Street BA2 4DL**
**email:** sales@bathwindsorguesthouse.com **web:** www.bathwindsorguesthouse.com

An easy two-minute walk from the city centre, shops, restaurants and attractions, The Windsor is set in a Grade I listed Georgian townhouse on Great Pulteney Street, one of the finest boulevards in Europe. Inside are 15 individually-styled, en suite bedrooms. Period features, free WiFi, air-conditioning, TVs, tea- and coffee-making facilities, hairdryer, mini-safe and ironing board come as standard. The addition of thick soft fluffy towels, cosy Dorma duvets, pillows and luxury Gilchrist and Soames toiletries complete the package. Breakfast offers a good selection of well-prepared, hot and cold dishes, and staff are very friendly and willing to help. Parking permits are available to purchase for the street outside.

**Rooms:** 15 en suite (1 fmly) **S** £69–£130; **D** £89–£200 (room only)*
**Facilities:** STV FTV DVD iPod docking station tea/coffee Direct dial Licensed WiFi **Extras:** Speciality toiletries, mini-bar, mini-safe **Parking:** 4

## Astor House

★★★★ BED AND BREAKFAST

**tel:** 01225 429134 & 07921 139558 **14 Oldfield Road BA2 3ND**
**email:** astorhouse.visitus@virgin.net **web:** www.astorhouse-bath.co.uk
**dir:** *A4 into Bath to lights, then follow A36 (avoiding city centre). Onto A367, then 2nd right*

Astor House offers very comfortable accommodation and personal, friendly service. Rooms are understatedly elegant, and equipped with a wealth of extras for the modern traveller. Hearty breakfasts are served in the light dining room. The location, in a quiet street, is within easy distance of all central attractions, making it an ideal base from which to explore the city.

**Rooms:** 7 en suite (3 fmly) **Facilities:** FTV Lounge TVL tea/coffee Direct dial WiFi ⌁ ⚓ **Parking:** 5

BATH *continued*

## The Bailbrook Lodge

★★★★ ⚏ GUEST HOUSE

**tel:** 01225 859090 **3537 London Road West BA1 7HZ**
**email:** hotel@bailbrooklodge.co.uk **web:** www.bailbrooklodge.co.uk
**dir:** *M4 junct 18, A46 S to A4 junct, left signed Batheaston. Lodge 1st on left*

Set in extensive gardens on the eastern edge of the city, this imposing Georgian building provides smart accommodation. The well-equipped bedrooms include some with four-poster beds and period furniture, and service is professional and efficient. The inviting lounge has a small bar, and light snacks are available from noon until evening. Breakfast is served in the elegant dining room.

**Rooms:** 15 rms (14 en suite) (1 pri facs) (5 fmly) (1 GF) **S** £79–£109; **D** £89–£119*
**Facilities:** FTV DVD iPod docking station Lounge tea/coffee Licensed WiFi ⚓
**Extras:** Mineral water, bath robes in some rooms **Conf:** Max 20 Thtr 20 Class 10 Board 12 **Parking:** 15 **Notes:** LB

## Marlborough House

★★★★ GUEST ACCOMMODATION

**tel:** 01225 318175 & 07960 907541 **1 Marlborough Lane BA1 2NQ**
**email:** mars@manque.dircon.co.uk **web:** www.marlborough-house.net
**dir:** *450yds W of city centre, at A4 junct with Marlborough Ln*

Marlborough House is situated opposite Royal Victoria Park and close to the Royal Crescent. Some original features remain and the rooms are decorated with period furniture and pictures. The atmosphere is relaxed, and service is attentive and friendly. The breakfast, served from an open-plan kitchen, is vegetarian and organic.

**Rooms:** 6 en suite (3 fmly) (1 GF) **S** £95–£145; **D** £95–£155 **Facilities:** FTV Lounge tea/coffee Direct dial Licensed WiFi ⚓ **Extras:** Organic toiletries, water; mini-bar – chargeable **Parking:** 3 **Notes:** LB Closed 24–26 Dec

## Villa Claudia

★★★★ BED AND BREAKFAST

**tel:** 01225 329670 **19 Forester Road, Bathwick BA2 6QE**
**email:** claudiaamato77@aol.com **web:** www.villaclaudia.co.uk
**dir:** *From A4 into Cleveland Place East (A36), at next rdbt 1st exit into Beckford Rd, left into Forester Rd*

Villa Claudia is a beautiful Victorian property located on a quiet, tree-lined residential street within easy walking distance of the city centre's attractions and restaurants. The Italian owners provide attentive and personal service. Bedrooms and bathrooms are beautifully decorated and very comfortable; a four-poster room is available. Delicious breakfasts are served in the charming dining room at a communal table.

**Rooms:** 3 rms (1 en suite) (2 pri facs) (1 fmly) **D** £125–£130* **Facilities:** FTV DVD tea/coffee WiFi **Extras:** Mineral water – complimentary **Parking:** 4 **Notes:** No children 5yrs Closed 21 Dec–1 Jan

## The Hollies

★★★★ GUEST ACCOMMODATION

**tel:** 01225 313366 **Hatfield Road BA2 2BD**
**email:** davcartwright@lineone.net **web:** www.theholliesbath.co.uk
**dir:** *A36 onto A367 Wells Rd & Wellsway, 0.7m right opposite Devonshire Arms*

This delightful house stands in impressive gardens overlooking a magnificent church, and is within easy reach of the city centre. The individually decorated, themed bedrooms are appointed to provide excellent levels of comfort and have good facilities. Breakfast in the elegant dining room is an enjoyable start to the day.

**Rooms:** 3 rms (2 en suite) (1 pri facs) **D** £115* **Facilities:** FTV Lounge tea/coffee WiFi ⚓ **Extras:** Sweets **Parking:** 3 **Notes:** No children 16yrs Closed 15 Dec–15 Jan

## Poplar House

★★★★ BED AND BREAKFAST

**tel:** 01225 852629 **9 The Batch BA1 7DR**
**email:** poplarhousebath@gmail.com **web:** www.poplarhousebath.co.uk
**dir:** *M4 junct 18 onto A46 (London Rd). Left at rdbt, located on left*

Located a short drive from the centre of Bath, Poplar House is a very well-maintained property that offers comfortable accommodation in a peaceful setting. Bedrooms offer a range of shapes and sizes, and guests are also welcome to use the comfortable lounge and outdoor seating terrace. Breakfast utilises good quality produce and is served around one large table in the very pleasant dining room.

**Rooms:** 3 en suite **Facilities:** FTV TVL tea/coffee WiFi ⚓ **Extras:** Robes, sweets – complimentary **Parking:** 6

## Brocks Guest House

★★★★ GUEST ACCOMMODATION

**tel:** 01225 338374 **32 Brock Street BA1 2LN**
**email:** brocks@brocksguesthouse.co.uk **web:** www.brocksguesthouse.co.uk
**dir:** *Just off A4 between Circus & Royal Crescent*

A warm welcome is extended at this delightful Georgian property, located in the heart of the city just a few hundred yards from Royal Crescent. All rooms reflect the comfortable elegance of the Georgian era. A traditional breakfast is served in the charming dining room, which also offers a lounge area with comfortable seating.

**Rooms:** 6 en suite (2 fmly) **Facilities:** FTV Lounge tea/coffee WiFi ⚓ **Notes:** Closed 24 Dec–1 Jan

## Milton House Bed & Breakfast

★★★★ BED AND BREAKFAST

**tel:** 01225 335632 & 07875 319567 **75 Wellsway BA2 4RU**
**email:** info@milton-house.co.uk **web:** www.milton-house.co.uk
**dir:** *A36 inner ring road onto A367 (Wells Road). After 0.5m, sharp right turn, Milton House 150 yards on left*

Located in a residential area just 15 minutes' walk from the centre of Bath, this comfortable establishment is run by Gibson and Blessing Mutandwa, who offer a very warm welcome to all guests. Bedrooms come in a range of shapes and sizes and are all well furnished and equipped. A carefully prepared breakfast is provided in the comfortable dining room. Parking is available on the side streets nearby, or on the main road outside.

**Rooms:** 4 en suite (1 fmly) **S** £65–£90; **D** £75–£95* **Facilities:** FTV tea/coffee WiFi ⚓ **Notes:** No children 8yrs

## Pulteney House

★★★★ GUEST ACCOMMODATION

**tel:** 01225 460991 **14 Pulteney Road BA2 4HA**
**email:** pulteneyhouse@gmail.com **web:** www.pulteneyhotel.co.uk
**dir:** *On A36*

This large detached property situated in a well-tended garden, is within walking distance of the city centre. Bedrooms vary in size including some annexe rooms, and are well equipped with useful facilities. Full English breakfasts are served in the dining room at individual tables. A guest lounge and car park are both welcome features.

**Rooms:** 12 rms (11 en suite) (1 pri facs) 5 annexe en suite (3 fmly) (2 GF)
**S** £65–£75; **D** £85–£180 **Facilities:** STV FTV TVL tea/coffee WiFi 🚲 **Parking:** 18
**Notes:** LB Closed 24-26 Dec

*See advert on following page*

## Wentworth House

★★★★ GUEST ACCOMMODATION

**tel:** 01225 339193 **106 Bloomfield Road BA2 2AP**
**email:** stay@wentworthhouse.co.uk **web:** www.wentworthhouse.co.uk
**dir:** *From city centre on A367 (signed Shepton Mallet), right into Bloomfield Rd*

Set in an elevated position above Bath with views over the city, Wentworth House is a comfortable establishment that includes a relaxing guest lounge, bar and garden with pool and hot tub in the summer. Bedrooms offer a range of shapes and sizes – some with four posters. Breakfast is served in the spacious dining room overlooking the garden.

**Rooms:** 19 rms (18 en suite) (1 pri facs) 1 annexe en suite (3 fmly) (9 GF)
**Facilities:** FTV TVL tea/coffee Direct dial Licensed WiFi ⚑ Hot tub **Conf:** Max 15
Class 15 Board 15 **Parking:** 15 **Notes:** LB

## The Rising Sun Inn

★★★ INN

**tel:** 01225 425918 & 07815 741764 **3–4 Grove Street BA2 6PJ**
**email:** therisingsunbath@gmail.com **web:** www.therisingsunbath.co.uk
**dir:** *From A46 into Bath. Left at lights, over Cleveland Bridge, 1st right into St John's Rd, leads into Grove St*

This inn has an excellent location, just a few minutes' stroll from central Bath and all its attractions. Bedrooms are comfortably furnished and come in a range of shapes and sizes. A good selection of real ales is offered at the bar along with traditional dishes and home-cooked specials.

**Rooms:** 6 en suite (2 fmly) **S** £65–£85; **D** £95–£135* **Facilities:** FTV tea/coffee
Dinner available WiFi

## Waltons Guest House

★★★ GUEST HOUSE

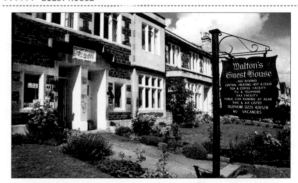

**tel:** 01225 426528 **17–19 Crescent Gardens, Upper Bristol Road BA1 2NA**
**email:** rose@waltonsguesthouse.co.uk **web:** www.bathguesthouse.com
**dir:** *On A4 350yds W of city centre*

There is a warm welcome at Waltons Guest House, situated within strolling distance of the centre of Bath. The cosy bedrooms come with useful extra facilities, and a traditional English breakfast is served at individual tables in the dining room.

**Rooms:** 7 en suite **S** £55–£85; **D** £85–£95* **Facilities:** FTV tea/coffee WiFi

*See advert on page 237*

## BRIDGWATER
Map 4 ST23

# Blackmore Farm
★★★★ FARMHOUSE

tel: 01278 653442 **Blackmore Lane, Cannington TA5 2NE**
email: dyerfarm@aol.com web: www.blackmorefarm.co.uk
dir: *3m W of Bridgwater. Follow brown tourist signs on A39, before Cannington*

Dating back to the 15th century, this Grade I listed manor house is truly unique; it has a wealth of original features such as oak beams, huge open fireplaces, stone archways and even a chapel. Bedrooms located in the main house are individual in style and one has a wonderful four-poster and a lofty, oak-beamed ceiling. Additionally, some bedrooms are located in a separate area, offering flexible accommodation with wonderful views across the rolling countryside. Breakfast is taken in the grandeur of the dining room around one incredibly long table – a truly memorable experience.

**Rooms:** 3 en suite 6 annexe en suite (1 fmly) (6 GF) **Facilities:** FTV TVL tea/coffee Licensed WiFi ⚓ ⚓18 Fishing ⚓ Farm shop café **Extras:** Fruit, bath robes in some rooms – complimentary **Conf:** Max 30 Board 30 **Parking:** 10 **Notes:** LB 900 acres dairy/arable

# Ash-Wembdon Farm
★★★★ FARMHOUSE

tel: 01278 453097 **Hollow Lane, Wembdon TA5 2BD**
email: mary.rowe@btinternet.com web: www.farmaccommodation.co.uk
dir: *M5, A38, A39 to Minehead, at rdbt 3rd exit into Homeburg Way, at lights take B3339, right into Hollow Ln*

Near the Quantock Hills, Ash-Wembdon Farm is a 17th-century farmhouse on a working beef and arable farm, offering homely and comfortable accommodation. All rooms have en suite showers or private bathrooms, and English or continental breakfasts are served in the guest dining room. Guests also have use of a lounge and landscaped garden.

**Rooms:** 3 rms (2 en suite) (1 pri facs) **S** £45–£50; **D** £65–£70 **Facilities:** FTV Lounge tea/coffee WiFi ⚓ **Parking:** 3 **Notes:** LB No children 12yrs Closed 22 Dec–3 Jan 340 acres arable/beef

## BROMPTON REGIS
Map 3 SS93

# Holworthy Farm
★★★★ ⚓ FARMHOUSE

tel: 01398 371244 **TA22 9NY**
email: holworthyfarm@aol.com web: www.holworthyfarm.co.uk
dir: *2m E of Brompton Regis. Exit A396 on E side of Wimbleball Lake*

Set in the south-east corner of Exmoor, this working livestock farm has spectacular views over Wimbleball Lake. Bedrooms are traditionally furnished and well equipped. The dining room overlooking the garden is an attractive setting for breakfast. Dinner is available by arrangement.

**Rooms:** 5 rms (3 en suite) (2 pri facs) (2 fmly) (1 GF) **Facilities:** FTV DVD Lounge TVL tea/coffee Dinner available WiFi ⚓ **Extras:** Bottled water – complimentary **Conf:** Max 20 Class 20 Board 20 **Parking:** 8 **Notes:** LB 200 acres beef/sheep

## CASTLE CARY
Map 4 ST63

# The Pilgrims
★★★★ ⚓⚓ ⚓ RESTAURANT WITH ROOMS

tel: 01963 240600 **Lovington BA7 7PT**
email: jools@thepilgrimsatlovington.co.uk web: www.thepilgrimsatlovington.co.uk
dir: *On B3153, 1.5m E of lights on A37 at Lydford*

The Pilgrims describes itself as 'the pub that thinks it's a restaurant', which is pretty accurate. With a real emphasis on fresh, local and carefully prepared produce, both dinner and breakfast are the focus of any stay here. In addition, the resident family proprietors provide a friendly and relaxed atmosphere. Comfortable and well-equipped bedrooms are available in the adjacent converted cider barn.

**Rooms:** 5 annexe en suite (5 GF) **S** £80–£130; **D** £100–£130* **Facilities:** FTV Lounge tea/coffee Dinner available WiFi **Extras:** Speciality toiletries **Parking:** 5 **Notes:** LB No children 14yrs RS Sun lunch–Tue lunch Restaurant & bar closed to non-residents

## CHARD                              Map 4 ST30

### Hornsbury Mill

★★★★ 🍴 GUEST ACCOMMODATION

**tel:** 01460 63317 **Eleighwater TA20 3AQ**
**email:** info@hornsburymill.co.uk **web:** www.hornsburymill.co.uk
**dir:** Off A358

Hornsbury Mill is a charming example of an early 19th-century corn mill, built of local flint with hamstone mullion windows. The waterwheel has been lovingly restored and turns during daylight hours; and there are four acres of beautiful gardens, making this a popular wedding venue. Bedrooms include a ground-floor room with good disabled access and facilities, and the delightful Crown Wheel Suite with four-poster bed and separate sitting room.

**Rooms:** 10 en suite (2 fmly) (1 GF) **S** £85; **D** £110* **Facilities:** FTV DVD Lounge tea/coffee Dinner available Direct dial Licensed WiFi 🔒 **Extras:** Speciality toiletries – complimentary **Conf:** Max 150 Thtr 150 Class 50 Board 50 **Parking:** 80 **Notes:** Closed 24 Dec–7 Jan Civ wed 130

## CHEDDAR                            Map 4 ST45

### The Bath Arms

[U]

**tel:** 01934 742425 **Bath Street BS27 3AA**
**email:** info@batharms.com **web:** www.batharms.com

Currently the rating for this establishment is not confirmed. This may be due to a change of ownership or because it has only recently joined the AA rating scheme.

**Rooms:** 6 en suite **S** £88–£145; **D** £95–£145* **Facilities:** FTV tea/coffee Dinner available WiFi **Extras:** Speciality toiletries, bottled water, snacks – complimentary **Parking:** 60

## CHEW MAGNA                         Map 4 ST56

### Premier Collection

### The Bear & Swan

★★★★★ 🍴 INN

**tel:** 01275 331100 **13 South Parade BS40 8PR**
**email:** thebearandswan@ohhcompany.co.uk **web:** www.ohhpubs.co.uk
**dir:** Chew Magna signed from A37 & A38, in centre of village

Part of a small and impressive collection of fine quality inns, this delightful village pub offers the best of traditional hospitality with an impressive range of dishes served throughout the day and evening. Newly refurbished bedrooms and bathrooms provide plenty of quality and comfort with sumptuous beds and bedding, and modern, spacious showers. All this along with a well-chosen selection of ales and wines will ensure a most relaxing stay.

**Rooms:** 4 en suite (1 fmly) **D** £90–£130* **Facilities:** FTV tea/coffee Dinner available Direct dial WiFi 🔒 **Extras:** Slippers **Parking:** 6 **Notes:** LB

## CLUTTON                            Map 4 ST65

### The Hunters Rest

★★★★ 🍴 INN

**tel:** 01761 452303 **King Lane, Clutton Hill BS39 5QL**
**email:** paul@huntersrest.co.uk **web:** www.huntersrest.co.uk
**dir:** Off A37 onto A368 towards Bath, 100yds right into lane, left at T-junct, inn 0.25m on left

The Hunters Rest was originally built around 1750 as a hunting lodge for the Earl of Warwick. Set in delightful countryside, it is ideally located for Bath, Bristol and Wells. Bedrooms and bathrooms are furnished and equipped to excellent standards, and the ground floor combines the character of a real country inn with an excellent range of home-cooked meals.

**Rooms:** 5 en suite (2 fmly) **Facilities:** FTV iPod docking station tea/coffee Dinner available Direct dial WiFi 🎣18 Fishing 🔒 **Conf:** Max 40 Thtr 40 Class 25 Board 25 **Parking:** 90 **Notes:** LB

## COMPTON MARTIN
Map 4 ST55

# Ring O Bells
★★★★ ☜ INN

**tel:** 01761 221284 **BS40 6JE**
**email:** ring_o_bells@btconnect.com **web:** www.ringobellscomptonmartin.co.uk
**dir:** *On A368 between Blagdon & Chew Valley*

The Ring O Bells is a delightful village inn that offers a rare combination of traditional character and hospitality with some more modern, quirky additions. The bar and dining areas are full of interest, and along with a good selection of real ales, a range of excellent dishes is offered. Bedrooms include very comfortable king-sized beds and quality showers in the bathrooms. Outdoor seating in the rear garden and car parking are both welcome features.

**Rooms:** 1 en suite 1 annexe en suite (2 GF) **Facilities:** FTV iPod docking station Lounge tea/coffee Dinner available WiFi ⚓18 🔒 **Parking:** 60 **Notes:** LB RS Mon—Wed closed 3—6pm

## CONGRESBURY
Map 4 ST46

# Mezzé at the Ship and Castle
★★★★ ☜ INN

**tel:** 01934 833535 **High Street BS49 5BN**
**email:** congresbury@mezzerestaurants.com **web:** www.mezzerestaurants.com

Part of the Mezzé chain, this pleasant inn offers good quality bedrooms and bathrooms in a range of shapes and sizes. The restaurant is very well decorated and furnished in a contemporary style, providing comfortable all-day dining. The extensive menu offers the popular range of tapas dishes in addition to a more traditional menu. The pleasant rear garden is especially popular for outdoor dining.

**Rooms:** 6 en suite (2 fmly) **S** £60—£65; **D** £70—£80* **Facilities:** FTV DVD iPod docking station tea/coffee Dinner available WiFi **Parking:** 60

## CORTON DENHAM
Map 4 ST62

### Premier Collection

# The Queens Arms
★★★★★ ◎◎ ☜ INN

**tel:** 01963 220317 **Corton Denham DT9 4LR**
**email:** relax@thequeensarms.com **web:** www.thequeensarms.com
**dir:** *A303 exit Chapel Cross signed South Cadbury & Corton Denham. Follow signs to South Cadbury. Through village, after 0.25m turn left up hill signed Sherborne & Corton Denham. Left at top of hill, pub at end of village on right*

This is a proper inn located in peaceful countryside. Staff are friendly and welcoming, and the pub dog can usually be found in front of the roaring log fire in the bar. Bedrooms and bathrooms offer impressive levels of comfort, style and quality. In addition to a very good selection of real ales, this is a paradise for bottled beer lovers with a great choice from around the world. Excellent quality local produce can be found in the choice of delicious dinners which may be enjoyed in the traditional bar or character restaurant.

**Rooms:** 5 en suite 3 annexe en suite (1 GF) **S** £95—£109; **D** £125—£150 **Facilities:** FTV DVD iPod docking station Lounge tea/coffee Dinner available Direct dial WiFi ⚓18 🔒 **Extras:** Speciality toiletries, robes/slippers, sweets **Conf:** Max 35 Thtr 35 Class 25 Board 30 **Parking:** 20 **Notes:** LB

*See advert opposite*

## CREWKERNE
Map 4 ST40

### Manor Farm

★★★★ GUEST ACCOMMODATION

tel: 01460 78865 & 07900 692070 **Wayford** TA18 8QL
email: theresaemery@hotmail.com **web:** www.manorfarm.biz
**dir:** *B3165 from Crewkerne to Lyme Regis. 3m, in Clapton right into Dunsham Ln, Manor Farm 0.5m up hill on right*

Just off the beaten track and well worth seeking out, this fine Victorian country house has extensive views over Clapton towards the Axe Valley. The comfortably furnished bedrooms are well equipped, and front-facing rooms enjoy splendid views. Breakfast is served at separate tables in the dining room, and a spacious lounge is also provided.

**Rooms:** 4 en suite 1 annexe en suite (2 fmly) **Facilities:** STV FTV TVL tea/coffee WiFi Fishing ⚓ **Parking:** 14

## EAST LYDFORD
Map 4 ST53

### Cross Keys Inn

★★★ INN

tel: 01963 240473 **TA11 7HA**
email: enquiries@crosskeysinn.info **web:** www.crosskeysinn.info
**dir:** *From A303 take A37 at Podimore Rdbt. Approx 5m to x-rds turn right, pub immediately on right. From Shepton Mallet take A37 to Lydford On Fosse. Left at x-roads pub on right*

Cross Keys Inn is a warm and welcoming establishment with a very relaxed and engaging atmosphere. There is plenty to admire with stone-flagged floors, original beams and a genuine sense of hospitality. Bedrooms offer contemporary comforts, and quality bathrooms. Food is honest and tasty and real ale lovers are very well looked after. There is also a lovely garden in which to sit, unwind, and enjoy the delights of this popular inn.

**Rooms:** 6 en suite (1 fmly) **D** £80–£95* **Facilities:** FTV tea/coffee Dinner available WiFi ⚓18 Camping site Skittle alley **Extras:** Speciality toiletries, bottled water – complimentary **Conf:** Max 100 Thtr 100 Class 75 Board 50 **Parking:** 50

## EXFORD
Map 3 SS83

### Stockleigh Lodge

★★★★ BED AND BREAKFAST

tel: 01643 831500 **TA24 7PZ**
email: stay@stockleighexford.co.uk **web:** www.stockleighexford.co.uk
**dir:** *On B3224 through Wheddon Cross to Exford. Over river bridge into Simonsbath Rd, up hill on right*

Situated at the very heart of Exmoor, Stockleigh Lodge dates from around 1900 and provides a perfect base from which to explore this spectacular area. Whether exploration is by car or cycle, on foot or on horseback, your hosts will be only too pleased to help with local information. The bedrooms are very comfortable and enjoy lovely views, while public areas include a spacious guest lounge warmed by a crackling fire in cooler months. Aga-cooked breakfasts will get the day off to a satisfying start. Stabling is also available for those wishing to bring their horses with them on holiday.

**Rooms:** 9 en suite (2 fmly) **S** £40–£45; **D** £80–£90* **Facilities:** TVL tea/coffee WiFi ⚓ Stabling available for guests' horses **Parking:** 10

---

# The Queens Arms

Corton Denham, Sherborne, Somerset DT9 4LR • Tel: 01963 220317
Website: www.thequeensarms.com • Email: relax@thequeensarms.com
Facebook: www.facebook.com/thequeensarms • Twitter: @queensarmspub

Taste Of The West Gold Winner 2016, Double Silver Winners, Best Tourism Pub and Best B&B Accommodation – South West Tourism Excellence Awards 2014–15. Taste of Somerset Best Pub 2013, Best National Freehouse 2012 and former AA Pub of the Year 2008–9. Quintessentially English Georgian Inn, in a gloriously rural setting, with the gently rolling landscape on the Dorset/Somerset Hills. A pilgrimage for Foodies – note their own smallholding (Pigs, Cows and Hens). Snuggle up in front of the roaring open fire with newspapers, pint and a homemade pork pie – oodles of rustic charm. Their eight en-suite rooms live up to the surroundings and wonderful views, and are all decorated with understated opulence.

## FITZHEAD     Map 3 ST12

### The Fitzhead Inn

★★★ INN

**tel:** 01823 400960 **TA4 3JP**
**email:** info@thefitzheadinn.co.uk **web:** www.thefitzheadinn.co.uk
**dir:** *From Taunton on B3227, through Norton Fitzwarren. After 4m turn right signed Fitzhead*

Located in the peaceful village of Fitzhead, this small traditional inn is popular with locals and visitors alike. Recently refurbished bedrooms and bathrooms offer a range of shapes and sizes and are located in a building adjacent to the inn across a small courtyard. Newly installed showers are especially good. Friendly and welcoming hospitality is a strength here and guests will enjoy the home cooked food at both dinner and breakfast. An outdoor patio with seating is a welcome addition in the warmer months.

**Rooms:** 5 en suite (3 GF) **S** £45–£60; **D** £55–£90* **Facilities:** FTV tea/coffee Dinner available WiFi **Notes:** No children 3yrs

## FIVEHEAD     Map 4 ST32

### Premier Collection

### Langford Fivehead

★★★★★ ◉◉ RESTAURANT WITH ROOMS

**tel:** 01460 282020 **Lower Swell TA3 6PH**
**email:** rebecca@thelangford.co **web:** www.langfordfivehead.co.uk

Documents indicate that there has been a house on this site since 1255 and the current property retains a significant proportion of a 15th-century hall house. In keeping with the grand character found throughout the building, guests can be assured of the most pleasant of welcomes and helpful, relaxing hospitality and service. Bedrooms offer a range of shapes and styles and are decorated and equipped to very high standards (although deliberately, no TVs in bedrooms). The restaurant is a delight of home-grown and local produce, providing delicious dining at both dinner and breakfast.

**Rooms:** 6 en suite **Facilities:** Dinner available **Notes:** Closed 25 Jul–7 Aug & 2–15 Jan

## FROME     Map 4 ST74

### Premier Collection

### Lullington House

★★★★★ BED AND BREAKFAST

**tel:** 01373 831406 & 07979 290146 **Lullington BA11 2PG**
**email:** info@lullingtonhouse.co.uk **web:** www.lullingtonhouse.co.uk
**dir:** *2.5m N of Frome. Off A36 into Lullington*

Built in 1866 as a rectory, this quintessentially English, stone-built country house stands in extensive grounds and gardens, which convey an air of peace, quiet and tranquillity. The luxurious large bedrooms, some with four-poster beds, are decorated to high standards using beautiful fabrics, fine antique furniture and many extras such as WiFi, decanters of sherry, fresh flowers and well-stocked beverage trays. Breakfast is served in the impressive dining room with an excellent selection of dishes available.

**Rooms:** 3 en suite **Facilities:** FTV tea/coffee WiFi ♨18 **Parking:** 4 **Notes:** Closed Xmas & New Year

### Archangel

★★★★ INN

**tel:** 01373 456111 **1 King Street BA11 1BH**
**email:** hello@archangelfrome.com **web:** www.archangelfrome.com
**dir:** *B3090 into Frome, into King St, just off market place*

With a history dating back many centuries, this fascinating and vibrant establishment is located in the heart of the bustling town of Frome. The style here is an engaging blend of old and new, a fusion which has broad appeal for those visiting for business or leisure. Stylish bedrooms are located within the main building and also within the courtyard, the former boasting such features like roll-top zinc baths and wall murals. The bar offers a range of cocktails in addition to real ales and an extensive wine list. Food is not to be missed, the menu featuring flavoursome, well-crafted dishes.

**Rooms:** 6 en suite 4 annexe en suite (1 fmly) (2 GF) **S** £70–£90; **D** £80–£160* **Facilities:** FTV DVD Lounge tea/coffee Dinner available Direct dial WiFi **Extras:** Bottled water **Conf:** Max 25 Thtr 25 Class 25 Board 16 **Notes:** LB

# Follow the AA

twitter: @TheAA_Lifestyle
facebook: www.facebook.com/TheAAUK

## Orchardleigh House

★★★★ GUEST ACCOMMODATION

**tel:** 01373 472550 & 07887 512450 **Orchardleigh BA11 2PH**
**email:** info@orchardleigh.net **web:** www.orchardleigh.net

Popular as a wedding venue, Orchardleigh House is a large imposing manor with a wealth of history and character. Guests can choose from a wide range of bedrooms and bathrooms, ranging from very large suites to more compact rooms, some including a bath or shower in the bedroom. Public areas are grand and include a formal dining room, billiard room and well furnished breakfast room. Delightful grounds surround the building including a full 18-hole golf course. The property can be hired for exclusive use, although regular bed and breakfast guests are also welcome.

**Rooms:** 43 rms (41 en suite) (7 fmly) (1 GF) **Facilities:** FTV Lounge TVL tea/coffee Licensed WiFi ⬥ ♨18 Fishing Snooker ♨ **Conf:** Max 165 **Parking:** 85 **Notes:** LB Civ wed 144

| GLASTONBURY | Map 4 ST53 |

*See also Somerton*

## The Glastonbury Town House

★★★★ BED AND BREAKFAST

**tel:** 01458 831040 & 07557 340247 **Hillclose, Street Road BA6 9EG**
**email:** stay@glastonburytownhouse.co.uk **web:** www.glastonburytownhouse.co.uk
**dir:** *M5 junct 23 towards Glastonbury. Continue on A39, at B&Q rdbt 3rd exit, 200yds on right*

A very warm welcome is guaranteed at The Glastonbury Town House where guests can expect to have a comfortable night's rest followed by a hearty breakfast. Recently refurbished throughout by the owners, bedrooms and bathrooms here are comfortable and well equipped. Centrally located with off-street parking, the house is well placed for exploring Glastonbury Tor and the Chalice Well.

**Rooms:** 3 en suite **S** £75–£130; **D** £89–£130* **Facilities:** FTV Lounge tea/coffee Dinner available WiFi ♨ **Extras:** Speciality toiletries, bottled water, fresh milk **Parking:** 3 **Notes:** No children 5yrs

| HATCH BEAUCHAMP | Map 4 ST32 |

### Premier Collection

## Frog Street Farmhouse

★★★★★ ⬥ BED AND BREAKFAST

**tel:** 01823 481883 **TA3 6AF**
**email:** frogstreet@hotmail.com **web:** www.frogstreet.co.uk
**dir:** *From A358, follow signs for Beercrocombe/Stewley. At T-junct (Elm Bridge Cottages) turn right, over bridge, driveway on right signed Frog Street Farmhouse*

Peacefully located on the edges of this pleasant village, this traditional Somerset longhouse is full of character with parts of the building dating back over 600 years. Bedrooms have been recently upgraded to offer well decorated, stylish and relaxing rooms with especially comfortable beds. Guests are welcome to use the large comfortable lounge with fireplace or sit in the pleasant surrounding gardens. Breakfast is a treat with high quality mainly local produce all cooked to order.

**Rooms:** 4 en suite (1 fmly) **S** £90–£130; **D** £90–£130 **Facilities:** STV TVL tea/coffee WiFi **Extras:** Speciality toiletries – complimentary **Parking:** 4 **Notes:** Closed Dec RS Jan Open weekends only

## The Hatch Inn

★★★★ ⬥ INN

**tel:** 01823 480245 **Village Road TA3 6SG**
**email:** info@thehatchinn.co.uk

Located in the historical village of Hatch Beauchamp, this popular inn welcomes guests and locals alike with friendly hospitality and a relaxed traditional inn style ambience. Bedrooms and bathrooms are all located in the main building and offer a range of shapes and sizes and are all comfortable and well equipped with plenty of welcome extras. Both dinner and breakfast utilise local quality produce and can be enjoyed in the characterful dining room.

**Rooms:** 5 en suite (2 fmly) **D** £65–£120 (room only)* **Facilities:** FTV tea/coffee Dinner available WiFi **Parking:** 10 **Notes:** Closed Sun eve & Mon

## HOLCOMBE
Map 4 ST64

### Premier Collection

## The Holcombe Inn
★★★★★  INN

**tel:** 01761 232478 **Stratton Road BA3 5EB**
**email:** bookings@holcombeinn.co.uk **web:** www. holcombeinn.co.uk
**dir:** *From Bath or Shepton Mallet take A367 (Fosse Way) to Stratton. Follow inn signs*

Dating back to the 16th century, this inn has views towards Downside Abbey in the distance. The attentive owners and pleasant staff create a friendly and relaxed atmosphere. Bedrooms are individually furnished and very comfortable. Real ales are served in the open-plan bar which has an attractive split-level restaurant.

**Rooms:** 8 en suite 2 annexe en suite (5 fmly) (2 GF) **Facilities:** FTV DVD Lounge tea/coffee Dinner available Direct dial WiFi **Extras:** Speciality toiletries – complimentary **Parking:** 40 **Notes:** LB

## ILCHESTER
Map 4 ST52

## Liongate House
★★★★ BED AND BREAKFAST

**tel:** 01935 841741 & 07951 538692 **Northover BA22 8NG**
**email:** info@liongatehouse.com **web:** www.liongatehouse.com
**dir:** *On B3151 opposite Texaco Petrol Station*

Located in the centre of this pleasant village and a short stroll from a selection of inns and restaurants, this very comfortable accommodation demonstrates high quality throughout its bedrooms and bathrooms. The proprietors offer a genuine welcome and are very focused on customer care. Breakfast offers a range of top local produce and includes home-made bread, alongside jams made with fruit from the garden.

**Rooms:** 3 en suite (1 fmly) (1 GF) **S** fr £75; **D** fr £85 **Facilities:** FTV DVD tea/coffee WiFi **Extras:** Fridge stocked with refreshments – complimentary **Parking:** 4 **Notes:** LB

## ILMINSTER
Map 4 ST31

## The New Inn
★★★★ INN

**tel:** 01460 52413 **Dowlish Wake TA19 0NZ**
**email:** newinn-ilminster@btconnect.com **web:** www.newinn-ilminster.co.uk
**dir:** *A358 or A303, follow signs for Perry's Cider, well-signed in village*

Situated in the tranquil and unspoilt village of Dowlish Wake, The New Inn is a proper local pub with a friendly welcome. All the bedrooms are on the ground floor; they are contemporary in style and located to the rear overlooking the garden. The menu offers a range of enduring favourites and daily specials, with good local produce used whenever possible. Breakfast is a substantial offering, just right for healthy appetites.

**Rooms:** 4 annexe en suite (4 GF) **Facilities:** FTV tea/coffee Dinner available **Parking:** 20 **Notes:** LB

## Square & Compass
★★★★ INN

**tel:** 01823 480467 **Windmill Hill, Ashill TA19 9NX**
**email:** squareandcompass@tiscali.co.uk **web:** www.squareandcompasspub.com
**dir:** *M5 junct 25 onto A358. After 5m, turn right into Wood Rd, signed Windmill Hill; From Ilminster, 2m N on A358*

This peacefully located inn provides a genuinely warm welcome and traditional hospitality. The bedrooms and modern bathrooms provide high standards of quality and comfort, and are situated in converted stables adjacent to the main building. In addition to a range of excellent home-cooked meals, a selection of real ales is also available. Outdoor seating is provided in the warmer months.

**Rooms:** 8 en suite (8 fmly) (8 GF) **Facilities:** FTV Lounge tea/coffee Dinner available WiFi **Conf:** Max 100 Class 100 Board 50 **Parking:** 50 **Notes:** Closed 24-26 Dec Civ wed 120

## KEYNSHAM
Map 4 ST66

## Grasmere Court
★★★★ GUEST ACCOMMODATION

**tel:** 0117 986 2662 **22–24 Bath Road BS31 1SN**
**email:** reception@grasmerecourt.co.uk **web:** www.grasmerecourthotel.com
**dir:** *On B3116 just off A4 between Bath & Bristol*

This very friendly establishment is located between Bath and Bristol. Bedrooms vary in size, with one room boasting a four-poster bed. A comfortable lounge and a well stocked bar are available, and good value, freshly prepared food is served in the attractive dining room overlooking the garden. Functions also catered for.

**Rooms:** 16 en suite (1 fmly) (4 GF) **Facilities:** FTV DVD TVL tea/coffee Dinner available Direct dial Licensed WiFi **Extras:** Bottled water **Conf:** Max 30 **Parking:** 13

## LOWER VOBSTER
Map 4 ST74

## The Vobster Inn
★★★★ INN

**tel:** 01373 812920 **BA3 5RJ**
**email:** rdavila@btinternet.com **web:** www.vobsterinn.co.uk
**dir:** *From A361 follow signs for Whatley & Mells, then Vobster*

Peacefully located in four acres, this is a village inn where the resident proprietors offer a genuine welcome and personal attention. Bedrooms and bathrooms provide high levels of quality and comfort. Dinner menus place an emphasis on good quality, simply prepared dishes with regular seasonal changes; several dishes demonstrate the Spanish heritage of the chef proprietor.

**Rooms:** 4 annexe en suite (2 fmly) (4 GF) **Facilities:** FTV tea/coffee Dinner available WiFi Petanque **Extras:** Home-made cookies – complimentary **Conf:** Max 40 Thtr 25 Class 32 Board 32 **Parking:** 60 **Notes:** LB RS Sun eve & Mon (ex BH lunch) No food or drinks available

### MILVERTON
Map 3 ST12

## The Globe
★★★ 🏵 INN

**tel:** 01823 400534 **Fore Street TA4 1JX**
**email:** adele@theglobemilverton.co.uk **web:** www.theglobemilverton.co.uk
**dir:** M5 junct 27 follow B3277 to Milverton. In village centre

This popular village local was once a coaching inn, and even though it has been given contemporary styling it still retains much traditional charm. The welcome is warm and genuine with a convivial atmosphere always guaranteed. Bedrooms are appointed in a similar modern style and have comfy beds. The hard-working kitchen is committed to quality, with excellent locally-sourced produce used in impressive dishes. Continental breakfast is served.

**Rooms:** 3 en suite (1 fmly) **Facilities:** tea/coffee Dinner available WiFi **Parking:** 4 **Notes:** LB Closed 20 Dec–2 Jan

### MINEHEAD
Map 3 SS94

## Alcombe House
★★★★ GUEST ACCOMMODATION

**tel:** 01643 705130 & 07549 887456 **Bircham Road, Alcombe TA24 6BG**
**email:** info@alcombehouse.co.uk **web:** www.alcombehouse.co.uk
**dir:** A39, pass junct for Dunster, straight over at floral rdbt. Alcombe House on left

This elegant period house is a perfect base from which to explore the many and varied delights of the area. The welcome is warm and genuine with plenty of attentive service. Bedrooms provide impressive levels of quality and comfort with ample space to relax and unwind. Public areas combine contemporary and traditional styling, and include a wonderful lounge where indulgent afternoon teas can be sampled. The attractive dining room is the venue for breakfast, and dinner (by prior arrangement).

**Rooms:** 7 en suite **Facilities:** FTV DVD Lounge TVL tea/coffee Dinner available Licensed WiFi ⌁ 🐾 **Parking:** 8 **Notes:** LB No children

## Kenella House
★★★★ GUEST ACCOMMODATION

**tel:** 01643 703128 & 07710 889079 **7 Tregonwell Road TA24 5DT**
**email:** kenellahouse@fsmail.net **web:** www.kenellahouse.co.uk
**dir:** Off A39 into Townsend Rd & right into Ponsford Rd & Tregonwell Rd

A warm welcome and a relaxed atmosphere are found at Kenella House, located close to the town centre, and also convenient for a visit to the steam railway. Walkers are welcomed and a heated boot cupboard is available for drying purposes. The well-maintained bedrooms are very comfortable and have many extras. Hearty breakfasts are served in the smart dining room.

**Rooms:** 6 en suite (1 GF) **S** £50–£70; **D** £60–£70* **Facilities:** FTV tea/coffee WiFi 🐾 **Parking:** 8 **Notes:** LB No children 14yrs Closed Nov–Feb

### MONKSILVER
Map 3 ST03

## The Notley Arms Inn
★★★★★ 🏵 🍴 INN

**tel:** 01984 656095 **Front Street TA4 4JB**
**email:** uksi@hotmail.com **web:** www.notleyarmsinn.co.uk
**dir:** From A358 at Bishop's Lydeard, onto B3224. After 5m right onto B3188 to Monksilver

The Notley Arms was re-built around 1870 and is a warm, friendly and inviting village inn. Crackling log fires, comfy sofas and attentive service all contribute to a relaxing atmosphere. Bedrooms are located in the adjacent coach house and all provide impressive levels of quality, comfort and sophistication. The bar comes well stocked with local ales; likewise the menu focuses on sourcing the best the region has to offer, with a range of flavoursome and thoroughly enjoyable dishes. A garden is also available.

**Rooms:** 6 en suite (2 fmly) (3 GF) **Facilities:** FTV Lounge tea/coffee Dinner available WiFi 🐾 Petanque court **Extras:** Speciality toiletries, home-made biscuits – complimentary **Parking:** 20 **Notes:** LB

### NORTH WOOTTON
Map 4 ST54

## Crossways
★★★★ 🏵 INN

**tel:** 01749 899000 **Stocks Lane BA4 4EU**
**email:** enquiries@thecrossways.co.uk **web:** www.thecrossways.co.uk
**dir:** Exit M5 junct 22 towards Shepton Mallet, 0.2m from Pilton

This family-run establishment is tucked away down a quiet lane, within easy reach of Wells and Glastonbury. The bedrooms and bathrooms are spacious, and provide high levels of quality and comfort. There is a large bar-restaurant and a smaller dining room where breakfast is served. The extensive menu (served Wednesday to Sunday) features high quality produce with a choice of traditional pub classics or à la carte options.

**Rooms:** 16 en suite (4 fmly) **Facilities:** FTV tea/coffee Dinner available WiFi Pool table 🐾 **Conf:** Max 150 Thtr 120 Class 60 Board 25 **Parking:** 100 **Notes:** Civ wed 150

### OAKHILL
Map 4 ST64

## The Oakhill Inn
★★★★ 🏵 INN

**tel:** 01749 840442 **Fosse Road BA3 5HU**
**email:** info@theoakhillinn.com **web:** www.theoakhillinn.com
**dir:** On A367 between Stratton-on-the-Fosse & Shepton Mallet

A welcoming country inn, offering warm hospitality, locally sourced food and a wide selection of fine ales from local microbreweries. The comfortable bedrooms include luxuries such as Egyptian cotton sheets and DVD players. In addition to lighter bar snacks, a full range of high-quality AA Rosette award-winning dishes, made with fresh local produce, is also available.

**Rooms:** 5 en suite (1 fmly) **S** £77.50–£85; **D** £85–£120* **Facilities:** FTV DVD Lounge tea/coffee Dinner available WiFi ⌁18 🐾 **Extras:** Mineral water – complimentary **Conf:** Max 30 Thtr 30 Class 30 Board 30 **Parking:** 12 **Notes:** LB RS 25 Dec no food, 26 Dec no dinner service

## PORLOCK
Map 3 SS84

### The Café Porlock Weir

★★★★ 🍴 GUEST ACCOMMODATION

**tel:** 01643 863300 **Porlock Weir TA24 8PB**
**email:** sarah@thecafeporlockweir.co.uk **web:** www.thecafeporlockweir.co.uk

With a delightful location in the centre of Porlock Weir and right next to the coast, this relaxing café offers high quality dishes throughout the day and evening. Guests can enjoy the splendid views from the dining room and lounges whether calling for coffee, lunch, afternoon tea or dinner. Bedrooms and bathrooms offer a range of shapes and sizes and are all very well decorated and furnished. A small car park and a well tended garden with outdoor seating are also available.

**Rooms:** 5 en suite **S** £50–£103.12; **D** £50–£137.50* **Facilities:** Dinner available Licensed **Parking:** 5

### Glen Lodge Country House

★★★★ 🍴 BED AND BREAKFAST

**tel:** 01643 863371 & 07786 118933 **Hawkcombe TA24 8LN**
**email:** glenlodge@gmail.com **web:** www.glenlodge.net
**dir:** A39 in Porlock, turn into Parsons St at church. After 0.5m turn left over small bridge, property drive opposite

The approach to this grand country house whets the appetite for some stunning views back down the densely wooded valley to the sea beyond. This is a perfect place to relax and unwind; a cup of tea and home-made cake on the deck sets the scene with helpful advice always readily offered. Bedrooms offer impressive levels of comfort and quality, with a number of thoughtful extras. Bathrooms come complete with robes and cosseting fluffy towels. Wonderful local and home-made produce features at breakfast. Additional facilities include a hot tub which enjoys wonderful views.

**Rooms:** 5 rms (3 en suite) (2 pri facs) **S** £70–£75; **D** £100–£110* **Facilities:** FTV DVD Lounge TVL tea/coffee WiFi 🌳 🍴 ⛳18 Fishing 🔒 Outdoor hot tub/jacuzzi **Extras:** Speciality toiletries, robes **Parking:** 6 **Notes:** Closed 23 Dec–5 Jan

### Tudor Cottage

★★★★ GUEST ACCOMMODATION

**tel:** 01643 862255 & 07703 464909 **Bossington TA24 8HQ**
**email:** tudorcottagebossington@btinternet.com
**dir:** From Porlock on A39, bear left signed Bossington. Continue to village centre, on left

Located in the centre of delightful village, Tudor Cottage is full of character and charm. Bedrooms and bathrooms are in keeping with the age and character of the building, while delicious breakfasts are cooked to order and served in the relaxing dining room. There is a cosy lounge where guests are served tea on arrival; alternatively this may be taken in the pleasant gardens during warmer months. Home-cooked dinners are also available by prior arrangement.

**Rooms:** 3 rms (1 en suite) (2 pri facs) **D** £80–£90* **Facilities:** FTV DVD TVL tea/coffee Dinner available Licensed WiFi 🔒 **Extras:** Mini-bar **Parking:** 3 **Notes:** No children

## RADSTOCK
Map 4 ST65

### The Redan Inn

★★★★★ 👁👁 INN

**tel:** 01761 258560 **Fry's Well, Chilcompton BA3 4HA**
**email:** info@theredaninn.co.uk **web:** www.theredaninn.co.uk
**dir:** From Radstock on A367, at rdbt exit signed Wells & Chilcompton (B3139). In village of Chilcompton, right into Frys Well, inn on right

Located just off the main road and an easy drive to Bath, this delightful property was originally a coaching inn but has been newly upgraded throughout to provide high quality contemporary bedrooms and bathrooms of various shapes and sizes. Carefully prepared dishes are available at lunch and dinner with a serious approach to utilising the finest quality produce. A pleasant garden with outdoor seating terrace plus a small car park are also available to guests.

**Rooms:** 7 en suite (1 fmly) **S** fr £85; **D** fr £95* **Facilities:** FTV tea/coffee Dinner available WiFi **Extras:** Speciality toiletries **Conf:** Max 12 Board 12 **Parking:** 15

## SHEPTON MALLET
Map 4 ST64

### Longbridge House Bed & Breakfast

★★★★ BED AND BREAKFAST

**tel:** 01749 572311 & 07809 437325 **78 Cowl Street BA4 5EP**
**email:** longbridgehouse@gmail.com **web:** www.longbridgehouse.co.uk

Guests who enjoy staying in a place with plenty of history will love this building, where the Duke of Monmouth is reputed to have stayed in 1685. The three individually designed bedrooms offer king-size beds with either en suite shower rooms, or an en suite bathroom with a roll-top bath. Thoughtful extras include fluffy robes, safes in each room, and ironing boards. Breakfast is a leisurely affair, as you watch your host prepare your food on a gorgeous red Aga, and is served either at one large table in the comfortable kitchen, or in the courtyard, weather permitting.

**Rooms:** 3 en suite **S** £70–£85; **D** £80–£110 **Facilities:** FTV tea/coffee WiFi 🔒 **Extras:** Bottled water, fluffy robes, ironing boards **Notes:** No children

### The Natterjack Inn

★★★★ 🍴 INN

**tel:** 01749 860253 **Evercreech Junction BA4 6NA**
**email:** natterjack@btconnect.com **web:** www.thenatterjackinn.co.uk
**dir:** On A371 between Bath & Castle Cary, 2m past Bath & West Showground heading towards Castle Cary

The Natterjack Inn offers plenty of traditional character and hospitality with a log fire, cosy seating and an excellent range of real ales and ciders. Dinner is another highlight with a varied menu to suit all tastes. Bedrooms are located in the adjacent converted cider barn, in a range of shapes and sizes that all come with very good quality bathrooms and showers. Breakfast is served in the pleasant dining room overlooking the large garden.

**Rooms:** 5 en suite (3 GF) **Facilities:** FTV tea/coffee Dinner available WiFi ⛳18 **Extras:** Speciality toiletries, home-made biscuits – complimentary **Parking:** 20

## Premier Collection

## Cartways Bed and Breakfast

★★★★★ ⬤ BED AND BREAKFAST

**tel:** 01458 223104 & 07704 776748 **High Street, Keinton Mandeville TA11 6EF**
**email:** cartways@outlook.com **web:** www.cartwaysbandb.co.uk
**dir:** *From Somerton E on B3151, through Kingweston into Keinton Mandeville. 3rd house on left on entering village*

Situated on the edge of the village of Keinton Mandeville, this grand house has much to offer, not least of which is the warm welcome from hosts, Judy and Tony. Given its location, this is a great base from which to explore the surrounding area, which includes many wonderful National Trust properties such as Montacute and Stourhead. Other local attractions include Haynes International Motor Museum, outlet shopping at Clarks Village and the legendary Glastonbury Tor. Bedrooms offer comfort and quality with a host of thoughtful extras, while bathrooms come complete with cosseting bath sheets, robes, slippers and pampering toiletries. Guests also have use of a wonderful drawing room with comfy sofas and a wood burner; there's also a snooker room with full-sized table. Breakfast is a generous and tasty offering, with eggs from the resident hens, served either in the dining room or the more informal breakfast room.

**Rooms:** 3 en suite **D** £70–£90* **Facilities:** FTV Lounge tea/coffee WiFi ⬤ ⬤18 Snooker ⬤ **Extras:** Speciality toiletries, bottled water, robe, slippers, fresh milk – complimentary **Parking:** 8 **Notes:** No children 10yrs

## The Devonshire Arms

★★★★ ⬤ INN

**tel:** 01458 241271 **Long Sutton TA10 9LP**
**email:** mail@thedevonshirearms.com **web:** www.thedevonshirearms.com
**dir:** *A303 onto A372 at Podimore rdbt. After 4m left onto B3165, signed Martock & Long Sutton*

This popular village inn offers an appealing blend of traditional and contemporary styling throughout its spacious public areas and accommodation. Bedrooms are individually designed, and provide impressive levels of comfort and quality. Public areas include a convivial bar and an elegant restaurant where excellent use is made of local produce in skilfully executed dishes.

**Rooms:** 7 en suite 2 annexe en suite (1 fmly) (2 GF) **S** £90–£150; **D** £100–£150*
**Facilities:** FTV tea/coffee Dinner available WiFi ⬤ ⬤18 ⬤ **Conf:** Max 14 Board 14
**Parking:** 6 **Notes:** LB Closed 25–26 Dec

## Somerton Court Country House

★★★★ GUEST ACCOMMODATION

**tel:** 01458 274694 **TA11 7AH**
**email:** enquiries@somertoncourt.com **web:** www.somertoncourt.com
**dir:** *From A303 onto A372 at Podimore rdbt. In 3m right onto B3151 to Somerton & follow signs*

Dating back to the 17th century and set in extensive gardens and grounds, this house provides a tranquil haven away from the pressures of modern life. The comfortable bedrooms have lovely views, and breakfast is served in a delightful dining room that overlooks the gardens.

**Rooms:** 4 en suite 2 annexe en suite (1 fmly) (2 GF) **S** fr £70; **D** fr £100*
**Facilities:** Lounge tea/coffee WiFi ⬤ **Parking:** 30 **Notes:** LB Closed Xmas & New Year

## New Farm Restaurant

★★★★ ⬤ GUEST ACCOMMODATION

**tel:** 01460 240584 & 07808 563885 **Over Stratton TA13 5LQ**
**email:** dine@newfarmrestaurant.co.uk **web:** www.newfarmrestaurant.co.uk
**dir:** *From A303, at South Petherton rdbt 4th exit (travelling E) or 2nd exit (travelling W), pass Esso garage on left. Turn next left, 500mtrs on right*

Situated in the picturesque village of Over Stratton, New Farm provides an ideal base from which to explore the many surrounding attractions of Somerset and Dorset, including several nearby National Trust properties. Bedrooms vary in size and all are comfortably furnished and decorated. Dinner (available Tuesday to Saturday and other times by prior arrangement) is a highlight, as is the range of well-cooked and presented dishes served at breakfast.

**Rooms:** 3 en suite **S** £55–£75; **D** £80–£110* **Facilities:** FTV Lounge tea/coffee Dinner available Licensed WiFi **Extras:** Mineral water – complimentary **Parking:** 11 **Notes:** LB

## Valley Farm

★★★★ BED AND BREAKFAST

**tel:** 01275 332723 & 07799 768161 **Sandy Lane BS39 4EL**
**email:** valleyfarm2010@btinternet.com
**dir:** *Exit B3130 into Stanton Drew, right into Sandy Ln*

Located on a quiet country lane, Valley Farm offers relaxing and friendly accommodation. All bedrooms are comfortable and well equipped, and each has pleasant views over the countryside. Breakfast is served around a communal table in the dining room and, although dinner is not available here, a number of village pubs are just a stroll away. Also conveniently located for Bath and Bristol.

**Rooms:** 3 en suite (1 fmly) **Facilities:** FTV TVL tea/coffee WiFi **Parking:** 6 **Notes:** No children 12yrs

## STOGUMBER
Map 3 ST03

# Wick House
★★★★ GUEST ACCOMMODATION

**tel:** 01984 656422 **Brook Street TA4 3SZ**
**email:** sheila@wickhouse.co.uk **web:** www.wickhouse.co.uk
**dir:** *Off A358 into village, left at x-rds, Wick House 3rd on left*

Wick House offers homely accommodation in a pretty village on the edge of Exmoor National Park. There is a cosy lounge with a wood-burning stove, a television room, and a pleasant dining room overlooking the garden. One bedroom is designed for easier access.

**Rooms:** 9 en suite (1 GF) **S** £45–£50; **D** £70–£90* **Facilities:** FTV Lounge TVL tea/coffee Licensed WiFi ✆ **Extras:** Sweets – complimentary **Parking:** 6 **Notes:** LB

## TAUNTON
Map 4 ST22

# Brookfield House
★★★★ GUEST HOUSE

**tel:** 01823 272786 **16 Wellington Road TA1 4EQ**
**email:** info@brookfieldguesthouse.uk.com **web:** www.brookfieldguesthouse.uk.com
**dir:** *From town centre follow signs to Musgrove Hospital, onto A38 (Wellington Rd), on right opposite turn to hospital*

This charming Grade II listed Georgian house is just a five-minute level walk from the town centre. The family take great pride in caring for guests, and the brightly decorated bedrooms are well equipped. Breakfast, featuring local produce, is served in the attractive dining room. The property is entirely non-smoking.

**Rooms:** 7 en suite (1 fmly) **S** £70–£80; **D** £85–£120* **Facilities:** FTV Lounge tea/coffee Dinner available WiFi ✆ **Extras:** Speciality toiletries **Parking:** 8 **Notes:** No children 7yrs

# Lower Marsh Farm
★★★★ FARMHOUSE

**tel:** 01823 451331 **Kingston St Mary TA2 8AB**
**email:** info@lowermarshfarm.co.uk **web:** www.lowermarshfarm.co.uk
**dir:** *M5 junct 25. B&B between Taunton & Kingston St Mary just past King's Hall School on right*

Located at the foot of the Quantock Hills, this delightful family-run farm provides a warm welcome with a pot of tea and a slice of cake ready and waiting. Bedrooms are individually styled and reflect the traditional charm of the house; an impressive level of quality is complemented by numerous thoughtful extras. The Aga-cooked breakfast is a real treat, served in the dining room around one grand table. There is a spacious lounge warmed by a crackling log fire in winter.

**Rooms:** 3 en suite (2 fmly) **S** fr £55; **D** fr £88 **Facilities:** TVL tea/coffee WiFi ✆ **Parking:** 6 **Notes:** 300 acres arable/sheep

| TINTINHULL | Map 4 ST41 |

## Crown & Victoria

★★★★  INN

**tel:** 01935 823341 **Farm Street BA22 8PZ**
**email:** info@thecrownandvictoria.co.uk **web:** www.thecrownandvictoria.co.uk
**dir:** *Off A303, signs for Tintinhull Gardens*

Appointed to a high standard, this light and airy property has very well-equipped bedrooms. The staff ensure guests are well cared for, and the contemporary bar and restaurant provide a good selection of carefully prepared dishes. The food here has been awarded an AA Rosette.

**Rooms:** 5 en suite **S** £75; **D** £95* **Facilities:** FTV DVD tea/coffee Dinner available WiFi
🔒 **Extras:** Bottled water **Parking:** 60

| WATCHET | Map 3 ST04 |

## The Georgian House

★★★★ GUEST HOUSE

**tel:** 01984 639279 **28 Swain Street TA23 0AD**
**email:** georgianhouse_watchet@virgin.net **web:** www.georgian-house.info
**dir:** *From A39 over railway bridge into main street*

This elegant Georgian property is situated in the heart of the increasingly popular coastal resort, and is within a short walk of the impressive marina. The comfortable bedrooms combine quality and individuality. Breakfast (and dinner by arrangement) is served in the well-appointed dining room. Additional facilities for guests include a lounge and the use of the garden.

**Rooms:** 3 en suite **Facilities:** Dinner available **Parking:** 2 **Notes:** LB

| WEDMORE | Map 4 ST44 |

## The George

★★★★ INN

**tel:** 01934 712124 **Church Street BS28 4AB**
**email:** info@thegeorgewedmore.co.uk **web:** www.thegeorgewedmore.co.uk
**dir:** *M5 junct 22, follow Bristol/Cheddar signs (A38). From dual carriageway right, follow signs for Mark, then Wedmore. In village centre*

The George is a traditional inn offering plenty of character, log fires and a fine selection of ales. Bedrooms come in a variety of shapes and sizes and are located on the first floor above the inn. A range of dishes is offered at lunch and dinner to suit all tastes, and may be taken in the cosy bar or more formal dining areas. Outdoor seating and car parking are also available.

**Rooms:** 4 en suite **S** £80–£100; **D** £100–£120 **Facilities:** FTV DVD iPod docking station Lounge tea/coffee Dinner available WiFi ⚓18 🔒 **Extras:** Speciality toiletries **Conf:** Max 60 Thtr 30 Class 30 Board 30 **Parking:** 30 **Notes:** Civ wed 100

| WELLINGTON | Map 3 ST12 |

## The Cleve Spa

★★★★ GUEST ACCOMMODATION

**tel:** 01823 662033 **Mantle Street TA21 8SN**
**email:** reception@clevehotel.com **web:** www.clevehotel.com
**dir:** *M5 junct 26 follow signs to Wellington town centre. Continue for 600mtrs, entrance on left*

This elegant Victorian country house is situated in an elevated position with commanding views. Bedrooms provide high levels of comfort and quality, with well appointed and stylish bathrooms. Dinner and breakfast are served in the attractive restaurant, after which a stroll around the extensive grounds is pleasant. An impressive array of leisure facilities is also offered, including indoor pool, spa bath, steam room and fully-equipped fitness studio.

**Rooms:** 21 en suite (3 GF) **S** £70–£120; **D** £80–£135* **Facilities:** FTV Lounge tea/coffee Dinner available Direct dial Licensed WiFi ⊗ Gym Spa beauty treatments **Conf:** Max 250 Thtr 250 Class 100 Board 60 **Parking:** 100 **Notes:** LB No children 16yrs Closed 25 Dec–2 Jan Civ wed 200

## WELLS
Map 4 ST54

## Double-Gate Farm

★★★★ FARMHOUSE

tel: 01458 832217 & 07843 924079 **Godney BA5 1RZ**
email: doublegatefarm@aol.com **web:** www.doublegatefarm.com
dir: *A39 from Wells towards Glastonbury, at Polsham right signed Godney/Polsham.
2m to x-rds, continue to farmhouse on left after inn*

Expect a warm welcome not only from the owners, but also their friendly Labradors.
Set on the banks of the River Sheppey in the Somerset Levels, this comfortable
farmhouse is well known for its attractive summer flower garden. Guests have use
of a games room and free internet access in the lounge.

**Rooms:** 1 en suite 7 annexe en suite (4 fmly) (5 GF) **S** £60–£85; **D** £80–£120*
**Facilities:** FTV DVD TVL tea/coffee Direct dial Licensed WiFi Fishing Snooker 🔒 Table
tennis **Extras:** Mini-fridges in some rooms, speciality toiletries **Parking:** 9 **Notes:** LB
RS 2 weeks Xmas accommodation only  8 acres non-working farm

*See advert opposite*

## Crapnell Farm

★★★★ FARMHOUSE

tel: 01749 342683 **Dinder BA5 3HG**
email: pamkeen@yahoo.com **web:** www.crapnellfarm.co.uk
dir: *M5 junct 23 signed Glastonbury/Wells. Onto A371 signed Shepton Mallet. Follow signs
for Dinder*

Crapnell Farm is a spacious 16th-century farmhouse located on the south side of
the Mendip Hills just three miles from the city of Wells; a peaceful and relaxing
location surrounded by rolling countryside. Traditionally furnished bedrooms and
bathrooms are spacious, and guests are also welcome to use the comfortable
lounge. Breakfast includes freshly-laid eggs from the farm's own hens.

**Rooms:** 3 en suite (2 fmly) **Facilities:** FTV TVL tea/coffee WiFi ⚲ ⚓18 🔒 **Parking:** 8
**Notes:** LB Closed 20 Dec–5 Jan

## The Crown at Wells

★★★★ 🍽 INN

tel: 01749 673457 **Market Place BA5 2RP**
email: stay@crownatwells.co.uk **web:** www.crownatwells.co.uk
dir: *On entering Wells follow signs for Hotels & Deliveries, in Market Place,
car park at rear*

Retaining its original features and period charm, this historic inn is situated in the
heart of the city, just a short stroll from the cathedral. The building's frontage has
been used in many films, most famously perhaps in 2007's *Hot Fuzz*. Bedrooms, all
with modern facilities, vary in size and style. Public areas focus around Anton's, the
popular bistro, which has a light, airy environment and relaxed atmosphere.
The Penn Bar offers an alternative eating option and real ales.

**Rooms:** 15 en suite (2 fmly) **S** £65; **D** £75–£115* **Facilities:** FTV Lounge TVL
tea/coffee Dinner available WiFi ⚓18 🔒 **Extras:** Speciality toiletries, filtered
water – complimentary **Parking:** 10 **Notes:** LB

## Highfield

★★★★ BED AND BREAKFAST

tel: 01749 675330 **93 Portway BA5 2BR**
email: steph@wellsbandb.com **web:** www.wellsbandb.com
dir: *Enter Wells & signs for A371 Cheddar, Highfield on Portway after last lights at top
of hill*

Within walking distance of the city and cathedral, this delightful home maintains
Edwardian style and provides comfortable accommodation. There are pleasant
views of the countryside and some bedrooms have balconies. A carefully prepared
breakfast is served around one large table in the well furnished breakfast room.
Welcome extra features include the well-tended garden and off-street parking.

**Rooms:** 3 en suite (1 fmly) **Facilities:** FTV tea/coffee WiFi ⚓18 **Parking:** 7 **Notes:** LB
No children 2yrs Closed 23 Dec–1 Jan

## WEST HUNTSPILL
Map 4 ST34

### Crossways Inn
★★★★ INN

tel: 01278 782500 **Withy Road TA9 3RA**
email: accommodation@crosswaysinn.com **web:** www.crosswaysinn.com
dir: *On main A38 between M5 junct 22 & 23*

Crossways is a traditional inn serving good food and offering a very high standard of accommodation accompanied by warm friendly service. Bedrooms are very comfortable, and offer a host of extras such as iPod docks and WiFi.

**Rooms:** 8 en suite (1 fmly) (2 GF) **Facilities:** FTV iPod docking station tea/coffee Dinner available Lift WiFi **Parking:** 72

## WESTON-SUPER-MARE
Map 4 ST36

### Premier Collection

### Church House
★★★★★ BED AND BREAKFAST

**tel:** 01934 633185 **27 Kewstoke Road, Kewstoke BS22 9YD**
**email:** info@churchhousekewstoke.co.uk **web:** www.churchhousekewstoke.co.uk
**dir:** *From M5 junct 21 follow signs for Kewstoke 2.5m, next to Kewstoke Church*

In a peaceful location at the foot of Monk's Hill, Church House is a delightful property that enjoys wonderful views of the Bristol Channel and as far as Wales on clear days. The bedrooms are stylish and spacious, with lots of thoughtful extras and well-appointed en suites. Public areas include a pleasant conservatory and an elegant dining room where impressive breakfasts are served.

**Rooms:** 5 en suite **S** £79–£95; **D** £89–£110* **Facilities:** FTV DVD iPod docking station Lounge tea/coffee WiFi ↓18 Extras: Home-made cake, sweets – complimentary **Parking:** 6

### Oakover Guest House
★★★★ GUEST HOUSE

**tel:** 01934 620125 & 07557 417208 **25 Clevedon Road BS23 1DA**
**email:** info@oakover.co.uk **web:** www.oakover.co.uk
**dir:** *M5 junct 21 onto A370 (Beach Rd), at 6th rdbt left onto A3033. 2nd right into Brighton Rd. Over T-lights into Clevedon Rd*

Located just a short walk from the seafront, this well-established quality accommodation has enthusiastic and welcoming proprietors. Bedrooms and bathrooms are decorated and maintained to high standards, and provide guests with plenty of quality and comfort throughout. A good range of breakfast dishes is offered and served in the stylish breakfast room. Parking is available to the rear via a fairly narrow entrance.

**Rooms:** 6 en suite (2 GF) **Facilities:** FTV DVD tea/coffee WiFi **Parking:** 6
**Notes:** No children 10yrs

WESTON-SUPER-MARE *continued*

## Camellia Lodge

★★★★ BED AND BREAKFAST

**tel:** 01934 613534 **76 Walliscote Road BS23 1ED**
**email:** dachefs@aol.com **web:** www.camellialodge.net
**dir:** *200yds from seafront*

Guests return regularly for the warm welcome at Camellia Lodge, an immaculate Victorian family home, which is just off the seafront and within walking distance of the town centre. Bedrooms have a range of thoughtful touches, and carefully prepared breakfasts are served in the relaxing dining room.

**Rooms:** 5 en suite (1 fmly) **S** £35–£45; **D** £70–£80* **Facilities:** FTV tea/coffee WiFi

## Jamesfield Guest House

★★★★ GUEST HOUSE

**tel:** 01934 642898 **1A Ellenborough Park North BS23 1XH**
**email:** jamesfield1@aol.com **web:** www.jamesfieldguesthouse.co.uk

A well-maintained property in an ideal location, Jamesfield Guest House is a short walk from the seafront and only a few minutes' stroll from town. The bedrooms are comfortably furnished and well decorated, and include rooms on the ground floor. Guests are welcome to use the relaxing lounge, and the property also benefits from its own car park.

**Rooms:** 7 rms (6 en suite) (1 pri facs) (1 fmly) (2 GF) **S** £45; **D** fr £70* **Facilities:** FTV TVL tea/coffee WiFi **Parking:** 9

## Linden Lodge Guest House

★★★★ ☕ GUEST ACCOMMODATION

**tel:** 01934 645797 **27 Clevedon Road BS23 1DA**
**email:** info@lindenlodge.com **web:** www.lindenlodge.com
**dir:** *Follow signs to seafront. 0.5m S of grand pier turn into Clevedon Rd*

Just a short walk from the town centre and the seafront, Linden Lodge offers welcoming hospitality and guest care in a traditional style. Bedrooms come in a range of shapes and sizes, and all are well decorated and equipped. A good selection is offered at breakfast including home-made bread and yogurts, all served in the pleasant conservatory.

**Rooms:** 5 en suite **Facilities:** FTV tea/coffee WiFi **Parking:** 3 **Notes:** LB No children 18yrs

## Goodrington Guest House

★★★ GUEST HOUSE

**tel:** 01934 623229 **23 Charlton Road BS23 4HB**
**email:** vera.bishop@talk21.com **web:** www.goodrington.info
**dir:** *A370 Beach Rd S onto Uphill Rd, left into Charlton Rd*

The owners of Goodrington Guest House make every effort to ensure guests enjoy their stay at this charming Victorian house, tucked away in a quiet residential area. The bedrooms are comfortably furnished, and there is an attractive lounge. Families are especially welcome and this makes a good holiday base.

**Rooms:** 3 rms (2 en suite) (1 pri facs) (1 fmly) (1 GF) **S** £45–£50; **D** £65–£70* **Facilities:** FTV DVD TVL tea/coffee WiFi **Notes:** LB Closed Oct–Easter

## Corbiere Guest House

★★★ GUEST HOUSE

**tel:** 01934 629607 & 429866 **24 Upper Church Road BS23 2DX**
**email:** corbierehotel@btinternet.com **web:** www.corbiereguesthouse.com
**dir:** *M5 junct 21, take 2nd exit to seafront*

Located on a residential street just a few minutes' walk from the seafront, this relaxed and welcoming accommodation offers rooms in a range of shapes and sizes. All are well furnished and have comfortable beds and bedding. Breakfast is served in the lower ground floor dining room and offers a good selection of hot and cold dishes.

**Rooms:** 10 en suite (4 fmly) (2 GF) **Facilities:** FTV DVD Lounge TVL tea/coffee Dinner available **Notes:** LB

## WHEDDON CROSS

Map 3 SS93

## The Rest and Be Thankful Inn

★★★★ INN

**tel:** 01643 841222 **TA24 7DR**
**email:** stay@restandbethankful.co.uk **web:** www.restandbethankful.co.uk
**dir:** *M5 junct 25, A358 to Minehead, left onto B3224 at Wheddon Cross sign*

The Rest and Be Thankful Inn is situated in the highest village on Exmoor, overlooking Dunkery Beacon. The comfortable bedrooms are extremely well equipped, with extras such as mini-bars and trouser presses. The convivial bar, complete with crackling log fires, is a popular meeting point for locals and visitors alike. A range of wholesome dishes is offered in the bar, the restaurant or outside on the patio, which enjoys some lovely countryside views.

**Rooms:** 8 en suite (1 fmly) **Facilities:** FTV tea/coffee Dinner available Direct dial WiFi Pool table Skittle alley Table Tennis **Extras:** Mini-bar – chargeable **Conf:** Max 50 Class 50 Board 50 **Parking:** 10 **Notes:** Closed 25 Dec

## WILLITON

Map 3 ST04

### Arden Cottage B&B

★★★★ BED AND BREAKFAST

**tel:** 01984 634090 & 07794 656484 **33 Long Street TA4 4QU**
**email:** enquiries@ardencottagewilliton.co.uk
**web:** www.ardencottagebedandbreakfast.co.uk
**dir:** M5 junct 23 to Bridgwater, then A39 signed Minehead. In Williton, over railway line, 0.5m on right

Located in the pleasant village of Williton, Arden Cottage is full of character and history. A warm, friendly welcome is assured along, with home-made cake and choice of tea or coffee all served in the conservatory. Bedrooms vary in size but all offer large comfortable beds and hospitality tray. Breakfast offers a good choice using a range of quality local ingredients plus the owners home-made granola and smoothies. Local pubs are all within easy walking distance for evening meals.

**Rooms:** 3 rms (2 en suite) (1 fmly) **S** £45–£55; **D** £77–£80* **Facilities:** iPod docking station TVL tea/coffee WiFi ♨ Shibashi Tai Chi Bowen Technique **Extras:** Home-made cake on arrival, speciality toiletries **Parking:** 3 **Notes:** LB

### The White House

★★★★ GUEST ACCOMMODATION

**tel:** 01984 632306 **11 Long Street TA4 4QW**
**email:** whitehouselive@btconnect.com **web:** www.whitehousewilliton.co.uk
**dir:** A39 Bridgwater to Minehead, in Williton on right prior to Watchet turning

This Grade II listed Georgian house is in the perfect location for guests wishing to explore the beautiful Somerset countryside and coast. Many original features have been retained and add to the character of the house. Rooms are well equipped, and guests can choose whether to stay in the main house or in a room off the courtyard. Additional facilities include a bar and lounge.

**Rooms:** 8 rms (7 en suite) (1 pri facs) 6 annexe en suite (2 fmly) (6 GF) **Facilities:** FTV TVL Licensed WiFi ♨ **Parking:** 12

## WINSFORD

Map 3 SS93

### The Royal Oak Exmoor

★★★★ 🍴 INN

**tel:** 01643 851455 **Halse Lane TA24 7JE**
**email:** enquiries@royaloakexmoor.co.uk **web:** www.royaloakexmoor.co.uk

Originally a farm, and dating back to the 12th century, this thatched pub is very much at the heart of this picturesque Exmoor village. Character abounds throughout public areas with lots of cosy areas to sit and sup a pint and enjoy the warm and convivial atmosphere. A range of skilfully-prepared dishes make use of local, seasonal produce. Bedrooms provide impressive levels of comfort, with quality linen and wonderful beds. Breakfast is the perfect start to a day exploring this stunning area.

The Royal Oak Exmoor

**Rooms:** 10 en suite 4 annexe en suite (2 GF) **Facilities:** STV Lounge tea/coffee Dinner available Direct dial WiFi **Conf:** Max 40 Thtr 40 Class 24 Board 12 **Parking:** 14

*See advert on following page*

## WITHYPOOL

Map 3 SS83

### Kings Farm

★★★★★ 🍴 BED AND BREAKFAST

**tel:** 01643 831381 **TA24 7RE**
**email:** info@kingsfarmexmoor.co.uk **web:** www.kingsfarmexmoor.co.uk
**dir:** Off B3223 to Withypool, over bridge & sharp left to farm

This delightful farmhouse is set in over two acres of landscaped gardens in an idyllic valley beside the River Barle. It combines the character and charm of its 19th-century origins with modern comforts. From the carefully planned bedrooms to the sumptuously furnished sitting room, delicious home-cooked breakfasts and the warmest of welcomes, top quality is most definitely the hallmark of Kings Farm. Both stabling and fishing are available.

**Rooms:** 2 rms (1 en suite) (1 pri facs) **S** £80; **D** £105–£115* **Facilities:** STV FTV Lounge tea/coffee WiFi Fishing ♨ **Extras:** Speciality toiletries, fruit, chocolates – complimentary **Parking:** 3 **Notes:** No children 14yrs

**Follow us on twitter**
@TheAA_Lifestyle

## WRAXALL

Map 4 ST47

### The Battleaxes

★★★★ 🍺 INN

**tel:** 01275 857473 **Bristol Road BS48 1LQ**
**email:** thebattleaxes@flatcappers.co.uk **web:** www.flatcappers.co.uk
**dir:** *From Bristol, A370 to Weston-Super-Mare, take Clevedon exit then follow signs for Nailsea. From M5, junct 19 to Portbury, then follow signs for Nailsea*

Part of the small local Flatcappers Group, this delightful inn offers a pleasing mix of traditional comfort and hospitality with some more contemporary features. Bedrooms are spacious and well equipped and free WiFi is included. Carefully prepared dishes are available throughout the day whether at breakfast, lunch or dinner. A good selection of real ales and wines by the glass adds to the relaxing ambience created throughout the bar and dining areas. A large car park is also available.

**Rooms:** 6 en suite **Facilities:** FTV iPod docking station Lounge tea/coffee Dinner available WiFi **Conf:** Max 30 Thtr 30 Class 30 Board 30 **Parking:** 50 **Notes:** Civ wed 90

## YEOVIL

Map 4 ST51

*See also Crewkerne*

### Little Barwick House

★★★★★ ◉◉◉ 🍴 RESTAURANT WITH ROOMS

**tel:** 01935 423902 **Barwick BA22 9TD**
**email:** littlebarwick@hotmail.com **web:** www.littlebarwickhouse.co.uk
**dir:** *From Yeovil A37 towards Dorchester, left at 1st rdbt, 1st left, 0.25m on left*

Situated in a quiet hamlet in three and half acres of gardens and grounds, this listed Georgian dower house is an ideal retreat for those seeking peaceful surroundings and good food. Just one of the highlights of a stay here is a meal in the restaurant, where good use is made of local ingredients. Each of the bedrooms has its own character, and a range of thoughtful extras such as fresh flowers, bottled water and magazines is provided.

**Rooms:** 6 en suite **Facilities:** FTV iPod docking station tea/coffee Dinner available Direct dial WiFi ⓧ **Parking:** 30 **Notes:** LB No children 5yrs RS Sun eve & Mon closed

## The Masons Arms

★★★★ ⚲ ⇔ INN

tel: 01935 862591 **41 Lower Odcombe BA22 8TX**
**email:** info@masonsarmsodcombe.co.uk **web:** www.masonsarmsodcombe.co.uk
**dir:** *From A303 take A3088 to Yeovil, follow signs to Montacute after village, 3rd right*

Dating back to the 16th century, The Masons Arms claims to be the oldest building in this small village on the outskirts of Yeovil. The spacious bedrooms are contemporary in style, with clean lines, a high level of comfort and a wide range of considerate extras. The friendly hosts run their own microbrewery, and their ales are available at the bar along with other brews. Public areas include a bar-restaurant, which offers a full menu of freshly prepared dishes, along with a choice of lighter snacks.

**Rooms:** 6 en suite (1 fmly) (6 GF) **Facilities:** FTV tea/coffee Dinner available Direct dial WiFi ⚲ **Extras:** Mineral water/beer in room fridge **Conf:** Max 15 Class 15 Board 15 **Parking:** 35

## The Halfway House Inn Country Lodge

★★★ INN

tel: 01935 840350 & 849005 **Ilchester Road BA22 8RE**
**email:** paul@halfwayhouseinn.com **web:** www.halfwayhotelyeovil.com
**dir:** *A303 onto A37 (Yeovil road) at Ilchester, inn 2m on left*

This roadside inn offers comfortable accommodation, which consists of bedrooms in the main house, in addition to contemporary annexe rooms, each with its own front door; all bedrooms are bright and well equipped. Meals are available in the cosy restaurant and bar, where friendly staff ensure a warm welcome.

**Rooms:** 10 en suite 9 annexe en suite (7 fmly) (8 GF) **Facilities:** FTV TVL tea/coffee Dinner available WiFi Fishing **Conf:** Max 90 Thtr 90 Class 60 Board 60 **Parking:** 49 **Notes:** LB

## At Your Service B&B

★★★ BED AND BREAKFAST

tel: 01935 706932 & 07957 473407 **102 West Coker Road BA20 2JG**
**email:** atyourserviceuk@gmail.com **web:** atyourserviceuk.wordpress.com

Conveniently located on the main through road, this relaxed bed and breakfast makes an ideal base from which to explore the various nearby attractions. Bedrooms come in a range of shapes and all are on the ground floor. There is a car park to the rear of the property.

**Rooms:** 4 en suite (4 GF) **S** £40; **D** £65* **Facilities:** FTV DVD tea/coffee WiFi ⚲ **Extras:** Bottled water – complimentary **Parking:** 4

## The Half Moon Inn

★★★ INN

tel: 01935 850289 **Main Street, Mudford BA21 5TF**
**email:** enquiries@thehalfmooninn.co.uk **web:** www.thehalfmooninn.co.uk
**dir:** *A303 at Sparkford onto A359 to Yeovil, 3.5m on left*

Situated north of Yeovil, this delightful village inn dates from the 17th century. It has a wealth of character including exposed beams and flagstone floors. The inn proves very popular for its extensive range of wholesome food, and there is a choice of bar and dining areas. Most of the spacious, well-equipped bedrooms are on the ground floor and are situated in an adjacent building.

**Rooms:** 14 en suite (4 fmly) (9 GF) **Facilities:** STV FTV tea/coffee Dinner available WiFi ⚲ **Parking:** 36 **Notes:** Closed 25–26 Dec

## STAFFORDSHIRE

### ADBASTON
Map 15 SJ72

## Offley Grove Farm

★★★ FARMHOUSE

tel: 01785 280205 & 07792 641984 **Eccleshall ST20 0QB**
**email:** enquiries@offleygrovefarm.co.uk **web:** www.offleygrovefarm.co.uk
**dir:** *3m from A519 between Shebdon & Adbaston*

This attractive farm dates back to the 1800s, and is quietly located between Eccleshall and Newport making it convenient for visiting attractions such as Alton Towers, Ironbridge and the Potteries. Bedrooms are traditional, comfortable and well equipped. The lounge and gardens also provide additional space for guests to relax in. A small conference room is available along with outdoor activities.

**Rooms:** 2 en suite (1 fmly) **S** £40; **D** £68* **Facilities:** FTV DVD TVL tea/coffee WiFi Fishing ⚲ 4x4 Land Rover courses Air rifle shooting **Conf:** Max 20 Thtr 20 Class 12 Board 12 **Parking:** 20 **Notes:** 45 acres sheep

### BARTON-UNDER-NEEDWOOD
Map 10 SK11

## The Three Horseshoes

★★★★ ⇔ INN

tel: 01283 716268 **2 Station Road DE13 8DR**
**email:** enquiries@3horseshoesbarton.co.uk **web:** www.3horseshoesbarton.co.uk

This popular inn has been lovingly transformed with a contemporary twist. Bedrooms are individually styled. Bit 'n' Cherry restaurant, located in a converted cobbler's workshop, offers a wide selection of imaginative meals.

**Rooms:** 3 en suite **S** £60–£65; **D** £70–£80* **Facilities:** FTV tea/coffee Dinner available WiFi **Parking:** 14

## ECCLESHALL
Map 15 SJ82

### Slindon House Farm
★★★★ ☆ FARMHOUSE

**tel:** 01782 791237 **Slindon ST21 6LX**
**email:** bonsall@btconnect.com **web:** www.slindonhousefarm.co.uk
**dir:** 2m N of Eccleshall on A519

This large, charming, Victorian farmhouse is fronted by a lovely garden and situated on a dairy, arable and livestock farm in the village of Slindon, some two miles from Eccleshall. It has one twin and one double room, both of which are thoughtfully equipped. Breakfast is served at individual tables in the traditionally furnished combined breakfast room and lounge.

**Rooms:** 2 rms (1 en suite) (1 pri facs) **S** £50–£55; **D** £70–£85* **Facilities:** FTV DVD TVL tea/coffee WiFi **Parking:** 4 **Notes:** Closed 23 Dec–3 Jan & 1–25 Apr 175 acres arable/dairy/sheep/beef

## FROGHALL
Map 10 SK04

### Hermitage Working Farm
★★★ FARMHOUSE

**tel:** 01538 266515 **ST10 2HQ**
**email:** gapfarm69@gmail.com **web:** www.hermitagefarm.co.uk

This family-run farm, peacefully located overlooking the picturesque Churnet Valley offers a warm welcome. Traditionally furnished; accommodation is split between the main house and converted farm buildings all are well equipped with stone barn conversions offering greater privacy and cooking facilities for the more independent guest. Full English breakfasts are served in the family dining room.

**Rooms:** 3 en suite 6 annexe en suite **Facilities:** FTV tea/coffee WiFi ▲ **Parking:** 10 **Notes:** LB 105 acres beef/poultry

## KINGSLEY
Map 10 SK04

### The Church Farm
★★★★ FARMHOUSE

**tel:** 01538 754759 **Holt Lane ST10 2BA**
**email:** thechurchfarm@yahoo.co.uk
**dir:** From A52 in Kingsley into Holt Ln, 150mtrs on right opposite school drive

A warm welcome is assured at this charming farmhouse. Thoughtfully equipped bedrooms with stylish furnishings are available in the main house. A hearty breakfast is served at individual tables overlooking the cottage gardens.

**Rooms:** 2 en suite **S** £45–£50; **D** £70–£80 **Facilities:** FTV DVD TVL tea/coffee WiFi **Extras:** Speciality toiletries, fruit tea – complimentary **Parking:** 6 **Notes:** LB Closed 23 Dec–2 Jan 100 acres beef/mixed

## LEEK
Map 16 SJ95

### Three Horseshoes Country Inn & Spa
★★★★ ◉◉ INN

**tel:** 01538 300296 **Buxton Road, Blackshaw Moor ST13 8TW**
**email:** enquiries@threeshoesinn.co.uk **web:** www.threeshoesinn.co.uk
**dir:** 2m N of Leek on A53

This traditional, family-owned hostelry provides stylish, individually designed, modern bedrooms, including several 'Garden rooms' with hot tubs. The smart brasserie, with an open kitchen and countryside views, offers modern English dishes using the best of seasonal ingredients. There is also a busy carvery, and the award-winning gardens and grounds are ideal for alfresco dining. The team are attentive and friendly. Spa facilities are available by prior arrangement.

**Rooms:** 26 en suite (2 fmly) (10 GF) **S** £110–£270; **D** £110–£270* **Facilities:** FTV tea/coffee Dinner available Lift WiFi **Parking:** 80 **Notes:** Closed 24 Dec–1 Jan Civ wed 220

## LICHFIELD
Map 10 SK10

### Premier Collection

### Pipe Hill House
★★★★★ BED AND BREAKFAST

**tel:** 01543 255751 & 07779 291219 **Walsall Road, Pipehill WS13 8JU**
**email:** nick@pipehillhouse.co.uk **web:** www.pipehillhouse.co.uk
**dir:** From A5 rdbt at junct with A461 towards Lichfield. 1m on right

Located two miles from the centre of the cathedral city of Lichfield, this beautiful 300-year-old Georgian house is personally run by owners Nick and Annmarie. Individually designed bedrooms offer high levels of comfort and warm hospitality ensures an enjoyable stay. The comprehensive breakfast features free-range eggs and locally sourced produce, while gluten free, dairy free, low sodium and diabetic diets are catered for. Full business services are available in an adjoining barn conversion.

**Rooms:** 3 en suite **D** £105–£130* **Facilities:** FTV DVD iPod docking station Lounge tea/coffee Licensed WiFi ▲ **Extras:** Speciality toiletries – complimentary; robes, slippers **Parking:** 6 **Notes:** No children 16yrs

### Premier Collection

### Netherstowe House
★★★★★ ◉ GUEST HOUSE

**tel:** 01543 254270 **Netherstowe Lane WS13 6AY**
**email:** hospitality@netherstowehouse.com **web:** www.netherstowehouse.com
**dir:** A38 onto A5192, 0.3m on right into Netherstowe Ln. 1st left, 1st right down private drive

Netherstowe House is located in a residential area a few minutes' drive from the city centre, and provides a range of bedrooms, some of which are quite spacious. Comprehensive breakfasts are taken in a cosy dining room and a comfortable guest lounge is also available, along with a well-equipped gym.

**Rooms:** 9 en suite 15 annexe en suite (8 fmly) (9 GF) **Facilities:** STV FTV DVD Lounge tea/coffee Dinner available Licensed WiFi ⚓18 Gym ▲ **Extras:** Robes, fruit, flowers – chargeable **Conf:** Max 14 Thtr 14 Class 14 Board 14 **Parking:** 45 **Notes:** LB No children 12yrs

## Innkeeper's Lodge Lichfield

★★★ INN

**tel:** 08451 551551 *(Calls cost 2p per minute plus your phone company's access charge)*
**Stafford Road WS13 8JB**
**email:** info@innkeeperslodge.com **web:** www.innkeeperslodge.com

Conveniently located close to the M6 Toll, M42 and Birmingham, and ideal for both the business and leisure traveller, this 18th-century property has been beautifully restored. Bedrooms are all attractively presented and are well-equipped — free WiFi is available. There is a very popular restaurant, with large gardens suitable for alfresco dining.

**Rooms:** 9 en suite (1 fmly) **Facilities:** FTV tea/coffee Dinner available WiFi

### UAKAMOOR · Map 10 SK04

## Crowtrees Farm

★★★★ FARMHOUSE

**tel:** 01538 702260 **Eaves Lane ST10 3DY**
**email:** dianne@crowtreesfarm.co.uk **web:** www.crowtreesfarm.co.uk
**dir:** *Exit B5417 in village N into Eaves Ln, farm 1m on left*

This impeccably maintained 200-year-old farmhouse is convenient for the Potteries, the Peak District and Alton Towers. Bedrooms are comfortable and well equipped. It is still a working farm and has splendid views. The friendly owners, along with their collection of pets, create a relaxing atmosphere.

**Rooms:** 5 annexe en suite (3 fmly) (5 GF) **Facilities:** FTV tea/coffee WiFi **Parking:** 8
**Notes:** LB Closed 25–26 Dec 70 acres sheep

### STAFFORD · Map 10 SJ92

## Rooks Nest

★★★★ FARMHOUSE

**tel:** 01889 270624 & 07966 732953 **Rooks Nest Farm, Weston ST18 0BA**
**email:** info@rooksnest.co.uk **web:** www.rooksnest.co.uk
**dir:** *From Stafford on A518 towards Weston. Left to Rooks Nest Farm, 1st property*

Rooks Nest is in a peaceful location with panoramic views over the Trent Valley and countryside. This modern farmhouse has comfortable bedrooms with homely extras. The establishment is handy for visiting the County Showground and Stafford University, with easy access to all Staffordshire's attractions.

**Rooms:** 2 en suite (1 fmly) **S** £39.50–£45; **D** £68–£75* **Facilities:** FTV DVD tea/coffee WiFi **Parking:** 4 **Notes:** 220 acres arable/beef

## Symbols and abbreviations
explained on pages 6–7

### STONE · Map 10 SJ93

## Field House

★★★ BED AND BREAKFAST

**tel:** 01785 605712 **59 Stafford Road ST15 0HE**
**email:** fieldhouse@ntlworld.com **web:** www.fieldhousehotel.co.uk
**dir:** *From A34, NW into town centre, right into Stafford Rd, opposite Walton Grange*

This family home stands in secluded, pretty gardens close to the town centre. The Georgian house has traditionally furnished bedrooms, some with family pieces. Guests breakfast together in the lounge-dining room, and hospitality is very welcoming.

**Rooms:** 2 rms (1 en suite) (1 pri facs) **Facilities:** STV FTV TVL tea/coffee Art tuition on request **Parking:** 4 **Notes:** LB

### TAMWORTH · Map 10 SK20

#### Premier Collection

## Oak Tree Farm

★★★★★ GUEST ACCOMMODATION

**tel:** 01827 56807 **Hints Road, Hopwas B78 3AA**
**email:** oaktreefarm1@aol.com **web:** www.oaktreefarmhotel.co.uk
**dir:** *2m NW of Tamworth. Off A51 in Hopwas*

A warm welcome is assured at this well-loved farmhouse, located in peaceful rural surroundings yet only a short drive from the NEC. Spacious bedrooms are filled with homely extras. The elegant dining room, adorned with Oriental artefacts, is the setting for memorable breakfasts.

**Rooms:** 4 en suite 10 annexe en suite (4 fmly) (7 GF) **Facilities:** FTV TVL tea/coffee WiFi ☒ **Parking:** 20 **Notes:** No children 16yrs

**TAMWORTH** *continued*

## The Gungate

★★★ ☕ GUEST ACCOMMODATION

**tel:** 01827 63120 & 07802 987283 **62 Upper Gungate B79 8AA**
**email:** suetipton@thegungate.co.uk **web:** www.thegungate.co.uk

The Gungate is just a moment's walk from the town centre and has on-site parking. Bedrooms and bathrooms have benefited from recent investment, showcasing the Victorian splendour of the main house, while the coach house rooms are more contemporary in their appeal. Families, leisure and business guests are well catered for. A number of popular visitor attractions are located nearby.

**Rooms:** 10 en suite (2 fmly) (1 GF) **Facilities:** FTV DVD TVL tea/coffee Direct dial Licensed WiFi ⚓ **Conf:** Max 30 Thtr 30 Class 20 Board 20 **Parking:** 10 **Notes:** LB

## Globe Inn

★★★ INN

**tel:** 01827 60455 **Lower Gungate B79 7AW**
**email:** info@theglobetamworth.com **web:** www.theglobetamworth.com

Located in the centre of Tamworth, this popular inn provides well-equipped and pleasantly decorated accommodation. The public areas include a spacious lounge bar and a relaxed dining area where a varied selection of dishes is available. There is also a function room and adjacent parking.

**Rooms:** 18 en suite (2 fmly) **S** £35–£50; **D** £55–£70* **Facilities:** STV FTV tea/coffee Dinner available WiFi ⚓ **Parking:** 30 **Notes:** Closed 25 Dec, 1 Jan

## SUFFOLK

▌ **BURY ST EDMUNDS** Map 13 TL86

### Premier Collection

## The Northgate

★★★★★ INN

**tel:** 01284 339604 **Northgate Street IP33 1HP**
**email:** info@thenorthgate.com **web:** www.thenorthgate.com
**dir:** A14 junct 43 onto A1101 towards town centre. 1st exit at rdbt into Northgate St

Recently reopened following extensive refurbishment, this historic house is situated a short stroll from the town centre and the Abbey with its beautiful grounds. The individually styled bedrooms are tastefully appointed and equipped with modern facilities (TVs and espresso coffee machines). The smartly presented public areas include a contemporary cocktail bar, conservatory, open plan restaurant and a separate Chef's Table in the heart of the kitchen; there is a heated outside terrace for alfresco dining.

**Rooms:** 9 en suite (1 fmly) **S** £115–£175; **D** £120–£210 **Facilities:** FTV tea/coffee Dinner available WiFi **Extras:** Nespresso coffee machine **Conf:** Max 25 Thtr 15 Class 18 Board 25 **Parking:** 10

### Premier Collection

## The Bannatyne Spa

★★★★★ ◎ GUEST ACCOMMODATION

**tel:** 01284 705550 **Horringer Court, Horringer Road IP29 5PH**
**email:** enquiries.claricebury@bannatyne.co.uk **web:** www.claricehouse.co.uk
**dir:** 1m SW from town centre on A143 towards Horringer

The Bannatyne Spa is a large country property set amid pretty landscaped grounds a short drive from the historic town centre. The spacious, well-equipped bedrooms have co-ordinated fabrics and many thoughtful touches. Public rooms have a wealth of charm and include a smart lounge bar, an intimate restaurant, a further lounge and a conservatory. The property also has superb leisure facilities.

**Rooms:** 13 en suite **Facilities:** FTV Lounge tea/coffee Dinner available Direct dial Lift Licensed WiFi 🏊 Gym Spa & Beauty facilities **Conf:** Max 50 Thtr 50 Class 50 Board 50 **Parking:** 85 **Notes:** LB No children 5yrs Closed 24–26 Dec & 31 Dec–1 Jan Civ wed 70

## The Chantry

★★★★ ☕ GUEST ACCOMMODATION

**tel:** 01284 767427 **8 Sparhawk Street IP33 1RY**
**email:** chantryhotel1@aol.com **web:** www.chantryhotel.com
**dir:** From cathedral S into Crown St, left into Honey Hill then right into Sparhawk St

The Chantry is an attractive Georgian property, just a short walk from the town centre. The individually decorated bedrooms are furnished with well-chosen pieces and have many extra thoughtful touches. Breakfast is served in the smart restaurant, and there is a cosy lounge-bar.

**Rooms:** 11 en suite 3 annexe en suite (1 fmly) (1 GF) **S** £89–£120; **D** £105–£165* **Facilities:** FTV Lounge tea/coffee Direct dial Licensed WiFi ⚓ **Parking:** 14 **Notes:** LB

## The Abbey

★★★★ GUEST ACCOMMODATION

**tel:** 01284 762020 **35 Southgate Street IP33 2AZ**
**email:** reception@abbeyhotel.co.uk **web:** www.abbeyhotel.co.uk
**dir:** A14 junct 44, A1302 to town centre, into Southgate St, premises 400yds

The Abbey is well placed for visiting the historic town centre. The property is split between several old buildings, the main core dating from the 15th century. The public rooms in the Tudor inn section feature a comfortable lounge and an informal dining area. Bedrooms vary in size and style, but all are comfortably furnished and well equipped.

**Rooms:** 12 en suite (2 GF) **S** £78–£118; **D** £103–£158* **Facilities:** FTV Lounge tea/coffee WiFi ⚓ **Parking:** 12 **Notes:** LB

## The Six Bells at Bardwell

★★★★ ⚏ INN

**tel:** 01359 250820 **The Green, Bardwell IP31 1AW**
**email:** sixbellsbardwell@aol.com **web:** www.sixbellsbardwell.co.uk
**dir:** *8m NE, off A143 on edge of village. Follow brown signs from A143*

This 16th-century inn lies in the peaceful village of Bardwell. The bedrooms, in a converted stable block next to the main building, are furnished in a country style and thoughtfully equipped. Public rooms have original character and provide a choice of areas in which to relax.

**Rooms:** 10 annexe en suite (1 fmly) (10 GF) **Facilities:** FTV Lounge tea/coffee Dinner available WiFi ⚓ **Parking:** 50 **Notes:** LB Closed 25 Dec–3 Jan

## Hamilton House

★★★ BED AND BREAKFAST

**tel:** 01284 703022 & 07787 146553 **4 Nelson Road IP33 3AG**
**email:** hamiltonhouse@hotmail.co.uk **web:** www.hamiltonhousebse.co.uk
**dir:** *A14 junct 42, follow A1302 across rdbt, then 1st right*

A warm welcome awaits at Hamilton House, a relaxing Edwardian villa, situated in a quiet side road just a short walk from the town centre. The bedrooms are brightly decorated with co-ordinated fabrics and have a good range of facilities. Breakfast is served at a large communal table in the dining room.

**Rooms:** 4 rms (2 en suite) (1 fmly) **S** £32.50–£40; **D** £57.50–£65* **Facilities:** FTV DVD tea/coffee WiFi ⚓

## The Old Cannon Brewery

★★★ ⚏ INN

**tel:** 01284 768769 **86 Cannon Street IP33 1JR**
**email:** info@oldcannonbrewery.co.uk **web:** www.oldcannonbrewery.co.uk
**dir:** *A14 junct 43, A134 towards town centre. At rdbt after Tesco left then sharp right into Cadney Ln, left into Cannon St, on left*

Originally a beer house and brewery, this delightful Victorian property is sure to please. The brewery's finished products can be sampled in the bar. The open-plan bar and dining area features the polished stainless steel mash tun and kettle. The well-equipped bedrooms are located in an adjacent building, and every visitor will find a bottle of beer waiting for them after they check in.

**Rooms:** 7 annexe en suite (3 GF) **Facilities:** STV tea/coffee Dinner available WiFi ⚓ **Parking:** 7 **Notes:** No children 10yrs

## 6 Orchard Street

★★★ BED AND BREAKFAST

**tel:** 07946 590265 **IP33 1EH**
**email:** mariellascarlett@me.com **web:** www.number6orchardstreet.co.uk
**dir:** *In town centre near St John's Church on one-way system; Northgate St turn right into Looms Ln, 2nd right into Well St, straight on into Orchard St*

Expect a warm welcome from the caring hosts at this terrace property, situated just a short walk from the town centre. The pleasant bedrooms are comfortably appointed and have a good range of useful extras. Breakfast is served at a large communal table in the cosy dining room.

**Rooms:** 3 rms (2 en suite) (1 pri facs) **S** £45–£50; **D** £60–£65* **Facilities:** FTV tea/coffee WiFi ⚓ **Notes:** No children 6yrs

## The Black Boy

★★★ INN

**tel:** 01284 752723 **69 Guildhall Street IP33 1QD**
**email:** enquiries@theblackboypublichouse.co.uk **web:** www.theblackboypublichouse.co.uk
**dir:** *Exit A14 to town centre*

The Black Boy is a popular inn situated in the centre of this historic town. The spacious bedrooms have co-ordinated fabrics, pine furniture and many thoughtful touches. Public areas feature a large open-plan bar with a good selection of ales. There is a wide variety of pubs and restaurants within a short walk. Breakfast is served daily in the bar.

**Rooms:** 5 en suite **S** £35–£40; **D** £60–£70* **Facilities:** FTV tea/coffee Dinner available WiFi Pool table **Parking:** 6 **Notes:** No children 5yrs

### CAVENDISH — Map 13 TL84

## The George

★★★★ ◉◉ ⚏ RESTAURANT WITH ROOMS

**tel:** 01787 280248 **The Green CO10 8BA**
**email:** thegeorgecavendish@gmail.com **web:** www.thecavendishgeorge.co.uk
**dir:** *A1092 into Cavendish, The George next to village green*

The George is situated in the heart of the pretty village of Cavendish and has five stylish bedrooms which have retained many of their original features, as well as being comfortable and spacious. The front-facing rooms overlook the village. The award-winning restaurant is very well appointed and dinner should not be missed. Guests are guaranteed to receive a warm welcome, attentive friendly service and great food.

**Rooms:** 5 en suite (1 fmly) **Facilities:** FTV DVD tea/coffee Dinner available WiFi ⚓ **Extras:** Speciality toiletries, mineral water, sweets **Notes:** Closed 25 Dec & 1 Jan

## DUNWICH | Map 13 TM47

### The Ship at Dunwich

★★★★ ⊛ INN

tel: 01728 648219 **St James Street IP17 3DT**
email: info@shipatdunwich.co.uk **web:** www.shipatdunwich.co.uk
**dir:** *From N: A12, exit at Blythburgh onto B1125, then left to village. Inn at end of road. From S: A12, turn right to Westleton. Follow signs for Dunwich*

The Ship is a delightful inn situated in the heart of this quiet village, surrounded by nature reserves and heathland, and just a short walk from the beach. Public rooms feature a smart lounge bar with an open fire and real ales on tap. The comfortable bedrooms are traditionally furnished; some rooms have lovely views across the sea or marshes.

**Rooms:** 11 en suite 5 annexe en suite (4 fmly) (5 GF) **D** £120–£140* **Facilities:** FTV tea/coffee Dinner available WiFi **Extras:** Speciality toiletries **Parking:** 10 **Notes:** LB

## ELMSWELL | Map 13 TL96

### Kiln Farm Guest House

★★★★ ⌙ GUEST HOUSE

tel: 01359 240442 **Kiln Lane IP30 9QR**
email: davejankilnfarm@btinternet.com **web:** www.kilnfarmguesthouse.com
**dir:** *A14 junct 47 onto A1088. Entrance to Kiln Ln off E'bound slip road*

Kiln Farm Guest House is a delightful Victorian farmhouse situated in a peaceful rural location amid three acres of landscaped grounds. The bedrooms are housed in converted farm buildings, and each one is smartly decorated and furnished in country style. Breakfast is served in the smart conservatory and there is also a cosy lounge and bar area.

**Rooms:** 2 en suite 6 annexe en suite (2 fmly) (6 GF) **Facilities:** FTV DVD Lounge TVL tea/coffee Dinner available Licensed WiFi ⌙ **Extras:** Fruit, snacks, chocolates **Parking:** 20

## ELVEDEN | Map 13 TL88

### Premier Collection

### The Elveden Inn

★★★★★ ⌙ INN

tel: 01842 890876 **Brandon Road IP24 3TP**
email: enquiries@elvedeninn.com **web:** www.elvedeninn.com
**dir:** *Off A11 (dual carriageway) onto B1106 (Brandon Road) towards Bury St Edmunds*

This charming country inn offers a range of beautifully presented bedrooms and sleek modern bathrooms. Enjoying a peaceful location in the heart of East Anglia, the inn is part of the Guinness family-owned Elveden Estate. The bar is full of character and the terrace is a popular dining venue on warmer days. The Elveden courtyard shops are nearby and the café is very popular. A Dinner Award has been given to this establishment for a very special dinner which has an emphasis on freshly prepared local ingredients.

**Rooms:** 6 en suite (2 fmly) **Facilities:** FTV tea/coffee Dinner available Direct dial WiFi **Extras:** Speciality toiletries, fruit, bottled water – complimentary **Parking:** 100 **Notes:** LB

## EYE | Map 13 TM17

### The White Horse Inn

★★★★ INN

tel: 01379 678222 **Stoke Ash IP23 7ET**
email: mail@whitehorse-suffolk.co.uk **web:** www.whitehorse-suffolk.co.uk
**dir:** *On A140 halfway between Ipswich & Norwich*

The White Horse Inn is a 17th-century coaching inn on the main A140 midway between Norwich and Ipswich. It has been run by the same family for over a decade, offering home-made, good quality food in a friendly and comfortable environment. This is complemented by well-kept local ales and cider. Comfortable bedrooms are found in the modern, purpose-built motel-style annexe. Some have air conditioning; all are well equipped. Complimentary WiFi is available in the public areas and bedrooms.

**Rooms:** 11 annexe en suite (1 fmly) (9 GF) **S** £60–£74; **D** £65–£84* **Facilities:** FTV tea/coffee Dinner available Direct dial WiFi **Conf:** Max 50 Thtr 50 Class 50 Board 20 **Parking:** 60 **Notes:** LB

## FRAMLINGHAM | Map 13 TM26

### Colston Hall

★★★★ ⌙ FARMHOUSE

tel: 01728 638375 **Badingham IP13 8LB**
email: liz@colstonhall.com **web:** www.colstonhall.com
**dir:** *On A1120 between Badingham & Peasenhall*

Set in a peaceful rural location, Colston Hall offers a range of individually designed spacious bedrooms. This Elizabethan farmhouse has many original features including brick floors and oak beams. Bedrooms have lovely countryside views, overlooking the lakes and the pretty kitchen garden. The hearty breakfasts are not to be missed and the home-made marmalade is rather special.

**Rooms:** 3 en suite 3 rms annexe (2 en suite) (1 pri facs) (3 GF) **Facilities:** FTV DVD Lounge TVL tea/coffee WiFi Fishing Snooker Pool table ⌙ **Conf:** Max 50 Thtr 50 Class 50 Board 50 **Parking:** 22 **Notes:** LB 27 acres sheep

## Church Farm

★★★★ FARMHOUSE

tel: 01728 723532 **Church Road, Kettleburgh IP13 7LF**
email: abater@suffolkonline.net **web:** www.churchfarmkettleburgh.co.uk
**dir:** *Off A12 to Wickham Market, signs to Easton Farm Park & Kettleburgh 1.25m, house behind church. Off A14, A1120 Earl Soham to Kettleburgh*

This is a charming 300-year-old farmhouse situated close to the village church surrounded by superb grounds that include a duck pond, mature shrubs and sweeping lawns. The property retains exposed beams and open fireplaces. Bedrooms are pleasantly decorated and equipped with useful extras, and ground-floor rooms are available.

**Rooms:** 2 rms (1 en suite) (1 pri facs) 2 rms annexe (1 en suite) (1 pri facs) (3 GF) **S** £40–£50; **D** fr £80* **Facilities:** TVL tea/coffee Dinner available WiFi Fishing
**Extras:** Home-made biscuits, chocolates – complimentary **Parking:** 10
**Notes:** 70 acres mixed

---

**INGHAM**      Map 13 TL87

## The Cadogan Arms

★★★★ ◉ INN

tel: 01284 728443 **The Street IP31 1NG**
email: info@thecadogan.co.uk **web:** www.thecadogan.co.uk
**dir:** *4m from Bury St Edmunds, follow A134 towards Thetford*

The Cadogan Arms is a popular inn situated four miles from the centre of Bury St Edmunds. The smartly appointed bedrooms have been thoughtfully designed and have many useful extras. The open-plan public rooms are contemporary in style and they include a range of seating areas with plush leather sofas and a smart restaurant.

**Rooms:** 7 en suite (7 fmly) **Facilities:** FTV tea/coffee Dinner available WiFi
**Extras:** Bottled water **Parking:** 30 **Notes:** LB

---

**IXWORTH**      Map 13 TL97

### Premier Collection

## Ixworth House

★★★★★ ◉ BED AND BREAKFAST

tel: 01359 230639 & 07887 903047 **St Edmund Close IP31 2HP**
email: sharyn@ixworthhouse.co.uk **web:** www.ixworthhouse.co.uk
**dir:** *A143 to Ixworth, opposite Fordhams Garage turn into St Edmund Close*

Built in 1908, this fine Edwardian house has been sympathetically restored and has retained many of its original features. Ixworth House enjoys a prominent position on a quiet cul de sac and is a short walk from the pretty village of Ixworth. The three spacious bedrooms are beautifully presented and there is a real sense of luxury. Hospitality is first class and freshly cooked breakfasts, served in the very well-appointed dining room, are not to be missed.

**Rooms:** 3 en suite (1 fmly) **S** £70–£80; **D** £90–£100* **Facilities:** FTV TVL tea/coffee WiFi **Parking:** 3

---

**KETTLEBASTON**      Map 13 TL95

## The Old Rectory

★★★★ BED AND BREAKFAST

tel: 01449 740400 & 07730 384495 **IP7 7QD**
email: theoldrectorykettlebaston@gmail.com **web:** www.theoldrectorykettlebaston.co.uk
**dir:** *From Lavenham onto A1141 towards Hadleigh, in Monks Fleigh left onto B1115. Turn immediately left to Kettlebaston, right at T-junct, over white bridge. The Old Rectory on left*

This fine house enjoys a peaceful rural setting among landscaped gardens, and enjoys lovely countryside views. Many original features have been retained, which add to the character of the house. There is a choice of two comfortable bedrooms, and guests can also relax in the spacious lounge, or make use of the tennis court. Delicious breakfasts are served in the light-filled breakfast room, and a warm welcome is assured from the friendly hosts. The historic towns of Lavenham and Long Melford are a short drive away, as is the popular market town of Bury St Edmunds. An ideal base for exploring Constable country.

**Rooms:** 2 rms (1 en suite) (1 pri facs) **S** £65–£100; **D** £100–£125* **Facilities:** TVL tea/coffee Dinner available **Parking:** 5

---

**LAVENHAM**      Map 13 TL94

### Premier Collection

## Lavenham Great House 'Restaurant With Rooms'

★★★★★ ◉◉◉ ◎ RESTAURANT WITH ROOMS

tel: 01787 247431 **Market Place CO10 9QZ**
email: info@greathouse.co.uk **web:** www.greathouse.co.uk
**dir:** *Exit A1141 into Market Ln, behind cross on Market Place*

The 18th-century frontage on Market Place conceals a 15th-century timber-framed building that is now a restaurant with rooms. Lavenham Great House is a little slice of France, offering high-quality rural cuisine served by French staff. The spacious bedrooms are individually decorated and thoughtfully equipped with many useful extras; some rooms have a separate lounge area.

**Rooms:** 5 en suite (1 fmly) **S** £105–£215; **D** £160–£215 (room only)*
**Facilities:** FTV DVD tea/coffee Dinner available Direct dial WiFi Free bicycle use for guests **Extras:** Mini-bar, fruit, sherry – complimentary **Notes:** LB Closed Jan RS Sun eve & Mon Restaurant closed

---

**LEISTON**      Map 13 TM46

## Field End

★★★★ GUEST HOUSE

tel: 01728 833527 & 07946 287451 **1 Kings Road IP16 4DA**
email: herbert@herbertwood.wanadoo.co.uk **web:** www.fieldendguesthouse.co.uk
**dir:** *In town centre off B1122*

This Edwardian house has been appointed to a high standard and is impeccably maintained by the present owners. Bedrooms have co-ordinated soft furnishings and many thoughtful touches. Breakfast is served in an attractive dining room, which has a large sofa and a range of puzzles and games.

**Rooms:** 5 rms (2 en suite) (1 pri facs) (1 fmly) (1 GF) **Facilities:** FTV DVD TVL tea/coffee WiFi **Extras:** Fridges **Parking:** 5 **Notes:** No children 6mths

## LONG MELFORD
Map 13 TL84

### Premier Collection

## Long Melford Swan
★★★★★ ◎◎ RESTAURANT WITH ROOMS

**tel:** 01787 464545 **Hall Street CO10 9JQ**
**email:** info@longmelfordswan.co.uk **web:** www.longmelfordswan.co.uk
**dir:** *From A134 into Long Melford, on main road through village*

Located in the very heart of Long Melford, bedrooms have all been completely refurbished with stylish decor and modern fixtures, home-made refreshments on arrival, turn-down service and feature bathrooms. All the rooms are located just next door in Melford House, adjacent to the main bar and restaurant. This family-run business offers an excellent restaurant with attentive service and a large alfresco dining area in the walled garden. Lunch and dinner are served daily, and a range of cooked and continental dishes are offered for breakfast in the restaurant.

**Rooms:** 3 en suite 4 annexe en suite (1 fmly) (2 GF) **S** £95–£120; **D** £155–£210*
**Facilities:** FTV DVD iPod docking station tea/coffee Dinner available Direct dial WiFi ↕18 Spa treatments by arrangement **Extras:** Speciality toiletries, fruit
**Notes:** LB

## MILDENHALL
Map 12 TL77

### Premier Collection

## The Bull Inn
★★★★★ ◎ INN

**tel:** 01638 711001 **The Street, Barton Mills IP28 6AA**
**email:** reception@bullinn-bartonmills.com **web:** www.bullinn-bartonmills.com
**dir:** *A11 between Newmarket & Mildenhall, signed Barton Mills. Inn by Five Ways rdbt*

This delightful 16th-century coaching inn is lovingly cared for by the owners. Public rooms offer a choice of bars, a brasserie-style restaurant and a further lounge area. The contemporary bedrooms are tastefully appointed with co-ordinated soft furnishings and many thoughtful touches. All are individually designed with designer wallpaper, bespoke glass walls and many other unique elements.

**Rooms:** 13 en suite 2 annexe en suite (1 fmly) (2 GF) **Facilities:** FTV Lounge tea/coffee Dinner available Direct dial WiFi 🛁 **Extras:** Speciality toiletries
**Conf:** Max 30 Thtr 30 Class 20 Board 20 **Parking:** 50 **Notes:** Closed 24–26 Dec

## NEWMARKET
Map 12 TL66

### Premier Collection

## The Packhorse Inn
★★★★★ ◎◎ INN

**tel:** 01638 751818 **Bridge Street, Moulton CB8 8SP**
**email:** info@thepackhorseinn.com **web:** www.thepackhorseinn.com
**dir:** *A14 junct 39 onto B1506. After 1.5m turn left at x-rds onto B1085 (Moulton Rd). In Moulton, left into Bridge St*

The Packhorse Inn is situated just a short drive from Newmarket in the heart of a village close to the River Kennet. The property has eight individually designed bedrooms, all tastefully appointed, with many thoughtful touches and views of the surrounding hills, after which the rooms are named. The open-plan public rooms include a choice of seating and dining areas with an eclectic collection of furniture.

**Rooms:** 4 en suite 4 annexe en suite (2 fmly) (4 GF) **S** £85–£100; **D** £100–£175*
**Facilities:** FTV Lounge TVL tea/coffee Dinner available WiFi ↕18 🛁
**Extras:** Speciality toiletries, mineral water, biscuits **Conf:** Max 30 Thtr 30 Class 20 Board 30 **Parking:** 30

## ORFORD
Map 13 TM45

### Premier Collection

## The Crown & Castle
★★★★★ ◎◎ RESTAURANT WITH ROOMS

**tel:** 01394 450205 **IP12 2LJ**
**email:** info@crownandcastle.co.uk **web:** www.crownandcastle.co.uk
**dir:** *Turn right from B1084 on entering village, towards castle*

The Crown & Castle is a delightful restaurant with rooms situated adjacent to the Norman castle keep. Contemporary style bedrooms are spilt between the main house and the garden wing; the latter are more spacious and have patios with access to the garden. The restaurant has an informal atmosphere with polished tables and local artwork, and a menu that features quality, locally sourced produce.

**Rooms:** 7 en suite 14 annexe en suite (2 fmly) (13 GF) **D** £140–£250*
**Facilities:** FTV DVD tea/coffee Dinner available Direct dial WiFi ↕18
**Extras:** Speciality toiletries, fresh milk **Notes:** LB No children 8yrs

SIBTON    Map 13 TM36

## Sibton White Horse Inn

★★★★  INN

**tel:** 01728 660337 **Halesworth Road IP17 2JJ**
**email:** info@sibtonwhitehorseinn.co.uk **web:** www. sibtonwhitehorseinn.co.uk
**dir:** *From A12 in Yoxford take A1120 signed Sibton & Peasenhall. 3m, in Peasenhall right opposite butcher's shop. White Horse 600mtrs*

Sibton White Horse Inn is a delightful Grade II listed 16th-century Tudor property set in open countryside, a few miles from the Suffolk coast. Public rooms include a traditional beamed bar with exposed brick fireplaces and a choice of dining areas. The attractive bedrooms are situated in a converted building adjacent to the inn.

**Rooms:** 6 annexe en suite (3 GF) **D** £90–£110* **Facilities:** FTV DVD tea/coffee Dinner available WiFi 🕯 **Extras:** Bottled water, speciality toiletries, cafetières **Parking:** 50 **Notes:** LB No children 12yrs Closed 26–27 Dec

SOUTHWOLD    Map 13 TM57

### Premier Collection

## Sutherland House

★★★★★  RESTAURANT WITH ROOMS

**tel.** 01502 724544 **56 High Street IP18 6DN**
**email:** enquiries@sutherlandhouse.co.uk **web:** www. sutherlandhouse.co.uk
**dir:** *A1095 into Southwold, on High St on left after Victoria St*

Situated in the heart of the bustling town centre, this delightful 16th-century house has a wealth of character – oak beams, exposed brickwork, open fireplaces and two superb ornate plasterwork ceilings. The stylish bedrooms are tastefully decorated using co-ordinated fabrics and include many thoughtful touches. Public rooms feature a large open-plan contemporary restaurant, which has been awarded two AA Rosettes. There's a modern British menu created with care, and the food miles are listed alongside each dish.

**Rooms:** 5 en suite (1 fmly) **S** £100* **Facilities:** FTV DVD tea/coffee Dinner available WiFi **Notes:** No children 10yrs RS Mon Restaurant closed in winter Oct–Mar

STOKE-BY-NAYLAND    Map 13 TL93

### Premier Collection

## The Angel Inn

★★★★★ ⚜ 🕯 INN

**tel:** 01206 263245 & 07748 484619 **Polstead Street CO6 4SA**
**email:** info@angelinnsuffolk.co.uk **web:** www.angelinnsuffolk.co.uk
**dir:** *From A134 onto Bear St (B1087), 2m on right in Stoke-by-Nayland*

This charming inn has welcomed guests since the 16th century. Still popular with the locals, it's well known for its food and ambience. Public areas have a wealth of character and offer a choice of dining rooms that include a smart restaurant with an original well. Bedrooms are pleasantly decorated and thoughtfully equipped.

**Rooms:** 6 en suite **Facilities:** FTV Lounge tea/coffee Dinner available WiFi 🕯 **Conf:** Max 25 Thtr 15 Class 18 Board 18 **Parking:** 12 **Notes:** LB

## SUDBURY
Map 13 TL84

# The Case Restaurant with Rooms
★★★★ ◉ RESTAURANT WITH ROOMS

**tel:** 01787 210483 **Further Street, Assington CO10 5LD**
**email:** restaurant@thecaserestaurantwithrooms.co.uk
**web:** www.thecaserestaurantwithrooms.co.uk
**dir:** *Exit A12 at Colchester onto A134 to Sudbury. 7m, establishment on left*

The Case Restaurant with Rooms offers dining in comfortable surroundings, along with luxurious accommodation in bedrooms that all enjoy independent access. Some bathrooms come complete with corner jacuzzi, while internet access comes as standard. In the restaurant, local produce is used in all dishes, and bread and delicious desserts are made fresh every day.

**Rooms:** 7 en suite (2 fmly) (7 GF) **Facilities:** FTV Lounge tea/coffee Dinner available WiFi **Extras:** Speciality toiletries – complimentary; snacks – chargeable **Parking:** 25 **Notes:** LB

## THORNHAM MAGNA
Map 13 TM17

### Premier Collection

# Thornham Hall
★★★★★ GUEST ACCOMMODATION

**tel:** 01379 783314 **IP23 8HA**
**email:** info@thornhamhall.com **web:** www.thornhamhall.com
**dir:** *Turn off A140 at Stoke Ash White Horse pub. After 350mtrs right before Four Horseshoes pub. Through village, pass church & into drive signed Thornham Hall*

Set in a formal park, Thornham Hall enjoys a picturesque setting and the comfortable, individually styled bedrooms overlook the extensive gardens. There is a choice of reception rooms in which to relax and the Thornham estate offers guests over ten miles of walks through ancient woodland and farmland. The walled garden contains many rare apple trees. The charming town of Eye is nearby and Framlingham is a short drive away.

**Rooms:** 3 en suite **Facilities:** Lounge TVL tea/coffee Licensed WiFi 🦢 🦢 Fishing 🔒 **Parking:** 10

## WINGFIELD
Map 13 TM27

# Holly Tree House
★★★★ 🍽 BED AND BREAKFAST

**tel:** 01379 384854 **Bleach Green IP21 5RG**
**email:** sharon@hollytreehousebandb.co.uk **web:** www.hollytreehousebandb.co.uk

This beautiful 16th-century timber-framed house enjoys a peaceful rural location on the Suffolk/Norfolk border. Guests are served refreshment on arrival in the garden or in the cosy lounge, depending on the weather. Bedrooms are beautifully presented and are very well equipped. The house has been sympathetically restored in recent years, and boasts many eye-catching original features as well as lovely gardens.

**Rooms:** 2 en suite **S** £70–£75; **D** £90–£105* **Facilities:** FTV DVD iPod docking station Lounge tea/coffee WiFi 🔒 **Extras:** Speciality toiletries, snacks **Parking:** 4

## WOODBRIDGE
Map 13 TM24

# Cherry Tree Inn
★★★★ 🍺 INN

**tel:** 01394 384627 & 385213 **73 Cumberland Street IP12 4AG**
**email:** info@thecherrytreepub.co.uk **web:** www.thecherrytreepub.co.uk

Cherry Tree Inn is a charming 17th-century inn located close to the town of Woodbridge. This authentic inn has many original features including oak beams, low ceilings and log fires. There is a great atmosphere in the bar and evening meals feature an extensive choice of freshly prepared traditional dishes. There is a good choice of cask ales available and the bedrooms are all spacious and very comfortable.

**Rooms:** 3 annexe en suite (1 fmly) (2 GF) **S** fr £90; **D** fr £100* **Facilities:** STV FTV DVD tea/coffee Dinner available Direct dial WiFi 🔒 **Extras:** Home-made biscuits, still/sparkling water **Parking:** 30

## YAXLEY
Map 13 TM17

### Premier Collection

## The Auberge
★★★★★ ◎◎ ⚲ RESTAURANT WITH ROOMS

**tel:** 01379 783604 **Ipswich Road IP23 8BZ**
**email:** aubmail@the-auberge.co.uk **web:** www.the-auberge.co.uk
**dir:** On A140 between Norwich & Ipswich at x-rds with B1117

A warm welcome awaits at The Auberge, a charming 15th-century property, which was once a rural pub but is now a smart restaurant with rooms. The restaurant has gained two AA Rosettes for the good use of fresh, quality produce in well-crafted dishes. The public areas have a wealth of character, such as exposed brickwork and beams, and the grounds are particularly well kept and attractive. The spacious bedrooms are tastefully appointed and have many thoughtful touches; one bedroom has a four-poster.

**Rooms:** 11 annexe en suite (2 fmly) (6 GF) **S** £75–£110* **Facilities:** FTV tea/coffee Dinner available Direct dial WiFi ⚲ **Conf:** Max 30 Thtr 30 Class 20 Board 12 **Parking:** 40 **Notes:** LB

## SURREY

## ALBURY
Map 6 TQ04

## The Drummond at Albury
★★★ ⚲ INN

**tel:** 01483 202039 **High Street GU5 9AG**
**web:** www.thedrummondarms.co.uk

The Drummond is centrally located in this picturesque village, with attractive gardens running down to a small river at the rear of the property. The bedrooms are individually appointed and offer all the modern comforts. Breakfast is served in the light and airy conservatory while the restaurant offers mouth-watering dishes.

**Rooms:** 9 en suite **Facilities:** Dinner available **Conf:** Max 40 Thtr 40 Class 40

## CAMBERLEY
Map 6 SU86

## Hatsue Guest House
★★★★ GUEST ACCOMMODATION

**tel:** 01276 22160 & 07791 267620 **17 Southwell Park Road GU15 3PU**
**email:** welcome@hatsueguesthouse.com **web:** www.hatsueguesthouse.com
**dir:** M3 junct 4, A331 N, A30 E, at Arena sports centre turn right. At T-junct, turn right, 2nd house on left before church

Hatsue Guest House offers comfortable, well-appointed accommodation in a period house, which has been sympathetically updated to meet the needs of the modern guest. TV and free WiFi are examples of the amenities provided. The breakfast room overlooks the quiet rear garden. Ample parking is available.

**Rooms:** 5 en suite **S** fr £60; **D** fr £70 **Facilities:** FTV tea/coffee WiFi **Parking:** 5

## CHARLWOOD

*See Gatwick Airport (Sussex, West)*

## CHIDDINGFOLD
Map 6 SU93

### Premier Collection

## The Crown Inn
★★★★★ INN

**tel:** 01428 682255 **The Green, Petworth Road GU8 4TX**
**email:** enquiries@thecrownchiddingfold.com **web:** www.thecrownchiddingfold.com

Set in a tranquil location in a picturesque village, the inn dates back to the early 13th century. This charming property offers stylish, modern accommodation that has been tastefully finished without losing any period features. Breakfast and dinner can be enjoyed in the oak-panelled dining room, and there is a spacious bar, outside seating and small courtyard.

**Rooms:** 8 en suite (4 fmly) **S** £95–£120; **D** £120–£210 **Facilities:** FTV Lounge tea/coffee Dinner available Direct dial WiFi ♪ 18 **Extras:** Speciality toiletries **Conf:** Max 40 Thtr 40 Class 25 Board 28 **Parking:** 15

## CRANLEIGH
Map 6 TQ03

## The Cranley
★★★ INN

**tel:** 01483 272827 **The Common GU6 8SQ**
**email:** thecranleyhotel@gmail.com **web:** www.thecranleyhotel.co.uk
**dir:** From Guildford on A281 left to Cranleigh

This traditional pub, located in the picturesque village of Cranleigh, offers freshly prepared food, at both lunch and dinner, using local produce. Regular entertainment is provided, and the rear garden is popular with families. The comfortable bedrooms have TVs and tea- and coffee-making facilities.

**Rooms:** 7 en suite **Facilities:** TVL tea/coffee Dinner available WiFi Pool table **Parking:** 50

## DORKING
Map 6 TQ14

## Denbies Farmhouse B&B
★★★★ FARMHOUSE

**tel:** 01306 876777 **London Road RH5 6AA**
**email:** bandb@denbiesvineyard.co.uk **web:** www.denbies.co.uk
**dir:** Off A24

Denbies Farmhouse enjoys a wonderful location in the heart of England's largest vineyard and is a short walk to the historic market town of Dorking. Very popular with ramblers, there are many beautiful walks nearby. Bedrooms are comfortable and breakfasts are served in the conservatory with its wonderful views of the vineyard.

**Rooms:** 7 en suite (2 fmly) (2 GF) **Facilities:** STV FTV tea/coffee Licensed WiFi ⚲ **Extras:** Speciality toiletries – complimentary **Parking:** 14 **Notes:** LB 650 acres wine

## EFFINGHAM  Map 6 TQ15

### Sir Douglas Haig

★★★ INN

**tel:** 01372 456886 **The Street KT24 5LU**
**email:** sirdouglashaig@hotmail.com **web:** www.sirdouglashaig.co.uk
**dir:** *M25 junct 9, A243 then A24, at rdbt take 2nd exit onto A246. Through Bookham, at lights with golf club on left, turn right. Pub on right*

A traditional public house located in the village centre, the Sir Douglas Haig has retained a country atmosphere and offers comfortable accommodation for the modern traveller. The bar is well stocked and provides regular entertainment while the restaurant serves a choice of traditional dishes. Ample parking is available.

**Rooms:** 7 en suite (1 fmly) **Facilities:** FTV DVD tea/coffee Dinner available WiFi
🔒 **Parking:** 15 **Notes:** LB

## GODALMING  Map 6 SU94

### Innkeeper's Lodge Godalming

★★★★ 🍺 INN

**tel:** 08451 551551 *(Calls cost 2p per minute plus your phone company's access charge)* **Ockford Road GU7 1RH**
**email:** info@innkeeperslodge.com **web:** www.innkeeperslodge.com

At Innkeeper's Lodge you'll find accommodation with comfort and character in equal measure, and everything needed for a relaxing stay, from easy check-in and free parking to complimentary breakfast and a cosy pub serving great value food and drink on the doorstep. Each Lodge has quality rooms, and there are Lodges in a variety of locations from towns and cities to countryside settings across the UK.

**Rooms:** 14 en suite (4 fmly) **Facilities:** FTV tea/coffee Dinner available Direct dial WiFi **Conf:** Max 28

## GUILDFORD  Map 6 SU94

### The Angel

★★★★ GUEST ACCOMMODATION

**tel:** 01483 564555 **91 High Street GU1 3DP**
**email:** reservations@angelpostinghouse.com **web:** www.angelpostinghouse.com
**dir:** *From A281 (Horsham Rd), turn left into High St. 200yds on left*

On the high street, in the heart of Guildford and within the popular Angel Gate area with its shops and restaurants, this historic property features a range of rooms including spacious suites and traditional doubles. All have TVs, free WiFi, and high-quality bathrooms with power showers, some with separate baths. Rates are room-only; breakfast is available in the adjacent 'Bills' restaurant, which is also open for lunch and dinner.

**Rooms:** 24 en suite **Facilities:** STV FTV Lounge tea/coffee Dinner available Licensed WiFi ⚓18 🔒 **Conf:** Max 60 Thtr 60 Class 30 Board 30 **Notes:** Civ wed 50

## HASLEMERE  Map 6 SU93

### The Wheatsheaf Inn

★★★ 🍺 INN

**tel:** 01428 644440 **Grayswood Road, Grayswood GU27 2DE**
**email:** ken@thewheatsheafgrayswood.co.uk **web:** www.thewheatsheafgrayswood.co.uk
**dir:** *1m N of Haslemere on A286 in Grayswood*

Situated in a small village just outside Haslemere, this well-presented inn has a friendly atmosphere. The smart conservatory restaurant, complements the attractive dining area and popular bar. Bedrooms are furnished to a good standard; all but one on the ground floor.

**Rooms:** 7 en suite (6 GF) **S** £59–£79* **Facilities:** FTV tea/coffee Dinner available Direct dial WiFi **Parking:** 21

## HORLEY

*See Gatwick Airport (Sussex, West)*

## MICKLEHAM  Map 6 TQ15

### Running Horses

★★★★ ◉ INN

**tel:** 01372 372279 **Old London Road RH5 6DU**
**email:** gm@therunninghorses.co.uk **web:** www.therunninghorses.co.uk
**dir:** *M25 junct 9 follow signs for Dorking, Sbound on A24. Left signed Mickleham, 200mtrs on right*

Located in the tranquil village of Mickleham, this renovated village pub offers modern and very comfortable accommodation, well equipped with up-to-date amenities ideal for both the leisure and corporate guest. The location is quiet yet with easy access to Dorking, Gatwick and the M25. The restaurant offers an excellent range of dishes and is open for breakfast, lunch and dinner.

**Rooms:** 5 en suite 1 annexe en suite (1 GF) **D** £79–£135* **Facilities:** FTV tea/coffee Dinner available WiFi 🔒

## RIPLEY  Map 6 TQ05

### The Talbot

★★★★ INN

**tel:** 01483 225188 **High Street GU23 6BB**
**email:** manager@the talbotripley.com **web:** www.bespokehotels.com/talbotinn
**dir:** *M25 junct 10 onto A3 (S), follow signs for Ripley. On left in High St*

The Talbot has lots of charm and character, and has retained many of its original features despite having undergone a major transformation. Public areas are very comfortable, with real ales and delicious, seasonal food on offer; alfresco dining is available in summer months. The Classic Rooms in the Ripley Wing are contemporary in design, and there are nine bedrooms in the main building. The inn also offers a number of rooms for meetings, private parties and weddings. The Wisley Suite accommodates up to 120 guests and comes equipped with the latest technology.

**Rooms:** 9 en suite 34 annexe en suite (15 GF) **Facilities:** FTV TVL tea/coffee Dinner available Direct dial WiFi 🐾 🔒 **Conf:** Max 100 Thtr 100 Class 60 Board 60 **Parking:** 43 **Notes:** LB Civ wed 100

## WEST END

Map 6 SU96

# The Inn West End

★★★★ ⬤ INN

**tel:** 01276 858652 & 485842 **GU24 9PW**
**email:** rooms@the-inn.co.uk **web:** www.the-inn.co.uk
**dir:** M3 junct 3, 3m on A322

A convenient location, attentive service, a traditional pub, a wine shop, a restaurant and 12 individually appointed and comfortable bedrooms are available at The Inn West End. The cottage-style bedrooms offer sumptuous beds, powerful showers and all the amenities expected by the modern traveller. The menu offers a range of dishes to meet the needs of a varied clientele with the focus on fresh and seasonal produce, locally sourced where possible. There is also a relaxing garden, ideal for barbecues during the summer months, and secure parking.

*The Inn West End*

**Rooms:** 12 annexe en suite (12 GF) **S** £95–£160; **D** £105–£170* **Facilities:** FTV tea/coffee Dinner available WiFi ⅃18 **Parking:** 35 **Notes:** No children 10yrs

*See advert below*

## WEYBRIDGE
Map 6 TQ06

### Innkeeper's Lodge Weybridge

★★★★ INN

**tel:** 08451 551551 *(Calls cost 2p per minute plus your phone company's access charge)*
**25 Oatlands Chase KT13 9RW**
**email:** info@innkeeperslodge.com **web:** www.innkeeperslodge.com

At Innkeeper's Lodge you'll find accommodation with comfort and character in equal measure, and everything needed for a relaxing stay, from easy check-in and free parking to complimentary breakfast and a cosy pub serving great value food and drink on the doorstep. Each Lodge has quality rooms, and there are Lodges in a variety of locations from towns and cities to countryside settings across the UK.

**Rooms:** 19 en suite (5 fmly) (2 GF) **Facilities:** FTV tea/coffee Dinner available WiFi Parking

## WOKING
Map 6 TQ05

### Innkeeper's Lodge Woking

★★★ INN

**tel:** 08451 551551 *(Calls cost 2p per minute plus your phone company's access charge)*
**Chobham Road, Horsell GU21 4AL**
**email:** info@innkeeperslodge.com **web:** www.innkeeperslodge.com

Just a short walk from Woking station, a 25-minute commute from central London, this establishment is ideal for both the business or leisure traveller. It offers comfortable en suite bedrooms and attractive public areas with cosy open fires and friendly, welcoming staff. Food is served daily in The Wheatsheaf. The free on-site parking is a plus.

**Rooms:** 33 en suite (3 fmly) (13 GF) **Facilities:** FTV tea/coffee Dinner available WiFi **Parking:** 28

### Made In Sud

★★★ GUEST ACCOMMODATION

**tel:** 01483 723080 **14 The Broadway GU21 5AP**
**email:** dminardi@btinternet.com **web:** www.madeinsudwoking.co.uk

A warm welcome is guaranteed, set within walking distance of Woking train station. All bedrooms are comfortably furnished, serviced to a high standard, and come equipped with a range of accessories. Breakfast is served in the light and airy café below. Free WiFi is accessible throughout.

**Rooms:** 8 en suite **Facilities:** WiFi

## EAST SUSSEX

## ALFRISTON
Map 6 TQ50

### The Star Inn

★★★★ INN

**tel:** 01323 870495 **High Street BN26 5TA**
**email:** julie.garvin@thestaralfriston.co.uk **web:** www.thestaralfriston.co.uk
**dir:** *At Beddingham rdbt stay on A27 towards Eastbourne, at next rdbt 3rd exit onto Alfriston Rd. Continue to High St, Star Inn on left*

Located in the very heart of Alfriston and conveniently located close to Glyndebourne, Eastbourne and Brighton, The Star Inn is a traditional inn with cosy public areas, serving lunch and dinner daily. All of the bedrooms offer stylish and very comfortable accommodation. Breakfast (both cooked and continental) is served daily in the restaurant. There is also on-site parking and WiFi.

**Rooms:** 13 en suite 24 annexe en suite (1 fmly) (12 GF) **Facilities:** FTV Lounge tea/coffee Dinner available Direct dial WiFi 🔒 **Conf:** Max 110 Thtr 110 Board 28 **Parking:** 30 **Notes:** Civ wed 110

## BOREHAM STREET
Map 6 TQ61

### Premier Collection

### Boreham House

★★★★★ 🍴 BED AND BREAKFAST

**tel:** 01323 833719 **Boreham Hill BN27 4SF**
**email:** enquiries@borehamhouse.com **web:** www.borehamhouse.com
**dir:** *On A271 between Herstmonceux & Battle, 100mtrs from Bull's Head pub*

This delightful Georgian manor is in a quiet location just a short drive from Bodiam Castle, Hastings and Pevensey Bay. Both sides of the property enjoy excellent views of the High Wield or across the Pevensey Marshes to the sea. Bedrooms and bathrooms are contemporary in style, yet retain many original features. There is a guest lounge, and an excellent pub just 100 metres away. Guests can enjoy a hearty cooked or continental breakfast served in the dining room, all items locally sourced.

**Rooms:** 3 en suite (1 fmly) **Facilities:** FTV Lounge tea/coffee WiFi 🔒 **Parking:** 3

## BRIGHTON & HOVE
Map 6 TQ30

### New Steine

★★★★ ⚲ ⚌ GUEST ACCOMMODATION

**tel:** 01273 681546 **10–11 New Steine BN2 1PB**
**email:** reservation@newsteinehotel.com **web:** www.newsteinehotel.com
**dir:** *A23 to Brighton Pier, left into Marine Parade, New Steine on left after Wentworth St*

Close to the seafront, off the Esplanade, the New Steine provides spacious and well-appointed accommodation. The Bistro offers simple yet appealing dishes with a French and British influence; produce from farms in Sussex is used for the breakfasts. There are two meeting rooms suitable for a variety of occasions. Street parking can be arranged.

**Rooms:** 20 rms (16 en suite) (4 pri facs) (4 fmly) (2 GF) **S** £62.50–£69;
**D** £89–£145* **Facilities:** FTV Lounge tea/coffee Dinner available Direct dial Licensed WiFi ♨ **Extras:** Speciality toiletries **Conf:** Max 50 Thtr 50 Class 20 Board 26 **Notes:** LB No children 4yrs

### Snooze

★★★★ GUEST ACCOMMODATION

**tel:** 01273 605797 **25 St George's Terrace BN2 1JJ**
**email:** info@snoozebrighton.com **web:** www.snoozebrighton.com
**dir:** *Follow A23 to seafront/pier. Turn left at mini rdbt opposite pier, then left into Bedford St, 2nd right into St George's Terrace*

This splendid Victorian terraced property is close to the beach and the popular Kemp Town bars and restaurants. Bedrooms have a distinctly 'retro' feel and all are comfortably presented. The spacious dining room with its large bay windows is the setting for a choice of hearty breakfasts. Snooze was the Winner of the AA Funkiest B&B of the Year Award 2016-2017.

**Rooms:** 8 en suite (2 GF) **Facilities:** FTV DVD iPod docking station tea/coffee WiFi **Extras:** Speciality toiletries

### Brighton House

★★★★ ⚲ GUEST ACCOMMODATION

**tel:** 01273 323282 **52 Regency Square BN1 2FF**
**email:** info@brighton-house.co.uk **web:** www.brighton-house.co.uk
**dir:** *Opposite West Pier*

Situated close to the seafront is the elegant and environmentally-friendly Brighton House. Comfortably appointed bedrooms and bathrooms come in a variety of sizes and are located on four floors. An impressively abundant, organic continental breakfast is served in the spacious and elegant dining room. Parking is in the nearby underground car park.

**Rooms:** 16 en suite (2 fmly) **Facilities:** FTV tea/coffee Licensed WiFi
**Notes:** No children 12yrs

### Gullivers

★★★★ GUEST ACCOMMODATION

**tel:** 01273 681546 & 695415 **12a New Steine BN2 1PB**
**email:** reservation@gullivershotel.com **web:** www.gullivershotel.com
**dir:** *A23 to Brighton Pier, left into Marine Parade, premises 300yds on left*

Situated in an impressive Regency square close to the town and seafront, Gullivers has much to offer. Compact rooms use clever design and contemporary colours to ensure comfort, and some have quality shower rooms en suite. The lounge and brasserie, decorated with fine art, are super areas in which to relax and dine.

**Rooms:** 12 rms (9 en suite) (3 pri facs) (2 GF) **S** £32.50–£64; **D** £69–£137.50*
**Facilities:** FTV Lounge tea/coffee Dinner available Direct dial Licensed WiFi
♨ **Extras:** Speciality toiletries – complimentary **Conf:** Max 30 Thtr 30 Class 10 Board 20 **Notes:** LB No children 4yrs

### Innkeeper's Lodge Brighton, Patcham

★★★★ INN

**tel:** 08451 551551 *(Calls cost 2p per minute plus your phone company's access charge)*
**Miller & Carter Brighton, London Road BN1 8YQ**
**email:** info@innkeeperslodge.com **web:** www.innkeeperslodge.com

At Innkeeper's Lodge you'll find accommodation with comfort and character in equal measure, and everything needed for a relaxing stay, from easy check-in and free parking to complimentary breakfast and a cosy pub serving great value food and drink on the doorstep. Each Lodge has quality rooms, and there are Lodges in a variety of locations from towns and cities to countryside settings across the UK.

**Rooms:** 17 en suite (6 fmly) (1 GF) **Facilities:** FTV tea/coffee Dinner available Direct dial WiFi

BRIGHTON & HOVE *continued*

## Marine View

★★★★ GUEST ACCOMMODATION

**tel:** 01273 603870 **24 New Steine BN2 1PD**
**email:** info@mvbrighton.co.uk **web:** www.mvbrighton.co.uk
**dir:** *From A23, left into Marine Pde, left into New Steine, 300mtrs*

Overlooking the elegant Steine Square with the sea just a glance away, this 18th-century property offers comfortable, well-designed accommodation. Plenty of accessories are provided, including free WiFi. A hearty breakfast is available in the bright lounge-dining room.

**Rooms:** 11 rms (8 en suite) (1 pri facs) (2 fmly) (2 GF) **S** £40–£80; **D** £60–£150*
**Facilities:** Lounge tea/coffee WiFi **Notes:** LB

## Regency Lansdowne Guest House

★★★ GUEST ACCOMMODATION

**tel:** 01273 321830 **45 Lansdowne Place BN3 1HF**
**email:** rlgh@btconnect.com **web:** www.regencylansdowne.co.uk
**dir:** *A23 to Brighton Pier, right onto A259, 1m right into Lansdowne Place, house on left before Western Rd*

A warm welcome is guaranteed at this Regency house, located only minutes from the seafront. Comfortable bedrooms are functionally equipped with a good range of facilities, and an extensive continental breakfast is served each day at a communal table overlooking attractive gardens. On-road parking is a short walk away.

**Rooms:** 7 rms (5 en suite) (2 pri facs) **Facilities:** FTV tea/coffee Lift WiFi
**Notes:** Closed 20–27 Dec

### BURWASH                                 Map 6 TQ62

## The Bear Inn & Burwash Motel

★★★ INN

**tel:** 01435 882540 **High Street TN19 7ET**
**email:** enquiries@bear-inn-hotel-burwash.co.uk **web:** www.bear-inn-hotel-burwash.co.uk

Located in the village of Burwash, this country inn offers en suite bedrooms with external access. The inn is traditional in style and benefits from uninterrupted views of the Sussex countryside. Traditional bar meals are available daily and guests can enjoy a cooked or continental breakfast in the restaurant.

**Rooms:** 8 en suite (8 GF) **Facilities:** FTV DVD TVL tea/coffee Dinner available WiFi 🏃
🏊36 Fishing Pool table 🅿 **Conf:** Max 50 Thtr 50 Class 35 Board 35 **Parking:** 8

### CAMBER                                   Map 7 TQ91

## The Gallivant

★★★★ ◎◎ RESTAURANT WITH ROOMS

**tel:** 01797 225057 **New Lydd Road TN31 7RB**
**email:** beachbistro@thegallivanthotel.com **web:** www.thegallivanthotel.com

The Gallivant is located right on the edge of Camber Sands, just a short drive from the historic town of Rye. The inn offers modern, coastal-styled accommodation with light airy decor and reconditioned driftwood furniture. Rooms are well equipped and ideal for both business and leisure guests. There's a bar and the award-winning Beach Bistro serves food daily. The large function suite is open year round and is perfect for parties or weddings. The sand dunes and beach are just across the road in front of the inn. The Gallivant was a finalist for the AA Restaurant with Rooms of the Year award 2017–18.

**Rooms:** 16 en suite 4 annexe en suite (4 fmly) (20 GF) **Facilities:** FTV DVD Lounge tea/coffee Dinner available Direct dial WiFi 🏊18 🅿 **Extras:** Speciality toiletries
**Conf:** Max 120 Thtr 120 Class 60 Board 40 **Parking:** 25 **Notes:** Civ wed 150

### DITCHLING                                 Map 6 TQ31

**Premier Collection**

## The Bull

★★★★★  INN

**tel:** 01273 843147 **2 High Street BN6 8TA**
**email:** info@thebullditchling.com **web:** www.thebullditchling.com
**dir:** *Exit A23 signed Pyecombe, left onto A273 signed Hassocks. Up hill, pass Pyecombe Golf Club on right, 2nd right into New Rd (B2112) to Ditchling. Right at mini rdbt, next left into car park*

Dating back to 1563, The Bull is one of the oldest buildings in this famously pretty Sussex village. First used as an overnight resting place for travelling monks, the inn has also served as a courthouse and a staging post for the London-Brighton coach. Accomplished dishes, using local produce together with local ales are available in the award-winning restaurant. There is a landscaped garden with seating that enjoys stunning views over the South Downs. Bedrooms are very comfortable, offering many stylish features and a range of amenities. An extensive cooked and continental breakfast is served daily in the restaurant.

**Rooms:** 4 en suite **D** £100–£180* **Facilities:** FTV DVD iPod docking station tea/coffee Dinner available WiFi 🏊18 🅿 **Extras:** Speciality toiletries, mineral water, mini-bar **Parking:** 30 **Notes:** LB

*See advert opposite*

## EASTBOURNE

Map 6 TV69

### Premier Collection

## Ocklynge Manor

★★★★★ BED AND BREAKFAST

**tel:** 01323 734121 & 07979 627172 **Mill Road BN21 2PG**
**email:** ocklyngemanor@hotmail.com **web:** www.ocklyngemanor.co.uk
**dir:** *From Eastbourne Hospital follow town centre/seafront sign, 1st right into Kings Av, Ocklynge Manor at top of road*

This charming home has seen a variety of uses since serving as a commanderie for the Knights of St John in the 12th century. An air of peace and relaxation is evident in the delightful public rooms, well-tended gardens and the spacious, comfortable bedrooms that come filled with thoughtful extras, including free WiFi. The hospitality is noteworthy, and home-baked bread is just one of the delights at breakfast.

**Rooms:** 3 rms (2 en suite) (1 pri facs) **S** £60–£125; **D** £110–£130* **Facilities:** FTV DVD Lounge tea/coffee WiFi ☕ **Extras:** Snacks – complimentary **Parking:** 3
**Notes:** No children 18yrs

## Gyves House Guesthouse

★★★★ GUEST ACCOMMODATION

**tel:** 01323 721709 **20 St Aubyns Road BN22 7AS**
**email:** book@gyveshouse.com **web:** www.gyvesguesthouse.co.uk
**dir:** *On seafront between Redoubt Fortress & pier, into St Aubyns Rd, 1st house*

This property is located just 30 metres from the seafront and within a short walking distance of the both the town centre and pier. Bedrooms are comfortably appointed throughout and are modern in style with high quality soft furnishings. Complimentary WiFi and digital TVs are provided in addition to well stocked beverage trays. A range of cooked and continental dishes are served daily in the main dining room.

**Rooms:** 6 en suite **S** £40–£45; **D** £70–£80* **Facilities:** FTV tea/coffee WiFi ⚡18
☕ **Extras:** Bottled water – complimentary

## The Mowbray

★★★★ ☕ GUEST ACCOMMODATION

**tel:** 01323 720012 **2 Lascelles Terrace BN21 4BJ**
**email:** info@themowbray.com **web:** www.themowbray.com
**dir:** *Opposite Devonshire Park Theatre*

The Mowbray is an elegant town house located opposite The Devonshire Park Theatre and a few minutes' walk from the seafront. Bedrooms are accessible by a lift to all floors, and vary in size, but all are attractively furnished and comfortable. Public areas include a spacious well presented lounge, small modern bar and a stylish dining room. Breakfast is home-cooked, as are evening meals, available by prior arrangement.

**Rooms:** 12 en suite (3 fmly) (1 GF) **Facilities:** FTV DVD iPod docking station Lounge TVL tea/coffee Dinner available Lift Licensed WiFi ☕ **Extras:** Superior rooms – fruit, bottled water, slippers **Conf:** Max 20 Thtr 20 Class 10 Board 10 **Notes:** LB

## The Berkeley Guest House

★★★★ GUEST ACCOMMODATION

**tel:** 01323 645055 **3 Lascelles Terrace BN21 4BJ**
**email:** info@theberkeley.net **web:** www.theberkeleyguesthouse.co.uk
**dir:** *Follow seafront from pier, take 7th turn on right*

The Berkeley Guest House is an attractive town house just a stone's throw from the seafront. Comfortable bedrooms are well equipped and all bathrooms are en suite. There is plenty of choice available at breakfast, in the spacious, contemporary dining room. A comfortable lounge is available for guest use, and WiFi is available throughout. Parking vouchers are available from reception.

**Rooms:** 13 en suite (2 fmly) (1 GF) **S** £30–£45; **D** £65–£95* **Facilities:** FTV DVD Lounge tea/coffee WiFi

## Bella Vista

★★★★ GUEST ACCOMMODATION

**tel:** 01323 724222 **30 Redoubt Road BN22 7DH**
**email:** stay@thebellavista.com **web:** www.thebellavista.com
**dir:** *500yds NE of town centre. Off A259 (Seaside Rd)*

Situated on the east side of town, just off the seafront, this is an attractive flint house with the bonus of a car park. Bedrooms are generally spacious, comfortable and neatly appointed with modern facilities including free WiFi. There is a large lounge and a dining room where dinner and breakfast is served.

**Rooms:** 9 en suite (3 GF) **Facilities:** FTV TVL tea/coffee Dinner available WiFi
**Parking:** 10 **Notes:** LB

## Far End Guest House

★★★★ GUEST ACCOMMODATION

**tel:** 01323 725666 **139 Royal Parade BN22 7LH**
**web:** www.farendhotel.co.uk
**dir:** *Phone for directions*

Located right on the seafront with excellent uninterrupted views, just one mile from the town centre, Far End is in the quieter area of Eastbourne. There's plenty of parking and a private, off-road car park for guests. Bedrooms and bathrooms are very traditional in style, many with excellent views. There is a guest lounge where guests can relax during their stay, and a dining room on the ground floor serving a cooked and continental breakfast.

**Rooms:** 10 rms (6 en suite) (1 pri facs) **S** £38; **D** £80* **Facilities:** Lounge tea/coffee
**Parking:** 5 **Notes:** No children 2yrs

## Ivydene

★★★★ GUEST HOUSE

**tel:** 01323 720547 **5–6 Hampden Terrace, Latimer Road BN22 7BL**
**email:** ivydenehotel@hotmail.co.uk **web:** www.ivydenehotel-eastbourne.co.uk
**dir:** *From town centre/pier NE along seafront, towards Redoubt Fortress, into St Aubyns Rd, 1st right into Hampden Terrace*

Ivydene is made up of two Victorian houses, 5 and 6 Hampden Terrace. With adjoining doors and the two staircases still in place, this traditional building is full of character. Darren and Martin are friendly and welcoming hosts.

**Rooms:** 14 en suite (1 GF) **S** £40; **D** £75–£85* **Facilities:** FTV TVL tea/coffee Licensed WiFi **Notes:** LB No children 16yrs Closed Oct–Mar

## The Royal

★★★★ GUEST ACCOMMODATION

**tel:** 01323 649222 **8-9 Marine Parade BN21 3DX**
**email:** info@royaleastbourne.org.uk **web:** www.royaleastbourne.org.uk
**dir:** *On seafront 100mtrs E of pier*

The Royal enjoys a central seafront location close to the pier and within easy walking distance of the town centre. Spectacular uninterrupted sea views are guaranteed. This eco-friendly property has comfortable modern bedrooms with TVs and free WiFi. One of the 10 rooms has private facilities, while the others are en suite. A substantial continental breakfast is served. The Royal offers a full pet-sitting service and dogs stay free of charge.

**Rooms:** 10 rms (9 en suite) (1 pri facs) (1 fmly) (1 GF) **Facilities:** STV FTV DVD tea/coffee WiFi ⌕18 ⬗ Free WiFi **Extras:** Speciality toiletries – complimentary **Notes:** LB No children 12yrs

## The Sherwood

★★★★ GUEST HOUSE

**tel:** 01323 724002 & 07851 716706 **7 Lascelles Terrace BN21 4BJ**
**email:** info@thesherwood.net **web:** www.thesherwood.net
**dir:** *Follow signs to seafront. At pier turn into Grand Parade (towards Beachy Head). Right into Lascelles Terrace*

The Sherwood is an attractive Victorian property just a minute's walk from the seafront, offering well-appointed bedrooms with comfortable, co-ordinated furnishings. The cosy lounge is great to relax in, and the attractive dining room serves a robust breakfast.

**Rooms:** 11 en suite (2 fmly) (1 GF) **Facilities:** FTV DVD TVL tea/coffee Licensed WiFi ⬗ **Extras:** Bottled water

## Beachy Rise Guest House

★★★ GUEST HOUSE

**tel:** 01323 639171 **5 Beachy Head Road BN20 7QN**
**email:** susanne234@hotmail.co.uk **web:** www.beachyrise.com
**dir:** *1m SW of town centre. Off B2103 Upper Dukes Rd*

This friendly, family-run guest house has a quiet residential location close to Meads. Bedrooms are individually styled with co-ordinated soft furnishings and feature some useful extras. Breakfast is served in the light and airy dining room overlooking the garden, where guests are free to wander.

**Rooms:** 4 en suite (2 fmly) **S** £40–£50; **D** £65–£70* **Facilities:** FTV tea/coffee WiFi

| HALLAND | Map 6 TQ41 |

## The BlackSmiths Arms

★★★ INN

**tel:** 01825 840304 **Lewes Road BN8 6PN**
**email:** nigel.fright@btconnect.com **web:** www.theblacklioninn-halland.co.uk

This traditional inn is located on the A22 between Eastbourne and Uckfield. There is a cosy restaurant and bar area with many original features and an open fireplace; traditional pub food is served daily. Bedrooms are modern and very comfortable with digital TV and free WiFi throughout. A cooked and continental breakfast is served in the bar area.

**Rooms:** 7 en suite **Facilities:** Dinner available WiFi

| HASTINGS & ST LEONARDS | Map 7 TQ80 |

**Premier Collection**

## Stream House

★★★★★ BED AND BREAKFAST

**tel:** 01424 814916 & 07941 911378 **Pett Level Road, Fairlight TN35 4ED**
**email:** info@stream-house.co.uk **web:** www.stream-house.co.uk
**dir:** *4m NE of Hastings. Exit A259 onto unclassified road between Fairlight & Cliff End*

Lovingly converted from three cottages, the Stream House stands in three acres of tranquil grounds, just one mile from Winchelsea beach. If you arrive before 6pm, you will be greeted with a complimentary cup of tea and slice of Sandra's home-made cake. The well-appointed bedrooms are beautifully decorated, and among the delightful extras provided are sherry and chocolates, along with speciality toiletries in the bathrooms. Delicious breakfasts are served in the lounge-dining room which has an original inglenook fireplace, and during warmer months you can enjoy the extensive garden with its rippling stream and Koi pond.

**Rooms:** 3 en suite (1 fmly) **S** £70–£85; **D** £90 £115* **Facilities:** STV Lounge tea/coffee WiFi ⬗ **Extras:** Speciality toiletries, Baileys, chocolates **Parking:** 4 **Notes:** LB No children 8yrs Closed Dec–Feb

HASTINGS & ST LEONARDS *continued*

## Premier Collection

## The Cloudesley

★★★★★ GUEST ACCOMMODATION

**tel:** 01424 722759 & 07507 000148 **7 Cloudesley Road TN37 6JN**
**email:** info@thecloudesley.co.uk **web:** www.thecloudesley.co.uk
**dir:** *A21 (London Rd) onto A2102, left into Tower Rd. Right into Cloudesley Rd, house on left*

The Cloudesley is located just minutes from Hastings in the quiet residential area of St Leonards, and offers high standards of quality and comfort. The bedrooms have been environmentally designed – the walls have been eco-limewashed, the hand-made beds have Siberian goosedown pillows, and the shampoos are free of parabens and sodiam lauryl sulphate. There is a treatment room for holistic therapies. The two guest lounges are stylish and decorated with photographs taken by the proprietor. An extensive selection of cooked and continental dishes is available for breakfast, which includes locally sourced, organic ingredients.

**Rooms:** 5 en suite **Facilities:** iPod docking station Lounge tea/coffee Dinner available Licensed WiFi Holistic therapies & massage **Extras:** Speciality toiletries, mini-fridge **Notes:** LB No children 6yrs

## Eagle House

★★★ GUEST ACCOMMODATION

**tel:** 01424 430535 **Pevensey Road TN38 0JZ**
**email:** info@eaglehousehotel.co.uk **web:** www.eaglehousehotel.co.uk
**dir:** *Exit seafront into London Rd, 5th turn on left into Pevensey Rd. 150mtrs on right*

Eagle House is a Victorian property situated in a peaceful residential area within easy walking distance of the shops, college and seafront. Public areas are sumptuously decorated in a traditional style and the spacious 'retro' bedrooms are simply furnished. A hearty breakfast can be enjoyed in the dining room, which overlooks the gardens.

**Rooms:** 22 rms (19 en suite) (3 fmly) (3 GF) **S** £45–£55; **D** £75–£100* **Facilities:** FTV TVL tea/coffee Dinner available Licensed WiFi **Parking:** 9

| HOVE |

*See Brighton & Hove*

| LEWES | Map 6 TQ41 |

## Premier Collection

## Broadacres

★★★★★ ⬤ ⬤ BED AND BREAKFAST

**tel:** 07568 083616 **Lewes Road, Whitesmith BN8 6JG**
**email:** joannawild@hotmail.co.uk **web:** www.broadacres-bandb.co.uk
**dir:** *A22 towards Eastbourne, right onto B2124 just before Golden Cross. 1m on left behind black metal gates*

This beautiful property, located very near to Lewes, has a single, spacious, self-contained suite for guest use. The richly decorated rooms are all well-equipped and the bedroom features a large TV, super king-size sleigh bed, and its own sitting area. There is also generous storage space. The luxurious and well-equipped bathroom has a rolltop bath and separate shower. Breakfast is a real treat and is served in the suite's own dining room. Dinner is also available on request. You can also expect WiFi, parking, all in extensive well-kept grounds.

**Rooms:** 1 en suite (1 GF) **S** £90–£120; **D** £90–£148* **Facilities:** FTV tea/coffee Dinner available WiFi ⬤ **Extras:** Speciality toiletries, home-made biscuits **Parking:** 4 **Notes:** LB No children 12yrs Closed 24–28 Dec ⬤

| NORTHIAM | Map 7 TQ82 |

## Premier Collection

## Knelle Dower B&B

★★★★★ ⬤ GUEST ACCOMMODATION

**tel:** 01797 253163 **Rye Road TN31 6NJ**
**email:** knelledower@btconnect.com **web:** www.knelledower.co.uk
**dir:** *A21 to Flimwell onto A268, then A28. In Northiam onto B2088 opposite primary school, on left between Talisman & Boundary House*

Located in a rural location close to both Rye and the village of Northiam, this converted barn hosts a prime location with uninterrupted countryside views. The accommodation is spacious with high-quality decor and furnishings, and there is a private terrace leading off the main living area for guests to enjoy during summer months. Breakfast can be served here or in the main house.

**Rooms:** 1 annexe en suite (1 GF) **Facilities:** FTV DVD iPod docking station tea/coffee WiFi ⬤⬤18 ⬤ **Parking:** 2 **Notes:** No children 3yrs Closed 21–28 Dec

## RYE
Map7 TQ92

*See also Hastings & St Leonards*

Premier Collection

### Jeake's House

★★★★★ ⌂ GUEST ACCOMMODATION

**tel:** 01797 222828 **Mermaid Street TN31 7ET**
**email:** stay@jeakeshouse.com **web:** www.jeakeshouse.com
**dir:** *Approach from High St or The Strand*

Previously a 16th-century wool store and then a 19th-century Baptist school, this delightful house stands on a cobbled street in one of the most beautiful parts of this small, bustling town. The individually decorated bedrooms combine elegance and comfort with modern facilities. Breakfast is served at separate tables in the galleried dining room, and there is an oak-beamed lounge as well as a stylish, book-lined bar complete with old pews.

**Rooms:** 11 rms (10 en suite) (1 pri facs) (2 fmly) **S** £80–£120; **D** £95–£150*
**Facilities:** FTV iPod docking station Lounge tea/coffee Licensed WiFi ♨
**Parking:** 20 **Notes:** LB No children 5yrs

*See advert on page 275*

### Manor Farm Oast

★★★★★ ⌂ BED AND BREAKFAST

**tel:** 01424 813787 & 07866 818952 **Windmill Lane TN36 4WL**
**email:** manor.farm.oast@lineone.net **web:** www.manorfarmoast.co.uk
**dir:** *4m SW of Rye. A259 W past Icklesham church, left at x rds into Windmill Ln, after sharp left bend, left (follow sign) into farmland*

Manor Farm Oast is a charming 19th-century environmentally-friendly oast house peacefully located amid orchards in open countryside. Spacious bedrooms are individually styled and include numerous thoughtful extras including free WiFi. A choice of lounges is available, one heated by a roaring log fire during the winter.

**Rooms:** 3 rms (2 en suite) (1 pri facs) (1 fmly) **S** £95–£105; **D** £105*
**Facilities:** FTV Lounge tea/coffee Licensed WiFi ♨ **Extras:** Speciality toiletries, fruit, chocolates **Conf:** Max 20 Thtr 20 Board 12 **Parking:** 8 **Notes:** LB No children 11yrs Closed 23–26 & 31 Dec

RYE *continued*

## The Kings Head Inn

★★★★ ⊜ INN

tel: 01797 225962 & 07762 404958 **Rye Hill TN31 7NH**
email: info@kingsheadrye.co.uk web: www. kingsheadrye.co.uk

This inn is located just a couple of miles from the centre of Rye. Bedrooms are stylish and contemporary in style and very comfortable and are split between the main pub and converted annexe rooms with private parking. The pub and restaurant is an ideal place to relax and enjoy a traditional pub lunch or dinner. Breakfast is served in this area daily.

**Rooms:** 5 en suite 6 annexe en suite (4 fmly) (5 GF) **Facilities:** FTV tea/coffee Dinner available WiFi **Parking:** 40

ST LEONARDS

*See also Hastings & St Leonards*

---

### Premier Collection

## Willow Tree House

★★★★★ GUEST ACCOMMODATION

tel: 01797 227820 & 07715 991325 **Winchelsea Road TN31 7EL**
email: info@willow-tree-house.com web: www.willow-tree-house.com
dir: *On A259, 500mtrs from town centre*

Willow Tree House is an early 17th-century farmhouse which has been sympathetically refurbished to retain many of its charming original features. There are six individually furnished bedrooms, all appointed to a high standard – four doubles, one four-poster bedroom and a king size/twin; each has an en suite shower room. There is also ample free parking in the secure on-site car park. Willow Tree House is only 10 minutes' walk away from Rye town centre with its antique shops restaurants, pubs, and cobbled streets.

**Rooms:** 6 en suite **S** £95–£110; **D** £95–£135* **Facilities:** FTV DVD iPod docking station Lounge tea/coffee WiFi ⊱18 ⬧ **Extras:** Speciality toiletries **Parking:** 6 **Notes:** LB No children 14yrs

## Strand House

★★★★ ⊜ GUEST ACCOMMODATION

tel: 01797 226276 **Tanyards Lane, Winchelsea TN36 4JT**
email: info@thestrandhouse.co.uk web: www.thestrandhouse.co.uk
dir: *M20 junct 10, A2070 to Lydd. A259 through Rye to Winchelsea, house in 2m*

This charming 15th-century house is just a few miles from Rye. Traditional character is maintained in comfortably appointed rooms and the public areas, while the annexe rooms offer a more contemporary style. Both the main house and the annexe rooms are available for exclusive use. The dining room is also open to the public on certain days of the week, where local produce is a feature of the well balanced menu. Home-made jams and marmalade, together with honey from the garden and other local produce are offered at breakfast. Secure parking available.

**Rooms:** 10 rms (9 en suite) (1 pri facs) 3 annexe en suite (4 fmly) (3 GF) **S** £65–£95; **D** £75–£195* **Facilities:** FTV DVD iPod docking station Lounge tea/coffee Dinner available Licensed WiFi ⬧ **Extras:** Mini-fridge in annexe rooms **Parking:** 15 **Notes:** LB No children 5yrs RS weekends (high season) 2 night bookings only Civ wed 30

## Ab Fab Rooms

★★★★   BED AND BREAKFAST

**tel:** 01323 895001 & 07713 197915 **11 Station Road, Bishopstone BN25 2RB**
**email:** stay@abfabrooms.co.uk **web:** www.abfabrooms.co.uk

Just a short walk from Bishopstone station and sandy beaches, this is a perfect base for visiting local sights and attractions. The three bedrooms are styled in a contemporary fashion and offer superior comfort and amenities – freshly-baked flapjacks are only one of the many baked goods offered. Breakfast, served in the garden conservatory, includes home-made jams and local Sussex produce. There is parking, and a rear garden to enjoy during the warmer months.

*Ab Fab Rooms*

**Rooms:** 3 en suite **Facilities:** STV DVD iPod docking station tea/coffee WiFi **Parking:** 2

---

# Jeake's House

Mermaid Street, Rye, East Sussex TN31 7ET
Tel: 01797 222828 · Email: stay@jeakeshouse.com
Website: www.jeakeshouse.com

Jeake's House provides outstanding accommodation in Rye. The 16th Century house plays host to the discerning guest who wants to recapture the feel of history while at the same time enjoying a high standard of modern comfort and relaxed hospitality. Rye accommodation is very special and Jeake's House certainly lives up to this reputation. Guests will be invariably welcomed by our flirtatious Tonkinese, Freddie and Monte, cordially complemented by the friendly service of the proprietors, Jenny Hadfield and Richard Martin. Breakfast is served in our galleried dining room and there is a booklined honesty bar to relax in.

Staying at Jeake's House also provides access to the surrounding countryside. There are many historical and beautiful villages and towns nearby. Jenny and Richard are always happy to advise on leisurely trips to historic castles, beautiful gardens and picturesque villages; and can recommend the best local restaurants and friendly inns.

Parking in this small town is notoriously difficult to find and we are happy to be some of the only accommodation in Rye to guarantee guests a space in our private car park. There is a small charge. Our car park is a three minute walk from Jeake's House and we advise that you park on Mermaid Street so that we can assist you with your luggage and provide you with a parking permit.

SEAFORD *continued*

## The Avondale

★★★ GUEST ACCOMMODATION

**tel:** 01323 890008 **Avondale Road BN25 1RJ**
**email:** info@theavondale.co.uk **web:** www.theavondale.co.uk
**dir:** *In town centre, off A259 behind war memorial*

A warm welcome is offered by the caring owners at this friendly, family-run guest accommodation which is ideally placed for the Newhaven to Dieppe ferry service. The bedrooms are pleasantly furnished and thoughtfully equipped. Breakfast is served in the attractive dining room and guests also have the use of a cosy lounge.

**Rooms:** 14 rms (8 en suite) (4 fmly) **Facilities:** FTV DVD TVL tea/coffee Lift Licensed WiFi **Conf:** Max 15 Class 15 Board 15 **Notes:** LB

### WADHURST                                    Map 6 TQ63

## Little Tidebrook Farm

★★★★ FARMHOUSE

**tel:** 01892 782688 & 07970 159988 **Riseden TN5 6NY**
**email:** info@littletidebrook.co.uk **web:** www.littletidebrook.co.uk
**dir:** *A267 from Tunbridge Wells to Mark Cross, left onto B2100, 2m, right at Best Beech Inn, left after 1m into Riseden Rd, farm on left*

This traditional farmhouse has cosy log fires in winter and wonderful garden dining can be arranged in warmer months. The imaginative decor sits well with modern amenities, such as WiFi, to provide both leisure and business guests with excellent accommodation. It is close to Bewl Water and Royal Tunbridge Wells.

**Rooms:** 3 rms (2 en suite) (1 pri facs) **Facilities:** FTV DVD TVL tea/coffee WiFi **Parking:** 8 **Notes:** No children 12yrs 50 acres horses

### WILMINGTON                                  Map 6 TQ50

## Crossways

★★★★ ◉◉ RESTAURANT WITH ROOMS

**tel:** 01323 482455 **Lewes Road BN26 5SG**
**email:** stay@crosswayshotel.co.uk **web:** www.crosswayshotel.co.uk
**dir:** *On A27 between Lewes & Polegate, 2m E of Alfriston rdbt*

Proprietors David Stott and Clive James have been welcoming guests to this elegant restaurant with rooms for over 25 years. Crossways sits amid stunning gardens and attractively tended grounds. The well-presented bedrooms are tastefully decorated and provide an abundance of thoughtful amenities including free WiFi. Guest comfort is paramount and the warm hospitality ensures guests often return.

**Rooms:** 7 en suite **S** £59–£85; **D** £145–£175* **Facilities:** FTV tea/coffee Dinner available Direct dial WiFi **Extras:** Speciality toiletries, mini-bar, fresh milk **Parking:** 30 **Notes:** LB No children 12yrs Closed 24 Dec–23 Jan

### WEST SUSSEX

### AMBERLEY                                    Map 6 TQ01

## Woody Banks Cottage

★★★★ BED AND BREAKFAST

**tel:** 01798 831295 & 07719 916703 **Crossgates BN18 9NR**
**email:** enquiries@woodybanks.co.uk **web:** www.woodybanks.co.uk
**dir:** *Off B2139 into village, right at Black Horse pub, Woody Banks 0.5m on left past Sportsman pub*

Located close to Arundel in an elevated position with stunning views over the Wildbrooks, this immaculately maintained house and gardens is very popular with walkers. It provides two comfortable, homely bedrooms filled with thoughtful extras. Imaginative breakfasts are served in the spacious lounge-dining room.

**Rooms:** 2 rms (1 pri facs) (1 fmly) **S** £45–£55; **D** £75–£85* **Facilities:** FTV DVD TVL tea/coffee WiFi **Extras:** Fruit teas **Parking:** 2 **Notes:** LB No children 6yrs Closed 24–27 Dec

### ANGMERING                                   Map 6 TQ00

## Angmering Manor

★★★★ ⬚ GUEST ACCOMMODATION

**tel:** 01903 859849 **High Street BN16 4AG**
**email:** angmeringmanor@thechapmansgroup.co.uk **web:** www.relaxinnz.co.uk
**dir:** *Follow A27 towards Portsmouth, exit A280, follow signs for Angmering*

This former manor house in the heart of the village has been stylishly appointed. It offers good food, a bar, an indoor pool, and good parking. Staff are friendly and helpful and rooms are very comfortable.

**Rooms:** 17 en suite (3 fmly) (4 GF) **Facilities:** FTV TVL tea/coffee Dinner available Direct dial Licensed WiFi ⊛ Gym Beauty salon **Parking:** 25 **Notes:** LB Civ wed 50

## ARUNDEL
Map 6 TQ00

*See also Amberley*

### Hanger Down House B&B

★★★★ BED AND BREAKFAST

**tel:** 01903 882904 & 07753 595191 **Priory Lane, Tortington BN18 0BG**
**email:** hangerdownhouse@btinternet.com **web:** www.hangerdownhouse.co.uk
**dir:** *A27 to Arundel, take road signed Ford/Climping at Arundel rdbt. Priory Ln 0.5m on right*

Set in picturesque Sussex countryside, Hanger Down House is conveniently and quietly located one mile from the historic town of Arundel. All three bedrooms are stylishly decorated and provide comfortable accommodation for guests. Bedrooms include king-size beds, a leather sofa, fridge, digital LCD TVs and free WiFi. There are great views of the local countryside and a walled garden which guests are free to use. A cooked or continental breakfast can be enjoyed in the dining room.

**Rooms:** 3 en suite (2 fmly) (1 GF) **S** £75–£95; **D** £95 **Facilities:** Lounge tea/coffee WiFi ↘ 🎾 🔒 Trampoline Football pitch Outdoor table tennis **Extras:** Speciality toiletries – complimentary; fridges **Parking:** 5 **Notes:** LB

### The Town House

★★★★ ⚜⚜ RESTAURANT WITH ROOMS

**tel:** 01903 883847 **65 High Street BN18 9AJ**
**email:** enquiries@thetownhouse.co.uk **web:** www.thetownhouse.co.uk
**dir:** *A27 to Arundel, into High Street, establishment on left at top of hill*

This is an elegant, Grade II listed Regency building overlooking Arundel Castle, just a short walk from the shops and centre of the town. Bedrooms and public areas retain the building's unspoilt character. The ceiling in the dining room is particularly spectacular and originated in Florence in the 16th century. The excellent food has been awarded two AA Rosettes.

**Rooms:** 5 en suite (1 fmly) **S** £75–£110; **D** £110–£150 **Facilities:** FTV iPod docking station Dinner available WiFi 🔒 **Extras:** Speciality toiletries **Notes:** Closed 2 weeks Easter & 2 weeks Oct RS Sun–Mon Restaurant closed

### White Swan

★★★★ ⚜ INN

**tel:** 01903 882677 **16 Chichester Road BN18 0AD**
**email:** thewhiteswan.arundel@pebblehotels.com **web:** www.pebblehotels.com
**dir:** *From Arundel follow A27 towards Chichester, premises on right hand side at top of hill*

The White Swan offers very comfortable and stylish accommodation. There is a character bar, a lounge and a restaurant, and informal service is provided by the friendly team. Substantial snacks and meals can be ordered throughout the day and evening. Complimentary WiFi is available in the public areas.

**Rooms:** 20 en suite (6 GF) **Facilities:** FTV TVL tea/coffee Dinner available Direct dial WiFi **Extras:** Speciality toiletries **Conf:** Max 100 Thtr 100 **Parking:** 100 **Notes:** Civ wed 70

## BOGNOR REGIS
Map 6 SZ99

### The Old Priory

★★★★ ⚜ GUEST HOUSE

**tel:** 01243 863580 & 07484 600297 **80 North Bersted Street PO22 9AQ**
**email:** bookings@old-priory.com **web:** www.old-priory.com
**dir:** *1.6m NW of Bognor. Off A259 (Chichester road) to North Bersted. Old Priory sign on left. Or A29 to rdbt (McDonalds). Turn right into Rowan Way, follow signs*

Located in the mainly residential area of North Bersted, this 400-year-old property retains many original features. Bedrooms, which are all individual in style, are homely, with a couple featuring four-poster beds and sunken jacuzzi baths. All have en suites or a private bathroom. Delicious breakfasts, featuring home-made jams and cake, as well as excellent cooked dishes, are served at an impressive communal table in the grand dining room. There is also an outdoor pool, hot tub and delightful grounds for guests to enjoy.

**Rooms:** 3 rms (2 en suite) (1 pri facs) 3 annexe en suite (3 GF) **S** £50–£60; **D** £72–£112 **Facilities:** STV tea/coffee WiFi ↘ 🔒 Hot tub **Parking:** 6

## BOLNEY
Map 6 TQ22

### 8 Bells Bed & Breakfast
★★★★ ⬭ INN

**tel:** 01444 881396 **The Long House, The Street RH17 5QP**
**email:** stay@8bellsbandb.com **web:** www.8bellsbandb.com
**dir:** A23/A272 junct. Village situated between Ansty & Cowfold on A272

This Tudor property is situated in a peaceful village, close to both Gatwick and Brighton. Many original features, including exposed beams, remain, along with high-quality, modern and comfortable accommodation. Guests check in at the pub located directly opposite and it is here that breakfast, lunch and dinner can be enjoyed.

**Rooms:** 3 en suite (1 fmly) (1 GF) **Facilities:** FTV DVD Lounge tea/coffee Dinner available WiFi Pool table **Extras:** Bottled water – complimentary **Parking:** 15 **Notes:** LB

## CHARLTON
Map 6 SU81

### The Fox Goes Free
★★★★ INN

**tel:** 01243 811461 **PO18 0HU**
**email:** enquiries@thefoxgoesfree.com **web:** www.thefoxgoesfree.com
**dir:** In village centre

This former hunting lodge has retained much original character and is located in lovely countryside at the foot of the South Downs National Park. The bedrooms are well appointed and the pub boasts low ceilings, brick floors and three inglenook fireplaces. The inn serves its own ale and has an inviting, daily-changing menu. During the summer months, guests can take advantage of the rear garden.

**Rooms:** 3 en suite 2 annexe en suite (3 fmly) (2 GF) **S** £73–£165; **D** £98–£190*
**Facilities:** FTV tea/coffee Dinner available WiFi ⚓ **Parking:** 50

## CHICHESTER
Map 5 SU80
*See also West Marden*

### Rooks Hill
★★★★★ ⬭ GUEST HOUSE

**tel:** 01243 528400 & 07802 415639 **Lavant Road, Lavant PO18 0BQ**
**email:** info@rookshill.co.uk **web:** www.rookshill.co.uk

This beautiful Grade II listed country house is at the foot of the South Downs yet is only a few minutes from Chichester. Goodwood is also close by and a 15-minute drive will take guests to the coast. The house is lovingly maintained with attractive rooms, all of which are presented in a way that balances the period features with contemporary style. All of them also feature modern en suites. The oak-beamed breakfast room and lounge is delightful and looks out to the wisteria-clad courtyard. Breakfasts are memorable for their quality, choice and the emphasis on local produce. Hospitality is also a highlight here.

**Rooms:** 4 en suite (1 GF) **Facilities:** FTV Lounge tea/coffee WiFi ⚓ **Parking:** 4 **Notes:** No children 14yrs

### Musgrove House
★★★★ ⬭ BED AND BREAKFAST

**tel:** 01243 790179 & 07885 586344 **63 Oving Road PO19 7EN**
**email:** enquiries@musgrovehouse.co.uk **web:** www.musgrovehouse.co.uk
**dir:** From A27 onto B2144 towards city centre, at corner of Oving Rd & St James Rd

Located just outside Chichester city centre, this establishment offers three stylish bedrooms with light, airy decor and modern fixtures and fittings, including free WiFi and digital TVs. Expect a friendly welcome on arrival and a choice of both cooked and continental dishes at breakfast, which makes good use of high-quality and locally sourced produce.

**Rooms:** 3 en suite **S** £75–£110; **D** £80–£115* **Facilities:** FTV DVD iPod docking station tea/coffee WiFi ⚓ **Extras:** Speciality toiletries **Parking:** 3 **Notes:** No children 12yrs

### The Bull's Head
★★★★ INN

**tel:** 01243 839895 **99 Fishbourne Road West PO19 3JP**
**email:** enquiries@bullsheadfishbourne.net **web:** www.bullsheadfishbourne.net
**dir:** A27 onto A259, 0.5m on left

Located in Fishbourne, yet just a short drive from the centre of Chichester, and within easy access of Portsmouth, The Bull's Head offers comfortably appointed bedrooms in a former coach house. The bedrooms are light and airy with modern decor and furnishings. The pub is traditional in style and offers a wide selection of home-cooked pub classics as well as a good range of cask ales. Breakfast is served in the restaurant.

**Rooms:** 4 annexe en suite (1 fmly) (4 GF) **Facilities:** FTV DVD tea/coffee Dinner available WiFi 🔒 **Parking:** 35

## 82 Fishbourne

★★★★ 🍷 ☕ BED AND BREAKFAST

**tel:** 07854 051013 **82 Fishbourne Road West PO19 3JL**
**email:** nik@nikwestacott.plus.com **web:** www.theoldgreenhouse.co.uk
**dir:** A27 at Chichester rdbt, towards Fishbourne & Bosham on A259. 0.5m on right diagonally opposite Woolpack pub

Warm and friendly hospitality abounds at 82 Fishbourne, which is just a short drive from historic Chichester. Accommodation is spacious and well equipped. Breakfast provides a substantial start to the day and includes delicious fresh eggs from the free-range hens that live in the back garden. Scheduled activities include 'mushroom hunts', and wine tastings are held throughout the year.

**Rooms:** 3 en suite (1 GF) **S** £55–£125; **D** £65–£175* **Facilities:** FTV tea/coffee Dinner available Licensed WiFi 🔒 Cookery lessons, fly fishing trips **Parking:** 3 **Notes:** LB

## The George & Dragon

★★★ ☕ INN

**tel:** 01243 785660 **51 North Street PO19 1NQ**
**email:** info@georgeanddragoninn.co.uk **web:** www.georgeanddragoninn.co.uk
**dir:** At top of North St, off A286, near Chichester Festival Theatre

This inn, located at one end of Chichester's high street boasts attractively styled rooms and a friendly atmosphere. Rooms are comfortable with all the amenities needed for a pleasant night's stay. There is a light and airy dining room set apart from the popular central bar area where dinner and breakfast is served. Regional ales are available.

**Rooms:** 10 annexe en suite (5 GF) **S** fr £60; **D** fr £80* **Facilities:** FTV tea/coffee Dinner available WiFi **Notes:** RS 25–26 Dec & 1 Jan No bkfst service & pub closed

CHILGROVE          Map 5 SU81

### Premier Collection

## The White Horse

★★★★★ ⊚ RESTAURANT WITH ROOMS

**tel:** 01243 519444 **High Street PO18 9HX**
**email:** info@thewhitehorse.co.uk **web:** www.thewhitehorse.co.uk
**dir:** From Chichester take A286 N, turn left onto B2141 to village

Part of The Epicurean Collection, this spacious property offers stylish and relaxed surroundings on the edge of the South Downs. The bar and dining areas have an opulent feel, with lots of quirky touches and interesting features. Guests are welcome to enjoy a pint and relax, or dine from the appealing and wide-ranging menus. The emphasis is on local produce and food is a highlight. Bedrooms offer an attractive blend of traditional and contemporary features, with wooden beams, sheepskin rugs and king-size beds. Most open out onto the private courtyard and feature either copper baths or large rain showers, with a couple even having hot tubs.

**Rooms:** 15 en suite **Facilities:** FTV Lounge tea/coffee Dinner available Direct dial WiFi Fishing **Conf:** Max 20 **Notes:** LB

COMPTON          Map 5 SU71

## Apiary Cottage

★★★★ BED AND BREAKFAST

**tel:** 023 9263 1306 **PO18 9EX**
**email:** janesmckellar1@hotmail.co.uk **web:** www.apiarycottagebandb.co.uk
**dir:** A3 at Horndean into Rowlands Castle road. Left into Finchdean road, left onto B1246 to West Marden, then Compton

This beautiful cottage near Chichester has two highly individual bedrooms with their own private bathrooms. The richly decorated rooms are well equipped and are ideal for business or leisure use. Public areas include a comfortable lounge and the dining area is a sociable setting for breakfast, which overlooks the gardens. There is also parking available.

**Rooms:** 2 rms (2 pri facs) **S** £65–£80; **D** £85–£120 **Facilities:** FTV TVL tea/coffee WiFi 🔒 **Extras:** Sweets, chocolate **Parking:** 6

CRAWLEY

*See Gatwick Airport*

GATWICK AIRPORT          Map 6 TQ24

## Old House Inn

★★★★ ☕ INN

**tel:** 01342 718529 **Effingham Road RH10 3JB**
**email:** info@theoldhouseinn.co.uk **web:** www.theoldhouseinn.co.uk
**dir:** On B2037

Part of The Epicurean Collection, and conveniently located just 10 minutes from Gatwick, this stylish inn offers a modern restaurant and bar, and has retained many original features. All of the bedrooms are en suite with stylish decor and very comfortable furnishings. There is plenty of parking on site and a large beer garden for guests to enjoy. Both cooked and continental breakfasts are served daily in the main restaurant.

**Rooms:** 6 annexe en suite (4 GF) **Facilities:** FTV Lounge tea/coffee Dinner available Direct dial WiFi ♿ ☂ 🔒 **Parking:** 50 **Notes:** LB

## Vulcan Lodge Guest House

★★★★ BED AND BREAKFAST

**tel:** 01293 771522 & 07980 576012 **27 Massetts Road RH6 7DQ**
**email:** reservations@vulcan-lodge.com **web:** www.vulcan-lodge.com
**dir:** M23 junct 9, A23 into Horley, off A23 Brighton Rd

A particularly warm and friendly welcome is offered by the hosts of Vulcan Lodge, a charming period house, which sits back from the main road and is convenient for Gatwick Airport. Bedrooms are well equipped and feature many thoughtful extras. A choice of breakfast is offered, including vegetarian, and is served in a delightful dining room.

**Rooms:** 4 rms (3 en suite) (1 pri facs) (1 fmly) **S** £59–£64; **D** fr £80* **Facilities:** FTV TVL tea/coffee WiFi **Extras:** Bottled water **Parking:** 13 **Notes:** Closed 23–27 Dec & 31 Dec–2 Jan

GATWICK AIRPORT *continued*

## Gainsborough Lodge

★★★ GUEST ACCOMMODATION

**tel:** 01293 783982 **39 Massetts Road RH6 7DT**
**email:** enquiries@gainsborough-lodge.co.uk **web:** www.gainsborough-lodge.co.uk
**dir:** *2m NE of airport off A23 (Brighton Rd)*

Close to Gatwick, this fine Edwardian house offers a courtesy service to and from the airport. The bright bedrooms are comfortably appointed, and a varied breakfast, including a vegetarian option is served in the cheerful conservatory-dining room. There is also an attractive lounge.

**Rooms:** 15 rms (14 en suite) (1 pri facs) 7 annexe en suite (2 fmly) (8 GF)
**S** £37–£47; **D** £39–£54 (room only) **Facilities:** FTV TVL tea/coffee Licensed WiFi
**Parking:** 20

## Gatwick White House

★★ GUEST ACCOMMODATION

**tel:** 01293 402777 & 0800 612 3605 **50–52 Church Road RH6 7EX**
**email:** hotel@gwhh.com **web:** www.gwhh.com
**dir:** *In Horley centre off A23 (Brighton Rd)*

Convenient for the airport and major routes, this establishment offers efficient and functional accommodation. There is a bar and a restaurant that serves good curries as well as traditional dishes. The house has ample parking, and a 24-hour transfer service to Gatwick is available on request.

**Rooms:** 27 en suite (2 fmly) (10 GF) **S** £39–£55; **D** £45–£65 **Facilities:** FTV TVL tea/coffee Dinner available Direct dial Licensed WiFi 🔒 **Parking:** 30

| HORSHAM | Map 6 TQ13 |

## Springfields

★★★★ GUEST ACCOMMODATION

**tel:** 01403 246770 **Springfield Park Road RH12 2PW**
**email:** enquiries@springfieldshotel.co.uk **web:** www.springfieldshotel.co.uk

This purpose-built guest accommodation is located in the very heart of Horsham, bedrooms are modern in style, spacious and come well equipped with stylish furnishings, free WiFi, digital TV and well stocked beverage trays. Breakfast is served in the main dining room on the ground floor and ample parking is available on site. There are a number of restaurants within walking distance including a good selection of traditional meals at the neighbouring pub.

**Rooms:** 11 en suite **Facilities:** WiFi **Parking**

| LITTLEHAMPTON | Map 6 TQ00 |

### Premier Collection

## Glendales

★★★★★ ⬤ BED AND BREAKFAST

**tel:** 01903 775383 & 07970 845689 **Pigeonhouse Lane, Rustington BN16 2AZ**
**email:** jenny@glendales.co.uk **web:** www.glendales.co.uk

Glendales is located in a quiet setting and is only a 10-minute walk away from the beach. The luxurious en suite accommodation is attractively presented and well-equipped. Guests have the use of the conservatory and attractive garden, and there is also off-street parking. Breakfast is also noteworthy and not to be missed.

**Rooms:** 1 en suite (1 GF) **Facilities:** FTV DVD tea/coffee WiFi **Extras:** Speciality toiletries, fruit, snacks – complimentary **Parking:** 2 **Notes:** No children

### Premier Collection

## Berry House

★★★★★ ⬤ GUEST ACCOMMODATION

**tel:** 01903 726260 & 07799 425136 **Berry Lane BN17 5HD**
**email:** info@berryhouse.biz **web:** www.berryhouse.biz

Berry House is located in the heart of Littlehampton and has spacious, modern and comfortably appointed accommodation. The house was built in 2012, so all rooms have modern facilities including complimentary WiFi and digital TV. Breakfast is served in the main dining room and there is a wide selection of both cooked and continental dishes. Secure off-road parking is provided, and there are gardens for guests to enjoy during the summer months.

**Rooms:** 4 en suite (1 fmly) (2 GF) **Facilities:** STV FTV tea/coffee WiFi ⬇18
🔒 **Extras:** Bottled water – complimentary; fruit, chocolates **Parking:** 7
**Notes:** No children 16yrs

## East Beach Guest House

★★★★ GUEST HOUSE

**tel:** 01903 714270 **71 South Terrace BN17 5LQ**
**email:** admin@eastbeachguesthouse.co.uk **web:** www.eastbeachguesthouse.co.uk
**dir:** *On South Terrace, opposite beach, 200mtrs from junct with Pier Rd*

This guest house offers individually styled and comfortable accommodation; all rooms are equipped with a good range of amenities including TVs and WiFi; some bedrooms have sea views. A freshly cooked breakfast, using local produce, is served in the first-floor breakfast room that overlooks the sea.

**Rooms:** 9 en suite (2 fmly) (2 GF) **Facilities:** FTV DVD TVL tea/coffee WiFi 🔒
**Extras:** Speciality toiletries – complimentary **Notes:** LB No children 3yrs

## Leeside

★★★★ GUEST ACCOMMODATION

**tel:** 01903 723666 & 07791 797131 **Rope Walk BN17 5DE**
**email:** leeside1@tiscali.co.uk **web:** www.leesidebandb.com
**dir:** *From A259 into Ferry Rd signed Rope Walk & West Beach. 1m, turn right into Rope Walk, Leeside on right*

Leeside is a bright bungalow, close to local sailing clubs, the River Arun and the beach. Visitors will enjoy a warm welcome, and comfortable modern bedrooms have flat-screen TVs and free WiFi. The hearty breakfasts make a good start to the day.

**Rooms:** 4 en suite (3 GF) **S** fr £43; **D** fr £75* **Facilities:** FTV TVL tea/coffee WiFi
🔒 **Parking:** 4 **Notes:** No children 14yrs

## LODSWORTH
Map 6 SU92

### Premier Collection

## The Halfway Bridge Inn

★★★★★ ◉ ♨ INN

**tel:** 01798 861281 & 07971 872655 **Halfway Bridge GU28 9BP**
**email:** enquiries@halfwaybridge.co.uk **web:** www.halfwaybridge.co.uk
**dir:** *From Petworth on A272 towards Midhurst, 3m on right*

This inn, located between Petworth and Midhurst, has attractively styled rooms in a converted barn setting; the spacious rooms, each with their own contemporary country-style decor, have many thoughtful extras. The popular inn offers warming fires, and intimate dining areas where guests can enjoy award-winning cuisine. The central bar is popular and guest ales feature strongly. The friendly team are key to the business here, making for a memorable stay.

**Rooms:** 7 en suite (1 fmly) (7 GF) **S** £90–£155; **D** £145–£230* **Facilities:** FTV DVD iPod docking station tea/coffee Dinner available WiFi **Extras:** Speciality toiletries, fresh milk – complimentary **Parking:** 30

## PETWORTH
Map 6 SU92

## The Old Railway Station

★★★★ ♨ GUEST ACCOMMODATION

**tel:** 01798 342346 **Station Road GU28 0JF**
**email:** info@old-station.co.uk **web:** www.old-station.co.uk
**dir:** *1.6m S of Petworth on A285*

This building, once the railway station for Petworth, retains much of its railway history and atmosphere. Guest rooms are available in both the Station House and the fully restored Edwardian Pullman railway carriages. The original ticket windows can still be seen in the reception area. Breakfast is served in the 'waiting room' which has a six-metre high vaulted ceiling; weather permitting, breakfast can be taken outside on the platform. Both WiFi and parking are available.

**Rooms:** 2 en suite 8 annexe en suite (1 GF) **S** £75–£120, **D** £100–£240*
**Facilities:** FTV Lounge tea/coffee Licensed WiFi 🔒 **Extras:** Speciality toiletries
**Parking:** 11 **Notes:** LB No children 10yrs Closed 23–26 Dec

## The Welldiggers Arms

★★★★ ⊜ INN

**tel:** 01798 344288 **Low Heath GU28 0HG**
**email:** enquiries@thewelldiggersarms.co.uk **web:** www.thewelldiggersarms.co.uk

Located just outside the historic town of Petworth, this recently refurbished country inn benefits from outstanding views of the South Downs. All bedrooms have been stylishly decorated with modern furnishings and offer excellent comfort for that night away. Breakfast, lunch and dinner are served daily in the main restaurant. Plenty of parking available and in a quiet location yet close to Petworth and Chichester.

**Rooms:** 14 en suite **Facilities:** Dinner available **Parking**

## Willow Barns

★★★★ BED AND BREAKFAST

**tel:** 01798 867493 & 07468 436167 **Graffham GU28 0NU**
**email:** infowillowbarns@aol.com **web:** www.willowbarns.co.uk

This bed and breakfast comprises five en suite bedrooms set in modern converted barns overlooking an RHS Silver Gilt awarded, professionally designed courtyard. This makes a fabulous choice for those walking the South Downs Way. Cyclists and horse riders are also welcomed, with stabling and turn-out facilities available by prior arrangement. Breakfast, lunch and dinner are served in the nearby inn, The White Horse.

**Rooms:** 5 en suite (2 fmly) (5 GF) **S** fr £110; **D** fr £110* **Facilities:** FTV DVD Lounge tea/coffee Dinner available Licensed WiFi **Parking:** 8 **Notes:** No children 12yrs Closed 2 weeks Xmas

## The Angel Inn

★★★★ ⊜ INN

**tel:** 01798 344445 & 342153 **Angel Street GU28 0BG**
**email:** reception@angelinnpetworth.co.uk **web:** www.angelinnpetworth.co.uk
**dir:** *Leave one-way system onto A283 E, 100yds on left*

Located in the heart of the historic town of Petworth, The Angel Inn has stylish yet traditionally decorated bedrooms and bathrooms. Guests can enjoy breakfast, lunch or dinner in the bar and restaurant area, and there is a large walled garden for alfresco dining during the warmer months. There is parking on site and the inn is just a two-minute walk from the town centre.

**Rooms:** 6 en suite **S** £100–£150; **D** £100–£160* **Facilities:** FTV tea/coffee Dinner available WiFi **Parking:** 15

## RUSTINGTON
Map 6 TQ00

## Kenmore Guest House

★★★★ GUEST ACCOMMODATION

**tel:** 01903 784634 **Claigmar Road BN16 2NL**
**email:** enquiries@kenmoreguesthouse.co.uk **web:** www.kenmoreguesthouse.com
**dir:** *A259 follow signs for Rustington, turn for Claigmar Rd by war memorial. Kenmore on right as Claigmar Rd bends*

A warm welcome is assured at this Edwardian house, located close to the sea and convenient for touring West Sussex. Spacious bedrooms, all individually decorated, are provided with many useful extras. There is a comfortable lounge in which to relax and a bright dining room where a good choice of breakfast is served.

**Rooms:** 8 rms (7 en suite) (1 pri facs) (1 fmly) (2 GF) **S** £47–£57; **D** £82–£87*
**Facilities:** FTV Lounge tea/coffee WiFi 🔒 **Parking:** 9 **Notes:** No children 6yrs

## Rustington Manor

★★★★ ⊜ GUEST ACCOMMODATION

**tel:** 01903 788782 **12 Broadmark Lane BN16 2HH**
**email:** enquiries@rustingtonmanor.com **web:** www.rustingtonmanor.co.uk

A warm welcome is assured at family-run Rustington Manor where guests are made to feel at home. Attentive service and excellent food make for a wonderful dining experience. Six comfortable, en suite rooms offer all the amenities that the modern guest requires. The property is just a short walk from the beach.

**Rooms:** 6 en suite **Facilities:** FTV DVD TVL tea/coffee Dinner available Direct dial Licensed WiFi ♨ 18 **Conf:** Max 40 Thtr 40 Class 40 Board 40 **Parking:** 14
**Notes:** No children 10yrs

## SIDLESHAM
Map 5 SZ89

### Premier Collection

## The Crab & Lobster
★★★★★ ⊛⊛ ⚲ RESTAURANT WITH ROOMS

**tel:** 01243 641233 **Mill Lane PO20 7NB**
**email:** enquiries@crab-lobster.co.uk **web:** www.crab-lobster.co.uk
**dir:** *A27 onto B2145 signed Selsey. 1st left after garage at Sidlesham into Rookery Ln to Crab & Lobster*

Hidden away on the south coast near Pagham Harbour and only a short drive from Chichester is the stylish Crab & Lobster. Bedrooms are superbly appointed, and bathrooms are a feature with luxury toiletries and powerful 'raindrop' showers. Guests can enjoy lunch or dinner in the smart restaurant where the menu offers a range of locally caught fresh fish together with other regionally-sourced, seasonal produce.

**Rooms:** 4 en suite **S** £100–£120; **D** £175–£205* **Facilities:** FTV DVD iPod docking station tea/coffee Dinner available WiFi **Extras:** Speciality toiletries, fresh milk **Parking:** 12

## STEYNING
Map 6 TQ11

## The Castle Inn
★★★ INN

**tel:** 01903 816629 **The Street, Bramber BN44 3WE**
**email:** steve@castleinnhotel.co.uk **web:** www.castleinnhotel.co.uk
**dir:** *A283 at rdbt take exit signed Bramber*

A family-run independent inn located in the quaint village of Bramber, just a stone's throw from the ruined medieval Bramber Castle. The inn has retained many of its original character, yet all rooms and public areas have been refurbished to meet the needs of modern guests. There is a range of well-appointed rooms to meet all budgets, as well as fine ales and an appealing menu with daily-changing dishes. There is a relaxing beer garden and a convenient car park to the rear of the property.

**Rooms:** 13 en suite (1 pri facs) 4 annexe en suite (5 fmly) (1 GF) **S** £35–£80; **D** £50–£100* **Facilities:** STV tea/coffee Dinner available WiFi **Extras:** Chocolates **Conf:** Max 40 Thtr 40 Class 30 Board 22 **Parking:** 18

## TILLINGTON
Map 6 SU92

## The Horse Guards Inn
★★★★ ⊛ ⚲ INN

**tel:** 01798 342332 **Upperton Road GU28 9AF**
**email:** info@thehorseguardsinn.co.uk **web:** www.thehorseguardsinn.co.uk
**dir:** *Off A272 to Tillington, up hill opposite All Hallows church*

This inn is conveniently located close to Petworth and Midhurst in a quiet village setting opposite the quaint church, and is perfect for exploring the beautiful surrounding countryside. The comfortable bedrooms are simply decorated, and delicious breakfasts are prepared to order using the finest local ingredients. The same principles apply to the substantial and flavoursome meals served in the cosy restaurant-bar dining areas.

**Rooms:** 2 en suite 1 annexe en suite (1 fmly) **S** £110–£140; **D** £110–£160* **Facilities:** FTV DVD tea/coffee Dinner available WiFi **Extras:** Speciality toiletries – complimentary **Notes:** Closed 25–26 Dec

## WEST MARDEN
Map 5 SU71

## Grandwood House
★★★★ GUEST ACCOMMODATION

**tel:** 07971 845153 & 023 9263 1436 **Watergate PO18 9EG**
**email:** info@grandwoodhouse.co.uk **web:** www.grandwoodhouse.co.uk

Set in the South Downs and built in 1907, Grandwood House was originally a lodge belonging to Watergate House, which was accidentally burnt down by troops during WWII. All rooms are en suite and enjoy views of the garden, open farmland or both. Large security gates leading onto the driveway ensure secure parking at all times. Only a short walk away, in nearby Walderton, is the local pub which serves lunches and evening meals.

**Rooms:** 4 annexe en suite (4 GF) **S** £75–£125; **D** £75–£125* **Facilities:** FTV DVD tea/coffee WiFi **Parking:** 8 **Notes:** LB

## WORTHING
Map 6 TQ10

## The Beacons
★★★★ GUEST ACCOMMODATION

**tel:** 01903 230948 **18 Shelley Road BN11 1TU**
**email:** thebeacons@btconnect.com **web:** www.beaconsworthing.com
**dir:** *0.5m W of town centre. Exit A259 Richmond Rd into Crescent Rd, 3rd left*

This splendid Edwardian property is ideally situated close to the shopping centre, marine garden and pier. Bedrooms are bright, spacious and attractively furnished with many thoughtful amenities, including free WiFi. Guests can enjoy the comfortable lounge with honesty bar, and breakfast is served in the sunny dining room.

**Rooms:** 8 en suite (1 fmly) (3 GF) **S** £55–£65; **D** £82–£90* **Facilities:** FTV Lounge tea/coffee Licensed WiFi **Parking:** 8

## The Burlington
★★★★ GUEST ACCOMMODATION

**tel:** 01903 211222 **Marine Parade BN11 3QL**
**email:** info@theburlington.net **web:** www.theburlington.net
**dir:** *On seafront 0.5m W of Worthing Pier, Wordsworth Rd junct opposite Heene Terrace*

This imposing seafront building has a modern contemporary look that appeals to a mainly youthful clientele. The light bar and terrace extends to a night club open at the weekends. Bedrooms are spacious and thoughtfully furnished, with some modern touches. The staff are friendly.

**Rooms:** 26 en suite (6 fmly) **Facilities:** FTV Lounge tea/coffee Dinner available Direct dial Licensed WiFi **Conf:** Max 100 Thtr 50 Class 35 Board 40

## Merton House
★★★★ GUEST ACCOMMODATION

**tel:** 01903 238222 & 07767 163059 **96 Broadwater Road BN14 8AW**
**email:** stay@mertonhouse.co.uk **web:** www.mertonhouse.co.uk
**dir:** *A24 into Worthing, on left past Manor Green*

This family run establishment is located on the A24 leading into Worthing, just a couple of minutes from the town centre and seafront. There are seven en suite bedrooms, all of a very traditional style yet providing up-to-date facilities including free WiFi and digital TV. A cooked and continental breakfast is served daily in the dining room. Parking available on site.

**Rooms:** 7 en suite (2 GF) **S** £50–£65; **D** £80–£90 **Facilities:** FTV Lounge tea/coffee WiFi **Extras:** Chocolates – complimentary **Parking:** 5 **Notes:** No children 12yrs

# Moorings

★★★★ GUEST ACCOMMODATION

**tel:** 01903 208882 **4 Selden Road BN11 2LL**
**email:** themooringsworthing@hotmail.co.uk **web:** www.mooringsworthing.co.uk
**dir:** *0.5m E of pier off A259 towards Brighton*

Moorings is a well-presented Victorian house, located in a quiet residential street just a short walk from the seafront and town centre. Bedrooms are attractively co-ordinated with plenty of extras such as WiFi and Freeview TV. Breakfast is served in a homely, traditional dining room and there is a very useful kitchenette with a microwave, fridge and crockery available. The friendly owners also offer secure parking for bicycles and motorcycles. On-street parking available.

**Rooms:** 6 en suite (1 fmly) **Facilities:** FTV DVD tea/coffee WiFi 🔒 **Notes:** LB
No children 5yrs

# High Beach Guest House

★★★ GUEST ACCOMMODATION

**tel:** 01903 236389 **201 Brighton Road BN11 2EX**
**email:** info@highbeachworthing.com **web:** www.highbeachworthing.com
**dir:** *On A259, 200yds past Splashpoint swimming pool*

High Beach Guest House is situated within a short walk of Worthing town centre, and its seafront location offers uninterrupted sea views from front-facing rooms and the breakfast room. Bedrooms are traditionally decorated and come well equipped. A conservatory with comfortable seating leads onto the front garden where guests can sit during summer months.

**Rooms:** 7 rms (3 en suite) (1 GF) **Facilities:** FTV Lounge tea/coffee WiFi 🔒 **Parking:** 3
**Notes:** No children 8yrs Closed 23 Dec–2 Jan

## TYNE & WEAR

### BIRTLEY                                                Map 19 NZ25

# Bowes Incline

★★★★ 🍺 INN

**tel:** 0191 410 2233 **Northside DH3 1RF**
**email:** info@thebowesinclinehotel.co.uk **web:** www.thebowesinclinehotel.co.uk
**dir:** *From rdbt on A1231 NE of Washington follow Wreckenton sign. Pass lakes on left, approx 0.5m 1st left (signed). Approx 0.5m*

Located just one mile from the A1 but surrounded by open countryside, close to the protective arms of the Angel of the North. The family-run inn takes its name from the Bowes Incline Railway & Museum located close by. Bedrooms are of a good size and very well appointed with modern en suites. The large bar and restaurant offers good food chosen from the large blackboards. The hands-on team are friendly and welcoming making this inn a perfect base to tour the North East.

**Rooms:** 18 en suite (2 fmly) (18 GF) **Facilities:** FTV tea/coffee Dinner available Direct dial WiFi **Parking:** 40 **Notes:** Closed 24 Dec–2 Jan

### SOUTH SHIELDS                                        Map 21 NZ36

# Forest Guest House

★★★★ 🍴 GUEST HOUSE

**tel:** 0191 454 8160 & 07834 690989 **117 Ocean Road NE33 2JL**
**email:** enquiries@forestguesthouse.com **web:** www.forestguesthouse.com

Forest Guest House is centrally located, close to both the beach and the town centre. It offers comfortable and modern bedrooms and many thoughtful extras provided as standard. The hospitable owners are always on hand to offer help and recommendations. A well-cooked breakfast is served on individual tables giving a great start to the day. Forest Guest House was a finalist for the AA Friendliest B&B of the Year award 2017–18.

**Rooms:** 6 en suite (2 fmly) **S** £40–£45; **D** £70–£74* **Facilities:** STV FTV DVD tea/coffee WiFi 🔒 **Extras:** Speciality toiletries, chocolates – complimentary

# The Sir William Fox

★★★ GUEST ACCOMMODATION

**tel:** 0191 456 4554 **5 Westoe Village NE33 3DZ**
**email:** enquiries@sirwilliamfoxhotel.com **web:** www.sirwilliamfoxhotel.com
**dir:** *A194 into John Reid Rd, then King George Rd into Sunderland Rd. Over rdbt, turn right & right again*

Located in the picturesque village of Westoe in the heart of South Shields, The Sir William Fox offers value-for-money accommodation. It benefits from some off-road parking and is within easy walking distance of the Metro, and South Tyneside College. Dinner is available and the property is fully licensed.

**Rooms:** 15 en suite (4 fmly) (2 GF) **Facilities:** FTV DVD TVL tea/coffee Dinner available Direct dial Licensed WiFi 🔒 **Parking:** 10

### SUNDERLAND                                           Map 19 NZ35

# Three Horseshoes

★★★★ INN

**tel:** 0191 519 2006 **Washington Road SR5 3HZ**
**email:** manager@threehorseshoeshotel.co.uk **web:** www.threehorseshoeshotel.co.uk
**dir:** *N of city on A19, follow signs for Transport Museum*

The Three Horseshoes now reopened after extensive refurbishment and investment, and benefits from ample seating inside and out. It also offers a large number of beers and ales some of which are brewed by the parent company Sonnet 43. Boutique-style bedrooms are well appointed and equipped in accord with the needs of the modern guest.

**Rooms:** 7 en suite **Facilities:** FTV iPod docking station tea/coffee Dinner available WiFi **Parking:** 20 **Notes:** LB

## WHITLEY BAY
Map 21 NZ37

### Park Lodge

★★★★  GUEST HOUSE

**tel:** 0191 253 0288 **158-160 Park Avenue NE26 1AU**
**email:** parklodgehotel@hotmail.com **web:** www.parklodgewhitleybay.com
**dir:** *From S A19 through Tyne Tunnel, right onto A1058 to seafront. Left, after 2m left at lights onto A191. On left*

Set on a leafy avenue, overlooking the park and just minutes from the town centre and coastline, you can expect a friendly atmosphere at this Victorian house. Bedrooms are very comfortable, stylishly furnished and feature homely extras. A hearty breakfast is served and free WiFi is available.

**Rooms:** 5 en suite (1 fmly) (2 GF) **S** £70; **D** £100* **Facilities:** FTV DVD iPod docking station TVL tea/coffee WiFi 🅿 **Parking:** 2

## WARWICKSHIRE

## ALDERMINSTER
Map 10 SP24

### The Bell at Alderminster

★★★★ ◎ INN

**tel:** 01789 450414 **Shipston Rd CV37 8NY**
**email:** info@thebellald.co.uk **web:** www.thebellald.co.uk

This former 18th-century coaching inn is situated in Alderminster just a few miles away from Stratford-upon-Avon. It's a warm and friendly place where guests can enjoy a range of AA Rosette-worthy, home-cooked dishes and a range of ales and fine wines. The accommodation is smart, stylish and contemporary in design and bedrooms offer a high level of comfort with many thoughtful extras.

**Rooms:** 4 en suite 5 annexe en suite (2 fmly) (3 GF) **S** £75; **D** £100–£170*
**Facilities:** FTV iPod docking station tea/coffee Dinner available Direct dial WiFi
**Extras:** Speciality toiletries, home-made biscuits, milk **Conf:** Max 12 Thtr 12 Class 12 Board 12 **Parking:** 50

## ARMSCOTE
Map 10 SP24

### The Fuzzy Duck

★★★★ ◎◎ INN

**tel:** 01608 682635 **Ilmington Road CV37 8DD**
**email:** info@fuzzyduckarmscote.com **web:** www.fuzzyduckarmscote.com

The Fuzzy Duck is an English country pub offering boutique bed and breakfast accommodation. The bedrooms are sumptuous, providing guests with lovely accessories such as luxury robes, and fluffy socks and slippers. Dinner can be enjoyed in the sophisticated restaurant where the chef uses only the finest quality and fresh ingredients.

**Rooms:** 4 en suite (2 fmly) **S** £110; **D** £110–£160* **Facilities:** FTV iPod docking station Lounge Dinner available Direct dial WiFi **Extras:** Robes, fruit, snacks, slippers **Conf:** Max 20 **Parking:** 15

## BAGINTON
Map 11 SP37

### The Oak

★★★ INN

**tel:** 024 7651 8855 **Coventry Road CV8 3AU**
**email:** thebagintonoak@aol.com **web:** www.thebagintonoak.co.uk

Located close to major road links, Coventry Airport and Stoneleigh Park, this popular inn serves a wide range of food throughout the open-plan public areas. Families are especially welcome. Situated in a separate building to the rear of the inn the recently refurbished bedrooms are modern and well-equipped.

**Rooms:** 13 annexe en suite (2 fmly) (6 GF) **S** £55–£70; **D** £55–£70 (room only)
**Facilities:** FTV tea/coffee Dinner available WiFi **Conf:** Max 40 Thtr 40 Class 40 Board 25 **Parking:** 110

## COLESHILL
Map 10 SP28

### Innkeeper's Lodge Birmingham (NEC) Coleshill

★★★ INN

**tel:** 08451 551551 *(Calls cost 2p per minute plus your phone company's access charge)* **High Street B46 3BL**
**email:** info@innkeeperslodge.com **web:** www.innkeeperslodge.com

At Innkeeper's Lodge you'll find accommodation with comfort and character in equal measure, and everything needed for a relaxing stay, from easy check-in and free parking to complimentary breakfast and a cosy pub serving great value food and drink on the doorstep. Each Lodge has quality rooms, and there are Lodges in a variety of locations from towns and cities to countryside settings across the UK.

**Rooms:** 33 en suite (7 fmly) (1 GF) **Facilities:** FTV tea/coffee Dinner available Direct dial WiFi **Parking:** 44

---

**EDGEHILL**                                      Map 11 SP34

## Castle at Edgehill

★★★★ ◉◉ ☐ RESTAURANT WITH ROOMS
- - - - - - - - - - - - - - - - - - - - - - - - - - - - - - - - - - - -
**tel:** 01295 670255 **Main Street OX15 6DJ**
**email:** enquiries@castleatedgehill.co.uk **web:** www.castleatedgehill.co.uk

Built in 1742 to mark the centenary of the battle of Edgehill, where Charles I raised his standard at the start of the Civil War, the building has a unique history. Many of the original features have been restored and the exposed stone walls, along with the wood-panelled restaurant, really add to the character of the building. The Tower bedrooms boast panoramic views from their elevated position and bedrooms are all well-appointed. Dinner is not to be missed in the two AA Rosette award-winning restaurant and breakfast features the best in local produce.

**Rooms:** 2 en suite 2 annexe en suite (1 fmly) (1 GF) **Facilities:** FTV tea/coffee Dinner available WiFi **Conf:** Max 30 Thtr 24 Class 30 Board 18 **Parking:** 22

---

**FILLONGLEY**                                    Map 10 SP28

## Heart of England Conference & Events Centre

★★★★ GUEST ACCOMMODATION
- - - - - - - - - - - - - - - - - - - - - - - - - - - - - - - - - - - -
**tel:** 01676 540333 **Meriden Road CV7 8DX**
**email:** pa@heartofengland.co.uk **web:** www.heartofengland.co.uk

The Heart of England Conference & Events Centre is a charming stone-built house that offers attractively presented, well-equipped bedrooms and sleek modern bathrooms. This fine old house has bags of character and the spacious, comfortable lounge has a wood-burning stove, which proves a real bonus on cooler evenings. Delicious hot breakfasts are served at individual tables in the well-appointed breakfast room. The nearby Quicken Tree restaurant serves an extensive choice of imaginative dishes and makes a good choice for evening meals. As the name implies, first-rate conference and business facilities are available on site.

**Rooms:** 7 en suite 3 rms annexe (1 en suite) (1 GF) **S** £45–£140; **D** £45–£140* **Facilities:** FTV TVL tea/coffee Dinner available Direct dial Licensed WiFi Fishing **Conf:** Max 600 Thtr 600 Class 200 Board 50 **Parking:** 36 **Notes:** LB Civ wed 260

---

**ILMINGTON**                                     Map 10 SP24

### Premier Collection

## The Howard Arms

★★★★★ ◉ INN
- - - - - - - - - - - - - - - - - - - - - - - - - - - - - - - - - - - -
**tel:** 01608 682226 **Lower Green CV36 4LT**
**email:** info@howardarms.com **web:** www.howardarms.com

This 400-year-old Cotswold stone former coaching inn enjoys a prominent position in the heart of the pretty village of Ilmington. The bar/restaurant has been sympathetically restored and many original features have been retained. Real fires burn bright, and there is a great range of local ales along with an award-winning restaurant.

**Rooms:** 8 en suite (2 fmly) (1 GF) **S** £88–£120; **D** £110–£150* **Facilities:** FTV tea/coffee Dinner available Direct dial WiFi **Extras:** Speciality toiletries **Parking:** 18

---

**KENILWORTH**                                    Map 10 SP27

## Ferndale House

★★★★ GUEST HOUSE
- - - - - - - - - - - - - - - - - - - - - - - - - - - - - - - - - - - -
**tel:** 01926 853214 **45 Priory Road CV8 1LL**
**email:** info@kenilworth-guesthouse-accommodation.com
**web:** www.kenilworth-guesthouse-accommodation.com
**dir:** From M40 junct 15 onto A46 towards Coventry, then onto A452, Priory Rd on right

Ferndale House is situated five minutes' walk from Kenilworth, and is on the local bus route close to the university. Each of the bedrooms is attractively designed and modern, and the beds provide a very good night's sleep. Both parking and WiFi are free of charge.

**Rooms:** 7 en suite (1 GF) **S** £39–£42; **D** £65–£75* **Facilities:** FTV TVL tea/coffee WiFi **Parking:** 4

---

## Stoneleigh Park Lodge

★★★★ GUEST HOUSE
- - - - - - - - - - - - - - - - - - - - - - - - - - - - - - - - - - - -
**tel:** 024 7669 0123 **Grandstand Stoneleigh Events, Stoneleigh Park CV8 2LZ**
**email:** info@stoneleighparklodge.com **web:** www.stoneleighparklodge.com
**dir:** 2m E of Kenilworth in Stoneleigh Park

This house lies within the grounds of the National Agricultural Centre and provides modern, well-equipped accommodation. Meals, using local produce, are served in the Park View Restaurant overlooking the showground. Various conference and meeting facilities are available.

**Rooms:** 58 en suite (4 fmly) (26 GF) **Facilities:** FTV TVL tea/coffee Dinner available Direct dial Licensed WiFi **Conf:** Max 12 Thtr 12 Class 12 Board 12 **Parking:** 60 **Notes:** Closed Xmas

---

**LONG COMPTON**                                  Map 10 SP23

## The Red Lion

★★★★ ◉ INN
- - - - - - - - - - - - - - - - - - - - - - - - - - - - - - - - - - - -
**tel:** 01608 684221 **Main Street CV36 5JS**
**email:** info@redlion-longcompton.co.uk **web:** www.redlion-longcompton.co.uk
**dir:** 5m S of Shipston on Stour on A3400

Located in the pretty rural village of Long Compton, this mid 18th-century posting house retains many original features which are complemented by rustic furniture in the public areas. A good range of ales is offered, and interesting menus capitalise on quality local produce. The bedrooms are well appointed, and have a good range of facilities.

**Rooms:** 5 en suite (1 fmly) **S** £60–£65; **D** £95–£150* **Facilities:** FTV tea/coffee Dinner available WiFi Pool table Children's play area **Extras:** Speciality toiletries, home-made biscuits **Parking:** 60

## RUGBY        Map 11 SP57

### Innkeeper's Lodge Rugby, Dunchurch

★★★ INN

**tel:** 08451 551551 *(Calls cost 2p per minute plus your phone company's access charge)*
**The Green, Dunchurch CV22 6NJ**
**email:** info@innkeeperslodge.com **web:** www.innkeeperslodge.com

At Innkeeper's Lodge you'll find accommodation with comfort and character in equal measure, and everything needed for a relaxing stay, from easy check-in and free parking to complimentary breakfast and a cosy pub serving great value food and drink on the doorstep. Each Lodge has quality rooms, and there are Lodges in a variety of locations from towns and cities to countryside settings across the UK.

**Rooms:** 16 en suite (2 fmly) (6 GF) **Facilities:** FTV tea/coffee Dinner available WiFi

## SHIPSTON ON STOUR        Map 10 SP24

### Holly End Bed & Breakfast

★★★★ ⌾ GUEST ACCOMMODATION

**tel:** 01608 664064 **London Road CV36 4EP**
**email:** hollyend.hunt@btinternet.com **web:** www.holly-end.co.uk
**dir:** *0.5m S of Shipston on Stour on A3400, just beyond Old Rd*

Located between Oxford and Stratford-upon-Avon and a short walk from the town centre, this immaculate detached house offers bedrooms with lots of thoughtful extras. Accommodation is all you would expect from a four-star establishment yet still manages to maintain a home-from-home atmosphere. Comprehensive breakfasts use the best of local produce and comprise an award-winning range of options, one of which is full English.

**Rooms:** 3 rms (2 en suite) (1 pri facs) (1 GF) **S** £75; **D** £90 **Facilities:** FTV iPod docking station tea/coffee WiFi ⌘18 ⌾ **Extras:** Speciality toiletries, bottled water – complimentary **Parking:** 6 **Notes:** LB No children 11yrs

### George Townhouse

★★★★ GUEST ACCOMMODATION

**tel:** 01608 661453 **8 High Street CV36 4AJ**
**email:** book@thegeorgeshipston.co.uk **web:** www.thegeorgeshipston.co.uk
**dir:** *In Market Square*

This distinctive 18th-century townhouse is the tallest building on the High Street and has been completely refurbished and has a feel of casual elegance. Rooms are attractively furnished and well appointed; all have modern en suite facilities supplied with luxurious toiletries. On the ground floor, the bar and dining area provide a relaxed and casual dining experience at breakfast and dinner. Local produce is used where possible to provide either pub-style dishes or an à la carte menu. Car parking is at the rear of the building. Complimentary WiFi is available throughout.

**Rooms:** 15 en suite **S** £70–£240; **D** £85–£240* **Facilities:** FTV tea/coffee Dinner available Licensed WiFi ⌘18 ⌾ **Extras:** Nespresso machines **Conf:** Max 24 Thtr 24 Class 12 Board 10 **Parking:** 13

## STRATFORD-UPON-AVON        Map 10 SP25

### Premier Collection

### Arden House

★★★★★ ⌾ GUEST ACCOMMODATION

**tel:** 01789 298682 & 206999 **58–59 Rother Street CV37 6LT**
**email:** info@theardenhotelstratford.com **web:** www.ardenhousestratford.com

Arden House set in the heart of this medieval market town provides an elegant, inviting and relaxed sanctuary. Bedrooms are thoughtfully equipped to the highest standard. Dedicated hosts are on hand to ensure your every need is taken care of; from afternoon tea to evening drinks, you are invited to make yourself at home. There is a welcoming guest lounge, and a small outdoor terrace for the warmer months. There are treats in The Pantry and 5pm is 'Gin o'clock'!

**Rooms:** 10 en suite **S** £164.50–£194.50; **D** £229–£289* **Facilities:** FTV Lounge TVL Direct dial Licensed WiFi **Extras:** Apple TV, fruit, afternoon tea pantry **Parking:** 8

## Adelphi Guest House

★★★★ ⬡ GUEST ACCOMMODATION

**tel:** 01789 204469 **39 Grove Road CV37 6PB**
**email:** info@adelphi-guesthouse.com **web:** www.adelphi-guesthouse.com
**dir:** *M40 junct 15 onto A46 towards Stratford, then A3400. Straight over at 2 rdbts, at lights right into Arden St (A4390). This becomes Grove Rd, on right opposite park*

Based in the centre of Stratford-upon-Avon, the Adelphi is ideally located for those visiting the Royal Shakespeare, Swan or Courtyard Theatres. The bedrooms offer comfort throughout and are all tastefully decorated in period design with many thoughtful extras. All guests will receive a warm and friendly welcome, and breakfast is not to be missed with a wide selection of high-quality dishes offered. Free parking and WiFi are also available.

**Rooms:** 6 rms (5 en suite) (1 pri facs) (1 fmly) (1 GF) **S** £50–£60; **D** £90–£110 **Facilities:** FTV DVD iPod docking station tea/coffee WiFi ⬧ **Parking:** 5 **Notes:** LB No children 10yrs

## Ambleside Guest House

★★★★ GUEST HOUSE

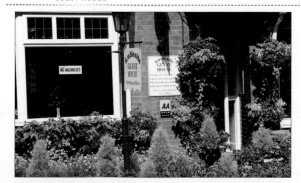

**tel:** 01789 297239 **41 Grove Road CV37 6PB**
**email:** peter@amblesideguesthouse.com **web:** www.amblesideguesthouse.com
**dir:** *250mtrs from town centre on A4390 opposite Firs Gdns*

Ambleside, situated less than five minutes' walk from the town centre, is very popular with theatre goers and tourists. It is tastefully decorated in a contemporary style and offers a choice of breakfasts in the bright and airy dining room which overlooks the small park opposite. Free on-site parking and WiFi are provided.

**Rooms:** 6 rms (5 en suite) (1 pri facs) (2 fmly) **S** £40–£45; **D** £75–£85 **Facilities:** FTV tea/coffee WiFi ⬧ **Parking:** 9 **Notes:** No children 7yrs

## Arden Way Guest House

★★★★ GUEST ACCOMMODATION

**tel:** 01789 205646 **22 Shipston Road CV37 7LP**
**email:** info@ardenwayguesthouse.co.uk **web:** www.ardenwayguesthouse.co.uk
**dir:** *On A3400, S of River Avon, 100mtrs on left*

A warm welcome is assured at this non-smoking house, located within easy walking distance of the Butterfly Farm and cricket ground. The homely bedrooms are filled with lots of thoughtful extras and an attractive dining room, overlooking the pretty rear garden, is the setting for comprehensive breakfasts.

**Rooms:** 6 en suite (1 fmly) (2 GF) **S** £50–£65; **D** £70–£82* **Facilities:** FTV DVD tea/coffee WiFi ⬧ **Parking:** 6 **Notes:** LB

## The Townhouse, Stratford

★★★★ GUEST ACCOMMODATION

**tel:** 01789 262222 **16 Church Street CV37 6HB**
**email:** book@churchstreettownhouse.co.uk **web:** www.churchst-th.co.uk

A striking and distinctive 400 year old, Grade II listed building that has been recently and very tastefully refurbished. All rooms are well-decorated and furnished and have a feel of quality to them. All have espresso machines, free WiFi and are modern but sympathetic to the age and style of the property. The downstairs is a bar and dining area that provides a casual and relaxed atmosphere; lunch, dinner or a pre-theatre meal can be enjoyed.

**Rooms:** 12 en suite (1 GF) **Facilities:** TVL tea/coffee Dinner available Licensed WiFi ⬧ **Extras:** Port, home-made biscuits, fresh milk

## Twelfth Night

★★★★ GUEST ACCOMMODATION

**tel:** 01789 414595 **13 Evesham Place CV37 6HT**
**email:** twelfthnight@gmail.com **web:** www.twelfthnight.co.uk
**dir:** *In town centre off A4390 Grove Rd*

This delightful Victorian villa is within easy walking distance of the town centre. Quality decor and furnishings enhance the charming original features, and the elegant dining room is the setting for delicious, imaginative English breakfasts. AA Friendliest B&B of the Year 2017–18 finalist.

**Rooms:** 7 rms (6 en suite) (1 pri facs) **Facilities:** tea/coffee **Parking:** 6 **Notes:** Closed 11–25 Feb

## Moonraker House

★★★★ GUEST ACCOMMODATION

**tel:** 01789 268774 **40 Alcester Road CV37 9DB**
**email:** info@moonrakerhouse.com **web:** www.moonrakerhouse.com
**dir:** *200yds from rail station on A422 (Alcester Rd)*

Just a short walk from the railway station and the central attractions, this establishment provides a range of comfortable bedrooms. Freshly cooked breakfasts are served in the sitting area. The attractive exterior is enhanced by a magnificent floral display during the warmer months.

**Rooms:** 7 en suite (1 fmly) (2 GF) **S** £60; **D** £84–£98* **Facilities:** FTV tea/coffee WiFi **Parking:** 7 **Notes:** LB No children 6yrs

## Stretton House

★★★ GUEST HOUSE

**tel:** 01789 268647 **38 Grove Road CV37 6PB**
**email:** shortpbshort@aol.com **web:** www.strettonhouse.co.uk
**dir:** *On A439 in town centre road behind police station*

This attractive, Edwardian terrace house is within easy walking distance of the railway station and Shakespeare's Birthplace. Bedrooms are carefully decorated, well equipped, and many have modern shower rooms en suite. The pretty front garden is a welcoming feature.

**Rooms:** 6 rms (5 en suite) (1 pri facs) (4 fmly) (1 GF) **Facilities:** FTV tea/coffee WiFi ⬧ **Parking:** 6

STRATFORD-UPON-AVON *continued*

## Salamander Guest House

★★★ Ⓐ GUEST HOUSE

**tel:** 01789 205728 **40 Grove Road CV37 6PB**
**email:** p.delin@btinternet.com **web:** www.salamanderguesthouse.co.uk
**dir:** *250yds W of town centre on A439 ring road, opposite Firs Garden*

Ideally located within easy walking distance of central attractions, this well-maintained Edwardian house provides a range of thoughtfully furnished bedrooms most with the benefit of modern and efficient en suite shower rooms. Breakfast is served in an attractive dining room overlooking a pretty park, and private parking is also available.

**Rooms:** 7 rms (6 en suite) (1 pri facs) (5 fmly) (1 GF) **Facilities:** FTV tea/coffee Dinner available WiFi **Parking:** 12 **Notes:** LB

---

| TEMPLE GRAFTON | Map 10 SP15 |

## The Blue Boar

★★★ INN

**tel:** 01789 750010 **B49 6NR**
**email:** info@theblueboar.co.uk **web:** www.theblueboar.co.uk
**dir:** *From A46 (Stratford-upon-Avon – Alcester), turn left, Blue Boar at 1st x-rds*

A warm welcome is guaranteed at this country inn. The bedrooms are comfortable and homely, and the dining room and bar menus offer extensive choice, plus additional specials. There is also a beer garden to sit in when the weather allows.

**Rooms:** 14 en suite (5 fmly) (1 GF) **Facilities:** FTV Dinner available WiFi **Conf:** Max 30 Thtr 30 Class 30 Board 30 **Parking:** 35

---

| WELLESBOURNE | Map 10 SP25 |

## Innkeeper's Lodge Stratford-upon-Avon

★★★ INN

**tel:** 08451 551551 *(Calls cost 2p per minute plus your phone company's access charge)*
**Warwick Road CV35 9LX**
**email:** info@innkeeperslodge.com **web:** www.innkeeperslodge.com

At Innkeeper's Lodge you'll find accommodation with comfort and character in equal measure, and everything needed for a relaxing stay, from easy check-in and free parking to complimentary breakfast and a cosy pub serving great value food and drink on the doorstep. Each Lodge has quality rooms, and there are Lodges in a variety of locations from towns and cities to countryside settings across the UK.

**Rooms:** 9 en suite (2 fmly) **Facilities:** FTV tea/coffee Dinner available WiFi **Parking:** 35

---

| WEST MIDLANDS |

| BIRMINGHAM | Map 10 SP08 |

## Tri-Star

★★★ GUEST ACCOMMODATION

**tel:** 0121 782 1010 & 782 6131 **Coventry Road, Elmdon B26 3QR**
**email:** info@tristarhotel.co.uk **web:** www.tristarhotel.co.uk
**dir:** *On A45*

Just a short drive from the airport, Birmingham International station and the NEC, this owner-managed property provides a range of thoughtfully furnished bedrooms with modern bathrooms. The open-plan ground-floor area includes a bright, attractive dining room and a comfortable lounge and bar. A separate room is available for conferences or functions.

**Rooms:** 15 en suite (3 fmly) (6 GF) **Facilities:** FTV TVL tea/coffee Dinner available Licensed WiFi Pool table Games room **Conf:** Max 20 Thtr 20 Class 10 Board 20 **Parking:** 25

---

## Innkeeper's Lodge Birmingham West (Quinton)

★★★ INN

**tel:** 08451 551551 *(Calls cost 2p per minute plus your phone company's access charge)*
**563 Hagley Road West, Quinton B32 1HP**
**email:** info@innkeeperslodge.com **web:** www.innkeeperslodge.com

At Innkeeper's Lodge you'll find accommodation with comfort and character in equal measure, and everything needed for a relaxing stay, from easy check-in and free parking to complimentary breakfast and a cosy pub serving great value food and drink on the doorstep. Each Lodge has quality rooms, and there are Lodges in a variety of locations from towns and cities to countryside settings across the UK.

**Rooms:** 24 en suite (8 fmly) (8 GF) **Facilities:** FTV tea/coffee Dinner available Direct dial WiFi

---

| BIRMINGHAM (NATIONAL EXHIBITION CENTRE) |
*See Solihull*

| COVENTRY | Map 10 SP37 |

## Innkeeper's Lodge Birmingham (NEC) Meriden

★★★★ INN

**tel:** 08451 551551 *(Calls cost 2p per minute plus your phone company's access charge)*
**Main Road, Meriden CV7 7NN**
**email:** info@innkeeperslodge.com **web:** www.innkeeperslodge.com

At Innkeeper's Lodge you'll find accommodation with comfort and character in equal measure, and everything needed for a relaxing stay, from easy check-in and free parking to complimentary breakfast and a cosy pub serving great value food and drink on the doorstep. Each Lodge has quality rooms, and there are Lodges in a variety of locations from towns and cities to countryside settings across the UK.

**Rooms:** 13 en suite (3 fmly) (4 GF) **Facilities:** FTV tea/coffee Dinner available Direct dial WiFi

## SOLIHULL — Map 10 SP17

### Premier Collection

## Hampton Manor

★★★★★ ◉◉◉◉ ♟ RESTAURANT WITH ROOMS

**tel:** 01675 446080 **Shadowbrook Lane, Hampton-in-Arden B92 0EN**
**email:** info@hamptonmanor.com **web:** www.hamptonmanor.com
**dir:** *M42 junct 6 follow signs for A45 (Birmingham). At 1st rdbt, 1st exit onto B4438 (Catherine de Barnes Ln). Left into Shadowbrook Ln*

Hampton Manor is set in 45 acres of mature woodland, only minutes from Birmingham's major air, rail and road links and the NEC. The manor offers luxurious accommodation with a contemporary and sophisticated style while still maintaining many of its original features and heritage. The bedrooms are all beautifully and uniquely designed and boast sumptuous beds. Fine dining can be enjoyed at Peel's restaurant, which is a fabulous venue for innovative cooking, and will prove the highlight of any stay.

**Rooms:** 15 en suite (3 fmly) (1 GF) **S** £160–£350; **D** £160–£350 (room only)*
**Facilities:** FTV DVD iPod docking station Lounge tea/coffee Dinner available Direct dial WiFi ♨ 18 Beauty treatments **Extras:** Bottled water, home-made cookies, fresh fruit **Conf:** Max 120 Thtr 120 Class 60 Board 35 **Parking:** 30
**Notes:** LB Civ wed 120

## Innkeeper's Lodge Solihull, Knowle

★★★ INN

**tel:** 08451 551551 *(Calls cost 2p per minute plus your phone company's access charge)*
**Warwick Road, Knowle B93 0EE**
**email:** info@innkeeperslodge.com **web:** www.innkeeperslodge.com

At Innkeeper's Lodge you'll find accommodation with comfort and character in equal measure, and everything needed for a relaxing stay, from easy check-in and free parking to complimentary breakfast and a cosy pub serving great value food and drink on the doorstep. Each Lodge has quality rooms, and there are Lodges in a variety of locations from towns and cities to countryside settings across the UK.

**Rooms:** 11 en suite (1 fmly) **Facilities:** FTV tea/coffee Dinner available WiFi

## WILTSHIRE

## AMESBURY — Map 5 SU14

## Park House Motel

★★★★ GUEST ACCOMMODATION

**tel:** 01980 629256 **SP4 0EG**
**email:** info@parkhousemotel.com **web:** www.parkhousemotel.co.uk
**dir:** *5m E of Amesbury. Junct A303 & A338*

Park House Motel is a family-run establishment that offers a warm welcome and is extremely convenient for the A303. Bedrooms are practically equipped with modern facilities and come in a variety of sizes. There is a large dining room where dinner is served during the week, and a cosy bar in which to relax.

**Rooms:** 30 rms (27 en suite) (1 pri facs) (9 fmly) (25 GF) **S** £62–£75; **D** fr £83*
**Facilities:** STV FTV TVL tea/coffee Dinner available Licensed WiFi **Parking:** 40

## BOWERCHALKE — Map 5 SU02

## Greenbank Bed & Breakfast

★★★★ BED AND BREAKFAST

**tel:** 01722 780350 & 07812 486045 **Church Street SP5 5BE**
**email:** enquiries@greenbank101.com **web:** www.greenbank101.com
**dir:** *A354 from Salisbury to Coombe Bissell. Right at 1st junct, follow signs for Broad Chalke. Left by public house & follow signs for Bowerchalke*

Located in the scenic Chalke Valley, a short drive out from Salisbury, Greenbank offers contemporary en suite accommodation. There is ample off-road parking and a warm welcome from your hosts Sue and Paul, who will ensure that your stay is a relaxing and pleasurable experience. Accommodation consists of two non-smoking, en suite double rooms. Guests also have use of a fridge and their own conservatory-lounge where there is access to all indoor and outdoor areas, games, magazines and items of local interest.

**Rooms:** 2 en suite (2 GF) **S** £60–£70; **D** £80–£90 **Facilities:** FTV Lounge tea/coffee WiFi **Extras:** Fruit, snacks – complimentary **Parking:** 4 **Notes:** No children 12yrs

## BOX — Map 4 ST86

### Premier Collection

## The Northey Arms

★★★★★ ◉ INN

**tel:** 01225 742333 **Bath Road SN13 8AE**
**email:** thenorthey@ohhcompany.co.uk **web:** www.ohhcompany.co.uk

This stylish inn combines modern facilities and quality with relaxed and welcoming hospitality. The bedrooms and bathrooms are especially comfortable and well equipped, with large walk-in showers, luxurious towels and toiletries. Food is served throughout the day and utilises high quality produce on a menu which has something for everyone.

**Rooms:** 5 en suite 5 annexe en suite (1 fmly) (5 GF) **S** £75–£150; **D** £75–£150
**Facilities:** STV tea/coffee Dinner available Direct dial WiFi **Conf:** Max 20 Thtr 20 Class 20 Board 12 **Parking:** 30

**Find out more**
about the AA's B&B rating scheme on pages 8–9

## BRADFORD-ON-AVON · Map 4 ST86

# The George

★★★★ ◉ INN

tel: 01225 865650 & 07511 662784 **67 Woolley Street BA15 1AQ**
email: thegeorgeatwoolley@gmail.com **web:** www.thegeorgebradfordonavon.co.uk
**dir:** *M4 junct 18 onto A46, A4 then A363 towards Bradford-on-Avon. Onto B3105 at Woolley Green, turn right into Woolley St*

Recently completely refurbished throughout, this village inn just outside Bradford-on-Avon, has been transformed into delightful accommodation combining friendly hospitality with quality and character throughout. Two very well equipped bedrooms with separate kitchen areas are available above the property. A good selection of ales, wines and a menu full of tempting dishes is available in the very well furnished yet relaxing dining areas.

**Rooms:** 2 en suite **S** £100–£120; **D** £110–£140* **Facilities:** FTV tea/coffee Dinner available Direct dial WiFi **Extras:** Fresh fruit, mineral water **Conf:** Max 26 Thtr 26 Class 18 Board 16 **Parking:** 11 **Notes:** LB

# Beeches Farmhouse

★★★★ BED AND BREAKFAST

tel: 01225 865170 **Holt Road BA15 1TS**
email: stay@beeches-farmhouse.co.uk **web:** www.beeches-farmhouse.co.uk
**dir:** *1m E of Bradford-on-Avon on B3107, on left just past garden centre*

Peacefully located and surrounded by delightful countryside, this relaxed and welcoming accommodation offers guest bedrooms in well furnished, converted barns and stables adjacent to the main building. There are various leisure facilities in the grounds including a games room. Breakfast is served in the conservatory of the main farmhouse.

**Rooms:** 1 en suite 4 annexe en suite (1 fmly) (4 GF) **S** £69–£129* **Facilities:** FTV DVD Lounge tea/coffee WiFi ⅃18 Pool table ⚓ **Extras:** Mineral water, fruit, local biscuits & fudge **Conf:** Max 8 Board 8 **Parking:** 11 **Notes:** LB RS Xmas & New Year room only (no breakfast)

# The Tollgate Inn

★★★★ ⊜ INN

tel: 01225 782326 **Ham Green, Holt BA14 6PX**
email: laura@tollgateinn.co.uk **web:** www.tollgateholt.co.uk
**dir:** *A363 Bradford-on-Avon turn left onto B3105, left onto B3107, 100yds on right at W end of Holt*

The Tollgate Inn combines the comforts of a traditional hostelry with excellent food, served in delightful surroundings. It stands near the village green in Holt, only a short drive from Bath. The bedrooms, varying in size, are comfortable and thoughtfully equipped with welcome extras. An on-site café, deli and farm shop provide lunches and interesting picnic items.

**Rooms:** 4 en suite 1 annexe en suite (1 GF) **Facilities:** FTV DVD tea/coffee Dinner available Direct dial WiFi Boules pitch **Extras:** Fresh fruit, still & sparkling mineral water **Parking:** 30

## BROAD HINTON · Map 5 SU17

# The Crown at Broad Hinton

★★★★ INN

tel: 01793 731302 **SN4 9PA**
email: enquiries@thecrownatbroadhinton.co.uk **web:** www.thecrownatbroadhinton.co.uk
**dir:** *M4 junct 16 follow signs for Wroughton, then Salthrop. A4361 right towards Devizes, next right to Broad Hinton. Left at T-junct, on right*

A warm welcome is guaranteed at this owner-run inn; traditional in style with a great range of ales on tap. Home-cooked pub fare is served, with specials changing daily. Located just moments from the M4 in a peaceful village, with good transport links, it's great for exploring the local area, including Avebury Stone Circles, Swindon and Devizes. Rooms are well designed and spacious with luxurious finishing touches; en suites are modern and finished to a high standard. Dylan and Flo (the pub dogs) are sure to greet all guests with a friendly wag of their tails.

**Rooms:** 2 en suite (1 fmly) **S** £75–£100; **D** £75–£100* **Facilities:** FTV iPod docking station Lounge tea/coffee Dinner available WiFi ⅃27 ⚓ **Conf:** Max 20 Board 12 **Parking:** 90 **Notes:** Closed 25 Dec

## BURCOMBE                  Map 5 SU03

### Burcombe Manor B&B

★★★★ BED AND BREAKFAST

**tel:** 01722 744288 & 07967 594449 **Burcombe Lane SP2 0EJ**
**email:** enquiries@burcombemanor.co.uk **web:** www.burcombemanor.co.uk
**dir:** A30 from Wilton, after 0.75m turn left over bridge. At T-junct turn right, 100mtrs on left

Located in the village of Burcombe, only five miles west of Salisbury, this family home is set at the edge of a 1300-acre farm with views out over the water meadows. Bedrooms, including two en suite rooms, offer comfortable accommodation. Breakfast is served in one of the drawing rooms and there is a spacious lounge for guests to relax in.

**Rooms:** 3 rms (2 en suite) (1 pri facs) **S** £70; **D** £85* **Facilities:** FTV Lounge tea/coffee WiFi **Parking:** 6

## BURTON                Map 4 ST87

### Premier Collection

### The Old House at Home

★★★★★ INN

**tel:** 01454 218227 **SN14 7LT**
**email:** office@ohhcompany.co.uk **web:** www.ohhcompany.co.uk
**dir:** M4 junct 18, A46, B4040 to Acton Turvill, right onto B4039. 1.5m to Burton

In a pleasant setting, just a couple of miles from the delightful village of Castle Combe, this well-established country inn is run personally by the resident proprietors and family. Six purpose-built, high-quality bedrooms and bathrooms provide plenty of welcome extras, and are located in a stylish block adjacent to the main building. Dinner here should not be missed, with a varied selection of carefully prepared ingredients used in the dishes, including the daily specials.

**Rooms:** 6 annexe en suite (6 GF) **S** £75–£120; **D** £75 £120 **Facilities:** FTV tea/coffee Dinner available Direct dial WiFi **Parking:** 20 **Notes:** LB Closed 25 Dec

## CALNE            Map 4 ST97

### The White Horse

★★★★★ INN

**tel:** 01249 813118 **Compton Bassett SN11 8RG**
**email:** info@whitehorse-comptonbassett.co.uk
**web:** www.whitehorse-comptonbassett.co.uk
**dir:** M4 junct 16 onto A3102, after Hilmarton village turn left to Compton Bassett

Nestled in the Wiltshire countryside, this free house offers a warm welcome and remains part of the local community. Inside the pub there is a modern, comfortable restaurant where high-quality food is served at breakfast, lunch and dinner. The bedrooms, located separately from the bar and restaurant areas, are individually styled.

**Rooms:** 8 annexe en suite (3 fmly) (6 GF) **S** £75–£90; **D** £85–£100* **Facilities:** FTV DVD tea/coffee Dinner available WiFi Boules **Extras:** Home-made cookies, bottled water – complimentary **Parking:** 40 **Notes:** Closed 25 Dec

### The Lansdowne

★★★ INN

**tel:** 01249 812488 **The Strand SN11 0EH**
**email:** lansdowne@arkells.com **web:** www.lansdownestrand.co.uk

Situated in a picturesque market town, The Lansdowne was built in the 16th century as a coaching inn, and it still retains much of the charm and character of that era. Under the new management of Arkells, this property is undergoing a full refurbishment project over the next couple of years. Public areas offer a comfortale and inviting space in which to relax and enjoy excellent food. Bedrooms are spacious and furnished in a traditional style at this time. Guests can enjoy a relaxed but memorable meal in The Strand Room or the bar areas. An outdoor courtyard seating area is also available.

**Rooms:** 21 en suite 4 annexe en suite (2 fmly) **Facilities:** FTV tea/coffee Dinner available WiFi **Conf:** Max 50 Thtr 45 Class 45 Board 50 **Parking:** 7

## CASTLE COMBE           Map 4 ST87

### Fosse Farmhouse Chambre d'Hote

★★★★ BED AND BREAKFAST

**tel:** 01249 782286 **Nettleton Shrub SN14 7NJ**
**email:** caroncooper@fossefarmhouse.com **web:** www.fossefarmhouse.com
**dir:** 1.5m N from Castle Combe on B4039, left at Gib, 1m on right

Set in quiet countryside not far from Castle Combe, this bed and breakfast has well-equipped bedrooms decorated in keeping with its 18th-century origins. Excellent dinners are served in the farmhouse, and cream teas can be enjoyed in the old stables or the delightful garden.

**Rooms:** 2 en suite (1 fmly) **S** £99–£110; **D** £110–£160* **Facilities:** FTV DVD TVL tea/coffee Dinner available Licensed WiFi ↓18 **Extras:** Speciality toiletries, bottled water, flowers **Conf:** Max 15 Thtr 10 Class 10 Board 10 **Parking:** 12 **Notes:** LB

## CHIPPENHAM          Map 4 ST97

### Diana Lodge Bed & Breakfast

★★★ BED AND BREAKFAST

**tel:** 01249 650306 **Grathie Cottage, 72 Marshfield Road SN15 1JR**
**email:** diana.lodge@talktalk.net **web:** www.dianalodgebedandbreakfast.co.uk
**dir:** 500yds NW of town centre on A420, into West End Club car park

A cheerful welcome awaits at Diana Lodge Bed & Breakfast, a late 19th-century cottage within walking distance of the town centre and the railway station. The comfortable bedrooms are well appointed, and there is a small, adjacent car park.

**Rooms:** 5 rms (3 en suite) (2 pri facs) (1 fmly) (2 GF) **Facilities:** FTV tea/coffee WiFi **Parking:** 1

## COLLINGBOURNE KINGSTON · Map 5 SU25

# Manor Farm B&B

★★★★ FARMHOUSE

**tel:** 01264 850859 **SN8 3SD**
**email:** stay@manorfm.com **web:** www.manorfm.com
**dir:** *Opposite church in centre of village*

An attractive, Grade II listed farmhouse with comfortable and spacious rooms on a working family farm, this is the ideal base from which to explore the surrounding countryside, whether walking or cycling, directly from the farm. All rooms have been individually appointed and offer a range of practical amenities. Sumptuous traditional, vegetarian and special diet breakfasts are served at the communal table in the dining room.

**Rooms:** 3 rms (2 en suite) (1 pri facs) (2 fmly) **S** £60–£70; **D** £70–£85 **Facilities:** FTV tea/coffee WiFi **Extras:** Speciality toiletries, bottled water – complimentary **Parking:** 6 **Notes:** LB No children 8yrs 550 acres arable

## CORSHAM · Map 4 ST87

### Premier Collection

# The Methuen Arms

★★★★★ ◎◎ INN

**tel:** 01249 717060 **2 High Street SN13 0HB**
**email:** info@themethuenarms.com **web:** www.themethuenarms.com
**dir:** *M4 junct 17, A350 towards Chippenham, at rdbt take A4 towards Bath. 1m after lights, at next rdbt sharp left into Pickwick Rd, establishment 0.5m on left*

This well-established inn, in the centre of the thriving town of Corsham, provides very high levels of quality and comfort. The bedrooms are modern and stylish with large comfortable beds and spacious, well-equipped bathrooms. Guests can enjoy a drink in the relaxing bar, a light snack in the day or evening, and should not miss the carefully prepared, award-winning dishes at dinner.

**Rooms:** 14 en suite (3 fmly) **S** £90–£155; **D** £120–£175* **Facilities:** FTV tea/coffee Dinner available WiFi ↓18 **Extras:** Speciality toiletries, digital radios **Conf:** Max 60 Thtr 50 Board 14 **Parking:** 40

# Pickwick Lodge Farm B&B

★★★★ FARMHOUSE

**tel:** 01249 712207 **Guyers Lane SN13 0PS**
**email:** bandb@pickwickfarm.co.uk **web:** www.pickwickfarm.co.uk
**dir:** *Exit A4, Bath side of Corsham, into Guyers Ln, farmhouse at end on right*

This Grade II listed, 17th-century farmhouse is peacefully located on a 300-acre beef and arable farm, within easy reach of Bath. The spacious bedrooms are well equipped with modern facilities and many thoughtful extras. A hearty breakfast, using the best local produce, is served at a communal table in the dining room.

**Rooms:** 3 rms (2 en suite) (1 pri facs) **Facilities:** FTV TVL tea/coffee WiFi Fishing **Extras:** Speciality toiletries, fruit, home-made cake **Parking:** 6 **Notes:** LB No children 12yrs 300 acres arable/beef

## CRICKLADE · Map 5 SU09

# The Red Lion Inn

★★★★ ◎ INN

**tel:** 01793 750776 **74 High Street SN6 6DD**
**email:** info@theredlioncricklade.co.uk **web:** www.theredlioncricklade.co.uk
**dir:** *Off A419*

This historic pub is proud to feature real ales from its very own microbrewery on site along with ciders and other guest ales. A range of menu options are available from pub classics to modern British dishes. There are five spacious en suite bedrooms, all designed individually and providing a high level of quality and comfort. Dogs are welcome in some of the accommodation.

**Rooms:** 5 annexe en suite (2 GF) **Facilities:** FTV DVD iPod docking station tea/coffee Dinner available WiFi

## DEVIZES · Map 4 SU06

### Premier Collection

# Blounts Court Farm

★★★★★ BED AND BREAKFAST

**tel:** 01380 727180 **Coxhill Lane, Potterne SN10 5PH**
**email:** carys@blountscourtfarm.co.uk **web:** www.blountscourtfarm.co.uk
**dir:** *A360 to Potterne, into Coxhill Ln opposite George & Dragon, at fork turn left, follow drive uphill to farmhouse*

A warm welcome is assured at this peacefully located, delightful arable farm, overlooking the village cricket field. The character barn has been converted to provide three attractive bedrooms on the ground floor – one has a four-poster bed. The elegant decor is in keeping with the character of the house. Breakfast, which features home-made and local produce, is served in the farmhouse dining room.

**Rooms:** 3 en suite (3 GF) **S** £56–£62; **D** £88–£98* **Facilities:** FTV DVD iPod docking station TVL tea/coffee WiFi **Extras:** Speciality toiletries, home-made biscuits – complimentary **Parking:** 5 **Notes:** No children 8yrs

## The Peppermill

★★★★★ ◉◉ RESTAURANT WITH ROOMS

**tel:** 01380 710407 **40 Saint John's Street SN10 1BL**
**email:** philip@peppermilldevizes.co.uk **web:** www.peppermilldevizes.co.uk
**dir:** *Situated in the market place*

Situated in the heart of Devizes, The Peppermill offers seven bedrooms located above the restaurant, in one of the oldest buildings in the town. The en suite bath/shower rooms have underfloor heating, limestone floors and heated mirrors. Hypnos Royal Lansdowne beds, three of which split into twins if needed, have goose-down bedding and Egyptian cotton bed linen to ensure a good night's sleep. The restaurant serves breakfast, lunch and dinner, all offered daily.

**Rooms:** 7 en suite **S** £95–£155; **D** £115–£175* **Facilities:** FTV iPod docking station TVL tea/coffee Dinner available WiFi ♨18 ☕ **Extras:** Robes **Notes:** LB

## Avalon Lodge

★★★★ BED AND BREAKFAST

**tel:** 01380 728189 **Devizes Road, Rowde SN10 2LU**
**email:** stay@avalonlodge.co.uk **web:** www.avalonlodge.co.uk
**dir:** *1m from Devizes on A342. On left*

Avalon Lodge, located on the outskirts of Devizes, offers a great base for visiting a host of local historical sites. Expect a very warm welcome from owners Nick and Jenny. Rooms are individually decorated, offering very good levels of comfort, with lots of thoughtful extras provided.

**Rooms:** 4 en suite **S** £60–£70; **D** £80–£95* **Facilities:** FTV DVD iPod docking station Lounge tea/coffee Dinner available Licensed WiFi ☕ **Extras:** Fresh milk – complimentary; snacks – chargeable **Parking:** 6 **Notes:** LB No children 12yrs

## Magnolia Tree Bed and Breakfast

★★★★ BED AND BREAKFAST

**tel:** 01380 738459 **27 Roundway Park SN10 2ED**
**email:** info@magnoliatreebedandbreakfast.co.uk
**web:** www.magnoliatreebedandbreakfast.co.uk
**dir:** *In centre of Devizes onto A361 (signed Swindon), pass Wiltshire Police Headquarters on left. Turn left into Roundway Park*

Located a short walk from the centre of the market town of Devizes, the Magnolia Tree is within easy reach of the Wessex Ridgeway and the Kennet and Avon Canal's Caen Hill flight of 29 locks. Salisbury, Stonehenge and Bath are also in close proximity. A warm welcome is guaranteed from Candy, Lloyd, and Daisy the dog. Bedrooms are comfortably furnished, serviced to a high standard, and come equipped with a range of accessories. Breakfast is served in the light and airy dining room. Free WiFi is accessible throughout.

**Rooms:** 3 en suite **S** £45; **D** £75* **Facilities:** FTV DVD tea/coffee WiFi ☕
**Extras:** Home-made biscuits, bottled water **Parking:** 6

---

**EDINGTON** Map 4 ST95

## The Three Daggers

★★★★★ ⬭ INN

**tel:** 01380 830940 **Westbury Road BA13 4PG**
**email:** hello@threedaggers.co.uk **web:** www.threedaggers.co.uk
**dir:** *A36 towards Warminster, A350 to Westbury, B3098 to Edington*

Stylishly refurbished to offer luxurious standards of quality and comfort throughout, The Three Daggers combines traditional hospitality with contemporary furnishings and decor. Bedrooms and bathrooms come in a range of shapes and sizes but all are appointed with high quality Egyptian cotton bedding, large shower heads and a generous range of welcome extras. The bar and dining area menus offer high quality, carefully prepared ingredients at both dinner and breakfast. A large lounge with a real fire and comfortable seating is also available to guests. Adjoining is a farm shop and brewery.

**Rooms:** 3 rms (2 en suite) (1 pri facs) (1 fmly) **Facilities:** FTV DVD iPod docking station TVL tea/coffee Dinner available WiFi ☕ **Extras:** Fruit, speciality toiletries, fresh flowers **Conf:** Max 16 Thtr 16 Class 16 Board 16 **Parking:** 45 **Notes:** LB

---

**FONTHILL BISHOP** Map 4 ST93

## The Riverbarn

★★★★ ◉◉ GUEST HOUSE

**tel:** 01747 820232 **SP3 5SF**
**email:** info@the riverbarn.org.uk **web:** www.theriverbarn.org.uk
**dir:** *From Wincanton towards Amesbury on A303 take B3089, through Hindon to Fonthill Bishop. Property on right. Or from Amesbury on A303 left onto unclassified road after Wylye signed Fonthill Bishop. Property on left*

Surrounded by lawns stretching down to the river, The Riverbarn is the central hub of the village of Fonthill Bishop. Parts of the barn are 600 years old and it has been operated as a business for the last 100 years. The annexe bedrooms are spacious and well appointed. The café-bar offers sumptuous cakes and cream teas, light lunches and evening meals.

**Rooms:** 4 annexe en suite (4 GF) **S** £75–£80; **D** £90–£195^ **Facilities:** FTV DVD tea/coffee Dinner available Licensed WiFi ☕ **Parking:** 20 **Notes:** LB No children 14yrs Closed 24 Dec–20 Jan

---

**FOXHAM** Map 4 ST97

## The Foxham Inn

★★★★ ◉ INN

**tel:** 01249 740665 **SN15 4NQ**
**email:** info@thefoxhaminn.co.uk **web:** www.thefoxhaminn.co.uk
**dir:** *Off B4069 between Sutton Benger & Lyneham*

The Foxham Inn is an unpretentious family-run country inn, which serves award-winning food, real ale and fine wines. The two rooms are well configured and have been completed to a very good standard, and both offer a range of amenities including free WiFi. The main restaurant is a versatile venue suitable for a range of different occasions.

**Rooms:** 2 en suite **S** £75; **D** £90 **Facilities:** FTV Lounge tea/coffee Dinner available WiFi Fishing ☕ **Conf:** Max 40 Thtr 40 Class 40 Board 20 **Parking:** 20 **Notes:** Closed 2–14 Jan RS Mon, Sun eve

## HORNINGSHAM
Map 4 ST84

### The Bath Arms at Longleat
★★★★  INN

tel: 01985 844308 **Longleat Estate BA12 7LY**
email: enquiries@batharms.co.uk **web:** www.batharms.co.uk
dir: *In Longleat village of Horningsham*

Peacefully located at the edges of the Longleat Estate, this delightful inn is perhaps best described as offering 'quirky luxury'. Bedrooms come in a variety of shapes and sizes; each individually decorated in a range of styles and designs. High-quality produce is used to prepare delicious, AA Rosette award-winning dinners which are served in the relaxed main restaurant.

**Rooms:** 9 en suite 8 annexe en suite (8 fmly) (8 GF) **S** £55–£135; **D** £75–£145*
**Facilities:** FTV DVD tea/coffee Dinner available Direct dial WiFi **Conf:** Max 30 Thtr 30 Class 30 Board 20 **Parking:** 6

## LACOCK
Map 4 ST96

### Sign of the Angel
★★★★ ◉◉ RESTAURANT WITH ROOMS

tel: 01249 730230 **6 Church Street SN15 2LB**
email: info@signoftheangel.co.uk **web:** www.signoftheangel.co.uk
dir: *M4 junct 17 onto A350 signed Poole. After 8m, left signed Lacock. Left into Church St*

This delightful 15th-century inn is located in the heart of the National Trust village of Lacock. Packed full of character, rooms vary in size according to the quirks of the building, but all offer very comfortable beds, quality bedding and a welcoming ambience. Guests are welcome to use the cosy bar and outdoor seating in the garden, while the dining room offers top quality British food, carefully sourced from local suppliers. Neither dinner nor breakfast should be missed here.

**Rooms:** 5 en suite (2 fmly) **S** £80–£110; **D** £110–£160 **Facilities:** Lounge tea/coffee Dinner available WiFi ♨9 **Extras:** Fudge, home-made cookies **Conf:** Max 16 Board 16 **Notes:** RS Sun eve & Mon closed

## LUDWELL
Map 4 ST92

### The Grove Arms
★★★★ INN

tel: 01747 828811 **SP7 9ND**
email: ninabartlett123@gmail.com **web:** www.grovearms-ludwell.co.uk
dir: *2m E of Shaftesbury on A30*

This 16th-century, Grade II listed building is located between Salisbury and Shaftesbury, and provides a great base for exploring the Wiltshire and Dorset countryside. The six en suite bedrooms are comfortable and well equipped.

Lunch and dinner menus offer a great choice, enhanced with daily specials; traditional ales are also available.

**Rooms:** 6 en suite (1 fmly) **Facilities:** FTV DVD Lounge tea/coffee Dinner available WiFi Pool table ♨ **Parking:** 35 **Notes:** LB

## MALMESBURY
Map 4 ST98

### Kings Arms
★★★ INN

tel: 01666 823383 **29 High Street SN16 9AA**
email: thekingsarms.malmesbury@arkells.com **web:** www.thekahotel.co.uk

Located on Malmesbury High Street, a stone's throw from the Abbey, this traditional coaching inn is split between either side of the original delivery passage. One side features a cosy bar, the ideal place to enjoy a pint of Arkell's ale; while the more contemporary restaurant is located opposite and is perfect for dining and breakfast. Bedrooms are en suite and located above the main pub building or in the former coach house and stables at the rear. Owned by the Arkell's family brewers, a great range of traditionally brewed beers are available.

**Rooms:** 12 en suite **Facilities:** Dinner available

## PEWSEY
Map 5 SU15

### Premier Collection

### Troutbeck Guest House at the Red Lion Freehouse
★★★★★ ◉◉◉ ▾ RESTAURANT WITH ROOMS

tel: 01980 671124 **East Chisenbury SN9 6AQ**
email: enquiries@redlionfreehouse.com **web:** www.redlionfreehouse.com
dir: *A345 to Upavon, left at T-junct, right signed East Chisenbury*

The Red Lion Freehouse at East Chisenbury offers an interesting blend of sumptuous accommodation and food, yet it retains the informality and laidback atmosphere of a traditional pub. Each of the five rooms have been individually appointed and offer plenty of in-room amenities coupled with beautiful views of the surrounding countryside. The cooking is confident and a particular flair is brought to the dishes based on seasonal, local ingredients. The pub rears its own pigs and keeps rescue hens. Tucked behind the Red Lion is a tranquil tree-shaded beer garden.

**Rooms:** 5 en suite (1 fmly) (5 GF) **S** £180–£260; **D** £180–£260* **Facilities:** FTV tea/coffee Dinner available WiFi ♨18 Fishing **Extras:** Speciality toiletries, snacks, robes – complimentary; mini-bar – chargeable **Conf:** Max 16 **Parking:** 5 **Notes:** LB

## RAMSBURY
Map 5 SU27

### The Bell at Ramsbury
★★★★★ ◉◉ INN

tel: 01672 520230 **The Square SN8 2PE**
email: thebell@thebellramsbury.com **web:** www.thebellramsbury.com
dir: *From Hungerford on B4192 towards Swindon. After 3.5m, left into Newton Rd. 1m on right*

Owned by the local Ramsbury Brewery, this inn offers excellent en suite accommodation. Various dining options are available; traditional pub classics served in the bar or garden for a relaxed experience, the more formal dining options in the restaurant, and also the Shaker-influenced Café Bella (open daily) offering delicious cakes and much more. AA Pub of the Year for England 2017–18.

**Rooms:** 6 en suite 3 annexe en suite **Facilities:** FTV tea/coffee Dinner available WiFi ♨18 ♨ **Conf:** Max 8 Board 8 **Parking:** 20 **Notes:** Closed 25 Dec

## ROWDE — Map 4 ST96

## The George & Dragon
★★★★ ⚜⚜ RESTAURANT WITH ROOMS

**tel:** 01380 723053 **High Street SN10 2PN**
**email:** gm@thegeorgeanddragonrowde.co.uk **web:** www.thegeorgeanddragonrowde.co.uk
**dir:** *1.5m from Devizes on A350 towards Chippenham*

The George & Dragon dates back to the 14th century when it was a meeting house. Exposed beams, wooden floors, antique rugs and open fires create a warm atmosphere in the bar and restaurant. Bedrooms and bathrooms are very well decorated and equipped with some welcome extras. Dining in the bar or restaurant should not be missed, as local produce and fresh fish deliveries from Cornwall are offercd on the daily-changing blackboard menu.

**Rooms:** 3 rms (2 en suite) (1 pri facs) (1 fmly) **S** £75–£125; **D** £75–£125*
**Facilities:** FTV DVD iPod docking station Lounge TVL tea/coffee Dinner available WiFi 🔒 **Extras:** Mini-bar, snacks, robes – complimentary **Parking:** 14

## SALISBURY — Map 5 SU12
*See also Amesbury*

## Websters
★★★★ GUEST HOUSE

**tel:** 01722 339779 **11 Hartington Road SP2 7LG**
**email:** enquiries@websters-bed-breakfast.com **web:** www.websters-bed-breakfast.com
**dir:** *From city centre onto A360 (Devizes Rd), 1st turn on left*

A warm welcome is assured at Websters, a delightful property, located in a quiet cul-de-sac close to the city centre. The charming, well-presented bedrooms are equipped with numerous extras including broadband. There is one ground-floor room with easier access.

**Rooms:** 5 en suite (1 GF) **S** £55–£75; **D** £65–£95* **Facilities:** FTV TVL tea/coffee WiFi **Parking:** 5 **Notes:** LB No children 12yrs Closed 31 Dec & 1 Jan RS Xmas & New Year continental breakfast only at Xmas

## Cricket Field House
★★★★ GUEST ACCOMMODATION

**tel:** 01722 322595 **Skew Bridge, Wilton Road SP2 9NS**
**email:** cricketfieldcottage@btinternet.com **web:** www.cricketfieldhouse.co.uk
**dir:** *A36, 1m W of Salisbury, towards Wilton & Warminster*

Cricket Field House is a 19th-century gamekeeper's cottage set in award-winning gardens overlooking the South Wiltshire Cricket Ground. It is within walking distance of the city centre and railway station, and provides high levels of accommodation, hospitality and customer care.

**Rooms:** 8 annexe en suite (4 GF) **Facilities:** FTV tea/coffee Licensed WiFi 🔒 **Parking:** 25 **Notes:** No children 14yrs Closed 21 Dec–4 Jan

## STOURTON — Map 4 ST73

## Spread Eagle Inn
★★★★ 🍺 INN

**tel:** 01747 840587 **Church Lawn BA12 6QE**
**email:** enquiries@spreadeagleinn.com **web:** www.spreadeagleinn.com
**dir:** *0.5m W off B3092 at entrance to Stourhead Gardens*

Set in the beautiful grounds of Stourhead House with its Palladian temples, lakes and inspiring vistas, the Spread Eagle Inn is an impressive red-brick building with a good reputation for simple, honest and locally-sourced food. In the bedrooms, National Trust antiques sit side by side with modern comforts. The large Georgian windows, low ceilings and uneven floors add to the authentic atmosphere of this delightful country house.

**Rooms:** 5 en suite **Facilities:** tea/coffee Dinner available Direct dial WiFi **Conf:** Max 30 Thtr 30 Board 20 **Notes:** LB

## SWINDON — Map 5 SU18

## Sun Inn
★★★★ INN

**tel:** 01793 523292 **Coate SN3 6AA**
**email:** sun-inn@arkells.com **web:** www.suninn-swindon.co.uk
**dir:** *M4 junct 15 onto A419, take 1st exit signed Swindon & hospital. 1st exit at rdbt, 1m on left*

Located on the outskirts of Swindon, adjacent to the popular Coate Water Country Park, the inn features a large garden and children's play area with a thatched summer house. Accommodation is suitable for both business and leisure guests, offering free WiFi throughout. A regularly-changing blackboard menu offers well-prepared dishes, available throughout the day and evening. The popular Sunday lunch should not be missed. Owned by the Arkell's family brewers, a great range of traditionally brewed beers are available.

**Rooms:** 10 en suite **Facilities:** FTV DVD tea/coffee Dinner available WiFi **Parking:** 80

## The Angel
★★★★ ⚜ INN

**tel:** 01793 851161 **47 High Street, Royal Wootton Bassett SN4 7AQ**
**email:** theangel.wbassett@arkells.com **web:** www.theangelhotelwoottonbassett.co.uk

Located directly on the high street of historic Royal Wootton Bassett, The Angel offers everything from morning coffee in the lounge, to a drink at the bar or a meal in the popular restaurant. Public areas are intimate and comfortably furnished. Accommodation is located at the rear of the property in a purpose-built wing overlooking the courtyard. Its location makes it ideal for corporate guests and those exploring the local area. The property also includes a boardroom and larger function room.

**Rooms:** 3 en suite 14 annexe en suite **Facilities:** FTV Lounge tea/coffee Dinner available WiFi **Conf:** Max 100 Thtr 100 Class 36 Board 14 **Notes:** Closed 26 Dec & 1 Jan RS 25 Dec

SWINDON *continued*

## Ardecca

★★★★ GUEST ACCOMMODATION

tel: 01793 721238 & 07791 120826 **Fieldrise Farm, Kingsdown Lane SN25 5DL**
email: chris-graham.ardecca@fsmail.net **web:** www.ardecca-bedandbreakfast.co.uk
dir: *A419 onto B4019 to Blunsdon/Highworth, then into Turnpike Rd at Cold Harbour pub,
left into Kingsdown Ln*

Ardecca is quietly located in 16 acres of pastureland with easy access to Swindon
and the Cotswolds. All bedrooms are on the ground floor and are well furnished and
equipped. An especially friendly welcome is provided and arts and crafts workshops
are available on site.

**Rooms:** 4 rms (4 pri facs) (1 fmly) (4 GF) **Facilities:** FTV tea/coffee WiFi
**Extras:** Bottled water, sweets **Parking:** 5 **Notes:** No children 6yrs

## The Old Post Office Guest House

★★★★ GUEST HOUSE

tel: 01793 823114 **Thornhill Road, South Marston SN3 4RY**
email: theoldpostofficeguesthouse@yahoo.co.uk
web: www.theoldpostofficeguesthouse.co.uk
dir: *M4 junct 15, A419 signed Cirencester/Swindon (East), approx 3m, left onto A420
towards Oxford, at next rdbt 2nd exit into Merlin Way, 0.3m, at White Hart rdbt 3rd exit
onto A420. At Gablecross rdbt follow South Marston signs*

This attractive property is about two miles from Swindon. Guests are welcomed by
the enthusiastic owner, a professional opera singer with a wonderful sense of
humour. The comfortable bedrooms vary in size, and all are equipped with
numerous facilities. An extensive choice is offered at breakfast, which is freshly
cooked and uses the best local produce.

**Rooms:** 5 en suite (1 fmly) **Facilities:** STV tea/coffee WiFi ♠ Use of nearby country
club **Extras:** Snacks, chocolate **Parking:** 6

## Tawny Owl

★★★★ INN

tel: 01793 706770 **Queen Elizabeth Drive, Taw Hill SN25 1WR**
email: thetawnyowl.swindon@arkells.com **web:** www.arkells.com
dir: *2.5m NW of town centre, signed from A419*

Expect a genuinely friendly welcome from the staff at this modern inn on the
northwest outskirts of Swindon. It has comfortable, well-equipped bedrooms and
bathrooms. A varied selection of enjoyable home-cooked meals is on offer at both
lunch and dinner, together with a range of Arkell's ales and wines. A private
function room is available.

**Rooms:** 5 en suite (2 fmly) **S** £50–£75; **D** £50–£89 (room only)* **Facilities:** TVL
tea/coffee Dinner available WiFi **Conf:** Max 55 Thtr 55 Class 55 Board 55 **Parking:** 75
**Notes:** RS Xmas/New Year

## The White Hart

★★★★ INN

tel: 01793 822272 & 07789 717368 **Oxford Road, Stratton St Margaret SN3 4JD**
email: info@whitehartstratton.co.uk **web:** www.whitehartstratton.co.uk
dir: *On White Hart rdbt, at intersection of A420 & A419*

Located on the outskirts of Swindon, with good access to the M4 just a five-minute
drive from junction 15, with its close links to Cirencester and the M5.
Accommodation has been purpose built, offering comfortable and spacious rooms,
suitable for both business and leisure guests. Free WiFi is available throughout,
and there's ample free parking. A classic pub menu offers well-prepared dishes,
available throughout the day and evening, and a popular carvery is available on
Sundays. Function rooms are available. Owned by the Arkell's family brewers, a
great range of traditionally brewed beers are available.

**Rooms:** 24 en suite (6 fmly) (12 GF) **Facilities:** FTV Lounge TVL tea/coffee Dinner
available WiFi Pool table ♠ **Extras:** Speciality toiletries **Conf:** Max 42 Thtr 42
Class 30 Board 20 **Parking:** 60

## Heart in Hand

★★★ INN

tel: 01793 721314 **43 High Street, Blunsdon SN26 7AG**
email: leppardsteve@aol.com **web:** www.heartinhand.co.uk
dir: *Exit A419 into High St, 200yds on right*

Right in the village centre, this family-run inn offers a friendly welcome together
with a wide selection of home-cooked food. Bedrooms are spacious, well equipped
and offer a number of useful extras. A pleasant patio and rear garden with seating
is also available.

**Rooms:** 4 en suite (1 fmly) **Facilities:** tea/coffee Dinner available **Parking:** 17
**Notes:** LB

## Saracens Head

★★ INN

tel: 01793 762284 **High Street, Highworth SN6 7AG**
email: saracenshead@arkells.com **web:** www.arkells.com
dir: *5m NE of Swindon*

The Saracens Head stands on the main street of a pleasant market town, close
to Swindon. It has lots of character, including a popular bar dating from 1828.
The fine selection of real ales, and some excellent home-cooked food are highlights.
Bedrooms, which vary in size, are generally compact. A rear car park and a patio
area are available.

**Rooms:** 12 en suite (1 fmly) **Facilities:** tea/coffee Dinner available WiFi **Conf:** Max 10
Thtr 10 Class 10 Board 10 **Parking:** 30 **Notes:** LB

## TISBURY
Map 4 ST92

### Hare Lodge Bed and Breakfast

★★★★ BED AND BREAKFAST

**tel:** 01747 870582 & 07754 044815 **Monmouth Road, Tuckingmill SP3 6NR**
**email:** harelodge@btinternet.com **web:** www.hare-lodge.co.uk
**dir:** *In Tisbury, at The Square, exit signed Semley/Newtown. Pass church on left, over mini rdbt. Into Tuckingmill, 3rd house on left*

Located on the edge of the village within an Area of Outstanding Natural Beauty, this Scandinavian-style house is a perfect base for exploring the area. A warm welcome is assured with every effort made to ensure a relaxing and rewarding stay. Bedrooms provide generous levels of space and comfort, one room having the benefit of a balcony, the other a suite with separate lounge area. Tasty breakfasts are served around the dining table, or outside in the summer if preferred. This is a popular area for walkers, and helpful advice is always on offer to help plans routes.

**Rooms:** 2 en suite (1 fmly) **S** fr £80; **D** fr £90* **Facilities:** FTV DVD tea/coffee WiFi **🔒 Extras:** Speciality toiletries, fresh milk **Parking:** 3 **Notes:** Closed 23 Dec–3 Jan

## TOLLARD ROYAL
Map 4 ST91

### King John Inn

★★★★ ❀❀ RESTAURANT WITH ROOMS

**tel:** 01725 516207 **SP5 5PS**
**email:** info@kingjohninn.co.uk **web:** www.kingjohninn.co.uk
**dir:** *From A354 or A350 onto B3081*

Part of The Epicurean Collection, the King John Inn is a traditional style country inn located in a country village. It has a Victorian-style garden pavilion serving seasonal classics such as chargrilled lobster and pigeon salad. The Dove Cottage offers three more en suite bedrooms to go with the five rooms at the inn. All have feature bathrooms. Food and wine is a real feature here with local ingredients much in evidence, alongside excellent levels of hospitality and customer care. Ample parking for residents.

**Rooms:** 5 en suite 3 annexe en suite (2 GF) **Facilities:** FTV Lounge tea/coffee Dinner available Direct dial WiFi **Parking:** 18 **Notes:** LB RS 25 Dec restaurant closed for dinner

## WESTBURY
Map 4 ST85

### The Hollies Inn

★★★★ INN

**tel:** 01373 864493 **55 Westbury Leigh BA13 3SF**
**email:** info@theholliesinn.com **web:** www.theholliesinn.com

This traditional style inn provides plenty of quality and comfort in both bedrooms and bathrooms, and throughout the public areas. The inn is open during the day when lighter meals are offered, and there is a full menu in the evening along with a good range of ales. Quiz nights and live music are regular features. A car park is available, together with outdoor seating for the warmer months.

**Rooms:** 3 en suite **Facilities:** Dinner available **Parking**

## WEST GRAFTON
Map 5 SU26

### Mayfield Bed & Breakfast

★★★★ 🛏 BED AND BREAKFAST

**tel:** 01672 810339 & 07771 996811 **SN8 3BY**
**email:** angela.orssich@gmail.com **web:** www.mayfieldbandb.com
**dir:** *M4 junct 14 onto A338, through Hungerford. Turn left to West Grafton, 300mtrs on right*

Dating from the 15th century, this cosy bed and breakfast is located in a quiet hamlet just seven miles from the famous market town of Marlborough. Bedrooms are comfortable with many thoughtful extras. Hearty breakfasts feature as much home-made produce as possible, and are served around a family-style table.

**Rooms:** 4 rms (2 en suite) (2 fmly) **Facilities:** STV FTV TVL tea/coffee WiFi ➚🛋🔒 **Extras:** Fruit, snacks – complimentary **Parking:** 8 **Notes:** Closed Xmas

# WORCESTERSHIRE

## ABBERLEY
Map 10 SO76

### Premier Collection

### The Manor Arms

★★★★★ ❀❀ INN

**tel:** 01299 890300 **The Village WR6 6BN**
**email:** enquiries@themanorarms.co.uk **web:** www.themanorarms.co.uk
**dir:** *N of Worcester on A443, onto B4202 signed Cleobury Mortimer. Follow brown tourist signs to Manor Arms*

This charming inn was totally refurbished in 2015 and offers guests a range of high quality, stylish bedrooms. The inn enjoys a prominent position in the heart of the pretty village of Abberley and many of the bedrooms have views overlooking the rolling countryside. The award-winning restaurant is very popular and the bar has been sympathetically restored, and many of the original features retained. The Manor Arms is an ideal base from which to explore the historic towns of Worcester and Malvern both of which are a short drive away.

**Rooms:** 6 en suite **D** £80–£130* **Facilities:** Dinner available WiFi ♿18 **Extras:** Speciality toiletries, robes, home-made biscuits, fresh milk **Conf:** Max 40 Thtr 40 Class 20 Board 20 **Parking:** 40 **Notes:** Civ wed 50

---

## Alcott Farm

★★★ BED AND BREAKFAST

---

**tel:** 01564 824051 & 07736 445188 **Icknield Street, Weatheroak B48 7EH**
**email:** alcottfarm@btinternet.com **web:** www.alcottfarm.co.uk
**dir:** *2m NE of Alvechurch. M42 junct 3, A435 for Birmingham, left signed Weatheroak, left at x-rds down steep hill, left opposite pub, farm 0.5m on right up long driveway*

Hidden away in the leafy Worcestershire countryside is Alcott Farm. A long drive leads to this red-brickfarmhouse which is surrounded by well-kept floral displays, making it very easy on the eye in summer months. The house is decorated in keeping with the age and style of the property and has a very homely feel. A warm welcome and hearty breakfast are assured here.

**Rooms:** 4 en suite 2 annexe en suite (1 GF) **S** £55; **D** £75* **Facilities:** FTV TVL tea/coffee WiFi Fishing **Extras:** Snacks **Parking:** 20 **Notes:** No children 10yrs

---

## Corner Cottage

★★★ BED AND BREAKFAST

---

**tel:** 01527 459122 & 07917 582884 **1194 Evesham Road B96 6AA**
**email:** marilyn_alan1194@hotmail.co.uk **web:** www.corner-cottagebb.co.uk
**dir:** *A441 through Astwood Bank, Corner Cottage at lights*

A warm welcome awaits you at Corner Cottage, a beautiful Victorian cottage set in a delightful village location within walking distance of pubs, shops and restaurants. Convenient for Stratford-upon-Avon, Evesham, Warwick, Birmingham and Worcester.

**Rooms:** 4 rms (3 en suite) (1 pri facs) **S** £45; **D** £65* **Facilities:** FTV TVL tea/coffee WiFi ⛔ **Notes:** LB

---

### Premier Collection

## Kateshill House

★★★★★ ⬤ GUEST ACCOMMODATION

---

**tel:** 01299 401563 **Red Hill DY12 2DR**
**email:** info@kateshillhouse.co.uk **web:** www.kateshillhouse.co.uk
**dir:** *A456 onto B4195 signed Bewdley. Bear left over bridge, 1st left into Severnside South. Right into Lax Ln, at T-junct turn left, up hill on right*

A very warm welcome awaits at Kateshill House, a Georgian manor house overlooking Bewdley. Two acres of landscaped gardens provide a dramatic backdrop to the house, as well as fruit for breakfasts and home-made jams. The elegant bedrooms are individually styled, sumptuously decorated with rich fabrics and period furniture, and equipped with a wealth of amenities for guests' use. Small private functions are also catered for. Kateshill House was the AA Guest Accommodation of the Year for England 2016-2017.

**Rooms:** 7 en suite **S** £75–£85; **D** £95–£105 **Facilities:** FTV Lounge TVL tea/coffee Licensed WiFi ⛔ **Parking:** 10 **Notes:** LB

## The Mug House Inn

★★★★ ⬤ INN

---

**tel:** 01299 402543 **12 Severnside North DY12 2EE**
**email:** drew@mughousebewdley.co.uk **web:** www.mughousebewdley.co.uk
**dir:** *In town centre on riverfront*

Located on the opposite side of the River Severn to Bewdley Rowing Club, this 18th-century inn combines high standards of comfort and facilities with many original features. Bedrooms are thoughtfully furnished, there is a separate breakfast room, and imaginative dinners are served in the restaurant.

**Rooms:** 4 en suite 3 annexe en suite (1 GF) **S** £70–£120; **D** £80–£120*
**Facilities:** FTV tea/coffee Dinner available WiFi **Notes:** No children 10yrs

## Royal Forester Country Inn

★★★★ ⬤ INN

---

**tel:** 01299 266286 **Callow Hill DY14 9XW**
**email:** royalforesterinn@btinternet.com **web:** www.royalforesterinn.co.uk

Located opposite the Wyre Forest on the town's outskirts, this inn dates back to 1411 and has been sympathetically restored to provide high standards of comfort. Stylish modern bedrooms are complemented by smart bathrooms, and equipped with many thoughtful extras. Decor styles throughout the public areas highlight the many period features, and the restaurant serves imaginative food featuring locally sourced produce.

**Rooms:** 7 en suite (2 fmly) **Facilities:** STV FTV TVL tea/coffee Dinner available WiFi **Parking:** 40 **Notes:** LB

## Welchgate Guest House

★★★★ GUEST HOUSE

---

**tel:** 01299 402655 **1 Welch Gate DY12 2AT**
**email:** info@welchgate-guesthouse.co.uk **web:** www.welchgate-guesthouse.co.uk

Welchgate Guest House is a 400-year-old former inn providing modern comfort and good facilities. Bedrooms are equipped with fine furnishings and thoughtful extras, and have smart, modern en suite shower rooms. Hearty breakfasts are taken in a rustic-look café, which is also open to the public during the day.

**Rooms:** 4 en suite **S** £35–£50; **D** £70–£90 (room only)* **Facilities:** tea/coffee Licensed WiFi ⛔ **Notes:** LB No children

## Bank House

★★★ BED AND BREAKFAST

---

**tel:** 01299 402652 **14 Lower Park DY12 2DP**
**email:** fleur.nightingale@virgin.net **web:** www.bewdley-accommodation.co.uk
**dir:** *In town centre. From junct High St & Lax Ln, Bank House after junct on left*

Once a private bank, this Victorian house retains many original features and offers comfortable accommodation. The cosy dining room is the setting for tasty English breakfasts served at one family table. Owner Mrs Nightingale has a comprehensive knowledge of the town and its history.

**Rooms:** 4 rms **S** £37–£40; **D** £62–£65* **Facilities:** FTV tea/coffee WiFi ⛔ **Parking:** 2 **Notes:** Closed 24–26 Dec

## BROADWAY
Map 10 SP03

### Abbots Grange
★★★★★ ♨ GUEST HOUSE

**tel:** 020 8133 8698 **Church Street WR12 7AE**
**email:** rooms@abbotsgrange.com **web:** www.abbotsgrange.com
**dir:** M5 junct 9 follow signs to Evesham & Broadway

A warm welcome awaits at Abbots Grange, a 14th-century monastic manor house believed to be the oldest dwelling in Broadway. A Grade II listed building, it stands in eight acres of grounds. The bedrooms are luxurious and comprise twin and four-poster suites. Among the thoughtful extras in the rooms are fruit bowls and a selection of alcoholic drinks. The stunning medieval Great Hall is the guests' lounge and makes a romantic setting with its log fire and candles. Tea and cake is offered on arrival, and quality breakfasts are served at the large communal table in the wood-panelled dining room. Abbots Grange has a tennis court and croquet lawn along with a helicopter landing pad.

**Rooms:** 6 rms (5 en suite) (1 pri facs) **Facilities:** STV FTV DVD iPod docking station Lounge tea/coffee WiFi ♨ ⚘ ⚘ **Extras:** Port, whisky, sherry, soft drinks, mineral water **Conf:** Max 12 Board 12 **Parking:** 10 **Notes:** No children 6yrs

### Mill Hay House
★★★★★ ♨ GUEST ACCOMMODATION

**tel:** 01386 852498 **Snowshill Road WR12 7JS**
**email:** info@millhay.co.uk **web:** www.millhay.co.uk
**dir:** 0.7m S of Broadway towards Snowshill, house on right

Set in three acres of immaculate grounds beside a medieval watermill, this impressive early 18th-century stone house has many original features complemented by quality decor, period furniture and works of art. The spacious bedrooms are filled with thoughtful extras and one has a balcony. Imaginative breakfasts are served in the elegant dining room, and there is a spacious drawing room.

**Rooms:** 3 en suite **S** £175–£235; **D** £195–£255 **Facilities:** FTV Lounge tea/coffee Direct dial WiFi ⚘ **Extras:** Mineral water – complimentary **Parking:** 10 **Notes:** LB No children 12yrs

### Russell's
★★★★★ ◎◎ ♨ RESTAURANT WITH ROOMS

**tel:** 01386 853555 **20 High Street WR12 7DT**
**email:** info@russellsofbroadway.co.uk **web:** www.russellsofbroadway.co.uk
**dir:** Opposite village green

Situated in the centre of picturesque Broadway, this restaurant with rooms makes a great base for exploring local attractions. The superbly appointed bedrooms, each with its own character, have air conditioning and a wide range of extras. The cuisine is a real draw here with skilful use made of freshly-prepared, local produce.

**Rooms:** 4 en suite 3 annexe en suite (4 fmly) (2 GF) **S** £130–£300; **D** £130–£300* **Facilities:** FTV DVD tea/coffee Dinner available Direct dial WiFi **Extras:** Honesty bar **Conf:** Max 12 Board 12 **Parking:** 7

## BROMSGROVE
Map 10 SO97

### The Vernon
★★★★ INN

**tel:** 01527 821236 **Droitwich Road, Hanbury B60 4DB**
**email:** info@thevernonhanbury.co.uk **web:** www.thevernonhanbury.co.uk
**dir:** M5 junct 5, A38 to Droitwich. Turn left into Bromsgrove Rd (B4065). Left into Hanbury Rd (B4090), opposite junction

Situated in the rural parish of Hanbury close to Bromsgrove and Droitwich, this 18th-century inn is sometimes known as the 'Birthplace of The Archers', because Godfrey Baseley, the original creator of the famous soap, was a regular. The inn boasts modern and comfortable accommodation, and fine dining can be enjoyed in the attractive restaurant.

**Rooms:** 5 en suite **S** £65; **D** £85–£105* **Facilities:** STV FTV Lounge TVL tea/coffee Dinner available Direct dial WiFi **Parking:** 74

## FLYFORD FLAVELL

Map 10 SO95

# The Boot Inn

★★★★ 🍴 INN

tel: 01386 462658 **Radford Road WR7 4BS**
email: enquiries@thebootinn.com **web:** www.thebootinn.com
dir: *In village centre, signed from A422*

An inn has occupied this site since the 13th century, though The Boot itself dates from the Georgian period. Much historic charm remains in the pub, while the bedrooms, furnished in antique pine, are equipped with practical extras and have modern bathrooms. A range of ales, wines and imaginative food is offered in the cosy public areas, which include an attractive conservatory and patio.

**Rooms:** 5 annexe en suite (2 GF) **S** £65–£85; **D** £75–£95 **Facilities:** FTV DVD iPod docking station Lounge tea/coffee Dinner available WiFi ♨27 Pool table **Parking:** 30 **Notes:** LB

## HIMBLETON

Map 10 SO95

# Phepson Farm

★★★★ 🍴 FARMHOUSE

tel: 01905 391205 **WR9 7JZ**
email: info@phepsonfarm.co.uk **web:** www.phepsonfarm.co.uk
dir: *M5 junct 5 onto A38 (Droitwich). Left at 1st lights, left at next lights onto B4090. After 2m right to Himbleton. Phepson Farm 2m on right*

Set in 50 acres of peaceful Worcestershire countryside, Phepson Farm has a one and a half acre coarse fishing lake. The family farm is run in an eco-friendly manner and guests are welcome to walk the wildlife route. There are four individually styled bedrooms; two large rooms are in the main farmhouse, and

two are in the converted stables that have their own entrances. Award-winning breakfasts include asparagus in season, damsons and plums from the farm, and locally sourced sausages and bacon. There are also three self-catering cottages on site.

**Rooms:** 2 en suite 2 annexe en suite (2 GF) **S** £55–£60; **D** £80–£85* **Facilities:** FTV TVL tea/coffee WiFi Fishing **Extras:** Bottled water **Parking:** 4 **Notes:** LB No children Closed Xmas & New Year 50 acres beef

## KEMPSEY

Map 10 SO84

# Walter de Cantelupe Inn

★★★ INN

tel: 01905 820572 **Main Road WR5 3NA**
email: info@walterdecantelupe.co.uk **web:** www.walterdecantelupe.co.uk
dir: *On A38 in village centre*

This inn provides cosy bedrooms with smart bathrooms, and is convenient for the M5 and Worcester. The intimate, open-plan public areas are the setting for a range of real ales, and imaginative food featuring local produce and a fine selection of British cheeses.

**Rooms:** 3 en suite **Facilities:** FTV DVD iPod docking station Lounge tea/coffee Dinner available WiFi **Parking:** 24 **Notes:** LB

## MALVERN

Map 10 SO74

# Ashbury Bed & Breakfast

★★★★ BED AND BREAKFAST

tel: 01684 574225 **Ashbury, Old Hollow WR14 4NP**
email: ashburybandb@btinternet.com **web:** www.ashburybedandbreakfast.co.uk
dir: *A449 onto B4053, 2nd left into Hornyold Rd. Right at T-junct into Cowleigh Rd, 250yds on left*

A warm and friendly welcome awaits you from Karen and Graham at Ashbury Bed & Breakfast. This beautiful and grand Victorian property offers modern, comfortable and stylish bedrooms; the many period features that have been retained add to the overall charm of the house. An enjoyable breakfast made with all fresh ingredients can be enjoyed with views across the Malvern countryside. This is a good location for those wishing to go walking in the Malvern area. Free WiFi is available. Ashbury B&B was a finalist for the AA Friendliest B&B of the Year award 2017–18.

**Rooms:** 3 en suite (2 GF) **S** £59–£125; **D** £79–£125* **Facilities:** FTV tea/coffee WiFi 🔒 **Extras:** Home-made biscuits, speciality toiletries – complimentary **Conf:** Max 10 Board 10 **Parking:** 4 **Notes:** LB No children 12yrs

# Cowleigh Park Farm

★★★★ 🍴 BED AND BREAKFAST

tel: 01684 566750 & 07954 121570 **Cowleigh Road WR13 5HJ**
email: info@cowleighparkfarm.co.uk **web:** www.cowleighparkfarm.co.uk
dir: *From A449 onto B4219 signed Bromyard. Take 1st right to stay on B4219 (Cowleigh Rd), driveway 0.5m on right*

A warm welcome is assured at this 400 year old timber-framed former farmhouse peacefully set in attractive and deceptively large gardens below The Malvern Hills. Carefully modernised over hundreds of years this property blends modern day comforts with period features in abundance. Comfortably furnished en suites are complemented by a large sitting room with wood-burning stove. Home-cooked breakfasts are served in the attractive dining room and make for an excellent start to the day ahead.

**Rooms:** 3 en suite **S** £60–£65; **D** £85–£95* **Facilities:** FTV DVD Lounge tea/coffee WiFi 🔒 **Parking:** 8

## The Dell House

★★★★ BED AND BREAKFAST

tel: 01684 564448 2 Green Lane WR14 4HU
email: stay@thedellhouse.co.uk web: www.thedellhouse.co.uk

This former rectory dates back to the 1820s and is quietly located in its own large garden. Retaining many original features, rooms are thoughtfully furnished and provide good levels of comfort with suitable extras, and each bedroom benefits from countryside views. The breakfast menu features a number of vegetarian options. This is a good location for those wishing to go walking in the Malverns, or to attend events at the Three Counties Showground.

Rooms: 4 en suite S £60–£75; D £85–£120* Facilities: Lounge TVL tea/coffee WiFi
🔒 Conf: Max 10 Thtr 10 Class 8 Board 8 Parking: 4 Notes: LB

## Wyche Inn

★★★★ INN

tel: 01684 575396 74 Wyche Road WR14 4EQ
email: thewycheinn@googlemail.com web: www.thewycheinn.co.uk
dir: 1.5m S of Malvern. On B4218 towards Malvern & Colwall. Off A449 (Worcester to Ross/Ledbury road)

Located in an elevated position on the outskirts of Malvern, this inn is popular with locals and visiting walkers. The thoughtfully furnished bedrooms provide good levels of comfort with suitable guest extras; all bathrooms have a bath and shower. Each bedroom benefits from stunning countryside views. The menus feature home-cooked dishes, including good-value options, and a comprehensive range of real ales is available from the bar.

Rooms: 4 en suite 2 annexe rms (2 pri facs) (1 GF) Facilities: FTV DVD tea/coffee
Dinner available WiFi Pool table Extras: Speciality toiletries, bottled mineral water
Parking: 6 Notes: LB

## Sidney House

★★★ BED AND BREAKFAST

tel: 01684 574994 40 Worcester Road WR14 4AA
email: info@sidneyhouse.co.uk web: www.sidneyhouse.co.uk
dir: On A449, 200yds N from town centre

Believed to have been purpose-built as a guest house in 1823, this Grade II listed property has a long history of welcoming visitors to Great Malvern. This tradition is continued today by Alexandra and Anthony, whose warm welcome is assured. Situated within easy walking distance of local attractions and restaurants, and within easy reach of the Malvern Hills, the property boasts enviable views across the Severn Vale and beyond. En suite rooms are comfortably furnished with a guest lounge, on-site parking and complimentary WiFi all provided.

Rooms: 6 en suite S £60–£65; D £75–£90* Facilities: FTV TVL tea/coffee Licensed
WiFi Discounts at local beauty salon Extras: Speciality toiletries, home-made brownies, cake Parking: 8 Notes: LB No children 16yrs

## The Pembridge

★★★ GUEST ACCOMMODATION

tel: 01684 574813 114 Graham Road WR14 2HX
email: info@thepembridge.co.uk web: www.thepembridge.co.uk
dir: From A449 into Church St, 1st left

Located on a leafy residential road close to the town centre, this large Victorian house retains many original features, including a superb staircase. Bedrooms are well equipped. Other areas include a comfortable sitting room and an elegant dining room.

Rooms: 7 en suite (1 fmly) S £48–£53; D £64–£69* Facilities: FTV TVL tea/coffee
Direct dial WiFi 🔒 Parking: 9 Notes: LB No children 7yrs RS 25–26 Dec No cooked
English breakfast

## Portocks End House

★★★ BED AND BREAKFAST

tel: 01684 310276 Little Clevelode WR13 6PE
email: email@portocksendbandb.co.uk web: www.portocksendbandb.co.uk
dir: On D4424, 4m N of Upton upon Severn, opposite Riverside Caravan Park

Peacefully located, yet convenient for the showground and major road links, this period house retains many original features; the traditional furnishings and decor highlight its intrinsic charm. The bedrooms are equipped with lots of thoughtful extras, and breakfasts are taken in a cosy dining room overlooking the garden.

Rooms: 3 rms (1 en suite) (2 pri facs) (1 fmly) S £35–£40; D £60–£65*
Facilities: Lounge tea/coffee WiFi 🔒 Extras: Speciality toiletries – complimentary
Parking: 4 Notes: Closed Dec–Feb

<table>
<tr><td>■ PERSHORE</td><td>Map 10 SO94</td></tr>
</table>

## Evesham Lodge Bed & Breakfast

★★★★ 🍴 BED AND BREAKFAST

tel: 01386 710285 & 07816 203960 Evesham Lodge, Bricklehampton WR10 3HQ
email: kerry@eveshamlodge.co.uk web: www.eveshamlodge.co.uk
dir: B4084 Pershore to Evesham road, exit signed Bricklehampton. At T-junct turn right, through village, road bears right, 2nd on right

Located in the Vale of Evesham and within easy reach of The Cotswolds, the historic city of Worcester and the Malvern Hills, this former gate house offers the best of both worlds; easily accessible from the motorway, yet peacefully nestled on the edge of the 30 acre Bricklehampton Hall estate. Both en suite rooms are very well appointed, one features a Juliet balcony with views across the garden and parkland beyond. A freshly cooked breakfast using free-range eggs and local produce is served in the dining room overlooking the garden.

Rooms: 2 en suite S £60–£70; D £75–£85* Facilities: FTV DVD Lounge tea/coffee
WiFi 🔒 Extras: Speciality toiletries, fridge, home-made biscuits Parking: 2 Notes: LB

| UPTON UPON SEVERN | Map 10 SO84 |

## The Swan

★★★★ INN

**tel:** 01684 594948 & 07501 223754 **Waterside WR8 0JD**
**email:** info@theswanhotelupton.co.uk **web:** www.theswanhotelupton.co.uk

Set in the historic riverside town of Upton upon Severn this 400-year-old inn offers plenty of charm and quirkiness. The bedrooms provide good comfort and practicality and are modern in design, with some having views of the river. Enjoy good quality bar meals and cask conditioned ales in the waterside bar. A separate restaurant is also available for functions.

**Rooms:** 6 en suite **S** £57.50–£97.50; **D** £75–£115* **Facilities:** FTV tea/coffee Dinner available Direct dial WiFi 🛏 **Extras:** Slippers

## The Star Inn

★★★ INN

**tel:** 01684 593432 & 07721 594001 **3 High Street WR8 0HQ**
**email:** info@richmondhillbreweries.co.uk **web:** www.thestarinnupton.co.uk
**dir:** *M5 junct 8 onto M50. Exit after 1m at junct 1, signed Malvern (A38). Continue on A38, after 6m left signed Upton & follow signs to town centre*

This charming property is located opposite one of the town's most famous landmarks known locally as 'The Pepperpot'; a copper-clad coppola which is a remnant of a former church that stands on the historic battle site. Run by a husband and wife team, The Star sits back from the riverbank and offers a range of comfortably furnished en suite rooms. There is a large sun terrace to the rear which overlooks the River Severn. Evening meals are served in the traditional dining room to the rear of the property.

**Rooms:** 17 en suite (3 fmly) **Facilities:** FTV DVD TVL tea/coffee Dinner available WiFi

| WORCESTER | Map 10 SO85 |

## Church House Bed & Breakfast

★★★★ FARMHOUSE

**tel:** 01905 452366 & 07909 968938 **Church House, Claines WR3 7RL**
**email:** wr37rl@btinternet.com **web:** www.churchhousebandb.co.uk
**dir:** *M5 junct 6 onto A449, after 3m at rdbt take 1st exit. 1st drive on right before Claines church*

Church House Bed & Breakfast is situated on a working farm in a peaceful area of Worcestershire, within easy reach of the motorway network. This Grade II listed Georgian building offers relaxing and comfortable accommodation. Each bedroom is en suite, with WiFi and large screen TVs. The comfortable beds offer a good night's sleep, and the enjoyable breakfast, with home-made produce from the farm, will provide a good start for the day.

**Rooms:** 2 en suite **Facilities:** FTV tea/coffee WiFi Fishing 🛏 **Extras:** Home-made biscuits – complimentary **Parking:** 10 **Notes:** No children 12yrs 600 acres mixed

## Wyatt Guest House

★★★★ GUEST HOUSE

**tel:** 01905 26311 **40 Barbourne Road WR1 1HU**
**email:** info@wyattguest.co.uk **web:** www.wyattguest.co.uk
**dir:** *On A38 0.5m N from city centre*

Located within easy walking distance of shops, restaurants and central attractions, this lovely Victorian house provides a range of thoughtfully furnished bedrooms. Breakfast is served in an attractive dining room, a warm welcome is assured, and the attractive frontage is a regular winner in Worcester's 'Britain in Bloom' competition.

**Rooms:** 8 rms (7 en suite) (1 fmly) (1 GF) **S** £50; **D** £75 **Facilities:** FTV DVD Lounge tea/coffee WiFi

| EAST RIDING OF YORKSHIRE |

| BEVERLEY | Map 17 TA03 |

| Premier Collection |

## Newbegin House

★★★★★ 🍴 BED AND BREAKFAST

**tel:** 01482 888880 **10 Newbegin HU17 8EG**
**email:** wsweeney@wsweeney.karoo.co.uk **web:** www.newbeginhousebbbeverley.co.uk
**dir:** *At end of M62 onto B1230 signed North Cave. Through North Cave & Walkington. Left at mini rdbt, 1st left at at next mini rdbt into Admiral Walker Rd. 5th right into Newbegin. House on left*

Newbegin House is a delightful Georgian manor house located on a quiet one way street in the centre of this historic market town. It is an impressive family home, very spacious and with many original period features and a homely, inviting feel. Excellent breakfasts are served in the grand dining room. The walled garden is also available for guests to enjoy and private parking is provided.

**Rooms:** 3 en suite (1 fmly) **Facilities:** FTV DVD iPod docking station TVL tea/coffee WiFi 🛏 **Conf:** Max 30 Thtr 30 Class 20 Board 12 **Parking:** 3 **Notes:** LB RS Closed owners' annual holiday

## Trinity Guest House

★★★★ GUEST HOUSE

**tel:** 01482 869537 **Trinity Lane, Station Square HU17 0AR**
**email:** trinity_house@hotmail.com **web:** www.trinityguesthouse.com
**dir:** *Opposite railway station*

This well presented Victorian town house is located next to the train station in the historic town centre. Guests simply need to cross the quiet street if they arrive by train. There is a convenient public car park opposite the house or permits are available for on-street parking. The house combines traditional and modern decor with a comfortable lounge also provided. WiFi access is also available. A secluded, walled garden provides additional space for guests to relax in warmer weather.

**Rooms:** 6 en suite (2 fmly) **S** £47–£54; **D** £67–£75* **Facilities:** FTV DVD TVL tea/coffee WiFi 🛏

## BRIDLINGTON                                      Map 17 TA16

### Premier Collection

## Marton Grange

★★★★★ GUEST ACCOMMODATION

tel: 01262 602034 & 07708 211071
**Flamborough Road, Marton cum Sewerby YO15 1DU**
email: info@marton-grange.co.uk web: www.martongrange.co.uk
*dir: 2m NE of Bridlington. On B1255, 600yds W of Links golf club*

This Grade II listed former farmhouse is set in well-maintained gardens and offers high levels of comfort, service and hospitality. Bedrooms are well appointed with quality fixtures and fittings and public areas offer wonderful views of the gardens. Thoughtful extras, provided as standard, help create a delightful guest experience.

**Rooms:** 11 en suite (3 GF) **S** £60–£90; **D** £80–£105* **Facilities:** FTV iPod docking station Lounge tea/coffee Lift Licensed WiFi ℄18 ⚓ **Extras:** Home-made shortbread, speciality toiletries, cream tea on arrival – complimentary **Parking:** 11 **Notes:** LB RS Jan–Feb restricted opening for refurbishments

## The Royal Bridlington

★★★★ GUEST ACCOMMODATION

tel: 01262 672433 **1 Shaftesbury Road YO15 3NP**
email: info@royalhotelbrid.co.uk web: www.royalhotelbrid.co.uk
*dir: A615 N to Bridlington (Kingsgate), right into Shaftesbury Rd*

Just off the promenade, this immaculate property has a range of thoughtfully furnished bedrooms with smart modern bathrooms. The spacious public areas include a large dining room, conservatory-sitting room, and a cosy TV lounge. Freshly-cooked dinners are a feature and a warm welcome is assured.

**Rooms:** 14 rms (13 en suite) (1 pri facs) 4 annexe en suite (7 fmly) (4 GF) **S** £41–£52; **D** £72–£84* **Facilities:** FTV DVD Lounge TVL tea/coffee Dinner available Licensed WiFi ℄18 ⚓ **Conf:** Max 85 Thtr 85 Class 20 Board 40 **Parking:** 7 **Notes:** LB No children 12yrs

## The Brockton

★★★★ GUEST ACCOMMODATION

tel: 01262 673967 & 401771 **4 Shaftesbury Road YO15 3NP**
email: brocktonhotel@yahoo.co.uk web: www.brockton-bridlington.co.uk
*dir: Off A167 coast road, right at golf course, through lights, 2nd on left*

Located close to the seafront, this family-run property offers comfortable bedrooms, some with sea views, and all with en suite shower rooms. A lounge and bar area is available, and dinner and breakfast are served in the dining room.

**Rooms:** 10 en suite (2 fmly) (2 GF) **Facilities:** FTV DVD Lounge TVL tea/coffee Dinner available Licensed WiFi ℄18 ⚓ **Conf:** Max 20 **Parking:** 10 **Notes:** LB

## Rosebery House

★★★★ GUEST HOUSE

tel: 01262 670336 **1 Belle Vue YO15 2ET**
email: info@rosebery-house.com web: www.rosebery-house.com
*dir: From B1254 (Promenade) into Tennyson Ave, Belle Vue on left*

This beautiful, quietly positioned Grade II listed Georgian house is only 100 metres from the seafront and promenade. The harbour is only a few minutes' walk and within five to 10 minutes guests can walk to a wide range of shops, restaurants and cafés or explore the historic Old Town. Private parking, parking permits and secure cycle storage are all provided as well as free WiFi access. Bedrooms are comfortable and the front rooms have views of the garden, public gardens and the sea beyond.

**Rooms:** 7 en suite **D** £62–£75* **Facilities:** FTV TVL tea/coffee WiFi ⚓ **Parking:** 6 **Notes:** No children 5yrs Closed Nov–Feb

## HUGGATE                                          Map 19 SE85

## The Wolds Inn

★★★ 🍴 INN

tel: 01377 288217 **Driffield Road YO42 1YH**
email: woldsinn@gmail.com web: www.woldsinn.co.uk
*dir: Huggate signed off A166 & brown signs to Wolds Inn*

At the end of the highest village in the Yorkshire Wolds, midway between York and the coast, this ancient inn is a rural haven beside the Wolds Way walk. Substantial meals are served in the dining room and a good range of well-kept beers is available in the bar. Bedrooms, varying in size, are well equipped and comfortable.

**Rooms:** 3 en suite **S** £53; **D** £81* **Facilities:** FTV tea/coffee Dinner available WiFi ⚓ **Extras:** Bottled water – complimentary **Parking:** 30

## SOUTH DALTON                                     Map 17 SE94

### Premier Collection

## The Pipe and Glass Inn

★★★★★  🍴 INN

tel: 01430 810246 **West End HU17 7PN**
email: email@pipeandglass.co.uk web: www.pipeandglass.co.uk

The former coaching inn stands on the site of the original gatehouse to Dalton Park on the beautiful Dalton Estate, with parts of the current building dating back to the 17th century. After an initial major refurbishment in 2006, James and Kate have updated the premises regularly, including an exclusive private dining suite. Three new accommodation rooms and a kitchen garden were added as part of an ambitious garden redesign. The restaurant is more contemporary in style and the conservatory looks out over the garden. James sources top-notch local and seasonal produce for a range of modern British menus.

**Rooms:** 5 annexe en suite (5 GF) **Facilities:** FTV DVD iPod docking station Lounge tea/coffee Dinner available Direct dial WiFi **Parking:** 60 **Notes:** Closed 2 weeks Jan RS Mon closed (ex BHs)

## WILLERBY
Map 17 TA03

### Innkeeper's Lodge Hull, Willerby

★★★ INN

**tel:** 08451 551551 *(Calls cost 2p per minute plus your phone company's access charge)*
**Beverley Road HU10 6NT**
**email:** info@innkeeperslodge.com **web:** www.innkeeperslodge.com

Conveniently located for the city centre which is just five minutes away and also close to the M62 and the Humber Bridge. Bedrooms are modern and offer good space and comfort. There is a Toby Carvery pub on site where guests can enjoy a wide range of drinks and food, including fresh roast dinners. Complimentary WiFi is provided and there is also on-site parking.

**Rooms:** 32 en suite (12 fmly) (8 GF) **Facilities:** FTV tea/coffee Dinner available WiFi
**Parking:** 70

## NORTH YORKSHIRE

## ALLERSTON
Map 19 SE88

### Rains Farm Holidays

★★★★ FARMHOUSE

**tel:** 01723 859333 **YO18 7PQ**
**email:** rainsholidays@btconnect.com **web:** www.rains-farm-holidays.co.uk
**dir:** *1.5m S of A170 Pickering to Scarborough road, through village, 1m on right between Allerston & Yedingham*

A warm welcome awaits you at Rains Farm Holidays situated a short drive from the popular town of Pickering. Bedrooms and bathrooms are comfortably appointed. A lounge area is available as well as a modern kitchen for guest use. Delicious hearty cooked breakfasts are served at a communal dining table. Gardens are an attractive feature with outdoor seating available in the summer months. Car parking is generous.

**Rooms:** 3 en suite (1 GF) **S** fr £60; **D** fr £90* **Facilities:** FTV TVL tea/coffee WiFi
**Extras:** Use of kitchen **Parking:** 6 **Notes:** LB No children 12yrs Closed Xmas & New Year 7 acres non-working

## AMPLEFORTH
Map 19 SE57

### Premier Collection

### Shallowdale House

★★★★★ ⬒ ⬚ GUEST ACCOMMODATION

**tel:** 01439 788325 **West End YO62 4DY**
**email:** stay@shallowdalehouse.co.uk **web:** www.shallowdalehouse.co.uk
**dir:** *Off A170 at W end of village, on turn to Hambleton*

An outstanding example of an architect-designed 1960s house, Shallowdale lies in two acres of hillside gardens. There are stunning views from every room, and the elegant public rooms include a choice of lounges. Spacious bedrooms blend traditional and 1960s style with many home comforts. Expect excellent service and genuine hospitality from Anton and Phillip. The very imaginative, freshly cooked dinners are not to be missed.

**Rooms:** 3 rms (2 en suite) (1 pri facs) **S** £105–£130; **D** £125–£160*
**Facilities:** FTV Lounge tea/coffee Dinner available Licensed WiFi ⬚
**Extras:** Speciality toiletries – complimentary **Parking:** 3 **Notes:** No children 12yrs Closed Xmas & New Year

## ARKENGARTHDALE
Map 18 NY90

### Charles Bathurst Inn

★★★★ ⬡ ⬚ INN

**tel:** 01748 884567 **DL11 6EN**
**email:** info@cbinn.co.uk **web:** www.cbinn.co.uk
**dir:** *B6270 to Reeth, at Buck Hotel turn N to Langthwaite, pass church on right, inn 0.5m on right*

The CB Inn, as it is known to locals, is surrounded by magnificent scenery high in the Dales. Food is the focus of the pub, where a choice of rustic eating areas makes for atmospheric dining. The well-equipped bedrooms blend contemporary and traditional styles, and cosy lounge areas are available. A function suite is also available.

**Rooms:** 19 en suite (3 fmly) (5 GF) **Facilities:** Lounge tea/coffee Dinner available Direct dial WiFi Fishing Pool table ⬚ **Extras:** Speciality toiletries, home-made shortbread **Conf:** Max 70 Thtr 70 Class 30 Board 30 **Parking:** 35 **Notes:** LB Closed 25 Dec Civ wed 70

| ASENBY | Map 19 SE37 |
| --- | --- |

## Crab Manor

★★★★★  RESTAURANT WITH ROOMS

**tel:** 01845 577286 **Dishforth Road YO7 3QL**
**web:** www.crabandlobster.co.uk
**dir:** A1(M) junct 49, on outskirts of village

This stunning 18th-century Grade II listed Georgian manor is located in the heart of the North Yorkshire Dales. Each bedroom is themed around the world's most famous hotels and has high-quality furnishings, beautiful wallpaper, and thoughtful extras. Scandinavian log cabins are also available in the grounds, which have their own terrace with hot tubs. There is a comfortable lounge bar where guests can relax in the Manor before enjoying dinner next door in the Crab & Lobster Restaurant, which specialises in fresh local seafood. The attractive gardens offer a lovely backdrop.

**Rooms:** 8 en suite 12 annexe en suite (3 fmly) **Facilities:** FTV iPod docking station Lounge tea/coffee Dinner available Direct dial WiFi **Conf:** Max 16 Board 16 **Parking:** 90 **Notes:** Civ wed 105

| AUSTWICK | Map 18 SD76 |
| --- | --- |

## The Traddock

★★★★★  RESTAURANT WITH ROOMS

**tel:** 015242 51224 **Settle LA2 8BY**
**email:** info@thetraddock.co.uk **web:** www.thetraddock.co.uk
**dir:** From Skipton take A65 towards Kendal, 3m after Settle turn right signed Austwick, cross hump back bridge, 100yds on left

Situated within the Yorkshire Dales National Park and a peaceful village environment, this fine Georgian country house with well-tended gardens offers a haven of calm and good hospitality. There are two comfortable lounges with real fires and fine furnishings, as well as a cosy bar and an elegant dining room serving fine cuisine. Bedrooms are individually styled with many homely touches.

**Rooms:** 12 en suite (2 fmly) (1 GF) **D** £95–£240* **Facilities:** FTV DVD Lounge tea/coffee Dinner available Direct dial WiFi 18 **Extras:** Speciality toiletries, fruit, home-made biscuits, bottled water – complimentary **Conf:** Max 24 Thtr 24 Class 16 Board 16 **Parking:** 20 **Notes:** LB

| AYSGARTH | Map 19 SE08 |
| --- | --- |

## The Aysgarth Falls

★★★★ INN

**tel:** 01969 663775 **DL8 3SR**
**email:** info@aysgarthfallshotel.com **web:** www.aysgarthfallshotel.com
**dir:** On A684 between Leyburn & Hawes

A friendly, high-quality inn, perfect for exploring the Yorkshire Dales, and the grounds lead down to Aysgarth Falls. Excellent meals are served throughout the bar and dining areas, and also on the outdoor terraces in warmer weather. Bedrooms are contemporary, featuring comfortable beds, TVs and luxurious en suites. Residents also have use of a drying room for waterproofs and boots.

**Rooms:** 11 en suite 2 annexe en suite (2 fmly) (2 GF) **D** £90–£120* **Facilities:** FTV DVD tea/coffee Dinner available WiFi **Conf:** Max 40 Thtr 40 Board 16 **Parking:** 30

| BAINBRIDGE | Map 18 SD99 |
| --- | --- |

## Yorebridge House

★★★★★ RESTAURANT WITH ROOMS

**tel:** 01969 652060 **DL8 3EE**
**email:** enquiries@yorebridgehouse.co.uk **web:** www.yorebridgehouse.co.uk
**dir:** A648 to Bainbridge. Yorebridge House N of centre on right before river

Yorebridge House is situated by the river on the edge of Bainbridge, in the heart of the North Yorkshire Dales. In the Victorian era this was a schoolmaster's house and school, the building now offers luxury boutique-style accommodation. Each bedroom is individually designed with high-quality furnishings and thoughtful extras. All rooms have stunning views of the Dales and some have their own terrace with hot tub. There is a comfortable lounge bar where guests can relax before enjoying an excellent, three AA Rosette award-winning dinner in the attractive and elegant dining room.

**Rooms:** 7 en suite 4 annexe en suite (11 fmly) (5 GF) **Facilities:** STV FTV DVD iPod docking station Lounge tea/coffee Dinner available Direct dial WiFi Fishing **Extras:** Speciality toiletries **Conf:** Max 70 Thtr 70 Class 60 Board 30 **Parking:** 30 **Notes:** LB Civ wed 100

## BIRSTWITH　　　　　　　　　Map 19 SE25

# The Station Hotel

★★★★ ◉ 🍷 INN

tel: 01423 770254 **Station Road HG3 3AG**
email: admin@station-hotel.net **web:** www.station-hotel.net
dir: *A59 Harrogate to Skipton road, turn into Chain Bar Ln, signed Hampsthwaite. At T-junct left into Hollins Ln, in 1m at next T-junct right into Hampsthwaite High St. 1.6m to Birstwith, right into Wreaks Rd. 0.5m on left*

The Station Hotel is a family-owned country inn in the village of Birstwith, on the edge of Nidderdale, which means stunning scenery and great walks right on the doorstep. The restaurant serves food daily and vegetarians are well catered for. There are four bedrooms on the first floor of the main pub building and there is also a ground floor room in a separate annexe. All rooms are furnished with traditional oak furniture and comfortable beds. There are also useful facilities such as tea- and coffee-making facilities, alarm clocks, free internet access and Freesat TVs. On-site parking and a hearty Yorkshire breakfast are included in the price.

**Rooms:** 4 en suite 1 annexe en suite (1 fmly) (1 GF) **S** £80–£110; **D** £100–£120
**Facilities:** STV FTV iPod docking station tea/coffee Dinner available WiFi 🅿
**Parking:** 25

## BOLTON ABBEY　　　　　　　　Map 19 SE05

# Howgill Lodge

★★★★ GUEST ACCOMMODATION

tel: 01756 720655 **Barden BD23 6DJ**
email: info@howgill-lodge.co.uk **web:** www.howgill-lodge.co.uk
dir: *B6160 from Bolton Abbey signed Burnsall, 3m right at Barden Tower signed Appletreewick, Howgill Lodge 1.25m on right at phone box*

In an idyllic position high above the valley, this converted stone granary provides a quality get-away. The stylish bedrooms provide a host of thoughtful touches and are designed to feature original stone walls, flagstone floors and timber beams. All of the rooms boast spectacular, memorable views. Breakfasts make excellent use of fresh local ingredients.

**Rooms:** 4 en suite (1 fmly) (4 GF) **S** £70–£85; **D** £85* **Facilities:** FTV tea/coffee
**Extras:** Fridge **Parking:** 6 **Notes:** LB Closed Nov & 24–26 Dec

## BOROUGHBRIDGE　　　　　　　Map 19 SE36

# The Crown Inn

★★★★ ◉◉ 🍷 RESTAURANT WITH ROOMS

tel: 01423 322300 **Roecliffe YO51 9LY**
email: info@crowninnroecliffe.co.uk **web:** www.crowninnroecliffe.co.uk
dir: *A1(M) junct 48, follow signs for Boroughbridge. At rdbt exit towards Roecliffe & brown tourist signs*

The Crown is a 16th-century coaching inn providing an excellent combination of traditional charm and modern comforts. Service is friendly and professional and food is a highlight of any stay. The kitchen team uses the finest of Yorkshire produce from the best local suppliers to create a weekly-changing seasonal menu. Bedrooms are attractively furnished with stylish en suite bathrooms.

**Rooms:** 4 en suite (1 fmly) **S** £80–£90; **D** £90–£120* **Facilities:** FTV DVD tea/coffee Dinner available WiFi 🅿 **Extras:** Sherry, espresso coffee machine, chocolate
**Conf:** Max 100 Thtr 100 Class 60 Board 30 **Parking:** 40 **Notes:** Civ wed 120

## BURNSALL　　　　　　　　　　Map 19 SE06

# The Devonshire Fell

★★★★ ◉ RESTAURANT WITH ROOMS

tel: 01756 729000 & 718111 **BD23 6BT**
email: manager@devonshirefell.co.uk **web:** www.devonshirefell.co.uk
dir: *On B6160, 6m from Bolton Abbey rdbt, A59 junct*

Located on the edge of the attractive village of Burnsall, The Devonshire Fell is colourful, contemporary and quirky. Originally a gentleman's club it enjoys what may be one of the finest locations in the country. A brasserie-style menu is served in the light and airy conservatory restaurant, with views of the Fells and Dales and original modern art work within. Intimate and friendly, The Devonshire Fell is a superb choice for those looking to escape from it all. Expect quality surroundings, home comforts and a friendly, warm welcome.

**Rooms:** 16 en suite (2 fmly) **Facilities:** STV FTV DVD tea/coffee Dinner available Direct dial WiFi 🅿 Fishing 🅿 Free use of spa facilities at sister hotel **Conf:** Max 50 Thtr 50 Class 30 Board 24 **Parking:** 40 **Notes:** LB Civ wed 80

## CLAPHAM　　　　　　　　　　Map 18 SD76

### Premier Collection

# The New Inn

★★★★★ 🍷 ◉ INN

tel: 015242 51203 **The Green LA2 8HH**
email: info@newinn-clapham.co.uk **web:** www.newinn-clapham.co.uk
dir: *From Skipton take A65 towards Kendal. Follow Clapham signs*

The New Inn has been in operation since 1745 and is ideally located in the heart of the conservation village of Clapham, beside Clapham Beck in the Yorkshire Dales National Park. The whole property has been refurbished to a very high standard that is sympathetic to the character of the building and to the environment. Fully en suite, bedrooms cater well for visitors to this lovely and peaceful village. There is a small but comfortable lounge on the first floor and the bars are full of charm and character enhanced with a log-burning stove. The restaurant and menus show imagination and flair, and an extensive and hearty breakfast is served.

**Rooms:** 15 en suite 5 annexe en suite (3 fmly) (2 GF) **S** £90–£115; **D** £115–£155*
**Facilities:** FTV DVD Lounge TVL tea/coffee Dinner available WiFi 🛝18 🅿 Seasonal game shooting **Extras:** Speciality toiletries, bottled water **Conf:** Max 30 Thtr 30 Class 25 Board 25 **Parking:** 40 **Notes:** LB

## Brookhouse Guest House

★★★★ 🍽 GUEST HOUSE

--------------------------------------------------

**tel:** 015242 51580 **Station Road LA2 8ER**
**email:** admin@brookhouseclapham.co.uk **web:** www.brookhouse-clapham.co.uk
**dir:** *Off A65 into village*

Beside the river, in the pretty conservation village of Clapham, this personally run guest house provides comfortable accommodation and warm hospitality. Brookhouse also provides an evening bistro, popular with locals, which offers an interesting selection of home-made meals. Secure storage for cycles is also available.

**Rooms:** 3 rms (2 en suite) (1 pri facs) (1 fmly) **Facilities:** FTV tea/coffee Dinner available Licensed WiFi 🛏 ♨18 **Notes:** LB

| CRAYKE | Map 19 SE57 |

### Premier Collection

## The Durham Ox

★★★★★ 🅰 RESTAURANT WITH ROOMS

--------------------------------------------------

**tel:** 01347 821506 **Westway YO61 4TE**
**email:** enquiries@thedurhamox.com **web:** www.thedurhamox.com
**dir:** *A19 to Easingwold. Through market place to Crayke, 1st left up hill*

The Durham Ox is some 300 years old. The owners pride themselves on offering a friendly and efficient service, plus traditional pub food using only the best local ingredients. The pub has breathtaking views over the Vale of York on three sides, and a charming view up the hill to the medieval church on the other.

Accommodation is mainly in four converted farm cottages. Crayke is in the heart of 'Herriot Country' and less than 20 minutes from York city centre.

*The Durham Ox*

**Rooms:** 1 en suite 5 annexe en suite (1 fmly) (3 GF) **Facilities:** FTV DVD iPod docking station tea/coffee Dinner available WiFi ♨18 ♨ Shooting, fishing, riding by arrangement **Extras:** Speciality toiletries, honesty bar **Conf:** Max 80 Thtr 80 Class 60 Board 30 **Parking:** 35 **Notes:** LB

| DANBY | Map 19 NZ70 |

## Church House Farm

★★★★ FARMHOUSE

--------------------------------------------------

**tel:** 01287 669303 & 07866 743331 **Danby Head YO21 2NH**
**email:** andrewdmorris@yahoo.co.uk **web:** www.churchhousefarmyorkshire.co.uk

Church House Farm is set in the beautiful Danby Dale on a working farm. The en suite accommodation is comfortable and homely with modern accessories such as flat-screen TVs and complimentary WiFi. Freshly cooked breakfasts are served in the spacious ground floor dining room at a communal dining table, which makes for a truly engaging breakfast experience.

**Rooms:** 2 en suite S £64–£69; D £74–£79* **Facilities:** FTV DVD TVL tea/coffee WiFi ♨ **Extras:** Fruit **Parking:** 2 **Notes:** LB No children 85 acres mixed

| EASINGWOLD | Map 19 SE56 |

## George at Easingwold

★★★★ 🍽 INN

--------------------------------------------------

**tel:** 01347 821698 **Market Place YO61 3AD**
**email:** info@the-george-hotel.co.uk **web:** www.the-george-hotel.co.uk
**dir:** *From A19 follow signs for Easingwold. Into Market Place, on right*

The George has a prominent position in the centre of the village and is only a 30-minute ride into York. The inn is very well managed and run by the owners Kay and Michael. Accommodation is comfortable, with modern en suite bathrooms, and public areas are quite spacious. Food is a must here; local produce, good sized portions and all freshly cooked. Hand-pulled beers and a good choice of wines are also available. There is some limited parking.

**Rooms:** 15 en suite (2 fmly) (6 GF) S £69–£85; D £79–£109* **Facilities:** FTV DVD Lounge tea/coffee Dinner available Direct dial WiFi ♨ Complimentary use of adjacent gymnasium **Extras:** Bottled water **Conf:** Max 40 Thtr 40 Class 20 Board 20 **Parking:** 8 **Notes:** LB Closed 24–25 Dec

## ELLERBY
Map 19 NZ71

### Ellerby Residential Country Inn
★★★★ ⊜ INN

**tel:** 01947 840342 **12–14 Ryeland Lane TS13 5LP**
**email:** relax@ellerbyhotel.co.uk **web:** www.ellerbyhotel.co.uk
**dir:** From A171 onto B1266, follow signs for Ellerby. Or from A174 (Whitby) follow signs for Ellerby

Located in the North York Moors National Park, this friendly, family-run inn is in a quiet country setting just eight miles from Whitby. There is a traditional bar with open fire and real ales as well as a spacious restaurant. There is also a beautiful secluded garden and a residents' conservatory lounge. A range of bedrooms is available including ground-floor rooms, family rooms and a disabled accessible room. Complimentary WiFi is also provided and there is secure bicycle storage.

**Rooms:** 10 en suite (4 fmly) (4 GF) **Facilities:** STV FTV Lounge tea/coffee Dinner available Direct dial WiFi 🔒 **Extras:** Fresh milk, fridge, robes **Parking:** 30 **Notes:** LB

## FILEY
Map 17 TA18

### Premier Collection

### All Seasons Guesthouse
★★★★★ ⊜ GUEST HOUSE

**tel:** 01723 515321 & 07870 267945 **11 Rutland Street YO14 9JA**
**email:** lesley@allseasonsfiley.co.uk **web:** www.allseasonsfiley.co.uk
**dir:** From A165 at rdbt follow signs for Filey. Continue to town centre, right into West Ave, 2nd left into Rutland St

This immaculately presented, contemporary guest house is a short stroll from the seafront and is also close to the Crescent Gardens and town centre. There is a friendly, welcoming atmosphere and a lovely lounge for guests to relax in. Bedrooms and bathrooms are stylish and very comfortable. They include a luxury suite, a king-size room, family and twin rooms. Breakfast is a highlight of any stay with all produce either locally sourced or home-made. Complimentary WiFi is also provided.

**Rooms:** 6 en suite (2 fmly) **Facilities:** FTV DVD TVL tea/coffee WiFi 🌳 ♨19 🔒
**Extras:** Dressing gowns, slippers – complimentary **Notes:** LB No children 10yrs

## FLIXTON
Map 17 TA07

### Orchard Lodge
★★★★ ⊜ GUEST ACCOMMODATION

**tel:** 01723 890202 & 07789 228682 **North Street YO11 3UA**
**email:** orchardlodgescarborough@gmail.com **web:** www.orchard-lodge.com
**dir:** Off A1039 in village centre

A warm welcome is guaranteed at this owner-run property situated in the small village of Flixton near the popular seaside resort of Scarborough. Bedrooms are comfortably appointed with modern accessories, including complimentary WiFi. Award-winning breakfasts are served in the spacious dining room which is also open as a tearoom throughout the afternoon. A focus on local and home-made produce means eggs are sourced from the resident hens and the fruit used for jams and juices is picked from the on-site orchard. Free parking is also available. Orchard Lodge was a finalist for the AA Friendliest B&B of the Year award 2017–18.

**Rooms:** 6 en suite (1 fmly) **S** £80–£120; **D** £90–£130* **Facilities:** FTV Lounge tea/coffee Licensed WiFi 🔒 **Extras:** Fridge **Conf:** Max 12 **Parking:** 6 **Notes:** LB No children 12yrs Closed 8–18 Nov, 8–30 Jan

## FYLINGTHORPE
Map 19 NZ90

### Flask Inn
★★★★ ⊜ INN

**tel:** 01947 880305 & 880592 **YO22 4QH**
**email:** info@flaskinn.com **web:** www.theflaskinn.co.uk
**dir:** On A171 from Whitby, on left

This traditional inn offers spacious bar and dining areas along with smart, contemporary bedrooms. The rooms are very well equipped and feature modern en suites. There is a friendly atmosphere and food is a highlight of any stay with a high standard of cooking and a wide choice on the appealing menus. The inn has a very convenient location, close to the main road offering a scenic drive between Whitby and Scarborough and set in the beautiful North Yorkshire countryside.

**Rooms:** 9 en suite (2 fmly) (3 GF) **S** £60; **D** £80* **Facilities:** FTV tea/coffee Dinner available WiFi Pool table 🔒 **Extras:** Bottled water **Parking:** 25 **Notes:** LB Closed 2 Jan–7 Feb

## GILLING EAST
Map 19 SE67

### The Fairfax Arms
★★★★ ⊛ INN

**tel:** 01439 788212 & 788819 **Main Street YO62 4JH**
**email:** info@thefairfaxarms.co.uk **web:** www.thefairfaxarms.co.uk
**dir:** From A170 turn right onto B1257, right again onto B1363 to Gilling East, pub on right

This independently owned inn is situated in the quiet village of Gilling East within easy driving distance of Helmsley. A perfect balance between the appeal of up-to-date facilities and original features such as wooden beams and open fires has been struck by the owners. Bedrooms are well appointed with comfortable beds guaranteed to provide a good night's sleep; a range of thoughtful accessories are provided such as iPod docking stations, TVs and luxurious toiletries. PlayStation consoles are also available on request. Award-winning dinners that focus on excellent quality local produce can be enjoyed both in the bar and restaurant areas. On-site parking is available.

**Rooms:** 8 en suite 4 annexe en suite (2 fmly) (3 GF) **S** fr £75; **D** fr £100*
**Facilities:** FTV DVD iPod docking station tea/coffee Dinner available Direct dial WiFi ♨10 🔒 **Extras:** Speciality toiletries **Parking:** 14 **Notes:** LB

**GOLDSBOROUGH** Map 19 SE35

## Premier Collection

# Goldsborough Hall

★★★★★  ≜ GUEST ACCOMMODATION

**tel:** 01423 867321 **Church Street HG5 8NR**
**email:** info@goldsboroughhall.com **web:** www.goldsboroughhall.com
**dir:** A1(M) junct 47, A59 to Knaresborough. 2nd left into Station Rd, at T-junct left into Church St

It's not every day that you get the chance to stay in the former residence of a Royal Princess, in this case HRH Princess Mary (1897–1965), who was one of the Queen's aunts. Hospitality at Goldsborough Hall is second to none. The luxury bedrooms are appointed to the highest standards, and the bathrooms have a real 'wow' factor. Some of the main house bedrooms feature hand-made mahogany four-poster beds, chesterfields and 60" TVs. The popular seasonal afternoon tea is served either in front of the roaring fire in the Jacobean Library or in the Dining Room. Reservations for dinner from non-residents are welcomed.

**Rooms:** 6 en suite 6 annexe en suite (4 fmly) **S** £95  £195; **D** £125–£225 (room only)* **Facilities:** FTV DVD iPod docking station Lounge tea/coffee Dinner available Direct dial Lift Licensed WiFi ◡ ♨18 ♨ Outdoor hot tub **Extras:** Speciality toiletries, fruit; mini-bar – chargeable **Conf:** Max 150 Thtr 150 Class 50 Board 30 **Parking:** 50 **Notes:** LB Closed 24–26 Dec Civ wed 150

**GRASSINGTON** Map 19 SE06

## Premier Collection

# Grassington House

★★★★★ ❀❀ ≜ RESTAURANT WITH ROOMS

**tel:** 01756 752406 **5 The Square BD23 5AQ**
**email:** bookings@grassingtonhouse.co.uk **web:** www.grassingtonhouse.co.uk
**dir:** A59 into Grassington, in town square opposite post office

Located in the square of the popular village of Grassington, this beautifully converted Georgian house is personally run by owners John and Sue. Delicious food, individually designed bedrooms and warm hospitality ensure an enjoyable stay. There is a stylish lounge bar looking out to the square and the restaurant is split between two rooms; here guests will find the emphasis is on fresh, local ingredients and attentive, friendly service.

**Rooms:** 9 en suite (2 fmly) **S** fr £107.50; **D** £125–£145* **Facilities:** STV FTV tea/coffee Dinner available Direct dial WiFi ♨ **Extras:** Speciality toiletries **Parking:** 25 **Notes:** LB Civ wed 44

## Premier Collection

# Ashfield House

★★★★★ ≜ GUEST ACCOMMODATION

**tel:** 01756 752584 **Summers Fold BD23 5AE**
**email:** sales@ashfieldhouse.co.uk **web:** www.ashfieldhouse.co.uk
**dir:** B6265 to village centre, from main street left into Summers Fold

Guests are greeted like old friends at this beautifully maintained 17th-century house, peacefully tucked away a few yards from the village square. The smart lounges offer a high level of comfort and an honesty bar. The attractive bedrooms are well furnished and thoughtfully equipped.

**Rooms:** 7 rms (6 en suite) (1 pri facs) 1 annexe en suite **Facilities:** FTV Lounge tea/coffee Licensed WiFi **Extras:** Home-baked cookies, speciality toiletries **Conf:** Max 8 Board 8 **Parking:** 8 **Notes:** LB No children 5yrs

**HARROGATE** Map 19 SE35

## Premier Collection

# The Grafton Boutique B&B

★★★★★ ≜ GUEST ACCOMMODATION

**tel:** 01423 508491 **1–3 Franklin Mount HG1 5EJ**
**email:** enquiries@graftonhotel.co.uk **web:** www.graftonhotel.co.uk
**dir:** Follow signs to International Centre, into Kings Rd (with Centre on left), Franklin Mount 450yds on right

The Grafton is a stylish townhouse, in a quiet location, just a short walk from the conference centre and town. It is a period property but with contemporary interior design throughout and a luxurious feel. There is a beautifully appointed lounge looking out to the garden, and breakfast is served in a spacious and striking dining room. Complimentary WiFi is provided.

**Rooms:** 13 en suite (1 GF) **D** £90–£140* **Facilities:** FTV Lounge tea/coffee Direct dial Licensed WiFi ♨18 ♨ **Parking:** 1 **Notes:** LB Closed 15 Dec–6 Jan

HARROGATE *continued*

## Shelbourne House

★★★★ ⌕ GUEST ACCOMMODATION

**tel:** 01423 504390 **78 Kings Road HG1 5JX**
**email:** sue@shelbournehouse.co.uk **web:** www.shelbournehouse.co.uk
**dir:** *Follow signs to International Centre, over lights by Holiday Inn, premises on right*

Situated opposite the conference centre and close to the town centre, this elegant Victorian house features attractive well-equipped bedrooms. There is a beautifully presented guest lounge and smart dining room. The friendly owners provide attentive service and offer a wide choice at breakfast, with emphasis on local ingredients. Complimentary WiFi access is provided.

**Rooms:** 8 en suite (2 fmly) **Facilities:** FTV DVD iPod docking station TVL tea/coffee WiFi **Parking:** 1 **Notes:** LB

## Harrogate Brasserie with Rooms

★★★★ ⇌ GUEST ACCOMMODATION

**tel:** 01423 505041 **28–30 Cheltenham Parade HG1 1DB**
**email:** info@harrogatebrasserie.co.uk **web:** www.harrogatebrasserie.co.uk
**dir:** *On A61 in town centre behind theatre*

This town centre establishment is distinctly continental in style. The brasserie covers three cosy dining areas, richly decorated and adorned with artefacts. Live jazz is featured every night except Saturdays. The individual bedrooms feature period collectibles; many rooms have DVD players and all have plentiful amounts of reading material.

**Rooms:** 13 en suite 3 annexe en suite (3 fmly) (1 GF) **Facilities:** FTV tea/coffee Dinner available Direct dial Licensed WiFi 🔒 **Parking:** 12 **Notes:** LB

## Innkeeper's Lodge Harrogate (West)

★★★★ INN

**tel:** 08451 551551 *(Calls cost 2p per minute plus your phone company's access charge)*
**Beckwith Knowle, Otley Road HG3 1UE**
**email:** info@innkeeperslodge.com **web:** www.innkeeperslodge.com

Located close to town in Beckwith Knowle, this period property is ideal for exploring historic and vibrant Harrogate and the Yorkshire Dales National Park. The spacious public areas are stylish and full of character. Seasonally-changing menus feature traditional favourites as well as Mediterranean influences and the chef's daily specials. Bedrooms are modern, spacious and well furnished. Complimentary WiFi is provided.

**Rooms:** 12 en suite (4 fmly) **Facilities:** FTV tea/coffee Dinner available WiFi **Parking:** 60

---

**HAWNBY** Map 19 SE58

## The Inn at Hawnby

★★★★ ⊕ INN

**tel:** 01439 798202 **YO62 5QS**
**email:** info@innathawnby.co.uk **web:** www.innathawnby.co.uk
**dir:** *Exit B1257 between Stokesley & Helmsley*

This charming 19th-century inn is located in a peaceful village. Service is attentive and friendly, with guests able to relax and browse menus in the cosy bar where there is a good wine list and range of ales. Delicious, home-cooked meals are served in the restaurant, overlooking the gardens and surrounding countryside. Bedrooms are well equipped, with some in the converted stables.

**Rooms:** 6 en suite 3 annexe en suite (1 fmly) (3 GF) **S** £79; **D** £99* **Facilities:** FTV DVD tea/coffee Dinner available Direct dial WiFi Fishing **Extras:** Speciality toiletries **Conf:** Max 20 Thtr 12 Class 20 **Parking:** 9 **Notes:** LB Closed 25 Dec RS Feb & Mar Restricted lunch service Mon & Tue

---

**HELMSLEY** Map 19 SE68

*See also Hawnby*

### Premier Collection

## Shallowdale House

★★★★★ ⌕ ⇌ GUEST ACCOMMODATION

**tel:** 01439 788325 **West End YO62 4DY**
**email:** stay@shallowdalehouse.co.uk **web:** www.shallowdalehouse.co.uk

*(For full entry see Ampleforth)*

## Plumpton Court

★★★★ GUEST ACCOMMODATION

**tel:** 01439 771223 **High Street, Nawton YO62 7TT**
**email:** mail@plumptoncourt.com **web:** www.plumptoncourt.com
**dir:** *2.5m E of Helmsley. Exit A170 in Nawton, signed*

Situated in the small village of Nawton between Helmsley and Kirkbymoorside, Plumpton Court has six modern and individually decorated bedrooms. Guests can relax in front of a real fire in the homely lounge with a bottle of wine from the well-stocked bar and enjoy a leisurely breakfast with locally sourced ingredients. Chris is a convivial host and takes delight in helping guests make the most of their visit to North Yorkshire. To the rear of the house is a private, secure car park and a secluded garden.

**Rooms:** 6 en suite (1 GF) **S** £65; **D** £78–£86* **Facilities:** FTV DVD Lounge tea/coffee Licensed WiFi ↧18 🔒 **Parking:** 7 **Notes:** No children 12yrs Closed 22–29 Dec & 4–31 Jan

## The Feathers

★★★★ ⇌ INN

**tel:** 01439 770275 **Market Place YO62 5BH**
**email:** feathers@innmail.co.uk **web:** www.feathershotelhelmsley.co.uk
**dir:** *A1(M) junct 49 onto A168 signed Thirsk. Bear left, then take 2nd exit at rdbt onto A170 to Helmsley. In Market Place*

This fine old property enjoys a prominent position overlooking the busy town square in pretty Helmsley. The bar and lounge areas are full of character and real fires glow on the cooler evenings. There is an extensive dinner menu along with a nightly specials board, which uses the best in local, seasonal produce. Bedrooms have been decorated to a high standard and are most comfortable. Some secure parking is available for guests at the rear of the inn. The Feathers is an ideal base from which to explore the North York Moors National Park, and Helmsley is situated on the Cleveland Way walk.

**Rooms:** 21 en suite 4 annexe en suite (2 fmly) (2 GF) **Facilities:** FTV tea/coffee Dinner available WiFi ⌁18 🍷 **Conf:** Max 100 Thtr 100 Class 70 Board 40 **Parking:** 15 **Notes:** LB

---

### HETTON
Map 18 SD95

#### Premier Collection

## The Angel Inn
★★★★★ ◉◉ 🍷 RESTAURANT WITH ROOMS

**tel:** 01756 730263 **BD23 6LT**
**email:** info@angelhetton.co.uk **web:** www.angelhetton.co.uk
**dir:** B6265 from Skipton towards Grassington. At Rylstone turn left by pond, follow signs to Hetton

This roadside inn is steeped in history; parts of the building go back more than 500 years. The restaurant and bar are in the main building, which has ivy and green canopies at the front. Food is a highlight of any stay, offering excellent ingredients, skilfully prepared and carefully presented. The large, stylish bedrooms are across the road in a converted barn which has great views of the Dales, private parking and its own wine cave.

**Rooms:** 9 en suite (3 GF) **Facilities:** FTV tea/coffee Dinner available Direct dial WiFi 🍷 Wine tasting cave **Conf:** Max 16 Board 14 **Parking:** 40 **Notes:** LB Closed 25 Dec & 1week Jan Civ wed 40

---

### HUNTON
Map 19 SE19

## The Countryman's Inn
★★★ 🍺 INN

**tel:** 01677 450554 & 07734 556845 **South View DL8 1PY**
**email:** tony@countrymansinn.co.uk **web:** www.countrymansinn.co.uk
**dir:** Exit A1(M) at Leeming Bar onto A684 towards Bedale/Leyburn. Through Patrick Brompton, right at x-rds. After 1.25m turn left signed Hunton

This traditional country pub offers a friendly atmosphere, cask ales and great food. The bar features a real fire and beamed ceiling and there is a beer garden for warmer weather. A wide choice of freshly prepared meals are served and there is a smartly presented dining room. Bedrooms and bathrooms are more contemporary with a fresh, bright style with good provision made for families and a designated 'pet friendly' room. Other facilities include complimentary WiFi and private parking.

**Rooms:** 4 en suite (2 fmly) **Facilities:** FTV DVD iPod docking station TVL tea/coffee Dinner available WiFi 🐾 🍷 **Extras:** Still & sparkling water **Parking:** 8 **Notes:** LB

---

### KETTLEWELL
Map 18 SD97

## Belk's Bed & Breakfast
★★★ 🍴 BED AND BREAKFAST

**tel:** 01756 761188 & 07538 566495 **Middle Lane BD23 5QX**
**email:** davidbelk23@gmail.com **web:** www.zarinaskettlewell.co.uk
**dir:** Into Kettlewell on B6160, turn opposite Racehorses Hotel, 200mtrs on right

Belk's Bed & Breakfast is located in the picturesque village of Kettlewell, and is popular with cyclists and walkers. The house provides guests with a warm and friendly welcome. Bedrooms are comfortable and well equipped with many thoughtful extras. Memorable breakfasts served in the pleasantly appointed tea room feature eggs from the Belk's own chickens, as well as home-made preserves. Outside garden seating area is available in warmer weather.

**Rooms:** 3 en suite **S** £49; **D** £89* **Facilities:** FTV DVD tea/coffee Licensed WiFi 🍷 **Extras:** Mini-bar **Parking:** 2 **Notes:** LB No children 18yrs Closed Jan

---

### KEXBY
Map 17 SE65

#### Premier Collection

## Kexby House
★★★★★ 🍴 GUEST ACCOMMODATION

**tel:** 01759 380254 **Kexby YO41 5LE**
**email:** info@bradfordowen.com **web:** www.kexbyhouse.co.uk
**dir:** On A1079, E of York

This beautifully presented 18th-century farmhouse is just a few miles outside of York, yet enjoys an idyllic setting in 13 acres of grounds, with 400 yards of private fishing. The marble-floored hall leads to an impressive and elegant dining room and the three bedrooms in the main house are individually furnished with bathrooms featuring cast iron roll top baths. The Cottage Room is located within the grounds and gives guests the added benefits of a kitchenette, living room and private patio. Delicious breakfasts feature free-range eggs from the owners' own hens.

**Rooms:** 3 en suite 1 annexe en suite (1 fmly) (1 GF) **Facilities:** DVD tea/coffee WiFi Fishing **Parking:** 8 **Notes:** No children 11yrs Closed 30 Nov–15 Jan

## KIRKBY FLEETHAM
Map 19 SE29

### Premier Collection

## Black Horse Inn
★★★★★ ⚜ INN

tel: 01609 749010 & 749011 **7 Lumley Lane DL7 0SH**
email: reservations@blackhorseinnkirkbyfleetham.com
web: www.blackhorseinnkirkbyfleetham.com
dir: *A1 onto A648 towards Northallerton. Left into Ham Hall Lane, through Scruton. At T-junction left into Fleetham Lane. Through Great Fencote to Kirkby Fleetham, into Lumley Lane, inn on left past post office*

The Black Horse Inn is set in the heart of Kirkby Fleetham, in North Yorkshire countryside. It offers free parking, free WiFi in public areas, a bar, a garden and a restaurant. Each of the seven bedrooms has been decorated in neutral colours and boast antique furniture, breakfast hamper, TV and mini fridge with fresh orange juice, milk and water. The en suite bathrooms feature bath and/or power shower with complimentary toiletries. Some bedrooms benefit from an in-room roll-top bath. Guests can relax in the bar or in the garden, and the restaurant serves traditional British dishes, all prepared using local produce. The Black Horse Inn is just 10 minutes' drive from Catterick Racecourse and 40 from Yorkshire Dales National Park.

**Rooms:** 7 en suite (1 fmly) (2 GF) **Facilities:** FTV tea/coffee Dinner available WiFi ⚓18 Fishing Quoits pitch **Extras:** Fridge, fresh milk, orange juice – complimentary **Conf:** Max 40 Thtr 40 Class 30 Board 24 **Parking:** 90 **Notes:** LB

## KIRKBY MALZEARD
Map 19 SE27

## The Moorhouse
★★★★ ⚽ BED AND BREAKFAST

tel: 01765 658371 **HG4 3RH**
email: enquiries@moorhousebnb.co.uk web: www.moorhousebnb.co.uk
dir: *From Ripon on B6265 to Pateley Bridge, turn right to Grantley. Left after pub to T-junct, turn right. On left after 1.5m*

A warm welcome is guaranteed along with afternoon tea, served by the open fire in the guest lounge, on colder days. This friendly B&B is situated in the countryside, with popular destinations such as Ripon and Harrogate easily reachable by car. Bedrooms are well appointed and comfortable. Thoughtful extras such as bathrobes, luxurious toiletries and well-stocked hospitality trays are provided. Hearty Yorkshire breakfasts are served in the dining room alongside more healthy options such as fresh fruit smoothies. Plenty of parking is provided.

**Rooms:** 5 en suite (2 GF) **Facilities:** FTV TVL tea/coffee Licensed WiFi **Parking:** 5 **Notes:** No children 12yrs Closed Aug–Mar

## KNARESBOROUGH
Map 19 SE35

### Premier Collection

## General Tarleton Inn
★★★★★ ⚜⚜ RESTAURANT WITH ROOMS

tel: 01423 340284 **Boroughbridge Road, Ferrensby HG5 0PZ**
email: gti@generaltarleton.co.uk web: www.generaltarleton.co.uk
dir: *A1(M) junct 48 at Boroughbridge, take A6055 to Knaresborough. 4m on right*

This 18th-century coaching inn is both beautiful and stylish. Though the physical aspects are impressive, the emphasis here is on food with high-quality, skilfully prepared dishes served in the smart bar-brasserie and in the Orangery. There is also a richly furnished cocktail lounge with a galleried private dining room above it. Bedrooms are very comfortable and business guests are also well catered for.

**Rooms:** 13 en suite (7 GF) **S** £75–£95; **D** £129–£150* **Facilities:** FTV Lounge tea/coffee Dinner available Direct dial WiFi ⚓ **Extras:** Speciality toiletries, home-made biscuits **Conf:** Max 40 Thtr 40 Class 35 Board 20 **Parking:** 40 **Notes:** LB Closed 24–26 Dec, 1 Jan

## Newton House
★★★★ ⚽ GUEST ACCOMMODATION

tel: 01423 863539 & 07801 557388 **5–7 York Place HG5 0AD**
email: info@newtonhouseyorkshire.com web: www.newtonhouseyorkshire.com
dir: *A1(M) junct 47 onto A59 towards Knaresborough. Right at 1st rdbt, continue to town centre, on right before lights*

This elegant Georgian guest accommodation is only a short walk from the river, castle and market square; the property is entered by an archway into the courtyard. Attractive, very well-equipped bedrooms include some four-poster beds and also king-sized double rooms. There is a comfortable lounge with honesty bar and memorable breakfasts are served in the attractive dining rooms.

**Rooms:** 9 rms (8 en suite) (1 pri facs) 3 annexe en suite (2 fmly) (4 GF) **S** fr £60; **D** £85–£125* **Facilities:** FTV DVD Lounge tea/coffee Licensed WiFi ⚓18 ⚓ Special arrangement for guests to use nearby spa **Extras:** Speciality toiletries, mini-bar in most rooms **Conf:** Max 20 Thtr 20 Board 12 **Parking:** 7 **Notes:** LB

## Innkeeper's Lodge Harrogate (East)
★★★ INN

tel: 08451 551551 *(Calls cost 2p per minute plus your phone company's access charge)* **Wetherby Road, Plompton HG5 8LY**
email: info@innkeeperslodge.com web: www.innkeeperslodge.com

This country pub and lodge is convenient for Harrogate, with its tourist attractions, shops and tearooms as well as the Conference Centre. It is also well located for visiting picturesque Knaresborough, Ripon and the Yorkshire Dales. Hearty, seasonal food and cask ales are noteworthy, along with real fires and a range of areas in which to relax. There is a lovely beer garden for when the weather's warmer. Bedrooms are comfortable. Complimentary WiFi and on-site parking are also provided.

**Rooms:** 10 en suite (2 fmly) **Facilities:** FTV tea/coffee Dinner available Direct dial WiFi

| LEEMING BAR | Map 19 SE28 |
|---|---|

## Little Holtby

★★★★★ ≋ BED AND BREAKFAST

tel: 01609 748762 **DL7 9LH**
email: littleholtby@yahoo.co.uk web: www.littleholtby.co.uk
dir: *0.5m N of A684 (junct with A1), on A6055 N*

Little Holtby is a charming farmhouse on land which used to form part of an estate that is mentioned in the Domesday Book, although the current house dates back to the late 17th century. Ideally located close to the A1 and convenient for Leeming Bar and Bedale, this is a great location for touring this part of North Yorkshire. A warm welcome awaits along with cakes and a drink. Bedrooms are generous in size with all necessary facilities including a well-stocked hospitality tray. The gardens and surrounding countryside add to the experience as do the open log fires which keep away the chill of outside. An award-winning breakfast will be sure to get your day off to the right start.

**Rooms:** 3 rms (2 en suite) (1 pri facs) **S** £50; **D** £90* **Facilities:** FTV DVD TVL tea/coffee WiFi ↓18 **Extras:** Speciality toiletries, fruit, snacks – complimentary **Parking:** 7 **Notes:** LB No children 12yrs

| LEVISHAM | Map 19 SE89 |
|---|---|

## The Horseshoe Inn

★★★★ ⇔ INN

tel: 01751 460240 **Main Street YO18 7NL**
email: info@horseshoelevisham.co.uk web: www.horseshoelevisham.co.uk
dir: *From Pickering on A169, after 4m past Fox & Rabbit Inn on right. 0.5m left to Lockton, then steep winding road to village*

The Horseshoe Inn is a charming 19th-century inn with a peaceful location in Levisham village. The spacious bar and dining area are traditionally furnished and food is a highlight with a wide choice and generous portions. The attractive bedrooms include seven garden rooms, and most rooms in the main house have lovely views of the village.

**Rooms:** 11 en suite (7 GF) **D** £85–£150* **Facilities:** FTV Lounge tea/coffee Dinner available WiFi **Parking:** 30 **Notes:** LB

| LEYBURN | Map 19 SE19 |
|---|---|

## Braithwaite Hall

★★★★★ ≋ BED AND BREAKFAST

tel: 01969 640287 **East Witton DL8 4SY**
email: info@braithwaitehall.co.uk web: www.braithwaitehall.co.uk
dir: *1.5m from East Witton on single track road*

This impressive 17th-century building is set in open farmland in Coverdale with views over the Pennines bordering Wensleydale. Inside are many period features including antique furnishings and a stunning oak staircase. The drawing room comes complete with oak panelling from the 1660s. Bedrooms are spacious and very comfortable. Delicious breakfasts are served in the elegant dining room and there is a friendly, welcoming atmosphere.

**Rooms:** 3 rms (2 en suite) (1 pri facs) **D** £95–£100* **Facilities:** FTV DVD tea/coffee ⊌ Fishing **Extras:** Speciality toiletries, fruit, port **Parking:** 7 **Notes:** No children 12yrs Closed Nov–Feb

## Low Mill Guest House

★★★★★ ⚲ ⇔ GUEST HOUSE

tel: 01969 650553 **Bainbridge DL8 3EF**
email: lowmillguesthouse@gmail.com web: www.lowmillguesthouse.co.uk
dir: *A1 junct 51 onto A684 towards Hawes. In Bainbridge turn right by junct on village green*

A truly unique, luxurious retreat tucked away in the beautiful Dales village of Bainbridge. Grade II listed, Low Mill Guest House has been refurbished to an impressive standard with the original mill works and waterwheel restored. Bedrooms are spacious with original features blended with stylish design. There is a stunning lounge with working range, and an attractive dining room where breakfast and candlelit evening meals are served.

**Rooms:** 3 en suite **S** £78–£135; **D** £110–£180* **Facilities:** FTV DVD iPod docking station TVL tea/coffee Dinner available Direct dial Licensed WiFi Fishing **Extras:** Speciality toiletries, home-made biscuits **Parking:** 3 **Notes:** LB No children 10yrs

## The Old Town Hall

★★★★★ ▲ GUEST ACCOMMODATION

tel: 01969 625641 **Priory Close, Redmire DL8 4ED**
email: enquiries@theoldtownhall.co.uk web: www.theoldtownhall.co.uk

Louise and David run this romantic, luxury B&B, which is set in stunning countryside between Leyburn and Aysgarth Falls. The three rooms are charming, and simply yet elegantly decorated. All have beamed ceilings and seating areas, while one has a double spa bath and body jet shower. Guests will enjoy the soft towels and bathrobes, luxury L'Occitane en Provence toiletries, and a well-stocked fridge with fresh milk, water and cordials. On arrival, tea or coffee with home-made cake and biscuits are offered in the guest lounge. Breakfast is cooked to order and features local produce as well as fresh, home-baked bread.

**Rooms:** 3 rms (2 en suite) (1 pri facs) **S** £90–£130; **D** £110–£150* **Facilities:** FTV DVD Lounge tea/coffee WiFi **Extras:** Speciality toiletries, home-made biscuits, silent fridge, fresh milk, chocolates – complimentary **Parking:** 3 **Notes:** No children 18yrs

LEYBURN *continued*

## The Queens Head

★★★★ ⬤ ⬤ INN

**tel:** 01677 450259 **Westmoor Lane, Finghall DL8 5ND**
**email:** enquiries@queensfinghall.co.uk **web:** www.queensfinghall.co.uk
**dir:** *From Bedale follow A684 W towards Leyburn, just after pub & caravan park turn left signed to Finghall. Follow road, on left*

Located in the quiet village of Finghall, this country inn dates back to the 18th century and has original oak beams. A wide choice of freshly prepared meals are served in either the bar or more contemporary restaurant, which has lovely views of the surrounding countryside. Bedrooms are spacious and located in an adjacent annexe.

**Rooms:** 3 annexe en suite (1 fmly) (3 GF) **Facilities:** FTV DVD tea/coffee Dinner available WiFi ⬤ **Parking:** 40 **Notes:** LB

---

| LOW ROW | Map 18 SD99 |

## The Punch Bowl Inn

★★★★ ⬤ ⬤ INN

**tel:** 03337 000779 **DL11 6PF**
**email:** info@pbinn.co.uk **web:** www.pbinn.co.uk
**dir:** *From Scotch Corner take A6108 to Richmond then B6270 to Low Row*

This friendly inn is appointed in a contemporary style. Real ales and freshly-cooked meals are served in either the spacious bar or dining room. The modern bedrooms are stylish yet simply furnished, with well-equipped bathrooms. Guests also have use of a lounge which has stunning views of the Dales.

**Rooms:** 9 en suite 2 annexe en suite (1 fmly) (1 GF) **Facilities:** FTV Lounge tea/coffee Dinner available Direct dial WiFi Fishing ⬤ **Extras:** Speciality toiletries, home-made shortbread **Parking:** 20 **Notes:** LB Closed 25 Dec

---

| MALHAM | Map 18 SD96 |

## The Lister Arms

★★★★ INN

**tel:** 01729 830330 **BD23 4DB**
**email:** relax@listerarms.co.uk **web:** www.listerarms.co.uk
**dir:** *From A59 into Malham, right in centre of village*

Located in Malham in the Yorkshire Dales National Park, The Lister Arms is a traditional country inn with wood beams and open fires. It is close to the village green and a babbling stream. The accommodation is comfortable and well equipped, and a wide selection of imaginative dishes, together with real ales and fine wines, are served in the busy bar and restaurant, where the atmosphere is relaxed and comfortable.

**Rooms:** 15 en suite (3 fmly) **Facilities:** FTV tea/coffee Dinner available WiFi **Parking:** 20 **Notes:** LB

---

| MIDDLEHAM | Map 19 SE18 |

| Premier Collection |

## The Saddle Room

★★★★★ ⬤ ⬤ GUEST ACCOMMODATION

**tel:** 01969 640596 **Tupgill Park, Coverdale DL8 4TJ**
**email:** info@thesaddleroom.co.uk **web:** www.thesaddleroom.co.uk

The Saddle Room is located in the idyllic Tupgill Park Estate in the heart of the Yorkshire Dales. High quality accommodation that caters well for the modern traveler with many thoughtful extras that are provided as standard. Hands-on team are proactive and show wonderful customer care awareness to their guests and seem to really go that extra mile on their behalf. The bar and restaurant actively promote quality local produce wherever possible and the setting of the old stables along with some fantastic horse racing objets d'art makes for a really unique location.

**Rooms:** 9 en suite (3 GF) **D** £90–£130* **Facilities:** FTV tea/coffee Dinner available Direct dial Lift Licensed WiFi Fishing ⬤ **Extras:** Mini-bar, Nespresso machine **Conf:** Max 100 Thtr 100 Class 100 Board 50 **Parking:** 200 **Notes:** Civ wed 100

---

# The Coach House at Middleton Lodge

Kneeton Lane, Middleton Tyas, Richmond, North Yorkshire DL10 6NJ

**Tel:** 01325 377 977

**Email:** info@middletonlodge.co.uk   **Web:** www.middletonlodge.co.uk

## MIDDLETON TYAS     Map 19 NZ20

### Premier Collection

## The Coach House

★★★★★ ◉◉◉   RESTAURANT WITH ROOMS

**tel:** 01325 377977 **Middleton Lodge DL10 6NJ**
**email:** info@middletonlodge.co.uk **web:** www.middletonlodge.co.uk

Nestled within a 200-acre estate, surrounded by tall trees and winding footpaths, this picturesque setting really sets the tone for your stay. Bedrooms are annexed in a courtyard style setting and are furnished to a luxurious standard. Traditional features such as exposed beams and high ceilings are coupled with a wide range of modern accessories such as flat-screen TV, Nespresso machines and complimentary WiFi. The kitchen takes a modern approach, using seasonal regional produce for an interesting range of meals that are served in the modern restaurant; a selection of cocktails is also offered. Beauty treatments are also available. Weddings and private functions can also be booked in the main house, Middleton Lodge.

**Rooms:** 9 en suite (6 GF) **S** £120–£170; **D** £140–£190* **Facilities:** STV FTV DVD Lounge tea/coffee Dinner available Direct dial WiFi ➳ ♨18 ♠ **Extras:** Snacks, juice – complimentary **Parking:** 70 **Notes:** LB Civ wed 100

*See advert opposite*

## NEWTON UNDER ROSEBERRY     Map 19 NZ51

## The Kings Head Inn

★★★ ⊜ INN

**tel:** 01642 722318 **The Green TS9 6QR**
**email:** info@kingsheadinn.co.uk **web:** www.kingsheadinn.co.uk
**dir:** *A171 towards Guisborough, at rdbt onto A173 to Newton under Roseberry, under Roseberry Topping landmark*

The Kings Head Inn enjoys a wonderful location with the Roseberry Topping providing an iconic back drop, and is located at the edge of the North York Moors within easy striking distance of Whitby, York and Newcastle. Comfortable bedrooms are located in the adjacent 17th-century cottages. The pub serves good, home-cooked food and the staff are friendly and welcoming.

**Rooms:** 12 annexe en suite (1 fmly) (6 GF) **Facilities:** tea/coffee Dinner available WiFi **Parking:** 50

## OLDSTEAD     Map 19 SE57

### Premier Collection

## The Black Swan at Oldstead

★★★★★ ◉◉◉◉ ⚑ RESTAURANT WITH ROOMS

**tel:** 01347 868387 **YO61 4BL**
**email:** enquiries@blackswanoldstead.co.uk **web:** www.blackswanoldstead.co.uk
**dir:** *Exit A19, 3m S Thirsk for Coxwold, left in Coxwold, left at Byland Abbey for Oldstead*

The Black Swan is set amidst the stunning scenery of the North York Moors National Park, and parts of the building date back to the 16th century. Well appointed, very comfortable bedrooms provide the perfect get-away; some are on the ground floor overlooking the kitchen garden, others are in the Georgian House and feature both baths and wet-room showers. These bedrooms, together with welcoming open fires, a traditional bar and an award-winning restaurant that has become a destination in its own right, all combine to make this a 'little gem' of a property.

**Rooms:** 4 en suite 5 annexe en suite (6 GF) **D** £330–£480* **Facilities:** FTV tea/coffee Dinner available WiFi **Extras:** Home-made biscuits, speciality toiletries **Parking:** 20 **Notes:** No children 18yrs

## OSMOTHERLEY     Map 19 SE49

### Premier Collection

## The Cleveland Tontine

★★★★★ ◉◉ ⚑ RESTAURANT WITH ROOMS

**tel:** 01609 882671 **Staddlebridge DL6 3JB**
**email:** bookings@theclevelandtontine.co.uk **web:** www.theclevelandtontine.co.uk
**dir:** *Just off A172 junct on A19 N'bound*

This iconic destination restaurant with rooms is a stunning place. Contemporary public areas sit alongside a traditional restaurant with open fires, tiled flooring and great food. Afternoon tea can be taken in the conservatory overlooking the gardens. Bedrooms are individually designed, with modern furniture and feature bathrooms. The service is friendly and relaxed, there is ample parking and major road links are close by.

**Rooms:** 7 en suite (4 fmly) **Facilities:** FTV Lounge tea/coffee Dinner available Direct dial WiFi **Extras:** Speciality toiletries **Conf:** Max 70 Thtr 56 Class 28 Board 38 **Parking:** 60 **Notes:** Civ wed 56

## PATELEY BRIDGE — Map 19 SE16

## Roslyn House

★★★★ ☻ GUEST ACCOMMODATION

**tel:** 01423 711374 **9 King St HG3 5AT**
**email:** enquiries@roslynhouse.co.uk **web:** www.roslynhouse.co.uk
**dir:** *B6165 into Pateley Bridge, right at end of High St at newsagents into King St, house 200yds on left*

You are assured of a warm welcome at well-maintained Roslyn House in the centre of the village. Bedrooms are attractively furnished, with homely touches and contemporary en suites. The lounge is comfortable, and hearty breakfasts will ensure you are set up for the day. Complimentary WiFi is also available. Cyclists and walkers on the famous Nidderdale Way are well catered for.

**Rooms:** 7 en suite **S** £80; **D** £90–£105* **Facilities:** FTV TVL tea/coffee WiFi ⛽
**Extras:** Chocolates, water, sweets – complimentary **Parking:** 6 **Notes:** LB
No children 3yrs

## PICKERING — Map 19 SE78

### Premier Collection

## 17 Burgate

★★★★★ ☻ GUEST ACCOMMODATION

**tel:** 01751 473463 **17 Burgate YO18 7AU**
**email:** info@17burgate.co.uk **web:** www.17burgate.co.uk
**dir:** *From A170 follow sign to Castle. 17 Burgate on right*

An elegant house close to the centre of Pickering and the castle, 17 Burgate offers comfortable, individually designed bedrooms with all modern facilities, including free broadband, iPod docks, DVD/CD player and comfy sofas. Public areas include a restful lounge, and breakfast features a wide choice of local, healthy foods. The proprietors here make every effort to maintain green and sustainable credentials.

**Rooms:** 3 en suite **S** £80–£95; **D** £95–£115 **Facilities:** FTV DVD iPod docking station Lounge tea/coffee WiFi ⛽ **Extras:** Chocolate, snacks – chargeable
**Conf:** Max 12 Thtr 12 Class 12 Board 12 **Parking:** 7 **Notes:** LB No children 10yrs
Closed 24 Oct–15 Mar RS 15–29 Dec

## Fox & Hounds Country Inn

★★★★ ⓢ INN

**tel:** 01751 431577 **Main Street, Sinnington YO62 6SQ**
**email:** fox.houndsinn@btconnect.com **web:** www.thefoxandhoundsinn.co.uk
**dir:** *3m W of Pickering. Off A170 between Pickering & Helmsley*

An attractive village inn offering smart, well-equipped bedrooms. The public areas include a bar, a cosy lounge and a restaurant which offers an impressive range of well presented and well cooked dishes. Food here has been awarded an AA Rosette.

**Rooms:** 10 en suite (4 GF) **S** £59–£94; **D** £70–£170* **Facilities:** FTV Lounge tea/coffee Dinner available Direct dial WiFi **Parking:** 40 **Notes:** LB Closed 25–27 Dec
Civ wed

## Grindale House

★★★★ 🅐 GUEST ACCOMMODATION

**tel:** 01751 476636 **123 Eastgate YO18 7DW**
**email:** info@grindalehouse.com **web:** www.grindalehouse.com

Close to the North York Moors National Park and North Riding Forest Park, Grindale House is a charming stone building with self-catering cottages to the side and behind. The guest accommodation is comfortable and attractive and breakfasts are memorable. Much of the produce that goes into it has come from local farms and suppliers. There is also on-site parking, WiFi, and secure bike lock-up.

**Rooms:** 6 rms (5 en suite) (1 pri facs) 3 annexe en suite (2 fmly) (3 GF)
**Facilities:** FTV TVL tea/coffee WiFi ⛽ **Parking:** 8 **Notes:** LB Closed mid Dec–Mar

## REETH — Map 19 SE09

## Arkleside Guesthouse Bed and Breakfast

★★★ GUEST HOUSE

**tel:** 01748 884200 **DL11 6SG**
**email:** enquiries@arklesidereeth.co.uk **web:** www.arklesidereeth.co.uk
**dir:** *From Richmond on A6108, right onto B6270 signed Reeth. In village bear right at village green*

Arkleside is located in a quiet courtyard in the peaceful village of Reeth, with stunning views of Swaledale and Fremington Edge. Bedrooms are well appointed and presented, and the high quality breakfast uses produce from local butchers and farmers, giving a great start to the day. Reeth is an ideal base for touring the Dales, for walking, or for cyclists to replicate the 2014 Tour de France stage.

**Rooms:** 4 en suite **S** £45–£65; **D** £55–£85* **Facilities:** FTV tea/coffee Licensed WiFi ⛽ **Parking:** 4

## RICCALL — Map 16 SE63

## White Rose Villa

★★★★ 🅐 BED AND BREAKFAST

**tel:** 01757 248115 **33 York Road YO19 6QG**
**email:** whiterosevilla@btinternet.com **web:** www.whiterosevilla.info
**dir:** *S of York, from A19, signed Riccall, 50mtrs on right*

Expect a warm and friendly welcome from Viv and Steve when visiting White Rose Villa. Conveniently located in the heart of the Yorkshire countryside, the popular village of Riccall is close to both York and Selby. All bedrooms are en suite and well equipped. There is a TV lounge to relax in, complete with a selection of DVDs, CDs, books and board games. Breakfast is served in the sunny dining room, and special diets are catered for by prior arrangement.

**Rooms:** 3 en suite (2 fmly) **S** £35–£40; **D** £65–£75* **Facilities:** FTV DVD TVL tea/coffee WiFi **Extras:** Speciality toiletries **Parking:** 4 **Notes:** LB Closed 24–26 & 31 Dec

## Per Bacco at The Park View

★★★ RESTAURANT WITH ROOMS

**tel:** 01757 249146 **20 Main Street YO19 6PX**
**email:** gianlucasechi@hotmail.co.uk **web:** www.per-bacco.co.uk
**dir:** *A19 from Selby, left for Riccall by water tower, house 100yds on right*

This spacious detached property is located in a quiet residential area and is convenient for York. The ground floor has been converted into an authentic Italian restaurant and there is a wide choice of fresh, home-made dishes, all in a friendly atmosphere. The restaurant is the main part of the business but there is also a range of comfortable en suite bedrooms. Ample parking is available.

**Rooms:** 4 en suite (2 fmly) **Facilities:** STV FTV iPod docking station Lounge TVL tea/coffee Dinner available WiFi ⅃ ⅄ **Parking:** 30 **Notes:** LB

### ▌ RICHMOND · Map 19 NZ10

## Whashton Springs Farm

★★★★ FARMHOUSE

**tel:** 01748 822884 **DL11 7JS**
**email:** thefarmhouse@whashtonsprings.co.uk **web:** www.whashtonsprings.co.uk
**dir:** In Richmond N at lights towards Ravensworth, 3m down steep hill, farm at bottom on left

A friendly welcome awaits at Whashton Springs Farm, situated in the heart of the countryside yet convenient for major routes. Bedrooms are split between the courtyard rooms and the main farmhouse. Traditional hearty breakfasts are served with free range eggs from the farms own hens as well as ample amounts of home-made and local produce. The spacious dining room overlooks the beautiful gardens.

**Rooms:** 3 en suite 5 annexe en suite (2 fmly) (5 GF) **Facilities:** FTV tea/coffee WiFi **Conf:** Max 16 Board 16 **Parking:** 10 **Notes:** LB No children 3yrs Closed late Dec-Jan 600 acres arable/beef/mixed/sheep

## The Frenchgate Guest House

★★★★ GUEST HOUSE

**tel:** 07889 768696 **66 Frenchgate DL10 7AG**
**email:** frenchgate66@icloud.com **web:** www.66frenchgate.co.uk
**dir:** From Scotch Corner, enter Richmond, straight over rdbt & lights. Left at 1st rdbt, turn sharp left after 100mtrs, drive to top of Frenchgate

Tucked away on a charming cobbled street in an historic market town, this attractively presented Victorian town house has an elevated position with stunning views. Bedrooms are comfortable and well equipped with complimentary WiFi access provided. The spacious conservatory-lounge and breakfast room has panoramic south-facing views of the Swale Valley and Easby Abbey.

**Rooms:** 8 rms (7 en suite) (1 pri facs) (3 fmly) (2 GF) **Facilities:** FTV Lounge tea/coffee WiFi ⅃18 ⅄ **Extras:** Fridges, bottled water, fruit, chocolates **Conf:** Max 20 Thtr 15 Class 15 Board 15 **Notes:** LB No children 5yrs

## Black Lion

★★★ INN

**tel:** 01748 826217 **12 Finkle Street DL10 4QB**
**email:** info@blacklionhotelrichmond.co.uk **web:** www.blacklionhotelrichmond.co.uk
**dir:** A1M take A1/A66. At rdbt take A6108 to Richmond

Nestled in the historic market town of Richmond, the Black Lion is a traditional family run inn which dates back to 1697. Bedrooms are well appointed and comfortable. Public areas are full of original character and charm and offer a range of seating areas including the snug. Menus offer a good selection of pub classics. Breakfasts are served in the Shiraz restaurant which is also available to hire as a function room. On-site car parking is available to the rear.

**Rooms:** 14 rms (13 en suite) (1 pri facs) (2 fmly) **Facilities:** FTV TVL tea/coffee Dinner available WiFi ⅃18 ⅄ **Conf:** Max 30 Class 30 Board 30 **Parking:** 10

## Farmers Arms

★★★ ⊜ INN

**tel:** 01748 818062 & 07966 984272 **Gatherley Road, Brompton-on-Swale DL10 7HZ**
**email:** info@farmersarmsyorkshire.com **web:** www.farmersarmsyorkshire.com
**dir:** From A1 junct 51 take A6136

This cosy inn is situated in the small village of Brompton-on-Swale, near Richmond with easy access to the A1. A warm welcome awaits at the Farmers Arms; a family-run inn full of original character and charm, dating back to 1700. Bedrooms are comfortable and well equipped with modern amenities such as large TVs and complimentary WiFi. Evening and lunch menus offer an interesting selection of modern dishes, coupled with traditional home-cooked classics.
An ample amount of on-site parking is available.

**Rooms:** 4 en suite (1 fmly) **Facilities:** FTV tea/coffee Dinner available WiFi ⅃18 Pool table ⅄ **Parking:** 40

### Premier Collection

## Mallard Grange

★★★★★ ≅ FARMHOUSE

**tel:** 01765 620242 & 07720 295918 **Aldfield HG4 3BE**
**email:** maggie@mallardgrange.co.uk **web:** www.mallardgrange.co.uk
**dir:** *B6265 W from Ripon, Mallard Grange 2.5m on right*

Located near Fountains Abbey, a genuine welcome is always guaranteed at Mallard Grange. The original features of this early 16th-century, Grade II listed farmhouse are highlighted by quality furnishings and decor. Bedrooms, two of which are in a converted smithy, are filled with a wealth of thoughtful extras, and comprehensive breakfasts feature home-reared and local produce.

**Rooms:** 2 en suite 2 annexe en suite (2 GF) **D** £80–£115* **Facilities:** FTV Lounge tea/coffee WiFi **Extras:** Speciality toiletries, home-made biscuits **Parking:** 6 **Notes:** No children 12yrs Closed Xmas & New Year 500 acres mixed/beef/sheep/arable

### Premier Collection

## The Old Coach House

★★★★★ ⒶGUEST ACCOMMODATION

**tel:** 07912 632296 & 01765 634900 **2 Stable Cottages, North Stainley HG4 3HT**
**email:** enquiries@oldcoachhouse.info **web:** www.oldcoachhouse.info
**dir:** *From Ripon take A6108 to Masham. Once in North Stainley, on left opposite Staveley Arms*

The Old Coach House has been part of the local community for over 20 years, so if you need information on the local area, don't hesitate to ask. This 18th-century building stands in the grounds of North Stainley Hall. All bedrooms are designed to a high specification and are individually decorated. Each room is named after a famous Yorkshire landmark or place and each offers a range of facilities. All rooms are en suite and some have wet rooms.

**Rooms:** 8 en suite (4 GF) **S** £75–£105; **D** £85–£115* **Facilities:** FTV iPod docking station Lounge tea/coffee Direct dial WiFi ⌁18 ☌ **Extras:** Speciality toiletries – complimentary **Parking:** 8 **Notes:** No children 14yrs

## St George's Court

★★★★ ≅ FARMHOUSE

**tel:** 01765 620618 **Old Home Farm, Grantley HG4 3PJ**
**email:** info@stgeorgescourt.co.uk **web:** www.stgeorgescourt.co.uk
**dir:** *B6265 W from Ripon, up hill 1m past Risplith sign & next right, 1m on right*

This renovated farmhouse is in a great location, in the delightful countryside close to Fountains Abbey. The attractive, well-equipped, ground-floor bedrooms are located around a central courtyard and provide modern accessories such as in-room fridges and TVs. Imaginative breakfasts are served in the breakfast room, and a guest lounge is available, both with views of the surrounding countryside.

**Rooms:** 4 en suite (1 fmly) (4 GF) **Facilities:** Lounge tea/coffee WiFi Fishing ☌ **Conf:** Max 12 **Parking:** 12 **Notes:** LB 20 acres beef/sheep/pigs

## The George at Wath

★★★★ ◉◉ INN

**tel:** 01765 641324 **Main Street, Wath HG4 5EN**
**email:** reception@thegeorgeatwath.co.uk **web:** www.thegeorgeatwath.co.uk
**dir:** *N of Ripon on A61, after rdbt turn left signed Wath. Continue for 3m, inn on right*

A warm welcome is guaranteed at this family-run establishment situated in a peaceful village. Bedrooms are well equipped and offer modern accessories such as TVs and complimentary WiFi. In-room beverage trays are well stocked and include home-made treats straight from the kitchen to enjoy on arrival. Dinner is served in the award-winning Harrison's Restaurant and will definitely be the highlight of any stay. Hearty breakfasts are also served using local produce. Complimentary on-site parking available.

**Rooms:** 5 en suite (1 fmly) **S** fr £65; **D** fr £85* **Facilities:** FTV iPod docking station tea/coffee Dinner available WiFi **Conf:** Max 40 Class 40 Board 40 **Parking:** 10 **Notes:** Closed 25 Dec

## The Firs

★★★★ ≅ GUEST HOUSE

**tel:** 01947 840433 **26 Hinderwell Lane TS13 5HR**
**email:** info@the-firs.co.uk **web:** www.the-firs.co.uk
**dir:** *From Whitby on A174, turn right signed Runswick. At T-junct turn left, 150yds on right*

The Firs is a spacious, family-run property located in the picturesque village of Runswick on the stunning North Yorkshire coast. The house is just eight miles north of Whitby and is on the edge of the North York Moors National Park. Free private parking, complimentary WiFi and comfortable bedrooms are offered along with a friendly welcome. The ground floor rooms are wheelchair accessible and have en suite wet rooms. (Please note credit cards may only be used for online transactions.)

**Rooms:** 9 en suite (3 fmly) (6 GF) **S** £75; **D** £95 **Facilities:** FTV DVD iPod docking station Lounge tea/coffee Direct dial WiFi ☌ **Extras:** Sweets, mineral water, home-made cake – complimentary **Parking:** 14 **Notes:** LB No children 2yrs Closed Nov-Mar

## Downe Arms Country Inn

★★★★ INN

tel: 01723 862471 **Main Road, Wykeham YO13 9QB**
email: info@downearmshotel.co.uk **web:** www.downearmshotel.co.uk
dir: *On A170 Pickering to Scarborough road in Wykeham*

Downe Arms Country Inn is a family-orientated inn on the doorstep of the North York Moors National Park and close to the coast and tourist areas in and around York. Part of the Dawnay estate, this 17th-century former farmhouse has been tastefully modernised. Expect comfortable public areas supported by good cooking, and well-appointed bedrooms with a contemporary feel. The property also caters well for functions and is a popular wedding venue. Ample car parking is available.

**Rooms:** 10 en suite (2 fmly) **Facilities:** FTV Lounge tea/coffee Dinner available WiFi Fishing 🔒 Pheasant & grouse shooting **Conf:** Max 150 Thtr 150 Class 90 Board 50 **Parking:** 85 **Notes:** Civ wed 120

## Paragon

★★★★ GUEST ACCOMMODATION

tel: 01723 372676 **123 Queens Parade YO12 7HU**
email: lynnandmike@paragonhotel.com **web:** www.paragonhotel.com
dir: *On A64, follow signs for North Bay. Establishment on clifftop*

This welcoming Victorian terraced house has been carefully renovated to provide stylish, thoughtfully equipped, non-smoking accommodation. Hearty English breakfasts are served in the attractive dining room and there is also a lounge bar with a fabulous sea view.

**Rooms:** 14 en suite (1 fmly) **S** £44–£46; **D** £68–£85* **Facilities:** FTV Lounge tea/coffee Licensed WiFi **Parking:** 6 **Notes:** LB No children 5yrs Closed 20 Nov–24 Jan

## The Whiteley

★★★★ GUEST ACCOMMODATION

tel: 01723 373514 **99–101 Queens Parade YO12 7HY**
email: thewhiteley@gmail.com **web:** www.yorkshirecoast.co.uk/whiteley
dir: *A64, A165 to North Bay & Peasholm Park, right into Peasholm Rd, 1st left*

The Whiteley is an immaculately run, sea-facing home-from-home. Bedrooms, though compact, are carefully decorated and have many thoughtful extras. There's a small garden at the rear and a choice of lounges. The establishment has superb views, and the owners provide personal attention and a substantial breakfast.

**Rooms:** 10 en suite (3 fmly) (1 GF) **S** £37.50–£39; **D** £63–£70* **Facilities:** Lounge TVL tea/coffee WiFi **Parking:** 8 **Notes:** LB No children 3yrs Closed 30 Nov–Jan

## The Albert

★★★ INN

tel: 01723 447260 **58 North Marine Road YO12 7PE**
email: alberthotel@btinternet.com **web:** www.thealbert-scarborough.co.uk
dir: *From rail station turn left onto Northway. Turn right at lights then straight on. At rdbt turn left, The Albert 100yds on left*

Located within a few minutes' walk of Scarborough's North Bay and the town centre, this traditional seaside pub offers a range of locally sourced dishes as well as a wide selection of real ales. The en suite accommodation is comfortable and offers a range of modern accessories such as TVs and complimentary WiFi.

**Rooms:** 3 en suite (2 fmly) **S** £45–£65; **D** £65–£85* **Facilities:** FTV tea/coffee Dinner available WiFi Pool table 🔒 **Extras:** Fruit tea **Parking:** 6 **Notes:** LB

## North End Farm Country Guesthouse

★★★ GUEST ACCOMMODATION

tel: 01723 862965 **88 Main Street, Seamer YO12 4RF**
email: northendfarm@tiscali.co.uk **web:** www.northendfarmseamer.co.uk
dir: *A64 N onto B1261 through Seamer, next to rdbt*

Located in Seamer, a village inland from Scarborough, this 18th-century property offers comfortable, well-equipped en suite bedrooms. Breakfast is served at individual tables in the smart dining room, and the cosy lounge has a large-screen TV.

**Rooms:** 3 en suite (1 fmly) **S** £45–£50; **D** £75–£80* **Facilities:** FTV TVL tea/coffee WiFi 🔒 **Parking:** 6

## The Phoenix Guest House

★★★ GUEST HOUSE

tel: 01723 368319 & 07847 102337 **157 Columbus Ravine YO12 7QZ**
email: jnnlms@aol.co.uk **web:** www.phoenixscarborough.wordpress.com
dir: *From railway station at junct of A64 & A165, take A165 signed North Bay. On right, 100mtrs from Peasholm Park*

Located close to Peasholm Park and just a few minutes' walk from the North Bay, this friendly guest house offers clean, comfortable bedrooms. There is a cosy lounge where guests can relax, exchange books or play games at the card table. Complimentary WiFi is provided and packed lunches can also be purchased.

**Rooms:** 6 en suite (2 fmly) **S** £30–£36; **D** £40–£46 (room only)* **Facilities:** FTV DVD TVL tea/coffee WiFi **Notes:** LB

## The Sheridan

★★★ 🅰 GUEST ACCOMMODATION

tel: 01723 372094 **108 Columbus Ravine YO12 7QZ**
email: kim@thesheridan.co.uk **web:** www.thesheridan.co.uk
dir: *From railway station left into Northway, over 2 mini rdbts, establishment 300yds on left*

Set on an attractive, tree-lined road close to all North Bay attractions, and only five minutes' walk away from the beach, The Sheridan is a welcoming place to stay. At breakfast, try a full English – special diets are catered for. Traditional Yorkshire cuisine is available in the evening.

**Rooms:** 9 en suite (2 fmly) (1 GF) **S** £40–£45; **D** £65–£75* **Facilities:** FTV tea/coffee Dinner available WiFi **Parking:** 5 **Notes:** LB No children 5yrs Closed Nov–Jan

## The Vintage

★★ 🅰 INN

tel: 01748 824424 **DL10 6NP**
email: thevintagescotchcorner@btinternet.com **web:** www.thevintagehotel.co.uk
dir: *Exit A1 at Scotch Corner onto A66 towards Penrith, premises 200yds on left*

A warm welcome and attentive service awaits you at The Vintage, a family-run establishment. Bedrooms come in a variety of styles and sizes and all are well equipped. You can choose either a continental or a cooked breakfast, and a tempting selection of evening meals is available either in the bar or restaurant.

**Rooms:** 8 rms (5 en suite) **S** £30–£45; **D** £45–£60 (room only)* **Facilities:** FTV TVL tea/coffee Dinner available WiFi **Extras:** Snacks – complimentary **Conf:** Max 40 Thtr 40 Class 24 Board 20 **Parking:** 40 **Notes:** LB Closed Xmas & New Year

## SEAMER
Map 17 TA08

### The Mayfield

★★★ GUEST ACCOMMODATION

**tel:** 01723 863160 **YO12 4RF**
**email:** info@themayfieldseamer.co.uk **web:** www.themayfieldseamer.co.uk
**dir:** *From Thirsk follow A170 to Seamer village. From York follow A64 to Staxton rdbt, turn left. At next rdbt turn left into Seamer village*

The Mayfield is set in the quiet village of Seamer near the popular seaside resort of Scarborough. The stylish accommodation boasts many modern extras such as complimentary WiFi, wine fridges and iPod docking stations. The bar is child friendly with family room and large soft play area. Menus offer a wide selection of home-made pub classics as well as a full carvery offering.

**Rooms:** 9 en suite 6 annexe en suite (1 fmly) **Facilities:** STV FTV DVD iPod docking station tea/coffee Dinner available Direct dial Licensed WiFi ⬢ **Extras:** Fridge, safe **Conf:** Max 70 Thtr 70 Class 48 Board 30 **Parking:** 24

## SETTLE
Map 18 SD86

*See also Clapham*

### The Lion at Settle

★★★★ INN

**tel:** 01729 822203 **Duke Street BD24 9DU**
**email:** relax@thelionsettle.co.uk **web:** www.thelionsettle.co.uk
**dir:** *In town centre opposite Barclays Bank*

Located in the heart of the market town of Settle, this is a traditional coaching inn with an inglenook fireplace. The accommodation is comfortable and well equipped. A wide selection of imaginative dishes, together with real ales and fine wines, is served in the busy bar, and also the restaurant where the atmosphere is relaxed and comfortable; alfresco dining is possible in the courtyard.

**Rooms:** 14 en suite (3 fmly) **Facilities:** FTV tea/coffee Dinner available WiFi ⬢
**Notes:** LB

## SKIPTON
Map 18 SD95

### The Woolly Sheep

★★★★ ⬢ INN

**tel:** 01756 700966 **38 Sheep Street BD23 1HY**
**email:** woolly.sheep@btconnect.com **web:** www.woollysheepinn.co.uk
**dir:** *At bottom of High St*

Situated right in the centre of Skipton's vibrant market town, close to the medieval castle and railway station, this popular inn offers good quality and comfortable accommodation. All bedrooms have a modern country feel and are en suite. They are also well equipped with well stocked beverage trays, TVs and complimentary WiFi. Good home-cooked food is served alongside a range of Timothy Taylor real ales. There is an attractive courtyard seating area and free, secure parking to the rear.

**Rooms:** 9 en suite (3 fmly) **Facilities:** FTV tea/coffee Dinner available WiFi
**Parking:** 14 **Notes:** LB

### Rockwood House

★★★ GUEST ACCOMMODATION

**tel:** 01756 799755 & 07976 314980 **14 Main Street, Embsay BD23 6RE**
**email:** rockwood@steadonline.com **web:** www.stayinyorkshire.co.uk
**dir:** *2m NE of Skipton. Off A59 into Embsay village centre*

This Victorian mid-terrace house has a peaceful location in the charming village of Embsay; great for walking, local attractions and of course the steam railway. Bedrooms are thoughtfully furnished, individually styled and reassuringly comfortable. The traditionally styled dining room is the venue for hearty breakfasts. Hospitality is a feature here with a genuine and friendly welcome.

**Rooms:** 3 en suite (1 fmly) (1 GF) **S** £50–£72; **D** £72–£80* **Facilities:** tea/coffee **Notes:** LB No children 3yrs

## STILLINGFLEET
Map 16 SE54

### Harmony House

★★★★ ⬢ GUEST ACCOMMODATION

**tel:** 01904 720933 & 07889 808749 **The Green YO19 6SH**
**email:** hilary@harmonyhouseyork.com **web:** www.harmonyhouseyork.com
**dir:** *From York on A19 towards Selby, through Escrick (on dual carriageway). Right onto B1222 signed Stillingfleet. 2m to village. Right signed Naburn. 1st left into The Green, house on right*

Harmony House is in a peaceful village setting, yet is just a short drive from York city centre. On arrival guests are served complimentary tea and home-made cake in the cosy lounge (between 3pm and 5pm). Bedrooms are homely and well equipped, with complimentary WiFi, fridges and TVs. Beverage trays are included, and breakfasts are guaranteed to set you up for the day. Evening meals can be arranged on request. Off-road parking is also available.

**Rooms:** 3 en suite **S** £55–£70; **D** £75–£90* **Facilities:** FTV iPod docking station TVL tea/coffee Dinner available WiFi ⬢ **Extras:** Speciality toiletries, mini-fridge, fresh milk, home-made biscuits, snacks, sweets **Conf:** Max 12 **Parking:** 6 **Notes:** LB Closed 23 Dec–2 Jan

## TADCASTER
Map 16 SE44

### The Old Presbytery Guest House

★★★ BED AND BREAKFAST

**tel:** 01937 557708 **London Road, Saxton LS24 9PU**
**email:** guest@presbytery.plus.com **web:** www.presbyteryguesthouse.co.uk
**dir:** *4m S of Tadcaster on A162. 100yds N of Barkston Ash on E side of road*

Dating from the 18th century, this former dower house has been modernised to provide comfortable accommodation, while retaining many original features. The hall lounge features a wood-burning stove, and delicious breakfasts are served at an old oak dining table in a cosy breakfast room. The beautiful gardens are a feature in their own right, with an attractive wooden bower providing sheltered outdoor seating space. Secure parking and complimentary WiFi are provided.

**Rooms:** 4 rms (3 en suite) (1 pri facs) (1 fmly) **S** £47–£67; **D** £88* **Facilities:** FTV TVL tea/coffee WiFi ⬢18 ⬢ **Parking:** 6 **Notes:** Closed 21 Dec–6 Jan

## THIRSK
Map 19 SE48

### Newsham Grange Farm Bed and Breakfast

★★★★ BED AND BREAKFAST

**tel:** 01845 588047 & 07808 903044 **Newsham Grange Farm YO7 4DF**
**email:** sue@newshamgrangefarm.co.uk **web:** www.newshamgrangefarm.co.uk
**dir:** A1(M) junct with A61, follow signs to Thirsk for 4m. Left at rdbt onto A167, 3m on left

This impressive Georgian farmhouse is set in extensive grounds on the outskirts of Thirsk. It's family run and the friendly owners have refurbished the property to a high standard. The four spacious bedrooms feature luxurious touches, such as under-floor heating, and can also be reconfigured to provide family rooms. The grounds are stunning with a decked terrace, outdoor swimming pool and hot tub adding to the idyllic setting overlooking the orchard. Secure parking with CCTV and lockable storage for bicycles add to the range of facilities. Complimentary WiFi is also available.

**Rooms:** 2 en suite 2 annexe rms (2 pri facs) (2 fmly) (4 GF) **Facilities:** FTV tea/coffee Licensed WiFi ↖ ⅃18 ⌂ Hot tub **Extras:** Bath robes, slippers **Parking:** 4 **Notes:** LB No children 7yrs

## WASS
Map 19 SE57

### The Stapylton Arms

★★★★ GUEST ACCOMMODATION

**tel:** 01347 868280 **YO61 4BE**
**email:** info@stapyltonarms.co.uk **web:** www.stapyltonarms.co.uk

This owner-run property is situated within the heart of the peaceful North Yorkshire village of Wass. The newly refurbished accommodation is decorated in a contemporary country style with all the amenities expected by modern day traveller provided. TVs, complimentary WiFi and well-stocked hospitality trays are all inlcuded. Dinner menus offer a good level of choice with daily changing specials and hearty breakfasts are also a highlight. On-site car parking available.

**Rooms:** 3 en suite **D** £100–£130* **Facilities:** tea/coffee WiFi **Parking**

## WESTOW
Map 19 SE76

### Woodhouse Farm

★★★★ FARMHOUSE

**tel:** 01653 618378 & 07904 293422 **YO60 7LL**
**email:** stay@wood-house-farm.co.uk **web:** www.wood-house-farm.co.uk
**dir:** Exit A64 to Kirkham Priory & Westow. Right at T-junct, farm drive 0.5m out of village on right

The owners of this house are a young farming family who offer caring hospitality in their rural home. Bedrooms are spacious and there is a comfortable lounge also available for guests. Complimentary WiFi is provided. Home-made bread, preserves and farm produce turn breakfast into a feast, and the views from the house across open fields are splendid.

**Rooms:** 2 en suite (1 fmly) **S** £40–£60; **D** £70–£90* **Facilities:** FTV DVD iPod docking station TVL tea/coffee WiFi Fishing ⌂ **Extras:** Robes **Parking:** 12 **Notes:** LB Closed Xmas, New Year & mid Mar–mid Apr 500 acres arable/sheep/beef

## WEST WITTON
Map 19 SE08

### Premier Collection

### The Wensleydale Heifer

★★★★★ ◉ ⌂ RESTAURANT WITH ROOMS

**tel:** 01969 622322 **Main Street DL8 4LS**
**email:** info@wensleydaleheifer.co.uk **web:** www.wensleydaleheifer.co.uk
**dir:** A1 to Leeming Bar junct, A684 towards Bedale for approx 10m to Leyburn, then towards Hawes 3.5m to West Witton

Describing itself as 'boutique style', this 17th-century former coaching inn is very much of the 21st century. The bedrooms, with Egyptian cotton linen and Molton Brown toiletries as standard, are each designed with an interesting theme – for example, Black Sheep, Night at the Movies, True Romantics and Shooters, and for chocolate lovers, there's a bedroom where you can eat as much chocolate as you like! The food is very much the focus here in both the informal fish bar and the contemporary style restaurant. The kitchen prides itself on sourcing the freshest fish and locally reared meats.

**Rooms:** 9 en suite 4 annexe en suite (2 fmly) (2 GF) **S** £80–£160; **D** £120–£200 **Facilities:** FTV DVD Lounge tea/coffee Dinner available Direct dial WiFi **Extras:** Speciality toiletries, fruit, snacks **Parking:** 30 **Notes:** LB

## WHITBY
Map 19 NZ81

### Abbotsleigh of Whitby

★★★★ ⌂ GUEST HOUSE

**tel:** 01947 606615 & 07866 880707 **5 Argyle Road YO21 3HS**
**email:** enquiries@abbotsleighofwhitby.co.uk **web:** www.abbotsleighofwhitby.co.uk
**dir:** From train station onto Bagdale. At mini rdbt turn right onto Chubb Hill. At next rdbt take 2nd exit & right at next rdbt. Right into Argyle Rd

Guests can be sure of friendly service at this immaculately presented Victorian house where tea and home-made cake are offered on arrival. The attractively furnished bedrooms, and stylish en suite wet rooms have a luxurious feel. Thoughtful accessories such as coffee machines, iPod docking stations and DVD players are provided. Complimentary WiFi is also available.

**Rooms:** 5 en suite (1 GF) **D** fr £95* **Facilities:** STV DVD iPod docking station tea/coffee WiFi **Extras:** Speciality toiletries, home-made biscuits, milk **Parking:** 3 **Notes:** LB No children 12yrs

### Estbek House

★★★★ ◉◉ ⌂ RESTAURANT WITH ROOMS

**tel.** 01947 893424 **East Row, Sandsend YO21 3SU**
**email:** info@estbekhouse.co.uk **web:** www.estbekhouse.co.uk
**dir:** From Whitby take A174. In Sandsend, left into East Row

The speciality seafood restaurant on the first floor is the focus of this listed building in a small coastal village north west of Whitby. The seasonal menu is based on fresh, local ingredients, and is overseen by Tim the chef, who has guided his team to two AA Rosettes. There is also a small bar and breakfast room, and four individually appointed bedrooms offering high levels of comfort.

**Rooms:** 4 rms (3 en suite) (1 pri facs) **Facilities:** tea/coffee Dinner available WiFi **Parking:** 6 **Notes:** LB No children 14yrs

WHITBY *continued*

## Netherby House

★★★★ ⚅ ☕ GUEST ACCOMMODATION

tel: 01947 810211 **90 Coach Road, Sleights YO22 5EQ**
email: info@netherby-house.co.uk web: www.netherby-house.co.uk
dir: *In village of Sleights, off A169 (Whitby-Pickering road)*

This fine Victorian house offers thoughtfully furnished, individually styled bedrooms together with delightful day rooms. There is a fine conservatory and the grounds are extensive, with exceptional views from the summer house at the bottom of the garden. Imaginative dinners feature produce from the extensive kitchen garden.

**Rooms:** 6 en suite 5 annexe en suite (1 fmly) (5 GF) **S** £43.50–£53.50; **D** £87–£107*
**Facilities:** FTV Lounge TVL tea/coffee Dinner available Licensed WiFi ⛄ 🔒
**Parking:** 17 **Notes:** LB No children 2yrs Closed 25–26 Dec

## Overdale Guest House

★★★★ GUEST HOUSE

tel: 01947 605612 & 07763 339818 **39 Prospect Hill YO21 1QE**
email: jayneoates@hotmail.co.uk web: www.overdaleguesthouse.co.uk
dir: *A171 to Whitby, onto A174 signed Town Centre. Guest house on left*

This fine Victorian terraced house has been sympathetically refurbished and offers guests four charming, very well appointed bedrooms. Built originally for a local sea captain, the house is a short walk from the town centre and Whitby's lovely beaches. Free WiFi is available throughout the house and parking is available. A warm welcome is guaranteed and breakfast is served at individual tables in the light-filled breakfast room.

**Rooms:** 4 en suite (1 fmly) **D** £95–£110* **Facilities:** FTV Lounge tea/coffee WiFi
🔒 **Parking:** 6

## Whitehaven Guest House

★★★★ GUEST ACCOMMODATION

tel: 01947 601569 & 07748 374683 **29 Crescent Avenue YO21 3EW**
email: simon@whitehavenguesthouse.co.uk web: www.whitehavenguesthouse.co.uk
dir: *Follow signs to West Cliff, A174 into Crescent Av*

A warm welcome awaits at this attractive, family-run Edwardian house. Occupying a corner position close to the sports complex and indoor swimming pool, Whitehaven Guest House is only a short walk from other local attractions. Bedrooms are modern and coordinated with a contemporary twist, and all have flat panel TVs with Freesat channel availability. DVD players are available on request. Freshly prepared breakfasts are served in the elegant ground-floor dining room. Complimentary WiFi is available throughout the building and there is free on-street parking.

**Rooms:** 4 rms (3 en suite) (1 pri facs) (1 fmly) **D** £75–£90* **Facilities:** STV FTV DVD tea/coffee WiFi 🔒 **Extras:** Speciality toiletries **Notes:** LB Closed 23–26 Dec

## Argyle House

★★★★ GUEST ACCOMMODATION

tel: 01947 821877 **18 Hudson Street YO21 3EP**
email: bill@argyle-house.co.uk web: www.argyle-house.co.uk
dir: *Follow signs for West Cliff & Whitby Pavilion, with the sea on left, turn into Royal Crescent & exit through the rear of crescent. Hudson St is also known as Abbey Terrace*

Built originally in the 1850s and enjoying a prominent position in a conservation area, Argyle House is a short walk from Whitby's town centre, harbour and beaches. There are a range of comfortable, well-appointed bedrooms. Guests are guaranteed a warm welcome from the friendly owners and delicious breakfast is served at individual tables in the light-filled breakfast room. Free WiFi is available throughout.

**Rooms:** 7 en suite (2 fmly) **Facilities:** STV FTV DVD iPod docking station tea/coffee WiFi **Extras:** Fruit **Notes:** LB No children 5yrs

## Boulmer Guest House

★★★★ GUEST HOUSE

**tel:** 01947 604284 **23 Crescent Avenue YO21 3ED**
**email:** info@boulmerguesthouse.co.uk **web:** www.boulmerguesthouse.co.uk
**dir:** *Follow signs for West Cliff, from Royal Crescent into Crescent Av, pass church on right. Road bears to right, 3rd house on left before sorting office*

This friendly guest house is just a short walk from the beautiful beach and Whitby Pavilion on the picturesque West Cliff, and is also convenient for shops, cafés and restaurants. The range of attractively presented bedrooms include family rooms, a twin, a single, and with prior arrangement, dog-friendly bedrooms. Modern facilities are provided including complimentary WiFi. Free on-street parking is available.

**Rooms:** 7 rms (5 en suite) (2 fmly) (1 GF) **S** £37.50; **D** £80–£105* **Facilities:** FTV DVD TVL tea/coffee WiFi ☕ **Notes:** LB

## Kimberley House

★★★★ GUEST ACCOMMODATION

**tel:** 01947 604125 **7 Havelock Place YO21 3ER**
**email:** enquiries@kimberleyhouse.com **web:** www.kimberleyhouse.com
**dir:** *Follow signs for West Cliff, close to Whalebone Arch and Captain Cook Monument, behind Royal Crescent at corner of Hudson St*

Warm and genuine hospitality is offered at this attractive house in the centre of Whitby, just a short stroll away from the local attractions. Bedrooms are pleasantly co-ordinated and comfortably furnished, with an attic family suite available. Freshly prepared breakfasts are served in the attractive ground floor dining room which has a cosy sitting area, where guests can enjoy complimentary teas and coffees.

**Rooms:** 8 rms (7 en suite) (1 pri facs) (1 fmly) (1 GF) **S** £35–£40; **D** £60–£80 **Facilities:** FTV DVD TVL tea/coffee WiFi ☕ **Extras:** Guest fridge **Notes:** Closed 15–27 Dec

| YORK | Map 16 SE65 |
| --- | --- |

### Premier Collection

## The Judge's Lodging

★★★★★ ⚜ INN

**tel:** 01904 638733 **9 Lendal YO1 8AQ**
**email:** relax@judgeslodgingyork.co.uk **web:** www.judgeslodgingyork.co.uk

The Judge's Lodging is a Grade I listed Georgian townhouse situated in the heart of the city centre, just a stone's throw from the Minster. The building has a wealth of charm and character throughout the public areas and in the well-equipped bedrooms. The public rooms include a cellar bar with original vaulted ceilings and cosy dining/drinking areas; a Cask Bar and a superb glass box, where you can dine inside yet still feel like you're outside. The property also has a choice of sun terraces for alfresco dining.

**Rooms:** 21 en suite **D** fr £115 **Facilities:** FTV tea/coffee Dinner available WiFi **Extras:** Fresh milk

## Ascot House

★★★★ GUEST ACCOMMODATION

**tel:** 01904 426826 **80 East Parade YO31 7YH**
**email:** admin@ascothouseyork.com **web:** www.ascothouseyork.com
**dir:** *0.5m NE of city centre. Exit A1036 (Heworth Green) into Mill Ln, 2nd left*

Ascot House is a 15-minute walk from York Minster. All bedrooms are en suite and the first-floor rooms all have four-poster or antique canopy beds and attractive period furniture, while those on the second floor have a more contemporary style. All rooms are well equipped with TV and free WiFi. The dining room offers a range of breakfast options including traditional English, vegetarian and continental. The comfortable residents' lounge is the ideal place to enjoy tea or coffee, or something stronger from the Butler's Pantry.

**Rooms:** 12 en suite (3 fmly) (2 GF) **S** £90–£110; **D** £104–£115* **Facilities:** FTV TVL tea/coffee Licensed WiFi ☕ **Extras:** Bottled water – complimentary **Parking:** 13 **Notes:** LB Closed 21–28 Dec

## Burswood Guest House

★★★★ ⚜ GUEST HOUSE

**tel:** 01904 702582 **68 Tadcaster Road, Dringhouses YO24 1LR**
**email:** info@burswoodguesthouse.co.uk **web:** www.burswoodguesthouse.co.uk
**dir:** *On A1036 Tadcaster Rd*

Located on the main Tadcaster Road just opposite York race course, this well presented accommodation offers very well equipped bedrooms and bathrooms including some on the ground floor. Breakfast is taken in the comfortable dining room and is freshly cooked to order using good quality ingredients. Off-street car parking is a welcome feature and a number of pubs and hotels are within easy walking distance for dinner.

**Rooms:** 6 en suite (1 fmly) (3 GF) **Facilities:** FTV Lounge tea/coffee WiFi ☕ **Extras:** Fresh milk, robes, slippers **Parking:** 6 **Notes:** LB

YORK *continued*

## Guy Fawkes Inn

★★★★  INN

**tel:** 01904 623716 & 466674 **25 High Petergate YO1 7HP**
**email:** reservations@guyfawkesinnyork.com **web:** www.guyfawkesinnyork.com
**dir:** *A64 onto A1036 signed York & inner ring road. Over bridge into Duncombe Place,*
*right into High Petergate*

The Guy Fawkes Inn stands next to York Minster and was the birthplace of the
notorious Gunpowder Plotter. The inn offers rooms with free WiFi and TVs, furnished
with antiques and Italian fabrics. Many rooms have views of the city or the
courtyard, and bathrooms have luxury toiletries from Aromatherapy Associates.
Old or original features include the timber staircase, gas lighting and real log fires.
The world-famous Guy Fawkes Ghost Walk leaves every night just around the corner.
Dine by candlelight in the restaurant, which serves traditional food from locally-
sourced ingredients. The bar stocks a wide range of real ales and a selection of
fruit wines.

**Rooms:** 13 en suite (1 fmly) (2 GF) **Facilities:** FTV tea/coffee Dinner available Direct
dial WiFi **Notes:** LB

## The Heathers Guest House

★★★★ GUEST ACCOMMODATION

**tel:** 01904 640989 **54 Shipton Rd, Clifton-Without YO30 5RQ**
**email:** aabbg@heathers-guest-house.co.uk **web:** www.heathers-guest-house.co.uk
**dir:** *N of York on A19, halfway between A1237 ring road & York city centre*

This spacious detached house offers off-street parking and a peaceful setting,
only a short drive or walk from the city centre. Each room is individually designed,
using quality fabrics. The light, airy breakfast room looks out onto the beautiful

large rear garden, which is visited daily by local wildlife. Complimentary WiFi
access is provided.

*The Heathers Guest House*

**Rooms:** 5 en suite **D** £92–£120 **Facilities:** FTV Lounge tea/coffee WiFi  **Parking:** 9
**Notes:** No children 12yrs Closed Xmas & Jan

## Lamb & Lion Inn

★★★★  INN

**tel:** 01904 612078 & 654112 **2–4 High Petergate YO1 7EH**
**email:** reservations@lambandlioninnyork.com **web:** www.lambandlioninnyork.com
**dir:** *A64 onto A1036. 3.5m, at rdbt 3rd exit, continue on A1036. 2m, right into*
*High Petergate*

In the heart of York, just beyond the entrance of Bootham Bar, the Lamb & Lion
Inn offers hearty food, real ales, and luxurious bedrooms, some with spa baths.
The bedrooms are beautifully decorated in earthy colours and all have en suite
bathrooms. Guests can also enjoy free WiFi, a TV and tea- and coffee-making
facilities. The restaurant serves authentic, rustic dishes, including a cooked
Yorkshire breakfast. A wide range of real ales and lagers is available at the bar.
York Minster is just close by, while the National Railway Museum is a 15-minute
walk, and Harrogate is a 40-minute drive.

**Rooms:** 12 en suite **S** fr £45; **D** fr £49* **Facilities:** FTV tea/coffee Dinner available
WiFi **Conf:** Max 20 Thtr 20 Class 20 Board 20

## Holmwood House

★★★★ GUEST ACCOMMODATION

**tel:** 01904 626183 **112/114 Holgate Road YO24 4BB**
**email:** info@holmwoodhousehotel.co.uk **web:** www.holmwoodhousehotel.co.uk
**dir:** *Phone for directions*

A 15-minute walk from Holmwood House takes you into the centre of York. The
individually styled bedrooms are richly decorated and smartly furnished with many
antiques. There is a comfortable lounge and a substantial breakfast is served in
the pleasant basement dining room. Some private parking and complimentary WiFi
are also available.

**Rooms:** 14 en suite 7 annexe en suite (1 fmly) (5 GF) **D** £65–£140* **Facilities:** FTV
Lounge tea/coffee WiFi  **Parking:** 8 **Notes:** LB Closed 24–27 Dec

## Ashley Guest House

★★★★  GUEST HOUSE

**tel:** 01904 647520 & 07955 250271 **76 Scott Street YO23 1NS**
**email:** stay@ashleyguesthouse.co.uk **web:** www.ashleyguesthouse.co.uk
**dir:** From A64 take York West exit onto A1036 (Tadcaster Rd) follow city centre signs.
After racecourse (on right) at 2nd lights right into Scarcroft Rd. Scott St 2nd last street
before lights

Ashley Guest House is a Victorian end-terrace that has been given modern
treatment resulting in stylish interiors and a distinctive character. Attractively
furnished bedrooms and caring hospitality are hallmarks of this well-located city
centre establishment.

**Rooms:** 6 rms (5 en suite) (1 pri facs) (1 fmly) **S** £60–£80; **D** £75–£95*
**Facilities:** FTV Lounge tea/coffee WiFi ⚓ **Notes:** No children 5yrs

## City Guest House

★★★★ GUEST ACCOMMODATION

**tel:** 01904 622483 **68 Monkgate YO31 7PF**
**email:** info@cityguesthouse.co.uk **web:** www.cityguesthouse.co.uk
**dir:** NE of city centre on B1036

Just a five-minute walk from York Minster and close to the city wall and other
sights, this charming Victorian town house is well located for business, shopping
and sightseeing. Carefully furnished bedrooms are attractively presented and offer
a range of thoughtful touches. The traditional and beautifully presented dining
room provides a pleasant venue for the hearty breakfast.

**Rooms:** 7 rms (6 en suite) (1 pri facs) (1 fmly) (1 GF) **S** £46–£48; **D** £70–£75*
**Facilities:** FTV iPod docking station Lounge tea/coffee WiFi ₺9 ⚓ **Parking:** 2
**Notes:** No children 8yrs Closed Xmas & 1st 2 weeks Jan

## Fifth Milestone Cottage

★★★★ GUEST HOUSE

**tel:** 01904 489361 & 07885 502420 **Hull Road YO19 5LR**
**email:** mrsmartyn@hotmail.com **web:** www.milestonecottage.co.uk
**dir:** From A64 onto A1079 towards Hull. On left after Philip Welch Garage

As the name suggests, this spacious cottage is just five miles from York centre.
The property is set in large, well-kept grounds with private parking. Guests can
relax in the pretty garden where there is also a large decked area. There is a wide
range of bedrooms available from doubles, including a four-poster room, to twins
and family rooms. Some also have their own terrace and several offer very good
disabled facilities and good access for wheelchair users.

**Rooms:** 3 en suite 3 annexe en suite (1 fmly) (3 GF) **S** £55–£65; **D** £75–£115*
**Facilities:** FTV DVD tea/coffee WiFi ⚓ Animal farm **Extras:** Hot tub in one room
**Parking:** 12 **Notes:** RS 25–26 Dec room only

## Greenside

★★★ GUEST HOUSE

**tel:** 01904 623631 **124 Clifton YO30 6BQ**
**email:** greenside@onebillnet.co.uk **web:** www.greensideguesthouse.co.uk
**dir:** A19 N towards city centre, over lights for Greenside, on left opposite Clifton Green

Overlooking Clifton Green, this charming detached conservation house is within
walking distance of the city centre. Accommodation consists of comfortably
furnished bedrooms and the traditional full English breakfast is served in the
dining room. Secure parking and WiFi are additional bonuses.

**Rooms:** 6 rms (3 en suite) 2 annexe rms (2 fmly) (3 GF) **S** £35–£37; **D** £64–£75
**Facilities:** FTV tea/coffee WiFi **Parking:** 6 **Notes:** LB Closed Xmas & New Year

## SOUTH YORKSHIRE

**DONCASTER** Map 16 SE50

## Innkeeper's Lodge Doncaster, Bessacarr

★★★ INN

**tel:** 08451 551551 *(Calls cost 2p per minute plus your phone company's access charge)*
**Bawtry Road, Bessacarr DN4 7BS**
**email:** info@innkeeperslodge.com **web:** www.innkeeperslodge.com

Comfortable, modern accommodation ideal for Doncaster racecourse and also
convenient for Doncaster airport. There is a Toby Carvery offering a friendly pub
atmosphere and roast dinners every day. There is also a pub menu, free WiFi
throughout and Sky Sports is shown in the bar. Ample on-site parking is also
available.

**Rooms:** 25 en suite (3 fmly) (6 GF) **Facilities:** FTV tea/coffee Dinner available
Direct dial WiFi

**SHEFFIELD** Map 16 SK38

## Cross Scythes

★★★★ INN

**tel:** 0114 236 0204 **Baslow Road, Totley S17 4AE**
**email:** enquiries@cross-scythes.com **web:** www.cross-scythes.com

Located approximately five miles south of Sheffield city centre and just 10 minutes'
drive from Chatsworth House, this 18th-century building has been sympathetically
renovated. There are four tastefully decorated double rooms and all are en suite.
Food is served all day throughout the spacious public areas.

**Rooms:** 4 en suite **D** £64 (room only)^ **Facilities:** FTV tea/coffee Dinner available
WiFi ₺18 **Parking:** 51

## Dog & Partridge

★★★★ INN

**tel:** 01226 763173 **Bord Hill, Flouch S36 4HH**
**email:** info@dogandpartridgeinn.co.uk **web:** www.dogandpartridgeinn.co.uk
**dir:** M1 junct 37 onto A628. At Flouch rdbt, straight over follow signs for Manchester.
1m on left

This comfortable family-run inn is located within the Peak District National Park.
Bedrooms are situated in the 18th-century barn adjoining the inn, all rooms are
comfortably furnished and some superior rooms are available. The beer garden has
stunning views of the surrounding moorland and a selection of real ales and
imaginative food is served in the public areas.

**Rooms:** 10 en suite (2 fmly) (7 GF) **S** £60–£85; **D** £70–£100* **Facilities:** FTV
tea/coffee Dinner available Direct dial WiFi ⚓ **Conf:** Max 50 Thtr 50 Class 36 Board
20 **Parking:** 70 **Notes:** Closed 25-27 Dec Civ wed 80

**SHEFFIELD** *continued*

## Innkeeper's Lodge Hathersage, Peak District

★★★ INN

**tel:** 08451 551551 *(Calls cost 2p per minute plus your phone company's access charge)*
**Hathersage Road, Longshaw S11 7TY**
**email:** info@innkeeperslodge.com **web:** www.innkeeperslodge.com

At Innkeeper's Lodge you'll find accommodation with comfort and character in equal measure, and everything needed for a relaxing stay, from easy check-in and free parking to complimentary breakfast and a cosy pub serving great value food and drink on the doorstep. Each Lodge has quality rooms, and there are Lodges in a variety of locations from towns and cities to countryside settings across the UK.

**Rooms:** 9 en suite (6 fmly) (4 GF) **Facilities:** FTV tea/coffee Dinner available WiFi

### WEST YORKSHIRE

| CASTLEFORD | Map 16 SE42 |

## The Wheldale

★★ INN

**tel:** 01977 553403 **Wheldon Road WF10 2SD**
**email:** wheldalecas@hotmail.co.uk **web:** www.wheldalehotel.co.uk
**dir:** *Opposite Castleford Tigers rugby stadium*

This inn is well established locally, and public areas are modern and provide spacious areas for families. The bar is very much a local's bar and has good real ales on offer. The Wheldale is situated opposite the Castleford Tigers Rugby ground so match days can be busy. Good parking is available and there is a very spacious beer garden where events are often held. Bedrooms are comfortable and offer both en suite and standard rooms.

**Rooms:** 10 rms (5 en suite) (1 fmly) **S** £21–£29; **D** £39–£65* **Facilities:** STV FTV Lounge TVL tea/coffee Dinner available WiFi ⅃18 Pool table 🏐 Bouncy castle at weekends **Parking:** 10 **Notes:** No children 12yrs

| HAWORTH | Map 19 SE03 |

### Premier Collection

## Ashmount Country House

★★★★★ 🍴 GUEST HOUSE

**tel:** 01535 645726 & 643822 **Mytholmes Lane BD22 8EZ**
**email:** info@ashmounthaworth.co.uk **web:** www.ashmounthaworth.co.uk
**dir:** *M65 junct 13A Laneshaw Bridge, turn right over moors to Haworth. Turn left after car park on right, 100yds on right*

Ashmount Country House is a stunning property in the heart of Brontë Country, just a short stroll from the centre of Haworth. It is an ideal location for those seeking a relaxing retreat with luxury touches. Each bedroom is designed with high-quality furnishings, attractive decor and many thoughtful extras; some have their own terrace with hot tub or sauna. There is also a comfortable lounge bar and an elegant dining room. Room service is available until 8.30pm. The landscaped gardens provide a lovely backdrop and a pleasant location to relax or enjoy afternoon tea on the lawn.

**Rooms:** 8 en suite (3 GF) **S** £79–£220; **D** £99–£220* **Facilities:** FTV iPod docking station Lounge tea/coffee Licensed WiFi 🌸 🏐 **Extras:** Fruit, home-made biscuits, sherry – complimentary **Conf:** Max 25 Thtr 20 Class 25 Board 15 **Parking:** 12 **Notes:** No children 10yrs Civ wed 40

| HOLMFIRTH | Map 16 SE10 |

## Rooms at the Nook

★★★★ GUEST ACCOMMODATION

**tel:** 01484 682373 & 07841 646308 **Victoria Square HD9 2DN**
**email:** office@thenookbrewhouse.co.uk **web:** www.roomsatthenook.co.uk
**dir:** *From A6024 in Holmfirth. On A635 (Victoria St), at bottom of Victoria St*

A warm welcome is assured at this centrally-located former 18th-century inn, which offers eight stylish bedrooms. The Nook pub retains many original features and benefits from an on-site microbrewery serving award-winning ales and a good wine selection. An adjacent bar and restaurant, known as The Tap House, specialises in tapas with a Yorkshire twist.

**Rooms:** 8 en suite (3 fmly) **Facilities:** FTV DVD TVL tea/coffee Dinner available Licensed WiFi ⅃18 Pool table 🏐

## Old Bridge Inn & Coffee House

★★★ INN

**tel:** 01484 681212 **Market Walk HD9 7DA**
**email:** oldbridge@innmail.co.uk **web:** www.oldbridgeholmfirth.co.uk

The Old Bridge Inn & Coffee House is a modern inn in the centre of the popular town of Holmfirth. Bedrooms are more traditional and offer good levels of comfort. Cocktails and drinks can be enjoyed in the stylish bar before dinner in the cosy restaurant with open fire. Menus offer an interesting choice. Home-made cakes can also been enjoyed throughout the day in the coffee shop bar area with a choice of comfortable sofas available. A large car park is available to all residents which is an asset.

**Rooms:** 21 en suite **S** £49–£99; **D** £69–£119* **Facilities:** STV tea/coffee Dinner available WiFi **Parking**

| HUDDERSFIELD | Map 16 SE11 |

### Premier Collection

## 315 Bar and Restaurant

★★★★★ 🏵🏵 RESTAURANT WITH ROOMS

**tel:** 01484 602613 **315 Wakefield Road, Lepton HD8 0LX**
**email:** info@315barandrestaurant.co.uk **web:** www.315barandrestaurant.co.uk
**dir:** *M1 junct 38, A637 towards Huddersfield. At rdbt take A642 towards Huddersfield. Establishment on right in Lepton*

In a wonderful setting, 315 Bar and Restaurant benefits from countryside views from the well-appointed dining room and conservatory areas. The interior is modern, with open fires that add character and ambiance, while the chef's table gives a real insight into the working of the two AA Rosette award-winning kitchen. Bedrooms are modern, and most have feature bathrooms. Air conditioning is also provided in some. Staff are friendly and attentive, and there are excellent parking facilities. New for 2017 is the addition of a fantastic spa facility. Treatments and use of facilities is at an extra charge.

**Rooms:** 10 en suite 8 annexe en suite (3 fmly) (8 GF) **S** £85; **D** £95–£145* **Facilities:** FTV DVD tea/coffee Dinner available Lift WiFi Spa facilities **Conf:** Max 150 Thtr 100 Class 75 Board 60 **Parking:** 97 **Notes:** Civ wed 120

## Woodman Inn

★★★★★ ⌂ INN

**tel:** 01484 605778 **Thunder Bridge Lane HD8 0PX**
**email:** info@woodman-inn.com **web:** www.woodman-inn.com

*(For full entry see Kirkburton)*

## Innkeeper's Lodge Huddersfield, Kirkburton

★★★ INN

**tel:** 08451 551551 *(Calls cost 2p per minute plus your phone company's access charge)*
**36a Penistone Road, Kirkburton HD8 0PQ**
**email:** info@innkeeperslodge.com **web:** www.innkeeperslodge.com

Situated on the Penistone Road, with easy reach of the National Coal Mining Museum and Huddersfield town centre. The lodge provides modern bedrooms and is attached to the Foxglove Vintage Inn; an attractive 19th-century building with real fires and spacious dining areas. A continental buffet breakfast is complimentary for all guests – a cooked option available at a supplement. Free WiFi is available throughout plus ample parking space.

**Rooms:** 23 en suite (3 fmly) (13 GF) **Facilities:** FTV tea/coffee Dinner available WiFi

| ILKLEY | Map 19 SE14 |
|---|---|

## Innkeeper's Lodge Ilkley

★★★ INN

**tel:** 08451 551551 *(Calls cost 2p per minute plus your phone company's access charge)*
**Hangingstone Road LS29 8BT**
**email:** info@innkeeperslodge.com **web:** www.innkeeperslodge.com

This Innkeeper's Lodge is a 19th-century Victorian property idyllically located in the Yorkshire Dales, with stunning views over Wharfedale. Perfect for walkers, browsing the spa town of Ilkley, close to Ben Rhydding golf course and only a short drive from Leeds and Bradford. There is lots of period charm in the inviting public areas, where hearty food and cask ales are served. The bedrooms are modern and comfortable. Complimentary WiFi is provided.

**Rooms:** 14 en suite (2 fmly) **Facilities:** FTV tea/coffee Dinner available WiFi

## Follow us on twitter
@TheAA_Lifestyle

| KIRKBURTON | Map 16 SE11 |
|---|---|

## Woodman Inn

★★★★★ ⌂ INN

**tel:** 01484 605778 **Thunder Bridge Lane HD8 0PX**
**email:** info@woodman-inn.com **web:** www.woodman-inn.com
**dir:** *1m SW of Kirkburton. Off A629 in Thunder Bridge*

The Woodman Inn is extremely popular with locals. The busy bar offers offers a wide range selection of ales, including Small World Beers brewed only one mile away. Bedrooms are comfortable and comprehensively furnished, making this an ideal place for walking, visiting the Yorkshire Dales, or simply escaping to the country. Weddings and functions are also well catered for.

**Rooms:** 13 en suite 6 annexe en suite (3 fmly) (6 GF) **S** £59–£85; **D** £79–£119*
**Facilities:** FTV Lounge tea/coffee Dinner available Direct dial WiFi ⌂18
**Extras:** Speciality toiletries **Conf:** Max 60 Thtr 50 Class 60 Board 30 **Parking:** 60
**Notes:** Civ wed 80

## LEEDS
Map 19 SE23

### Hinsley Hall

★★★ GUEST ACCOMMODATION

**tel:** 0113 261 8000 **62 Headingley Lane LS6 2BX**
**email:** info@hinsley-hall.co.uk **web:** www.hinsley-hall.co.uk
**dir:** *On A660 Leeds to Skipton road, past university & Hyde Park lights. Turn right into Oakfield*

Set in extensive landscaped gardens, Hinsley Hall enjoys a peaceful setting just a short drive from Leeds city centre and the nearby university. Bedrooms are all comfortable, well equipped and well appointed. A lounge is available for guests along with a small bar area. There are large conferencing facilities on site along with a number of meeting rooms. Headingley Stadium is a 10-minute walk away.

**Rooms:** 50 rms (47 en suite) (3 pri facs) (1 fmly) (4 GF) **S** £49.95–£55; **D** £65–£75
**Facilities:** FTV Lounge TVL tea/coffee Dinner available Lift Licensed WiFi 🔔
**Conf:** Max 90 Thtr 90 Class 50 Board 36 **Parking:** 100 **Notes:** Closed 24 Dec–2 Jan

### Innkeeper's Lodge Leeds Calverley

★★★ INN

**tel:** 08451 551551 *(Calls cost 2p per minute plus your phone company's access charge)*
**Calverley Lane, Pudsey LS28 5QQ**
**email:** info@innkeeperslodge.com **web:** www.innkeeperslodge.com

A striking 19th-century Victorian lodge peacefully located in the picturesque village of Calverley, yet very convenient for Bradford and Leeds and only six miles from Leeds Bradford International Airport. The spacious bar and dining areas are comfortable, with cask ales and a wide choice of food offered. Bedrooms are spacious and suitably equipped, and there is a large garden with outside seating. Complimentary WiFi is also provided.

**Rooms:** 14 en suite (5 fmly) **Facilities:** FTV tea/coffee Dinner available WiFi

## LINTON
Map 16 SE34

### The Windmill Inn

★★★★ 🔔 INN

**tel:** 01937 582209 **Main Street LS22 4HT**
**email:** enquiries@thewindmillinnlinton.co.uk **web:** www.thewindmillinnlinton.co.uk
**dir:** *A1(M) junct 45, then 2nd exit at Moore Grange rdbt. Left on A58, right onto A659. Right into Linton Ln, follow road into Main St*

The Windmill is a beautiful, traditional country inn tucked away in a charming village. Food is locally sourced and the two rooms are converted outbuildings that are just across the car park. They are spacious suites with lounge areas, WiFi, TVs and modern bathrooms. There is ample car parking and an award-winning beer garden. Families are very welcome in the pub.

**Rooms:** 2 annexe en suite (1 GF) **D** fr £100* **Facilities:** FTV DVD Lounge TVL tea/coffee Dinner available WiFi ⚓18 Access to Wood Hall Spa & Swimming Pool
**Parking:** 48 **Notes:** No children Closed 1 Jan Civ wed 80

## MIRFIELD
Map 16 SE21

### Mirfield Monastery B&B

★★ GUEST ACCOMMODATION

**tel:** 01924 483346 & 494318 **Stocks Bank Road WF14 0BN**
**email:** enquiries@mirfield.org.uk **web:** www.mirfield.org.uk
**dir:** *M62 junct 25 towards Mirfield. At rdbt, fork left onto A62 (Leeds). 1st right at lights, 0.5m*

This is a quiet haven; set within the walls of Mirfield Monastery, in beautiful gardens tended by the resident monks. Rooms are modestly appointed and decorated in calming neutral tones. WiFi is available. A continental breakfast is provided on a self-service basis. The emphasis is on peace and quiet, with guests welcome to attend services if they wish.

**Rooms:** 8 en suite **S** £43–£55; **D** £53–£65 **Facilities:** FTV Lounge tea/coffee Licensed WiFi **Conf:** Max 70 Thtr 70 Class 40 Board 25 **Parking:** 10 **Notes:** No children 5yrs

## NORMANTON
Map 16 SE32

### The Grange

★★★★ BED AND BREAKFAST

**tel:** 01924 892203 & 07970 505157 **2 Snydale Road WF6 1NT**
**email:** enquiries@thegrangenormanton.co.uk **web:** www.thegrangenormanton.co.uk

The house has been in Sarah's family for over 100 years, and is a well maintained property with gardens that were designed by 2002 Chelsea Flower Show winner, Peter Garnett-Orme. The individually styled bedrooms are well appointed and have many thoughtful extras. Guests have use of the lounge with large screen TV. Full English breakfast is served in the dining room.

**Rooms:** 3 rms (2 en suite) (1 pri facs) (1 fmly) **Facilities:** FTV TVL tea/coffee Dinner available WiFi 🔔 **Extras:** Fruit juice, bottled water **Parking:** 4 **Notes:** LB No children 18mths Closed 24–29 Dec

## CHANNEL ISLANDS
## JERSEY

**ST AUBIN**       Map 24

### Premier Collection

## The Panorama

★★★★★ 🏵 GUEST ACCOMMODATION

**tel:** 01534 742429 & 07797 742429 **La Rue du Crocquet JE3 8BZ**
**email:** info@panoramajersey.com **web:** www.panoramajersey.com
**dir:** *In village centre*

Enjoying spectacular views across St Aubin's Bay, The Panorama is a long-established favourite with visitors. The welcome is genuine and many of the well-equipped bedrooms have wonderful views; the bathrooms are finished to a high standard. Public areas also look seaward and have attractive antique fireplaces. Breakfast is excellent and served in two dining areas.

**Rooms:** 14 en suite (3 GF) S £50–£90; D £100–£178* **Facilities:** STV Lounge tea/coffee WiFi 🔒 **Extras:** Robes, slippers, fridge **Notes:** No children 18yrs Closed mid Oct–mid Apr

## Harbour View

★★★★ GUEST ACCOMMODATION

**tel:** 01534 741585 **Le Boulevard JE3 8AB**
**email:** harbourview@localdial.com **web:** www.harbourviewjersey.com

Harbour View is situated in a beautiful location overlooking St Aubin harbour. The guest house has been lovingly restored and it retains many original features. Bedrooms are all smartly presented and come with a host of facilities. Food can be taken at 'Danny's at the Harbour View' and parking is an added bonus. A substantial continental breakfast, along with cooked options, is available in the well-appointed breakfast room.

**Rooms:** 16 en suite (4 fmly) (2 GF) **Facilities:** STV TVL tea/coffee Licensed WiFi ♿18 **Parking:** 8 **Notes:** LB Closed Dec–Feb

**ST HELIER**       Map 24

## Bay View Guest House

★★★★ GUEST ACCOMMODATION

**tel:** 01534 720950 & 07700 720100 **12 Havre des Pas JE2 4UQ**
**email:** enquiries@bayviewjersey.com **web:** www.bayviewjersey.com
**dir:** *Through tunnel, right at rdbt, down Green St & left, 100yds on left*

The Bay View is just across the road from the Havre des Pas Lido and beach, and a 10-minute walk from the centre of St Helier. The bedrooms are well equipped, and extra facilities include a bar and a TV lounge both with Sky TV. Free WiFi is available throughout the property. There is a small patio garden to the front of the establishment, and at the rear, another secluded terrace and a hot tub.

**Rooms:** 12 rms (12 pri facs) (3 fmly) S £38–£54; D £76–£108* **Facilities:** FTV DVD iPod docking station TVL tea/coffee Licensed WiFi 🔒 Hot tub **Extras:** Speciality toiletries, robes, fridge **Notes:** LB

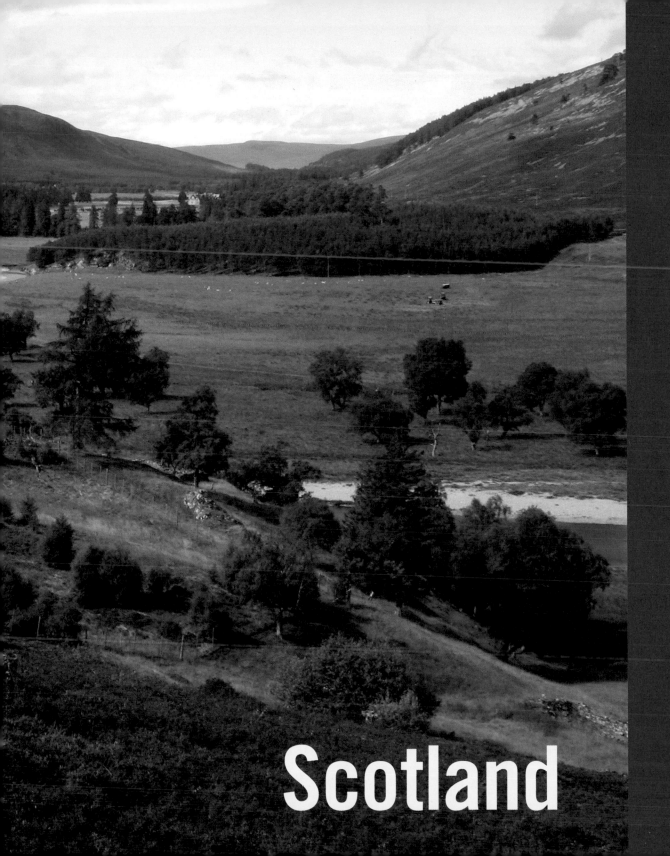

# Scotland

## ABERDEENSHIRE

### ABOYNE
Map 23 NO59

## The Lodge on the Loch of Aboyne

★★★★ 🛏 GUEST ACCOMMODATION

**tel:** 013398 86444 **Aboyne Loch Golf Centre AB34 5BR**
**email:** info@thelodgeontheloch.com **web:** www.thelodgeontheloch.com
**dir:** *1m E of Aboyne on A93*

The beautiful location of this lochside property ensures stunning views and a peaceful stay. The wide range of facilities include a nine-hole golf centre with driving range, osprey viewing deck, fitness centre and a wide range of treatments offered in the Reflect Spa. Dining options include the restaurant and the bistro bar, with very good function and wedding facilities also available.

**Rooms:** 14 en suite (2 fmly) (7 GF) **S** £85–£140; **D** £115–£200* **Facilities:** FTV tea/coffee Dinner available Direct dial Licensed WiFi ♨9 ◾ Hot tub Holistic spa treatments **Conf:** Max 80 Thtr 80 Class 40 Board 25 **Parking:** 30 **Notes:** LB Civ wed 120

### BALLATER
Map 23 NO39

## Deeside Inn

★★★★ INN

**tel:** 01339 755413 **13–15 Victoria Road AB35 5RA**
**email:** deeside@crerarhotels.com **web:** www.crerarhotels.com/the-deeside-inn
**dir:** *On A93 (Braemar Rd)*

Located in the Royal Deeside village of Ballater, in the heart of the Grampian Highlands, Deeside Inn is a great base from which to explore the area. Relax in the stylish bar or public lounge with its large open fires. Comfortable accommodation is provided in the spacious bedrooms.

**Rooms:** 25 en suite (2 fmly) **Facilities:** STV FTV tea/coffee Dinner available Direct dial WiFi

### ELLON
Map 23 NU93

## Premier Collection

## Aikenshill House

★★★★★ FARMHOUSE

**tel:** 01358 742990 **Aikenshill, Foveran AB41 6AT**
**email:** enquiries@aikenshill.co.uk **web:** www.aikenshill.co.uk
**dir:** *From Aberdeen N on A90, pass Cock & Bull restaurant & Trump International Golf Links. Turn left signed Aikenshill, 500mtrs at end of road*

This farmhouse enjoys spectacular views from its elevated position overlooking Donald Trump's golf course and the Aberdeenshire coastline beyond. Located close to Aberdeen, the house is well situated for either a peaceful getaway or a city break. Decorated and furnished to an impressive standard, the modern feel of the property is complemented by friendly hospitality from the whole family. Memorable breakfasts include the best ingredients, and dinners by request are also available.

**Rooms:** 4 en suite **Facilities:** FTV TVL Dinner available WiFi ⛳◾
**Notes:** 300 acres arable

### KILDRUMMY
Map 23 NJ41

## Kildrummy Inn

★★★★  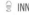 🍽 INN

**tel:** 01975 571227 **AB33 8QS**
**email:** enquiries@kildrummyinn.co.uk **web:** www.kildrummyinn.co.uk
**dir:** *On A97, 2m from junct with A944 at Mossat in direction of Strathdon & Cairngorms National Park*

Located in the heart of rural Aberdeenshire, this popular inn is the perfect base for touring the Grampian Mountains and beyond. Personally run and with a unique history, Kildrummy Inn provides four comfortable bedrooms, all en suite and featuring TV, DVD player and free WiFi. The lounge bar with roaring fire and a good selection of beers and whiskies is a great place in which to while away the time. No visit would be complete without sampling the food on offer with skilfully created dishes highlighting the best in local produce.

**Rooms:** 4 en suite **S** £89–£99; **D** £89–£99* **Facilities:** FTV DVD Lounge tea/coffee Dinner available WiFi Fishing ◾ **Extras:** Speciality toiletries **Conf:** Max 12 Board 12 **Parking:** 20 **Notes:** Closed Jan Civ wed 70

### STONEHAVEN
Map 23 NO88

## The Ship Inn

★★★ INN

**tel:** 01569 762617 **5 Shorehead AB39 2JY**
**email:** enquiries@shipinnstonehaven.com **web:** www.shipinnstonehaven.com
**dir:** *From A90 follow signs to Stonehaven, then signs to harbour*

This popular inn overlooks the harbour in Stonehaven, and has been a fixture since 1771. Bedrooms and bathrooms offer good levels of comfort; many with views of the harbour. The Lounge Bar serves a host of whiskies and real ales, while the Captain's Table restaurant specialises in fresh local fish and some spectacular meats. Close to Aberdeen and the A90, the property is in an excellent location for those looking for some peace and tranquillity.

**Rooms:** 11 en suite (2 fmly) **S** £80–£105; **D** £110–£140* **Facilities:** FTV tea/coffee Dinner available WiFi

### TARLAND
Map 23 NJ40

## The Commercial

★★★★ INN

**tel:** 01339 881922 **The Square AB34 4TX**
**email:** info@thecommerical-hotel.co.uk **web:** www.thecommerical-hotel.co.uk
**dir:** *From Aboyne on A93 follow signs for Tarland. In village turn left into The Square, on right by monument*

This property benefits from a stunning location in the heart of Royal Deeside in the 'Howe O' Cromar'. Near to Aberdeen, the Grampian Mountains and the Cairngorm National Park, The Commercial is ideally located, family-run and offers comfortable accommodation and a range of dining options, including the cosy lounge bar or the more formal Cromar restaurant.

**Rooms:** 9 en suite **S** £50–£75; **D** £80–£115 (room only)* **Facilities:** FTV DVD iPod docking station Lounge tea/coffee Dinner available WiFi Pool table ◾
**Extras:** Bottled water – complimentary **Parking:** 17 **Notes:** LB

## ANGUS

### INVERKEILOR
Map 23 NO64

#### Premier Collection

### Gordon's
★★★★★ ◉◉◉ RESTAURANT WITH ROOMS

tel: 01241 830364 **Main Road DD11 5RN**
email: gordonsrest@aol.com web: www.gordonsrestaurant.co.uk
dir: *Exit A92 between Arbroath & Montrose into Inverkeilor*

It's worth a detour off the main road to this family-run restaurant with rooms set in the centre of the village. The food in the restaurant has been awarded three AA Rosettes, and the excellent breakfasts are equally memorable. A huge fire dominates the restaurant on cooler evenings. Individually designed rooms all come with contemporary wenge furniture, oversized headboards, chandeliers, high decorative cornice and designer wallpaper. The showcase Thistle Suite is in purple, stone and lavender and has an en suite bathroom with roll-top bath and monsoon shower.

**Rooms:** 4 en suite 1 annexe en suite (1 GF) **S** £110; **D** £110–£160*
**Facilities:** tea/coffee Dinner available WiFi ⚓ **Extras:** Speciality toiletries – complimentary **Parking:** 6 **Notes:** No children 12yrs Closed Jan

### MONTROSE
Map 23 NO75

### Oaklands Guest House
★★★ GUEST HOUSE

tel: 01674 672018 **10 Rossie Island Road DD10 9NN**
email: oaklands1@btopenworld.com web: www.oaklands.sm4.biz
dir: *On A92 at S end of town*

A genuine welcome and attentive service are assured at Oaklands Guest House, a smart, detached house situated on the south side of the town. Bedrooms come in a variety of sizes and are neatly presented. There is a lounge on the ground floor next to the attractive dining room, where hearty breakfasts are served. Motorcycle guided tours can be arranged for those travelling with their own motorbikes.

**Rooms:** 7 en suite (1 fmly) (1 GF) **S** £35–£45; **D** £60–£75 **Facilities:** FTV TVL tea/coffee WiFi ⚓ **Extras:** Mints – complimentary **Parking:** 8

## ARGYLL & BUTE

### APPIN
Map 20 NM94

### Pineapple House
★★★★ GUEST HOUSE

tel: 01631 740350 **Duror PA38 4BP**
email: info@pineapplehouse.co.uk web: www.pineapplehouse.co.uk
dir: *In Duror, off A828. 5m S of A82*

Situated in the pretty village of Duror on the Argyll Coastal Route, Pineapple House is within easy reach of both Fort William and Oban. The property is in an excellent location for tourists, walkers and cyclists who wish to explore the Highlands. Appointed to a very high standard, the guest house is family-run and all bedrooms have en suite facilities. Bike storage and drying facilities are also available. The hearty breakfasts and warm hospitality make for a memorable stay.

**Rooms:** 6 en suite (1 fmly) **S** £50; **D** £80–£95* **Facilities:** FTV TVL tea/coffee WiFi ⚓ **Extras:** Sweets, bottled water, speciality toiletries **Parking:** 8
**Notes:** No children 7yrs Closed mid Nov–mid Mar

### BARCALDINE
Map 20 NM94

#### Premier Collection

### Ardtorna
★★★★★ 🍴 BED AND BREAKFAST

tel: 01631 720125 & 07867 785524 **Mill Farm PA37 1SE**
email: info@ardtorna.co.uk web: www.ardtorna.co.uk
dir: *N from Connel on A828, 0.5m from Scottish Sea Life Sanctuary*

Purpose-built as a luxury bed and breakfast, Ardtorna enjoys a commanding position overlooking the Firth of Lorn near Oban. Warm hospitality can always be found here. Floor-to-ceiling windows in the bedrooms let you watch the glorious sunsets in comfort, and the excellent king-size beds will provide a great night's sleep. Bathrooms have luxury toiletries and huge towels. Breakfast will leave you spoilt for choice. 'Butler' and 'romantic' packages are also available for those wishing to be pampered further.

**Rooms:** 4 en suite (4 GF) **Facilities:** FTV DVD iPod docking station tea/coffee WiFi ⚓ ♨9 ⚓ Leisure facilities available at nearby hotel **Extras:** Fresh fruit, flowers, malt whisky, Baileys **Parking:** 10 **Notes:** LB No children 12yrs

### CAIRNDOW
Map 20 NN11

### Cairndow Stagecoach Inn
★★★ INN

tel: 01499 600286 & 600252 **PA26 8BN**
email: enq@cairndowinn.com web: www.cairndowinn.com
dir: *From N, take either A82 to Tarbet, A83 to Cairndow, or A85 to Dalmally, A819 to Inveraray & A83 to Cairndow*

A relaxed, friendly atmosphere prevails at the 18th-century Cairndow Stagecoach Inn, overlooking the beautiful Loch Fyne. Bedrooms offer individual decor and thoughtful extras. Traditional public areas include a comfortable beamed lounge, a well-stocked bar where food is served all day, and a spacious restaurant with conservatory extension. Deluxe bedrooms offer more space and luxury.

**Rooms:** 13 en suite 5 annexe en suite (2 fmly) (5 GF) **Facilities:** STV FTV Lounge tea/coffee Dinner available Direct dial WiFi ♨9 Pool table ⚓ **Conf:** Max 30 Thtr 30 Class 30 Board 30 **Parking:** 30 **Notes:** LB

### LUSS
Map 20 NS39

### The Inn on Loch Lomond
★★★★ 🍴 INN

tel: 01436 860678 **Inverbeg G83 8PD**
email: res@innonlochlomond.co.uk web: www.innonlochlomond.co.uk
dir: *A82 N of Balloch*

Dating back to the 18th century, this inn offers very stylish, comfortable bedrooms (many with stunning views), bathrooms, and equally attractive public areas that boast open fires and cow hide sofas. Food is as much of a feature as the property itself, with a varied menu offered. The inn has its own chip shop fryer which proves most popular. The Beach House accommodation, just a short walk from the inn, is a real treat for those looking for a little more privacy.

**Rooms:** 25 en suite 8 annexe en suite (1 fmly) (6 GF) **D** £104–£194* **Facilities:** TVL tea/coffee Dinner available WiFi ⚓ **Parking:** 60 **Notes:** LB Civ wed 60

## OBAN
Map 20 NM82

### Premier Collection

## Blarcreen House

★★★★★ GUEST HOUSE

**tel:** 01631 750272 & 07557 977225 **Ardchattan, Connel PA37 1RG**
**email:** info@blarcreenhouse.com **web:** www.blarcreenhouse.com
**dir:** *N over Connel Bridge, turn right signed Bonawe, 6.7m to Blarcreen*

This elegant Victorian mansion house on the side of Loch Etive is the ideal base for exploring the Highlands. Warm hospitality and log fires await guests arriving at this property, where they can relax and enjoy comfortable bedrooms and fantastic views. Evening meals are also available by prior arrangement.

**Rooms:** 3 en suite **S** £120–£140; **D** £120–£140* **Facilities:** FTV DVD iPod docking station TVL tea/coffee Dinner available Licensed WiFi ⚓ **Extras:** Speciality toiletries, chocolates – complimentary **Parking:** 5 **Notes:** No children 16yrs Closed Dec–Jan

## MacKay's Guest House

★★★★ ⌬ GUEST HOUSE

**tel:** 01631 563121 & 566356 **Corran Esplanade PA34 5AQ**
**email:** info@mackaysguesthouse.co.uk **web:** www.mackaysguesthouse.co.uk
**dir:** *A85 into town, at rdbt 2nd exit to seafront (Corran Esplanade). Pass Cathedral, 300yds on right*

Boasting fantastic views across Oban Bay, this property offers comfort and quality as well as warm traditional hospitality. All front-facing bedrooms are spacious and very well appointed. Award winning breakfast is served in the bright conservatory and breakfast room. Dedicated off-road parking and outdoor seating overlooking the bay add to this wonderful guest experience.

**Rooms:** 8 en suite (2 GF) **D** £100–£130* **Facilities:** FTV DVD iPod docking station tea/coffee WiFi **Extras:** Robes, snacks, water, sherry – complimentary **Parking:** 10 **Notes:** No children 15yrs Closed 13 Nov–21 Mar

## Barriemore Guest House

★★★★ GUEST HOUSE

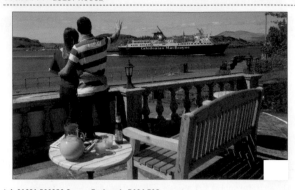

**tel:** 01631 566356 **Corran Esplanade PA34 5AQ**
**email:** info@barriemore.co.uk **web:** www.barriemore.co.uk
**dir:** *A85 into Oban, 1st rdbt exit towards sea. Right at 2nd rdbt, continue with sea on left, last guest house on right*

This splendid three-storey Victorian town house is in a fantastic location on Oban's seafront and enjoys great views over Oban Bay. Friendly service and spacious rooms with modern decor can be found at this family-run property. A hearty Scottish breakfast will set guests up for the day ahead.

**Rooms:** 15 en suite (2 fmly) (2 GF) **D** £85–£165* **Facilities:** FTV DVD iPod docking station Lounge tea/coffee WiFi **Extras:** Fruit, bottled water, sherry, robes, slippers, speciality toiletries **Parking:** 14 **Notes:** Closed Nov–Apr

## Glenrigh Guest House

★★★★ GUEST HOUSE

**tel:** 01631 562991 **Corran Esplanade PA34 5AQ**
**email:** info@glenrigh.co.uk **web:** www.glenrigh.co.uk
**dir:** *Down hill into Oban, turn right (with sea on left), along esplanade*

This former Victorian mansion has fantastic views of Oban Bay and the far away islands, and has the added bonus of on-site parking. Close to the heart of Oban town centre, it is also within walking distance of local amenities. Glenrigh offers comfortable bedrooms, impressive bathrooms and a hearty breakfast. A friendly team are waiting to make your stay memorable.

**Rooms:** 15 en suite (1 fmly) (5 GF) **S** £58–£65; **D** £90–£150* **Facilities:** FTV DVD iPod docking station TVL tea/coffee WiFi ⚓ **Extras:** Snacks, drinks **Parking:** 20 **Notes:** No children 13yrs Closed Nov–Mar

## TAYNUILT                                    Map 20 NN03

### The Taynuilt Etive

★★★   ⚑ INN

**tel:** 01866 822437 **PA35 1JN**
**email:** enquiries@taynuilthotel.co.uk **web:** www.taynuilthotel.co.uk
**dir:** *In Taynuilt, on A85*

This small inn enjoys a great location in the heart of stunning Highland countryside, not far from Oban. Accommodation has been offered on this site for centuries, and it continues to provide comfortable bedrooms, and cosy public areas including the main restaurant, snug restaurant and lounge bar. A stay here would not be complete without sampling the quality cuisine on offer; Scottish produce treated with respect. Craft ales and a great selection of whiskies are also features of the inn.

**Rooms:** 9 en suite (1 fmly) **Facilities:** FTV DVD iPod docking station tea/coffee Dinner available WiFi ⚑9 ⚓ **Conf:** Max 50 Thtr 50 Class 30 Board 28 **Parking:** 15

## NORTH AYRSHIRE

## WEST KILBRIDE                              Map 20 NS24

### Carlton Seamill B&B

AA ADVERTISED

**tel:** 01294 822075 & 07887 611738 **53 Ardrossan Road, Seamill KA23 9NE**
**email:** stay@carlton-seamill.co.uk **web:** www.carlton-seamill.co.uk
**dir:** *On A78 coastal road*

Carlton Seamill is an impressive, stone-built Victorian house, set in an ideal location at Seamill, on the Ayrshire coast. It enjoys commanding views to the Firth of Clyde and the Isle of Arran. The Rennie family have been at Carlton for over 60 years, and provide a relaxing atmosphere. On the ground floor, the handsome reception room has magnificent views over the Rose Garden and Croquet Lawn; and the elegant Victorian staircase leads up to the comfortable, first-floor accommodation. Carlton's garden gate leads to the sandy beach, so guests can enjoy a walk before heading to a local hostelry for dinner.

**Rooms:** 3 rms **D** £65–£75* **Facilities:** FTV DVD tea/coffee WiFi ⚓ **Extras:** Mini-fridge **Parking:** 6

## DUMFRIES & GALLOWAY

## CASTLE DOUGLAS                             Map 21 NX76

### Craigadam

★★★★ ⚑  GUEST HOUSE

**tel:** 01556 650233 & 650100 **Craigadam DG7 3HU**
**email:** inquiry@craigadam.com **web:** www.craigadam.com
**dir:** *From Castle Douglas E on A75 to Crocketford. In Crocketford turn left on A712 for 2m. House on hill*

Set on a farm, this elegant country house offers gracious living in a relaxed environment. The large bedrooms, most set around a courtyard, are strikingly individual in style. Public areas include a billiard room, and the panelled dining room which features a magnificent 15-seater table, the setting for Celia Pickup's delightful meals.

**Rooms:** 10 en suite (2 fmly) (7 GF) **Facilities:** FTV DVD Lounge tea/coffee Dinner available Licensed WiFi ⚑ Fishing Snooker ⚓ Shooting **Extras:** Speciality toiletries **Conf:** Max 22 **Parking:** 12 **Notes:** LB Closed Xmas & New Year Civ wed 150

## DUMFRIES                                   Map 21 NX97

### Wallamhill House

★★★★ BED AND BREAKFAST

**tel:** 01387 248249 **Kirkton DG1 1SL**
**email:** wallamhill@aol.com **web:** www.wallamhill.co.uk
**dir:** *3m N of Dumfries. Off A701 signed Kirkton, 1.5m on right*

Wallamhill House is set in well-tended gardens, in a delightful rural area three miles from Dumfries. Bedrooms are spacious and extremely well equipped. Beds feature luxurious Egyptian linens while bathrooms have underfloor heating. There is a peaceful drawing room, and a mini health club with sauna, steam shower and gym equipment.

**Rooms:** 3 en suite (1 fmly) (3 GF) **Facilities:** FTV TVL tea/coffee WiFi ⚑ Gym ⚓ Steam room Hot tub **Extras:** Fridge **Parking:** 6 **Notes:** LB

DUMFRIES continued

## Southpark House

★★★★ GUEST ACCOMMODATION

**tel:** 01387 711188 & 0800 970 1588 **Quarry Road, Locharbriggs DG1 1FA**
**email:** info@southparkhouse.co.uk **web:** www.southparkhouse.co.uk
**dir:** 3.5m NE of Dumfries. Exit A701 in Locharbriggs into Quarry Rd, last house on left

With a peaceful location commanding stunning views, this well-maintained property offers comfortable, attractive and well-equipped bedrooms. The peaceful lounge has a log fire on colder evenings. Friendly proprietor Ewan Maxwell personally oversees the hearty Scottish breakfasts served in the conservatory breakfast room.

**Rooms:** 4 en suite (1 fmly) **Facilities:** STV FTV Lounge TVL tea/coffee WiFi 2 acres of garden **Parking:** 13 **Notes:** LB

## Rivendell

★★★★ GUEST HOUSE

**tel:** 01387 252251 **105 Edinburgh Road DG1 1JX**
**email:** info@rivendellbnb.co.uk **web:** www.rivendellbnb.co.uk
**dir:** On A701 Edinburgh Rd, 400yds S of A75 junct

Situated just north of the town and close to the bypass, this lovely Charles Rennie Mackintosh inspired 1920s house, standing in extensive landscaped gardens, has been restored to reflect the period style of the property. Bedrooms are thoughtfully equipped, many are spacious and all offer modern facilities. Traditional breakfasts are served in the elegant dining room.

**Rooms:** 7 rms (6 en suite) (1 pri facs) 3 annexe en suite (2 fmly) (5 GF) **Facilities:** FTV iPod docking station tea/coffee WiFi **Parking:** 12 **Notes:** LB

### GRETNA (WITH GRETNA GREEN)      Map 21 NY36

## Surrone House

★★★★ GUEST ACCOMMODATION

**tel:** 01461 338341 **Annan Road DG16 5DL**
**email:** enquiries@surronehouse.co.uk **web:** www.surronehouse.co.uk
**dir:** In town centre on B721

Guests are assured of a warm welcome at this well-maintained property in attractive gardens set back from the road. Bedrooms are sensibly furnished and include a delightful honeymoon suite. The property is located only 500 yards from the centre of Gretna. Complimentary parking is available on site.

**Rooms:** 6 en suite (3 fmly) (1 GF) **S** £55; **D** £75* **Facilities:** FTV TVL tea/coffee WiFi **Extras:** Speciality toiletries – complimentary **Parking:** 10

### MOFFAT      Map 21 NT00

## Bridge House Moffat

★★★★ GUEST HOUSE

**tel:** 01683 220558 **Well Road DG10 9JT**
**email:** bookings@bridgehousemoffat.scot **web:** www.bridgehousemoffat.scot
**dir:** Exit A708 (The Holm) into Burnside, bear right into Well Rd, house opposite Ballplay Rd

This luxury Victorian guest house is situated on the outskirts of Moffat, within a short walk of the town centre. It enjoys views of the Moffat hills, and has easy access to a network of walking and cycling routes. All rooms feature complimentary toiletries, Freeview TV and a refreshment tray. Four-poster and superior rooms also have fluffy bathrobes and Egyptian cotton bedding. Well-behaved dogs are welcome and doggy day care or boarding is available. The bar has a fine selection of Scottish whiskies and gins.

**Rooms:** 7 en suite (1 fmly) **S** £56–£94; **D** £75–£125 **Facilities:** FTV Lounge tea/coffee Licensed WiFi ✿ **Parking:** 7 **Notes:** LB

### PORTPATRICK      Map 20 NW95

### Premier Collection

## Knockinaam Lodge

★★★★★ ⚫⚫⚫ RESTAURANT WITH ROOMS

**tel:** 01776 810471 **DG9 9AD**
**email:** reservations@knockinaamlodge.com **web:** www.knockinaamlodge.com
**dir:** From A77 or A75 follow signs to Portpatrick. Through Lochans. After 2m left at signs for hotel

Any tour of Dumfries and Galloway wouldn't be complete without a stay at this haven of tranquillity and relaxation. Knockinaam Lodge is an extended Victorian house set in an idyllic cove with its own pebble beach (ideal for a private swim in the summer) and sheltered by majestic cliffs and woodlands. Surrounded by 30 acres of delightful grounds, the lodge was the location for a meeting between Churchill and General Eisenhower in World War II. Today, a warm welcome is assured from the proprietors and their committed team, and much emphasis is placed on providing a sophisticated but intimate home-from-home experience. There are just ten suites – each individually designed and all with flat-screen TVs with DVD players, luxury toiletries and complimentary bottled water. The cooking is a real treat and showcases prime Scottish produce on the daily-changing, four-course set menus; guests can always discuss the choices in advance if they wish.

**Rooms:** 10 en suite (1 fmly) **S** £175–£325; **D** £290–£450* **Facilities:** Dinner available ⚓ Fishing Shooting Walking Sea fishing Clay pigeon shooting **Notes:** Civ wed 40

### SANQUHAR
Map 21 NS70

## Blackaddie House

★★★★ ◉◉ RESTAURANT WITH ROOMS

**tel:** 01659 50270 **Blackaddie Road DG4 6JJ**
**email:** ian@blackaddiehotel.co.uk **web:** www.blackaddiehotel.co.uk
**dir:** *300 yds from A76 on N side of Sanquhar*

Overlooking the River Nith, in two acres of secluded gardens, this family-run country house offers friendly and attentive hands-on service. The bedrooms and suites are all well-presented and comfortable, with many useful extras provided as standard. The award-winning food, served in the restaurant, with its lovely garden views, is based on prime Scottish ingredients.

**Rooms:** 6 en suite 1 annexe en suite (1 GF) **S** £105–£225; **D** £125–£235*
**Facilities:** FTV DVD Lounge tea/coffee Dinner available Direct dial WiFi ⅃9 ⚓
**Extras:** Speciality toiletries, mineral water, home-made shortbread **Conf:** Max 16 Thtr 16 Class 16 Board 12 **Parking:** 20 **Notes:** LB Civ wed 24

## WEST DUNBARTONSHIRE

### BALLOCH
Map 20 NS38

## The Waterhouse Inn

★★★★ INN

**tel:** 01389 752120 **34 Balloch Road G83 8LE**
**email:** info@waterhouseinn.co.uk **web:** www.waterhouseinn.co.uk
**dir:** *M8 junct 30 onto M898. Over Erskine bridge, take exit for Crianlarich onto A82 head towards Loch Lomond. Right at rdbt onto A811*

The Waterhouse Inn is located on the high street of Balloch, close to the park and the mouth of Loch Lomond. Bedrooms are well equipped and spacious, with modern bright bathrooms. The inn is welcoming and friendly, with a café that serves home-cooked food throughout the day, and is a perfect base for touring Loch Lomond and the Trossachs National Park.

**Rooms:** 7 en suite (2 fmly) **Facilities:** STV FTV Lounge TVL tea/coffee Dinner available WiFi ⚓

## Innkeeper's Lodge Loch Lomond

★★★ INN

**tel:** 08451 551551 *(Calls cost 2p per minute plus your phone company's access charge)* **Balloch Road G83 8LQ**
**email:** info@innkeeperslodge.com **web:** www.innkeeperslodge.com

This property enjoys an excellent location, a stone's throw from Loch Lomond and the nearby Balloch Castle Country Park. The historic lodge provides modern, spacious accommodation. The cosy and welcoming lounge bar is a popular place to

dine below the exposed wooden beams. Enjoy a cask ale by the open fire or a dish from their vast and varying menu. Parking available on site.

**Rooms:** 11 en suite (3 fmly) **Facilities:** FTV tea/coffee Dinner available WiFi **Parking:** 52

## CITY OF EDINBURGH

### EDINBURGH
Map 21 NT27

*See also Livingston (West Lothian)*

### Premier Collection

## Kew House

★★★★★ ⚑ GUEST ACCOMMODATION

**tel:** 0131 313 0700 **1 Kew Terrace, Murrayfield EH12 5JE**
**email:** info@kewhouse.com **web:** www.kewhouse.com
**dir:** *1m W of Princes St*

Forming part of a listed Victorian terrace, Kew House lies within walking distance of the city centre, and is convenient for Murrayfield Stadium and tourist attractions. Meticulously maintained in contemporary style throughout, it offers attractive bedrooms in a variety of sizes, all thoughtfully equipped to suit business and leisure guests. There is a comfortable lounge. Both parking and WiFi are complimentary.

**Rooms:** 6 en suite (1 fmly) (2 GF) **S** £89–£105; **D** £99–£185* **Facilities:** FTV Lounge tea/coffee Direct dial WiFi ⚓ **Extras:** Speciality toiletries, sherry, chocolates, fridge **Parking:** 6 **Notes:** LB Closed approximately 5–31 Jan

**EDINBURGH** *continued*

## Premier Collection

### 21212

★★★★★ ◉◉◉◉ RESTAURANT WITH ROOMS

**tel:** 0131 523 1030 **3 Royal Terrace EH7 5AB**
**email:** reservations@21212restaurant.co.uk **web:** www.21212restaurant.co.uk
**dir:** *Calton Hill, city centre*

A real jewel in Edinburgh's crown, this establishment takes its name from the number of choices at each course on the five-course dinner menu. Located on the prestigious Royal Terrace this light and airy, renovated Georgian town house stretches over four floors. The four individually-designed bedrooms epitomise luxury living and the bathrooms certainly have the wow factor. At the heart of this restaurant with rooms is the creative and impressive four AA Rosette award-winning cooking of Paul Kitching. Service throughout is friendly and very attentive.

**Rooms:** 4 en suite **S** £95–£325; **D** £95–£325 **Facilities:** STV FTV iPod docking station Lounge Dinner available WiFi **Extras:** Speciality toiletries, mineral water, sloe gin **Notes:** No children 5yrs Closed 1 week Jan & 1 week Autumn RS Sun & Mon restaurant closed

## Premier Collection

### The Witchery by the Castle

★★★★★ ◉ ≊ RESTAURANT WITH ROOMS

**tel:** 0131 225 5613 **Castlehill, The Royal Mile EH1 2NF**
**email:** mail@thewitchery.com **web:** www.thewitchery.com
**dir:** *Top of Royal Mile at gates of Edinburgh Castle*

Originally built in 1595, The Witchery by the Castle is situated in a historic building at the gates of Edinburgh Castle. The two luxurious and theatrically decorated suites, known as the Inner Sanctum and the Old Rectory, are located above the restaurant and are reached via a winding stone staircase. Filled with antiques, opulently draped beds, large roll-top baths and a plethora of memorabilia, this ancient and exciting establishment is often described as one of the country's most romantic destinations.

**Rooms:** 4 en suite 5 annexe en suite (1 GF) **Facilities:** STV FTV DVD tea/coffee Dinner available Direct dial WiFi **Extras:** Bottled water – complimentary **Notes:** No children 12yrs Closed 25–26 Dec

### Bonnington Guest House

★★★★ GUEST HOUSE

**tel:** 0131 554 7610 & 07880 312820 **202 Ferry Road EH6 4NW**
**email:** booking@thebonningtonguesthouse.com
**web:** www.thebonningtonguesthouse.com
**dir:** *On A902, near corner of Ferry Rd & Newhaven Rd*

This delightful Georgian house offers individually furnished bedrooms on two floors that retain many of their original features. A family room is also available. A substantial freshly prepared breakfast is served in the dining room. Off-street parking is an added bonus.

**Rooms:** 5 rms (4 en suite) (1 pri facs) (1 fmly) **S** £70–£85; **D** £80–£143 **Facilities:** FTV tea/coffee WiFi **Extras:** Speciality toiletries, sherry – complimentary; robes **Parking:** 9 **Notes:** Closed Nov–Mar RS 27 Dec–2 Jan Open for New Year & certain wknds Nov–Mar

### Fraoch House

★★★★ ≊ GUEST ACCOMMODATION

**tel:** 0131 554 1353 **66 Pilrig Street EH6 5AS**
**email:** info@fraochhouse.com **web:** www.fraochhouse.com
**dir:** *1m from Princes St*

Situated within walking distance of the city centre and convenient for many attractions, Fraoch House, which dates from the 1900s, has been appointed to offer well-equipped and thoughtfully furnished bedrooms. Delicious, freshly cooked breakfasts are served in the charming dining room on the ground floor.

**Rooms:** 9 rms (7 en suite) (2 pri facs) (1 fmly) (1 GF) **Facilities:** FTV tea/coffee WiFi Free use of DVDs and CDs & internet access

### Kingsway Guest House

★★★★ ≊ GUEST HOUSE

**tel:** 0131 667 5029 **5 East Mayfield EH9 1SD**
**email:** booking@kingswayguesthouse.com **web:** www.edinburgh-guesthouse.com
**dir:** *A701 to city centre, after 4m road name changes to Mayfield Gdns. Right at lights into East Mayfield*

Well situated for the city centre and with off-road parking, this well-presented Victorian building maintains a number of original features, and genuine and warm hospitality is assured. All the bedrooms are comfortable, and the quality Scottish breakfasts make an excellent start to the day.

**Rooms:** 7 rms (6 en suite) (1 pri facs) (2 fmly) **S** from £50; **D** from £70* **Facilities:** FTV DVD iPod docking station tea/coffee WiFi �room18 **Extras:** Speciality toiletries – complimentary **Parking:** 4

### Southside Guest House

★★★★ ≊ GUEST HOUSE

**tel:** 0131 668 4422 **8 Newington Road EH9 1QS**
**email:** info@southsideguesthouse.co.uk **web:** www.southsideguesthouse.co.uk
**dir:** *E end of Princes St into North Bridge to Royal Mile, continue S, 0.5m, house on right*

Situated within easy reach of the city centre and convenient for the major attractions, Southside Guest House is an elegant sandstone building. Bedrooms are individually styled, comfortable and thoughtfully equipped. Traditional, freshly cooked Scottish breakfasts are served at individual tables in the smart, ground-floor dining room.

**Rooms:** 8 en suite (2 fmly) (1 GF) **S** £80–£100; **D** £120–£190* **Facilities:** FTV DVD tea/coffee Direct dial Licensed WiFi **Extras:** Speciality toiletries **Notes:** LB No children 10yrs

### Sherwood Guest House

★★★★ GUEST HOUSE

**tel:** 0131 667 1200 **42 Minto Street EH9 2BR**
**email:** vivienne@sherwood-edinburgh.com **web:** www.sherwood-edinburgh.com
**dir:** *On A701, S of city centre*

The Sherwood Guest House is located on the south side of the city, and is well served by buses. Bedrooms vary in size, and the smaller ones are thoughtfully appointed to make the best use of space. Many thoughtful extras are provided and a continental breakfast is served in the bright and welcoming dining room. The property has limited parking space on a first come first served basis.

**Rooms:** 6 rms (5 en suite) (1 pri facs) (2 fmly) (1 GF) **S** £60–£80; **D** £80–£150* **Facilities:** FTV iPod docking station tea/coffee WiFi **Extras:** Fridge **Parking:** 3 **Notes:** Closed Jan

## Ashlyn Guest House

★★★★ GUEST HOUSE

tel: 0131 552 2954 **42 Inverleith Row EH3 5PY**
email: info@ashlynguesthouse.com **web:** www.ashlynguesthouse.com
dir: *Adjacent to Edinburgh Botanic Gardens. Follow signs for North Edinburgh & Botanics*

The Ashlyn Guest House is a warm and friendly Georgian home, ideally located to take advantage of Edinburgh's attractions. The city centre is within walking distance and the Royal Botanical Gardens are minutes away. Bedrooms are all individually decorated and furnished to a high standard. A generous and hearty breakfast gives a great start to the day.

**Rooms:** 3 rms (2 en suite) (1 pri facs) **D** £75–£95* **Facilities:** FTV Lounge tea/coffee WiFi ♨ **Extras:** Mineral water **Notes:** No children 10yrs Closed 23–28 Dec

## Elder York Guest House

★★★ GUEST HOUSE

tel: 0131 556 1926 **38 Elder Street EH1 3DX**
email: reception@elderyork.co.uk **web:** www.elderyork.co.uk
dir: *Close to Princes St, next to bus station*

Elder York Guest House is centrally located just minutes from the bus station, Harvey Nichols and the St James Shopping Centre. Accommodation is situated up flights of stairs and all bedrooms are well appointed with many thoughtful extras including WiFi. Quality breakfast is served on individual tables overlooking Queen Street.

**Rooms:** 12 rms (11 en suite) (1 pri facs) (1 fmly) **Facilities:** FTV tea/coffee WiFi

## Innkeeper's Lodge Edinburgh, Corstorphine

★★★ INN

tel: 08451 551551 *(Calls cost 2p per minute plus your phone company's access charge)*
**St Johns Road, Corstorphine EH12 8AX**
email: info@innkeeperslodge.com **web:** www.innkeeperslodge.com

At Innkeeper's Lodge you'll find accommodation with comfort and character in equal measure, and everything needed for a relaxing stay, from easy check-in and free parking to complimentary breakfast and a cosy pub serving great value food and drink on the doorstep. Each Lodge has quality rooms, and there are Lodges in a variety of locations from towns and cities to countryside settings across the UK.

**Rooms:** 28 en suite (4 fmly) (6 GF) **Facilities:** FTV tea/coffee Dinner available Direct dial WiFi **Parking:** 46

## Averon Guest House

★★★ GUEST HOUSE

tel: 0131 229 9932 **44 Gilmore Place EH3 9NQ**
email: info@averon.co.uk **web:** www.averon.co.uk
dir: *From W end of Princes St onto A702, right at Kings Theatre*

Situated within walking distance of the west end of the city and close to the Kings Theatre, Averon Guest House offers comfortable, good-value accommodation, with a secure car park to the rear.

**Rooms:** 10 rms (6 en suite) (1 pri facs) (3 fmly) (5 GF) **S** £32–£60; **D** £64–£130*
**Facilities:** tea/coffee **Parking:** 19

## Halcyon House

★★★ GUEST HOUSE

tel: 0131 556 1033 & 556 1032 **8 Royal Terrace EH7 5AB**
email: patricia@halcyon-hotel.com **web:** www.halcyon-hotel.com

Halcyon House benefits from a fantastic location, and has retained many of its original Georgian features. It is within easy walking distance of the theatre and the centre of Edinburgh. Rooms are split over three floors, come in a variety of sizes, and are decorated in a basic but comfortable fashion. Front or back rooms offer wonderful views of the gardens or views across to the Forth.

**Rooms:** 14 rms (11 en suite) (1 pri facs) (7 fmly) (2 GF) **S** £70–£110; **D** £91–£210*
**Facilities:** TVL tea/coffee WiFi **Notes:** LB

| RATHO | Map 21 NT17 |

## The Bridge Inn at Ratho

★★★★ ◉ ♨ INN

tel: 0131 333 1320 **27 Baird Road EH28 8RA**
email: info@bridgeinn.com **web:** www.bridgeinn.com

Located beside the Union Canal and in use as a hostelry since the 19th century, this inn offers modern, spacious and well-furnished bedrooms with views of the canal. The busy bistro's kitchen uses home-grown produce to create award-winning food. Outdoor seating is an added bonus as are the two restaurant barges that serve lunch, afternoon tea and dinner.

**Rooms:** 4 en suite **S** £70–£140; **D** £80–£150* **Facilities:** FTV iPod docking station tea/coffee Dinner available WiFi ♨ **Extras:** Speciality toiletries – complimentary **Parking:** 40 **Notes:** Closed 25 Dec Civ wed 80

| SOUTH QUEENSFERRY | Map 21 NT17 |

## Innkeeper's Lodge Edinburgh South Queensferry

★★★ INN

tel: 08451 551551 *(Calls cost 2p per minute plus your phone company's access charge)*
**7 Newhalls Road EH30 9TA**
email: info@innkeeperslodge.com **web:** www.innkeeperslodge.com

At Innkeeper's Lodge you'll find accommodation with comfort and character in equal measure, and everything needed for a relaxing stay, from easy check-in and free parking to complimentary breakfast and a cosy pub serving great value food and drink on the doorstep. Each Lodge has quality rooms, and there are Lodges in a variety of locations from towns and cities to countryside settings across the UK.

**Rooms:** 14 en suite (5 fmly) (3 GF) **Facilities:** FTV tea/coffee Dinner available Direct dial WiFi **Parking:** 40

## FIFE

### ANSTRUTHER
Map 21 NO50

# The Spindrift

★★★★ ≘ GUEST HOUSE

tel: 01333 310573 & 07713 597996 **Pittenweem Road KY10 3DT**
**email:** info@thespindrift.co.uk **web:** www.thespindrift.co.uk
**dir:** *Enter town from W on A917, 1st building on left*

This immaculate Victorian villa stands on the western edge of the village. The attractive bedrooms offer a wide range of extra touches; the Captain's Room, a replica of a wood-panelled cabin, is a particular feature. The inviting lounge has an honesty bar, while imaginative breakfasts are served in the cheerful dining room. This is also the venue, by arrangement, for dinners that use the best in fresh local produce. Free WiFi is available throughout.

**Rooms:** 8 rms (7 en suite) (1 pri facs) (2 fmly) **S** £50–£70; **D** £66–£110
**Facilities:** FTV DVD iPod docking station TVL tea/coffee Dinner available Direct dial Licensed WiFi ↯18 **Extras:** Speciality toiletries, shortbread, chocolates – complimentary **Parking:** 9 **Notes:** LB No children 10yrs Closed Xmas–late Jan

# The Bank

★★★★ INN

tel: 01333 310189 **23-25 High Street East KY10 3DQ**
**email:** enquiries@thebank-anstruther.co.uk **web:** www.thebank-anstruther.co.uk
**dir:** *From St Andrews, in Anstruther turn right towards Pittenweem. 50mtrs on left*

Located in the heart of Anstruther where the Dreel Burn meets the Forth, this friendly inn serves real ales and great pub food; there is a separate building next door for the accommodation. Modern, high quality, en suite bedrooms cater well for guests' needs and some offer great views. The beer garden is a real suntrap and has a children's play area.

**Rooms:** 13 en suite (1 fmly) (1 GF) **Facilities:** STV FTV iPod docking station tea/coffee Dinner available Direct dial WiFi ↯18 Pool table **Extras:** Bottled water – complimentary; fridge, safe **Parking:** 3 **Notes:** LB

# The Waterfront

★★★★ ≘ RESTAURANT WITH ROOMS

tel: 01333 312200 **18–20 Shore Street KY10 3EA**
**email:** info@anstruther-waterfront.co.uk **web:** www.anstruther-waterfront.co.uk
**dir:** *Off A917 opposite marina*

Situated overlooking the harbour, The Waterfront offers spacious, stylish, contemporary accommodation, with bedrooms located in lovingly restored buildings in a courtyard behind the restaurant. There is a comfortable lounge with a smartly fitted kitchen and dining room, and laundry facilities are available in the granary. Dinner and breakfast are served in the attractive restaurant that offers a comprehensive menu featuring the best of local produce.

**Rooms:** 10 en suite (3 fmly) (2 GF) **Facilities:** FTV DVD Lounge tea/coffee Dinner available WiFi ↯ Pool table **Extras:** Mineral water **Notes:** LB

### ELIE
Map 21 NO40

# The Ship Inn

★★★★ ≘ INN

tel: 01333 330246 **The Toft KY9 1DT**
**email:** info@shipinn.scot **web:** www.shipinn.scot

You'd have to travel a long way to find views better than the ones from this inn. Overlooking the harbour in Elie, The Ship Inn has a beer garden and views over the sea and beach. They even organise cricket matches on the beach when the weather and tides allow. A comfortable lounge bar and expansive dining space enjoy beautiful views and sunsets when weather permits. Bedrooms and bathrooms continue the quality theme with Egyptian linens, coffee machines and beautiful toiletries a feature. No visit would be complete without sampling the food or trying one of the cask ales.

**Rooms:** 6 en suite (1 GF) **Facilities:** FTV iPod docking station tea/coffee Dinner available WiFi ↯18 **Extras:** Nespresso coffee machine

## INVERKEITHING
Map 21 NT18

# The Roods

★★★★ BED AND BREAKFAST

**tel:** 01383 415049 **16 Bannerman Avenue KY11 1NG**
**email:** isobelmarley@hotmail.com **web:** www.the-roods.co.uk
**dir:** *N of town centre off B981(Church St/Chapel Place)*

This charming house stands in secluded, well-tended gardens close to the train station. Bedrooms are individually styled and have state-of-the-art bathrooms. There is an inviting lounge, and breakfast is served at a large shared table in an attractive conservatory.

**Rooms:** 3 en suite (2 GF) **Facilities:** FTV DVD iPod docking station TVL tea/coffee Direct dial WiFi **Parking:** 4 **Notes:** LB

## NEWPORT-ON-TAY
Map 21 NO42

# The Newport Restaurant

★★★★ ◎◎ RESTAURANT WITH ROOMS

**tel:** 01382 541449 **1 High Street DD6 8AB**
**email:** info@thenewportrestaurant.co.uk **web:** www.thenewportrestaurant.co.uk

Jamie Scotts' restaurant with rooms is situated shore side in Newport looking over the Tay to Dundee. The modern restaurant is set over two floors both enjoying panoramic views. Style is modern with a nod to the local maritime and fishing history. Four bedrooms are spacious and well equipped for the modern traveller with comfortable beds and a few added luxuries.

**Rooms:** 4 en suite (2 fmly) **S** £140–£160; **D** £160–£210* **Facilities:** FTV iPod docking station Dinner available WiFi **Parking:** 10 **Notes:** Closed 24 Dec–9 Jan

## PEAT INN
Map 21 NO40

### Premier Collection

# The Peat Inn

★★★★★ ◎◎◎ RESTAURANT WITH ROOMS

**tel:** 01334 840206 **KY15 5LH**
**email:** stay@thepeatinn.co.uk **web:** www.thepeatinn.co.uk
**dir:** *At junct of B940 & B941, 5m SW of St Andrews*

This 300-year-old former coaching inn enjoys a rural location is close to St Andrews. The Peat Inn is spacious, very well appointed, and offers rooms that all have lounge areas. The inn is steeped in history and for years has proved a real haven for food lovers. The three dining areas create a romantic setting, and chef/owner Geoffrey Smeddle produces excellent, award-winning dishes. Expect welcoming open fires and a relaxed ambiance. An extensive continental breakfast selection is served to guests in their bedrooms each morning.

**Rooms:** 8 annexe en suite (3 fmly) (8 GF) **Facilities:** FTV Lounge tea/coffee Dinner available Direct dial WiFi **Extras:** Speciality toiletries, fruit, sherry – complimentary **Parking:** 24 **Notes:** LB Closed 25–26 Dec, 2 weeks Jan, 1 week Nov RS Sun–Mon closed

## ST ANDREWS
Map 21 NO51

# Lorimer House

★★★★ A GUEST HOUSE

**tel:** 01334 476599 **19 Murray Park KY16 9AW**
**email:** info@lorimerhouse.com **web:** www.lorimerhouse.com
**dir:** *A91 to St Andrews, left into Golf Place, right into The Scores, right into Murray Park*

A warm and friendly welcome is assured at Lorimer House, set in a delightful Victorian terrace, situated within easy reach of the famous Old Course, the seafront and town centre. Bedrooms are attractive, comfortably furnished and well equipped. Freshly prepared Scottish breakfasts are served in the stylish dining room, which also has a lounge area and offers free broadband internet access.

**Rooms:** 5 en suite (1 GF) **S** £62–£90; **D** £92–£110 **Facilities:** STV FTV TVL tea/coffee WiFi **Extras:** Chilled water, use of fridge **Notes:** No children 12yrs

### GLASGOW

## GLASGOW
Map 20 NS56

# ABode Glasgow

★★★★ GUEST ACCOMMODATION

**tel:** 0141 221 6789 **129 Bath Street G2 2SZ**
**email:** info@abodeglasgow.co.uk **web:** www.abodeglasgow.co.uk

Located a moment's walk from Glasgow's shopping centres and central transport links, this impressive building provides comfortable luxury accommodation with a boutique feel. Bedrooms are all tastefully appointed; many with high ceilings that allude to the fantastic history of the property. Bedrooms feature air conditioning and 32" TVs as standard. The modern restaurant offers an interesting range of dishes, and a hearty traditional Scottish breakfast sets you up for the day ahead.

**Rooms:** 59 en suite

GLASGOW *continued*

## Georgian House

★★ GUEST HOUSE

**tel:** 0141 339 0008 & 07973 971563 **29 Buckingham Terrace,
Great Western Road G12 8ED**
**email:** thegeorgianhouse@yahoo.com **web:** www.thegeorgianhousehotel.com
**dir:** *M8 junct 17 towards Dumbarton, through 4 sets of lights & right into
Queen Margaret Dr, then right into Buckingham Terrace*

Georgian House offers good-value accommodation and is situated at the west end
of the city in a peaceful tree-lined Victorian terrace near the Botanic Gardens.
Bedrooms vary in size and are furnished in a modern style. A continental style
breakfast is served in the first-floor lounge-dining room.

**Rooms:** 11 rms (10 en suite) (1 pri facs) (4 fmly) (3 GF) **Facilities:** FTV tea/coffee
WiFi **Parking:** 6 **Notes:** LB

## HIGHLAND

### ACHARACLE | Map 22 NM66

## Mingarry Park

★★★★ ☞ RESTAURANT WITH ROOMS

**tel:** 01967 431202 & 07791 115467 **Mingarry PH36 4JX**
**email:** info@mingarryparkhouse.co.uk **web:** www.mingarryparkhouse.co.uk

Set in some breath-taking scenery, Mingarry Park offers individually and
contemporary-styled bedrooms. Each offers great views across the deer park and
surrounding countryside. Some rooms have balconies and decked areas to relax in.
Diners are treated to the best local produce in creative dishes with a roaring log
burner the centre piece of the restaurant.

**Rooms:** 6 en suite (3 GF) **S** £75–£130; **D** £95–£140* **Facilities:** FTV DVD
iPod docking station tea/coffee Dinner available WiFi 🔒 **Notes:** Closed Feb–Mar

### AVIEMORE | Map 23 NH81

## Eriskay Bed & Breakfast

★★★ BED AND BREAKFAST

**tel:** 01479 810717 & 07702 009614 **Craig Na Gower Avenue PH22 1RW**
**email:** enquiries@eriskay-aviemore.co.uk **web:** www.eriskay-aviemore.co.uk
**dir:** *From S turn left into Craig Na Gower Av, follow signs to Aviemore dental practice. At
end of lane next to dentist*

This family-run B&B enjoys a quiet location close to the centre of Aviemore and
is a great base for exploring the Cairngorms National Park and further afield.
All bedrooms have en suite facilities and provide comfortable accommodation.
Warm hospitality and a hearty breakfast are major aspects of any stay here. Newly
built, self-contained ecopods in the grounds of the property are an alternative to
the main accommodation.

**Rooms:** 3 en suite (1 fmly) (3 GF) **S** £45–£80; **D** £60–£80 (room only)* **Facilities:** FTV
tea/coffee WiFi **Parking:** 3 **Notes:** LB

### BRACHLA | Map 23 NH53

### Premier Collection

## Loch Ness Lodge

★★★★★ GUEST ACCOMMODATION

**tel:** 01456 459469 **Loch Ness-Side IV3 8LA**
**email:** escape@loch-ness-lodge.com **web:** www.loch-ness-lodge.com
**dir:** *A9 from Inverness onto A82 signed Fort William, 9m, at 30mph sign. Lodge on
right immediately after Clansman Hotel*

This house enjoys a prominent position overlooking Loch Ness, and each of the
individually designed bedrooms enjoys views of the loch. The bedrooms are of
the highest standard, and are beautifully presented with a mix of traditional
luxury and up-to-date technology, including WiFi. There is a spa with a hot tub,
sauna and a therapy room offering a variety of treatments. Guests have a choice
of attractive lounges which feature real fires in the colder months and where
decadent afternoon teas are served.

**Rooms:** 7 en suite (1 GF) **S** £105–£260; **D** £175–£330* **Facilities:** FTV
DVD Lounge Direct dial Licensed WiFi 🔒 18 Fishing Hot tub Therapy room
**Extras:** Speciality toiletries **Conf:** Max 14 Thtr 14 Class 10 Board 14 **Parking:** 10
**Notes:** LB No children 10yrs Closed 2 Nov–27 Mar (dates may vary)
Civ wed 14

### CARRBRIDGE | Map 23 NH92

## Cairn

★★★ INN

**tel:** 01479 841212 **Main Road PH23 3AS**
**email:** info@cairnhotel.co.uk **web:** www.cairnhotel.co.uk

Conveniently located in the centre of the Cairngorms National Park, this property is
the hub of the local community. The traditional bar and restaurant are
complemented by a range of cosy bedrooms featuring modern touches. Guests can
relax in front of the log fire with a cask ale or local malt whisky. The inn is an ideal
base from which to participate in a number of outdoor activities with activity
breaks and packages available to book.

**Rooms:** 7 rms **Facilities:** Dinner available

## CROMARTY                                                    Map 23 NH76

### The Factor's House

★★★★★ ◉ ⚲ GUEST ACCOMMODATION

**tel:** 01381 600394 & 07917 799143 **Denny Road IV11 8YT**
**email:** info@thefactorshouse.com **web:** www.thefactorshouse.com
**dir:** *Situated on A832 as you approach Cromarty on left from Fortrose*

Situated overlooking the historic town of Cromarty and only a short drive from Inverness, this refurbished house provides luxury accommodation in a secluded and peaceful setting. Spacious bedrooms feature Egyptian linens, a host of thoughtful touches and even home-made soaps to complement an impressive range of toiletries. Award-winning dinners and breakfasts are available; both making good use of the best of local produce, including fruit from the garden and eggs from the resident hens. Dinner must be booked 24 hours in advance.

**Rooms:** 3 en suite (1 GF) **S** £100–£110; **D** £130–£140* **Facilities:** FTV DVD iPod docking station Lounge tea/coffee Dinner available Licensed WiFi 🔓 **Extras:** Speciality toiletries, home-made soap, fresh fruit **Parking:** 3 **Notes:** LB No children 5yrs Closed 20 Dec–5 Jan

## DORNOCH                                                    Map 23 NH78

### Links House at Royal Dornoch

★★★★★ ◉◉ ⚲ GUEST ACCOMMODATION

**tel:** 01862 810279 **Links House, Golf Road IV25 3LW**
**email:** info@linkshousedornoch.com **web:** www.linkshousedornoch.com
**dir:** *From A9 onto A949 into Dornoch. From Castle St, right into Church Street then left into Golf Rd. House at junct of Golf Rd & Kennedy Ave*

This beautifully restored former manse house enjoys a stunning setting overlooking the famous Royal Dornoch Golf Course. The property provides an exceptional level of accommodation with stunning bedrooms and bathrooms, as well as delightful public areas including a wood-panelled library and a drawing room both with open fires; also an outside patio with a fire. The small dining room has a peat fire and provides the backdrop for memorable service, whether enjoying an elaborate evening meal or a sumptuous breakfast. Afternoon teas are also available by prior booking. The property is not just a great base for golf but also for shooting, fishing, stalking and a host of other activities in this beautiful part of the Highlands.

**Rooms:** 5 en suite 9 annexe en suite (4 GF) **D** £320–£365* **Facilities:** STV Lounge TVL Dinner available Licensed WiFi ⬇18 🔓 Leisure activities can be booked in advance **Extras:** Speciality toiletries, fruit – complimentary **Conf:** Max 12 Thtr 12 Class 12 Board 12 **Parking:** 12 **Notes:** Closed 25–27 Dec & 4 Jan–18 Mar

### 2 Quail

★★★★★ ⚲ ⬛ GUEST ACCOMMODATION

**tel:** 01862 811811 **Castle Street IV25 3SN**
**email:** theaa@2quail.com **web:** www.2quail.com
**dir:** *On main street, 200yds from cathedral*

The saying 'small is beautiful' applies to this property set in the main street. The cosy public rooms are ideal for conversation, but there are masses of books for those just wishing to relax. The stylish, individual bedrooms match the character of the house and are thoughtfully equipped with a number of thoughtful touches. Dinner and breakfast are both worth sampling at the property.

**Rooms:** 3 en suite **S** £80–£108; **D** £90–£125* **Facilities:** FTV DVD Lounge tea/coffee Dinner available Direct dial Licensed WiFi ⬇ **Extras:** Speciality toiletries **Notes:** No children 8yrs Closed Xmas & 2 weeks Feb/Mar RS Nov–Mar winter hours – check when booking

## FORT WILLIAM                                                Map 22 NN17

*See also Spean Bridge*

### Mansefield Guest House

★★★★ GUEST HOUSE

**tel:** 01397 772262 **Corpach PH33 7LT**
**email:** mansefield@btinternet.com **web:** www.fortwilliamaccommodation.com
**dir:** *2m N of Fort William. A82 onto A830, house 2m on A830 in Corpach*

Peacefully set in its own well-tended garden, this friendly, family-run guest house provides comfortable, attractively decorated and well-equipped accommodation. There is a cosy lounge, where a roaring coal fire burns on cold evenings, and an attractive dining room where delicious, home-cooked evening meals and breakfasts are served at individual tables.

**Rooms:** 6 en suite (1 GF) **Facilities:** FTV DVD TVL tea/coffee Dinner available WiFi ⬇18 🔓 **Parking:** 7 **Notes:** LB No children 12yrs

## FOYERS
Map 23 NH42

### The Craigdarroch Inn
★★★★ INN

tel: 01456 486400 **IV2 6XU**
email: info@hotel-loch-ness.co.uk web: www.thecraigdarrochinn.co.uk
dir: *Take B862 from either end of loch, then B852 signed Foyers*

Craigdarroch Inn is located in an elevated position, high above Loch Ness on the south side. Bedrooms vary in style and size but all are comfortable and well equipped; those that are front-facing have wonderful views. This friendly inn offers relaxed dining, many tables have loch views, and the staff are friendly and welcoming.

**Rooms:** 8 en suite (1 fmly) **S** £70–£120; **D** £80–£140 (room only)* **Facilities:** FTV Lounge TVL tea/coffee Dinner available WiFi  **Conf:** Max 30 Thtr 30 Class 30 Board 30 **Parking:** 24

### Foyers Bay Country House
★★★ GUEST HOUSE

tel: 01456 486624 **Lochness IV2 6YB**
email: info@foyersbay.co.uk web: www.foyersbay.co.uk
dir: *Off B852 into Lower Foyers*

Situated in sloping grounds with pines and abundant colourful rhododendrons, this delightful Victorian villa has stunning views of Loch Ness. The attractive bedrooms vary in size and are well equipped. There is a comfortable lounge next to the plant-filled conservatory-café, where traditional breakfasts are served.

**Rooms:** 7 en suite (1 GF) **D** £90–£130* **Facilities:** FTV TVL tea/coffee Licensed WiFi  **Parking:** 7 **Notes:** No children 16yrs

## GLENCOE
Map 22 NN15

### The Glencoe Inn
★★★★ INN

tel: 01855 811245 & 811625 **Tyndrum Road PH49 4HP**
email: glencoe@crerarhotels.com web: www.crerarhotels.com/theglencoe-inn

This welcoming inn has a stunning location in the shadow of the Pap of Glencoe, overlooking Loch Leven. The Glencoe Inn is all about traditional Scottish hospitality, complemented by the nature and adventure that awaits outdoors. The public areas are comfy and rustic, and very dog-friendly. An ideal base for those who want to explore Glencoe, walk the West Highland Way or climb the remote Munros of 'Meall a' Bhùiridh' and 'Bidean Nam-Bain'. After a hard day exploring visit the Glencoe Gathering, a retro fish and chip bar located next door.

**Rooms:** 15 en suite (2 fmly) **Facilities:** STV FTV Lounge tea/coffee Dinner available WiFi  **Extras:** Speciality toiletries **Parking:** 40

## GRANTOWN-ON-SPEY
Map 23 NJ02

### Premier Collection

### The Dulaig
★★★★★  BED AND BREAKFAST

tel: 01479 872065 **Seafield Avenue, Aviemore PH26 3JF**
email: enquiries@thedulaig.com web: www.thedulaig.com
dir: *A9 onto A95 to B9102. Into High St, left into Seafield Av for 200mtrs, past Rhuarden Court, The Dulaig on left*

Presented to an exceptional standard, this bed and breakfast benefits from a tranquil setting in 1.5 acres of stunning gardens. Featuring a summer house, duck pond and plenty of wildlife, the grounds provide a relaxing backdrop to the house. Located only a short walk from the centre of the town, features include luxurious, spacious bedrooms with Arts and Crafts antique furniture, and immaculately presented bathrooms with luxury toiletries. A welcoming drawing room is available and memorable breakfasts are served around a large shared table, making use of the best local produce and including eggs from the collection of hens. Carol and Gordon provide memorable hospitality which is appreciated by their many regular guests. The Dulaig was AA Guest Accommodation of the Year for Scotland 2016-2017.

**Rooms:** 3 en suite **S** £125–£145; **D** £165–£185 **Facilities:** STV DVD Lounge tea/coffee WiFi  **Extras:** Speciality toiletries, fruit, chocolates – complimentary **Parking:** 6 **Notes:** LB  No children 12yrs Closed 11 Dec–8 Jan

## INVERNESS
Map 23 NH64

### Premier Collection

### Daviot Lodge
★★★★★  GUEST ACCOMMODATION

tel: 01463 772215 **Daviot Mains IV2 5ER**
email: margaret.hutcheson@btopenworld.com web: www.daviotlodge.co.uk
dir: *Exit A9 5m S of Inverness onto B851 signed Croy. 1m on left*

Standing in 80 acres of peaceful pasture land, this impressive establishment offers attractive, well-appointed and well-equipped bedrooms. The master bedroom is furnished with a four-poster bed. There is a tranquil lounge with deep sofas and a real fire, and a peaceful dining room where hearty breakfasts featuring the best of local produce are served. Full disabled access for wheelchairs is provided.

**Rooms:** 6 en suite (1 GF) **Facilities:** FTV DVD Lounge TVL tea/coffee Licensed WiFi **Extras:** Speciality toiletries, snacks **Parking:** 10 **Notes:** LB No children 10yrs Closed 23 Dec–2 Jan

## Trafford Bank

★★★★★ 🛎 GUEST HOUSE

**tel:** 01463 241414 **96 Fairfield Road IV3 5LL**
**email:** info@traffordbankhotel.co.uk **web:** www.traffordbankhotel.co.uk
**dir:** *Exit A82 at Kenneth St, 2nd left into Fairfield Rd, 600yds on right*

This impressive Victorian house lies in a residential area close to the canal. Lorraine Pun has made great use of her interior design skills to blend the best in contemporary styles with the house's period character and the results are simply stunning. Delightful public areas offer a choice of lounges, while breakfast is taken in a beautiful conservatory featuring eye-catching wrought-iron chairs. Each bedroom is unique in design and has TV, DVD and CDs, sherry, silent mini-fridges and much more.

**Rooms:** 5 en suite (2 fmly) **Facilities:** STV FTV TVL tea/coffee WiFi **Parking:** 10
**Notes:** LB

*See advert on following page*

## Avalon Guest House

★★★★ GUEST HOUSE

**tel:** 01463 239075 & 07936 226241 **79 Glenurquhart Road IV3 5PB**
**email:** avalon@inverness-loch-ness.co.uk **web:** www.inverness-loch-ness.co.uk

Avalon Guest House is just a short walk from the city centre, and five minutes' drive from Loch Ness. Breakfast can be taken in the well-appointed dining room where fresh local produce is the highlight of the menu. Bedrooms are spacious with a host of thoughtful extras including WiFi, fridges, fluffy towels and complimentary toiletries. A guest lounge is also provided.

**Rooms:** 6 rms (5 en suite) (1 pri facs) (4 GF) **D** £65–£95* **Facilities:** FTV DVD iPod docking station TVL tea/coffee WiFi **Extras:** Fridge, chocolates, flowers **Parking:** 10 **Notes:** No children 14yrs

## Ballifeary Guest House

★★★★ 🛎 GUEST HOUSE

**tel:** 01463 235572 **10 Ballifeary Road IV3 5PJ**
**email:** info@ballifearyguesthouse.co.uk **web:** www.ballifearyguesthouse.co.uk
**dir:** *Exit A82, 0.5m from town centre, left into Bishops Rd, sharp right into Ballifeary Rd*

This charming detached house has a peaceful residential location within easy walking distance of the town centre and Eden Court Theatre. The attractive bedrooms are carefully appointed and well equipped. There is an elegant ground-floor drawing room and a comfortable dining room, where delicious breakfasts, featuring the best of local produce, are served at individual tables.

**Rooms:** 6 en suite (1 GF) **S** £50–£70; **D** £70–£90 **Facilities:** FTV DVD Lounge tea/coffee WiFi 🛎 **Extras:** Mineral water – complimentary **Parking:** 6 **Notes:** LB No children 15yrs Closed 24–28 Dec

## Moyness House

★★★★ GUEST HOUSE

**tel:** 01463 233836 & 236624 **6 Bruce Gardens IV3 5EN**
**email:** info@moyness.co.uk **web:** www.moyness.co.uk
**dir:** *Off A82 (Fort William road), almost opposite Highland Regional Council headquarters*

Situated in a quiet residential area just a short distance from the city centre, this elegant Victorian villa dates from 1880 and offers beautifully decorated, comfortable bedrooms and well-appointed bathrooms. There is an attractive sitting room and an inviting dining room, where traditional Scottish breakfasts are served. Guests are welcome to use the secluded and well-maintained back garden.

**Rooms:** 6 en suite (1 fmly) (2 GF) **Facilities:** FTV Lounge tea/coffee WiFi **Extras:** Speciality toiletries, robes **Parking:** 10 **Notes:** LB

# Trafford Bank
## Guest House

Koshal and Lorraine Pun purchased Trafford Bank in 2002 with the vision to make it into one of the top boutique guest houses in Scotland.

From the paintings on our walls to the cushions on our beds, these are all from local highland businesses. Our breakfast menu is all locally sourced, we have a variety of options which caters for all guests.

This former Bishop's home has been refurbished from top to bottom and mixes antique and contemporary furniture, some of which has been designed by Lorraine herself — an accomplished interior designer.

The guest house is non-smoking throughout, and is surrounded by mature gardens that the guests can enjoy and has ample parking.

AA
Breakfast
Award

AA ★★★★★

Trafford Bank Guest House
96 Fairfield Road, Inverness, Highland IV3 5LL
Tel: 01463 241414
www.traffordbankhotel.co.uk
E-Mail: info@traffordbankhotel.co.uk

INVERNESS *continued*

## Dunhallin Guest House

★★★★ GUEST HOUSE

**tel:** 01463 220824 **164 Culduthel Road IV2 4BH**
**email:** relax@dunhallin.co.uk **web:** www.dunhallin.co.uk
**dir:** *From city centre follow Castle St then Culduthel Rd for 1m. At mini rdbt take 1st exit, right at lights. 100mtrs on right*

Located in the Highland capital, this comfortable guest house offers a relaxing home-from-home. Margaret and Sandy love what they do and this shows in the friendly hospitality and helpful service they provide to all guests. Breakfasts are a feature of any stay here with a wide range of dishes offering something for everybody. Bedrooms are spaciously appointed with a great range of modern accessories including TVs, DVD players and iPod docks. Complimentary parking is available on site.

**Rooms:** 5 en suite **S** £49–£135; **D** £59–£145* **Facilities:** FTV DVD iPod docking station Lounge tea/coffee WiFi 🛁 **Extras:** Fridges in rooms **Parking:** 5 **Notes:** LB No children 12yrs

## Heathcote B&B

★★★★ BED AND BREAKFAST

**tel:** 01463 236596 & 07833 730849 **59 Glenurquhart Road IV3 5PB**
**email:** info@heathcotebandb.co.uk **web:** www.heathcotebandb.co.uk
**dir:** *On A82, 1m from city centre*

Only a few minutes' walk from the Eden Court Theatre and the centre of Inverness, this Victorian townhouse is ideally situated for touring the city and beyond, whether you are searching for the Loch Ness Monster or just castle-hunting. Modern bedrooms and bathrooms offer spacious and comfortable accommodation. Friendly hospitality and memorable breakfasts are also features here. Ample off-street, private parking is provided.

**Rooms:** 3 en suite **S** £40–£90; **D** £48–£98* **Facilities:** FTV tea/coffee WiFi 🛁 **Extras:** Bottled water **Parking:** 6

## Lyndon Guest House

★★★★ GUEST HOUSE

**tel:** 01463 232551 **50 Telford Street IV3 5LE**
**email:** lyndon@invernessbedandbreakfast.com
**web:** www.invernessbedandbreakfast.com
**dir:** *A9 onto A82, over Friars Bridge, right at rdbt into Telford St. House on right*

A warm Highland welcome awaits at Lyndon Guest House, family-run accommodation close to the centre of Inverness. All bedrooms are en suite and are equipped with plenty of useful facilities including full internet access. Gaelic is spoken here.

**Rooms:** 6 en suite (2 fmly) (2 GF) **S** £35–£50; **D** £60–£100* **Facilities:** FTV TVL tea/coffee WiFi 🛁 **Parking:** 7 **Notes:** Closed 20 Dec–5 Jan

## Sunnyholm

★★★ GUEST ACCOMMODATION

**tel:** 01463 231336 **12 Mayfield Road IV2 4AE**
**email:** sunnyholm@invernessguesthouse.com **web:** www.invernessguesthouse.com
**dir:** *500yds SE of town centre. Exit B861 (Culduthel Rd) into Mayfield Rd*

Situated in a peaceful residential area within easy walking distance of the city centre, Sunnyholm offers comfortably proportioned and well-equipped bedrooms. A spacious conservatory-lounge overlooks the beautiful rear gardens, and there is another lounge next to the bright, airy dining room. Off-street parking is available to all guests.

**Rooms:** 4 en suite (4 GF) **S** fr £45; **D** fr £75* **Facilities:** FTV DVD Lounge tea/coffee WiFi 🛁 **Extras:** Snacks – complimentary **Parking:** 6 **Notes:** No children 3yrs

## Fraser House

★★★ GUEST ACCOMMODATION

**tel:** 01463 716488 & 07502 980034 **49 Huntly Street IV3 5HS**
**email:** fraserlea@btconnect.com **web:** www.fraserhouse.co.uk
**dir:** *A82 W over bridge, left into Wells St leading into Huntly St, house in 100yds*

Situated on the west bank of the River Ness, Fraser House has a commanding position overlooking the city, and is within easy walking distance of the central amenities. Bedrooms, all en suite, vary in size and are comfortably furnished and well equipped. The ground-floor dining room is the setting for freshly cooked Scottish breakfasts.

**Rooms:** 5 en suite (2 fmly) **S** £45–£60; **D** £60–£90* **Facilities:** FTV DVD iPod docking station tea/coffee WiFi 🛁 **Notes:** Closed Feb–Mar

| KINGUSSIE | Map 23 NH70 |

## The Cross

★★★★ ⊛⊛⊛ 🍽 RESTAURANT WITH ROOMS

**tel:** 01540 661166 **Tweed Mill Brae, Ardbrollach Road PH21 1LB**
**email:** relax@thecross.co.uk **web:** www.thecross.co.uk
**dir:** *From lights in Kingussie centre take Ardbroilach Rd, 300yds left into Tweed Mill Brae*

Built as a water-powered tweed mill in the late 19th century, The Cross is situated in the picturesque Cairngorms National Park and surrounded by four acres of riverside grounds that teem with an abundance of wildlife, including red squirrels. Comfortable lounges and a selection of well-appointed bedrooms are offered, and award-winning dinners are served by an open fire in the stone-walled and wood-beamed restaurant.

**Rooms:** 8 en suite **S** £90–£150; **D** £110–£180* **Facilities:** FTV DVD Lounge tea/coffee Dinner available Direct dial WiFi 🛁 **Extras:** Bottled water, speciality toiletries **Conf:** Max 20 Thtr 20 Class 20 Board 20 **Parking:** 20 **Notes:** LB Closed Jan

| LAGGAN | Map 22 NN29 |
|---|---|

## The Rumblie Guest House

★★★★ ☟ GUEST HOUSE

**tel:** 01528 544766 **Gergask Avenue PH20 1AH**
**email:** mail@rumblie.com **web:** www.rumblie.com
**dir:** *A9 at Dalwhinnie onto A889. Right on A86, left at church after bridge, follow sign*

Comfortable eco-friendly accommodation and a warm welcome await you here, with evening meals available if pre-booked. The guest house is licensed, giving you a chance to try some of the wide range of whiskies available. In the morning, a fine breakfast will set you up for the day, making good use of local organic produce. The Rumblie is situated in the Cairngorm National Park, and on the long-distance East Highland Way.

**Rooms:** 3 en suite (1 GF) **D** £90–£110 **Facilities:** FTV DVD Lounge tea/coffee Dinner available Licensed WiFi ☂ **Extras:** Fruit, flowers, home-made shortbread, filtered water **Parking:** 5 **Notes:** No children 10yrs Closed 20 Nov–27 Dec

| NAIRN | Map 23 NH85 |
|---|---|

### Premier Collection

## Boath House

★★★★★ ◉◉◉◉ ☟ RESTAURANT WITH ROOMS

**tel:** 01667 454896 **Auldearn IV12 5TE**
**email:** info@boath-house.com **web:** www.boath-house.com
**dir:** *2m past Nairn on A96, E towards Forres, signed on main road*

Standing in its own 20-acre grounds, with an ornamental lake, walled garden and secluded seating areas, this splendid Georgian mansion was built in 1825 for the Dunbar family, but there has been occupation on the site since the 16th century. Hospitality here is first class; the owners are passionate about what they do, and have a real ability to establish a special relationship with their guests. The food is memorable; head chef Charlie Lockley is a devotee of slow and organic cooking which also includes using foraged produce. The five-course dinners are a culinary adventure, matched only by the excellence of breakfasts. The house itself is delightful, with inviting lounges and a dining room overlooking a trout loch. The bedrooms, with lake and woodland views, are striking and very comfortable; Orangerie Rooms have their own conservatory.

**Rooms:** 9 en suite (2 GF) **S** £235–£305; **D** £380–£450* **Facilities:** FTV DVD Lounge tea/coffee Dinner available Direct dial WiFi ☘ Fishing **Parking:** 20 **Notes:** Civ wed 32

| POOLEWE | Map 22 NG88 |
|---|---|

### AA GUEST ACCOMMODATION OF THE YEAR FOR SCOTLAND 2017–18

### Premier Collection

## Pool House

★★★★★ ☟ 🍴 GUEST HOUSE

**tel:** 01445 781272 **IV22 2LD**
**email:** stay@pool-house.co.uk **web:** www.pool-house.co.uk
**dir:** *6m N of Gairloch on A832 in the centre of village by bridge*

Set on the shores of Loch Ewe where the river meets the bay, the understated roadside façade gives little hint of its splendid interior, nor of the views facing the bay. Memorable features include delightful public rooms and stunningly romantic suites, each individually designed and with feature bathrooms. Pool House is run very much as a country house – the hospitality and guest care by the Harrison family are second to none.

**Rooms:** 4 en suite **S** £125–£180; **D** £195–£295 **Facilities:** FTV DVD iPod docking station Lounge tea/coffee Dinner available Direct dial Licensed WiFi Snooker **Extras:** Sherry, speciality toiletries – complimentary **Parking:** 10 **Notes:** LB No children 12yrs Closed Nov–mid Mar

| ROY BRIDGE | Map 22 NN28 |
|---|---|

## Homagen

★★★★ BED AND BREAKFAST

**tel:** 01397 712411 **PH31 4AN**
**email:** stay@homagen.co.uk **web:** www.homagen.co.uk
**dir:** *On A86, opposite Roy Bridge Hotel*

Homagen is a family-run property in a great location for touring the Highlands, with links to Fort William, Aviemore and beyond. Bedrooms feature modern decor and comfortable beds. Hearty breakfasts are served in the dining room at a communal table. Free WiFi is provided. Packed lunches are available for making day trips.

**Rooms:** 4 rms (3 en suite) (1 pri facs) (4 GF) **S** £45; **D** £85 **Facilities:** FTV Lounge tea/coffee WiFi Fishing ☂ **Parking:** 6 **Notes:** LB No children 10yrs Closed 23 Dec–3 Jan

## SPEAN BRIDGE                                    Map 22 NN28

# Smiddy House

★★★★ ◉◉ ☕ RESTAURANT WITH ROOMS

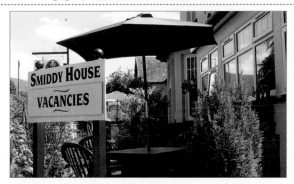

**tel:** 01397 712335 **Roy Bridge Road PH34 4EU**
**email:** enquiry@smiddyhouse.com **web:** www.smiddyhouse.com
**dir:** *In village centre, A82 onto A86*

Set in the Great Glen which stretches from Fort William to Inverness, this was once the village smithy, and is now a very friendly restaurant with rooms. The attractive bedrooms, named after places in Scotland, are comfortably furnished and well equipped. A relaxing garden room is available for guest use. Delicious evening meals are served in Russell's restaurant.

**Rooms:** 4 en suite 1 annexe en suite (1 GF) **S** £90–£130; **D** £115–£195*
**Facilities:** FTV Lounge tea/coffee Dinner available WiFi **Extras:** Speciality toiletries, mineral water – complimentary **Parking:** 15 **Notes:** No children 12yrs Closed Mon RS Nov–Mar limited opening

# Distant Hills Guest House

★★★★ ☕ GUEST HOUSE

**tel:** 01397 712452 **Roy Bridge Road PH34 4EU**
**email:** enquiry@distanthills.com **web:** www.distanthillsspeanbridge.co.uk
**dir:** *From A82 onto A86 signed Newtonmore. 0.5m on right*

Distant Hills Guest House in the heart of the Highlands offers stylish bedrooms, award-winning breakfasts and friendly hospitality. Set amongst wonderful scenery, the house enjoys a quiet setting in its own impressive grounds. An ideal base for touring Fort William, Oban, Inverness and the Highlands whether walking, climbing or driving. Off-road parking and free WiFi are some of the numerous features of the house.

**Rooms:** 7 en suite (7 GF) **S** fr £73; **D** fr £88 **Facilities:** FTV DVD TVL tea/coffee WiFi ♨9 **Extras:** Speciality toiletries **Parking:** 10 **Notes:** No children 12yrs Closed 15 Nov–1 Mar

## STRATHPEFFER                                    Map 23 NH45

# Inver Lodge

★★★ GUEST HOUSE

**tel:** 01997 421392 & 07895 030713 **IV14 9DL**
**email:** inverlodgebandb@gmail.com **web:** www.inverlodgestrathpeffer.com
**dir:** *A834 through Strathpeffer centre, turn beside Spa Pavilion signed Bowling Green, Inver Lodge on right*

You are assured of a warm welcome at this Victorian lodge, secluded in its own tree-studded gardens yet within easy walking distance of the town centre. Bedrooms are comfortable and well equipped, and the cosy lounge is ideal for relaxation. Breakfasts, and evening meals (by arrangement), are served at a communal table.

**Rooms:** 2 rms (1 fmly) **S** £35–£37; **D** £52* **Facilities:** FTV Lounge tea/coffee Dinner available WiFi ♨18 **Parking:** 2 **Notes:** LB Closed Xmas & New Year

## TORRIDON                                        Map 22 NG95

# The Torridon Inn

★★★★ 🍽 INN

**tel:** 01445 791242 **IV22 2EY**
**email:** inn@thetorridon.com **web:** www.thetorridon.com/inn

The Torridon Inn enjoys an idyllic location and is set in 58 acres of parkland, overlooking Loch Torridon and surrounded by steep mountains on all sides. Bedrooms are lodge style with adjacent parking and are smartly appointed with comfy beds and modern facilities. Freshly prepared food is served in the adjacent inn, where over 80 whiskies, and several real ales, including a local Torridon Ale, are firm favourites.

**Rooms:** 12 en suite (3 fmly) (5 GF) **S** £120–£130; **D** £120–£130* **Facilities:** STV tea/coffee Dinner available WiFi ⛷ Fishing Pool table **Outdoor adventure activities available **Parking:** 12 **Notes:** LB Closed Jan Civ wed 55

## ULLAPOOL
Map 22 NH19

### The Arch Inn
★★★ ☐ INN

tel: 01854 612454 **10–11 West Shore Street IV26 2UR**
email: info@thearchinn.co.uk web: www.thearchinn.co.uk
dir: *Into Ullapool, continue along Shore St. Pass pier, inn on right*

The Arch Inn is situated on Ullapool waterfront on the shores of Loch Broom, only a two-minute walk from the Outer Hebrides ferry terminal. The accommodation provided is comfortable, and most rooms have stunning views over the loch to the mountains in the distance. The relaxed bar and grill offers a selection of fresh local produce including seafood.

**Rooms:** 10 en suite (1 fmly) (2 GF) **S** £50–£95; **D** £80–£95* **Facilities:** STV FTV tea/coffee Dinner available WiFi Pool table **Extras:** Sweets **Conf:** Max 60 Thtr 40 Class 30 Board 35 **Parking:** 5

## INVERCLYDE

## INVERKIP
Map 20 NS27

### The Inverkip
★★★ ☐ INN

tel: 01475 521478 **Main Street PA16 0AS**
email: hello@inverkip.co.uk web: www.inverkip.co.uk
dir: *Just off A78, near Inverkip Marina*

This family-run property enjoys a great location at the centre of the historic village of Inverkip and is only a short stroll from the popular Inverkip Marina. This is a great place for those with an interest in great pub food and a passion for cask ales, whiskies (over 200) and gin. A small public bar and a larger restaurant are most atmospheric, and a friendly face is always present with staff eager to please. Bedrooms and bathrooms are modern and well presented. Ample parking on site.

**Rooms:** 5 en suite (2 fmly) **S** £65–£75; **D** £89–£98* **Facilities:** STV FTV Lounge tea/coffee Dinner available WiFi ⌚18 ☗ **Parking:** 33 **Notes:** Closed 24–25 & 31 Dec–1 Jan (accommodation) RS 1–2 Jan & 25 Dec closed for accommodation & food

# Silver Stars
The AA Silver Star rating denotes a B&B that we highly recommend. They have a superior level of quality within their star rating, high standards of hospitality, service and cleanliness.

## NORTH LANARKSHIRE

## MOTHERWELL
Map 20 NS75

### Innkeeper's Lodge Glasgow
★★★ INN

tel: 08451 551551 *(Calls cost 2p per minute plus your phone company's access charge)*
**1 Hamilton Road ML1 3RB**
email: info@innkeeperslodge.com web: www.innkeeperslodge.com

This property enjoys an excellent location for those travelling to and from Scotland, or as a base for visiting anywhere in the central belt. The inn is located just off the M74 with links to nearby Glasgow and Edinburgh. Modern, spacious bedrooms occupy an attractive building, where friendly service, wide-ranging breakfasts, free WiFi and complimentary parking are also available. Next door is the ever-popular Toby Carvery where food and real ales are available all day.

**Rooms:** 28 en suite (13 fmly) (14 GF) **Facilities:** FTV tea/coffee Dinner available WiFi **Conf:** Max 35 **Parking:** 150

## SOUTH LANARKSHIRE

## STRATHAVEN
Map 20 NS74

### Rissons at Springvale
★★★ ◉ RESTAURANT WITH ROOMS

tel: 01357 521131 & 520234 **18 Lethame Road ML10 6AD**
email: info@rissons.co.uk web: www.rissonsrestaurant.co.uk
dir: *A71 into Strathaven, W of town centre off Townhead St*

Guests are assured of a warm welcome at this charming establishment close to the town centre. The bedrooms and bathrooms are stylish and well equipped. The main attraction here is the food –a range of interesting, well-prepared dishes served in Rissons Restaurant.

**Rooms:** 9 en suite (1 fmly) (1 GF) **S** £50; **D** £85–£90* **Facilities:** FTV Lounge TVL tea/coffee Dinner available WiFi ⌚ ⌚18 Fishing ☗ **Parking:** 10 **Notes:** Closed 1st week Jan

## EAST LOTHIAN

## ABERLADY
Map 21 NT47

### Ducks Inn
★★★★ ◉◉ RESTAURANT WITH ROOMS

tel: 01875 870682 **Main Street EH32 0RE**
email: info@ducks.co.uk web: www.ducks.co.uk
dir: *A1 (Bankton junct) take 1st exit to North Berwick. At next rdbt 3rd exit onto A198 signed Longniddry, left towards Aberlady. At T-junct, facing river, right to Aberlady*

The name of this restaurant with rooms is referenced around the building — Ducks Restaurant for award-winning cuisine; Donald's Bistro and the Ducklings informal coffee shop. The warm and welcoming public areas include a great bar offering real ales and various objets d'art. The bedrooms are comfortable and well-appointed with stylish en suites. The team are informal and friendly, taking the time to chat to their guests.

**Rooms:** 23 en suite (1 fmly) (6 GF) **S** £50–£110; **D** £70–£140* **Facilities:** STV FTV Lounge TVL tea/coffee Dinner available Direct dial WiFi ⌚18 ☗ **Conf:** Max 100 Thtr 100 Class 60 Board 30 **Parking:** 15

## WEST LOTHIAN

### EAST CALDER
Map 21 NT06

## Ashcroft Farmhouse

★★★★ 🍴 GUEST HOUSE

**tel:** 01506 881810 & 07788 926239 **EH53 0ET**
**email:** ashcroftinfo@aol.com **web:** www.ashcroftfarmhouse.com

*(For full entry see Livingston)*

## Whitecroft Bed & Breakfast

★★★★ BED AND BREAKFAST

**tel:** 01506 882494 **7 Raw Holdings EH53 0ET**
**email:** lornascot@aol.com **web:** www.whitecroftbandb.co.uk

*(For full entry see Livingston)*

### LINLITHGOW
Map 21 NS97

### Premier Collection

## Arden Country House

★★★★★ 🍴 GUEST ACCOMMODATION

**tel:** 01506 670172 **Belsyde EH49 6QE**
**email:** info@ardencountryhouse.com **web:** www.ardencountryhouse.com
**dir:** *1.3m SW of Linlithgow. A706 over Union Canal, entrance 200yds on left at Lodge Cottage*

Situated in the picturesque grounds of the Belsyde country estate and close to the Royal Burgh of Linlithgow, Arden Country House offers immaculate, stylishly furnished and spacious bedrooms. There is a cosy ground-floor lounge and a charming dining room where delicious breakfasts feature the best of local produce.

**Rooms:** 3 en suite (1 GF) **S** £70–£110; **D** £85–£110 (room only)* **Facilities:** FTV DVD iPod docking station Lounge tea/coffee WiFi **Extras:** Savoury snacks, chocolates **Parking:** 4 **Notes:** LB No children 12yrs Closed 25–26 Dec

## Bomains Farm Guest House

★★★★ GUEST HOUSE

**tel:** 01506 822188 & 07974 736480 **Bo'ness EH49 7RQ**
**email:** bunty.kirk@onetel.net **web:** www.bomains.co.uk
**dir:** *A706, 1.5m N towards Bo'ness, left at golf course x-rds, 1st farm on right*

From its elevated location this friendly farmhouse has stunning views of the Firth of Forth. The bedrooms, which vary in size, are beautifully decorated and well-equipped with many thoughtful extra touches. Delicious home-cooked fare, featuring the best local produce, is served in a stylish lounge-dining room.

**Rooms:** 6 rms (4 en suite) (1 pri facs) (1 fmly) (2 GF) **Facilities:** STV FTV DVD Lounge TVL tea/coffee WiFi ⅃18 Fishing 🛁 **Extras:** Sweets **Parking:** 12

## Kirkland House

★★★★ BED AND BREAKFAST

**tel:** 01506 822188 & 07974 736480 **Bomains Farm EH49 7RQ**
**email:** bunty.kirk@onetel.net **web:** www.bomains.co.uk
**dir:** *A706, 1.5m N towards Bo'ness, left at golf course x-rds, 1st farm on right*

Kirkland House is a purpose-built property adjacent to the family-run Bomains Farm Guest House, where a number of guest services are provided. Large bedrooms come with high quality fixtures and fittings, and patio doors that lead onto the garden which has a children's play area and views onto the River Forth. A peaceful location within striking distance of Linlithgow, Edinburgh and the Central Belt.

**Rooms:** 3 en suite (1 fmly) (3 GF) **Facilities:** FTV TVL tea/coffee WiFi ⅃18 Fishing **Parking:** 6

## LIVINGSTON
Map 21 NT06

# Ashcroft Farmhouse

★★★★ 🏠 GUEST HOUSE

**tel:** 01506 881810 & 07788 926239 **East Calder EH53 0ET**
**email:** ashcroftinfo@aol.com **web:** www.ashcroftfarmhouse.com
**dir:** *On B7015, off A71, 0.5m E of East Calder, near Almondell Country Park*

With over 40 years' experience in caring for guests, Derek and Elizabeth Scott ensure a stay at Ashcroft will be memorable. Their modern home sits in lovely, award-winning landscaped gardens, and provides attractive and well-equipped ground-floor bedrooms. The comfortable lounge includes a video and DVD library. Breakfast, featuring home-made sausages and the best of local produce, is served at individual tables in the stylish dining room. Free WiFi is available, and a Park & Ride facility is nearby. Ashcroft Farmhouse was a finalist for the AA B&B Story of the Year award 2017–18.

**Rooms:** 6 en suite (2 fmly) (6 GF) **D** £80–£90* **Facilities:** FTV TVL tea/coffee WiFi
🅿 **Parking:** 8

# Whitecroft Bed & Breakfast

★★★★ BED AND BREAKFAST

**tel:** 01506 882494 **7 Raw Holdings, East Calder EH53 0ET**
**email:** lornascot@aol.com **web:** www.whitecroftbandb.co.uk
**dir:** *A71 onto B7015, establishment on right*

A relaxed and friendly atmosphere prevails at Whitecroft, a charming, modern bed and breakfast. The bedrooms, all of which are on the ground floor, are

attractively colour co-ordinated, well-equipped and contain many thoughtful extra touches. Breakfast is served at individual tables in the smart dining room.

*Whitecroft Bed & Breakfast*

**Rooms:** 3 en suite (3 GF) **Facilities:** FTV DVD tea/coffee WiFi **Parking:** 5
**Notes:** No children 12yrs

## MIDLOTHIAN

## DALKEITH
Map 21 NT36

# The Sun Inn

★★★★ 🌸 🍴 INN

**tel:** 0131 663 2456 **Lothian Bridge EH22 4TR**
**email:** thesuninn@live.com **web:** www.thesuninnedinburgh.co.uk
**dir:** *On A7 towards Galashiels, opposite Newbattle Viaduct*

The Sun Inn dates back to 1697 and is situated within easy striking distance of Edinburgh. It has boutique-style bedrooms (one featuring a copper bath) and modern bathrooms. High quality, award-winning food is served in stylish surroundings; drinks can be enjoyed in the terraced garden area.

**Rooms:** 5 en suite **S** £75; **D** £95–£150* **Facilities:** STV FTV Lounge tea/coffee Dinner available WiFi ⚓18 Fishing **Conf:** Max 80 Thtr 80 Class 50 Board 40 **Parking:** 100
**Notes:** LB

## ROSLIN
Map 21 NT26

# The Original Rosslyn Inn

★★★★ INN

**tel:** 0131 440 2384 **4 Main Street EH25 9LE**
**email:** enquiries@theoriginalhotel.co.uk **web:** www.theoriginalhotel.co.uk
**dir:** *From A701 at rdbt take B7003 signed Roslin & Rosewell, into Roslin. At T-junct, inn opposite. Or from mini rdbt on A701 at Bilston take B7006 to Roslin. Inn on left*

Whether on *The Da Vinci Code* trail or in the area on business, this property is ideally placed for a visit to the famous Rosslyn Chapel, which is just a short walk away. It is a delightful village inn that offers well-equipped bedrooms with en suites; four of the bedrooms have four-poster beds. The Grail Restaurant, the lounge and conservatory offer a comprehensive selection of dining options.

**Rooms:** 7 en suite (2 fmly) **Facilities:** FTV DVD Lounge tea/coffee Dinner available WiFi 🅿 **Conf:** Max 130 Thtr 130 Class 80 Board 60 **Parking:** 8 **Notes:** LB Civ wed 180

## MORAY

### FORRES
Map 23 NJ05

## Cluny Bank

★★★★ ◉ RESTAURANT WITH ROOMS

**tel:** 01309 674304 **69 St Leonards Road IV36 1DW**
**email:** info@clunybankhotel.co.uk **web:** www.clunybankhotel.co.uk

Historic, listed Cluny Bank occupies a quiet location within walking distance of the centre of Forres, and is an ideal base for exploring the northeast of Scotland. Family-run, the building retains many original architectural features. Public areas include the Altyre Bar with a wide range of whiskies, and Franklin's Restaurant where a real taste of Moray can be experienced. Room service, complimentary WiFi and memorable breakfasts are also provided for guests.

**Rooms:** 6 en suite 1 annexe en suite (2 GF) **S** £85–£90; **D** £122.50–£165*
**Facilities:** FTV iPod docking station Lounge tea/coffee Dinner available Direct dial WiFi **Parking:** 7 **Notes:** LB

## PERTH & KINROSS

### ALYTH
Map 21 NO24

### Premier Collection

## Tigh Na Leigh Guesthouse

★★★★★ ◉ ⊜ GUEST ACCOMMODATION

**tel:** 01828 632372 **22–24 Airlie Street PH11 8AJ**
**email:** book@tighnaleigh.com **web:** www.tighnaleigh.co.uk
**dir:** In town centre on B952

Situated in the heart of this charming country town, Tigh Na Leigh (Gaelic for 'The House of the Doctor') is an equally charming property. It has an imposing, yet welcoming appearance, and inside has been completely restored to blend its Victorian architecture with contemporary interior design. Bedrooms, including a superb suite, have state-of-the-art bathrooms and spa baths. There are three lounges, and delicious meals are served in the conservatory/dining room overlooking a spectacular landscaped garden. Free WiFi is provided.

**Rooms:** 5 en suite (1 GF) **S** £55; **D** £94–£133* **Facilities:** FTV DVD iPod docking station Lounge TVL tea/coffee Dinner available Licensed WiFi ♨18 ♨ **Extras:** Fruit, mineral water **Parking:** 5 **Notes:** No children 12yrs Closed Dec–Jan

### BLAIR ATHOLL
Map 23 NN86

## The Firs

★★★★ GUEST HOUSE

**tel:** 01796 481256 **PH18 5TA**
**email:** kirstie@firs-blairatholl.co.uk **web:** www.firs-blairatholl.co.uk
**dir:** A9 follow signs to Blair Atholl, 1st left after Blair Atholl garage

The Firs is located in the peaceful village of Blair Atholl, home of Europe's only legal private army, the Atholl Highlanders. This is a well-presented property with lovely gardens. Bedrooms are comfortable and have quality decor. Public areas are warm and welcoming, and are enhanced by a log fire, while breakfast is served in the conservatory at individual tables.

**Rooms:** 6 en suite (3 fmly) (2 GF) **S** £55–£65; **D** £75–£105* **Facilities:** FTV DVD Lounge tea/coffee WiFi ♨ **Extras:** Speciality toiletries **Parking:** 7 **Notes:** LB Closed Nov–Feb

### CALVINE
Map 23 NN86

## The Struan Inn

★★★★ GUEST ACCOMMODATION

**tel:** 01796 483714 **PH18 5UB**
**email:** thestruan.calvine@btinternet.com **web:** www.thestruan-inn.co.uk
**dir:** From N : A9 turn right onto B847, turn right for Kinloch Rannoch. Under bridge, 1st right. From S: A9 turn left onto B847, turn right for Kinloch Rannoch, then as above

Located on the edge of the Cairngorms National Park in a peaceful location yet just two minutes from the A9, this historic inn is comfortable and welcoming. Inside there is a residents' bar with a log fire, comfortable lounge, and a restaurant serving hearty dinners. Bedrooms are well appointed with modern features. Hospitality is warm and friendly.

**Rooms:** 5 en suite (2 fmly) (1 GF) **S** £60–£80; **D** £75–£100* **Facilities:** STV DVD iPod docking station TVL tea/coffee Dinner available Licensed WiFi ♨ **Parking:** 8 **Notes:** Closed 18 Dec–13 Jan

### MEIKLEOUR
Map 21 NO13

## Meikleour Arms

★★★★ INN

**tel:** 01250 883206 & 883406 **PH2 6EB**
**email:** contact@meikleourarms.co.uk **web:** www.meikleourarms.co.uk
**dir:** N of Perth on A93

This family-run country inn has been a popular venue for almost 200 years. It was first established as a coach and posting house. Today it welcomes both locals and visitors who come to the area for fishing and shooting. Bedrooms are spacious and comfortable with impressive bathrooms. An attractive restaurant serves high quality local produce, and the lounge bar is a cosy area where beer connoisseurs can sample the property's own real ale.

**Rooms:** 11 en suite 4 annexe en suite (2 fmly) (11 GF) **S** £65–£150; **D** £75–£180 **Facilities:** FTV Lounge tea/coffee Dinner available WiFi ♨45 Fishing ♨ Drying room for anglers **Extras:** Speciality toiletries, bottled water, sherry, fruit – complimentary **Parking:** 40

## PERTH
Map 21 NO12

### The Townhouse
★★★★★ GUEST HOUSE

**tel:** 01738 446179 **17 Marshall Place PH2 8AG**
**email:** info@thetownhouseperth.co.uk **web:** www.thetownhouseperth.co.uk
**dir:** *M90 junct 10 towards Perth. Into centre of town, left into Marshall Place*

This traditional, Georgian terraced property enjoys a great location in the heart of Perth city centre, and several of the large beautifully appointed rooms benefit from great views over picturesque South Inch Park. Luxurious beds and antique furniture sit alongside contemporary design. Breakfasts feature local and home-made produce. Complimentary parking and WiFi are provided.

**Rooms:** 5 en suite (1 fmly) (1 GF) **S** £65–£75; **D** £85–£135* **Facilities:** STV FTV DVD iPod docking station tea/coffee Direct dial WiFi 🔒 **Parking:** 5

## SCOTTISH BORDERS

## EDDLESTON
Map 21 NT24

### The Horseshoe Restaurant with Rooms
★★★★ 🍴 RESTAURANT WITH ROOMS

**tel:** 01721 730225 **Edinburgh Road EH45 8QP**
**email:** reservations@horseshoeinn.co.uk **web:** www.horseshoeinn.co.uk
**dir:** *A703, 5m N of Peebles*

The Horseshoe is five miles north of Peebles and only 18 miles south of Edinburgh. Originally a blacksmith's shop, it has a very good reputation for its delightful atmosphere and excellent cuisine. There are eight luxuriously appointed and individually designed bedrooms. Please note: children are welcome, but dinner is not served to under fives except in the private dining room.

**Rooms:** 8 en suite (1 fmly) (6 GF) **Facilities:** FTV Lounge tea/coffee Dinner available Direct dial WiFi **Extras:** Speciality toiletries, fruit, mineral water - complimentary **Parking:** 20 **Notes:** LB Closed 25 Dec, 1st 2 weeks Jan & 2 weeks Jul RS Mon & Tue closed

## INNERLEITHEN
Map 21 NT33

### Caddon View
★★★★ 🍴 🍽 GUEST ACCOMMODATION

**tel:** 01896 830208 **14 Pirn Road EH44 6HH**
**email:** stay@caddonview.co.uk **web:** www.caddonview.co.uk
**dir:** *Signed from A72 in Innerleithen*

Set in its own well maintained gardens this well-presented Victorian house was originally built in the 1850s. Caddon View offers high standards of accommodation along with wonderful hospitality and customer care awareness. Located in the beautiful Tweed Valley, it's ideally located for all the border areas as well as Edinburgh. The property is licensed and serves quality evening meals (by prior arrangement), in a bright, welcoming and well-appointed dining room.

**Rooms:** 8 rms (7 en suite) (1 pri facs) (2 fmly) (2 GF) **S** £50–£60; **D** £70–£120* **Facilities:** FTV DVD Lounge tea/coffee Dinner available Licensed WiFi 🔒 **Parking:** 7 **Notes:** Closed 25–26 Dec RS Sun & Mon no dinner available

## JEDBURGH
Map 21 NT62

### Ferniehirst Mill Lodge
★★ GUEST HOUSE

**tel:** 01835 863279 **TD8 6PQ**
**email:** ferniehirstmill@aol.com **web:** www.ferniehirstmill.co.uk
**dir:** *2.5m S of Jedburgh on A68, onto private track to end*

Reached by a narrow farm track and a rustic wooden bridge, this chalet-style house has a secluded setting by the River Jed. Bedrooms are small and functional, and there is a comfortable lounge in which to relax. Home-cooked and hearty breakfasts are served in the cosy dining room.

**Rooms:** 7 en suite (1 GF) **S** £30; **D** £60* **Facilities:** TVL tea/coffee WiFi Fishing 🔒 **Parking:** 10

## MELROSE
Map 21 NT53

### Fauhope Country House
★★★★★ 🍴 GUEST HOUSE

**tel:** 01896 823184 & 07906 184266 **Gattonside TD6 9LU**
**email:** info@fauhopehouse.com **web:** www.fauhopehouse.com
**dir:** *0.7m N of Melrose over River Tweed. N off B6360 at Gattonside 30mph sign (E), along long driveway*

It's hard to imagine a more complete experience than a stay at Fauhope Country House, set high on a hillside on the north-east edge of the village. Hospitality is first class, breakfasts are excellent, and the delightful country house has a splendid interior. Bedrooms are luxurious, each individual and superbly equipped. Public areas are elegantly decorated and furnished, and enhanced by beautiful floral arrangements; the dining room is particularly stunning.

**Rooms:** 3 en suite **Facilities:** FTV DVD Lounge tea/coffee Dinner available WiFi 🏌 ⛳ Treatment room **Extras:** Speciality toiletries, fruit, sherry – complimentary **Parking:** 10 **Notes:** LB

## PEEBLES
Map 21 NT24

### Premier Collection

# Kingsmuir House

★★★★★ 🍴 BED AND BREAKFAST

tel: 01721 724413 & 07776 405842 **Springhill Road EH45 9EP**
email: malcolm@kingsmuirhouse.co.uk **web:** www.kingsmuirhouse.co.uk
**dir:** *From High St, over bridge then 2nd right into Springhill Rd.*
*0.25m opposite tennis court*

Kingsmuir House was built in 1855 and is set in a slightly elevated position to the south of Peebles, just a few minutes' walk from the high street. This period building still boasts many of the original features, and the decor and furnishings are in keeping with its character. Hospitality is warm and genuine; and the bedroom suites are generous in size and beautifully presented with many thoughtful extras provided as standard. The en suites are also a feature, with walk-in showers and free-standing roll-top baths available. Gardens are pleasing to the eye, and include a delightful summer house.

*Kingsmuir House*

**Rooms:** 2 en suite **S** £90; **D** £140 **Facilities:** FTV DVD iPod docking station t ea/coffee WiFi ⅃18 🔒 **Extras:** Home-made shortbread & truffles, fruit **Parking:** 5 **Notes:** No children 12yrs

***See advert below***

## STIRLING

### STIRLING
Map 21 NS79

#### Premier Collection

## Victoria Square Guest House

★★★★★ **A** GUEST HOUSE

**tel:** 01786 473920 **12 Victoria Square FK8 2QZ**
**email:** info@vsgh.co.uk **web:** www.victoriasquareguesthouse.com
**dir:** *M9 junct 10 into Stirling, at Smith Museum 1st right into Victoria Place. 1st left into Victoria Square*

This classic Victorian building is situated in the peaceful and prestigious Kings Park area of Stirling, just a short walk away from Stirling Castle, Stirling Golf Club, the Smith Museum & Art Gallery and other attractions. Bedrooms are spacious and well-appointed and offer the space and comfort to ensure a peaceful and relaxing stay. Combining contemporary elegance with a strong sense of history, each room's decor and facilities enhance Victoria Square Guest House's welcome.

**Rooms:** 10 en suite (1 GF) **S** £69–£82; **D** £84–£140 **Facilities:** FTV iPod docking station Lounge tea/coffee WiFi ♨18 **Extras:** Speciality toiletries, mini-fridge, robes **Parking:** 5 **Notes:** No children 12yrs Closed 23–29 Dec

### STRATHYRE
Map 20 NN51

#### Premier Collection

## Creagan House

★★★★★ ♨ RESTAURANT WITH ROOMS

**tel:** 01877 384638 **FK18 8ND**
**email:** eatandstay@creaganhouse.co.uk **web:** www.creaganhouse.co.uk
**dir:** *0.25m N of Strathyre on A84*

Originally a farmhouse dating from the 17th century, Creagan House has operated as a restaurant with rooms for many years. The baronial-style dining room provides a wonderful setting for the classic French and Scottish cuisine. The warm hospitality and attentive service are noteworthy.

**Rooms:** 5 en suite (1 fmly) (1 GF) **S** £90–£110; **D** £135–£155* **Facilities:** FTV Lounge tea/coffee Dinner available WiFi ♨ **Extras:** Speciality toiletries **Conf:** Max 35 Thtr 35 Class 12 Board 35 **Parking:** 16 **Notes:** LB Closed 26 Oct–6 Apr RS Wed & Thu closed

## SCOTTISH ISLANDS

### ISLE OF ARRAN

### BRODICK
Map 20 NS03

## Dunvegan House

★★★★ GUEST HOUSE

**tel:** 01770 302811 **Dunvegan Shore Road KA27 8AJ**
**email:** dunveganhouse1@hotmail.com **web:** www.dunveganhouse-arran.co.uk
**dir:** *Turn right from ferry terminal, 500yds along Shore Rd*

Situated close to the shore and enjoying spectacular views of the bay, this establishment is a popular choice for visitors to the island. The property benefits from having a hands-on approach from the friendly owner while public areas and bedrooms have great views.

**Rooms:** 9 en suite (3 GF) **S** £60; **D** £85* **Facilities:** FTV Lounge tea/coffee Dinner available Licensed WiFi ♨ **Parking:** 8 **Notes:** Closed 23 Dec–3 Jan

### ISLE OF ISLAY

### GLENEGEDALE
Map 20 NR35

#### AA FRIENDLIEST B&B OF THE YEAR 2017–18

#### Premier Collection

## Glenegedale House

★★★★★ ♨ GUEST HOUSE

**tel:** 01496 300400 & 07554 669664 **PA42 7AS**
**email:** info@glenegedalehouse.co.uk **web:** www.glenegedalehouse.co.uk

Situated halfway between Bowmore and Port Ellen, this luxury guest house enjoys some of the best views on the island with the Mull of Oa and the glory of the Atlantic Ocean in full view. Modern accommodation is complemented by a range of comfortable lounges. The strength here lies with the hosts who go out of their way to ensure guests enjoy both the house and all the island has to offer. Memorable breakfasts served in the stunning dining room are not to be missed.

**Rooms:** 4 en suite (1 GF) **S** £90–£110; **D** £130–£160 **Facilities:** FTV Lounge tea/coffee WiFi ♨18 Fishing ♨ **Parking:** 8 **Notes:** LB No children 12yrs Closed Dec

## ISLE OF MULL

### TOBERMORY
Map 22 NM55

# Highland Cottage
★★★★ ◉◉ ☐ RESTAURANT WITH ROOMS

**tel:** 01688 302030 **24 Breadalbane Street PA75 6PD**
**email:** davidandjo@highlandcottage.co.uk **web:** www.highlandcottage.co.uk
**dir:** *A848 Craignure/Fishnish ferry terminal, pass Tobermory signs, straight on at mini rdbt across narrow bridge, turn right. Highland Cottage on right opposite fire station*

Providing the highest level of natural and unassuming hospitality, this delightful little gem lies high above the island's capital. Don't be fooled by its side street location, a stunning view over the bay is just a few metres away. 'A country house in town' it is an Aladdin's Cave of collectables and treasures, as well as masses of books and magazines. There is an honesty bar in the first-floor lounge. The cosy dining room offers memorable dinners and splendid breakfasts. Bedrooms are individual; some have four-posters and all are comprehensively equipped to include TVs and music centres.

**Rooms:** 6 en suite (1 GF) **S** £125–£155; **D** £155–£170* **Facilities.** FTV Dinner available Direct dial WiFi **Notes:** No children 10yrs Closed Nov–Mar

## SHETLAND

### LERWICK
Map 24 HU44

# Glen Orchy House
★★★★ ☐ GUEST HOUSE

**tel:** 01595 692031 **20 Knab Road ZE1 0AX**
**email:** glenorchy.house@virgin.net **web:** www.guesthouselerwick.com
**dir:** *Next to coastguard station*

This welcoming and well-presented house lies above the town with views over the Knab, and is within easy walking distance of the town centre. Bedrooms are modern in design and there is a choice of lounges with books and board games, one with an honesty bar. Substantial breakfasts are served, and the restaurant offers a delicious Thai menu.

**Rooms:** 24 en suite (4 fmly) (4 GF) **Facilities:** STV FTV DVD Lounge TVL tea/coffee Dinner available Licensed WiFi **Extras:** Locally made fudge **Parking:** 10

## ISLE OF SKYE

### STRUAN
Map 22 NG35

#### Premier Collection

# Ullinish Country Lodge
★★★★★ ◉◉◉ ☐ RESTAURANT WITH ROOMS

**tel:** 01470 572214 **IV56 8FD**
**email:** ullinish@theisleofskye.co.uk **web:** www.theisleofskye.co.uk
**dir:** *Take A863 N. Lodge signed on left*

Set in some of Scotland's most dramatic landscape, with views of the Black Cuillin and MacLeod's Tables, this lodge has lochs on three sides. Samuel Johnson and James Boswell stayed here in 1773 and were impressed with the hospitality even then. Hosts Brian and Pam hope to extend the same welcome to their guests today. As you would expect, all bedrooms have amazing views, and come with half-tester beds.

**Rooms:** 6 en suite **S** £120–£190; **D** £180–£270* **Facilities:** FTV Lounge tea/coffee Dinner available WiFi **Extras:** Sherry, sweets, mineral water – complimentary **Parking:** 8 **Notes:** LB No children 16yrs Closed 24 Dec–Jan

### UIG
Map 22 NG36

# Woodbine House
★★★★ GUEST ACCOMMODATION

**tel:** 01470 542243 & 07904 267561 **IV51 9XP**
**email:** contact@woodbineskye.co.uk **web:** www.woodbineskye.co.uk
**dir:** *From Portree into Uig Bay, pass Ferry Inn, right onto A855 (Staffin road), house 300yds on right*

Built in the late 19th century, Woodbine House occupies an elevated position overlooking Uig Bay and the surrounding countryside, and is well suited for walking and bird-watching enthusiasts. The ground-floor dining room has lovely sea views, as do the front-facing bedrooms.

**Rooms:** 5 en suite (1 fmly) (1 GF) **S** £50–£68; **D** £70–£88* **Facilities:** FTV Lounge tea/coffee WiFi Sea kayak hire Boat trips **Parking:** 5 **Notes:** LB RS Nov–Feb long stays or group bookings only

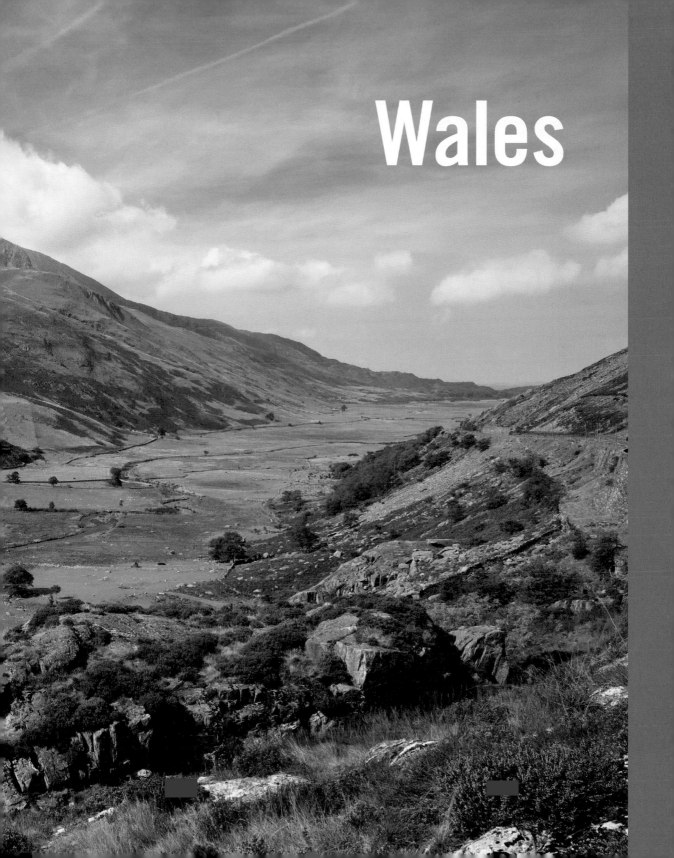

# Wales

## ISLE OF ANGLESEY

### Premier Collection

#### The Bull – Beaumaris
★★★★★ ◉◉ INN

**tel:** 01248 810329 **Castle Street LL58 8AP**
**email:** info@bullsheadinn.co.uk **web:** www.bullsheadinn.co.uk
**dir:** *Located on Main St in town centre*

Both Charles Dickens and Samuel Johnson visited this inn, and the interior still features exposed beams and antique weaponry. Bedrooms are richly decorated and traditional, while The Townhouse, just across a side street, offers additional boutique bedrooms, each with vibrant decor. The food continues to attract high praise in both the Loft Restaurant and the less formal Brasserie, and cask-conditioned ales are served in the traditional bar. Meeting and functions can be catered for.

**Rooms:** 25 en suite (2 fmly) (5 GF) **S** £85–£152.50; **D** £110–£180* **Facilities:** FTV Lounge tea/coffee Dinner available Direct dial Lift WiFi ⅄18 **Extras:** Speciality locally made Beaumaris toiletries, Welsh cakes, Aberffraw biscuits – complimentary **Parking:** 1 **Notes:** LB Closed 24–26 Dec

#### Blackthorn Farm
★★★★ ⒶGUEST ACCOMMODATION

**tel:** 01407 765262 **Penrhosfeilw, Trearddur Bay LL65 2LT**
**email:** enquiries@blackthornfarm.co.uk **web:** www.blackthornleisure.co.uk
**dir:** *A55 to Holyhead, take 1st exit at rdbt, turn immediately right between two pubs. At end of road, turn right, 0.5m on left*

Blackthorn Farm is a family-run establishment that is also a camping and touring site. Set in 18 peaceful acres on Holy Island, the farm enjoys outstanding panoramic views of the Irish Sea, Snowdonia, and coastal views of Anglesey. There is a beach, and coastal trails, within easy reach. A full Welsh breakfast is served. Please note pets are welcome.

**Rooms:** 8 rms (6 en suite) (3 fmly) (1 GF) **Facilities:** FTV DVD tea/coffee Licensed WiFi ⛅ **Parking:** 10 **Notes:** LB Closed 22–31 Dec

#### Black Lion Inn
★★★★ ◉ INN

**tel:** 01407 730718 **Llanfaethlu LL65 4NL**
**email:** info@blacklionanglesey.co.uk **web:** www.blacklionanglesey.com
**dir:** *A55 junct 3, A5025 (follow Wylfa Power Station signs). Right at lights. 6m to inn*

After being derelict for many years, this inn has been lovingly brought back to life. The smartly whitewashed rural property stands on the main road between Valley and Cemaes Bay. Two spacious, modern bedrooms offer enhanced comfort for guests and are complemented by bathrooms complete with oversized rain showers. The busy and vibrant restaurant focuses on local produce, with the meat coming directly from the family farm. The bar also concentrates on local ales.

**Rooms:** 2 en suite (1 fmly) **S** £90–£110; **D** £115–£130 **Facilities:** DVD tea/coffee Dinner available WiFi **Extras:** Speciality toiletries, home-made biscuits **Conf:** Max 30 Thtr 28 Class 28 Board 28 **Parking:** 38 **Notes:** Closed 5–15 Jan RS Out of season closed Sun–Tue

#### Bulkeley Arms
★★★ INN

**tel:** 01248 712715 **Uxbridge Square LL59 5DF**
**email:** tafarnwr@gmail.com **web:** www.bulkeleyarms.com
**dir:** *From A5, 2nd exit at rdbt, follow signs to town centre. Opposite Dale St*

This family-run, friendly pub is easy to locate with its whitewashed walls standing prominently amongst the high street shops. A smart bar on the ground floor offers good quality dining and there is a separate area with pool tables and large-screen TVs. Bedrooms are spacious and well equipped, all with en suite shower rooms. The small car park is a welcome addition.

**Rooms:** 3 en suite (1 fmly) **S** £50–£60; **D** £60–£70* **Facilities:** FTV tea/coffee Dinner available Direct dial WiFi Pool table ⛅ **Parking:** 6 **Notes:** LB

#### Cefn Dref
★★★★ ⬙ BED AND BREAKFAST

**tel:** 01407 810714 & 07834 340854 **LL64 5JH**
**email:** bookings@cefndref.co.uk **web:** www.cefndref.co.uk
**dir:** *A55 junct 5 (signed Rhosneigr), onto A4080 to Llanfaelog. Turn right signed Rhosneigr, 1st house on right after 30mph sign*

Enjoying stunning coastal views, this welcoming Edwardian shooting lodge has been transformed into a very comfortable and inviting bed and breakfast. Bedrooms, complemented by smart, stylish bathrooms, are very well equipped with extras including WiFi and luxury toiletries. Breakfast is a memorable experience, with home-made or locally sourced produce from an extensive and imaginative menu. The town centre, with many dining options, is a short walk away, as is the sea.

**Rooms:** 3 en suite (1 fmly) **S** £75–£115; **D** £95–£130* **Facilities:** FTV DVD iPod docking station tea/coffee WiFi ⅄18 ⛅ **Extras:** Speciality toiletries, fridges in rooms **Parking:** 10 **Notes:** Closed Nov–Easter

## BRIDGEND

### BRIDGEND
Map 9 SS97

## Hazelwood Guest House
★★★★ GUEST HOUSE

**tel:** 01656 647780 **Tondu Road CF31 4LJ**
**email:** info@hazelwood-house.co.uk **web:** www.hazelwood-house.co.uk

Located just outside Bridgend, this popular guest house offers a range of well-equipped bedrooms and bathrooms including some on the ground floor. Breakfast is taken in the comfortable conservatory and a large car park is also provided. There are a range of options for dinner, all within a short walk of the accommodation, including a pleasant inn.

**Rooms:** 8 en suite (3 GF) **S** £45–£60; **D** £60–£80 (room only)* **Facilities:** FTV TVL tea/coffee WiFi 🛇 **Parking:** 14 **Notes:** LB Closed 24–27 Dec

## CARDIFF

### CARDIFF
Map 9 ST17

## Innkeeper's Lodge Cardiff
★★★★ INN

**tel:** 08451 551551 *(Calls cost 2p per minute plus your phone company's access charge)*
**The Beverley Hotel, 75–77 Cathedral Road CF11 9PG**
**email:** info@innkeeperslodge.com **web:** www.innkeeperslodge.com
**dir:** M4 junct 29 (from E) onto A48. Left onto A4119, 0.5m left again (Cathedral Rd). Lodge on right

Located in the Pontcanna district of Cardiff, this former Victorian villa has been tastefully restored as an inn. The modern bedrooms are equipped to a good standard, offering a range of extras for both the business and leisure traveller. The popular bar and restaurant offers home-cooked classics, with a number of real ales on tap. Just a short walk away are the Swalec Stadium, Cardiff University and the Millennium Centre.

**Rooms:** 17 en suite (9 fmly) **Facilities:** FTV tea/coffee Dinner available WiFi

## Silver Stars

The AA Silver Star rating denotes a B&B that we highly recommend. They have a superior level of quality within their star rating, high standards of hospitality, service and cleanliness.

## CARMARTHENSHIRE

### FELINGWM UCHAF
Map 8 SN52

## Allt Y Golau Farmhouse
★★★★ ⬮ FARMHOUSE

**tel:** 01267 290455 **Allt Y Golau Uchaf SA32 7BB**
**email:** alltygolau@btinternet.com **web:** www.alltygolau.com
**dir:** A40 onto B4310, N for 2m. 1st on left after Felingwm Uchaf

This delightful Georgian farmhouse has been furnished and decorated to a high standard by the present owners, and enjoys panoramic views over the Tywi Valley to the Black Mountains beyond. Guests are welcome to take a relaxing walk through the two acres of mature garden. Many thoughtful extras are provided in the comfortable bedrooms, and there is a separate lounge. Breakfast is provided in the cosy dining room and served around a communal table.

**Rooms:** 3 rms (2 en suite) (1 pri facs) (2 GF) **S** £45; **D** £70 **Facilities:** TVL tea/coffee WiFi 🛇 **Extras:** Speciality toiletries, snacks – complimentary **Parking:** 3 **Notes:** No children 12yrs Closed 20 Dec–2 Jan 2 acres small holding

### LLANARTHNE
Map 8 SN31

### Premier Collection

## Llwyn Helyg Country House
★★★★★ ⬮ BED AND BREAKFAST

**tel:** 01558 668778 & 07464 106085 **SA32 8HJ**
**email:** enquiries@llwynhelygcountryhouse.co.uk
**web:** www.llwynhelygcountryhouse.co.uk
**dir:** A48 onto B4310, at rdbt at entrance of National Botanic Gardens of Wales take 1st exit (B4310). After 0.3m turn right at farm along lane then sharp left, 1m on left

The owners of Llwyn Helyg, a modern country house, have used the finest quality materials to create this luxury bed and breakfast accommodation. Situated in three acres of landscaped gardens and surrounded by countryside, it's on the outskirts of Llanarthne, midway between Carmarthen and Llandeilo. All the individually designed, en suite bedrooms have 6-foot wide beds and luxurious Vi-Spring mattresses. Private parking is available.

**Rooms:** 3 en suite **S** £99–£115; **D** £129–£149* **Facilities:** FTV DVD iPod docking station Lounge TVL tea/coffee WiFi ♨18 🛇 Therapy/Holistic treatment room **Extras:** Speciality toiletries, fruit, snacks – complimentary **Conf:** Max 6 Board 6 **Parking:** 10 **Notes:** LB No children 16yrs Closed Xmas & New Year

## LLANDOVERY
Map 9 SN73

# Llanerchindda Farm

★★★ 🛏 GUEST HOUSE

tel: 01550 750274 **Cynghordy SA20 0NB**
email: info@cambrianway.com web: www.cambrianway.com
dir: *A483 (Llandovery to Builth Wells road) after 40mph sign turn left at brown tourist sign (Llanerchindda), 2.75m to farm*

Set in 50 acres of Welsh countryside with spectacular views over the Black Mountains and the Brecon Beacons, this farmhouse-style accommodation is the ideal base for various activities including walking, fishing, quad-bike riding and bird watching. Bedrooms and bathrooms are comfortable and guests also have use of the lounge. In addition to a substantial breakfast, dinner is available by prior arrangement and features delicious home cooking.

**Rooms:** 9 en suite (1 fmly) (2 GF) **S** £41–£45; **D** £82–£90* **Facilities:** FTV Lounge TVL tea/coffee Dinner available Licensed WiFi ⳩18 Fishing 🔒 Clay pigeon shooting 4x4 driving experience **Parking:** 31 **Notes:** LB Closed 2–16 Jan

*See advert opposite*

## LLANSTEFFAN
Map 8 SN31

### AA GUEST ACCOMMODATION OF THE YEAR FOR WALES 2017–18

# Mansion House Llansteffan

★★★★  RESTAURANT WITH ROOMS

tel: 01267 241515 & 07768 194539 **Pantyrathro SA33 5AJ**
email: info@mansionhousellansteffan.co.uk web: www.mansionhousellansteffan.co.uk
dir: *From Carmarthen on B4312 towards Llansteffan, follow brown signs*

Mansion House has been lovingly restored by the current owners, and is set in five acres of grounds with enviable views over the Towy Estuary and Carmarthen Bay. While bedrooms differ in size and style, all are well-equipped and complemented by smart bathrooms. With a wealth of quality produce right on the doorstep it's not surprising that the head chef focuses on using seasonal, local, and home-grown produce on the constantly changing, interesting menu. Pre-dinner drinks can be taken in the bar, where there is an excellent range of gins.

**Rooms:** 9 en suite (1 fmly) **S** £110–£190; **D** £120–£200* **Facilities:** FTV DVD iPod docking station Lounge tea/coffee Dinner available Direct dial WiFi ⳩18 🔒 **Extras:** Speciality toiletries, robes, home-made cookies **Conf:** Max 200 Thtr 150 Class 80 Board 40 **Parking:** 50 **Notes:** LB Civ wed 120

## LLANYBYDDER
Map 8 SN54

# Glasfryn Guest House

★★★★ GUEST HOUSE

tel: 01570 481400 & 07398 139084 **Glasfryn SA40 9TY**
email: ron@glasfrynguesthouse.co.uk web: www.glasfrynguesthouse.co.uk
dir: *On A485. On entering Llanybydder from Carmarthen located on right*

Glasfryn is a spacious, double-fronted Victorian villa standing in the centre of market town of Llanybydder. Renowned for its livestock markets and monthly pony sales, the location is ideal for exploring the nearby Cardigan Bay, the Brecon Beacons, and shopping centres of Carmarthen and Aberystwyth. The friendly owners welcome you into their home, and bedrooms are of a good size. Most have en suite facilities. A wealth of original features have been retained, with high ceilings and original woodwork and architrave. Dinners can be provided on request, or there are a number of good quality eating places within a short drive.

**Rooms:** 4 rms (3 en suite) (1 pri facs) (1 fmly) **S** £48–£50; **D** £68–£100* **Facilities:** FTV DVD tea/coffee Dinner available WiFi 🔒 **Parking:** 6

## ST CLEARS — Map 8 SN21

### Premier Collection

## Coedllys Country House

★★★★ ⓦ BED AND BREAKFAST

**tel:** 01994 231455 **Coedllys Uchaf, Llangynin SA33 4JY**
**email:** coedllys@btinternet.com **web:** www.coedllyscountryhouse.co.uk
**dir:** *A40 St Clears rdbt, take 3rd exit, at lights turn left. After 100yds turn right, 3m to Llangynin, pass village sign. 30mph sign on left, turn immediately down track (private drive)*

Set in a peaceful valley, Coedllys is the home of the Harbers, who make visitors feel like honoured guests. Bedrooms are lavishly furnished, and the thoughtful and useful extras make a stay most memorable. There is a cosy, well-furnished lounge, and an extensive breakfast choice is served in the pleasant dining room. A further cottage-style annexe, suitable as a self-catering let, is also available.

**Rooms:** 2 en suite (1 GF) **S** £80–£85; **D** £90–£110* **Facilities:** FTV DVD iPod docking station Lounge tea/coffee WiFi ☕ **Extras:** Speciality toiletries, home-made biscuits – complimentary **Parking:** 6 **Notes:** LB No children 12yrs Closed 22–28 Dec

### CEREDIGION

## ABERAERON — Map 8 SN46

### Premier Collection

## Feathers Royal

★★★★★ ⊜ INN

**tel:** 01545 571750 **Alban Square SA46 0AQ**
**email:** enquiries@feathersroyal.co.uk **web:** www.feathersroyal.co.uk
**dir:** *A482, Lampeter Road, Feathers Royal opposite recreation grounds*

This is a family-run inn, ideally located in the picturesque Georgian town of Aberaeron. It is a charming Grade II listed property, built in 1815 as a traditional coaching house, and later transformed to coincide with the town's bicentenary celebrations. Accommodation is very comfortable with modern fittings and accessories provided, and the public areas are well appointed. There is a large suite available for private or business functions.

**Rooms:** 13 en suite (2 fmly) **S** fr £79; **D** fr £130* **Facilities:** FTV Lounge tea/coffee Dinner available Direct dial WiFi ☕ **Conf:** Max 200 Thtr 200 Class 100 Board 50 **Parking:** 20 **Notes:** LB Civ wed 200

## The Castle

★★★★ ⊜ INN

**tel:** 01545 570205 **Market Street SA46 0AU**
**email:** castle_hotel@btconnect.com **web:** www.the-castlehotel.co.uk
**dir:** *On A487, in centre of town*

The Castle is a Grade II listed building right in the centre of the pretty harbour town of Aberaeron. Pastel coloured houses are a feature of this Georgian town, ideally situated for many walks, including the Llanerchaeron Trail and Wales Coastal Path. A smart café bar serves very good quality home cooked dishes throughout the day. The modern bedrooms have TVs, WiFi, Egyptian linen and duck-down duvets.

**Rooms:** 8 en suite (1 fmly) **Facilities:** FTV tea/coffee Dinner available WiFi ☕ **Conf:** Max 45 Thtr 30 Class 40 Board 20 **Notes:** LB

## ABERYSTWYTH — Map 8 SN58

### Premier Collection

## Awel-Deg

★★★★★ BED AND BREAKFAST

**tel:** 01970 880681 **Capel Bangor SY23 3LR**
**email:** awel-deg@tiscali.co.uk **web:** www.awel-deg.co.uk
**dir:** *5m E of Aberystwyth. On A44 in Capel Bangor*

Located five miles from the historic university town of Aberystwyth, this attractive bungalow, set in pretty gardens, provides high standards of hospitality, comfort and facilities. Immaculately maintained throughout, spacious bedrooms are equipped with a wealth of thoughtful extras and smart, modern en suite shower rooms. Comprehensive breakfasts are served at one table in the elegant dining room and a choice of lounges is available.

**Rooms:** 2 en suite (2 GF) **D** £59* **Facilities:** FTV TVL tea/coffee WiFi **Parking:** 8 **Notes:** LB No children 11yrs Closed 2030 Dec

ABERYSTWYTH *continued*

## Bodalwyn Guest House

★★★★ GUEST HOUSE

**tel:** 01970 612578 **Queen's Avenue SY23 2EG**
**email:** enquiries@bodalwyn.co.uk **web:** www.bodalwyn.co.uk
**dir:** *500yds N of town centre. Exit A487 (Northgate St) into North Rd to end*

Located a short walk from the promenade, this imposing Edwardian house, built for a college professor, has been appointed to provide high standards of comfort and good facilities. Smart modern bathrooms complement the spacious bedrooms, which are equipped with a wealth of thoughtful extras; family rooms are available. Welsh breakfasts are served in the elegant conservatory-dining room.

**Rooms:** 7 en suite (2 fmly) **S** £48–£59; **D** £75–£88 **Facilities:** FTV DVD tea/coffee WiFi **Notes:** Closed 22 Dec–2 Jan

## Glyn-Garth

★★★★ GUEST HOUSE

**tel:** 01970 615050 & 07890 401498 **South Road SY23 1JS**
**email:** glyngarth@aol.com **web:** www.glyngarth.pages.qpg.com
**dir:** *In town centre. Off A487 into South Rd, off South Promenade*

Privately owned and personally run by the same family for over 50 years, this immaculately maintained guest house provides a range of thoughtfully furnished bedrooms with smart modern bathrooms. Breakfast is served in the attractive dining room and a lounge is also available.

**Rooms:** 10 rms (6 en suite) (2 fmly) (1 GF) **Facilities:** STV FTV TVL tea/coffee WiFi ⌴18 🅿 **Parking:** 2

## Yr Hafod

★★★★ GUEST HOUSE

**tel:** 01970 617579 **1 South Marine Terrace SY23 1JX**
**email:** johnyrhafod@aol.com **web:** www.yrhafod.co.uk
**dir:** *On south promenade between harbour & castle*

Yr Hafod is an immaculately maintained end of terrace Victorian house with a commanding location overlooking South Bay. The spacious bedrooms are comfortable, some with delightful sea views and many have particularly well-appointed bathrooms. Breakfast is served in the front-facing dining room.

**Rooms:** 6 rms (3 en suite) **S** £37–£38; **D** £74–£92* **Facilities:** STV FTV TVL tea/coffee WiFi 🅿 **Extras:** Chocolates, mineral water – complimentary **Parking:** 1 **Notes:** Closed Xmas & Jan

## Y Gelli

★★★ GUEST HOUSE

**tel:** 01970 617834 **Dolau, Lovesgrove SY23 3HP**
**email:** pat@plasdolau.co.uk **web:** www.plasdolau.co.uk
**dir:** *Off A44 2.75m E of town centre*

Set in spacious grounds on the town's outskirts, this modern detached house contains a range of practical furnished bedrooms, with three further rooms available in an adjacent Victorian property. Comprehensive breakfasts are served in the attractive dining room with evening meals available on request. A comfortable lounge is also available for guests' use.

**Rooms:** 6 rms (3 en suite) 3 rms annexe (1 en suite) (3 fmly) (1 GF) **Facilities:** TVL tea/coffee Dinner available Snooker Pool table Table tennis Stabling can be provided **Parking:** 20 **Notes:** LB

### CARDIGAN      Map 8 SN14

### Premier Collection

## Caemorgan Mansion

★★★★★ 🏵 🥂 GUEST HOUSE

**tel:** 01239 613297 **Caemorgan Road SA43 1QU**
**email:** guest@caemorgan.com **web:** www.caemorgan.com
**dir:** *N of Cardigan on A487 towards Aberporth. Left into Caemorgan Rd, entrance 200mtrs*

Caemorgan Mansion stands in its own peaceful grounds, a haven for local wildlife, on the fringes of Cardigan, and is ideally located for visiting the glorious local beaches. Bought in a derelict state, the owners have breathed new life into the property, now fully refurbished. Bedrooms are spacious, with high quality bathrooms; several have feature showers and baths. The smart dining room overlooking the gardens is the ideal place to sample the innovative cuisine made from locally sourced produce at breakfast and dinner. The friendly hosts are on hand to offer suggestions for places to visit during your stay. Caemorgan Mansion was the AA Guest Accommodation of the Year for Wales 2016-2017.

**Rooms:** 5 en suite **D** £90–£120* **Facilities:** FTV DVD iPod docking station Lounge tea/coffee Dinner available Licensed WiFi 🅿 **Extras:** Robes, slippers, speciality toiletries, safe **Conf:** Max 20 Thtr 20 Class 10 Board 10 **Parking:** 10 **Notes:** No children 15yrs Closed 23–29 Dec

## EGLWYS FACH                    Map 14 SN69

### Premier Collection

# Ynyshir
★★★★★ ◎◎◎◎◎ RESTAURANT WITH ROOMS

**tel:** 01654 781209 **SY20 8TA**
**email:** info@ynyshir.co.uk **web:** www.ynyshir.co.uk
**dir:** Exit A487, 5.5m S of Machynlleth, signed from main road

Set in beautifully landscaped grounds and surrounded by the RSPB Ynys-hir Nature Reserve, Ynyshir is a haven of calm. The house was once owned by Queen Victoria and is surrounded by mountain scenery. Lavishly styled bedrooms, each individually themed around a great painter, provide high standards of luxury and comfort. The lounge and bar, adorned with an abundance of fresh flowers, have different moods. The dining room offers highly accomplished cooking using the best, locally sourced ingredients including herbs, soft fruit and vegetables from the hotel's own kitchen garden, and wild foods gathered nearby. This restaurant with rooms makes an idyllic location for weddings. AA Wine Award Winner for Wales and the Overall winner 2017–18.

**Rooms:** 7 en suite 3 annexe en suite (4 GF) **S** £120–£296; **D** £150–£370*
**Facilities:** FTV DVD Lounge tea/coffee Dinner available Direct dial WiFi ⬤ RSPB Bird Reserve **Extras:** Speciality toiletries, bottled water **Parking:** 15
**Notes:** Civ wed 40

## LLECHRYD                    Map 8 SN24

# Hammet House
★★★★ ◎◎ 🍴 GUEST ACCOMMODATION

**tel:** 01239 682382 & 07866 682451 **SA43 2QA**
**email:** mail@hammethouse.co.uk **web:** www.hammethouse.co.uk
**dir:** From A40 in St Clears at Penblewin rdbt, take A478 towards Cardigan. Right on B4332 signed Boncath. Left signed Llechryd. Left before river bridge in Llechryd

An eclectic mix awaits guests at this impressive accommodation, from the sweeping drive up to the main house, the surrounding grounds, and the imposing exterior of the building, to the contemporary styling of the interior. There are plenty of areas to relax and enjoy a drink, or a meal from the all-day dining menus. Bedrooms offer a range of shapes and sizes, and all are stylishly furnished to provide very comfortable beds and bedding. To accompany the fine selection of award-winning dishes at dinner, an impressive wine list with the emphasis on organic and bio-dynamic wines is offered. Hammet House is also available for exclusive use, and has the flexibility to cater for a range of private events.

**Rooms:** 15 en suite (1 fmly) **Facilities:** FTV Lounge TVL tea/coffee Dinner available Direct dial Licensed WiFi ⬤ Fishing **Parking:** 40 **Notes:** LB Civ wed 150

## NEW QUAY                    Map 8 SN35

# The Swallows Bed and Breakfast
★★★★ BED AND BREAKFAST

**tel:** 07516 905548 **Blaenwaun Fawr SA44 6JD**
**email:** theswallowsbandb@gmail.com **web:** www.the-swallows-bed-and-breakfast.com
**dir:** S of New Quay on A487. Through Synod Inn hamlet turn opposite parking sign for layby

The Swallows Bed and Breakfast is set just off the main coast road with stunning views over the countryside of Cardigan Bay, and a short distance from the coast. This relaxed and friendly property offers three spacious bedrooms located apart from the main house, allowing guests total privacy and their own front door. Each room has a conservatory which acts as a dining room for breakfast and dinner. Hearty homemade dinners after a day exploring the nearby coastal path, or spotting dolphins, are delivered to your door to enjoy at your leisure. Large modern walk-in wet rooms complement these three ground floor rooms for easy access and use.

**Rooms:** 3 annexe en suite (3 fmly) (3 GF) **Facilities:** FTV DVD tea/coffee Dinner available WiFi ⬤ **Extras:** Fresh milk, fruit – complimentary **Parking:** 3

# Cambrian Inn & Restaurant
★★★ INN

**tel:** 01545 560295 **New Road SA45 9SE**
**email:** cambrianhotel@gmail.com **web:** www.cambrianhotel-newquay.co.uk
**dir:** From A487 at Llanarth onto B4342 for 2m

Situated in a quiet location on the outskirts of popular New Quay, this family-run inn offers a good selection of dishes at both lunch and dinner. Bedrooms include a range of sizes and are all located on the first floor. Breakfast is served in the conservatory restaurant, and a garden with outdoor seating is also available.

**Rooms:** 4 en suite **Facilities:** FTV TVL tea/coffee Dinner available WiFi ⬤ **Extras:** Trouser press **Parking:** 9 **Notes:** LB RS Dec–Mar bar & restaurant closed

## TREGARON                    Map 9 SN65

# Y Talbot
★★★★ ◎◎ INN

**tel:** 01974 298208 **The Square SY25 6JL**
**email:** info@ytalbot.com **web:** www.ytalbot.com
**dir:** From Lampeter or Aberystwyth on A485, in Tregaron turn opposite NatWest, 100yds in Square

Located in the heart of this quiet town, Y Talbot has been appointed to provide a range of very high-quality bedrooms and bathrooms with luxury showers. Some smaller standard rooms are also available. There is a traditional bar serving real ales and a contemporary-style main restaurant and lounge. Dinner offers a very good selection of dishes using quality produce.

**Rooms:** 11 en suite 2 annexe en suite (3 fmly) (1 GF) **S** £65–£100; **D** £110–£140*
**Facilities:** FTV iPod docking station Lounge tea/coffee Dinner available WiFi ⬤9 ⬤ Drying room **Extras:** Speciality toiletries, mineral water, cafetiere **Conf:** Max 120 Thtr 80 Class 120 Board 40 **Parking:** 7 **Notes:** LB Civ wed 140

## CONWY

### ABERGELE
Map 14 SH97

### Premier Collection

## The Kinmel Arms

★★★★★ ◎◎ RESTAURANT WITH ROOMS

**tel:** 01745 832207 **The Village, St George LL22 9BP**
**email:** info@thekinmelarms.co.uk **web:** www.thekinmelarms.co.uk
**dir:** *From A55 junct 24a to St George. E on A55, junct 24. 1st left to Rhuddlan, 1st right into St George. 2nd right*

This converted 17th-century coaching inn stands close to the church in the village of St George. The restaurant specialises in skilfully prepared produce from Wales and north-west England. Friendly, helpful staff will ensure you have a relaxing stay, in one of four attractive suites. All are kitted out with small kitchenettes where continental breakfasts are placed each day to enjoy at your leisure. Each suite is individually designed in a clean, natural style with luxurious bathrooms to match.

**Rooms:** 4 en suite (2 GF) **S** £115–£155; **D** £115–£175 **Facilities:** STV Lounge tea/coffee Dinner available ⌂18 **Extras:** Speciality toiletries, fruit, snacks, bottled water – complimentary **Conf:** Max 10 Board 10 **Parking:** 50 **Notes:** LB No children 16yrs Closed 25 Dec & 1 Jan RS Sun & Mon closed (ex BHs)

### BETWS-Y-COED
Map 14 SH75

### Premier Collection

## Penmachno Hall

★★★★★ ⊖ GUEST ACCOMMODATION

**tel:** 01690 760410 **Penmachno LL24 0PU**
**email:** stay@penmachnohall.co.uk **web:** www.penmachnohall.co.uk
**dir:** *4m S of Betws-y-Coed. A5 onto B4406 to Penmachno, over bridge, right at Eagles pub signed Ty Mawr. 500yds at stone bridge*

Set in more than two acres of mature grounds including a mountain stream and woodland, this impressive Victorian rectory provides high standards of comfort and good facilities. Stylish decor and quality furnishings highlight the many original features throughout the ground-floor areas, and the bedrooms have a wealth of thoughtful extras. Alongside the main building is a superb two-bedroom, self-catering unit in a former coach house. Pre-booked set menu, party-style evening meals are served on Saturday nights, while buffet-style meals are served Tuesday through Friday.

**Rooms:** 3 en suite **D** £95–£100 **Facilities:** STV DVD Lounge tea/coffee Dinner available Licensed WiFi **Extras:** Fruit – complimentary, robes **Parking:** 5 **Notes:** LB Closed Xmas & New Year RS Sun–Mon no evening meals

## Afon View Guest House

★★★★ GUEST HOUSE

**tel:** 01690 710726 **Holyhead Road LL24 0AN**
**email:** welcome@afon-view.co.uk **web:** www.afon-view.co.uk
**dir:** *On A5, 60yds W of Rockbottom Shop*

A warm welcome is assured at this elegant Victorian house, located between Waterloo Bridge and the village centre. Bedrooms are equipped with lots of thoughtful extras, and day rooms include an attractive dining room and comfortable guest lounge.

**Rooms:** 7 en suite (1 fmly) **S** £60–£75; **D** £75–£120* **Facilities:** FTV Lounge tea/coffee WiFi **Parking:** 7 **Notes:** LB No children 8yrs Closed 20–27 Dec

## Bryn Bella Guest House

★★★★ GUEST HOUSE

**tel:** 01690 710627 **Lon Muriau, Llanrwst Road LL24 0HD**
**email:** welcome@bryn-bella.co.uk **web:** www.bryn-bella.co.uk
**dir:** *A5 onto A470, 0.5m right onto driveway signed Bryn Bella*

Located in an elevated position on the outskirts of the village, with stunning views of the surrounding countryside, this elegant Victorian house provides a range of thoughtfully equipped bedrooms and smart, modern bathrooms. An eco-friendly approach is to be commended and this ethos runs through the whole operation from local sourcing to reduce food-miles to water reclamation. A warm welcome is assured and guest services include a daily weather forecast.

**Rooms:** 5 en suite (1 GF) **S** fr £80; **D** fr £80* **Facilities:** FTV DVD TVL tea/coffee WiFi **Extras:** Robes, microwave **Parking:** 6 **Notes:** LB No children 16yrs

## Cwmanog Isaf Farm

★★★★ FARMHOUSE

**tel:** 01690 710225 & 07808 421634 **Fairy Glen LL24 0SL**
**email:** h.hughes165@btinternet.com **web:** www.cwmanogisaffarmholidays.co.uk
**dir:** *1m S of Betws-y-Coed off A470 before stone bridge, 500yds on farm lane*

Peacefully located in 30 acres of undulating land, where the Fairy Glen (a well known beauty spot on the River Conwy) can be found, this 200-year-old house on a working livestock farm has been restored to provide comfortable, thoughtfully furnished bedrooms. Breakfasts use home-reared or organic produce. The property's elevated position provides stunning views of the surrounding countryside.

**Rooms:** 3 en suite (1 GF) **S** £45–£75; **D** £65–£80* **Facilities:** STV Lounge tea/coffee **Parking:** 4 **Notes:** No children 15yrs Closed Nov–Easter 30 acres sheep

## Park Hill

★★★★ GUEST HOUSE

**tel:** 01690 710540 **Llanrwst Road LL24 0HD**
**email:** welcome@park-hill.co.uk **web:** www.park-hill.co.uk
**dir:** *0.5m N of Betws-y-Coed on A470 (Llanrwst road)*

A warm welcome is assured at this guest house, which benefits from a peaceful location overlooking the village of Betws-y-Coed and valley beyond. Well-equipped bedrooms, including one with a four-poster, offer comfortable beds and modern extras. There is a sun lounge to the front, a heated swimming pool, sauna and whirlpool bath for guests' use. Ample parking onsite.

**Rooms:** 8 en suite **S** £73–£97; **D** £76–£100 **Facilities:** FTV Lounge tea/coffee WiFi ⌂9 **Parking:** 11 **Notes:** LB No children 8yrs

## CAPEL CURIG
Map 14 SH75

# Bryn Tyrch Inn
★★★★ ⚜ INN

**tel:** 01690 720223 & 07855 762791 **LL24 0EL**
**email:** info@bryntyrchinn.co.uk **web:** www.bryntyrchinn.co.uk
**dir:** *On A5 at top end of village*

Dating from the 19th century, this former posting house has been sympathetically refurbished to provide public areas of real character and stylish modern bedrooms with smart en suite bathrooms. Hog and lamb roasts are a feature on certain days throughout the year and the award-winning restaurant also impresses. The enthusiastic proprietors, assisted by a friendly team are constantly making improvements to ensure a visit to Bryn Tyrch is worth the trip. AA Pub of the Year 2017–18.

**Rooms:** 11 en suite **Facilities:** FTV Lounge tea/coffee Dinner available WiFi ⚓9 Drying facilities **Extras:** Home-made biscuits **Parking:** 30 **Notes:** LB Closed 15–27 Dec & 3–20 Jan RS Feb–Mar open wknds only & school hols Civ wed 75

## COLWYN BAY
Map 14 SH87

# The Northwood
★★★★ GUEST HOUSE

**tel:** 01492 549931 **47 Rhos Road, Rhos-on-Sea LL28 4RS**
**email:** welcome@thenorthwood.co.uk **web:** www.thenorthwood.co.uk
**dir:** *Exit at A55 junct 22 (Old Colwyn). At T-junct right, to next T-junct (facing sea). Left, pass pier, opposite harbour left into Rhos Rd. On left adjacent to church*

A short walk from the seafront and shops, this constantly improving guest house has a warm and friendly atmosphere and welcomes back many regular guests. The bedrooms are en suite, comfortable and well equipped for the modern traveller.

**Rooms:** 9 en suite (4 fmly) (2 GF) **S** £30–£60; **D** £60–£120* **Facilities:** FTV DVD TVL tea/coffee Licensed WiFi ⚓ **Conf:** Max 20 Class 20 Board 20 **Parking:** 12 **Notes:** LB No children 16yrs

## CONWY
Map 14 SH77

# The Groes Inn
★★★★★ ⚜ INN

**tel:** 01492 650545 **Tyn-y-Groes LL32 8TN**
**email:** enquiries@thegroes.com **web:** www.groesinn.com
**dir:** *A55, over Old Conwy Bridge, 1st left through Castle Walls on B5106 (Trefriw Road), 2m on right*

Located in the picturesque Conwy Valley, this historic inn dates from 1573 and was the first licensed house in Wales. The exterior and gardens have an abundance of shrubs and seasonal flowers that create an impressive welcome, which is matched by the friendly and professional staff. Public areas are decorated and furnished with flair to highlight the many period features. The spacious bedrooms, in renovated outbuildings, are equipped with a wealth of thoughtful extras; many have balconies overlooking the countryside.

**Rooms:** 14 en suite (1 fmly) (6 GF) **Facilities:** FTV tea/coffee Dinner available Direct dial WiFi ⚓18 Petanque **Conf:** Max 20 Thtr 20 Class 20 Board 20 **Parking:** 100 **Notes:** LB Civ wed 100

# Sychnant Pass Country House
★★★★★ ⚑ GUEST ACCOMMODATION

**tel:** 01492 596868 **Sychnant Pass Road LL32 8BJ**
**email:** office@sychnantpasscountryhouse.co.uk **web:** www.sychnant-pass-house.co.uk

A warm welcome is assured on arrival at Sychnant Pass Country House from the friendly team here. Located just on the northern edge of the Snowdonia National Park and within minutes of Conwy and Llandudno. It enjoys a secluded position in this Area of Outstanding Natural Beauty, and is ideally located for visiting the many attractions in North Wales. There is a relaxing comfortable lounge, or for the more energetic guests there is an indoor swimming pool, sauna and gym. Guests can enjoy dinner served in the smart dining room overlooking the gardens, feasting on the finest local seasonal produce. A range of bedrooms styles are offered, including one room with its own private hot tub.

**Rooms:** 12 en suite (4 fmly) (2 GF) **S** £85–£120; **D** £105–£195 **Facilities:** FTV Lounge tea/coffee Dinner available Licensed WiFi ⚓ Gym ♨ Outside heated hot tub **Parking:** 20 **Notes:** Civ wed 45

## DWYGYFYLCHI
Map 14 SH77

# The Gladstone
★★★★ INN

**tel:** 01492 623231 **Ygborwen Road LL34 6PS**
**email:** thegladstonepub@hotmail.co.uk **web:** www.thegladstone.co.uk
**dir:** *A55 junct 16 turn left, then left again towards Dwygyfylchi, 0.25m on right*

The Gladstone is first and foremost a great pub enjoying a superb sea-facing outlook with views of Puffin Island and Great Orme. Guests can sit inside or out to take in the sunset with drinks and an extensive menu served in a friendly, informal style. Comfortable, stylish bedrooms are individually designed, equipped with plenty of modern extras and luxurious bathrooms. Off-road parking is available.

**Rooms:** 6 en suite **Facilities:** FTV Lounge TVL tea/coffee Dinner available WiFi ♨ **Conf:** Max 20 Board 20 **Parking:** 25 **Notes:** LB Civ wed 40

## LLANDUDNO
Map 14 SH78

# Bryn Derwen
★★★★★ BED AND BREAKFAST

**tel:** 01492 876804 **34 Abbey Road LL30 2EE**
**email:** brynderwen34@btinternet.com **web:** www.bryn-derwen.co.uk
**dir:** *A470 into Llandudno, left at The Parade promenade to cenotaph, left, over rdbt, 4th right into York Rd, Bryn Derwen at top*

Bryn Derwen is located in a quiet area of Llandudno, just a short walk from the main shopping area and local restaurants. A friendly welcome is assured at this impressive Victorian house, which retains many original features such as tiled floors and fine stained-glass windows. Decor and furnishings highlight the historic charm of the property, which is most apparent in the sumptuous lounges and attractive dining room. A choice of individually styled bedrooms are available and these are equipped with many thoughtful extras.

**Rooms:** 9 en suite (1 fmly) **Facilities:** FTV DVD iPod docking station Lounge TVL tea/coffee Licensed WiFi ⚓18 ♨ **Extras:** Speciality toiletries, water, chocolates — complimentary **Parking:** 9 **Notes:** LB No children 12yrs Closed mid Dec–mid Jan

**LLANDUDNO** *continued*

## Brigstock House

★★★★ GUEST HOUSE

**tel:** 01492 876416 **1 St David's Place LL30 2UG**
**email:** brigstockguesthouse@gmail.com **web:** www.brigstockhouse.co.uk
**dir:** *A470 into Llandudno, left into The Parade promenade, left into Lloyd St, left into St David's Rd & left into St David's Place*

This impressive Edwardian property in a quiet residential corner of the town is within easy walking distance of the seafront and central shopping area. The atmosphere is relaxed and refined. Attractive, modern bedrooms are tastefully decorated with suites available for those who like to spread out. A comfortable lounge is also available with honesty bar. Substantial breakfasts are served in the elegant dining room.

**Rooms:** 8 en suite **Facilities:** FTV DVD TVL tea/coffee Licensed WiFi 🐾 **Parking:** 6
**Notes:** LB No children 12yrs Closed Dec—Jan

## The Cliffbury

★★★★ GUEST ACCOMMODATION

**tel:** 01492 877224 **34 St David's Road LL30 2UH**
**email:** info@thecliffbury.co.uk **web:** www.thecliffbury.co.uk

Located on a leafy avenue within easy walking distance of the town centre, this elegant Edwardian house sets high standards. Bedrooms, furnished in a bright, modern style, provide a range of practical and thoughtful extras. Two popular suites are available. A warm welcome is assured for all with comfort at the heart of everything the hosts provide. Off-street parking available.

**Rooms:** 6 en suite **D** £70—£84* **Facilities:** FTV DVD tea/coffee WiFi **Parking:** 6
**Notes:** LB No children 14yrs Closed Jan

## St Hilary Guest House

★★★★ GUEST ACCOMMODATION

**tel:** 01492 875551 **16 Craig-y-Don Parade, The Promenade LL30 1BG**
**email:** info@sthilaryguesthouse.co.uk **web:** www.sthilaryguesthouse.co.uk
**dir:** *0.5m E of town centre. On B5115 (seafront road) near Venue Cymru*

Anne-Marie and Howard offer a warm and personal welcome in their guest house sitting at the more peaceful Craig-y-Don end of The Promenade. Many of the elegant bedrooms have sea views and are all equipped with modern facilities such as WiFi and large TVs. The attractive front-facing dining room is the scene for hearty breakfasts. A bright and comfortable guest lounge, with an honesty bar, is also available.

**Rooms:** 9 en suite (1 GF) **S** £55—£83; **D** £73—£93* **Facilities:** FTV DVD iPod docking station Lounge tea/coffee Licensed WiFi **Notes:** LB No children 18yrs Closed mid Dec—mid Jan

## Stratford House

★★★★ GUEST ACCOMMODATION

**tel:** 01492 877962 **8 Craig-y-Don Parade, The Promenade LL30 1BG**
**email:** stratfordhtl@aol.com **web:** www.thestratfordbandb.com
**dir:** *A470 at rdbt take 4th exit, on Queens Rd to promenade, on right*

This immaculately presented spacious house is located on the seafront with spectacular views. Bedrooms are attractively decorated, some with four-poster beds, and all have an excellent range of accessories, including TVs. The traditionally decorated dining room is also beautifully presented. The friendly owners are very welcoming.

**Rooms:** 9 en suite (1 fmly) (1 GF) **S** £55—£80; **D** £60—£85* **Facilities:** FTV tea/coffee WiFi **Extras:** Chocolates, Bottled water — complimentary **Notes:** LB No children 10yrs Closed Jan—Feb RS Dec & Mar

## Britannia Guest House

★★★★ GUEST HOUSE

**tel:** 01492 877185 & 07890 765071 **15 Craig-y-Don Parade, The Promenade LL30 1BG**
**email:** info@thebritanniaguesthouse.co.uk **web:** www.thebritanniaguesthouse.co.uk
**dir:** *A55 onto A470 to Llandudno, at rdbt take 4th exit signed Craig-y-Don, right at promenade*

This family-run Victorian guest house offers a warm welcome and friendly service. The bedrooms are very comfortable and well equipped, and many have fantastic views of Llandudno's bay. Ground-floor rooms are available, and hearty breakfasts are served in the dining room that has sea views.

**Rooms:** 10 en suite (2 GF) **D** £69—£96* **Facilities:** FTV tea/coffee WiFi **Extras:** Speciality toiletries **Notes:** LB No children 10yrs Closed 28 Oct—10 Mar

## Can-Y-Bae

★★★★ GUEST ACCOMMODATION

**tel:** 01492 874188 **10 Mostyn Crescent, Central Promenade LL30 1AR**
**email:** canybae@btconnect.com **web:** www.can-y-baehotel.com
**dir:** *A55 junct 19, A470, signed Llandudno/Promenade. Can-Y-Bae on seafront promenade between Venue Cymru Theatre & band stand*

A warm welcome is assured at this tastefully renovated house, centrally located on the Promenade. Bedrooms are equipped with both practical and homely extras and upper floors are serviced by a modern lift. Public rooms include a panoramic lounge, cosy bar with souvenirs of famous guests and an attractive ground floor dining room.

**Rooms:** 16 en suite (2 GF) **S** £40—£60; **D** £80—£90 **Facilities:** FTV Lounge tea/coffee Dinner available Direct dial Lift Licensed WiFi **Extras:** Speciality toiletries, mineral water — complimentary **Notes:** LB No children 12yrs

## The Epperstone

★★★★ GUEST ACCOMMODATION

**tel:** 01492 878746 & 07749 304394 **15 Abbey Road LL30 2EE**
**email:** epperstonehotel@btconnect.com **web:** www.theepperstone.co.uk
**dir:** *A550, A470 to Mostyn St. Left at rdbt, 4th right into York Rd. Epperstone at junct of York Rd & Abbey Rd*

This delightful property is located in wonderful gardens in a residential part of town, within easy walking distance of the seafront and shopping area. Bedrooms are attractively decorated and thoughtfully equipped. Two lounges and a Victorian-style conservatory are available.

**Rooms:** 8 en suite (5 fmly) (1 GF) **Facilities:** FTV Lounge tea/coffee Dinner available Direct dial Licensed WiFi 🔒 **Parking:** 7 **Notes:** LB No children 6yrs Closed Jan–Apr

## Glenavon Guest House

★★★★ GUEST HOUSE

**tel:** 01492 877687 **27 St Mary's Road LL30 2UB**
**email:** postmaster@glenavon.plus.com **web:** www.glenavon-llandudno.co.uk
**dir:** *From A470 signed Llandudno, left at lights into Trinity Av. 3rd right into St Mary's Rd. Glenavon on right*

Supporters of Liverpool Football Club are especially welcome here and they can admire the extensive range of memorabilia throughout the comfortable day rooms. Bedrooms are equipped with thoughtful extras and Welsh breakfasts provide a good start to the day.

**Rooms:** 7 en suite (1 fmly) **Facilities:** FTV TVL tea/coffee WiFi 🔒 **Parking:** 4 **Notes:** LB

## The Lilly Restaurant with Rooms

★★★★ ◉ 🍷 RESTAURANT WITH ROOMS

**tel:** 01492 876513 **West Parade, West Shore LL30 2BD**
**email:** thelilly@live.co.uk **web:** www.thelilly.co.uk
**dir:** *Phone for detailed directions*

Located on the seafront on the West Shore with views over the Great Orme, this establishment has bedrooms that offer high standards of comfort, and good facilities. Children are very welcome here, and a relaxed atmosphere is found in Madhatter's Brasserie, which takes its name from Lewis Carroll's *Alice in Wonderland*, some of which may have been written while the author was staying on the West Shore. A fine dining restaurant is also available.

**Rooms:** 5 en suite **Facilities:** FTV iPod docking station Lounge tea/coffee Dinner available Direct dial WiFi **Extras:** Speciality toiletries **Conf:** Max 35 Thtr 25 Board 20 **Notes:** LB

## The Oasis

★★★★ BED AND BREAKFAST

**tel:** 01492 877822 **LL30 1AT**
**email:** info@theoasiswales.co.uk **web:** www.theoasiswales.co.uk
**dir:** *A470 to Llandudno, right at rdbt onto B5115 (Clarence Crescent). On Promenade*

The Oasis is a family-run bed and breakfast and hosts Carole and Ed, very much look forward to welcoming their guests. Situated on the main promenade with beautiful views of the Great Orme, the Victorian Pier and the Irish Sea, a stay here will prove relaxing and enjoyable. Refurbished in early 2017, the en suite bedrooms are tastefully decorated and equipped with tea- and coffee-making facilities and hairdryers. Free WiFi is available. A home-cooked full English breakfast is served.

**Rooms:** 15 en suite (5 fmly) (3 GF) **Facilities:** FTV TVL tea/coffee WiFi 🔒 **Parking:** 1

## No. 9 Guest House

★★★ BED AND BREAKFAST

**tel:** 01492 877251 & 07950 445524 **9 Chapel Street LL30 2SY**
**email:** m.hartill69@gmail.com **web:** www.no9llandudno.co.uk
**dir:** *See website for detailed directions*

No. 9 Guest House is centrally located in Llandudno with the promenade, shopping areas and restaurants all within a few minutes' walk. This Victorian building is traditionally styled, with a warm welcome assured from the friendly owner. Bedrooms vary in size and offer comfortable facilities for guests. A hearty breakfast is provided including homemade jams and seasonal special dishes in addition to the traditional breakfast.

**Rooms:** 8 en suite (2 fmly) **S** £32–£36; **D** £60–£78* **Facilities:** FTV DVD TVL WiFi 🔒

## Cae Mor

★★★ GUEST ACCOMMODATION

**tel:** 01492 878101 **5–6 Penrhyn Crescent LL30 1BA**
**email:** info@caemorhotel.co.uk **web:** www.caemorhotel.co.uk
**dir:** *Exit A55 junct 19, follow A470/Llandudno/Town Centre signs. Straight on at 3 rdbts, right at 4th. Into right lane, right at next rdbt, follow Promenade signs. Straight on at next rdbt, left at next rdbt onto Promenade. Adjacent to Venue Cymru*

Located in a stunning seafront position adjacent to Venue Cymru, this tastefully renovated Victorian property provides a range of thoughtfully furnished bedrooms in minimalist style with smart modern bathrooms. Public areas include a choice of lounges and a stylish restaurant, the setting for imaginative dinners featuring the best of local seasonal produce.

**Rooms:** 23 en suite (2 fmly) (2 GF) **Facilities:** Lift WiFi **Parking**

## The Trevone

★★★ GUEST ACCOMMODATION

**tel:** 01492 876314 **10 St Georges Crescent LL30 2LF**
**email:** info@trevone.net **web:** www.trevone.net
**dir:** *A55 follow signs for Llandudno & central promenade*

The Trevone is in a splendid location at the heart of the Llandudno seafront and a friendly welcome and service is assured. Bedrooms and bathrooms come in a range of shapes and sizes; some have excellent sea views. Guests can relax in a choice of lounges and a well-stocked bar is provided.

**Rooms:** 24 en suite (5 fmly) (1 GF) **S** £42–£46; **D** £84–£120* **Facilities:** FTV Lounge TVL tea/coffee Lift Licensed WiFi 🔒 **Notes:** LB Closed Dec–Feb

## LLANDUDNO JUNCTION       Map 14 SH77

### Premier Collection

## Queens Head

★★★★★   ⊛   INN

**tel:** 01492 546570 **Glanwydden LL31 9JP**
**email:** enquiries@queensheadglanwydden.co.uk
**web:** www.queensheadglanwydden.co.uk
**dir:** A55 onto A470 towards Llandudno. At 3rd rdbt right towards Penrhyn Bay, 2nd right into Glanwydden, on left

Queens Head is an attractive stone inn located in a small village just a couple of miles from both Llandudno and Colwyn Bay. The friendly team ensure all guests are well cared for during their stay. Storehouse Cottage stands just a few steps away from the inn and offers quaint, cosy accommodation. With a smart fully equipped kitchen, lounge, bedroom and dressing room, there is plenty of space to relax and unwind after a busy day. There is a small sun-trap garden with seating area. A substantial continental breakfast is provided for guests in the cottage. Other meals are available in the inn or can be delivered to the cottage on request. There is a minimum two-night stay for bed and breakfast.

**Rooms:** 1 annexe en suite **Facilities:** FTV DVD Dinner available WiFi 🛁
**Extras:** Sherry, fruit – complimentary **Parking:** 40 **Notes:** LB

## RHOS-ON-SEA       Map 14 SH88

*See also Colwyn Bay*

### Premier Collection

## Plas Rhos

★★★★★   ⊜   GUEST ACCOMMODATION

**tel:** 01492 543698 **Cayley Promenade LL28 4EP**
**email:** info@plasrhos.co.uk **web:** www.plasrhos.co.uk
**dir:** A55 junct 20 onto B5115 for Rhos-on-Sea, right at rdbt into Whitehall Rd to promenade

Stunning sea views are a feature of this lovely Victorian house, which provides high standards of comfort and hospitality. Cosy bedrooms are filled with a wealth of thoughtful extras, and public areas include a choice of sumptuous lounges featuring smart decor, quality soft furnishings and memorabilia. Breakfast is served in the attractive dining room, overlooking the patio garden.

**Rooms:** 5 en suite **S** £70–£85; **D** £85–£110 **Facilities:** FTV Lounge TVL tea/coffee Licensed WiFi 🛁 **Parking:** 4 **Notes:** LB No children 12yrs Closed Nov–Mar

## Whitehall Guest House

★★★★   GUEST HOUSE

**tel:** 01492 547296 **51 Cayley Promenade LL28 4EP**
**email:** tony@whitehall-hotel.co.uk **web:** www.whitehall-hotel.co.uk
**dir:** A55 onto B5115 (Brompton Av), right at rdbt into Whitehall Rd to seafront

Overlooking the Rhos-on-Sea promenade, this popular, family-run establishment is convenient for the shops and local amenities. Attractively appointed bedrooms include family rooms and a room on the ground floor; all benefit from an excellent range of facilities such as video and CD players as well as air-conditioning. Facilities include a bar and a foyer lounge.

**Rooms:** 12 en suite (4 fmly) (1 GF) **S** £25–£36; **D** £50–£85* **Facilities:** FTV DVD Lounge TVL tea/coffee Direct dial Licensed WiFi 🛁 **Parking:** 5 **Notes:** LB

## TAL-Y-CAFN       Map 14 SH77

### Premier Collection

## Bodnant Welsh Food Centre

★★★★★   ⊜   RESTAURANT WITH ROOMS

**tel:** 01492 651100 & 651102 **Furnace Farm LL28 5RP**
**email:** reception@bodnant-welshfood.co.uk **web:** www.bodnant-welshfood.co.uk
**dir:** Off A470, 4m from A55 junct 19, follow signs for A470

Overlooking the River Conwy and neighbouring Bodnant Gardens, this 18th-century farm has been fully restored and is now the home to Bodnant Welsh Food Centre. It is ideally placed to explore the North Wales coastline, Snowdonia, and the nearby surf park. The buildings have been transformed into a tea room, farm shop and wine merchants with a focus on Welsh products. The Hayloft Restaurant serves interesting lunches and dinners, including a seven-course tasting menu. A range of room types and sizes can be found in the comfortable accommodation, with a guest lounge and kitchen also available. There is a cookery school on-site, and small conferences and weddings can be accommodated here.

**Rooms:** 6 en suite (1 GF) **Facilities:** FTV Lounge TVL tea/coffee Dinner available Lift WiFi **Parking:** 80 **Notes:** LB Closed 25–26 Dec Civ wed 80

## TREFRIW       Map 14 SH76

### Premier Collection

## Yr Hafod Country House

★★★★★   ⊜   BED AND BREAKFAST

**tel:** 01492 642444 **LL27 0RQ**
**email:** enquiries@hafod-house.co.uk **web:** www.hafod-house.co.uk
**dir:** From N: A470 onto B5279, after 1m left onto B5106. 5.5m to Trefriw, over bridge 200mtrs on left. From S: A470 into Llanrwst, left over bridge onto B5106. 1.5m on right

Situated in tranquil countryside and ideally located for the Conwy Valley and Snowdonia National Park, this cosy, family run B&B offers four smartly appointed bedrooms, which are tastefully designed and comfortable; each has separate access and its own balcony. A hearty breakfast is served in the traditional dining room and, not to be missed, dishes are freshly prepared using as much home-grown and local produce as possible. The well-stocked bar and lounge are also part of the package. Bespoke dinner menus are designed on request for groups of 6-12 people, when three or more bedrooms are booked. There are a number of quality local eating establishments, some within easy walking distance. Yr Hafod Country House was a finalist for the AA Friendliest B&B of the Year award 2017–18.

**Rooms:** 4 en suite **S** £72.50–£75; **D** £90–£100* **Facilities:** FTV DVD TVL tea/coffee Licensed WiFi 🔒 **Extras:** Speciality toiletries, sweets, bottled water **Parking:** 4 **Notes:** Closed Dec–13 Feb

## Ty Newydd B&B

★★★ GUEST ACCOMMODATION

**tel:** 01492 641210 **Conwy Road LL27 0JH**
**email:** tynewyddtrefriw@aol.com **web:** www.tynewyddtrefriw.co.uk
**dir:** *In village centre, near post office*

Nestled in a small village in the unspoilt Conwy Valley, Ty Newydd is just a short drive from Llandudno. The hosts of this large Victorian house offer a genuine warm Welsh welcome on arrival. Comfortable rooms are well equipped, and the property is within easy walking distance of a number of pubs and restaurants.

**Rooms:** 4 rms (2 en suite) (2 pri facs) (1 fmly) **S** fr £35; **D** fr £70 **Facilities:** STV FTV TVL tea/coffee WiFi ⚓9 🔒 **Extras:** Safe **Notes:** LB

## DENBIGHSHIRE

### CORWEN     Map 15 SJ04

## Bron-y-Graig

★★★★ GUEST HOUSE

**tel:** 01490 413007 **LL21 0DR**
**email:** info@north-wales-hotel.co.uk **web:** www.north-wales-hotel.co.uk
**dir:** *On A5 on E edge of Corwen*

A short walk from the town centre, Bron-y-Graig is an impressive Victorian house that has retained many original features including fireplaces, stained glass, and a tiled floor in the entrance hall. Bedrooms, complemented by luxurious bathrooms, are thoughtfully furnished; two are to be found in a coach house. Ground-floor areas include a traditionally furnished dining room and a comfortable lounge. A warm welcome and attentive service are assured.

**Rooms:** 7 en suite 2 annexe en suite (4 fmly) **S** £40–£49; **D** £60–£79 **Facilities:** STV FTV DVD Lounge tea/coffee Direct dial Licensed WiFi 🔒 **Conf:** Max 20 Class 20 Board 15 **Parking:** 15 **Notes:** LB

## Plas Derwen Country House

★★★★ GUEST ACCOMMODATION

**tel:** 01490 412742 & 07773 965874 **London Road LL21 0DR**
**email:** bandb@plasderwen.supanet.com **web:** www.plasderwen.co.uk
**dir:** *On A5, 0.5m E of Corwen*

Set in an elevated position within four acres of mature gardens and natural meadow, this elegant late 18th-century house has been restored to provide top-notch levels of comfort and facilities. Quality furnishings and stylish decor highlight the many original features, and a warm and personal welcome is assured. An extensive continental or locally sourced full Welsh breakfast is served.

**Rooms:** 2 en suite (2 fmly) **Facilities:** FTV TVL tea/coffee WiFi 🔒 **Parking:** 6 **Notes:** Closed Dec–Jan

### DENBIGH     Map 15 SJ06

## Guildhall Tavern

★★★★ INN

**tel:** 01745 816533 **Hall Square LL16 3NU**
**email:** info@guildhalltavernhotel.co.uk **web:** www.guildhalltavernhotel.co.uk

Standing in the centre of this historic medieval town, this 16th-century inn has had a number of different uses including a stint as a military HQ in 1646, when it was taken over by Generals Mytton and Myddleton. A wealth of historic features are still evident throughout, including the ornate carved staircases. Rooms are individually decorated and complemented by good quality bathrooms, many with feature baths or showers. There is a friendly bar area frequented by guests and locals, serving a range of local ales and ciders, alongside home-cooked dishes.

**Rooms:** 10 rms **Facilities:** Dinner available

## LLANDYRNOG
Map 15 SJ16

### Premier Collection

## Pentre Mawr Country House

★★★★★ GUEST ACCOMMODATION

**tel:** 01824 790732 **LL16 4LA**
**email:** info@pentremawrcountryhouse.co.uk **web:** www.pentremawrcountryhouse.co.uk
**dir:** From Denbigh follow Bodfari/Llandyrnog signs. Left at rdbt to Bodfari, 50yds, left into country lane, Pentre Mawr on left

Expect a warm welcome from Graham and Bre at this superb family country house, set in nearly 200 acres of meadows, park and woodland. The property has been in Graham's family for over 400 years. Bedrooms are individually decorated, very spacious, and each is thoughtfully equipped. Breakfast is served in the conservatory-restaurant overlooking the salt water swimming pool on the terrace. A formal private dining room is available for larger parties. There is a range of diverse accommodation options in addition to the main house, including six luxury Safari lodges and two suites, all with private hot tubs.

**Rooms:** 3 en suite 8 annexe en suite (7 GF) **Facilities:** FTV DVD iPod docking station Lounge tea/coffee Dinner available Licensed WiFi ↝ ⅏ ➹ Fishing ⬩ **Extras:** Robes **Conf:** Max 20 Class 20 Board 20 **Parking:** 14 **Notes:** LB No children 13yrs

## LLANGOLLEN
Map 15 SJ24

*See also Corwen*

## Tyn Celyn Farmhouse

★★★★ BED AND BREAKFAST

**tel:** 01978 861117 **Tyndwr LL20 8AR**
**email:** j.m.bather-tyncelyn@talk21.com **web:** www.tyncelyn-bnb-llangollen.co.uk
**dir:** A5 to Llangollen, pass golf club on right, next left signed Tyndwr outdoor centre, 0.5m sharp left into Tyndwr Rd, past Tyndwr Hall on left. Tyn Celyn 0.5m on left

This 300-year-old timber-framed farmhouse has stunning views over the Vale of Llangollen. Bedrooms, one of which is located on the ground floor, provide a range of thoughtful extras in addition to fine period furniture. Breakfast is served at a magnificent carved table in a spacious sitting-dining room.

**Rooms:** 3 en suite (1 fmly) (1 GF) **D** £70–£75* **Facilities:** DVD TVL tea/coffee WiFi ⬩ **Parking:** 5 **Notes:** LB

## RUTHIN
Map 15 SJ15

### Premier Collection

## Firgrove Country House B&B

★★★★★ ⬩ ➾ BED AND BREAKFAST

**tel:** 01824 702677 & 07710 251606 **Firgrove, Llanfwrog LL15 2LL**
**email:** meadway@firgrovecountryhouse.co.uk **web:** www.firgrovecountryhouse.co.uk
**dir:** 0.5m SW of Ruthin. A494 onto B5105, 0.25m past Llanfwrog church on right

Standing in immaculate mature gardens in a peaceful rural location, this well-proportioned house retains many original features, highlighted by the quality decor and furnishings throughout. Bedrooms, complemented by smart modern bathrooms, are equipped with a wealth of thoughtful extras. Memorable breakfasts, using home-made or local produce, are served in an elegant dining room. Imaginative dinners are also available by prior arrangement and a warm welcome is assured.

**Rooms:** 2 en suite 1 annexe en suite (1 GF) **S** £80–£120; **D** £100–£120* **Facilities:** FTV Lounge tea/coffee Dinner available WiFi ⬩ **Extras:** Mineral water, fresh milk – complimentary; fridge **Parking:** 4 **Notes:** No children Closed Dec–Feb

## ST ASAPH
Map 15 SJ07

### Tan-Yr-Onnen Guest House
★★★★★ 🍵 GUEST HOUSE

**tel:** 01745 583821 **Waen LL17 0DU**
**email:** tanyronnenvisit@aol.com **web:** www.northwalesbreaks.co.uk
**dir:** W on A55 junct 28, turn left in 300yds

A warm welcome is assured at Tan-Yr-Onnen Guest House, which is quietly located in six acres of gardens, conveniently close to the A55. The very well-equipped accommodation includes four ground-floor rooms with French windows that open onto the terrace. Upstairs, there are two luxury suites with lounge areas. Hearty breakfasts are served in the dining room overlooking the gardens, and a conservatory-lounge and WiFi access are also available.

**Rooms:** 6 en suite (1 fmly) (4 GF) **Facilities:** FTV Lounge tea/coffee Licensed WiFi
🔒 **Parking:** 8

## GWYNEDD

### ABERDYFI
Map 14 SN69

### Penhelig Arms
★★★★★ 🌸 INN

**tel:** 01654 767215 **Terrace Road LL35 0LT**
**email:** info@penheligarms.com **web:** www.penheligarms.com

Originally a collection of fishermen's cottages, the charming Penhelig Arms overlooks the picturesque Dyfi Estuary within the Snowdonia National Park. Bedrooms in the main house are charming, with many taking in the impressive views. Award-winning cuisine is a real feature at the inn; local produce is a key factor in the popular dining room and bar, where bookings are essential to avoid disappointment.

**Rooms:** 11 en suite 4 annexe en suite **D** £99–£180 **Facilities:** Dinner available WiFi **Parking:** 5

### BARMOUTH
Map 14 SH61

*See also Dyffryn Ardudwy*

### Llwyndu Farmhouse
★★★★ 🍵 🍴 GUEST ACCOMMODATION

**tel:** 01341 280144 **Llanaber LL42 1RR**
**email:** intouch@llwyndu-farmhouse.co.uk **web:** www.llwyndu-farmhouse.co.uk
**dir:** A496 towards Harlech where street lights end, on outskirts of Barmouth, next right

This converted 16th-century farmhouse offers warm hospitality and traditional guest accommodation. Many original features have been retained, including inglenook fireplaces, exposed beams and timbers. There is a cosy lounge and meals can be enjoyed in the licensed restaurant. Bedrooms are and well equipped; some have four-poster beds and extraordinary views over Cardigan Bay. Four bedrooms are in the old dairy building.

**Rooms:** 3 en suite 4 annexe en suite (2 fmly) **D** £96–£130* **Facilities:** FTV TVL tea/coffee Dinner available Licensed WiFi 🔒 **Extras:** Speciality toiletries, fruit, snacks – complimentary **Conf:** Max 10 **Parking:** 10 **Notes:** LB Closed 24–27 Dec RS Sun & Wed no dinner

### BEDDGELERT
Map 14 SH54

### Tanronnen Inn
★★★★ INN

**tel:** 01766 890347 **LL55 4YB**
**email:** tanbedd@12freeukisp.co.uk **web:** www.tanronnen.co.uk
**dir:** In village centre opposite river bridge

This delightful village inn offers comfortable, modern and attractively appointed accommodation, including rooms suitable for families. There is a selection of pleasant and relaxing public areas. The wide range of bar food is popular with tourists and locals alike. More formal meals are served in the restaurant. Real ales are another draw here with a good selection available.

**Rooms:** 7 en suite (3 fmly) **S** £60–£70; **D** £110* **Facilities:** FTV tea/coffee Dinner available Direct dial 🔒 **Parking:** 9 **Notes:** LB

## CAERNARFON Map 14 SH46

### Premier Collection

## Plas Dinas Country House

★★★★★ GUEST ACCOMMODATION

**tel:** 01286 830214 **Bontnewydd LL54 7YF**
**email:** info@plasdinas.co.uk **web:** www.plasdinas.co.uk
**dir:** 3m S of Caernarfon, off A487, 0.5m down private drive

Situated in 15 acres of beautiful grounds in Snowdonia, this delightful Grade II listed building dates back to the mid-17th century, but has many Victorian additions. It was once the home of the Armstrong-Jones family, and there are many family portraits, memorabilia and original pieces of furniture on view. The bedrooms are individually decorated and include four-poster beds along with modern facilities. There is a stylish drawing room where a fire burns in the winter, and fresh local produce features on the dinner menu. Plas Dinas was a finalist for the AA Friendliest B&B of the Year award 2017–18.

**Rooms:** 10 en suite (2 fmly) (1 GF) **Facilities:** FTV Lounge tea/coffee Dinner available Licensed WiFi **Extras:** Speciality toiletries, mini-bar **Conf:** Max 14 Board 14 **Parking:** 16 **Notes:** No children 12yrs Civ wed 32

## Black Boy Inn

★★★★ INN

**tel:** 01286 673604 **LL55 1RW**
**email:** office@black-boy-inn.com **web:** www.black-boy-inn.com
**dir:** A55 junct 9, A487, follow signs for Caernarfon. Inn within town walls between castle & Victoria Dock

Located within Caernarfon's historic town walls, this fine 16th-century inn has low ceilings, narrow staircases and thick wooden beams originally from old ships. It is one of the oldest inns in north Wales, and has a wealth of charm and character. The bedrooms provide modern accommodation, and hearty meals are available in both the restaurant and bar area. On-site parking is available.

**Rooms:** 16 en suite 10 annexe en suite (5 fmly) (3 GF) **Facilities:** FTV tea/coffee Dinner available Direct dial WiFi ♿18 ❄ **Conf:** Max 40 Thtr 40 Class 20 Board 30 **Parking:** 26 **Notes:** LB

## CRICCIETH Map 14 SH43

## Bron Rhiw

★★★★ GUEST ACCOMMODATION

**tel:** 01766 522257 **Caernarfon Road LL52 0AP**
**email:** clairecriccieth@yahoo.co.uk **web:** www. bronrhiwhotel.co.uk
**dir:** From High St onto B4411 & Bron Rhiw is 300yds on right

A warm welcome, and high standards of comfort and facilities are assured at Bron Rhiw, a constantly improving Victorian property, just a short walk from the seafront. Bedrooms are equipped with lots of thoughtful extras and ground-floor areas include a sumptuous lounge, a cosy bar, and an elegant dining room, the setting for imaginative breakfasts.

**Rooms:** 9 en suite **S** £51–£61; **D** £80–£83* **Facilities:** FTV Lounge tea/coffee Licensed WiFi ❄ **Parking:** 3 **Notes:** LB No children 10yrs Closed Nov–Feb

## Premier Collection

## Tyddynmawr Farmhouse

★★★★★ FARMHOUSE

**tel:** 01341 422331 **Cader Road, Islawrdref LL40 1TL**
**email:** olwynevans@btconnect.com **web:** www.wales-guesthouse.co.uk
**dir:** *From town centre left at top of square, left at garage into Cader Rd for 3m. 1st farm on left after Gwernan Lake*

A warm welcome is assured at this 18th-century farmhouse which lies at the foot of Cader Idris amid breathtaking scenery. The bedrooms are spacious and have Welsh oak furniture; the upper room has a balcony and the ground-floor room has a patio area. The bathrooms are large and luxurious. Breakfast offers an excellent choice of home-made items including bread, preserves, muesli or smoked fish. Self-catering cottages are also available.

**Rooms:** 2 en suite (1 GF) **S** £65; **D** £86* **Facilities:** Lounge TVL tea/coffee WiFi
⚓ **Parking:** 8 **Notes:** No children Closed Dec–Jan 800 acres beef/sheep

## Dolgun Uchaf Guesthouse

★★★★ GUEST HOUSE

**tel:** 01341 422269 **Dolgun Uchaf LL40 2AB**
**email:** dolgunuchaf@aol.com **web:** www.guesthousessnowdonia.com
**dir:** *Exit A470 at Little Chef just S of Dolgellau. Dolgun Uchaf 1st property on right*

Located in a peaceful area with stunning views of the surrounding countryside this 500-year-old was a rich history as a Quaker meeting place. The house retains many original features including exposed beams and open fireplaces. The bedrooms, some in the house and others with external access are well-equipped. Ample parking onsite, a lounge for guests and a spacious breakfast room complete the facilities.

**Rooms:** 3 en suite 1 annexe en suite (1 GF) **Facilities:** TVL tea/coffee Dinner available WiFi ⚓ **Parking:** 6 **Notes:** No children 5yrs

## Cadwgan Inn

★★★★ INN

**tel:** 01341 247240 **LL44 2HA**
**email:** cadwgan.hotel@virgin.net **web:** www.cadwganhotel.co.uk
**dir:** *In Dyffryn Ardudwy into Station Rd, over railway crossing*

Privately-owned Cadwgan Inn stands in its own grounds, a stone's throw from Dyffryn Ardudwy station, between Barmouth and Harlech. With the beach just a short walk away, this well-equipped and modern accommodation includes family rooms and a luxury four-poster bedroom. Public areas include an attractive dining room and popular bar, serving honest pub food. Families are ably catered for.

**Rooms:** 6 en suite (3 fmly) **Facilities:** TVL tea/coffee Dinner available Gym Pool table
**Notes:** LB Civ wed 60

## LLANBEDR
Map 14 SH52

### Victoria Inn
★★★★ INN

tel: 01341 241213 **LL45 2LD**
email: junevicinn@aol.com web: www.vic-inn.co.uk
dir: *In village centre*

A former coaching inn, the Victoria Inn lies beside the River Artro in a very pretty village. Many original features remain, including the Settle bar with its flagstone floor, black polished fireplace and unusual circular wooden settle. The menu is extensive and is supplemented by blackboard specials. Bedrooms are spacious and thoughtfully furnished.

**Rooms:** 5 en suite (1 fmly) **Facilities:** FTV tea/coffee Dinner available 🛇
**Conf:** Max 40 **Parking:** 75 **Notes:** LB

## PORTHMADOG
Map 14 SH53

### Tudor Lodge
★★★★ GUEST ACCOMMODATION

tel: 01766 515530 **Tan-Yr-Onnen, Penamser Road LL49 9NY**
email: res@tudorlodge.co.uk web: www.tudorlodge.co.uk
dir: *From main Porthmadog rdbt into Criccieth Rd, house 40mtrs on left*

Tudor Lodge is a large property conveniently situated within a short walk of the town centre. It has good quality, modern accommodation. Separate tables are provided in the breakfast room, where a substantial self-service continental breakfast buffet is provided. There is also a pleasant garden for guests to use.

**Rooms:** 13 en suite (6 GF) **S** £54–£59; **D** £84–£110 **Facilities:** STV tea/coffee WiFi
⚡18 🛇 **Parking:** 25 **Notes:** LB No children 14yrs

## PWLLHELI
Map 14 SH33

### Premier Collection

### The Old Rectory
★★★★★ BED AND BREAKFAST

tel: 01758 721519 **Boduan LL53 6DT**
email: theashcrofts@theoldrectory.net web: www.theoldrectory.net
dir: *From Pwllheli take A497 signed Nefyn. Continue 3m, after villlage sign for Boduan turn left. 1st house on right*

The Old Rectory is a lovely Georgian property set in delightful grounds. Ideally located for the marina in Abersoch, it is centrally placed for walkers on the Welsh Coast Path. The proprietors take great pride in their home and provide very well appointed bedrooms, spacious public areas and super gardens.

Breakfast is also a delight, featuring local produce and taken at a large communal table in the dining room.

**Rooms:** 4 en suite (1 fmly) **S** £80–£95; **D** £90–£115* **Facilities:** FTV TVL tea/coffee WiFi ⚡18 🛇 **Extras:** Chocolates, sherry **Conf:** Max 8 Board 8 **Parking:** 6
**Notes:** LB Closed 24–27 Dec

## MERTHYR TYDFIL

### MERTHYR TYDFIL
Map 9 SO00

### The Mount Pleasant Inn
★★★★ GUEST HOUSE

tel: 01443 693555 & 07918 763640 **Mount Pleasant CF48 4TD**
email: jwacmorgan@aol.com web: www.themountpleasantinn.co.uk
dir: *A470 at Abercynnon rdbt onto A4054 towards Aberfan. 2.5m to Mount Pleasant*

With pleasant views across the valley, this friendly and welcoming guest house provides a relaxed and homely ambience. Bedrooms offer a range of shapes and sizes and are well equipped. Mount Pleasant is fully licensed, and dinner is available to residents; good quality, home-cooked dishes are on offer. Guests may enjoy a drink on the outdoor seating terrace to the rear of the property or choose to laze in the outdoor spa pool.

**Rooms:** 5 en suite (1 fmly) **Facilities:** STV FTV DVD Lounge TVL tea/coffee Dinner available Licensed WiFi 🛇 Heated spa pool **Extras:** Speciality toiletries – complimentary **Notes:** Closed 23 Dec–2 Jan

## PONTSTICILL
Map 9 SO01

### Penrhadw Farm
★★★★ GUEST HOUSE

tel: 01685 723481 & 07733 327871 **CF48 2TU**
email: treghotel@aol.com web: www.penrhadwfarm.co.uk
dir: *5m N of Merthyr Tydfil*

Expect a warm welcome at this 19th-century former farmhouse in the glorious Brecon Beacons National Park. The house is appointed to provide quality modern accommodation. The well-equipped, spacious bedrooms include two large suites in cottages adjacent to the main building. There is also a comfortable lounge. Separate tables are provided in the cosy breakfast room.

**Rooms:** 5 en suite 5 annexe en suite (5 fmly) (1 GF) **S** £45–£55* **Facilities:** FTV TVL tea/coffee Dinner available WiFi ⚡18 🛇 **Conf:** Max 10 Thtr 10 Class 10 **Parking:** 22
**Notes:** LB

## MONMOUTHSHIRE

### ABERGAVENNY
Map 9 SO21

### The Abergavenny
★★★★ GUEST ACCOMMODATION

tel: 01873 859050 **21 Monmouth Road NP7 5HF**
email: mail@abergavennyhotel.com web: www.abergavennyhotel.com

Located just a few minutes' stroll from the sister accommodation (the popular Angel Hotel), this relaxing guest accommodation offers high quality bedrooms and bathrooms in a range of shapes and sizes. Guests may enjoy a drink in the bar where a good selection of wines, beers and cocktails are available before wandering up the High Street where an array of local restaurants are available. Breakfast here is a self-service continental-style operation. The adjacent car park is a welcome addition.

**Rooms:** 20 en suite **Facilities:** Licensed

## LLANDOGO
Map 4 SO50

## The Sloop Inn
★★★★ INN

**tel:** 01594 530291 **NP25 4TW**
**email:** thesloopinn@btinternet.com **web:** www.thesloopinn.co.uk
**dir:** On A466 in village centre

This welcoming inn is centrally located in the village of Llandogo, close to the River Wye in an outstandingly beautiful valley. The Sloop Inn offers a selection of traditional food, as well as friendly hospitality. The dining room has delightful views over the valley, and the spacious bedrooms and bathrooms are equipped for both business and leisure guests.

**Rooms:** 4 en suite (1 fmly) **Facilities:** tea/coffee Dinner available Pool table **Parking:** 50 **Notes:** LB RS Mon–Fri closed between 3pm–6pm

## MONMOUTH
Map 10 SO51

## Inn at Penallt
★★★★ INN

**tel:** 01600 772765 **Penallt NP25 4SE**
**email:** cnquiries@theinnatpenallt.co.uk **web:** www.theinnatpenallt.co.uk

Now under new management this village inn offers a traditional style pub with relaxed and welcoming hospitality and a good range of real ales and ciders. Popular themed or village menus are often available providing a range of tempting dishes which can be enjoyed in the bar or the conservatory. Bedrooms are well decorated and are all located above the inn. The pleasant rear garden includes seating where the delightful views over the surrounding countryside can be enjoyed.

**Rooms:** 4 en suite **Facilities:** Dinner available

## #7 Church Street
★★★★ ◉◉ RESTAURANT WITH ROOMS

**tel:** 01600 712600 **7 Church Street NP25 3BX**
**email:** enquiries@numbersevenchurchstreet.co.uk
**web:** www.numbersevenchurchstreet.co.uk
**dir:** From S on A40, at lights left turn, at T-junct left turn, 2nd right, at rear of car park

Located in the centre of Monmouth #7 Church Street is open for light lunches and dinner and is popular with both guests and locals. Award-winning food is prepared with care and an emphasis on local sourcing and seasonality. Rooms are located above the restaurant and vary in size and shape, a comfortable private guest lounge is also available.

**Rooms:** 8 en suite (2 fmly) **Facilities:** FTV DVD TVL tea/coffee Dinner available WiFi 🔒 **Notes:** Closed 25–26 Dec

## Church Farm Guest House
★★★ GUEST HOUSE

**tel:** 01600 712176 **Mitchel Troy NP25 4HZ**
**email:** info@churchfarmguesthouse.eclipse.co.uk
**web:** www.churchfarmmitcheltroy.co.uk
**dir:** From A40 S, left onto B4293 for Trelleck before tunnel, 150yds turn left and follow signs to Mitchel Troy. Guest House on main road on left, 200yds beyond campsite

Located in the village of Mitchel Troy, this 16th-century former farmhouse retains many original features including exposed beams and open fireplaces. There is a range of bedrooms and a spacious lounge, and breakfast is served in the traditionally furnished dining room. Dinner is available by prior arrangement.

**Rooms:** 8 rms (6 en suite) (2 pri facs) (3 fmly) **S** £37–£38; **D** £74–£76 **Facilities:** FTV Lounge TVL tea/coffee Dinner available WiFi 🔒 **Parking:** 12 **Notes:** LB Closed Xmas

## ROCKFIELD
Map 9 SO41

## The Stonemill & Steppes Farm Cottages
★★★★ ◉◉ RESTAURANT WITH ROOMS

**tel:** 01600 775424 **NP25 5SW**
**email:** bookings@thestonemill.co.uk **web:** www.steppesfarmcottages.co.uk
**dir:** A48 to Monmouth, take B4233 to Rockfield. 2.6m

Located in a small hamlet just west of Monmouth, close to the Forest of Dean and the Wye Valley, this operation offers accommodation comprising six very well-appointed cottages. The comfortable rooms (available for self-catering or on a B&B basis) have been lovingly restored to retain many original features. In a separate, converted 16th-century barn is Stonemill Restaurant with oak beams, vaulted ceilings and an old cider press. Breakfast is served in the cottages on request. This establishment's location proves handy for golfers, with a choice of many courses in the area.

**Rooms:** 6 en suite (6 fmly) (6 GF) **Facilities:** FTV DVD TVL tea/coffee Dinner available WiFi ⚓18 (Free golf) 🔒 **Conf:** Max 60 Thtr 60 Class 56 Board 40 **Parking:** 53 **Notes:** LB Civ wed 120

## TINTERN PARVA — Map 4 SO50

### Parva Farmhouse Riverside Guest House

★★★★ 🏠 GUEST HOUSE

tel: 01291 689411 **Monmouth Road NP16 6SQ**
email: parvahoteltintern@hotmail.co.uk **web:** www.parvafarmhouse.co.uk
dir: *On A466 at N edge of Tintern. Next to St Michael's Church on the riverside*

Parva Farmhouse is a relaxed and friendly family-run guest house, situated on a sweep of the River Wye with far-reaching views of the valley. Dating from the 17th century, this establishment has many excellent features, providing character and comfort in an informal atmosphere. The cosy Inglenook Restaurant is the place for quality ingredients at breakfast and dinner. The individually designed bedrooms are tastefully decorated and enjoy pleasant views; one has a four-poster.

**Rooms:** 8 en suite (2 fmly) **S** £68–£80; **D** £80–£95* **Facilities:** FTV Lounge tea/coffee Dinner available Licensed WiFi 🐾 **Parking:** 8 **Notes:** No children 12yrs

## USK — Map 9 SO30

### Premier Collection

### Newbridge on Usk

★★★★★ 🌹🌹 🍴 RESTAURANT WITH ROOMS

tel: 01633 451000 & 410262 **Tredunnock NP15 1LY**
email: bookings@celtic-manor.com **web:** www.celtic-manor.com
dir: *M4 junct 24, signed Newport, onto B4236. At Ship Inn turn right, over mini rdbt onto Llangybi/Usk road. Turn right opposite Cwrt Bleddyn Hotel, signed Tredunnock, through village & down hill*

This cosy country house is tucked away in a beautiful village setting alongside the River Usk. The well-equipped bedrooms, in a separate building, provide comfort and a good range of extras. Guests can eat at rustic tables around the bar or in the upstairs dining room where award-winning, seasonal food is served; there is also a small private dining room. Breakfast is one of the highlights of a stay with quality local ingredients offered in abundance.

**Rooms:** 6 en suite (2 fmly) (4 GF) **S** fr £60; **D** fr £89 (room only)* **Facilities:** STV FTV DVD tea/coffee Dinner available Direct dial WiFi 🐾 ⛳ ⚓18 Fishing Gym Facilities available at Celtic Manor Resort **Extras:** Speciality toiletries – complimentary **Conf:** Max 14 Thtr 14 Class 14 Board 14 **Parking:** 60 **Notes:** LB Civ wed 80

## WHITEBROOK — Map 4 SO50

### Premier Collection

### The Whitebrook

★★★★★ 🌹🌹🌹🌹 🍴 RESTAURANT WITH ROOMS

tel: 01600 860254 **NP25 4TX**
email: info@thewhitebrook.co.uk **web:** www.thewhitebrook.co.uk
dir: *4m from Monmouth on B4293, left at sign to Whitebrook, 2m on unclassified road, The Whitebook on right*

Peacefully located and surrounded by woods and rivers, this delightful restaurant with rooms offers a peaceful escape. All the bedrooms are located above the main restaurant and come in a range of shapes and sizes. All are very comfortably decorated and furnished. The four AA Rosette award-winning food makes great use of the finest local produce and the relaxing surroundings and friendly service provide a memorable dining experience.

**Rooms:** 8 en suite **S** £105–£190; **D** £130–£215* **Facilities:** FTV Lounge tea/coffee Dinner available Direct dial WiFi **Extras:** Speciality toiletries, Welsh cakes **Parking:** 20 **Notes:** No children 12yrs Closed 2–15 Jan

## NEATH PORT TALBOT

## NEATH — Map 9 SS79

### Cwmbach Cottages Guest House

★★★★ GUEST HOUSE

tel: 01639 639825 **Cwmbach Road, Cadoxton SA10 8AH**
email: l.morgan5@btinternet.com **web:** www.cwmbachguesthouse.co.uk
dir: *1.5m NE of Neath. A465 onto A474 & A4230 towards Aberdulais, left opposite Cadoxton church, guest house signed*

This terrace of former miners' cottages has been restored to provide a range of thoughtfully furnished bedrooms, with one on the ground floor for easier access. Spacious public areas include a comfortable lounge and a pleasant breakfast room with separate tables. A superb decked patio overlooks a wooded hillside rich with wildlife.

**Rooms:** 5 en suite (2 fmly) (1 GF) **S** £44–£94* **Facilities:** FTV DVD iPod docking station Lounge TVL tea/coffee WiFi ⚓18 🐾 **Parking:** 13 **Notes:** LB

## PEMBROKESHIRE

### EGLWYSWRW
Map 8 SN13

#### Premier Collection

## Ael y Bryn
★★★★★ ⬕ ⬤ BED AND BREAKFAST

**tel:** 01239 891411 **SA41 3UL**
**email:** stay@aelybrynpembrokeshire.co.uk **web:** www.aelybrynpembrokeshire.co.uk
**dir:** *In Eglwyswrw at junct of B4332 & A487 turn right signed Cardigan. Left after car park, 0.5 on left*

Set in beautiful countryside between Cardigan and Fishguard, a mere four miles from the coastal path, Ael y Bryn is a long, single-storey building that offers impressive levels of accommodation. Obviously, all rooms are on the ground floor, meaning access is easy for all. Alongside the four luxurious bedrooms, guests have use of a conservatory, a lounge/music room, a library, an inner courtyard and a delightful garden. Breakfast and evening meals – available with prior notice - are served in the attractive dining room. Cyclists and walkers are welcome and safe storage and drying space is provided. Ael y Bryn was a finalist for the AA Friendliest B&B of the Year award 2017–18.

**Rooms:** 4 en suite (4 GF) **D** £105–£140* **Facilities:** FTV Lounge tea/coffee Dinner available WiFi 🛇 **Extras:** Fresh milk, mini-fridge – complimentary **Parking:** 4 **Notes:** No children 14yrs Closed mid Dec–mid Jan

### FISHGUARD
Map 8 SM93

#### Premier Collection

## Erw-Lon Farm
★★★★★ ⬕ FARMHOUSE

**tel:** 01348 881297 **Pontfaen SA65 9TS**
**email:** lilwenmcallister@btinternet.com **web:** www.erwlonfarm.co.uk
**dir:** *5.5m SE of Fishguard on B4313*

Located in the Pembrokeshire Coast National Park, with stunning views of the Gwaun Valley, this attractive farmhouse has been converted to provide modern well-equipped bedrooms with a wealth of homely extras. The McAllisters give the warmest of welcomes, and their memorable dinners feature the finest local produce.

**Rooms:** 3 en suite **S** £55–£60; **D** £75–£80* **Facilities:** FTV TVL tea/coffee Dinner available WiFi 🛇 **Parking:** 5 **Notes:** LB No children 10yrs Closed Dec–Mar 128 acres beef/sheep

## Cefn-y-Dre
★★★★ ⬕ BED AND BREAKFAST

**tel:** 01348 875663 **Cefyn-y-Dre House SA65 9QS**
**email:** welcome@cefnydre.co.uk **web:** www.cefnydre.co.uk
**dir:** *On A40 in Scleddau turn opposite Gate Inn. Pass garden centre on left, 200yds turn right into No Through Rd*

Perched in delightful countryside along the end of a winding lane, this peaceful accommodation is located approximately a mile above the town and harbour of Fishguard. Bedrooms and bathrooms are very well decorated and furnished and include some welcome extras. Breakfast makes use of high quality ingredients and offers a number of daily specials. The owners offer a very friendly and relaxed style of accommodation with tea and cake offered on arrival. Guests are welcome to use the lounge and play the piano if the mood takes them.

**Rooms:** 3 rms (2 en suite) (1 pri facs) **S** £70; **D** £99–£109* **Facilities:** FTV Lounge tea/coffee Dinner available Licensed WiFi 🐾 🛇 **Parking:** 8 **Notes:** LB

## HAVERFORDWEST
Map 8 SM91

### Premier Collection

## Roch Castle

★★★★★ ⊕ GUEST ACCOMMODATION

tel: 01437 725566 **Roch SA62 6AQ**
email: stay@rochcastle.com **web:** www.rochcastle.com

Be the king of the castle at Roch Castle, a unique property dating back to the 12th century. Ideally located with 360-degree views over St Brides Bay and the Preselli Hills, its just a short drive from the smallest city in Wales, St Davids and the larger town of Haverfordwest. Sympathetically restored, the quality here is unrivalled, its fully hypo allergenic throughout. Staying at Roch Castle is an experience and the professional team are on hand to make the most of your stay. Included in the stay are transfers to the sister property Twr Y Felin with its excellent restaurant.

*Roch Castle*

**Rooms:** 6 en suite **D** £210–£250* **Facilities:** STV FTV DVD iPod docking station Lounge TVL tea/coffee Direct dial Licensed WiFi **Extras:** Speciality toiletries – complimentary; honesty bar – chargeable **Conf:** Max 18 Class 12 Board 18 **Parking:** 10 **Notes:** LB No children 12yrs Civ wed 18

---

## Premier Collection

### Slebech Park Estate

★★★★★  RESTAURANT WITH ROOMS

**tel:** 01437 752000 & 752002 **SA62 4AX**
**email:** enquiries@slebech.co.uk **web:** www.slebech.co.uk
**dir:** E of Haverfordwest on A40, take exit signed Picton Castle

A delightful and peaceful retreat located on the shores of Dau Cleddau Estuary
– one of Europe's largest natural harbours. The estate covers 650 acres, with an
array of walks from the door through meadows, woodlands and the riverside.
Guests are ensured a warm welcome and excellent service throughout their stay.
Bedrooms offer a range of shapes and sizes – all full of quality. Both the award-
winning dinner and breakfast are served in the separate restaurant, and offer a
range of carefully prepared dishes making use of top quality local produce.
Lunch and afternoon tea are also available.

**Rooms:** 19 en suite (5 fmly) (7 GF) **S** £72.95–£142.50; **D** £85–£180*
**Facilities:** STV FTV Lounge tea/coffee Dinner available Direct dial WiFi 🦢 🦆 ⚓18
Fishing 🔫 Shooting **Extras:** Speciality toiletries, home-made cakes **Conf:** Max 200
Thtr 200 Class 180 Board 160 **Parking:** 60 **Notes:** LB Civ wed 120

*See advert opposite*

### College Guest House

★★★★ GUEST HOUSE

**tel:** 01437 763710 **93 Hill Street, St Thomas Green SA61 1QL**
**email:** colinlarby@aol.com **web:** www.collegeguesthouse.com
**dir:** In town centre, along High St, pass church, keep in left lane. 1st exit by Stonemason
Arms pub, follow signs for St Thomas Green/Leisure Centre/Police Station. 300mtrs on left
by No Entry sign

Situated in a mainly residential area within easy walking distance of
Haverdfordwest's attractions, this impressive Georgian house offers good levels of
comfort and facilities. There is a range of practically equipped bedrooms, along
with public areas that include a spacious lounge (with internet access) and an
attractive pine-furnished dining room – the setting for comprehensive breakfasts.

**Rooms:** 8 en suite (4 fmly) **Facilities:** FTV DVD TVL tea/coffee WiFi

**KILGETTY** | Map 8 SN10

### The Begelly Arms

★★★ INN

**tel:** 01834 812601 **New Road SA68 0YF**
**email:** info@begellyarms.co.uk **web:** www.begellyarms.co.uk
**dir:** On A40 at St Clears rdbt onto A477, signed Tenby/Pembroke Dock. At next rdbt take
3rd exit signed Kilgetty, into village, on left

Being located very close to Oakwood Theme Park, this is a popular inn with
families. Rooms are located in two areas – some above the main inn and others in
an adjacent block. Food is served throughout the day and children are well catered
for in terms of menus and the garden to the rear of the building. Function rooms
are also available and a large car park is provided.

**Rooms:** 7 en suite (1 fmly) **S** fr £60; **D** £70–£80* **Facilities:** STV FTV DVD tea/coffee
Dinner available WiFi ⚓18 Pool table 🅿 **Parking:** 60 **Notes:** LB

## MANORBIER
Map 8 SS09

### Castlemead
★★★★ 🍴 RESTAURANT WITH ROOMS

**tel:** 01834 871358 **SA70 7TA**
**email:** castlemeadhotel@aol.com **web:** www.castlemeadhotel.com
**dir:** *A4139 towards Pembroke, B4585 into village, follow signs to beach & castle, establishment on left*

Benefiting from a superb location with spectacular views of the bay, the Norman church and Manorbier Castle, this family-run business is friendly and welcoming. Bedrooms, which include some in a converted former coach house at ground floor level, are generally quite spacious and have modern facilities. Public areas include a sea-view residents' lounge and a restaurant accessed by stairs, which is open to non-residents, along with a cosy bar. There are extensive gardens to the rear of the property.

**Rooms:** 5 en suite 3 annexe en suite (2 fmly) (3 GF) **Facilities:** FTV Lounge tea/coffee Dinner available Direct dial WiFi 🔒 **Parking:** 20 **Notes:** Closed Jan–Feb RS Nov maybe B&B only

## NEWPORT
Map 8 SN03

### Llys Meddyg
★★★★ ❁❁ 🍷 RESTAURANT WITH ROOMS

**tel:** 01239 820008 **East Street SA42 0SY**
**email:** info@llysmeddyg.com **web:** www.llysmeddyg.com
**dir:** *On A487 in centre of town*

Llys Meddyg is a Georgian town house offering a blend of old and new, with elegant furnishings, deep sofas and a welcoming fire. The owners of the property employed local craftsmen to create a lovely interior that has an eclectic style. The focus of the quality restaurant menu is on fresh, seasonal, locally sourced ingredients. The spacious bedrooms are comfortable and contemporary in design; bathrooms vary in style.

**Rooms:** 5 en suite 3 annexe en suite (3 fmly) (1 GF) **Facilities:** FTV DVD iPod docking station Lounge tea/coffee Dinner available WiFi ⚓18 🔒 **Extras:** Speciality toiletries, mini-bar **Conf:** Max 20 Class 20 Board 20 **Parking:** 8 **Notes:** LB Civ wed 90

### Salutation Inn
★★★ ⓐ INN

**tel:** 01239 820564 & 07793 488262 **Filindre Farchog SA41 3UY**
**email:** johndenley@aol.com **web:** www.salutationcountryhotel.co.uk
**dir:** *On A487 between Cardigan & Fishguard. 3m N of Newport*

John and Gwawr Denley offer a warm welcome at this 16th-century coaching inn in the heart of the Pembrokeshire Coast National Park. The old part of the inn blends well with the modern and well equipped bedrooms. The two bars have oak beams and an old country atmosphere. The inn overlooks lawned gardens that lead down to the river. All bedrooms are on the ground floor, en suite, and equipped with TV.

**Rooms:** 8 en suite (2 fmly) (8 GF) **Facilities:** FTV tea/coffee Dinner available Direct dial WiFi ⚓18 Pool table **Conf:** Max 25 Thtr 25 Class 12 Board 12 **Parking:** 60 **Notes:** LB

## ST DAVIDS
Map 8 SM72

### Penrhiw
★★★★★ GUEST ACCOMMODATION

**tel:** 01437 725588 & 725555 **SA62 6PG**
**email:** stay@penrhiwhotel.com **web:** www.penrhiwhotel.com

Penrhiw was originally built as a Vicarage for the Church of Wales in 1884. This property is a fine example of Victorian architecture and over the years has been used for many things from a Priory to a Retreat. Ideally located in the centre of St Davids, the smallest city in Wales, the property has now been fully refurbished and offers a calming and relaxing luxury accommodation. The property has been designed to be completely hypoallergenic. Transfers are offered from the property to the sister Hotel Twr Y Felin where guests can enjoy an excellent dining experience before being driven back. Breakfast is a treat not be missed and an excellent end to a stay.

**Rooms:** 6 en suite 2 annexe en suite (1 GF) **D** £190–£240* **Facilities:** STV FTV DVD iPod docking station Lounge TVL tea/coffee Direct dial Licensed WiFi **Extras:** Speciality toiletries, fridge – complimentary; honesty bar – chargeable **Conf:** Max 18 Thtr 18 Class 18 Board 18 **Parking:** 8 **Notes:** LB No children 12yrs Civ wed

## Premier Collection

## Ramsey House
★★★★★ 🕯 GUEST HOUSE

**tel:** 01437 720321 & 07795 575005 **Lower Moor SA62 6RP**
**email:** info@ramseyhouse.co.uk **web:** www.ramseyhouse.co.uk
**dir:** *From Cross Sq in St Davids towards Porthclais, house 0.25m on left*

This pleasant guest house, under the ownership of Suzanne and Shaun Ellison, offers the ideal combination of professional management and the warmth of a family-run guest house. The property is quietly located on the outskirts of St Davids, and is surrounded by unspoilt countryside. It provides modern, well-equipped bedrooms, most with en suite bathrooms, along with a good range of welcome extras. Breakfast provides a choice of home-made items, including breads and preserves. Ramsey House was a finalist for the AA Friendliest B&B of the Year award 2017–18.

**Rooms:** 6 rms (5 en suite) (1 pri facs) (3 GF) **S** £70–£120; **D** £100–£130*
**Facilities:** FTV Lounge tea/coffee Licensed WiFi 🔔 **Extras:** Speciality toiletries – complimentary: Fruit, wine, flowers – chargeable **Parking:** 10 **Notes:** LB No children 16yrs Closed Nov–13 Feb

## The Waterings
★★★★ BED AND BREAKFAST

**tel:** 01437 720876 **Anchor Drive, High Street SA62 6QH**
**email:** enquiries@waterings.co.uk **web:** www.watcrings.co.uk
**dir:** *On A487 on E edge of St Davids*

Situated a short walk from the centre of St Davids, The Waterings offers spacious bedrooms that are accessed from a courtyard garden; most bedrooms have their own separate seating area. Breakfast, made from a good selection of local produce, is served in a smart dining room in the main house.

**Rooms:** 2 en suite 5 annexe en suite (4 fmly) (5 GF) **S** £55–£80; **D** £75–£100*
**Facilities:** FTV tea/coffee Licensed WiFi 🔔 ♿9 **Conf:** Max 15 Board 15 **Parking:** 20
**Notes:** No children 5yrs

## The City Inn
★★★ INN

**tel:** 0845 347 3102 *(Calls cost 7p per minute plus your phone company's access charge)*
& 01437 720829 **New Street SA62 6SU**
**email:** info@cityinnstdavids.co.uk **web:** www.cityinnstdavids.co.uk

Located just 10 minutes' walk from St Davids Cathedral and even closer to the main town, this well-furnished accommodation provides a relaxed and informal atmosphere. Guests can choose from a range of bar and restaurant menus at both dinner and lunch. Meals are served in the spacious lounge or the main dining room. The car park is a welcome feature.

**Rooms:** 9 en suite (5 fmly) **Facilities:** FTV Dinner available WiFi ♿9 Pool table
🔔 **Parking:** 12 **Notes:** Closed 23–26 Dec

## SOLVA                                        Map 8 SM82

### Premier Collection

## Crug Glas Country House

★★★★★ ◉ ⌣ RESTAURANT WITH ROOMS

**tel:** 01348 831302 **Abereiddy SA62 6XX**
**email:** janet@crug-glas.co.uk **web:** www.crug-glas.co.uk
**dir:** *From Solva to St Davids on A487. From St Davids take A487 towards Fishguard. 1st left after Carnhedryn, house signed*

This house, on a dairy, beef and cereal farm of approximately 600 acres, is situated about a mile from the coast on the St Davids Peninsula. Comfort, relaxation and flawless attention to detail are provided by the charming host, Janet Evans. Each spacious bedroom has the hallmark of assured design plus a luxury bathroom with both bath and shower; one suite on the top floor has great views. In addition there are two suites in separate buildings.

**Rooms:** 7 en suite (1 fmly) (2 GF) **Facilities:** FTV Lounge tea/coffee Dinner available WiFi ⚓ **Extras:** Speciality toiletries **Conf:** Max 200 Thtr 200 Class 200 Board 200 **Parking:** 10 **Notes:** No children 12yrs Closed 22–29 Dec Civ wed 220

## TENBY                                        Map 8 SN10

### Premier Collection

## Trefloyne Manor

★★★★★ ◉ GUEST ACCOMMODATION

**tel:** 01834 842165 & 844429 **Trefloyne Lane, Penally SA70 7RG**
**email:** tom.benyon@trefloyne.com **web:** www.trefloyne.com
**dir:** *A478 to Tenby onto A4139 signed Penally. Turn right opposite Kiln Park Garage, then 1st right to Trefloyne, 150 mtrs along Trefloyne Ln turn left into Trefloyne Manor*

Delightfully located in a peaceful valley, surrounded by an 18-hole golf course, this relaxing accommodation offers an excellent range of high quality bedrooms and bathrooms. Some rooms are in the main house while others are in an adjacent coach house – decorated to very high standards including a number of suites. Both dinner and breakfast use local produce and are served in the light and airy conservatory overlooking the golf course.

**Rooms:** 5 en suite 7 annexe en suite (4 fmly) (3 GF) **Facilities:** FTV iPod docking station Lounge TVL tea/coffee Dinner available Licensed WiFi ♪18 ⚓ **Extras:** Speciality toiletries, home-made biscuits **Conf:** Max 60 Thtr 60 Class 60 Board 40 **Parking:** 150 **Notes:** LB Closed 25 Dec Civ wed 110

## Esplanade

★★★★ GUEST ACCOMMODATION

**tel:** 01834 842760 & 843333 **1 The Esplanade SA70 7DU**
**email:** esplanadetenby@googlemail.com **web:** www.esplanadetenby.co.uk
**dir:** *Follow signs to South Beach, exit South Parade into St Florence Parade. Premises on seafront adjacent to town walls*

Located beside the historic town walls of Tenby, with stunning views over the sea to Caldey Island, the Esplanade provides a range of standard and luxury bedrooms, some ideal for families. Breakfast is offered in the elegant front-facing dining room, which contains a comfortable lounge-bar area.

**Rooms:** 14 en suite (4 fmly) (1 GF) **S** £55–£120; **D** £75–£130* **Facilities:** FTV DVD Lounge tea/coffee Direct dial Licensed WiFi ⚓ **Extras:** Mineral water – complimentary **Notes:** LB Closed 15 Dec–6 Jan

## POWYS

## BRECON                                        Map 9 S002

### Premier Collection

## Peterstone Court

★★★★★ ◉ ⌣ RESTAURANT WITH ROOMS

**tel:** 01874 665387 **Llanhamlach LD3 7YB**
**email:** info@peterstone-court.com **web:** www.peterstone-court.com
**dir:** *3m from Brecon on A40 towards Abergavenny*

Situated on the edge of the Brecon Beacons, this establishment affords stunning views overlooking the River Usk. The atmosphere is friendly and informal, with no unnecessary fuss. No two bedrooms are alike, but all share comparable levels of comfort, quality and elegance. Public areas reflect similar standards, eclectically styled with a blend of the contemporary and the traditional. Quality produce is cooked with care in a range of enjoyable dishes.

**Rooms:** 8 en suite 4 annexe en suite (2 fmly) **Facilities:** FTV DVD iPod docking station Lounge tea/coffee Dinner available Direct dial WiFi ⌁ Fishing Gym ⚓ Pool open mid Apr-1 Oct Spa facilities **Conf:** Max 100 Thtr 100 Class 100 Board 60 **Parking:** 60 **Notes:** LB Civ wed

## BUILTH WELLS                                        Map 9 S005

## Rhedyn Guest House

★★★★ ⌣ ⌣ GUEST HOUSE

**tel:** 01982 551944 & 07703 209721 **Rhedyn, Cilmery LD2 3LH**
**email:** info@rhedynguesthouse.co.uk **web:** www.rhedynguesthouse.co.uk
**dir:** *From Builth Wells on A483 towards Garth. Rhedyn Guest House on right, through farm gate, closing all gates once through*

This detached property stands just off the main road outside Cilmery, which is a short drive from Builth Wells. Three comfortable bedrooms provide all the modern facilities including WiFi and a range of guest extras. Two bedrooms are on the ground floor with their own entrances. Dinner, bookable at the time of reservation, offers imaginative menus. A hearty breakfast, including a selection of home-made preserves, is served in the delightful dining room around a communal table. Access to the guest house is via two gates through a field.

**Rooms:** 1 en suite 2 annexe en suite (2 GF) **S** £85; **D** £95 **Facilities:** STV FTV DVD Lounge tea/coffee Dinner available WiFi ⚓ **Extras:** Sherry, Welsh cakes – complimentary **Parking:** 3 **Notes:** No children except babies

## CEMMAES — Map 14 SH80

### The Penrhos Arms

★★★★ INN

**tel:** 01650 511243 & 07808 589349 **SY20 9PR**
**email:** dawndavies8@hotmail.com **web:** www.penrhosarms.com

The Penrhos Arms provides a warm welcome to new and returning guests alike, an historic inn with a charming and comfortable interior. Bedrooms are smartly appointed and have very comfortable beds. A hearty range of menu choices are offered, using local produce where possible.

**Rooms:** 5 en suite 2 annexe en suite (1 fmly) **Facilities:** FTV DVD TVL tea/coffee Dinner available WiFi ⅃ Pool table 🔒 **Conf:** Max 40 **Notes:** LB Civ wed 50

## CRICKHOWELL — Map 9 SO21

### The Bear

★★★★ ◉ INN

**tel:** 01873 810408 **High Street NP8 1BW**
**email:** info@bearhotel.co.uk **web:** www.bearhotel.co.uk
**dir:** Town centre, off A40 (Brecon road). 6m from Abergavenny

The Bear is a favourite with locals as well as visitors; the character and friendliness of this 15th-century coaching inn are renowned. The bedrooms come in a variety of sizes and include some with four-posters. The bar and restaurant are furnished in keeping with the style of the building, and provide comfortable areas in which to enjoy some of the very popular dishes that use the finest locally-sourced ingredients, served from a menu to suit all tastes.

**Rooms:** 34 en suite (4 fmly) (6 GF) **Facilities:** FTV Lounge tea/coffee Dinner available Direct dial WiFi Fishing 🔒 **Parking:** 40

## CRIGGION — Map 15 SJ21

### Brimford House

★★★★ FARMHOUSE

**tel:** 01938 570235 **SY5 9AU**
**email:** info@brimford.co.uk **web:** www.brimford.co.uk
**dir:** Exit B4393 after Crew Green left for Criggion, Brimford 1st on left after pub

This elegant Georgian house stands in lovely open countryside and is a good base for touring central Wales and the Marches. The bedrooms are spacious, and thoughtful extras enhance guest comfort. A cheery log fire burns in the lounge during colder weather; the hospitality is equally warm and creates a relaxing atmosphere throughout.

**Rooms:** 3 en suite **S** £50; **D** £75–£85* **Facilities:** FTV TVL tea/coffee WiFi Fishing **Parking:** 4 **Notes:** LB 250 acres arable/beef/sheep

## ERWOOD — Map 9 SO04

### Hafod-y-Garreg

★★★★ ☕ BED AND BREAKFAST

**tel:** 01982 560400 **LD2 3TQ**
**email:** john-annie@hafod-y.wanadoo.co.uk **web:** www.hafodygarreg.co.uk
**dir:** 1m S of Erwood. Off A470 at Trericket Mill, sharp right, up track past cream farmhouse towards pine forest, through gate

This remote Grade II listed farmhouse dates in part from 1401 and has been confirmed, by dendrochronology, as the 'oldest dwelling in Wales'. As you would expect, the house has tremendous character, and is decorated and furnished to befit its age; even so, the bedrooms have all the modern facilities. There is an impressive dining room and a lounge with an open fireplace. Warm hospitality from John and Annie is a major strength here.

**Rooms:** 2 en suite **Facilities:** STV iPod docking station tea/coffee Dinner available WiFi 🔒 **Extras:** Speciality toiletries, sherry, magazines, books – complimentary **Parking:** 6 **Notes:** No children Closed Xmas

## HAY-ON-WYE — Map 9 SO24

*See also Erwood*

### Old Black Lion Inn

★★★★ ◉ INN

**tel:** 01497 820841 **26 Lion Street HR3 5AD**
**email:** info@oldblacklion.co.uk **web:** www.oldblacklion.co.uk
**dir:** From B4348 in Hay-on-Wye into Lion St. Inn on right

This fine old coaching inn, with a history stretching back several centuries, has a wealth of charm and character. It was occupied by Oliver Cromwell during the siege of Hay Castle. Privately owned and personally-run, it provides cosy and well-equipped bedrooms, some located in an adjacent building. A wide range of well-prepared food is provided, and the service is relaxed and friendly.

**Rooms:** 6 rms (5 en suite) (1 pri facs) 4 annexe en suite (2 GF) **S** £55–£66; **D** £89–£125* **Facilities:** FTV Lounge TVL tea/coffee Dinner available Direct dial WiFi 🔒 **Parking:** 12 **Notes:** RS 3–12 Jan Limited services

## LLANDRINDOD WELLS — Map 9 SO06

### Holly Farm

★★★★ FARMHOUSE

**tel:** 01597 822402 **Holly Lane, Howey LD1 5PP**
**email:** ruth@hollyfarmbandb.co.uk **web:** www.hollyfarmbandb.co.uk
**dir:** 2m S on A483 of Llandrindod Wells near Howey

This working farm dates from Tudor times, and is situated with easy access to the larger towns of Builth Wells and Llandrindod Wells. The bedrooms are homely and full of character. A comfortable lounge has a warming log fire in cooler months and pleasant gardens offer a peaceful area to sit in the warmer summer months. A hearty farmhouse breakfast can be enjoyed in the quaint dining room.

**Rooms:** 3 en suite (1 fmly) **S** £44–£48; **D** £72–£76* **Facilities:** FTV DVD TVL tea/coffee WiFi 🔒 **Parking:** 4 **Notes:** LB 70 acres beef/sheep

## LLANGAMMARCH WELLS | Map 9 SN94

### The Cammarch

★★★★ GUEST ACCOMMODATION

**tel:** 01591 620545 **LD4 4BY**
**email:** mail@cammarch.com **web:** www.cammarch.com
**dir:** *Exit A483 at Garth, signed Llangammarch Wells, opposite T-junct*

This property dates from the 1850s and was built as a railway hotel. Owner Kathryn Dangerfield offers a warm welcome to all guests and the establishment provides modern, well-equipped bedrooms that are tastefully decorated. There is a comfortable spacious bar and lounge, with a log-burning fire, ideal for colder evenings. The conservatory dining room, overlooking the attractive gardens and pond, offers fresh local produce on the dinner menu and the hearty Welsh breakfast makes a good start to the day. Parking is provided at the side of the property.

**Rooms:** 12 en suite (3 fmly) **S** £69; **D** £95* **Facilities:** FTV DVD Lounge TVL tea/coffee Dinner available Licensed WiFi Fishing **Extras:** Speciality toiletries **Conf:** Max 20 Thtr 20 Class 15 Board 15 **Parking:** 16 **Notes:** LB RS Xmas-New Year

## LLANGEDWYN | Map 15 SJ12

### Plas Uchaf Country House

★★★★ GUEST HOUSE

**tel:** 01691 780588 & 07817 419747 **SY10 9LD**
**email:** info@plasuchaf.com **web:** www.plasuchaf.com
**dir:** *Mile End services Oswestry A483/Welshpool. After 2m right at White Lion public house, 4.5m Llangedwyn. 150yds after school on right*

Located in an elevated position in extensive mature parkland, this elegant Queen Anne house provides high standards of comfort and facilities. The interior flooring was created from recycled ship timbers taken from the Armada fleet of 1588, and furnishing styles highlight the many period features. Imaginative dinners are available, and a warm welcome is assured.

**Rooms:** 6 en suite (1 fmly) (1 GF) **S** £71.25; **D** £100–£115* **Facilities:** FTV iPod docking station Lounge tea/coffee Dinner available Licensed WiFi **Extras:** Speciality toiletries – complimentary **Conf:** Max 15 Thtr 15 Class 15 Board 15 **Parking:** 30 **Notes:** LB

## LLANGURIG | Map 9 SN97

### The Old Vicarage

★★★★ GUEST HOUSE

**tel:** 01686 440280 **SY18 6RN**
**email:** info@theoldvicaragellangurig.co.uk **web:** www.theoldvicaragellangurig.co.uk
**dir:** *A470 onto A44, signed*

Located in pretty, mature grounds, which feature a magnificent holly tree, this elegant Victorian house provides a range of thoughtfully furnished bedrooms, some with fine period objects. Breakfast is served in a spacious dining room, and a comfortable guest lounge is also available.

**Rooms:** 4 en suite (1 fmly) **Facilities:** DVD TVL tea/coffee Licensed WiFi **Parking:** 6 **Notes:** LB No children 6yrs

## LLANWRTYD WELLS | Map 9 SN84

### Lasswade Country House

★★★★ RESTAURANT WITH ROOMS

**tel:** 01591 610515 **Station Road LD5 4RW**
**email:** info@lasswadehotel.co.uk **web:** www.lasswadehotel.co.uk
**dir:** *Exit A483 into Irfon Terrace, right into Station Rd, 350yds on right*

This friendly establishment on the edge of the town has impressive views over the countryside. Bedrooms are comfortably furnished and well equipped, while the public areas consist of a tastefully decorated lounge, an elegant restaurant with a bar, and an airy conservatory which looks towards the neighbouring hills. The kitchen makes good use of fresh, local produce to provide an enjoyable, award-winning dining experience.

**Rooms:** 8 en suite (1 fmly) **S** £60–£80; **D** £90–£125 **Facilities:** FTV Lounge TVL tea/coffee Dinner available WiFi **Conf:** Max 20 Thtr 20 Class 20 Board 20 **Parking:** 6 **Notes:** LB

## Carlton Riverside

★★★★ ◉◉ RESTAURANT WITH ROOMS

tel: 01591 610248 **Irfon Crescent LD5 4SP**
email: carltonriverside@hotmail.co.uk **web:** www.carltonriverside.co.uk

Located as the name suggests, this pleasant restaurant with rooms offers friendly and personal hospitality and service in a relaxed and comfortable setting. Bedrooms include a range of shapes and sizes and are all comfortably furnished. The real highlight here however is the food; carefully sourced, mainly local and seasonal produce is expertly combined under the guidance of talented new Head Chef Luke Roberts. An interesting wine list accompanies the menu with an especially good selection by the half bottle.

**Rooms:** 4 en suite **Facilities:** FTV Lounge tea/coffee Dinner available WiFi
**Notes:** LB Closed 15–30 Dec

| MONTGOMERY | Map 15 SO29 |
| --- | --- |

### Premier Collection

## The Nags Head Inn

★★★★★ ◉ ⚲ INN

tel: 01686 640600 **Garthmyl SY15 6RS**
email: jdrestaurantsltd@outlook.com **web:** www.nagsheadgarthmyl.co.uk
**dir:** On A483 between Welshpool & Newtown

Once a former coaching inn, The Nags Head continues to offer accommodation for guests but has been bought right up to date. A warm welcome is assured from the friendly team here in this busy inn. Log fires for the winter and a sun soaked terrace for alfresco dining make this a great destination at all times of the year. Dining is not to be missed with a range of imaginative dishes, sitting aside their own take on pub classics. To complement dining, a range of local beers are stocked in addition to a well-chosen wine list.

**Rooms:** 4 en suite **Facilities:** FTV Lounge TVL tea/coffee Dinner available WiFi ♨9
**Conf:** Max 16 **Parking:** 40

| SWANSEA | |
| --- | --- |

| LLANGENNITH | Map 8 SS49 |
| --- | --- |

## Kings Head

★★★★ INN

tel: 01792 386212 **Town House SA3 1HX**
email: info@kingsheadgower.co.uk **web:** www.kingsheadgower.co.uk
**dir:** M4 junct 47 follow signs for Gower A483. At next rdbt, 2nd left follow signs to Gowerton. At lights right onto B495, through old walls, keep left at fork. Kings Head on right

The Kings Head is made up of three 17th-century buildings set behind a splendid rough stone wall; it stands opposite the church in this coastal village. The well-equipped bedrooms, including some on the ground floor, are in two of the buildings. This is an ideal base for exploring the Gower Peninsula, whether for walking, cycling or surfing. Evening meals and breakfasts can be taken in the inn.

**Rooms:** 27 en suite (3 fmly) (14 GF) **S** £99–£150; **D** £99–£150 **Facilities:** FTV tea/coffee Dinner available Direct dial WiFi Pool table ⚐ **Conf:** Max 50 **Parking:** 35
**Notes:** LB Closed 25 Dec RS 24 Dec Closed for check-in

| PARKMILL (NEAR SWANSEA) | Map 8 SS58 |
| --- | --- |

## Parc-le-Breos House

★★★★ FARMHOUSE

tel: 01792 371636 **SA3 2HA**
email: info@parclebreos.co.uk **web:** www.parc-le-breos.co.uk
**dir:** On A4118, right 300yds after Shepherds shop, next left, signed

This imposing, early 19th-century house is at the end of a forest drive and set in over 60 acres of delightful grounds. Many charming original features have been retained in the public rooms, which include a lounge and a games room. The bedrooms have comfortable furnishings, and many are suitable for families. Freshly prepared dinners are not to be missed and afternoon tea on the terrace is a highlight during summer months.

**Rooms:** 10 en suite (7 fmly) (1 GF) **Facilities:** FTV Lounge TVL tea/coffee Dinner available Licensed WiFi Fishing Pool table **Conf:** Max 30 Thtr 30 **Parking:** 12
**Notes:** LB Closed 25–26 Dec 65 acres arable/horses/pigs/chickens

## REYNOLDSTON
Map 8 SS48

### Premier Collection

## Fairyhill

 RESTAURANT WITH ROOMS

**tel:** 01792 390139 **SA3 1BS**
**email:** postbox@fairyhill.net **web:** www.fairyhill.co.uk
**dir:** *M4 junct 47, A483, at next rdbt right onto A484. At Gowerton take B4295 for 10m*

Peace and tranquillity are never far away at this charming Georgian mansion set in the heart of the beautiful Gower Peninsula. Bedrooms are furnished with care and are filled with many thoughtful extras. There is also a range of comfortable seating areas, with crackling log fires, to choose from. The smart restaurant offers menus based on local produce that are complemented by an excellent wine list.

**Rooms:** 8 en suite (8 fmly) **S** fr £200; **D** fr £200 (room only)* **Facilities:** FTV DVD iPod docking station Lounge tea/coffee Dinner available Direct dial WiFi 🕊
**Extras:** Speciality toiletries, home-made Welsh cakes, fruit – complimentary
**Conf:** Max 32 Thtr 32 Board 16 **Parking:** 40 **Notes:** LB Civ wed 100

## Silver Stars

The AA Silver Star rating denotes a B&B that we highly recommend. They have a superior level of quality within their star rating, high standards of hospitality, service and cleanliness.

## SWANSEA
Map 9 SS69

## Hurst Dene Guest House

★★★ GUEST HOUSE

**tel:** 01792 280920 **10 Sketty Road, Uplands SA2 0LJ**
**email:** hurstdenehotel@yahoo.co.uk **web:** www.hurstdene.co.uk
**dir:** *1m W of city centre. A4118 through Uplands shopping area into Sketty Rd, Hurst Dene on right*

This friendly guest house has a private car park and provides soundly maintained bedrooms with modern furnishings and equipment. Facilities include an attractive breakfast room with separate tables and a small comfortable lounge.

**Rooms:** 10 rms (8 en suite) (3 fmly) (1 GF) **Facilities:** FTV TVL tea/coffee WiFi
**Parking:** 7 **Notes:** Closed 22 Dec–1 Jan

## TORFAEN

### PONTYPOOL
Map 9 SO20

## The Lion
★★★★ Ⓐ INN

**tel:** 01495 792516 **41 Broad Street, Blaenavon NP4 9NH**
**email:** info@thelionhotelblaenavon.co.uk **web:** www.thelionhotelblaenavon.co.uk
**dir:** *N of Pontypool, in centre of Blaenavon*

The Lion is set in the beautiful village of Blaenavon, part of a UNESCO World Heritage Site, ideally located for walking and mountain biking in the Brecon Beacons. The restaurant offers a full service from breakfast to dinner, and prides itself on using the best of Welsh produce in its cooking. Rooms at The Lion fuse contemporary chic with classic luxury. Bedrooms all feature en suite bathroom or shower and a wide range of amenities including Freeview TV/DVD, hairdryer, alarm clock, tea- and coffee-making facilities, free WiFi and a choice of pillows.

**Rooms:** 12 en suite (2 fmly) **Facilities:** FTV DVD TVL tea/coffee Dinner available Direct dial WiFi steam room **Notes:** LB

## VALE OF GLAMORGAN

### HENSOL
Map 9 ST07

#### Premier Collection

## Llanerch Vineyard
★★★★★ Ⓐ 🍴 GUEST ACCOMMODATION

**tel:** 01443 222716 **CF72 8GG**
**email:** info@llanerch-vineyard.co.uk **web:** www.llanerch-vineyard.co.uk
**dir:** *M4 junct 34, follow brown tourist signs*

Llanerch Vineyard is delightfully set on a working Welsh vineyard with views over the vines to the countryside beyond. Bedrooms and bathrooms come in a range of shapes and sizes including sumptuously appointed suites in the main building. The Cariad Restaurant & Bistro is open for lunch, afternoon tea and dinner, with outdoor seating on the terrace in the warmer months. The vineyard's own wines are available to purchase in the small shop area, and are also on the wine list at dinner.

**Rooms:** 3 en suite 8 annexe en suite (4 fmly) (7 GF) **D** £125–£200* **Facilities:** FTV TVL tea/coffee Dinner available Direct dial Licensed WiFi ⚓18 Wine tasting & vineyard tour **Extras:** Bottled water – complimentary **Conf:** Max 150 Thtr 150 Class 80 Board 40 **Parking:** 100 **Notes:** LB Civ wed 150

### LLANCARFAN
Map 9 ST07

## The Fox & Hounds
★★★★ INN

**tel:** 01446 781287 **CF62 3AD**
**email:** enquiries@fandhllancarfan.co.uk **web:** www.fandhllancarfan.co.uk
**dir:** *A48, E of Cardiff, towards Cowbridge. Through St Nicholas village, left at lights onto A4226 signed Barry. After 1.5m turn right signed Llancarfan & follow brown tourist sign to Fox & Hounds, over ford on right*

This whitewashed inn has a picture postcard setting in the centre of the village; next to the stream and overlooking the church. The smart terrace is ideal for alfresco dining in the summer, in the winter the log fires inside the pub equally inviting. Dinner, served by the friendly team, showcases locally-sourced ingredients. The bedrooms are tastefully decorated and well equipped for the modern traveller.

**Rooms:** 8 en suite **D** £75–£105* **Facilities:** FTV Dinner available WiFi **Extras:** Speciality toiletries, robes, fresh milk **Conf:** Max 20 **Parking:** 20

### PENARTH
Map 9 ST17

#### Premier Collection

## Restaurant James Sommerin
★★★★★ 🏅🏅🏅 RESTAURANT WITH ROOMS

**tel:** 029 2070 6559 **The Esplanade CF64 3AU**
**email:** info@jamessommerinrestaurant.co.uk
**web:** www.jamessommerinrestaurant.co.uk

Restaurant James Sommerin stands proudly by the Pier in Penarth with unrivalled views across the Bay, just a short distance from Cardiff centre. Cuisine is accomplished and exciting with three different tasting menus offered in addition to the à la carte, showcasing the passion for food from this innovative chef and his team. The latest addition is the accommodation, which offers comfortable, quality facilities for guests wanting to take full advantage of the interesting and extensive wine list. This is truly a family business; the friendly front of house team are under the watchful eye of Louise Sommerin and often their oldest daughter can be seen assisting in the kitchen.

**Rooms:** 9 en suite **S** £120–£150; **D** £150–£170* **Facilities:** FTV tea/coffee Dinner available Direct dial Lift WiFi **Extras:** Bottled water **Conf:** Max 60 **Notes:** LB RS Mon closed

*See advert on following page*

# Restaurant James Sommerin with Rooms

The restaurant opened in May 2014 with its 9 bedrooms only opening in February 2016.

The family run Restaurant with Rooms is situated on the Esplanade in Penarth with panoramic views over the Severn Estuary. James and eldest daughter, Georgia, can be found cooking up a storm in the kitchen and Louise, front of house.

There are 9 en-suite bedrooms, elegantly decorated with 5 benefiting from unobstructed sea views and 4 with views over the courtyard. All rooms benefit from flat screen Freeview TVs, hot drinks tray, complimentary water and toiletries. All rooms are accessible via a lift, one room has complete disabled access and facilities, and another is dog friendly (there is an additional £25 charge per dog staying in the room).

The restaurant offers A la Carte and Tasting Menus, all dietary requirements are catered for.

Free wifi access available.

**The Esplanade, Penarth CF64 3AU    Tel: 029 2070 6559**
jamessommerinrestaurant.co.uk    info@jamessommerinrestaurant.co.uk

## WREXHAM

### LLANARMON DYFFRYN CEIRIOG                Map 15 SJ13

## The Hand at Llanarmon

★★★★ @@ INN

**tel:** 01691 600666 **Ceiriog Valley LL20 7LD**
**email:** reception@thehandhotel.co.uk **web:** www.thehandhotel.co.uk
**dir:** *Exit A5 at Chirk onto B4500 signed Ceiriog Valley, 11m to village*

Appointed to a high standard, this inn provides a range of thoughtfully furnished bedrooms, with smart modern bathrooms. Public areas retain many original features including exposed beams and open fires. Imaginative food makes great use of the finest local produce. A warm welcome and attentive service ensure a memorable guest experience.

**Rooms:** 13 en suite (4 GF) **S** £60–£95; **D** £95–£150* **Facilities:** STV FTV Lounge tea/coffee Dinner available Direct dial WiFi Pool table **Conf:** Max 15 Thtr 10 Class 10 Board 15 **Parking:** 19 **Notes:** LB

### WREXHAM                Map 15 SJ35

## The Lemon Tree

★★★ ⊜ RESTAURANT WITH ROOMS

**tel:** 01978 261211 **29 Rhosddu Road LL11 2LP**
**email:** info@thelemontree.org.uk **web:** www.thelemontree.org.uk
**dir:** *A483 junct 5 follow signs for town centre, pass university & football stadium. Keep left, left at 1st rdbt*

A modern and stylish restaurant setting awaits within this unassuming Gothic, Grade II listed building in the heart of Wrexham. The owners have a relaxed approach and offer locally sourced, modern British cuisine in the evenings. Straightforward and good value bedrooms are smartly appointed and comfortable; available in a range of sizes.

**Rooms:** 12 en suite **Facilities:** FTV TVL tea/coffee Dinner available WiFi **Conf:** Max 40 Thtr 40 Class 20 Board 20 **Parking:** 15 **Notes:** LB

*Below: Llynnau Mymbyr, Capel Curig, with the Snowdonia mountain range in the background*

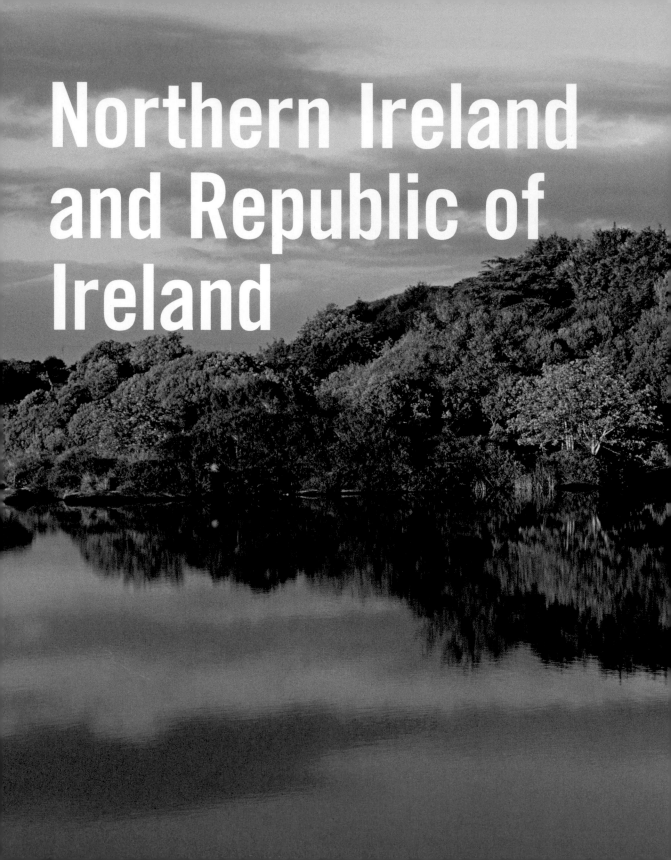

# Northern Ireland and Republic of Ireland

## NORTHERN IRELAND

## COUNTY ANTRIM

| BUSHMILLS | Map 1 C6 |

### Premier Collection

## Causeway Lodge

★★★★★ ♨ GUEST HOUSE

**tel:** 028 2073 0333 **52 Moycraig Road, Dunseverick BT57 8TB**
**email:** stay@causewaylodge.com **web:** www.causewaylodge.com

Causeway Lodge offers high-quality, contemporary accommodation in an idyllic setting on the north Antrim coast. Each of the individually designed bedrooms is thoughtfully presented and the Causeway Suite is very stylish. The house is close to the Giant's Causeway, Carrick-A-Rede rope bridge and the famous Bushmills Distillery. WiFi is available and a warm welcome is assured from the friendly owners.

**Rooms:** 4 en suite 1 annexe en suite (2 fmly) (1 GF) **Facilities:** STV FTV iPod docking station TVL tea/coffee WiFi Gym 🛁 Hot tub **Extras:** Speciality toiletries, fridge, bottled water, fresh milk, robes, slippers **Parking:** 6

### Premier Collection

## Whitepark House

★★★★★ ♨ GUEST ACCOMMODATION

**tel:** 028 2073 1482 **150 Whitepark Road, Ballintoy BT54 6NH**
**email:** bob@whiteparkhouse.com **web:** www.whiteparkhouse.com
**dir:** On A2 at Whitepark Bay, 6m E of Bushmills

Whitepark House nestles above a sandy beach and has super views of the ocean and Scotland's Western Isles. The house features objets d'art gathered from Far Eastern travels, while the traditional bedrooms are homely. Breakfasts are served around a central table in the open-plan hallway, and hospitality is warm and memorable.

**Rooms:** 3 en suite S £80; D £130* **Facilities:** Lounge tea/coffee WiFi
**Extras:** Bottled water, robes **Parking:** 6 **Notes:** No children 10yrs Closed Dec-Feb

## BELFAST

| BELFAST | Map 1 D5 |

## Tara Lodge

★★★★ GUEST ACCOMMODATION

**tel:** 028 9059 0900 **36 Cromwell Road BT7 1JW**
**email:** sinead@taralodge.com **web:** www.taralodge.com
**dir:** M1 onto A55, left onto A1, right into Fitzwilliam St, left into University Rd, proceed to Botanic Ave

Friendly staff and comfortable bedrooms make Tara Lodge popular for leisure or business guests. The stylish dining room is the scene for memorable breakfasts, while secure off-road parking is a bonus so close to the city centre.

**Rooms:** 19 en suite 15 annexe en suite (3 GF) S £75–£115; D £80–£145*
**Facilities:** STV FTV DVD TVL tea/coffee Direct dial Lift WiFi **Parking:** 19 **Notes:** LB Closed 24–28 Dec

## Springfield B&B

★★★ BED AND BREAKFAST

**tel:** 07711 971188 **16 Springfield Road BT12 7AG**
**email:** k.obrien@live.co.uk **web:** www.bnbbelfast.com

Located just 10–15 minutes' walk from the city centre, Springfield B&B offers budget accommodation and genuine hospitality. Bedrooms and en suites are generally compact but cater well for the guest. Complimentary super-fast WiFi and good-sized TVs feature throughout. Breakfast offers a great start to the day with the traditional Ulster Fry – not for the faint-hearted, but not to be missed.

**Rooms:** 5 en suite **Facilities:** WiFi

## COUNTY DOWN

## AA GUEST ACCOMMODATION OF THE YEAR FOR NORTHERN IRELAND 2017–18

| COMBER | Map 1 D5 |

## The Old Schoolhouse Inn

★★★★ ◉◉ ♨ RESTAURANT WITH ROOMS

**tel:** 028 9754 1182 **100 Ballydrain Road BT23 6EA**
**email:** info@theoldschoolhouseinn.com **web:** www.theoldschoolhouseinn.com
**dir:** A22 to Comber, right at end of road. 0.5m past Castle Espie to property

Located close to the shore of Strangford Lough, The Old Schoolhouse Inn enjoys a peaceful rural location, and is just a short drive from Comber and 20 minutes from Belfast. This family-run operation is in the capable hands of Will Brown who has learnt his trade in some of London's best kitchens and in establishments closer to home. Bedrooms are spacious and well appointed, while service is warm and genuine. The refurbished restaurant has been awarded 2 AA Rosettes and serves local produce with flair and imagination.

**Rooms:** 12 en suite (12 GF) **Facilities:** TVL tea/coffee Dinner available Direct dial
**Conf:** Max 60 Thtr 60 Class 30 Board 30 **Parking:** 100

## DONAGHADEE — Map 1 D5

### Pier 36
★★★★ Ⓐ GUEST HOUSE

**tel:** 028 9188 4466 **36 The Parade BT21 0HE**
**email:** info@pier36.co.uk **web:** www.pier36.co.uk
**dir:** A2 left onto flyover before Bangor, follow signs for Donaghadee (right across bridge). In 3m take 3rd exit at rdbt towards harbour. Pier 36 on right

Pier 36 is right on the quayside of Donaghadee Harbour. The en suite bedrooms are well furnished, and both superior and standard rooms are available, all with fabulous views over the harbour and Copeland Islands. The breakfast menu is extensive, and there's is also a restaurant where guests can enjoy anything from sirloin and fillet steaks to a wide range of seafood, or a home-made scone beside the fire. Entertainment is offered most weekends.

**Rooms:** 6 en suite (2 fmly) **Facilities:** STV FTV TVL tea/coffee Dinner available Licensed WiFi ♨18 🔒 **Extras:** Bottled water **Conf:** Max 36 Thtr 28 Class 20 Board 16 **Notes:** LB

## COUNTY FERMANAGH

### ENNISKILLEN — Map 1 C5

### Belmore Court & Motel
★★★★ GUEST ACCOMMODATION

**tel:** 028 6632 6633 **Tempo Road BT74 6HX**
**email:** info@motel.co.uk **web:** www.motel.co.uk
**dir:** On A4, opposite Tesco on corner of Tempo Rd (B80)

Situated in the centre of Enniskillen, the Belmore Court offers an ideal location for visiting the northwest and Fermanagh lakes. The accommodation offered has a range of styles from rooms with small kitchen areas to executive suites. All are stylish and have TVs and free WiFi. Some also come with coffee makers. The public areas are also modern, and the breakfast room catches all the morning sun. Parking is available.

**Rooms:** 30 en suite 30 annexe en suite (17 fmly) (12 GF) **Facilities:** FTV DVD iPod docking station TVL tea/coffee Direct dial Lift WiFi ♨18 🔒 **Extras:** Speciality toiletries **Conf:** Max 45 Thtr 45 Class 25 Board 16 **Parking:** 60 **Notes:** LB Closed 24–28 Dec

## COUNTY LONDONDERRY

### MAGHERA — Map 1 C5

### Ardtara Country House
★★★★ ⊛⊛ RESTAURANT WITH ROOMS

**tel:** 028 7964 4490 **8 Gorteade Road BT46 5SA**
**email:** info@ardtara.com **web:** www.ardtara.com

Set in its own extensive gardens Ardtara Country House enjoys a secluded location just a short drive from the beautiful North Antrim Coast and the famous Giant's Causeway. This fine 19th-century house offers guests spacious bedrooms with views over the landscaped gardens. There is a comfortable lounge, a cosy bar and many of the original features have been sympathetically restored. The award-winning restaurant offers the best in fresh seasonal produce and the hearty breakfasts served in the conservatory are not to be missed. The city is of Derry is a short drive away as is the challenging Royal Portrush golf course. Ardtara Country House was the AA Guest Accommodation of the Year for Northern Ireland 2016–17.

**Rooms:** 9 en suite (1 GF) S £89–£139; D £99–£159* **Facilities:** Lounge tea/coffee Dinner available Direct dial WiFi ♨18 Fishing **Extras:** Robes, slippers **Conf:** Max 50 **Parking:** 100 **Notes:** LB Civ wed 65

## REPUBLIC OF IRELAND

## COUNTY CARLOW

### CARLOW — Map 1 C3

### Barrowville Town House
★★★★ GUEST HOUSE

**tel:** 059 9143324 & 086 2520013 **Kilkenny Road**
**email:** barrowvilletownhouse@eircom.net **web:** www.barrowville.com
**dir:** N9 (Kilkenny Rd) near Institute of Technology

The Smyths are the friendly owners of this carefully maintained 18th-century town house. Many of the very comfortable bedrooms are spacious, and the public rooms are elegant and relaxing. The conservatory, with its fruiting vine, is where breakfasts are served, overlooking well tended gardens. Ample parking is available.

**Rooms:** 7 en suite (3 fmly) **Facilities:** STV TVL tea/coffee Direct dial WiFi **Parking:** 11 **Notes:** LB Closed 24-26 Dec

## COUNTY CLARE

### BALLYVAUGHAN — Map 1 B3

### Hazelwood Lodge
★★★★ ⬠ GUEST ACCOMMODATION

**tel:** 065 7077092
**email:** info@hazelwoodlodge.ie **web:** www.hazelwoodlodge.ie
**dir:** 1km from village, S on N67. 1st property on left

Located just 1km south of the coastal village of Ballyvaughan, Hazelwood Lodge is the family home of three generations of the Sweeney family, and their dog Donny. The unassuming frontage belies the airiness and quality that lies within. Bedrooms are spacious, with high quality furnishings and wonderfully comfortable beds. There is a relaxing lounge area, with a terrace at the rear to catch the last of the evening sun. Having two experienced chefs in the family ensures that breakfast here is a real highlight, featuring some interesting and healthy options, together with home baking and hand-made preserves. Dinner can be served to groups with prior arrangement.

**Rooms:** 8 en suite (4 fmly) (2 GF) **S** €65–€80; **D** €90–€100 (room only)* **Facilities:** STV FTV Lounge tea/coffee 🔒 **Extras:** Still water, fresh milk in fridge, home-made biscuits **Parking:** 10 **Notes:** Closed 31 Oct–10 Feb

BALLYVAUGHAN *continued*

## Ballyvaughan Lodge

★★★ ☙ GUEST HOUSE

**tel:** 065 7077292 & 086 2511512
**email:** ballyvaughanlodge@yahoo.ie **web:** www.ballyvaughanlodge.com
**dir:** *From Galway take N6. Exit at junct 19 onto N18 (Oranmore). In Kilcolgan right onto N69 signed Ennistimon. Lodge on right on entering Ballyvaughan*

The warm and welcoming home of the O'Sullivans is the ideal base for touring the wonderful Burren region and Galway Bay. The village has a number of craft shops and atmospheric pubs, most of which serve evening meals. Bedrooms are comfortably appointed and the relaxing lounges include a sun room, with reading material, guides and some interesting pieces of original art. Breakfast is a delight; an array of fresh and poached fruits and local farmhouse cheeses followed by a selection of options cooked to order by Pauline.

**Rooms:** 11 en suite (1 fmly) (5 GF) **S** €50–€65; **D** €100* **Facilities:** FTV Lounge TVL tea/coffee Direct dial WiFi ❦ **Extras:** Bottled water, snacks, chocolates **Parking:** 11 **Notes:** Closed 23–28 Dec

---

### DOOLIN                                                                Map 1 B3

## Cullinan's Seafood Restaurant & Guest House

★★★ ◉◉ ☙ GUEST HOUSE

**tel:** 065 7074183
**email:** info@cullinansdoolin.com **web:** www.cullinansdoolin.com
**dir:** *In town centre at x-rds between McGanns Pub & O'Connors Pub*

A charming guest house and restaurant, where award-winning food is served in the conservatory dining room (in season; closed Wed and Sun) overlooking the River Aille. Chef-patron James Cullinan features locally caught fresh fish on the dinner menu, which also includes steaks, lamb and vegetarian dishes, and there is a popular Early Bird menu. Bedrooms are attractively decorated in a traditional style. There is a cosy guest lounge and ample off-street parking.

**Rooms:** 8 en suite 2 annexe en suite (3 fmly) (3 GF) **Facilities:** STV FTV Lounge TVL tea/coffee Dinner available Direct dial WiFi **Parking:** 15 **Notes:** No children 4yrs Closed mid Dec–mid Feb

---

### LAHINCH                                                              Map 1 B3

### Premier Collection

## Moy House

★★★★★ ◉◉ ☙ GUEST HOUSE

**tel:** 065 7082800
**email:** moyhouse@eircom.net **web:** www.moyhouse.com
**dir:** *1km from Lahinch on Miltown Malbay Rd, signed from Lahinch N67*

Moy House, an 18th-century former hunting lodge, overlooks Lahinch Bay, the world-famous surfing beach and championship golf links. Individually designed bedrooms and suites are decorated with luxurious fabrics and fine antique furniture. The elegant drawing room has an open turf fire and guests can enjoy breathtaking views of the ocean while enjoying a pre-dinner drink from the honesty bar. The Conservatory Restaurant adjoins the elegant dining room and features award-winning cookery. The menu is based on local seafood and seasonal produce from small independent farmers. A gourmet tasting menu is served on selected nights. Dinner must be pre-booked. Breakfast is also a treat, with a number of healthy options on offer together with the traditional Irish selection.

**Rooms:** 9 en suite (2 fmly) (4 GF) **S** €130–€200; **D** €165–€395* **Facilities:** STV FTV DVD Lounge Dinner available Direct dial Licensed WiFi ☕ ❦ Private access to beach **Extras:** Speciality toiletries **Conf:** Max 16 Board 16 **Parking:** 30 **Notes:** LB Closed Nov–Feb Civ wed 35

---

### LISDOONVARNA                                                         Map 1 B3

## Wild Honey Inn

★★★★ ◉◉ RESTAURANT WITH ROOMS

**tel:** 065 7074300 **Kincora**
**email:** info@wildhoneyinn.com **web:** www.wildhoneyinn.com
**dir:** *N18 from Ennis to Ennistymon. Continue through Ennistymon towards Lisdoonvarna, located on the right at edge of town*

Set in a former hotel dating from the 1860s, when the town prospered as a spa, the Wild Honey Inn has created a solid reputation for its two AA Rosette award-winning cuisine. 'Modern bistro style' is Aidan McGrath's description of the food on offer, served in the comfortable atmospheric bar at both lunch and dinner. Great attention is paid to the provenance of the ingredients, most of which are organic and sourced as close to County Clare as possible. Reservations are not taken. Bedrooms come in a number of styles, and the garden rooms have private patios. Residents have the use of a relaxing lounge, filled with reading material, not surprisingly featuring food and cookery. Breakfast is also a highlight of any visit, with a range of interesting options.

**Rooms:** 14 en suite (3 GF) **S** €80–€100; **D** €110–€130 **Facilities:** STV Lounge Dinner available Direct dial WiFi ❦ **Extras:** Bottled water, speciality toiletries, robes, slippers **Notes:** LB No children 12yrs Closed Nov–Feb RS Mar–Apr & Oct Open Thu–Sun

## COUNTY CORK

### BALTIMORE
Map 1 B1

## Rolfs Country House

★★★ ◎ RESTAURANT WITH ROOMS

**tel:** 028 20289 **Baltimore Hill**
**email:** info@rolfscountryhouse.com **web:** www.rolfscountryhouse.com
**dir:** *Before village turn sharp left up hill. House signed*

Situated on a hill above the fishing village of Baltimore, these 400-year-old stone buildings have been successfully converted by the Haffner family. There are ten traditionally furnished en suite bedrooms in an annexe, a cosy bar with an open fire, and a rustic restaurant on two levels. Dinner is served nightly during the high season and at weekends in the winter; the menu features quality meats, artisan cheeses and fish landed at the busy pier. This is a lovely place to stay and the hosts are very friendly.

**Rooms:** 10 annexe en suite (4 GF) **S** €59–€79; **D** €79–€99* **Facilities:** FTV Lounge tea/coffee Dinner available WiFi **Parking:** 60 **Notes:** LB Closed 20–26 Dec

### CLONAKILTY
Map 1 B2

## Duvane House

★★★★ ◎ FARMHOUSE

**tel:** 023 8833129 **Ballyduvane**
**email:** duvanefarm@eircom.net **web:** www.duvanehouse.com
**dir:** *1km SW from Clonakilty on N71*

This Georgian farmhouse is on the N71 Skibbereen road. Bedrooms are comfortable and include four-poster and brass beds. There is a lovely sitting room and dining room, and a wide choice is available at breakfast (dinner is available by arrangement). Local amenities include Blue Flag beaches, riding and golf.

**Rooms:** 4 en suite (1 fmly) **Facilities:** TVL tea/coffee Dinner available WiFi ♨9 Fishing Pool table **Parking:** 20 **Notes:** LB Closed Nov–Mar 100 acres beef/dairy/mixed/sheep/horses

### DURRUS
Map 1 B2

## Blairscove House & Restaurant

★★★★ ◎◎ RESTAURANT WITH ROOMS

**tel:** 027 61127
**email:** mail@blairscove.ie **web:** www.blairscove.ie
**dir:** *From Durrus on R591 towards Crookhaven, 2.4km, blue gate on right*

Blairscove comprises four elegant suites located in the courtyard of a Georgian country house outside the pretty village of Durrus near Bantry; each room is individually decorated in a contemporary style and has stunning views over Dunmanus Bay and the mountains. The restaurant is renowned for its wide range of hors d'oeuvres and its open wood-fire grill. The piano-playing and candlelight add to a unique dining experience.

**Rooms:** 4 annexe en suite (1 fmly) **S** €150–€260, **D** €150–€260* **Facilities:** FTV DVD tea/coffee Dinner available Direct dial WiFi **Extras:** Speciality toiletries, sherry – complimentary; wine – chargeable **Parking:** 30 **Notes:** Closed Nov-mid Mar Civ wed 35

### GOLEEN
Map 1 A1

## The Heron's Cove

★★★★ ◎ ≋ BED AND BREAKFAST

**tel:** 028 35225 & 0868 073072 **The Harbour**
**email:** suehill@eircom.net **web:** www.heronscove.com
**dir:** *By harbour in Goleen*

There are charming views of the harbour, fast-flowing stream and inland hills from The Heron's Cove, at Ireland's most south-westerly point, near Mizen Head. Bedrooms are comfortably furnished, some with balconies. The restaurant and wine bar is run by chef-patron Sue Hill, where the freshest fish and local produce feature and guests can choose their own wines from the cocktail bar shelves. Breakfast is a special treat and the best of West Cork ingredients can be enjoyed while watching the famous herons.

**Rooms:** 5 en suite (2 fmly) **S** €60–€100; **D** €80–€100 **Facilities:** STV tea/coffee Dinner available Direct dial Licensed WiFi **Extras:** Bottled water **Parking:** 10 **Notes:** LB Closed Xmas & New Year RS Oct–Apr bookings essential

### KINSALE
Map 1 B2

## Friar's Lodge

★★★★★ GUEST HOUSE

**tel:** 086 2895075 & 021 4777384 **5 Friars Street**
**email:** mtierney@indigo.ie **web:** www.friars-lodge.com
**dir:** *In town centre next to parish church*

This family-run and owned lodge was purpose-built and is near the Friary, on a quiet street just a short walk from Kinsale, renowned for its restaurants and bars. Bedrooms and suites are particularly spacious and furnished with comfort in mind. Being close to The Old Head Golf Club, and many others, there is storage for clubs and a drying room available, with secure parking to the rear. A wine and snack menu is available. The elegant dining room is the setting for imaginative Irish breakfasts.

**Rooms:** 18 en suite (2 fmly) (4 GF) **S** €65–€80; **D** €80–€120* **Facilities:** STV tea/coffee Direct dial Lift WiFi **Parking:** 20 **Notes:** Closed Xmas

KINSALE *continued*

## Long Quay House

★★★★ GUEST ACCOMMODATION

**tel:** 021 4709833 **Long Quay**
**email:** info@longquayhousekinsale.com **web:** www.longquayhousekinsale.com
**dir:** *Follow R600 from Cork to Kinsale, on entering the town house on right*

Located at the entrance to the picturesque coastal town of Kinsale, Long Quay House is a Georgian residence and the home of Rasa and Peter Deasy. Many of the comfortable rooms retain the original proportions of the building, but don't miss out on today's creature comforts. Breakfast is a particular feature; beautiful presentation of interesting options. Kinsale is renowned for its restaurants, and is also an ideal base for touring West Cork

**Rooms:** 8 en suite (2 fmly) (1 GF) **D** €110–€220 **Facilities:** FTV TVL Direct dial WiFi ⌁ 🔒 **Notes:** Closed 15 Nov–27 Dec

## The White House

★★★★ ⊚ RESTAURANT WITH ROOMS

**tel:** 021 4772125 **Pearse Street, The Glen**
**email:** info@whitehouse-kinsale.ie **web:** www.whitehouse-kinsale.ie
**dir:** *In town centre*

Centrally located among the narrow, twisting streets of the charming maritime town of Kinsale, this restaurant with rooms dates from 1850. It is a welcoming hostelry with smart, comfortably appointed contemporary bedrooms. The atmospheric bar and bistro are open for lunch and dinner, with Restaurant d'Antibes also open during the evenings. The varied menu features local fish and beef. The courtyard at the rear makes a perfect setting in summer and there is regular entertainment in the bar.

**Rooms:** 10 en suite (2 fmly) **Facilities:** STV tea/coffee Dinner available Direct dial WiFi **Notes:** LB Closed 24–25 Dec

## The Old Bank House

🇺

**tel:** 021 4772206 **10/11 Pearse Street**
**email:** info@oldbankhousekinsale.com **web:** www.oldbankhousekinsale.com
**dir:** *On main road into Kinsale from Cork Airport (R600). House on right at start of Kinsale, next to Post Office*

Currently the rating for this establishment is not confirmed. This may be due to a change of ownership or because it has only recently joined the AA rating scheme.

**Rooms:** 17 en suite (3 fmly) **D** €75–€250* **Facilities:** FTV TVL tea/coffee Direct dial Lift WiFi 🔒 **Conf:** Max 15 Thtr 15 Class 10 Board 12 **Notes:** LB Closed 25 Dec

---

**SHANAGARRY**     Map 1 C2

## Ballymaloe House

★★★★★ ⊚⊚  GUEST HOUSE

**tel:** 021 4652531
**email:** res@ballymaloe.ie **web:** www.ballymaloe.ie
**dir:** *N25 onto R630 at Midleton rdbt. After 0.5m, left onto R631 to Cloyne. 2m after Cloyne on Ballycotton road*

This charming country house is on a 400-acre farm, part of the Geraldine estate in east Cork. Bedrooms upstairs in the main house retain many original features, and the ground floor and courtyard rooms have garden patios. The relaxing drawing room and dining rooms have enchanting old-world charm. Ballymaloe House is renowned for excellent meals, many of which are created using ingredients produced on the farm. There is a craft shop, café, tennis and small golf course on the estate.

**Rooms:** 20 en suite 9 annexe en suite (2 fmly) (3 GF) **S** €155–€205; **D** €215–€315 **Facilities:** Lounge TVL Dinner available Direct dial Licensed WiFi ⚲ ⌁ ⌁ ⌁9 🔒 Children's sand pit/slide **Conf:** Max 200 Thtr 200 Class 50 Board 50 **Parking:** 50 **Notes:** LB Closed 23–26 Dec, 8–28 Jan RS Jan–Feb Closed Sun–Tue rooms & dinner Civ wed 170

---

**COUNTY DONEGAL**

**BALLYLIFFIN**     Map 1 C6

## Ballyliffin TownHouse

★★★★ ⌁ GUEST ACCOMMODATION

**tel:** 074 9378300
**email:** info@ballyliffintownhouse.ie **web:** www.ballyliffintownhouse.ie

A popular spot with golfers, this warm and welcoming property is located at the top of the village of Ballyliffin on the Inishowen Peninsula. Family-owned and operated, one is assured of a friendly welcome. Bedrooms and en suites are high quality, spacious and all very comfortably appointed. There is a large lounge for guests, together with an atmospheric pub for a night-cap before retiring. Breakfast is a highlight, featuring an attractive and appetising cold buffet selection and a good choice of hot options.

**Rooms:** 13 en suite (5 fmly) **S** €65–€85; **D** €80–€125* **Facilities:** STV FTV DVD Lounge TVL tea/coffee Direct dial Lift Licensed WiFi ⌁18 Pool table 🔒 **Extras:** Home-made cakes & biscuits **Parking:** 31 **Notes:** LB

## CARRIGANS
Map 1 C5

### Mount Royd Country Home
★★★★ ⚲ BED AND BREAKFAST

tel: 074 9140163
email: jmartin@mountroyd.com web: www.mountroyd.com
dir: *From Letterkenny on N14. At Dry Arch rdbt 2nd exit onto N13. At next rdbt 2nd exit onto N14 towards Lifford. Left at R236 to Carrigans. Or from Derry take A40 to Carrigans*

Mount Royd is a creeper-clad house with beautifully maintained gardens in the pretty village of Carrigans, a short distance from Derry City. The friendly Martins have brought hospitality to new heights – nothing is too much trouble for them. It is no wonder so many of their visitors are return guests. Breakfast is a feast of choices including home-baking and eggs from their own hens. Each of the individually designed bedrooms are very comfortable, with lots of personal touches.

Rooms: 4 en suite (1 fmly) (1 GF) Facilities: FTV TVL tea/coffee WiFi Parking: 7 Notes: LB No children 12yrs RS Nov–Feb

## DONEGAL
Map 1 B5

### The Red Door Country House
★★★★ ◉ RESTAURANT WITH ROOMS

tel: 074 9360289 Fahan, Inishowen
email: info@thereddoor.ie web: www.thereddoor.ie
dir: *In Fahan, church on right, The Red Door Country House signed on left*

Nestled among mature trees and landscaped gardens, this warm and welcoming restaurant with rooms stands proudly on the shore of Lough Swilly, in the historic village of Fahan, just south of Buncrana. Dating from 1789, the original features of the house are cleverly combined with contemporary styling. Bedrooms are cosy and comfortable, each individually decorated and all en suite. The house has a fine reputation in the region for the quality of its restaurant for evening dining, and alfresco lunches. Breakfast is also a highlight and is designed to be lingered over.

Rooms: 4 en suite Facilities: FTV Lounge tea/coffee Dinner available WiFi ⚓18 Conf: Max 100 Thtr 100 Board 100 Parking: 40 Notes: RS Mon & Tue closed Civ wed 160

# DUBLIN

## DUBLIN
Map 1 D4

## Premier Collection

### Glenogra Town House
★★★★★ GUEST HOUSE

tel: 01 6683661 64 Merrion Road, Ballsbridge
email: info@glenogra.com web: www.glenogra.com
dir: *Opposite Royal Dublin Showgrounds & Intercontinental Hotel*

This fine 19th-century red brick house is situated across from the RDS and close to the Aviva Stadium. The bedrooms are comfortably appointed and include many thoughtful extras; three bedrooms are on the ground floor. There is an elegant drawing room and dining room, and the interesting breakfast menu offers a range of dishes. Secure parking is available, and The Aircoach and city-centre buses stop in Merrion Road; the DART rail is around the corner.

Rooms: 13 en suite (1 fmly) (3 GF) S €69–€149; D €99–€299* Facilities: STV TVL tea/coffee Direct dial WiFi ⚓ Parking: 10 Notes: LB Closed 23–28 Dec

## Premier Collection

### Harrington Hall
★★★★★ GUEST HOUSE

tel: 01 4753497 69–70 Harcourt Street
email: harringtonhall@eircom.net web: www.harringtonhall.com
dir: *St Stephen's Green via O'Connell St, in Earlsfort Terrace, pass National Concert Hall, right into Hatch St, right into Harcourt St*

Harrington Hall is a Georgian house on a one-way street, just off St Stephen's Green in the centre of the city. The spacious bedrooms are well appointed and include comfortable suites. A lovely plasterwork ceiling adorns the relaxing drawing room, and an extensive breakfast menu is served in the basement dining room. A lift, porter service and limited off-street parking are available.

Rooms: 28 en suite (3 fmly) (3 GF) Facilities: STV FTV tea/coffee Direct dial Lift Licensed WiFi ⚓ Parking: 14 Notes: LB Closed 24–26 Dec

### Charleville Lodge Guest House
★★★★ GUEST HOUSE

tel: 01 8386633 268/272 North Circular Road, Phibsborough
email: info@charlevillelodge.ie web: www.charlevillelodge.ie
dir: *N from O'Connell St to Phibsborough, left fork at St Peter's Church, house 250mtrs on left*

Situated close to the city centre near Phoenix Park, this elegant terrace of Victorian houses provides accommodation of a high standard. The two interconnecting lounges are welcoming, and the smart dining room offers a choice of breakfasts. Bedrooms are very comfortable with pleasant decor, and there is a secure car park.

Rooms: 30 en suite (2 fmly) (4 GF) S €55–€150; D €70–€300 (room only) Facilities: STV FTV Lounge TVL tea/coffee Direct dial Licensed WiFi ⚓18 Conf: Max 10 Thtr 10 Class 10 Board 10 Parking: 18 Notes: LB

### Ardagh House
★★★ GUEST HOUSE

tel: 01 4977068 1 Highfield Road, Rathgar
email: enquiries@ardahouse.com web: www.ardahouse.com
dir: *S of city centre through Rathmines*

Ardagh House is an early 19th-century house with modern additions, and stands in a premier residential area on the outskirts of the city, close to local restaurants and pubs. It retains many original features and has a relaxing lounge that overlooks a delightful garden. There is an attractive dining room where hearty breakfasts are served at individual tables. The comfortable bedrooms vary in size. Ample off-street parking is available.

Rooms: 19 en suite (4 fmly) (1 GF) S €65–€110; D €80–€160* Facilities: FTV TVL tea/coffee Direct dial WiFi Parking: 20 Notes: Closed 22 Dec–3 Jan

DUBLIN *continued*

## Leeson Bridge Guest House

★★★ GUEST HOUSE

**tel:** 01 6681000 & 6682255 **1 Upper Leeson Street**
**email:** info@leesonbridgehouse.ie **web:** www.leesonbridgehouse.ie
**dir:** *At junct of N11 & N7, Leeson St*

This guest house is located right by Leeson Street Bridge, close to the city centre and is easily accessible from the ferry ports. Centred around a Georgian house, many of its original architectural features are retained. It offers a range of en suite bedroom styles, some with spa baths, sauna or galley kitchenette. Residents have access to ample parking at the rear. A take-away breakfast is offered to guests departing early in the morning.

**Rooms:** 20 en suite (1 fmly) (2 GF) **Facilities:** STV FTV TVL tea/coffee Direct dial Lift WiFi Fishing **Parking:** 18 **Notes:** LB

## COUNTY GALWAY

| CLIFDEN | Map 1 A4 |

## Ardmore House

★★★★ FARMHOUSE

**tel:** 095 21221 & 076 6030227 **Sky Road**
**email:** info@ardmore-house.com **web:** www.ardmore-house.com
**dir:** *N59 from Galway to Clifden. Just N of Clifden centre follow signs on left for 'Sky Road', 5km, house on left*

Ardmore House is set among the wild scenery of Connemara, between hills and the sea on the Sky Road. Bedrooms are attractively decorated and the house is very comfortable throughout. A path leads from the house to the coast. A good hearty breakfast is provided featuring home baking.

**Rooms:** 6 en suite (1 fmly) (5 GF) **S** €45–€60; **D** €80–€90 **Facilities:** STV FTV Lounge tea/coffee WiFi **Parking:** 8 **Notes:** LB Closed Oct–Mar 25 acres non-working

## Faul House

★★★★ FARMHOUSE

**tel:** 095 21239 & 087 9285287 **Ballyconneely Road**
**email:** info@ireland.com **web:** www.faulhouse.com
**dir:** *1.5km from town right at rugby pitch*

Faul House, a fine modern farmhouse, stands on a quiet and secluded road overlooking Clifden Bay. It is smart and comfortable with large bedrooms, all well furnished and with good views. Kathleen offers a hearty breakfast with home baking. There are Connemara ponies available for trekking.

**Rooms:** 6 en suite (3 fmly) (3 GF) **S** €50–€60; **D** €80–€90 **Facilities:** FTV Lounge TVL tea/coffee WiFi **Parking:** 10 **Notes:** Closed Nov–26 Mar 35 acres sheep/ponies/hens/ducks

## Mallmore House

★★★★ BED AND BREAKFAST

**tel:** 095 21460 **Ballyconneely Road**
**email:** info@mallmore.com **web:** www.mallmorecountryhouse.com
**dir:** *1.5km from Clifden towards Ballyconneely take 1st right*

Mallmore House is a charming and lovingly maintained 17th-century house. It is situated close to the town and has a beautiful garden and mature woodland, and overlooks Clifden Bay. Bedrooms are spacious and very well appointed with antique furniture. The drawing room is delightfully relaxing with a turf fire. There is a wide choice available at breakfast including home baking and locally smoked fish. Mallmore is a lovely place to stay and enjoy the peace and quiet of Connemara.

**Rooms:** 6 en suite (1 fmly) (6 GF) **D** €90–€100 **Facilities:** FTV DVD Lounge tea/coffee WiFi 🔒 **Parking:** 15 **Notes:** Closed Oct–1 Apr

## Ben View House

★★★ GUEST HOUSE

**tel:** 095 21256 **Bridge Street**
**email:** benviewhouse@ireland.com **web:** www.benviewhouse.com
**dir:** *Enter town on N59, opposite Esso fuel station*

This house is well located in the centre of the town with ample on-street parking. Dating from 1824, it offers good quality accommodation at a moderate cost. The breakfast room and lounge feature an old world atmosphere, with antique furniture and sparkling silverware in everyday use.

**Rooms:** 10 rms (9 en suite) (3 fmly) **Facilities:** TVL tea/coffee **Notes:** LB

| GALWAY | Map 1 B3 |

## Marian Lodge Guest House

★★★★ GUEST HOUSE

**tel:** 091 521678 **Knocknacarra Road, Salthill Upper**
**email:** celine@iol.ie **web:** www.marian-lodge.com
**dir:** *From Galway to Salthill on R336, through Salthill, 1st right after Spinnaker Hotel into Knocknacarra Rd*

This large modern house just 50 metres from the seafront, is an ideal base for both Galway City and the wilderness of Connemara. The comfortable bedrooms have orthopaedic beds and en suite facilities. There is also a cosy lounge and separate breakfast room where your welcoming host Celine is on hand to make recommendations for what to do with your day. There's plenty of parking available.

**Rooms:** 6 en suite (4 fmly) **Facilities:** STV TVL tea/coffee Direct dial **Parking:** 10 **Notes:** LB No children 3yrs Closed 23-28 Dec

## Screebe House

★★★★ ◎◎ RESTAURANT WITH ROOMS

**tel:** 091 574110 **Rosmuc**
**email:** booking@screebe.com **web:** screebe.com

This house was a hunting and fishing lodge in the 19th century, and following a sympathetic renovation programme is now once again caring for visitors. Situated right on the edge of Camus Bay, it cannot get any closer to the Atlantic. Each of the spacious rooms is designed with relaxation and comfort in mind. Unusually there are no TVs in rooms, so one is sure to switch off and relax. The public rooms all retain their original charm and features, most with real fires. Dinner is a particular highlight; the daily-changed seven course set menu is driven by the season and the market. Breakfast is also noteworthy for its range and quality. An ideal base for country pursuits, with an adjacent pool and sauna for the less sporty.

**Rooms:** 10 rms (8 en suite) (2 pri facs) (2 GF) **S** €120–€135; **D** €170–€320
**Facilities:** Lounge TVL Dinner available Direct dial WiFi ⟳ Fishing Gym
**Conf:** Max 20 Thtr 20 Class 20 Board 20 **Parking:** 10 **Notes:** No children 16yrs Closed 30 Nov–10 Feb RS Mon & Tue closed

## COUNTY KERRY

### DINGLE (AN DAINGEAN) — Map 1 A2

### Premier Collection

## Castlewood House

★★★★★ ☺ GUEST HOUSE

**tel:** 066 9152788 **The Wood**
**web:** www.castlewooddingle.com
**dir:** R559 from Dingle, 0.5km from Aquarium

Less than a 10-minute stroll from the bustling centre of Dingle, Castlewood House is the perfect place to park the car and take in all the delights the town has to offer. Quality standards exceed the expectations of many a hotel, but it is the personal attention that proprietors Helen and Brian give their guests that really impresses here. Wonderfully spacious bedrooms are well-appointed and accessed by lift. Breakfast is a real highlight; so many options are available that choosing is difficult. The drawing room is a great place to relax after a day's walking and plan the next day's activities.

**Rooms:** 12 en suite (3 fmly) (4 GF) **S** €85–€125; **D** €99–€220 **Facilities:** STV tea/coffee Direct dial Lift **Parking:** 15 **Notes:** LB Closed 4–27 Dec & 4 Jan–4 Feb Civ wed 20

### Premier Collection

## Gormans Clifftop House & Restaurant

★★★★★ ◎ GUEST HOUSE

**tel:** 066 9155162 & 083 0033133 **Glaise Bheag, Ballydavid**
**email:** info@gormans-clifftophouse.com **web:** www.gormans-clifftophouse.com
**dir:** R559 to An Mhuirioch, turn right at T-junct, N for 3km

Sile and Vincent Gorman's guest house and restaurant is perched over the cliffs on the western tip of the Slea Head Peninsula near Ballydavid village. The beauty of the rugged coastline, rhythm of the sea and the sun going down on Smerwick Harbour can be enjoyed over a delicious dinner in the smart dining room. The menu includes produce from the garden, local seafood and lamb. Bedrooms are comfortably proportioned and thoughtfully equipped and have breathtaking views of the ocean or mountains, the ground-floor rooms are adapted for the less mobile. Bracing cliff walks can be accessed across from the house.

**Rooms:** 8 en suite (2 fmly) (4 GF) **S** €95–€125; **D** €110–€175*
**Facilities:** tea/coffee Dinner available Direct dial Licensed WiFi Cycle hire
**Parking:** 15 **Notes:** LB Closed 24–26 Dec RS Oct–Mar reservation only

### KENMARE — Map 1 B2

## Muxnaw Lodge

★★★★ BED AND BREAKFAST

**tel:** 064 6641252 & 087 2922895 **Casletownbere Road**
**email:** muxnaw@eircom.net **web:** www.muxnawlodge.ie

Located on the Castletownbere Road, within easy walking distance of Kenmare town, this warm and friendly house is a former hunting lodge dating from the early 19th century. It is set on an elevated site in mature gardens. Bedrooms and en suites are individually decorated, with some enjoying views of the Kenmare River. The lounge retains much of its original character, in addition to the bright and airy sun room. Ample parking is available to the rear.

**Rooms:** 5 en suite (2 fmly) **D** €100* **Facilities:** STV DVD TVL tea/coffee WiFi ⌣ ♨ **Parking:** 5 **Notes:** Closed 24–25 Dec

## Sea Shore Farm Guest House

★★★★ GUEST HOUSE

**tel:** 064 6641270 & 6641675 **Tubrid**
**email:** seashore@eircom.net **web:** www.seashorekenmare.com
**dir:** 1.6km from Kenmare off N70 Ring of Kerry /Sneem road. Signed at junct N70 & N71

Overlooking Kenmare Bay on the Ring of Kerry road, this modern farm guest house is close to town and has spacious bedrooms. Ground-floor rooms open onto the patio and have easier access. Guests are welcome to enjoy the farm walks through the fields to the shore, and nearby salmon and trout fishing on the Roughty River. There is a comfortable sitting room and dining room and a delightful garden.

**Rooms:** 6 en suite (2 fmly) (2 GF) **Facilities:** FTV Lounge tea/coffee Direct dial WiFi ⌕18 ♨ **Extras:** Speciality toiletries, snacks – complimentary **Parking:** 10 **Notes:** No children 5yrs Closed Nov–19 Mar

## KILLARNEY — Map 1 B2

### Premier Collection

## Fairview Guest House

★★★★★ GUEST HOUSE

**tel:** 064 6634164 **College Street**
**email:** info@fairviewkillarney.com **web:** www.killarneyfairview.com
**dir:** *In town centre off College St*

Great attention to detail is demonstrated in the design of this smart guest house, handily located in the town centre close to the bus/railway station. Bedrooms include some with air conditioning and jacuzzi baths, and all are comfortable, with quality furnishings and fittings. There is a lift to all floors, and the impressive penthouse suite enjoys views over the town towards the Kerry mountains. There is a relaxing sitting area and the breakfast menu offers a selection of dishes cooked to order. Local activities and excursions include lake cruises, championship golf courses and the Killarney National Park.

**Rooms:** 29 en suite (2 fmly) (1 GF) **Facilities:** STV DVD TVL tea/coffee Dinner available Direct dial Lift Licensed WiFi ♨18 Jacuzzi suites available **Parking:** 11 **Notes:** LB

## Ashville House

★★★★ GUEST HOUSE

**tel:** 064 6636405 & 6636778 **Rock Road**
**email:** info@ashvillekillarney.com **web:** www.ashvillekillarney.com
**dir:** *In town centre. Exit at N end of High St into Rock Rd*

This inviting house is just a stroll from the town centre and near the N22 (Tralee road). Bedrooms are comfortably furnished, and there is a pleasant sitting room and dining room. There is a private car park, and tours can be arranged.

**Rooms:** 12 en suite (4 GF) **S** €50–€110; **D** €70–€200 **Facilities:** STV FTV TVL tea/coffee Direct dial WiFi ♨18 🐾 **Parking:** 13 **Notes:** LB Closed Nov–1 Mar

## Kingfisher Lodge Bed & Breakfast

★★★★ GUEST HOUSE

**tel:** 064 6637131 & 086 3741379 **Lewis Road**
**email:** info@kingfisherlodgekillarney.com **web:** www.kingfisherlodgekillarney.com
**dir:** *Dublin link straight through 1st rdbt. Right at next rdbt towards town centre, Lodge on left*

This welcoming, modern guest house is home to the Carroll family. It is situated within walking distance of the town centre, and has comfortable and well-appointed bedrooms, all of which are en suite. Breakfast is served in the attractively decorated dining room and there is also a relaxing lounge and conservatory with WiFi. A drying room is available for fishing and wet gear. Golf, walking and fishing trips can be arranged. There is ample parking, and complimentary pick-up from the bus and train station are offered.

**Rooms:** 10 en suite (1 fmly) (2 GF) **S** €40–€75; **D** €70–€120* **Facilities:** STV FTV Lounge TVL tea/coffee Direct dial WiFi ♨18 🐾 Walking Fishing Horseriding Golf can be booked **Parking:** 12 **Notes:** LB Closed 31 Oct–9 Mar

## KILLORGLIN — Map 1 A2

### Premier Collection

## Carrig House Country House & Restaurant

★★★★★ ◉◉ GUEST HOUSE

**tel:** 066 9769100 **Caragh Lake**
**email:** info@carrighouse.com **web:** www.carrighouse.com
**dir:** *N70 to Killorglin*

Located on the shores of Lake Caragh a short drive from Killorglin, amid natural green woodlands, this family-run house is the perfect retreat for a relaxing break. There is a range of room styles on offer, with some having lake views. Each is decorated to a high standard, with guest comfort in mind. Public rooms include elegant drawing rooms and cosy nooks. There is a true passion for food in evidence at dinner, where local seafood and seasonal produce is cooked and presented with care in the Lakeshore Restaurant. With over 15 golf courses and a range of other outdoor pursuits available, there is something to suit all tastes.

**Rooms:** 16 en suite **Facilities:** Lounge TVL Dinner available Direct dial Licensed WiFi 🐾 ♨18 Fishing **Extras:** Bottled water **Parking:** 20 **Notes:** LB No children 8yrs Closed Oct–Feb Civ wed 63

## COUNTY KILKENNY

## KILKENNY — Map 1 C3

## Butler House

★★★★ GUEST HOUSE

**tel:** 056 7765707 & 7722828 **Patrick Street**
**email:** res@butler.ie **web:** www.butler.ie
**dir:** *In centre near Kilkenny Castle*

Once the dower house of Kilkenny Castle, this fine Georgian building fronts onto the main street, with wonderful secluded gardens at the rear, through which you stroll to take breakfast in the Kilkenny Design Centre. Many of the spacious bedrooms retain some of the architectural features of the period, together with contemporary furnishings and minimalist decor. There is a comfortable foyer lounge and a number of conference and event spaces. Secure car parking to the rear.

**Rooms:** 13 en suite (4 fmly) **Facilities:** STV FTV Lounge tea/coffee Direct dial WiFi 🐾 **Extras:** Bottled water – complimentary; safe in all rooms **Conf:** Max 120 Thtr 120 Class 40 Board 40 **Parking:** 24 **Notes:** LB Closed 24–29 Dec Civ wed 80

## COUNTY LAOIS

### PORTLAOISE
Map 1 C3

## Mahers B&B

★★★★ BED AND BREAKFAST

**tel:** 087 2129236 **Beech Avenue, Rathleague**
**email:** mahersbandb@rathleague.com **web:** www.mahers-bnb.com

This Georgian home has been creatively renovated with attention to every detail, keeping original features where possible, together with every modern facility. Built in the late 18th century, it has been in the Maher family for over 100 years. Outbuildings include storage for bikes, fishing tackle and hiking gear, and there is even an ornamental plant nursery on the site. Above all, it is the natural warm welcome from the family that endears visitors to this fine family home. There is a comfortable guest lounge, and breakfast is a real treat with a number of options available.

**Rooms:** 4 rms (2 en suite) (2 pri facs) (3 fmly) **Facilities:** STV FTV TVL tea/coffee WiFi ⚓18 🔒 **Conf:** Max 20 Thtr 20 Class 16 Board 20 **Parking:** 10

## COUNTY LOUTH

### CARLINGFORD
Map 1 D4

## Ghan House

★★★★ ◉◉ 🍷 GUEST ACCOMMODATION

**tel:** 042 9373682
**email:** info@ghanhouse.com **web:** www.ghanhouse.com
**dir:** *M1 junct 18 signed Carlingford, 5mtrs on left after 50kph speed sign*

Dating from 1727, Ghan House oozes charm and comfort. Set in two acres of walled gardens, the house is within 50 metres of the centre of the medieval village of Carlingford, making it an ideal base for walking and touring the Cooley peninsula. Bedrooms are warm and well appointed, either in the house itself or in a converted barn in the grounds. Comfortable public rooms feature log fires and relaxing armchairs. Food is an important element of the business, and a successful cookery school has operated here for many years. Dinner has an emphasis on artisan produce and the renowned Cooley lamb. Breakfast is a treat, with a choice of fruit compôtes and preserves.

**Rooms:** 4 en suite 8 annexe en suite (3 fmly) (4 GF) **S** €80–€95; **D** €160–€250 **Facilities:** FTV iPod docking station Lounge tea/coffee Dinner available Licensed WiFi ⚓18 🔒 **Extras:** Home-made biscuits **Conf:** Max 50 Thtr 50 Class 26 Board 32 **Parking:** 35 **Notes:** LB Civ wed 50

## COUNTY MAYO

### CASTLEBAR
Map 1 B4

## Lough Lannagh Lodge

★★★ GUEST ACCOMMODATION

**tel:** 094 9027111 **Old Westport Road**
**email:** info@loughlannagh.ie **web:** www.loughlannagh.ie
**dir:** *N5/N60/N84 to Castlebar. At ring road follow signs for N5 Westport, signed Lough Lannagh village approaching Westport rdbt*

Lough Lannagh Lodge is in a delightful wooded area within walking distance of Castlebar. There is a conference centre, fitness centre, tennis, table tennis, laundry and drying facilities, a private kitchen, and many activities for children. Bedrooms are well appointed and breakfast is served in the café. Dinner is available by appointment for groups.

**Rooms:** 24 en suite (24 fmly) (12 GF) **S** €74; **D** €94 **Facilities:** FTV Lounge TVL Dinner available Direct dial WiFi 🏊⚓18 🔒 Bicycle hire, water sports **Conf:** Max 100 Thtr 100 Class 54 Board 34 **Parking:** 24 **Notes:** LB Closed mid Dec–mid Jan RS Sun no arrivals Civ wed 100

### WESTPORT
Map 1 B4

## Bertra House

★★★ FARMHOUSE

**tel:** 098 64833 & 086 0667233 **Thornhill, Murrisk**
**email:** bertrahse@eircom.net **web:** www.bertrahouse.com
**dir:** *W of Westport off R335, near Croagh Patrick on L1833*

This attractive bungalow overlooks the Bertra beach of Clew Bay, at the foot of Croagh Patrick, locally known as 'The Reek'. Located about a 10-minute drive from Westport, it is an ideal location for browsing the shops and touring the north Mayo. Four bedrooms are en suite with the fifth having a dedicated bathroom. Breakfast is generous and features Margaret Gill's home baking, some of which might just be available with a cup of tea on your arrival in the cosy lounge!

**Rooms:** 5 rms (4 en suite) (1 pri facs) (1 fmly) (5 GF) **S** €40–€50; **D** €70–€75 **Facilities:** FTV Lounge TVL tea/coffee WiFi **Parking:** 7 **Notes:** LB No children 6yrs Closed 15 Nov–15 Mar 40 acres beef/sheep

## COUNTY MEATH

### SLANE
Map 1 D4

#### Premier Collection

## Tankardstown
★★★★★ @@ ⌂ GUEST ACCOMMODATION

**tel:** 041 9824621
**email:** info@tankardstown.ie **web:** www.tankardstown.ie
**dir:** *N51 (Navan-Slane road), take turn directly opposite main entrance to Slane Castle, signed Kells. Continue for 5km*

Tankardstown is a magical place. Set in 80 acres of parkland, it has many strings to its bow. The main house is host to elegant rooms, with others in cottages in the converted stableyard. Each is individually decorated to a very high standard. The cottages have the benefit of spacious kitchens and living areas, ideal for longer stays. The property is also host to the award-winning Brabazon, a fine dining restaurant, and there's a bistro for more casual fare. Excellent breakfasts are served in the main house, with the option of having it delivered to the cottages. This fine property is ideal for family gatherings and intimate wedding celebrations.

**Rooms:** 7 en suite 15 annexe en suite (6 fmly) (2 GF) **S** €105–€180; **D** €210–€360 **Facilities:** STV FTV DVD Lounge TVL tea/coffee Dinner available Direct dial Licensed WiFi ⌡36 Fishing ⌂ Hot tub **Extras:** Still water – complimentary; mini-bar – chargeable **Conf:** Max 150 Thtr 150 Class 80 Board 50 **Parking:** 200 **Notes:** Civ wed 200

## COUNTY MONAGHAN

### GLASLOUGH
Map 1 C5

#### Premier Collection

## The Castle at Castle Leslie Estate
★★★★★ GUEST HOUSE

**tel:** 047 88100
**email:** info@castleleslie.com **web:** www.castleleslie.com
**dir:** *M1 junct 14, N2 to Monaghan then N12 onto R185 for Glaslough*

Set in 1000 acres of rolling countryside, The Castle is the centre of the Leslie Estate which has been in the family since the 1660s. Bedrooms are all decorated in keeping with the age and style of the period, and are ideal for relaxing breaks where guests enjoy the peace and tranquillity of the property without any interference from televisions or other distractions. With a successful equestrian centre and a private fishing lake, this is an ideal location for those who enjoy country pursuits.

**Rooms:** 20 rms (19 en suite) (1 pri facs) **Facilities:** Lounge TVL Direct dial Lift Licensed WiFi ⌂ ⌡18 Fishing Snooker Private cinema Falconry Clay pigeon shooting **Extras:** Speciality toiletries **Conf:** Max 280 Thtr 260 Class 150 Board 65 **Parking:** 100 **Notes:** LB Closed 22–27 Dec Civ wed 90

## COUNTY SLIGO

### BALLYSADARE
Map 1 B5

## Seashore House
★★★ BED AND BREAKFAST

**tel:** 071 9167827 & 086 2224842 **Lisduff**
**email:** info@seashoreguests.com **web:** www.seashoreguests.com
**dir:** *N4 onto N59 W at Ballisadore, in 4km Seashore signed on right. Turn down road, 600mtrs on right*

Seashore House is an attractive dormer bungalow in a quiet seashore location. A comfortable lounge with open turf fire and sunny conservatory-dining room look out over attractive landscaped gardens and further sea and mountain views. Bedrooms are attractively appointed and comfortable, and there is also a tennis court and bicycle storage. Credit cards only accepted during high season.

**Rooms:** 4 en suite (2 fmly) (2 GF) **S** €45–€55; **D** €75–€80 **Facilities:** STV FTV TVL WiFi ⌂ ⌡18 ⌂ **Parking:** 6 **Notes:** LB No children

# Follow the AA
twitter: @TheAA_Lifestyle
facebook: www.facebook.com/TheAAUK

## ENNISCRONE (INISHCRONE) Map 1 B5

## Waterfront House

★★★★ @ RESTAURANT WITH ROOMS

**tel:** 096 37120 **Sea Front, Cliff Road**
**email:** relax@waterfronthouse.ie **web:** www.waterfronthouse.ie

Located less than a five minute stroll from the town, Waterfront House has great views of the beach and Killalla Bay. This is a warm and friendly place, with proprietor Martina and her loyal team going to great lengths to ensure guests enjoy their stay. Bedrooms are spacious and very comfortably appointed. The award-winning restaurant has a well-deserved reputation, where the menu features fresh seafood, but there are plenty of other options available. Breakfast is a particular highlight in terms of range and food quality. This is an ideal location for the golf and surfing facilities in the area, or the famed Warm Seaweed Baths!

**Rooms:** 11 en suite **Facilities:** STV tea/coffee Dinner available Lift WiFi ♨18
**Parking:** 16 **Notes:** LB

## STRANDHILL Map 1 B5

## Strandhill Lodge and Suites

★★★★ GUEST HOUSE

**tel:** 071 9122122 **Top Road**
**email:** info@strandhilllodgeandsuites.com **web:** strandhilllodgeandsuites.com
**dir:** From Sligo onto R292 for Strandhill

Located in the centre of Strandhill village, just five kilometres from Sligo, this property offers particularly spacious accommodation, finished to a very high standard. Many of the rooms have stunning views of the bay. Public areas are open plan in design, with a bright and airy breakfast room where continental breakfast is served. This is an ideal property for those playing golf or participating in the many other pursuits available in the region. There is a meeting room on the first floor, and ample parking to the rear. A number of cosy pubs and quality restaurants are located in the village.

**Rooms:** 21 en suite 1 annexe en suite (7 fmly) (8 GF) **Facilities:** STV FTV DVD iPod docking station Lounge TVL tea/coffee Direct dial Lift WiFi ♨18 Fishing
🔒 **Extras:** Bottled water **Conf:** Max 20 Thtr 20 Class 10 Board 8 **Parking:** 22
**Notes:** LB Closed Jan–5 Feb

## COUNTY TIPPERARY

## CASHEL Map 1 C3

## Ashmore House

★★★ BED AND BREAKFAST

**tel:** 062 61286 & 0861 037010 **John Street**
**email:** info@ashmorehouse.com **web:** www.ashmorehouse.com
**dir:** M8 exit 8 to town centre, into John St opposite Cashel Palace Hotel, house 100mtrs on right

Ashmore House is a Georgian building set in a colourfully planted walled garden, right in the centre of the town, within walking distance of the Rock of Cashel. There is secure parking at the rear. Guests have use of a large sitting and dining room, and bedrooms come in a variety of sizes from big family rooms to a more compact double. Children are welcome and guests have WiFi access.

**Rooms:** 5 en suite (2 fmly) **S** fr €50; **D** €75–€80* **Facilities:** FTV TVL tea/coffee Dinner available WiFi **Parking:** 10

## THURLES Map 1 3

### Premier Collection

## The Castle

★★★★★ BED AND BREAKFAST

**tel:** 0504 44324 **Twomileborris**
**email:** bandb@thecastletmb.com **web:** www.thecastletmb.com
**dir:** 7km E of Thurles. On N75 200mtrs W of Twomileborris at Castle

Pierce and Joan are very welcoming hosts. Their fascinating house, sheltered by a 16th-century tower house, has been in the Duggan family for 200 years. Bedrooms are comfortable and spacious, there is a relaxing lounge, and the dining room overlooks the delightful garden. Golf, fishing, hill walking, and traditional pubs and restaurants are all nearby. Dinner is available by arrangement.

**Rooms:** 4 en suite (3 fmly) **Facilities:** STV FTV TVL tea/coffee Dinner available
WiFi ♨ ♨ ♨18 Fishing Pool table 🔒 **Conf:** Max 40 Board 20 **Parking:** 30
**Notes:** LB

## TIPPERARY Map 1 C3

## Aisling

★★★ BED AND BREAKFAST

**tel:** 087 2278230 **Glen of Aherlow**
**email:** ladygreg@oceanfree.net **web:** www.aislingbedandbreakfast.com
**dir:** From town centre take R664 for 2.4km, past golf club

Aisling is close to Tipperary on the R664, Glen of Aherlow road. The bedrooms are well furnished and attractively decorated. There is a comfortable guest sitting room and a delightful garden with patio seating. Marian and Bob are helpful hosts, happy to arrange day trips, and provide maps and information on the locality.

**Rooms:** 5 rms (3 en suite) (2 pri facs) (2 fmly) (5 GF) **D** fr €80 **Facilities:** STV FTV Lounge TVL WiFi ♨ 🔒 **Extras:** Snacks on arrival – complimentary **Parking:** 5
**Notes:** LB

## COUNTY WATERFORD

## TRAMORE Map 1 C2

## Seacourt

★★★★ BED AND BREAKFAST

**tel:** 051 386244 **Tivoli Road**
**email:** seacourthouse@gmail.com **web:** www.seacourt.ie
**dir:** Leave Waterford City on R675 to Tramore. Over 2 rdbts, at 3rd rdbt (boat in middle) straight over, 1st B&B on left

Seacourt is a very comfortable house situated in the seaside town close to Splashworld, the beach and Tramore Race Course, with many other tourist attractions available locally. Bedrooms are comfortably furnished with a spacious family room on the ground floor. There is a cosy guest sitting room, a wide choice of cooked breakfast served in the dining room, and ample off-street parking is available.

**Rooms:** 5 rms (5 pri facs) (1 fmly) (1 GF) **Facilities:** STV TVL tea/coffee WiFi ♨18
🔒 **Parking:** 10 **Notes:** No children 6yrs Closed Oct–2 Apr

**TRAMORE** *continued*

## Westcliff House

★★★★ GUEST ACCOMMODATION

**tel:** 051 381365 & 0876 655723 **5 Newtown Hill**
**web:** www.westcliffhouse.ie
**dir:** *Just off R675 (coast road)*

Westcliff House is the warm and inviting home of Evelyne Power and her family. Located in a quiet elevated position in a residential area a short drive from the town centre. Each of the bedrooms is comfortably appointed, and includes a triple suite; there are no family rooms. Guests are welcome to make themselves at home in the cosy sitting room or the bright and airy sunroom at the rear overlooking the gardens...just the place to enjoy some refreshments and Evelyne's renowned home baking.

**Rooms:** 4 en suite **D** fr €90* **Facilities:** FTV Lounge TVL tea/coffee WiFi 🅿 **Parking:** 4 **Notes:** No children Closed 30 Sep–1 Apr

---

| WATERFORD | Map 1 C2 |

## Belmont House

★★★ BED AND BREAKFAST

**tel:** 051 832174 **Belmont Road, Rosslare Road**
**email:** belmonthouse@eircom.net
**dir:** *Exit N25 at Luffany rdbt onto N29. At Slieverue rdbt follow R711 (Waterford N). Belmont House 4km from junct, 2nd B&B on left after service station*

This comfortable bed and breakfast is within walking distance of the city centre. A hospitality tray is available in the relaxing guest sitting room and a hearty breakfast is served in the dining room at separate tables. Bedrooms are well appointed and offer good quality and space.

**Rooms:** 6 rms (4 en suite) (3 fmly) **Facilities:** TVL WiFi **Parking:** 6 **Notes:** No children 7yrs Closed Nov-Apr

# COUNTY WEXFORD

| GOREY | Map 1 D3 |

### Premier Collection

## Clonganny House

★★★★★ ◎◎ GUEST ACCOMMODATION

**tel:** 053 948 2111 **Ballygarrett**
**email:** info@clonganny.com **web:** www.clonganny.com
**dir:** *Just off R742 between Ballygarrett & Kilmuckridge*

Located three kilometres south of Ballygarrett, Clonganny House was painstakingly restored to its former glory by Brona and Phillippe Brillant, who had run a similar property in England for a number of years. The breakfast room and lounge retain many of the original architectural features, and are beautifully presented with guest comfort and relaxation in mind. The accommodation features four individually decorated double rooms all at ground floor level, some with French windows overlooking the walled garden. There are walks set among the 10 acres of woodland grounds. The breakfast menu reveals some real treats, with options sure to please the most discerning palates. Dinner is available on some dates with advance notice.

**Rooms:** 4 annexe en suite (4 GF) **D** €180–€200 **Facilities:** FTV iPod docking station Lounge tea/coffee Dinner available Licensed WiFi 18 🅿 **Parking:** 13 **Notes:** No children 16yrs Civ wed 20

---

| WEXFORD | Map 1 D3 |

### Premier Collection

## Killiane Castle Country House & Farm

★★★★★ 🌾 FARMHOUSE

**tel:** 053 9158885 **Drinagh**
**email:** info@killianecastle.com **web:** www.killianecastle.com
**dir:** *Off N25 between Wexford and Rosslare*

This 17th-century house is run by the Mernagh family on a working dairy farm at Drinagh south of Wexford town. The house is part of a 13th-century Norman castle. The comfortable reception rooms and bedrooms are beautifully furnished. Many have been recently refurbished to a very high standard, in classic decor schemes. Breakfast is a real treat and includes farm produce and home-made baking and preserves.

**Rooms:** 9 en suite (2 fmly) (2 GF) **S** €75–€90; **D** €115–€145 **Facilities:** STV FTV DVD iPod docking station Lounge TVL Dinner available Licensed WiFi 🏊 🕙 ⛳18 🅿 Driving range 18-hole pitch & putt **Extras:** Speciality toiletries, honesty bar **Parking:** 10 **Notes:** Closed Dec–Feb 230 acres dairy/sheep

## Aldridge Lodge Restaurant and Guesthouse

★★★★ ◎◎ RESTAURANT WITH ROOMS

**tel:** 051 389116 **Duncannon**
**email:** info@aldridgelodge.com **web:** www.aldridgelodge.com

Just a 45-minute drive from the Ferryport at Rosslare, Aldridge Lodge is an ideal first night stop-off following an afternoon sailing from the UK, and it's tempting to return for the final night of a visit to Ireland given the warm welcome. It makes a great base for exploring the many attractions and activities of The Hook Peninsula. Hosts Joanne and Billy, who is also the chef, take a keen interest in their guests – it's no wonder so many of them return, making advance weekend reservations essential. While each of the three guest rooms is warm and cosy, what brings most visitors here is the food. Billy has a strong reputation for his use of local ingredients and seasonality is also very much to the fore. The breakfast experience is also a feature – quality ingredients cooked with skill and care in a relaxed environment.

**Rooms:** 3 en suite **S** €45–€55; **D** €90–€100 **Facilities:** FTV tea/coffee Dinner available WiFi 🅿 **Parking:** 20 **Notes:** No children Closed 6 Jan-1 Feb RS Mon–Tue closed Civ wed 30

---

## Who are the AA's award-winning B&Bs?
– see pages 12–15

*Oppposite: The Long Room Library in Trinity College, Dublin*

## COUNTY WICKLOW

### DUNLAVIN
Map 1 C3

## Tynte House
★★★★ FARMHOUSE

- - - - - - - - - - - - - - - - - - - - - - - - - - - - - - - - - - - - - - - - - - - - - - - - -

**tel:** 045 401561
**email:** info@tyntehouse.com **web:** www.tyntehouse.com
**dir:** *N81 at Hollywood Cross, right at Dunlavin, follow finger signs for Tynte House,*
*past market house in town centre*

This 19th-century farmhouse stands in the square of the quiet country village of
Dunlavin, in the west of County Wicklow. The friendly hosts have carried out a lot of
restoration resulting in cosy bedrooms and a relaxing guest sitting room.
Breakfast, featuring Caroline's home baking, is a highlight of a visit to this house.
An all-weather tennis court is located in the grounds, together with an indoor
games room. This house is an ideal base for touring the Wicklow and Kildare areas
with their many sporting attractions.

**Rooms:** 7 en suite (2 fmly) **Facilities:** Lounge TVL tea/coffee Direct dial WiFi ☺ ⅃18
Playground Games room **Parking:** 16 **Notes:** LB Closed 16 Dec–9 Jan 200 acres
beef/arable

# COUNTY MAPS

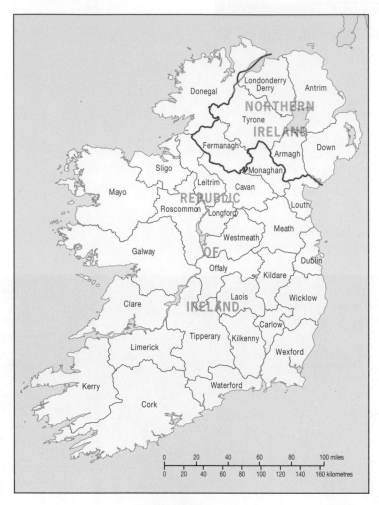

## England

1  Bedfordshire
2  Berkshire
3  Bristol
4  Buckinghamshire
5  Cambridgeshire
6  Greater Manchester
7  Herefordshire
8  Hertfordshire
9  Leicestershire
10 Northamptonshire
11 Nottinghamshire
12 Rutland
13 Staffordshire
14 Warwickshire
15 West Midlands
16 Worcestershire

## Scotland

17 City of Glasgow
18 Clackmannanshire
19 East Ayrshire
20 East Dunbartonshire
21 East Renfrewshire
22 Perth & Kinross
23 Renfrewshire
24 South Lanarkshire
25 West Dunbartonshire

## Wales

26 Blaenau Gwent
27 Bridgend
28 Caerphilly
29 Denbighshire
30 Flintshire
31 Merthyr Tydfil
32 Monmouthshire
33 Neath Port Talbot
34 Newport
35 Rhondda Cynon Taff
36 Torfaen
37 Vale of Glamorgan
38 Wrexham

Na h-Eileanan
an Iar

Highland

Moray

Aberdeenshire

City of
Aberdeen

SCOTLAND

Angus

Argyll
& Bute

Perth &
Kinross

City of
Dundee

Stirling

Fife

East
Lothian

North
Ayrshire

24

19

Scottish
Borders

South
Ayrshire

Dumfries &
Galloway

Northumberland

Tyne & Wear

Cumbria

Durham

Isle
of Man

North
Yorkshire

East Riding
of Yorkshire

Lancashire

West
Yorkshire

Isle of
Anglesey

Merseyside

6

South
Yorkshire

Lincolnshire

Conwy

30

Cheshire

Derbyshire

11

29

38

Gwynedd

13

ENGLAND

Norfolk

Shropshire

9

12

WALES

5

Ceredigion

Powys

15

Suffolk

14

10

Pembrokeshire

16

1

Carmarthenshire

7

Swansea

Gloucestershire

4

8

Essex

Oxfordshire

Greater
London

3

2

Wiltshire

Surrey

Kent

Somerset

Hampshire

West
Sussex

East
Sussex

Devon

Dorset

Cornwall

Isle of
Wight

Isles of
Scilly

Orkney Islands

Shetland Islands

Argyll
& Bute

Stirling

18

22

Fife

Inverclyde

25

20

Falkirk

City of
Edinburgh

23

17

North
Lanarkshire

West
Lothian

Midlothian

North
Ayrshire

21

Scottish
Borders

19

South Lanarkshire

31

26

32

33

36

35

28

27

34

37

Cardiff

Guernsey

Jersey

| 0 | 20 | 40 | 60 | 80 | 100 miles |

| 0 | 20 | 40 | 60 | 80 | 100 | 120 | 140 | 160 kilometres |

# KEY TO ATLAS

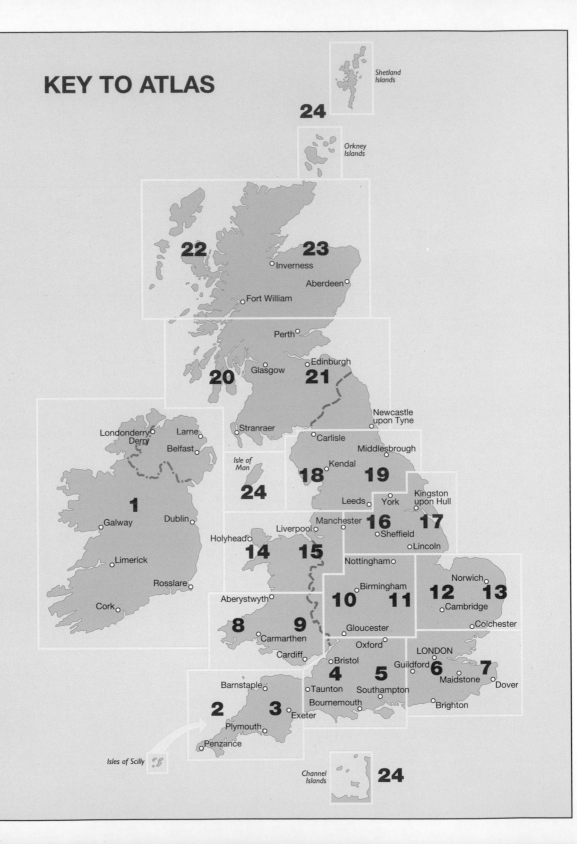

Shetland Islands — 24

Orkney Islands

22

23
Inverness
Aberdeen
Fort William

Perth

20
Glasgow
21
Edinburgh

Stranraer
Newcastle upon Tyne

Carlisle
Middlesbrough

Londonderry Derry
Larne
Belfast

Isle of Man
24

18
Kendal
19

1
Galway
Dublin
Leeds
York
Kingston upon Hull

Limerick
Rosslare
Cork

Holyhead
Liverpool
Manchester
16
Sheffield
17
Lincoln

14
15
Nottingham

Aberystwyth
10
Birmingham
11
12
Norwich
13
Cambridge
Colchester

8
Carmarthen
9
Cardiff
Gloucester
Oxford
LONDON
Guildford
6
Maidstone
7
Dover

Bristol
4
5
Southampton
Brighton
Taunton
Bournemouth

Barnstaple
2
3
Exeter
Plymouth
Penzance

Isles of Scilly

Channel Islands — 24

**2**

### Legend

| | |
|---|---|
| M6 | Motorway/toll motorway |
| ⑧ ⑱ Ⓢ | Motorway junction full/restricted. Service area |
| A33 | Primary route single/dual carriageway |
| A34 | Other A road single/dual carriageway |
| B3400 | B road |
| | Unclassified road |
| — V — | Vehicle ferry |
| — C — | Fast vehicle ferry or catamaran |

| | |
|---|---|
| ● Stamford | Guest Accommodation |
| ● Padstow | AA Guest Accommodation Award Winners |
| ○ King's Cliffe | Town/Village name |
| | National boundary |
| **ESSEX** | English county name & boundary |
| **CONWY** | Welsh county name & boundary |
| **MORAY** | Scottish county name & boundary |
| | National Park |

**ISLES OF SCILLY**

Bryher · New Grimsby · **Tresco** · St Martin's · Higher Town · **St Mary's** · Hugh Town · Old Town · *ISLES OF SCILLY (ST MARY'S)* · Middle Town · St Agnes

**SV**

**SW**

Lundy

Hartland Point · Hartland

**Meddon**

**Morwenstow**

Kilkhampton

*Bude* · **Bude** · Stratton

*Bude Bay*

Widemouth Bay

Crackington Haven · Week St Mary

Boscastle

Tintagel

Delabole · Bolventor · *BODMIN MOOR* · Blisland

**Port Gaverne** · Port Isaac · Pendoggett · St Tudy · **Camelford**

Polzeath · **St Kew** · **CORNWALL** · St Cleer

Rock · **Padstow** · **Wadebridge** · Lanivet · **Bodmin** · Dobwalls · **Liskeard** · St Keyne

Harlyn · **Port Gaverne**

Porthcothan

Mawgan Porth · St Mawgan · St Columb Major · Roche · Bugle · **Luxulyan** · St Blazey · **Lostwithiel** · Pelynt · Wide

**Newquay** · West Pentire · Summercourt · **St Austell** · Par · **Bodinnick** · **Looe**

Perranporth · **Mitchell** · Ladock · St Stephen · Fowey · Polruan · **Polperro**

**St Agnes**

Porthtowan · Marazanvose · Grampound · Pentewan · **Mevagissey**

Portreath · **Truro** · Tregony · Gorran Haven

St Day · Carnon Downs · **Redruth** · **Ruan High Lanes** · **Portloe**

**St Ives** · *St Ives Bay* · Gwithian · **Camborne** · St Just-in-Roseland · **Veryan** · Portscatho

Zennor · Lelant · **Hayle** · **Penryn** · St Mawes

**Leedstown** · **Falmouth**

St Just · **Penzance** · **Marazion** · Constantine · Mawnan Smith

*LAND'S END* · Newlyn · **Perranuthnoe** · Helston · **Gweek** · Manaccan

Land's End · Sennen · **St Buryan** · Mousehole · Praa Sands · **Porthleven** · **St Keverne**

Porthcurno · Treen · *Mount's Bay*

Mullion

Coverack

Cadgwith

Lizard · Lizard Point

7

**Guest Accommodation**
**AA Guest Accommodation Award Winners**
Town/Village name

0        10 miles
0          10        20 kilometres

Aberdyfi
Borth
Llandre
Aberystwyth
Llanfarian
CERED
Llanrhystud
Llansantffraid
Aberarth
New Quay
Aberaeron
CARDIGAN BAY
Llangranog
Aberporth
Temple Bar
Tan-y-groes
Blaenporth
Lampeter
St Dogmaels
Cardigan
Rhydowen
Llanybydder
Llechryd
Llandysul
Newcastle Emlyn
Strumble Head
Nevern
Newport
Eglwyswrw
Llangeler
SM
Fishguard
PEMBROKESHIRE COAST NATIONAL PARK
MYNYDD PRESELI
Llansawe
Talley
SN
Letterston
Wolf's Castle
Brechfa
St David's Head
St Davids
Solva
PEMBROKESHIRE
Llandissilio
Cynwyl Elfed
Felingwm Uchaf
Newgale
Roch
CARMARTHENSHIRE
Nantgaredig
Llandeilo
St Brides Bay
PEMBROKESHIRE COAST NATIONAL PARK
Broad Haven
Haverfordwest
Roberston Wathen
Narberth
Carmarthen
Llanarthne
Llandybie
Whitland
St Clears
Llanddarog
Cross Hands
Johnston
Red Roses
Laugharne
Llansteffan
Pontyberem
Ammanf
Broad Sound
Marloes
Milford Haven
Neyland
Carew
Kilgetty
Amroth
Pendine
Carmarthen Bay
Kidwelly
Pontyates
Hendy
Pontarddul
Dale
Angle
Pembroke Dock
Pembroke
St Florence
Saundersfoot
Tenby
Swansea (West)
M4
Castlemartin
PEMBROKESHIRE COAST NATIONAL PARK
Penally
Manorbier
Pembrey
Bury Port
Llanelli
Gorseinon
Bosherston
Gowerton
Dunvant
Llanrhidian
Llangennith
Reynoldston
SWANSEA
Bishopston
Rhossili
Worms Head
Parkmill
Oxwich
SS
Port Einon
SR

Guest Accommodation
AA Guest Accommodation Award Winners
Town/Village name
0                    10 miles
0          10          20 kilometres

Lundy
Ilfracombe
Combe Martin
Mortehoe   Lee

**Guest Accommodation**
● **AA Guest Accommodation Award Winners**
○ Town/Village name

| | | |
|---|---|---|
| 0 | 10 miles | |
| 0 | 10 | 20 kilometres |

ISLE OF
ANGLESEY

Cemaes
Amlwch
Llanerchymedd
Holyhead
Llanfachraeth
Benllech
Red
Wharf Bay
Llangoed
Trearddur Bay
Pentraeth
Holy
Island
Llangefni
Rhosneigr
Menai
Bridge Bangor
Beaumaris
Llanfairfechan
Aberffraw
Y Felinheli
Newborough
Caernarfon
Llanrug
Llanberis
Bethnewydd
Llanwnda
Llandwrog
Caernarfon
Bay
Penygroes
Rhyd-Ddu
Clynnog-fawr

Llandudno
Deganwy
Llandudno
Junction
Rhôs-
on-Sea
Colwyn Bay
Rhy
Abergel
Conwy
Dwygyfylchi
Penmaenmawr
Llanddulas
Llansanffraid
Glan Conwy
Betws-yn-Rhos
Llanfairfechan
Tal-y-Cafn
Llan
Llanfair
Talhaiarn
Llansannan
Trefriw
Llanrwst
Bylchau
CONWY
Capel Curig
Betws-y-Coed
Dolwyddelan
Penmachno
Pentrefoelas
Cerrigydrudion
Y Maer

SH

Beddgelert
Blaenau Ffestiniog
Prenteg
Tremadog
Maentwrog
Ffestiniog
Morfa Nefyn
Nefyn
Llanystumdwy
Porthmadog
Penrhyndeudraeth
PENINSULA
Bodfuan
Criccieth
Borth-y-Gest
Talsarnau
Trawsfynydd
Balg
LLEYN
Pwllheli
Harlech
G W Y N E D D
Llanddec
Sarn
SNOWDONIA
Llanbedrog
NATIONAL
Llanuwchllyn
Llanw
Aberdaron
Y Rhiw
Abersoch
Llanbedr
PARK
Ganllwyd
Bardsey
Island
Dyffryn Ardudwy
Tal-y-bont
A470
Dinas-Mawddwy
Barmouth
Dolgellau
A458
Llangadfa
Fairbourne
Mallwyd
Llwyngwril
Corris
Cemmaes
Road
Cemmaes
Llanbrynmair
Bryncrug
Pennal
Tywyn
Machynlleth
Carno

SN

Aberdyfi
Eglwys
Fach
Borth
Tal-y-bont
Llandre
Capel
Bangor
Aberystwyth
Ponterwyd
Goginan
Llanidloes

9

For continuation pages refer to numbered arrows

**20**

**22**

PERTH
KINR

ARGYLL AND
BUTE

STIRLING

AND THE TROSSACHS

NATIONAL PARK

LOCH LOMOND

ISLE
OF
MULL

JURA

ISLAY

KINTYRE

ARRAN

NORTH AYRSHIRE

GREENOCK

INVER

GLASGOW

C GLAS

PAISLEY

RENS

E RENS

EAST
KILBRIDE

KILMARNOCK

SO
LANA

EAST
AYRSHIRE

SOUTH
AYRSHIRE

DUMFR
GAL

NX

NW

North Channel

NM

NN

NR

NS

| | |
|---|---|
| **C EDIN** | City of Edinburgh |
| **C GLAS** | City of Glasgow |
| **CLACKS** | Clackmannanshire |
| **C DUND** | City of Dundee |
| **E DUNS** | East Dunbartonshire |
| **E RENS** | East Renfrewshire |
| **INVER** | Inverclyde |
| **MDLOTH** | Midlothian |
| **N LANS** | North Lanarkshire |
| **RENS** | Renfrewshire |
| **W DUNS** | West Dunbartonshire |
| **W LOTH** | West Lothian |

Coll
Arinagour
Tiree
Scarinish
Tobermory
Ulva
Iona
Fionnphort
Kerrera
Oban
Luing
Scarba
Colonsay
Scalasaig
Oronsay
Port Askaig
Portnahaven
Glenegedale
Port Ellen
Gigha
Kennacraig
Claonaig
Tarbert
Lochgilphead
Campbeltown
Mull of Kintyre
Ailsa Craig
Brodick
Lamlash
Acharacle
Point of Ardnamurchan
Fort William
Kinlochleven
Glencoe
Ballachulish
Lochaline
Appin
Barcaldine
Taynuilt
Dalmally
Crianlarich
Tyndrum
Lochearnhead
Strathyre
Killin
Callander
Inveraray
Cairndow
Luss
Helensburgh
Balloch
Dumbarton
Dunoon
Colintraive
Rothesay
Bute
Inverkip
Kilsyth
W DUNS
E DUNS
Largs
Great Cumbrae Island
West Kilbride
Stewarton
Ardrossan
Kilwinning
Beith
Kilbirnie
Strathaven
Irvine
Galston
Troon
Prestwick
Ayr
Cumnock
Maybole
Girvan
Ballantrae
Cairnyan
Newton Stewart
Stranraer
Portpatrick
Wigtown
Gatehouse of Fleet
Kirkcudbright
Wigtown Bay
Luce Bay
Drummore
Whithorn
Burrow Head
Mull of Galloway
New Galloway
Strathaven
Galashiels

Firth of Lorne
Sound of Jura
Sound of Bute
Kilbrannan Sound
(May-Sept)
(Oct-Mar)

NA

NB

Cape Wrath

Scourie

A894

Inchnadamph

Lochinver

A837

A835

Rudha Rhobhanais
(Butt of Lewis)

Port Nis
(Port of Ness)

Cellar
Head

A857

LEWIS

Great
Bernera

Carlabhagh
(Carloway)

A858

ISLE

OF

A859

Steornabhagh
(Stornoway)

A858

A866

Tiumpan
Head

STORNOWAY

THE MINCH

Scarp

NA H–EILEANAN
AN IAR

Taransay

Tairbeart
(Tarbert)

A859

HARRIS

Scalpay

A859

Gruinard
Bay

Ullapool

A832

Pabbay

Boreray

Berneray

THE LITTLE MINCH

Pooleeve

A835

HIGHLANDS

Gairloch

A832

NORTH UIST

A865

Loch nam Madadh
(Lochmaddy)

A867

Uig

A855

Kinlochewe

A832

Torridon

Achnasheen

A832

NF

Benbecula

A865

Ronay

Wiay

Dunvegan

A863

A850

ISLE

NG

Portree

A896

A890

WEST

Gannich

SOUTH
UIST

Struan

OF

A87

Raasay

Inner Sound

A896

A865

Drynoch

SKYE

Scalpay

Kyle of
Lochalsh

A890

Loch Baghasdail
(Lochboisdale)

Soay

A87

A87

A887

BARRA

Eriskay

Canna

Cuillin Sound

Ardvasar

A851

Sound of Sleet

NORTH

A82

Invergarry

A888

Bagh a Chaisteil
(Castlebay)

Rùm

Mallaig

Laggan

Sandray

Eigg

A830

Spean
Bridge

A82

Roy
Bridge

Mingulay

INNER HEBRIDES

Muck

A861

A830

A861

Fort William

(Ardnamurchan)

Point of
Ardnamurchan

NM

Acharacle

Kinlochleven

NL

Coll

Arinagour

Tobermory

A861

A884

A82

Glencoe

Ballachulish

A828

Tiree

Scarinish

ISLE

A849

Lochaline

A828

Appin

Barcaldine

20

Ulva

OF

Kerrera

Taynuilt

A85

Tyn

Iona

MULL

Oban

Dalmally

A816

Crianlarich

Fionnphort

A849

Lorne

A85

OUTER HEBRIDES

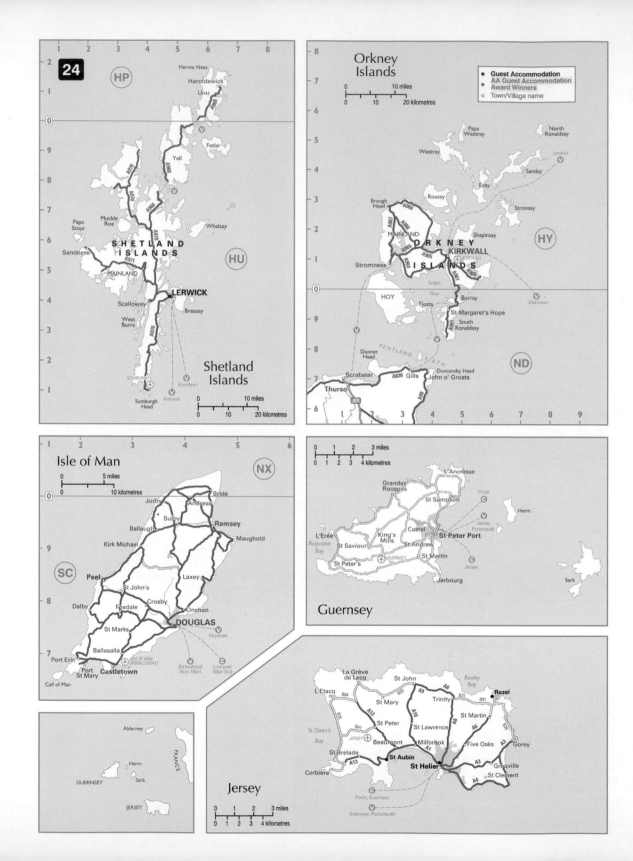

**24**

HP

Herma Ness
Haroldswick
Unst
A968

Fetlar

Yell
A970
A968
A969

Papa Stour
Muckle Roe
Whalsay

SHETLAND
ISLANDS
Sandness
A971
MAINLAND
A970

Scalloway
West Burra
Bressay
LERWICK

SUMBURGH
Aberdeen
Kirkwall
Sumburgh Head

HU

## Shetland Islands

0      10 miles
0   10   20 kilometres

## Orkney Islands

**Guest Accommodation**
**AA Guest Accommodation Award Winners**
○ Town/Village name

0      10 miles
0   10   20 kilometres

Papa Westray
North Ronaldsay
Westray
Rousay
Eday
Sanday
Stronsay
Lerwick
Brough Head
A966
A967
A986
MAINLAND
ORKNEY
Shapinsay
Stromness
A965
A960
KIRKWALL
A961
ISLANDS
Scapa Flow
HOY
Flotta
Burray
St Margaret's Hope
South Ronaldsay
Aberdeen

HY

ND

Dunnet Head
PENTLAND FIRTH
Scrabster    A836    Gills    Duncansby Head    John o' Groats
Thurso    A9
A99

## Isle of Man

NX

0      5 miles
0   10 kilometres

Bride
Jurby    Andreas
Sulby
Ballaugh    Ramsey
Kirk Michael    Maughold
SC
Peel    Laxey
St John's
Dalby    Crosby
Foxdale    Onchan
St Marks    DOUGLAS
Ballasalla    Heysham
Port Erin
Port St Mary    Castletown    ISLE OF MAN (RONALDSWAY)
Calf of Man    Birkenhead (Nov-Mar)    Liverpool (Mar-Oct)

0      1      2      3 miles
0   1   2   3   4 kilometres

L'Ancresse
Grandes Rocques
St Sampson    Poole
Herm
Jersey Portsmouth
L'Erée    King's Mills    Castel    St Peter Port
Rocquaine Bay    St Saviour    St Andrew
St Peter's    GUERNSEY    St Martin    Jersey
Jerbourg    Sark

## Guernsey

Alderney
Herm
FRANCE
GUERNSEY    Sark
JERSEY

La Grève de Lecq    St John    A8    Bouley Bay
L'Etacq    B64    St Mary    B30    A9    Trinity    B31    B81    **Rozel**
A12    St Peter    A10    St Lawrence    St Martin    A8    A6    B26
B41    Beaumont    Millbrook    Five Oaks    A3    Gorey
St Ouen's Bay    JERSEY    A1    Grouville
St Brelade    **St Aubin**    **St Helier**    A3    St Clement
Corbière    A13    A4
Poole, Guernsey
Guernsey, Portsmouth

## Jersey

0      1      2      3 miles
0   1   2   3   4 kilometres

# Central London

**KEY TO B&B LOCATIONS**

Each B&B in London has a map reference, eg C2. The letter 'C' refers to the grid square located at the left hand edge of the map. The figure '2' refers to the grid square located at the bottom of the map. For example, where these two intersect, Buckingham Palace can be found. Due to the scale of the map, only a rough guide to the location of a B&B can be given. A more detailed map will be necessary to be precise.

Congestion Charging Zone boundary

# Index of Bed & Breakfasts

# Readers' Report Form

Please send this form to:–
Editor, The B&B Guide,
Lifestyle Guides,
AA Media,
Fanum House,
Basingstoke RG21 4EA

e-mail: lifestyleguides@theAA.com

Please use this form to recommend any guest house, farmhouse or inn where you have stayed, that is not currently listed in the guide. If you have any comments about your stay at an establishment listed in the guide, please let us know, as feedback from readers helps to keep our Guide accurate and up to date. If you have a complaint during your stay, we recommend that you discuss the matter with the establishment.

**Please note** that the AA does not undertake to arbitrate between you and the establishment, or to obtain compensation or engage in protracted correspondence.

Date
Your name (BLOCK CAPITALS)
Your address (BLOCK CAPITALS)

Post code
E-mail address

Name of establishment
Location
Comments

(please attach a separate sheet if necessary)

Please tick here ☐ if you DO NOT wish to receive details of AA offers or products

# Readers' Report Form *continued*

Have you bought this guide before?  ☐ YES  ☐ NO

Do you regularly use any other accommodation, restaurant, pub or food guides?  ☐ YES  ☐ NO
If YES, which ones?

_____

_____

Why did you buy this guide? (tick all that apply)
Holiday ☐                    Short break ☐              Business travel ☐           Special occasion ☐
Overnight stop ☐             Find a venue for an event e.g. conference ☐
Other (please state)

How often do you stay in B&Bs? (tick one choice)
More than once a month ☐                    Once a month ☐              Once in 2-3 months ☐
Once in six months ☐        Once a year ☐              Less than once a year ☐
Other (please state)

**Please answer these questions to help us make improvements to the guide:**
Which of these factors are the most important when choosing a B&B? (tick all that apply)
Price ☐                      Location ☐                 Awards/ratings ☐            Service ☐
Decor/surroundings ☐         Previous experience ☐      Recommendation ☐
Other (please state)

Do you use the location atlas?  ☐ YES  ☐ NO

What elements of the guide do you find most useful when choosing somewhere to stay? (tick all that apply)
Description ☐                Photo ☐                    Advertisement ☐             Star rating ☐

Is there any other information you would like to see added to this guide?

_____

_____

_____

_____

_____

_____